Wirth/Arnold/Morshäuser/Carl/Greene
Corporate Law in Germany

Corporate Law in Germany

Gerhard Wirth

Michael Arnold

Ralf Morshäuser

Steffen Carl

in cooperation with
Mark Greene

Revised 3rd edition
2017

C.H.BECK

Authors

Rechtsanwalt **Dr. Gerhard Wirth**, born 1944, studied law at the Universities of Tübingen and Hamburg. After having gained a post-graduate degree at the College of Business Administration in Speyer, he went on to do further studies in economics/tax law at the University of Mannheim. He was admitted to the bar in 1972 and is now a senior partner of Gleiss Lutz in Stuttgart. Gerhard Wirth practices corporate law and mergers & acquisitions. He acts for many major listed companies. In recent years he has advised a number of German stock corporations in connection with important mergers. Gerhard Wirth is a member of the German Bar Association. He sits on the supervisory boards and advisory boards of a number of companies and has written several publications on corporate law.

Rechtsanwalt **Prof. Dr. Michael Arnold**, born 1969, studied law at the Universities of Tübingen, Geneva/Switzerland and Heidelberg. He was admitted to the bar in 1999 and is now a partner of Gleiss Lutz in Stuttgart. Michael Arnold specializes in corporate law, takeover law and mergers & acquisitions. He advises many German and international clients in connection with mergers, takeovers and general corporate work. Michael Arnold is a member of the German Bar Association. As a legal author he has written several publications in the field of corporate law and mergers & acquisitions.

Rechtsanwalt **Dr. Ralf Morshäuser**, born 1972, studied law at the Universities of Regensburg and Munich. He was admitted to the bar in 2001 and is now a partner of Gleiss Lutz in Munich. Ralf Morshäuser specializes in mergers & acquisitions and corporate law. He has represented many strategic and financial investors in cross-border M&A transactions and advises German and foreign clients in matters of German corporate law. Ralf Morshäuser is a member of the German Bar Association. He regularly teaches seminars on corporate and M&A topics and has written several publications in the field of M&A and corporate law.

Rechtsanwalt **Steffen Carl**, born 1968, studied law at the Universities of Freiburg and Hamburg. He was admitted to the bar in 1999 and is now a partner of Gleiss Lutz in Munich. Steffen Carl focuses on corporate law and complex transactions. He advises many German and foreign clients in mergers & acquisitions as well as matters of German corporate and securities law. Steffen Carl is a member of the German Bar Association. He has written several publications in the field of German and international corporate law.

Mark I. Greene is a partner at Cravath, Swaine & Moore LLP in New York. He received a B.A. from Cornell University in 1989 and a J.D. from the University of Pennsylvania in 1993. At the University of Pennsylvania, he was an Associate Editor of the Law Review. After a clerkship with Charles Legge (U.S. District Court for the Northern District of California), he joined Cravath in 1994 and was elected a partner in 2000. Mark Greene is extensively involved in mergers and acquisitions, corporate governance and securities matters, including advising cross–border transactions, private equity deals, complex restructuring transactions, proxy fights, takeover defense and global securities offerings.

www.beck.de

ISBN 978 3 406 69202 4

© 2017 Verlag C.H.Beck oHG
Wilhelmstraße 9, 80801 München
Druck: Beltz Bad Langensalza GmbH
Neustädter Straße 1–4, 99947 Bad Langensalza
Satz: Fotosatz Buck
Zweikirchener Str. 7, 84036 Kumhausen
Umschlaggestaltung: Bütefisch Marketing und Kommunikation,
Schlaitdorf

Gedruckt auf säurefreiem, alterungsbeständigem Papier
(hergestellt aus chlorfrei gebleichtem Zellstoff)

Preface

When we discussed the scope of the first edition of this book in 2001, we focused on a translation of the most important German corporate law statutes into (American) English. In addition, we intended to provide an overview of major principles of German corporate law in order to facilitate access to the statutes.

It quickly became apparent that we would have to concentrate on the most important statutes, namely the Limited Liability Company Act (*Gesetz betreffend die Gesellschaften mit beschränkter Haftung*) and the Stock Corporation Act (*Aktiengesetz*). Apart from providing as direct and precise a translation as possible, our primary goal was to use the terminology consistently as used throughout both statutes.

We quickly discovered that describing only the major principles of the Limited Liability Company Act and the Stock Corporation Act in isolation is almost impossible. Accordingly, the "Introduction" took on more and more the character of a real description of most of the aspects of those complex statutes.

Where appropriate, we use charts to summarize certain topics. We have also attached a glossary of some of the most important legal terms in both English and German. We have also attached a list, prepared for our internal use, with relevant legal vocabulary.

The second edition has taken into account the many changes to the Limited Liability Company Act and the Stock Corporation Act as well as the case law, in particular the Law on the Modernization of the Law of Limited Liability Companies and the Prevention of Misuse (*MoMiG*), which significantly changed the law on Limited Liability Companies, and the amendments to the law on stock corporations, in particular the Shareholders' Rights Act (*Gesetz zur Umsetzung der Aktionärsrechterichtlinie – ARUG*) and the Act on the Reasonableness of the Remuneration of the Management Board (*VorstAG*).

This third edition includes recent changes in the laws of the limited liability company and the stock corporation due to changes in statutory law, to wit the Act for the Equal Participation of Women and Men in Leadership Positions in the Private and Public Sector (*Gesetz für die gleichberechtigte Teilhabe von Frauen und Männern an Führungspositionen in der Privatwirtschaft und im öffentlichen Dienst – BGleiNRG*), the Accounting Directive Implementation Act (*Bilanzrichtlinie-Umsetzungsgesetz – BilRUG*), the Audit Law Reform Act (*Abschlussprüfungsreformgesetz – AReG*) and the Stock Corporation Law Amendment 2016 (*Gesetz zur Änderung des Aktiengesetzes – Aktienrechtsnovelle 2016*).

We are very thankful to Dr. Verena Koppmann, Dr. Johannes Wittmann, Vera Richter, Dr. Bernd Fluck and Lennart Laude for their contributions to the form and contents of the book.

September 2016   *The authors*

Dr. Gerhard Wirth
Gleiss Lutz Rechtsanwälte
Lautenschlagerstraße 21
D-70173 Stuttgart
Germany
gerhard.wirth@gleisslutz.com

Dr. Ralf Morshäuser
Gleiss Lutz Rechtsanwälte
Karl-Scharnagl-Ring 6
D-80539 Munich
Germany
ralf.morshaeuser@gleisslutz.com

Mark Greene
Cravath, Swaine & Moore LLP
Worldwide Plaza
825 Eighth Avenue
New York, NY 10019
U.S.A.
MGreene@cravath.com

Prof. Dr. Michael Arnold
Gleiss Lutz Rechtsanwälte
Lautenschlagerstraße 21
D-70173 Stuttgart
Germany
michael.arnold@gleisslutz.com

Steffen Carl
Gleiss Lutz Rechtsanwälte
Karl-Scharnagl-Ring 6
D-80539 Munich
Germany
steffen.carl@gleisslutz.com

Summary Table of Contents

Preface	V
Table of Abbreviations	XIX

Part 1: Introduction to Limited Liability Company Law and Stock Corporation Law

A. The Limited Liability Company	1
I. Introduction	1
II. Formation	2
III. Legal Position of the Shareholders	17
IV. Transfer of Shares	26
V. Shareholder Meeting	28
VI. Management of the Company	36
VII. Supervisory Board and Codetermination	46
VIII. Financial System	50
IX. Dissolution and Liquidation of the Company	64
X. Limited Partnership with a *GmbH* as the Personally Liable Shareholder (*GmbH & Co. KG*)	66
B. Stock Corporation	68
I. Introduction	68
II. Overview	69
III. Formation	74
IV. Legal Position of the Shareholders	86
V. Constitution of the *AG*	95
VI. Financial System	167
VII. Dissolution and Liquidation of the Company	193
VIII. Accounting	197
IX. Group of Companies	202
X. Listed Companies	213
C. Taxation of German Limited Liability Companies and Stock Corporations	224
I. Income Taxes	224
II. Other Taxes	226

Part 2: Relevant Statutes

A. Limited Liability Company Act	227
B. Stock Corporation Act	296

List of Tables

Table 1: The Formation of a *GmbH* 15

Table 2: Important (Minority) Shareholder Rights of a *GmbH* 33

Table 3: The Formation of a Stock Corporation 84

Table 4: Important (Minority) Shareholder Rights on a *AG* 158

Table 5: Forms of Affiliation 204

Appendix 1: Comparison between the Legal Forms of an *AG* and a *GmbH* 583

Appendix 2: Glossary 595

Table of Contents

Preface V
Table of Abbreviations XIX

Part 1: Introduction to Limited Liability Company Law and Stock Corporation Law

A. The Limited Liability Company 1
   I. Introduction 1
      1. The Significance of Limited Liability Companies in the German Business World 1
      2. Structure and Corporate Bodies of the *GmbH* 1
   II. Formation 2
      1. Steps of Formation 2
         a) Overview 2
         b) Articles of Association 3
            aa) Execution 3
            bb) Shareholders 3
            cc) Contents 4
         c) Appointment of Managing Directors 5
         d) The Raising of Capital (Cash Formation/Formation through Contributions in Kind) 5
            aa) Cash Formation 5
            bb) Formation through Contributions in Kind 5
         e) Application with the Commercial Register 6
            aa) General Requirements 6
            bb) Special Requirements in Case of Contributions in Kind .. 7
            cc) Liability for False Information 7
         f) Examination by the Register Court 8
         g) Registration 9
      2. Nominee Formation 9
      3. Simplified Formation Proceedings 10
      4. Formation of an Entrepreneur Company *(UG)* 10
      5. Shelf Companies 11
      6. Hidden Contributions in Kind 11
      7. Pre-Registered Company 13
         a) Legal Nature 13
         b) Internal Relations 13
         c) External Relations 13
         d) Liability of the Company and the Shareholders 14
         e) Liability of the Persons Acting 15
         f) Principles regarding Defective Companies 15
      8. Overview: The Formation of a *GmbH* 15

Table of Contents

- III. Legal Position of the Shareholders 17
  - 1. Membership Rights and Membership Duties 17
  - 2. Membership Rights 18
    - a) Distinction between Membership Rights and Special Rights 18
    - b) Right to Information and Right of Inspection 18
    - c) Shareholder Lawsuit 19
  - 3. Membership Duties 19
    - a) Duty to Render Contributions 19
    - b) Ancillary Duties 21
    - c) Duty to Render Additional Contributions 21
    - d) Fiduciary Duty Pursuant to Corporate Law 22
    - e) Non-Compete Obligations 22
    - f) The Requirement of Equal Treatment 23
  - 4. Liability of a Shareholder of a Limited Liability Company 23
    - a) Generally No Shareholder Liability 23
    - b) Contractual Shareholder Liability 23
    - c) Capital Preservation 23
    - d) Insolvency Law Liability 24
    - e) Destruction of the Economic Basis of the Company 24
    - f) Other Exemptions 25
  - 5. Redemption of a Share 25
  - 6. Withdrawal and Expulsion of a Shareholder 26
- IV. Transfer of Shares 26
  - 1. Disposal and Transfer of the Shares 26
  - 2. Notarial Form 27
  - 3. Restriction on Transferability 28
  - 4. Shareholder List 28
- V. Shareholder Meeting 28
  - 1. Competence of the Shareholder Meeting 28
  - 2. The Convening of a Shareholder Meeting 29
  - 3. Proceedings of the Shareholder Meeting 30
  - 4. Voting and Shareholder Resolutions 31
  - 5. Exclusion of Voting Rights 32
  - 6. Nullity of Shareholder Resolutions and Action to Set Aside Resolutions 32
  - 7. Important (Minority) Shareholder Rights (Overview) 33
- VI. Management of the Company 36
  - 1. Management and Representation of the Company 36
    - a) Management by Managing Directors 36
    - b) Duties of the Managing Directors 36
    - c) Authority of the Managing Directors to Represent the Company 37
    - d) Restrictions in Internal Relations 38
  - 2. Appointment and Dismissal of the Managing Directors 38
    - a) Personal Requirements for Appointment as Managing Director 38
    - b) Corporate Act of Appointment 40
    - c) Dismissal 40
  - 3. Service Contracts with Managing Directors 41

	a) Legal Nature of the Service Contract	41
	b) Parties to the Service Contract	41
	c) Form and Content of the Service Contract	42
	d) Termination of the Service Contract	43
4.	Liability of the Managing Director	44
	a) Prerequisites of the Liability of the Managing Director	44
	b) Consequences of the Liability of the Managing Director	45
	c) Third-Party Claims	46

VII. Supervisory Board and Codetermination 46
    1. Overview 46
    2. The Optional Supervisory Board 47
    3. Advisory Board 47
    4. Supervisory Board according to One-Third Participation Act .. 48
    5. Supervisory Board according to Codetermination Act 48

VIII. Financial System 50
    1. Bookkeeping and Accounting 50
        a) Overview 50
        b) Annual Financial Statements 51
        c) Preparation of the Annual Financial Statements 51
        d) Audit of the Annual Financial Statements 52
        e) Formal Approval of the Annual Financial Statements .. 53
    2. Allocation of the Annual Net Income 53
        a) Right to Participate in the Profits and Right to the Distribution of Profits 53
        b) Calculation 53
        c) Provisions of the Articles of Association 54
    3. The Maintenance of the Registered Share Capital 54
        a) Introduction 54
        b) Restrictions on Payments of Capital to Shareholders .. 55
        c) Exceptions to the Prohibition against Refunding of Contributions 57
        d) Acquisition of Company's Own Shares 57
        e) Shareholder Loans 58
    4. Increase of the Registered Share Capital 59
        a) Overview 59
        b) Ordinary Capital Increase 60
        c) Capital Increase from Company Resources 61
        d) Capital Increase from Authorized Capital 62
    5. Reduction of the Registered Share Capital 63

IX. Dissolution and Liquidation of the Company 64
    1. Overview 64
    2. Dissolution and Grounds for Dissolution 64
    3. Liquidation 65
    4. Completion of Liquidation 66

X. Limited Partnership with a *GmbH* as the Personally Liable Shareholder (*GmbH & Co. KG*) 66
    1. Definition 66
    2. Legal Particularities 66
    3. The Legal Position of the General Partner *GmbH* 67
    4. Codetermination 68

B. Stock Corporation 68
  I. Introduction 68
    1. The Significance of *AGs* in the German Business World 68
    2. Structure and Legal Bodies of the Company 69
  II. Overview 69
    1. The AG 69
    2. The Share 70
      a) Fraction of the Registered Share Capital 70
      b) Right of Membership 71
      c) Share Certificates 73
    3. Other Securities Governed by Corporate Law 73
    4. Protection of Shareholders in a Stock Corporation 73
  III. Formation 74
    1. Steps of Formation and Stages of the Company during the
       Formation Process 74
      a) Overview 74
      b) Subscription to Shares 75
      c) Appointment of the Formation Bodies 76
      d) Formation Report 76
      e) Raising of the Registered Share Capital 76
      f) Formation Audit 78
      g) Application for Registration in the Commercial Register ... 79
      h) Inspection by the Register Court 80
      i) Registration and Notification 81
    2. Post-Formation Acquisitions 81
    3. The Pre-Registered Company 82
    4. Defects Relating to Formation 82
    5. Overview: The Formation of a Stock Corporation 84
  IV. Legal Position of the Shareholders 86
    1. Introduction 86
    2. Membership Rights 86
      a) Administrative Rights 87
      b) Property Rights 87
      c) Prohibition of Separation 87
      d) Special Rights 88
      e) Shareholders' Rights to File a Lawsuit 88
    3. Membership Duties 89
      a) The Duty to Pay Contributions 89
      b) Ancillary Obligations 90
      c) Fiduciary Duty 90
    4. Principle of Equal Treatment 91
    5. Change in Membership 92
      a) Introduction 92
      b) Sale and Transfer of Shares 92
        aa) Transfer of Bearer Shares 92
        bb) Transfer of Registered Shares 93
      c) Peculiarities regarding Registered Shares 93
      d) Restrictions on Transferability 93
      e) Restricted Property Rights 94
      f) Transfer by Way of Security 94

	g) Inheritance	94
V. Constitution of the *AG*		95
1. Introduction		95
2. Management Board		96
	a) Management of the Company	96
	b) Representation of the Company	98
	c) Appointment of the Members of the Management Board	100
	d) Chairman/Spokesman of the Management Board	102
	e) Dismissal of Members of the Management Board	103
	f) Service Contracts with Members of the Management Board	104
	g) Rights and Duties of Members of the Management Board	106
	h) Liability of Members of the Management Board	109
3. Supervisory Board		113
	a) Introduction	113
	b) Overview of the Statutory Supervisory Board Models	114
	c) Gender Quota	115
	d) Appointment and Dismissal of Members of the Supervisory Board	116
	e) Responsibilities of the Supervisory Board	119
	f) Supervisory Board Procedures	122
	g) Supervisory Board Committees	124
	h) Duties of Members of the Supervisory Board	125
	i) Remuneration	126
	j) Confidentiality Obligation	127
	k) Liability of Members of the Supervisory Board	128
4. General Meeting		130
	a) Introduction	130
	b) Statutory Competency of the General Meeting	130
	aa) Routine Matters	131
	bb) Fundamental Decisions	132
	cc) Resolutions on Matters relating to the Management of the Company	132
	dd) Other Cases Regulated by Law	133
	ee) Unwritten Competencies of the General Meeting	133
	c) Convening of the General Meeting	134
	d) The Course of the General Meeting	138
	e) The Right to Information	140
	f) Resolutions of the General Meeting and Voting	142
	g) Provisions of the Articles of Association on Voting	143
	h) Voting Right	143
	i) Prohibition of Voting	144
	j) Voting Agreements	145
	k) Exercise of Voting Rights by Proxy	146
	l) Proxy Voting Rights for Deposited Shares	147
5. Actions against Resolutions of the General Meeting		149
	a) Overview	149
	b) Nullity of Resolutions	151
	aa) Overview	151
	bb) Violation of Provisions relating to Form and Procedure	151
	cc) Other Violations of Law	153

				dd) Cured Defects	154

- dd) Cured Defects 154
- c) Action to Set Aside a Resolution 155
  - aa) Reasons for Setting Aside Resolutions 155
  - bb) Procedure 156
- d) Release (Fast-track) Proceedings 157
6. Overview: Important (Minority) Shareholder Rights 158
7. Corporate Governance Code 163
   - a) Development of Voluntary Codes of Governance Best Practices 163
   - b) Is the German Corporate Governance Code Statutory Law? 164
   - c) Major Content of the German Corporate Governance Code 164
   - d) Level of Acceptance of the German Corporate Governance Code 166
8. Impact of the Sarbanes-Oxley Act (SOA) on German Corporate Governance 166

VI. Financial System 167
1. The Registered Share Capital/The Principle of Capital Maintenance 167
2. Appropriation of Profits 169
   - a) Overview 169
   - b) Creation of Reserves 169
   - c) Appropriation of the Balance Sheet Profit 170
   - d) Distribution of Profits 170
   - e) Claim to the Profit 170
3. Equity Financing 171
   - a) Forms of Capital Increase 171
   - b) Capital Increase against Contributions 171
     - aa) Overview 171
     - bb) Resolution on the Capital Increase 171
       - aaa) General Requirements 171
       - bbb) Resolution on the Capital Increase 172
     - cc) Contributions in Kind 173
     - dd) Subscription Right 175
       - aaa) The Subscription Right 175
       - bbb) Exclusion of Subscription Rights 175
       - ccc) *De facto* Exclusion of Subscription Rights 177
       - ddd) Indirect Subscription Right 177
     - ee) Defects relating to the Adoption of the Resolution on the Capital Increase 177
     - ff) Subscription 177
     - gg) Application and Registration of the Resolution and the Implementation of the Capital Increase 178
   - c) Contingent Capital Increase 179
     - aa) General Requirements 179
     - bb) Resolution on the Contingent Capital Increase 179
     - cc) Subscription Rights 180
     - dd) Effectiveness of the Contingent Capital Increase ... 180
     - ee) Application, Registration and Announcement of the Issue of Shares 181
   - d) Authorized Capital 181

		aa) General Requirements	181
		bb) Authorization of the Management Board	182
		cc) Contents and Limits of the Authorization	182
		dd) Exclusion of Subscription Rights	183
		ee) Implementation of the Capital Increase by the Management Board	184
		ff) Subscription, Payment of the Contribution and Registration of the Implementation of the Capital Increase	185
	e)	Capital Increase from Company Resources	185
		aa) Overview	185
		bb) Resolution on the Capital Increase	185
		cc) Application, Registration and Effectiveness of the Capital Increase	185
		dd) Entitlement of Shareholders to New Shares	186
4.	The Capital Reduction		186
	a)	Forms of Capital Reduction	186
	b)	Ordinary Capital Reduction	187
	c)	Simplified Capital Reduction	187
	d)	Redemption of Shares	188
5.	Debt Financing		188
	a)	Convertible Bonds and Warrant-Linked Bonds	188
		aa) Contents and Economic Significance	188
		bb) Resolution of the General Meeting and Issue of the Bonds	189
		cc) Shareholders' Subscription Rights	190
		dd) Rights arising from Convertible or Warrant-Linked Bonds	190
		ee) Securing the Conversion or Option Right	190
		ff) Special Forms	191
		aaa) Naked Warrants	191
		bbb) Stock Options	191
		gg) Conversion and Option Rights for Bonds from Other Entities	192
	b)	Dividend Bonds	192
	c)	Jouissance Rights	193
VII. Dissolution and Liquidation of the Company			193
1. Dissolution and Grounds for Dissolution			193
	a)	Expiration of a Period of Time	193
	b)	Dissolution Resolution	193
	c)	Defect of the Articles of Association	193
	d)	Insolvency	194
	e)	Deletion Due to Lack of Assets	194
2. Declaration of Nullity by a Court upon Application			194
3. Liquidation			194
	a)	Liquidators	195
	b)	Duties of the Liquidators	195
	c)	Accounting	196
	d)	Completion of Liquidation	196
	e)	Continuation of a Dissolved Company	196

VIII. Accounting	197
1. Introduction	197
2. Annual Financial Statements	197
a) Preparation of the Annual Financial Statements	197
b) Audit of the Annual Financial Statements	198
c) Formal Approval of the Annual Financial Statements	200
d) Contestation of the Annual Financial Statements	200
3. Consolidated Financial Statements	201
a) Introduction	201
b) Obligation to draw up Consolidated Financial Statements	201
c) Content, Preparation and Approval of the Consolidated Financial Statements	202
IX. Group of Companies	202
1. Purpose of the Law	202
2. Legal Form of Affiliated Enterprises	203
3. Forms of Affiliation	203
a) Overview	203
b) Majority Ownership	205
c) Control	205
d) Group of Companies	205
e) Enterprise Agreements	206
aa) Profit and Loss Transfer Agreement	206
bb) Domination Agreement	207
cc) Other Enterprise Agreements	207
f) Integration of *AGs*	207
4. Consequences of Affiliation and Control	208
a) Affiliation	208
b) Control	208
c) Groups of Companies	210
d) *GmbH* Group of Companies	210
aa) Overview	210
bb) Contract-Based *GmbH* Group of Companies	211
e) *De facto* GmbH Group	212
f) Rules on the Conflict of Laws with respect to Groups of Companies	213
X. Listed Companies	213
1. Applicable Laws	213
2. Securities Trading Act	213
a) Insider Law	214
b) *Ad Hoc* Disclosure Requirements	215
c) Disclosure of Significant Shareholdings	216
d) Information regarding Shares and the Company	219
e) Financial Reports	219
3. Securities Acquisition and Takeover Act	219
4. Stock Exchange Act	222
5. Securities Prospectus Act	222
6. Provisions of the Stock Corporation Act	222
C. Taxation of German Limited Liability Companies and Stock Corporations	**224**
I. Income Taxes	224

	1. Corporate Income Tax	224
	2. Trade Tax	225
	3. Dividend Distributions	225
II.	Other Taxes	226
	1. Value-Added Tax	226
	2. Real Estate Transfer Tax	226

Part 2: Relevant Statutes

A. Limited Liability Company Act 227

B. Stock Corporation Act 296

List of Tables

Table 1: The Formation of a *GmbH*	15
Table 2: Important (Minority) Shareholder Rights of a *GmbH*	33
Table 3: The Formation of a Stock Corporation	84
Table 4: Important (Minority) Shareholder Rights on a *AG*	158
Table 5: Forms of Affiliation	204
Appendix 1: Comparison between the Legal Forms of an *AG* and a *GmbH*	583
Appendix 2: Glossary	595

Table of Abbreviations

	German	English
AG	Aktiengesellschaft	Stock corporation
ARUG	Gesetz zur Umsetzung der Aktionärsrechterichtlinie	Shareholders' Rights Act
BaFin	Bundesanstalt für Finanzdienstleistungsaufsicht	Federal Financial Supervisory Authority
BayObLG	Bayerisches Oberstes Landgericht	Supreme Regional Court of Bavaria
BB	Der Betriebs-Berater	The Business Advisor (journal)
BGB	Bürgerliches Gesetzbuch	German Civil Code
BGHZ	Entscheidungen des Bundesgerichtshofs in Zivilsachen	Decisions of the Federal Supreme Court in civil matters
BörsG	Börsengesetz	Stock Exchange Act
DAX	Deutscher Aktienindex	German Stock Index
DB	Der Betrieb	The Business (journal)
DStR	Deutsches Steuerrecht	German Tax Law (journal)
GmbH	Gesellschaft mit beschränkter Haftung	Limited liability company
GmbHG	Gesetz betreffend die Gesellschaften mit beschränkter Haftung	Limited Liability Company Act
GmbHR	GmbH-Rundschau	GmbH Review (journal)
IPRspr	Die deutsche Rechtsprechung auf dem Gebiete des Internationalen Privatrechts	German Case Law concerning the Conflict of Laws (compilation of court decisions)
KG	Kommanditgesellschaft	Limited partnership
KGaA	Kommanditgesellschaft auf Aktien	Partnership limited by shares
MoMiG	Gesetz zur Modernisierung des GmbH-Rechts und zur Bekämpfung von Missbräuchen	Law on the Modernization of the Law of Limited Liability Companies and the Prevention of Misuse
NJW	Neue Juristische Wochenschrift	New Weekly Law Journal
NJW-RR	NJW-Rechtsprechungsreport Zivilrecht	NJW-Report on Case Law in Civil Matters
NZG	Neue Zeitschrift für Gesellschaftsrecht	New Journal of Company Law
OHG	Offene Handelsgesellschaft	General commercial partnership
PCAOB	–	Public Company Accounting Oversight Board

	German	English
RGZ	Entscheidungen des Reichsgerichts in Zivilsachen	Decisions of the Supreme Court of the German Reich in civil matters
SE	Societas Europaea	European company
SOA	–	Sarbanes-Oxley Act
UG	Unternehmergesellschaft	Entrepreneur company
VorstAG	Gesetz zur Angemessenheit der Vorstandsvergütung	Act on the Reasonableness of the Remuneration of the Management Board
WM	Zeitschrift für Wirtschafts- und Bankrecht	Journal of Commercial and Banking Law
WpHG	Wertpapierhandelsgesetz	Securities Trading Act
WpPG	Wertpapierprospektgesetz	Securities Prospectus Act
WpÜG	Wertpapiererwerbs- und Übernahmegesetz	Securities Acquisition and Takeover Act
ZIP	Zeitschrift für Wirtschaftsrecht	Journal of Commercial Law

Part 1: Introduction to Limited Liability Company Law and Stock Corporation Law

A. The Limited Liability Company

I. Introduction

1. The Significance of Limited Liability Companies in the German Business World

The Limited Liability Company (*Gesellschaft mit beschränkter Haftung – GmbH*) is the most widespread form of corporation in Germany and can be set up for any legally permissible purpose[1], e.g., for economic, non-economic, social, sporting, cultural, charitable, political and religious purposes. The *GmbH* can also be a suitable form of organization for certain freelance professionals such as tax consultants, business auditors, lawyers or patent attorneys. Most of the *GmbHs* engage in the fields of production, trade, and services. Public authorities use *GmbHs* to operate public transport companies, housing construction enterprises or other public utilities.

Due to the far-reaching autonomy afforded to its shareholders, as well as its flexibility, the *GmbH* is a widespread legal form for small and medium-sized companies. Another reason for the *GmbH's* popularity is the low requirement established for the minimum registered share capital (*Stammkapital*), which must generally be at least EUR 25,000.[2] Many entrepreneurs choose to organize their business under the legal form of a *GmbH* because they consider it a great advantage that liability is limited to the company's assets.

2. Structure and Corporate Bodies of the *GmbH*

The *GmbH* is a **legal entity** in which, in general, only the assets of the company are available to satisfy its liabilities to creditors. It has a registered share capital that is split into shares (*Geschäftsanteile*).

The *GmbH* is a **corporation**. Under German law, the basic form of a corporation is an association under civil law (*Verein*). The general provisions of the Civil Code (*Bürgerliches Gesetzbuch – BGB*) concerning unincorporated associations[3] apply mutatis mutandis to the *GmbH,* unless the Limited Liability Company Act contains special provisions.

The corporate bodies of the *GmbH* are the shareholders, who regularly adopt resolutions at the shareholder meeting (*Gesellschafterversammlung*), the managing directors (*Geschäftsführer*), and, if either exist, the supervisory board (*Aufsichtsrat*)

---

[1] Sec. 1 of the Limited Liability Company Act.
[2] Sec. 5a of the Limited Liability Company Act now also provides for the formation of limited liability companies with a registered share capital of less than EUR 25,000 – the so called "Entrepreneur Company" (*Unternehmergesellschaft – UG*). For details *cf.* A.II.4.
[3] Sec. 21 et seq. of the Civil Code.

and the advisory board (*Beirat*). The shareholder meeting is the highest corporate body for determining the objectives and purpose of the company. The managing directors carry on the management and representation of the company in legal relations. They are obliged to follow instructions issued by the shareholder meeting. If a supervisory board is in existence, it is entitled to perform certain monitoring functions.

II. Formation

1. Steps of Formation

a) Overview

GmbHs come into existence either through **formation** (*Gründung*) or through **conversion** of legal entities of another legal form into a *GmbH* (*Umwandlung*).

The vast majority of *GmbHs* come into existence through formation. *GmbHs* can be formed for any legally permissible purpose by one or more persons.[4] The formation process of the *GmbH* begins with the execution of the articles of association (*Gesellschaftsvertrag*). Upon the execution of the articles of association by the shareholders, the company is established. It now exists as a so-called "**pre-registered company**" or "**pre-GmbH**" (*Vorgesellschaft or Vor-GmbH*). As such, it has only limited legal capacity. The shareholders are liable for the debts of the company to the extent that they have consented to the conduct of business prior to registration.[5] Such liability is a liability vis-à-vis the company. The company achieves legal capacity **upon registration** in the commercial register (*Handelsregister*) and thereby becomes a *GmbH*.[6]

The **articles of association** (*Gesellschaftsvertrag*) must be notarized and contain:
- the name (*Firma*) and registered office (*Satzungssitz*) of the company;[7]
- the object of the company (*Gegenstand des Unternehmens*);[8]
- the amount of the registered share capital (*Stammkapital*);[9] and
- the number and nominal amounts of the shares to which each of the shareholders has subscribed for (*Stammeinlage*) in the company's registered share capital.[10]

The participation acquired through the subscription to a part of the registered share capital is described by the term **"share"** (*Geschäftsanteil*). In general, the registered share capital of a *GmbH* must amount to at least EUR 25,000.[11] If the company's registered share capital is below EUR 25,000, special provisions apply with regard to formation and appropriation of profits. Furthermore, the company name in this case must include the designation "*Unternehmergesellschaft (haftungsbeschränkt)*" or "*UG (haftungsbeschränkt)*" instead of "*GmbH*".[12]

Each shareholder may subscribe to more than one share, including at the time of the formation of the company.[13] The nominal amounts of the individual shares

---

[4] Sec. 1 of the Limited Liability Company Act.
[5] Decision of the Federal Supreme Court, published in BGHZ, vol. 134, pp. 333 et seq.
[6] Sec. 11 of the Limited Liability Company Act.
[7] Sec. 3 para. 1 no. 1 of the Limited Liability Company Act.
[8] Sec. 3 para. 1 no. 2 of the Limited Liability Company Act.
[9] Sec. 3 para. 1 no. 3 of the Limited Liability Company Act.
[10] Sec. 3 para. 1 no. 4 of the Limited Liability Company Act.
[11] Sec. 5 para. 1 of the Limited Liability Company Act.
[12] Sec. 5 para. 1 and sec. 5a para. 1 of the Limited Liability Company Act. *Cf.* A.II.4 for more details on the Entrepreneur Company.
[13] Sec. 5 para. 2 of the Limited Liability Company Act.

may differ from each other. There are no restrictions on the individual nominal amount, such as a minimum amount, or such amount's divisibility, except that it must be an even euro amount. The sum of the nominal amount of the shares must equal the registered share capital.[14] The sum of the nominal amounts of the shares held by the individual shareholders represents the extent of their respective participation in the company.

On the basis of the documents submitted, the register court has to examine whether the company has been properly formed and has applied for registration.[15] If these prerequisites are not fulfilled, the court will reject the registration.[16] Otherwise, the company will be registered in the commercial register (*Handelsregister*); by virtue of such registration the company obtains legal capacity and becomes a *GmbH*.[17]

b) Articles of Association

aa) Execution. With the execution of the articles of association, the actual formation process begins. The articles of association need to be notarized.[18] The notarization generally has to be carried out by a German notary; notarization by German consulates abroad is also possible.[19] It is disputed whether notarization by a foreign notary is sufficient. If at all, this requires that the notarization corresponds to a notarization in Germany in terms of the professional legal education and standing of the notary and the notarization procedure. These requirements are fairly stringent. Since German register courts are very reluctant to accept foreign notarizations of formation documents, in practice, the formation documents are usually notarized by German notaries.

The articles of association have to be signed by all shareholders.[20] The declarations of the shareholders can also be issued in front of different notaries. Declarations by proxy are possible, provided there is a power of attorney that was drawn up or certified by a notary.[21] If the power of attorney is certified by a foreign notary, the register courts require that the power of attorney is apostilled or, if the Hague Convention Abolishing the Requirement of Legalization for Foreign Public Documents does not apply, legalized by a German consulate.

With the execution of the articles of association, the **pre-*GmbH*** comes into existence. It corresponds to the future *GmbH*, which only comes into existence upon registration in the commercial register.[22] Upon such registration, any rights and obligations created by the *pre-GmbH* transfer automatically to the *GmbH*.

bb) Shareholders. A *GmbH* can be established by one or more shareholders. Legal entities and partnerships can also become shareholders of a *GmbH* or a pre-*GmbH*.

As far as minors are concerned, the consent of their legal representative is required.[23] If the *GmbH's* purpose is directed toward the operation of a for-profit

---

[14] Sec. 5 para. 3 of the Limited Liability Company Act.
[15] Sec. 9c para. 1 of the Limited Liability Company Act.
[16] Sec. 9c para. 1 of the Limited Liability Company Act.
[17] Sec. 11 of the Limited Liability Company Act.
[18] Sec. 2 para. 1 of the Limited Liability Company Act.
[19] Sec. 10 para. 1 no. 1 of the Act on Consular Officials, Their Tasks and Competencies.
[20] Sec. 2 para. 1 sentence 2 of the Limited Liability Company Act.
[21] Sec. 2 para. 2 of the Limited Liability Company Act.
[22] Sec. 11 para. 1 of the Limited Liability Company Act.
[23] *Cf.* sec. 105 et. seq. of the Civil Code.

business, in addition, the approval of the family court (*Familiengericht*) is required.[24]

cc) Contents. Mandatory contents of the articles of association are the name (even imaginative names) and registered office (*Satzungssitz*) of the company, the object of the company, the amount of the registered share capital and the number and nominal amounts of the shares (*Geschäftsanteile*) to which each of the shareholders subscribes.[25] The company name needs to contain the designation *"Gesellschaft mit beschränkter Haftung"* or a generally comprehensible abbreviation of this designation, such as the abbreviation *"GmbH"*.[26] If the company exclusively and directly pursues purposes that are tax-privileged according to sec. 51 to sec. 68 of the General Tax Code (*Abgabenordnung*), it may also use the abbreviated designation *"gGmbH"*.[27] Any provisions that limit the duration of the company or impose special obligations on the shareholders also need to be included in the articles of association.[28]

Optional contents of the articles of association are, for example, agreements regarding contributions in kind,[29] restrictions on the transferability of shares,[30] the establishment of duties to render additional contributions[31] and the redemption of shares.[32] In contrast to the Stock Corporation Act, the Limited Liability Company Act largely contains provisions which can be opted out of or modified. This is also why the articles of association of *GmbHs* regularly go beyond the minimum information legally required. Usually, they include provisions concerning the managing directors,[33] the assignment of responsibilities to the managing directors and to the shareholder meeting,[34] the shareholder meeting in general and the procedure it uses to adopt resolutions,[35] the appropriation of profits,[36] the supervisory board or advisory board[37] and the withdrawal or expulsion of shareholders.

All of these (mandatory and optional) provisions have a **corporate character** and are genuine elements of the articles of association which can only be amended by an amendment of the articles of association. Such genuine elements have to be distinguished from agreements between shareholders that merely fall under the law of obligations. Such agreements can either be incorporated into the articles of association or be the subject of a **separate shareholder agreement** under the law of obligations. This applies, for example, to agreements binding a party to exercise its voting rights in a prescribed manner. The advantage of such shareholder agreements is that they do not need to be made public because they do not need to be filed with the commercial register.

---

[24] Sec. 1643, 1822 no. 3 of the Civil Code.
[25] Sec. 3 para. 1 of the Limited Liability Company Act.
[26] Sec. 4 sentence 1 of the Limited Liability Company Act.
[27] Sec. 4 sentence 2 of the Limited Liability Company Act.
[28] Sec. 3 para. 2 of the Limited Liability Company Act.
[29] Sec. 5 para. 4 of the Limited Liability Company Act.
[30] Sec. 15 para. 5 of the Limited Liability Company Act.
[31] Sec. 26 of the Limited Liability Company Act.
[32] Sec. 34 para. 1 of the Limited Liability Company Act.
[33] Sec. 6 para. 3 of the Limited Liability Company Act.
[34] Sec. 37, 45 of the Limited Liability Company Act.
[35] Sec. 47 of the Limited Liability Company Act.
[36] Sec. 29 of the Limited Liability Company Act.
[37] Sec. 52 of the Limited Liability Company Act.

c) Appointment of Managing Directors

The next step in the formation process is the appointment of the company's initial managing directors (*Geschäftsführer*), if they have not already been appointed in the articles of association (see below).

d) The Raising of Capital (Cash Formation/Formation through Contributions in Kind)

According to statutory law, a certain minimum amount of the registered share capital must be raised before the company can apply for registration in the commercial register.

aa) Cash Formation. To the extent that contributions are to be rendered in cash, at least one-fourth of the respective cash amount must be paid in on each share.[38]

In addition, the total amount of cash contributed and the nominal amounts of the shares on which contributions in kind are to be rendered taken together must add up to at least half of the minimum registered share capital, i.e., EUR 12,500.[39] A *GmbH* can therefore be formed with as little as EUR 6,250 in cash provided additional capital of EUR 6,250 is raised in the form of contributions in kind.

Cash contributions must be made in such a way that they are **at the free disposal of the managing directors**.[40] Apart from handing over physical currency, the unconditional wiring and crediting of funds to an account of the pre-registered company or to an escrow account of one of the managing directors or of a third party is sufficient. On the other hand, a set-off against a debt that the company owes a founding shareholder does not constitute effective payment, unless the shareholder's respective claim arose out of an acquisition of assets (*Sachübernahme*) by the company from the shareholder in accordance with the provisions governing contributions in kind (see below). Neither does the payment of a debt that the company owes a third party, unless the company has instructed the shareholder to make the payment to the third party, and the third party claim is mature and liquid and has value that is not impaired.[41]

The money paid must be available, in terms of value, at the time the company is registered. Thus, there is no general prohibition against spending contributed cash prior to registration of the company, as long as the asset acquired with the cash is still available, in terms of value, at the time of registration. For example, the managing directors may acquire goods for a price equal to the fair value of those goods at the time of registration.

bb) Formation through Contributions in Kind. The capital allocated to a share may be raised not only in cash but also through a transfer of other assets. The latter constitutes a **contribution in kind** (*Sacheinlage*). In a **formation through contributions in kind** (*Sachgründung*), the capital relating to at least one share is contributed in kind. Such formation is subject to special provisions.

A shareholder who, according to the articles of association, has to render a cash contribution may enter into an agreement with the company whereby the company acquires certain assets from him and credits the company's claim against the shareholder's obligation to render his cash contribution. Such an **acquisition**

---

[38] Sec. 7 para. 2 sentence 1 of the Limited Liability Company Act.
[39] Sec. 7 para. 2 sentence 2 of the Limited Liability Company Act. Different amounts apply with respect to Entrepreneur Companies.
[40] Sec. 8 para. 2 of the Limited Liability Company Act.
[41] Decision of the Federal Supreme Court, published in NJW 1986, pp. 989 et seq.

of assets (*Sachübernahme*) is permitted as long as the provisions on contributions in kind, which also apply to this arrangement, are observed.[42] If an agreement of the kind previously mentioned exists but is not openly acknowledged, the respective cash contribution may be deemed a **hidden contribution in kind** (*verdeckte Sacheinlage*).[43]

All items of property that can effectively be transferred to the company and that have an ascertainable value can be used as contributions in kind.[44] This includes, for instance, real estate, goods, securities and intellectual property rights. Claims of shareholders against third parties can also be contributed to the company if they are assignable. Even claims of shareholders against the company itself can be contributed if the claims are due, liquid and fully recoverable. Shares in other companies can also be contributed.

For reasons of **creditor protection**, it needs to be ensured that the registered share capital is raised. It is therefore of particular importance that each contribution in kind that is rendered fully corresponds to the value of the respective share. Various special legal regulations ensure that the contribution requirements are met:

- The object of the contribution in kind and the nominal amount of the share to which the contribution in kind relates need to be stipulated in the articles of association.[45]
- The shareholders have to prepare a **report on the formation through contributions in kind** (*Sachgründungsbericht*)[46]. Such report must set forth all information which is of importance for the valuation of the contribution in kind. If an enterprise is contributed, the annual earnings for the last two fiscal years must be stated. The report on formation through contributions in kind needs to be signed by all persons who are shareholders at the time the company is registered.
- Contributions in kind need to be made to the company, prior to the application for registration in the commercial register, in such a way that they are at the free disposal of the managing directors.[47] Further requirements exist with respect to the application with the commercial register (see below). If the fair value of the assets contributed falls short of the amount of registered share capital allocated to them, the contributing shareholder is liable to the company to pay the difference in cash (*Differenzhaftung*).[48]

e) Application with the Commercial Register

aa) General Requirements. After the minimum contributions have been made, the **managing directors can apply for registration** of the company with the commercial register. The following items need to be attached to the application:[49]

- the articles of association and, if the shareholders have provided their signature by proxy, their powers of attorney in original form or as certified copies;

---

[42] Sec. 19 para. 2 sentence 2 of the Limited Liability Company Act.
[43] *Cf.* A.II.6.
[44] Sec. 27 para. 2 of the Stock Corporation Act.
[45] Sec. 5 para. 4 sentence 1 of the Limited Liability Company Act.
[46] Sec. 5 para. 4 sentence 2 of the Limited Liability Company Act.
[47] Sec. 7 para. 3 of the Limited Liability Company Act.
[48] Sec. 9 of the Limited Liability Company Act.
[49] Sec. 8 of the Limited Liability Company Act.

II. Formation

- the documents evidencing the appointment of the managing directors (for example, the minutes of the shareholder meeting in which the managing directors were appointed); and
- a list of shareholders, signed by the newly appointed managing directors, showing the surname, first name, date of birth and place of residence of the shareholders, and the serial numbers and nominal amounts of the shares subscribed to by each shareholder.

The **application for registration** of the company must be made by all managing directors[50] and needs to be notarized.[51] It will then be submitted by the notary to the commercial register electronically.[52] The application for registration needs to contain:

- a confirmation of the managing directors that the minimum payments towards the cash contributions have been made, that the contributions in kind have been rendered and that all contributions are at their free disposal;[53]
- a confirmation of the managing directors that there are no circumstances barring their appointment and that they were notified of their unlimited duty to provide information to the court;[54]
- a business address of the company in Germany;[55] and
- the specification of the power of representation of the managing directors[56] (for example whether they are entitled to represent the company alone or only together with another managing director or a procuration officer).

bb) Special Requirements in Case of Contributions in Kind. If contributions in kind are made, the application has to include, in addition to the documents mentioned above, documents evidencing that the value of the contributions in kind reaches the nominal amounts of the shares for which they are made. The nature of such documentation depends on the type of contribution in kind. It may be in the form of stock exchange lists, price lists, receipts, recent purchase agreements, etc. In the case of a contribution of a business, as a rule, the submission of an audited contribution balance sheet and/or an expert valuation is required. An expert valuation may also be appropriate in the case of contributions of intellectual property or land.

cc) Liability for False Information. If a managing director, a shareholder or other persons (such as valuation experts or tax advisors) provide **false information** during the registration proceedings or otherwise in connection with the formation of the company and for the purpose of setting up the company, all managing directors and shareholders are jointly and severally liable to the company for any damages resulting from such false information, so-called **founding liability** (*Gründungshaftung*).[57]

Examples of information that can lead to founding liability are the value of contributions in kind, whether or not contributions have in fact been rendered, the managing directors' free disposal of the contributions, as well as a person's ability to serve as managing director.

---

[50] Sec. 78 of the Limited Liability Company Act.
[51] Sec. 12 para. 1 of the Commercial Code.
[52] Sec. 8 para. 5 of the Limited Liability Company Act, sec. 12 para. 2 of the Commercial Code.
[53] Sec. 8 para. 2 of the Limited Liability Company Act.
[54] Sec. 8 para. 3 of the Limited Liability Company Act.
[55] Sec. 8 para. 4 no. 1 of the Limited Liability Company Act.
[56] Sec. 8 para. 4 no. 2 of the Limited Liability Company Act.
[57] Sec. 9a para. 1 of the Limited Liability Company Act.

Managing directors and shareholders are not liable to the extent they neither knew nor should have known the underlying facts.[58] If shareholders or managing directors subsequently become aware of false information, they have a duty to correct it.

In the case of founding liability, the company must be put in the position it would be in had the information provided been correct. Damages may include the value of the minimum cash contributions and of contributions in kind that were not fully rendered at the time of registration. In addition to such civil liability, there may also be criminal liability.[59]

The company itself is entitled to claim the above-mentioned damages; however, these damage claims can only be asserted if there has been a correspondent shareholders' resolution.[60] If creditors have suffered damages themselves in connection with the formation of a company, they can assert damage claims in tort, but only if the requirements for such liability are fulfilled.[61]

A waiver or settlement of damage claims is invalid to the extent that the compensation for such damage is required to satisfy the creditors.[62] This does not apply if (i) the party obligated to pay compensation is insolvent and settles with its creditors in order to avert insolvency proceedings, or (ii) the obligation to pay compensation is governed by an insolvency plan concerning the company.[63] To a certain extent, this removes the damage claims from the company's control.

f) Examination by the Register Court

The register court examines whether the company is set up properly and has properly applied for registration.[64] The court reviews compliance with the **formal registration requirements** (e.g., the notarization of the articles of association) as well as **compliance with substantive law**.

In the latter case, the court will review whether the **articles of association** contain the information required by statutory law and whether the individual provisions comply with legal requirements. However, only certain severe defects will prevent the register court from registering the company, such as, in particular, defects of mandatory provisions of the articles of association or violations of legal provisions which are in the public interest.[65] For **cash formations**, documentation of payment as well as account statements will be examined. In the event of **contributions in kind**, the register court will also review whether the contribution was substantially overvalued.[66]

The register judge can carry out the necessary investigations and collect suitable evidence *ex officio*. For example, the judge can appoint independent experts to examine whether the contribution has been properly rendered. If the registration

---

[58] Sec. 9a para. 3 of the Limited Liability Company Act.
[59] Sec. 82 para. 1 of the Limited Liability Company Act.
[60] Sec. 46 no. 8 of the Limited Liability Company Act.
[61] Sec. 823 para. 2 of the Civil Code in connection with sec. 82 para. 1 of the Limited Liability Company Act; sec. 826 of the Civil Code.
[62] Sec. 9b para. 1 sentence 1 of the Limited Liability Company Act.
[63] Sec. 9b para. 1 sentence 2 of the Limited Liability Company Act.
[64] Sec. 9c para. 1 of the Limited Liability Company Act.
[65] Sec. 9c para. 2 of the Limited Liability Company Act.
[66] Sec. 9c para. 1 of the Limited Liability Company Act.

requirements are not fulfilled, the court will reject the registration.[67] An appeal and a further appeal can be lodged against such decision.[68]

If the company has not been duly established and filed for registration, the register court must **refuse registration**.[69] In practice, the register court issues an **interim court order** (*Zwischenverfügung*), thereby giving the opportunity to correct mistakes. If the judge registers the company, even though formal registration requirements have not been fulfilled, the company comes into existence but may be nullified by court action at a later stage.

g) Registration

As a result of the company's registration in the commercial register, the pre-*GmbH* is transformed into a legal entity by operation of law and gains full **legal capacity**.[70] The company's name, registered office, the company's object, the amount of the registered share capital, the date of execution of the articles of association and the identity and powers of representation of the managing directors have to be registered in the commercial register.[71] The registration of a domestic business address is also obligatory and in particular important if a company has its place of effective management (*Verwaltungssitz*) outside Germany, which is generally allowable since 2008.

If the articles of association contain provisions regarding the duration of the company or the creation of authorized shares, such provisions must be registered as well.[72] The **registration is published** in an electronic information and communication system designated by the German federal states.[73] At present, the **Company Register** (*Unternehmensregister*) serves this function.[74] The filed documents are publicly available.

Upon registration of the company in the commercial register, the act of formation comes to a close.

Once the company is **registered in the commercial register** as a *GmbH*, most defects that may have occurred during the formation process no longer affect the company's existence. Only the occurrence of certain severe defects within the articles of association, such as missing provisions regarding the amount of the registered share capital or the company's object, enables any shareholder, managing director or supervisory board member to initiate a court **action for the declaration of nullity** (*Nichtigkeitsklage*).[75] The register court may also decide to delete a company *ex officio* in such cases.[76]

2. Nominee Formation

A *GmbH* may also be established by one or more trustees in a so-called **nominee formation**. In this event, one or more nominees may establish a *GmbH* for the

---

[67] Sec. 9c para. 1 of the Limited Liability Company Act.
[68] Sec. 58, 70 of the Act on Procedure in Family Matters and Matters of Non-Contentious Jurisdiction.
[69] Sec. 9c para. 1 of the Limited Liability Company Act.
[70] Sec. 11 para. 1 of the Limited Liability Company Act.
[71] Sec. 10 para. 1 of the Limited Liability Company Act.
[72] Sec. 10 para. 2 sentence 1 of the Limited Liability Company Act.
[73] Sec. 10 of the Commercial Code.
[74] www.unternehmensregister.de (also accessible in English).
[75] Sec. 75 of the Limited Liability Company Act.
[76] Sec. 397 of the Act on Procedure in Family Matters and Matters of Non-Contentious Jurisdiction.

trustor on the basis of a trust agreement. Upon registration of the company, the trustee becomes a shareholder with all rights and duties. The trustor does not, on the other hand, acquire any membership rights at this stage. However, under the trust agreement, the trustee will generally be obliged to assign the shares to the trustor. A trust agreement which imposes such duty on the trustee has to be notarized.[77] Irrespective of the above, any founding liability will apply to both the trustor and the trustee.[78] The same holds true for a number of other duties.[79]

3. Simplified Formation Proceedings

A *GmbH* may be **formed in simplified proceedings** if the following conditions are met:[80]
- there are no more than three shareholders and only one managing director;
- the deed of formation conforms to a template which is attached to the Limited Liability Company Act; and
- the articles of association conform to a template which is attached to the Limited Liability Company Act. In particular, contributions to shares have to be made in cash and cannot be made in kind.

A deed of formation modeled on the template will at the same time also embody the articles of association and the list of shareholders.

The simplified formation proceedings yield few benefits in practice. While there is no need to draft customized articles of association, the deed of formation must still be notarized. Notarization and filing fees may be reduced. The disadvantage is that the founders have to use a standard formation protocol provided in the Limited Liability Company Act which may not be amended or supplemented. The protocol only allows for one managing director and does not contain any provisions as to the relationship between the shareholders or between the different bodies of the company. Special issues cannot be addressed, protective provisions cannot be implemented. Therefore, in practice, the use of customized articles of association instead of the simplified formation procedure is often advisable.

4. Formation of an Entrepreneur Company *(UG)*

Until November 2008, the registered share capital of a *GmbH* could not fall short of EUR 25,000. Under the revised Limited Liability Company Act, *GmbHs* can now be founded with a registered share capital of as little as EUR 1. Such companies are, however, subject to special provisions. In particular, their company name must include the designation "Entrepreneur Company (with limited liability)", i.e. *"Unternehmergesellschaft (haftungsbeschränkt)"* or *"UG (haftungsbeschränkt)"*[81]. The founders of these companies may only apply for registration with the commercial register when the company's registered share capital has been contributed in

---

[77] Sec. 15 para. 4 of the Limited Liability Company Act.
[78] Sec. 9a para. 4 of the Limited Liability Company Act; also *cf.* A.II.1.e.cc.
[79] For contingent liability pursuant to sec. 24 of the Limited Liability Company Act, for the claim to non-refundable repayments pursuant to sec. 30, 31 of the Limited Liability Company Act and for the prohibition against waiving or deferring original contributions pursuant to sec. 19 para. 2 of the Limited Liability Company Act.
[80] Sec. 2 para. 1a of the Limited Liability Company Act.
[81] Sec. 5a para. 1 of the Limited Liability Company Act.

full.[82] Contributions in kind are not allowed.[83] In the balance sheet of the annual financial statements, a statutory reserve needs to be created to which one-fourth of the annual profits, reduced by losses from the previous year, needs to be contributed.[84] Furthermore, such reserve may be used for special purposes only. The reserve may, in particular, be used to increase the registered share capital to EUR 25,000 or more.

The *UG* seems to have established itself as an attractive alternative to the *GmbH* for small businesses: As of November 2014, more than 100,000 *UGs* have been registered in the German commercial register.

5. Shelf Companies

The time-consuming registration procedure as well as liability risks related to the commencement of business operations prior to the company's registration can be avoided by using already existing companies. One possibility is to use so-called **shelf companies** or **shells**. Their name derives from the fact that these companies are formed by a professional service provider and initially assume no business operations but merely exist "on the shelf". The use of already existing, but currently dormant companies is also possible, but bears significantly higher liability risks due to the longer "pre-existence" of the companies before activation. However, both procedures are legally permissible.[85]

The Federal Supreme Court has held that from an economic point of view the activation of a (shelf or dormant) company for business is identical to the formation of a company. Therefore, the provisions of the Limited Liability Company Act concerning the raising of the registered share capital apply.[86] As a practical consequence, the **managing directors** must disclose the **"economic re-establishment"** (*wirtschaftliche Neugründung*) **to the register court**[87] and need to **affirm with the register court** that the relevant contributions have been made[88] and are still at their free disposal.[89] If the economic re-establishment is not disclosed to the register court, the shareholders of the *GmbH* are **liable for any deficiency of the registered share capital** (*Unterbilanzhaftung*) at the time of the economic re-establishment. This means that they are obligated vis-à-vis the company to compensate all losses that occurred up to the economic re-establishment and to increase the equity of the company to the level of the registered share capital.

6. Hidden Contributions in Kind

The shareholders may raise capital through **contributions in kind** (*Sacheinlagen*) and the **acquisition of assets** (*Sachübernahme*). Special provisions are meant to ensure that the true value of the assets contributed corresponds to the nominal

---

[82] Sec. 5a para. 2 sentence 1 of the Limited Liability Company Act.
[83] Sec. 5a para. 2 sentence 2 of the Limited Liability Company Act.
[84] Sec. 5a para. 3 sentence 1 of the Limited Liability Company Act.
[85] Decision of the Federal Supreme Court, published in BGHZ, vol. 117, pp. 323 et seq.
[86] Decisions of the Federal Supreme Court, published in BGHZ, vol. 153, pp. 158 et seq. and in ZIP 2011, p. 1761 recital 9.
[87] Decision of the Federal Supreme Court, published in BGHZ vol. 192, pp. 341 et seq. and in NJW pp. 2012, 1875 et seq.
[88] Sec. 8 para. 2 of the Limited Liability Company Act.
[89] Decision of the Federal Supreme Court, published in ZIP 2011, p. 1761 recital 9.

value of the respective portions of the registered share capital.[90] Shareholders who undertake to render cash contributions sometimes enter into arrangements with the *GmbH* which, in economic terms, lead to the equivalent of a contribution in kind without observing the formalities concerning contributions in kind. Such arrangements are called **hidden contributions in kind** (*verdeckte Sacheinlagen*).[91]

The Federal Supreme Court presumes a hidden contribution in kind if it finds a **substantive and temporal connection** between the contribution of cash to the company and the arrangement leading to the economic effect of a contribution in kind.[92] A substantive connection is indicated by an equal amount of the cash contribution and the consideration for the transfer of assets or the absence of plausible reasons for the combination of cash contribution and asset transfer other than to perform a hidden contribution in kind. A temporal connection is usually not presumed for transactions that are carried out at least one year after the registration of the company. The Federal Supreme Court even rejected a temporal connection in a case where only eight months had passed.[93] However, if there is a substantive and temporal connection, no further subjective requirements for a hidden contribution in kind are necessary. In particular, it is of no significance whether or not the shareholder intended to circumvent the provisions on contributions in kind.

The law disfavors hidden contributions in kind because the proper procedure for making contributions in kind is circumvented and there is a risk that the value of the contributed assets does not reach the nominal value of the respective share capital. Although the underlying agreements concerning the transfer of the assets are valid and binding,[94] the shareholder is generally not released from his obligation to render the cash contribution.[95] Additionally, the register court may refuse to register the company. If, however, the register court registers the company,[96] the company's claim against the shareholder to render the cash contribution is reduced by the fair value of the assets that have actually been contributed.[97] The value of the assets is determined as of the time of their transfer to the company but in no event as of an earlier date than that of the company's application for registration.[98] The shareholder remains liable to the company for any difference between the value of the assets and the nominal amount of the committed cash contribution (*Differenzhaftung*).

If a managing director incorrectly declares in the company's application for registration that the claim for cash contribution has been satisfied, he may be subject to criminal sanctions. Furthermore, all managing directors and shareholders may be liable to the company for damages.[99]

A **situation similar to a hidden contribution in kind** arises where a shareholder renders the stipulated cash contribution and the company subsequently repays him a corresponding amount. This typically takes place in connection with a loan by the company to the shareholder. In such case, the money is **paid**

---

[90] *Cf.* A.II.1.d.bb.
[91] Sec. 19 para. 4 sentence 1 of the Limited Liability Company Act.
[92] Decisions of the Federal Supreme Court, published in BGHZ, vol. 153, pp. 107 et seq. and in BGHZ, vol. 175, pp. 265 et seq.
[93] Decision of the Federal Supreme Court, published in BGHZ, vol. 152, pp. 37, 45.
[94] Sec. 19 para. 4 sentence 2 of the Limited Liability Company Act.
[95] Sec. 19 para. 4 sentence 1 of the Limited Liability Company Act.
[96] Sec. 19 para. 4 sentence 4 of the Limited Liability Company Act.
[97] Sec. 19 para. 4 sentence 3 of the Limited Liability Company Act.
[98] Sec. 19 para. 4 sentence 3 of the Limited Liability Company Act.
[99] *Cf.* A.II.1.e.cc.

back and forth (*Hin- und Herzahlen*).[100] As a consequence, the cash contribution is not at the free disposal of the managing directors and is therefore deemed to not have been made.[101] The company thus generally retains its claim against the shareholder for payment of the cash contribution, unless the requirements for a permitted, so-called "back and forth payment" have been met. A permitted back and forth payment requires in particular that the shareholder and the company have agreed upon the repayment prior to the contribution of cash and that the company has a fully recoverable repayment claim against the shareholder that can be enforced at any time. In this case the obligation to render the cash contribution is fulfilled.[102] Additionally, the agreement regarding the back and forth payment has to be disclosed in the application to the commercial register.[103] The Federal Supreme Court has indicated that the correct disclosure to the commercial register constitutes an additional requirement for the fulfillment of the obligation to render the cash contribution.[104] The requirements for a permitted back and forth payment are of particular importance if the newly formed company is to be included in a cash-pooling system. In this context, it is of further importance that the Federal Supreme Court only acknowledges a back and forth payment if the cash pool account is either balanced or in favor of the company; if there is a negative balance (i.e. the shareholder has a claim against the company), the Federal Supreme Court assumes a hidden contribution in kind.[105]

7. Pre-Registered Company

a) Legal Nature

The pre-registered company or pre-*GmbH* comes into existence with the execution of the articles of association. The pre-*GmbH* is a *sui generis* association of persons that corresponds to the future *GmbH*. The articles of association and limited liability company law generally already apply to the pre-*GmbH*, unless the respective provisions require full legal capacity or are for other reasons not suitable before registration.[106]

b) Internal Relations

The rights and duties of the shareholders to each other (internal relations) are determined by the articles of association and the purpose of the pre-registered company, which is for the company to obtain legal capacity. Every business activity that goes beyond the purpose of forming the company therefore requires the consent of all shareholders.[107]

c) External Relations

In its external relations with third parties, the pre-*GmbH* has preliminary legal capacity. It can, for example, open bank accounts, be registered in the land register,

---

[100] Decision of the Federal Supreme Court, published in BGHZ, vol. 165, pp. 113 et seq.
[101] Sec. 7 para. 3 of the Limited Liability Company Act; also *cf.* A.II.1.d.aa.
[102] Sec. 19 para. 5 sentence 1 of the Limited Liability Company Act.
[103] Sec. 19 para. 5 sentence 2 of the Limited Liability Company Act.
[104] Decisions of the Federal Supreme Court, published in ZIP 2009, pp. 713, 715 and in GmbHR 2009, pp. 926 et seq.
[105] Decision of the Federal Supreme Court, published in GmbHR 2009, pp. 926 et seq.
[106] Decision of the Federal Supreme Court, published in BGHZ, vol. 134, pp. 333 et seq.
[107] Decision of the Federal Supreme Court, published in BGHZ, vol. 80, pp. 129, 139.

write checks, sue or be sued, become insolvent, and in any other way participate in business dealings. The pre-*GmbH* is represented by the managing directors, whose power of representation is generally limited by the purposes of achieving the formation of the company and of managing the assets contributed thus far.[108] In the event of a cash formation, the power of representation is restricted to transactions which are necessary for the company's registration. In the event of a formation through contributions in kind, the managing directors may also represent the company in acquiring the assets to be contributed by entering into agreements with the respective shareholders. The shareholders may jointly authorize the pre-*GmbH* to start business operations prior to registration. In this case, the managing directors possess unlimited power of representation.

d) Liability of the Company and the Shareholders

The pre-*GmbH* itself acquires rights and obligations and thus incurs liability on the basis of transactions lawfully entered into on behalf of the *GmbH*. The shareholders are **liable to cover all losses** (*Verlustdeckungshaftung*) of the pre-*GmbH* but such liability exists only vis-à-vis the company but not vis-à-vis third parties.[109] The liability of each shareholder is initially capped pro rata to his stake in the company. However, in the event that a shareholder is unable to pay, the other shareholders become **contingently liable** (*Ausfallhaftung*).

The pre-*GmbH*'s claim against its shareholders for coverage of losses arises **when registration in the commercial register has failed:**[110] if the application for registration is withdrawn, if the register court declines registration, if the shareholders resolve to liquidate the company or if the managing directors file for insolvency.[111] The company's creditors may seize the company's claim for coverage of losses and enforce it against the shareholders.[112]

If, following the failure of registration, the shareholders do not immediately liquidate the pre-*GmbH* but instead cause it to continue its business operations, they incur personal and unlimited liability for all debts of the pre-*GmbH* as if it was a general partnership.[113]

Upon registration of the *GmbH* in the commercial register, the rights and obligations of the pre-registered company become the rights and obligations of the *GmbH* by operation of law.[114] The pre-registered company and the registered *GmbH* become the same legal entity. The previous personal liability of shareholders to cover losses expires and the shareholders are **liable for any deficiency of the registered share capital** (*Vorbelastungshaftung*) at the time of the company's registration.[115] This means that they are obligated vis-à-vis the company to compensate all losses that occurred up to the time of registration (with the exception of formation costs) and to increase the equity of the company to the level of the registered share capital. Here, too, individual shareholders may become **contingently liable** (*Ausfallhaftung*) for the obligations of illiquid shareholders.[116]

---

[108] Decision of the Federal Supreme Court, published in BGHZ, vol. 80, pp. 129, 139.
[109] Decision of the Federal Supreme Court, published in BGHZ, vol. 134, pp. 333 et seq.
[110] Decision of the Federal Supreme Court, published in BGHZ, vol. 134, pp. 333 et seq.
[111] Decision of the Federal Supreme Court, published in NJW 2003, pp. 429, 430.
[112] Decision of the Federal Supreme Court, published in BGHZ, vol. 134, pp. 333 et seq.
[113] Decision of the Federal Supreme Court, published in NJW 2003, pp. 429, 430.
[114] Decision of the Federal Supreme Court, published in BGHZ, vol. 80, pp. 129, 137.
[115] Decisions of the Federal Supreme Court, published in BGHZ, vol. 80, pp. 129 et seq. and in BGHZ, vol. 165, pp. 391 et seq.
[116] Decision of the Federal Supreme Court, published in BGHZ, vol. 80, pp. 129 et seq.

II. Formation

e) Liability of the Persons Acting

If actions are performed in the name of the company prior to its registration, the acting persons are personally, jointly and severally liable.[117] Acting persons in this respect are not only the managing directors of the pre-*GmbH* but also such persons who behave like managing directors without corresponding appointment. Such liability expires as soon as the company is registered and consequently assumes the rights and duties of the pre-registered company.

f) Principles regarding Defective Companies

In case of a defective formation and/or registration of a company, the register court may *ex officio* refuse the registration of the company.[118]

Special rules apply after a defective formation if the company in question is not yet registered with the commercial register but has already been **actually implemented** (*in Vollzug gesetzt*). In this case, the so-called **principles regarding defective companies** (*Grundsätze der fehlerhaften Gesellschaft*) prevent the company from being unwound with retroactive effect but allow for liquidation with effect for the future.[119] The liquidation can be initiated by any shareholder by way of simple declaration towards the remaining shareholders; a court action for the declaration of nullity (see above)[120] is not required. A company is deemed "actually implemented" if (i) contributions with regard to the subscribed share capital have been made or (ii) (preparatory) business activities have been commenced. Once the company is registered, however, most defects of the formation would no longer affect the company's existence.[121]

8. Overview: The Formation of a *GmbH*[122]

	Signing of the articles of association by the shareholders
	– Notarization required
	Shareholders
Possible shareholders	– Natural persons – Legal entities – Partnerships
Number of shareholders	– One or more shareholders
	Raising of the registered share capital
Minimum amount of registered share capital	– EUR 25,000 – EUR 1 in case of an *UG* ("Entrepreneur Company")

---

[117] Sec. 11 para. 2 of the Limited Liability Company Act.
[118] Sec. 9c para. 1 sentence 1 of the Limited Liability Company Act.
[119] Decision of the Federal Supreme Court, published in BGHZ, vol. 13, pp. 320 et seq.
[120] *Cf.* A.II.1.g.
[121] *Cf.* A.II.1.g.
[122] The overview refers to the most common creation of a *GmbH* by way of formation.

Minimum amount of a shareholder's contribution	– EUR 1
Cash contributions	– Prior to application with the commercial register, a contribution of one-fourth needs to be paid in for each share. – Altogether, at least half of the minimum registered share capital, i.e., in general EUR 12,500, must be paid in.
Contributions in kind	– Contributions in kind are permitted for formation of a regular GmbH but not in case of formation of an *UG*. – Items of property that have an ascertainable economic value can be contributed as contributions in kind. – Shareholders have to indicate the fair value of the contributions in kind in a report on formation through contributions in kind.
Managing directors	
	– The company can have one or more managing directors. – They are appointed either by means of a special shareholder resolution or in the articles of association. – Unless otherwise provided for in the articles of association, all managing directors have to act jointly to represent the company. In practice, managing directors are either granted power to represent the company alone or (more common) to represent the company together with one other managing director or a procuration officer (*Prokurist*). – Managing directors are generally not entitled to enter into transactions with themselves on their own behalf or as a representative of third parties. Full or partial relief from this prohibition may be granted by way of a shareholder resolution or in the articles of association.
Application for registration in the commercial register	
	– Registration of the *GmbH* in the commercial register needs to be applied for. – The application, which needs to be certified by a notary, is to be made by the managing directors. – The application needs to contain the articles of association, proof of appointment of the managing directors, shareholder list, report on contributions in kind, if any, and underlying agreements as well as proof of value of the contributions in kind, if any. – The managing directors have to ensure that the minimum registered share capital has been paid into the company's account and is at their free disposal.

Registration in the commercial register	
	The following information is registered in the commercial register: – name, registered office and domestic business address of the company and of any branches – name and address of a person authorized to receive declarations (if applicable) – object of the company – amount of the registered share capital – date of execution and, if applicable, amendment of the articles of association – managing directors and procuration officers (*Prokuristen*) and their respective powers of representation – provisions of the articles of association concerning the duration of the company or authorized capital (if applicable)
Legal effect of registration in the commercial register	
	– The *GmbH* comes into existence as a legal entity.

Table 1: The Formation of a *GmbH*

III. Legal Position of the Shareholders

1. Membership Rights and Membership Duties

Membership in the *GmbH* is embodied through the share. The *GmbH*, in contrast to the *AG*, exhibits some characteristics of a partnership structure. The shareholders have significant latitude to provide for rules in the articles of association that differ from the provisions of the Limited Liability Company Act. The membership rights and duties of the shareholders are correspondingly diverse.

Membership rights can be divided into administrative rights and property rights:

- **Administrative rights** include the right to demand that the shareholder meeting be convened, the right to participate in the shareholder meeting, the right to vote and the right to information.
- **Property rights** include the entitlement to share in annual profits, the right to dispose of and bequeath the share and the entitlement to share in liquidation proceeds.

The most important **membership duties** are the duty to render contributions, the fiduciary duty and the duties to secure the registered share capital. Membership duties can be expanded, restricted or excluded in the articles of association, as long as this is not in conflict with mandatory law.

Some of the membership rights and duties will be referred to in the following paragraphs, others, in particular property rights, will be described at the respective provisions below.[123]

---

[123] *Cf.* A.VIII.2.a.

2. Membership Rights

a) Distinction between Membership Rights and Special Rights

Special rights (*Sonderrechte*)[124] grant individual shareholders unique privileges as compared to the other shareholders. Therefore, in contrast to general **membership rights**, not all shareholders are equally entitled to special rights. Examples of possible special rights include: entitlement to preferred dividends, purchase of the company's goods or services at a discount, consent rights regarding the assignment of shares, rights to issue instructions to the managing directors and the right to appoint managing directors or to serve as a managing director oneself.

Special rights can be **established only in the articles of association**. In order to introduce special rights at a later stage, the articles of association need to be amended and all shareholders without special rights must give their consent. The revocation of or change in a special right requires, in addition to an amendment of the articles of association, the consent of the party who has the right.[125] As the special right pertains to membership, if the share is assigned, the special right passes over to the acquirer, provided it is not specifically tied to the person having the right.

b) Right to Information and Right of Inspection

The **managing directors** must provide every shareholder with **information** about the affairs of the company immediately upon such shareholder's request and must allow shareholders to **inspect the books and records** of the company.[126] This extensive right to information and inspection is generally unrestricted and is not limited to certain purposes. However, the right may not be misused.[127] The shareholder's right to information covers all affairs of the company, including all data essential for determining profits or for composing the tax balance sheet. The same applies to the right of inspection of every shareholder with respect to the company's books and records.

Courts held that a shareholder may only require such information which is necessary to satisfy his need for information and that he must acquire the information in the way least burdensome to the company.[128] Therefore, the more intrusive right of inspection may be avoided where the shareholder can obtain sufficient information simply by attending the shareholders meeting or asserting his right to information.

Information and inspection may be **refused by the managing directors** if there is a threat that the information will be used for purposes which are not related to the proper conduct of a shareholder, thereby causing substantial harm to the company or an affiliated company.[129] This is the case, for example, when the shareholder operates a **competing enterprise** or otherwise does not maintain the usual confidentiality. Such refusal by the managing directors requires a **resolution of the shareholder meeting**. The shareholder requesting information is not entitled to vote in the meeting. In the event that the request for information

---

[124] Sec. 35 of the Civil Code.
[125] Sec. 35 of the Civil Code.
[126] Sec. 51a para. 1 of the Limited Liability Company Act.
[127] Decisions of the Federal Supreme Court, published in BGHZ, vol. 135, pp. 48 et seq. and in BGHZ, vol. 152, pp. 339, 344 et seq.
[128] Decision of the Higher Regional Court of Jena, published in NZG 2004, p. 1156.
[129] Sec. 51a para. 2 of the Limited Liability Company Act.

is refused, the shareholder may ask a court to force the managing directors to furnish the information.[130]

The rights to information and inspection are inalienable and may not be restricted in the articles of association.[131] The rights may be exercised by proxy.

c) Shareholder Lawsuit

The term "shareholder lawsuit" is used for different scenarios:

Firstly, the term describes **claims of shareholders against co-shareholders**. A shareholder may have a claim against co-shareholders on account of them violating their fiduciary duty.[132] This right cannot be excluded by the articles of association. If harm caused to a shareholder can be remedied by paying compensation to the company, the shareholder can demand payment only to the company and not to himself. In this respect, the shareholder exercises his own rights; the shareholder does not act on behalf of the company.

Secondly, "shareholder lawsuit" can also mean **claims of the company against shareholders**. As a rule, such a shareholder lawsuit is used to assert claims for damages and reimbursement based on other shareholders' violation of their membership duties: claims regarding liability for overvaluation of contributions in kind[133] and founding liability[134] or claims in connection with the violation of non-compete provisions or the general fiduciary duty. It is, however, the company who is entitled to these claims in principle; thus, the claims are generally pursued by the managing directors, for which pursuit a shareholder resolution is a precondition.[135] Despite the in-principle competence of the company, represented by its managing directors, the shareholder lawsuit (*actio pro socio*) is usually deemed admissible. The shareholders can, for example, sue their co-shareholders without a prior shareholder resolution if the managing directors cannot be expected to pursue the claim on behalf of the company.[136]

The right of individual shareholders to file an action **against the managing directors** in connection with illegal actions or omissions by them is generally not permitted under the prevailing view. The reason is that no legal relationship exists between the shareholders and the managing directors. Though, there can be a claim against the managing directors on the basis of tort law, if the managing directors act outside of their competence and infringe membership duties.[137]

3. Membership Duties

a) Duty to Render Contributions

The essential duty of the shareholders is to render the agreed contribution. It serves the fulfillment of the articles of association, but also the protection of creditors. At the time of the formation (see above) or of a capital increase, **con-**

---

[130] Sec. 51b of the Limited Liability Company Act, sec. 132 paras. 1, 3 and 5 of the Stock Corporation Act.
[131] Sec. 51a para. 3 of the Limited Liability Company Act.
[132] Decisions of the Federal Supreme Court, published in BGHZ, vol. 65, pp. 15 et seq., in BGHZ, vol. 95, 330 et seq. and in NJW 2007, p. 917.
[133] Sec. 9 of the Limited Liability Company Act.
[134] Sec. 9a of the Limited Liability Company Act.
[135] Sec. 46 no. 8 of the Limited Liability Company Act.
[136] Decision of the Federal Supreme Court, published in NJW 1990, pp. 2627 et seq.
[137] *Cf.* decisions of the Federal Supreme Court, published in NJW 1982, pp. 1703, 1706 and in NJW 1990, pp. 2877, 2880 et seq.

tributions in kind** need to be rendered in full and **cash contributions** at least to one-fourth.[138] To the extent the contribution requirement has not been fulfilled at the time of registration in the commercial register (of the formation or the capital increase), the **company has a contribution claim** that can be entered as an asset on the balance sheet. The claim can be asserted, if necessary, before a court by the company, represented by its managing directors, or by the shareholders by way of the shareholder lawsuit (see above). Creditors of the company can seize this claim. Contribution claims of the company generally become time-barred ten years after the claim came into existence.[139]

To ensure that the registered share capital is effectively raised, the payment on the contribution must in fact go to the company, i.e., be at the free disposal of the managing directors. This is not the case, for example, if the payment is made conditionally or if the company or a controlled company grants a loan to the shareholder to finance the contribution.[140] Payment to a creditor of the company fulfills the requirement of effectively raising the registered share capital if and to the extent that the creditor's claim is mature, liquid and the value is not impaired, and the shareholder has rendered the payment upon request of the company.[141]

The **shareholders cannot be released** from the obligation to render a contribution.[142] Thus, waiver, deferment and other transactions reducing the contribution duty are not permitted. Furthermore, a shareholder may not set off claims against the company's claim for contribution unless the respective claim arose out of an acquisition of assets (*Sachübernahme*) by the company from the shareholder according to sec. 5 para. 4 of the Limited Liability Company Act.[143]

The **company**, by contrast, **can set off claims**, but only to the extent that the shareholder's claim is mature, liquid and unimpaired[144] or, exceptionally, if the company would otherwise incur harm on account of the poor economic situation of the debtor.[145]

The Limited Liability Company Act contains complicated provisions that are designed to prevent circumvention of the rules on contributions in kind.[146] A shareholder's contribution in kind releases the shareholder from the contribution obligation only if the object to be contributed and the nominal amount of the contribution are already laid down as a contribution in kind in the articles of association[147] or in the resolution on the capital increase.[148] However, the fair value of the contributed asset may be deducted from the outstanding obligation to render the contribution in cash.

Contribution claims of the company against shareholders may be assigned[149] or pledged[150] if the company receives consideration of equal value in return.

---

[138] Sec. 7 paras. 2 and 3, sec. 56a of the Limited Liability Company Act.
[139] Sec. 19 para. 6 of the Limited Liability Company Act.
[140] Concerning the requirements of a permitted payment back and forth cf. A.II.6 above.
[141] Decision of the Federal Supreme Court, published in NJW 1986, pp. 989 et seq.; cf. decision of the Federal Supreme Court, published in NZG 2011, pp. 667, 668.
[142] Sec. 19 para. 2 sentence 1 of the Limited Liability Company Act.
[143] Sec. 19 para. 2 sentence 2 of the Limited Liability Company Act.
[144] Decision of the Federal Supreme Court, published in BGHZ, vol. 125, pp. 141, 143.
[145] Decision of the Federal Supreme Court, published in BGHZ, vol. 15, pp. 52, 57 et seq.
[146] Sec. 19 para. 4 of the Limited Liability Company Act.
[147] Sec. 5 para. 4 of the Limited Liability Company Act.
[148] Sec. 56 para. 1 of the Limited Liability Company Act.
[149] Decision of the Federal Supreme Court, published in BGHZ, vol. 69, pp. 274, 282.
[150] Decision of the Federal Supreme Court, published in NJW 1992, p. 2229.

If the contribution is not rendered or not rendered on time, the shareholder has to pay **interest** until the contribution is rendered.[151] Further damages to the company are to be calculated according to the general law on damages (*Schadensersatzrecht*). As an additional possible sanction, the defaulting shareholder may forfeit his membership and contributions already made.[152] The shareholders may also resolve to dissolve the company.[153]

If these sanctions remain unsuccessful and the outstanding amount can be collected neither from the expelled shareholder nor from his predecessors in title, the relevant amounts may be raised by a sale of the share. If such sale also fails to cover the shortfall, the **remaining shareholders are liable** to the company in proportion to their shareholdings, i.e., the amounts that cannot be obtained from individual shareholders are allocated to the remaining shareholders pro rata.[154] This **contingent liability** also includes liability for any difference in value in the event that a contribution in kind is overvalued (*Differenzhaftung*),[155] liability in the event of legal or factual defects in a contribution in kind and liability for any deficiency of the registered share capital upon commencement of business prior to the registration of the company.[156] In such cases, the remaining shareholders must make up the full difference between the equity of the company and the amount of the registered share capital. Such difference may exceed the value of the contribution that was defaulted on.

b) Ancillary Duties

It is common for the **articles of association** to stipulate **ancillary duties** (*Nebenpflichten*) for the shareholders. Such duties include ancillary financial duties (e.g., the duty to grant a loan to the company) and obligations to deliver goods and services to the company. Also possible is the obligation to serve as managing director of the company. These duties must be distinguished from duties based on the law of obligations which are not stipulated in the articles of association and therefore do not pass to the acquirer of the share.

c) Duty to Render Additional Contributions

One ancillary duty that is regulated by statutory law is the optional **duty to render additional contributions** (*Nachschusspflicht*).[157] The articles of association can provide that the shareholders may resolve to call in further payments beyond the original contributions on the shares, so-called additional contributions (*Nachschüsse*).[158] Additional contributions must then be rendered in proportion to the shareholdings and[159] may be capped at a certain amount[160] or be unrestricted.[161]

---

[151] Sec. 20 of the Limited Liability Company Act.
[152] Sec. 21 para. 2 of the Limited Liability Company Act.
[153] Sec. 60 para. 1 no. 2 of the Limited Liability Company Act.
[154] Sec. 24 of the Limited Liability Company Act.
[155] Sec. 9 of the Limited Liability Company Act.
[156] *Cf.* A.II.7.d.
[157] Sec. 26 to 28 of the Limited Liability Company Act.
[158] Sec. 26 para. 1 of the Limited Liability Company Act.
[159] Sec. 26 para. 2 of the Limited Liability Company Act.
[160] Sec. 26 para. 3 of the Limited Liability Company Act.
[161] Sec. 27 of the Limited Liability Company Act.

d) Fiduciary Duty Pursuant to Corporate Law

The shareholders are subject to a **general fiduciary duty**. The shareholders have to be loyal to the company, actively promote its objectives and keep it from harm. These duties also exist, to a certain extent, in relation to co-shareholders. They are not explicitly stipulated by statutory law, but are recognized by the courts.[162] The content and scope of the fiduciary duty depends on **the structure of the company**. For example, in a company with two shareholders, such shareholders must show more consideration for each other than when there is a multitude of shareholders.

Fiduciary duties have an effect in many areas, such as the exercise of voting rights[163], restraints on competition (see below) and the exercise of the right to issue instructions in a group of companies.[164]

Fiduciary duties can comprise **duties to act**, for example to vote in a specific way, as well as duties to forebear from acting. The violation of fiduciary duties can give rise not only to damage claims, but also to claims to compel a certain act or forbearance. Also possible is the action for dissolution of the company[165] or the expulsion for good cause of the shareholder who has committed a breach of duty. If a voting right is exercised in breach of the fiduciary duty, the vote is null and void.[166] The relevant resolution may be contested.[167]

e) Non-Compete Obligations

The shareholders are, as a general rule, not prohibited from competing with the *GmbH*. The Limited Liability Company Act primarily views them as capital providers. In contrast, partners are prohibited from competing with their partnership which is oriented towards its members even more than a *GmbH*.[168]

A shareholder may, however, be subject to an obligation not to compete with the *GmbH* based on his **fiduciary duty** towards the *GmbH* if he is able to exert a dominating influence on the company by virtue of majority share ownership or special rights provided for in the articles of association.[169] A shareholder who owns all shares in a *GmbH* is, on the other hand, not restrained from competition because he could at any time grant himself an exemption from such restraint.

Shareholders who serve as managing directors are prohibited from competing with the company based on the specific **fiduciary duty of managing directors**.

The shareholders may agree on a non-compete obligation in a **contract** or in the **articles of association**. Such restraints must not contravene mandatory law and must in particular observe the limits set by antitrust law.[170] Non-compete obligations are compatible with the **Act against Restraints on Competition**[171] to the extent they are necessary to prevent the company from being undermined or even destroyed from the inside by a shareholder seeking to promote his own

---

[162] Decisions of the Federal Supreme Court, published in BGHZ, vol. 65, pp. 15, 20 et seq. and in NJW 2007, p. 917.
[163] Decision of the Federal Supreme Court, published in NJW 2010, pp. 65, 67.
[164] Decisions of the Federal Supreme Court, published in BGHZ, vol. 89, pp. 162, 166 and in BGHZ, vol. 150, pp. 61, 68.
[165] Sec. 61 of the Limited Liability Company Act.
[166] Decision of the Federal Supreme Court, published in GmbHR 1993, pp. 579, 581.
[167] Decisions of the Federal Supreme Court, published in BGHZ, vol. 103, pp. 184, 193 et seq. and in NZG 2005, pp. 551, 553.
[168] Sec. 112 para. 1 of the Commercial Code.
[169] Decision of the Federal Supreme Court, published in BGHZ, vol. 89, pp. 162, 166 et seq.
[170] Sec. 138 of the Civil Code, sec. 1 of the Act against Restraints on Competition.
[171] Sec. 1 of the Act against Restraints on Competition.

competing business.[172] Accordingly, a non-compete obligation may – from an antitrust perspective – typically only be imposed on shareholders who could exert significant influence on the management and the market behavior of the company. Furthermore, a non-compete obligation must in general remain limited to the products or services offered by the company and the geographic area in which the company is active.[173]

In the event that a shareholder violates the prohibition on competition, the general legal consequences for breaches of fiduciary duties apply (see above). The company may also demand that the transactions entered into by the shareholder be deemed to have been made for the account of the company.[174]

f) The Requirement of Equal Treatment

In contrast to stock corporation law,[175] the Limited Liability Company Act does not contain any regulation that requires equal treatment of shareholders; there is contractual freedom such that the rights and duties of individual shareholders can be structured differently. Beyond that, however, shareholders may not be treated unequally unless there is a material reason for doing so.

4. Liability of a Shareholder of a Limited Liability Company

a) Generally No Shareholder Liability

The Limited Liability Company Act treats a *GmbH* as a **corporate entity separate from its shareholders**. If the *GmbH* enters into legal transactions or takes other measures, such measures take effect only in favor or to the detriment of the *GmbH* itself. The shareholders of a *GmbH* are in principle not liable for debts of the *GmbH*. Only the company's assets are available to the creditors of the company.[176] There are only a few exemptions from this general rule.

b) Contractual Shareholder Liability

Shareholders of a limited liability company may be liable for debts or losses of the company if they undertake a respective contractual obligation towards the company's creditors or the company. This, for example, applies if the shareholder has issued a guarantee to certain creditors or a "hard" comfort letter (i.e., containing an undertaking to pay for outstanding debts) to the company. Under corporate law, an obligation of the shareholder to cover losses of the company exists if the shareholder has entered into a profit transfer agreement with the company.

c) Capital Preservation

A shareholder may be personally liable to the company for repayment of payments to him to the extent such payments cause the equity of the company to **fall short of the registered share capital**.[177] The term "payment" encompasses all benefits granted to a shareholder without adequate compensation. Therefore, the

---

[172] Decisions of the Federal Supreme Court, published in BGHZ, vol. 70, pp. 331 et seq. and in BGHZ, vol. 104, pp. 246 et seq.
[173] Decision of the Higher Regional Court of Frankfurt, published in DB 2009, pp. 1640 et seq.
[174] Sec. 113 of the Commercial Code analogously.
[175] Sec. 53a of the Stock Corporation Act.
[176] Sec. 13 para. 2 of the Limited Liability Company Act.
[177] Sec. 30, 31 of the Limited Liability Company Act; *cf.* A.VIII.3.

shareholder may be under a repayment obligation if he entered into transactions with the company which have not been at arm's length. If the shareholder receiving the payment is not in a position to render the repayment to the company, the remaining shareholders have to render the repayment pro rata to their participation in the company if such repayment is required to fulfill debts of the company vis-à-vis third parties.[178]

d) Insolvency Law Liability

Once the company gets into economic trouble a shareholder is expected to either (i) inject new equity into the company, (ii) liquidate the company or (iii) cause the management to commence insolvency proceedings. It is not uncommon that shareholders, instead of injecting equity into the company, grant loans to the company. German insolvency law treats all repayment claims from shareholder loans – except for certain restructuring loans – as subordinate to all claims of other creditors in case of an insolvency of the company, provided that the relevant shareholder holds more than 10% of the share capital.[179] If the shareholder has received a repayment for such loan within the last year prior to the filing of insolvency by the company, the insolvency administrator may claim repayment to the company.[180]

e) Destruction of the Economic Basis of the Company

Additionally, shareholders may be held liable by the company if, **disregarding the purpose of the company's assets to serve as collateral for its creditors**, they intentionally abuse their control to remove assets or business opportunities from the company, rendering it unable to satisfy its debts (so-called **destruction of the economic basis of the company**). The shareholder liability only applies if the company falls into insolvency. This does not only apply to going-concern companies but also to companies in liquidation.[181]

Such liability was introduced by the Federal Supreme Court in the landmark case *"Bremer Vulkan"*. The court held that, in the event that a sole shareholder of a *GmbH* causes the *GmbH* to enter into a group-wide cash pool, such shareholder has to observe the interests of the company, including its ability to fulfill its obligations. In particular, the cash-pooling arrangement must not endanger the existence of the company.[182]

The Federal Supreme Court has, in the past, held shareholders liable directly to the creditors of the company.[183] Subsequently, however, the court has held in the *"Trihotel"* decision that **only the company may claim damages from the shareholders**.[184] The creditors cannot directly hold the shareholders liable but must instead seize the company's claim for damages. In insolvency proceedings over the assets of the company, the insolvency administrator will enforce the claim against the shareholder; the creditors do not have access to the shareholder's assets.

---

[178] Sec. 31 para. 3 of the Limited Liability Company Act.
[179] Sec. 39 para. 1 no. 5, paras. 4, 5 of the Insolvency Code.
[180] Sec. 135 para. 1 no. 2 of the Insolvency Code.
[181] Decision of the Federal Supreme Court, published in NZG 2009, pp. 545, 548.
[182] Decision of the Federal Supreme Court, published in BGHZ, vol. 149, pp. 10 et seq.
[183] Decision of the Federal Supreme Court, published in BGHZ, vol. 151, pp. 181 et seq.
[184] Decision of the Federal Supreme Court, published in BGHZ, vol. 173, pp. 246, 258; decision of the Higher Regional Court of Munich, published in ZInsO 2013, pp. 1693 et seq.

III. Legal Position of the Shareholders

The claim of the company for damages based on a destruction of its economic basis is currently based in tort law.[185] It requires in particular that the shareholder in question **acts with intent** and with the knowledge that the economic existence of the company will be at risk.[186] These requirements are not easily satisfied, limiting the scope of such liability. However, the exact limits of liability are not yet fully shaped.

f) Other Exemptions

Apart from these exceptions there are only a few scenarios of shareholder liability in literature and court practice. One is the so-called **intermingling of assets**.

A shareholder may become personally liable towards the company's creditors if the assets are not clearly designated to the shareholders or the company in the books of the company and such designation is further not indicated through, for example, physical separation.[187] In such a case, the shareholders are, like partners, liable directly vis-à-vis the creditors of the company.[188] Mere transactions between the company and a shareholder as such do not constitute an intermingling of assets. The courts seldom invoke this doctrine in practice.

The Limited Liability Company Act does not provide that a *GmbH* must be furnished with an amount of capital adequate to conduct its business. It is sufficient for the shareholders to raise and maintain the registered share capital.[189] Parts of legal literature, however, argue for liability of the shareholders in the event of an **undercapitalization** of the company. Still, the Federal Supreme Court has recently denied a proposed duty of the shareholders of a *GmbH* to provide it with sufficient funds for its business.[190] In particular, undercapitalization does not as such constitute a destruction of the economic basis of the company.[191]

5. Redemption of a Share

The Limited Liability Company Act does not comprehensively govern the withdrawal and the expulsion of a shareholder. One way of exiting a company is the **redemption** (*Einziehung*) of a shareholder's share. The redemption is possible only if it is provided for in the articles of association[192] and the original contribution has been paid in full. A redemption cannot be carried out if the compensation payment would cause the remaining assets to fall short of the registered share capital.[193]

The articles of association usually provide for the redemption of a share with the **consent of the shareholder** concerned. The articles of association can also declare a redemption permissible **against a shareholder's will** (so-called **compulsory redemption**). In this event, however, the articles of association must set forth the grounds for redemption. In most cases, compulsory redemption is provided for in the event that shares are attached or the shareholder becomes insolvent.

---

[185] Sec. 826 of the Civil Code.
[186] Decision of the Federal Supreme Court, published in BGHZ, vol. 173, pp. 246, 251 et seq.
[187] Decisions of the Federal Supreme Court, published in BGHZ, vol. 95, pp. 330, 341 et seq., in BGHZ, vol. 165, pp. 85 et seq. and in NJW-RR 2008, pp. 629, 630.
[188] Decision of the Federal Supreme Court, published in BGHZ, vol. 165, pp. 85 et seq.
[189] *Cf.* A.II.1.d and A.VIII.3.
[190] Decision of the Federal Supreme Court, published in BGHZ, vol. 176, pp. 204, 212 et seq.
[191] *Cf.* A.III.4.e.
[192] Sec. 34 para. 1 of the Limited Liability Company Act.
[193] Sec. 34 para. 3 of the Limited Liability Company Act.

Frequently, compulsory redemption is also allowed by the articles of association if *good cause* is present in the person of the shareholder that justifies his expulsion. The shareholder whose share shall be redeemed is generally entitled to participate in the vote unless the redemption shall be effected due to good cause in the person of the shareholder.[194]

The redemption takes place by means of a **majority vote of the shareholders**.[195] The shareholder is to be informed of the redemption through an informal statement by the managing directors. The redemption leads to the termination of the membership of the shareholder concerned.

The articles of association can stipulate the **conditions of the redemption**. If such stipulation is missing, the withdrawing shareholder has a claim for **compensation** in the amount of the full value of the redeemed share. The articles of association can also provide for a lesser amount. However, the courts do not allow such restrictions of compensation without any limits. Compensation below the full value can be null and void depending on the circumstances of the particular case. The courts have developed standards in this regard.[196]

6. Withdrawal and Expulsion of a Shareholder

A shareholder can voluntarily leave the company by **disposing of his share** (see below). If provided for in the articles of association, the **redemption of his share** may even be possible with or without his consent (see above).

If the articles of association remain silent, the general principle of civil law that long-term legal relationships can always be **terminated for** *good cause* applies. Accordingly, a shareholder has the right to withdraw from the company if there is good cause as well as the right to demand **compensation** for his share. Conversely, the company can exclude the shareholder if good cause is present (e.g., his remaining in the company no longer appears to be acceptable).

Withdrawal and expulsion for good cause are each, however, the *ultima ratio* to remedy the situation, and are permissible only if no less intrusive measures are available.

IV. Transfer of Shares

1. Disposal and Transfer of the Shares

Shares in a *GmbH* may be freely disposed of and are transferable by inheritance.[197] **Notarial form** is required for a contractual obligation to assign, as well as for the assignment itself.[198] The **division of a share** does not require the consent of the company.

It is possible under certain circumstances to **acquire shares in good faith** from unauthorized persons if the shareholder list kept by the commercial register has

---

[194] Decisions of the Federal Supreme Court, published in BGHZ, vol. 9, pp. 157, 178, in GmbHR 1977, pp. 81, 82, in NZG 2003, pp. 284, 285 and in NZG 2003, pp. 286 et. seq.
[195] Sec. 46 no. 4 of the Limited Liability Company Act.
[196] Decisions of the Federal Supreme Court, published in BGHZ, vol. 116, pp. 359, 368 et seq. and in BGHZ, vol. 126, pp. 226, 241 et seq.
[197] Sec. 15 para. 1 of the Limited Liability Company Act.
[198] Sec. 15 paras. 3, 4 of the Limited Liability Company Act.

been incorrect for at least three years or if the reason for the incorrectness of the shareholder list is attributable to the real shareholder.[199]

A shareholder can **acquire one or more additional shares** besides his existing share. Each of the shares remains independent, i.e., no accumulation takes place.[200] The shareholder meeting can, however, with the consent of the shareholder concerned, resolve that the shares be consolidated into one share.[201]

2. Notarial Form

A **purchase agreement** concerning a share in a *GmbH* needs to be **notarized**.[202] The same applies to other contracts which establish the obligation to assign a *GmbH* share, e.g., option or preemption rights concerning *GmbH* shares. Without notarization, such contract is **null and void**.

Moreover, the **assignment of the share itself** (*transfer in rem*) needs to be notarized.[203] If the assignment is performed in accordance with the notarial form, the lack of notarization of the underlying contractual obligation to assign (e.g., the share purchase agreement) is cured.[204] However, in M&A transactions concerning shares in a *GmbH* it is usually not appropriate to rely on the curing effect of a notarization of the share transfer since a purchase agreement which is null and void due to a lack of notarization leads to transaction uncertainty between signing and closing of the transaction.

The requirement of notarial form is fulfilled by means of notarization before a German notary. In the early years of the decade it had become common for share purchase agreements concerning *GmbH* shares to be notarized before Swiss notaries (in particular notaries in the city of Basel) in order to save notarial fees, which used to be very high in Germany, in the event of high-value M&A transactions. This development had its origins in a decision of the Federal Supreme Court of 1981 pursuant to which a notarization by a foreign notary may be valid if such notarization is equivalent to a notarization in Germany.[205] Various courts have held that a notarization by certain Swiss notaries (in particular in the city of Basel) is equivalent to a notarization in Germany.[206] Since the Law on the Modernization of the Law of Limited Liability Companies and the Prevention of Misuse (*MoMiG*) entered into force in 2008, it has become highly disputed whether the transfer of shares can still be notarized by a foreign notary. As a consequence, notarizations before foreign notaries have almost disappeared. Even though the Federal Supreme Court in 2013 upheld its earlier decision of 1981 notwithstanding the 2008 legislation,[207] the court did not explicitly acknowledge notarization by notaries in the city of Basel, and so some uncertainty remains. Since the fees

---

[199] Sec. 16 para. 3 of the Limited Liability Company Act.
[200] Sec. 15 para. 2 of the Limited Liability Company Act.
[201] Decision of the Supreme Court of the German Reich, published in RGZ, vol. 142, pp. 36, 39 et seq.
[202] Sec. 15 para. 4 of the Limited Liability Company Act.
[203] Sec. 15 para. 3 of the Limited Liability Company Act.
[204] Sec. 15 para. 4 sentence 2 of the Limited Liability Company Act.
[205] Decision of the Federal Supreme Court, published in BGHZ, vol. 70, pp. 76 et seq.
[206] Decision of the Federal Supreme Court, published in BGHZ, vol. 70, pp. 76 et seq.; decision of the Higher Regional Court of Frankfurt, published in NZG 2005, p. 820; decision of the Higher Regional Court of Munich, published in NJW-RR 1998, p. 758; decision of the Higher Regional Court of Hamburg, published in IPRspr 1979 No. 9; decision of the Regional Court of Stuttgart, published in IPRspr 1976 no. 5A.
[207] Decision of the Federal Supreme Court, published in NZG 2014, pp. 219 *et seq.*

of German notaries are now capped at approximately EUR 60,000 for a single notarization (in the German language), notarizations by foreign notaries are less attractive. In most cases, a notarization before a German notary will remain the most convenient solution.

3. Restriction on Transferability

In principle, shares are **freely assignable**. However, the articles of association can make the **assignment contingent upon** the approval by the company, the shareholder meeting or individual shareholders, the supervisory board, the advisory board or even third parties. The articles of association can further specify the approval requirement, limit it to specific cases, stipulate criteria for selection of new shareholders or exempt specific cases from the approval requirement.[208]

If the transferability of shares is dependent upon the approval of the company, the managing directors are responsible for granting the approval. In internal relations, however, the managing directors are bound by the decision of the shareholder meeting.

4. Shareholder List

The notary notarizing a share assignment must file a revised shareholder list with the commercial register and with a copy to the company. The same duty applies to the managing directors if they are notified of a change in the shareholder structure. The filing of the new shareholder list is not, however, a prerequisite for the validity of the assignment of the share, but serves to authorize the new shareholder's standing with the company.[209] Until the new shareholder list has been filed with the commercial register, only the previously registered shareholder is authorized to exercise shareholder rights and receive profits.

V. Shareholder Meeting

1. Competence of the Shareholder Meeting

The shareholder meeting is the *GmbH's* **ultimate decision-making authority**. Shareholders usually exercise their rights in the shareholder meeting. The articles of association often determine the authority and the rules of procedure of the shareholder meeting. To the extent that the articles of association do not contain specific provisions regarding the shareholder meeting, sections 46 through 51 of the Limited Liability Company Act apply as the model framework.[210]

The **shareholder meeting is exclusively responsible** for:
- amendments to the articles of association[211];
- the calling in of additional contributions[212];
- the dissolution of the company and the appointment and revocation of the appointment of the liquidators[213]; and

---

[208] Sec. 15 para. 5 of the Limited Liability Company Act.
[209] Sec. 16 para. 1 of the Limited Liability Company Act.
[210] Sec. 45 para. 2 of the Limited Liability Company Act.
[211] Sec. 53 to 58f of the Limited Liability Company Act.
[212] Sec. 26 of the Limited Liability Company Act.
[213] Sec. 60 para. 1 no. 2, 66 of the Limited Liability Company Act.

- resolutions regarding measures pursuant to the Transformation Act such as mergers, spin-offs and changes of the legal form.[214]

Except as otherwise stipulated in the articles of association, the shareholders decide on:[215]
- the formal approval of individual and consolidated annual financial statements and the appropriation of profits;
- the demand that payment be made in respect of the shares;
- the repayment of additional contributions;
- the division, consolidation and redemption of shares;
- the appointment and dismissal of managing directors, as well as the ratification of their acts;
- the execution and termination of service agreements with managing directors;
- the assertion of damage claims to which the company is entitled against managing directors or shareholders, as well as the representation of the company in litigation proceedings against the managing directors;
- the rules of procedure for the management; and
- the appointment of procuration officers and authorized signatories.

In addition, the shareholder meeting has the right to issue **instructions to the management board**, to **appoint or dismiss members of an optional supervisory board or advisory board** and to grant its **consent to the assignment of shares**.

In the articles of association, the shareholders may grant comprehensive rights to the shareholder meeting subject, however, to certain restrictions: the fiduciary duty, the requirement of equal treatment, the prohibition of misuse, and the protection of minorities impose limits on the shareholders' freedom of contract. The same applies to the question of the extent to which the validity of shareholder resolutions can be made subject to the consent of third parties outside the company or voting rights granted to them.

As a rule, **shareholders decide in a meeting by majority vote**.[216] Under certain circumstances, shareholder resolutions may also be taken without a physical meeting. In particular, a meeting is not necessary if all the shareholders indicate in text form that they are in agreement with a measure to be taken or with casting their votes in writing.[217] A physical meeting is not required if there is only one shareholder. In this event, however, the single shareholder must, immediately after the passing of a resolution, take down minutes of the resolution and sign them.[218]

2. The Convening of a Shareholder Meeting

Shareholder meetings are convened by one or more of the **managing directors**. In the case of codetermined companies, the **supervisory board** also has the right to convene shareholder meetings whenever the interest of the company so requires. The articles of association can also grant the right to convene shareholder meetings to other corporate bodies (such as an optional supervisory board or advisory board), as well as to a single shareholder. **Shareholders whose shares together correspond to at least 10%** of the registered share capital also have the right to de-

---

[214] Sec. 13, 50 et seq., 125, 193, 226 et seq. of the Transformation Act.
[215] Sec. 46 no. 1 to 8 of the Limited Liability Company Act.
[216] Sec. 47, 48 of the Limited Liability Company Act.
[217] Sec. 48 para. 2 of the Limited Liability Company Act.
[218] Sec. 48 para. 3 of the Limited Liability Company Act.

mand the convening of the shareholder meeting, which demand needs to indicate the purpose of and reasons for the meeting.[219] This right cannot be excluded by the articles of association. The same holds for the right to have items announced that are to be resolved on by the shareholder meeting.[220] If those demands are not fulfilled, the authorized shareholders can convene or announce the shareholder meeting themselves.[221]

If it seems **necessary in the interest of the company**, the shareholder meeting has to be convened.[222] This may, for example, be the case for decisions on extraordinary business transactions or on measures to deal with a company crisis. If a decision is to be made that falls within the competence of the shareholder meeting (see above), the shareholder meeting has to be convened as well. The shareholder meeting has to be convened immediately if the annual balance sheet or a balance sheet prepared in the course of the fiscal year shows that **half of the registered share capital has been lost**.[223] The violation of the respective reporting duty of the managing directors is a criminal offense.[224]

The Limited Liability Company Act provides that the convening of the shareholder meeting takes place by means of a registered letter to all shareholders.[225] It must set forth the details (place and time) of the meeting, as well as the **agenda**. Advance notice of at least one week has to be given.[226] Items can be added to the agenda by means of registered letter at the latest three days prior to the meeting.[227] The articles of association may provide for different rules.

If the **meeting has not been properly convened** (i.e., if there have been formal defects in convening the meeting), resolutions can be passed only if all shareholders are present.[228]

In practice, there are often **plenary meetings** where all shareholders gather while consciously disregarding the formalities for the convening of a shareholder meeting. The shareholders unanimously waive such formalities in order to cure any potential formal defects of the resolutions that are adopted at the meeting.

3. Proceedings of the Shareholder Meeting

Shareholder resolutions **amending the articles of association** need to be **notarized**.[229] Beyond this, the Limited Liability Company Act contains no regulations on the course of the shareholder meeting. As a rule, a chairman of the meeting is appointed and the passed resolutions are formally approved and recorded. The shareholder meeting is not public. **All shareholders** are entitled to participate, regardless of whether they have voting rights or not. The articles of association often contain specific provisions with respect to representation (for example, that shareholders can only be represented by other shareholders, or that certain shareholders have to appoint a joint representative). Insolvency administrators

---

[219] Sec. 50 para. 1 of the Limited Liability Company Act.
[220] Sec. 50 para. 2 of the Limited Liability Company Act.
[221] Sec. 50 para. 3 of the Limited Liability Company Act.
[222] Sec. 49 para. 2 of the Limited Liability Company Act.
[223] Sec. 49 para. 3 of the Limited Liability Company Act.
[224] Sec. 84 para. 1 of the Limited Liability Company Act.
[225] Sec. 51 para. 1 of the Limited Liability Company Act.
[226] Sec. 51 para. 1 of the Limited Liability Company Act.
[227] Sec. 51 para. 4 of the Limited Liability Company Act.
[228] Sec. 51 para. 3 of the Limited Liability Company Act.
[229] Sec. 53 para. 2 of the Limited Liability Company Act.

and executors of a will (*Testamentsvollstrecker*) are entitled to participate instead of the underlying shareholder. **Managing directors** and **members of the supervisory board**, on the other hand, are not entitled to participate unless codetermination law requires the company to establish a supervisory board[230] or unless the articles of association or a shareholder resolution grants them participation rights. In practice, the participation of managing directors in the meeting is often helpful and sometimes even mandatory with regard to certain agenda items. The shareholders will in such cases instruct the managing directors to be present at the meeting. Advisors are to be admitted if this is required by the nature of the matters considered at the meeting.

4. Voting and Shareholder Resolutions

The shareholder meeting decides by way of resolution. Subject to specific provisions in the articles of association, the **majority of the votes cast** is decisive.[231] The presence of even one voting shareholder constitutes a quorum. The chairman of the meeting determines the voting process. The chairman of the shareholder meeting formally determines and announces that the shareholder resolution has been adopted. However, this is no prerequisite for a valid resolution.[232]

Votes are either affirmative or negative; abstentions are not counted.[233] The **voting right** based on a share can be exercised only **uniformly**. A shareholder who has more than one share can vote differently with each share. The right to vote can be exercised by proxy unless the articles of association provide otherwise. The proxy always has to be in text form.[234]

A **qualified majority of three-quarters** of the votes cast is, for example, required for amendments to the articles of association,[235] the dissolution of the company,[236] resolutions on mergers, spin-offs and other measures under the Transformation Act, as well as for granting consent to the execution of domination and profit and loss transfer agreements. Apart from the qualified majority, an amendment to the articles of association requires notarization and registration in the commercial register.[237]

A shareholder resolution that **goes beyond the articles of association** (*satzungsdurchbrechender Gesellschafterbeschluss*) without formally amending the articles of association also requires a qualified majority of three quarters of the votes cast. By transcending the articles of association, the shareholders deviate from the articles of association in a particular case. It is disputed whether such action also needs to be notarized and registered in the commercial register.

---

[230] Sec. 118 para. 2 of the Stock Corporation Act together with sec. 25 para. 1 sentence 1 no. 2 of the Codetermination Act, sec. 1 para. 1 no. 3 of the One-Third Participation Act, sec. 3 para. 2 of the Coal, Iron and Steel Codetermination Act.
[231] Sec. 47 para. 1 of the Limited Liability Company Act.
[232] Decisions of the Federal Supreme Court, published in NJW 1980, pp. 1527 et. seq., in NJW 1984, pp. 489, 491 and in NJW 2007, pp. 917, 918.
[233] Decision of the Federal Supreme Court, published in NJW 1988, pp. 1844, 1845; decision of the Higher Regional Court of Celle, published in NZG 1998, pp. 29, 30 et seq.
[234] Sec. 47 para. 3 of the Limited Liability Company Act.
[235] Sec. 53 para. 2 of the Limited Liability Company Act.
[236] Sec. 60 para. 1 no. 2 of the Limited Liability Company Act.
[237] Sec. 54 of the Limited Liability Company Act.

5. Exclusion of Voting Rights

Where a resolution is to be passed to approve a shareholder's actions or to release him from liability, the shareholder concerned has **no right to vote** or to exercise voting rights on behalf of others.[238] The same applies with respect to resolutions relating to entering into legal transactions or the initiation or settlement of litigation regarding a particular shareholder.[239] The purpose of excluding the shareholder from casting his vote is to avoid a potential **conflict of interest**. Apart from the aforementioned situations, a shareholder's voting rights are also excluded where the shareholder meeting is to resolve on measures against him for good cause (e.g., dismissal as managing director for good cause).[240]

A **non-shareholder who represents or acts as trustee** for a shareholder whose voting right is excluded is also considered conflicted and therefore excluded from voting.[241] The same applies to the legal representative of a legal entity whose voting rights as shareholder are excluded. If the representative of a shareholder is conflicted himself, he is barred from exercising his principal's voting right even if there is no reason to exclude the voting right of the shareholder itself.[242]

Exclusion of voting rights **does not apply in single-shareholder companies** because the purpose of the exclusion of voting rights is to protect the company's assets vis-à-vis a single shareholder in favor of the other shareholders, but not in favor of the company's creditors.[243]

The mere risk that a shareholder may pursue his own interests instead of those of the company **does not trigger an exclusion of voting rights**. Consequently, a shareholder retains his voting right where the vote concerns his appointment as managing director or as a member of the supervisory or advisory board. The same applies where the vote concerns his dismissal, unless the dismissal would be for good cause.[244] There is no exclusion of a shareholder's voting rights with respect to votes on the execution or termination of his managing director's service contract.[245] Furthermore, both the assignor and the assignee of a share may take part in voting regarding the company's consent to dispose of the share in question.[246]

6. Nullity of Shareholder Resolutions and Action to Set Aside Resolutions

Limited liability company law does not regulate under what circumstances shareholder resolutions are null and void or can be challenged. However, the **provisions of the Stock Corporation Act** relating to the nullity of resolutions of general meetings and on actions to set aside such resolutions[247] apply by way of analogy

---

[238] Sec. 47 para. 4 sentence 1 of the Limited Liability Company Act.
[239] Sec. 47 para. 4 sentence 2 of the Limited Liability Company Act.
[240] Decisions of the Supreme Court of the German Reich, published in RGZ, vol. 124, pp. 371, 378 and in RGZ, vol. 138, pp. 98 et seq.
[241] Decision of the Higher Regional Court of Munich, published in GmbHR 1995, p. 231.
[242] Sec. 47 para. 4 sentence 1, second alternative of the Limited Liability Company Act.
[243] Decisions of the Federal Supreme Court, published in BGHZ, vol. 105, pp. 324, 333 and in NZG 2011, pp. 950, 951.
[244] Decision of the Federal Supreme Court, published in NJW 1987, p. 1889.
[245] Decisions of the Federal Supreme Court, published in BGHZ, vol. 18, pp. 205, 210 et seq. and in BGHZ, vol. 51, pp. 209, 215 et seq.
[246] Decision of the Federal Supreme Court, published in BGHZ, vol. 48, pp. 163 et seq.
[247] Sec. 241 et seq. of the Stock Corporation Act.

V. Shareholder Meeting

to the extent that the peculiarities of the *GmbH* itself do not require a deviation from such provisions.[248]

Particular rules apply with regard to the authorization to file an action to set aside a resolution. In the case of a *GmbH*, **every shareholder** is entitled to file such action regardless of whether he participated in the shareholder meeting, unless he consented to the resolution knowing the defect or subsequently waived the right to bring an action. **Managing directors**, by contrast (unlike the management board of an *AG*),[249] are generally not entitled to bring an action to set aside resolutions.[250] An exception is made where a managing director could be criminally or civilly liable if he implemented the resolution.[251] The same applies to members of the **supervisory board**.

The action to set aside needs to be brought reasonably quickly and generally within the **contestation period** of one month set forth in sec. 246 para. 1 of the Stock Corporation Act.[252] The action may be brought after this contestation period only if the plaintiff can show a compelling reason for why it was not brought earlier.[253] The articles of association may set forth the contestation period which may not, however, be shorter than one month.[254]

7. Important (Minority) Shareholder Rights (Overview)

Legal Provision	Rights Resulting from the Participation
One Share	
Sec. 51a para. 1 of the Limited Liability Company Act	Right to request information regarding the affairs of the company and right to inspect accounts and records
Sec. 51b sentence 2 of the Limited Liability Company Act	Right to bring an action against the refusal of a request for information or inspection of accounts or records
Sec. 75 para. 1 of the Limited Liability Company Act	Right to bring an action to declare the company null and void if the articles of association do not contain provisions regarding the amount of the registered share capital or the object of the company
Sec. 35 of the Civil Code	Right to prevent the revocation of a special right established in the articles of association in favor of the shareholder
Decision of the Federal Supreme Court	Right to assert claims against co-shareholders or managing directors (by way of an *actio pro socio*) for violating their membership duties or their duties as part of a company body (shareholder lawsuit)

---

[248] Decision of the Supreme Court of the German Reich, published in RGZ, vol. 166, pp. 129 et seq.; decisions of the Federal Supreme Court, published in BGHZ, vol. 111, pp. 224 et seq. and in NJW 1997, pp. 1510, 1511.
[249] Sec. 245 no. 4 of the Stock Corporation Act.
[250] Decision of the Federal Supreme Court, published in BGHZ, vol. 76, pp. 154, 159 et seq.
[251] Sec. 245 no. 5 of the Stock Corporation Act analogously.
[252] Decisions of the Federal Supreme Court, published in DStR 2009, p. 2113 and in NZG 2005, pp. 479, 480 et seq.
[253] Decision of the Federal Supreme Court, published in NZG 2005, pp. 551, 553.
[254] Decision of the Federal Supreme Court, published in BGHZ, vol. 104, pp. 66, 73 et seq.

A. The Limited Liability Company

Legal Provision	Rights Resulting from the Participation
Decision of the Federal Supreme Court	Right to bring an action to set aside a resolution and right to bring an action for the declaration of nullity of a resolution
10% of the registered share capital	
Sec. 50 para. 1 of the Limited Liability Company Act	Right to request the convening of a shareholder meeting
Sec. 50 para. 2 of the Limited Liability Company Act	Right to request that items to be resolved by the meeting be announced
Sec. 61 para. 2 sentence 2 of the Limited Liability Company Act	Right to bring an action for dissolution of the company if the object of the company can no longer be achieved, or if other good causes for dissolution pertaining to the circumstances of the company exist
Sec. 66 para. 2, 3 sentence 1 of the Limited Liability Company Act	Right to request the court to appoint liquidators or to dismiss them for good cause
» 25% of the votes cast	
(see below)	Blocking minority for resolutions for which a majority of 75% is required (see below)
» 50% of the votes cast	
Sec. 47 para. 1 of the Limited Liability Company Act	A simple majority of the votes cast (more than 50%) is required for all resolutions for which statutory law or the articles of association do not stipulate a different majority requirement, e.g.:
Sec. 46 no. 1, sec. 42a para. 2 of the Limited Liability Company Act	– formal approval of the annual financial statements
Sec. 46 no. 1, sec. 29 of the Limited Liability Company Act	– appropriation of profits
Sec. 46 no. 2, sec. 19 of the Limited Liability Company Act	– demand that the contributions on shares be rendered
Sec. 46 no. 3, sec. 30 para. 2 of the Limited Liability Company Act	– repayment of additional contributions
Sec. 46 no. 4, sec. 34 of the Limited Liability Company Act	– redemption of shares
Sec. 46 no. 5, sec. 6 para. 3, sec. 38 of the Limited Liability Company Act	– appointment and dismissal of managing directors
Sec. 46 no. 5 of the Limited Liability Company Act	– ratification of acts of the managing directors

V. Shareholder Meeting

Legal Provision	Rights Resulting from the Participation
Sec. 46 no. 6 of the Limited Liability Company Act	– measures for reviewing and supervising the management of the company
Sec. 46 no. 7 of the Limited Liability Company Act, sec. 48 para. 1, sec. 54 para. 1 of the Commercial Code	– appointment of procuration officers (*Prokuristen*) and authorized signatories
Sec. 46 no. 8, sec. 9a, sec. 43 of the Limited Liability Company Act	– assertion of indemnification claims against managing directors or shareholders to which the company is entitled on the basis of the way the company was founded or managed
Sec. 46 no. 8 of the Limited Liability Company Act	– representation of the company in lawsuits against the managing directors
Sec. 15 para. 5 of the Limited Liability Company Act	– consent to the assignment of shares with restricted transferability
Sec. 26 para. 1 of the Limited Liability Company Act	– demand that payment be made in respect of additional contributions
Sec. 66 para. 1, 3 sentence 2 of the Limited Liability Company Act	– appointment and dismissal of liquidators
Sec. 74 para. 2 sentence 2 of the Limited Liability Company Act	– resolution on which shareholder or third party is to retain the books and records of the company after completion of the liquidation
Sec. 318 para. 1 sentence 1 of the Commercial Code	– appointment of the auditors of the annual financial statements
75% of the votes cast	
	A qualified majority of 75% is required for a number of fundamental resolutions, e.g.:
Sec. 53 para. 2 sentence 1 of the Limited Liability Company Act	– amendments to the articles of association
Sec. 55 para. 1, sec. 3 para. 1 no. 3, sec. 53 para. 2 sentence 1 of the Limited Liability Company Act	– capital increases
Sec. 58 para. 1, sec. 3 para. 1 no. 3, sec. 53 para. 2 sentence 1 of the Limited Liability Company Act	– capital reductions
Sec. 60 para. 1 no. 2 of the Limited Liability Company Act	– dissolution of the company
Unanimity	
Sec. 48 para. 2 of the Limited Liability Company Act	Waiver as to the requirement of a resolution being passed within the proper course of a shareholder meeting

Legal Provision	Rights Resulting from the Participation
Sec. 53 para. 3 of the Limited Liability Company Act	Augmentation of the payments or performances which the shareholders must render pursuant to the articles of association
Sec. 76 of the Limited Liability Company Act	Cure of a defect relating to the provisions of the articles of association regarding the object of the company
Decision of the Federal Supreme Court	Waiver of proper form and notice for convening a shareholder meeting

Table 2: Important (Minority) Shareholder Rights

VI. Management of the Company

1. Management and Representation of the Company

a) Management by Managing Directors

Management conducts the day-to-day activities of the company. Such activities may be of a legal or factual nature. They include the establishment of a business organization and short-term planning. Not included, however, are changes to the constitution of the company and variations in the general direction of the company. Such "basic" or "structural" measures are reserved for the shareholders.

A *GmbH* can have one or more **managing directors** (*Geschäftsführer*).[255] The managing directors perform management in the aforementioned sense and represent the company in legal transactions.[256] The law also allows for management by either shareholder or third-party managing directors.[257]

b) Duties of the Managing Directors

The **managing directors have a duty to act on behalf of the company**. While doing so, they must exercise the **care of a prudent businessman**.[258] More specifically, the statute explicitly assigns the managing directors a large number of special duties which they must personally fulfill. The managing directors must, for example, ensure that the accounts are kept properly and balance sheets are drawn up properly.[259] They must submit tax returns in the name of the company at the appropriate times.[260] The shareholder meeting is convened by the managing directors;[261] it must be convened immediately if the annual balance sheet or a balance sheet prepared in the course of the fiscal year shows that half of the registered share capital has been lost.[262] The managing directors must file the necessary applications with the commercial register.[263] If the company becomes

---

[255] Sec. 6 para. 1 of the Limited Liability Company Act.
[256] Sec. 35 para. 1 sentence 1 of the Limited Liability Company Act.
[257] Sec. 6 para. 3 sentence 1 of the Limited Liability Company Act.
[258] Sec. 43 para. 1 of the Limited Liability Company Act.
[259] Sec. 41, 42 of the Limited Liability Company Act.
[260] Sec. 34 of the General Tax Code (*Abgabenordnung*).
[261] Sec. 49 para. 1 of the Limited Liability Company Act.
[262] Sec. 49 para. 3, 84 para. 1 of the Limited Liability Company Act.
[263] Sec. 78 of the Limited Liability Company Act.

illiquid or over-indebted, they must, without undue delay, but at the latest within three weeks, apply for the opening of insolvency proceedings.[264]

Further, the managing directors have a duty to ensure **compliance** of the *GmbH's* activities with applicable laws. They must install an effective **compliance-system** with risk control functions, appropriate for the size of the *GmbH* and the industry in which it is active. Certain tasks can be delegated to a compliance officer; however, this does not relieve the managing directors from their duty to monitor the compliance system and its effectiveness and to become active once compliance failures have become apparent. Violations of these duties may expose the managing directors to personal liability to the *GmbH*.

c) Authority of the Managing Directors to Represent the Company

The managing directors have **authority to represent** and act on behalf of the company in all legal transactions in and out of court.[265] The **scope of the authority is unlimited** and cannot be limited in relation to third parties either in the articles of association or by shareholder resolution.[266] The purpose of this rule is to protect third parties, who need to rely on the power of a managing director to bind the company.

The scope of the authority to represent the company may, however, be limited in individual cases where the respective third party is not entitled to rely on unlimited authority. Such limitation occurs in particular where a managing director **abuses his authority to represent the company** and the third party knows of or deliberately ignores the abuse.[267] It may constitute an abuse for a managing director simply to exceed the authority granted to him internally by the shareholder meeting (see below). An abuse is definitely present where a managing director and a third party deliberately act to harm the company.

The scope of the authority of the managing directors to represent the company is further limited by the **prohibitions against self-dealing and multiple representations**.[268] A managing director cannot in general enter into legal transactions on behalf of the company with himself (self-dealing) or as the representative of a third party (multiple representations) unless the transaction serves only to fulfill an existing obligation or only bestows a legal advantage upon the company. The managing director can be **exempted** from the prohibitions against self-dealing and multiple representations. Such exemption may be granted in the articles of association or, if the articles of association allow it, by the shareholder meeting or another competent appointing body. If a managing director is also the sole shareholder of a *GmbH*, an exemption can only be granted in the articles of association.[269] In addition, he must record every transaction between himself and the company for reasons of legal certainty.[270]

Unless the articles of association provide otherwise, the managing directors are only **jointly authorized to represent** the company.[271] Alternatively, the articles of association may provide that a managing director has **authority to represent**

---

[264] Sec. 15a para. 1 of the Insolvency Code.
[265] Sec. 35 para. 1 sentence 1 of the Limited Liability Company Act.
[266] Sec. 37 para. 2 of the Limited Liability Company Act.
[267] Decision of the Federal Supreme Court, published in NZG 2004, pp. 139, 140.
[268] Sec. 181 of the Civil Code.
[269] Decision of the Federal Supreme Court, published in BGHZ, vol. 87, pp. 59, 60 et seq.
[270] Sec. 35 para. 3 sentence 2 of the Limited Liability Company Act.
[271] Sec. 35 para. 2 sentence 1 of the Limited Liability Company Act.

the company alone (**sole power of representation**) or that he may represent the company **together with another managing director or a procuration officer (joint power of representation)**. The articles of association may also allow the shareholder meeting or another body such as a supervisory board or advisory board to determine the managing directors' sole or joint powers of representation. In any event, the manner in which the managing directors are entitled to represent the company and every change to it must be **registered in the commercial register**[272] so that third parties can determine and rely on the power of representation of the managing directors.

Legal declarations are deemed received by the company as soon as they have reached just one managing director, irrespective of his power of representation.[273] Similarly and insofar as legal consequences are tied to knowledge, the **knowledge of each managing director is imputed independently to the company**.

d) Restrictions in Internal Relations

In internal relations, the **managing directors have to observe the restrictions** contained in the articles of association, in resolutions of the shareholders, in their service contracts or in rules of procedure for the managing directors. In contrast to an *AG*, the managing directors in a *GmbH* are **subject to instructions by the shareholder meeting** or, in single-shareholder companies, by the **sole shareholder**.[274] The shareholders can issue instructions *ad hoc* or in a general way by establishing **rules of procedure** which provide for general restrictions on management (e.g., make certain kind of transactions subject to the consent of the shareholder meeting). Even if there are no formal restrictions, the managing directors may not override the recognizable or presumed will of the shareholder meeting. They have to obtain the consent of the shareholder meeting for **extraordinary measures**.[275] If the managing directors do not comply with internal restrictions, they are obligated to compensate the company for any damages incurred.[276]

2. Appointment and Dismissal of the Managing Directors

a) Personal Requirements for Appointment as Managing Director

Only natural persons of full legal capacity can become managing directors.[277] It does not matter whether the managing director is a **German** or **foreign citizen,** as long as the (German or foreign) managing director is at all times able to fulfill his statutory duties as a managing director, in particular the duty to keep accounts. Neither knowledge of German nor a place of residence in Germany is required.[278] In the past, some courts held that managing directors had to be able to enter Germany at any time in order to fulfill their statutory duties.[279] As a consequence, it was necessary for managing directors of countries outside the European Union to

---

[272] Sec. 39 of the Limited Liability Company Act.
[273] Sec. 35 para. 2 sentence 2 of the Limited Liability Company Act.
[274] Sec. 37 para. 1, 45 of the Limited Liability Company Act.
[275] Decision of the Federal Supreme Court, published in GmbHR 1991, p. 197.
[276] Sec. 37 para. 1, 43 para. 2 of the Limited Liability Company Act.
[277] Sec. 6 para. 2 sentence 1 of the Limited Liability Company Act.
[278] Decision of the Higher Regional Court of Cologne, published in GmbHR 1999, pp. 182 et seq.
[279] Decision of the Higher Regional Court of Hamm, published in ZIP 1999, pp. 1919 et seq; decision of the Higher Regional Court of Stuttgart, published in NZG 2006, pp. 789 et seq.

VI. Management of the Company

possess a residence permit for Germany[280] or be entitled to enter Germany without visa requirements for a short time period.[281] With modern means of communication, the presence of a managing director in Germany becomes less important. It seems that since sec. 4a of the Limited Liability Company Act[282] allows a *GmbH* to set up a place of effective management (*Verwaltungssitz*) outside Germany, courts no longer require that the managing director of a *GmbH* be able to enter Germany at any time.[283] However, the residence of a managing director outside Germany could result in a change of place of effective management (*Verwaltungssitz*) of the *GmbH*, which could, in particular, trigger tax consequences.

The statute provides for legal **grounds for exclusion** that make an appointment null and void.[284] In particular, persons who were convicted in Germany or abroad of certain **white-collar crimes** (e.g., fraud, making false statements, breach of trust or criminal offenses related to insolvency) are barred for five years from serving as managing directors.[285] Also barred are persons who are **prohibited from practicing a profession** or a trade that matches the object of the company in whole or in part.[286] The managing directors must **disclose any information** relating to such grounds of exclusion to the register court. They must be instructed of this duty of disclosure in writing, for example by the court, by a German or foreign notary, by a representative of a similar legal profession or a consular officer. In the notification to the commercial register, the managing directors must confirm that they were so instructed and that there are no circumstances that would preclude their appointment.[287] If they provide false information, they may be prosecuted for a criminal offense and may also become liable for damages.[288]

Since the beginning of 2016, new rules **concerning the diversity and gender quotas for managing directors** and senior management-level employees apply to *GmbHs* that are subject to **codetermination**.[289] If a *GmbH* is subject to the One-Third Participation Act, the shareholder meeting must determine target figures for the **proportion of women** amongst the **managing directors**.[290] If a *GmbH* is subject to the Codetermination Act, this responsibility rests with the supervisory board.[291]

---

[280] Decision of the Higher Regional Court of Celle, published in ZIP 2007, p. 1157, decision of the Higher Regional Court of Cologne, published in GmbHR 1999, pp. 182 et seq. and decision of the Higher Regional Court of Hamm, published in ZIP 1999, pp. 1919 et seq.

[281] I.e., be resident in countries listed in Annex II of the Directive EC No. 539/2001 of March 15, 2001, OJ L 81 of March 21, 2001 ("Visa Directive"), in the version of Directive EC 509/2014 of May 15, 2014, OJ L 149/67 of May 20, 2014.

[282] Sec. 4a of the Limited Liability Company Act has been amended by the Law on the Modernization of the Law of Limited Liability Companies and the prevention of Misuse (*MoMiG*), dated October 23, 2008, Federal Law Gazette (*Bundesanzeiger*), Vol. I pp. 2026 et seq.

[283] No residence permit is required according to the decision of the Higher Regional Court of Düsseldorf, published in ZIP 2009, p. 1074, the decision of the Higher Regional Court of Munich, published in NJW-RR 2010, pp. 338 et. seq., the decision of the Higher Regional Court of Zweibrücken, published in GmbHR 2010, pp. 1260 et seq. and the decision of the Higher Regional Court of Frankfurt, 12 November 2010, ref. no. 20 W 370/10 (juris).

[284] Sec. 6 para. 2 of the Limited Liability Company Act; sec. 134 of the Civil Code.

[285] Sec. 6 para. 2 no. 3 of the Limited Liability Company Act.

[286] Sec. 6 para. 2 no. 2 of the Limited Liability Company Act.

[287] Sec. 8 para. 3 of the Limited Liability Company Act.

[288] Sec. 9a para. 1, 82 para. 1 of the Limited Liability Company Act.

[289] Act for the Equal Participation of Women and Men in Leadership Positions in the Private and Public Sector (*Gesetz für die gleichberechtigte Teilhabe von Frauen und Männern an Führungspositionen in der Privatwirtschaft und im öffentlichen Dienst – BGleiNRG*), dated April 24, 2015, Federal Law Gazette (*Bundesanzeiger*), Vol. I pp. 642 et seq.

[290] Sec. 52 para. 2 sentence 1 of the Limited Liability Company Act.

[291] Sec. 52 para. 2 sentence 2 of the Limited Liability Company Act.

Similarly, in codetermined *GmbHs* the managing directors are required to set target figures for the proportion of women in the **two levels of senior management** below the managing directors.[292] The law, however, allows for a large degree of flexibility in setting these target figures and in defining the two levels of senior management below the managing directors. When setting the target figures, even „0% representation" would be legally permissible if and for as long as women are not represented amongst the managing directors and in senior management. However, codetermined *GmbHs* are prohibited from setting target figures for the proportion of women amongst the managing directors or at the senior management level which would fall short of the current composition, unless women already account for at least 30% of the managing directors or management level. Codetermined *GmbHs* are required to report on the targets set on an annual basis and need to disclose whether targets were met or not.[293] However, the failure to meet a target for women's representation amongst the managing directors or senior management level does not have any immediate legal consequences.[294]

The articles of association may stipulate any further personal criteria for the appointment of managing directors, e.g., a minimum age or membership in a family or group of shareholders.

b) Corporate Act of Appointment

The law distinguishes between the corporate act of **appointment** of a managing director and the related **service contract**.[295] The appointment takes place by means of majority resolution of the shareholders; a managing director may also be appointed in the articles of association.[296] A sole shareholder can appoint him or herself as managing director.

In practice, the articles of association often provide for rights of a shareholder or a group of shareholders to appoint a managing director or to propose him to the shareholder meeting with binding effect. The articles of association can also provide for a different appointment procedure. For example, they may transfer the shareholder meeting's authority to appoint managing directors to a supervisory board or advisory board.

c) Dismissal

The term of office of the managing director is in general **indefinite**. The articles of association or the shareholder resolution concerning the appointment may provide for a time limitation or a condition subsequent.[297]

With regard to the termination of a managing director, it is necessary to distinguish between revocation of the corporate appointment to management (dismissal) and termination of the service contract. **Dismissal** is possible at any time, without giving notice or reasons.[298] A majority resolution of the shareholders suffices.[299] In this respect, the legal situation is different from the *AG*, where members of the management board may be dismissed only for good cause.

---

[292] Sec. 36 of the Limited Liability Company Act.
[293] Sec. 289a para. 4 sentence 1 of the Commercial Code.
[294] For gender quota in the supervisory board of co-determined *GmbHs* cf. A.VII.4 and 5.
[295] Sec. 38 para. 1 of the Limited Liability Company Act.
[296] Sec. 6 para. 3 sentence 2, 46 no. 5 of the Limited Liability Company Act.
[297] Decision of the Federal Supreme Court, published in NZG 2006, pp. 62, 63.
[298] Sec. 38 para. 1 of the Limited Liability Company Act.
[299] Sec. 46 no. 5, sec. 47 para. 1 of the Limited Liability Company Act.

If a managing director is also a shareholder, the managing director can participate both in the vote on his appointment and in the vote on his dismissal. This does not apply if the dismissal is being demanded for good cause, in which case the managing director is excluded from voting.

If a shareholder-managing director has been granted a **special right to management** in the articles of association, the dismissal becomes effective only if the director consents or if there is good cause for the dismissal. If there is good cause for dismissal, even a shareholder-managing director with a special right to management can be dismissed. In this case, the shareholder-managing director concerned has no right to vote.[300]

A managing director can **resign from office** at any time and without giving notice, even without good cause. Resignation from office can be ineffective, however, if the timing is inappropriate or if the company is in an emergency situation.

The **articles of association** can provide for different rules governing the appointment and dismissal of managing directors. In particular, they **can transfer responsibility to the supervisory board or advisory board** (if any). In case of doubt, the same corporate body which is authorized to appoint managing directors is also authorized to dismiss them. It is also permissible to limit the right to dismiss managing directors to certain grounds or to good cause. The right to issue a dismissal for good cause is mandatory, however, and cannot be excluded or limited by the articles of association.

With respect to companies subject to the Codetermination Act (see below), the **supervisory board** is responsible for the appointment and dismissal of managing directors. The term of office, as in the case of the *AG*, is limited to five years.[301]

3. Service Contracts with Managing Directors

a) Legal Nature of the Service Contract

The **employment contract of the managing director** is a service contract. It is not a genuine employment contract because the managing director carries out employer functions. Important provisions of general employment law are not applicable to managing directors (e.g., provisions on dismissal protection, working hours, election of works council, etc.). The courts, however, apply individual provisions of labor law to managing directors since their position is at least partly similar to that of employees (e.g., they are entitled to a job reference).

b) Parties to the Service Contract

The service contract is entered into between the managing director and the *GmbH*, which is represented by the shareholder meeting (or the sole shareholder) if the articles of association do not designate another corporate body as responsible.[302] In practice, service contracts are also entered into between the managing director and third parties such as the parent company of the group.

Although the law is not explicit in this regard, the responsible corporate body for the execution and termination of the service contract with the *GmbH* is the corporate body which is also responsible for the appointment and dismissal of the

---

[300] Decision of the Federal Supreme Court, published in BGHZ, vol. 97, pp. 28, 34 et seq.
[301] Sec. 31 para. 1 sentence 1 of the Codetermination Act, sec. 84 para. 1 sentence 1 of the Stock Corporation Act.
[302] Sec. 46 no. 5 of the Limited Liability Company Act.

managing director (so-called **annexed responsibility** (*Annexzuständigkeit*)). As a rule, this is the shareholder meeting (or the sole shareholder), unless the articles of association provide otherwise. If the company is codetermined pursuant to the Codetermination Act (see below), the supervisory board is responsible for the execution of the service contract with the managing director.

A managing director who is also a shareholder may vote in the shareholder meeting on his service contract or on its termination.[303]

c) Form and Content of the Service Contract

The service contract need not take a specific form. Since the corporate duties of a managing director towards the company come into being upon his appointment (see above), it is not strictly necessary for him to have a managing director's service contract. In practice, however, such an agreement usually exists in order to set out any additional **terms of the employment relationship** such as remuneration, retirement benefits and prohibitions on competition. Care must be taken that the provisions themselves do not overstep the company's articles of association since the latter, as the legal basis of the company, take precedence.

A managing director's service contract usually stipulates the **remuneration** due to him (there being no general entitlement to remuneration by law). Unlike the Stock Corporation Act, which states that the overall compensation due to the managing director must be reasonably related to his responsibilities and the situation of the company,[304] the Limited Liability Company Act is silent with regard to the extent of remuneration due to a managing director. The general law of obligations concerning service contracts provides that reasonable remuneration for services is deemed to have been agreed if, under the circumstances, such services cannot be expected to be provided for free.[305] However, there may be circumstances which suggest that the managing director should not receive any remuneration, such as where the company is a non-profit organization or the managing director is entitled to a share in its profits by reason of share ownership[306] or otherwise.

Hidden distributions of profits to a shareholder-managing director by way of an inappropriately high salary are prohibited.[307] If there is a significant deterioration in the situation of the company after execution of the service contract and the salary payment would threaten its existence, courts have held that a managing director can be obliged to agree to an appropriate **reduction in salary** based on his corporate fiduciary duty.[308] Conversely, in exceptional cases, the courts have taken the view that there may be a right to an increase in remuneration if the profits of the company have risen in an entirely unforeseen manner since the managing director's service contract was entered into.[309]

The company is only obliged to pay a **pension** to a managing director and benefits to his surviving dependents if his service contract so provides. The company is free to determine whether and to what extent it wishes to promise such benefit payments.

---

[303] Decisions of the Federal Supreme Court, published in BGHZ, vol. 18, pp. 205, 210 et seq., in NJW 1991, pp. 172 et. seq. and in NJW-RR 2011, pp. 1117 et seq.
[304] Sec. 87 para. 1 of the Stock Corporation Act.
[305] Sec. 612 of the Civil Code.
[306] Decision of the Higher Regional Court of Frankfurt, published in DStR 1993, p. 659.
[307] Decision of the Federal Supreme Court, published in BGHZ, vol. 111, pp. 224, 227 et seq.
[308] Decision of the Federal Supreme Court, published in GmbHR 1992, pp. 605, 607 et seq.; decision of the Higher Regional Court of Düsseldorf, published in GmbHR 2012, pp. 332, 335.
[309] Decision of the Federal Supreme Court, published in GmbHR 1978, pp. 12, 13.

Even if his service contract contains no explicit provisions in this regard, a managing director is subject to a **prohibition on competition** for the duration of his service contract. He may not compete with the company or exploit any of the company's business opportunities personally.

d) Termination of the Service Contract

Termination of a managing director's service contract takes place in accordance with the general provisions of the Civil Code governing service contracts.[310] The dismissal of a managing director or his resignation from office do not, as such, terminate his service contract but may be cause for **ordinary termination with notice period** (*ordentliche Kündigung*) or **termination without notice period** (*außerordentliche Kündigung*).

A service contract with a limited term ends upon expiration of the agreed period. In practice, **fixed-term service contracts** with a term of three to five years are often agreed upon in accordance with the standard practice for stock corporations. It is also commonplace to provide for significantly **longer ordinary notice periods** than required by statute (e.g., one year or longer). According to case law, if the **service contract is for an indefinite term** and contains no indication as to notice period, the general provisions of the Civil Code[311] apply.[312] These provide that ordinary termination is permissible for both parties on four weeks' notice to the 15th or to the end of a month. This period increases according to how long the managing director's service contract has subsisted.[313]

Termination without notice is possible at any time for **good cause**.[314] The courts recognize several grounds for good cause, such as criminal actions, self-interested transactions by the managing director, the acceptance of bribes, failure as a businessman and violation of shareholder instructions. Notice of termination must be given **within two weeks** after the shareholder meeting (or in case the supervisory board is responsible, the supervisory board) having adequate knowledge of the facts on which the termination of the service contract shall be based.[315] According to the Federal Supreme Court, the two week period only begins to run once the shareholder meeting has assembled and its members have gained knowledge of the relevant facts after such assembly.[316] Every shareholder and every co-managing director is obligated to convene a shareholder meeting in due course after having gained knowledge of facts justifying the termination of the service contract for good cause.

The corporate body **authorized** to enter into the service contract (see above) is also authorized to issue a termination notice.

Upon termination of his service contract, the managing director must **return all business documents to the company**. A **post-contractual prohibition on competition** applies only if his service contract contains a provision to this effect. In this event, however, the withdrawing managing director must be paid a certain amount of compensation by the company. Where there is no provision regarding a prohibition on competition, there may nevertheless be a fiduciary duty prohib-

---

[310] Sec. 620 et seq. of the Civil Code.
[311] Sec. 622 para. 1 of the Civil Code.
[312] Decision of the Federal Supreme Court, published in BGHZ, vol. 91, p. 217 et seq.
[313] Sec. 622 para. 2 of the Civil Code.
[314] Sec. 626 of the Civil Code.
[315] Sec. 626 para. 2 of the Civil Code.
[316] Decision of the Federal Supreme Court, published in NJW 1998, p. 3274.

iting him from later exploiting business opportunities that became known to him during his term of office as managing director for personal gain.[317]

4. Liability of the Managing Director

a) Prerequisites of the Liability of the Managing Director

The Limited Liability Company Act provides that the managing directors of a *GmbH* must always act with the **due care of a prudent businessman**.[318] If a managing director violates this duty, he may be liable to the company for damages. In addition to this general liability provision, the Limited Liability Company Act contains various other provisions under which a managing director can be held liable, in particular in connection with the repayment of registered share capital to shareholders.[319]

Managing directors have to make sure that they possess the **knowledge and ability** which is objectively required to properly fulfill the obligations of a managing director. Even though it is possible for the managing directors to **allocate certain areas of responsibility** to individual managing directors, each managing director remains obligated to monitor whether the other managing directors are fulfilling their obligations.

If the company has incurred damages as a consequence of managing directors breaching their duties, the **burden of proof** with respect to the respective breach of duty and fault is reversed. The managing director has to prove that he acted in accordance with his duty.[320] If, for example, he alleges that he was only following an instruction of the shareholder meeting, he must prove that such an instruction was in fact issued.

Attempts have been made to **substantiate the managing director's duty of care** by enumerating certain **individual duties of conduct**. They include:
- observance of the law;
- observance of the articles of association and rules of procedure;
- observance of the provisions of the service contract;
- compliance with the instructions of the shareholders;
- proper organization of the company;
- monitoring of the organization of the company;
- regular monitoring of the liquidity and financial situation of the company;
- avoidance of excessive risks;
- avoidance, or at least disclosure, of all conflicts between the interests of the company and the personal interests of the managing director; and
- careful preparation of business and entrepreneurial decisions.

In addition to the general duty of care, there are a number of **individual legal duties** that the managing directors must abide by. These include the:
- duty to properly keep accounts and prepare balance sheets;
- prohibition on hidden distributions of profits;
- duty to convene the shareholder meeting in the event that half of the registered share capital is lost;
- duty to file for insolvency in the event of illiquidity or over-indebtedness;

---

[317] Decision of the Federal Supreme Court, published in GmbHR 1977, p. 43.
[318] Sec. 43 para. 1 of the Limited Liability Company Act.
[319] Sec. 43 para. 3 of the Limited Liability Company Act.
[320] Decision of the Federal Supreme Court, published in BGHZ, vol. 152, pp. 280 et seq., decision of the Higher Regional Court of Koblenz, published in NZG 2015, p. 272.

- duty to pay taxes and social insurance contributions; and
- duty to observe penal, labor, trade, and environmental regulations.

Insofar as these duties are imposed on the company itself, the managing directors must ensure that they are fulfilled. The managing directors are subject to liability if the company suffers damages as a result of the non-fulfillment of such duties.

The managing directors are further subject to **fiduciary duties**. From this follows – though not explicitly mentioned in the law – the **obligation to keep secret the company's confidential information and business secrets**. The managing directors are also subject to a **prohibition on competition**[321] which prohibits the managing directors from entering into personal transactions in the company's area of activity. Beyond this prohibition on competition, the fiduciary duties prohibit managing directors from exploiting the company's business opportunities for their personal benefit. For managing directors whose main occupation is their position as managing director, this would generally mean an obligation not to take up any other professional or commercial activity.

The courts recognize that certain **entrepreneurial decisions** made by the managing directors may be mistaken and that, while the company may suffer damages, the managing directors should not be liable for them. In its *"ARAG"* decision, the Federal Supreme Court held that the management is granted a **broad scope of action**.[322] This includes the deliberate taking of business risks and, in general, covers the danger of mistaken judgments and assessments. The Federal Supreme Court thereby borrowed from the U.S. business judgment rule, which has since become reflected in sec. 93 para. 1 of the Stock Corporation Act.[323] The broad **entrepreneurial discretion** granted to management is not unlimited, however. The managing directors may not have any personal interest in the decision reached, they have to carefully determine the grounds for the decision, they must act in the interest of the company and in good faith, and they may not take any irresponsible entrepreneurial risks.

b) Consequences of the Liability of the Managing Director

If a managing director violates the aforementioned duties, the company can claim **compensation for damages** from the managing director concerned. The shareholder meeting decides by simple majority whether the claim will be asserted;[324] in codetermined companies, this decision is made by the supervisory board. If the managing director concerned is a shareholder, he is excluded from the vote.[325]

Unlike an *AG*, a *GmbH* can **waive** the claim for damages or agree on a settlement. If the company **ratifies** the acts of the managing director (*Entlastung*), this entails a waiver of claims to damages to the extent such claims were known to the shareholder meeting (or the supervisory board, if competent) or could have been known after due analysis of all management reports and other management submissions. Private knowledge of all shareholders may be sufficient.[326]

---

[321] Decision of the Federal Supreme Court, published in BB 1989, pp. 1637 et seq.
[322] Decision of the Federal Supreme Court, published in BGHZ, vol. 135, pp. 244, 253 et seq.
[323] *Cf.* B.V.2.h.
[324] Sec. 46 no. 8, 47 para. 1 of the Limited Liability Company Act.
[325] Sec. 47 para. 4 of the Limited Liability Company Act.
[326] Decision of the Federal Supreme Court, published in WM 1976, pp. 736 et seq.

The limitation period for claims for damages is **five years**.[327] This limitation period begins when the claim comes into existence, i.e., when the breach of duty is committed and the company incurs the damage.

c) Third-Party Claims

The managing directors **are liable to third parties only in exceptional cases**. They are liable when they have **personally committed a tortious act** and thereby have inflicted damages on a third party (e.g., by causing a traffic accident on a business trip). In these cases, the company is also liable insofar as the managing director was conducting company business.[328] Furthermore, the managing directors are liable to third parties when they have violated a **protective law** within the meaning of sec. 823 para. 2 of the Civil Code. In particular, the duty to file for insolvency,[329] the provisions of the Criminal Code regarding fraud and embezzlement, and the duty to pay social insurance contributions have been recognized as protective laws for the benefit of companies' creditors. Sec. 43 of the Limited Liability Company Act, which sets forth the managing director's duty of care, is, however, not considered as a protective law in this context.[330] Personal liability on the part of a managing director can result from an **intentional act that is unethical and against public policy** and harms a business partner of the company.[331] If a managing director, in **contract negotiations**, deliberately conceals the economically catastrophic situation of the company and thereby induces a third party to enter into a contract, there can be personal liability for the managing director to that other party. The **shareholders** are treated as third parties and, therefore, generally have no direct damage claims against the managing directors.

VII. Supervisory Board and Codetermination

1. Overview

In contrast to an *AG*, the law on *GmbHs* does not, as a rule, require an obligatory supervisory board for a *GmbH*. It allows the formation of a supervisory board through the articles of association (**optional supervisory board**). However, a *GmbH* is **obliged** to form a supervisory board pursuant to codetermination law where:
- the *GmbH* regularly employs more than 500 employees. In this event, according to the **One-Third Participation Act** (*Drittelbeteiligungsgesetz*), a supervisory board consisting of at least three members has to be formed. The number of supervisory board members has to be divisible by three. One-third of the members of the supervisory board are elected by the employees and two-thirds by the shareholder meeting or another authorized corporate body determined by the articles of association.
- the *GmbH* regularly employs more than 2,000 employees. In this event, according to the **Codetermination Act** (*Mitbestimmungsgesetz*), a supervisory board must be formed. Its size varies according to the number of employees (at least 12 members; if there are more than 10,000 employees, at least 16 members; if

---

[327] Sec. 43 para. 4 of the Limited Liability Company Act.
[328] Sec. 31 of the Civil Code.
[329] Sec. 15a para. 1 of the Insolvency Code.
[330] Decision of the Federal Supreme Court, published in BGHZ, vol. 194, pp. 26 et seq.
[331] Sec. 826 of the Civil Code.

there are more than 20,000 employees, at least 20 members). One-half of the supervisory board members are elected by the shareholder meeting or another competent corporate body determined by the articles of association, the other half by the employees.
- the *GmbH* regularly employs more than 1,000 employees and operates in the coal, iron or steel sector. In this case, according to the **Coal, Iron and Steel Codetermination Act** (*Montanmitbestimmungsgesetz*), a supervisory board with 11 members must be established. Five members are elected by the shareholder meeting or any other authorized corporate body as determined by the articles of association; five members are elected by the employees; one member (the so-called neutral member) is determined in a rather complicated mediation procedure. The size of the supervisory board can vary if the registered share capital of the company exceeds certain threshold values.

2. The Optional Supervisory Board

In companies with up to 500 employees, no supervisory board needs to be established. However, the articles of association can provide for the formation of a supervisory board (**optional supervisory board**). In this event, the articles of association can stipulate the optional supervisory board's composition, competencies and mode of procedure. The rules for an optional supervisory board of a *GmbH* can therefore differ quite substantially from the rules for a legally mandated supervisory board of an *AG*.

The Limited Liability Company Act provides that the most important **stock corporation regulations** concerning supervisory boards generally apply to optional supervisory boards.[332] However, the reference to the stock corporation regulations applies only if the optional supervisory board in question carries out **monitoring responsibilities** with respect to the managing directors, i.e., not in the case of an optional supervisory board that only has advisory responsibilities. The rules for stock corporations that apply accordingly to optional supervisory boards (with a monitoring function) include, in particular, provisions regarding reporting, the number of supervisory board members, the personal prerequisites for supervisory board members, their dismissal and the initiation of transactions requiring consent. However, such rules may be modified or excluded in the *GmbH's* articles of association, except for a few mandatory rules, e.g., those that concern liability of the supervisory board members, criminal offences of supervisory board members and requirements for business letters.

3. Advisory Board

It is often the case that, in addition to the shareholder meeting and the managing directors, a further corporate body is set up, e.g., an **advisory board** (*Beirat*), **administrative board** (*Verwaltungsrat*) or **shareholders' committee** (*Gesellschafterausschuss*). This optional corporate body can take the place of a supervisory board or it can **coexist with a supervisory board**.

The law assumes the permissibility of such corporate bodies but does not contain any regulations on them. Such boards may have a purely **advisory function** or may be made to **closely resemble supervisory boards**. The responsibilities

---

[332] Sec. 52 para. 1 of the Limited Liability Company Act.

of the advisory board are determined exclusively by the articles of association of the company together with the rules of procedure for the advisory board, if any. Even management responsibilities may be partly transferred to the advisory board. However, the advisory board may not be granted responsibilities which pertain to the core competencies of the managing directors (e.g., representation of the company as corporate body, duties regarding bookkeeping, preservation of capital and filing for insolvency) or the shareholders (e.g., amendments to the articles of association, structural measures, liquidation of the company, right to reclaim responsibilities from the advisory board). The same applies to other optional corporate bodies.

4. Supervisory Board according to One-Third Participation Act

The One-Third Participation Act (*Drittelbeteiligungsgesetz*) applies to companies which regularly employ more than 500 (and fewer than 2,000) employees. The **employees of companies that the *GmbH* controls** through a domination agreement and of companies that are integrated into the *GmbH* also count towards these limits.

If these prerequisites are fulfilled, the management structure of the *GmbH* is modified and the formation of a supervisory board having between three and twenty-one members, depending on the amount of the registered share capital, becomes mandatory.[333] Shareholders are represented by two-thirds of the members of the supervisory board, employees by one-third. The representatives of the shareholders are **elected** by the shareholder meeting or another competent corporate body determined in the articles of association.

The shareholder meeting further determines target figures for the **proportion of women** in the **supervisory board**.[334] If the existing proportion of women is below 30%, the target figures to be determined may not be lower than the status quo.[335] *GmbHs* subject to the One-Third Participation Act are required to report on the targets set on an annual basis and need to disclose whether targets were met or not.[336] However, the failure to meet a target for women's representation does not have any immediate legal consequence.

The supervisory board is tasked with **monitoring** the managing directors. It is obligated to make certain kinds of transactions subject to its consent.[337] However, the **right of the shareholders to issue binding instructions** to the managing directors **remains unaffected**. In other respects, as well, the rights of such supervisory board are weaker than those of an *AG's* supervisory board. The shareholder meeting remains competent for the appointment, dismissal, and service contract of each managing director. The same applies to formal approval of the annual financial statements.

5. Supervisory Board according to Codetermination Act

If a company regularly employs more than 2,000 employees, a mandatory supervisory board pursuant to the Codetermination Act (*Mitbestimmungsgesetz*) must

---

[333] Sec. 95 sentence 4 of the Stock Corporation Act.
[334] Sec. 52 para. 2 sentence 1 of the Limited Liability Company Act.
[335] Sec. 111 para 5 of the Stock Corporation Act.
[336] Sec. 289a para. 4 sentence 1 of the Commercial Code.
[337] Sec. 111 para. 4 of the Stock Corporation Act.

be formed.[338] If the *GmbH* controls a group of companies, the **employees of group companies** controlled by the *GmbH* count as employees of the *GmbH*.[339] Control can be exercised through an enterprise agreement (e.g., domination agreement) or *de facto*. If the *GmbH* holds the majority of votes or share capital of a particular company, such company is presumed to be controlled by the *GmbH*. Thus, even a mere holding *GmbH* without any employees of its own may have to form a mandatory supervisory board.

The supervisory board generally consists of **12 members**.[340] If more than 10,000 employees are employed, the supervisory board must consist of **16 members**;[341] if more than 20,000 are employed, the required number of supervisory board members is **20**.[342]

Furthermore, the supervisory board determines target figures for the **proportion of women** in the **supervisory board**.[343] If the existing proportion of women is below 30%, the target figures to be determined may not be lower than the status quo.[344] Codetermined *GmbHs* are required to report on the targets set on an annual basis and need to disclose whether targets were met or not.[345] However, the failure to meet a target for women's representation does not have any immediate legal consequence.

Half of the supervisory board members are **elected** by the employees and half are elected by the shareholders or the authorized corporate body determined by the articles of association. A **majority** can be reached for the shareholders' side through the fact that the **chairman of the supervisory board**, who can be determined by the shareholders, has a right to cast a second vote under certain conditions.[346]

The **responsibilities** of the codetermined supervisory board have been made to largely resemble those in an *AG*. In contrast to the supervisory board formed pursuant to the One-Third Participation Act (see above), the codetermined supervisory board has the responsibility of **appointing and removing the managing directors** of the *GmbH* and of executing and terminating their **service contracts**. Thus the managing directors are largely independent of the shareholders; this strengthens their position vis-à-vis the shareholders. The Codetermination Act provides for a special **three-stage voting procedure for the appointment and dismissal of managing directors**.[347] During the first vote, a majority of at least two thirds of all supervisory board members is required. If such a majority does not come about, a special mediation committee is required to make a proposal within a month. During the subsequent second vote, a simple majority of the votes of all supervisory board members is sufficient. If the necessary majority is again not reached, the chairman of the supervisory board has two votes during a third voting procedure. In this case, too, an absolute majority of all votes is necessary.

In contrast to the *AG*, important responsibilities are reserved for **the shareholder meeting** (and not the supervisory board), namely: the formal approval of the

---

[338] Sec. 1 of the Codetermination Act.
[339] Sec. 5 of the Codetermination Act.
[340] Sec. 7 para. 1 sentence 1 no. 1 of the Codetermination Act.
[341] Sec. 7 para. 1 sentence 1 no. 2 of the Codetermination Act.
[342] Sec. 7 para. 1 sentence 1 no. 3 of the Codetermination Act.
[343] Sec. 52 para. 2 sentence 2 of the Limited Liability Company Act.
[344] Sec. 111 para 5 Stock of the Corporation Act.
[345] Sec. 289a para. 4 sentence 1 of the Commercial Code.
[346] Sec. 29 of the Codetermination Act.
[347] Sec. 31 of the Codetermination Act.

annual financial statements and the **right to issue instructions** to the managing directors.

VIII. Financial System

1. Bookkeeping and Accounting

a) Overview

The bookkeeping and accounting requirements pertaining to *GmbHs* are mainly covered by the **Commercial Code**. The relevant provisions set out the general rules for bookkeeping, inventory, annual financial statements and preservation of documents for all persons and entities conducting business (*Kaufleute*).[348] There are also supplementary provisions for companies and corporations.[349] A number of special regulations are dependent on the **size of the corporation**. The Commercial Code defines three sizes of corporation (small corporations, medium-sized corporations, large corporations), categorized according to their balance sheet totals, turnover and number of employees:[350]

- **small corporations** are those which do not exceed at least two of the following three thresholds: balance sheet total of EUR 6,000,000, turnover of EUR 12,000,000 and an annual average of 50 employees.[351]
- **medium-sized corporations** are those which exceed at least two of the thresholds characterizing small corporations and do not exceed at least two of the three thresholds for large corporations.
- **large corporations** are those which exceed at least two of the following three thresholds: balance sheet total of EUR 20,000,000, turnover of EUR 40,000,000 and an annual average of 250 employees.

In 2012, the concept of **tiny corporations** (*Kleinstkapitalgesellschaften*) as a sub-category of small corporations has been introduced in the Commercial Code. Tiny corporations are **small corporations** which do not exceed at least two of the following three thresholds: balance sheet total of EUR 350,000, turnover of EUR 700,000 and annual average of 10 employees.[352]

The Limited Liability Company Act contains very **few additional provisions with respect to accounting**. It is stipulated that proper bookkeeping falls under the duties of the managing director.[353] Furthermore, it is provided that the registered share capital has to be reported in the annual financial statements as subscribed capital.[354] Claims against shareholders for additional contributions have to be capitalized under certain circumstances. Loans, receivables and liabilities to shareholders each have to be reported separately or listed in the notes to the financial statements. The annual financial statements have to be formally approved at the shareholder meeting.[355]

---

[348] Sec. 238 to 263 of the Commercial Code.
[349] Sec. 264 to 342e of the Commercial Code.
[350] Sec. 267 of the Commercial Code.
[351] Sec. 267 para. 1 of the Commercial Code.
[352] Sec. 267a of the Commercial Code.
[353] Sec. 41 of the Limited Liability Company Act.
[354] Sec. 42 para. 1 of the Limited Liability Company Act.
[355] Sec. 42a, 46 no. 1 of the Limited Liability Company Act.

b) Annual Financial Statements

The company must prepare the annual financial statements (*Jahresabschluss*) each year, comprising the **balance sheet** (*Bilanz*), the **profit and loss statement** (*Gewinn- und Verlustrechnung*) and the **notes** (*Anhang*). Further, a **management report** (*Lagebericht*) has to be prepared by all companies, except tiny and small corporations,[356] describing the course of business and the economic situation of the company, as well as its anticipated development, its research and development activities and other transactions of particular importance which have occurred until the end of the fiscal year. There are several ways in which this process is made easier for tiny, small and medium-sized companies, e.g., with respect to the layout of the balance sheet and profit and loss statement or the information which needs to be provided in the notes, if required at all.

The annual financial statements, the management report and the proposal for the appropriation of profits for the year have to **be submitted to the Federal Gazette** (*Bundesanzeiger*) without undue delay following the presentation of the annual financial statements to the shareholders, but at the latest prior to the end of the 12th month of the fiscal year following the reporting date of the annual financial statements.[357] The managing directors must cause the documents submitted to the Federal Gazette to be published without undue delay. This achieves the goal of strict disclosure of the annual financial statements and the other documents submitted. For tiny, small and medium-sized companies, certain facilitating provisions apply. Large and medium-sized companies may choose to publish annual financial statements drawn up pursuant to International Accounting Standards.[358] This does not, however, relieve them of the obligation to also draw up annual financial statements pursuant to the Commercial Code for purposes of, inter alia, profit distribution and taxation.

These disclosure regulations are enforced by civil law and criminal penalty provisions.[359] Moreover, the Federal Office of Justice (*Bundesamt für Justiz*) may open proceedings ex officio and may impose fines on the managing directors of a *GmbH* and on the *GmbH* itself in case of insufficient compliance with the aforementioned disclosure requirements.[360]

c) Preparation of the Annual Financial Statements

The **managing directors** have to prepare the annual financial statements.[361] They have a period of three months from the beginning of the subsequent fiscal year to do so, or up to six months in the case of tiny or small companies.[362] The subsequent proceedings leading up to formal approval of the annual financial statements by the shareholder meeting depends on whether the company has a supervisory board and whether or not the annual financial statements are to be audited.

- In the case of **tiny** or **small companies** without a supervisory board, the managing directors present the annual financial statements directly to the shareholders[363] who then decide whether or not to formally approve them.

---

[356] Sec. 264 para. 1 sentence 4, 267a para. 2 of the Commercial Code.
[357] Sec. 325 para. 1 of the Commercial Code.
[358] Sec. 325 para. 2a of the Commercial Code.
[359] Sec. 331 to 335b of the Commercial Code.
[360] Sec. 335 para. 1 of the Commercial Code.
[361] Sec. 41 of the Limited Liability Company Act; sec. 242 para. 1 of the Commercial Code.
[362] Sec. 264, 267a para. 2 of the Commercial Code.
[363] Sec. 42a of the Limited Liability Company Act.

If the company has a supervisory board, the annual financial statements are first presented to the supervisory board which has to audit them, prepare a report on them and return the documents with its audit report to the managing directors.[364] The managing directors then present these documents to the shareholder meeting for adoption of a resolution on formal approval.[365]

- In the case of **medium-sized and large companies** without a supervisory board, the managing directors must first present the annual financial statements and the management report to the auditor of annual financial statements.[366] The auditor then returns these documents together with its audit report to the managing directors. Finally, the managing directors present the annual financial statements, including the audit report, to the shareholder meeting. If a supervisory board exists, the annual financial statements with the audit report of the auditor must also be passed on to the supervisory board. Afterwards, the documents with the supervisory board's own audit report are passed back to the managing directors, who then present the documents to the shareholder meeting for the adoption of a resolution.

d) Audit of the Annual Financial Statements

If the annual financial statements have to be **examined by an auditor of annual financial statements**,[367] the audit covers the annual financial statements and the management report, including bookkeeping. The audit has to review whether the legal regulations and any supplementary provisions of the articles of association have been observed.[368] The management report has to be examined to determine whether it is in accordance with the annual financial statements and the findings the auditor of annual financial statements has gained in the course of the examination and whether the report as a whole conveys an accurate picture of the state of the company. The auditor of annual financial statements further has to determine whether the risks associated with future developments have been accurately represented.[369] The auditor of annual financial statements has to **report in writing** and with the necessary detail on the type, scope, and results of his examination.[370] Further, he has to comment on the managing directors' assessment of the condition of the company.[371] The auditor then summarizes the results of the audit in an "auditor's certificate of the annual financial statements".[372] If the supervisory board has to review the annual financial statements, its review not only covers the results of the auditor but also the question whether the annual financial statements have been prepared in the appropriate way, i.e. whether the financial accounting election rights and the retention or distribution of earnings serve the interests of the company.

---

[364] Sec. 52 para. 1 of the Limited Liability Company Act in connection with sec. 170, 171 of the Stock Corporation Act; sec. 1 para. 1 no. 3 of the One-Third Participation Act in connection with sec. 170, 171 of the Stock Corporation Act; sec. 25 para. 1 no. 2 of the Codetermination Act in connection with sec. 170, 171 of the Stock Corporation Act.
[365] Sec. 42a of the Limited Liability Company Act.
[366] Sec. 320 para. 1 of the Commercial Code.
[367] Sec. 316 para. 1 of the Commercial Code.
[368] Sec. 317 para. 1 of the Commercial Code.
[369] Sec. 317 para. 1 and 2 of the Commercial Code.
[370] Sec. 321 of the Commercial Code.
[371] Sec. 321 para. 1 sentence 2 of the Commercial Code.
[372] Sec. 322 para. 1 of the Commercial Code.

VIII. Financial System

e) Formal Approval of the Annual Financial Statements

In a *GmbH*, unlike an *AG*, financial sovereignty rests with the shareholders. It is their responsibility to **formally approve the annual financial statements by adopting a shareholder resolution**.[373] Formal approval of the annual financial statements by the shareholder meeting renders the annual financial statements legally binding. The shareholders reach their decision by a simple majority. They may amend the annual financial statements within the bounds of the statutory accounting regulations. However, if the statements were previously examined by an auditor of annual financial statements, they will have to be audited again following an amendment.[374]

2. Allocation of the Annual Net Income

a) Right to Participate in the Profits and Right to the Distribution of Profits

The shareholders have a **right to participate in the profits**.[375] The shareholders generally have a claim to the annual net income plus profits carried forward, minus losses carried forward, unless otherwise provided by law, the articles of association or the **shareholder resolution on the appropriation of profits**. In particular, the resolution on the appropriation of profits may transfer funds to revenue reserves or carry them forward as profits. The allocation of profits is carried out in proportion to the shares held, unless otherwise provided in the articles of association.[376]

The general right of shareholders to participate in the profits is inseparably linked to their membership, which means that it cannot be the subject of an independent disposition. By the resolution on the appropriation of profits, this right is given the concrete form of a **claim to the distribution of profits**.[377] This claim can be assigned, attached and pledged even before the resolution has been adopted. The resolution brings the right to the distribution of profits into being.

The shareholders' claim to the distribution of profits has to be **satisfied in cash**. Unlike the laws governing *AGs*[378], the laws governing limited liability companies do not provide for dividends in kind.

b) Calculation

The appropriation of profits is resolved by the *GmbH's* shareholder meeting by simple majority.[379] As a rule, the shareholder meeting has to decide whether to **distribute** the profits or **retain** them for investment in the company. Generally, the shareholders are entitled to a complete distribution of the profits.[380] This right can be overcome by a resolution to retain the profits adopted by a majority of the shareholders. However, the power to reinvest the profits is not unlimited. If the majority of the shareholders wrongfully withhold profits from the minority shareholders by adopting such a resolution on the appropriation of profits, a minority shareholder is able to contest this resolution under certain circumstances. If the

---

[373] Sec. 42a, 46 no. 1 of the Limited Liability Company Act.
[374] Sec. 316 para. 3 of the Commercial Code.
[375] Sec. 29 para. 1 of the Limited Liability Company Act.
[376] Sec. 29 para. 3 of the Limited Liability Company Act.
[377] Decisions of the Federal Supreme Court, published in BGHZ, vol. 139, pp. 299, 302 et seq.
[378] Sec. 58 para. 5, 174 para. 2 no. 2 of the Stock Corporation Act.
[379] Sec. 46 no. 1, 47 para. 1 of the Limited Liability Company Act.
[380] Sec. 29 para. 1 of the Limited Liability Company Act.

shareholders fail to adopt a resolution on the appropriation of profits within a time period of eight months (11 months in case of tiny or small companies) after the end of the fiscal year,[381] the minority shareholders can bring an action to force the distribution of the profits.

c) Provisions of the Articles of Association

The provisions of the Limited Liability Company Act regarding the distribution of profits are not mandatory. Rather, the **articles of association** can determine the conditions under which revenue reserves are to be created or profits carried forward. The same applies to the formula on the allocation of profits among the shareholders. The articles of association can even exclude certain shareholders from the right to participate in the profits; amendments of the articles of association to that effect require the consent of the affected shareholders.[382] The company's own shares are not entitled to participate in the profits. Portions of the profits can also be paid out to third parties if so provided in the articles of association. It is further possible for third parties to have silent participations which may lead to a claim for a share in the profits. Profit and loss transfer agreements are frequently entered into and are governed by the law governing groups of companies,[383] since the Limited Liability Company Act does not govern this issue. Interim dividends or advance payments are also possible, provided that a shareholder resolution to that effect has been adopted[384] and that the equity of the company will not fall short of the amount of registered share capital set forth in the articles of association.[385]

3. The Maintenance of the Registered Share Capital

a) Introduction

Since, in general, only the company's assets are available to satisfy the creditors, it is necessary to ensure that the registered share capital is available to the creditors to cover liabilities. The Limited Liability Company Act ensures **the maintenance of the registered share capital** through various statutory provisions:
- The company assets necessary to maintain the registered share capital may in general not be paid out to the shareholders.[386]
- The company may not acquire its own shares if it cannot (theoretically) provide for a balance sheet reserve in the amount of the consideration without diminishing the registered share capital (see below for details).[387]
- The amount of the registered share capital is to be shown as subscribed capital on the liabilities section of the balance sheet.[388]

It should be noted that the registered share capital is only a (theoretical) calculation figure once the shareholders have made their respective contributions to the company. There is no obligation of the company to retain the same funds or

---

[381] Sec. 42a para. 2 sentence 1 of the Limited Liability Company Act.
[382] Analogy to sec. 53 para. 3 of the Limited Liability Company Act.
[383] Sec. 291 et. seq. of the Stock Corporation Act.
[384] Sec. 46 no. 1 of the Limited Liability Company Act.
[385] Sec. 30 para. 1 sentence 1 of the Limited Liability Company Act.
[386] Sec. 30 to 32 of the Limited Liability Company Act.
[387] Sec. 33 para. 2 of the Limited Liability Company Act.
[388] Sec. 42 para. 1 of the Limited Liability Company Act in connection with sec. 266 para. 3 A.I. of the Commercial Code.

assets which have been contributed, e.g., cash on a separate account, as long as other assets sufficiently cover the liabilities. The respective funds may be used up in the business.

The protection of registered share capital afforded by the **Limited Liability Company Act** falls short of the protection of capital provided by the **Stock Corporation Act**. Only the assets necessary to preserve the registered share capital are bound and not the entire company assets, as is the case with an *AG*. Furthermore, the Stock Corporation Act contains more stringent regulations[389] regarding a company's acquisition of its own shares than the corresponding provisions in the Limited Liability Company Act.[390] However, in another sense, the Stock Corporation Act is less stringent than the Limited Liability Company Act. For example, the Stock Corporation Act has no provisions comparable to sec. 31 para. 3 of the Limited Liability Company Act, under which the other shareholders are subject to contingent liability in the event that the recipient of a prohibited payment cannot refund it.

The regulations on capital maintenance are **supplemented by general provisions** on the protection of the company's assets. For example, a managing director could be subject to prosecution for breach of fiduciary duty[391] if he makes payments to a shareholder which put the company's economic existence at risk, in particular if he has violated the capital maintenance regulations.

b) Restrictions on Payments of Capital to Shareholders

The Limited Liability Company Act provides that the assets of the company necessary for the maintenance of the registered share capital may in general not be paid out to the shareholders.[392] The relevant sum is the amount of registered share capital set forth in the articles of association and recorded in the commercial register. Where the assets in the balance sheet minus liabilities (including accruals) no longer reach the amount of the registered share capital, i.e., there is an **"adverse balance"**, the registered share capital is no longer being "maintained". The same applies in the event of **over-indebtedness**, i.e., when the liabilities exceed the sum of the assets and the registered share capital.

Any allocation to the shareholders that would cause the equity to fall short of the registered share capital or that is made when the equity is already below the registered share capital is prohibited. Such an allocation may come in the form of a straightforward **payment of cash** to a shareholder. However, an allocation may also be made through a transaction with a shareholder in which the company renders a performance but does not receive sufficient value in return, contravening the **arm's-length principle**.

The prohibition of payments also applies to the **creation of security interests in the company's assets** for third-party claims against a shareholder or a shareholder's claims against a third party. However, it is controversial whether the mere creation of the security interest or only the realization of the security should be understood as a payment that can bring about an adverse balance.

Payments to non-shareholders do not automatically conflict with the principle of capital maintenance. However, there is a conflict if **a payment is made to a third party in lieu of a shareholder** and thus is to be ascribed to the shareholder. This

---

[389] Sec. 71 et seq. of the Stock Corporation Act.
[390] Sec. 33 of the Limited Liability Company Act.
[391] Sec. 266 of the Criminal Code.
[392] Sec. 30 of the Limited Liability Company Act.

could be the case, for example, where payments are made to persons close to the shareholders, such as spouses or children.

A prohibited allocation to a shareholder may result in the **liability** of both the shareholders and the managing directors of the company.

At first, the prohibition of payments set forth in the Limited Liability Company Act[393] means that the **company can and must refuse to render the payment** to the shareholder. Any shareholder resolution calling for such payment is null and void.

Payments that were rendered in contravention have to be **reimbursed to the company**.[394] This constitutes an independent reimbursement claim under corporate law. This reimbursement claim is due and payable immediately, without a shareholder resolution being necessary. The claim may not be deferred[395] or waived.[396] If the recipient has accepted the payment in **good faith**, reimbursement may only be demanded to the extent necessary to satisfy the claims of the company's creditors.[397] The defense of reliance in good faith is not available in the case of intent or gross negligence of the recipient. Also, the reimbursement claim remains unaffected even if the registered share capital is subsequently restored and the adverse balance has disappeared.[398]

The primary debtor of the reimbursement claim is the recipient of the prohibited funds, i.e., the **shareholder involved** or, in exceptional cases, a third party that received the payment.

If the sum to be repaid cannot be obtained from the recipient, the **other shareholders** will be liable for this sum in proportion to their shareholdings and to the extent necessary to satisfy the company's creditors.[399] Pursuant to case law, this contingent liability only exists up to the amount of the registered share capital.[400]

Managing directors who have made prohibited payments in breach of their duty are liable to the company for damages.[401] Shareholders who have provided compensation due to their contingent liability[402] can demand reimbursement from a managing director if he culpably made the prohibited payments.[403]

Furthermore, under the Limited Liability Company Act, **additional contributions** paid in can be refunded to the shareholders as long as they are not needed to cover a deficiency in the registered share capital.[404] Even if the registered share capital would be maintained after the repayment, such repayments may not be effected until three months have elapsed since the repayment resolution was published in the company's designated journals.[405]

---

[393] Sec. 30 para. 1 sentence 1 of the Limited Liability Company Act.
[394] Sec. 31 para. 1 of the Limited Liability Company Act.
[395] Decision of the Federal Supreme Court, published in NJW 2004, pp. 1111, 1112.
[396] Sec. 31 para. 4 of the Limited Liability Company Act.
[397] Sec. 31 para. 2 of the Limited Liability Company Act.
[398] Decision of the Federal Supreme Court, published in BGHZ, vol. 144, pp. 336, 340 et seq.
[399] Sec. 31 para. 3 of the Limited Liability Company Act.
[400] Decisions of the Federal Supreme Court, published in BGHZ, vol. 60, pp. 324, 331 et seq. and in BGHZ, vol. 150, 61, 64 et seq.
[401] Sec. 43 para. 3 of the Limited Liability Company Act.
[402] Sec. 31 para. 3 of the Limited Liability Company Act.
[403] Sec. 31 para. 6 of the Limited Liability Company Act.
[404] Sec. 30 para. 2 of the Limited Liability Company Act.
[405] Sec. 30 para. 2 sentence 2 to 4, sec. 12 of the Limited Liability Company Act.

c) Exceptions to the Prohibition against Refunding of Contributions

The Limited Liability Company Act provides for a number of exceptions to the general prohibition against allocations to shareholders that cause the equity to fall short of the registered share capital. In this case, the law deems the company to be sufficiently protected by other means or it intends to permit economically useful behavior.

As long as payments are made on the basis of a **profit and loss transfer agreement** between the company and the respective shareholder, the capital maintenance regulations do not apply.[406] The economic survival of the company is ensured through the duty of the dominating party to compensate losses of the company.[407]

Payments are also exempted from the general prohibition if they are matched by a fully recoverable, i.e., unimpaired, **claim for repayment or retransfer** of the company against the shareholder.[408] This exception in principle permits the granting of loans to a shareholder, e.g., in the context of **cash-pooling** systems. It embodies a so-called "accounting view" of capital maintenance. Previously, the Federal Supreme Court had held that loans could not be granted to shareholders if the equity – disregarding the repayment claim against the shareholder – fell short of the registered share capital. It only considered that a loan may be permissible if there could be no reasonable doubt as to the creditworthiness of the shareholder or if repayment was fully secured by valuable collateral.[409] Now, the statute permits loans to shareholders provided that the claim for repayment can be recovered in full.[410] However, the managing director is obliged to constantly review whether the shareholder remains creditworthy and whether the claim for repayment or retransfer remains fully recoverable and unimpaired. In order to meet this obligation, the management of the company may have to install an internal system securing adequate information and early warning. If the requirements for the making of a loan are no longer met, the managing director has a duty of care to make the claim for repayment or retransfer due and to enforce it against the shareholder. If he fails to do so, he may be liable to the company for damages.[411]

Finally, an exception provides that the company may repay **shareholder loans** and may satisfy claims of shareholders arising from economically equivalent transactions without regard to capital maintenance rules.[412] The creditors are still protected to some extent since an insolvency administrator may reclaim such payments in insolvency proceedings over the assets of the company subject to certain time limitations.[413]

d) Acquisition of Company's Own Shares

In principle, a *GmbH* **can acquire or pledge its own shares**.

The Limited Liability Company Act merely **prohibits** the company's acquisition of its own shares or taking them in pledge where the **capital contribution has**

---

[406] Sec. 30 para. 1 sentence 2 of the Limited Liability Company Act.
[407] Sec. 302 para. 2 of the Stock Corporation Act analogously.
[408] Sec. 30 para. 1 sentence 2 of the Limited Liability Company Act.
[409] Decision of the Federal Supreme Court, published in NJW 2004, pp. 1111, 1112.
[410] Sec. 30 para. 2 sentence 1 of the Limited Liability Company Act.
[411] Sec. 43 para. 2 of the Limited Liability Company Act.
[412] Sec. 30 para. 1 sentence 3 of the Limited Liability Company Act.
[413] Cf. A.VIII.3.e.

not yet been fully paid in.[414] If, despite this prohibition, the company acquires shares that have not been fully paid in, the assignment of such shares as well as the obligation to assign are null and void. Without this prohibition, the outstanding claim for contributions would be directed against the company itself. For this reason, the company also cannot subscribe to its own shares in the course of a capital increase, the only exception being in the case of a capital increase from company resources.[415]

The **conditions for a company's acquisition of its own shares** are that the company could (theoretically) provide for a balance sheet reserve in the amount of the consideration without diminishing either (i) the registered share capital or (ii) a reserve to be created pursuant to the articles of association which must not be used for payments to the shareholders.[416] Under certain circumstances, a company can acquire its own shares in connection with a merger, change of legal form or spin-off.[417] If the shares were acquired in violation of the aforementioned requirements, only the obligation to assign but not the assignment of the shares itself will be null and void.[418]

Generally, **membership rights** arising from shares held by the company itself are **suspended**. This applies in particular to voting rights and the right to participate in the profits. Once the company assigns the share to a third party, the rights are revived.

There is **no upper limit** on a company's acquisition of its own shares. This can in fact lead to a situation in which the company temporarily acquires all shares in the company itself.

e) Shareholder Loans

The majority of German *GmbHs* only have registered share capital in the minimum amount of EUR 25,000. However, a company's financing needs are generally much greater. These needs are often satisfied either by outside capital (bank loans or other outside funds) or by way of loans granted by the shareholders.

Loans granted by shareholders are **generally permissible**. However, they are subject to **special regulations** which were recently simplified. Until 2008, if a shareholder granted or did not reclaim a loan at a time when the company was over-indebted or illiquid or when it was not in a position to obtain new loans from its banks at customary rates ("crisis"), such shareholder loan was considered as equity-replacing. It was argued that a shareholder is responsible for ensuring proper corporate financing.[419] Thus, if a shareholder provided a loan to the company instead of equity, it was justified to treat such outside capital in a manner similar to equity during a corporate crisis. If such a shareholder loan had been repaid to the shareholder, an insolvency administrator of the company could claim from the shareholder to repay such loan to the company. Additional repayment claims of the company – irrespective of insolvency – existed if the repayment of the loan was made from the registered share capital.

---

[414] Sec. 33 para. 1 of the Limited Liability Company Act.
[415] Sec. 57c para. 1, sec. 57l para.1 of the Limited Liability Company Act.
[416] Sec. 33 para. 2 of the Limited Liability Company Act.
[417] Sec. 33 para. 3 of the Limited Liability Company Act.
[418] Sec. 33 para. 2 sentence 3 of the Limited Liability Company Act.
[419] Decisions of the Federal Supreme Court, published in BGHZ, vol. 90, pp. 381, 389 and in BGHZ, vol. 105, pp. 168, 175 et seq.

VIII. Financial System

This dual system has recently been abolished. The Insolvency Code now provides that in insolvency proceedings, shareholders may claim repayment of their loans only as **subordinate insolvency creditors,** regardless of whether the company was in a "crisis" at the time the respective loan was made.[420] Such loan repayment claims are only to be notified to the insolvency administrator as subordinate claims if the insolvency court makes a special call for notification of such subordinated claims.[421] They then have the lowest priority, below all other subordinate claims.

Claims of third parties are subordinated if the underlying transactions are economically equivalent to a loan granted by a shareholder.[422] This would be the case, for example, if close relatives receive funds from a shareholder and turn them over to the company. Case law on the former provisions concerning shareholder loans further requires an economic unity between the lender and the shareholder.[423]

If the **company repays a shareholder loan or satisfies an equivalent claim during the year preceding the filing to initiate insolvency proceedings**, the insolvency administrator may contest such repayment or satisfaction and demand reimbursement to the company.[424] The same applies to security interests or sureties granted during the ten year period preceding the filing to initiate insolvency proceedings.[425]

Loan repayment claims of **shareholders who are not managing directors** and who **hold 10% or less of the shares** in the registered share capital are not subordinated (so-called **small shareholders privilege**).[426] The same applies to loan repayment claims of shareholders who acquired their shares when the company was over-indebted, illiquid or about to become illiquid, and who made the acquisition for the purpose of restructuring the company (so-called **restructuring privilege**).[427]

If **third parties** grant loans to a company or undertake corresponding legal actions and a shareholder provides the third party with a security interest for the repayment of the loan, the repayment claim of the third party can be notified to the insolvency table in its full amount. However, the third party can only demand satisfaction from the insolvency estate to the extent that it did not first obtain satisfaction from the realization of the security interest created by the shareholder.[428]

4. Increase of the Registered Share Capital

a) Overview

The Limited Liability Company Act provides for three forms of registered share capital increases: the **capital increase against contributions** (ordinary capital

---

[420] Sec. 39 para. 1 no. 5 of the Insolvency Code.
[421] Sec. 174 para. 3 sentence 1 of the Insolvency Code.
[422] Sec. 39 para. 1 no. 5 of the Insolvency Code.
[423] Decisions of the Federal Supreme Court, published in BGHZ, vol. 81, pp. 311, 315, in BGHZ, vol. 105, pp. 168, 177 and in GmbHR 2001, p. 106.
[424] Sec. 135 para. 1 no. 2 of the Insolvency Code.
[425] Sec. 135 para. 1 no. 1 of the Insolvency Code.
[426] Sec. 39 para. 5 of the Insolvency Code.
[427] Sec. 39 para. 4 sentence 2 of the Insolvency Code.
[428] Sec. 44a of the Insolvency Code.

increase),[429] the **capital increase from company resources**[430] and the **capital increase from authorized capital**.[431] In contrast to the laws governing *AGs*, the Limited Liability Company Act does not provide for contingent capital.

The following steps are to be taken to increase the registered share capital against contributions or from company resources:
- the shareholder meeting adopts a resolution to amend the articles of association;
- a resolution determining the subscribers is adopted[432];
- the subscription agreements between the subscribers and the company are entered into[433];
- the contributions for the new shares are paid in by the subscribers; and
- an application is submitted for registration of the capital increase in the commercial register, and such registration is effected[434].

b) Ordinary Capital Increase

An ordinary capital increase first requires a **resolution by the shareholder meeting** to amend the articles of association. The resolution must state the increased amount of the registered share capital and the premium to be paid by the subscribers, if any. The resolution requires a majority of **three-quarters** of the votes cast and must be **notarized**.[435] The articles of association can also impose additional requirements.[436]

Generally, the shareholders have a **subscription right** to the new shares (although this right is not regulated by statute). However, third parties may also be permitted to subscribe. It has to be **determined in a resolution** whether the new shares are to be issued only to shareholders or to third parties as well.[437]

In order for third parties to be permitted to subscribe to new shares, the **shareholders' subscription rights** must be excluded. The exclusion has to be resolved upon in connection with the resolution on the capital increase. According to the prevailing view, the exclusion of the subscription rights requires a **majority of three-quarters of the votes cast**, i.e., the same majority which is required for the resolution on the capital increase. Additionally, an exclusion of subscription rights is only permissible if (i) the exclusion is justified because it is in the interest of the company, (ii) there is no other way to achieve the interests of the company with lesser encroachment of shareholder rights, and (iii) the encroachment of shareholder rights is not disproportionate compared to the advantage of the company. An exclusion of subscription rights not meeting such requirements may be challenged by the shareholders. No justification is necessary if all affected shareholders agree to the exclusion of the subscription rights.

Each subscriber enters into an agreement with the company for the subscription to the new shares (**subscription agreement**). The subscriber must then pay the new contribution and fulfill the duties associated with the share. The subscrip-

---

[429] Sec. 55, 56 to 57a of the Limited Liability Company Act.
[430] Sec. 57c to 57o of the Limited Liability Company Act.
[431] Sec. 55a of the Limited Liability Company Act.
[432] Sec. 55 para. 2 of the Limited Liability Company Act.
[433] Sec. 55 para. 1 of the Limited Liability Company Act.
[434] Sec. 57, 54 para. 3 of the Limited Liability Company Act.
[435] Sec. 53 para. 2 sentence 1 of the Limited Liability Company Act.
[436] Sec. 53 para. 2 sentence 2 of the Limited Liability Company Act.
[437] Sec. 55 para. 2 of the Limited Liability Company Act.

tion declaration by the subscriber has to be recorded or certified by a notary.[438] It may also be rendered prior to the capital increase resolution. The company may not itself subscribe to any shares of its own in the course of an ordinary capital increase.[439] According to legal literature, the same applies to enterprises controlled by the company.

New shares may be subscribed to in **any amount**. If an existing shareholder subscribes to a new share, the new share will not be combined with the existing shares.[440] Alternatively, it is possible to increase the nominal value of the existing shares held by the shareholders (*Aufstockung*); generally, this requires that the respective shares have been fully paid in.

The increased registered share capital must actually be **paid in**. In this respect, the law governing the capital increase makes reference to the legal requirements regarding the formation of a *GmbH*. A report on the value of contributions which is required in case of a formation against contributions in kind (see above) is not mandatory in case of a capital increase against contributions in kind but is generally requested by the register court. In all other respects, reference is made to the discussion of the legal requirements for forming a *GmbH* (see above).

The capital increase must be filed **for registration in the commercial register**.[441] The capital increase becomes effective upon registration.[442]

c) Capital Increase from Company Resources

The registered share capital may also be increased **by converting reserves into registered share capital**.[443] No new resources are contributed to the company for this capital increase; instead, reserves are converted into registered share capital by way of an exchange of equity items on the balance sheet.

A capital increase from company resources requires a **resolution** by the shareholder meeting which amends the articles of association.[444] Another requirement is the **formal approval of the annual financial statements** for the last fiscal year completed prior to the adoption of the capital increase resolution and a **resolution on the appropriation of profits**. The capital increase resolution has to be based on a balance sheet.[445]

Only capital and revenue reserves that have **been shown in the balance sheet as such** can be converted into registered share capital.[446] Reserves cannot be converted as long as the balance sheet on which they are based shows a loss, including a loss carried forward.[447] Other revenue reserves may only be converted to the extent compatible with the purpose of such resources.[448] Hidden reserves cannot be converted into registered share capital. The underlying balance sheet[449] must be **audited** by an auditor.[450] It is also possible to increase the capital from

---

[438] Sec. 55 para. 1, 2 sentence 2 of the Limited Liability Company Act.
[439] Decision of the Federal Supreme Court, published in BGHZ, vol. 15, pp. 391, 393.
[440] Sec. 55 para. 3 of the Limited Liability Company Act.
[441] Sec. 57 para. 1 of the Limited Liability Company Act.
[442] Sec. 54 para. 3 of the Limited Liability Company Act.
[443] Sec. 57c para. 1 of the Limited Liability Company Act.
[444] Sec. 57c para. 4, 53 of the Limited Liability Company Act.
[445] Sec. 57c para. 2, 3 of the Limited Liability Company Act.
[446] Sec. 57d para. 1 of the Limited Liability Company Act.
[447] Sec. 57d para. 2 of the Limited Liability Company Act.
[448] Sec. 57d para. 3 of the Limited Liability Company Act.
[449] Sec. 57c para. 3 of the Limited Liability Company Act.
[450] Sec. 57e, 57f of the Limited Liability Company Act.

company resources on the basis of the company's annual balance sheet, provided that the reference date of the annual balance sheet is not older than eight months and the auditor has not raised any objections against the annual balance sheet in its audit certification.[451]

The capital increase may only be effected by either **creating new shares** or **increasing the nominal value of the existing shares**. The new shares and the shares whose nominal value is increased may be set at any even euro amount.[452] The shareholders are entitled to the new shares in proportion to their holdings in the previous registered share capital.[453]

d) Capital Increase from Authorized Capital

The Limited Liability Company Act was recently amended to allow the creation of authorized capital. Such authorization may be included in the articles of association upon formation of the company[454] or be introduced later on by way of amendment to the articles in a shareholder resolution requiring a majority of **three-quarters** of the votes cast.[455] The articles of association must set forth a maximum amount for the authorized capital increase.[456] The maximum amount may not exceed half of the registered share capital present at the time of authorization.[457] The articles must also provide for the duration of the authorization, which may be up to five years from the registration of the authorization in the commercial register.[458] The articles may provide that the subscription rights of the existing shareholders are excluded or that the managing directors have the power to exclude them. It can be assumed that the principles regarding the justification of an exclusion of subscription rights in case of a capital increase from authorized capital which have been developed by the Federal Supreme Court for stock corporations[459] will also be applied in the case of a *GmbH*.

The authorization in the articles may determine the terms and conditions of the future capital increase. It may, in particular, limit the authorization to certain purposes or provide for additional contributions. To the extent such determination is not made, the managing directors have to exercise reasonable discretion.

Once the managing directors have resolved to make use of the authorization and increase the registered share capital, the subscribers have to issue notarized subscription declarations and to render the appropriate contributions.[460] Contributions in kind are permitted only if the authorization so provides.[461] Finally, the use of the authorization and the corresponding change in the articles of association regarding the amount of the registered share capital have to be filed with the commercial register.[462]

---

[451] Sec. 57e para. 2 of the Limited Liability Company Act.
[452] Sec. 57h para. 1 of the Limited Liability Company Act.
[453] Sec. 57j sentence 1 of the Limited Liability Company Act.
[454] Sec. 55a para. 1 sentence 1 of the Limited Liability Company Act.
[455] Sec. 55a para. 2, sec. 53 para. 2 sentence 1 of the Limited Liability Company Act.
[456] Sec. 55a para. 1 sentence 1 of the Limited Liability Company Act.
[457] Sec. 55a para. 1 sentence 2 of the Limited Liability Company Act.
[458] Sec. 55a para. 1 sentence 1 of the Limited Liability Company Act.
[459] *Cf.* B.VI.3.b.dd.bbb. below.
[460] Sec. 55 para. 1, 56a of the Limited Liability Company Act.
[461] Sec. 55a para. 3 of the Limited Liability Company Act.
[462] Sec. 57 of the Limited Liability Company Act.

5. Reduction of the Registered Share Capital

A reduction of the registered share capital usually will be conducted for one of the following reasons: (i) to allow **distribution of parts of the registered share capital to the shareholders** or (ii) to **adjust the registered share capital** to equalize losses or an adverse balance. In both cases, the reduction of the registered share capital is generally subject to the following prerequisites:[463]

- adoption of a resolution by the shareholder meeting for the capital reduction;
- announcement of the capital reduction in the company's designated journals calling the creditors to give notice to the company;
- satisfaction of the creditors that do not agree to the reduction of the share capital or securing of their claims;
- submission of an application for registration of the capital reduction in the commercial register following a one-year waiting period; and
- registration of the capital reduction in the commercial register.

The resolution on the capital reduction has to be adopted by a **majority of three-quarters** of the votes cast and needs to be taken in a **notarized form**.[464] The capital reduction is usually carried out by way of a proportional reduction of the nominal amounts of the shares unless the shareholders agree on a disproportionate reduction. Once the registered share capital reduction has been effected, the amount that has been released has to be shown on the balance sheet as a revenue reserve or profit carried forward (if it is not necessary to equalize losses or an adverse balance) and may be **distributed** to the shareholders. The distribution of the "released" share capital is not mandatory, though. The amounts may also be retained in the company's revenue reserves, which is customary in a restructuring context. A third way to effect the adjustment of the shareholdings to the decreased registered share capital is the **redemption of the shares** of one or more shareholders.[465] In this case, the relevant shareholder ceases to be a shareholder and is **compensated** from the proceeds of the capital reduction.

The ordinary capital reduction is subject to certain requirements designed to **protect the creditors**. The managing directors have to publish an announcement of the reduction resolution, in which the creditors are called upon, in the company's designated journals.[466] If the creditors do not agree to the reduction, their asserted claims have to be satisfied or secured.[467] When applying for registration of the reduction resolution in the commercial register after the one-year waiting period has elapsed, the managing directors have to assure that the creditors who have notified the company have either agreed to the reduction or been satisfied or secured.[468] Managing directors who violate their duties in this respect or make a false statement may be subject to claims for damages by the company[469] or creditors who suffered a loss,[470] or even criminal prosecution.[471]

---

[463] Sec. 58 of the Limited Liability Company Act.
[464] Sec. 53 of the Limited Liability Company Act.
[465] Sec. 34 of the Limited Liability Company Act.
[466] Sec. 58 para. 1 no. 1 of the Limited Liability Company Act.
[467] Sec. 58 para. 1 no. 2 of the Limited Liability Company Act.
[468] Sec. 58 para. 1 no. 4 of the Limited Liability Company Act.
[469] Sec. 43 para. 1 of the Limited Liability Company Act.
[470] Decision of the Supreme Regional Court of Bavaria, published in BB 1974, pp. 1362, 1363.
[471] Sec. 82 para. 2 no. 1 of the Limited Liability Company Act.

If the capital reduction is conducted to equalize losses or an adverse balance (i.e. for restructuring purposes), a so-called **simplified capital reduction** is possible.[472] This means that the company's creditors do not have to be notified by announcement in the company's designated journals and that the one-year waiting period does not apply. Furthermore, there is no obligation to satisfy creditors who do not agree to the capital reduction or to grant security to them. Instead, the creditors are protected by restrictions on the future distribution of profits[473] and restrictions on the use of the company's revenue reserves.[474]

IX. Dissolution and Liquidation of the Company

1. Overview

Termination of a *GmbH* is usually effected through the **dissolution** of the company, followed by its **liquidation**. Once the liquidation has been completed, the **company is cancelled in the commercial register**. There are also other ways of terminating a company, such as by merging it with another company (if the other company is the acquiring company) or by spinning it off into another company.

2. Dissolution and Grounds for Dissolution

The law sets forth the possible grounds for dissolution, the most important of which are the following:
- The articles of association can provide that the company will be dissolved after a certain **period of time has elapsed**.[475] This seldom occurs in practice, since *GmbHs* generally tend to be formed for an unlimited period of time.
- If the articles of association do not contain a special provision, the shareholders can at any time **adopt a resolution** to dissolve the company with a majority of three-quarters of the votes cast.[476] No specific grounds for the dissolution need to be given. The Federal Supreme Court has always declined to review the justification for a resolution to dissolve a company.[477]
- A minority of shareholders who hold an aggregate of at least 10% of the registered share capital may file **an action for dissolution** of the company if **good cause** for dissolution can be found in the company's affairs.[478] The statute identifies one case of such good cause: when it is impossible to achieve the purpose of the company.[479] Good cause would also include an irreconcilable rift among the shareholders which jeopardizes the continuation of the company. In any case, an action for dissolution would be the last resort. If it is justified to exclude the "disruptive" shareholder, this method must be employed first.

---

[472] Sec. 58a of the Limited Liability Company Act.
[473] Sec. 58d of the Limited Liability Company Act.
[474] Sec. 58b, 58c of the Limited Liability Company Act.
[475] Sec. 60 para. 1 no. 1 of the Limited Liability Company Act.
[476] Sec. 60 para. 1 no. 2 of the Limited Liability Company Act.
[477] Decision of the Federal Supreme Court, published in BGHZ, vol. 76, pp. 352, 353 et seq.
[478] Sec. 60 para. 1 no. 3 of the Limited Liability Company Act in connection with sec. 61 para. 2 sentence 2 of the Limited Liability Company Act.
[479] Sec. 61 para. 1 of the Limited Liability Company Act.

- The **commencement of insolvency proceedings against the company's assets** leads to the company's dissolution;[480] the same applies if the court refuses to commence insolvency proceedings due to insufficient assets.[481]
- The **register court may order the dissolution** of the company if the articles of association contain serious defects.[482]
- The **register court can also order the company's dissolution** if it no longer has any assets.[483]
- Additionally, **dissolution orders may be issued by the administrative court** if a company endangers the public interest,[484] violates the constitutional order or if its purposes or activities violate provisions of criminal law intended to protect the security of the state.[485]

The dissolution of the company has to be registered in the commercial register and be publicly announced.[486] A liquidation suffix must be added to the company's name, normally the abbreviation *"i.L."*.[487]

3. Liquidation

Following dissolution, the company enters the liquidation stage. The **legal identity** of the company remains intact, but the previous business purpose is now replaced by the purpose of liquidation.

The statutory **liquidators** are the managing directors.[488] They need not be specially appointed to this position. However, the position of liquidator can be transferred to other persons by virtue of the articles of association or a shareholder resolution. Upon the request of a minority of shareholders holding at least 10% of the registered share capital, the register court may appoint liquidators if there is good cause to do so.[489] The liquidators' power to represent the company externally is, like that of the managing directors, unrestricted and not capable of being restricted.

The **liquidation commences** once the liquidators have published a notice of the dissolution in the company's designated journals and have called upon the creditors to register with the company.[490] Additionally, the liquidators have to prepare an opening balance sheet and a report explaining the opening balance sheet. If the liquidation process goes on for several years, annual financial statements for the liquidation also have to be prepared. Proper accounting further requires a final balance sheet once the liquidation is concluded.

The liquidators **must convert the entire assets of the company into cash**.[491] To this end, they have to conclude the day-to-day business, collect the company's receivables and fulfill its obligations. Once all the company's **creditors** have been satisfied or secured, the company's remaining assets are **distributed to the**

---

[480] Sec. 60 para. 1 no. 4 of the Limited Liability Company Act.
[481] Sec. 60 para. 1 no. 5 of the Limited Liability Company Act.
[482] Sec. 60 para. 1 no. 6 of the Limited Liability Company Act.
[483] Sec. 60 para. 1 no. 7 of the Limited Liability Company Act.
[484] Sec. 62 of the Limited Liability Company Act.
[485] Sec. 17 of the Association Act (*Vereinsgesetz*).
[486] Sec. 65 of the Limited Liability Company Act.
[487] Sec. 68 para. 2 of the Limited Liability Company Act.
[488] Sec. 66 para. 1 of the Limited Liability Company Act.
[489] Sec. 66 para. 2 of the Limited Liability Company Act.
[490] Sec. 65 para. 2 of the Limited Liability Company Act.
[491] Sec. 70 of the Limited Liability Company Act.

shareholders. This distribution may not be performed until the one-year waiting period after the third public call to the creditors has elapsed.[492]

4. Completion of Liquidation

Upon completion of the liquidation, the company **ceases to exist**. The liquidators must apply for **registration** of the company's termination in the commercial register.[493] Once the liquidation is completed, the company's books and correspondence are to be placed in the custody of one of the shareholders or a third party for a period of ten years.[494]

X. Limited Partnership with a *GmbH* as the Personally Liable Shareholder (*GmbH & Co. KG*)

1. Definition

A *GmbH & Co. KG* is a limited partnership with one or more limited partners and a **general partner** (with unlimited personal liability), which is not a natural person but a ***GmbH*** (general partner *GmbH*). The particularity about this kind of limited partnership is that no natural person is liable without limitation to the company's creditors. Claims of creditors will generally be satisfied only from the assets of the limited partnership; additionally, the general partner *GmbH* is directly liable to the *GmbH & Co. KG*'s creditors with all its assets. The limited partners of the *GmbH & Co. KG* and the shareholders of the *GmbH* generally do not face personal liability. Today, the *GmbH & Co. KG* is recognized not only by case law but also by more recent statutes. Since the manner in which the liability is structured resembles that of a corporation, a number of statutory provisions which otherwise only apply to corporations are also applicable to *GmbH & Co. KGs*.

2. Legal Particularities

Often, the shareholding structure in a *GmbH & Co. KG* is fashioned such that the limited partners hold shares in the general partner *GmbH* in proportion to their shareholdings in the limited partnership. However, this is not mandated by law.

Another possible structure is a **single-shareholder *GmbH & Co. KG*** where the identical person is at the same time both the sole limited partner and the sole shareholder of the general partner *GmbH*. Finally, the relationship between the limited partnership and the general partner *GmbH* is closest in a "**consolidated limited partnership**" (*Einheitsgesellschaft*) where all of the shares in the general partner *GmbH* have been assigned to the limited partnership, which then becomes the sole shareholder in the general partner *GmbH*.

Newer statutes have recognized the permissibility of *GmbH & Co. KGs* in a number of individual statutory provisions, but there is **no comprehensive regulatory treatment** of this structure. The legislature has neglected to put this structure on its own legal footing. However, certain provisions governing *GmbH & Co. KGs* move this legal form closer to that of a corporation. For example, a *GmbH & Co. KG*

---

[492] Sec. 73 para. 1 of the Limited Liability Company Act.
[493] Sec. 74 para. 1 of the Limited Liability Company Act.
[494] Sec. 74 para. 2 of the Limited Liability Company Act.

must provide the same information on its business letters as a *GmbH*.[495] It must, like a *GmbH*, apply for the commencement of insolvency proceedings in case of illiquidity or over-indebtedness.[496] Certain provisions on accounting and disclosure applicable to *GmbHs* are also applied to *GmbH & Co. KGs*.[497]

As a limited partnership, a *GmbH & Co. KG* is subject to the **laws governing partnerships**, while the general partner *GmbH* is governed **by limited liability company law**. It is essential in practice to include complicated provisions into the articles of association in order to achieve the necessary harmonization of both corporate forms.

3. The Legal Position of the General Partner *GmbH*

The **general partner *GmbH* runs the business** of the *GmbH & Co. KG* (limited partnership) and represents it in relation to third parties. Since the general partner *GmbH* itself is not a natural person and therefore not able to act by itself, it is **represented by its managing directors**. These managing directors are therefore indirectly the managing directors and representatives of the *GmbH & Co. KG*. In order to achieve the necessary transparency for legal transactions, the *GmbH & Co. KG* must state on its business letters not only its own legal form, register court and registration number, but also those of the general partner *GmbH* (including the names of its managing directors).[498]

The **appointment of the managing directors** of the general partner *GmbH* is governed by limited liability company law, which means that it is the responsibility of the shareholders of the general partner *GmbH*.[499] Any third party, as well as shareholders in the general partner *GmbH* or limited partners of the *GmbH & Co. KG*, may be appointed managing directors. The limited partners do not need to give their consent to the appointment of a managing director of the general partner *GmbH*. However, the *GmbH's* shareholders have to take into account the interests of the limited partners when appointing or dismissing managing directors.

As a rule, the **service contracts with the managing directors** are also entered into with the general partner *GmbH*. However, it may also be entered into between the managing directors and the *GmbH & Co. KG* directly. In this case, the managing directors' remuneration claim will be against the limited partnership, which will also be able to issue instructions to the managing directors.

If the limited partnership is not involved in the service contract, it will not have the right to issue instructions to the managing directors. However, the managing directors have a duty to safeguard the interests of the limited partnership and its limited partners. Case law deems a service contract between managing directors and the general partner *GmbH* to constitute a contract with protective effect for the limited partnership such that the latter will have damage claims of its own if the managing directors breach their duties.[500] The managing directors are then liable toward the limited partnership for applying the care of a prudent businessman.[501]

---

[495] Sec. 125a of the Commercial Code.
[496] Sec. 15a para. 1 sentence 2 of the Insolvency Code.
[497] Sec. 264a of the Commercial Code.
[498] Sec. 125a of the Commercial Code.
[499] Sec. 46 no. 5 of the Limited Liability Company Act.
[500] Decisions of the Federal Supreme Court, published in BGHZ, vol. 76 pp. 326, 337 et seq., in BGHZ, vol. 100, pp. 190 et seq. and in NZG 2002, pp. 568, 569.
[501] Sec. 43 of the Limited Liability Company Act.

The **dismissal of a managing director** of a general partner *GmbH* for breach of his duties to the limited partnership is not always straightforward. The dismissal is carried out by the shareholders of the general partner *GmbH*. However, if the shareholder meeting of the general partner *GmbH* refuses to dismiss the managing director – even in the event of a breach of duty – the limited partnership may remove the general partner *GmbH*'s power to manage and represent the company for good cause or exclude it from the limited partnership for good cause.

4. Codetermination

The Codetermination Act also applies to *GmbH & Co. KGs*. Codetermination is achieved by attributing the employees of the limited partnership to the general partner *GmbH*.[502] However, this requires that the majority of the limited partners also are majority shareholders of the general partner *GmbH* and that the general partner *GmbH* does not have a business operation of its own with more than 500 employees.

If the number of employees who normally work for the general partner *GmbH* and who are ascribed to it pursuant to sec. 4 of the Codetermination Act reaches 2,000 in the aggregate, the general partner *GmbH* must establish a supervisory board governed by the rules of the Codetermination Act. Half of its members are elected by the shareholders of the general partner *GmbH* or the competent corporate body pursuant to its articles of association and the other half are elected by the employees. In all other respects, the same rules which apply to *GmbHs* that are subject to codetermination regulations apply here as well (see above).

B. Stock Corporation

I. Introduction

1. The Significance of *AGs* in the German Business World

The legal form of the stock corporation (*Aktiengesellschaft* or *AG*) was originally intended for larger (public) companies. Today, there are both large public companies as well as smaller companies that are organized in the legal form "*AG*".

An *AG* can be established for any object allowed by law; generally an *AG* is used to conduct business. The Stock Corporation Act provides for detailed and highly complex rules for the organization of an *AG*. As opposed to the largely non-mandatory rules of the Limited Liability Company Act, most of the rules of the Stock Corporation Act are mandatory. Therefore, an *AG* **has to meet strict demands in terms of organization, accounting and legal housekeeping**. Considering these time-consuming and costly requirements, smaller companies in particular should give careful thought to the question whether or not to organize themselves in the legal form of an *AG*.

However, if a company intends to have its shares admitted to the stock exchange, the legal form of an *AG* is frequently chosen. While the shares in a partnership limited by shares (*Kommanditgesellschaft auf Aktien* or *KGaA*) and shares in

---

[502] Sec. 4 of the Codetermination Act.

a European Company (*societas europaea* or *SE*) can also be **admitted to the stock exchange**, these forms of companies carry special limitations and are therefore still rare. Shares in a *GmbH* cannot be traded on a stock exchange.

2. Structure and Legal Bodies of the Company

Like a *GmbH*, an *AG* is a **company with an own legal personality** (**legal entity**). Only the company's assets are available to the creditors to satisfy their claims against the company. An *AG* has a registered share capital (*Grundkapital*), which is divided into shares.[503]

An *AG* is a **corporation**. Irrespective of the object of the company, an *AG*, like a *GmbH*, is a commercial company by virtue of its legal form.[504] Like a *GmbH*, the AG is a special form of the so-called association (*Verein*) defined by sec. 21 et seq. of the Civil Code. As a result, these basic civil law provisions also generally apply to *AGs* unless they are superseded by more specific provisions in the Stock Corporation Act.

An *AG* has three corporate bodies: the general meeting (*Hauptversammlung*), the management board (*Vorstand*) and the supervisory board (*Aufsichtsrat*). Fundamental corporate decisions are taken by the general meeting. The members of the management board assume responsibility for the management and representation of the company. As opposed to the *GmbH*, the members of the management board of an *AG* are not bound by instructions issued by the general meeting. The supervisory board reviews and controls the work of the management board and reports to the general meeting. Hence, corporate governance in a German *AG* is characterized by a two-tier system: instead of being directed by a single board, an *AG* has a **management body** (management board) and a **control body** (supervisory board).

II. Overview

1. The AG

As a corporation, an *AG* owns all the company's assets and assumes all rights and obligations arising out of its business. An *AG* enters into contracts in its own name. An *AG* can initiate lawsuits and can be sued under its company name. The company is represented by one or more members of the management board (according to its articles of association) vis-à-vis third parties, in normal business and before the courts.

Only the company's assets are available to creditors to satisfy their claims against the company. In general, neither the shareholders nor the members of the management board are held personally liable for the debts of an *AG*.

As compensation for the missing personal liability of the shareholders, the *AG* must have a **registered share capital** (*Grundkapital*) of at least EUR 50,000.[505] However, this registered share capital does not need to be "frozen" for the creditors' benefit but may be used by the company in its regular business. The registered share capital is divided into shares (*Aktien*).[506]

---

[503] Sec. 1 of the Stock Corporation Act.
[504] Sec. 3 para. 1 of the Stock Corporation Act.
[505] Sec. 7 of the Stock Corporation Act.
[506] Sec. 1 para. 2 of the Stock Corporation Act.

The shareholders may be liable to the company for certain breaches of duties, e.g., if the founding shareholders made incorrect statements concerning the initial contributions[507] or if a shareholder has forced its subsidiary to incur disadvantages without compensation.[508] However, this does not give the company's creditors a direct claim against the shareholders. Unless expressly agreed otherwise (e.g., in the articles of association), the shareholders are also not obliged to render additional contributions or to assume the company's losses.

As an *AG* conducts business in its own name, the *AG* is generally the holder of all rights and obligations associated therewith. For example, an *AG* can be the owner of assets, a custodian, a creditor, a debtor, the holder of public permits and the holder of (certain) fundamental rights under the German Basic Constitutional Law (*Grundgesetz*).

On the other hand, the *AG* is obliged to comply with all duties relating to its business such as contractual duties as well as public law duties. Furthermore, an *AG* has to ensure, for example, that its premises are safe for use. In the case of a breach of such duties, the *AG* is liable for damages. Additionally, an *AG* is considered to constitute a manufacturer within the meaning of sec. 1 of the Product Liability Act and is therefore liable for claims under the Product Liability Act.

Subject to the requirements stipulated in sec. 31 of the Civil Code, an *AG* is generally liable for all actions taken by the bodies of the *AG* in breach of the *AG's* duties. This also includes the *AG's* liability for torts committed by members of the management board. Moreover, the knowledge of (former) management board members is also attributed to the company, i.e., treated as the *AG's* own knowledge.[509]

This said, the *AG* as a legal entity cannot be subject to criminal punishment (although the members of the management and/or the supervisory board may themselves be punished). However, the *AG* can be subject to fines imposed under the Administrative Offenses Act (*Ordnungswidrigkeitengesetz*) or under tax law.[510]

2. The Share

The term "share" has three different meanings:

a) Fraction of the Registered Share Capital

Each share represents a **fraction of the registered share capital**.[511] The shares may be issued as either par value or non-par value shares.[512] The registered share capital may not be divided into both par value and non-par value shares.

Par value shares (*Nennbetragsaktien*) must have a value of at least one euro. Shares with a lower par value are invalid.[513] The issued shares do not necessarily have identical par values. It is permissible to divide the registered share capital into shares with different par values.

---

[507] Sec. 46 para. 2 of the Stock Corporation Act.
[508] Sec. 311 of the Stock Corporation Act.
[509] Decisions of the Federal Supreme Court, published in BGHZ, vol. 132, pp. 30, 37 and in BGHZ, vol. 140, pp. 54, 61.
[510] Sec. 30 of the Administrative Offenses Act, sec. 377 of the Tax Code.
[511] Sec. 1 para. 2 of the Stock Corporation Act.
[512] Sec. 8 para. 1 of the Stock Corporation Act.
[513] Sec. 8 para. 2 of the Stock Corporation Act.

Non-par value shares (*Stückaktien*) do not have a specific nominal value. All non-par value shares in a company participate equally in the registered share capital. If the total amount of the registered share capital is divided by the number of non-par value shares, the registered share capital per share may not be less than one euro.[514]

The part of the registered share capital attributable to each share is determined for par value shares on the basis of the ratio of their par value to the registered share capital and for non-par value shares according to the number of the shares.[515] A share cannot be divided into more than one share.[516]

The articles of association (*Satzung*) have to specify how the registered share capital is allocated to the individual shares.[517] In case of par value shares, the articles of association have to state the par value of the shares and the number of shares issued for each par value. In case of non-par value shares, the articles of association have to state the number of issued shares. If different classes of shares are issued, the articles of association have to stipulate the class of the respective shares and the number of the shares in each class.

It is **not permitted** to issue shares for an amount below their par value or the part of the registered share capital attributable to the individual non-par value shares (**under-par issue**). This is because an under-par issue would jeopardize the actual contribution of the full registered share capital.[518] Shares may, however, be issued for a higher amount than their par value or the part of the registered share capital attributable to the individual non-par value shares (**over-par issue**).[519] In case of an over-par issue, the company receives more capital than required for the full payment of the registered share capital. The **premium** is to be allocated to the capital reserves.[520] Shareholders may also render additional contributions to the capital reserves of the company at a later stage, either on a capital increase (where the premium would be a payment into capital reserves) or as an isolated contribution to the capital reserves.

b) Right of Membership

The share also represents **membership** in the *AG*. Accordingly, it is the embodiment of the rights and duties associated with the position of a shareholder (see below for details).

The *AG's* structure is more capital-focused than that of a *GmbH*. Each share constitutes an independent right of membership. If several shares are acquired by one person, the person acquires several membership rights without the shares being amalgamated.

In principle, each share grants a voting right in the general meeting.[521] However, the law also allows for the issuance of shares without voting rights provided these shares confer preferential rights relating to the distribution of profits as compensation (**preference shares without a voting right**).[522] **Multiple voting rights**, i.e., provisions in the articles of association that grant a number of voting

---

[514] Sec. 8 para. 3 of the Stock Corporation Act.
[515] Sec. 8 para. 4 of the Stock Corporation Act.
[516] Sec. 8 para. 5 of the Stock Corporation Act.
[517] Sec. 23 para. 3 no. 4 of the Stock Corporation Act.
[518] Sec. 9 para. 1 of the Stock Corporation Act.
[519] Sec. 9 para. 2, 182 para. 3 of the Stock Corporation Act.
[520] Sec. 272 para. 2 no. 1 of the Commercial Code.
[521] Sec. 12 para. 1 sentence 1, sec. 134 para. 1 of the Stock Corporation Act.
[522] Sec. 12 para. 1 sentence 2, sec. 139 et seq. of the Stock Corporation Act.

rights to a shareholder that exceeds his pro-rata share in the registered share capital, are not permitted.[523]

The most recent legislative reform of the Stock Corporation Act[524] has brought about significant changes with regard to preference shares. Formerly the issuance of preference shares without voting rights was only permissible if the shares were endowed with a subsequent preference right with regard to the distribution of profits and if the voting right preclusion was justified on the basis of the preference shareholders' right to an advance dividend payable with priority. From 2016 on, preference shares without voting rights can be issued without such obligatory subsequent preferential rights in the distribution of profits.[525] Furthermore, a preference right can consist of either an advance dividend *(Vorabdividende)* or an additional dividend *(Mehrdividende)*.[526]

In case the preferential amount is not paid or not fully paid within one year, the voting rights of preference shares which do not carry subsequent preferential rights in the distribution of profits are reinstated. These shares then carry voting rights until the full preferential amount is paid within one year.[527]

The aforementioned most recent legislative reform of the Stock Corporation Act by a law called *Aktienrechtsnovelle 2016*[528] has brought about another significant change: from now on, shares generally shall be issued as **registered shares** *(Namensaktien)*.[529] Shares may only be issued as **bearer shares** *(Inhaberaktien)*, if the company is listed on a stock exchange or if the entitlement of the shareholders to the individual certification of their shares is excluded and the global certificate is deposited with one of the qualified depositories named in sec. 10 para. 1 sentence 2 no. 2 of the Stock Corporation Act.[530] If the company issues registered shares or if, in case of bearer shares, it has not yet deposited the global certificate,[531] it is obliged to draw up a share register stating the name, date of birth and address of each shareholder, the number of shares held or the identification number of the share and, in case of par value shares, the par value.[532] If a share is transferred to another person, the share register has to be amended upon the submission of notification and evidence to this effect.[533] In relation to the company, only those persons shall be deemed shareholders who are registered as such in the share register (e. g., in order to have voting rights at the general meeting).[534] The articles of association have to stipulate whether the shares are bearer shares or registered shares.[535] For a long time, registered shares were mainly used by family-run companies. However, in recent years more and more publicly traded companies have introduced registered shares. The registration of the shareholders gives the company an overview of the current shareholder structure and enables it to get in touch with the investors if required.

---

[523] Sec. 12 para. 2 of the Stock Corporation Act.
[524] By a law called „*Aktienrechtsnovelle 2016*", published in BGBl. I, pp. 2565 et seq.
[525] Sec. 139 para. 1 sentence 1 of the Stock Corporation Act.
[526] Sec. 139 para. 1 sentence 2 of the Stock Corporation Act.
[527] Sec. 140 para. 2 sentence 2 of the Stock Corporation Act.
[528] Published in BGBl. I pp. 2565 et. seq.
[529] Sec. 10 para. 1 sentence 1 of the Stock Corporation Act.
[530] Sec. 10 para. 1 sentence 2 of the Stock Corporation Act.
[531] Sec. 10 para. 1 sentence 3 of the Stock Corporation Act.
[532] Sec. 67 para. 1 sentence 1 of the Stock Corporation Act.
[533] Sec. 67 para. 3 of the Stock Corporation Act.
[534] Sec. 67 para. 2 of the Stock Corporation Act.
[535] Sec. 23 para. 3 no. 5 of the Stock Corporation Act.

c) Share Certificates

Finally, the term "share" also designates the share certificate which certifies membership in the *AG*.[536] In theory, each shareholder is entitled to an issued share certificate (**certification**). In practice, however, the shareholder's right to have a share certificate issued for his particular share is either excluded or at least restricted by the articles of association.[537]

Irrespective of restrictions contained in the articles of association concerning the certification of shares, each shareholder has a right to demand that a certification is effected in the form of one or several global share certificates (*Globalurkunde*). In this case, all shares of the *AG* are certified in one global share certificate. A global share certificate is used by most listed stock corporations. The global certificate is commonly deposited with Clearstream Banking AG in Frankfurt and is the basis for trading on the stock exchange.

3. Other Securities Governed by Corporate Law

The Stock Corporation Act also recognizes other forms of securities, not merely shares. **Interim share certificates** (*Zwischenscheine*) are issued as a temporary means of certifying membership if shares cannot yet be allocated. An interim share certificate must state the name of the person entitled under the interim share certificate; interim share certificates issued for the bearer are void.[538] **Dividend coupons** (*Gewinnanteilsscheine*) represent the annual claim to profits and facilitate the payment of profits and the separate transfer thereof. **Renewal coupons** (*Erneuerungsscheine*) represent rights to the allocation of new shares or dividend coupons.[539] **Participating certificates** represent participation rights (see below).

4. Protection of Shareholders in a Stock Corporation

Most provisions of the Stock Corporation Act are mandatory. According to sec. 23 para. 5 sentence 1 of the Stock Corporation Act, an *AG's* articles of association may only deviate from the rules of the Stock Corporation Act if this is explicitly permitted (**stringency of stock corporation law**). The aim is to protect shareholders and parties acquiring new shares by guaranteeing a fixed framework of rules applicable to all stock corporations. In contrast to a *GmbH*, there is **hardly any scope for deviation in the articles of association**.

Supplementary provisions in the articles of association are permitted pursuant to sec. 23 para. 5 sentence 2 of the Stock Corporation Act if the law does not conclusively deal with the matter in question, i.e., if the law has intentionally left a gap or if the matter has been left entirely unregulated. As the law of stock corporations is highly regulated, this only applies to few cases. Supplementary provisions in the articles of association include, for example, specific personal requirements to be met by members of the management board (maximum age, nationality, etc.), creation of the position of a management board spokesman or extensions to the shareholders' right to receive information.

---

[536] Sec. 10 of the Stock Corporation Act.
[537] Sec. 10 para. 5 of the Stock Corporation Act.
[538] Sec. 8 para. 6, sec. 10 para. 3, 4, sec. 41 para. 4, sec. 67 para. 7, sec. 68 para. 4, sec. 191 of the Stock Corporation Act.
[539] Sec. 75 of the Stock Corporation Act.

III. Formation

1. Steps of Formation and Stages of the Company during the Formation Process

a) Overview

AGs are either created via **formation** or via the **transformation of legal entities** having a different legal form into an **AG**. Usually, AGs are created via formation. AGs may be established by one or more persons for any purpose allowed by law.[540]

The formation of an AG commences with establishing the articles of association.[541] However, the establishment of the articles of association as such is not sufficient. Additionally, the founders must subscribe to the shares in the formation deed and thereby undertake to render the required contributions to the company.[542] An establishment of the articles without a subscription to all shares is not permitted.

The articles of association have to be established by notarial deed. If authorized representatives act for one or more of the founders, the representatives must each have been provided with a power of attorney certified by a notary.[543]

The **deed of formation** has to state the following:[544]
- the names of the founders;
- for par value shares: the par value; for non-par value shares: the number of shares;
- the issue price of the shares;
- if there is more than one class of shares, the class of the shares subscribed to by the respective founder; and
- the paid up amount of the registered share capital.

The **articles of association** have to state the following:[545]
- the name and registered office of the company;
- the company's object; in case of industrial and commercial companies, details must be provided as to the type of products and goods to be manufactured and traded;
- the amount of the registered share capital;
- whether the registered share capital is divided into par value shares or non-par value shares. In case of par value shares, the par value of the shares and – if shares with different par values are issued – the number of shares issued for each par value need to be stated; in case of non-par value shares, the number of shares needs to be stated. If there is more than one class of shares, the respective class of shares and the number of shares in each class need to be specified;
- whether the shares are issued as bearer shares or registered shares; and

---

[540] Sec. 2 of the Stock Corporation Act.
[541] Sec. 2 of the Stock Corporation Act.
[542] Sec. 2, 23 of the Stock Corporation Act.
[543] Sec. 23 para. 1 of the Stock Corporation Act.
[544] Sec. 23 para. 2 of the Stock Corporation Act.
[545] Sec. 23 para. 3 of the Stock Corporation Act.

- the number of members of the management board or the rules pursuant to which this number is determined.

Wherever the law or the articles of association call for a company announcement to be published in the company's designated journals *(Gesellschaftsblätter)*, the announcement has to be published online in the Federal Gazette.[546]

If applicable, the following additional provisions have to be included in the articles of association:

- **special benefits** granted to an individual shareholder or a third party have to be set forth in the articles of association stating the name of the person who is to receive such benefits.[547] Contracts or arrangements to implement a special benefit are not binding for the company if the articles of association do not provide for the specific special benefit.[548] Examples of special benefits are rights to receive goods from the company, rights to commission and – according to the prevailing opinion in legal literature – the right to delegate members of the supervisory board as well as special rights to information;
- the total expenses to be paid by the company to shareholders or to other persons as compensation or remuneration for the formation of the company or the preparation for such formation (**formation expenses** *(Gründungsaufwand)*) are to be stipulated in the articles of association;[549] and
- if shares are to be issued against **contributions in kind**, the articles of association have to contain certain details concerning the intended contributions in kind (see below); the same applies in case of intended **acquisitions in kind**,[550] i.e., if the company is to take over assets against remuneration other than shares.

The Federal Supreme Court has recently decided that the articles of association may even allow for a foreign location for the general meeting. However, any such provision in the articles of association must take into account the shareholders' interest in attending the general meeting. A provision which enables the person convening the general meeting to choose between several far-flung foreign locations does not meet these standards set forth by the Federal Supreme Court.[551]

An *AG* only comes into existence upon registration in the commercial register.[552] It is possible to start business activities even before the registration of the *AG* (in the state of the so-called pre-*AG* *(Vor-AG)*); in this case, however, persons acting on behalf of the company are personally liable for debts incurred by the company prior to its registration in the commercial register.[553] Moreover, the founders will be liable to the company for any losses incurred prior to registration.

b) Subscription to Shares

In the same notarial deed in which the articles of association are established, the founders have to **subscribe to the shares**, i.e. **acquire the shares** in exchange for the promised contribution.[554] The company cannot subscribe to its own shares.[555]

---

[546] Sec. 25 of the Stock Corporation Act.
[547] Sec. 26 para. 1 of the Stock Corporation Act.
[548] Sec. 26 para. 3 sentence 1 of the Stock Corporation Act.
[549] Sec. 26 para. 2 of the Stock Corporation Act.
[550] Sec. 27 para. 1 of the Stock Corporation Act
[551] Decision of the Federal Supreme Court, published in BGHZ, vol. 203, pp. 68 et seq.
[552] Sec. 39, 41 para. 1 of the Stock Corporation Act.
[553] Sec. 41 para. 1 sentence 2 of the Stock Corporation Act.
[554] Sec. 23 para. 2 no. 2 of the Stock Corporation Act.
[555] Sec. 56 para. 1 of the Stock Corporation Act.

Upon subscription to all shares (i.e., with the conclusion of the formation deed), the company is established.[556] However, before the registration with the commercial register has been completed, the company only exists as a **pre-AG**.

c) Appointment of the Formation Bodies

After having both determined the articles of association and subscribed to the shares, the founders have to **appoint the first supervisory board** and the first auditors of the company. The term of appointment is limited until the end of the general meeting resolving upon the annual accounts for the first full or partial fiscal year. The appointments of the supervisory board and the auditors have to be notarized.[557] These appointments are usually included within the same notarial deed in which the company is formed.

The first supervisory board exclusively consists of representatives of the shareholders; the provisions on codetermination of the supervisory board (i.e., the election of employee representatives) do not apply to the first supervisory board.[558] Only the supervisory board to be elected after the expiry of the term of the first supervisory board has to be elected in accordance with the applicable codetermination laws.[559]

The first supervisory board appoints the first management board.[560]

d) Formation Report

The founders have to submit a written report on the formation of the company (**formation report** – *Gründungsbericht*).[561] The formation report must set out the material circumstances upon which the fairness of the consideration for contributions in kind or acquisitions in kind depends. This includes, for example, previous legal transactions seeking to enable the company to undertake the acquisition in kind[562] and, in the event of the acquisition of an entity by the company, the earnings of the acquired entity in the two preceding fiscal years.[563]

e) Raising of the Registered Share Capital

In a next step, the founders render the **contributions** which they undertook to render when subscribing to the shares. The issue price of the shares must be at least equal to the nominal value (for par value shares) or the proportionate amount of the registered share capital allocated to each share (for non-par value shares), the so-called **lowest issue price** (*geringster Ausgabebetrag*). Shares may not be issued for an amount lower than the lowest issue price.[564] However, shares may be issued with a **premium** which has to be paid in addition to the lowest issue price.[565]

In case of **cash contributions**, at least one quarter of the lowest issue price of the shares subscribed to, plus the whole premium for the respective shares, has to

---

[556] Sec. 29 of the Stock Corporation Act.
[557] Sec. 30 para. 1 of the Stock Corporation Act.
[558] Sec. 30 para. 2 of the Stock Corporation Act.
[559] Sec. 30 para. 3 of the Stock Corporation Act.
[560] Sec. 30 para. 4 of the Stock Corporation Act.
[561] Sec. 32 para. 1 of the Stock Corporation Act.
[562] Sec. 32 para. 2 sentence 2 no. 1 of the Stock Corporation Act.
[563] Sec. 32 para. 2 sentence 2 no. 3 of the Stock Corporation Act.
[564] Sec. 9 para. 1 of the Stock Corporation Act.
[565] Sec. 9 para. 2 of the Stock Corporation Act.

III. Formation

be paid-in.[566] Cash contributions can only be made by cash payment in euros or by crediting a bank account belonging to the company or the management board. The amount has to be paid unconditionally and has to be at the free disposal of the management board.[567]

Contributions in kind are to be made in full, generally prior to the application for registration of the company. However, if the contribution in kind consists of an obligation to transfer assets to the company, the transfer *in rem* of the respective assets must be effected within five years after the registration of the company in the commercial register.[568] This five-year period makes it considerably easier for capital to be raised, in particular if other enterprises are to be contributed to the company.

The Federal Supreme Court[569] has ruled that the company's own shares must not constitute contributions in kind. If a shareholder waives his claim for restitution of shares that he had previously transferred to the company as a loan, such waiver is deemed an (attempted) contribution in kind in the context of a capital increase.

The value of the contribution in kind has to be at least equal to the lowest issue price plus the agreed premium, if any.[570] If the value of the contribution in kind is not sufficient, the founder is obliged to pay to the company the difference in cash (so-called **liability for difference**), if necessary retrospectively. According to the court rulings of the Federal Supreme Court, a subscription to shares against contribution in kind always contains the obligation to cover the subscribed capital.[571]

The issues relating to a so-called **hidden contribution in kind** as described in the context of the *GmbH*[572] also apply in the case of an *AG*. The Shareholders' Rights Act (*Gesetz zur Umsetzung der Aktionärsrechterichtlinie – ARUG*) has improved the legal position of a shareholder rendering a hidden contribution in kind. Whereas previously the contribution was not considered to have been rendered, which, in consequence, obliged the shareholder to render the contribution again in full, the law now provides – in line with the situation in case of a *GmbH* – that the fair value of the contribution in kind shall be deducted from the still-outstanding obligation of the shareholder to make his cash contribution.[573] The deduction is not effective prior to the company's registration in the commercial register.[574] The relevant point in time for determining the value of the contributed assets is the date of the company's application for registration to the commercial register or, if the assets have been transferred to the company afterwards, the date of their transfer to the company.[575] The contributing shareholder remains liable to the company for any difference between the assets' fair value and the nominal amount of the cash contribution (*Differenzhaftung*). The agreements underlying the transfer of the assets in connection with the hidden contribution in kind are valid.[576] If a member of the management board incorrectly declares in the company's application for

---

[566] Sec. 36a para. 1 of the Stock Corporation Act.
[567] Sec. 36 para. 2, 54 para. 3 of the Stock Corporation Act.
[568] Sec. 36a para. 2 sentence 1, 2 of the Stock Corporation Act.
[569] Decision of the Federal Supreme Court, published in NZG 2011, pp. 1271 et seq.
[570] Sec. 36a para. 2 sentence 3 of the Stock Corporation Act.
[571] Decision of the Federal Supreme Court, published in BGHZ, vol. 64, pp. 52, 62.
[572] *Cf.* A.II.7.
[573] Sec. 27 para. 3 sentence 3 of the Stock Corporation Act.
[574] Sec. 27 para. 3 sentence 4 of the Stock Corporation Act.
[575] Sec. 27 para. 3 sentence 3 of the Stock Corporation Act.
[576] Sec. 27 para. 3 sentence 2 of the Stock Corporation Act.

registration that the claim for the cash contribution has been satisfied, he may be subject to criminal sanctions and all managing directors and founders may be liable to the company for damages.[577] In addition, the register court may refuse to register the company.

A hidden contribution in kind with its legal consequences outlined above can only be assumed if there has been an agreement between the company and the shareholder in question according to which – from an economic point of view – his cash contribution was to be substituted by a contribution in kind.[578] The Federal Supreme Court presumes such an agreement if it finds both a **substantive and temporal connection** between the contribution of cash and the arrangement leading to the economic effect of a contribution in kind.[579] A substantive connection is indicated if the amount of the cash contribution and the consideration for the transfer of assets correspond to each other or if there is no plausible motive for the transaction other than to perform a hidden contribution in kind. A lack of a temporal connection is presumed starting from one year after registration of the company, potentially even earlier. The Federal Supreme Court rejected a temporal connection in a case where eight months had passed.[580]

There are no subjective requirements for a hidden contribution in kind. Thus, the shareholder does not need to have intended the substantive and temporal connection or to circumvent the provisions on contributions in kind.

A situation similar to a hidden contribution in kind arises where a shareholder renders the stipulated cash contribution and subsequently the company repays him a corresponding amount. Typically, the repayment is a loan made by the company to the shareholder. In such case, the money is **paid back and forth** (*Hin- und Herzahlen*).[581] As a consequence, the cash contribution is not at the management board's free disposal. Hence, it is deemed to not have been made.[582] The company thus retains its claim against the shareholder for payment of the cash contribution. If, however, the payment to the shareholder was agreed upon prior to the contribution of cash and if the company has a fully recoverable, i.e., unimpaired, repayment claim against the shareholder that can be enforced at any time, the obligation to render the cash contribution is satisfied.[583] This provision of the law is useful especially where a newly formed company is to be incorporated in a cash-pooling system.

f) Formation Audit

The members of the management board and the supervisory board have to audit the formation procedure.[584] If (i) one of the founders is a member of the management board or the supervisory board, (ii) shares have been subscribed to at formation for the account of a member of the management board or the supervisory board, (iii) a member of the management board or the supervisory board has been granted a special benefit for the formation or preparation of the formation or (iv) the formation was effected by way of contributions in kind, an audit

---

[577] *Cf.* B.V.2.h.
[578] Sec. 27 para. 3 sentence 1 of the Stock Corporation Act.
[579] Decisions of the Federal Supreme Court, published in BGHZ, vol. 153, pp. 107 et seq. and in BGHZ, vol. 175, pp. 265 et seq.
[580] Decision of the Federal Supreme Court, published in BGHZ, vol. 152, pp. 37, 45.
[581] Decision of the Federal Supreme Court, published in BGHZ, vol. 165, pp. 113 et seq.
[582] Sec. 36 para. 2 of the Stock Corporation Act.
[583] Sec. 27 para. 4 of the Stock Corporation Act.
[584] Sec. 33 para. 1 of the Stock Corporation Act.

has to be carried out by one or more external **formation auditors** (*Gründungsprüfer*). The formation auditors act in addition to the management board and the supervisory board and are appointed by the court. Usually an audit firm is appointed as formation auditor.[585] In the aforementioned cases (i) and (ii), the formation audit can also be conducted by the notary who notarized the formation deed.[586] However, if a formation is effected against contributions in kind, such a notarial audit is never sufficient.

The audit conducted by the members of the management board and the supervisory board and the audit conducted by the formation auditors has to address the following issues:
- whether the statements of the founders concerning the subscription to the shares and the contributions to the registered share capital and the stipulations in the articles of association concerning special benefits and contributions in kind are complete and correct[587]; and
- whether the value of the contributions or acquisitions in kind does at least equal the lowest issue price of the shares issued in exchange for the contribution or the value of the consideration to be paid in exchange for the contribution.[588]

A **written report** is to be provided on the formation audit. The report has to be submitted to the court and the management board. Everyone is entitled to inspect the report at the court.[589]

According to the Shareholders' Rights Act, an audit by external formation auditors may be omitted under certain circumstances in case of a formation against contributions in kind, in particular in case of a contribution of publicly traded shares.[590]

g) Application for Registration in the Commercial Register

After the formation audit has been completed, all founders, all members of the management board and all members of the supervisory board have to apply for registration of the company with the commercial register.[591] The application can only be filed after all contributions (except for contributions in kind) have been made to the extent called by the company. The application has to state that the payments on the registered share capital which have been called have been effected. Additionally, evidence has to be provided that the amount that has been paid in is unconditionally at the free disposal of the management board.[592]

The following documents have to be attached to the application:
- the articles of association and the deeds in which the articles of association have been established and the shares have been subscribed to by the founders;
- in the event of contributions and/or acquisitions in kind or in the event that special benefits have been granted, the underlying contracts and a calculation of the formation expenses incurred by the company;
- the deeds on the appointment of the management board and the supervisory board;

---

[585] Sec. 33 para. 2, 3 sentence 2 of the Stock Corporation Act.
[586] Sec. 33 para. 3 sentence 1 of the Stock Corporation Act.
[587] Sec. 34 para. 1 no. 1 of the Stock Corporation Act.
[588] Sec. 34 para. 1 no. 2 of the Stock Corporation Act.
[589] Sec. 34 para. 2, 3 of the Stock Corporation Act.
[590] Sec. 33a of the Stock Corporation Act.
[591] Sec. 36 para. 1 of the Stock Corporation Act.
[592] Sec. 37 para. 1 of the Stock Corporation Act.

- a list of the members of the supervisory board stating the surname, first name, occupation held and place of residence of each member of the supervisory board; and
- the formation report and the audit reports by the members of the management board, the supervisory board and, if applicable, the formation auditors, each including their documentary records.[593]

The application also has to state a business address within Germany and the power of representation of each member of the management board,[594] i.e., whether they possess the sole power of representation or whether they are only authorized to represent the company jointly with another member of the management board or a procuration officer (*Prokurist*). The members of the management board also have to confirm that there are no circumstances which prevent them from being appointed as members of the management board,[595] for example, having been sentenced for an insolvency offense or certain other white-collar crimes.[596] The documents have to be electronically filed with the commercial register by the notary.[597] Special provisions apply in case of a formation against contributions in kind if an external audit has been omitted.[598]

h) Inspection by the Register Court

The register court has to **examine** whether the company has been duly established and the application has been duly made. If these requirements have not been fulfilled, the court has to reject the application.[599] The court has to examine whether the formal requirements for the formation of an *AG* have been complied with and whether the articles of association are in accordance with substantive law.

The court will generally also decline to enter the company in the commercial register if the formation report or the audit report prepared by the members of the management board and the supervisory board are obviously incorrect or incomplete or if one of the reports fails to comply with the legal requirements.[600] Nonetheless, the court does not review whether the formation of the company is feasible from an economic point of view.

However, the register court has to refuse the registration of the company if the formation auditors declare or the court is of the opinion that the value of the contributions or acquisitions in kind is significantly lower than the lowest issue price of the shares or the consideration to be given in exchange for the contribution in kind.[601] If a formation audit is not required by law,[602] the register court generally only examines whether the requirements for an omission of the formation audit are fulfilled. In this case, the registration of the company can only be rejected in case of an obvious and significant overvaluation of the contributed assets.[603]

In the event of defective, missing or invalid provisions in the articles of association, the register court may only refuse registration under certain circumstances,

---

[593] Sec. 37 para. 4 of the Stock Corporation Act.
[594] Sec. 37 para. 3 of the Stock Corporation Act.
[595] Sec. 37 para. 2 of the Stock Corporation Act.
[596] Sec. 76 para. 3 sentence 2 no. 3 of the Stock Corporation Act.
[597] Sec. 37 para. 5 of the Stock Corporation Act, sec. 12 para. 2 of the Commercial Code.
[598] Sec. 37a of the Stock Corporation Act.
[599] Sec. 38 para. 1 of the Stock Corporation Act.
[600] Sec. 38 para. 2 sentence 1 of the Stock Corporation Act.
[601] Sec. 38 para. 2 sentence 2 of the Stock Corporation Act.
[602] Sec. 33a of the Stock Corporation Act.
[603] Sec. 38 para. 3 sentence 2 of the Stock Corporation Act.

for example if the articles of association violate provisions of statutory law which are intended to protect the company's creditors or which are otherwise in the public interest.[604]

i) Registration and Notification

Once the company has been duly founded, it is registered in the commercial register. The *AG* obtains its legal capacity as an *AG* upon registration.[605] The registration in the commercial register contains the following information:
- the name and registered office of the company;
- domestic business address within Germany;
- the object of the company;
- the amount of the registered share capital;
- the date the articles of association were established;
- the members of the management board and their powers of representation; and
- if applicable, the domestic address of the company's authorized recipient for declarations and service of process.

If the articles of association provide for the company to have a fixed term or if they contain provisions concerning authorized capital, such information forms part of the entry in the commercial register as well.[606]

Shares cannot be transferred and share certificates and interim share certificates cannot be issued prior to the registration of the company in the commercial register.[607] Prior to the registration, a change of shareholders requires a unanimous amendment of the articles of association.

2. Post-Formation Acquisitions

The strict formation requirements concerning contributions in kind could be circumvented if a company established by means of cash formation could acquire assets from the founders or shareholders without restrictions after being registered in the commercial register, using the cash contributions to pay for such assets.

This scenario is referred to as **post-formation acquisition** (*Nachgründung*). The Stock Corporation Act addresses this issue in sec. 52 et seq. Contracts between the company and founders or shareholders having an interest in the company accounting for more than 10% of the registered share capital only become effective upon the approval of the general meeting and the registration of the contract with the commercial register if:
- the company is to acquire assets in return for remuneration exceeding 10% of the registered share capital; and
- such contracts are entered into in the first two years following the registration of the company in the commercial register.

Any actions taken to consummate such contracts are invalid unless the contracts have been approved by the general meeting and registered in the commercial register.[608]

Contracts with founders or shareholders constituting post-formation acquisitions must be entered into in writing. The company has special information

---

[604] Sec. 38 para. 4 of the Stock Corporation Act.
[605] Sec. 41 para. 1 sentence 1 of the Stock Corporation Act.
[606] Sec. 39 para. 2 of the Stock Corporation Act.
[607] Sec. 41 para. 4 sentence 1 of the Stock Corporation Act.
[608] Sec. 52 para. 1 sentence 2 of the Stock Corporation Act.

obligations vis-à-vis the shareholders in connection with the general meeting when the approval of contracts is on the agenda.[609] The supervisory board has to inspect the contract and submit a written report (so-called **post-formation report** – *Nachgründungsbericht*).[610] In addition, an inspection must be carried out by one or more formation auditors before a resolution of the general meeting can be adopted.[611] The Shareholders' Rights Act provides that such inspection by external formation auditors may be omitted under the same circumstances as in the case of a formation against contributions in kind.[612] After approval by the general meeting, the management board has to apply for registration of the contract with the commercial register.[613] The register court can decline registration if the formation auditors have stated or it is apparent that the post-formation report is incorrect, incomplete or fails to comply with the relevant legal requirements or that the remuneration granted for the assets which are to be acquired is inappropriately high.[614] If a post-formation audit is not required, the register court generally only examines whether the requirements for an omission of the post-formation audit are fulfilled. In this case, the registration can only be rejected in case of an obvious and significant overvaluation of the acquired assets.[615] The rules on post-formation acquisition do not apply if the assets are acquired in the company's normal course of business, during enforcement proceedings or on the stock exchange.[616]

The post-formation acquisition provisions do not only apply to the **formation** of a company, but also to **capital increases by way of contributions in kind** and certain **procedures under the law regulating the transformation of companies** within two years after the registration of the company in the commercial register.[617]

3. The Pre-Registered Company

The so-called **pre-AG** comes into existence upon the assumption of all shares by the founders; it automatically converts into an *AG* upon registration of the *AG* in the commercial register.

Anyone acting in the name of the company before the company is registered in the commercial register is personally liable (**liability of the acting persons**).[618] The liability ceases upon registration of the *AG* in the commercial register. In addition, the founders are liable to the company for any losses incurred prior to registration.

4. Defects Relating to Formation

Defects in the formation procedure may concern formal registration requirements, the establishing of the articles of association or the payment of contributions which have been called in.

---

[609] Sec. 52 para. 2 of the Stock Corporation Act.
[610] Sec. 52 para. 3 of the Stock Corporation Act.
[611] Sec. 52 para. 4 sentence 1 of the Stock Corporation Act.
[612] Sec. 52 para. 4 sentence 2, sec. 33a of the Stock Corporation Act.
[613] Sec. 52 para. 6 of the Stock Corporation Act.
[614] Sec. 52 para. 7 of the Stock Corporation Act.
[615] Sec. 52 para. 7 sentence 2, sec. 38 para. 3 sentence 2 of the Stock Corporation Act.
[616] Sec. 52 para. 9 of the Stock Corporation Act.
[617] Change of form, sec. 197 Transformation Act; merger of one company with another, sec. 67 of the Transformation Act.
[618] Sec. 41 para. 1 sentence 2 of the Stock Corporation Act.

If the company has not been duly established or an application for registration has not been duly filed, the register court has to decline registration.[619] If the defect is not discovered until after the company's registration, the register court can delete the company if certain requirements are met (e.g., in the event of invalid provisions concerning the amount of the registered share capital or the object of the company).[620] However, the company has to be granted an appropriate time period to cure the defects in the articles of association.

In the time period between the company's formation and its registration with the commercial register, defects relating to the establishment of the articles of association are to be treated in accordance with the rules on **defective companies** which have commenced operation (see below). This means that the company may be dissolved at the request of a founder.

Once the company has been registered in the commercial register, defects relating to the establishment of the articles of association can only be asserted to the extent that they constitute a reason to declare the company void. The company is declared void by the court if the articles of association do not contain provisions on the amount of the registered share capital or the object of the company or if the provisions concerning the object of the company are void.[621] Before initiating a lawsuit, the potential claimant has to request the company to cure the defect, if this is possible. The lawsuit can only be initiated within three years from the date of the company's registration with the commercial register. If the court declares the company void, the company enters into liquidation (but ceases to exist only after finalization of the liquidation proceedings).[622]

If only individual provisions of the articles of association are invalid (except for the ones previously mentioned), the invalidity is cured if three years have passed since the date of registration.[623]

According to sec. 46 para. 1 of the Stock Corporation Act, the founders have to ensure that their statements relating to the formation are correct and complete (e.g., towards the register court or public officers who have to grant approvals). They are also responsible for ensuring that the contributions are at the management board's free disposal. A breach of such duties may give rise to damage claims by the company against the founders. Each founder is additionally liable for any shortfall in contributions if another founder is unable to pay his contribution and the respective founder was aware of the other founder's inability to render the contribution.[624] The founders' liability also extends to damage to the company caused by intentional or grossly negligent conduct of the founders relating to contributions, acquisitions in kind and the formation expenditure.[625]

Furthermore, incorrect statements (e.g., in the formation report, the post-formation report or the audit report) for the purpose of having the company registered in the commercial register are penal offenses punishable with up to three years of imprisonment. The same applies to issuers (*Emittenten*) if they make

---

[619] Sec. 38 para. 1 of the Stock Corporation Act.
[620] Sec. 397 sentence 1, 399 of the Act on Procedure in Family Matters and Matters of Non-Contentious Jurisdiction.
[621] Sec. 275 et seq. of the Stock Corporation Act.
[622] Sec. 277 of the Stock Corporation Act.
[623] Application of sec. 242 para. 2 of the Stock Corporation Act by way of analogy.
[624] Sec. 46 para. 4 of the Stock Corporation Act.
[625] Sec. 46 para. 2, 3 of the Stock Corporation Act.

false statements or fail to disclose relevant circumstances in the public announcement pursuant to sec. 47 no. 3 of the Stock Corporation Act.[626]

5. Overview: The Formation of a Stock Corporation[627]

Establishment of the articles of association by the founders	
	The articles of association must be established in the form of a notarial deed.
Founders	
Possible founders	– Natural persons – Legal entities – Partnerships
Number of founders	One or more shareholders
Subscription to shares	
	The subscription to shares by the founders has to be recorded within the same notarial deed as the articles of association.
Appointment of formation bodies	
	– Appointment of the first supervisory board and the auditors for the first annual financial statements by the founders in a notarial deed. – First supervisory board consists exclusively of representatives of the shareholders (no employee representatives). – Appointment of the first management board by the first supervisory board. – Unless provided otherwise by the articles of association, all members of the management board have to act jointly to represent the company. In practice, members of the management board are either granted power to represent the company alone or (more common) to represent the company together with one other member of the management board or a procuration officer (*Prokurist*). – Members of the management board are generally not entitled to enter into transactions with themselves on their own behalf or as a representative of third parties. They may be relieved from the prohibition to enter in transactions as a representative of third parties (not on their own behalf!) by way of a shareholder resolution or in the articles of association.
Raising of the registered share capital	
Minimum nominal value of registered share capital	EUR 50,000

---

[626] Sec. 399 para. 1 no. 3, sec. 47 no. 3 of the Stock Corporation Act.
[627] The overview relates to the most common creation of an *AG* via formation.

III. Formation

Minimum value of shares	– Nominal value of a par value share: EUR 1 – Part of the registered share capital attributable to a non-par value share: EUR 1
Cash contributions	– Prior to application to the commercial register, the amount called in by the company for each share has to be duly paid in and has to be at the free disposal of the management board. – The amount of the cash contributions called in must be at least one quarter of the lowest issue price. – In the event of a formation by only one founder, the shareholder has to provide additional security for the part of the cash contributions exceeding the amount called in.
Contributions in kind	– Contributions in kind are permissible. – Contributions in kind generally have to be made in full. – The value of the contributions in kind must be at least equal to the lowest issue price and the premium, if any, which has been agreed. – In the event that the contribution in kind is to be effected by way of a transfer of assets, the transfer has to be implemented within five years after the registration of the company.
Formation report	
	– Description of the formation process. – Indication of the fair value of the contributions in kind or acquisitions in kind.
Formation audit	
	– Audit of the formation procedure by the members of the management board and the supervisory board. – In certain cases, an additional audit has to be conducted by court-appointed formation auditors.
Application for registration in the commercial register	
	– Registration of the *AG* in the commercial register has to be applied for by all founders and members of the management board and supervisory board. – The application has to be certified by a notary. – The application has to state inter alia that the contributions towards the registered share capital have been called in and paid in and are at the free disposal of the management board. – The application has to contain as annexes, among others, the articles of association, the deeds containing the appointment of the management board and supervisory board, the formation report and the report on the formation audit.

Hidden contributions in kind	
	– A hidden contribution is assumed if cash contributions are supposed to be rendered but instead, in terms of the economic result, contributions in kind are in fact rendered. – As a result, the obligation to render the cash contribution remains in existence but is reduced by the fair value of the hidden contribution in kind. – This does not apply if the formalities of a post-formation acquisition are complied with.
Registration in the commercial register	
	The following information is registered in the commercial register: – name, registered office and domestic business address of the company and of any branches – details of a person who is authorized to receive declarations and notices of service (if applicable) – object of the company – amount of the registered share capital – date of establishment and, if applicable, amendments of the articles of association – members of the management board and procuration officers (*Prokuristen*) and their respective powers of representation – provisions of the articles of association on the duration of the company or on authorized capital (if applicable)
Legal effect of the registration in the commercial register	
	The *AG* comes into existence as a legal entity.

Table 3: The Formation of a Stock Corporation

IV. Legal Position of the Shareholders

1. Introduction

The membership of the shareholder in the *AG* is represented by the share (see above). Membership in the *AG* is a lasting legal relationship between the company in its capacity as a legal entity and the shareholders. It encompasses a variety of individual rights and duties. Membership also constitutes a right of each shareholder. Claims for damages may be asserted and protection against infringement may be sought by the shareholder in case of violation of such right.[628]

The content and scope of the rights and duties relating to the membership in an *AG* are mainly stipulated by law. The majority of such provisions are mandatory.

2. Membership Rights

Membership rights are divided into **administrative rights** and **property rights**.

---

[628] Decisions of the Federal Supreme Court, published in BGHZ, vol. 90, pp. 92, 95 and in BGHZ, vol. 110 pp. 323, 327 et seq.

a) Administrative Rights

Administrative rights concern the capacity of the shareholder to influence the decision-making of the company or to avert the influence of others. In principle, the shareholders exercise their administrative rights in the general meeting.[629] The administrative rights of the shareholders include in particular:
- the right to attend and to speak at the general meeting;
- the right to receive information at the general meeting;[630]
- the voting right;[631]
- the right to contest the validity of resolutions passed by the general meeting;[632]
- the right of shareholders having an aggregate shareholding amounting to 5% of the registered share capital to request that the management board convene a general meeting;[633]
- the right of shareholders having an aggregate shareholding amounting to 5% of the registered share capital or a nominal value of EUR 500,000 to request that items are announced as agenda items for a resolution of the general meeting;[634] and
- the right of shareholders having an aggregate shareholding amounting to 1% of the registered share capital or a nominal value of EUR 100,000 to apply to the courts to assert certain claims of the company for damages.[635]

b) Property Rights

The main property rights of the shareholders are:
- the right to participate in the balance sheet profit (**dividends**);[636]
- the right to subscribe to new shares in the case of a capital increase;[637]
- the right to participate in the proceeds in the case of liquidation of the company;[638] and
- the right to receive consideration and compensation in the event of a merger, split or change of form of the company, in the case of the execution of a domination or profit and loss transfer agreement between the company and the main shareholder, and in case of a squeeze-out of minority shareholders (see below).[639]

c) Prohibition of Separation

The rights of a shareholder arising from his membership may not be separated from such membership, i.e., may only be exercised by the shareholder (or his representatives). This is referred to as the **prohibition of separation** (*Abspaltungsverbot*).

The prohibition of separation also covers property rights of the shareholder, in particular the right to share in the company's profits. However, the right to receive

---

[629] Sec. 118 para. 1 of the Stock Corporation Act.
[630] Sec. 131 of the Stock Corporation Act.
[631] Sec. 134 of the Stock Corporation Act.
[632] Sec. 245 nos. 1, 2 and 3, 249 of the Stock Corporation Act.
[633] Sec. 122 para. 1 sentence 1 of the Stock Corporation Act.
[634] Sec. 122 para. 2 of the Stock Corporation Act.
[635] Sec. 148 of the Stock Corporation Act.
[636] Sec. 58 para. 4, sec. 60 of the Stock Corporation Act.
[637] Sec. 186 para. 1, sec. 212 of the Stock Corporation Act.
[638] Sec. 271 of the Stock Corporation Act.
[639] Sec. 2, 15, 25, 123, 125, 196, 205, 207 of the Transformation Act, sec. 304, 320b, 327a et seq. of the Stock Corporation Act.

the actual payment of the dividend after the resolution on the appropriation of profits has been adopted may be separated from the membership and may be disposed of independently.[640]

The encumbrance of shares, e. g., a pledge of the shares, is not prohibited as such.

d) Special Rights

In addition to the general membership rights, the articles of association may grant **special rights** (*Sonderrechte*) for the benefit of individual shareholders or groups of shareholders.[641] The following special rights are commonly granted: shares without a voting right but with a preference in profits,[642] the right to delegate members to the supervisory board,[643] rights to use the company's facilities.

e) Shareholders' Rights to File a Lawsuit

Any shareholder may **initiate lawsuits** relating to his membership rights, in particular the rights to attend the general meeting, to obtain information or to be paid dividends. Shareholders can also challenge shareholder resolutions adopted by the general meeting, either by way of an **action for the declaration of nullity** (*Nichtigkeitsklage*) (in case of severe breaches listed in the Stock Corporation Act) or by way of an **action to set aside the resolution** (*Anfechtungsklage*) in other cases. Each of these actions is to be brought **against the company**.

However, **individual shareholders** are generally **not entitled** to assert claims for damages against members of the management board and the supervisory board who fail to act in accordance with their duties. Such claims may only be raised by the company (or by shareholders in the name of the company after approval of the court, or by shareholders to the effect that performance is to be made to the company). Shareholders may, however, in some instances have personal claims based on tort law.

The general meeting may request the company, by way of a simple majority resolution, to assert claims for damages against (i) a founder concerning claims arising out of the formation process, (ii) a member of the management board or a member of the supervisory board for breach of duties in the management of the company or (iii) another person (including another shareholder) who has used his influence on the company to cause the management or representatives of the company to act to the detriment of the company.[644] The general meeting may also appoint a special representative to assert such claims on behalf of the company. If the general meeting does not appoint a special representative, a minority of shareholders holding an aggregate of 10% of the registered share capital or shares in a nominal amount of EUR 1,000,000 may apply to the court to appoint such special representative.[645]

Instead, shareholders holding shares with an aggregate nominal amount of at least EUR 100,000 or of at least 1% of the registered share capital may apply to the court to be authorized to assert damage claims on behalf of the company.[646] The

---

[640] Decision of the Federal Supreme Court, published in BGHZ, vol. 139, pp. 299, 302 et seq.
[641] Sec. 26 para. 1 of the Stock Corporation Act.
[642] Sec. 12 para. 1 sentence 2, sec. 139 et seq. of the Stock Corporation Act.
[643] Sec. 101 para. 2 of the Stock Corporation Act.
[644] Sec. 147 para. 1 of the Stock Corporation Act.
[645] Sec. 147 para. 2 of the Stock Corporation Act.
[646] Sec. 148 of the Stock Corporation Act.

company may at any time decide to pursue its claims for damages itself, leading to the dismissal of the shareholder action. The approval of the action by the court as well as the circumstances of its settlement have to be published in the company's designated journals.

Actions for a declaratory judgment are generally permitted, provided the plaintiff can prove a legitimate legal interest.[647]

3. Membership Duties

a) The Duty to Pay Contributions

The shareholders' main duty is the **duty to pay the called contributions**.[648] Unless the articles of association provide for contributions in kind, the shareholders have to pay the issue price in cash.[649] The amount due is the issue price of the shares, i.e., the lowest issue price (in the case of par value shares the nominal value and in the case of non-par value shares the proportionate amount of the registered share capital[650]) plus any premium which may have been agreed upon.[651] The shareholders are **not obliged to render additional contributions**.

Shareholders may not be released from their obligation to render a contribution. The obligation to render a contribution may not be set off by the shareholder against any claims the shareholder has against the company.[652] Because contributions generally have to be made in cash,[653] a set off by the company against claims for contribution is generally neither permitted. Accordingly, the shareholder is not entitled to assert a right of retention regarding the objects of a contribution in kind.

There are comprehensive statutory provisions ensuring that the shareholders comply with their obligation to render contributions. Only registered shares may be issued before the full issue price has been paid in[654] so that the company can easily find out the debtor of the contribution. Shareholders who fail to pay an amount which has been called by the company have to pay interest on the outstanding amount and compensation for additional damages.[655] The articles of association may provide for contractual penalties in the event that payment is not made on time.[656] Additionally, shares of shareholders may be forfeited (**forfeiture of shares**) if the shareholder does not make payments on called contributions on time; this requires, however, that the shareholder has been granted a grace period for payment accompanied by the warning that his shares will be forfeited after lapse of this grace period.[657] Each previous bearer of the share is liable for the contribution in arrears for up to two years.[658] If the arrears cannot be paid by the previous bearers of the share, the share has to be sold on the stock exchange or in

---

[647] Sec. 256 of the Code of Civil Procedure.
[648] Sec. 54 of the Stock Corporation Act.
[649] Sec. 54 para. 2 of the Stock Corporation Act.
[650] Sec. 9 para. 1 of the Stock Corporation Act.
[651] Sec. 54 para. 1 of the Stock Corporation Act.
[652] Sec. 66 para. 1 of the Stock Corporation Act.
[653] Sec. 54 para. 3 of the Stock Corporation Act.
[654] Sec. 10 para. 2 of the Stock Corporation Act.
[655] Sec. 63 para. 2 of the Stock Corporation Act.
[656] Sec. 63 para. 3 of the Stock Corporation Act.
[657] Sec. 64 of the Stock Corporation Act.
[658] Sec. 65 para. 1, 2 of the Stock Corporation Act.

a public auction.[659] By contrast to *GmbH* law,[660] the stock corporation law does not stipulate that the other remaining shareholders are generally liable for paying the amount in arrears, but only under certain circumstances.[661]

b) Ancillary Obligations

In the event of registered shares whose transfer requires the approval of the company, the articles of association can provide that the shareholders are obliged to render additional recurring contributions (apart from the obligation to render the initial contributions), so-called **ancillary obligations**, which may not consist of monetary payments.[662] Ancillary obligations are used mainly in connection with agricultural companies which are organized similarly to a co-operative (*Genossenschaft*), and create obligations of the shareholders, e. g., to deliver certain raw materials to the company.

c) Fiduciary Duty

Shareholders have a general fiduciary duty to the company and to the other shareholders. Due to the capitalist structure of *AGs*, the existence of fiduciary duties has only been recognized fairly recently with regard to them, whereas it has long been recognized with regard to partnerships and limited liability companies.

The law indicates the existence of fiduciary duties in the liability clause in sec. 117 of the Stock Corporation Act and the provisions of sec. 243 para. 2 of the Stock Corporation Act, according to which the validity of resolutions of the general meeting may be contested if voting rights have been exercised by a shareholder in order to acquire special benefits for himself or a third party to the detriment of the company or the other shareholders. Also, provisions governing the relationship of affiliated companies recognize the principle of fiduciary duties.[663]

In particular, sec. 117 of the Stock Corporation Act grants claims to the company in case of specific cases of a breach of fiduciary duties. Anyone – shareholder or a third party – who has intentionally exerted his influence over the company to induce a member of the company's management to act to the detriment of the company or its shareholders is liable for damages. Damage claims may be asserted by the company as well as by individual shareholders if such shareholders have suffered damage exceeding the damage suffered by the company. In addition, the members of the management board or supervisory board who have breached their duties are also jointly and severally liable for such damages. This does, however, not apply if the influence was exerted under a domination agreement or in case of an integrated company within the meaning of sec. 319 of the Stock Corporation Act.[664] In practice, damage claims pursuant to sec. 117 of the Stock Corporation Act are only awarded in exceptional cases.

The courts and legal literature have extended the scope of fiduciary duties beyond the statutory provisions and developed **general principles concerning**

---

[659] Sec. 65 para. 3 of the Stock Corporation Act.
[660] Sec. 24 of the Limited Liability Company Act.
[661] *Cf.* sec. 46 para. 4 of the Stock Corporation Act.
[662] Sec. 55 of the Stock Corporation Act.
[663] Sec. 309 of the Stock Corporation Act: liability of the legal representatives of a controlling enterprise in the case of a domination agreement; sec. 317 of the Stock Corporation Act: responsibility of the controlling enterprise and its legal representatives in a de facto group of companies.
[664] Sec. 117 para. 7 of the Stock Corporation Act.

fiduciary duties. The scope of fiduciary duties in case of an *AG* is essentially the same as in case of a *GmbH* (see above). Typical fiduciary duties are, for example:
- an obligation to promote the common goal, i.e., the business operated by the *AG*;
- an obligation not to cause damage to the company;
- an obligation to take into account the interests of the other shareholders; and
- an obligation to exercise rights and exert influence on the company in a responsible way.

The following examples show how fiduciary duties are applied in practice:
- It constitutes a breach of the fiduciary duty if shareholders file an action to set aside a resolution if such action is brought with the aim of receiving unjustified benefits from the company (e. g., payments in return for a stop of the action).[665]
- Minority shareholders who hold a minority position which enables them to block certain resolutions of the general meeting (e. g., a capital increase with more than 25% of the registered share capital) are not allowed to block resolutions of the general meeting if such resolution is necessary to ensure the future existence or success of the company.[666]
- Subscription rights of shareholders in the event of a capital increase may only be excluded if such exclusion is justified by facts.[667]

Depending on the violation, a breach of fiduciary duties may lead to claims of the company for performance, for information and/or for damages. If the company becomes aware of a threatening breach of fiduciary duties, the company may have the right to apply for injunctive relief. A breach of fiduciary duties may finally be a reason for other shareholders to bring an action to set aside a resolution of the general meeting.

4. Principle of Equal Treatment

Shareholders are to be treated equally in the same circumstances.[668] This **principle of equal treatment** means that shareholders may not be discriminated against arbitrarily, i.e., without a justifying reason. The criterion for applying the principle of equal treatment is the amount of the shareholder's capital interest, i.e., his share in the registered share capital.[669] The greater the extent to which membership or property rights of this shareholder are affected by the unequal treatment, the stricter the requirements regarding justification of any discrimination.[670]

If a resolution of the general meeting breaches the principle of equal treatment, an action may be brought to set aside the resolution pursuant to sec. 243 para. 1 of the Stock Corporation Act. The shareholder may also assert a claim against the company for equality to be restored.[671]

---

[665] Decision of the Federal Supreme Court, published in BGHZ, vol. 107, pp. 296, 313 et seq.
[666] Decision of the Federal Supreme Court, published in BGHZ, vol. 129, pp. 136, 142 et seq.
[667] Decision of the Federal Supreme Court, published in BGHZ, vol. 71, pp. 40, 44 et seq. and in BGHZ, vol. 125, pp. 239, 244.
[668] Sec. 53a of the Stock Corporation Act.
[669] Sec. 60 para. 1, 134 para. 1, 186 para. 1, 212 of the Stock Corporation Act.
[670] Decision of the Federal Supreme Court, published in BGHZ, vol. 71, pp. 40, 45.
[671] Decision of the Federal Supreme Court, published in GmbHR 1972, pp. 224, 225.

5. Change in Membership

a) Introduction

The share, which represents membership in the *AG*, may generally be freely sold and transferred by inheritance.

The Stock Corporation Act does not provide for a **general right of withdrawal and expulsion** of shareholders. Rights of a shareholder to withdraw from the company (other than by selling his shares) only apply in the event that a domination agreement or a profit and loss transfer agreement is entered into[672] and – in certain cases – of mergers or changes of the legal form of the company.[673]

A shareholder may be expelled from the company by way of the forfeiture of shares procedure pursuant to sec. 64 of the Stock Corporation Act or as a result of shares being redeemed pursuant to sec. 237 of the Stock Corporation Act.

Pursuant to sec. 327a et seq. of the Stock Corporation Act, a majority shareholder holding more than 95% of the registered share capital is entitled to request the expulsion of the minority shareholders in return for reasonable cash compensation. The expulsion is resolved upon by the general meeting and then registered in the commercial register (a so-called **squeeze-out**). The reasonable cash compensation is determined by the average market value during a three-month reference period starting from the date of disclosure of the planned squeeze-out.[674]

If a majority shareholder has reached a participation of more than 95% of the registered share capital in the course of a public takeover offer or mandatory offer, the majority shareholder may, within three months, alternatively apply to the Regional Court (*Landgericht*) of Frankfurt am Main to expel the minority shareholders by court decision.[675]

A similar effect is achieved by a **majority integration** (*Eingliederung*).[676]

b) Sale and Transfer of Shares

In contrast to the sale and assignment of shares in a *GmbH*,[677] the sale and transfer of shares in an *AG* does not require a specific form. The way in which shares are transferred mainly depends on whether the shares to be transferred are bearer shares or registered shares.

aa) Transfer of Bearer Shares

- Bearer shares are generally transferred by **transferring title to the share certificate** pursuant to sec. 929 et seq. of the German Civil Code. This means that the parties need to agree on the transfer of title and need to hand over the share certificate. If the owner is not able to hand over the share certificate because a third party has it in its possession, the handing over might be substituted by an assignment of the owner's claim for return of the share certificate against the person possessing the share certificate.
- The transfer may also be executed by **assigning the membership** resulting from the share.[678]

---

[672] Sec. 305 para. 1 of the Stock Corporation Act.
[673] Sec. 29, sec. 207 of the Transformation Act.
[674] Decision of the Federal Supreme Court, published in BGHZ, vol. 186, pp. 229 et seq.
[675] Sec. 39a et seq. of the Securities Acquisition and Takeover Act.
[676] Sec. 319 et seq. of the Stock Corporation Act.
[677] Sec. 15 of the Limited Liability Company Act.
[678] Sec. 398, sec. 413 of the Civil Code.

- If bearer shares are held in **separate custody**, generally in **jacket custody** (*Streifbandverwahrung*), or if they are held in **collective custody** (*Sammelverwahrung*), the transfer of the bearer shares can also be executed according to the provisions of the German Securities Deposit Act. In practice, collective custody prevails because jacket custody entails a greater administrative effort.

bb) Transfer of Registered Shares
- Registered shares are generally transferred by assigning the rights resulting from the shares according to sec. 413, 398 of the German Civil Code. The agreement regarding the assignment does not require a specific form. It is not necessary for the share certificate to be delivered to the assignee.
- Registered shares may also be transferred by way of **endorsement**.[679] The endorsement has to be put on the registered share certificate itself or on a paper connected to the share certificate. It is also necessary for the transferor and the transferee to agree upon the transfer of title and for the share certificate to be handed over or for handing over to be substituted, e. g., by assigning the claims for return of the share certificate to the acquirer.
- Registered shares may also be held in collective custody if they are provided with a blank endorsement (*Blankoindossament*) and are fully paid in. Registered shares endorsed in blank can be transferred like bearer shares (see above).

c) Peculiarities regarding Registered Shares

Registered shares have to be entered in the company's **share register**, stating the name, date of birth and address of the holder, the number of shares held or the identification number of the share and, in the case of par value shares, the nominal value thereof.[680] The articles of association may determine under what circumstances a shareholder may be registered in his own name with respect to shares which are owned by a third party.

Only those persons entered in the share register are considered to be a shareholder vis-à-vis the company.[681] If the registered share is transferred to another person, the deletion and renewed entry in the share register is effected upon the submission of notification and evidence to the company.[682] If the new shareholder is not entered into the share register, he cannot exercise his membership rights vis-à-vis the company. This applies, in particular, to the voting right in the general meeting and the right to receive dividends, provided the claim to dividends is not embodied in a separate certificate. The shareholder may demand information from the company as to what data relating to his person has been entered into the share register.[683] The shareholders are not entitled to obtain information relating to the other persons entered in the share register.

d) Restrictions on Transferability

The articles of association may make the transfer of registered shares subject to the consent of the company (**registered shares with restricted transferability**).[684] Consent is granted by the management board. However, the articles of association

---

[679] Sec. 68 para. 1 of the Stock Corporation Act.
[680] Sec. 67 para. 1 sentence 1 of the Stock Corporation Act.
[681] Sec. 67 para. 2 of the Stock Corporation Act.
[682] Sec. 67 para. 3 of the Stock Corporation Act.
[683] Sec. 67 para. 6 sentence 1 of the Stock Corporation Act.
[684] Sec. 68 para. 2 sentence 1 of the Stock Corporation Act.

may provide that the supervisory board or the general meeting have to adopt a resolution granting such consent. The articles of association can stipulate reasons for which consent may be withheld.[685] The restrictions on transferability (*Vinkulierung*) must not be so stringent that it is practically impossible to transfer the share.

If the articles of association do not provide details concerning reasons to grant or withhold consent, the management board decides in its own discretion whether consent may be or has to be withheld, e. g., because the company wishes to maintain its commercial independence or does not wish to be influenced by a specific shareholder.[686]

A refusal to grant consent renders the transfer of shares invalid. The obligation of the seller to transfer the shares, however, remains in force. Accordingly, claims for damages against the seller may be asserted by the purchaser in this case.

e) Restricted Property Rights

Shares may be encumbered with a **usufruct** or may be **pledged** or **attached**. In the case of registered shares with restricted transferability, the company's consent is required for such encumbrance to take legal effect. The usufruct or the pledge is created in accordance with general civil law provisions. The usufruct entitles the entitled party to exploit the benefits entailed by the share.[687] This covers the claim to dividends, but not a claim to the proceeds of liquidation or to a price gain obtained when the share is sold. In relation to the company, the shareholder (and not the usufructuary) is entitled to exercise the voting rights and other administrative rights.

In the case of a pledge, the administrative rights remain with the shareholder. The pledgee is generally not entitled to dividends, unless a special form of pledge (*Nutzungspfandrecht*)[688] has been explicitly agreed upon. An ordinary pledge only extends to the dividend right retained by the shareholder.[689]

f) Transfer by Way of Security

In practice, shares are often **transferred by way of security** instead of being pledged. The creditor becomes a shareholder and exercises the membership rights attached to the shares. As between the creditor and the debtor, the creditor is bound by the security agreement and is obliged to follow the instructions of the debtor, provided they do not contradict the duties entailed by membership.[690] The creditor may authorize the debtor to exercise the rights on his behalf.

g) Inheritance

In case of a shareholder's death, his shares are transferred by virtue of law to his heir(s). If they are registered shares, the heir has to be entered into the share register in order to be acknowledged by the company as a shareholder. In the event that there is more than one heir, the community of heirs takes the place of the shareholder in accordance with general provisions of the law of succession.

---

[685] Sec. 68 para. 2 sentence 2 to 4 of the Stock Corporation Act.
[686] Decision of the Regional Court of Aachen, published in ZIP 1992, pp. 924 et seq.
[687] Sec. 1068, 1030, 100 of the Civil Code.
[688] Sec. 1213 of the Civil Code.
[689] Analogy to sec. 1289 of the Civil Code.
[690] Sec. 665 et seq. of the Civil Code.

In this case, the rights arising from the share may only be exercised by a common representative.[691] He is appointed by the heirs as their attorney-in-fact.

V. Constitution of the *AG*

1. Introduction

The *AG* is designed as a legal form for large companies with a multitude of shareholders. The Stock Corporation Act, however, explicitly recognizes that an *AG* may also act as part of a group of companies, not exclusively as an independent company. As a result, not only shareholders with different shareholdings and possibilities for exerting influence but also the *AG's* employees, its creditors and – if it has been admitted to stock exchange trading – the capital market all participate in the business dealings of the *AG*. The management of the *AG* has to juggle all these differing interests.

Typical for the *AG* – in contrast to all other company forms in Germany (unless they are subject to codetermination) – is the mandatory **two-tier management system**. Alongside the meeting of shareholders (the so-called general meeting), there is the management board and, as a third mandatory corporate body, the supervisory board. In contrast, in particular Anglo-American laws, French law and Swiss law, observe in principle a one-tier management system with only one board of directors consisting of executive and non-executive members. In contrast to the German supervisory board system, these systems are referred to as **board systems**.

The management board manages the *AG* on its own responsibility, i.e., independently of instructions by the general meeting and the supervisory board.[692] Accordingly, it is the corporate body which is actually responsible for the management of the company. The general meeting decides on a number of measures listed individually in the Stock Corporation Act or other statutes, the most important of which are amendments to the articles of association, capital increases and reductions, the election of shareholder representatives to the supervisory board, consent to enterprise agreements, mergers and other corporate restructuring measures and the distribution of the balance sheet profit for the year.

The supervisory board supervises the management of the company by the management board. For this reason, there is a strict **incompatibility** between the membership in the management board and the supervisory board.[693] Additionally, in case of a listed company, a person who has been member of the management board within the last two years cannot be a member of the supervisory board unless he is elected upon proposal of shareholders in the aggregate holding more than 25% of the voting rights.[694] The supervisory board is not authorized to manage the company.[695] Neither may the supervisory board issue instructions to the management board. However, the Stock Corporation Act explicitly provides that either the articles of association or the supervisory board have to determine certain kinds of actions whose implementation requires the supervisory board's

---

[691] Sec. 69 para. 1 of the Stock Corporation Act.
[692] Sec. 76 para. 1 of the Stock Corporation Act.
[693] Sec. 105 of the Stock Corporation Act.
[694] Sec. 100 para. 2 no. 4 of the Stock Corporation Act.
[695] Sec. 111 para. 4 sentence 1 of the Stock Corporation Act.

consent.[696] The supervisory board is also involved in the granting of formal approval for the annual financial statements.[697]

In **practice**, it depends to a great extent on the shareholder structure how much influence is actually exercised by the management board on the one hand and the supervisory board and the shareholder(s) on the other hand. The management board of public companies with a large number of shareholders (without a majority shareholder) usually has an extraordinarily strong position. The members of the supervisory board are nominated *de facto* (not *de jure*) by the management board and are then elected by the general meeting. If there is a majority shareholder, the management board is generally unable to break away from the majority shareholder's influence despite the fact that the supervisory board and the general meeting are not entitled to issue orders. This is because the majority shareholder is able to influence the composition of the management board indirectly via the composition of the supervisory board.

A further peculiarity of German law is the **codetermination** of the employees in the supervisory board (see below). If an *AG* employs at least 500 employees, one-third of the members of the supervisory board are to be elected by the employees.[698] If the *AG* employs 2,000 employees or more, the Codetermination Act stipulates that a supervisory board is to be formed with half its members elected by the shareholders and half by the employees. Nevertheless, there is no genuine equality of representation since if there is a parity of votes, a further round of voting will be conducted in which the chairman of the supervisory board (who is a representative of the shareholders) has the right to cast two votes.

2. Management Board

a) Management of the Company

The management board (*Vorstand*) **manages** the *AG* on its own responsibility.[699] This means that it not only conducts the company's affairs and represents the *AG* but also determines company policy guidelines, including corporate planning, coordination and controlling of the company, and is further responsible for filling the leading positions.

Managing the company **on its own responsibility** means that the management board is not bound by instructions. Neither the general meeting nor the supervisory board may issue instructions to the management board. The supervisory board is – as indicated by its name – limited to a supervisory role.[700] While the supervisory board may generally prevent the management board from taking any action by denying its consent in certain types of transactions that require its consent,[701] it is never permitted to instruct the management board to have certain measures implemented. The general meeting is neither permitted to give instructions to the management board concerning the company's management, unless the management board has requested that a decision be made by the general meeting.[702] Even a majority shareholder may not give instructions to the manage-

---

[696] Sec. 111 para. 4 sentence 2 of the Stock Corporation Act.
[697] Sec. 172 of the Stock Corporation Act.
[698] Sec. 1 para. 1 no. 1 of the One-Third Participation Act.
[699] Sec. 76 para. 1 of the Stock Corporation Act.
[700] Sec. 111 of the Stock Corporation Act.
[701] Sec. 111 para. 4 of the Stock Corporation Act.
[702] Sec. 119 para. 2 of the Stock Corporation Act.

ment board, except in the event that the company has entered into a domination agreement (*Beherrschungsvertrag*) the majority shareholder.

The management board is obliged to comply with the statutory **regulations concerning competencies** within the AG, namely the competencies of the supervisory board and the general meeting. It is also obliged to act within the scope of the articles of association. The management board may not extend its corporate activities to areas which are not covered by the **object of the company** (*Unternehmensgegenstand*), which is mandatorily determined in the articles of association. The management board is entitled to pursue the object of the company by acquiring other companies, by founding subsidiaries or by disposing of company divisions and subsidiaries. However, according to the *"Holzmüller"* and *"Gelatine"* decisions of the Federal Supreme Court,[703] in order to conduct **fundamental alterations to the company structure** which in fact equate an amendment to the company's articles of association, the management board has to previously obtain the consent of the general meeting.

If the management board has more than one member, the law provides that the members of the management board **shall manage the company jointly** (*gemeinschaftliche Geschäftsführung*).[704] This provision is optional, though, and usually not practicable for larger companies. The articles of association or the rules of procedure of the management board may provide otherwise. In practice, the **rules of procedure of the management board** (*Geschäftsordnung*) usually contain provisions concerning the management competencies of the members of the management board.

It is primarily the supervisory board that is responsible for issuing rules of procedure of the management board.[705] The management board may itself issue rules of procedure if neither the supervisory board has yet issued such rules nor do the articles of association stipulate that the responsibility for issuing rules of procedure lies exclusively with the supervisory board. In this case, the management board must pass a unanimous written resolution on the rules of procedure.

Typically, the rules of procedure provide that the management board passes decisions with a **majority of the votes cast**. The rules of procedure may stipulate either a simple majority or a qualified majority; a sliding scale according to the nature or importance of the matter on which a resolution is to be passed may also be used. The chairman of the management board may be permitted to have the deciding vote in the event of a tie. However, the rules of procedure cannot provide that one or more management board members can take valid decisions contrary to the dissenting vote of the majority of the management board members.[706] As a result, the rules of procedure cannot provide for an exclusive right of decision of the management board's chairman. It is a matter in dispute whether a veto right for certain members of the management board can be implemented. For companies which are codetermined pursuant to the Codetermination Act, this is definitely inadmissible. It is also common for the rules of procedure to stipulate that individual members of the management board are responsible for a certain business division or carry out a certain function (e. g., production, sales, etc.). As a consequence of this allocation of **departmental responsibility**,

---

[703] Decisions of the Federal Supreme Court, published in BGHZ, vol. 83, pp. 122, 131, in BGHZ, vol. 159, pp. 30 et seq. and in ZIP 2007, p. 24.
[704] Sec. 77 para. 1 sentence 1 of the Stock Corporation Act.
[705] Sec. 77 para. 2 of the Stock Corporation Act.
[706] Sec. 77 para. 1 sentence 2 of the Stock Corporation Act.

the management board member in question essentially has the exclusive right to make decisions pertaining to his own department. However, even if a company has such a departmental structure, each member of the management board is nevertheless obligated to monitor activities in the other departments and to intervene if anything detrimental to the company as a whole is happening in any of the other departments.

Furthermore, the **management board as a whole** carries the responsibility for the actual managing of the company, namely the essential issues of company policy, corporate planning and controlling of the company. This general management responsibility may not be delegated to individual members of the management board. The responsibility also lies with the entire management board as far as statutory provisions allocate to the management board particular tasks and authorities concerning other corporate bodies, e.g., the convening of the general meeting.[707] In these instances, the management board must act as a collective body. Individual members may only be charged with the preparation of these tasks, but not with their actual implementation.

In companies with extremely diverse business divisions, a functional division between the strategic and operating management of the company is often achieved by incorporating the individual business divisions into subsidiaries which are managed by a **management holding company**. In this case, the operating business is in the hands of legally independent subsidiaries, while the chairmen of the management boards of such subsidiaries also have a seat on the management board of the management holding company and are therefore also involved in the overall strategic planning of the group. If a holding structure cannot be implemented for legal or economic reasons, the so-called **virtual holding** is becoming increasingly popular in practice. This is a company which is (legally) a single company but in which each of the individual divisions is managed by one member of the management board and other executives, often bearing the title "divisional management board" (without being such in a legal sense). The function of the management board as a whole is restricted – comparable to the management holding company – to the strategic management of the company as a whole. The legal assessment of this managerial structure has not yet been finalized in detail.

b) Representation of the Company

The *AG* is represented by the management board both in and out of court.[708] Unless otherwise provided in the articles of association, all members of the management board are only authorized to represent the company jointly (**joint representation**).[709] If a declaration of intent is to be submitted to the company, however, it suffices for such declaration to be submitted to one of the members of the management board (so-called passive representation).[710] Joint representation means that declarations in the name of the company have to be submitted either jointly by all members of the management board or separately but with identical content. The principle of joint representation does not apply to filing for insolvency of the company; each member of the management board is entitled to file for insolvency (and may be obliged to do so if the company is illiquid or

---

[707] Sec. 121 para. 2 sentence 1 of the Stock Corporation Act.
[708] Sec. 78 of the Stock Corporation Act.
[709] Sec. 78 para. 2 of the Stock Corporation Act.
[710] Sec. 78 para. 2 of the Stock Corporation Act.

over-indebted).[711] Neither does the principle of joint representation apply to the **attribution of knowledge**: the knowledge or lack of knowledge due to negligence of even one member of the management board is deemed to constitute knowledge or negligent lack of knowledge of the corporation as a whole.

The articles of association usually provide for a deviation from the statutory requirement of joint representation. The articles of association may also authorize the supervisory board to determine how the company is to be represented by passing a resolution.[712] In **practice**, the most common scenario is that the company is jointly represented by two members of the management board or by one member of the management board together with a procuration officer (*Prokurist*).[713] Nonetheless, it is also possible to grant a single member of the management board the right to represent the company alone.

Particular rules apply regarding the company's representation whenever an action to set aside a resolution of the general meeting or for declaration of nullity of a resolution is brought against the company. Here, the company is generally represented by the management board and the supervisory board[714] in court proceedings.

A further special provision applies if the company needs to be **represented with regard to a matter concerning the members of the management board** themselves. In this case, the AG is represented by the supervisory board.[715] This also ensures that a member of the management board is not able to enter into a transaction with himself in the name of the AG (self-contracting). According to case law, the special provision stipulated in sec. 112 of the Stock Corporation Act does not only apply to members of the management board who are currently in office, but also to former members who have since retired.[716] Going beyond the wording of sec. 112 of the Stock Corporation Act, it is also assumed that the supervisory board has responsibility for representing the company in the event of claims arising from a pension agreement with a deceased member of the management board, asserted, for example, by his widow.[717]

The management board's powers of representation **may not be made subject to any restrictions in its dealings with third parties**.[718] On an internal level, however, the management board is obliged to comply with restrictions arising from the articles of association, the responsibilities of the supervisory board, the general meeting as well as the rules of procedure of the management board.[719] These restrictions do not affect, however, the management board's (generally unrestricted) power of representation in its dealings with third parties except in case of an **abuse of power of representation**. According to case law, such an abuse of power of representation is to be assumed if the management board goes beyond the limits of its authority to manage the company and this fact is known by, or at least objectively evident to, the party to the respective transaction.[720] It has not yet been definitively determined whether these rules also apply if the partner to the

---

[711] Sec. 15 of the Insolvency Act.
[712] Sec. 78 para. 3 of the Stock Corporation Act.
[713] Sec. 78 para. 3 of the Stock Corporation Act.
[714] Sec. 246 para. 2 sentence 2, sec. 249 of the Stock Corporation Act.
[715] Sec. 112 of the Stock Corporation Act.
[716] Decision of the Federal Supreme Court, published in BGHZ, vol. 130, pp. 108, 114.
[717] Decision of the Federal Supreme Court, published in NZG 2007, pp. 31.
[718] Sec. 82 para. 1 of the Stock Corporation Act.
[719] Sec. 82 para. 2 of the Stock Corporation Act.
[720] Decision of the Federal Supreme Court, published in NJW 2006, pp. 2776.

transaction only remained ignorant of the abuse of the power of representation due to negligence.

A further restriction on the powers of representation is stipulated in sec. 181 of the Civil Code: the **prohibition of multiple representation**. This means that the management board may not enter into a transaction with the *AG* in the name of the corporation and at the same time in the name of a third party. The articles of association or the supervisory board may, however, provide for a release from this prohibition provided that it is so authorized by the articles of association.[721]

Sec. 32 of the **Codetermination Act** sets forth another restriction on the powers of representation of the management board: if the corporation is subject to codetermination, the management board may exercise rights of the corporation as a shareholder (at least 25%) in other companies which are also subject to codetermination only on the basis of supervisory board resolutions if certain topics are concerned, e.g., the appointment, dismissal or approval of actions of members of the management board or the supervisory board and certain measures relating to the structure of the company such as enterprise agreements, dissolution or transformation. Without the consent of the supervisory board, any actions taken by the management board in representation of the company are null and void.

The names of the members of the management board, their power of representation and any changes thereto are to be filed for registration in the commercial register.[722] In addition, (amongst others) the names of all members of the management board and the company's register number have to be stated on all business letters. This allows all parties doing business with the company to ascertain the names and powers of representation of the members of the management board who are entitled to represent the company.

c) Appointment of the Members of the Management Board

Only a natural person of unrestricted legal capacity may be a member of the management board. However German citizenship is no requirement, i.e. the management board may be composed entirely of non-German citizens. Members of the supervisory board must not be members of the management board at the same time (incompatibility).[723] The supervisory board may appoint certain of its members as deputies for vacancies on the management board for a maximum period of one year. During this term of office, the member of the supervisory board must not engage in any activities as a member of the supervisory board.[724]

Anyone convicted of a criminal offense relating to certain white-collar crimes (e.g., fraud, breach of trust, criminal offenses related to insolvency) may not be a member of the management board and anyone who has been prohibited from exercising a profession or trade relating to the object of the company may not be a member of the management board for the duration of such prohibition.[725] These cases are statutory reasons for exclusion which render the appointment null and void. The members of the management board are obliged to provide the register court with information as to such prohibitions. They are to be advised of their unrestricted obligation to provide this information by the court or a notary. They have to assure in their application to the commercial register that they have been

---

[721] Sec. 78 para. 3 of the Stock Corporation Act.
[722] Sec. 81 para. 1 of the Stock Corporation Act.
[723] Sec. 105 para. 1 of the Stock Corporation Act.
[724] Sec. 105 para. 2 of the Stock Corporation Act.
[725] Sec. 76 para. 3 sentence 2 nos. 2 and 3 of the Stock Corporation Act.

properly advised and that there are no circumstances which would constitute an obstacle to their appointment.[726] If they give false information, they are subject to prosecution and damages.[727]

According to the prevailing opinion in literature, the articles of association may stipulate personal or professional requirements for members of the management board, provided the supervisory board's wide discretion concerning the election of members of the management board is thereby not restricted disproportionately. Particularly for *AGs* which are subject to codetermination, however, such stipulations in the articles of association have to meet far stricter criteria; partly it is even argued that the discretion of the supervisory board of codetermined *AGs* cannot be limited at all.

Since the beginning of 2016, new rules concerning the **diversity of and gender quotas for management board members** and senior management-level employees apply to certain *AGs*. The supervisory boards of all German listed companies, regardless of size or number of employees, as well as of the supervisory boards of companies subject to codetermination are required to set target figures for the participation of women in the management board.[728]

Similarly, in such companies the management board is required to set target figures for the participation of women in the two levels of senior management below the management board.[729] Generally, the law allows for a large degree of flexibility in setting these target figures and in defining the two levels of senior management below the management board. Such obligation affects only the company itself, not any subsidiaries. When setting the target figure, even „0% representation" would be legally permitted if and for as long as women are not represented on the board. However, companies are prohibited from setting target figures for the proportion of women on each board or on management level which would fall short of the current composition unless women already account for at least 30% of the members of the respective board or management level. Companies are required to report on the target figures set on an annual basis and need to disclose whether targets were met or not. Failure to meet a target for women's representation on the management board or management level does not have any immediate legal consequences, but the supervisory board and the management board will be required to explain the steps that have been taken and why the targets were not reached.

The law differentiates between the **corporate act of appointing** a member of the management board and the relevant **service contract**.[730] It is mandatory that the appointment be made exclusively by the supervisory board. Responsibility lies with the supervisory board as a whole; the decision may not be delegated to a supervisory board committee; the same applies to decisions on the remuneration of the members of the management board or the reduction of such remuneration.[731] The supervisory board decides by way of resolution with a simple majority of the votes cast. If the company is subject to the **Codetermination Act**, the appointment of a member of the management board requires a majority of at least two thirds of all supervisory board members. If such a majority is not

---

[726] Sec. 37 para. 2, sec. 81 para. 3 of the Stock Corporation Act.
[727] Sec. 399 para. 1, sec. 46, sec. 48 of the Stock Corporation Act.
[728] Sec. 111 para. 5 of the Stock Corporation Act.
[729] Sec. 76 para. 4 of the Stock Corporation Act
[730] Sec. 84 of the Stock Corporation Act.
[731] Sec. 107 para. 3 sentence 3 of the Stock Corporation Act.

obtained, a special mediation committee has to make a proposal within a period of one month. In an ensuing second round of voting, the person who obtains the majority of the members of the supervisory board is elected to the management board.[732] If the necessary majority fails to be achieved once more, the chairman of the supervisory board has two votes in a third round of voting.

In addition to ordinary members of the management board, the supervisory board may also appoint so-called **deputy management board members**. In spite of their misleading title, such members are, in a legal sense, genuine members of the management board with all the rights and obligations of a management board member. In practice, however, they have a slightly lower standing. For example, younger executives may be appointed deputy management board members if they are to be given the opportunity to grow into the new office and prove that they are capable of dealing with the demands posed by such a position.

The **term of office** of management board members is mandatorily limited to five years.[733] Management board members may be appointed for another term of office, whose duration is again limited to five years at most. Such reappointment requires a further supervisory board resolution which may not be passed any earlier than one year before the date the previous term of office is due to end.[734] However, according to the Federal Supreme Court[735], in case a management board member has resigned from his office in mutual consent with the supervisory board, his reappointment for another term of (at the most) five years by supervisory board resolution is admissible even if this reappointment resolution was taken earlier than one year before the date the original previous term of office would have been due to end. The supervisory board need not name any special reasons to justify this reappointment procedure; this approach is admissible as long as it has not been chosen with the sole intention to abuse the law.

d) Chairman/Spokesman of the Management Board

If the management board consists of more than one member, the supervisory board may appoint a **chairman of the management board**.[736] This requires a resolution of the entire supervisory board; the decision may not be delegated to a supervisory board committee.[737] The supervisory board resolution is passed with a simple majority of votes cast even if the *AG* is subject to codetermination.

The legal position of the management board chairman is not comprehensively defined by law. The position is not comparable to a **Chief Executive Officer** (CEO) in the U.S. The chairman represents the management board as a collective body. He chairs management board meetings and coordinates the work of the management board. The articles of association or the rules of procedure for the management board can grant the chairman the right to cast a decisive vote in the event of a parity of votes on the management board. It is doubtful, though, whether he may also be given a veto right against majority decisions of the management board. If the *AG* is subject to codetermination, a veto right is not permitted according to the Federal Supreme Court.[738] The name of the chairman

---

[732] Sec. 31 of the Codetermination Act.
[733] Sec. 84 para. 1 sentence 1 of the Stock Corporation Act.
[734] Sec. 84 para. 1 sentence 3 of the Stock Corporation Act.
[735] Decision of the Federal Supreme Court, published in NZG 2012, pp. 1027 et seq.
[736] Sec. 84 para. 2 of the Stock Corporation Act.
[737] Sec. 107 para. 3 sentence 3 of the Stock Corporation Act.
[738] Decision of the Federal Supreme Court, published in BGHZ, vol. 89, pp. 48, 58 et seq.

of the management board is to be stated on business letters[739] and in the notes to the annual financial statements.[740]

If the supervisory board does not appoint a chairman of the management board, the members of the management board may themselves appoint a **management board spokesman** (*Vorstandssprecher*). The authority to do so arises from the management board's responsibility to impose rules of procedure which comes into effect, however, if the supervisory board does not make use of its authority to impose rules of procedure and the articles of association do not stipulate that such powers are held exclusively by the supervisory board.[741] The management board spokesman may be granted responsibility for chairing management board meetings, taking the lead in dealings with the supervisory board and representing the management board. Responsibility for directing and coordinating the work of the management board may, however, not be delegated to the spokesman since this would give him the status of a chairman of the management board.

e) Dismissal of Members of the Management Board

The supervisory board may dismiss a member of the management board before the end of his term of office **for good cause**. Examples of such good cause are gross breach of duty, inability to manage the company properly or a vote of no confidence passed by the general meeting.[742] In summary, there is good cause for dismissal if it would be unbearable for the company to allow the management board member in question to continue in office until the end of his term of office. Instances in which this would be the case include criminal offenses, incorrect accounting, violations of statutory provisions, illness or unwillingness to co-operate within the management board.

A **withdrawal of confidence** by the general meeting requires a general meeting resolution that is passed with a simple majority of the votes cast. The supervisory board is not bound by the resolution of the general meeting. It decides at its own discretion whether or not to dismiss the management board member in question on the basis of the resolution passed by the general meeting. Nevertheless, the resolution passed by the general meeting as such generally constitutes "good cause" without further requirements unless such withdrawal of confidence by the general meeting was made for "obviously arbitrary reasons".[743]

The dismissal is made on the basis of a majority resolution passed by the supervisory board. Responsibility for passing such resolution lies with the supervisory board and must not be delegated to a committee.[744] If the company is subject to the **Codetermination Act** – as is the case when appointing members of the management board – a three-tiered procedure applies.[745] Generally, a majority of two thirds of the votes of all supervisory board members is required. If this majority is not obtained, however, a proposal is to be made by a special mediation committee. In a following round of voting, the simple majority of the votes of all supervisory board members is required. If this majority also fails to be obtained, the chairman of the supervisory board has two votes in a third round of voting.

---

[739] Sec. 80 para. 1 of the Stock Corporation Act.
[740] Sec. 285 no. 10 of the Commercial Code.
[741] Sec. 77 para. 2 of the Stock Corporation Act.
[742] Sec. 84 para. 3 of the Stock Corporation Act.
[743] Sec. 84 para. 3 of the Stock Corporation Act.
[744] Sec. 84 para. 3 sentence 1, sec. 107 para. 3 sentence 3 of the Stock Corporation Act.
[745] Sec. 31 of the Codetermination Act.

The dismissal resolution remains in effect until a court has established the invalidity thereof by unappealable decision.[746] Accordingly, bringing an action against the resolution does not lead to a suspension of the dismissal resolution.

Each member of the management board may resign from office for good cause. A member of the management board may withdraw from office by common consent at any time. On the part of the company, this requires a resolution passed by the entire supervisory board, not only by a committee.[747]

f) Service Contracts with Members of the Management Board

As mentioned above, there is a difference between the appointment and dismissal (under corporate law) of a member of the management board on the one hand and his service contract with the company on the other. From a legal point of view, such contract is not actually an employment contract since the member of the management board is not an employee of the company but rather performs the functions of an employer. Instead, it is a service contract within the meaning of sec. 611 et seq., 675 of the Civil Code.

The other party to the service contract is the *AG*, which is **represented by the supervisory board** when entering into the service contract with the member of the management board. The supervisory board is responsible not only for entering into the contract, but also for amending and terminating it. The supervisory board takes its decisions on the basis of resolutions. It can – and in practice generally does – delegate responsibility for the decision to a supervisory board committee. Additionally, the decision on the remuneration of the management board members and a reduction of the remuneration cannot be delegated to a supervisory board committee.[748] However, the committee as such may not decide on the appointment of the management board member, as this is the responsibility of the supervisory board as a whole. Hence, the service contract is usually entered into on the condition that the person in question will be appointed as a member of the management board by the supervisory board.

Like the appointment, the service contract may only have a maximum duration of five years[749]; however, it can provide for the case that the management board member's term of office is prolonged that the service contract shall remain in force until the final termination of his term of office.

In the service contract, the management board member undertakes to fulfill the tasks entailed by his position and to act exclusively in the interests of the company. The management board member is subject to a statutory prohibition of competition for the duration of his term of office.[750] The management board member may not be another company's management board member, managing director or personally liable shareholder at the same time unless the supervisory board grants its consent.[751] A post-contractual prohibition on competition requires a specific agreement to this effect in the service contract.

The **remuneration** for management board members generally consists of a fixed amount and a profit-related bonus. In addition, management board members are usually entitled to a pension as well as a widow's and orphan's pension. Stock

---

[746] Sec. 84 para. 3 sentence 4 of the Stock Corporation Act.
[747] Decision of the Federal Supreme Court, published in BGHZ, vol. 79, pp. 38, 41.
[748] Sec. 107 para. 3 sentence 3 of the Stock Corporation Act.
[749] Sec. 84 para. 1 sentence 5 in connection with sentence 1 of the Stock Corporation Act.
[750] Sec. 88 of the Stock Corporation Act.
[751] Sec. 88 para. 1 sentence 2 of the Stock Corporation Act.

options are also increasingly offered as part of the remuneration for management board members. Over the last years, there have been legal efforts to achieve increased transparency with regard to the remuneration of management board members of German corporations. As a consequence, the overall remuneration for current and former management board members (including fixed salaries, bonuses and stock-based remuneration) must be detailed separately in the notes to the annual financial statements.[752] If the *AG* is listed, not only the overall remuneration granted to all management board members but also the remuneration paid to individual members needs to be set forth in the notes to the annual financial statements.

When determining the overall remuneration for the individual management board members, the supervisory board is obligated to ensure that such remuneration is reasonable in relation to the management board member's duties and the company's (economic) situation.[753] Additionally, the remuneration must not exceed the customary remuneration in comparable companies unless there are special reasons.[754] In case of listed companies, the variable remuneration components shall take into account the company's long-term development, e. g., by using reference periods of more than one year. Additionally, the service contract shall provide for means to cap the variable remuneration in case of unforeseen developments.[755] A violation of this provision does not, however, render the service contract invalid. The supervisory board can be held liable, however, if it has granted a disproportionately high remuneration.[756] Moreover, if the company's situation deteriorates after the conclusion of the service contract and the agreed remuneration is therefore deemed unreasonable, the supervisory board is supposed to reduce the overall remuneration.[757] Pension claims and similar claims can only be reduced within a period of three years after the respective management board member's resignation from office.[758] The reduction is implemented by unilateral declaration of the supervisory board. The consent of the respective management board member is not required.

The dismissal of a management board member does not automatically affect his service contract. In practice, however, the appointment to the management board and the service contract are often connected by a provision stipulating that the service contract will terminate upon dismissal from the management board. In this instance, the statutory notice periods apply to the termination of the service contract.

The service contract may also be **terminated for good cause without notice period**. However, the requirements for such good cause with regard to the service contract are stricter than those for dismissal pursuant to sec. 84 para. 3 of the Stock Corporation Act. As a result, in practice it may occur that a management board member is dismissed prematurely, while his service contract remains in force and his remuneration is continually paid until the date of the regular termination of his term of office. Examples for good cause with regard to the termination of the service contract are: committing a criminal offense, violating reporting duties

---

[752] Sec. 285 no. 9 of the Commercial Code.
[753] Sec. 87 para. 1 sentence 1 of the Stock Corporation Act.
[754] Sec. 87 para. 1 sentence 1 of the Stock Corporation Act.
[755] Sec. 87 para. 1 sentences 2 and 3 of the Stock Corporation Act.
[756] Sec. 116 sentence 3 of the Stock Corporation Act.
[757] Sec. 87 para. 2 sentence 1 of the Stock Corporation Act.
[758] Sec. 87 para. 2 sentence 2 of the Stock Corporation Act.

owed to the supervisory board, entering into transactions in breach of duty, going beyond the limits of responsibilities or ignoring the requirement to obtain the consent of the supervisory board with respect to certain business measures. The termination for good cause without notice period must be implemented within two weeks of the date on which the party which is entitled to terminate the contract has become aware of such cause.[759] This provision often leads to difficulties in practice. Since the supervisory board is competent to terminate the service contract on behalf of the *AG*, its knowledge is decisive for the beginning of the two-week period. Such knowledge of the supervisory board is not deemed to have been obtained before the relevant facts have been announced in a supervisory board meeting. Any supervisory board member who obtains the relevant knowledge is obligated to arrange for a supervisory board meeting to be convened immediately. Yet unresolved problems arise as a result of the two-week period for *AGs* which are subject to codetermination: it is doubtful whether the three-tiered termination procedure pursuant to sec. 31 of the Codetermination Act has to be carried out within the two-week period, as this would entail a deviation from the periods stipulated in the Codetermination Act.

g) Rights and Duties of Members of the Management Board

It is not only a right, but also a **duty** of the management board **to manage the company** on its own responsibility. The management board is not allowed to delegate this management responsibility to any other party. Outside the scope of the law governing groups of companies, the management board must not enter into contracts with a third party in which the management board undertakes to follow a certain corporate policy or in which it agrees to alter the organizational structure of the company.

The management board must always act in the **best interest of the company** and ensure the lasting existence and success of the company. The management board is also responsible for ensuring an appropriate profitability of the capital invested in the company.

The management board is the trustee for the company's assets. It is therefore subject to comprehensive **fiduciary and loyalty duties** owed to the company. This goes far beyond the statutory non-compete obligation.[760] The core of the fiduciary duty is the management board members' obligation to seize business opportunities for the company (so-called **corporate opportunity doctrine**) and not to exploit them for their own interests. The management board is obligated to avoid any conflicts between the interests of the company and its own interests.

The management board is obliged to ensure that the **company complies with all applicable laws** (for example, labor law, environmental law, administrative law, competition law, tax law) and does not suffer any disadvantage in connection with a breach of law (liability for damages, penalties, fines, etc.). This also includes compliance with foreign laws if the company conducts business abroad.

The Stock Corporation Act stipulates various **internal duties** of the management board. The most important is the management board's obligation to ensure that the accounting books and records are properly kept.[761] If it becomes apparent when the annual financial statements or interim financial statements are prepared,

---

[759] Sec. 626 para. 2 of the Civil Code.
[760] Sec. 88 of the Stock Corporation Act.
[761] Sec. 91 of the Stock Corporation Act.

V. Constitution of the AG

or if it is to be assumed at the management board's dutiful discretion that a loss amounting to one half of the registered share capital has been incurred, the management board is obligated to convene an (if necessary extraordinary) general meeting and notify the general meeting of this loss.[762] If the company is illiquid or over-indebted, the management board has to apply for the opening of insolvency proceedings.[763] Sec. 93 para. 3 of the Stock Corporation Act lists a number of obligations which are designed to ensure that the registered share capital is properly raised and maintained.

The management board is obliged to duly organize the company in order to avoid unnecessary damage and risks. This includes controlling the company on a regular basis and monitoring its solvency and financial situation. Moreover, the management board is obliged to introduce appropriate measures in order to ensure that any developments endangering the company's continued existence will be early identified, in particular by introducing an appropriate monitoring system (so-called early warning system).[764]

The management board manages the company on its own responsibility and is therefore generally not obligated to follow any instructions concerning its management of the company. However, at the request of the general meeting, the management board has to prepare any matter falling within the authority of the general meeting.[765] It is also obligated to implement resolutions which have been lawfully passed by the general meeting.[766]

The management board is bound by the statutory allocation of responsibilities within the company. It must respect the authorities of the general meeting and the supervisory board as stipulated by law and in the articles of association.[767] In addition, it also fulfills a control function. The management board has to check the lawfulness of the resolutions passed by the other corporate bodies, namely the general meeting and the supervisory board. The law grants the management board the right to bring an action to challenge resolutions passed by the general meeting.[768]

The management board is subject to a number of **reporting requirements** which are crucial for the co-operation between the management board, the supervisory board and the general meeting. The management board is generally only obligated to give information to shareholders in the general meeting upon the shareholders' request if the requested information concerns items on the agenda.[769] The law provides with regard to certain fundamental decisions to be taken by the general meeting (for example, decisions concerning enterprise agreements, mergers, spin-offs, changes of legal form) that the management board is required to submit to the general meeting a comprehensive written report explaining the measure concerned. Additionally, the management board is subject to particular reporting obligations under capital market law (if the *AG* is listed) and reporting requirements vis-à-vis the corporation's employees, works council and economic committee.

---

[762] Sec. 92 of the Stock Corporation Act.
[763] Section 15a para. 1 of the Insolvency Code.
[764] Sec. 91 para. 2 of the Stock Corporation Act.
[765] Sec. 83 para. 1 sentence 1 of the Stock Corporation Act.
[766] Sec. 83 para 2 of the Stock Corporation Act.
[767] Sec. 82 para. 2 of the Stock Corporation Act.
[768] Sec. 245 no. 4, 249 of the Stock Corporation Act.
[769] Sec. 131 of the Stock Corporation Act.

The reports that the management board has to submit to the supervisory board are of particular importance.[770] They serve to give the supervisory board a comprehensive picture of the company's situation. These reports do not only refer to the past, but also to the "intended corporate policy" and other fundamental issues relating to the company's future management.[771] The law differentiates between reports submitted to the supervisory board as a whole, reports submitted only to the chairman of the supervisory board or to individual members of the supervisory board respectively. At least once a quarter, a report has to be submitted to the entire supervisory board. In case of transactions of considerable importance, a specific report has to be submitted to the supervisory board timely enough to give the supervisory board the opportunity to comment on the transaction in question before it is implemented.[772] At any time, the supervisory board as a whole but also each single supervisory board member can request information to be delivered to the supervisory board on any matter of considerable importance.[773] Moreover, irrespective of such request, the management board has to report any significant developments to the chairman of the supervisory board.[774]

Apart from these reporting requirements, the management board members are subject to a strict **confidentiality obligation**. They must neither disclose confidential information nor trade or business secrets of the company that they have obtained knowledge about as a result of their position.[775] Failure to comply with this confidentiality obligation entails liability for damages.

Compliance, the scope and set-up of compliance organizations and the consequences of compliance failures have been a hot topic in German corporate law since 2010. Based on the statutory duty to act lawfully and to control the lawfulness of the *AG's* activities, it is established doctrine that the management board of an *AG* has the obligation to organize the *AG*, its business and the business of any subsidiaries to be in compliance with applicable laws. Recent compliance cases have included German blue chip companies being involved in bribery activities in certain countries.

In a landmark decision in 2014, the Regional Court of Munich[776] had to deal with the personal liability of a management board member, who was aware of non-compliance and a group-wide system of bribery activities, but did not actively stop all these activities. The court upheld that such management board member violated his duties to organize an effective compliance-system. Although the management board member had never suggested to the use of bribery and had never been actively involved in the bribery system, the court stated that such management board member was nonetheless personally liable because he failed to organize the business of the *AG* in a way so that unlawful activities of employees were avoided. In case the business of an *AG* is active in sectors or countries that generally show a higher risk-profile in corruption indices, the management board is obliged to establish a compliance-system with appropriate risk control functions. Furthermore, if unlawful business practices are detected and become known to the management board, it has to take appropriate measures to investigate the matter,

---

[770] Sec. 90 of the Stock Corporation Act.
[771] Sec. 90 para. 1 of the Stock Corporation Act.
[772] Sec. 90 of the Stock Corporation Act.
[773] Sec. 90 para. 3 of the Stock Corporation Act.
[774] Sec. 90 para. 1 sentence 3 of the Stock Corporation Act.
[775] Sec. 93 para. 1 sentence 3 of the Stock Corporation Act.
[776] Regional court of Munich I, published in NZG 2014, pp. 345 et seq.

to stop the non-compliance and to take adequate corrective actions to prevent further incidents in the organization. The responsibility for compliance investigations lies primarily with the management board, provided that the supervisory board must monitor such investigations. If a management board member ist implicated in any wrong doing the supervisory board also must make sure that it receives the necessary information on which decisions can be based. This could even lead to separate investigations by the supervisory board. Finally, the court upheld that the management board must monitor the effectiveness of a compliance systems on an ongoing basis and correct, update or improve such systems when necessary.

The responsibility for effective compliance in general lies with all management board members. Certain functions and tasks may be delegated to a compliance organization or to a chief compliance officer, but this does not relieve the management board from the duty to monitor the compliance system and its effectiveness and to become active once compliance failures have become apparent. Violations of these duties may expose the management board members to personal liability to the *AG*.

h) Liability of Members of the Management Board

Civil law liability of management board members for damage they caused to the company while exercising their duties used to be of little importance in practice. In recent years, spectacular collapses of companies and erroneous management decisions with far-reaching economic implications have led to a change of view.

The Stock Corporation Act contains stipulations regarding the liability of the management board to the company (so-called **internal liability**). In exceptional cases such as fraud, the management may also be held liable to the shareholders or to the company's creditors. Claims of the company against management board members are generally asserted by the company's supervisory board.

The *"ARAG"* decision of the Federal Supreme Court defined guidelines for the assertion of damage claims by the supervisory board. According to the Federal Supreme Court, the supervisory board of an *AG* is obliged to assert claims for damages against management board members unless the protection of specific overriding company interests requires the supervisory board to abstain from such a course of action.[777] In addition to an increased public awareness concerning errors made by management board members, this case law has led to an increasing number of claims by *AGs* against current or former management board members.

Management board members are obliged to apply the **due care of a diligent and conscientious manager** when managing the company.[778] Management board members who fail to comply with their duties are liable for damage resulting from the breach of their duties. Sec. 93 of the Stock Corporation Act contains a general definition of liability, which applies to all management board members as a general clause.

Sec. 93 para. 2 of the Stock Corporation Act stipulates a partial **reversal of the burden of proof** in deviation from general law principles. According to this provision, the company only has to prove (i) that it has suffered damage, (ii) that there was an action or omission by the respective member of the management board and (iii) that the company has suffered damage as the result of the action or omission by the management board member. If the company has proven the

---

[777] Decision of the Federal Supreme Court, published in BGHZ, vol. 135, pp. 244, 255.
[778] Sec. 93 para. 1 sentence 1 of the Stock Corporation Act.

aforementioned facts, in order to avoid liability the management board member has to prove (i) that his action or omission did not constitute a breach of duties, (ii) that a breach of duties was not culpable or (iii) that the company would have suffered the same damage if the member of the management board had acted in accordance with his duties.

Whether or not the management board member acted in accordance with his duties is to be determined from an **objective point of view**. This means that the duty of care is deemed to have been breached if the standard of care used by an average management board member in a comparable company is not complied with. Personal deficiencies in the respective management board member's ability to fulfill such duties are irrelevant; the law assumes that each management board member must have the knowledge and skills that his position requires. Of course, the required standards can differ depending on the company's operations and the size and importance of the business. Hence, the management board of a large bank may have to meet higher standards than the management board of a small manufacturing company.

The liability risk for management board members may be reduced by implementing **departmental responsibility** for the individual members of the management board. In this case, members of the management board are generally only obliged to monitor the other members of the management board conducting business in their respective field of responsibility. However, there may be a duty to step in if a member of the management board has reason to believe that another member is not properly fulfilling his duties.

Besides the general rules stipulated in sec. 93 para. 1 and 2 of the Stock Corporation Act, the Stock Corporation Act provides for a number of specific duties of the management board which lead to a liability of the management board in case of a breach. These duties include, among others, the supervision of the maintenance of the company's capital including the prohibition of repayment of contributions,[779] prohibitions regarding the acquisition of the company's own shares[780] and the prohibition to make any payments once the company has become illiquid or over-indebted.[781]

The company is obliged to comply with all provisions applicable to the company, in particular civil law rules, competition law, labor law, criminal law, the law relating to administrative offenses, tax law and social law. The management board is obliged to take care that the company complies with these duties in order to prevent the company from suffering disadvantages such as damage claims by third parties, fines and the like. If the management board has doubts concerning the legal situation, it generally has to seek external legal advice in order to avoid personal liability. In its *"ISION"* decision[782], the Federal Supreme Court stated the following strict requirements that a management board member has to meet in case of ambiguous legal situations in order to avoid personal liability: The management board member has to seek professional and qualified advice by an independent expert to whom he or she discloses all relevant company information. Furthermore, the management board member has to carry out a plausibility check concerning any legal advice obtained. Thereafter, the Federal Supreme

---

[779] Sec. 93 para. 3 no. 1 of the Stock Corporation Act.
[780] Sec. 93 para. 3 no. 3 of the Stock Corporation Act.
[781] Sec. 93 para. 3 no. 6, sec. 92 para. 2 of the Stock Corporation Act.
[782] Decision of the Federal Supreme Court, published in in NZG 2011, pp. 1271 et seq.

Court[783] has more precisely defined the management board's duty to undertake such a plausibility check. The court held that the requirements for a plausibility check have been properly fulfilled when the management board has provided the knowledgeable expert with all relevant information and the knowledgeable expert has processed all this information and has given a consistent answer to all questions that a legal layman would pose. From this follows that the management board's duty to carry out a plausibility check is limited insofar as it does generally not comprise the duty to explicitly verify the legal correctness of the legal advice obtained by the expert, because otherwise, the management board had to be a legal expert itself.

The management board is generally not liable for unlawful actions of the company's **employees**. Nonetheless, the personal liability of the management board may very well apply if a member of the management board ordered or tolerated such actions by employees or if it failed to take the necessary measures to prevent them.

Most measures taken by the company's management relate to **business issues**, e.g., the introduction of a new product, the opening of a branch office or the acquisition of another company. All of these business measures and decisions entail risks which could lead to economic disadvantages for the company if the measure turned out to be unsuccessful. The Federal Supreme Court established in the *"ARAG"* decision[784] that the management board has **wide-ranging discretionary powers** regarding the company's management and administration. According to the Federal Supreme Court, such powers include the taking of business risks, including the risk of making a false assessment or miscalculation.

Meanwhile, these principles of the Federal Supreme Court have been adopted in sec. 93 para. 1 sentence 2 of the Stock Corporation Act. Pursuant to this provision, a management board member does not violate his duty of care (and can therefore not be held liable pursuant to sec. 93 para. 2 of the Stock Corporation Act) if, on the basis of appropriate information, he could assume that the business measure taken was in the interest of the company. The management board member can only rely on this privilege, however, if all of the following conditions are fulfilled (so-called "**safe harbor rule**"):

(i) the measure in question is a business measure;
(ii) the management board member was acting in good faith when taking the business decisions, i.e.:
   – he was acting free of any own or third party interests;
   – he was acting in the interests of the company; and
   – he was acting on the basis of sufficient information, thereby taking into account the importance of the business measure in question.

The fact that the supervisory board has approved an action of the management board does not automatically eliminate potential liability risks of the management.[785] Only if the action was based on a lawful resolution of the general meeting, the management board cannot be held liable. Hence, the law grants the management board the right to submit management measures to the general meeting for approval.[786]

---

[783] Decision of the Federal Supreme Court, published in NZG 2015, pp. 792 et seq.
[784] Decision of the Federal Supreme Court, published in BGHZ, vol. 135, pp. 244 et seq.
[785] Sec. 93 para. 4 sentence 2 of the Stock Corporation Act.
[786] Sec. 119 para. 2 of the Stock Corporation Act.

The Stock Corporation Act restricts the company's right to **waive** or **settle** claims for damages against management board members. The company may only waive or settle claims for damages three years after such claims have arisen with the approval of the general meeting; additionally, no objection may have been raised in the minutes of the general meeting by a minority of shareholders holding at least 10% of the registered share capital. This time limit does not apply if the management board member in question is insolvent and enters into a settlement with his creditors in order to avert insolvency proceedings or if the liability for damages is regulated in an insolvency plan.[787]

The **supervisory board** is generally **responsible** and competent for asserting the company's claims for damages against members of the management board.[788] The members of the supervisory board are obliged to further investigate if there is a likelihood that the company may be able to assert damage claims against members of the management board. Hence, the supervisory board has to establish whether the management board members have acted in breach of their duties. In the *"ARAG"* decision, the Federal Supreme Court held that the supervisory board is generally obliged to pursue claims for damages against management board members. The supervisory board may only refrain from asserting claims in the exceptional event that significant interests of the company outweigh the company's interest to receive compensation from the respective management board members, e.g., because a lawsuit against the management board would have severe effects on the company's business activities or its reputation. According to the apparently (still) prevailing opinion in legal literature, the supervisory board has no discretion whether or not to pursue claims against the management board: Thus, if the aforementioned conditions are fulfilled, the supervisory board is obliged to assert the claims against the respective management board members. If the supervisory board does not comply with this obligation, the members of the supervisory board themselves may be personally liable to the company for damages because of a breach of their duties.[789]

The **general meeting** may force the supervisory board to assert claims for damages against members of the management board by adopting a resolution with a simple majority of the votes cast.[790] The resolution has to precisely state the damage claims which shall be asserted. If the general meeting has requested the assertion of claims, the supervisory board is obliged to take appropriate actions within six months from the date of the general meeting.

The general meeting can also appoint, with a simple majority of the votes cast, a **special representative** of the company for the purpose of asserting the claims against the management board members.[791] The special representative can review books and records of the company as well as request information from the company. At the **request of a shareholder minority** holding an aggregate of at least 10% of the registered share capital or shares with a nominal value of at least EUR 1,000,000, the court may appoint a special representative if the general meeting has decided to assert claims against members of the management board.[792]

---

[787] Sec. 93 para. 4 sentence 4 of the Stock Corporation Act.
[788] Sec. 112 of the Stock Corporation Act.
[789] Sec. 116 sentence 1, sec. 93 para. 2 of the Stock Corporation Act.
[790] Sec. 147 para. 1 of the Stock Corporation Act.
[791] Sec. 147 para. 2 sentence 1 of the Stock Corporation Act.
[792] Sec. 147 para. 2 sentence 2 of the Stock Corporation Act.

Minority shareholders holding an aggregate of at least 1% of the registered share capital or shares with a nominal value of at least EUR 100,000 may apply to the court to be authorized to assert the damage claims against the members of the management board in their own name but for the benefit of the company.[793] The court will grant such authorization if (i) the shareholders prove that they (or their legal predecessors) acquired the shares before they could have known of the breach of duties or the damage to the company, (ii) the shareholders prove that the company refused to assert the claims despite a request by the shareholders to do so, (iii) there are facts justifying the suspicion that the company has suffered damage due to a severe breach of the law or the articles of association, and (iv) there are no overriding interests of the company which outweigh the interests in asserting the claim against the management board members. A judgment is binding in favor of or against the company and all shareholders.

The principles outlined above relate to so-called internal liability, i.e., the liability of the management board with regard to the company. **Regarding third parties**, such as the shareholders and the company's creditors, the management board is only liable in accordance with the general provisions stipulated under tort law,[794] in particular in case of criminal offenses like fraud and in the event of a breach of fiduciary duty or false representations concerning the company's situation.[795] In this case, the injured party can assert claims for damages directly against the relevant member of the management board.

Companies increasingly acquire liability insurance against financial loss in connection with the actions of management board members (**D&O insurance**). Usually, the company is the policy holder and the management board members are the insured persons. The premium payments are made by the company. In most cases, the D&O insurance covers potential claims of the company against the management board members. The company's decision to offer D&O insurance to its management board members is to be taken by the supervisory board because it affects the employment relationship with the members of the management board. The German tax authorities do not consider the premiums for D&O insurance as being taxable remuneration of the management board members provided that the D&O insurance is arranged in such a way that it predominantly serves the *AG*'s own interests and the calculation of the premium is not based on individual characteristics of the insured management board members. According to latest legislation, it is mandatory that the D&O insurance policy provides for a deductible which is to be personally borne by the member of the management board of at least 10% up to an amount equal to at least 1.5 annual fixed salaries of the respective management board member.[796]

3. Supervisory Board

a) Introduction

The main task of the supervisory board (*Aufsichtsrat*) is to **supervise** the management of the company. The supervisory board is responsible for the appointment of the management board members. Furthermore, it is involved in transactions which are subject to supervisory board approval and makes proposals for reso-

---

[793] Sec. 148 para. 1 sentence 1 of the Stock Corporation Act.
[794] Sec. 823 et seq. of the Civil Code.
[795] Sec. 400 of the Stock Corporation Act.
[796] Sec. 93 para. 2 sentence 3 of the Stock Corporation Act.

lutions to be passed by the general meeting. The composition of the supervisory board depends on the shareholder structure to a large extent. In the case of public companies, the candidates for the supervisory board are *de facto* selected and nominated by the management board. Former members of the company's management board (subject to the restrictions pursuant to sec. 100 para. 2 no. 4 of the Stock Corporation Act),[797] and management board members of "friendly" companies, banks or insurance companies are often elected as members of the supervisory board. If there are majority shareholders, the composition of the supervisory board generally reflects the weighting of each group of shareholders. If the company has subsidiaries, the management board members of the parent company are often also represented in the supervisory board of the subsidiary.

In recent years, the functioning of supervisory boards has been subject to increasing criticism since in numerous instances the intended control function of the supervisory board has failed to prevent companies from seriously going off course. Therefore, the law has been changed several times in an attempt to strengthen the position of the supervisory board and to improve the efficiency of its supervisory activities. As a consequence, the supervisory board is now obligated by law to make certain transactions subject to its consent, to hold a minimum number of meetings, to become informed about the corporate planning and to appoint the auditor of the annual financial statements as well as to ensure that the auditor attends the supervisory board's proceedings regarding the annual financial statements. If a company is listed on a stock exchange or has applied for a stock exchange listing (so-called capital market-oriented corporation (*kapitalmarktorientierte Kapitalgesellschaft*)), at least one member of its supervisory board must have expert knowledge in the field of accounting or auditing of financial statements.[798]

However, one fundamental obstacle to the efficiency of the supervisory board has been left untouched: the **Codetermination Act** stipulates that supervisory boards of large companies have to consist of twenty members, half of whom are to be employee representatives. The supervisory board's size and the differing qualifications and interests represented by the individual members is peculiar to Germany, and is legitimately open to criticism.

b) Overview of the Statutory Supervisory Board Models

In contrast to *GmbHs*, a supervisory board is mandatory under the Stock Corporation Act. Depending on the number of employees and the amount of the registered share capital, however, the size and composition of the supervisory board can vary considerably. The most important statutory supervisory board models are as follows:
- For *AGs* which as a rule employ **fewer than 500 employees** in Germany, only corporate law applies to the supervisory board. In this case, no employee representatives have to be elected to the supervisory board. The Stock Corporation Act provides that the supervisory board has to have at least three members. The articles of association may, however, stipulate a higher number: if the registered share capital is EUR 1,500,000 or less, the supervisory board may have no more than nine members; if the registered share capital is higher than EUR 1,500,000, there may be no more than 15 members and if the regis-

---

[797] *Cf.* B.V.3.d.
[798] Sec. 100 para. 5 of the Stock Corporation Act.

tered share capital is higher than EUR 10,000,000, the maximum number of supervisory board members is 21.[799]
- If an AG employs as a rule **more than 500 employees** in Germany, according to the **One-Third Participation Act**, one third of the supervisory board has to consist of employee representatives.[800] Furthermore, the law provides that in this case, the number of supervisory board members has to be divisible by three.[801] The employee representatives are elected by the employees working in the company's domestic facilities. In all other respects, the provisions of the Stock Corporation Act apply with regard to the size of the supervisory board, its responsibilities and its proceedings.
- If an *AG* employs as a rule **more than 2,000 employees** in Germany, the **Codetermination Act** applies. In this case, the supervisory board must consist of[802]: (i) twelve members if there are no more than 10,000 employees; (ii) sixteen members if there are more than 10,000 employees; and (iii) twenty members if there are more than 20,000 employees. Half of the supervisory board members are elected by the general meeting and half by the employees employed in the stock corporation's domestic facilities.
- Special rules apply if the stock corporation employs as a rule more than 1,000 employees in Germany and is active in the **coal, iron and steel industries**. In this case, the Coal, Iron and Steel Codetermination Act stipulates that a supervisory board with eleven members is to be appointed. Five members are elected by the general meeting, five by the employees and one (the so-called neutral member) is elected by means of a complicated mediation procedure. The articles of association may provide that the supervisory board may have more members if the registered share capital of the stock corporation exceeds certain thresholds.

c) Gender Quota

For a long time, the representation of women on supervisory boards and management boards of large listed German *AGs* has been below 10%. Both on executive and supervisory boards, female chairpersons have remained the exception. German legislators adopted in 2015 an act on equality for women and men in managerial positions, both at private companies and in the public sector. This legislation came into effect on January 1, 2016. German law now imposes a binding gender quota on the supervisory boards of large public companies and requires all listed German companies to set target figures for the gender diversity of their supervisory boards and management boards.

Listed AGs that are subject to codetermination (2,000 or more employees) or that have been created by a cross-border merger must ensure that at least **30% of supervisory board seats** are held by members of each gender.[803] Figures are to be rounded up or down according to mathematical rules. Companies affected by this legislation are not required to immediately adapt the composition of their supervisory boards; rather they are required to fulfill the gender quota when the terms of current board members expire.

---

[799] Sec. 95 sentence 4 of the Stock Corporation Act.
[800] Sec. 1 no. 1, sec. 4 para. 1 of the One Third Participation Act.
[801] Sec. 95 sentence 3 of the Stock Corporation Act in connection with sec. 4 para. 1 of the One-Third Participation Act.
[802] *Cf.* sec. 7 para. 1 of the Codetermination Act.
[803] Sec. 96 para. 2, 3 of the Stock Corporation Act.

In principle, the gender quota is intended to apply to the composition of the supervisory board as a whole. However, the shareholder representatives and employee representatives on a fully codetermined supervisory board (composed of an equal number of shareholder and employee representatives) may object to the overall fulfillment provision in advance of an election, subsequent to a resolution adopted by the majority of either group.[804] In such case, the shareholder representatives and employee representatives will be required to each meet the 30% quota separately. When companies subject to these new rules propose elections to the supervisory board, they will be required to disclose in the notice of meeting the minimum number of supervisory board seats that must be filled by members of each gender in order to comply with the legislation, as well as whether an objection has been lodged to meet separate quotas for shareholder and employee representatives on the supervisory board.

The gender quota in listed codetermined *AGs* is mandatory and non-fulfillment has severe legal consequences. If future elections by the general meeting or appointments to the supervisory board do not meet the quota, they will be legally invalid and the required position on the supervisory board will remain vacant ("empty seat" provision).[805] Such a seat must be staffed with a person of the underrepresented gender in a subsequent election.

AGs or *SEs* which are not subject to full codetermination, but that are either listed or subject to employee codetermination pursuant to the German One Third Participation Act, must set target figures for the proportion of women on the supervisory board and deadlines for fulfillment of such target figures. Should the existing proportion of women be below 30%, the target figure to be determined may not be lower than the status quo.[806] The first deadline for reaching the target figures must not extend beyond 30 June 2017. The supervisory board must state in its report on the annual financial statements whether the target figures have been reached or not and, if applicable, which new target figures have been set. Unlike in a full codetermined AG, the failure to fulfill the target figures does not have any immediate legal consequences and does not cause any elections of the general meeting to be invalid.

d) Appointment and Dismissal of Members of the Supervisory Board

Supervisory board members are personally responsible for the fulfillment of their duties. Accordingly, only a natural person with full legal capacity may become a supervisory board member.[807]

In a listed company, the supervisory board members, taken as a whole, must be familiar with the sector in which the company operates.

The Stock Corporation Act contains a number of **incompatibility provisions,** the purpose of which is to separate the supervision task from the management of the company.

Neither a member of the management board nor a procuration officer nor an authorized signatory of the company may be a member of the supervisory board.[808] This rule is slightly modified if the Codetermination Act applies: procuration officers may be elected as employee representatives to the supervisory

---

[804] Sec. 96 para. 2 sentences 2 and 3 of the Stock Corporation Act.
[805] Sec. 96 para. 2 sentence 6 of the Stock Corporation Act.
[806] Sec. 111 para. 5 of the Stock Corporation Act.
[807] Sec. 100 para. 1 of the Stock Corporation Act.
[808] Sec. 105 para. 1 of the Stock Corporation Act.

board unless they report directly to the management board and their powers are similar to those of a member of the management board.[809] Additionally, in case of a listed company, a former member of the management board cannot be a member of the supervisory board unless he is elected upon proposal of shareholders which in the aggregate hold more than 25% of the voting rights.[810]

The legal representatives of a subsidiary may not be elected to the supervisory board of the controlling entity since this would result in the representative of the subsidiary exerting control over the subsidiary in his position as a supervisory board member of the parent.[811]

The legal representatives of another corporation on the supervisory board of which a member of the company's management board serves may not be appointed to the company's supervisory board.[812]

In order to maintain the efficiency of the supervisory board, the law provides for a **maximum number of seats on supervisory boards** which may be held by one person. A person who is already a member of the supervisory boards of ten different companies which are under a legal obligation to form a supervisory board may not be elected to the supervisory board.[813] If the member has been elected to the position of chairman in any of these supervisory boards, such seats are counted twice when determining the maximum permissible number of seats that individual may hold. If the member holds supervisory board seats in several group companies which are controlled by one entity, up to five seats held in the group companies are not taken into account when determining the maximum number of seats.[814]

The codetermination laws provide for particular requirements for the eligibility of **employee representatives** (e.g., membership of a trade union). We refrain from going into detail on this topic.

The members of the supervisory board (other than the employee representatives) are elected by the **general meeting** with a simple majority of the votes cast after proposal by the supervisory board. The general meeting is not obliged to follow the proposal made by the supervisory board (if the Coal, Iron and Steel Codetermination Act does not apply).

The majority principle leads to the result that the majority shareholder or a group of shareholders who together hold the majority are in a position to occupy all seats on the supervisory board. Minority shareholders are not entitled to claim a proportionate number of supervisory board seats. The majority shareholder's power to elect all supervisory board members (or in the case of codetermined companies all shareholder representatives) at his discretion is the most important tool for **controlling the company,** since the election of the supervisory board is (in absence of a domination agreement) the only way to indirectly influence the management board.

The articles of association can either tighten the majority requirement, for example by providing for a qualified majority, or they may conversely allow a relative majority to suffice. The chairman of the general meeting is responsible for determining the voting procedure. If several supervisory board members are to

---

[809] Sec. 6 para. 2 of the Codetermination Act.
[810] Sec. 100 para. 2 no. 4 of the Stock Corporation Act.
[811] Sec. 100 para. 2 sentence 1 no. 2 of the Stock Corporation Act.
[812] Sec. 100 para. 2 sentence 1 no. 3 of the Stock Corporation Act.
[813] Sec. 100 para. 2 sentence 1 no. 1 of the Stock Corporation Act.
[814] Sec. 100 para. 2 sentence 2 of the Stock Corporation Act.

be elected, the chairman of the meeting may order either an **individual election** or a **list election**, in which case all candidates on the list may only be accepted or rejected as a whole. If a list election is held, the chairman of the general meeting needs to mention before voting is commenced that shareholders who do not agree with the choice of even one single shareholder have to reject the list as a whole. The German Corporate Governance Code recommends an individual election for listed companies.[815]

The election of employee representatives to the supervisory board is very complicated and technical. The applicable provisions stipulate in detail which employees are entitled to vote and the manner in which the seats are to be distributed between employees belonging to the company and trade union members. We refrain from going into detail here.

Instead of an election, the articles of association may make up to one third of the seats on the supervisory board held by the shareholder representatives subject to a **right of appointment** by certain shareholders.[816] A supervisory board member who has been appointed under such a right of appointment can be removed from office and substituted by another member at any time by the person(s) entitled to make the appointment.[817]

Deputy members (i.e., members who attend supervisory board meetings in the case of a temporary unavailability of the respective supervisory board member) may not be appointed.[818] However, substitute members may be appointed to take the place of a member of the supervisory board who permanently ceases to hold office (e.g., by death or withdrawal from office) before the official end of his term of office.[819] Substitute members are usually elected in large companies, especially if the company is subject to the Codetermination Act. This ensures that the balance in the supervisory board is not disrupted in the period between the time a member ceases to hold office and the time a new member is elected.

Appointment of supervisory board members by court order is possible if the supervisory board no longer possesses the number of members required to constitute a quorum.[820] A member may also be appointed by court order if the supervisory board has fewer members than the number stipulated by law or the articles of association for more than three months, or less in urgent cases. An urgent case is deemed to exist if important supervisory board decisions are imminent. In companies subject to codetermination, it is always deemed an urgent case if the supervisory board is no longer complete since such a situation leads to a disruption of the balance between shareholder representatives and employee representatives provided by law.[821] The term of office of the member appointed by the court terminates as soon as this shortcoming has been remedied.[822] An application to the court can be filed by the management board, single members of the supervisory board, shareholder(s) or, if the company is subject to codetermination, by larger groups of employees or their organizations.

The **term of office** for supervisory board members is limited by law. They may not be appointed for a period longer than until the end of the general meeting

---

[815] Sec. 5.4.3 of the German Corporate Governance Code.
[816] Sec. 101 para. 2 of the Stock Corporation Act.
[817] Sec. 103 para. 2 of the Stock Corporation Act.
[818] Sec. 101 para. 3 of the Stock Corporation Act.
[819] Sec. 101 para. 3 of the Stock Corporation Act.
[820] Sec. 104 para. 1 of the Stock Corporation Act.
[821] Sec. 104 para. 3 of the Stock Corporation Act.
[822] Sec. 104 para. 6 of the Stock Corporation Act.

which passes a resolution on ratification of their actions in the fourth fiscal year following the commencement of their term of office. The fiscal year in which the term of office commences is not counted.[823] As the ordinary general meeting is regularly held in the spring or summer (if the fiscal year is equivalent to the calendar year), the term of office lasts for approximately five years at most. The articles of association may stipulate a shorter term of office and different terms of office for different members of the supervisory board. Employee representatives may not be discriminated against. There are no restrictions on re-election.

The office of a member of the supervisory board terminates upon the expiry of the term of office and also terminates if the statutory eligibility requirements are no longer met. A member of the supervisory board may **resign from office** before the end of his or her term of office. The articles of association often stipulate time periods within which the resignation from office takes effect.

Supervisory board members who have been elected by the general meeting may be **removed from office** by the general meeting prior to expiry of their term of office. A majority of three quarters of the votes cast is required for removal.[824] The articles of association may stipulate a simple majority, and in practice often do. This is extremely significant in the event that the company undergoes a change of control; a new majority shareholder will be keen to fill the supervisory board with persons he or she trusts as soon as possible.

A member of the supervisory board may be removed from office by a court upon application by the supervisory board if there is **good cause** relating to the supervisory board member in question.[825] Good cause is interpreted in the same way as with respect to the dismissal of a member of the management board. The decisive criterion is whether it is unreasonable to expect the company to allow the respective supervisory board member to continue in office until the end of the regular term of office. The most common examples of good cause are failure to comply with the statutory confidentiality obligations or a continuing conflict of interest.

e) Responsibilities of the Supervisory Board

One of the supervisory board's main tasks is the **supervision** of the management board.[826] This supervision task consists primarily of a **retrospective control** of the management board's conduct of business and the manner in which it is performing its duties. For this purpose, the supervisory board has the right to inspect and audit the company books and accounts or to commission one of its members or experts, in particular chartered accountants, to do so. Moreover, the supervisory board is obliged to monitor managerial decisions relating to the **future**, in particular corporate planning and the filling of managerial positions. If the stock corporation is the controlling entity of a group of companies, the supervision also extends to monitoring the **group management** and actions taken in controlled companies to the extent that they are subject to management measures of the controlling company.

The supervision does not only relate to the lawfulness but also to the expediency and economic efficiency of decisions taken by the management board. The supervisory board has to check whether the members of the management board

---

[823] Sec. 102 of the Stock Corporation Act.
[824] Sec. 103 para. 1 of the Stock Corporation Act.
[825] Sec. 103 para. 3 of the Stock Corporation Act.
[826] Sec. 111 para. 1 of the Stock Corporation Act.

are acting with the due care of a diligent and conscientious manager and whether the corporate policy is plausible and consistent.

The **management board** is subject to comprehensive **reporting obligations** in order to enable the supervisory board to carry out its duties. The management board is obliged to provide the supervisory board with reports on a regular basis, in particular on intended corporate policy and corporate planning, the profitability of the company and the progress of business (standard reports).[827] The management board is further obliged to immediately report to the supervisory board about transactions of considerable importance and other significant developments (*ad hoc* reports).[828] In addition to the reports which the management board has to submit, the supervisory board can at any time request reports on matters relating to the company (requested reports). Even a single member of the supervisory board may request that such a report shall be submitted to the supervisory board.[829]

The supervisory board is not allowed to manage the company. The articles of association or the supervisory board itself (by way of resolution) must, however, stipulate certain types of transactions that may only be implemented if the supervisory board grants its consent.[830] These **catalogues of measures requiring supervisory board consent** are important in practice. They are seldom found in the articles of association. Instead, due to the greater degree of flexibility, they are generally determined in the form of a supervisory board resolution or rules of procedure for the management set up or agreed to by the supervisory board. Nevertheless, passing a catalogue of measures requiring supervisory board consent only enables the supervisory board to prevent certain transactions from being implemented. The supervisory board cannot actively direct the management board to implement a specific transaction, because the initiative to take a management measure always remains with the management board. If the management board comes to the conclusion that a certain measure is not advisable any more, it is entitled to refrain from its implementation even though the supervisory board has granted its consent.

Pursuant to sec. 111 para. 4 of the Stock Corporation Act, the above-mentioned catalogue of measures has to specify **certain types of transactions** requiring supervisory board consent. The consent requirements must not be so tight that the management board can no longer fulfill its duty to manage the company on its own authority. Furthermore, the kinds of transactions which are to be subject to the consent of the supervisory board have to be determined specifically. A wide general clause, e.g. referring to "important transactions", would not suffice. Generally, significant transactions such as the acquisition and sale of companies or of major assets will be made subject to the supervisory board's consent. Furthermore, it is common to state value thresholds in order to ensure that only financially significant transactions will be subject to consent. Case law also allows the supervisory board to *ad hoc* impose a requirement for consent on an individual transaction if the transaction in question is of particular importance.[831] The supervisory board can implement a consent requirement in its due discretion. If the supervisory board learns that the management board intends to implement

---

[827] Sec. 90 para. 1 sentence 1 nos. 1 to 3 of the Stock Corporation Act.
[828] Sec. 90 para. 1 sentence 1 no. 4 of the Stock Corporation Act.
[829] Sec. 90 para. 3 of the Stock Corporation Act.
[830] Sec. 111 para. 4 of the Stock Corporation Act.
[831] Decision of the Federal Supreme Court, published in BGHZ, vol. 124, pp. 111, 127.

V. Constitution of the AG

an illegal measure, it may be obliged to adopt an *ad hoc* resolution that imposes a requirement for supervisory board consent on this measure in order to prevent such measure from being taken.

The supervisory board has the duty to **inspect** the **annual financial statements** prepared by the management board (and audited by the auditor of annual financial statements), the management report and the proposal for the appropriation of the annual balance sheet profit.[832] The supervisory board has to provide the general meeting with a written report on the results of its review. Such report, amongst others, needs to contain sufficient information as to what extent the supervisory board has supervised the management of the company in the past fiscal year.[833] If the supervisory board has consented to the annual financial statements, they are formally approved.[834] The annual financial statements are then legally binding. The general meeting can no longer amend the annual financial statements and can only pass a resolution concerning the appropriation of the balance sheet profit shown in the annual financial statements. The law has strengthened the position of the supervisory board regarding the inspection of the annual financial statements by stipulating that the auditor of annual financial statements now has to attend the supervisory board meeting (or meeting of the audit committee) in which the annual financial statements are dealt with and has to report about the key results, in particular about potential weaknesses of the internal control and risk management system.[835] In addition, the supervisory board is responsible for mandating the auditor of annual financial statements with conducting the audit.[836] The purpose behind these provisions is to prevent the management board from exerting influence on the auditor of annual financial statements.

Another major task of the supervisory board is the **responsibility to appoint and dismiss the members of the management board**.[837] The supervisory board is also responsible for entering into, amending and terminating the service contract with the management board members. The supervisory board also fixes the remuneration for the management board members. Recently, the Federal Supreme Court has decided[838] that the supervisory board is responsible for entering into an agreement concerning the remuneration of a management board member even if the contract is concluded between the company and a third party, i.e. the management board member itself is not a party to this contract (*Drittanstellung*). According to this court decision, the conclusion of such a remuneration agreement falls within the supervisory board's competency pursuant to Sec. 84 para. 1 sentence 5, sec. 87, sec. 112 sentence 1 of the Stock Corporation Act.

Furthermore, the supervisory board decides on whether or not to take out D&O insurance for the management board members, the premiums of which are paid by the company. The supervisory board **represents the company with respect to all legal actions vis-à-vis the management board members**.[839] This power of representation also applies vis-à-vis retired members of the management board. The supervisory board is also responsible for deciding on and asserting claims for damages against current and former members of the management board.

---

[832] Sec. 170 et seq. of the Stock Corporation Act.
[833] Sec. 171 para. 2 sentence 2 of the Stock Corporation Act.
[834] Sec. 172 of the Stock Corporation Act.
[835] Sec. 171 para. 1 of the Stock Corporation Act.
[836] Sec. 318 para. 1 of the Commercial Code.
[837] Sec. 84 of the Stock Corporation Act.
[838] Decision of the Federal Supreme Court, published in NZG 2015, pp. 792 et seq.
[839] Sec. 112 of the Stock Corporation Act.

f) Supervisory Board Procedures

The supervisory board **elects a chairman** and one or more **co-chairmen** from amidst its members.[840] Unless stipulated otherwise in the articles of association, such election requires the simple majority of votes cast. A special election procedure applies to companies subject to **codetermination**. A majority of two thirds of all members is required in the first round of voting. If this majority is not obtained, two separate elections are held: the shareholder representatives in the supervisory board elect the chairman, and the employee representatives the co-chairman, in each case with a majority of the votes cast.[841] Since the chairman of the supervisory board in companies subject to codetermination has a second vote in the event of a tie,[842] the shareholder representatives control the supervisory board in spite of the fact that each side holds an equal number of seats.

The **chairman of the supervisory board prepares, convenes and chairs the supervisory board meetings**. The co-chairman only has the rights and duties of the chairman if the chairman is prevented from acting.[843] However, the co-chairman is not entitled to the second vote pursuant to the Codetermination Act.

The supervisory board must hold **at least two meetings in each six-month period** (i.e., four meetings per year).[844] In a non-listed company, the supervisory board can pass a resolution stipulating that only one meeting is to be held every six months.[845] Each member of the supervisory board and the management board can, stating the purpose and reasons for such request, request the chairman of the supervisory board to convene a meeting of the supervisory board without delay.[846]

The supervisory board **meetings are not public**. Only members of the supervisory board and the management board shall attend. Experts and persons required to give information may be invited to attend for specific items on the agenda.[847]

The supervisory board decides by way of **resolution**.[848] A formal voting procedure is required; tacit or implied decisions are prohibited for reasons of legal clarity. The resolutions are usually passed during supervisory board meetings. Nonetheless, it is permissible for resolutions to be passed outside of meetings in writing, by telephone or in a comparable form if the articles of association and the rules of procedure of the supervisory board contain a provision to that effect or if no member of the supervisory board objects.[849]

The supervisory board has a **quorum** if at least half of the number of members required by law or pursuant to the articles of association, but at least three members, participate in voting.[850] This means that a supervisory board consisting of three members already does not have a quorum if only one member is absent. Open voting is the usual procedure. According to the prevailing, but nevertheless controversial, view, secret voting is allowed.

---

[840] Sec. 107 para. 1 sentence 1 of the Stock Corporation Act.
[841] Sec. 27 of the Codetermination Act.
[842] Sec. 29 para. 2 of the Codetermination Act.
[843] Sec. 107 para. 1 sentence 3 of the Stock Corporation Act.
[844] Sec. 110 para. 3 sentence 1 of the Stock Corporation Act.
[845] Sec. 110 para. 3 sentence 2 of the Stock Corporation Act.
[846] Sec. 110 para. 1 sentence 1 of the Stock Corporation Act.
[847] Sec. 109 para. 1 of the Stock Corporation Act.
[848] Sec. 108 para. 1 of the Stock Corporation Act.
[849] Sec. 108 para. 4 of the Stock Corporation Act.
[850] Sec. 108 para. 2 of the Stock Corporation Act.

V. Constitution of the AG

Supervisory board resolutions generally require a **simple majority** of the votes cast. Abstentions and invalid votes do not count. In the event of a tie, the application is rejected. Special rules apply if the **Codetermination Act** applies: in the event of a tie, a second round of voting is held on the same subject in which the chairman of the supervisory board has two votes.[851]

The articles of association can stipulate a qualified majority requirement for individual items. This is not possible, though, if the corporation is subject to codetermination. In this case, the requirement of a simple majority is obligatory (unless, as an exception, other majorities are prescribed by law).

The law does not provide for an explicit **prohibition against voting** with regard to the supervisory board. In accordance with sec. 34 of the Civil Code, however, it is to be assumed that a member of the supervisory board may not participate in voting if the resolution in question concerns a legal transaction with him/her or the commencement or conclusion of litigation against him/her. There is no general prohibition of voting due to a conflict of interest. However, the German Corporate Governance Code recommends that members of the supervisory board should disclose potential conflicts of interest and provide information relating to such conflicts of interest in the supervisory board's written report to the general meeting. In the event of fundamental and not only temporary conflicts of interest, the supervisory board member concerned should resign from office.[852]

A supervisory board member cannot arrange for a proxy to vote in his place. However, absent members of the supervisory board are permitted by law to request other participants in the supervisory board meeting to submit their written vote (**voting by messenger**).[853] If a vote is submitted in this manner, the absent supervisory board member has to take his/her own decision and may not transfer responsibility for the decision to the messenger.

Minutes are to be kept on the meetings of the supervisory board. They have to be signed by the chairman of the supervisory board.[854]

The law does not explicitly stipulate the legal consequences of **defective supervisory board resolutions**. The German Federal Supreme Court has held that supervisory board resolutions which are not adopted in accordance with the law and the articles of association or supervisory board resolutions whose contents violate the law or the articles of association are null and void.[855] The details have not been clarified in all respects, however. In particular, with regard to procedural errors which are not severe, the prevailing view in legal literature advocates that such resolutions be only deemed challengeable but not automatically null and void.

The Federal Supreme Court[856] had to deal with the question which effect a shareholder's successful challenge of a supervisory board member's election has on the resolutions that the supervisory board has taken in the meantime since the supervisory board member in question has been elected. The court answered this question, which is of great practical significance, by ruling that principally, whenever a court declares a supervisory board member's election to be void, this court declaration has retroactive effect to the date of the member's election. Hence, in a legal sense, the person in question is deemed to never have been a member of

---

[851] Sec. 29 para. 2 of the Codetermination Act.
[852] Sec. 5.5 of the German Corporate Governance Code.
[853] Sec. 108 para. 3 of the Stock Corporation Act.
[854] Sec. 107 para. 2 of the Stock Corporation Act.
[855] Decision of the Federal Supreme Court, published in BGHZ, vol. 122, pp. 342, 351.
[856] Decision of the Federal Supreme Court, published in BGHZ, vol. 196, pp. 195 et seq.

the supervisory board, i.e. the supervisory board has had fewer members during the relevant span of time. However, third parties who have been affected by the execution of a supervisory board resolution but did not and could not have any knowledge of its nullity may rely upon the competence to act of the person who is executing the resolution.[857]

g) Supervisory Board Committees

The supervisory board can establish one or more committees from among its members to which it can delegate certain of its tasks.[858] Committees prepare the resolutions of the supervisory board. Committees may also be furnished with the **authority to pass resolutions** in their area of responsibility in place of the supervisory board as a whole. However, the supervisory board is not allowed to delegate the authority to pass resolutions for its overall area of responsibility to a committee. Furthermore, pursuant to sec. 107 para. 3 of the Stock Corporation Act, the supervisory board as a whole is solely responsible for passing resolutions on the following items (and may not delegate any of these to a committee):
- appointment and dismissal of the chairman and the co-chairman of the supervisory board;
- appointment and dismissal of members of the management board;
- decisions on the remuneration of management board members and on the reduction of such remuneration;
- adoption of rules of procedure for the management board;
- making certain transactions subject to the consent of the supervisory board pursuant to sec. 111 para. 4 of the Stock Corporation Act; and
- the review of the annual financial statements pursuant to sec. 171 of the Stock Corporation Act and the report thereon to the general meeting.

Responsibility for selection of members of the management board and negotiating the service contracts may be transferred to a **personnel committee** (*Personalausschuss*). The personnel committee may, however, not prejudice the supervisory board by its decisions concerning the service contract with the management board since responsibility for appointing and dismissing management board members rests with the supervisory board as a whole. In view of the importance of the personnel committee, it is common for the chairman of the supervisory board to also be the chairman of the personnel committee.

Particularly for large companies, the formation of supervisory board committees is an important means of making the work of the supervisory board more efficient. The most common committees are: personnel committees, which prepare the selection and appointment of management board members and settle the terms of the service contract with them; finance committees (*Finanzausschuss*); investment committees (*Investitionsausschuss*) and, in case of banks, credit committees (*Kreditausschuss*). A special function is often performed in large companies by a general committee (*Präsidialausschuss* or *Aufsichtsratspräsidium*) which acts as an interface between the supervisory board and the management board and coordinates the work within the supervisory board. Audit committees (*Prüfungsausschuss*) dealing with monitoring the accounts and the control system of the company are increasingly common, following the example of audit committees in the US. The German Corporate Governance Code explicitly recommends forming

---

[857] Decision of the Federal Supreme Court, published in BGHZ, vol. 196, pp. 195 et seq.
[858] Sec. 107 para. 3 of the Stock Corporation Act.

an audit committee and states that its chairman should not be a former member of the company's management board.[859] If an audit committee is established in a company which is listed on a stock exchange or has applied for a listing on a stock exchange, at least one member of the audit committee must have expert knowledge in the field of accounting or auditing of financial statements.[860]

In companies subject to **codetermination**, a so-called mediation committee is prescribed by law which shall be composed of the chairman of the supervisory board, the co-chairman, one additional member elected by the shareholder representatives and one elected by the employee representatives.[861] The mediation committee intervenes if the required two-thirds majority fails to be reached in the first round of voting for the appointment of a member of the management board.[862]

The decision as to whether a committee is established, who its members are and which responsibilities it has lies with the supervisory board as a whole.[863] Committees with the authority to pass resolutions must have at least three members.[864] Particular provisions apply to companies subject to **codetermination**: the employee representatives may not be discriminated against when appointing the members of the committees. In general, at least one employee representative is required to sit on each committee.

Supervisory board committees have a **quorum** if at least three members participate in the passing of the resolution. Decisions are made on the basis of the simple majority of votes cast. The articles of association or the rules of procedure for the supervisory board may grant the chairman of a committee the right to a second vote in the event of a tie.[865]

Members of the supervisory board who do not belong to the committee may attend the committee meetings only if the chairman of the committee does not decide otherwise.[866] The committees are obligated to provide the supervisory board as a whole with regular reports of their work.[867] This means that the supervisory board as a whole must be informed of at least the essential contents, if not all the specific details, of the work carried out by the committees.

h) Duties of Members of the Supervisory Board

All members of the supervisory board – irrespective of whether they are shareholder representatives or employee representatives – have the **same** rights and duties. They have to perform their duties **personally**[868] and in the best interest of the company.

A supervisory board member is not allowed to hold an "**imperative**" mandate in which he or she is committed to follow instructions. The supervisory board members are neither bound by instructions nor can they legally undertake to exercise their duties in accordance with instructions issued by third parties. The foregoing also applies without restriction to supervisory board members of

---

[859] Sec. 5.3.2 of the German Corporate Governance Code.
[860] Sec. 107 para. 4 of the Stock Corporation Act.
[861] Sec. 27 para. 3 of the Codetermination Act.
[862] Sec. 31 para. 3 of the Codetermination Act.
[863] Sec. 107 para. 3 of the Stock Corporation Act.
[864] Decision of the Federal Supreme Court, published in BGHZ, vol. 65, pp. 190, 191 et seq.
[865] Decision of the Federal Supreme Court, published in BGHZ, vol. 83, pp. 106, 120 et seq.
[866] Sec. 109 para. 2 of the Stock Corporation Act.
[867] Sec. 107 para. 3 sentence 4 of the Stock Corporation Act.
[868] Sec. 111 para. 6 of the Stock Corporation Act.

companies which are partly or wholly owned by the government and in which civil servants have been appointed to the supervisory board. A member of the supervisory board cannot enter into an agreement with a third party which obliges him or her to withdraw from office if he or she fails to comply with the third party's instructions and wishes (in particular if the third party is a shareholder). An agreement to that effect would be null and void.

The fact that none of the supervisory board members is obliged to follow instructions while exercising his or her duties can pose considerable difficulties for the majority shareholder in exercising control over the company. This applies in particular to companies which are codetermined pursuant to the Codetermination Act since the shareholder representatives can overrule the employee representatives with the second vote of the chairman of the supervisory board. This second vote generally only applies if all shareholder representatives have voted unanimously (leading to equal votes with the employee representatives).

The fact that supervisory board members are not obliged to follow instructions also makes it difficult for shareholders of a stock corporation to agree in syndicate agreements with regard to the manner in which their representatives on the supervisory board shall exercise their vote. While a representative may be instructed to exercise his or her voting right in a specified manner in the general meeting, and instructions to this effect may even be enforced by a court, the members of the supervisory board may only be "encouraged" by the shareholders to vote in a certain way.

i) Remuneration

The members of the supervisory board are only entitled to **remuneration** if this has been stipulated in the articles of association or approved by the general meeting.[869] The remuneration shall be reasonable in relation to the duties of the supervisory board member and the situation of the company.[870] In practice, the combination of a fixed amount and a profit-related variable amount is most common. The German Corporate Governance Code states that in case a performance-related remuneration is paid, it should be oriented towards the long-term success of the company.[871] Stock options may not be granted to supervisory board members.[872]

In principle, all members of the supervisory board are entitled to the same remuneration. No differentiation may be made between shareholder representatives and employee representatives. However, the chairman of the supervisory board and the co-chairman may be paid a higher remuneration than an ordinary member of the supervisory board (the chairman of the supervisory board is generally paid twice the normal remuneration, although this is actually less than he deserves in view of the importance of his position). Additional remuneration may be paid for being a member of a committee. The German Corporate Governance Code explicitly recommends that the position of chairman and co-chairman of the supervisory board, as well as the position of chair and membership in committees, should be considered when determining the remuneration.[873]

In addition, the members of the supervisory board are also entitled to **reimbursement of expenses** regardless of an express stipulation in the articles of

---

[869] Sec. 113 para. 1 of the Stock Corporation Act.
[870] Sec. 113 para. 1 sentence 3 of the Stock Corporation Act.
[871] Sec. 5.4.6 of the German Corporate Governance Code.
[872] Decision of the Federal Supreme Court, published in BGHZ, vol. 158 pp. 122 et seq.
[873] Sec. 5.4.6 of the German Corporate Governance Code.

association or resolution of the general meeting. Such expenses are in particular expenses incurred for travel, overnight stays and similar outlays which a supervisory board member is entitled to view as necessary.

Contracts for works and services, in particular **advisory agreements** between a member of the supervisory board and the company, require the consent of the supervisory board in order to be valid. Advisory agreements with a member of the supervisory board which involve advisory activities not going beyond the scope of those owed anyway by the supervisory board member in fulfillment of his duties are deemed invalid since this may in essence be a hidden increase of the supervisory board member's remuneration, which can only be decided upon by the general meeting.[874] The German Federal Supreme Court held that the same rules apply to advisory agreements between a company in which a supervisory board member is a shareholder or partner on the one hand and the company on the other.[875] This court ruling is of some significance since it makes it harder for professional service firms to act for companies in which one of its partners is a supervisory board member.

j) Confidentiality Obligation

The members of the supervisory board are subject to a **confidentiality obligation**.[876] Accordingly, they are obligated not only not to disclose the company's trade and company secrets, but also not to disclose any details concerning the confidential reports submitted to them and the confidential discussions held within the supervisory board. The confidentiality obligation covers the course of discussions, the opinions of individual members of the supervisory board and other participants (e. g., members of the management board) as well as the results of voting and the manner in which individual members voted. Violation of this duty is a punishable offense.[877] The confidentiality obligation applies equally to shareholder and employee representatives on the supervisory board. Consequently, the employee representatives are not entitled to forward confidential information to trade unions, works councils or the like.

The law recognizes an **exception to the confidentiality obligation** for members of the supervisory board elected or delegated to the supervisory board at the instigation of a regional authority, although only if such persons are under an obligation to report to the regional authority on the basis of statutory provisions under public law.[878] A further exception to the confidentiality obligation applies in a group of companies. Members of the supervisory board of a group subsidiary who are at the same time members of the management board or employees of the parent company are entitled to forward confidential information to other legal bodies and employees of the parent company if this serves the purpose of the proper management of the group. This exception applies to both a genuine group of companies and a *de facto* group of companies (see below on groups of companies).

The question as to whether a certain fact or piece of information must be kept secret is determined on the basis of whether or not there is an objective requirement for it to be kept secret in the interest of the company. None of the articles

---

[874] Decision of the Federal Supreme Court, published in BGHZ, vol. 114, pp. 127, 129.
[875] Decision of the Federal Supreme Court, published in NZG 2007, pp. 103 et seq.
[876] Sec. 116 of the Stock Corporation Act.
[877] Sec. 404 of the Stock Corporation Act.
[878] Sec. 394 of the Stock Corporation Act.

of association, the rules of procedure for the supervisory board, the supervisory board itself or the management board can give a binding definition of what must be kept secret since the scope of the statutory confidentiality obligation may be neither extended nor restricted. In practice, however, it has proven useful for the articles of association or the rules of procedure for the supervisory board to include guidelines which ensure that a member of the supervisory board seeks confirmation from the chairman of the supervisory board if there is doubt as to whether or not a piece of information is confidential.

k) Liability of Members of the Supervisory Board

The liability of supervisory board members largely corresponds to the rules which apply to management board members. Sec. 116 of the Stock Corporation Act explicitly refers to the rules governing the liability of management board members.[879] Reference is therefore made to the comments on the reversal of the burden of proof and the difficulties of waiving claims with regard to management board members (see above).

As sec. 93 para. 1 of the Stock Corporation Act applies accordingly, the members of the supervisory board are obligated to apply the due care of a diligent and conscientious manager. Since they are not managers in the true sense of the word, this reference is to be interpreted as meaning that they are to apply the care which is required in order for the duties of the supervisory board (in particular regarding the supervision of the company) to be performed in a diligent and conscientious manner. Members of the supervisory board are, in particular, liable if they grant the management board an inappropriate remuneration.[880]

All members of the supervisory board are subject to the **same duty of due care**. The Federal Supreme Court has decided that each supervisory board member – including each of the employee representatives – must have or acquire the minimum knowledge and skills required to understand and assess all issues arising in the ordinary course of business without seeking assistance from a third party.[881] The necessary knowledge and skills may, of course, differ considerably depending on the nature and size of the company. If a supervisory board member is elected to sit on a committee because he or she has special skills and knowledge (e. g., a banking specialist elected to the credit committee of a bank), such member of the supervisory board is liable for his/her particular individual skills. The other members of the supervisory board may rely on the assessment of the "specialist". A supervisory board member who has professionally acquired special knowledge is subject to a stricter standard of care as far as his or her area of expertise is concerned.[882]

Supervisory board members are often members of the management board, employees or supervisory board members of other companies at the same time. It is therefore not uncommon that a **conflict of interest** arises. Conflicts of interest are a consequence of the fact that the law allows that the position on the supervisory board is a secondary office which can be performed in addition to other duties and that several positions on supervisory boards may generally be held at the same time.[883] For activities within the supervisory board, however, in the

---

[879] Sec. 93 of the Stock Corporation Act.
[880] Sec. 116 sentence 3 of the Stock Corporation Act.
[881] Decision of the Federal Supreme Court, published in BGHZ, vol. 85, pp. 293, 295 et seq.
[882] Decision of the Federal Supreme Court, published in NZG 2011, pp. 1271 et seq.
[883] Sec. 100 para. 2 of the Stock Corporation Act.

event of a conflict of interest each member of the supervisory board is obligated to give preference to the company's interests. If no other solution can be found to resolve a conflict of interests, a supervisory board member may be obligated to resign from office.

If the supervisory board is involved in **business decisions** taken by the management board (e.g., by granting consent for a transaction for which the supervisory board's consent is required), it has the same wide discretion as the management board. If it properly exercises its discretion, the supervisory board is not liable even if its decision leads to the company suffering damage (e.g., due to an erroneous assessment of future developments). There is, however, no discretion concerning the duty to properly supervise the management board of the company. In this respect, the supervisory board is obligated to look into any identifiable issues and to avoid damage. This was explicitly decided by the Federal Supreme Court in connection with the assertion of damage claims against members of the management board.[884] The examination and assertion of damage claims against members of the management board who fail to comply with their duties is part of the supervisory board's supervision task with regard to the management board. In this respect, the supervisory board has generally no discretion.

The members of the supervisory board have **joint responsibility**. Even if they are not a member of a committee and have not attended the meetings of such committee, they must nevertheless satisfy themselves that the committees are working properly.

Responsibility for asserting claims for damages against the supervisory board lies with the **management board**. In all other respects, the same sanction system which applies to management board members equally applies to supervisory board members. They may, in particular, become liable to the company for damages (see above). Shareholders holding shares with an aggregate nominal amount of at least EUR 100,000 or the equivalent to at least 1% of the registered share capital may, with court approval, bring an action for damages on behalf of the company. In addition, the same principles that apply to management board members equally apply to supervisory board members with regard to supervisory board members' liability towards third parties (e.g., towards shareholders and creditors of the company).

The supervisory board members are usually included in the cover provided by **D&O insurance policies**. It is doubtful whether the premiums for the D&O insurance borne by the company are deemed to form part of the remuneration of the supervisory board members. If this were the case, a resolution of the general meeting approving the D&O insurance as part of the remuneration (or a provision in the articles of association to that effect) would be required. Views on this are still divided. The tax authorities are of the opinion that taking out such an insurance policy is usually in the interest of the company and that it does therefore not constitute remuneration, provided that the premium payments are not governed by individual characteristics of the respective supervisory board member. The rules concerning the deductible for management board members[885] do not apply to D&O insurance policies for supervisory board members.[886]

---

[884] Decision of the Federal Supreme Court, published in BGHZ, vol. 135, pp. 244, 256.
[885] Sec. 93 para. 2 sentence 3 of the Stock Corporation Act; *cf.* B.V.2.h.
[886] Sec. 116 sentence 1 of the Stock Corporation Act.

4. General Meeting

a) Introduction

The general meeting (*Hauptversammlung*) is the corporate body in which the shareholders exercise their rights relating to the concerns of the company.[887] Unless otherwise stipulated by law, shareholders are only entitled to exercise these rights in the general meeting.[888] The general meeting is often referred to as the company's highest corporate body. It decides on the composition of the supervisory board (in case of codetermination only about the representatives of the shareholders), which in turn appoints the management board.[889] Furthermore, the general meeting can withdraw its confidence in the members of the management board and therefore enable the supervisory board to revoke the appointment of members of the management board.[890] The general meeting also votes on matters of fundamental importance for the company, in particular amendments to the articles of association, corporate measures relating to the share capital, the dissolution of the company and management measures having serious implications. It is doubtful, however, whether the general meeting can in fact be referred to as the company's highest body. The management board is not obliged to follow the instructions of the general meeting,[891] and the articles of association may not include a general provision rendering management measures subject to the consent of the general meeting.[892]

The Shareholders' Rights Act (*Gesetz zur Umsetzung der Aktionärsrechterichtlinie – ARUG*) also implemented important changes relating to the convening and conduct of the general meeting, in particular with respect to shareholder voting rights. These are discussed where applicable.

The company's articles of association may provide or may authorize the management board to decide on shareholders being allowed to participate in the general meeting without being physically present at the actual location, to be represented by a proxy, to exercise certain or all of their rights by means of electronic communication or to exercise their voting right in writing.[893]

b) Statutory Competency of the General Meeting

In principle, the general meeting only passes resolutions in the cases expressly stipulated by law or in the articles of association.[894] Sec. 119 para. 1 of the Stock Corporation Act explicitly states a catalog of several cases for which the general meeting is responsible, which concern both routine matters and fundamental decisions. Alongside the matters for which the general meeting is responsible pursuant to the catalog under sec. 119 para. 1 of the Stock Corporation Act, the general meeting is also responsible for approving management decisions when asked to do so by the management board.[895] In addition, there are additional cases stipulated by law and unregulated competencies are also recognized by court decisions.

---

[887] Sec. 118 para. 1 of the Stock Corporation Act.
[888] Sec. 118 para. 1 sentence 1 of the Stock Corporation Act.
[889] Sec. 84 para. 1 sentence 1 of the Stock Corporation Act.
[890] Sec. 84 para. 3 of the Stock Corporation Act.
[891] Sec. 76 para. 1 of the Stock Corporation Act.
[892] Sec. 23 para. 5 of the Stock Corporation Act.
[893] Sec. 118 paras. 1 and 2 of the Stock Corporation Act.
[894] Sec. 119 para. 1 of the Stock Corporation Act.
[895] Sec. 119 para. 2 of the Stock Corporation Act.

aa) Routine Matters. The general meeting is responsible for **appointing the members of the supervisory board**.[896] This only applies, however, to members who are not delegated to the supervisory board by a certain shareholder and to members who are not elected by the employees in the case of codetermination.[897]

The general meeting also decides on the **appropriation of the balance sheet profit**.[898] The annual financial statements are generally prepared by the management board and need to be approved by the supervisory board.[899] As a result, the general meeting usually has no influence on the amount of profit shown on the balance sheet. The general meeting decides (merely) on the appropriation thereof.[900]

The general meeting also resolves on **the ratification (formal approval) of the acts of the members of the management board and the supervisory board**.[901] A decision to this effect indicates the approval of the general meeting for the manner in which the company has been administered by the members of the management board and the supervisory board. However, ratification does not entail a waiver of claims for damages.[902] Accordingly, ratification is only of symbolic significance. If ratification is withheld, however, the position of the member of the management in question is weakened; withholding the ratification might under certain circumstances be an indication that the general meeting has lost its confidence in such member of the management board. The next step in the general meeting often is a formal resolution of non-confidence which allows the supervisory board to prematurely dismiss the member of the management board in question.[903] Separate votes are held regarding the ratification of the acts of the supervisory board and the ratification of the acts of the management board, in each case often for the corporate body as a whole. A separate vote is to be held on the ratification of the acts of an individual member if so decided by the general meeting or requested by a minority having an aggregate shareholding of at least 10% of the registered share capital or the proportionate amount of EUR 1,000,000 in the registered share capital.[904] Additionally, the chairman of the meeting may order a vote regarding ratification of the acts of individual members if he believes it is appropriate. The general meeting has to adopt a resolution on the ratification in the first eight months of each fiscal year.[905] In a listed company, the general meeting also may vote on the approval of the remuneration system for the members of the management board; such vote, however, has no legal consequences and does not release the supervisory board from its obligation to implement an appropriate remuneration for the members of the management board.[906]

The general meeting also passes a resolution concerning the **election and appointment of the auditor of the annual financial statements**.[907] Only a certified public accountant (*Wirtschaftsprüfer*) or a firm of certified public accountants

---

[896] Sec. 119 para. 1 no. 1 of the Stock Corporation Act.
[897] Sec. 101 para. 1 sentence 1, sec. 119 para. 1 no. 1 of the Stock Corporation Act.
[898] Sec. 119 para. 1 no. 2 of the Stock Corporation Act.
[899] Sec. 172 of the Stock Corporation Act.
[900] Sec. 174 of the Stock Corporation Act.
[901] Sec. 119 para. 1 no. 3 of the Stock Corporation Act.
[902] Sec. 120 para. 2 sentence 2 of the Stock Corporation Act.
[903] Sec. 84 para. 3 of the Stock Corporation Act.
[904] Sec. 120 para. 1 sentence 2 of the Stock Corporation Act.
[905] Sec. 120 para. 1 sentence 1 of the Stock Corporation Act.
[906] Sec. 120 para. 4 of the Stock Corporation Act.
[907] Sec. 119 para. 1 no. 4 of the Stock Corporation Act, sec. 318 of the Commercial Code.

which is not affiliated with the company may be elected.[908] If there are any objective reasons for dismissal of the auditor, another auditor may be appointed by a court upon application by the management board, the supervisory board or a minority of shareholders holding at least 5% of the registered share capital or the proportionate amount of EUR 500,000 in the registered share capital.[909]

bb) Fundamental Decisions. The general meeting also decides in matters in which the **fundamentals of the company** are altered. This concerns, in particular:
- amendments to the articles of association;[910]
- measures to reduce or increase the registered share capital;[911]
- measures governed by the Transformation Act (such as a merger, spin-off or change of legal form);
- the transfer of the entire assets of the company;[912]
- approval for enterprise agreements;[913] and
- integration[914] and dissolution of the company.[915]

In order for such resolutions to be effective, the law generally requires a qualified majority of at least three-quarters of the registered share capital represented at the passing of the resolution and registration of the resolution in the commercial register. In certain cases – such as amendment of the articles of association – the company's articles of association may provide for a lower majority requirement.[916]

cc) Resolutions on Matters relating to the Management of the Company. The general meeting may be involved in the management of the company only under certain circumstances. If the supervisory board does not grant a necessary consent for a matter relating to the management of the company, the management board is entitled to call upon the general meeting.[917]

Furthermore, sec. 119 para. 2 of the Stock Corporation Act states that the general meeting has to decide on matters relating to the management of the company if requested to do so by the management board. It lies at the management board's sole discretion whether or not it calls upon the general meeting to decide on a certain management measure. In practice, this happens seldom. The measure in question has to be a management measure; the management board cannot bring a supervisory board decision to the general meeting. The management board as a whole convenes the general meeting unless the statutes of the company provide for a majority decision. If the general meeting declines to deal with the application brought to it by the management board pursuant to sec. 119 para. 2 of the Stock Corporation Act, the management board has to decide on the matter by itself. If the general meeting makes a decision (i.e., approves or rejects the measure), however, the management board is obliged to follow this decision,[918] even if the decision differs from its proposal. If the management board fails to follow the decision, it may be held liable for damages by the company.

---

[908] Sec. 319 of the Commercial Code.
[909] Sec. 318 para. 3 of the Commercial Code.
[910] Sec. 119 para. 1 no. 5, 179 of the Stock Corporation Act.
[911] Sec. 119 para. 1 no. 6 of the Stock Corporation Act.
[912] Sec. 179a of the Stock Corporation Act.
[913] Sec. 293 et seq. of the Stock Corporation Act.
[914] Sec. 319 et seq. of the Stock Corporation Act.
[915] Sec. 119 para. 1 no. 8, 262 et seq. of the Stock Corporation Act.
[916] Sec. 179 para. 2 sentence 2 of the Stock Corporation Act.
[917] Sec. 111 para. 4 sentence 3 of the Stock Corporation Act.
[918] Sec. 83 para. 2 of the Stock Corporation Act.

The general meeting may not take the initiative to decide on a measure relating to the management of the company itself. It only becomes responsible for doing so after being called upon by the management board. The management board retains the **right of initiative** in any event.

dd) Other Cases Regulated by Law. The Stock Corporation Act identifies a number of specific cases for which the general meeting is responsible, e.g., the following:
- determining remuneration for members of the supervisory board;[919]
- dismissal of shareholder representatives on the supervisory board;[920]
- resolution on squeeze-out of minority shareholders;[921]
- appointment of special auditors;[922] and
- deciding on asserting and waiving certain claims for damages.[923]

ee) Unwritten Competencies of the General Meeting. The decisions enumerated in sec. 119 para. 1 of the Stock Corporation Act do not cover all decisions which may have significant impact on the company. In particular, measures having a material impact on the structure of the company or being of material economic importance for the company are not all covered by sec. 119 para. 1 of the Stock Corporation Act.

Against this background, the Federal Supreme Court recognized in the *"Holzmüller"*-decision[924] certain unwritten authorities of the general meeting. This decision was later confirmed in the Federal Supreme Court's *"Gelatine"*-decision.[925] These two decisions together established the so-called *Holzmüller*-doctrine, which applies where material structural measures within a company have a significant economic impact on the company's business. According to the doctrine, any matter relating to the management of the company which *"affects the membership rights of the shareholders and their property interest embodied in title to the share to such an extent that the management board cannot sensibly expect to have the exclusive responsibility for making such a decision without involving the general meeting"*[926] is to be submitted to the general meeting. This only applies, however, if the existing business of the company is restructured (without being sold) in a way which heavily impacts on the shareholders' possibility to exert an influence on the company's business. This relates in particular to management board decisions to transfer major assets or divisions of the company's business to a subsidiary since, after the transfer, the parent company's shareholders cannot directly participate in the decision-making in the subsidiary. The *"Gelatine"*-decision indicates that such a transfer would have to affect at least a portion of 75% of the balance sheet assets.

In order to protect the shareholders, the management board in such cases is not only entitled pursuant to sec. 119 para. 2 of the Stock Corporation Act, but rather obliged to submit the measure in question to the general meeting for consent, which requires a majority of 75% of the votes cast.

Even if *Holzmüller* measures are concerned, the management board has full power of representation with regard to third parties. If the management board

---

[919] Sec. 113 of the Stock Corporation Act.
[920] Sec. 103 of the Stock Corporation Act.
[921] Sec. 327a et seq. of the Stock Corporation Act.
[922] Sec. 142 of the Stock Corporation Act.
[923] Sec. 50, 93 para. 4 sentence 3, 116, 117 para. 4, 147 of the Stock Corporation Act.
[924] Decision of the Federal Supreme Court, published in BGHZ, vol. 83, pp. 122 et seq.
[925] Decision of the Federal Supreme Court, published in BGHZ, vol. 159, pp. 30 et seq.
[926] Decision of the Federal Supreme Court, published in BGHZ, vol. 83, pp. 122, 131.

acts without the necessary resolution granting consent, any declarations it may have made to third parties regarding the transaction remain valid. However, the management board may have acted in breach of its duties, in which case claims for damages may arise. There may also be an obligation of the management to refrain from further consummation of the measure or to undo the measure.[927]

If the general meeting approves the *Holzmüller* measure, it has to be implemented by the management board.[928] The general meeting cannot, however, instruct the management board on its own initiative to prepare and implement a *Holzmüller* measure. Again, the management board has the exclusive **right of initiative**.

The delisting of a listed company does not require the approval of the general meeting[929]; however, pursuant to stock exchange laws, a delisting from a regulated market requires a simultaneous cash offer to all (minority) shareholders to purchase their shares.

c) Convening of the General Meeting

Comprehensive provisions govern the procedure to be followed when convening the general meeting of a stock corporation.[930] Accordingly, preparing for the general meeting involves a considerable effort. Only if all shareholders either attend or are represented (plenary meeting), the general meeting is entitled to adopt resolutions without complying with the provisions in sec. 121 et seq. of the Stock Corporation Act, provided none of the shareholders raises an objection to the resolution.[931] Therefore, the convening of general meetings in the case of single shareholder companies or companies without external shareholders entails a lesser degree of effort.

According to sec. 121 et seq. of the Stock Corporation Act, the following applies to the convening of the general meeting:

The general meeting is to be convened in the cases provided for by law or in the articles of association and whenever required in the interests of the company.[932] At least one general meeting must be held every year; this is referred to as the **ordinary or annual general meeting** and is held within eight months of the conclusion of the fiscal year (see, for example, sec. 120 para. 1 sentence 1 of the Stock Corporation Act). In addition, **extraordinary general meetings** are to be convened under certain circumstances. The law does not differentiate between ordinary and extraordinary general meetings; each general meeting, whether ordinary or extraordinary, follows the same rules.

The general meeting is convened by the **management board** which decides whether to convene a general meeting with a simple majority of votes cast.[933] However, the supervisory board is obliged to convene a general meeting whenever required by the interests of the company.[934] A minority of shareholders having an aggregate shareholding of 5% of the registered share capital may request the management board to convene the general meeting,[935] if they can prove that they

---

[927] Decision of the Federal Supreme Court, published in BGHZ, vol. 83, pp. 122, 132 et seq.
[928] Sec. 83 para. 2 of the Stock Corporation Act.
[929] Decision of the Federal Supreme Court, published in NZG 2013, pp. 1342 et seq.
[930] Sec. 121 et seq. of the Stock Corporation Act.
[931] Sec. 121 para. 6 of the Stock Corporation Act.
[932] Sec. 121 para. 1 of the Stock Corporation Act.
[933] Sec. 121 para. 2 sentence 1 of the Stock Corporation Act.
[934] Sec. 111 para. 3 sentence 1 of the Stock Corporation Act.
[935] Sec. 122 para. 1 sentence 1 of the Stock Corporation Act.

have owned the shares for at least 90 days before the date at which their request reaches the management board and that they will hold these shares until the date of the management board's decision about their request.[936] If the general meeting is not convened, the shareholders may be authorized by the court to convene the general meeting.[937] The shareholders have to prove, however, that they will hold the shares until the date of the court's decision.[938]

In principle, the general meeting must be convened at least **30 days before the date of the general meeting**.[939] The day the meeting is convened[940] and the day the general meeting is held[941] are not to be included when calculating such period. If the day calculated in this manner is a Sunday or public holiday, the authoritative date is **not shifted** to the previous or following working day.[942] The decisive date to determine whether the meeting has been properly convened is when the convening is published in the company's designated journals[943] (see below).

Unless otherwise provided for in the articles of association, the general meeting is to be held at the **registered office of the company**. In the case of listed *AGs*, it may also be held at the seat of the stock exchange.[944] Clauses in the articles of association which leave the determination of the location of the general meeting at the sole discretion of the person responsible for the convening of the general meeting are not permissible.[945]

The convening of the general meeting is to be published in the company's designated journals, i.e. online in the Federal Gazette.[946] Such announcement must state the name and registered offices of the company, the time and place of the general meeting. In addition, the agenda of the general meeting must be announced.[947] If the election of supervisory board members is on the agenda, the announcement has to state the statutory provisions according to which the supervisory board is composed and whether or not the general meeting is obligated to follow nominations of candidates. If the general meeting is to resolve on an amendment to the articles of association or a contract which is only valid if the general meeting grants its consent – for example a merger agreement or an enterprise agreement – the text of the proposed amendment to the articles of association or the essential contents of the contract are to be announced.[948] If consent is required for *Holzmüller* measures, an outline of the corporate concept and the essential steps leading to its implementation have to be announced.[949]

Listed companies additionally have to provide more detailed information in the announcement, in particular concerning (i) the participation in the meeting, including the record date and a description of its meaning and consequences, (ii) the voting procedure by proxy, by written vote or by means of electronic communication, (iii) certain rights of shareholders, in particular the right to request

---

[936] Sec. 122 para. 1 sentence 3 of the Stock Corporation Act.
[937] Sec. 122 para. 3 of the Stock Corporation Act.
[938] Sec. 122 para. 3 sentence 5 of the Stock Corporation Act.
[939] Sec. 123 para. 1 of the Stock Corporation Act.
[940] Sec. 123 para. 1 sentence 2 of the Stock Corporation Act.
[941] Sec. 121 para. 7 sentence 1 of the Stock Corporation Act.
[942] Sec. 121 para. 7 sentences 2 and 3 of the Stock Corporation Act.
[943] Sec. 121 para. 4 sentence 1 of the Stock Corporation Act.
[944] Sec. 121 para. 5 of the Stock Corporation Act.
[945] Decision of the Federal Supreme Court, published in BGHZ, vol. 203, pp. 68.
[946] Sec. 121 para. 4 sentence 1, sec. 25 of the Stock Corporation Act.
[947] Sec. 121 para. 3 sentence 2 of the Stock Corporation Act.
[948] Sec. 124 para. 2 sentence 3 of the Stock Corporation Act.
[949] Decision of the Federal Supreme Court, published in BGHZ, vol. 146, pp. 288, 294.

information and to make voting proposals which have to be made available, and (iv) the website on which information about the general meeting is available.[950] Listed companies furthermore have to release the announcement of the general meeting to the media for public dissemination throughout Europe if they have issued not only registered shares,[951] and to publish it and certain other information concerning the general meeting on its website, in particular the documents which have to be made available to the shareholders prior to the meeting and forms for the instruction of proxies.[952]

The management board and the supervisory board – in case of the election of supervisory board members and of auditors only the supervisory board – have to make voting **proposals** for each agenda item.[953] The management board and the supervisory board each have to adopt a majority decision regarding such proposals. In companies subject to the Codetermination Act (or other laws regarding codetermination), the proposals for the election of supervisory board members only need to be approved by the majority of the shareholder representatives on the supervisory board.[954]

If agenda items are not duly announced or if a voting proposal has not been made for a certain resolution by the supervisory board or the management board, any resolution passed on this matter may be set aside pursuant to sec. 243 para. 1 of the Stock Corporation Act. If the general meeting is not properly convened on the basis of a decision of the management board, the convening notice does not contain the information pursuant to sec. 121 para. 3 sentence 1 of the Stock Corporation Act or the convening is not properly announced, resolutions adopted at the meeting are null and void.[955]

Shareholders with an aggregate shareholding of at least 5% of the registered share capital or the proportionate amount of EUR 500,000 may request that certain items be put on the agenda for resolutions to be passed by the general meeting.[956] If such a minority application is filed, the company has to publish the items in question either together with the convening of the general meeting or, if this has already taken place, without undue delay after receipt of the minority request.[957]

It is common for the articles of association to contain provisions stipulating that attendance at the general meeting or the exercising of the voting right are conditional upon the shareholders registering to attend the meeting by a certain date before the date the general meeting is held. In this case, subject to sec. 123 para. 2 sentence 1 of the Stock Corporation Act, the shareholders have to register no later than six days (not working days) prior to the general meeting. The articles of association may provide for a shorter period or authorize the management board to announce such shorter period.[958] The minimum time period for the convening of the meeting (ordinarily 30 days) in this case is prolonged by the time period during which shareholders may no longer register to attend.[959]

---

[950] Sec. 121 para. 3 sentence 3 of the Stock Corporation Act.
[951] Sec. 121 para. 4a of the Stock Corporation Act.
[952] Sec. 124a of the Stock Corporation Act.
[953] Sec. 124 para. 3 of the Stock Corporation Act.
[954] Sec. 124 para. 3 sentence 5 of the Stock Corporation Act.
[955] Sec. 241 no. 1 of the Stock Corporation Act.
[956] Sec. 122 para. 2 of the Stock Corporation Act.
[957] Sec. 124 para. 1 sentence 1 of the Stock Corporation Act.
[958] Sec. 123 para. 2 sentence 3 of the Stock Corporation Act.
[959] Sec. 123 para. 2 sentence 5 of the Stock Corporation Act.

V. Constitution of the AG

Furthermore, the company's articles of association may regulate how the shareholding and, therefore, the right to attend the general meeting or to exercise the voting right, must be proven.[960] For bearer shares of listed companies, a certificate issued in textual form by the depository institution confirming the shareholder's share ownership constitutes sufficient evidence.[961] In the case of companies whose shares are listed on a stock exchange, such certificate shall make reference to the 21st day prior to the shareholders' meeting and must be delivered to the company within, at least, six days prior to the shareholders' meeting at the address specified in the notice calling the shareholders' meeting (the day of receipt is not included in this calculation).[962] The articles of association or the notice if authorised by the articles may provide for a shorter time limit which is to be calculated in days.[963]

Companies listed on a stock exchange have to provide additional information on their website immediately after the convening of the general meeting:[964]
- the content of the notice of convening of the general meeting;
- an explanation if no resolution shall be adopted for a certain agenda item (e.g., concerning the presentation of the annual accounts);
- the documents which are to be made available to the general meeting;
- the total number of shares and voting rights at the time of the convening of the meeting, separated by classes of shares;
- if applicable, forms for proxies and participation by written vote;
- requests of shareholders to place certain items on the agenda of the meeting.

In addition to the public announcement, **special notifications** have to be made pursuant to sec. 125 to 127 of the Stock Corporation Act. Shareholders who request so or who are registered as shareholders in the company's share register at the beginning of the fourteenth day before the date of the general meeting have to be informed separately by the management board that the general meeting has been convened and informed as to the agenda.[965] The same notification must also be sent to banks and shareholder associations which exercised voting rights for shareholders in the previous general meeting or have otherwise requested such notification in order to forward this information to the shareholders they deal with; if the agenda is amended upon request of shareholders (sec. 122 para. 2 of the Stock Corporation Act) in case of listed companies, the amended agenda is to be made available as well.[966] Such information must be given at least 21 days prior to the general meeting regarding banks and shareholder associations. With respect to individual shareholders, the notification has to be released after the fourteenth day prior to the meeting; the articles of association may provide that the notification will be made by means of electronic communication only.[967] The members of the supervisory board have the same right to information.[968] In the case of listed companies, information concerning membership of nominated supervisory board members in other supervisory boards has to be attached to a nomination of supervisory board members.[969]

---

[960] Sec. 123 para. 3 of the Stock Corporation Act.
[961] Sec. 123 para. 4 sentence 1 of the Stock Corporation Act.
[962] Sec. 123 para. 4 sentences 2, 4 of the Stock Corporation Act.
[963] Sec. 123 para. 4 sentence 3 of the Stock Corporation Act.
[964] Sec. 124a of the Stock Corporation Act.
[965] Sec. 125 para. 2 of the Stock Corporation Act.
[966] Sec. 125 para. 1 of the Stock Corporation Act.
[967] Sec. 125 para. 2 sentence 2 of the Stock Corporation Act.
[968] Sec. 125 para. 3 of the Stock Corporation Act.
[969] Sec. 125 para. 1 sentence 5 of the Stock Corporation Act.

Counter-proposals submitted by a shareholder must be made available (for example, via the internet) to those parties entitled to notification pursuant to sec. 126 Stock Corporation Act, provided that the proposals as well as an explanatory statement have been submitted to the company not later than 14 days before the date of the general meeting (not including the day of receipt). For listed companies, the law stipulates that the counter-proposal has to be made available on the company´s website.[970]

This applies accordingly – albeit with modifications – to proposals for the election of supervisory board members and auditors.[971] One of these modifications is, for example, that the shareholder does not have to give reasons for his/her election proposal.[972] Furthermore, specific additional information has to be published by the management board together with the shareholder's election proposal if the company is subject to codetermination.[973]

The Federal Gazette provides for a website, the so-called "shareholder forum" (*Aktionärsforum*), where shareholders can solicit other shareholders to vote together in a certain way, to grant proxies or to make certain requests or applications to the general meeting.[974] The shareholder forum is supposed to strengthen the position of minority shareholders, but is up to now of limited importance.

d) The Course of the General Meeting

There are only a few statutory provisions regulating the course of the general meeting. It is possible, however, for the general meeting to adopt **rules of procedure** providing for rules for the preparation and conduct of the general meeting by a three-quarters majority.[975]

The general meeting is presided over by its chairman.[976] The law does not stipulate who the chairman is. The articles of association usually appoint the chairman of the supervisory board or his deputy to the position of chairman of the general meeting. A provision to this effect in the articles of association may, in the case of codetermination, lead to an employee representative on the supervisory board being obligated to chair the general meeting by virtue of his position as the deputy chairman of the supervisory board. The chairman is in control of the proceedings of the general meeting.

At the beginning, the chairman opens the general meeting and asserts that it has been duly convened. If the articles of association make attendance or the exercise of the voting right conditional upon an application or providing proof of being a shareholder, the chairman is also required to ensure that the relevant requirements have been met. In addition, the **list of attendees** must be duly drawn up and made accessible to all attendees before the first votes are cast. Each shareholder is allowed to inspect this list of attendees upon request within two years of the relevant general meeting.[977] All agenda items have to be dealt with in a proper manner. After the debate on the points on the agenda has been completed, voting must be commenced, the votes counted, the result established and announced.

---

[970] Sec. 126 para. 1 sentence 3 of the Stock Corporation Act.
[971] Sec. 127 sentence 1 of the Stock Corporation Act.
[972] Sec. 127 sentence 2 of the Stock Corporation Act.
[973] Sec. 127 sentence 4 of the Stock Corporation Act.
[974] Sec. 127a of the Stock Corporation Act.
[975] Sec. 129 para. 1 of the Stock Corporation Act.
[976] *Cf.* sec. 130 of the Stock Corporation Act.
[977] Sec. 129 para. 4 of the Stock Corporation Act.

V. Constitution of the AG

The chairman is responsible for **maintaining order** in the general meeting. He also may, if necessary, impose limits on the time taken for speeches, or restrict the right to ask questions.[978] He may also order a shareholder to leave the room if the shareholder considerably disturbs the orderly conduct of the general meeting. Such measures are subject to strict requirements, however.[979]

Until the Shareholders' Rights Act came into effect, shareholders who wanted to exercise their rights at the general meeting had to be present at the venue or needed to be represented by proxy. Meanwhile, the articles of association of the company may provide or may authorize the management board to decide on shareholders being allowed to participate in the general meeting without being physically present at the actual location or to be represented by a proxy, to exercise certain or all of their rights by means of electronic communication or to exercise their voting right by way of written vote.[980]

The general meeting is **not public**. In general, the shareholders and their representatives are entitled to attend. In addition, the members of the management board and the supervisory board, including the employee representatives on the supervisory board, are supposed to attend the meeting. The articles of association may stipulate particular cases in which the members of the supervisory board may participate via audio-visual transmission.[981] Guests may be permitted to attend. The same also applies to press, radio and television. However, guests and the media have no enforceable claim to be admitted to the general meeting. The articles of association or the rules of procedure pursuant to sec. 129 para. 1 of the Stock Corporation Act may provide or authorize the management board or the chairman of the general meeting to allow that the general meeting may be broadcasted audio-visually.[982]

Each resolution passed by the general meeting is to be recorded in **minutes** of the proceedings in the form of a notarial deed. In the case of non-listed companies, it is sufficient for the minutes to be signed by the chairman of the supervisory board, provided that no resolutions are passed for which a majority of three-quarters or greater is required by law.[983] The documents relating to the convening of the general meeting are to be appended to the minutes if the contents thereof have not been recorded in the minutes.[984] Immediately following the general meeting, the management board has to submit a copy of the minutes and the appendices attested by a notary or, if applicable, signed by the chairman of the supervisory board, to the commercial register.[985] Additionally, listed companies have to publish – inter alia – the voting results on their website within seven days after the general meeting.[986]

---

[978] Sec. 131 para. 2 of the Stock Corporation Act.
[979] Decision of the Federal Constitutional Court, published in ZIP 1999, pp. 1798 et seq.
[980] Sec. 118 para. 1 and 2 of the Stock Corporation Act.
[981] Sec. 118 para. 3 of the Stock Corporation Act.
[982] Sec. 118 para. 4 of the Stock Corporation Act.
[983] Sec. 130 para. 1 of the Stock Corporation Act.
[984] Sec. 130 para. 3 of the Stock Corporation Act.
[985] Sec. 130 para. 5 of the Stock Corporation Act.
[986] Sec. 130 para. 6 of the Stock Corporation Act.

e) The Right to Information

In contrast to the law governing partnerships[987] and the *GmbH*,[988] the Stock Corporation Act does not grant the shareholders a right to inspect and review the company's books and records. All they are allowed to review are the annual financial statements, the management report and, if applicable, interim reports.

However, each shareholder has the right to **request information** from the management board **in the general meeting** regarding the company's affairs to the extent required to allow a proper assessment of an item on the agenda.[989] The obligation to provide information also extends to the legal and business relationships between the company and an affiliate.[990] Restricting the shareholder's right to information which is pertinent to items on the agenda shall avoid abusive and irrelevant questions. According to the Federal Supreme Court, this restriction of the shareholder's right to information set out in sec. 131 para. 1 sentence 1 of the Stock Corporation Act is a permissible measure pursuant to Art. 9 para. 2 sentence 1 of the Shareholders' Rights Directive. Also, the managing directors may refuse to answer on questions regarding confidential events in supervisory board meetings or committees subject to sec. 107 para. 3 sentence 1 of the Stock Corporation Act.[991]

The claim to information is an **individual right** of each shareholder, including shareholders without a voting right. Only the management board is addressee of the duty to provide information, not the supervisory board or any third party. As a rule, the information is given orally. If subsequent investigations have to be carried out to answer the question, the management board is obligated to take the necessary measures.[992]

The obligation to give information in the general meeting is subject to the requirement that the information is necessary to allow a **proper assessment of an item on the agenda**. This is determined based on the objective needs of an average shareholder whose knowledge of the company is based on generally known facts. For example, the debate on whether or not to grant ratification of the acts of the members of the management board and the supervisory board can extend to all aspects relating to the management of the company which may, if assessed objectively, be of relevance for the decision regarding ratification. With regard to the submission of the annual financial statements, questions concerning valuations and methods of calculation, etc., may be considered.

However, the right to information does also implicate certain duties for the shareholder asking for information, such as to clarify by means of a further inquiry to the management board that his information needs were aimed at specific information.

The information provided by the management board has to comply with the principles of conscientious and true accounting.[993] It has to be complete and correct.

Sec. 131 para. 3 of the Stock Corporation Act stipulates certain instances in which the management board may **refuse to provide information**:

---

[987] Sec. 118, 166 of the Commercial Code.
[988] Sec. 51a of the Limited Liability Company Act.
[989] Sec. 131 para. 1 of the Stock Corporation Act.
[990] Sec. 131 para. 1 sentence 2 of the Stock Corporation Act.
[991] Decision of the Federal Supreme Court, published in BGHZ, vol. 198, pp. 354 et seq.
[992] Decision of the Federal Supreme Court, published in BGHZ, vol. 32, pp. 159, 165 et seq.
[993] Sec. 131 para. 2 of the Stock Corporation Act.

V. Constitution of the AG

- The most important case is the possibility to refuse information to the extent the provision of such information – according to reasonable business judgment – is likely to cause **considerable damage** to the company or an affiliate, e.g., if confidential information would come to the attention of competitors. The interests of the company in keeping the information confidential and the shareholder's interest in receiving information have to be balanced. The burden of proving that the information should be kept confidential rests with the company.
- The reason for refusing information stipulated in sec. 131 para. 3 sentence 1 no. 2 of the Stock Corporation Act is to maintain **tax secrecy** in the relationship between the company and the shareholders. The cases stipulated in sec. 131 para. 3 sentence 1 nos. 3, 4 of the Stock Corporation Act concern information on **hidden reserves**. Sec. 131 para. 3 sentence 1 no. 5 of the Stock Corporation Act is predominantly of relevance if the management board would violate **confidentiality provisions** by providing the information.[994]
- According to Sec. 131 para. 3 sentence 1 no. 6 of the Stock Corporation Act, the management board of a credit institution or a financial services institution can deny to give information to shareholders to the extent that it does not have to lay open the applied accounting and valuation methods or calculations made in the annual accounts, management report, consolidated financial statements or group management report.
- In order to save time during the general meeting, the management may publish information on the company's website prior to the general meeting. If and to the extent information has continuously been made accessible on the company's website throughout at least the seven days prior to the beginning of and during the general meeting, the management board may refuse to provide such information in the general meeting again.[995]
- Information may not be refused for any reasons other than those stated in sec. 131 para. 3 sentence 1 of the Stock Corporation Act.[996]
- If a shareholder has been given information outside the general meeting as in their function as a shareholder, such information must be provided to any other shareholder in the general meeting upon request, even if such information is not necessary for a proper assessment of the item on the agenda.[997]

If information is denied, a shareholder may request that his question and the reason given for the refusal of the information be recorded in the minutes of the meeting.[998]

If information requested by a shareholder is denied, he may initiate court **proceedings to enforce the right to information**.[999] The validity of resolutions may be contested pursuant to sec. 243 para. 1 of the Stock Corporation Act, if information which was denied concerns the subject of the challenged resolution.[1000] If damage is caused to the company as a result of the information being withheld, the members of the management board are liable to the company for damages. Providing incorrect information or concealing it may constitute a punishable

---

[994] Sec. 404 of the Stock Corporation Act.
[995] Sec. 131 para. 3 no. 7 of the Stock Corporation Act.
[996] Sec. 131 para. 3 sentence 2 of the Stock Corporation Act.
[997] Sec. 131 para. 4 of the Stock Corporation Act.
[998] Sec. 131 para. 5 of the Stock Corporation Act.
[999] Sec. 132 of the Stock Corporation Act.
[1000] Decision of the Federal Supreme Court, published in BGHZ, vol. 119, pp. 1, 13 et seq.

offense.[1001] If damage is caused to a shareholder after he was given defective information, he may also claim damages from the company.

f) Resolutions of the General Meeting and Voting

The general meeting decides by resolution. There are no specific legal requirements relating to when the general meeting has a quorum. However, the articles of association can provide for a minimum number of shareholders which have to be present in order to pass a resolution.[1002]

The Stock Corporation Act does not contain any provisions regarding the **resolution procedure**. A motion brought by a person entitled to do so is first debated and then the chairman submits the motion to the general meeting for a vote to be cast. The order in which the items on the agenda are dealt with is at the discretion of the chairman. In case of the election of supervisory board members, however, under certain conditions a particular order has to be kept: If so requested by a shareholder minority holding an aggregate of 10% of the registered share capital represented at the general meeting, a nomination made by a shareholder[1003] has to be put to the vote first before votes may be cast on the nominations made by the supervisory board.[1004]

The law does not provide for a certain **voting procedure**. The manner in which the voting right is exercised depends on the articles of association.[1005] Usually, such provisions in the articles of association grant the chairman the right to determine the manner in which votes are cast. Votes are usually cast in open ballot. In large general meetings, vote slips are submitted. After the votes have been counted, the result is to be determined and announced by the chairman. In addition, the resolution has to be recorded in the minutes of the general meeting by the attending notary.[1006] Certain resolutions passed by the general meeting (e.g., amendments to the articles of association) need to be registered in the commercial register in order to become effective.[1007] The company's articles of association may allow voting by letter or by means of electronic communication.[1008] A listed company is obliged to publish the voting results on its website within seven days after the general meeting.[1009]

Resolutions of the general meeting generally require a **simple majority** of votes cast, unless the law or the articles of association provide for a larger majority or further requirements.[1010] Neither invalid votes nor abstentions count. The motion is rejected if there is a tie. Amendments to the articles of association[1011] and all other fundamental resolutions (dissolution of the company, execution and amendment of enterprise agreements, integration, transfer of assets and transformations) require, in addition to the majority of votes cast, a majority of three-quarters of the registered share capital represented at the voting. Accordingly, shareholders holding at least 25% of the registered share capital represent a **blocking minority**;

[1001] Sec. 400 para. 1 no. 1 of the Stock Corporation Act.
[1002] Sec. 133 para. 1 of the Stock Corporation Act.
[1003] *Cf.* Sec. 127 of the Stock Corporation Act.
[1004] Sec. 137 of the Stock Corporation Act.
[1005] Sec. 134 para. 4 of the Stock Corporation Act.
[1006] Sec. 130 para. 1 sentence 1 of the Stock Corporation Act.
[1007] Sec. 181 para. 3 of the Stock Corporation Act.
[1008] Sec. 118 para. 2 of the Stock Corporation Act.
[1009] Sec. 130 para. 6 of the Stock Corporation Act.
[1010] Sec. 133 para. 1 of the Stock Corporation Act.
[1011] Sec. 179 para. 2 of the Stock Corporation Act.

fundamental resolutions cannot be passed without the consent of the respective shareholder if he is present at the general meeting. In certain instances, the consent of individual shareholders or groups of shareholders is required. This is the case, for example, with encroachment on special rights granted to a shareholder.[1012] It may also apply to resolutions of the general meeting amending the relation between several classes of shares to the detriment of a particular class[1013] or – in the case of preference shares – canceling or restricting the preferential rights.[1014]

g) Provisions of the Articles of Association on Voting

The articles of association may deviate from the statutory majority requirements and impose more stringent requirements.[1015] They may even stipulate unanimity. It is possible for the articles of association to require the consent of certain shareholders or the supervisory board, but not external third parties, for certain resolutions. They may also deviate in certain instances from the qualified capital majority and demand a smaller capital majority; this applies, for example, to amendments to the articles of association[1016], capital increases[1017] and the dismissal of members of the supervisory board.[1018] The statutory qualified majority may not be deviated from, however, if the resolution concerns alterations to the company object[1019], capital reductions[1020], approval for an enterprise agreement[1021] and cases involving the transformation of the enterprise.[1022]

The articles of association may stipulate more lenient or more stringent provisions for **elections**.[1023] For example, an election by proportional representation could be stipulated when electing the supervisory board.

h) Voting Right

The voting right is exercised according to the nominal value of the shares in the case of par value shares, or according to the number of shares in the case of non-par value shares.[1024] If there are no preference shares, each share grants a right to vote.[1025] Entitlement to the voting right generally commences upon the contribution being paid in full.[1026] However, in case of a contribution in kind, the voting right is not suspended if the value of the contribution rendered by a shareholder does not fully match the nominal value of his share unless the shortfall was obvious.[1027] If there are various nominal values, the voting rights are allocated in proportion to the nominal values; for example, if the registered share capital is composed of shares with a par value of EUR 50 and shares with a par value of EUR 100, the share with a par value of EUR 100 grants twice as many voting rights

---

[1012] Sec. 35 of the Civil Code.
[1013] Sec. 179 para. 3 of the Stock Corporation Act.
[1014] Sec. 141 para. 1 of the Stock Corporation Act.
[1015] Sec. 133 para. 1, 179 para. 2 sentence 2 of the Stock Corporation Act.
[1016] Sec. 179 para. 2 sentence 2 of the Stock Corporation Act.
[1017] Sec. 182 para. 1 sentence 1 of the Stock Corporation Act.
[1018] Decision of the Federal Supreme Court, published in BGHZ, vol. 99, pp. 211, 215.
[1019] Sec. 179 para. 2 sentence 2 of the Stock Corporation Act.
[1020] Sec. 222 para. 1 of the Stock Corporation Act.
[1021] Sec. 293 para. 1 of the Stock Corporation Act.
[1022] Sec. 65 para. 1 of the Transformation Act.
[1023] Sec. 133 para. 2 of the Stock Corporation Act.
[1024] Sec. 134 para. 1 sentence 1 of the Stock Corporation Act.
[1025] Sec. 12, sec. 134 para. 1, sec. 139 et seq. of the Stock Corporation Act.
[1026] Sec. 134 para. 2 sentence 1 of the Stock Corporation Act.
[1027] Sec. 134 para. 2 sentence 2 of the Stock Corporation Act.

as the share with a par value of EUR 50. If various shares are held by one person, the voting rights allocated to each share may be exercised differently.

In the case of a non-listed company, the articles of association may limit voting rights by stipulating a **maximum nominal value** or a **sliding scale**.[1028] **Multiple voting rights** are not permitted.[1029]

i) Prohibition of Voting

The **exercise of the voting right** is prohibited by law in certain instances. This applies to shares belonging to the company itself, a controlled enterprise or a third party acting for account of the company or a controlled enterprise.[1030] The voting right is also suspended if and as long as the notification obligations pursuant to sec. 20, 21 of the Stock Corporation Act upon the acquisition of one quarter or one-half of the registered share capital have not been complied with.[1031] The same applies to voting rights of a bidder who fails to launch a mandatory tender offer when obligated to do so under Takeover Law.[1032] In addition, in the case of listed corporations, the notification obligations pursuant to sec. 21 of the Securities Trading Act are to be observed.[1033] A non-compliance with the notification obligations pursuant to sec. 21 of the Securities Trading Act results in a suspension of voting rights not only until such time as the notification obligations have been complied with but for an additional six-month period from when the notification obligation has been complied with, unless the non-compliance does not result from intent or gross negligence.[1034] In the case of cross-shareholdings, the voting right can only be exercised for up to one quarter of the registered share capital.[1035]

In sec. 136 para. 1 of the Stock Corporation Act, the voting right is excluded in some events of a **conflict of interest**. The Stock Corporation Act does not, however, recognize a general statutory exclusion of the voting right if the company's interests conflict with the personal interests of a shareholder. Rather, sec. 136 para. 1 of the Stock Corporation Act excludes voting rights only in the following cases:

- No person may exercise voting rights for himself or another person if a resolution is being passed as to whether ratification **is to be granted for his actions**. This predominantly entails ratification for the actions of the members of the management board and the supervisory board, provided they themselves are shareholders in the company.
- The same prohibition on voting applies if a resolution is to be passed on releasing a certain person from an obligation. This concerns the waiver of claims for damages due to failure to comply with duties brought against founders and members of the legal bodies[1036] and due to someone exerting an influence upon members of the legal bodies to the detriment of the company pursuant to sec. 117 of the Stock Corporation Act.
- A prohibition on voting also applies when passing a resolution on whether or not the company has to assert a claim against the shareholder in question. This

---

[1028] Sec. 134 para. 1 sentence 2 of the Stock Corporation Act.
[1029] Sec. 12 para. 2 of the Stock Corporation Act.
[1030] Sec. 71b, 71d sentence 4 of the Stock Corporation Act.
[1031] Sec. 20 para. 7 sentence 1, sec. 21 para. 4 of the Stock Corporation Act.
[1032] Sec. 59 of the Securities Acquisition and Takeover Act.
[1033] Sec. 28 of the Securities Trading Act.
[1034] Sec. 28 of the Securities Trading Act.
[1035] Sec. 328 para. 1 sentence 1 of the Stock Corporation Act.
[1036] Sec. 46 to 48, 93 para. 4, 116 of the Stock Corporation Act.

concerns the assertion of all claims relating to membership, contractual claims and claims in tort.

In addition to the exclusion of the voting right pursuant to sec. 136 of the Stock Corporation Act, a member of the management board or the supervisory board is not entitled to vote when the general meeting passes a resolution concerning the **appointment of a special auditor**.[1037]

If a shareholder is prohibited from exercising the voting right pursuant to sec. 136 para. 1 sentence 1 of the Stock Corporation Act, the voting right for the shares in question may not be exercised by a third person.[1038] This provision is intended to avoid circumvention of the prohibition of voting. Statutory and legal representatives are excluded, both if the prohibition of voting applies to the person who is represented and if it applies to the representative himself. The same applies to veiled representation and the transfer of the right to vote to a third person.[1039] Problems arise in cases where shareholders of a partnership or corporation are affected by the prohibition on voting in particular as a majority or sole shareholder and the question at issue is whether the voting right arising from the shares held by the company may be exercised. Similar problems arise relating to votes cast by employees and other persons who are bound to follow instructions of the company.

Sec. 136 para. 1 of the Stock Corporation Act does not contain a general prohibition of voting in the event that the resolution concerns a legal transaction with the shareholder. It is therefore highly debatable whether sec. 34 of the Civil Code and the general principles contained therein may be applied to stock corporation law.

j) Voting Agreements

Voting agreements are agreements in which a shareholder pledges to another shareholder or a third person his voting right in the general meeting in a certain manner. Voting agreements take various forms: either one party agrees to follow the instructions of the other party regarding the vote or the shareholders merely undertake to agree on joint votes in which case the manner in which the voting right is to be exercised is generally determined before the votes are cast on the basis of a majority decision taken by the concerned parties.

Voting agreements only concern the internal relationship between the participating shareholders. They have no external effect. If a shareholder votes in violation of the voting agreement, his vote remains valid, but the other parties to the voting agreement may have claims for damages.[1040]

The Stock Corporation Act considers voting agreements between the shareholders generally permissible.[1041] Agreements of this nature can be entered into concerning all kinds of resolutions. They are of particular importance when they involve the obligation to elect certain people, proposed by one of the parties to the contract, to the supervisory board. The **extent to which the parties to the voting agreement are bound** is determined by the voting agreement. In case of listed companies, voting agreements may trigger notification duties[1042] or even

---

[1037] Sec. 142 para. 1 sentence 2 of the Stock Corporation Act.
[1038] Sec. 136 para. 1 sentence 2 of the Stock Corporation Act.
[1039] Sec. 135 para. 3 sentence 2, sec. 129 para. 3 of the Stock Corporation Act.
[1040] Decision of the Supreme Court of the German Reich, published in RGZ, vol. 119, pp. 386, 388; decision of the Federal Supreme Court, published in DB 1987, p. 157 et seq.
[1041] Sec. 136 para. 2, 405 para. 3 no. 6, 7 of the Stock Corporation Act.
[1042] Sec. 22 para. 2 of the Securities Trading Act.

an obligation to make a mandatory takeover offer[1043] if the relevant thresholds of voting rights are exceeded by the involved parties.

Only in cases involving a **"purchase of votes"**, i.e., voting agreements in return for payment, the contract is deemed an administrative offense[1044] and is therefore null and void.[1045] Furthermore, sec. 136 para. 2 of the Stock Corporation Act prohibits voting agreements which oblige a shareholder to exercise his voting right in accordance with instructions issued by the company, the management board or the supervisory board of a controlled enterprise or in accordance with the proposals made by the management board or the supervisory board. In addition, no shareholder can legally undertake to vote in such a manner as to render the resolution invalid or voidable pursuant to sec. 241, 243 of the Stock Corporation Act.

A shareholder is not allowed to vote in accordance with his obligations under the voting agreement if the interests of the parties to the agreement to comply with such obligations are outweighed by the interests of the company not to do so. This is the case, for example, if a shareholder bound by a voting agreement believes that the candidate for the supervisory board for whom he is obliged to vote is not capable of fulfilling his duties properly or if the agreed vote would lead to an insolvency of the company.

Voting agreements are generally **long-term agreements**. They may be terminated without notice for good cause. A lawsuit may be filed to enforce the contract; a judgment to this effect, is – pursuant to the Federal Supreme Court – enforced pursuant to sec. 894 of the Code of Civil Procedure, i.e., the judgment replaces the owed declaration of intent represented by the casting of the vote (although this does not appear to be appropriate because votes have to be cast in the general meeting and the court decision will be late in such cases anyway). Generally, it appears to be reasonable to prevent a vote in violation of the voting agreement by means of a preliminary injunction.

It is common for voting agreements to include provisions stipulating **contractual penalties**.

k) Exercise of Voting Rights by Proxy

The voting right may be exercised by **proxy**.[1046] There are no restrictions regarding the person of the proxy. Other shareholders, third parties, members of the management board and the supervisory board may all act as a proxy. However, the prohibition of voting pursuant to sec. 136 para. 1 of the Stock Corporation Act must be complied with in all instances. The voting right may not be entirely separated from the ownership of shares[1047], i.e., the voting right may not be transferred in isolation from the share. In practice, companies often name certain persons who can be authorized by individual shareholders to exercise the shareholders' voting rights. In this case, the company has to keep the declaration of proxy available for inspection for a period of three years.[1048]

The authorization to act as a proxy has to be granted before casting the vote. Such authorization (as well as evidence for authorization and revocation of the authorization) must be given **in text form** (e. g., facsimile, copy, e-mail), unless

---

[1043] Sec. 35 para. 2 sentence 1 of the Securities Acquisition and Takeover Act.
[1044] Sec. 405 para. 3 no. 6, 7 of the Stock Corporation Act.
[1045] Sec. 134 of the Civil Code.
[1046] Sec. 134 para. 3 sentence 1 of the Stock Corporation Act.
[1047] Decision of the Federal Supreme Court, published in NJW 1987, p. 780 et seq.
[1048] Sec. 134 para. 3 sentence 5 of the Stock Corporation Act.

the articles of association or the notice of convening of the general meeting upon authorization in the articles of association provide differently.[1049] In the case of listed companies, the formal requirements may not be more stringent than text form (i.e., a requirement of written form is not permissible) and at least one way for electronic transmission of evidence for the authorization must be offered.[1050]

Each shareholder may also allow a third party to exercise the voting right in his own name (**transfer of the right to vote to a third party**).[1051] Accordingly, the genuine shareholder may still have his vote cast for him even if he chooses not to reveal his identity. This procedure requires a legal authorization in favor of the party to whom the right to vote is transferred. The third party who is permitted by a shareholder to exercise the voting right in his own name for shares which he does not hold must state the nominal amount in the case of par value shares and the number and class of the shares in the case of non-par value shares for inclusion in the list of attendees. The foregoing also applies to registered shares for which the holder of the authorization is entered in the share register as the shareholder.[1052]

l) Proxy Voting Rights for Deposited Shares

The **law governing proxy voting rights for deposited shares** was reformed in order to increase the generally low attendance at the general meetings of large *AGs*. The provisions in sec. 125 to 128 and 135 of the Stock Corporation Act are intended to prevent banks from being suspected of promoting their own interests by exercising the voting rights of shares they hold in custody for customers. In addition, they – now – provide the shareholder with the opportunity to issue instructions to the bank as to how to use the shareholder's voting rights held by the bank.

The proxy voting rights for deposited shares may only be exercised if **proxy** has been granted.[1053] Such proxy has to be recorded by the bank in a verifiable way.[1054] Therefore, even if the articles of association allow for less rigid formal requirements, in practice such proxy is usually granted in writing. Accordingly, the proxy can also be given by electronic data transfer. If not indicated differently on the proxy form, the bank may act in the name of the person concerned.[1055] In this case, it is sufficient if the bank complies with the requirements provided in the company's articles of association for the exercising of voting rights. If the articles of association do not contain such provision, it suffices to submit a special proof of share ownership issued by the custodian bank.[1056] The actual shareholder is therefore not necessarily required to appear in the company's share register. This even applies to registered shares, provided the bank has been entered into the share register as the holder of the shares. In this case, the proxy is replaced by an authorization.[1057]

[1049] Sec. 134 para. 3 sentence 3 of the Stock Corporation Act.
[1050] Sec. 134 para. 3 sentences 3 and 4 of the Stock Corporation Act.
[1051] Sec. 129 para. 3 sentence 1 of the Stock Corporation Act.
[1052] Sec. 129 para. 3 sentence 2 of the Stock Corporation Act.
[1053] Sec. 135 para. 1 sentence 1 of the Stock Corporation Act.
[1054] Sec. 135 para. 1 sentence 2 of the Stock Corporation Act.
[1055] Sec. 135 para. 5 sentence 2 of the Stock Corporation Act.
[1056] Sec. 135 para. 5 sentence 4, sec. 123 para. 3 of the Stock Corporation Act.
[1057] Sec. 67 para. 2, 135 para. 6 sentence 1 of the Stock Corporation Act.

The proxy may only be issued for one particular **bank**.[1058] The bank must inform the shareholder clearly and explicitly each year of the right to revoke the proxy at any time and of other possibilities for representation.[1059] The declaration of proxy must be complete and may only include declarations relating to the exercise of the voting right.[1060] It must be retained by the bank for the case of inspection.[1061] Blank proxies are not permitted. A bank proxy may not be included in general terms and conditions of the bank. A substitute power of attorney by the bank may generally only be granted to bank employees; a substitute power of attorney for third parties is only permissible if expressly provided for in the original power of attorney.[1062]

Shareholders who have granted a power of attorney to a bank have to be provided with specific information. In order to ensure that they are provided with adequate information prior to the general meeting, the management board is obliged to inform all banks that exercised proxy voting rights for deposited shares in the previous general meeting or which have requested that they be so informed of the convening of the general meeting and the agenda at least 21 days prior to the general meeting.[1063] The bank itself is obligated to forward this notification immediately to the shareholders whose shares it has in custody or for whom it is entered in the share register.[1064] The company's articles of association may provide that forwarding in electronic form is sufficient.[1065] Additionally, the bank has to provide the shareholders with proposals for the exercise of the voting rights concerning each agenda item.[1066] These proposals may coincide with the proposals made by the management board and the supervisory board, but must have been made independently by the bank. The bank has to make this proposal in consideration of the shareholder rights and has to ensure that its own interests do not influence the proposal. The bank has to appoint a member of the management which supervises the compliance with these rules and the proper exercise of the voting right and the documentation thereof.[1067] The bank has to request the shareholder to issue instructions regarding the manner in which the voting right is to be exercised and to inform the shareholder that it will vote in accordance with its proposals if not instructed otherwise.[1068] If the shareholder does not issue specific instructions, the general authorization in favor of the bank may only provide for (i) voting in accordance with the proposals made available to the shareholder or (ii) voting in accordance with the proposals of the management or the supervisory board of the company (in case of dissenting proposals the ones of the supervisory board).[1069] The shareholder is to be provided with a form or online form on which he can authorize the bank, amend the authorization, issue instructions or withdraw the authorization of the bank.[1070]

[1058] Sec. 135 para. 1 sentence 2 of the Stock Corporation Act.
[1059] Sec. 135 para. 1 sentence 6 of the Stock Corporation Act.
[1060] Sec. 135 para. 1 sentence 3 of the Stock Corporation Act.
[1061] Sec. 135 para. 1 sentence 2 of the Stock Corporation Act.
[1062] Sec. 135 para. 5 sentence 1 of the Stock Corporation Act.
[1063] Sec. 125 para. 1 sentence 1 of the Stock Corporation Act.
[1064] Sec. 128 para. 1 sentence 1 of the Stock Corporation Act.
[1065] Sec. 128 para. 1 sentence 2 of the Stock Corporation Act.
[1066] Sec. 135 para. 2 sentence 1 of the Stock Corporation Act.
[1067] Sec. 135 para. 2 sentence 2 of the Stock Corporation Act.
[1068] Sec. 135 para. 2 sentence 3 of the Stock Corporation Act.
[1069] Sec. 135 para. 1 sentence 4 of the Stock Corporation Act.
[1070] Sec. 135 para. 1 sentence 7 of the Stock Corporation Act.

If the shareholder issues instructions, the bank must **vote in accordance with the instructions**. If the shareholder fails to issue instructions as to how to exercise the voting right, the bank has to exercise the voting right in accordance with the proposals as set forth in the notice to shareholders.[1071] This does not apply if the bank may assume in the light of the prevailing circumstances that the shareholder, if he had knowledge of the facts, would approve the voting rights being exercised differently.[1072] This also applies if the bank has not followed instructions. The bank has to inform the shareholder retrospectively of its decision to deviate from the instructions or proposals by the shareholders, stating the reasons for such course of action.[1073]

Stricter rules apply for the exercise of the proxy voting right for deposited shares in the **bank's own general meeting**.[1074] In this case, the vote may only be exercised by proxy of the bank if the shareholder has given specific instructions regarding each of the agenda items. The Shareholders' Rights Act extends these strict rules to general meetings of companies in which the respective bank holds, directly or indirectly, more than 20% of the shares.[1075] However, indirect holdings pursuant to sec. 22a para. 3 to 6 of the Securities Trading Act are not included in the calculation of this participation threshold.[1076]

The rules concerning the exercise of voting rights also apply to shareholder associations, other professional agents who offer to exercise the voting right in the general meeting and financial service providers.[1077]

If a bank (or shareholder association) fails to comply with its obligations to the shareholders, claims for damages under the law of obligations may arise. Claims under tort may also be considered, as sec. 135 of the Stock Corporation Act is deemed to be a protective provision benefiting the shareholder within the meaning of sec. 823 para. 2 of the Civil Code. The bank may neither exclude nor restrict the liability for damages to the shareholder in advance.[1078] A vote which is cast in violation of the aforementioned requirements is generally not invalid, however. It is only invalid if the proxy or the authorization fails to comply with sec. 135 para. 1 sentence 1 of the Stock Corporation Act.[1079] Even if the votes cast by the bank are invalid, the shareholder resolutions may only be successfully challenged if the majority of votes have been carried by the invalid votes.

5. Actions against Resolutions of the General Meeting

a) Overview

The general meeting is the shareholders' **decision-making body**. Decisions are taken by the general meeting in the form of **resolutions**. The effort entailed in preparing and conducting a general meeting is substantial, especially in the case of listed *AGs*. Resolutions passed by the general meeting, especially resolutions concerning matters of fundamental importance for the company, have far-reaching implications. Accordingly, it is in the interest of the company that such reso-

---

[1071] Sec. 135 para. 3 sentence 1 of the Stock Corporation Act.
[1072] Sec. 135 para. 3 sentence 1 of the Stock Corporation Act.
[1073] Sec. 135 para. 3 sentence 2 of the Stock Corporation Act.
[1074] Sec. 135 para. 3 sentence 3 of the Stock Corporation Act.
[1075] Sec. 135 para. 3 sentence 4 of the Stock Corporation Act.
[1076] Sec. 135 para. 3 sentence 4 of the Stock Corporation Act.
[1077] Sec. 135 para. 8 of the Stock Corporation Act.
[1078] Sec. 128 para. 2, sec. 135 para. 9 of the Stock Corporation Act.
[1079] Sec. 135 para. 7 of the Stock Corporation Act.

lutions become and remain valid as soon as possible. However, the protection of the company regarding the validity of shareholder resolutions cannot be entirely unrestricted, for, on the other side, minority shareholders need to be protected in the event of a majority decision in order to avoid an abuse of majority power. Taking legal actions is the essential means by which an outvoted minority of shareholders can defend itself against a majority resolution passed by the general meeting.

Sec. 241 et seq. of the Stock Corporation Act contain provisions on the basis of which action may be taken against resolutions passed by the general meeting which have not been adopted in accordance with the law or the company's articles of association.

The Stock Corporation Act distinguishes among three basic **categories of defective resolutions**:

- the resolution passed by the general meeting may be null and **void**. Nullity describes the absence of the legal effects intended by the parties to the resolution on account of such resolution being illegal. Anyone can invoke the nullity of a void resolution.
- A resolution passed by the general meeting may be **ineffective**. Ineffectiveness does not necessarily result from a violation of the law. Certain resolutions (like resolutions altering the articles of association) need to be registered with the commercial register in order to become effective.[1080] Resolutions may be **temporarily** or **finally ineffective**. They are finally ineffective if the additional requirements for effectiveness can no longer be met. A resolution is temporarily ineffective if the additional requirements for effectiveness may yet be met, for example if the consent of certain persons or groups of persons or the required official permission are still to be granted and if it is to be expected that such consent or permission will indeed be granted. Once the additional requirements are met, the resolution is fully effective.
- A resolution of the general meeting may be contestable. It then has to be challenged by **an action to set aside the resolution**. A resolution which is contestable is – although it is violating legal provisions – generally valid but can be declared null and void if an action is brought and a corresponding final judgment is passed.[1081] If such action to set aside is not brought to the court within one month after the resolution has been adopted, the resolution remains valid.[1082]

A further topic under discussion is whether **non-resolutions** or **quasi-resolutions** exist, if, for example, the general meeting is convened by persons who are not authorized to do so. In fact, there is no need for such a category because the three abovementioned categories provide sufficient protection. A resolution which has been passed under the aforementioned circumstances is null and void.

Resolutions of the general meeting which are null and void or contestable are to be distinguished from **individual votes which are null and void or contestable**. Individual votes being void or having been contested only affect the validity of the resolution if the required majority is no longer attained. Then, the minority shareholders can bring an action to the court for the reason of false documentation of the outcome of the resolution.

[1080] Sec. 181 para. 3 of the Stock Corporation Act.
[1081] Sec. 243, 248 para. 1 sentence 1 of the Stock Corporation Act.
[1082] Sec. 246 para. 1 of the Stock Corporation Act.

b) Nullity of Resolutions

aa) Overview. Nullity applies by virtue of law whenever one of the requirements for nullity as listed in the Stock Corporation Act is met. It may be asserted by anyone without any restrictions as to time.[1083] It may also be established as a preliminary issue in a lawsuit concerning another matter. Null and void resolutions of the general meeting may neither be registered in the commercial register nor implemented by the management board or the supervisory board. They cannot be confirmed by a new resolution of the general meeting (with the consequence that pending lawsuits challenging the shareholder resolution would be dismissed).[1084] Instead, the resolution on the subject in question needs to be adopted once again (and pending lawsuits against the original resolutions will be successful). This, however, is only possible if the reason for nullity can be cured. If a resolution, for example, does not comply with the company's articles of association because of its content, the second resolution will also be null and void for the same reason as the first one. In exceptional cases, the law permits a void resolution to be cured. This is the case if the resolution was registered in the commercial register despite the resolution being null and void and a certain period of time has expired since the registration in the commercial register or the publication of the annual financial statement.[1085]

It is possible to file an **action for the declaration of nullity** with a court,[1086] which is, however, not a precondition for the resolution being null and void. A general action for a declaratory judgment may not be filed by the shareholders, the management board, managing directors or members of the supervisory board. For these persons, the action subject to Sec. 249 para. 1 sentence 1 of the Stock Corporation Act preceeds.

The legal reasons for a resolution being null and void may be divided into four categories:
- violation of rules relating to form and procedure (sec. 241 no. 1, 2 of the Stock Corporation Act);
- violation of fundamental provisions of substantive law;
- violation of the general clauses pursuant to sec. 241 nos. 3, 4 of the Stock Corporation Act; and
- the resolution has been declared void by *res judicata* judgment in an action to set aside or by a court of the Non-Contentious Jurisdiction (sec. 241 no. 5, 6 of the Stock Corporation Act).[1087]

bb) Violation of Provisions relating to Form and Procedure. The most common violations of rules relating to form and procedure are defects relating to the convening of the meeting and the notarization of resolutions and failure to adhere to the specified time limits for registration in the commercial register:
- **Defects relating to the convening of the general meeting** which render the resolution null and void arise if the general meeting is convened by a person who is not authorized to do so or if the convening of the general meeting is not properly announced, unless the meeting is a plenary meeting and no share-

---

[1083] Sec. 249 para. 1 sentence 2 of the Stock Corporation Act.
[1084] Sec. 244 sentence 1 of the Stock Corporation Act.
[1085] Sec. 242, 253 para. 1, 256 para. 6 of the Stock Corporation Act.
[1086] Sec. 249 of the Stock Corporation Act.
[1087] Sec. 241 no. 5 of the Stock Corporation Act.

holder objects to the voting.[1088] The defects relating to the convening of the general meeting which render the resolution null and void are listed in full in sec. 121 para. 2, 3 sentence 1 and para. 4 of the Stock Corporation Act.[1089] It had been disputed whether a wrong description of the formalities for granting a power of attorney when convening the general meeting renders a resolution void. After a change of law such formalities are mentioned in sec. 121 para. 3 sentence 3 no. 2 of the Stock Corporation Act; a violation does, therefore, not render the resolution null and void. Sec. 250 para. 1 of the Stock Corporation Act contains special provisions regarding the voidness of an election of members of the supervisory board. Annual financial statements which have been formally approved by the general meeting are also null and void if the general meeting, in which formal approval was granted, had been convened in violation of sec. 121 para. 2, 3 sentence 1 or para. 4 of the Stock Corporation Act.[1090]

- **Notarization defects** render a resolution null and void. It is deemed to constitute a defect if the minutes of the general meeting pursuant to sec. 130 para. 2 sentence 1 of the Stock Corporation Act are not complete or have not been signed by a notary (or by the chairman of the supervisory board in case of a non-listed stock corporation). In this event, the resolution of the general meeting is null and void pursuant to sec. 241 no. 2 of the Stock Corporation Act. In contrast, the omission of additional information to be included in the minutes in case of listed companies pursuant to sec. 130 para. 2 sentence 2 of the Stock Corporation Act does not render the resolution null and void.[1091] Special provisions regarding the election of supervisory board members are included in sec. 250 para. 1 no. 1-5 of the Stock Corporation Act. Annual financial statements which have been formally approved by the general meeting are also null and void if such formal approval has not been recorded in accordance with sec. 130 para. 1, 2 sentence 1 and para. 4 of the Stock Corporation Act.[1092]

- In certain cases, a resolution of the general meeting must be **registered** in the commercial register within a **certain period of time**. If the registration is not effected within this period, the resolution of the general meeting becomes void.[1093] This, under certain circumstances, applies to a resolution of the general meeting concerning a capital increase from company resources.[1094] Similar provisions apply under certain circumstances to resolutions on an ordinary capital reduction[1095] and a simplified capital reduction.[1096]

- If the general meeting has resolved upon a **contingent capital increase**, resolutions of the general meeting which (after the registration of the contingent capital with the commercial register) oppose such capital increase are also null and void.[1097] This applies in particular to resolutions cancelling a resolution stipulating a contingent capital increase which has been registered in the commercial register.

[1088] Sec. 121 para. 6 of the Stock Corporation Act.
[1089] Sec. 241 no. 1 of the Stock Corporation Act.
[1090] Sec. 256 para. 3 no. 1 of the Stock Corporation Act.
[1091] Sec. 241 no. 2 of the Stock Corporation Act.
[1092] Sec. 256 para. 3 no. 2 of the Stock Corporation Act.
[1093] Sec. 241 of the Stock Corporation Act.
[1094] Sec. 217 para. 2 sentence 4 of the Stock Corporation Act.
[1095] Sec. 228 para. 2 of the Stock Corporation Act.
[1096] Sec. 234 para. 3, 235 para. 2 of the Stock Corporation Act.
[1097] Sec. 192 para. 4 of the Stock Corporation Act.

cc) Other Violations of Law. Important examples for **breaches** of **fundamental provisions of substantive law** are the following:
- Violations of the shareholders' right to receive shares pro rata to their current participation in the event of a capital increase from company resources.[1098]
- The election of members of the supervisory board is void if the supervisory board has not been composed correctly, if the general meeting fails to follow the nominations made by the employees within the scope of the Coal, Iron and Steel Codetermination Act, if the maximum statutory number of members of the supervisory board pursuant to sec. 95 of the Stock Corporation Act has been exceeded, if the elected person fails to meet the requirements stipulated in sec. 100 para. 1, 2 of the Stock Corporation Act or if the election violates sec. 96 para. 2 of the Stock Corporation Act, i.e. contravenes the obligatory gender quota (colloquially called *"Frauenquote"*).[1099] This provision applies *mutatis mutandis* to the employee members of the supervisory board.
- Special provisions apply to the approval of the annual financial statements and the distribution of the balance sheet profit.[1100] If the general meeting approves the annual financial statements but alters the version of the financial statements previously audited by an auditor, the amendment proposed by the general meeting needs to be audited and confirmed by the auditor anew. If the confirmation of the auditor is not granted within two weeks after the resolution of the general meeting has been adopted, the resolution is deemed to be null and void.[1101]

A resolution of the general meeting may also be null and void if the requirements of one of the **general clauses** in sec. 241 nos. 3, 4 of the Stock Corporation Act are met:
- The resolution passed by the general meeting is deemed to be void if it cannot be reconciled with the nature of an *AG* or if it violates regulations which exclusively or primarily serve to protect creditors of the company or otherwise serve the public interest.[1102]
- The same applies to resolutions of the general meeting which violate public policy.[1103]

The resolution of the general meeting is also null and void if the resolution is deleted from the commercial register because its contents violate mandatory statutory provisions and it appears to be in the public interest for them to be deleted.[1104]

Relevant cases mainly relate to provisions for the protection of creditors (capital reductions;[1105] termination of domination or profit and loss transfer agreements;[1106] integration;[1107] cases involving the transformation of the company).[1108] The same applies to violations of provisions of the Stock Corporation Act regulating the principle of capital maintenance (*Kapitalbindung*).[1109] Amendments to the

---
[1098] Sec. 212, 241 para. 1 of the Stock Corporation Act.
[1099] Sec. 250 para. 1 of the Stock Corporation Act.
[1100] Sec. 253, 256 of the Stock Corporation Act.
[1101] Sec. 173 para. 3 sentence 2 of the Stock Corporation Act.
[1102] Sec. 241 no. 3 of the Stock Corporation Act.
[1103] Sec. 241 no. 4 of the Stock Corporation Act.
[1104] Sec. 241 no. 6 of the Stock Corporation Act, sec. 398 Act on Procedure in Family Matters and Matters of Non-Contentious Jurisdiction.
[1105] Sec. 225, 233 of the Stock Corporation Act.
[1106] Sec. 303 of the Stock Corporation Act.
[1107] Sec. 321 of the Stock Corporation Act.
[1108] Sec. 22, 133 et seq., 204 of the Transformation Act.
[1109] Sec. 57, 58 para. 4, 5, 71 et seq. of the Stock Corporation Act.

articles of association which violate the Codetermination Act are also null and void pursuant to sec. 241 no. 3 of the Stock Corporation Act as this act serves the public interest (employee participation).[1110] Violations of provisions of criminal or administrative law may also be considered as rendering a resolution of the general meeting void. If the prohibition of unlawful restraints on competition pursuant to sec. 1 of the Act against Restraints on Competition or Art. 102 of the Treaty on the Functioning of the European Union is violated, resolutions of the general meeting are also null and void pursuant to sec. 241 no. 3 of the Stock Corporation Act.

It is debatable whether **resolutions amending the articles of association** are null and void if they go beyond the restrictions of the Stock Corporation Act.[1111] This would mean that each resolution amending the articles of association which violates any mandatory provision of the Stock Corporation Act is void in principle. A more flexible interpretation is preferable. This means that a violation of provisions of the Stock Corporation Act which are not essential for the constitution of an *AG* merely renders contestable the resolution in question. In contrast, those resolutions in which the general meeting exceeds its competencies, for example by taking decisions relating to the management of the company, are null and void, as the provisions which will be infringed by such decisions concern the structure of the *AG* and the compliance with such provisions is predominantly in the public interest.

If resolutions of the general meeting are deleted on the grounds of being null and void based on a judicial decision pursuant to sec. 398 of the Act on Procedure in Family Matters and Matters of Non-Contentious Jurisdiction, this automatically renders the resolution in question void.[1112] For this to be the case, it is required that the contents of the resolution in question violate mandatory statutory law and that the elimination of the resolution appears to be necessary to serve the public interest. The **register court** examines independently whether such requirements are met. In many cases, the reasons for a deletion will be identical with the reasons causing a nullity pursuant to sec. 241 no. 3 of the Stock Corporation Act.

dd) Cured Defects. Void resolutions may be **cured** if certain requirements are met.
- Curing is based on the principle of legal certainty and only applies in certain cases specified by the Stock Corporation Act. Recording defects can no longer be asserted once the resolution has been registered in the commercial register.[1113] The respective resolution cannot be deleted *ex officio* either since such a deletion would require a defect relating to the contents of the resolution which is not available in case of mere (formal) recording defects.
- Defects relating to the convening of the general meeting and to the contents of a resolution are cured if the resolution has been registered in the commercial register and three years have passed since the date of registration.[1114] According to sec. 242 para. 3 of the Stock Corporation Act, the provision for curing a defect extends to cases in which capital alterations have not been registered within the period of time required by law but are registered thereafter and remain registered for three years. The same applies if invalid resolutions are registered

---

[1110] Decisions of the Federal Supreme Court, published in BGHZ, vol. 83, pp. 106, 110 and in BGHZ, vol. 89, pp. 48, 50.
[1111] Sec. 23 para. 5 of the Stock Corporation Act.
[1112] Sec. 241 no. 6 of the Stock Corporation Act.
[1113] Sec. 242 para. 1 of the Stock Corporation Act.
[1114] Sec. 242 para. 2 of the Stock Corporation Act.

erroneously.[1115] However, if the contents of the resolution violate mandatory statutory provisions, the resolution may be deleted from the commercial register *ex officio* despite the expiry of the cure period.[1116] The court will, however, need to consider whether the public interest still requires the deletion after expiry of the cure period.
- The curing of a defect **removes the** illegality of the resolution *ex tunc* with effect for and against all parties under substantive law. After expiry of the cure period, the management board and the supervisory board are obliged to implement the relevant resolutions (but may be liable for not having pursued the deletion of the resolution in time).

c) Action to Set Aside a Resolution

If a resolution of the general meeting is passed in violation of the law or the articles of association and this violation does not constitute a reason for nullity, the resolution is contestable and may be subject to an **action to set aside a resolution**.

aa) Reasons for Setting Aside Resolutions. The legal reasons for a resolution to be subject to an action to set aside a resolution may be divided into two categories:
- Violations of rules relating to **form and procedure** about the adoption of resolutions.
  As mentioned above with respect to the nullity of a resolution, the most common violations of rules relating to form and procedure are defects relating to the convening and conduct of the general meeting. If such defects do not render the resolution null and void, the resolution is contestable and may thus be subject to an action to set aside. The defect must have been capable of having influenced the resolution (e.g., because a person participated who was not entitled to attend the general meeting if his vote was decisive for the outcome of the resolution).
  Such defects may include, for example, convening the general meeting at an inadmissible place, failing to observe the notice period for convening the general meeting or non-compliance with publication requirements according to sec. 124 para. 1 to 3 of the Stock Corporation Act. Common errors are failures to adequately publish the agenda or violations of the shareholders' right to receive information at the general meeting[1117] or the shareholders' right to attend the general meeting and to speak in the general meeting.[1118]
- Violation of provisions regarding the **contents of the resolution**.
  An action to set aside a resolution may also be based on the claim that, when exercising the voting right, a shareholder was seeking to **acquire special benefits** for himself or a third party to the detriment of the company, and the resolution was suitable to serve this purpose.[1119]
  The prohibition to allow improper special benefits limits the power of a majority shareholder in a stock corporation. However, the majority principle applies to anybody having a shareholding in the *AG*. Consequently, a shareholder is generally obligated to accept all resolutions passed with the necessary majority by the general meeting even if he did not cast a consenting vote or if the

---
[1115] Decision of the Higher Regional Court of Hamburg, published in AG 1970, pp. 230 et seq.
[1116] Sec. 242 para. 2 sentence 3 of the Stock Corporation Act.
[1117] Sec. 131 of the Stock Corporation Act.
[1118] Sec. 118 of the Stock Corporation Act.
[1119] Sec. 243 para. 2 sentence 1 of the Stock Corporation Act.

resolution is detrimental to him. Nevertheless, the majority needs to take the interests of minority shareholders into consideration. The **majority** is deemed to be **making improper use of its power** if it tries to assert its interests by impairing the interests of the minority shareholders to a considerable extent and if the impairment of the interests of the minority shareholders is more severe than necessary for the purposes of the majority shareholder. In this event, such resolutions may also be subject to an action to set aside.[1120]

Resolutions may also be subject to an action to set aside if they violate the principle of **equal treatment of shareholders**.[1121]

Since the shareholders are increasingly granted more rights which may be exercised by way of electronic communication or data transfer, the law expressly provides that certain violations of such rights do not constitute a reason to set aside a resolution of the general meeting:

- violations of rights to participate in the general meeting by means of electronic communication[1122] or by written vote[1123] if such violation results from a technical failure and the company has not acted intentionally or with gross negligence (the articles of association may provide for stricter level of negligence);
- the violation of the duty to submit the convening of the general meeting to the Federal Gazette;[1124]
- the violation of the duty to publish certain information regarding the general meeting on the company's website;[1125]
- the violation of the bank's obligation to forward information concerning the general meeting to the shareholders who have deposited shares at the bank;[1126] and
- reasons which allow the initiation of proceedings pursuant to sec. 318 para. 3 of the German Commercial Code.[1127]

bb) Procedure. The resolution of the general meeting can only be set aside on the basis of an **action filed within one month** after the moment at which the resolution has been adopted.[1128] After the expiration of this time period, the resolution becomes binding despite potential deficiencies which may have occurred. The lawsuit has to be filed against the company, represented by the management board and the supervisory board.[1129] The Stock Corporation Act stipulates that only certain shareholders, the management board and single members of the management board and the supervisory board are authorized to contest the validity of a resolution.[1130] Pursuant to sec. 245 no. 1 of the Stock Corporation Act, only those shareholders who have been present at the general meeting and who have had their objections to the resolution recorded in the minutes of the general meeting are granted a right to set aside. Shareholders who were not present at the meeting have a right to file an action to set aside a resolution if they were not admitted to the general meeting wrongfully or if the general meeting was not

---

[1120] Sec. 243 para. 1 of the Stock Corporation Act.
[1121] Sec. 53a of the Stock Corporation Act.
[1122] Sec. 243 para. 3 no. 1, sec. 118 para. 1 sentence 2 of the Stock Corporation Act.
[1123] Sec. 243 para. 3 no. 1, sec. 118 para. 2 of the Stock Corporation Act.
[1124] Sec. 243 para. 3 no. 2, sec. 121 para. 4a of the Stock Corporation Act.
[1125] Sec. 243 para. 3. no. 2, sec. 124a of the Stock Corporation Act.
[1126] Sec. 243 para. 3 no. 2, sec. 128 of the Stock Corporation Act.
[1127] Sec. 243 para. 3 no. 3 of the Stock Corporation Act.
[1128] Sec. 246 para. 1 of the Stock Corporation Act.
[1129] Sec. 246 para. 2 of the Stock Corporation Act.
[1130] Sec. 245 no. 1 to 5 of the Stock Corporation Act.

convened properly or if an item of the agenda was not announced properly.[1131] The management board is always entitled to file an action to set aside a resolution.[1132] Each single member of the management board and supervisory board has a right to file an action to set aside a resolution, if the member, by implementing the resolution, would be committing punishable offenses or violating an ordinance, or would be liable for damages.[1133]

The lawsuit has to be filed with the **regional court** (*Landgericht*) in whose district the *AG* has its registered office.[1134] The management board is obligated to **announce the filing** of the lawsuit in the company's designated journals.[1135]

In order to accelerate the proceedings, the company is entitled to review and take copies of submitted applications immediately after the one-month period, even before they have formally been delivered to the company by the court.[1136]

If the court comes to the conclusion that the resolution is to be declared null and void, such judgment is **effective in favor of and against all shareholders** as well as **members of the management board** and **supervisory board**, even if they were not parties to the lawsuit.[1137] The judgment has to be submitted to the commercial register by the management board without undue delay.[1138] In the event that the resolution was registered in the commercial register, the judgment has to be registered as well.[1139] Furthermore, the registration of the judgment has to be announced in the same manner as the registration of the resolution.[1140]

In the event that the resolution contained an amendment to the articles of association, the judgment has to be submitted to the commercial register together with the complete text of the articles of association taking into consideration the judgment and all previous amendments to the articles, certified by a notary to that effect.[1141]

d) Release (Fast-track) Proceedings

In practice, the initiation of an action to set aside a resolution is particularly important if the respective resolution needs to be registered with the commercial register in order to be effective (e.g., capital increase, enterprise agreements, merger and other structural measures, squeeze-out). The register judge will most likely not register the resolution as long as lawsuits are pending. This can lead to significant delays given the fact that a binding judgment on an action to set aside a resolution may take several years.

The German Stock Corporation Act and the German Transformation Act contain provisions on so-called release or fast-track proceedings (*Freigabeverfahren*), pursuant to which the company can apply for a court decision that the **pending lawsuits do not obstruct the registration of the resolution**. In particular, this opportunity exists in relation to capital measures and enterprise agreements,[1142]

[1131] Sec. 245 no. 2 of the Stock Corporation Act.
[1132] Sec. 245 no. 4 of the Stock Corporation Act.
[1133] Sec. 245 no. 5 of the Stock Corporation Act.
[1134] Sec. 246 para. 3 sentence 1 of the Stock Corporation Act.
[1135] Sec. 246 para. 4 sentence 1 of the Stock Corporation Act.
[1136] Sec. 246 para. 3 sentence 5 of the Stock Corporation Act.
[1137] Sec. 248 para. 1 sentence 1 of the Stock Corporation Act.
[1138] Sec. 248 para 1 sentence 2 of the Stock Corporation Act.
[1139] Sec. 248 para 1 sentence 3 of the Stock Corporation Act.
[1140] Sec. 248 para. 1 sentence 4 of the Stock Corporation Act.
[1141] Sec. 248 para. 2 of the Stock Corporation Act.
[1142] Sec. 246a of the Stock Corporation Act.

squeeze-outs,[1143] mergers and other structural measures.[1144] Release proceedings are not available, however, in case of amendments to the articles of association.

In release proceedings, the court makes a preliminary assessment whether the claim to set aside the resolution is valid. The court will hold that the resolution may be registered if (i) the action is inadmissible, (ii) the action is obviously unfounded, (iii) the claimant has not proven that he holds shares in a nominal amount of at least EUR 1,000 or (iv) despite the action not being obviously unfounded, the interests of the company or the other shareholders in registration outweigh the interests of the shareholders in avoiding registration and there is no severe breach of law.[1145] Whereas formerly there was a two stage procedure before the Regional Court (*Landgericht*) and the Higher Regional Court (*Oberlandesgericht*), the Shareholders' Rights Act centralized the authority with the **Higher Regional Courts whose decisions are unappealable.**[1146] It can be assumed that the duration of the proceedings (formerly three to twelve months) will be significantly reduced.

6. Overview: Important (Minority) Shareholder Rights

Legal Provision	Rights Resulting from the Participation
One Share	
Sec. 118 para. 1, sec. 134 para. 1 sentence 1 of the Stock Corporation Act	Right to participate and to vote in the general meeting
Sec. 125 para. 4 of the Stock Corporation Act	Right to receive notice of the resolutions adopted at the general meeting
Sec. 126, sec. 127 of the Stock Corporation Act	Right to have published counter-motions and nominations concerning the election of supervisory board members or auditors
Sec. 131 of the Stock Corporation Act	Right to information in the general meeting
Sec. 145 para. 6 sentence 4 of the Stock Corporation Act	Right to request a copy of the audit report in case of a special audit
Sec. 275 para. 1 sentence 1 of the Stock Corporation Act	Right to bring an action for the declaration of nullity of the stock corporation
Sec. 245 no. 1 to 3 of the Stock Corporation Act	Right to bring an action to set aside resolutions of the general meeting
Sec. 249 para. 1 of the Stock Corporation Act	Right to bring an action for the declaration of nullity of resolutions of the general meeting

---

[1143] Sec. 327e para. 2, 319 para. 6 sentence 1 of the Stock Corporation Act.
[1144] Sec. 16 para. 3 sentence 1 of the Transformation Act.
[1145] Sec. 246a para. 2, 319 para. 6 sentence 3, sec. 327e para. 2 of the Stock Corporation Act, sec. 16 para. 3 sentence 3 of the Transformation Act.
[1146] Sec. 246a para. 1 sentence 3, para. 3 sentence 4, sec. 319 para. 6 sentences 7 and 9, sec. 327e para. 2 of the Stock Corporation Act, sec. 16 para. 3 sentence 7 and 9 of the Transformation Act.

Legal Provision	Rights Resulting from the Participation
Sec. 315 sentence 1 of the Stock Corporation Act	Right of the shareholder in a controlled enterprise to demand a special audit in certain cases
1% of the registered share capital or nominally EUR 100,000	
Sec. 142 para. 2 sentence 1 of the Stock Corporation Act	Right to apply for court decision to appoint a special auditor to examine matters relating to the formation of the company or the management of the company's business, in particular measures taken in relation to capital increases or capital reductions, if the general meeting rejected an application for the appointment
Sec. 148 para. 1 sentence 1 of the Stock Corporation Act	Right to apply for admission of a lawsuit to claim damages in favor of the company
Sec. 258 para. 1 sentence 1, para. 2 sentence 3 of the Stock Corporation Act	Right to apply for the appointment of a special auditor who will examine: – (i) allegedly undervalued items of the formally approved financial statements – (ii) the notes, in order to determine whether they contain the prescribed information, or, should the notes not contain such information, whether the management board has not, notwithstanding a question relating thereto, supplied the missing information at the general meeting and whether the recording of the question in the minutes of the general meeting was formally requested
Sec. 315 sentence 2 of the Stock Corporation Act	Right to demand a special audit in a controlled company in order to review whether there are facts which justify the suspicion that the company was harmed
5% of the registered share capital or nominally EUR 500,000	
Sec. 122 para. 2 of the Stock Corporation Act	Right to request that items are put on the agenda of the general meeting and are announced
Sec. 254 para. 1, 2 sentence 3 of the Stock Corporation Act	Right to bring an action against the resolution on the appropriation of the balance sheet profit if: – the general meeting transfers amounts to revenue reserves or carries such amounts forward as profit and – due to this, no dividend of 4% or more of the registered share capital will be paid
Sec. 260 para. 1 sentence 1 of the Stock Corporation Act	Right to bring a motion to the court for a decision against the findings of the special auditor
Sec. 265 para. 3 sentence 1 of the Stock Corporation Act	Right to demand the appointment or dismissal of liquidators for good cause by the court
Sec. 318 para. 3 sentence 1 of the Commercial Code	Right to demand the appointment of another auditor of annual financial statements by the court

Legal Provision	Rights Resulting from the Participation
5% of the registered share capital	
Sec. 122 para. 1 of the Stock Corporation Act	Right to request the convening of an extraordinary general meeting
Sec. 183a para. 3 of the Stock Corporation Act	Right to petition a court to appoint auditors in case of a capital increase from contributions in kind
>> 5% of the registered share capital	
Sec. 320 para. 1 sentence 1 of the Stock Corporation Act	Blocking minority against an integration by majority resolution
Sec. 327a para. 1 sentence 1 of the Stock Corporation Act	Blocking minority against a squeeze-out
10% of the registered share capital or nominally EUR 1,000,000	
Sec. 103 para. 3 sentence 3 of the Stock Corporation Act	Right to request the dismissal of a member of the supervisory board if such member was appointed on basis of the articles of association and if there is good cause for dismissal of the concerned person
Sec. 120 para. 1 sentence 2 of the Stock Corporation Act	Right to request a separate vote concerning the ratification of the acts of one individual member of the management board or the supervisory board
Sec. 147 para. 2 sentence 2 of the Stock Corporation Act	Right to apply for the appointment of a special representative to assert claims for damages of the company against a member of the management board or the supervisory board
10% of the registered share capital	
Sec. 50 sentence 1 of the Stock Corporation Act	Right to object to a waiver or a composition entered into by the company with respect to claims for damages in connection with the formation of the company
Sec. 93 para. 4 sentence 3 of the Stock Corporation Act	Right to object to a waiver or a composition entered into by the company with respect to claims for damages against members of the management board
Sec. 116 sentence 1, sec. 93 para. 4 sentence 3 of the Stock Corporation Act	Right to object to a waiver or a composition entered into by the company with respect to claims for damages against members of the supervisory board
Sec. 117 para. 4, sec. 93 para. 4 sentence 3 of the Stock Corporation Act	Right to object to a waiver or a composition entered into by the company with respect to claims for damages for exerting detrimental influence on the company by third persons
10% of the registered share capital represented at the adoption of the resolution	
Sec. 302 para. 3 sentence 3 of the Stock Corporation Act	Right to object to a waiver or a composition entered into by the company with respect to the loss of compensation due from the controlling enterprise

V. Constitution of the AG

Legal Provision	Rights Resulting from the Participation
Sec. 309 para. 3 sentence 1 of the Stock Corporation Act	Right to object to a waiver or a composition entered into by the company with respect to the claims for damages due from the legal representative of the controlling enterprise
>> 25% of the votes cast, of the registered share capital, of the registered share capital represented in the general meeting	
(see below)	Blocking minority for resolutions for which a majority of 75% is required (see below)
>> 50% of the votes cast	
Sec. 133 para. 1 of the Stock Corporation Act	A simple majority of the votes cast (more than 50%) is required for all resolutions for which statutory law or the articles of association do not stipulate a different majority requirement, such as:
Sec. 119 para. 1 no. 1, sec. 101 para. 1 sentence 1 of the Stock Corporation Act	– appointment of members of the supervisory board, unless such members are to be determined by the employees under a codetermination regime or appointed outside the general meeting by a single shareholder under an exclusive right of appointment
Sec. 119 para. 1 no. 2, sec. 174 para. 1 of the Stock Corporation Act	– appropriation of the balance sheet profit
Sec. 119 para. 1 no. 3, sec. 120 para. 1 of the Stock Corporation Act	– ratification of the acts of the members of the management board and the supervisory board
Sec. 119 para. 1 no. 4 of the Stock Corporation Act, sec. 318 para. 1 sentence 1 of the Commercial Code	– appointment of the auditors of the annual financial statements
Sec. 119 para. 1 no. 7, sec. 142 of the Stock Corporation Act	– appointment of a special auditor for the examination of specific matters relating to the formation of the company or the management of the company's business
Sec. 50 sentence 1, sec. 93 para. 4, sec. 116 sentence 1 of the Stock Corporation Act	– waiver or a composition with respect to claims for damages (minority of 10% may raise formal objection and stop the waiver, sec. 50 sentence 1 of the Stock Corporation Act)
Sec. 71 para. 1 no. 8 of the Stock Corporation Act	– authorization to acquire own shares
Sec. 84 para. 3 sentence 2 of the Stock Corporation Act	– motion of no-confidence regarding a member of the management board
Sec. 113 para.1 sentence 2 of the Stock Corporation Act	– remuneration for the services of the members of the supervisory board

B. Stock Corporation

Legal Provision	Rights Resulting from the Participation
Sec. 147 para. 1 sentence 1 of the Stock Corporation Act	– decision to bring an action against a member of the management board, the supervisory board or the founders with respect to claims for damages
Sec. 237 para. 4 of the Stock Corporation Act	– vote on simplified capital decrease against redemption of shares
Sec. 265 para. 2 of the Stock Corporation Act	– appointment of the liquidators
75% of the votes cast	
Sec. 103 para. 1 sentence 2 of the Stock Corporation Act	Dismissal of the supervisory board (the articles of association may only stipulate a higher majority)
Sec. 111 para. 4 sentence 3, 4 of the Stock Corporation Act	Consent to management measures if the supervisory board, which is normally competent to grant such consent, does not grant the consent and the management board therefore brings the matter to the general meeting for its consent
75% of the registered share capital represented at the adoption of the resolution	
	A qualified majority of 75% is required for a number of fundamental resolutions, such as:
Sec. 52 para. 5 sentence 1 of the Stock Corporation Act	– consent to agreements relating to a post-formation acquisition (the articles of association may only stipulate a higher majority)
Sec. 179 para. 2 of the Stock Corporation Act	– amendment of the articles of association (the articles of association may also stipulate a lower majority unless the object of the enterprise is to be amended)
Sec. 179a para. 1 of the Stock Corporation Act	– obligation of the company to transfer its entire assets (the articles of association may only stipulate a higher majority)
Sec. 182 para. 1 sentence 1 of the Stock Corporation Act	– registered share capital increase (the articles of association may also stipulate a lower majority except for preference shares)
Sec. 186 para. 3 sentence 2 of the Stock Corporation Act	– restriction of subscription rights in a registered share capital increase (the articles of association may only stipulate a higher majority)
Sec. 193 para. 1 sentence 1 of the Stock Corporation Act	– contingent registered share capital increase (the articles of association may only stipulate a higher majority)
Sec. 202 para. 2 sentence 2 of the Stock Corporation Act	– authorized capital (the articles of association may only stipulate a higher majority)
Sec. 221 para. 1 sentence 2 of the Stock Corporation Act	– issue of convertible bonds and dividend bonds (the articles may also stipulate a lower majority)

Legal Provision	Rights Resulting from the Participation
Sec. 222 para. 1 sentence 1 of the Stock Corporation Act	– registered share capital reduction (the articles of association may only stipulate a higher majority)
Sec. 262 para. 1 no. 2 of the Stock Corporation Act	– dissolution of the stock corporation (the articles of association may only stipulate a higher majority)
Sec. 274 para. 1 sentence 2 of the Stock Corporation Act	– continuation of the dissolved company (the articles of association may only stipulate a higher majority)
Sec. 293 para. 1 sentence 2 of the Stock Corporation Act	– approval of a domination agreement or a profit and loss transfer agreement (the articles of association may only stipulate a higher majority)
Sec. 65 para. 1 of the Transformation Act	– Resolution on mergers and splits of companies pursuant to the Transformation Act (the articles of association may only stipulate a higher majority)
95% of the registered share capital	
Sec. 320 para. 1 sentence 1 of the Stock Corporation Act	Integration by majority resolution
Sec. 327a para.1 sentence 1 of the Stock Corporation Act, sec. 39a para. 1 of the Securities Acquisition and Takeover Act	Squeeze-out of minority shareholders

Table 4: Important (Minority) Shareholder Rights

7. Corporate Governance Code

a) Development of Voluntary Codes of Governance Best Practices

The development of voluntary codes of governance best practices goes back to the year 2000 when the Code of Best Practice/Corporate Governance Principles by the German Panel on Corporate Governance (*Grundsatzkommission Corporate Governance: Corporate Governance Grundsätze für börsennotierte Gesellschaften*) and the German Code of Corporate Governance by the *Berliner Initiativkreis* were presented. In the same year, the German government appointed a commission (led by Professor Baums) to evaluate whether corporate governance principles should be introduced. The Baums Commission recommended the introduction of corporate governance rules and the appointment of a new commission to elaborate those rules. In September 2001, the Minister of Justice appointed such a commission on the German Corporate Governance Code (the "Government Commission"). The Government Commission adopted the German Corporate Governance Code on February 26, 2002 (the "Code"). Currently, the German Corporate Governance Code as amended on May 5, 2015 applies.

According to the Government Commission, the Code aims at making Germany's corporate governance rules transparent for both national and international investors, thus strengthening confidence in the management of German corpor-

ations. The Code addresses all major criticisms leveled against the preexisting German corporate governance system, namely inadequate focus on shareholder interests, the two-tier system of management board and supervisory board, inadequate transparency of German corporate governance, inadequate independence of German supervisory boards, and the limited independence of auditors of annual financial statements.

b) Is the German Corporate Governance Code Statutory Law?

The Code is not statutory law. It contains recommendations, identified in the text by the use of the word "shall". Furthermore, the Code contains suggestions by using terms such as "should" or "can". The remaining passages of the Code not marked by these terms contain provisions that corporations are compelled to observe under applicable law. Primarily, the Code addresses listed corporations. It is recommended, however, that non-listed corporations also adhere to the Code.

Pursuant to sec. 161 of the Stock Corporation Act, the management board and the supervisory board of listed corporations are obliged to declare once every year that the Code's recommendations have been and will be complied with and which of the Code's recommendations have not been or will not be followed and why such recommendations have not been or will not be followed. The declaration of the management board and the supervisory board has to be permanently available on the company's website.[1147] This principle of "comply or explain" only applies to *recommendations* of the Code. Deviations from the Code's *suggestions* do not have to be disclosed in the declaration of compliance. According to a recent decision of the Federal Supreme Court, approval given for the actions of the management board and the supervisory board may be set aside by the court if an incorrect declaration of compliance with the German Corporate Governance Code has been issued.[1148] The court also noted that, if recommendations of the Code are no longer complied with, the declaration has to be amended at once.

c) Major Content of the German Corporate Governance Code

The most relevant recommendations of the Code are:
- The management board shall publish reports and documents required by law for the general meeting on the corporation's website, together with the agenda.
- The management board shall conduct the business with a view to sustainable value creation and in the corporate interest which includes the interests of shareholders, employees and other stakeholders.
- If the corporation takes out a D&O policy for the management board and/or the supervisory board, a suitable deductible shall be agreed upon which shall not fall short of the higher of ten percent of the respective damages and one-and-a-half times the fixed yearly compensation of the respective board member.
- The overall compensation for members of the management board shall comprise a fixed salary and variable components. The chairman of the supervisory board shall outline the salient points of the compensation system and any changes thereto to the general meeting. The compensation paid to the members of the management board shall be disclosed in the notes or the management report. The figures shall be individualized.

[1147] Sec. 161 para. 2 of the Stock Corporation Act.
[1148] Decision of the Federal Supreme Court, published in NZG 2009, p. 342.

- When entering into new agreements with the members of the management board, severance payments to them upon termination of their management agreements shall be limited to (i) two times their annual salary and (ii) not more than the salary due for the remaining term of the management agreement.
- The supervisory board shall set up an audit committee which, in particular, shall handle issues concerning the accounting and risk management, the necessary independence required of the auditor, the issuing of the audit mandate to the auditor, the determination of auditing focal points and the fee agreement.
- Not more than two former members of the management board shall be members of the supervisory board and supervisory board members shall not exercise directorships or similar positions for important competitors of the corporation.
- The chairman of the management board or a member of the management board cannot switch to the supervisory board within two years after their leaving office unless the appointment was proposed by shareholders having more than 25% of the voting rights. In that case, the reasons for the switch shall be explained to the general meeting.
- Diversity shall be taken into account when appointing members of the management and supervisory boards. In listed companies for which the Codeterminaton Act, the Codetermination Act for the Iron and Steel Industry or the Codetermination Extension Act apply, the Supervisory Board shall comprise at least 30 percent women and at least 30 percent men. In the other companies covered by the Equality Act, the Supervisory Board shall determine targets for the share of women.
- Supervisory board members shall receive a remuneration which is reasonable in relation to their duties and to the company's situation. If the supervisory board members are paid a performance-related compensation, it shall be oriented towards the long-term success of the company. The compensation of the members of the supervisory board shall be reported in the notes to the consolidated financial statements.
- The shareholdings, including options and derivatives, held by individual members of the management board and the supervisory board shall be reported if these directly or indirectly exceed 1% of the shares issued by the corporation.
- Shareholders and third parties shall be kept informed during the fiscal year by means of interim reports.
- The Corporate Governance Report shall contain concrete information on stock option programs and similar securities-based incentive schemes of the corporation, insofar as this information has not been comprised by the annual financial statement, the consolidated financial statement or the compensation report.
- Prior to submitting a proposal for election, the supervisory board or, respectively, the audit committee, shall obtain a statement from the proposed auditor stating whether and, where applicable, which professional, financial and other relationships exist between the auditor on the one hand and the corporation and the members of its executive bodies on the other hand that could call its independence into question.

d) Level of Acceptance of the German Corporate Governance Code

The Code has been widely accepted among German listed corporations according to an annual study last published in June 2015.[1149] On average, every corporation listed in the DAX complies with about 95% of recommendations.

However, several suggestions and recommendations are obeyed by less than 90% of the affected corporations. Suggestions that have particularly low rates of implementation are that companies should make it possible for shareholders to follow general meetings using modern communication media, e.g. the Internet (30.8%); that in the case of a takeover offer, the management board should convene an extraordinary general meeting at which shareholders discuss the takeover offer and may decide on corporate actions (62.9%); and that in addition to their annual Corporate Governance Report, companies should provide comments on their compliance with the Code's suggestions (49.5%).

Recommendations that have particularly low rates of implementation include the recommendations that a deductible similar to the (obligatory) deductible of the management board shall be agreed upon in any D&O insurance for the supervisory board (67.6%); that when determining the management board's compensation, the supervisory board shall consider the relationship between the compensation of the management board and that of senior management and the staff overall, particularly in terms of its development over time, and that the supervisory board shall determine how senior managers and the relevant staff are to be differentiated (70.5%); that for pension schemes, the supervisory board shall establish the level of provision aimed for in each case, thereby also considering the length of time for which the individual has been a management board member (67.8%); and that an age limit for members of the management board shall be specified (74.1%).

8. Impact of the Sarbanes-Oxley Act (SOA) on German Corporate Governance

The main changes introduced by the SOA which affect German corporations are the following:
- certification of periodically filed reports by both the CEO and CFO;
- installation of an audit committee with independent members; and
- audit by independent statutory auditors.

While the SOA is a part of the U.S. regulatory framework, it also regulates foreign corporations that are subject to U.S. securities laws due to the "interstate commerce clause" of the U.S. Constitution, in particular corporations listed on exchanges in the United States. However, the SEC may – subject to certain restrictions – grant specific exemptions on a case by case basis.

There is an ongoing discussion in Germany as to how a German corporation can comply with both the SOA and the German regulatory framework. Some examples include:
- A German stock corporation is in compliance with German corporate governance provisions if its CFO and CEO certify periodically filed reports with the SEC. The only issue is what the consequences of the breach of a duty in connection with the filing would be, in particular whether a German investor could assert a claim for damages.

[1149] Report on the Acceptance and Application of the German Corporate Governance Code, published in DB 2015, pp. 1357 et seq.

- As recommended by the German Corporate Governance Code, the supervisory board of a German stock corporation may install an audit committee. The SOA requires all members of an audit committee to be independent. However, employees of the corporation are considered not to be independent. This would exclude employee representatives of German codetermined supervisory boards from serving on SOA-compliant audit committees. The SEC has taken account of the peculiarities of German codetermination law and, in principle, has acknowledged the independence of the employee representatives on the supervisory board.
- The Public Company Accounting Oversight Board (PCAOB) has issued rules regulating non-U.S. public accounting firms. These rules require such firms to register with the PCAOB and impose other obligations, such as to provide working documents, etc. The rules allow accounting firms to withhold information if submission would violate non-U.S. laws. This eases concerns with respect to the requirement to disclose information protected by German data protection laws.

The SOA created additional requirements with which German corporations listed in the U.S. must comply. However, certain concepts introduced by the SOA have also found their way into German corporate law. For example

- The independence of the auditors of financial statements was strengthened by the Financial Accounting Reform Act of 2004.[1150]
- An assurance similar to a balance sheet oath was introduced by the European Transparency Directive (2004/109/EC) and implemented into German law in 2007.[1151]
- The Financial Accounting Modernization Act of 2009 requires both auditors of financial statements and the management board to evaluate the internal control and risk management system of a company. However, there is not yet a requirement to establish such a system.[1152]

The Financial Accounting Modernization Act further requires that with respect to the supervisory board or audit committee of a stock corporation that is listed on a stock exchange or has applied for such listing, at least one member must be independent and have financial expertise.[1153]

VI. Financial System

1. The Registered Share Capital/The Principle of Capital Maintenance

One of the guiding principles of the German Stock Corporation Act is the **maintenance of the registered share capital**. This means that the registered share capital actually has to be **paid** in and that it **must not be repaid** to the shareholders. The shareholders are obliged to **pay the contributions** set by the issue price of the shares. Unless contributions in kind are stipulated in the articles of

---

[1150] Sec. 319, 319a of the Commercial Code.
[1151] Sec. 264 para. 2 sentence 3, 289 para. 1 sentence 5, 297 para. 2 sentence 4, 315 para. 1 sentence 6 of the Commercial Code.
[1152] Sec. 171 para. 1 sentence 2 of the Stock Corporation Act, Sec. 289 para. 5 of the Commercial Code.
[1153] Sec. 107 para. 4, 100 para. 5 of the Stock Corporation Act.

association, the shareholders have to pay in the issue price of the shares as cash contribution.[1154]

In the case of par value shares, the contribution of the shareholders has to equal at least the nominal value of the shares. Non-par value shares have no nominal value. The non-par value shares of a company participate equally in the registered share capital. The part of the registered share capital attributable to an individual non-par value share must not be less than one euro. Hence, a shareholder's minimum contribution has to amount to one euro. Generally, shares must not be issued for an amount below the nominal value or below the part of the registered share capital attributable to the individual non-par value shares (lowest issue price).[1155]

If shareholders fail to pay the called amount on time after having been granted a grace period accompanied by a warning that their shares and any contributions already made will be declared forfeited upon the expiration of such period, their shares and any contributions already made have to be declared forfeited for the company's benefit by announcement in the company's designated journals.[1156]

Each predecessor of such expelled shareholder listed in the share register is obliged to pay the company the contribution and arrears to the extent that his successors are unable to do so. The payment obligations of predecessors are limited to a time period of two years, commencing on the date of the application for the transfer of the share to be entered in the company's share register.[1157]

The Stock Corporation Act prohibits **releasing shareholders** and their **predecessors from their payment obligations** described above. Furthermore, claims of the shareholders against the company may not be set off against these payment obligations.[1158]

Furthermore, capital maintenance means that **reimbursements to the shareholders** are generally prohibited. The Stock Corporation Act explicitly prohibits contributions being repaid to shareholders. Interest may neither be promised nor paid to shareholders. Prior to the company's dissolution, only the balance sheet profit may be distributed among the shareholders.[1159] However, the articles of association may authorize the management board to pay the shareholders an interim dividend from the expected balance sheet profit after the end of the fiscal year, provided that interim financial statements for the preceding fiscal year show a balance sheet profit for the year.[1160]

In 2011, the Federal Supreme Court ruled that a company must not assume the prospectus risk for a selling shareholder in a secondary offering at the stock exchange, as it constitutes a reimbursement of capital to the shareholder, which is prohibited by sec. 57 para. 1 sentence 1 of the Stock Corporation Act.[1161]

Finally, the Stock Corporation Act restricts the ability of a company to acquire its own shares.[1162] The acquisition of own shares is generally only permitted for certain purposes expressly mentioned in the law. Without such special purpose, own shares may only be acquired upon authorization by the general meeting and only up to an amount of 10% of the registered share capital. The authorization may

---

[1154] Sec. 54 para. 2 of the Stock Corporation Act.
[1155] Sec. 9 para. 1 of the Stock Corporation Act.
[1156] Sec. 64 of the Stock Corporation Act.
[1157] Sec. 65 of the Stock Corporation Act.
[1158] Sec. 66 of the Stock Corporation Act.
[1159] Sec. 57 of the Stock Corporation Act.
[1160] Sec. 59 of the Stock Corporation Act.
[1161] Decision of the Federal Supreme Court, published in BGHZ, vol. 179, pp. 71 et seq.
[1162] Sec. 71 et seq. of the Stock Corporation Act.

only be granted for up to five years.[1163] Furthermore, the acquisition of own shares is only permitted if a reserve can be provided for in the balance sheet covering the costs for the acquisition of its own shares.[1164]

2. Appropriation of Profits

a) Overview

The general meeting is authorized to resolve on the **appropriation of the balance sheet profit**. The general meeting, however, is bound to the formally approved annual financial statements.[1165] This means that if the annual financial statements do not show a balance sheet profit, but only a balance sheet loss or an equilibrated balance sheet, the general meeting cannot create a distributable balance sheet profit by withdrawing amounts from the revenue reserves. The annual financial statements are generally approved by the management board and the supervisory board[1166] unless the management board and the supervisory board have decided to leave the approval with the general meeting or the supervisory board has not approved the annual financial statements.[1167]

A balance sheet profit or loss in the audited annual financial statements may deviate considerably from the achieved annual net income or loss according to the profit and loss statement. Before the general meeting resolves on the appropriation of a balance sheet profit, the management board and the supervisory board resolve on the appropriation of the annual net income according to sec. 58 of the Stock Corporation Act, which means that up to 50% of such income can be put into the reserves of the company and will therefore not be available for distribution to the shareholders.

b) Creation of Reserves

The Stock Corporation Act stipulates that **statutory reserves** have to be created on the balance sheet on the basis of the annual financial statements. Five percent of the annual net income, after deduction of any loss carried forward from the previous year, must be allocated to such reserves until the statutory reserves and the capital reserves pursuant to sec. 272 para. 2 no. 1 to 3 of the Commercial Code together reach 10% or a higher proportion of the registered share capital stipulated in the articles of association.[1168]

Unlike the articles of association of a *GmbH*, the **articles of association** of an *AG* may generally not stipulate the **extent of the creation of other reserves** out of the annual net income. Only if the annual financial statements are approved by the general meeting, the articles of association may stipulate that certain amounts of the annual net income be allocated to other revenue reserves.[1169]

If the annual financial statements are formally approved by the management board and the supervisory board, the management board and the supervisory board may allocate part of the annual net income to other revenue reserves. This authorization is limited to 50% of the annual net income unless the articles

---

[1163] Sec. 71 para. 1 sentence 1 no. 8 of the Stock Corporation Act.
[1164] Sec. 71 para. 2 sentence 2 of the Stock Corporation Act.
[1165] Sec. 174 para. 1 of the Stock Corporation Act.
[1166] Sec. 172 of the Stock Corporation Act.
[1167] Sec. 173 of the Stock Corporation Act.
[1168] Sec. 150 of the Stock Corporation Act.
[1169] Sec. 58 para. 1 sentence 1 of the Stock Corporation Act.

of association authorize the management board and the supervisory board to allocate a larger or smaller part of the annual net income to revenue reserves.[1170] Thus, the articles of association could stipulate that the management board and the supervisory board are authorized to allocate the total net income to revenue reserves.[1171]

The Stock Corporation Act also authorizes the management board and the supervisory board to transfer to other revenue reserves the equity portion of any restoration in the original value (*Wertaufholung*) of fixed assets and current assets.[1172]

c) Appropriation of the Balance Sheet Profit

The general meeting **resolves on the appropriation** of the balance sheet profit shown in the audited annual financial statements. The general meeting is not bound by the proposal of the management board for the appropriation of the balance sheet profit which is presented to the general meeting. Thus, the general meeting may resolve to distribute the total balance sheet profit to the shareholders, to allocate it to the revenue reserves or to carry it forward as profit.[1173]

d) Distribution of Profits

The **shareholders' share in the profits** is generally determined pro rata to the **participation** they have in the registered share capital.[1174] If, however, the contributions to the registered share capital have not been made in the same ratio for all shares, this principle does not apply. In this case, the shareholders initially receive from the distributable profit an amount equal to 4% of the contributions made.[1175] The articles of association, however, may set forth a different method for the distribution of profit.[1176]

e) Claim to the Profit

The shareholders have a claim to receive the balance sheet profit to the extent that such profit is not excluded from distribution to shareholders by law, by the articles of association, by a resolution of the general meeting or due to additional expense pursuant to the resolution concerning the appropriation of the balance sheet profit.

The shareholders' **claim** for payment of the balance sheet profits **arises** upon the resolution of the general meeting on the appropriation of the balance sheet profit. At that time, the claim also becomes **due**. In practice, the payment is effected one or two days after the general meeting. The articles of association may stipulate that the claim of the shareholders to payment becomes due on a later date or that the due date is determined by the resolution on the appropriation of the balance sheet profit.

[1170] Sec. 58 para. 2 of the Stock Corporation Act.
[1171] Decision of the Federal Supreme Court, published in BGHZ, vol. 55, pp. 359, 360 et seq.
[1172] Sec. 58 para. 2a of the Stock Corporation Act.
[1173] Sec. 174 para. 2, sec. 58 para. 3 of the Stock Corporation Act.
[1174] Sec. 60 para. 1 of the Stock Corporation Act.
[1175] Sec. 60 para. 2 of the Stock Corporation Act.
[1176] Sec. 60 para. 3 of the Stock Corporation Act.

3. Equity Financing

a) Forms of Capital Increase

The Stock Corporation Act recognizes four forms of an increase of the registered share capital:
- the ordinary capital increase against contributions (*Kapitalerhöhung gegen Einlagen*);[1177]
- the contingent capital increase (*bedingte Kapitalerhöhung*);[1178]
- the capital increase from authorized capital (*Kapitalerhöhung aus genehmigtem Kapital*)[1179] and
- the capital increase from company resources (*Kapitalerhöhung aus Gesellschaftsmitteln*).[1180]

Only the first three forms of a capital increase lead to an increase of the company's equity, while a capital increase from company resources merely shifts reserves provided for on the balance sheet into subscribed capital of the company.

Although the ordinary capital increase is foreseen as the standard type of capital increase according to the Stock Corporation Act, the capital increase from **authorized capital** is much **more common in practice**. This is because a capital increase from authorized capital can be used more flexibly by the company. The authorized capital can be created by the general meeting for a term of five years. Within this term, the management board may increase the share capital on the basis of the authorized capital when required without the need of convening a further general meeting. In addition, the management may be authorized by the articles of association to partially exclude the statutory subscription rights of the shareholders when exercising the authorization to increase the registered share capital.

b) Capital Increase against Contributions

aa) Overview. In the case of an ordinary capital increase against contributions, the *AG*'s registered share capital is increased by issuing new shares against contributions in cash or in kind rendered by the existing shareholders or by new shareholders.

The following steps are required to carry out an ordinary capital increase:
- resolution of the general meeting on the capital increase;
- application for registration of the resolution on the capital increase with the commercial register;
- subscription of the new shares;
- payment of the contributions;
- application for registration of the implementation of the capital increase with the commercial register; and
- issue of the new shares.

bb) Resolution on the Capital Increase

aaa) General Requirements. The **general meeting** is responsible for deciding on an ordinary capital increase. The resolution of the general meeting requires

---
[1177] Sec. 182 et seq. of the Stock Corporation Act.
[1178] Sec. 192 et seq. of the Stock Corporation Act.
[1179] Sec. 202 et seq. of the Stock Corporation Act.
[1180] Sec. 207 et seq. of the Stock Corporation Act.

a **majority of at least three quarters** of the registered share capital represented when voting on the capital increase.[1181] The articles of association may provide for a higher or a lower capital majority which, in any event, must be at least equivalent to a simple majority of the votes cast. The articles of association may also stipulate additional requirements.[1182]

If there are several classes of shares with voting rights, the resolution on the capital increase requires the consent of the shareholders of each class of shares.[1183] A separate resolution granting consent (**special resolution**) has to be passed for each class of shares.[1184] Such resolution is subject to the same requirements as the resolution on the capital increase itself.[1185] The resolution on the capital increase only becomes valid once all necessary special resolutions have been passed. If the shareholders of one particular class of shares refuse to grant their consent, the resolution becomes permanently invalid. A special resolution may be passed by way of a separate vote during the same general meeting,[1186] provided this separate vote has been duly announced as an agenda item for the general meeting.[1187] Otherwise, the special resolutions are to be passed in a separate meeting of the shareholders of each class of shares. The provisions relating to the general meeting apply accordingly to the convening and conducting of such separate meeting.[1188]

If **preference shares** exist at the time the resolution on the capital increase is passed, a special resolution granting the consent of the holders of the existing preference shares is required if preference shares with equal or superior preferential rights with respect to the distribution of profits or corporate assets are to be issued.[1189] A consent of the preference shareholders is not required if (i) the right to issue such shares was expressly reserved when (x) the preference rights were granted or, (y) the voting rights were excluded (if this happened at a later date) and (ii) the subscription rights of the holders of the existing preference shares are not excluded.[1190] This is normally the case in practice.

bbb) Resolution on the Capital Increase. The resolution has to stipulate the **essential contents** of the capital increase. The general meeting may, however, authorize the management board to determine the details. Such authorization may be granted subject to the supervisory board's consent.

The resolution on the capital increase must stipulate the **amount** by which the registered share capital is to be increased. It is sufficient, however, for the general meeting to determine either a **minimum** and a **maximum limit** or only a maximum limit for the capital increase. In this case, the **criteria for determining the final amount** by which the capital is to be increased need to be provided for in the shareholder resolution in sufficient detail so that the management board does **not** have its own discretion concerning the amount of the capital increase. Usually a minimum and maximum amount are used if it is uncertain whether all new shares will be subscribed to.

[1181] Sec. 182 para. 1 sentence 1 of the Stock Corporation Act.
[1182] Sec. 182 para. 1 sentence 3 of the Stock Corporation Act.
[1183] Sec. 182 para. 2 sentence 1 of the Stock Corporation Act.
[1184] Sec. 182 para. 2 sentence 2 of the Stock Corporation Act.
[1185] Sec. 182 para. 2 sentence 3 of the Stock Corporation Act.
[1186] Sec. 138 sentence 1 of the Stock Corporation Act.
[1187] Sec. 138 sentence 2, sec. 124 para. 1 sentence 1 of the Stock Corporation Act.
[1188] Sec. 138 sentence 2 of the Stock Corporation Act.
[1189] Sec. 141 para. 2 sentence 1 of the Stock Corporation Act.
[1190] Sec. 141 para. 2 sentence 2 of the Stock Corporation Act.

The resolution on the capital increase also needs to stipulate the **number of new shares** and, in the case of par value shares, the **nominal values** and the **type of new shares**, i.e., bearer or registered shares. If various classes of shares exist or if various classes of shares are to be created, the resolution also needs to stipulate the **classes** of the new shares and the number of new shares issued for each class.

The **issue price** of the new shares may be determined by the general meeting. The issue price must at least be equal to the par value or the proportionate amount of the registered share capital (**prohibition of issue below par**).[1191] The issue price should not be inappropriately high, as this could be deemed a *de facto* exclusion of the shareholders' statutory subscription rights (see below). Alternatively, the general meeting may provide for a minimum and maximum price and authorize the management board to determine the exact issue price.

The resolution on the capital increase may contain further details on the implementation of the capital increase, e.g., specify a time period in which the capital increase needs to be implemented. If no such provisions are stated in the resolution, the management board will implement the capital increase in accordance with applicable statutory law.

If applicable, the resolution of the general meeting has to include details regarding **contributions in kind** and an exclusion of the subscription right (see below).

cc) Contributions in Kind. In the event of a capital increase against contributions in kind, the contributions are not made via a cash payment of the issue price but instead are made **by transferring assets to the company**.[1192] A capital increase against contributions in kind requires complying with certain additional requirements. The purpose of such requirements is to ensure that the contributed assets have a value at least equivalent to the lowest issue price for the new shares in order to protect the other shareholders against dilution and to protect the company's creditors. Generally, any object with determinable value can be contributed to the company in a capital increase against contributions in kind. However, the company's own shares or an obligation to render services cannot be the object of a contribution in kind.[1193] In its *"Eurobike"* decision[1194], the Federal Supreme Court held that the principles concerning hidden contributions in kind[1195] do not apply to services that the recipient of new shares has provided to the company in return for payment in temporal cohesion with a capital increase. Service contracts against payment between the *AG* and the subscriber are not prohibited. If a company paid for consulting services provided by the subscriber before the subscriber made his contribution to the company, this will not constitute a payment back and forth *(Hin- und Herzahlen)* within the meaning of sec. 27 para. 4 sentence 1 of the Stock Corporation Act, according to the court, provided that the company paid for a service actually rendered, the compensation complied with the arm's-length principle and the service had an intrinsic value by objective standards and was not useless and consequently valueless for the company in question.

In practice, a capital increase against contribution in kind is often used to contribute companies, parts of companies or shareholdings in companies into the stock corporation.

[1191] Sec. 9 para. 1 of the Stock Corporation Act.
[1192] Sec. 183, sec. 27 para. 1 sentence 2 of the Stock Corporation Act.
[1193] Sec. 183, sec. 27 para. 2 of the Stock Corporation Act.
[1194] Decision of the Federal Supreme Court, published in in BGHZ, vol. 184, pp. 158 et seq.
[1195] *Cf.* sec. 27 para. 3 of the Stock Corporation Act.

In the case of a capital increase against contribution in kind, the **resolution** on the capital increase must state the object of the contribution in kind, the person making the contribution and the par value, or in the case of non-par value shares, the number of the shares to be granted in return.[1196] The fact that the registered share capital is to be increased against contributions in kind as well as the aforementioned content of the resolution has to be **explicitly announced**[1197] together with the agenda when the general meeting in which the resolution is to be adopted is convened.

The objects of the contribution in kind have to be inspected by an **auditor**.[1198] This auditor examines whether the value of the contribution in kind is at least equivalent to the lowest issue price[1199] for the new shares. In all other respects, the provisions relating to the formation audit apply accordingly to this inspection.[1200] An audit by external auditors may be omitted under certain circumstances.[1201] In this case, the register court may refuse the registration of the capital increase if the contribution in kind is obviously and substantially overvalued.[1202]

According to the Federal Supreme Court,[1203] in case the value of the contribution in kind reaches the lowest issue price but does not cover the premium,[1204] the contributing shareholder will be liable to the company for the difference pursuant to para. 9 sec. 1 of the Limited Liability Company Act analogously *(gesetzlicher Differenzhaftungsanspruch)*. The Federal Supreme Court also ruled in this so-called *Babcock*-decision that the management board may enter into a settlement agreement with the liable shareholder concerning this claim of the company without having to obtain the consent of the general meeting beforehand.[1205]

Normally, an **agreement on a contribution in kind (contribution agreement)** is entered into between the *AG* and the contributor before the contribution in kind is made. This agreement defines the contribution in kind in detail and contains the conditions of the contribution. From a legal point of view it is, however, not necessary for the *AG* and the contributor to enter into a contribution agreement. In straightforward cases, the subscription agreement and its execution may suffice.

The regulations governing a capital increase against contributions in kind lead to a more complicated and time-consuming procedure compared to a capital increase against cash contributions. Therefore, the parties involved may wish to avoid those regulations. A usual way is that the registered share capital is formally increased against cash contribution, but in the context of the capital increase agreements are entered into between the company and the contributor pursuant to which the company is obliged to use the cash contribution, e. g., for the purchase of assets from the contributor. The economic result of such **hidden contributions in kind** is that the company does not receive cash for its free disposal, but assets.

The rules on a capital increase against contributions in kind also apply to hidden contributions in kind, i.e., if an asset purchase can be regarded as being made in connection with the cash contribution. The principles set out in connection with

---

[1196] Sec. 183 para. 1 sentence 1 of the Stock Corporation Act.
[1197] Sec. 183 para. 1 sentence 2 of the Stock Corporation Act.
[1198] Sec. 183 para. 3 of the Stock Corporation Act.
[1199] Sec. 9 para. 1 of the Stock Corporation Act.
[1200] Sec. 183 para. 3 sentence 2, sec. 33 para. 3-5, sec. 34, sec. 35 of the Stock Corporation Act.
[1201] Sec. 183a of the Stock Corporation Act.
[1202] Sec. 184 para. 3 sentence 2, 38 para. 3 of the Stock Corporation Act.
[1203] Decision of the Federal Supreme Court, published in BGHZ, vol. 191, pp. 364 et seq.
[1204] *Cf.* Para. 9 sec. 2 of the Stock Corporation Act.
[1205] Decision of the Federal Supreme Court, published in BGHZ, vol. 191, pp. 364 et seq.

the formation of the company[1206] also apply in case of a hidden contribution in kind in connection with a capital increase.

In the past, a capital increase in which the contributions were to be made by leaving distributed dividends with the company or by paying them back to the company (the so-called "**pay out, take back procedure**" (*Schütt-aus-hol-zurück-Verfahren*)) was only considered possible if the provisions on contributions in kind were complied with. In the meantime, however, the Federal Supreme Court has held that, as an alternative, a capital increase by means of the "pay out, take back procedure" may be implemented in line with the regulations governing a **capital increase from company resources** (see below).[1207]

dd) Subscription Right

aaa) The Subscription Right. Pursuant to sec. 186 para. 1 of the Stock Corporation Act, each shareholder has a right to obtain new shares in the event of a capital increase pro rata to its previous participation in the registered share capital (**subscription right**).

All shareholders of the *AG* have a subscription right at the time the resolution on the capital increase takes effect. The class of shares they hold at that time is irrelevant. Also, holders of preference shares without voting rights generally have a subscription right with regard to the new shares. However, the company's own shares do not carry a subscription right. This also applies in the event that such shares are held by third parties for the account of the *AG*.[1208]

The subscription rights are **exercised** by way of a **declaration to exercise the subscription right**. Such declaration, which does not require a specific form, has to be submitted to the *AG*. The declaration to exercise the subscription right calls on the *AG* either to make an offer to the holder of the subscription right in question to subscribe to the new share or to provide the information and documents allowing these persons to submit a declaration of subscription to the new share to the company.

If the subscription rights are not excluded, the resolution on the capital increase contains a time period within which the shareholders have to exercise their subscription rights. Such period may not be less than two weeks.[1209] If the shareholders do not exercise the subscription right within this period, the subscription right is forfeited. Usually, the management board sells shares for which subscription rights were not exercised to third parties.

bbb) Exclusion of Subscription Rights. The Stock Corporation Act allows the subscription right to be wholly or partially excluded in the resolution on the capital increase.

The exclusion of subscription rights is a **serious encroachment on the shareholders' membership rights** as it leads to a dilution of their shareholdings. Therefore, the Federal Supreme Court has held in its "*Kali und Salz*" and "*Siemens/Nold*" decisions that the exclusion of subscription rights needs to be **justified by specific facts**.[1210] The Federal Supreme Court considers the exclusion of subscription rights justified if it (i) serves a purpose which is in the **company's interests**,

---

[1206] *Cf.* B.III.1.e.
[1207] Decision of the Federal Supreme Court, published in BGHZ, vol. 135, pp. 381, 384 et seq.
[1208] Sec. 71d sentence 4, 71b of the Stock Corporation Act.
[1209] Sec. 186 para. 1 sentence 2 of the Stock Corporation Act.
[1210] Decisions of the Federal Supreme Court, published in BGHZ, vol. 71, pp. 40, 46 and in BGHZ, vol. 136, pp. 133, 139.

(ii) is **suitable** for attaining the intended purpose and both (iii) **necessary** and (iv) **appropriate**. No justification is necessary if all affected shareholders agree to the exclusion of the subscription rights.

Excluding the subscription rights is deemed to be in the company's interests if the exclusion is intended to promote the object of the company. It is suitable if the intended purpose can be attained by excluding the subscription rights. It is necessary if there is no other alternative to achieve the purpose or, if there are several alternatives, the purpose can be best achieved by excluding the subscription rights. The exclusion of subscription rights is appropriate if the company's interests outweigh the shareholders' interests in retaining their legal position.

In court precedents, an exclusion of subscription rights has been considered justified in the **following cases**: to avoid the creation of fractional shares due to the capital increase, to issue shares to employees, to service convertible bonds or warrant-linked bonds, in the case of an intended listing at a stock exchange or in connection with a restructuring of the company (e.g., if a potential investor claims a majority share in the company). Furthermore, the exclusion of subscription rights is generally justified in the case of a so-called "cross-exclusion of subscription rights" which is required if several classes of shares exist, further shares of each class have to be issued and the subscription right of a shareholder has to be excluded with respect to the class of shares he does not own.

The exclusion of the subscription right has become easier in the case of authorized capital following the *"Siemens/Nold"* decision of the Federal Supreme Court (see below). However, the principles established in the *"Siemens/Nold"* decision do not apply to the ordinary capital increase.

The exclusion of the subscription right is notably permitted if the capital increase against cash contribution does not exceed **10%** of the current registered share capital and the issue price is not substantially below the price on the stock exchange.[1211]

The subscription right may only be excluded in the **resolution on the capital increase**.[1212] The resolution requires in any event a majority of three quarters of the registered share capital represented at the passing of the resolution. The articles of association may only determine a greater capital majority and further requirements for the exclusion of the subscription right.[1213] Unlike in the case of an authorized capital, it is not possible to just authorize the management board to exclude the subscription rights.

An additional formal requirement for the subscription rights to be excluded is that the intended exclusion of the subscription rights has been properly **announced** in the company's designated journals, i.e., in the Federal Gazette. This announcement generally happens simultaneously with the convening of the general meeting and the announcement of the agenda.[1214]

The management board has to submit a **written report** to the general meeting in which it presents the reasons for the exclusion of the subscription rights and justifies the proposed issue price. The report must be made available during the general meeting.[1215] Furthermore, the report needs to be available for inspection in the company's offices from the date the general meeting was convened until the

---

[1211] Sec. 186 para. 3 sentence 4 of the Stock Corporation Act.
[1212] Sec. 186 para. 3 sentence 1 of the Stock Corporation Act.
[1213] Sec. 186 para. 3 sentences 1 to 3 of the Stock Corporation Act.
[1214] Sec. 186 para. 4 sentence 1 of the Stock Corporation Act.
[1215] Sec. 186 para. 4 sentence 2 of the Stock Corporation Act.

date of the general meeting.[1216] Each shareholder is entitled to request a copy of the report.[1217] The company is not obliged to keep the document available in the company's offices or to send copies to shareholders if the documents are available on the company's website from the convening of the general meeting until the general meeting.[1218]

The report must comprehensively and accurately describe the facts that justify the exclusion of the subscription rights. The proposed issue price must be justified by presenting the figures on which calculation of the issue price was based and the criteria taken into account for the valuation. It is not sufficient if the report merely refers to general valuation principles; the report needs to describe the specific situation of the company. If the general meeting is not to determine an issue price or is to only stipulate a minimum or maximum amount, reasons for this are to be given as well. As the report must take the written form, an insufficient report cannot be improved retrospectively by an oral explanation during the general meeting.

ccc) De facto Exclusion of Subscription Rights. If the exercise of the subscription rights is rendered inappropriately difficult as a result of provisions included in the resolution on the capital increase, this may be deemed a **"*de facto* exclusion of subscription rights"**. This may be the case, for example, if the issue price is considerably higher than the value of the shares. A *de facto* exclusion of subscription rights is only allowed if the requirements for a formal exclusion of the subscription rights are met or if all shareholders agree. This is usually not the case. Therefore, in most cases, resolutions on the capital increase will be subject to an action to set aside the resolution if they lead to a *de facto* exclusion of subscription rights.

ddd) Indirect Subscription Right. In practice, registered share capital increases of *AGs* listed on a stock exchange are normally handled by banks. In such cases, the company does not issue the new shares to the shareholders themselves, but commissions an underwriting agent or an underwriting syndicate to subscribe to all shares arising from the capital increase. The underwriting agent is obliged to offer shares to the shareholders who are entitled to receive the shares. The shareholders have an **indirect subscription right** which can be exercised through the underwriting agent.[1219]

A formal exclusion of subscription rights is not required in such cases.[1220] However, the resolution on the capital increase must stipulate the indirect subscription rights of the shareholders.

ee) Defects relating to the Adoption of the Resolution on the Capital Increase. In case of defects of the resolution on the capital increase, the general provisions concerning the nullity and setting aside of resolutions passed by the general meeting (see above) apply.[1221]

ff) Subscription. The new shares resulting from the capital increase are acquired by way of **subscription**. This applies to both a capital increase against cash contributions and a capital increase against contributions in kind.

[1216] Analogy to sec. 175 para. 2 sentence 1 of the Stock Corporation Act.
[1217] Analogy to sec. 175 para. 2 sentence 2 of the Stock Corporation Act.
[1218] Analogy to sec. 175 para. 2 sentence 4 of the Stock Corporation Act.
[1219] Sec. 186 para. 5 sentence 1 of the Stock Corporation Act.
[1220] Sec. 186 para. 5 sentence 1 of the Stock Corporation Act.
[1221] Sec. 241 et seq., 255 of the Stock Corporation Act.

The new shares are subscribed to by means of **subscription certificates** (*Zeichnungsscheine*). Such certificates contain **the declaration of subscription** (*Zeichnungserklärung*), i.e., the declaration that the holder intends to acquire shares from the capital increase. The certificate needs to be executed in writing and has to be issued in duplicate.[1222] According to mandatory law, certain details need to be stated on the certificate, such as the date of the resolution on the capital increase, the issue price of the shares, the amount of the stipulated payments and the scope of ancillary obligations.

With the acceptance of the declaration of subscription by the *AG*, a **subscription agreement** (*Zeichnungsvertrag*) between the shareholder and the *AG* is entered into. The subscription agreement stipulates that new shares are to be issued to the subscriber in return for the payment of cash contributions or the making of contributions in kind. The new shares enter into existence once the implementation of the capital increase is registered in the commercial register. If more shares are subscribed to than are available from the capital increase, this is referred to as **over-subscription** (*Überzeichnung*). In case of an over-subscription, the company has to fulfill the subscription rights of the existing shareholders first prior to issuing shares to third parties, unless this has been validly excluded. Otherwise, the distribution of the available shares is at the discretion of the management board, although the principle of equal treatment[1223] of shareholders may apply.

gg) Application and Registration of the Resolution and the Implementation of the Capital Increase. The management board and the chairman of the supervisory board have to apply jointly for registration of the **resolution** on the capital increase in the commercial register.[1224] The application has to be certified by a notary before being filed with the commercial register. The application needs to contain all documents required by the register court to determine the validity of the resolution on the capital increase. In particular, the minutes of the general meeting containing the resolution on the capital increase, the minutes of any necessary special resolutions and, if applicable, the report on the auditing of contributions in kind are to be attached to the application.[1225] The application has to state whether and, if applicable, which contributions have not yet been rendered on the current registered share capital and must contain an explanation as to why such contributions cannot be obtained.[1226] In case of a capital increase against contributions in kind, the commercial register may refuse the registration if the value of the contributed assets falls significantly short of the lowest issue price of the new shares.[1227]

Once the new shares have been subscribed to, the management board and the chairman of the supervisory board have to apply for **registration of the implementation** of the capital increase in the commercial register.[1228] The registration of the implementation of the capital increase effectuates the capital increase.

[1222] Sec. 185 para. 1 of the Stock Corporation Act.
[1223] Sec. 53a of the Stock Corporation Act.
[1224] Sec. 184 para. 1 sentence 1 of the Stock Corporation Act.
[1225] Sec. 184 para. 1, para. 2 of the Stock Corporation Act.
[1226] Sec. 184 para. 1 sentence 2 of the Stock Corporation Act.
[1227] Sec. 184 para. 3 sentence 1 of the Stock Corporation Act.
[1228] Sec. 188 para. 1 of the Stock Corporation Act.

c) Contingent Capital Increase

aa) General Requirements. The general meeting can resolve upon a contingent capital increase. In this case, the increase of the registered share capital will only be implemented to the extent that conversion rights or subscription rights for **new shares** (preemptive shares) granted by the *AG* are exercised.[1229]

The contingent capital increase is generally **only allowed for the following purposes**:

- granting **conversion rights or subscription rights** on the basis of convertible bonds;
- preparing **combinations of several entities**; and
- granting **subscription rights to employees and members of the management** of the company or an affiliated enterprise, often as part of stock option programs.[1230]

Additionally, a contingent capital increase may also be permissible in comparable situations which have similar effects. For example, not only convertible bonds and warrant-linked bonds may be serviced by a contingent capital increase but also other rights granting conversion or subscription rights such as convertible or warrant-linked jouissance rights.

bb) Resolution on the Contingent Capital Increase. A contingent capital increase is resolved upon by the general meeting. The resolution requires a **majority** of at least **three quarters** of the registered share capital represented at the passing of the resolution.[1231] The articles of association may only stipulate a higher capital majority and additional requirements for the adoption of the resolution.[1232]

The resolution has to stipulate the **amount of the increase**, i.e., the maximum amount up to which the registered share capital can be increased. The total amount of all contingent capital of the company must not exceed 50% of the registered share capital. (An exception to this rule applies where a contingent capital increase is resolved upon solely in order to enable the company to carry out a conversion which the company is entitled to in the case of impending insolvency or for avoidance of over-indebtedness.) The resolution on the capital increase has to further state the **nominal values** of the new shares in the case of par value shares and the **number** of shares in the case of non-par value shares. If there are different classes of shares or if different classes of shares are to be created, the **classes** of the new shares must also be stated.[1233]

In addition, the resolution on the capital increase has to stipulate the **purpose** of the contingent capital increase.[1234] Specific details must be provided. For example, in the case of a combination of business entities, the entity which is to be combined and, as far as possible, details concerning the intended combination must be stated. The resolution also has to identify the **holders of the subscription rights**.[1235] However, the holders of subscription rights do not need to be stated by name. For instance, in the case of a contingent capital increase for granting conversion rights or subscription rights to the holders of convertible bonds, it is

---

[1229] Sec. 192 et seq. of the Stock Corporation Act.
[1230] Sec. 192 para. 2 of the Stock Corporation Act.
[1231] Sec. 193 para. 1 sentence 1 of the Stock Corporation Act.
[1232] Sec. 193 para. 1 sentence 2 of the Stock Corporation Act.
[1233] Sec. 23 para. 3 no. 4 of the Stock Corporation Act.
[1234] Sec. 193 para. 2 no. 1 of the Stock Corporation Act.
[1235] Sec. 193 para. 2 no. 2 of the Stock Corporation Act.

sufficient if the resolution clearly identifies the bondholders who are entitled to the subscription or conversion rights.

Furthermore, the resolution must stipulate the **issue price** of the shares or the basis upon which the issue price is to be calculated.[1236] The prohibition of issue below par applies.[1237] If the contingent capital increase is used to service convertible bonds, it is sufficient if the minimum issue price or the principles for the determination of the (minimum) issue price are stated.

In the case of a contingent capital increase for granting **subscription rights to employees and members of the management**,[1238] the resolution on the capital increase must also stipulate the allocation of subscription rights to members of the management and employees, performance targets, acquisition and option periods, and the waiting period prior to the initial exercise of rights.[1239] The minimum waiting period is four years.

Like the resolution on an ordinary capital increase, the resolution on the contingent capital increase needs to be filed for registration with the commercial register by the management board and the chairman of the supervisory board.[1240] The register court may refuse registration of the capital increase if the value of a contribution in kind falls substantially short of the lowest issue price of the new shares.[1241]

The rules concerning the audit in case of a contribution in kind and concerning hidden contributions in kind also apply in principle in case of a contingent capital increase.

cc) Subscription Rights. There are **no subscription rights for the existing shareholders** in the event of a contingent capital increase. The resolution on the capital increase identifies the persons entitled to subscribe to new shares. The subscription rights are based on a separate agreement between the person having the subscription right and the company; the subscription rights do not directly originate from the resolution on the contingent capital increase. The separate agreement, however, may only grant subscription rights within the framework of the resolution on the contingent capital increase and only for the purpose stipulated therein.

The subscription rights are exercised by virtue of a formal declaration in which the holder of the subscription right declares that he intends to acquire the new shares (**exercise notice**, *Bezugserklärung*).[1242] The exercise notice has to be given in writing and must be issued in duplicate.[1243] The effect of the exercise notice is identical with the effect of the declaration of subscription in the case of an ordinary capital increase. It leads to the execution of a subscription agreement. Under the subscription agreement, the company is obliged to issue the preemptive shares and the subscriber is obliged to render the relevant contribution.

dd) Effectiveness of the Contingent Capital Increase. The contingent capital increase enters into effect upon the **issuing of the preemptive shares**.[1244] Therefore, the registered share capital is amended every time new shares are issued;

[1236] Sec. 193 para. 2 no. 3 of the Stock Corporation Act.
[1237] Sec. 9 para. 1 of the Stock Corporation Act.
[1238] Sec. 192 para. 2 no. 3 of the Stock Corporation Act.
[1239] Sec. 193 para. 2 no. 4 of the Stock Corporation Act.
[1240] Sec. 195 para. 1 of the Stock Corporation Act.
[1241] Sec. 195 para. 3 of the Stock Corporation Act.
[1242] Sec. 198 para. 1 sentence 1 of the Stock Corporation Act.
[1243] Sec. 198 para. 1 sentences 1 and 2 of the Stock Corporation Act.
[1244] Sec. 200 of the Stock Corporation Act.

the share book of the company is to be corrected accordingly. If convertible bonds are converted, the amount relating to the bonds needs to be corrected accordingly. Unlike an ordinary capital increase, the subsequent registration of the consummation of the contingent capital increase has only **declaratory** effect, i.e., it is not a prerequisite for the effectiveness of the capital increase.

ee) Application, Registration and Announcement of the Issue of Shares. At least once a year, until the end of one month after the end of the fiscal year at the latest, the management board has to **apply** for **registration with the commercial register** in order to register preemptive shares that have been issued.[1245] Unlike the ordinary capital increase, the chairman of the supervisory board does not need to be involved in the application. The provisions of the articles of association which have become incorrect as a result of the capital increase do not necessarily have to be amended from a legal point of view. The *AG* may delay amending the articles of association until the subscription period has fully expired. Thereafter, however, the wording of the articles of association regarding the amount of the registered share capital, the number of the shares, etc., need to be amended to reflect the new circumstances.[1246] It is advisable that the supervisory board be authorized to make such amendments in order to avoid having to convene a general meeting for this purpose.[1247]

d) Authorized Capital

aa) General Requirements. The original articles of association or the general meeting by way of a resolution amending the articles of association may authorize the management board, for a period that must not exceed five years, to increase the registered share capital up to a specified nominal amount by issuing new shares against contributions.[1248] The total amount of all authorized capital of the company must not exceed 50% of the registered share capital.

In connection with the creation of authorized registered share capital, the general meeting may also authorize the management board to exclude the subscription rights of the shareholders.

Authorized capital is very common for German *AGs*. The **advantage** of authorized capital is that new shares can be issued without having to go through the complex and time-consuming procedure of conducting a general meeting every time a capital increase is required. Instead, the authorized capital is created once or annually at the general meeting and may be used by the management if required. This gives the management board the flexibility required, for example, to issue new shares in connection with the acquisition of other companies or to make use of favorable situations in the capital markets. Compared to contingent capital, authorized capital has the additional advantage that the details of an intended combination of businesses do not need to be announced at the time the resolution of the general meeting on the creation of the authorized registered share capital is passed. The authorized capital may even be created without any specific target in mind at the time of creation.

AGs usually have more than one batch of authorized capital in existence at one time (for example, **authorized capital I and II**) which may differ with respect to

---

[1245] Sec. 201 para. 1 of the Stock Corporation Act.
[1246] Analogy to sec. 181 para. 1 sentence 2 of the Stock Corporation Act.
[1247] Sec. 179 para. 1 sentence 2 of the Stock Corporation Act.
[1248] Sec. 202 paras. 1 and 2 of the Stock Corporation Act.

their purposes, terms and other conditions. If there is more than one batch of authorized capital, at least one of such batches of authorized capital will in practice authorize the management to exclude the subscription rights. There are no legal restrictions on creating more than one batch of authorized capital, provided they do not in aggregate amount to more than 50% of registered share capital.

The creation of authorized capital also has to be registered with the commercial register. The register court may refuse registration of the capital increase if the value of a contribution in kind falls substantially short of the lowest issue price of the new shares.[1249]

The rules concerning the audit in case of a contribution in kind and concerning hidden contributions in kind also apply in principle in case of an authorized capital increase.

bb) Authorization of the Management Board. The authorization of the management board to increase capital needs to be included in the articles of association of the company. It may be included in the **original articles of association**[1250] or granted through a **subsequent amendment to the articles of association** resolved by the general meeting.[1251]

Only the general meeting may amend the articles of association in order to grant such authorization to the management board. The **resolution** of the general meeting requires a **majority of at least three quarters** of the registered share capital represented at the passing of the resolution.[1252] The articles of association may only provide for a higher capital majority or stipulate further requirements for the resolution of the general meeting. Unlike in the case of an ordinary capital increase, the articles of association cannot permit a smaller capital majority.[1253]

cc) Contents and Limits of the Authorization. The authorization allows the management board to increase the registered share capital up to a certain amount within the period of time specified by the authorization with the consent of the supervisory board. The time period may **not exceed five years** from registration of the amendment to the articles of association with the commercial register. The resolution in which the authorization is granted has to explicitly state such time period. Otherwise the resolution is null and void.

The authorization also has to stipulate the **maximum nominal amount** up to which the management board is entitled to increase the registered share capital.[1254] The resolution is null and void without this provision.

Like contingent capital, authorized capital is **limited** to a maximum of **50% of the registered share capital** available at the date of the authorization's registration with the commercial register.[1255] When determining the nominal amount of the authorized capital, any existing authorized capital which has not yet been used is to be included in the calculations. This also applies to any further authorized capital which may be decided upon at the same time. If there is contingent capital besides the authorized capital, such contingent capital does not count in determining the threshold.

[1249] Sec. 205 para. 7 of the Stock Corporation Act.
[1250] Sec. 202 para. 1 of the Stock Corporation Act.
[1251] Sec. 202 para. 2 of the Stock Corporation Act.
[1252] Sec. 202 para. 2 sentence 2 of the Stock Corporation Act.
[1253] Sec. 202 para. 2 sentence 3 of the Stock Corporation Act.
[1254] Sec. 202 para. 1 of the Stock Corporation Act.
[1255] Sec. 202 para. 3 sentence 1 of the Stock Corporation Act.

If the management board is to be authorized to implement a capital increase in return for **contributions in kind**, the authorization by the general meeting has to expressly encompass a capital increase against contributions in kind; however, the specific form of the contribution in kind does not need to be mentioned.[1256] All further specifications required in connection with a capital increase against contributions in kind (see above), such as the determination of the object of the contribution in kind and the person making the contribution, will usually be made by the management board with the consent of the supervisory board when the authorization is exercised; however, the resolution of the general meeting can also include such specifications.[1257]

If the management board is to be authorized to issue **preference shares**, this needs to be expressly stipulated in the resolution on the capital increase.[1258] The management board may also be authorized to issue all or part of the new shares to company employees.[1259]

Furthermore, the resolution on the authorization may include provisions stipulating the **purpose** for which the authorized capital is to be used and **further provisions** relating to the contents of the share rights and the **conditions governing the issuing of the shares**. If the general meeting does not specify the conditions governing the issuing of the shares, the decisions on these matters are taken by the management board with the supervisory board's consent.

dd) Exclusion of Subscription Rights. As in the case of an ordinary capital increase, the shareholders generally also have subscription rights pro rata to their current shareholding in the case of a capital increase by way of authorized capital. The subscription rights may, however, be excluded. The exclusion can be resolved upon by the general meeting itself.[1260] In practice, however, the **general meeting authorizes the management board** to exclude the subscription rights in connection with the exercise of the authorization.

As mentioned above, there are strict requirements for the exclusion of the subscription rights by the general meeting in the case of an ordinary capital increase. In particular, the exclusion of the subscription rights has to be justified.[1261] In case of a capital increase from authorized capital, the **requirements** for an exclusion of subscription rights **are lower**.

In the *"Siemens/Nold"* decision, the Federal Supreme Court held that an exclusion of the subscription rights by the general meeting itself as well as an authorization of the management board to exclude the subscription rights are possible if (i) the exclusion of the subscription rights is in the **interest of the company** and (ii) the reason for the exclusion of the subscription rights is **presented to the general meeting in an abstract and general way**.[1262]

The *"Siemens/Nold"* decision significantly facilitates the exclusion of the subscription rights in the case of capital increases from authorized capital. The **report** of the management board which is also required in the case of authorized capital[1263] may be limited to an abstract description of the measures the authorized

---

[1256] Sec. 205 para. 1 of the Stock Corporation Act.
[1257] Sec. 205 para. 2 of the Stock Corporation Act.
[1258] Sec. 204 para. 2 of the Stock Corporation Act.
[1259] Sec. 202 para. 4 of the Stock Corporation Act.
[1260] Sec. 203 para. 1, 186 para. 3 of the Stock Corporation Act.
[1261] Decision of the Federal Supreme Court, published in BGHZ, vol. 71, pp. 40, 46.
[1262] Decision of the Federal Supreme Court, published in BGHZ, vol. 136, pp. 133, 136 et seq.
[1263] Sec. 203 para. 2, 186 para. 4 sentence 2 of the Stock Corporation Act.

capital must be used for (e. g., acquisition of other companies). If such measures are considered to be in the interest of the company, the exclusion of the subscription right or the authorization of the management board to exclude the subscription right is justified.

As compensation for the limitation of shareholders' rights in the general meeting, the management board is obliged to review the justification for exclusion of the subscription rights when implementing the capital increase (see below).

The intended exclusion of the subscription rights or the authorization of the management has to be **properly announced** when convening the general meeting and announcing the agenda.[1264]

The exclusion of subscription rights is deemed permitted if the capital increase against cash contribution does not exceed **10%** of current registered share capital and the issue price is not substantially below the price on the stock exchange (see above).[1265]

The *"Siemens/Nold"* decision was issued in connection with a **capital increase against contributions in kind**. It is therefore not clear whether the principles established in the case also apply to the exclusion of subscription rights in case of a **capital increase against cash contributions**.

ee) Implementation of the Capital Increase by the Management Board. The management board decides at its **own discretion** after a due assessment of the circumstances whether, when and to what extent it utilizes the authorization to increase the registered share capital. The decision is a **management measure**, i.e., does not need to be approved by the general meeting.

Nevertheless, the management board should only issue the new shares with the **consent of the supervisory board**.[1266] The supervisory board has to grant its consent for each individual resolution on a capital increase passed by the management board. The supervisory board may not approve in advance all or several capital increases to be decided by the management by adopting a general consent resolution. However, a missing approval by the supervisory board does not affect the resolutions passed by the management board or the implementation measures effected by the management board. The register court, however, must not register the capital increase if it is aware that consent has not been granted.

If the general meeting has resolved to exclude subscription rights or has authorized the management to do so, the management is entitled to exclude the subscription rights when the capital increase is implemented. The **exclusion of the subscription right** is subject to the consent of the supervisory board (see below). When excluding the subscription right, the management board has to review whether the **exclusion is factually justified**. In principle, the same criteria apply as in the case of an exclusion of the subscription right in an ordinary capital increase (see above). The management board has to check whether the exclusion of the subscription right is in the company's interest, suitable for attaining the intended purpose and both necessary and appropriate. The *"Siemens/Nold"* decision did not change these requirements. If the management board excludes the subscription rights unlawfully, shareholders may have damage claims against the *AG*. The *AG* may have recourse claims against the members of the management board and the supervisory board. Furthermore, if the shareholders notice the

---

[1264] Sec. 203 para. 2, 186 para. 4 sentence 1 of the Stock Corporation Act.
[1265] Sec. 186 para. 3 sentence 4 of the Stock Corporation Act.
[1266] Sec. 202 para. 3 sentence 2 of the Stock Corporation Act.

unlawfulness prior to the implementation of the capital increase, they may file a claim for forbearance against the company.[1267]

The wording of the articles of association concerning the amount of the registered capital, the number of shares and the authorized capital becomes incorrect once the capital increase takes effect. The articles of association need to be corrected. This requires a separate resolution to be adopted by the general meeting unless (as is usual in practice) the supervisory board is authorized to amend the wording of the articles of association.[1268]

ff) Subscription, Payment of the Contribution and Registration of the Implementation of the Capital Increase. After the management board has decided upon the implementation of the capital increase, the new shares can be subscribed to. The same principles as in the case of an ordinary capital increase apply. Once the shares are subscribed to and the contributions are paid, an application is made for the implementation of the capital increase to be registered in the commercial register. The capital increase takes effect when the implementation is registered in the commercial register.[1269]

e) Capital Increase from Company Resources

aa) Overview. The capital increase from company resources[1270] has a different economic basis. As **capital reserves** and/or **revenue reserves** of the *AG* are **converted into registered share capital**, a capital increase from company resources does **not** lead to a **gain in funds** for the company. Instead, existing funds are converted into registered share capital.

bb) Resolution on the Capital Increase. The general meeting resolves on a capital increase from company resources with a majority of at least **three quarters** of the registered share capital represented at the passing of the resolution. The articles of association may, however, increase or reduce the required majorities and may also stipulate further requirements.[1271]

The resolution on the capital increase has to be based on a **balance sheet** having a record date at most eight months before the date at which the application for the resolution is filed with the commercial register.[1272] This may be either the last annual balance sheet or a separate interim balance sheet, the latter of which has to be drawn up by the management board and audited by an auditor.[1273]

The resolution has to stipulate the exact **amount** by which the registered share capital will be increased. The resolution also has to state that the **capital increase is to be effected by converting** capital reserves and/or revenue reserves. It must furthermore stipulate **which reserves** are to be converted and **which balance sheet** is to be taken as the basis.[1274]

cc) Application, Registration and Effectiveness of the Capital Increase. The management board and the chairman of the supervisory board have to apply jointly for the resolution on the capital increase to be registered in the commer-

---

[1267] Decision of the Federal Supreme Court, published in BGHZ, vol. 136, pp. 133, 140 et seq.
[1268] Sec. 179 para. 1 sentences 1 and 2 of the Stock Corporation Act.
[1269] Sec. 203 para. 1, 189 of the Stock Corporation Act.
[1270] Sec. 207 of the Stock Corporation Act.
[1271] Sec. 207 para. 2, 182 para. 1 of the Stock Corporation Act.
[1272] Sec. 207 para. 3, sec. 209 paras. 1 and 2 sentence 2 of the Stock Corporation Act.
[1273] Sec. 209 paras. 1, 2 and 3 of the Stock Corporation Act.
[1274] Sec. 207 para. 3, sec. 209 of the Stock Corporation Act.

cial register.[1275] The application must include the minutes of the general meeting which adopted the resolution, the revised version of the articles of association and the balance sheet upon which the capital increase is based.[1276] The parties filing the application have to declare to the commercial register that, to their knowledge, no reduction in the value of company assets has occurred between the record date of the relevant balance sheet and the date of the application to such extent as would preclude the capital increase if such resolution were to be adopted on the date of application.[1277] The capital increase becomes effective upon the registration of the resolution on the capital increase.[1278]

dd) Entitlement of Shareholders to New Shares. The capital increase from company resources is not intended to change the participation ratio of the shareholders in the company. Therefore, the existing shareholders are entitled to acquire new shares in accordance with their participation.[1279]

When distributing the new shares among the shareholders, there may be **fractional amounts** which are not sufficient to reach the par value or, in the case of non-par value shares, the proportionate amount of the registered share capital accounted for by a new share. The Stock Corporation Act provides that **fractional shares** are created in such a case. These are independent membership rights which only differ from a full share in terms of quantity. Although the fractional shares entail membership rights, such rights cannot be exercised independently. They can only be exercised if fractional shares sufficient to comprise a full share are consolidated in the hands of a single owner or if several entitled persons whose fractional shares together result in a full share join together to exercise the rights.[1280]

Unless otherwise provided in the resolution on the capital increase, the new shares **participate in the profits** of the company starting from the fiscal year in which the capital increase was resolved upon.

4. The Capital Reduction

a) Forms of Capital Reduction

The Stock Corporation Act provides for three different forms of capital reduction:
- the **ordinary capital reduction;**[1281]
- the **simplified capital reduction;**[1282] and
- the capital reduction by **redemption of shares**.[1283]

Capital reductions may be used to pay back portions of the registered share capital to the company's shareholders, a move which would otherwise not be possible due to the stringent capital preservation rules concerning stock corporations (see above). These cases, however, are very rare in practice. Typically, capital reductions are used during a **company crisis** to adjust the registered share capital as compensation for losses. A capital reduction is usually conducted in case of an

---

[1275] Sec. 207 para. 2 sentence 1, 184 para. 1 sentence 1 of the Stock Corporation Act.
[1276] Sec. 210 para. 1 sentence 1 of the Stock Corporation Act.
[1277] Sec. 210 para. 1 sentence 2 of the Stock Corporation Act.
[1278] Sec. 211 of the Stock Corporation Act.
[1279] Sec. 212 sentence 1 of the Stock Corporation Act.
[1280] Sec. 213 of the Stock Corporation Act.
[1281] Sec. 222 et seq. of the Stock Corporation Act.
[1282] Sec. 229 et seq. of the Stock Corporation Act.
[1283] Sec. 237 et seq. of the Stock Corporation Act.

adverse balance, i.e., if the equity of the company is lower than the registered share capital. Such an adverse balance may be compensated by a capital reduction. If the capital reduction is conducted during a company crisis, the **simplified capital reduction** may be used.

b) Ordinary Capital Reduction

The ordinary capital reduction is the basic type of capital reduction. There is no restriction in the Stock Corporation Act as to the purpose of an ordinary capital reduction. In particular, the ordinary capital reduction can be used to pay back equity to the shareholders.

The general meeting resolves on the reduction of the registered share capital with a **majority of at least three quarters** of the registered share capital represented at the passing of the resolution.[1284] The resolution has to contain information regarding the **purpose** and the **amount** of the capital reduction. The company's articles of association can provide for a higher capital majority and impose further requirements.

The capital reduction can be implemented either by a reduction of the par value of shares or, in the case of non-par value shares, by a reduction of the registered share capital or, in the case of par value and non-par value shares, by consolidation or redemption of shares. The resolution must state how the capital reduction is to be implemented.

The resolution on the capital reduction needs to be filed for registration in the commercial register.[1285] The reduction of the registered share capital becomes effective upon registration of the resolution.[1286]

The ordinary capital reduction releases registered share capital, which is normally preserved[1287] in favor of the **company's creditors**, to the shareholders. For this reason, the Stock Corporation Act provides that the creditors may claim security from the company unless their claims have been satisfied.[1288] Payments to shareholders may only be made six months after the announcement of the registration of the capital reduction and after creditors who claimed security have been paid or have been granted security.[1289]

c) Simplified Capital Reduction

If the registered share capital is to be reduced to adjust for a decline in value of assets, to offset other losses, or to transfer amounts from the registered share capital to the capital reserves, the registered share capital reduction may be executed through a simplified procedure.[1290] This method of reducing the registered share capital is called "simplified" because the provisions regarding the protection of creditors as stipulated in sec. 225 of the Stock Corporation Act do not apply.

The required resolution of the general meeting has to stipulate that the reduction is being made for one of the permitted purposes mentioned above. The simplified capital reduction is only permissible once there has been a release of any amount by which the statutory reserves and the capital reserves exceed 10%

[1284] Sec. 222 para. 1 sentence 1 of the Stock Corporation Act.
[1285] Sec. 223 of the Stock Corporation Act.
[1286] Sec. 224 of the Stock Corporation Act.
[1287] Sec. 57, 62, 71 of the Stock Corporation Act.
[1288] Sec. 225 of the Stock Corporation Act.
[1289] Sec. 225 para. 2 sentence 1 of the Stock Corporation Act.
[1290] Sec. 229 para. 1 sentence 1 of the Stock Corporation Act.

of the registered share capital remaining after such reduction and any amounts in the revenue reserves. A simplified capital reduction is not permissible as long as there is any profit carried forward.[1291]

The free capital obtained from the release of the capital reserves and revenue reserves and from the capital reduction may only be used to compensate for the decline in the value of assets, to offset other losses, and to transfer amounts to the capital reserves or the statutory reserves. Payments to shareholders are prohibited.[1292]

As a consequence of the simplified capital reduction, dividends must not be paid until the combined total of statutory reserves and the capital reserves has (once again) reached the level of 10% of the registered share capital.[1293] Additionally, the payment of dividends which are higher than 4% of the registered share capital is permissible only for a fiscal year which commences more than two years after the resolution on the simplified capital reduction has been adopted.

In company reorganizations, simplified capital reductions are often combined with a capital increase. In such cases, the capital reduction is necessary to make an investment attractive for a new investor or to set aside an existing adverse balance which would prohibit the capital increase because of the prohibition of an issue of shares below par.

d) Redemption of Shares

The registered share capital may also be reduced by redemption of shares. The capital reduction by redemption of shares may be used for the same purposes as the ordinary capital reduction, i.e., for repayment of registered share capital to the shareholders and for restructuring the company. In contrast to the ordinary capital reduction and the simplified capital reduction, it is possible to cancel individual shares by way of redemption. The rules concerning an ordinary capital reduction apply accordingly.

5. Debt Financing

In addition to the general means of obtaining financing, *AGs* also have the option of obtaining financing via debt capital.

a) Convertible Bonds and Warrant-Linked Bonds

aa) Contents and Economic Significance. According to sec. 221 of the Stock Corporation Act, convertible bonds are bonds which grant the creditors a conversion or subscription right with regard to shares in the company. Most recently, sec. 192, 194 and 221 of the Stock Corporation Act have been changed in order to allow for convertible bonds with a conversion right for the stock corporation itself.[1294]

A distinction needs to be made between the following forms of bonds:
- **convertible bond** (*Wandelschuldverschreibung* or *Wandelanleihe*); and
- **warrant-linked bond** (*Optionsschuldverschreibung* or *Optionsanleihe*).

[1291] Sec. 229 para. 2 of the Stock Corporation Act.
[1292] Sec. 230 of the Stock Corporation Act.
[1293] Sec. 233 para. 1 of the Stock Corporation Act.
[1294] Sec. 192 para. 2 no. 1, sec. 194 para. 1 sentence 2, sec. 221 para. 1 sentence 1 of the Stock Corporation Act.

Convertible bonds and warrant-linked bonds typically represent the right to repayment of the nominal value after reaching maturity. They are generally subject to a fixed rate of interest during their term.
- In the case of **convertible bonds**, the holder, instead of requesting repayment of the securitized claim, has the right to convert the bond into a certain number of shares after the bond reaches maturity.
- In the case of **warrant-linked bonds**, alongside the claim to interest and repayment, the holder is granted the right to acquire a certain number of shares within a certain time period for a certain price. This right may be made dependent upon further conditions. The option rights are generally securitized in separate warrants and may be separated from the actual warrant-linked bond after a certain time and transferred independently.

The legal details relating to the bonds are usually set forth in the **terms and conditions for the bond** set up by the *AG*. The conversion and option right may entail the right to acquire ordinary shares or the right to subscribe to shares of a particular class.

The economic advantage of convertible and warrant-linked bonds for the investor is the combination of fixed interest payments and the repayment of the nominal value with the prospect of being able to use the conversion or option right if the share price develops favorably. The opportunity for the investor to make a profit by way of the conversion into shares means that convertible and warrant-linked bonds are subject to a relatively low fixed rate of interest, allowing the company to benefit from this method of raising capital as well.

bb) Resolution of the General Meeting and Issue of the Bonds. Convertible and warrant-linked bonds may only be issued on the basis of a **resolution of the general meeting**.[1295] The resolution requires a majority of at least **three quarters** of the capital represented at the passing of the resolution.[1296] The articles of association may stipulate a higher or lower capital majority and further requirements.[1297] If there are several classes of shares, the resolution requires the consent of the shareholders of each class of shares by way of a special resolution.[1298]

In practice, the general meeting usually authorizes the management board to issue convertible and warrant-linked bonds. The authorization may be granted to the management board for a maximum period of five years.[1299] The authorization of the management board is only effective if the period of authorization is expressly mentioned in the resolution. Otherwise, the authorization is null and void. The prevailing view is that the total nominal value of the bonds to be issued is to be stated in the resolution granting authorization. It is, however, disputed whether or not further information needs to be given when preparing the respective shareholder resolution, such as information relating to the terms and conditions for conversion and subscription. In practice, at least the essential terms and conditions for the bonds are described in the resolution of the general meeting.

The decision to issue the bonds rests with the management board. This issuing of the bonds constitutes a management measure. The bond needs to be put into a certificate and signed by the members of the management board.[1300] Bond issues

---

[1295] Sec. 221 para. 1 sentence 1 of the Stock Corporation Act.
[1296] Sec. 221 para. 1 sentence 2 of the Stock Corporation Act.
[1297] Sec. 221 para. 1 sentence 3 of the Stock Corporation Act.
[1298] Sec. 221 para. 1 sentence 4, sec. 182 para. 2 of the Stock Corporation Act.
[1299] Sec. 221 para. 2 sentence 1 of the Stock Corporation Act.
[1300] Sec. 793 paras. 1 and 2 of the Civil Code.

are regularly conducted with the participation of an underwriting consortium; in this case the shareholders only acquire an indirect subscription right.

If the management board has been authorized to issue bonds, the management board decides in its due discretion whether and to what extent to make use of such authorization. Defects in the resolution adopted by the general meeting or the lack of such a resolution do not render the issue of the bonds invalid. However, there may be a right to damages on the part of the company against the members of the management board and the supervisory board.[1301]

The management board and the chairman of the supervisory board have to deposit the resolution adopted by the general meeting and a declaration concerning the issue of the bonds with the commercial register.[1302]

cc) Shareholders' Subscription Rights. The shareholders of a company have a **subscription right** to convertible and warrant-linked bonds. The rules concerning subscription rights in the case of a capital increase (see above) also apply in this case.[1303]

A resolution **excluding subscription rights** may be adopted by the general meeting. Alternatively, as in the case of authorized capital, the general meeting may **authorize the management board to exclude the subscription rights**. In practice, the authorization of the management is more common. The rules concerning the exclusion of subscription rights or the authorization of the management to exclude subscription rights in the case of authorized capital (see above) also apply in the case of convertible and warrant-linked bonds.

dd) Rights arising from Convertible or Warrant-Linked Bonds. The holder of a bond can exercise the subscription right by making a declaration (**conversion** or **option declaration**) in accordance with the requirements stipulated in the terms and conditions of bonds and options established by the company. The declaration is usually submitted in writing to a bank, which acts as the receiving agent.

If the shares for the conversion are made available on the basis of **contingent capital**, a formal exercise notice pursuant to sec. 198 of the Stock Corporation Act is required.

Shares may also be made available via an **ordinary capital increase** or from **authorized capital** (although the use of contingent capital is more common in practice). In this case, a formal subscription is required in addition to the conversion or option declaration.

The company may also use **own shares** for distribution to the holders of conversion rights.[1304]

ee) Securing the Conversion or Option Right. In order to ensure that the company is able to meet its obligations to the holders of the conversion and option rights, the issue of convertible and warrant-linked bonds is generally linked to the creation of **contingent capital**. Sec. 192 para. 4 of the Stock Corporation Act ensures that sufficient shares can be made available. According to this provision, any resolution passed by the general meeting contradicting the resolution on the contingent capital increase is null and void. However, if the shares required to

---

[1301] Sec. 93, 116 of the Stock Corporation Act.
[1302] Sec. 221 para. 2 sentence 2 of the Stock Corporation Act.
[1303] Sec. 221 para. 4 sentence 2, 186 of the Stock Corporation Act.
[1304] Sec. 71 para. 1 sentence 1 no. 8 of the Stock Corporation Act.

service the bonds are made available via a **regular capital increase** or via **authorized capital**, the bondholders are not protected by this provision.

As **protection against dilution** of the conversion and option rights resulting from a capital increase from company resources, the law provides that the conversion or option rights are automatically increased in the event of a capital increase from company resources.[1305] For all other cases (issue of further convertible and warrant-linked bonds, **capital increases other than from company resources**) however, there is no special protection for the holders of bonds and warrants. Therefore, the terms and conditions of the bond should contain protection of the holders of bonds and warrants against dilution. Usually, the company undertakes to reduce the original conversion or option price in the event of subsequent capital increases or the issue of further convertible or warrant-linked bonds.

In the event of **transformation measures** (e.g., mergers or spin-offs), the holders of convertible and warrant-linked bonds are generally granted equivalent rights in the acquiring entity.[1306]

ff) Special Forms

aaa) Naked Warrants. Naked warrants represent a subscription right to shares of the issuer which are neither linked to a bond nor are in combination with another means of financing. Accordingly, in return for the payment of a certain option price, the acquirer obtains the chance to make a profit if the price of the share rises. A strong opinion considers naked warrants as inadmissible except as set forth in sec. 192 para. 2 no. 3 of the Stock Corporation Act.

bbb) Stock Options. Stock option programs offer a certain group of people (in **particular, members of the management board and employees**) subscription rights to shares which are usually provided from contingent capital.

Convertible and warrant-linked bonds may be issued to the participants in a stock option program. Such bonds can be exercised after a certain increase in the stock price has occurred (or other targets have been reached) and a certain waiting period has expired. The price for the exercising of the right is either determined according to the stock exchange price at the time the option is granted or the stock exchange price at the time the option is exercised after a performance-related deduction has been made.

Stock option programs are predominantly offered to **members of the management board**, but they may also be offered to **employees below management board level** as well as to management board members and employees of affiliated companies. It was usual practice to offer stock option plans also to **members of the supervisory board**. In 2004, the Federal Supreme Court decided that it is unlawful to grant stock options to members of the supervisory board of the company or of affiliated companies. Stock options which are nevertheless granted are null and void.[1307]

The implementation of a stock option plan requires that the shareholders' **statutory subscription rights** are **excluded**. The exclusion of the subscription rights is deemed justified if the conditions and the volume of the stock option program are appropriate.

It is also possible to issue **independent subscription rights** through the creation of contingent capital in the form of **naked warrants** which can be exercised

---

[1305] Sec. 216 para. 3, sec. 218 of the Stock Corporation Act.
[1306] Sec. 23, sec. 36 para. 1, sec. 125, sec. 204 of the Transformation Act.
[1307] Decision of the Federal Supreme Court, published in BGHZ, vol. 158, pp. 122 et seq.

once certain predetermined performance targets have been met and waiting periods have expired.[1308] The holders can then acquire an agreed number of shares in the issuing entity for a certain price within a certain predetermined exercise period. Pursuant to sec. 192 para. 2 no. 3 of the Stock Corporation Act, these independent subscription rights can be issued to **employees** and **members of the management** (including those in affiliated companies). The law does **not** provide for such rights to be issued to members of the **supervisory board**.

Contingent capital is created in accordance with the general requirements for the passing of a resolution on a contingent capital increase (see above). However, the nominal amount of contingent capital for the purpose of stock option plans may not exceed 10% of the registered share capital which is available at the time the relevant resolution is passed.[1309] The resolution has to state the issue amount, the people to whom the plan is addressed, the performance targets, acquisition and exercise periods and the waiting period with respect to the initial exercise (which must be at least four years).[1310] In the case of contingent capital, there is no need to exclude the shareholders' subscription rights. In practice, companies have in many cases granted independent subscription rights as part of a stock option plan.

In addition, companies also have the opportunity of servicing a stock option program for members of the **management board** and **employees** by using **own shares**.[1311]

gg) Conversion and Option Rights for Bonds from Other Entities.

Conversion and option rights may also be issued for **shares in other entities**. In this case, sec. 221 of the Stock Corporation Act does not apply. In such cases, there is no requirement for authorization by the general meeting of the issuing entity or for the shareholders' subscription rights to be excluded.

If, however, the other company whose shares are the subject of the conversion or option rights is to **guarantee** performance of the bond, sec. 221 of the Stock Corporation Act applies accordingly. Such arrangements are often found in the case of **foreign subsidiaries** of German parent companies. As a rule, the parent company issues the warrants which grant the holders the right to subscribe to shares. These warrants are attached to the bonds issued by the subsidiary. The German parent company creates contingent capital for the purpose of meeting its obligations. Views differ whether it is necessary for the companies to be affiliated within a group of companies in order to be entitled to enter into such an arrangement.

b) Dividend Bonds

Pursuant to sec. 221 para. 1 sentence 1 of the Stock Corporation Act, dividend bonds are bonds which promise additional benefits to the respective holder. Such benefits are not membership rights under stock corporation law, but rather contractual claims against the company, the value of which depends on the profit made by the company. The company is free to determine the terms of a dividend bond. The resolution is passed by the general meeting and the dividend bonds are issued in accordance with the same rules as apply to convertible and warrant-linked bonds. In practice, dividend bonds are of almost no significance.

[1308] Sec. 192 para. 2 no. 3 of the Stock Corporation Act.
[1309] Sec. 192 para. 3 sentence 1 of the Stock Corporation Act.
[1310] Sec. 193 para. 2 no. 4 of the Stock Corporation Act.
[1311] Sec. 71 para. 1 sentence 1 no. 8 of the Stock Corporation Act.

c) Jouissance Rights

Jouissance rights may provide rights to participate in profits or in the distribution of assets remaining after liquidation, but also rights to benefits of widely varying types. Jouissance rights are claims under contract, not membership rights. Jouissance rights are normally embodied in **jouissance certificates**.

The company is largely free to establish jouissance rights as it wishes. Issuing jouissance rights usually serves to grant advantages to the founders of the *AG*, provide remuneration for licenses and render compensation to shareholders whose shares are redeemed. Today, jouissance rights are mainly issued as a means of **employee participation** or for the purposes of **generating additional capital**.

Jouissance rights can be **issued** in return for a cash payment, in return for the transfer of assets or gratuitously. The resolution passed by the general meeting and the shareholders' subscription rights are governed by the same rules as apply to convertible and warrant-linked bonds.[1312]

VII. Dissolution and Liquidation of the Company

The dissolution of a company is implemented in two steps: first the company is dissolved by a resolution of the general meeting or declared to be null and void; afterwards, the company undergoes the liquidation procedure until it finally ceases to exist.

1. Dissolution and Grounds for Dissolution

Upon dissolution, the object of the *AG* changes from doing business and generating profits to liquidation, i.e., liquidating the company's assets, satisfying claims of the creditors and distributing the excess assets to the shareholders. The reasons for dissolution are essentially as follows:

a) Expiration of a Period of Time

If the articles of association stipulate a certain period of time for the duration of the *AG*, the *AG* is dissolved upon the expiration of such period unless the shareholders agree on a continuation.[1313]

b) Dissolution Resolution

The *AG* may be dissolved at any time by way of a resolution adopted by the general meeting.[1314] The resolution requires a majority of at least three quarters of the registered share capital represented at the passing of the resolution. This majority requirement may be increased by the articles of association. Foreign relocation of the administration of the company no longer leads to a dissolution of the company; however, the registered office of the company must remain in Germany.[1315]

c) Defect of the Articles of Association

If the register court declares, pursuant to sec. 399 of the Act on Procedure in Family Matters and Matters of Non-Contentious Jurisdiction, that certain essential

---

[1312] Sec. 221 para. 3, 221 para. 1 of the Stock Corporation Act.
[1313] Sec. 262 para. 1 no. 1 of the Stock Corporation Act.
[1314] Sec. 262 para. 1 no. 2 of the Stock Corporation Act.
[1315] Sec. 5 of the Stock Corporation Act.

provisions in the articles of association are missing or null and void, the *AG* is dissolved once the official declaration to this effect has become legally binding.[1316] Before making such a declaration, however, the register court has to issue a notice of defect in order to give the company the opportunity to remedy the defect in question.

d) Insolvency

The institution of insolvency proceedings against the *AG's* assets and the binding rejection of the institution of such proceedings due to a lack of assets constitute a reason for the dissolution of the company.[1317] Insolvency proceedings are to be instituted if a company is illiquid or over-indebted.[1318] Insolvency proceedings may only be instituted if the remaining assets of the debtor will probably suffice to cover the costs of the proceedings.[1319] If this is not the case, the institution of such proceedings is rejected. The dissolution will be registered in the commercial register *ex officio* by the court.

e) Deletion Due to Lack of Assets

Sec. 394 of the Act on Procedure in Family Matters and Matters of Non-Contentious Jurisdiction allows for the deletion of an *AG* which does not possess any assets from the commercial register. The deletion leads to the dissolution of the *AG*.[1320]

The management board is obliged to apply for the **dissolution** to be **registered in the commercial register**. The deletion may also be initiated ex officio by the court.[1321]

2. Declaration of Nullity by a Court upon Application

Shareholders and members of the management board may bring an action to declare the company null and void.[1322] A prerequisite for such an action is that the articles of association do not contain any provisions relating to the amount of the registered share capital or the object of the company or that the provisions in the articles of association concerning the object of the company are null and void. Furthermore, the claim can only be brought within three years of the company being registered in the commercial register.[1323]

3. Liquidation

In principle, the dissolution of the *AG* leads to the initiation of liquidation proceedings conducted by the liquidators.[1324] The only exception to this rule applies in the event of the institution of insolvency proceedings or deletion as a result of a lack of assets. In the first case, insolvency proceedings take place instead of

---

[1316] Sec. 262 para. 1 no. 5 of the Stock Corporation Act.
[1317] Sec. 262 para. 1 nos. 3 and 4 of the Stock Corporation Act.
[1318] Sec. 17 et seq. of the Insolvency Act.
[1319] Sec. 26 para. 1 sentence 1 of the Insolvency Act.
[1320] Sec. 262 para. 1 no. 6 of the Stock Corporation Act.
[1321] Sec. 263 of the Stock Corporation Act.
[1322] Sec. 275 para. 1 of the Stock Corporation Act.
[1323] Sec. 275 para. 3 of the Stock Corporation Act.
[1324] Sec. 264 para. 1 of the Stock Corporation Act.

VII. Dissolution and Liquidation of the Company

liquidation; after the finalization of the insolvency proceedings, which are run by the court-appointed insolvency administrator, the company ceases to exist. In the second instance, liquidation only takes place if it becomes apparent after the deletion that distributable assets are available despite the deletion.[1325]

Liquidation also takes place if the nullity of a company is registered in the commercial register on the basis of a final, binding judgment or a register court decision.[1326] The provisions concerning the liquidation in the event of dissolution also apply to the liquidation in case of the nullity of the company.[1327]

a) Liquidators

The liquidation is conducted by so-called liquidators, who act in place of the management board. Generally, the liquidators are identical to the former members of the management board.[1328] The articles of association or a resolution of the general meeting may appoint other persons as liquidators.

In addition, the liquidators may be appointed and dismissed by a court, which is only possible for cause. The application can be filed by the supervisory board or a qualified minority of shareholders (at least 5% of the registered share capital or a proportionate amount of EUR 500,000).[1329]

The service contracts of the members of the management board continue to apply while they are performing their duties as liquidators. The members of the management board are generally obliged to accept the duties they have as liquidators of the company.

Because the liquidators act on behalf of the company instead of the management board, the liquidators have to be **registered** in the **commercial register**.[1330] The application for registration of the initial liquidators is to be filed by the management board. Any applications regarding subsequent changes in the person of the liquidators are to be filed by the liquidators.

b) Duties of the Liquidators

In general, the liquidators are responsible for winding up current transactions, collecting claims, turning the remaining assets into cash and satisfying the claims of the creditors.[1331] Apart from that, they have the same rights and duties as the management board. They manage the company at their own discretion within the limits imposed by the objective of liquidation.[1332] The purpose of liquidation forces the liquidators to act in the interests of the creditors and of the shareholders to accumulate the largest possible amount of distributable assets.

The liquidators represent the company both in and out of court.[1333] Like the management board of the company, the liquidators are subject to supervision by the supervisory board.[1334]

[1325] Sec. 264 para. 2 of the Stock Corporation Act.
[1326] Sec. 277 para. 1 of the Stock Corporation Act.
[1327] Sec. 277 para. 1 of the Stock Corporation Act.
[1328] Sec. 265 para. 1 of the Stock Corporation Act.
[1329] Sec. 265 para. 3 of the Stock Corporation Act.
[1330] Sec. 266 of the Stock Corporation Act.
[1331] Sec. 268 of the Stock Corporation Act.
[1332] Analogy to sec. 76 of the Stock Corporation Act.
[1333] Sec. 269 of the Stock Corporation Act.
[1334] Sec. 268 para. 2 of the Stock Corporation Act.

Immediately following the dissolution, the liquidators have to call upon the creditors to **register** their **claims** referring to the dissolution of the company. Such call is to be published electronically in the Federal Gazette.[1335]

The company assets remaining after all liabilities have been settled are distributed among the shareholders.[1336] Such distribution is effected in accordance with the percentage held by each of the shareholders in the registered share capital. A deviation from this rule can only apply if there are shares granting different rights relating to the distribution of the company's assets.[1337]

The assets may not be distributed earlier than one year after the date on which the call to the creditors was published.[1338]

c) Accounting

The liquidators have to draw up a balance sheet as of the opening of the liquidation proceedings (opening balance sheet) and a report explaining the opening balance sheet. The provisions governing the annual financial statements apply accordingly to the opening balance sheet and the explanatory report.[1339] In contrast to a normal balance sheet, fixed assets have to be treated as current assets, provided they are intended to be sold within a foreseeable period or are no longer required for the operation of the business. The liquidators are also obligated to draw up annual financial statements for the liquidation and the management reports. The provisions governing the annual financial statements apply accordingly.

In addition, the liquidators have to submit final accounts prior to the conclusion of the liquidation proceedings.[1340] The Stock Corporation Act does not provide further details regarding the contents of such final accounts. As this obligation concerns the general duty to render accounts, a balance sheet is not necessary. Instead, it is sufficient for a proper compilation of receipts and expenses to be submitted together with the appropriate documents.

d) Completion of Liquidation

The liquidators have to apply for the completion of liquidation to be registered in the commercial register as soon as the liquidation has been completed and the final accounts have been rendered. The liquidation is deemed to be complete once all current transactions have been concluded, the creditors have been satisfied and the remaining assets have been distributed amongst the shareholders. If the requirements for registration are met, the register court orders the registration of the completion of liquidation and the **deletion** of the company.[1341]

e) Continuation of a Dissolved Company

The general meeting may interrupt liquidation proceedings at any time and adopt a resolution stipulating the continuation of the company provided the liquidators have not yet begun to distribute the remaining assets among the shareholders. A continuation of the company by way of shareholder resolution is, however, only

---

[1335] Sec. 267 of the Stock Corporation Act.
[1336] Sec. 271 para. 1 of the Stock Corporation Act.
[1337] Sec. 271 para. 2 of the Stock Corporation Act.
[1338] Sec. 272 para. 1 of the Stock Corporation Act.
[1339] Sec. 270 para. 2 of the Stock Corporation Act.
[1340] Sec. 273 para. 1 of the Stock Corporation Act.
[1341] Sec. 273 para. 1 of the Stock Corporation Act.

possible if the company was dissolved as a result of the expiration of a fixed period of time or on the basis of a resolution passed by the general meeting.

VIII. Accounting

1. Introduction

Accounting in *AGs* only differs from accounting in limited liability companies in a few aspects. Generally, the accounting provisions stipulated in the Commercial Code apply. In particular, *AGs* are also divided into three categories depending on size (small, medium-sized and large corporations) (see above). Special provisions stipulated in the Stock Corporation Act apply in addition to the general provisions of the Commercial Code.

As companies become more and more interconnected, it is common for an *AG* to be subject to the provisions applicable to groups of companies. If it is a controlled company, the *AG* may be obligated to draw up a report on relations with the controlling company[1342] and if it is a controlling company, it may be subject to the accounting provisions applicable to groups of companies.[1343]

2. Annual Financial Statements

a) Preparation of the Annual Financial Statements

The annual financial statements of an *AG* consist of the balance sheet, the profit and loss statement and the notes.[1344] The management report provides information concerning the course of business of the *AG* and also includes prognoses for the future.[1345] The annual financial statements of a capital market-oriented *AG* must include a cash flow statement and a statement of stockholders' equity, and they may include a segment report.[1346]

The management board is responsible for drawing up the annual financial statements and the management report.[1347] The annual financial statements and the management report have to be drawn up within three months of the end of the fiscal year.[1348] Special terms apply to small corporations. They are not obligated to draw up a management report and are generally also allowed to draw up the annual financial statements within six months of the end of the fiscal year.[1349]

The Stock Corporation Act contains several special provisions regarding the drawing up of the annual financial statements that differ from the provisions which apply according to commercial law:

- The *AG* is subject to a further obligation to create **statutory reserves**.[1350] Five percent of the annual net income after deduction of any loss carried forward from the previous year is to be allocated to the statutory reserves. This obligation applies until the statutory reserves and the capital reserves reach 10%

[1342] Sec. 312 et seq. of the Stock Corporation Act.
[1343] Sec. 290 et seq. of the Commercial Code.
[1344] Sec. 242, 264 para. 1 sentence 1 of the Commercial Code.
[1345] Sec. 289 of the Commercial Code.
[1346] Sec. 264 para. 1 sentence 2 of the Commercial Code.
[1347] Sec. 264 para. 1 sentence 1 of the Commercial Code, sec. 78 para. 1 of the Stock Corporation Act.
[1348] Sec. 264 para. 1 sentence 3 of the Commercial Code.
[1349] Sec. 264 para. 1 sentence 4 of the Commercial Code.
[1350] Sec. 150 para. 1 of the Stock Corporation Act.

of the registered share capital.[1351] The articles of association may stipulate a higher percentage.
- The registered capital of an *AG* is to be shown as subscribed capital on the **balance sheet**.[1352] The amount of the registered share capital accounted for by each class of shares has to be stated separately.[1353] Contingent capital has to be shown at its nominal value.[1354] If there are multiple voting shares, their respective voting rights have to be stated separately.[1355] Exceptions to these rules apply under certain circumstances to very small AGs *("Kleinstkapitalgesellschaften")* as defined by sec. 267a of the Commercial Code.[1356]
- If the management board and the supervisory board jointly approve the annual financial statements, they have far-reaching discretion regarding the appropriation of the annual net income while drawing up the annual financial statements (see above). As a consequence, the following positions have to be added to the **profit and loss statement**: profit or loss carried forward from the previous year, withdrawals from the capital reserves, withdrawals from revenue reserves and the balance sheet profit or balance sheet loss.[1357] Alternatively, the company may provide this information in the notes.[1358] Exceptions to these rules apply under certain circumstances to very small AGs *("Kleinstkapitalgesellschaften")* as defined by sec. 267a of the Commercial Code.[1359]
- In addition to the general provisions stipulated in the Commercial Code,[1360] stock corporation law includes provisions regarding the contents of the **notes**. In this regard, detailed information has to be given concerning treasury stock, the company's own shares, classes of shares, authorized capital, the number of subscription rights according to sec. 192 para. 2 no. 3 of the Stock Corporation Act, cross-shareholdings and certain participations which are subject to disclosure under *AG* or securities trading law.[1361] Exceptions to these rules apply under certain circumstances to very small AGs *("Kleinstkapitalgesellschaften")* as defined by sec. 267a of the Commercial Code.[1362]

b) Audit of the Annual Financial Statements

The annual financial statements are to be audited by an **auditor of annual financial statements** and the **supervisory board**. As the audit conducted by the auditor largely corresponds to the audit of a limited liability company as described above, the following merely describes certain peculiarities relating to the Stock Corporation Act.

The **auditor** of annual financial statements for the following fiscal year is appointed by the general meeting.[1363] It is, however, the supervisory board which

---

[1351] Sec. 150 para. 2 of the Stock Corporation Act.
[1352] Sec. 152 para. 1 sentence 1 of the Stock Corporation Act.
[1353] Sec. 152 para. 1 sentence 2 of the Stock Corporation Act.
[1354] Sec. 152 para. 1 sentence 3 of the Stock Corporation Act.
[1355] Sec. 152 para. 1 sentence 4 of the Stock Corporation Act.
[1356] Sec. 152 para. 4 sentence 1 of the Stock Corporation Act.
[1357] Sec. 158 para. 1 sentence 1 of the Stock Corporation Act.
[1358] Sec. 158 para. 1 sentence 2 of the Stock Corporation Act.
[1359] Sec. 158 para. 3 of the Stock Corporation Act.
[1360] Sec. 284 et seq. of the Commercial Code.
[1361] Sec. 160 para. 1 of the Stock Corporation Act.
[1362] Sec. 160 para. 3 of the Stock Corporation Act.
[1363] Sec. 119 para. 1 no. 4 of the Stock Corporation Act.

commissions the audit.[1364] The auditor of annual financial statements forwards the audit report to the supervisory board after having given the management board the opportunity to comment.[1365]

The management board submits the annual financial statements and the management report to the supervisory board without undue delay.[1366] At the same time, it also provides the supervisory board with a proposal for the appropriation of the balance sheet profit, which must also be submitted to the general meeting.[1367] The law stipulates the following format for such proposal:[1368] (1) distribution to shareholders, (2) allocation to revenue reserves, (3) profit carried forward, and (4) balance sheet profit. Every member of the supervisory board is entitled to take note of the proposal submitted by the management board and the audit report submitted by the auditor of annual financial statements.[1369]

The **supervisory board** has to inspect the annual financial statements, the management report and the proposal for the appropriation of profits within one month of their receipt.[1370] The supervisory board may delegate the responsibility for such inspection to a committee for preparatory purposes, but in no event for the purpose of passing a resolution.[1371] The supervisory board must examine independently whether the accounts submitted by the management board are lawful and appropriate. With regard to the legality of the accounts, the task to be met by the supervisory board overlaps with that of the auditor of annual financial statements. This does not, however, mean that the supervisory board is obliged to audit the annual financial statements as intensely as the auditor. As a rule, the supervisory board, which generally does not have extensive specialist knowledge regarding accounting, can rely on the audit conducted by the expert auditor. It is only obliged to conduct a more extensive investigation if reservations are made in the auditor's report. The personal requirements for members of the supervisory board in capital market-oriented corporations, however, have recently been enhanced. One member of the supervisory board must have expert knowledge in the field of accounting or auditing of financial statements; if an audit committee is established, at least one of its members must have such expert knowledge as well.[1372]

In contrast to the auditors, the supervisory board not only reviews the legality but also the appropriateness of the annual accounts, e. g., checks the discretionary decisions taken by the management board regarding balance sheet policy in light of the company's interests. The supervisory board has to provide the general meeting with a written report on the results of the inspection.[1373] This report must state in what manner and to what extent the management of the company has been inspected during the fiscal year, include a comment on the results of the audit of the annual financial statements conducted by the auditor of annual financial statements and give a final declaration as to whether or not the supervisory board approves the annual financial statements. In the case of listed companies,

---

[1364] Sec. 111 para. 2 sentence 3 of the Stock Corporation Act.
[1365] Sec. 321 para. 5 sentence 2 of the Commercial Code.
[1366] Sec. 170 para. 1 sentence 1 of the Stock Corporation Act.
[1367] Sec. 170 para. 2 sentence 1 of the Stock Corporation Act.
[1368] Sec. 170 para. 2 sentence 2 of the Stock Corporation Act.
[1369] Sec. 170 para. 3 sentence 1 of the Stock Corporation Act.
[1370] Sec. 171 para. 1 sentence 1, para. 3 sentence 1 of the Stock Corporation Act.
[1371] Sec. 107 para. 3 sentence 2 and 3 of the Stock Corporation Act.
[1372] Sec. 100 para. 5, 107 para. 4 of the Stock Corporation Act.
[1373] Sec. 171 para. 2 sentence 1 of the Stock Corporation Act.

c) Formal Approval of the Annual Financial Statements

Once the annual financial statements have been drawn up, they must be formally approved. The Stock Corporation Act offers **two alternatives** for approval: the formal approval granted jointly by the management board and the supervisory board and the formal approval granted by the general meeting.

Formal approval by the management board and the supervisory board is the rule. In this case, the supervisory board approves the proposal made by the management board.[1375] The resolution granting approval is passed by a plenary session of the supervisory board. The annual financial statements are formally approved once such approval has been given.

The **general meeting** is only responsible for granting formal approval for the annual financial statements in exceptional cases, namely if the supervisory board does not approve the management board's proposal or if the management board and supervisory board have decided to seek formal approval from the general meeting.[1376]

The **decision regarding the appropriation of the balance sheet profit** is in all instances the responsibility of the general meeting (see above).[1377] Within the framework of the decision regarding the appropriation of the balance sheet profit, further amounts may be allocated to the revenue reserves or carried forward as profit.[1378]

Regarding the submission of the annual financial statements and related documents to the electronic Federal Gazette and publication, the same principles as in the case of a limited liability company apply (see above). However, certain capital market-oriented corporations have to disclose the annual financial statements within four months after the end of the fiscal year.[1379]

d) Contestation of the Annual Financial Statements

If the annual financial statements are formally approved by the general meeting, the rules concerning the setting aside of resolutions passed by the general meeting apply (see above).[1380] Furthermore, the Stock Corporation Act contains a special provision regarding the assertion of nullity which also applies if the financial statements are formally approved by the management board and the supervisory board jointly.[1381] In both instances, however, only certain violations of the law or the articles of association, which are expressly mentioned in the law, lead to the annual financial statements being declared invalid.[1382]

[1374] Sec. 171 para. 2 of the Stock Corporation Act.
[1375] Sec. 172 sentence 1 of the Stock Corporation Act.
[1376] Sec. 173 para. 1 sentence 1 of the Stock Corporation Act.
[1377] Sec. 119 para. 1 no. 2, sec. 174 para. 1 sentence 1 of the Stock Corporation Act.
[1378] Sec. 174 para. 2 of the Stock Corporation Act.
[1379] Sec. 325 para. 4 sentence 1 of the Commercial Code.
[1380] Sec. 257 para. 1 sentence 1, 243 of the Stock Corporation Act.
[1381] Sec. 256 of the Stock Corporation Act.
[1382] Sec. 256 of the Stock Corporation Act.

3. Consolidated Financial Statements

a) Introduction

The annual financial statements of individual affiliated companies often present an inadequate picture of the financial situation and profitability of the parent company or the subsidiary. In order to obtain a more realistic picture, the groups of companies are obligated to draw up consolidated financial statements.

The law governing consolidated financial statements was originally included in stock corporation law. Since 1985, however, uniform rules applicable to all corporations (not only *AGs*) have been stipulated in the Commercial Code.[1383]

b) Obligation to draw up Consolidated Financial Statements

The **obligation** to draw up consolidated financial statements applies with respect to German parent entities who can exert, directly or indirectly, a dominating influence on one or more subsidiaries.[1384] A dominating influence is deemed to be present whenever the parent company (1) holds the majority of voting rights in a subsidiary,[1385] (2) is a shareholder in the subsidiary and is entitled to appoint or dismiss the majority of the members of the administrative, management or supervisory legal bodies which determine financial and business policy,[1386] (3) is entitled to determine financial and business policy on the basis of a domination agreement entered into with the entity in question or on the basis of the articles of association of such entity,[1387] or (4) in an economic sense bears the risks and rewards of a company which serves a limited and specific purpose of the parent entity.[1388] The influence can be exercised either directly by the parent entity itself or indirectly by subsidiaries or other persons or entities acting on behalf of the parent entity.[1389]

There are certain **exemptions from the obligation** to draw up consolidated financial statements. In particular, the obligation may not apply **due to the size of the group** if the following thresholds are not exceeded: (1) balance sheet total of the affiliated enterprises (in case of individual financial statements) of EUR 24,000,000, (2) total turnover of the affiliated enterprises (in case of individual financial statements) of EUR 48,000,000 or (3) 250 employees in the group on a yearly average[1390] or, alternatively, if the following thresholds are not exceeded: (1) balance sheet total of the group (in case of consolidated financial statements) of EUR 20,000,000, (2) turnover of the group (in case of consolidated financial statements) of EUR 40,000,000 or (3) 250 employees in the group on a yearly average.[1391] Such exemptions do not apply if the parent entity or one of the entities to be included in the consolidated financial statements is a capital market-oriented corporation, i.e., either participates in an organized market for securities or has applied for admission to such a market.[1392]

[1383] Sec. 290 to 315a of the Commercial Code.
[1384] Sec. 290 para. 1 of the Commercial Code.
[1385] Sec. 290 para. 2 no. 1 of the Commercial Code.
[1386] Sec. 290 para. 2 no. 2 of the Commercial Code.
[1387] Sec. 290 para. 2 no. 3 of the Commercial Code.
[1388] Sec. 290 para. 2 no. 4 of the Commercial Code.
[1389] Sec. 290 para. 3 sentence 1 of the Commercial Code.
[1390] Sec. 293 para. 1 sentence 1 no. 1 of the Commercial Code.
[1391] Sec. 293 para. 1 sentence 1 no. 2 of the Commercial Code.
[1392] Sec. 293 para. 5 of the Commercial Code.

Furthermore, there are exemptions due to the **preparation of financial statements in accordance with IAS**. An entity the securities of which are admitted for trading in an organized market in the European Union or which has applied for admission to such a market must draw up the consolidated financial statements and the consolidated management report in accordance with IAS and is exempt from drawing up consolidated financial statements in accordance with the Commercial Code.[1393] Other entities may choose to draw up their consolidated financial statements and the management report in accordance with IAS instead of with the Commercial Code.[1394]

c) Content, Preparation and Approval of the Consolidated Financial Statements

The consolidated financial statements consist of a **consolidated balance sheet**, a **consolidated profit and loss statement, consolidated notes**, a **capital flow calculation** and an **equity statement**.[1395] The consolidated financial statements may include a segment report.[1396] Furthermore, a **consolidated management report** has to be drawn up.[1397] This corresponds to the management report, but refers to the situation of the group. The consolidated financial statements ought to present the financial situation and profitability of the group entities as though they formed a single entity.[1398]

If the obligation to draw up consolidated financial statements applies, the **management board** of the parent company is obligated to draw up consolidated financial statements and a consolidated management report within the first five months of the group fiscal year, or, in case of certain capital market-oriented corporations, generally within four months.[1399] The consolidated financial statements are audited by **an auditor of annual financial statements**.[1400] Together with the ordinary annual financial statements, the consolidated financial statements are examined by the **supervisory board**[1401] which **approves** the consolidated financial statements if there are no objections.[1402] In contrast to the ordinary financial statements, the consolidated financial statements are not formally determined (*festgestellt*). The general disclosure requirements in the electronic Federal Gazette also apply to the consolidated financial statements.[1403]

IX. Group of Companies

1. Purpose of the Law

Germany has a codified law governing groups of companies. The relevant statutory provisions were adopted in 1965 as part of a reform of the Stock Corporation Act. By creating these new regulations, the legislature sought to take account of

---

[1393] Sec. 315a paras. 1 and 2 of the Commercial Code.
[1394] Sec. 315a para. 3 of the Commercial Code.
[1395] Sec. 297 para. 1 sentence 1 of the Commercial Code.
[1396] Sec. 297 para. 1 sentence 2 of the Commercial Code.
[1397] Sec. 315 of the Commercial Code.
[1398] Sec. 297 para. 3 sentence 1 of the Commercial Code.
[1399] Sec. 290 para. 1 of the Commercial Code.
[1400] Sec. 316 para. 2 of the Commercial Code.
[1401] Sec. 171 para. 1 sentence 1 of the Stock Corporation Act.
[1402] Sec. 171 para. 2 sentences 4 and 5 of the Stock Corporation Act.
[1403] Sec. 325 para. 3 of the Commercial Code.

the increasing concentration of companies. More and more companies are not independent, but are majority-owned by another company or contractually bound to a group of companies (*Konzern*). The provisions governing groups of companies attempt to resolve the conflict between the interests of the dependent company and those of the controlling company and the group of companies. These provisions primarily deal with the protection of the minority shareholders and the creditors of the controlled enterprise.

2. Legal Form of Affiliated Enterprises

The Stock Corporation Act sets forth general definitions concerning affiliation, control and company groups. These definitions are not specific to *AGs* but apply to all kinds of entities.[1404] Apart from that, the Act directly regulates the consequences of a relationship of control only for situations in which the controlled enterprise is an *AG* or a partnership limited by shares (*KGaA*). The legal form of the controlling enterprise is irrelevant. In fact, the term "enterprise" is neutral as far as legal form is concerned. A **controlling entity** can be a corporation, a partnership, a cooperative (*Genossenschaft*), a foundation (*Stiftung*) and the like, as well as a natural person or a non-commercial partnership. The Federal Supreme Court has recognized the Federal Republic of Germany as an enterprise with respect to its shareholding in the former VEBA AG, as well as the State of Lower Saxony with respect to its shareholding in Volkswagen AG.[1405] In both cases, the Federal Supreme Court found that these entities constituted publicly-owned enterprises, because they pursued their own entrepreneurial interests above and beyond those of their shareholders, resulting in the typical conflict situations against which the law on groups of companies sought to provide protection.

If the **controlled entity** is not an *AG* or a *KGaA*, but rather a *GmbH* or a partnership, it is subject to the provisions relevant to the respective legal form. In the case of a *GmbH* and of partnerships (*OHG*, *KG*), however, there is no codified law governing company groups, but merely rules developed from the case law, some of which have been developed from the provisions governing groups of *AGs*.

3. Forms of Affiliation

a) Overview

Companies are considered to be affiliated (*verbunden*) in each of the cases outlined below pursuant to sec. 15 of the Stock Corporation Act. Legal documents frequently define the term "affiliate" or "affiliated enterprise" by referring to "sec. 15 et seq. of the Stock Corporation Act".

Many provisions in the Stock Corporation Act, the Commercial Code and in other statutes attach legal consequences based upon affiliation in general. Frequently, however, the statutes refer only to certain forms of affiliation.

[1404] Sec. 15 et seq. of the Stock Corporation Act.
[1405] Decisions of the Federal Supreme Court, published in BGHZ, vol. 69, pp. 334 et seq. and in BGHZ, vol. 135 pp. 107 et seq.

Term	Definition	Stock Corporation Act
Majority-held and majority holding companies	Majority holdings calculated based on the registered share capital or the voting rights	Sec. 16
Controlled and controlling enterprises	The controlling enterprise can, directly or indirectly, exert a dominant influence over the controlled enterprise. If an enterprise holds a majority in another, it is presumed that the latter is controlled by the former.	Sec. 17
Group companies	Either a controlling and one or more controlled enterprises are subject to the uniform control of the controlling enterprise (*Unterordnungskonzern*) or legally separate enterprises not controlled by another enterprise but are affiliated under uniform control (*Gleichordnungskonzern*)	Sec. 18
Enterprises with cross-shareholdings	The enterprises (which must be corporations with their registered office in Germany) are affiliated with each other in such manner that each of them holds more than 25% of the shares in the other enterprise.	Sec. 19
Parties to an enterprise agreement	Enterprise agreements within the meaning of the law governing groups of companies are:	Sec. 15
	– **Domination Agreement** The company submits to the direction of another enterprise which can issue directives to it	Sec. 291
	– **Profit and Loss Transfer Agreement** The company undertakes to pay its entire profit to another enterprise	Sec. 291
	– **Profit Pool** The company undertakes to pool in whole or in part its profits or the profits of certain of its operations with the profits of other enterprises or certain operations of other enterprises with a view to sharing pooled profits	Sec. 292 para. 1 no. 1
	– **Partial Profit Transfer Agreement** The company undertakes to transfer, in whole or in part, a share of its profit or the profit of certain of its businesses to another person	Sec. 292 para. 1 no. 2
	– **Lease of Undertaking, Agreement to relinquish Undertaking** The company grants a lease or otherwise relinquishes the operation of its undertaking to another person	Sec. 292 para. 1 no. 3

Table 5: Forms of Affiliation

b) Majority Ownership

Affiliation between companies is frequently based on majority ownership. This requires that the parent entity either holds the majority of shares or the majority of voting rights.[1406] There are only a few legal consequences attached directly to majority ownership, most importantly:
- Once an enterprise acquires a majority holding in an *AG*, it has to inform the *AG* thereof without undue delay.[1407]
- It is **presumed** that a majority-held entity is controlled by the majority shareholder.[1408] The presumption is refutable; the burden of proof is on the entity that invokes the absence of control. For example, if a majority-held *AG* does not wish to prepare a report on intra-group relations pursuant to sec. 312 of the Stock Corporation Act, the *AG* will bear the burden of proof that it is not a controlled enterprise.

Additional duties arise in connection with listed companies (see below).

c) Control

A company is deemed a controlled enterprise (*abhängiges Unternehmen*) if another enterprise (the controlling enterprise (*herrschendes Unternehmen*)) can directly or indirectly exert a controlling influence on it.[1409] Such controlling influence must be based on corporate law. If a company is majority-held by another entity, it is presumed that it is dependent on the enterprise with the majority shareholding.[1410] Even a minority shareholding can suffice for control if, due to other circumstances, a controlling influence exists. This was the finding of the Federal Supreme Court in the case of *VEBA v. Gelsenberg*.[1411] Even though the controlling shareholder (the Federal Republic of Germany) only held 43.7% of the *AG*'s registered share capital, such shareholding was, in view of the normally low attendance at general meetings, deemed sufficient to determine the outcome of shareholder votes.

d) Group of Companies

The group of companies (*Konzern*) is the most important subcategory of affiliated enterprises (*verbundene Unternehmen*). It involves a particularly close connection between enterprises. According to the statute, a group of companies exists when one or more controlled enterprises are consolidated under the **common management** (*einheitliche Leitung*) of a controlling enterprise.[1412] Mere control is in general not sufficient to create a group of companies in a legal sense. However, there exists a statutory presumption that a controlled enterprise forms a group of companies with the controlling enterprise.[1413] This presumption may be refuted. Since a majority-held enterprise is in turn presumed to be controlled, majority ownership usually leads to the creation of a so-called ***de facto* group of companies** (*faktischer Konzern*).

The Stock Corporation Act does not explicitly define the term **"uniform control"**. Although the majority shareholder of an *AG* can control the general meeting

---

[1406] Sec. 16 para. 1 of the Stock Corporation Act.
[1407] Sec. 20 para. 4 of the Stock Corporation Act.
[1408] Sec. 17 para. 2 of the Stock Corporation Act.
[1409] Sec. 17 para. 1 of the Stock Corporation Act.
[1410] Sec. 17 para. 2 of the Stock Corporation Act.
[1411] Decision of the Federal Supreme Court, published in BGHZ, vol. 69, pp. 334 et seq.
[1412] Sec. 18 para. 1 of the Stock Corporation Act.
[1413] Sec. 18 para. 1 sentence 3 of the Stock Corporation Act.

of the controlled *AG*, it does not have the right to issue directives directly to the controlled *AG's* management board and supervisory board. In practice, it can only exercise its uniform control in consensus with the controlled *AG*, or at most by bringing indirect pressure to bear (e.g., in the general meeting the majority shareholder may elect the supervisory board members who in turn appoint and dismiss the management board members; this affords the majority shareholder an indirect influence on the composition of the management board and thereby on its decision making). Uniform control is deemed to exist if the controlling enterprise works out an overall concept for the group of companies and implements it, at least in essential areas of the controlled *AG's* management (in particular the financial area). In practice, uniform control is frequently carried out through informal meetings and consultations between the majority shareholder and the management board of the controlled *AG*, by creating common governing bodies which formulate recommendations or through the setting of goals. Often, interlocking directorates between the management board of the majority shareholder and that of the controlled *AG de facto* lead to a uniform control for both enterprises.

e) Enterprise Agreements

The reasons for affiliation outlined above are based on factual circumstances like majority ownership of shares or the existence of a controlling influence or of uniform control. Enterprises may also choose to determine the nature of their affiliation by entering into enterprise agreements. The two most important types are the profit and loss transfer agreement and the domination agreement.[1414] Both types are often combined into a "domination and profit and loss transfer agreement". Less frequently, enterprises agree to pool their profits, to transfer profits only partially or to lease or relinquish their undertaking.[1415]

Enterprise agreements must be approved by the general meeting of the *AG* in a resolution passed by a majority of at least three quarters of the stock capital represented at the passing of the resolution.[1416] Furthermore, an enterprise agreement becomes effective only upon registration in the commercial register.[1417] Entities who are party to an enterprise agreement are considered to be affiliated (*verbunden*) with one another.[1418]

The law assumes that enterprise agreements fundamentally influence the purpose and organization of the enterprises involved. This is why it provides for the protection of minority shareholders and creditors (see below).

aa) Profit and Loss Transfer Agreement.

A company may agree in a profit and loss transfer agreement (more commonly called profit transfer agreement, *Gewinnabführungsvertrag*) to surrender its entire balance sheet profit to another company.[1419] The courts have not ruled on whether the execution of a profit transfer agreement by itself leads to the first company being controlled by the second. However, such an agreement will usually only be entered into if the entity entitled to receive the profits already controls the company.

[1414] Sec. 291 of the Stock Corporation Act.
[1415] Sec. 292 of the Stock Corporation Act.
[1416] Sec. 293 para. 1 of the Stock Corporation Act.
[1417] Sec. 294 of the Stock Corporation Act.
[1418] Sec. 15 of the Stock Corporation Act.
[1419] Sec. 291 para. 1 sentence 1 of the Stock Corporation Act.

The law protects minority shareholders through a formal reporting and review process involving independent auditors.[1420] Additionally, the agreement must stipulate a **reasonable compensation**, consisting of a certain annual share in profits.[1421] Finally, the enterprise entitled to receive the profits has to acquire a minority shareholder's shares upon his/her request in return for **reasonable consideration** stipulated in the agreement.[1422]

As a means to protect the creditors, the company that is entitled to receive the profits is obliged to **compensate the transferring company for any balance sheet losses** (*Verlustübernahme*).[1423]

bb) Domination Agreement. By entering into a domination agreement (*Beherrschungsvertrag*), an *AG* places itself under the direction of another entity. The controlling entity is entitled to issue **binding instructions** directly to the management board of the controlled *AG*.[1424] Such instructions may even be detrimental to the controlled *AG* as long as they serve the interests of either the controlling enterprise or of other enterprises which are affiliated with both the controlling and the controlled enterprise.[1425] However, the right to issue instructions does not extend to measures that are illegal or would endanger the existence of the controlled *AG*. In order to protect the controlled entity's shareholders and creditors, protective means applying in case of a profit and loss transfer agreement equally apply in case of a domination agreement.[1426] In particular, the controlling enterprise is obliged to compensate any annual net loss incurred during the term of the agreement to the dependent company.[1427] The parties to a domination agreement are irrefutably presumed to form a so-called **contract-based group of companies** (*Vertragskonzern*).[1428]

cc) Other Enterprise Agreements. As far as the other types of enterprise agreements are concerned, only the partial profit transfer agreement (*Teilgewinnabführungsvertrag*) is of high importance.[1429] The Federal Supreme Court holds that a **silent partnership** (*stille Gesellschaft*) in a stock corporation constitutes a partial profit transfer agreement.[1430] This means that silent partnerships in a stock corporation are only valid with the approval of the general meeting and registration in the commercial register.

f) Integration of *AGs*

A contract-based group of companies can be created through a domination agreement but also by way of a so-called **integration** (*Eingliederung*) of an *AG* into another *AG*.[1431] Integrations are extremely rare in practice. A requirement for integration is that the controlling enterprise – referred to as the principal enterprise – holds at least 95% of the stock capital of the *AG* which shall be integrated. A reso-

---

[1420] Sec. 293a et seq. of the Stock Corporation Act.
[1421] Sec. 304 of the Stock Corporation Act.
[1422] Sec. 305 of the Stock Corporation Act.
[1423] Sec. 302 of the Stock Corporation Act.
[1424] Sec. 308 para. 1 sentence 1 of the Stock Corporation Act.
[1425] Sec. 308 para. 1 sentence 2 of the Stock Corporation Act.
[1426] Sec. 293a et seq., 304 et seq. of the Stock Corporation Act.
[1427] Sec. 302 of the Stock Corporation Act.
[1428] Sec. 18 para. 1 sentence 3 of the Stock Corporation Act.
[1429] Sec. 292 para. 1 no. 2 of the Stock Corporation Act.
[1430] Decision of the Federal Supreme Court, published in BGHZ, vol. 156, pp. 38 et seq.
[1431] Sec. 319 et seq. of the Stock Corporation Act.

lution has to be passed by the controlled *AG's* general meeting before integration can take place. Upon registration in the commercial register, the shares held by the external shareholders are transferred to the controlling enterprise. In return, the former shareholders are entitled to a reasonable consideration, which as a rule takes the form of shares in the controlling enterprise.[1432] In the case of integration, the controlling enterprise's right to issue instructions is even more extensive than in the case of a domination agreement: not only detrimental instructions but even instructions endangering the existence of the controlled enterprise may be issued.[1433] This is justified because the controlling enterprise is liable to the creditors of the integrated *AG* for all of the integrated *AG's* liabilities.[1434]

4. Consequences of Affiliation and Control

a) Affiliation

Affiliated enterprises are subject to special regulation. Many provisions apply to all affiliated enterprises regardless of the particular form of affiliation. The most important general provisions with respect to *AGs* are the following:
- The management board of the controlling entity has to report to the supervisory board not only regarding the company itself, but also regarding affiliated enterprises.[1435]
- The shareholders' right to information in the general meeting also extends to the company's legal and business relationships with an affiliated enterprise.[1436]
- Stock options may be issued to members of the management and the employees of an affiliated enterprise.[1437]
- The auditor of the annual financial statements cannot be a legal representative or member of the supervisory board of a separate legal entity, shareholder of a partnership or owner of an enterprise if such separate legal entity, partnership or enterprise is affiliated with the company to be audited.[1438]

b) Control

The most important legal consequences of control are:
- There is a (refutable) presumption that the controlled enterprise forms a **group of companies** with the controlling enterprise.[1439]
- Certain **incompatibilities** arise: a person cannot be a member of the supervisory board of an *AG* if he is, at the same time, the legal representative (management board member, managing director) of an enterprise controlled by the company[1440] or the legal representative of another corporation on whose supervisory board a member of the company's management board is serving ("prohibition of interlocking directorates").[1441] The same applies to a *GmbH*

[1432] Sec. 320b of the Stock Corporation Act.
[1433] Sec. 323 of the Stock Corporation Act.
[1434] Sec. 322 of the Stock Corporation Act.
[1435] Sec. 90 para. 1 sentence 3 of the Stock Corporation Act.
[1436] Sec. 131 para. 1 sentence 2 of the Stock Corporation Act.
[1437] Sec. 192 para. 2 no. 3 of the Stock Corporation Act.
[1438] Sec. 319 para. 3 no. 2 of the Commercial Code.
[1439] Sec. 18 para. 1 sentence 3 of the Stock Corporation Act.
[1440] Sec. 100 para. 2 no. 2 of the Stock Corporation Act.
[1441] Sec. 100 para. 2 no. 3 of the Stock Corporation Act.

with a codetermined supervisory board[1442] or an optional supervisory board for which the articles of association do not provide otherwise.[1443]
- The controlling enterprise may not use its influence to cause a controlled *AG* to enter into legal transactions that would be detrimental to it or to take **measures to the disadvantage of the controlled *AG***, unless there is a domination agreement in place or the controlling enterprise compensates for the individual disadvantages.[1444] This **compensation of disadvantages** (*Nachteilsausgleich*) is of far-reaching importance as it forces the controlling enterprise to enter into transactions with the dependent *AG* on an **arm's-length basis**. If the two enterprises have entered into a domination agreement, the controlling enterprise must, in any event, cover all balance sheet losses of the controlled *AG*, making a compensation for individual disadvantages redundant. With regard to this obligation to compensate the controlled *AG* for disadvantages, which is set forth in sec. 311 of the Stock Corporation Act *(Nachteilsausgleich)*, the Federal Supreme Court[1445] has ruled that in case the general meeting of the controlled enterprise approves a detrimental legal transaction of the controlling enterprise by majority vote, this same resolution of the general meeting must also stipulate the compensation for disadvantages. Hence, it is no longer possible for the controlling enterprise to only commit to compensate the controlled enterprise for disadvantages on the condition that a court will decide upon the necessity and amount of the compensation. In the same decision, the court further held that if the disadvantage incurred by the controlled enterprise at the instigation of the controlling enterprise is quantifiable, a compensatory arrangement according to sec. 311 para. 2 of the Stock Corporation Act, which creates a payment claim, must put a precise figure on the compensation claim and must not be made dependent on a determination of the disadvantage in retrospect.
- Within the first three months of the fiscal year, the management board of the controlled *AG* must prepare a report on its relationships with affiliated enterprises (**"report on intra-group relations"**, *Abhängigkeitsbericht*).[1446] This report has to specify all transactions the company has entered into during the past fiscal year with the controlling enterprise or any enterprise affiliated with the controlling enterprise or upon instruction or in the interest of any such enterprise, as well as all other measures it has taken, or has refrained from taking, upon instruction or in the interest of any such enterprise in the past business year. For all such transactions, the report on intra-group relations has to specify the consideration given or received, the reasons for the measure as well as its advantages and disadvantages for the company.
- The report on intra-group relations must be submitted to the **auditor** of the *AG* for examination.[1447] The auditor prepares a report on the audit which has to be presented to the *AG's* supervisory board. If the auditor does not raise any objections, he confirms the propriety of the report on intra-group relations in a special certificate.[1448] If the auditor does raise any objections, he has to restrict his auditor's certificate or refuse to issue one.

[1442] Sec. 6 para. 2 sentence 1 of the Codetermination Act, sec. 3 para. 2 of the Coal, Iron and Steel Codetermination Act, sec. 1 para. 1 no. 3 of the One-Third Participation Act.
[1443] Sec. 52 para. 1 of the Limited Liability Company Act.
[1444] Sec. 311 of the Stock Corporation Act.
[1445] Decision of the Federal Supreme Court, published in NZG 2012, pp. 1030 et seq.
[1446] Sec. 312 of the Stock Corporation Act.
[1447] Sec. 313 of the Stock Corporation Act.
[1448] Sec. 313 para. 3 of the Stock Corporation Act.

- The report on intra-group relations of the management board is submitted to the supervisory board together with the auditor's audit report. The **supervisory board** has to **examine** the report on intra-group relations and subsequently has to report on this examination in its report to the general meeting.[1449] At the end of its report, the supervisory board must state whether it raises any objections to the report on intra-group relations.[1450]
- The provisions concerning the report on intra-group relations of the management board do not apply if the respective controlled and controlling enterprises have entered into a **domination agreement** or if there are two *AGs* one of which is **integrated** into the other.[1451]

All these requirements lead to an intensive review of all transactions and measures entered into between a controlling and a controlled enterprise, at least in case the controlled enterprise is an *AG*.

c) Groups of Companies

The existence of a group of companies entails the following consequences in particular:
- Special provisions apply with respect to accounting: the controlling enterprise must draw up **consolidated annual group financial statements**.[1452]
- Special rules governing the **codetermination** of employees in the supervisory board apply to a group of companies. The employees of the subordinate group enterprises may be attributed to the controlling enterprise.[1453] As a result, a codetermined supervisory board may need to be formed in the controlling enterprise as well as in the individual group enterprises, which means that codetermined supervisory boards may exist at various levels within the group.

d) *GmbH* Group of Companies

aa) Overview. In contrast to the Stock Corporation Act, the Limited Liability Company Act does not contain a codified law on groups of companies. The **general conceptual definitions of stock corporation law** regarding affiliated enterprises, majority shareholdings, controlled enterprises, and groups of companies apply to *GmbHs* as well.[1454] Attempts to further regulate *GmbH* groups of companies did not advance beyond the draft stage. At present, the law on *GmbH* groups of companies is being shaped by the courts. In the process, analogies are sometimes drawn to the codified law on *AG* groups of companies in order to protect outside *GmbH* shareholders and creditors of the *GmbH*.

Due to the nature of corporate governance in a *GmbH*, the majority shareholder has greater influence on the company than in case of an *AG*. In contrast to the majority shareholder of an *AG*, the majority shareholder of a *GmbH* can directly issue instructions to the *GmbH's* managing directors by means of shareholder resolution, thereby determining not only the guidelines of the business policy but also intervening in individual transactions. This opportunity to exercise immediate influence on the *GmbH's* management has led to the situation that in

---

[1449] Sec. 314 para. 2 sentence 1 of the Stock Corporation Act.
[1450] Sec. 314 para. 3 of the Stock Corporation Act.
[1451] Sec. 312 para. 1 sentence 1, 323 para. 1 sentence 3 of the Stock Corporation Act.
[1452] Sec. 290 et seq. of the Commercial Code.
[1453] Sec. 5 of the Codetermination Act, sec. 2 para. 2 of the One-Third Participation Act.
[1454] Sec. 15 et seq. of the Stock Corporation Act.

many groups of companies the subordinate level of the group consists of *GmbHs* rather than *AGs*.

Such consequences of a ***de facto* group of companies** – i.e., the unified management of one or more *GmbHs* through *de facto* instruments of control, especially through majority holdings – have proved to be particularly problematic. This is why, in a series of decisions, the courts have set up protective mechanisms for the benefit of outside *GmbH* shareholders and the *GmbH's* creditors, which apply when the majority shareholder intervenes in a damaging way in the *GmbH* he controls.

bb) Contract-Based *GmbH* Group of Companies. Contract-based groups of companies come about through **enterprise agreements** defined in stock corporation law (domination agreement, profit and loss transfer agreement, profit pool, partial profit transfer agreement, lease of undertaking, agreement to relinquish undertaking).[1455] It is also acknowledged that enterprise agreements defined under stock corporation law[1456] can be entered into between *GmbHs* or between another kind of enterprise and a *GmbH*. Many issues in this regard have been clarified by the courts. In practice, the most common are **profit-transfer agreements**, entered into in order to have both companies treated as one for tax purposes. These are often linked to domination agreements.

The Federal Supreme Court assumes that an enterprise agreement is a special organizational contract under corporate law altering the legal status of the controlled *GmbH*.[1457] The enterprise agreement is entered into by the managing directors of the *GmbH*. Written form suffices. In order for such a contract to be effective, the controlled *GmbH* has to give its approval in the form of a shareholder resolution. According to the prevailing view, the majority shareholder with whom the enterprise agreement is to be entered into is allowed to participate in voting. The prohibition of voting which applies in the event of other legal transactions that are entered into between the company and a shareholder[1458] does not apply in this case. It has not yet been decided, however, whether the shareholder resolution of the controlled *GmbH* requires the **consent of all shareholders** or whether a majority required for amendments to the articles of association (in accordance with statutory provisions a three-quarters majority) suffices. The prevailing view is that the resolution granting approval has to be passed unanimously. Accordingly, in practice it is generally recommended that the consent of all shareholders shall be obtained.

Additionally, the enterprise agreement needs to be filed for **registration with the commercial register**. The resolution granting the approval of the shareholder meeting and the enterprise agreement are to be attached to the application for registration. The enterprise agreement takes effect upon being registered in the commercial register.

A **domination agreement may be advantageous** for the controlling entity although the shareholder meeting of a GmbH already has a statutory right to issue instructions to the *GmbH*. If a domination agreement exists, it is possible to issue instructions directly from the controlling entity's management to the *GmbH's* management. If there is no domination agreement, instructions may only be issued as a shareholder resolution, i.e., in compliance with all the formalities and

---

[1455] Sec. 291, 292 of the Stock Corporation Act.
[1456] Sec. 291, 292 of the Stock Corporation Act.
[1457] Decision of the Federal Supreme Court, published in BGHZ, vol. 105, pp. 324, 331.
[1458] Sec. 47 para. 4 of the Limited Liability Company Act.

time periods applicable for convening a shareholder meeting (if the controlling entity is not the sole shareholder). Additionally, a **domination agreement** gives the controlling enterprise the right to issue instructions concerning the management of the company to the *GmbH's* managing directors. Instructions to the detriment of the company are also permitted,[1459] but the existence of the controlled *GmbH* may not be jeopardized. Instructions violating mandatory statutory provisions (including, for example, the provisions regarding the maintenance of capital) or instructions which are not within the scope of the object of the *GmbH* as defined in the articles of association are not permitted.

In the case of a **profit and loss transfer agreement**, special tax law provisions must be complied with to ensure that the special arrangement whereby both companies are treated as one for tax purposes is recognized by the tax authorities.

If a domination agreement or a profit and loss transfer agreement exists, the controlling enterprise has to compensate for all annual net losses incurred during the term of the agreement (application of sec. 302 of the Stock Corporation Act by way of analogy). This **obligation to assume losses** exists by virtue of law. However, the tax authorities may only acknowledge the agreement if the obligation to assume losses is expressly stated in the agreement.[1460] The obligation to assume losses applies irrespective of whether or not a loss was specifically caused by implementing orders issued by the controlling enterprise.

As all shareholders of the controlled *GmbH* are required to approve the execution of an enterprise agreement, the external shareholders of the *GmbH* do not require a protection mechanism of settlement and compensation like the one provided for in the Stock Corporation Law. Whether or not they make their consent for the enterprise agreement contingent upon such settlement or compensation is in their own discretion.

e) *De facto* GmbH Group

In case of a *de facto* **group**, the controlled enterprise is placed under uniform control by way of *de facto* control mechanisms rather than a domination agreement. This generally takes the form of a majority shareholding which generally enables the majority shareholder to prevail in the shareholder meeting.

In its *"Bremer Vulkan"*-decision of 2001,[1461] the Federal Supreme Court ruled that the protection of a *de facto*-controlled *GmbH* against (detrimental) interventions by its sole shareholder is not accomplished by an analogous application of the liability provisions governing the group law of Stock Corporations.[1462] Rather, the protection of a de facto-controlled GmbH is limited to the protection ensured by the provisions governing the preservation of the share capital[1463] as well as the *GmbH's* right of continuance according to which the sole shareholder is obliged to take into account the *GmbH's* interests appropriately.[1464]

In its *"TRIHOTEL"*-decision of 2007,[1465] the Federal Supreme Court ruled that in order to appropriately take into account the *GmbH's* interests with regard to its right of continuance, the shareholders have to make sure that the *GmbH* remains

---

[1459] Sec. 308 para. 1 of the Stock Corporation Act.
[1460] Sec. 17 sentence 2 no. 2 of the Corporation Tax Act.
[1461] Decision of the Federal Supreme Court, published in BGHZ, vol. 149, pp. 10 et seq.
[1462] i.e. sec. 291 et seq., sec. 311 et seq. of the Stock Corporation Act.
[1463] i.e. sec. 30 et seq. of the Limited Liability Company Act.
[1464] Decision of the Federal Supreme Court, published in BGHZ, vol. 149, pp. 10 et seq.
[1465] Decision of the Federal Supreme Court, published in BGHZ, vol. 173, pp. 246 et seq.

able to service its financial liabilities. In case the shareholders withdraw the financial resources necessary to meet the company's financial obligations from the *GmbH*, this may constitute a so-called "existence-destroying encroachment". According to the Federal Supreme Court's ruling in the *"TRIHOTEL"*-decision, a controlling shareholder who undertook such an existence-destroying encroachment will be liable in tort pursuant to sec. 826 of the Civil Code.[1466] As a result, the dependent *GmbH* potentially has a claim against its shareholder for damages.[1467]

f) Rules on the Conflict of Laws with respect to Groups of Companies

In practice, **international groups of companies** are common. The prevailing view is that international domination or profit and loss transfer agreements in which a German *AG* or *GmbH* becomes a controlled enterprise may be entered into. However, German law governing groups of companies applies to such contracts as – according to German conflict of laws provisions – the registered office of the controlled company is decisive when determining which substantive law governing groups of companies is to apply.

The same applies to *de facto* groups of companies. If the controlled *AG* or *GmbH* has its registered office in Germany and the controlling enterprise has its registered office abroad, German law governing groups of companies applies for the protection of the external shareholders in the controlled *AG/GmbH* and their creditors. However, it is doubtful whether the competent foreign courts will recognize the applicability of German law governing groups of companies in the event of a lawsuit against the foreign parent company before a foreign court.

X. Listed Companies

1. Applicable Laws

The Stock Corporation Act contains only a few provisions which relate specifically to listed companies (*börsennotierte Gesellschaften*). German listed companies can be incorporated in the form of an *AG* or a partnership limited by shares (*KGaA*).

There are a number of specific laws which apply to listed companies which are of great relevance in practice. These regulations aim at protecting investors and the capital market as a whole. A brief overview of the following laws is provided below: the Securities Trading Act (*WpHG*), the Securities Acquisition and Takeover Act (*WpÜG*), the Stock Exchange Act (*BörsG*) and the Securities Prospectus Act (*WpPG*).

2. Securities Trading Act

The Securities Trading Act has traditionally contained important provisions relating to the prohibition of insider trading, disclosure requirements (including the so-called *ad hoc* disclosure procedure regarding facts of relevance to the stock exchange price) and publication requirements in the event of changes to the composition of the shareholders of a listed company. On July 3, 2016, a new EU-regulation, the so-called **Market Abuse Regulation (MAR)**[1468] came into force. This

---

[1466] *Cf.* A.III.4.e.
[1467] Decision of the Federal Supreme Court, published in BGHZ, vol. 173, pp. 246, 252 et seq.
[1468] Regulation (EU) 596/24 of April 16, 2014, OG L 173 of June 12, 2014.

regulation contains important provisions with regard to securities trading that are directly applicable to EU member states and partly replace the national rules set forth in the German Securities Trading Act.

a) Insider Law

Articles 8, 10 and 14 of the new MAR contain provisions dealing with inside information. Art. 14 of the MAR explicitly prohibits **insider dealings** (*Insidergeschäfte*). The purposes of this prohibition are to protect confidence in the integrity of the capital markets and to ensure equal treatment of all trading parties.

Anyone who possesses so-called inside information is deemed to be an **insider** and is subject to the prohibition against insider dealings. According to Art. 18 of the MAR, issuers or any person acting on their behalf or on their account shall draw up a list of all persons who have access to inside information and who are working for them under a contract of employment, or otherwise performing tasks through which they have access to inside information, such as advisers, accountants or credit rating agencies (so-called insider list).[1469] The issuers also have to promptly update the insider list in case of specifically defined events and also have to provide the insider list to the competent authority as soon as possible upon its request.[1470]

Inside information is defined in Art. 7 of the MAR. According to Art. 7 para. 1(a) of the MAR, one – particularly important – type of inside information is "information of a precise nature, which has not been made public, relating, directly or indirectly, to one or more issuers or to one or more financial instruments, and which, if it were made public, would be likely to have a significant effect on the prices of those financial instruments or on the price of related derivative financial instruments."[1471] Art. 7 para. 1(b)-(d) of the MAR contain definitions of more specific types of inside information. Art. 7 para. 2 of the MAR gives a definition as to when information is to be deemed specific: "For the purposes of paragraph 1, information shall be deemed to be of a precise nature if it indicates a set of circumstances which exists or which may reasonably be expected to come into existence, or an event which has occurred or which may reasonably be expected to occur, where it is specific enough to enable a conclusion to be drawn as to the possible effect of that set of circumstances or event on the prices of the financial instruments or the related derivative financial instrument, the related spot commodity contracts, or the auctioned products based on the emission allowances. In this respect in the case of a protracted process that is intended to bring about, or that results in, particular circumstances or a particular event, those future circumstances or that future event, and also the intermediate steps of that process which are connected with bringing about or resulting in those future circumstances or that future event, may be deemed to be precise information."[1472] According to Art. 7 para. 3 of the MAR, "An intermediate step in a protracted process shall be deemed to be inside information if, by itself, it satisfies the criteria of inside information as referred to in this Article."[1473]

[1469] Art. 18 para. 1 (a) of the MAR.
[1470] Art. 18 para. 1 (b), (c) of the MAR.
[1471] Art. 7 para. 1 (a) of the MAR.
[1472] Art. 7 para. 2 of the MAR.
[1473] Art. 7 para. 3 of the MAR.

It is **prohibited to engage or attempt to engage in insider dealing**.[1474] It is furthermore **prohibited to recommend that another person engage in insider dealing or induce another person to engage in insider dealing**.[1475] Finally, it is **prohibited to unlawfully disclose inside information**.[1476]

A breach of the prohibitions regarding insider trading is a **criminal offense** and may be sanctioned with imprisonment of up to five years or a fine.

b) *Ad Hoc* Disclosure Requirements

Very important in practice are the rules concerning the so-called duty of *ad hoc* **disclosure**. This duty aims to provide equal information to all market participants and to minimize opportunities for insider trading.

Pursuant to Art. 17 of the MAR, an issuer of securities admitted to the stock exchange (i.e., the listed company) has to inform the public as soon as possible of inside information which directly concerns that issuer.[1477] Examples of insider information that might have to be published include the making of an offer to acquire a target company, the sale of a core business, the setting up of accruals or the modification of a forecast based on an unfavorable court decision, the suspicion of fraudulent accounting practices or the announcement of a management board member that he wishes to resign. On the other hand, general market statistics, interest rate developments, general business news or changes in the situation of a competitor do usually not constitute insider information that directly concerns the issuer.

It is still unclear whether a **multi-stage decision-making process** can produce several instances of insider information over its course or only one piece of insider information at the end. Two higher regional courts have issued contradictory decisions on this question.[1478] According to the guidelines published by the Federal Financial Supervisory Authority (*BaFin*), insider information exists at the latest as soon as the management board has made its decision.

In order to comply with the *ad hoc* disclosure rules, the information must also be published in the **company register**. The issuer's failure to accurately publish insider information may give rise to damage claims of third parties who traded its securities pursuant to sec. 37b and 37c of the Securities Trading Act.[1479] If incorrect information was published in an *ad hoc* announcement, the publication must be corrected as soon as the error becomes known.

An issuer may, on its own responsibility, **delay disclosure to the public of inside information** provided that (i) immediate disclosure is likely to prejudice the legitimate interests of the issuer or emission allowance market participant, (ii) delay of disclosure is not likely to mislead the public and (iii) the issuer or emission allowance market participant is able to ensure the confidentiality of that information (so-called **self-exemption**).[1480] Particular rules and conditions regarding the self-exemption apply if the issuer is a credit institution or a financial

---

[1474] Art. 14 lit. (a) of the MAR.
[1475] Art. 14 lit. (b) of the MAR.
[1476] Art. 14 lit. (c) of the MAR.
[1477] Art. 17 para.1 of the MAR.
[1478] Decisions of the Higher Regional Court of Frankfurt, published in NZG 2009, p. 391 and of the Higher Regional Court of Stuttgart, published in NZG 2009, p. 624.
[1479] Sec. 15 para. 3 Securities Trading Act in connection with sec. 15 para. 1 Securities Trading Act and/or in connection with Art. 17 para. 1, 7 or 8 of the MAR.
[1480] Art. 17 para. 4 lit. (a) to (c) of the MAR.

institution and the self-exemption is made use of in order to preserve the stability of the financial system.[1481]

Until 2004, such an exemption had to be granted by the Federal Financial Supervisory Authority. Nowadays, the management of the issuer must, according to the clearly prevailing opinion, formally resolve to claim the self-exemption.

If disclosure of inside information has been delayed according to the self-exemption provisions and the confidentiality of that inside information is no longer ensured, the issuer has to disclose that inside information to the public as soon as possible.[1482] This also applies to situations where a rumor explicitly relates to inside information the disclosure of which has been delayed according to the self-exemption provisions, and where that rumor is sufficiently accurate to indicate that the confidentiality of that information is no longer ensured.[1483] The issuer must also inform the competent authority specified under Art. 17 para. 3 of the MAR about the self-exemption at the date and under the conditions set forth by Art. 17 para. 4 and/or para. 6 of the MAR.

The ability to delay the publication of insider information is of particular information in the context of **M&A transactions**. According to **guidelines** published by the Federal Financial Supervisory Authority, the execution of a customary letter of intent or the start of exclusive negotiations generally requires a review whether any insider information exists. However, the guidelines also indicate that it qualifies for a legitimate interest that is required for a self-exemption if the publication would be detrimental to the transaction.

Specific rules apply with regard to so-called **directors' dealings** (the MAR refers to "managers' transactions"). According to Art. 19 para. 1 of the MAR, persons discharging managerial responsibilities, as well as persons closely associated with them, shall notify the issuer and the (yet to be defined) competent authority of every transaction conducted on their own accounts relating to the shares or debt instruments of that issuer or to derivatives or other financial instruments linked thereto.[1484] This obligation exists as soon as all transactions within a calendar year added together, without netting, exceed a specific threshold yet to be defined by the competent authority.[1485] Similar rules apply to emission allowance market participants.[1486] Such notifications shall be made promptly and no later than three business days after the date of the transaction.[1487]

c) Disclosure of Significant Shareholdings

Shareholders in a listed stock corporation whose home member state is Germany **must notify** both the **company and the Federal Financial Supervisory Authority** (*Bundesanstalt für Finanzdienstleistungen – BaFin*) when their stake in the voting rights derived from their shares in a stock corporation directly or indirectly reaches, exceeds or falls below the thresholds of 3%, 5%, 10%, 15%, 20%, 25%, 30%, 50% or 75%.[1488] The notification needs to be made without delay, but at the latest within four trading days after the relevant threshold has been met. A "trading day" is

---

[1481] Art. 17 para. 5 of the MAR.
[1482] Art. 17 para. 7 of the MAR.
[1483] Art. 17 para. 7 of the MAR.
[1484] Art. 19 para. 1(a) of the MAR.
[1485] According to Art. 19 para. 8, para. 9 of the MAR, the lower limit for the threshold is EUR 5,000.
[1486] Art. 19 para. 1(b) of the MAR.
[1487] Art. 19 para. 1 of the MAR.
[1488] Sec. 21 para. 1 sentence 1 of the Securities Trading Act.

each calendar day other than a Saturday, Sunday or any other day declared to be a public holiday in at least one German federal state.[1489] The target company **has to publish** the notification without delay, but at the latest within three trading days.[1490] In practice, such publication is generally made by passing the notification on to a recognised information distribution system and on the company's website.

Such notification duties under sec. 21 of the Securities Trading Act may be triggered by direct ownership of shares and by **attribution of voting rights** to the notifying party under sec. 22 of the Securities Trading Act.[1491] Most recently, these attribution rules have been extended by the German Transparency Directive Amendment Directive Implementation Act *(Gesetz zur Umsetzung der Transparenzrichtlinie-Änderungsrichtlinie).*[1492] The notification regime has been changed such that notification obligations exist for voting rights (sec. 21 of the Securities Trading Act), certain related instruments (sec. 25 of the Securities Trading Act) and the aggregate of voting rights and certan related instruments (sec. 25a of the Securities Trading Act).

As far as voting rights are concerned, the following rules apply: Particularly if the company holding the shares is a direct or indirect subsidiary, its voting rights will be fully attributed to the respective **parent company**.[1493] Pursuant to the Security Trading Act, a company is deemed to be a subsidiary of another entity/person if such entity/person holds the majority of the voting rights in the company; has the right to appoint or dismiss the majority of the members of the administrative, management, or supervisory body of the company and, at the same time, is a shareholder of the company; or is otherwise able to exercise a dominating influence over the company. If a group of companies has several levels, it has to be determined for each entity/person at each level whether the company which directly holds the shares in the target company is a direct or indirect subsidiary of the respective entity/person. Accordingly, the voting rights arising from the shares in the target company held by the Investor would be attributed to all persons directly or indirectly controlling the Investor (including any individual(s) ultimately controlling the Investor, if any) and would lead to respective disclosure obligations.

Two new additional rules have been recently introduced in sec. 22 of the Securities Trading Act.[1494] They lay down the attribution of voting rights that have been transferred separately from the underlying shares and of shares which are subject to certain security arrangements.

Another reason for an attribution of voting rights is the so-called **"acting in concert"**, i.e., the collaboration of different shareholders with regard to the exercise of voting rights or a change of the long-term business strategy of the company (except for collaborations in an individual case).[1495]

Sec. 25 of the Securities Trading Act has also been recently amended by the above-mentioned German Transparency Directive Amendment Directive Implementation Act. This provision imposes notification obligations for instruments that (i) provide for an unconditional right to acquire, or the acquirer's discretion

---

[1489] Sec. 30 para. 1 of the Securities Trading Act.
[1490] Sec. 26 para. 1 sentence 1 of the Securities Trading Act.
[1491] Sec. 22 of the Securities Trading Act.
[1492] BGBl. I 2015, Nr. 46, pp. 2029 et seq.
[1493] Sec. 22 para. 1 sentence 1 no. 1 of the Securities Trading Act.
[1494] *Cf.* sec. 22 para. 1 sentence 1 no. 7 and no. 8 of the Securities Trading Act.
[1495] Sec. 22 para. 2 of the Securities Trading Act.

as to its right to acquire, shares already issued, or (ii) have "a similar economic effect" to the aforementioned instruments. Thus, all types of instruments subject to notification obligations are aggregated in sec. 25 of the Securities Trading Act. According to the legislature's explanatory statements, no changes to the previous scope of the instruments that trigger a notification obligation are intended.

The amended sec. 25a of the Securities Trading Act stipulates a further notification requirement for the aggregate of holdings of voting rights (sec. 21, 22 of the Securities Trading Act) and instruments within the meaning of the amended sec. 25 of the Securities Trading Act. Based on the wording of the amended sec. 25a of the Securities Trading Act, it is not entirely clear whether the notification obligation arises irrespectively of whether an additional threshold is reached or crossed.

If the Investor, or any person to which the shares held by the Investor are attributed, **failed to make a notification** required pursuant to sec. 21, 22 of the Securities Trading Act, its voting and other shareholder rights in the *AG* are suspended (i) until the disclosure obligations have been complied with[1496] and (ii), if the notification requirements were intentionally or grossly negligently violated with respect to the percentage of the voting rights, for a period of six months after the omitted notification has been made.[1497] Its dividend right may be irreversibly forfeited, if a notification was deliberately omitted.[1498]

Additionally, the Federal Financial Supervisory Authority *(BaFin)* can impose an administrative fine for each violation of sec. 21, 25 or 25a of the Securities Trading Act.[1499] The (maximum) amount of these administrative fines has recently been significantly increased to fines of up to EUR 2 million for natural persons, up to EUR 10 million or 5% of the annual (group) turnover for legal entities or up to twice the amount of profits gained or losses avoided because of the breach (whichever is the highest).[1500]

Furthermore, under the recently amended sec. 40c of the Securities Trading Act, the Federal Financial Supervisory Authority *(BaFin)* has to publish every decision on sanctions and measures that are imposed for a breach of the notification requirements without undue delay, including at least information on the type and nature of the breach and the identity of the natural persons or legal entities responsible for it (so-called "naming and shaming"). The obligation to publish applies irrespective of a potential appeal. However, in case the decision has not yet become final, this has to be mentioned in the *BaFin's* publication. Where an appeal has been filed, this fact also needs to be published.[1501]

Investors reaching or **exceeding the threshold of 10%** of the voting rights in a listed target company have to comply with **additional disclosure obligations**. Unless an exception applies[1502], such investor is obliged to notify, within 20 trading days, whether (i) the investment serves the implementation of strategic objectives or the generation of trading profits; (ii) the investor intends to obtain further voting rights by acquisition or otherwise within the next 12 months; (iii) the investor aims at an influence on the composition of the administrative,

---

[1496] Sec. 28 para. 1 sentence 1 of the Securities Trading Act.
[1497] Sec. 28 para. 1 sentence 3 of the Securities Trading Act.
[1498] Sec. 28 para. 1 sentence 1 and sentence 2 of the Securities Trading Act.
[1499] Sec. 39 para. 2 no. 2 lit. f) and lit. g) of the Securities Trading Act.
[1500] Sec. 39 para. 4 of the Securities Trading Act.
[1501] Sec. 40c para. 1 and 2 of the Securities Trading Act.
[1502] *Cf.* sec. 27a para. 1 sentence 5 and 6 and para. 3 of the Securities Trading Act for exceptions.

management or supervisory bodies of the issuer; and (iv) the investor aims at a significant change to the company's capital structure, in particular with respect to the ratio of equity and debt financing and the dividend policy. In addition to the aforementioned objectives pursued by the acquisition, with respect to the source of the used funds the investor has to indicate if these funds are (i) internal funds or (ii) external funds that the investor has taken out to finance the acquisition of the shares.[1503] The target company has to publish (i) the information received from the investor or (ii) the fact that the disclosure obligation was not complied with by the investor.[1504] The law does not explicitly provide for any other sanctions. However, non-compliance with this provisions may – depending on the circumstances in the individual case – result in a violation of the prohibition of market manipulation and insider trading. These additional disclosure obligations only apply to investors that have reached or exceeded the 10% threshold after May 31, 2009 (i.e., not to investors which already held 10% or more at that time).

d) Information regarding Shares and the Company

Pursuant to sec. 30a et seq. of the Securities Trading Act, the company is obliged to immediately publicize in the Federal Gazette certain information regarding the shares and the company, e.g., concerning the general meeting, dividends, option and subscription rights, changes to the rights granted by the shares, the issuance of bonds and information which has been made publicly available in another country if the information may be relevant for the public in the European Economic Area.

e) Financial Reports

Sec. 37v et seq. of the Securities Trading Act provide that listed stock corporations have to comply with extended financial reporting obligations, meaning that the company has to disclose half-yearly financial statements. Additionally, sec. 37n et seq. of the Securities Trading Act authorize the Federal Financial Supervisory Authority (*Bundesanstalt für Finanzdienstleistungen – BaFin*) to review the annual accounts and to determine and if necessary publicize that the annual financial statements of the respective company have been incorrect.

3. Securities Acquisition and Takeover Act

The Securities Acquisition and Takeover Act came into effect on January 1, 2002. It replaced the voluntary Takeover Code which previously applied. Responsibility for supervising the offer procedure has been transferred to a government agency, the Federal Financial Supervisory Authority (*Bundesanstalt für Finanzdienstleistungen – BaFin*).

The Securities Acquisition and Takeover Act **regulates all public offers** for the acquisition of securities in a target company (i) registered in Germany whose shares are admitted to trading in an organized market in Germany (even if the company is also listed in another member state of the European Economic Area), and (ii) – to the extent provisions regarding remuneration, content of the offer document and the offer procedure are concerned – registered in another member state of the European Economic Area but (y) solely listed in Germany or (z) listed

---

[1503] Sec. 27a para. 1 of the Securities Trading Act.
[1504] Sec. 27a para. 2 of the Securities Trading Act.

in Germany and in another member state of the European Economic Area (except for the country of registration) if Germany has been the first place of listing or – in case of contemporaneous listings in multiple countries – the company has elected for the Federal Financial Supervisory Authority (*Bundesanstalt für Finanzdienstleistungen – BaFin*) as its supervisory authority.[1505] If the target company is registered in Germany but listed only in another member state of the European Economic Area, the takeover procedure is generally governed by the law of the country in which the company is listed; in this case, only certain provisions of the Securities Acquisition and Takeover Act apply, in particular regarding employee participation and permitted actions of the corporate bodies of the target company.[1506]

The Securities Acquisition and Takeover Act establishes the principle that all holders of securities in the target company shall be treated equally. The management board and supervisory board of the target company have to act in the target company's interests.

The Securities Acquisition and Takeover Act differentiates between
- **acquisition offers**, aimed at the acquisition of securities without obtaining control over the company;
- **takeover offers**, aimed at the obtaining of control over the company; and
- **mandatory offers**, which are to be made after acquisition of control over the company.

According to the Securities Acquisition and Takeover Act, control is defined as holding at least 30% of the voting rights in the target company, these being either voting rights attached to the offeror's own shares of the target company or voting rights that are attributed to the offeror according to sec. 30 of the Securities Acquisition and Takeover Act.[1507] If a shareholder exceeds this control threshold, he is subsequently obligated to publish that fact without undue delay and within seven calendar days at the latest, stating his percentage of voting rights.[1508] Additionally, he has to submit a mandatory offer to all outstanding shareholders.[1509]

In case of acquisition offers, the offeror is free to determine the price as he wishes. In the case of takeover offers and mandatory offers, appropriate compensation has to be offered in return, the **minimum prices** of which are stipulated by law. The minimum amount is the higher of (i) the weighted average share price of the three months prior to the decision to launch the offer (or the announcement the control has been obtained in case of a mandatory offer) has been announced[1510] and (ii) the highest price paid for shares of the target by the bidder (or companies attributable to him) in the six months prior to the publication of the offer document.[1511] If within one year after the end of the offer has been announced the offeror (or a company attributable to him) acquires shares in the target outside the stock exchange for a higher price than the offer price, all shareholders who accepted the offer are entitled to an add-on payment in an amount equal to the balance between the offer price and the higher price paid later on.[1512]

In order to safeguard the outstanding shareholders, the offeror must take the steps necessary to ensure that he **has at his disposal**, at the time at which the

---

[1505] Sec. 1 para. 3 of the Securities Acquisition and Takeover Act.
[1506] Sec. 1 para. 2 of the Securities Acquisition and Takeover Act.
[1507] Sec. 29 para. 2 sentence 1 of the Securities Acquisition and Takeover Act.
[1508] Sec. 35 para. 1 sentence 1 of the Securities Acquisition and Takeover Act.
[1509] Sec. 35 para. 2 of the Securities Acquisition and Takeover Act.
[1510] Sec. 5 of the Ordinance on Takeover Offers.
[1511] Sec. 4 of the Ordinance on Takeover Offers.
[1512] Sec. 31 para. 5 sentence 1 of the Securities Acquisition and Takeover Act.

claim for consideration becomes dues, **the necessary means for performing the offer in full**. Where the offer provides for a cash payment as consideration, an independent securities service provider has to confirm in writing that the required measures have been taken.[1513] If the offeror cannot fulfill his obligations, the securities services provider issuing the confirmation will be liable for the shortfall.[1514]

The **offer procedure** involves the following steps:
- notification of the Federal Financial Supervisory Authority (*Bundesanstalt für Finanzdienstleistungen – BaFin*) and the relevant stock exchange about the intended offer prior to its public announcement;[1515]
- announcement of the intention to launch the offer;[1516]
- preparation of the offer document and submission to Federal Financial Supervisory Authority (*Bundesanstalt für Finanzdienstleistungen – BaFin*) for approval within four weeks;[1517]
- publication of the offer document after approval of Federal Financial Supervisory Authority (*Bundesanstalt für Finanzdienstleistungen – BaFin*) or lapse of objection period;[1518]
- offer period of four to ten weeks;[1519] regular announcements of number of shares held by the offeror (generally weekly, daily in the last week)[1520]; the offer period is extended by two weeks if the offer is amended in the last two weeks of the offer.[1521] In case of a competing offer, the offer period is aligned with the offer period of the competing offer;[1522]
- announcement of end of offer period;[1523] in case of a takeover offer: start additional offer period of two weeks after the end of the offer period for all shareholders who have not accepted the offer (only in case of a successful offer);[1524] and
- announcement of end of additional offer period (in case of a takeover offer).[1525]

Under German takeover law – compared to other jurisdictions – the management board and the supervisory board of the target company are allowed to take relatively far-reaching defensive action against takeover offers.[1526] In view of recent European legislation, new provisions limiting the competencies of the management to defend against takeover offers have been included in sec. 33a et seq. of the Securities Acquisition and Takeover Act. However, such rules only apply if the articles of association of the target provide accordingly ("opt-in").

Finally, the Securities Acquisition and Takeover Act contains provisions on a squeeze-out following a takeover offer or a mandatory offer.[1527] If the offeror has reached a participation of at least 95% of the voting rights following the offer, he can apply to the Regional Court of Frankfurt/Main (*Landgericht Frankfurt am*

[1513] Sec. 13 para. 1 of the Securities Acquisition and Takeover Act.
[1514] Sec. 13 para. 2 of the Securities Acquisition and Takeover Act.
[1515] Sec. 10 para. 2 of the Securities Acquisition and Takeover Act.
[1516] Sec. 10 para. 1 of the Securities Acquisition and Takeover Act.
[1517] Sec. 14 para. 1 of the Securities Acquisition and Takeover Act.
[1518] Sec. 14 para. 2 of the Securities Acquisition and Takeover Act.
[1519] Section 16 para. 1 of the Securities Acquisition and Takeover Act.
[1520] Sec. 23 para. 1 of the Securities Acquisition and Takeover Act.
[1521] Sec. 21 para. 5 of the Securities Acquisition and Takeover Act.
[1522] Sec. 22 para. 2 of the Securities Acquisition and Takeover Act.
[1523] Sec. 23 para. 1 sentence 1 no. 2 of the Securities Acquisition and Trading Act.
[1524] Sec. 16 para. 2 of the Securities Acquisition and Takeover Act.
[1525] Sec. 23 para. 1 sentence 1 no. 3 of the Securities Acquisition and Takeover Act.
[1526] Sec. 33 of the Securities Acquisition and Takeover Act.
[1527] Sec. 39a of the Securities Acquisition and Takeover Act.

Main) to decide that the remaining outstanding shareholders be excluded in return for compensation.[1528] If 90% of the outstanding shareholders had accepted the takeover offer or mandatory offer, the offer price is deemed to be adequate and no additional valuation of the company needs to take place.[1529] The minority shareholders are excluded once the court decision becomes final and binding.[1530] The possibility to initiate a squeeze-out pursuant to the Securities Acquisition and Takeover Act does not prevent the offeror from initiating a squeeze-out pursuant to the Stock Corporation Act. However, a squeeze-out pursuant to the Stock Corporation Act is not permitted while a squeeze-out procedure pursuant to the Securities Acquisition and Takeover Act is pending. If a squeeze-out pursuant to the Securities Acquisition and Takeover Act is possible, the outstanding shareholders who did not accept the offer have the right to accept the offer within an additional period of three months after the offer has ended.[1531]

4. Stock Exchange Act

The Stock Exchange Act provides the legal basis for comprehensive state supervision of securities exchanges and over-the-counter trading. It includes general provisions relating to the stock exchanges, their legal bodies, the pertinent supervisory agencies and their powers as well as regulations regarding the determining of the stock exchange price for securities. Furthermore, the Stock Exchange Act also stipulates the provisions concerning the admission of securities to stock exchange trading in the official or regulated markets.

5. Securities Prospectus Act

The Securities Prospectus Act is aimed at improving the protection of investors by ensuring that the public is informed about securities on offer and the issuers thereof. It applies when securities are placed on public offer or are to be admitted to trading on a German stock exchange. Whenever this is the case, the party offering the securities has to publish a sales prospectus.

The Securities Prospectus Act stipulates the required contents of the sales prospectus. In addition, the law governs the publication of the sales prospectus and the liability for the prospectus. Liability for the prospectus applies if information given in a sales prospectus which is essential for assessing the securities on offer is either incorrect or incomplete.

6. Provisions of the Stock Corporation Act

The Stock Corporation Act differentiates in various instances between *AGs* which are admitted to stock exchange trading and those which are not. In some instances, the Stock Corporation Act stipulates stricter provisions for listed *AGs* than for unlisted *AGs*.

Sec. 3 para. 2 of the Stock Corporation Act gives a **definition** of a listed *AG* within the meaning of the Stock Corporation Act. A listed *AG* is a company "whose shares are admitted to a market which is regulated and monitored by

---

[1528] Sec. 39b of the Securities Acquisition and Takeover Act.
[1529] Sec. 39a para. 3 sentence 3 of the Securities Acquisition and Takeover Act.
[1530] Sec. 39b para. 5 sentence 1 of the Securities Acquisition and Takeover Act.
[1531] Sec. 39c of the Securities Acquisition and Takeover Act.

state-recognized authorities, takes place regularly and is accessible directly or indirectly to the public".

The market described in sec. 3 para. 2 of the Stock Corporation Act covers the **regulated market** (*regulierter Handel*)[1532] but not the unofficial market (*Freiverkehr*).[1533]

Most differences between listed and non-listed *AGs* are found in the provisions of the Stock Corporation Act relating to the **constitution of the *AG***:

- The **supervisory board** must hold two **meetings** every six months, except in the case of non-listed *AGs* where the supervisory board may pass a resolution stipulating that only one meeting is to be held every calendar year.[1534]
- When **members of the supervisory board** are to be **elected** by the general meeting, listed *AGs* are obliged to provide information on other seats in supervisory boards held by the nominated candidate.[1535] The purpose of this provision is to disclose potential interlocking between the personnel of listed *AGs*.
- The articles of association may provide how the **right to attend the general meeting** shall be proven.[1536] However, for bearer shares of listed companies, a proof of share ownership issued in text form by the custodian bank is in any case sufficient.[1537] For holders of registered shares of listed companies, the right to attend the general meeting and to exercise their voting rights follows from their registration in the share register according to sec. 67 para. 2 sentence 1 of the Stock Corporation Act.[1538]
- Each resolution adopted by the general meeting has to be recorded in the minutes of the general meeting.[1539] It is generally sufficient for the minutes to be signed by the chairman of the supervisory board, provided no resolutions are passed which require by law a majority of three quarters or more.

In the case of listed companies, however, each resolution adopted by the general meeting has to be recorded in **minutes** taken by a notary in the form of a **notarial deed**.[1540]

- The principle "one share, one vote" applies. Only the articles of association of a non-listed *AG* may **limit voting rights** by stipulating a maximum par value or a sliding scale in the case that a shareholder is the owner of several shares.[1541]
- A shareholder is obliged to **disclose** to a non-listed *AG* if he has acquired more than 25% or more than 50%.[1542] In case of a listed *AG*, whose shares are admitted to trading on an organized market, only the special publicity obligations stipulated in the Securities Trading Act apply in order to avoid double disclosure obligations.[1543]
- Pursuant to **sec. 161 of the Stock Corporation Act**, the management board and the supervisory board of listed companies have to declare annually to what extent the recommendations of the Corporate Governance Code have been

---

[1532] Sec. 32 et seq. of the Stock Exchange Act.
[1533] Sec. 48 of the Stock Exchange Act.
[1534] Sec. 110 para. 3 of the Stock Corporation Act.
[1535] Sec. 125 para. 1 sentence 5 of the Stock Corporation Act.
[1536] Sec. 123 para. 3 sentence 2 of the Stock Corporation Act.
[1537] Sec. 123 para. 4 sentence 1 of the Stock Corporation Act.
[1538] Sec. 123 para. 5 of the Stock Corporation Act.
[1539] Sec. 130 para. 1 sentence 1 of the Stock Corporation Act.
[1540] Sec. 130 para. 1 sentences 1 and 3 of the Stock Corporation Act.
[1541] Sec. 134 para. 1 of the Stock Corporation Act.
[1542] Sec. 20, 21 of the Stock Corporation Act.
[1543] Sec. 20 para. 8, sec. 21 para. 5 of the Stock Corporation Act in connection with sec. 21 para. 2 of the Securities Trading Act.

and are being complied with or which recommendations have not been or are not applied and for what reasons (so-called **Compliance Declaration**). The Corporate Governance Code contains both an overview of the applicable rules of conduct for the management of listed *AGs* and recommendations for good practice. Sec. 161 of the Stock Corporation Act serves the purpose to establish recognized standards of conduct for the management of listed *AGs* and to support the confidence of domestic and foreign investors.

- The supervisory board is obliged to inspect the annual financial statements, the management report and the proposal for the distribution of the balance sheet profit, as well as the consolidated financial statements and the consolidated group management report in the case of a parent company of a group of companies. The **supervisory board reports** to the general meeting in writing on the results of its inspection.[1544] In the case of listed *AGs*, the report also has to state which supervisory board committees have been formed and the number of meetings held by the supervisory board and its committees.

C. Taxation of German Limited Liability Companies and Stock Corporations

As corporations, both the *AG* and the *GmbH* are subject to various taxes under German law.

From a practical point of view, the most important taxes applicable to *AGs* and *GmbHs* are corporate income tax (*Körperschaftsteuer*), the solidarity surcharge (*Solidaritätszuschlag*) on corporate income tax, trade tax (*Gewerbesteuer*), value-added tax (*Umsatzsteuer*), and real estate transfer tax (*Grunderwerbsteuer*).

I. Income Taxes

1. Corporate Income Tax

Any income derived by a *GmbH* or an *AG* that is tax resident in Germany is generally subject to corporate income tax. The taxable income has to be determined in accordance with the provisions of the German Corporate Income Tax Act (*Körperschaftsteuergesetz*) and the German Income Tax Act (*Einkommensteuergesetz*).[1545] These provisions stipulate that the tax assessment basis is determined by the **profit** as shown in the **local GAAP financial statements** of the company. Such profit is, however, amended (due to particular concerns of German tax law) by special tax accounting rules which lead to a modified **profit for tax purposes**. This ensures a unified tax basis.

The tax rate is 1% for any profits (whether retained or distributed).[1546] A **solidarity surcharge**[1547] of 5.5% is levied on the resulting corporate income tax, thus leading to an aggregate tax rate of 15.825%.

[1544] Sec. 171 paras. 1 and 2 of the Stock Corporation Act.
[1545] Sec. 8 of the Corporate Income Tax Act in connection with sec.4 para. 1 and sec. 5 of the Income Tax Act.
[1546] Sec. 23 para. 1 of the Corporate Income Tax Act.
[1547] The solidarity surcharge was introduced for the purpose of financing the reunification of Germany of 1990.

The tax **assessment period** is the calendar year if the fiscal year (*Wirtschaftsjahr*) of the company corresponds to the calendar year. With the consent of the tax authorities, the company may elect a fiscal year that deviates from the calendar year, in which case this differing fiscal year forms the tax assessment period.

Corporate income tax returns have to be filed by May 31 of the calendar year following the end of the relevant tax assessment period.[1548] However, with the consent of the tax authorities, an extension of this period is possible upon request.

AGs and *GmbHs* are in principle required to make **advance payments** on their annual corporate income tax liability. The advance payments are determined once a year and paid by the corporation quarterly (March 10, June 10, September 10 and December 10). The quarterly amount due is determined by the tax authorities based on the corporate income tax liability of the previous assessment period.

2. Trade Tax

The income of a corporation is also subject to trade tax which is levied by the German municipalities (*Gemeinden*) where the business is conducted. The income subject to trade tax is determined on the basis of the profit as calculated for corporate income purposes, adjusted by specific additions and reductions for trade tax purposes.[1549]

The trade tax rate ranges between 7% and 17.5%, depending on the local multiplier applicable in the relevant municipality. Based on an average multiplier for Germany of 400%, the trade tax rate would be 14%, thus leading to an **average combined tax rate** for corporate income tax and trade tax of **29.825%**.

Like corporate income tax, trade tax is assessed based on the profit of the relevant fiscal year for which quarterly advance payments are due and an annual tax return has to be filed.

3. Dividend Distributions

Dividends distributed by a *GmbH* or an *AG* are generally subject to **withholding tax** of 26.375% (including a solidarity surcharge of 5.5%) which has to be deducted by the company from the gross dividend and paid directly to the tax authorities.

At the **shareholder level**, such withholding tax is creditable against the individual income tax liability of shareholders resident in Germany (or refundable in case of an overpayment). However, for individual shareholders holding the shares as non-business assets, a general flat-rate tax corresponding to the amount of the withholding tax (i.e., 26.375%) generally applies as definitive withholding tax. In the case of corporate shareholders, 95% of the dividend is tax exempt in principle (i.e., only 5% of the dividend is subject to income taxation) provided that the corporate shareholder holds a participation in the company of at least 15%.

Shareholders who are not resident in Germany may be entitled to a reduction of, or exemption from the withholding tax liability under certain conditions, in particular pursuant to a double taxation treaty or the EU Parent Subsidiary Directive.[1550]

[1548] Sec. 149 para. 2 of the General Tax Code (Abgabenordnung).
[1549] Sec. 7 through 9 German Trade Tax Act (*Gewerbesteuergesestz*). For example, 25% of any interest paid on loans extended to the company have to be added back for trade tax purposes.
[1550] Sec. 43b, 44a para. 9 and sec. 50d of the Income Tax Act.

II. Other Taxes

1. Value-Added Tax

Generally, supplies rendered or received by a *GmbH* or an *AG* are subject to value-added tax at a rate of 19%. In principle, the value-added tax has to be paid to the tax authorities by the entrepreneur rendering the supply. The recipient is entitled to deduct the respective input value-added tax if it is an entrepreneur (which is usually true, in principle, for a *GmbH* and an *AG*).

2. Real Estate Transfer Tax

The sale of German real estate by way of an asset deal is subject to real estate transfer tax at a tax rate of up to 6.5%[1551] of the purchase price, depending on the German state which levies the tax. Real estate transfer tax is triggered, as a general rule, also if a *GmbH* or an *AG* holds German real estate and 95% or more of the shares in such company are transferred to one acquirer (or a group of dominating and controlled acquirers). In this case, the real estate transfer tax amounts to up to 6.5% of the tax value of the properties owned by the company (which very roughly corresponds to the fair market value of the property).

[1551] Baden-Württemberg 5,0%; Bayern 3.5%; Berlin 6.0%; Brandenburg 6.5%; Bremen 5.0%; Hamburg 4.5%; Hessen 6.0%; Mecklenburg-Vorpommern 5.0%; Niedersachsen 5.0%; Nordrhein-Westfalen 6.5%; Rheinland-Pfalz 5.0%; Saarland 6.5%; Sachsen 3.5%; Sachsen-Anhalt 5.0%; Schleswig-Holstein 6.5%; Thüringen 5.0% (as of January 2016).

Part 2: Relevant Statutes

A. Limited Liability Company Act

<table>
<tr><td>

Gesetz betreffend die
Gesellschaften mit beschränkter
Haftung
Vom 20. April 1892 (RGBl. S. 477)
in der Fassung der Bekannt-
machung vom 20. Mai 1898
(RGBl. S. 846)

BGBl. III/FNA 4123-1

</td><td>

Enacted on April 20, 1892
(Reich Law Gazette, p. 477)
in the announcement of
May 20, 1898
(Reich Law Gazette, p. 846)

Federal Law Gazette,
Vol. III/FNA 4123-1

</td></tr>
</table>

Zuletzt geändert durch Art. 8 des Gesetzes zur Umsetzung der prüfungsbezogenen Regelungen der Richtlinie 2014/56/EU sowie zur Ausführung der entsprechenden Vorgaben der Verordnung (EU) Nr. 537/2014 im Hinblick auf die Abschlussprüfung bei Unternehmen von öffentlichem Interesse vom 10. Mai 2016.

Last amended by Art. 8 of the Act to Implement the Provisions of Directive 2014/56/EU and enforce the Corresponding Provisions of Regulation 537/2014/EU with regard to the Audit of Public-Interest Entities, dated May 10, 2016 (Federal Law Gazette, Vol. I p. 1142).

Inhaltsübersicht	§§	Summary of Contents	§§
Erster Abschnitt. Errichtung der Gesellschaft	1–12	Part One. Establishment of the Company	1–12
Zweiter Abschnitt. Rechtsverhältnisse der Gesellschaft und der Gesellschafter	13–34	Part Two. Legal Relationships of the Company and the Shareholders	13–34
Dritter Abschnitt. Vertretung und Geschäftsführung	35–52	Part Three. Representation and Management	35–52
Vierter Abschnitt. Abänderungen des Gesellschaftsvertrages	53–59	Part Four. Amendments to the Articles of Association	53–59
Fünfter Abschnitt. Auflösung und Nichtigkeit der Gesellschaft	60–77	Part Five. Dissolution and Nullity of the Company	60–77
Sechster Abschnitt. Ordnungs-, Straf- und Bußgeldvorschriften	78–88	Part Six. Administrative, Penal and Administrative Fine Provisions	78–88

Abschnitt 1. Errichtung der Gesellschaft

§ 1 Zweck; Gründerzahl.

Gesellschaften mit beschränkter Haftung können nach Maßgabe der Bestimmungen dieses Gesetzes zu jedem gesetzlich zulässigen Zweck durch eine oder mehrere Personen errichtet werden.

§ 2 Form des Gesellschaftsvertrags.

(1) ^{1}Der Gesellschaftsvertrag bedarf notarieller Form. ^{2}Er ist von sämtlichen Gesellschaftern zu unterzeichnen.

(1a) ^{1}Die Gesellschaft kann in einem vereinfachten Verfahren gegründet werden, wenn sie höchstens drei Gesellschafter und einen Geschäftsführer hat. ^{2}Für die Gründung im vereinfachten Verfahren ist das in der Anlage bestimmte Musterprotokoll zu verwenden. ^{3}Darüber hinaus dürfen keine vom Gesetz abweichenden Bestimmungen getroffen werden. ^{4}Das Musterprotokoll gilt zugleich als Gesellschafterliste. ^{5}Im Übrigen finden auf das Musterprotokoll die Vorschriften dieses Gesetzes über den Gesellschaftsvertrag entsprechende Anwendung.

(2) Die Unterzeichnung durch Bevollmächtigte ist nur auf Grund einer notariell errichteten oder beglaubigten Vollmacht zulässig.

§ 3 Inhalt des Gesellschaftsvertrags.

(1) Der Gesellschaftsvertrag muß enthalten:

1. die Firma und den Sitz der Gesellschaft,
2. den Gegenstand des Unternehmens,
3. den Betrag des Stammkapitals,
4. die Zahl und die Nennbeträge der Geschäftsanteile, die jeder Gesellschafter gegen Einlage auf das

Part 1. Establishment of the Company

§ 1 Purpose; Number of Founders.

Limited liability companies can be established for any legally permissible purpose by one or more persons, in accordance with the provisions of this Act.

§ 2 Form of the articles of association.

(1) ^{1}The articles of association shall be notarized. ^{2}They shall be signed by all the shareholders.

(1a) ^{1}The company may be incorporated in a simplified proceeding if it has at most three shareholders and one managing director. ^{2}For incorporation in the simplified proceeding, the model protocol attached hereto shall be used. ^{3}Furthermore, the provisions of this Act may not be modified. ^{4}The model protocol shall at the same time be deemed the shareholder list. ^{5}Apart from that, the provisions of this Act on the articles of association shall apply accordingly.

(2) Signing by authorized representatives is permissible only on the basis of a power of attorney drawn up or certified by a notary.

§ 3 Contents of the articles of association.

(1) The articles of association shall contain:

1. the name and the registered office of the company,
2. the object of the enterprise,
3. the amount of the registered share capital,
4. the number and the nominal amounts of the shares which each shareholder subscribes to against

Stammkapital (Stammeinlage) übernimmt.

(2) Soll das Unternehmen auf eine gewisse Zeit beschränkt sein oder sollen den Gesellschaftern außer der Leistung von Kapitaleinlagen noch andere Verpflichtungen gegenüber der Gesellschaft auferlegt werden, so bedürfen auch diese Bestimmungen der Aufnahme in den Gesellschaftsvertrag.

§ 4 Firma.

¹Die Firma der Gesellschaft muß, auch wenn sie nach § 22 des Handelsgesetzbuchs oder nach anderen gesetzlichen Vorschriften fortgeführt wird, die Bezeichnung „Gesellschaft mit beschränkter Haftung" oder eine allgemein verständliche Abkürzung dieser Bezeichnung enthalten. ²Verfolgt die Gesellschaft ausschließlich und unmittelbar steuerbegünstigte Zwecke nach den §§ 51 bis 68 der Abgabenordnung kann die Abkürzung „gGmbH" lauten.

§ 4a Sitz der Gesellschaft.

Sitz der Gesellschaft ist der Ort im Inland, den der Gesellschaftsvertrag bestimmt.

§ 5 Stammkapital; Geschäftsanteil.

(1) Das Stammkapital der Gesellschaft muß mindestens fünfundzwanzigtausend Euro betragen.

(2) ¹Der Nennbetrag jedes Geschäftsanteils muss auf volle Euro lauten. ²Ein Gesellschafter kann bei Errichtung der Gesellschaft mehrere Geschäftsanteile übernehmen.

(3) ¹Die Höhe der Nennbeträge der einzelnen Geschäftsanteile kann verschieden bestimmt werden. ²Die Summe der Nennbeträge aller Geschäftsanteile muss mit dem Stammkapital übereinstimmen.

(4) ¹Sollen Sacheinlagen geleistet werden, so müssen der Gegenstand der

contribution to the registered share capital (original contribution).

(2) Should the enterprise be limited to a certain time or should other obligations vis-à-vis the company be imposed on the shareholders other than the payment of capital contributions, then these provisions shall also be included in the articles of association.

§ 4 Name.

¹The name of the company shall contain the designation "limited liability company" or a generally understandable abbreviation of this designation, even if the name is continued according to sec. 22 of the Commercial Code or other legal regulations. ²If the company exclusively and directly pursues tax-privileged purposes in accordance with sec. 51 to 68 of the Fiscal Code, the abbreviation "gGmbH" may be used.

§ 4a Registered office of the company.

The registered office of the company is the location in Germany determined by the articles of association.

§ 5 Registered share capital; share.

(1) The registered share capital of the company shall amount to at least twenty-five thousand euros.

(2) ¹The nominal amount of each share shall be an even euro amount. ²A shareholder may subscribe to more than one share at the time of establishment of the company.

(3) ¹The nominal amounts of the individual shares may differ from each other. ²The sum of the nominal amounts of all shares shall correspond to the registered share capital.

(4) ¹If contributions in kind are to be made, the items comprising the contri-

Sacheinlage und der Nennbetrag des Geschäftsanteils, auf den sich die Sacheinlage bezieht, im Gesellschaftsvertrag festgesetzt werden. ²Die Gesellschafter haben in einem Sachgründungsbericht die für die Angemessenheit der Leistungen für Sacheinlagen wesentlichen Umstände darzulegen und beim Übergang eines Unternehmens auf die Gesellschaft die Jahresergebnisse der beiden letzten Geschäftsjahre anzugeben.

§ 5a Unternehmergesellschaft.

(1) Eine Gesellschaft, die mit einem Stammkapital gegründet wird, das den Betrag des Mindeststammkapitals nach § 5 Abs. 1 unterschreitet, muss in der Firma abweichend von § 4 die Bezeichnung „Unternehmergesellschaft (haftungsbeschränkt)" oder „UG (haftungsbeschränkt)" führen.

(2) ¹Abweichend von § 7 Abs. 2 darf die Anmeldung erst erfolgen, wenn das Stammkapital in voller Höhe eingezahlt ist. ²Sacheinlagen sind ausgeschlossen.

(3) ¹In der Bilanz des nach den §§ 242, 264 des Handelsgesetzbuchs aufzustellenden Jahresabschlusses ist eine gesetzliche Rücklage zu bilden, in die ein Viertel des um einen Verlustvortrag aus dem Vorjahr geminderten Jahresüberschusses einzustellen ist. ²Die Rücklage darf nur verwandt werden

1. für Zwecke des § 57c;
2. zum Ausgleich eines Jahresfehlbetrags, soweit er nicht durch einen Gewinnvortrag aus dem Vorjahr gedeckt ist;
3. zum Ausgleich eines Verlustvortrags aus dem Vorjahr, soweit er nicht durch einen Jahresüberschuss gedeckt ist.

(4) Abweichend von § 49 Abs. 3 muss die Versammlung der Gesellschafter bei drohender Zahlungsunfähigkeit unverzüglich einberufen werden.

bution in kind and the nominal amount of the share the contribution in kind represents shall be stipulated in the articles of association. ²The shareholders shall, in a report on formation through contributions in kind, describe the main considerations for the fairness of the valuation of the contributions in kind, and, in the case of the transfer of an enterprise to the company, indicate the annual earnings of such enterprise during the last two fiscal years.

§ 5a Entrepreneur company.

(1) A company established with a registered share capital that falls short of the minimum registered share capital set forth in sec. 5 para. 1 shall, sec. 4 notwithstanding, include the designation "Unternehmergesellschaft (with limited liability)" or "UG (with limited liability)" in its company name.

(2) ¹Sec. 7 para. 2 notwithstanding, the application for registration shall be made only when the registered share capital has been contributed in full. ²Contributions in kind are excluded.

(3) ¹In the balance sheet of the annual financial statements to be drawn up pursuant to sec. 242, 264 of the Commercial Code, a statutory reserve must be created to which one fourth of the annual net income, reduced by losses carried forward from the previous year, shall be contributed. ²The reserve may only be used:

1. for the purposes of sec. 57c;
2. for compensation of annual net losses to the extent they are not covered by profits carried forward from the previous year;
3. for compensation of losses carried forward from the previous year to the extent they are not covered by annual net profits.

(4) Sec. 49 para. 3 notwithstanding, the meeting of the shareholders shall be convened without undue delay in the case of imminent illiquidity.

(5) Erhöht die Gesellschaft ihr Stammkapital so, dass es den Betrag des Mindeststammkapitals nach § 5 Abs. 1 erreicht oder übersteigt, finden die Absätze 1 bis 4 keine Anwendung mehr; die Firma nach Absatz 1 darf beibehalten werden.

§ 6 Geschäftsführer.

(1) Die Gesellschaft muß einen oder mehrere Geschäftsführer haben.

(2) ¹Geschäftsführer kann nur eine natürliche, unbeschränkt geschäftsfähige Person sein. ²Geschäftsführer kann nicht sein, wer

1. als Betreuter bei der Besorgung seiner Vermögensangelegenheiten ganz oder teilweise einem Einwilligungsvorbehalt (§ 1903 des Bürgerlichen Gesetzbuchs) unterliegt,

2. aufgrund eines gerichtlichen Urteils oder einer vollziehbaren Entscheidung einer Verwaltungsbehörde einen Beruf, einen Berufszweig, ein Gewerbe oder einen Gewerbezweig nicht ausüben darf, sofern der Unternehmensgegenstand ganz oder teilweise mit dem Gegenstand des Verbots übereinstimmt,
3. wegen einer oder mehrerer vorsätzlich begangener Straftaten
    a) des Unterlassens der Stellung des Antrags auf Eröffnung des Insolvenzverfahrens (Insolvenzverschleppung),
    b) nach den §§ 283 bis 283d des Strafgesetzbuchs (Insolvenzstraftaten),
    c) der falschen Angaben nach § 82 dieses Gesetzes oder § 399 des Aktiengesetzes,
    d) der unrichtigen Darstellung nach § 400 des Aktiengesetzes, § 331 des Handelsgesetzbuchs, § 313 des Umwandlungsgesetzes oder § 17 des Publizitätsgesetzes oder

(5) If the company increases its registered share capital such that it reaches or exceeds the amount of the minimum registered share capital pursuant to sec. 5 para. 1, para. 1 to 4 shall no longer apply; the company name pursuant to para. 1 may be retained.

§ 6 Managing directors.

(1) The company shall have one or more managing directors.

(2) ¹Only a natural person with full legal capacity may be managing director. ²A managing director cannot be an individual who,

1. as a ward, with regard to the handling of his financial affairs, is partially or completely subject to a requirement that any transactions entered into by him be approved by a third party (sec. 1903 of the Civil Code).

2. is, due to a court judgment or by an enforceable decision of an administrative body, prohibited from engaging in a profession, a branch of a profession, a trade or a branch of a trade to the extent that the object of the enterprise matches the subject matter of the prohibition in whole or in part.
3. has been convicted of one or more intentionally committed criminal offenses
    a) of failure to file the application for the commencement of insolvency proceedings (delay in filing a petition in insolvency),
    b) pursuant to sec. 283 to 283d of the Criminal Code (criminal offenses related to insolvency),
    c) of making false statements pursuant to sec. 82 of this Act or sec. 399 of the Stock Corporation Act,
    d) of misrepresentation pursuant to sec. 400 of the Stock Corporation Act, sec. 331 of the Commercial Code, sec. 313 of the Transforma-

e) nach den §§ 263 bis 264a oder den §§ 265b bis 266a des Strafgesetzbuchs zu einer Freiheitsstrafe von mindestens einem Jahr verurteilt worden ist; dieser Ausschluss gilt für die Dauer von fünf Jahren seit der Rechtskraft des Urteils, wobei die Zeit nicht eingerechnet wird, in welcher der Täter auf behördliche Anordnung in einer Anstalt verwahrt worden ist.

³Satz 2 Nr. 3 gilt entsprechend bei einer Verurteilung im Ausland wegen einer Tat, die mit den in Satz 2 Nr. 3 genannten Taten vergleichbar ist.

(3) ¹Zu Geschäftsführern können Gesellschafter oder andere Personen bestellt werden. ²Die Bestellung erfolgt entweder im Gesellschaftsvertrag oder nach Maßgabe der Bestimmungen des dritten Abschnitts.

(4) Ist im Gesellschaftsvertrag bestimmt, daß sämtliche Gesellschafter zur Geschäftsführung berechtigt sein sollen, so gelten nur die der Gesellschaft bei Festsetzung dieser Bestimmung angehörenden Personen als die bestellten Geschäftsführer.

(5) Gesellschafter, die vorsätzlich oder grob fahrlässig einer Person, die nicht Geschäftsführer sein kann, die Führung der Geschäfte überlassen, haften der Gesellschaft solidarisch für den Schaden, der dadurch entsteht, dass diese Person die ihr gegenüber der Gesellschaft bestehenden Obliegenheiten verletzt.

§ 7 Anmeldung der Gesellschaft.

(1) Die Gesellschaft ist bei dem Gericht, in dessen Bezirk sie ihren Sitz hat, zur Eintragung in das Handelsregister anzumelden.

e) pursuant to sec. 263 to 264a or sec. 265b to 266a of the Criminal Code resulting in a prison sentence of one year or longer; this exclusion shall apply for five years from when the conviction has become res judicata excluding the period of time during which the offender was confined to an institution by official order.

³Sentence 2 no. 3 shall apply accordingly in the case of a conviction abroad of an offense which is comparable to the offenses mentioned in sentence 2 no. 3.

(3) ¹Shareholders or other persons may be appointed as managing directors. ²The appointment shall be made either in the articles of association or according to the provisions of Part Three herein.

(4) If it is stipulated in the articles of association that all the shareholders are authorized to manage the company, only the persons belonging to the company at the time of the adoption of such stipulation shall be deemed to be the appointed managing directors.

(5) Shareholders who intentionally or grossly negligently surrender the management of the business to someone who may not be a managing director are jointly and severally liable to the company for any damages caused by this person through violation of his obligations to the company.

§ 7 Application for registration of the company.

(1) An application shall be made for the company to be registered with the commercial register of the court in the district where the company has its registered office.

(2) ¹Die Anmeldung darf erst erfolgen, wenn auf jeden Geschäftsanteil, soweit nicht Sacheinlagen vereinbart sind, ein Viertel des Nennbetrags eingezahlt ist. ²Insgesamt muß auf das Stammkapital mindestens soviel eingezahlt sein, daß der Gesamtbetrag der eingezahlten Geldeinlagen zuzüglich des Gesamtnennbetrags der Geschäftsanteile, für die Sacheinlagen zu leisten sind, die Hälfte des Mindeststammkapitals gemäß § 5 Abs. 1 erreicht.

(3) Die Sacheinlagen sind vor der Anmeldung der Gesellschaft zur Eintragung in das Handelsregister so an die Gesellschaft zu bewirken, daß sie endgültig zur freien Verfügung der Geschäftsführer stehen.

§ 8 Inhalt der Anmeldung.

(1) Der Anmeldung müssen beigefügt sein:

1. der Gesellschaftsvertrag und im Fall des § 2 Abs. 2 die Vollmachten der Vertreter, welche den Gesellschaftsvertrag unterzeichnet haben, oder eine beglaubigte Abschrift dieser Urkunden,
2. die Legitimation der Geschäftsführer, sofern dieselben nicht im Gesellschaftsvertrag bestellt sind,
3. eine von den Anmeldenden unterschriebene Liste der Gesellschafter, aus welcher Name, Vorname, Geburtsdatum und Wohnort der letzteren sowie die Nennbeträge und die laufenden Nummern der von einem jeden derselben übernommenen Geschäftsanteile ersichtlich sind,
4. im Fall des § 5 Abs. 4 die Verträge, die den Festsetzungen zugrunde liegen oder zu ihrer Ausführung geschlossen worden sind, und der Sachgründungsbericht,
5. wenn Sacheinlagen vereinbart sind, Unterlagen darüber, daß der Wert der Sacheinlagen den Nennbetrag

(2) ¹The application may not be made until, if no contributions in kind have been agreed, at least one fourth of the nominal amount of every share has been paid in by each of the shareholders. ²The total amount of the cash contributions paid in plus the total nominal amount of the shares for which contributions in kind are to be made shall at least be equal to one half of the required minimum registered share capital pursuant to sec. 5 para. 1.

(3) The contributions in kind are to be effected prior to the application for the company's registration with the commercial register, in such a way that they are definitively at the free disposal of the managing directors.

§ 8 Contents of the application.

(1) Along with the application shall be enclosed:

1. the articles of association and, if sec. 2 para. 2 applies, the powers of attorney of the representatives who have signed the articles of association, or a certified copy of such documents,
2. the proof of appointment for the managing directors, if they are not appointed in the articles of association,
3. a list of shareholders, signed by the applicants, specifying for each shareholder surname, first name, date of birth and place of residence, as well as the nominal amounts and the serial numbers of the shares to which each shareholder has subscribed,
4. if sec. 5 para. 4 applies, the contracts on which the stipulation are based or which were concluded for their implementation, and the report on formation through contributions in kind,
5. if contributions in kind have been agreed, documents showing that the value of the contributions in kind

der dafür übernommenen Geschäftsanteile erreicht.

(2) ¹In der Anmeldung ist die Versicherung abzugeben, daß die in § 7 Abs. 2 und 3 bezeichneten Leistungen auf die Geschäftsanteile bewirkt sind und daß der Gegenstand der Leistungen sich endgültig in der freien Verfügung der Geschäftsführer befindet. ²Das Gericht kann bei erheblichen Zweifeln an der Richtigkeit der Versicherung Nachweise (unter anderem Einzahlungsbelege) verlangen.

(3) ¹In der Anmeldung haben die Geschäftsführer zu versichern, daß keine Umstände vorliegen, die ihrer Bestellung nach § 6 Abs. 2 Satz 2 Nr. 2 und 3 sowie Satz 3 entgegenstehen, und daß sie über ihre unbeschränkte Auskunftspflicht gegenüber dem Gericht belehrt worden sind. ²Die Belehrung nach § 53 Abs. 2 des Bundeszentralregistergesetzes kann schriftlich vorgenommen werden; sie kann auch durch einen Notar oder einen im Ausland bestellten Notar, durch einen Vertreter eines vergleichbaren rechtsberatenden Berufs oder einen Konsularbeamten erfolgen.

(4) In der Anmeldung sind ferner anzugeben

1. eine inländische Geschäftsanschrift,
2. Art und Umfang der Vertretungsbefugnis der Geschäftsführer.

(5) Für die Einreichung von Unterlagen nach diesem Gesetz gilt § 12 Abs. 2 des Handelsgesetzbuchs entsprechend.

§ 9 Überbewertung der Sacheinlagen.

(1) ¹Erreicht der Wert einer Sacheinlage im Zeitpunkt der Anmeldung der Gesellschaft zur Eintragung in das Handelsregister nicht den Nennbetrag des dafür übernommenen Geschäftsanteils, hat der Gesellschafter in Höhe des Fehl-

equals the nominal amount of the subscribed shares.

(2) ¹In the application, assurance shall be provided that the considerations indicated in sec. 7 paras. 2 and 3 in respect to the shares have been effected and that the assets comprising the consideration are definitively at the free disposal of the managing directors. ²If there are substantial doubts concerning the truthfulness of the assurance, the court may request proof (inter alia deposit receipts).

(3) ¹In the application, the managing directors shall provide assurance that no circumstances exist that, according to sec. 6 para. 2 sentence 2 nos. 2 and 3 as well as sentence 3 present an obstacle to their appointment, and that they have been advised of their unlimited duty to furnish information to the court. ²Such advisement pursuant to sec. 53 para. 2 of the Federal Central Register Act may be performed in writing; it may also be performed by a notary or a notary appointed in a foreign country, by a representative of a comparable profession providing legal advice or by a consular officer.

(4) The application shall further state

1. a business address in Germany,
2. the nature and extent of the power of representation of the managing directors.

(5) Sec. 12 para. 2 of the Commercial Code shall apply accordingly to the submission of documents pursuant to this Act.

§ 9 Overvaluation of the contributions in kind.

(1) ¹If, at the time the application is made for the company's registration in the commercial register, the value of any contribution in kind does not equal the nominal amount of the respective share subscribed to, the shareholder

betrags eine Einlage in Geld zu leisten. ²Sonstige Ansprüche bleiben unberührt.

(2) Der Anspruch der Gesellschaft nach Absatz 1 Satz 1 verjährt in zehn Jahren seit der Eintragung der Gesellschaft in das Handelsregister.

§ 9a Ersatzansprüche der Gesellschaft.

(1) Werden zum Zweck der Errichtung der Gesellschaft falsche Angaben gemacht, so haben die Gesellschafter und Geschäftsführer der Gesellschaft als Gesamtschuldner fehlende Einzahlungen zu leisten, eine Vergütung, die nicht unter den Gründungsaufwand aufgenommen ist, zu ersetzen und für den sonst entstehenden Schaden Ersatz zu leisten.

(2) Wird die Gesellschaft von Gesellschaftern durch Einlagen oder Gründungsaufwand vorsätzlich oder aus grober Fahrlässigkeit geschädigt, so sind ihr alle Gesellschafter als Gesamtschuldner zum Ersatz verpflichtet.

(3) Von diesen Verpflichtungen ist ein Gesellschafter oder ein Geschäftsführer befreit, wenn er die die Ersatzpflicht begründenden Tatsachen weder kannte noch bei Anwendung der Sorgfalt eines ordentlichen Geschäftsmannes kennen mußte.

(4) ¹Neben den Gesellschaftern sind in gleicher Weise Personen verantwortlich, für deren Rechnung die Gesellschafter Geschäftsanteile übernommen haben. ²Sie können sich auf ihre eigene Unkenntnis nicht wegen solcher Umstände berufen, die ein für ihre Rechnung handelnder Gesellschafter kannte oder bei Anwendung der Sorgfalt eines ordentlichen Geschäftsmannes kennen mußte.

shall make a contribution in cash in the amount of the deficiency. ²Further claims shall remain unaffected.

(2) The claim of the company pursuant to sec. 1 sentence 1 shall become time-barred ten years after registration of the company in the commercial register.

§ 9a Claims to damages of the company.

(1) If false information is provided for purposes of the establishment of the company, the shareholders and managing directors of the company as joint and several debtors shall make the outstanding payments, pay any compensation not included in the expenses for the formation and indemnify the company for damages arising otherwise.

(2) If through contributions or expenses for the formation the company is harmed by shareholders intentionally or by gross negligence, all shareholders, as joint and several debtors, are obligated to indemnify the company.

(3) A shareholder or a managing director is released from such obligations if such shareholder, or managing director, as the case may be, was not actually aware of the facts warranting the duty to indemnify, nor should have been aware of such facts had such shareholder, or managing director, as the case may be, exercised the care of a prudent businessman.

(4) ¹In addition to the shareholders, those persons are liable in the same way for whose account the shareholders subscribed to shares. ²Those persons cannot plead their own ignorance regarding such circumstances that a shareholder acting for their account was aware or should have been aware of had he applied the care of a prudent businessman.

§ 9b Verzicht auf Ersatzansprüche.

(1) ¹Ein Verzicht der Gesellschaft auf Ersatzansprüche nach § 9a oder ein Vergleich der Gesellschaft über diese Ansprüche ist unwirksam, soweit der Ersatz zur Befriedigung der Gläubiger der Gesellschaft erforderlich ist. ²Dies gilt nicht, wenn der Ersatzpflichtige zahlungsunfähig ist und sich zur Abwendung des Insolvenzverfahrens mit seinen Gläubigern vergleicht oder wenn die Ersatzpflicht in einem Insolvenzplan geregelt wird.

(2) ¹Ersatzansprüche der Gesellschaft nach § 9a verjähren in fünf Jahren. ²Die Verjährung beginnt mit der Eintragung der Gesellschaft in das Handelsregister oder, wenn die zum Ersatz verpflichtende Handlung später begangen worden ist, mit der Vornahme der Handlung.

§ 9c Ablehnung der Eintragung.

(1) ¹Ist die Gesellschaft nicht ordnungsgemäß errichtet und angemeldet, so hat das Gericht die Eintragung abzulehnen. ²Dies gilt auch, wenn Sacheinlagen nicht unwesentlich überbewertet worden sind.

(2) Wegen einer mangelhaften, fehlenden oder nichtigen Bestimmung des Gesellschaftsvertrages darf das Gericht die Eintragung nach Absatz 1 nur ablehnen, soweit diese Bestimmung, ihr Fehlen oder ihre Nichtigkeit

1. Tatsachen oder Rechtsverhältnisse betrifft, die nach § 3 Abs. 1 oder auf Grund anderer zwingender gesetzlicher Vorschriften in dem Gesellschaftsvertrag bestimmt sein müssen oder die in das Handelsregister einzutragen oder von dem Gericht bekanntzumachen sind,
2. Vorschriften verletzt, die ausschließlich oder überwiegend zum Schutze der Gläubiger der Gesellschaft oder sonst im öffentlichen Interesse gegeben sind, oder

§ 9b Waiver of claims to damages.

(1) ¹A waiver by the company of claims to damages pursuant to sec. 9a or a composition by the company regarding these claims is invalid to the extent the indemnity is required to satisfy the claims of creditors of the company. ²This does not apply if the person having the duty to indemnify is illiquid and is reaching a composition with his creditors to avoid insolvency proceedings, or if the duty to indemnify is being determined pursuant to an insolvency plan.

(2) ¹The company's claims for damages pursuant to sec. 9a become time-barred after five years. ²The period of limitation commences upon registration of the company in the commercial register or, if the action obligating the indemnification was committed later, with the performance of the action.

§ 9c Rejection of registration.

(1) ¹The court shall refuse to register the company if the establishment of the company and the application for registration are not properly effected. ²This also applies where contributions in kind are materially overvalued.

(2) The court may reject registration according to para. 1 because of a defective, missing, or void provision of the articles of association only to the extent such provision, its absence, or its nullity

1. pertains to facts or legal matters that, according to sec. 3 para. 1 or due to other mandatory statutory provisions, have to be determined in the articles of association, or that have to be registered in the commercial register or made public by the court,
2. violates regulations that are exclusively or primarily for the protection of the creditors of the company or are otherwise in the public interest, or

3. die Nichtigkeit des Gesellschaftsvertrages zur Folge hat.

§ 10 Inhalt der Eintragung.

(1) ¹Bei der Eintragung in das Handelsregister sind die Firma und der Sitz der Gesellschaft, eine inländische Geschäftsanschrift, der Gegenstand des Unternehmens, die Höhe des Stammkapitals, der Tag des Abschlusses des Gesellschaftsvertrages und die Personen der Geschäftsführer anzugeben. ²Ferner ist einzutragen, welche Vertretungsbefugnis die Geschäftsführer haben.

(2) ¹Enthält der Gesellschaftsvertrag Bestimmungen über die Zeitdauer der Gesellschaft oder über das genehmigte Kapital, so sind auch diese Bestimmungen einzutragen. ²Wenn eine Person, die für Willenserklärungen und Zustellungen an die Gesellschaft empfangsberechtigt ist, mit einer inländischen Anschrift zur Eintragung in das Handelsregister angemeldet wird, sind auch diese Angaben einzutragen; Dritten gegenüber gilt die Empfangsberechtigung als fortbestehend, bis sie im Handelsregister gelöscht und die Löschung bekannt gemacht worden ist, es sei denn, dass die fehlende Empfangsberechtigung dem Dritten bekannt war.

§ 11 Rechtszustand vor der Eintragung.

(1) Vor der Eintragung in das Handelsregister des Sitzes der Gesellschaft besteht die Gesellschaft mit beschränkter Haftung als solche nicht.

(2) Ist vor der Eintragung im Namen der Gesellschaft gehandelt worden, so haften die Handelnden persönlich und solidarisch.

§ 12 Bekanntmachungen der Gesellschaft.

¹Bestimmt das Gesetz oder der Gesellschaftsvertrag, dass von der Gesell-

3. has the nullity of the articles of association as a consequence.

§ 10 Content of the registration.

(1) ¹For the registration in the commercial register, the name and registered office of the company, a business address in Germany, the object of the enterprise, the amount of the registered share capital, the date the articles of association were concluded and the identities of the managing directors shall be stated. ²Furthermore, the extent to which the managing directors have representative authority shall be entered.

(2) ¹If the articles of association contain provisions regarding the duration of the company or regarding the authorized capital, such provisions shall also be registered in the commercial register. ²If a person who is authorized to receive declarations of intent and deliveries addressed to the company is filed for registration in the commercial register with a business address in Germany, this information shall be registered as well; in relation to third parties, the authorization to receive shall be deemed to continue until it is deleted from the commercial register and the deletion has been announced, unless the third party was aware of the lack of authorization to receive.

§ 11 Legal status prior to registration.

(1) Prior to registration in the commercial register of the registered office of the company, the limited liability company does not exist as such.

(2) If business is transacted in the name of the company prior to the registration, the persons acting are subject to joint and several personal liability.

§ 12 Announcements of the company.

¹If the law or the articles of association stipulate that the company must an-

schaft etwas bekannt zu machen ist, so erfolgt die Bekanntmachung im Bundesanzeiger (Gesellschaftsblatt). ²Daneben kann der Gesellschaftsvertrag andere öffentliche Blätter oder elektronische Informationsmedien als Gesellschaftsblätter bezeichnen.

nounce something to the public, such announcement shall be effected in the Federal Gazette (company's designated journal). ²The articles of association may in addition designate other public journals or electronic information media as the company's designated journals.

Abschnitt 2. Rechtsverhältnisse der Gesellschaft und der Gesellschafter

Part 2. Legal Relationships of the Company and the Shareholders

§ 13 Juristische Person; Handelsgesellschaft.

§ 13 Legal entity; commercial company.

(1) Die Gesellschaft mit beschränkter Haftung als solche hat selbständig ihre Rechte und Pflichten; sie kann Eigentum und andere dingliche Rechte an Grundstücken erwerben, vor Gericht klagen und verklagt werden.

(1) The limited liability company as such has independent rights and duties; it can acquire property and other rights to real property, bring a legal action before a court and be sued in court.

(2) Für die Verbindlichkeiten der Gesellschaft haftet den Gläubigern derselben nur das Gesellschaftsvermögen.

(2) Only the corporate assets are available to satisfy the liabilities of the company to its creditors.

(3) Die Gesellschaft gilt als Handelsgesellschaft im Sinne des Handelsgesetzbuchs.

(3) The company shall be deemed a commercial company within the meaning of the Commercial Code

§ 14 Einlagepflicht.

§ 14 Obligation to render contributions.

¹Auf jeden Geschäftsanteil ist eine Einlage zu leisten. ²Die Höhe der zu leistenden Einlage richtet sich nach dem bei der Errichtung der Gesellschaft im Gesellschaftsvertrag festgesetzten Nennbetrag des Geschäftsanteils. ³Im Fall der Kapitalerhöhung bestimmt sich die Höhe der zu leistenden Einlage nach dem in der Übernahmeerklärung festgesetzten Nennbetrag des Geschäftsanteils.

¹Towards each share a contribution must be rendered. ²The amount of the contribution to be rendered is determined by the nominal amount of the share set forth in the articles of association at the time of establishment of the company. ³In case of a capital increase, the amount of the contribution to be rendered is determined by the nominal amount of the share set forth in the declaration of subscription.

§ 15 Übertragung von Geschäftsanteilen.

§ 15 Assignment of shares.

(1) Die Geschäftsanteile sind veräußerlich und vererblich.

(1) Shares are alienable and inheritable.

(2) Erwirbt ein Gesellschafter zu seinem ursprünglichen Geschäftsanteil weitere Geschäftsanteile, so behalten dieselben ihre Selbständigkeit.

(2) If a shareholder acquires additional shares to his original share, these retain their separateness.

(3) Zur Abtretung von Geschäftsanteilen durch Gesellschafter bedarf es eines in notarieller Form geschlossenen Vertrages.

(4) ¹Der notariellen Form bedarf auch eine Vereinbarung, durch welche die Verpflichtung eines Gesellschafters zur Abtretung eines Geschäftsanteils begründet wird. ²Eine ohne diese Form getroffene Vereinbarung wird jedoch durch den nach Maßgabe des vorigen Absatzes geschlossenen Abtretungsvertrag gültig.

(5) Durch den Gesellschaftsvertrag kann die Abtretung der Geschäftsanteile an weitere Voraussetzungen geknüpft, insbesondere von der Genehmigung der Gesellschaft abhängig gemacht werden.

§ 16 Rechtsstellung bei Wechsel der Gesellschafter oder Veränderung des Umfangs ihrer Beteiligung; Erwerb vom Nichtberechtigten.

(1) ¹Im Verhältnis zur Gesellschaft gilt im Fall einer Veränderung in den Personen der Gesellschafter oder des Umfangs ihrer Beteiligung als Inhaber eines Geschäftsanteils nur, wer als solcher in der im Handelsregister aufgenommenen Gesellschafterliste (§ 40) eingetragen ist. ²Eine vom Erwerber in Bezug auf das Gesellschaftsverhältnis vorgenommene Rechtshandlung gilt als von Anfang an wirksam, wenn die Liste unverzüglich nach Vornahme der Rechtshandlung in das Handelsregister aufgenommen wird.

(2) Für Einlageverpflichtungen, die in dem Zeitpunkt rückständig sind, ab dem der Erwerber gemäß Absatz 1 Satz 1 im Verhältnis zur Gesellschaft als Inhaber des Geschäftsanteils gilt, haftet der Erwerber neben dem Veräußerer.

(3) ¹Der Erwerber kann einen Geschäftsanteil oder ein Recht daran durch Rechtsgeschäft wirksam vom Nichtberechtigten erwerben, wenn der Veräußerer als Inhaber des Geschäftsanteils

(3) A notarized contract is required for the assignment of shares by shareholders.

(4) ¹An agreement creating the obligation of a shareholder to assign any shares is also required to be notarized. ²An agreement that is not notarized will nevertheless become valid through a contract of assignment concluded in accordance with the preceding paragraph.

(5) The articles of association may specify additional requirements that shall be met for the assignment of shares, in particular approval by the company.

§ 16 Legal position in case of a change of the shareholders or a change in the size of their shareholding; acquisition from an unauthorized person.

(1) ¹In the case of a change of shareholders or in the size of their shareholdings, only he who is registered as such in the list of shareholders recorded with the commercial register (sec. 40) of the company is deemed to be holder of a share. ²A legal act performed by the acquirer in respect of the corporate relationship is deemed to be effective from the start if the list is recorded with the commercial register without undue delay after the performance of the legal act.

(2) Concerning obligations to render contributions which are in arrears at the time the acquirer is deemed to be the holder of the share pursuant to para. 1 sentence 1, the acquirer shall be liable in addition to the assignor.

(3) ¹The acquirer may validly acquire a share or a right in a share by legal transaction from an unauthorized person if the assignor is registered in the shareholder list recorded with the commer-

in der im Handelsregister aufgenommenen Gesellschafterliste eingetragen ist. ²Dies gilt nicht, wenn die Liste zum Zeitpunkt des Erwerbs hinsichtlich des Geschäftsanteils weniger als drei Jahre unrichtig und die Unrichtigkeit dem Berechtigten nicht zuzurechnen ist. ³Ein gutgläubiger Erwerb ist ferner nicht möglich, wenn dem Erwerber die mangelnde Berechtigung bekannt oder infolge grober Fahrlässigkeit unbekannt ist oder der Liste ein Widerspruch zugeordnet ist. ⁴Die Zuordnung eines Widerspruchs erfolgt aufgrund einer einstweiligen Verfügung oder aufgrund einer Bewilligung desjenigen, gegen dessen Berechtigung sich der Widerspruch richtet. ⁵Eine Gefährdung des Rechts des Widersprechenden muss nicht glaubhaft gemacht werden.

cial register as holder of the share. ²This shall not apply if the list was incorrect at the time of acquisition with respect to the share for less than three years and the incorrectness is not attributable to the authorized person. ³An acquisition in good faith is furthermore not possible if the acquirer was aware of the lack of authorization or was not aware of it due to his gross negligence or if there is an objection assigned to the list. ⁴The assignment of an objection results from a temporary injunction or the approval of the person against whose authorization the objection is directed. ⁵A threat to the right of the person making the objection need not be made credible.

§ 17 *(aufgehoben)*

§ 17 *(repealed)*

§ 18 Mitberechtigung am Geschäftsanteil.

§ 18 Joint entitlement to a share.

(1) Steht ein Geschäftsanteil mehreren Mitberechtigten ungeteilt zu, so können sie die Rechte aus demselben nur gemeinschaftlich ausüben.

(1) If several persons are jointly entitled to an undivided share, the rights arising with respect to such share may be exercised only jointly.

(2) Für die auf den Geschäftsanteil zu bewirkenden Leistungen haften sie der Gesellschaft solidarisch.

(2) Such persons are jointly and severally liable to the company for the contributions to be made to the share.

(3) ¹Rechtshandlungen, welche die Gesellschaft gegenüber dem Inhaber des Anteils vorzunehmen hat, sind, sofern nicht ein gemeinsamer Vertreter der Mitberechtigten vorhanden ist, wirksam, wenn sie auch nur gegenüber einem Mitberechtigten vorgenommen werden. ²Gegenüber mehreren Erben eines Gesellschafters findet diese Bestimmung nur in bezug auf Rechtshandlungen Anwendung, welche nach Ablauf eines Monats seit dem Anfall der Erbschaft vorgenommen werden.

(3) ¹Legal actions that the company has to take vis-à-vis the person entitled to the share are valid even if they are taken vis-à-vis only one of the jointly entitled persons, unless a common representative of the jointly entitled persons exists. ²Vis-à-vis multiple heirs of a shareholder, this provision applies only in relation to legal actions that are performed after the expiration of one month after the devolution of the inheritance.

§ 19 Leistung der Einlagen.

§ 19 Rendering of the contributions.

(1) Die Einzahlungen auf die Geschäftsanteile sind nach dem Verhältnis der Geldeinlagen zu leisten.

(1) The payments on the shares shall be rendered according to the ratio of the cash contributions.

A. Limited Liability Company Act

(2) ¹Von der Verpflichtung zur Leistung der Einlagen können die Gesellschafter nicht befreit werden. ²Gegen den Anspruch der Gesellschaft ist die Aufrechnung nur zulässig mit einer Forderung aus der Überlassung von Vermögensgegenständen, deren Anrechnung auf die Einlageverpflichtung nach § 5 Abs. 4 Satz 1 vereinbart worden ist. ³An dem Gegenstand einer Sacheinlage kann wegen Forderungen, welche sich nicht auf den Gegenstand beziehen, kein Zurückbehaltungsrecht geltend gemacht werden.

(3) Durch eine Kapitalherabsetzung können die Gesellschafter von der Verpflichtung zur Leistung von Einlagen höchstens in Höhe des Betrags befreit werden, um den das Stammkapital herabgesetzt worden ist.

(4) ¹Ist eine Geldeinlage eines Gesellschafters bei wirtschaftlicher Betrachtung und aufgrund einer im Zusammenhang mit der Übernahme der Geldeinlage getroffenen Abrede vollständig oder teilweise als Sacheinlage zu bewerten (verdeckte Sacheinlage), so befreit dies den Gesellschafter nicht von seiner Einlageverpflichtung. ²Jedoch sind die Verträge über die Sacheinlage und die Rechtshandlungen zu ihrer Ausführung nicht unwirksam. ³Auf die fortbestehende Geldeinlagepflicht des Gesellschafters wird der Wert des Vermögensgegenstandes im Zeitpunkt der Anmeldung der Gesellschaft zur Eintragung in das Handelsregister oder im Zeitpunkt seiner Überlassung an die Gesellschaft, falls diese später erfolgt, angerechnet. ⁴Die Anrechnung erfolgt nicht vor Eintragung der Gesellschaft in das Handelsregister. ⁵Die Beweislast für die Werthaltigkeit des Vermögensgegenstandes trägt der Gesellschafter.

(5) ¹Ist vor der Einlage eine Leistung an den Gesellschafter vereinbart worden, die wirtschaftlich einer Rückzahlung der Einlage entspricht und die nicht als verdeckte Sacheinlage im Sinne

(2) ¹The shareholders cannot be released from the obligation to render the contributions. ²A set-off against a claim of the company is only permissible with a claim resulting from a transfer of assets the deduction of which from the obligation to render the contribution has been agreed on pursuant to sec. 5 para. 4 sentence 1. ³A right of retention with respect to the object of a contribution in kind cannot be asserted on account of claims not related to such object.

(3) Through a reduction of the registered share capital, the shareholders may only be released from the obligation to render contributions up to the amount by which the registered share capital was reduced.

(4) ¹If a cash contribution of a shareholder is, from an economic point of view and based on an understanding reached in connection with the promise of the contribution in cash, in fact a contribution in kind in whole or in part (hidden contribution in kind) then the shareholder shall not be released from his obligation to render a contribution. ²However, the contracts concerning the contribution in kind and the legal acts for its consummation shall not be invalid. ³The value of the asset at the time the application for registration of the company in the commercial register is made or at the time the asset is transferred to the company, if such transfer occurs later, shall be deducted from the continuing obligation of the shareholder to render the cash contribution. ⁴The deduction shall not take place prior to the registration of the company in the commercial register. ⁵The burden of proof to establish the value of the asset is on the shareholder.

(5) ¹If, prior to the contribution, a performance to the shareholder was agreed upon which economically corresponds to a repayment of the contribution and which cannot be judged a hidden con-

von Absatz 4 zu beurteilen ist, so befreit dies den Gesellschafter von seiner Einlageverpflichtung nur dann, wenn die Leistung durch einen vollwertigen Rückgewähranspruch gedeckt ist, der jederzeit fällig ist oder durch fristlose Kündigung durch die Gesellschaft fällig werden kann. ²Eine solche Leistung oder die Vereinbarung einer solchen Leistung ist in der Anmeldung nach § 8 anzugeben.

(6) ¹Der Anspruch der Gesellschaft auf Leistung der Einlagen verjährt in zehn Jahren von seiner Entstehung an. ²Wird das Insolvenzverfahren über das Vermögen der Gesellschaft eröffnet, so tritt die Verjährung nicht vor Ablauf von sechs Monaten ab dem Zeitpunkt der Eröffnung ein.

§ 20 Verzugszinsen.

Ein Gesellschafter, welcher den auf die Stammeinlage eingeforderten Betrag nicht zur rechten Zeit einzahlt, ist zur Entrichtung von Verzugszinsen von Rechts wegen verpflichtet.

§ 21 Kaduzierung.

(1) ¹Im Fall verzögerter Einzahlung kann an den säumigen Gesellschafter eine erneute Aufforderung zur Zahlung binnen einer zu bestimmenden Nachfrist unter Androhung seines Ausschlusses mit dem Geschäftsanteil, auf welchen die Zahlung zu erfolgen hat, erlassen werden. ²Die Aufforderung erfolgt mittels eingeschriebenen Briefes. ³Die Nachfrist muß mindestens einen Monat betragen.

(2) ¹Nach fruchtlosem Ablauf der Frist ist der säumige Gesellschafter seines Geschäftsanteils und der geleisteten Teilzahlungen zugunsten der Gesellschaft verlustig zu erklären. ²Die Erklärung erfolgt mittels eingeschriebenen Briefes.

(3) Wegen des Ausfalls, welchen die Gesellschaft an dem rückständigen Betrag

tribution in kind pursuant to para. 4, the shareholder is only released from his obligation to render the contribution if the performance is matched by an unimpaired claim for return which is due at any time or which can be made due by termination without notice by the company. ²Such performance or the agreement on such performance must be declared in the application pursuant to sec. 8.

(6) ¹The claim of the company to the rendering of the contributions shall become time-barred ten years after the claim has come into being. ²If insolvency proceedings are commenced over the assets of the company, the claim shall not become time-barred during the six months following the commencement of the proceedings.

§ 20 Interest on arrears.

A shareholder who does not pay the amount demanded on the original contribution when due is legally obligated to pay interest on arrears.

§ 21 Forfeiture of shares.

(1) ¹In the event of delayed payment, the defaulting shareholder can be issued a renewed demand for payment within a grace period to be determined, under threat of his expulsion with respect to the share on which payment has to be made. ²The demand shall be effected by means of registered letter. ³The grace period shall be at least one month.

(2) ¹Upon expiration of the grace period without payment, the defaulting shareholder shall be declared to have forfeited his share and the rendered partial payments for the benefit of the company. ²The declaration shall be effected by means of registered letter.

(3) The expelled shareholder remains liable to the company for any loss in-

oder den später auf den Geschäftsanteil eingeforderten Beträgen der Stammeinlage erleidet, bleibt ihr der ausgeschlossene Gesellschafter verhaftet.

§ 22 Haftung der Rechtsvorgänger.

(1) Für eine von dem ausgeschlossenen Gesellschafter nicht erfüllte Einlageverpflichtung haftet der Gesellschaft auch der letzte und jeder frühere Rechtsvorgänger des Ausgeschlossenen, der im Verhältnis zu ihr als Inhaber des Geschäftsanteils gilt.

(2) Ein früherer Rechtsvorgänger haftet nur, soweit die Zahlung von dessen Rechtsnachfolger nicht zu erlangen ist; dies ist bis zum Beweis des Gegenteils anzunehmen, wenn der letztere die Zahlung nicht bis zum Ablauf eines Monats geleistet hat, nachdem an ihn die Zahlungsaufforderung und an den Rechtsvorgänger die Benachrichtigung von derselben erfolgt ist.

(3) ¹Die Haftung des Rechtsvorgängers ist auf die innerhalb der Frist von fünf Jahren auf die Einlageverpflichtung eingeforderten Leistungen beschränkt. ²Die Frist beginnt mit dem Tag, ab welchem der Rechtsnachfolger im Verhältnis zur Gesellschaft als Inhaber des Geschäftsanteils gilt.

(4) Der Rechtsvorgänger erwirbt gegen Zahlung des rückständigen Betrages den Geschäftsanteil des ausgeschlossenen Gesellschafters.

§ 23 Versteigerung des Geschäftsanteils.

¹Ist die Zahlung des rückständigen Betrages von Rechtsvorgängern nicht zu erlangen, so kann die Gesellschaft den Geschäftsanteil im Wege öffentlicher Versteigerung verkaufen lassen. ²Eine andere Art des Verkaufs ist nur mit Zustimmung des ausgeschlossenen Gesellschafters zulässig.

curred by the company due to the outstanding amount or the amounts of the original contribution later demanded on the share.

§ 22 Liability of predecessors in title.

(1) Each predecessor in title of the expelled shareholder, who is deemed a holder of the share, is liable to the company for the obligation to render a contribution that was not fulfilled by the expelled shareholder.

(2) A former predecessor in title is liable to the extent payment cannot be obtained from his successor in title; this is to be assumed until the contrary is proven if the successor did not make the payment by the expiration of one month after payment was demanded from him and the predecessor in title was notified of such demand.

(3) ¹The liability of the predecessor in title is limited to the performances which have been demanded on the obligation to render contribution within a period of five years. ²The period begins on the day on which the predecessor in title is deemed a holder of the share in relation to the company.

(4) The predecessor in title acquires the share of the expelled shareholder upon payment of the outstanding amount.

§ 23 Auctioning of the share.

¹If payment of the outstanding amount cannot be obtained from predecessors in title, the company may have the share sold at a public auction. ²Any other kind of sale is permissible only with the consent of the expelled shareholder.

§ 24 Aufbringung von Fehlbeträgen.

¹Soweit eine Stammeinlage weder von den Zahlungspflichtigen eingezogen, noch durch Verkauf des Geschäftsanteils gedeckt werden kann, haben die übrigen Gesellschafter den Fehlbetrag nach Verhältnis ihrer Geschäftsanteile aufzubringen. ²Beiträge, welche von einzelnen Gesellschaftern nicht zu erlangen sind, werden nach dem bezeichneten Verhältnis auf die übrigen verteilt.

§ 25 Zwingende Vorschriften.

Von den in den §§ 21 bis 24 bezeichneten Rechtsfolgen können die Gesellschafter nicht befreit werden.

§ 26 Nachschusspflicht.

(1) Im Gesellschaftsvertrag kann bestimmt werden, daß die Gesellschafter über die Nennbeträge der Geschäftsanteile hinaus die Einforderung von weiteren Einzahlungen (Nachschüssen) beschließen können.

(2) Die Einzahlung der Nachschüsse hat nach Verhältnis der Geschäftsanteile zu erfolgen.

(3) Die Nachschußpflicht kann im Gesellschaftsvertrag auf einen bestimmten, nach Verhältnis der Geschäftsanteile festzusetzenden Betrag beschränkt werden.

§ 27 Unbeschränkte Nachschusspflicht.

(1) ¹Ist die Nachschußpflicht nicht auf einen bestimmten Betrag beschränkt, so hat jeder Gesellschafter, falls er die Stammeinlage vollständig eingezahlt hat, das Recht, sich von der Zahlung des auf den Geschäftsanteil eingeforderten Nachschusses dadurch zu befreien, daß er innerhalb eines Monats nach der Aufforderung zur Einzahlung den Geschäftsanteil der Gesellschaft zur Befriedigung aus demselben zur Verfügung stellt. ²Ebenso kann die Gesell-

§ 24 Raising of outstanding amounts.

¹To the extent an original contribution cannot be collected from those liable to pay nor can be covered via sale of the share, the remaining shareholders shall contribute the outstanding amount on a pro rata basis in proportion to their shares. ²Amounts that cannot be obtained from individual shareholders will be allocated to the remaining shareholders in the proportion indicated.

§ 25 Mandatory provisions.

The shareholders cannot be released from the legal consequences indicated in sec. 21 to 24.

§ 26 Obligation to make additional contributions.

(1) The articles of association may specify that the shareholders may pass resolutions calling in further payment (additional contributions) in addition to the nominal amounts of the shares.

(2) The payment of the additional contributions shall be rendered in proportion to the shares held.

(3) The obligation to render additional contributions may be limited in the articles of association to a specific amount proportionate to the shares held.

§ 27 Obligation to make unlimited additional contributions.

(1) ¹If the obligation to render additional contributions is not limited to a specific amount, each shareholder, provided he has paid the original contribution in full, has the right to exempt himself from payment of the additional contribution called on the share by placing the share at the disposal of the company for its satisfaction within a month of the call for payment. ²Likewise, if the shareholder neither makes use of the right indicated above nor makes the payment

schaft, wenn der Gesellschafter binnen der angegebenen Frist weder von der bezeichneten Befugnis Gebrauch macht, noch die Einzahlung leistet, demselben mittels eingeschriebenen Briefes erklären, daß sie den Geschäftsanteil als zur Verfügung gestellt betrachte.

(2) ¹Die Gesellschaft hat den Geschäftsanteil innerhalb eines Monats nach der Erklärung des Gesellschafters oder der Gesellschaft im Wege öffentlicher Versteigerung verkaufen zu lassen. ²Eine andere Art des Verkaufs ist nur mit Zustimmung des Gesellschafters zulässig. ³Ein nach Deckung der Verkaufskosten und des rückständigen Nachschusses verbleibender Überschuß gebührt dem Gesellschafter.

(3) ¹Ist die Befriedigung der Gesellschaft durch den Verkauf nicht zu erlangen, so fällt der Geschäftsanteil der Gesellschaft zu. ²Dieselbe ist befugt, den Anteil für eigene Rechnung zu veräußern.

(4) Im Gesellschaftsvertrag kann die Anwendung der vorstehenden Bestimmungen auf den Fall beschränkt werden, daß die auf den Geschäftsanteil eingeforderten Nachschüsse einen bestimmten Betrag überschreiten.

§ 28 Beschränkte Nachschusspflicht.

(1) ¹Ist die Nachschußpflicht auf einen bestimmten Betrag beschränkt, so finden, wenn im Gesellschaftsvertrag nicht ein anderes festgesetzt ist, im Fall verzögerter Einzahlung von Nachschüssen die auf die Einzahlung der Stammeinlagen bezüglichen Vorschriften der §§ 21 bis 23 entsprechende Anwendung. ²Das gleiche gilt im Fall des § 27 Abs. 4 auch bei unbeschränkter Nachschußpflicht, soweit die Nachschüsse den im Gesellschaftsvertrag festgesetzten Betrag nicht überschreiten.

(2) Im Gesellschaftsvertrag kann bestimmt werden, daß die Einforderung von Nachschüssen, auf deren Zahlung

within the specified period, the company may declare to the same by means of registered letter that it regards the share as having been placed at its disposal.

(2) ¹The company shall have the share sold at public auction within one month of such declaration of the shareholder or the company. ²Any other kind of sale is permissible only with the consent of the shareholder. ³Any excess sale proceeds after payment of the costs of the sale and the outstanding additional contribution are payable to the shareholder.

(3) ¹If the company cannot be satisfied by means of the sale, the share falls to the company. ²The same is authorized to dispose of the share for its own account.

(4) The articles of association may limit the application of the preceding provisions to circumstances where additional contributions called in on the share exceed a specified amount.

§ 28 Obligation to make limited additional contributions.

(1) ¹If the obligation to render additional contributions is limited to a specific amount, the provisions of sec. 21 to 23 pertaining to the payment of original contributions apply accordingly in the case of the delayed payment of additional contributions, unless otherwise provided in the articles of association. ²The same applies in the case of sec. 27 para. 4 for the obligation to render unlimited additional contributions, to the extent the additional contributions do not exceed the amount stipulated in the articles of association.

(2) The articles of association may set forth that the calling in of additional contributions, to the payment of which

die Vorschriften der §§ 21 bis 23 Anwendung finden, schon vor vollständiger Einforderung der Stammeinlagen zulässig ist.

§ 29 Ergebnisverwendung.

(1) ¹Die Gesellschafter haben Anspruch auf den Jahresüberschuß zuzüglich eines Gewinnvortrags und abzüglich eines Verlustvortrags, soweit der sich ergebende Betrag nicht nach Gesetz oder Gesellschaftsvertrag, durch Beschluß nach Absatz 2 oder als zusätzlicher Aufwand auf Grund des Beschlusses über die Verwendung des Ergebnisses von der Verteilung unter die Gesellschafter ausgeschlossen ist. ²Wird die Bilanz unter Berücksichtigung der teilweisen Ergebnisverwendung aufgestellt oder werden Rücklagen aufgelöst, so haben die Gesellschafter abweichend von Satz 1 Anspruch auf den Bilanzgewinn.

(2) Im Beschluß über die Verwendung des Ergebnisses können die Gesellschafter, wenn der Gesellschaftsvertrag nichts anderes bestimmt, Beträge in Gewinnrücklagen einstellen oder als Gewinn vortragen.

(3) ¹Die Verteilung erfolgt nach Verhältnis der Geschäftsanteile. ²Im Gesellschaftsvertrag kann ein anderer Maßstab der Verteilung festgesetzt werden.

(4) ¹Unbeschadet der Absätze 1 und 2 und abweichender Gewinnverteilungsabreden nach Absatz 3 Satz 2 können die Geschäftsführer mit Zustimmung des Aufsichtsrats oder der Gesellschafter den Eigenkapitalanteil von Wertaufholungen bei Vermögensgegenständen des Anlage- und Umlaufvermögens in andere Gewinnrücklagen einstellen. ²Der Betrag dieser Rücklagen ist in der Bilanz gesondert auszuweisen; er kann auch im Anhang angegeben werden.

the provisions of sec. 21 to 23 apply, is permissible even prior to the time that all the original contributions have been called in.

§ 29 Appropriation of profits and losses.

(1) ¹The shareholders are entitled to the annual net income plus profit carried forward minus any loss carried forward, to the extent that such sum is not excluded from being distributed among the shareholders by law or the company's articles of association, by resolution in accordance with para. 2, or as additional expenses based on the resolution concerning the appropriation of profits. ²If the balance sheet is prepared to reflect the partial appropriation of profits, or if reserves are released, the shareholders are, in deviation from sentence 1, entitled to the balance sheet profit.

(2) Unless the articles of association provide otherwise, the shareholders may elect, by a resolution concerning the appropriation of profits, to allocate amounts to the revenue reserves or carry them forward as profits.

(3) ¹Profits are distributed on a pro rata basis in proportion to the shares held. ²A different standard for distribution may be set forth in the articles of association.

(4) ¹Without prejudice to paras. 1 and 2 and any alternate distribution of profits arrangements in accordance with para. 3 sentence 2, the managing directors may, with the consent of the supervisory board or the shareholders, allocate the capitalized part of restorations in value of fixed assets and current assets to other revenue reserves. ²The amount of these reserves is to be shown separately in the balance sheet. It may also be indicated in the notes.

§ 30 Kapitalerhaltung.

(1) ¹Das zur Erhaltung des Stammkapitals erforderliche Vermögen der Gesellschaft darf an die Gesellschafter nicht ausgezahlt werden. ²Satz 1 gilt nicht bei Leistungen, die bei Bestehen eines Beherrschungs- oder Gewinnabführungsvertrags (§ 291 des Aktiengesetzes) erfolgen, oder durch einen vollwertigen Gegenleistungs- oder Rückgewähranspruch gegen den Gesellschafter gedeckt sind. ³Satz 1 ist zudem nicht anzuwenden auf die Rückgewähr eines Gesellschafterdarlehens und Leistungen auf Forderungen aus Rechtshandlungen, die einem Gesellschafterdarlehen wirtschaftlich entsprechen.

(2) ¹Eingezahlte Nachschüsse können, soweit sie nicht zur Deckung eines Verlustes am Stammkapital erforderlich sind, an die Gesellschafter zurückgezahlt werden. ²Die Zurückzahlung darf nicht vor Ablauf von drei Monaten erfolgen, nachdem der Rückzahlungsbeschluß nach § 12 bekanntgemacht ist. ³Im Fall des § 28 Abs. 2 ist die Zurückzahlung von Nachschüssen vor der Volleinzahlung des Stammkapitals unzulässig. ⁴Zurückgezahlte Nachschüsse gelten als nicht eingezogen.

§ 31 Erstattung verbotener Rückzahlungen.

(1) Zahlungen, welche den Vorschriften des § 30 zuwider geleistet sind, müssen der Gesellschaft erstattet werden.

(2) War der Empfänger in gutem Glauben, so kann die Erstattung nur insoweit verlangt werden, als sie zur Befriedigung der Gesellschaftsgläubiger erforderlich ist.

(3) ¹Ist die Erstattung von dem Empfänger nicht zu erlangen, so haften für den zu erstattenden Betrag, soweit er zur Befriedigung der Gesellschaftsgläubiger erforderlich ist, die übrigen Gesellschafter nach Verhältnis ihrer Geschäftsanteile. ²Beiträge, welche von einzelnen

§ 30 Capital maintenance.

(1) ¹The corporate assets that are required to maintain the registered share capital may not be repaid to the shareholders. ²Sentence 1 shall not apply to transactions which are made while a domination or profit transfer agreement (sec. 291 Stock Corporation Act) is in existence or which are matched by an unimpaired claim against the shareholder for consideration or for return. ³Sentence 1 also shall not apply to the repayment of a shareholder loan and to performances on claims resulting from legal acts which correspond in economic terms to a shareholder loan.

(2) ¹Any additional contributions that have been paid can be repaid to the shareholders to the extent such contributions are not required to cover a loss of registered share capital. ²Such repayment may not be effected until the expiration of three months after the shareholders resolution on the repayment is announced pursuant to sec. 12. ³In case of sec. 28 para. 2, the repayment of additional contributions prior to the registered share capital has been fully paid is impermissible. ⁴Repaid additional contributions are deemed not collected.

§ 31 Reimbursement of prohibited repayments.

(1) Payments that are made in violation of the provisions of sec. 30 shall be reimbursed to the company.

(2) If the recipient acted in good faith, the reimbursement may be demanded only to the extent required to satisfy the company's creditors.

(3) ¹If reimbursement cannot be obtained from the recipient, the other shareholders are liable on a pro rata basis in proportion to their shares for the amount to be reimbursed, to the extent required for the satisfaction of the company's creditors. ²Amounts that cannot be obtained

Gesellschaftern nicht zu erlangen sind, werden nach dem bezeichneten Verhältnis auf die übrigen verteilt.

(4) Zahlungen, welche auf Grund der vorstehenden Bestimmungen zu leisten sind, können den Verpflichteten nicht erlassen werden.

(5) ¹Die Ansprüche der Gesellschaft verjähren in den Fällen des Absatzes 1 in zehn Jahren sowie in den Fällen des Absatzes 3 in fünf Jahren. ²Die Verjährung beginnt mit dem Ablauf des Tages, an welchem die Zahlung, deren Erstattung beansprucht wird, geleistet ist. ³In den Fällen des Absatzes 1 findet § 19 Abs. 6 Satz 2 entsprechende Anwendung.

(6) ¹Für die in den Fällen des Absatzes 3 geleistete Erstattung einer Zahlung sind den Gesellschaftern die Geschäftsführer, welchen in betreff der geleisteten Zahlung ein Verschulden zur Last fällt, solidarisch zum Ersatz verpflichtet. ²Die Bestimmungen in § 43 Abs. 1 und 4 finden entsprechende Anwendung.

§ 32 Rückzahlung von Gewinn.

Liegt die in § 31 Abs. 1 bezeichnete Voraussetzung nicht vor, so sind die Gesellschafter in keinem Fall verpflichtet, Beträge, welche sie in gutem Glauben als Gewinnanteile bezogen haben, zurückzuzahlen.

§§ 32a, 32b *(aufgehoben)*

§ 33 Erwerb eigener Geschäftsanteile.

(1) Die Gesellschaft kann eigene Geschäftsanteile, auf welche die Einlagen noch nicht vollständig geleistet sind, nicht erwerben oder als Pfand nehmen.

(2) ¹Eigene Geschäftsanteile, auf welche die Einlage vollständig geleistet ist, darf sie nur erwerben, sofern sie im Zeitpunkt des Erwerbs eine Rücklage in Höhe der Aufwendungen für den Erwerb bilden könnte, ohne das Stammkapital oder eine nach dem Gesellschaftsvertrag zu bildende Rückla-

from individual shareholders shall be distributed to the other shareholders in the proportion indicated.

(4) Those liable to pay on the basis of the above provisions cannot be exempted from the payments required.

(5) ¹The claims of the company shall become time-barred in the cases of para. 1 in ten years and in the cases of para. 3 in five years. ²The period of limitation begins with the expiration of the date on which the payment was made for which reimbursement is claimed. ³In the cases of para. 1, sec. 19 para. 6 sentence 2 shall apply accordingly.

(6) ¹With respect to a reimbursement of a payment made pursuant to para. 3, managing directors who are at fault with regard to the payment rendered are jointly and severally liable to the shareholders. ²The provisions of sec. 43 paras. 1 and 4 shall apply accordingly.

§ 32 Repayment of profits.

If the condition set forth in sec. 31 para. 1 is not met, the shareholders are in no case liable to repay amounts that they received in good faith as shares in the profits.

§§ 32a, 32b *(repealed)*

§ 33 Acquisition of own shares.

(1) The company cannot acquire or take in pledge its own shares on which the contributions have not yet been fully made.

(2) ¹The company may acquire its own shares on which the contribution has been paid in full only to the extent it could, at the time of the acquisition, provide for a reserve in the amount of the expenditures for the acquisition without diminishing the registered share capital or any reserve that shall be provided

ge zu mindern, die nicht zur Zahlung an die Gesellschafter verwandt werden darf. ²Als Pfand nehmen darf sie solche Geschäftsanteile nur, soweit der Gesamtbetrag der durch Inpfandnahme eigener Geschäftsanteile gesicherten Forderungen oder, wenn der Wert der als Pfand genommenen Geschäftsanteile niedriger ist, dieser Betrag nicht höher ist als das über das Stammkapital hinaus vorhandene Vermögen. ³Ein Verstoß gegen die Sätze 1 und 2 macht den Erwerb oder die Inpfandnahme der Geschäftsanteile nicht unwirksam; jedoch ist das schuldrechtliche Geschäft über einen verbotswidrigen Erwerb oder eine verbotswidrige Inpfandnahme nichtig.

(3) Der Erwerb eigener Geschäftsanteile ist ferner zulässig zur Abfindung von Gesellschaftern nach § 29 Abs. 1, § 122i Abs. 1 Satz 2, § 125 Satz 1 in Verbindung mit § 29 Abs. 1, § 207 Abs. 1 des Umwandlungsgesetzes, sofern der Erwerb binnen sechs Monaten nach dem Wirksamwerden der Umwandlung oder nach der Rechtskraft der gerichtlichen Entscheidung erfolgt und die Gesellschaft im Zeitpunkt des Erwerbs eine Rücklage in Höhe der Aufwendungen für den Erwerb bilden könnte, ohne das Stammkapital oder eine nach dem Gesellschaftsvertrag zu bildende Rücklage zu mindern, die nicht zur Zahlung an die Gesellschafter verwandt werden darf.

§ 34 Einziehung von Geschäftsanteilen.

(1) Die Einziehung (Amortisation) von Geschäftsanteilen darf nur erfolgen, soweit sie im Gesellschaftsvertrag zugelassen ist.

(2) Ohne die Zustimmung des Anteilsberechtigten findet die Einziehung nur statt, wenn die Voraussetzungen derselben vor dem Zeitpunkt, in welchem der Berechtigte den Geschäftsanteil erworben hat, im Gesellschaftsvertrag festgesetzt waren.

pursuant to the articles of association and that may not be used for payment to the shareholders. ²The company may take such shares in pledge only to the extent the total amount of the claims secured by taking its own shares in pledge, or the value of shares taken in pledge if this amount is lower, does not exceed the assets held in excess of the registered share capital. ³A violation of sentences 1 and 2 does not invalidate the acquisition or the taking in pledge of the shares; however, the transaction creating the obligation relating to a prohibited acquisition or a prohibited taking in pledge is null and void.

(3) The company's acquisition of its own shares is further permissible for the compensation of shareholders pursuant to sec. 29 para. 1, sec. 122i para. 1 sentence 2, sec. 125 sentence 1 in connection with sec. 29 para. 1 and sec. 207 para. 1 of the Transformation Act, if the acquisition takes place within six months after the transformation has taken effect or after the court decision has become res judicata, and the company could, at the time of the acquisition, provide for a reserve in the amount of the expenditures for the acquisition without diminishing the registered share capital or any reserve that shall be established pursuant to the articles of association and that may not be used for payment to the shareholders.

§ 34 Redemption of shares.

(1) The redemption of shares (amortization) may only be effected to the extent permitted in the articles of association.

(2) Without the consent of the person entitled to the share, redemption may occur only if the conditions therefor were specified in the articles of association prior to the time at which the entitled person acquired the share.

(3) Die Bestimmung in § 30 Abs. 1 bleibt unberührt.

Abschnitt 3. Vertretung und Geschäftsführung

§ 35 Vertretung der Gesellschaft.

(1) ¹Die Gesellschaft wird durch die Geschäftsführer gerichtlich und außergerichtlich vertreten. ²Hat eine Gesellschaft keinen Geschäftsführer (Führungslosigkeit), wird die Gesellschaft für den Fall, dass ihr gegenüber Willenserklärungen abgegeben oder Schriftstücke zugestellt werden, durch die Gesellschafter vertreten.

(2) ¹Sind mehrere Geschäftsführer bestellt, sind sie alle nur gemeinschaftlich zur Vertretung der Gesellschaft befugt, es sei denn, dass der Gesellschaftsvertrag etwas anderes bestimmt. ²Ist der Gesellschaft gegenüber eine Willenserklärung abzugeben, genügt die Abgabe gegenüber einem Vertreter der Gesellschaft nach Absatz 1. ³An die Vertreter der Gesellschaft nach Absatz 1 können unter der im Handelsregister eingetragenen Geschäftsanschrift Willenserklärungen abgegeben und Schriftstücke für die Gesellschaft zugestellt werden. ⁴Unabhängig hiervon können die Abgabe und die Zustellung auch unter der eingetragenen Anschrift der empfangsberechtigten Person nach § 10 Abs. 2 Satz 2 erfolgen.

(3) ¹Befinden sich alle Geschäftsanteile der Gesellschaft in der Hand eines Gesellschafters oder daneben in der Hand der Gesellschaft und ist er zugleich deren alleiniger Geschäftsführer, so ist auf seine Rechtsgeschäfte mit der Gesellschaft § 181 des Bürgerlichen Gesetzbuchs anzuwenden. ²Rechtsgeschäfte zwischen ihm und der von ihm vertretenen Gesellschaft sind, auch wenn er nicht alleiniger Geschäftsführer ist, unverzüglich nach ihrer Vornahme in eine Niederschrift aufzunehmen.

(3) The provision in sec. 30 para. 1 remains unaffected.

Part 3. Representation and Management

§ 35 Representation of the company.

(1) ¹The company is represented by the managing directors in and out of court. ²If a company does not have a managing director (lack of leadership), it is represented by the shareholders in the case that declarations of intent are made vis-à-vis the company or written documents are delivered to the company.

(2) ¹If several managing directors are appointed, they are only authorized to jointly represent the company unless the articles of association provide otherwise. ²If a declaration of intent is to be made vis-à-vis the company, it is sufficient to make such declaration vis-à-vis one of the representatives of the company pursuant to para. 1. ³Declarations of intent may be made and written documents may be delivered for the company to the representatives of the company pursuant to para. 1 at the business address registered in the commercial register. ⁴Independent of this, declarations may also be made and deliveries may also be effected to the registered address of the person authorized to receive pursuant to sec. 10 para. 2 sentence 2.

(3) ¹If all the shares of the company are in the ownership of one shareholder or of one shareholder and the company, and if such shareholder is at the same time its sole managing director, then sec. 181 of the Civil Code is to be applied to such shareholder's legal transactions with the company. ²Legal transactions between such shareholder and the company represented by such shareholder shall be recorded without undue delay after their performance, even if such shareholder is not the sole managing director.

§ 35a Angaben auf Geschäftsbriefen.

(1) ¹Auf allen Geschäftsbriefen gleichviel welcher Form, die an einen bestimmten Empfänger gerichtet werden, müssen die Rechtsform und der Sitz der Gesellschaft, das Registergericht des Sitzes der Gesellschaft und die Nummer, unter der die Gesellschaft in das Handelsregister eingetragen ist, sowie alle Geschäftsführer und, sofern die Gesellschaft einen Aufsichtsrat gebildet und dieser einen Vorsitzenden hat, der Vorsitzende des Aufsichtsrats mit dem Familiennamen und mindestens einem ausgeschriebenen Vornamen angegeben werden. ²Werden Angaben über das Kapital der Gesellschaft gemacht, so müssen in jedem Falle das Stammkapital sowie, wenn nicht alle in Geld zu leistenden Einlagen eingezahlt sind, der Gesamtbetrag der ausstehenden Einlagen angegeben werden.

(2) Der Angaben nach Absatz 1 Satz 1 bedarf es nicht bei Mitteilungen oder Berichten, die im Rahmen einer bestehenden Geschäftsverbindung ergehen und für die üblicherweise Vordrucke verwendet werden, in denen lediglich die im Einzelfall erforderlichen besonderen Angaben eingefügt zu werden brauchen.

(3) ¹Bestellscheine gelten als Geschäftsbriefe im Sinne des Absatzes 1. ²Absatz 2 ist auf sie nicht anzuwenden.

(4) ¹Auf allen Geschäftsbriefen und Bestellscheinen, die von einer Zweigniederlassung einer Gesellschaft mit beschränkter Haftung mit Sitz im Ausland verwendet werden, müssen das Register, bei dem die Zweigniederlassung geführt wird, und die Nummer des Registereintrags angegeben werden; im übrigen gelten die Vorschriften der Absätze 1 bis 3 für die Angaben bezüglich der Haupt- und der Zweigniederlassung, soweit nicht das ausländische Recht Abweichungen nötig macht. ²Befindet sich die ausländische Gesell-

§ 35a Information on business letters.

(1) ¹All business letters, regardless of their form, addressed to a specific recipient shall contain the legal form, the registered office of the company, the register court of the registered office of the company, and the number under which the company is registered in the commercial register, as well as all managing directors, and, if the company has established a supervisory board and the supervisory board has a chairman, the chairman of the supervisory board with surname and at least one first name written in full. ²If information is provided regarding the capital of the company, the registered share capital shall be indicated in any case, as well as the total amount of the outstanding contributions if not all the contributions to be made in cash have been paid.

(2) The information in accordance with para. 1 sentence 1 is not required for communications or reports that are sent pursuant to an existing business relationship and for which forms are generally used in which only the special information required in the individual case needs to be included.

(3) ¹Order forms are deemed business letters within the meaning of para. 1. ²Para. 2 does not apply to them.

(4) ¹All business letters and order forms used by a branch office of a limited liability company with its registered office abroad shall contain the commercial register of the location where the branch office is run and the number of its registration; in other respects, the provisions of paras. 1 to 3 shall apply to information with respect to the head office and the branch office, to the extent that foreign law does not require deviations. ²If the foreign company is in the process of liquidation, this fact shall also be indicated, along with all the liquidators.

schaft in Liquidation, so sind auch diese Tatsache sowie alle Liquidatoren anzugeben.

§ 36 Zielgrößen und Fristen zur gleichberechtigten Teilhabe von Frauen und Männern.

[1]Die Geschäftsführer einer Gesellschaft, die der Mitbestimmung unterliegt, legen für den Frauenanteil in den beiden Führungsebenen unterhalb der Geschäftsführer Zielgrößen fest. [2]Liegt der Frauenanteil bei Festlegung der Zielgrößen unter 30 Prozent, so dürfen die Zielgrößen den jeweils erreichten Anteil nicht mehr unterschreiten. [3]Gleichzeitig sind Fristen zur Erreichung der Zielgrößen festzulegen. [4]Die Fristen dürfen jeweils nicht länger als fünf Jahre sein.

§ 37 Beschränkungen der Vertretungsbefugnis.

(1) Die Geschäftsführer sind der Gesellschaft gegenüber verpflichtet, die Beschränkungen einzuhalten, welche für den Umfang ihrer Befugnis, die Gesellschaft zu vertreten, durch den Gesellschaftsvertrag oder, soweit dieser nicht ein anderes bestimmt, durch die Beschlüsse der Gesellschafter festgesetzt sind.

(2) [1]Gegen dritte Personen hat eine Beschränkung der Befugnis der Geschäftsführer, die Gesellschaft zu vertreten, keine rechtliche Wirkung. [2]Dies gilt insbesondere für den Fall, daß die Vertretung sich nur auf gewisse Geschäfte oder Arten von Geschäften erstrecken oder nur unter gewissen Umständen oder für eine gewisse Zeit oder an einzelnen Orten stattfinden soll, oder daß die Zustimmung der Gesellschafter oder eines Organs der Gesellschaft für einzelne Geschäfte erforderlich ist.

§ 38 Widerruf der Bestellung.

(1) Die Bestellung der Geschäftsführer ist zu jeder Zeit widerruflich, unbeschadet der Entschädigungsansprüche aus bestehenden Verträgen.

§ 36 Targets and deadlines for the equal participation of women and men

[1]The managing directors of a company that is subject to codetermination shall set the targets for the proportion of women in the two management tiers below the managing directors. [2]If the proportion of women is below 30 percent at the time the targets are determined, the targets may not fall below the achieved percentage in each case. [3]At the same time, deadlines for achieving the targets are to be set. [4]None of these deadlines may exceed five years.

§ 37 Restrictions of the power of representation.

(1) Vis-à-vis the company, the managing directors shall observe the restrictions regarding the scope of the authority of the managing directors to act on behalf of the company provided for in the articles of association, or, unless the articles of association provide otherwise, in the resolutions of the shareholders.

(2) [1]Vis-à-vis third parties, a restriction of the authority of the managing directors to represent the company has no legal effect. [2] This applies especially in cases in which the representation extends only to certain transactions or types of transactions, or is supposed to take place only under certain circumstances or for a certain time or in certain locations, or in which the consent of the shareholders or a corporate body of the company is required for individual transactions.

§ 38 Revocation of the appointment.

(1) The appointment of the managing directors is revocable at any time, without prejudice to claims for damages based on existing contracts.

(2) ¹Im Gesellschaftsvertrag kann die Zulässigkeit des Widerrufs auf den Fall beschränkt werden, daß wichtige Gründe denselben notwendig machen. ²Als solche Gründe sind insbesondere grobe Pflichtverletzung oder Unfähigkeit zur ordnungsmäßigen Geschäftsführung anzusehen.

§ 39 Anmeldung der Geschäftsführer.

(1) Jede Änderung in den Personen der Geschäftsführer sowie die Beendigung der Vertretungsbefugnis eines Geschäftsführers ist zur Eintragung in das Handelsregister anzumelden.

(2) Der Anmeldung sind die Urkunden über die Bestellung der Geschäftsführer oder über die Beendigung der Vertretungsbefugnis in Urschrift oder öffentlich beglaubigter Abschrift beizufügen.

(3) ¹Die neuen Geschäftsführer haben in der Anmeldung zu versichern, daß keine Umstände vorliegen, die ihrer Bestellung nach § 6 Abs. 2 Satz 2 Nr. 2 und 3 sowie Satz 3 entgegenstehen und daß sie über ihre unbeschränkte Auskunftspflicht gegenüber dem Gericht belehrt worden sind. ²§ 8 Abs. 3 Satz 2 ist anzuwenden.

§ 40 Liste der Gesellschafter.

(1) ¹Die Geschäftsführer haben unverzüglich nach Wirksamwerden jeder Veränderung in den Personen der Gesellschafter oder des Umfangs ihrer Beteiligung eine von ihnen unterschriebene Liste der Gesellschafter zum Handelsregister einzureichen, aus welcher Name, Vorname, Geburtsdatum und Wohnort der letzteren sowie die Nennbeträge und die laufenden Nummern der von einem jeden derselben übernommenen Geschäftsanteile zu entnehmen sind. ²Die Änderung der Liste durch die Geschäftsführer erfolgt auf Mitteilung und Nachweis.

(2) ¹ The articles of association may restrict the right to revoke to the case in which good cause makes the same necessary. ²In particular, gross breaches of duty and inability to properly manage the business are to be regarded as such reasons.

§ 39 Filing for registration of the managing directors.

(1) An application shall be made for every change in the identity of the managing directors, as well as the termination of a managing director's representative authority, to be registered in the commercial register.

(2) The documents regarding the appointment of the managing directors or regarding the termination of their representative authority are to be attached in original or in certified copy to the application.

(3) ¹The new managing directors shall provide assurance in the application that there exist no circumstances that oppose their appointment pursuant to sec. 6 para. 2 sentence 2 nos. 2 and 3, as well as sentence 3, and that they have been informed of their unlimited duty to furnish information to the court. ²Sec. 8 para. 3 sentence 2 shall apply.

§ 40 List of shareholders.

(1) ¹Without undue delay after the entry into force of every change of shareholders or the size of their shareholdings, the managing directors shall submit to the commercial register a list of shareholders signed by the managing directors providing the surname, first name, date of birth and place of residence of the shareholders, as well as the nominal amounts and the serial numbers of the shares subscribed by them. ²The amendment of the list by the managing directors is effected upon notification and verification.

(2) ¹Hat ein Notar an Veränderungen nach Absatz 1 Satz 1 mitgewirkt, hat er unverzüglich nach deren Wirksamwerden ohne Rücksicht auf etwaige später eintretende Unwirksamkeitsgründe die Liste anstelle der Geschäftsführer zu unterschreiben, zum Handelsregister einzureichen und eine Abschrift der geänderten Liste an die Gesellschaft zu übermitteln. ²Die Liste muss mit der Bescheinigung des Notars versehen sein, dass die geänderten Eintragungen den Veränderungen entsprechen, an denen er mitgewirkt hat, und die übrigen Eintragungen mit dem Inhalt der zuletzt im Handelsregister aufgenommenen Liste übereinstimmen.

(3) Geschäftsführer, welche die ihnen nach Absatz 1 obliegende Pflicht verletzen, haften denjenigen, deren Beteiligung sich geändert hat, und den Gläubigern der Gesellschaft für den daraus entstandenen Schaden als Gesamtschuldner.

§ 41 Buchführung.

Die Geschäftsführer sind verpflichtet, für die ordnungsmäßige Buchführung der Gesellschaft zu sorgen.

§ 42 Bilanz.

(1) In der Bilanz des nach den §§ 242, 264 des Handelsgesetzbuchs aufzustellenden Jahresabschlusses ist das Stammkapital als gezeichnetes Kapital auszuweisen.

(2) ¹Das Recht der Gesellschaft zur Einziehung von Nachschüssen der Gesellschafter ist in der Bilanz insoweit zu aktivieren, als die Einziehung bereits beschlossen ist und den Gesellschaftern ein Recht, durch Verweisung auf den Geschäftsanteil sich von der Zahlung der Nachschüsse zu befreien, nicht zusteht. ²Der nachzuschießende Betrag ist auf der Aktivseite unter den Forderungen gesondert unter der Bezeichnung „Eingeforderte Nachschüsse" auszuweisen, soweit mit der Zahlung gerechnet

(2) ¹If a notary has participated in changes pursuant to para. 1 sentence 1, he shall sign the list instead of the shareholders, submit it to the commercial register and send a copy of the amended list to the company without undue delay after the changes have entered into force and regardless of any potential grounds for ineffectiveness occurring later. ²The list shall be furnished with the certificate of the notary that the amended entries correspond to the changes in which the notary participated and that the other entries correspond with the content of the list last recorded in the commercial register.

(3) Managing directors who violate their duties pursuant to para. 1 shall be jointly and severally liable to the persons whose shareholding has changed and to the creditors of the company for the damages arising therefrom.

§ 41 Accounting.

The managing directors are obligated to ensure that the company maintains proper accounting records.

§ 42 Balance sheet.

(1) On the balance sheet of the annual financial statements to be prepared pursuant to sec. 242 and 264 of the Commercial Code, the registered share capital shall be reported as subscribed capital.

(2) ¹The right of the company to demand additional contributions of the shareholders shall be entered as an asset on the balance sheet to the extent the demand has already been approved by resolution and the shareholders are not entitled, by referring to the share, to a right to be exempted from payment of the additional contributions. ²The additional amount to be paid is to be shown on the assets side among the receivables, separately under the designation "Additional Contributions Called In", to the

werden kann. ³Ein dem Aktivposten entsprechender Betrag ist auf der Passivseite in dem Posten „Kapitalrücklage" gesondert auszuweisen.

(3) Ausleihungen, Forderungen und Verbindlichkeiten gegenüber Gesellschaftern sind in der Regel als solche jeweils gesondert auszuweisen oder im Anhang anzugeben; werden sie unter anderen Posten ausgewiesen, so muß diese Eigenschaft vermerkt werden.

§ 42a Vorlage des Jahresabschlusses und des Lageberichts.

(1) ¹Die Geschäftsführer haben den Jahresabschluß und den Lagebericht unverzüglich nach der Aufstellung den Gesellschaftern zum Zwecke der Feststellung des Jahresabschlusses vorzulegen. ²Ist der Jahresabschluß durch einen Abschlußprüfer zu prüfen, so haben die Geschäftsführer ihn zusammen mit dem Lagebericht und dem Prüfungsbericht des Abschlußprüfers unverzüglich nach Eingang des Prüfungsberichts vorzulegen. ³Hat die Gesellschaft einen Aufsichtsrat, so ist dessen Bericht über das Ergebnis seiner Prüfung ebenfalls unverzüglich vorzulegen.

(2) ¹Die Gesellschafter haben spätestens bis zum Ablauf der ersten acht Monate oder, wenn es sich um eine kleine Gesellschaft handelt (§ 267 Abs. 1 des Handelsgesetzbuchs), bis zum Ablauf der ersten elf Monate des Geschäftsjahrs über die Feststellung des Jahresabschlusses und über die Ergebnisverwendung zu beschließen. ²Der Gesellschaftsvertrag kann die Frist nicht verlängern. ³Auf den Jahresabschluß sind bei der Feststellung die für seine Aufstellung geltenden Vorschriften anzuwenden.

(3) Hat ein Abschlußprüfer den Jahresabschluß geprüft, so hat er auf Verlangen eines Gesellschafters an den Ver-

extent payment can be expected. ³An amount corresponding to the asset item is to be reported separately on the liabilities side in the item "Capital Reserves".

(3) Capital financing, receivables and liabilities vis-à-vis shareholders are, as a rule, to be shown as such, in each case separately, or to be indicated in the notes; if they are shown under other items, this fact shall be noted.

§ 42a Submission of annual financial statements and management report.

(1) ¹The managing directors shall submit the annual financial statements and the management report to the shareholders for their formal approval without undue delay after their preparation. ²If the annual financial statements are to be audited by an auditor of annual financial statements, the managing directors shall submit the annual financial statements together with the management report and the report of the auditor of annual financial statements without undue delay upon receipt of the report of the auditor of annual financial statements. ³If the company has a supervisory board, its report regarding the results of its audit shall also be submitted without undue delay.

(2) ¹The shareholders shall adopt resolutions concerning the formal approval of the annual financial statements and the appropriation of profits at the latest by the expiration of the first eight months of the fiscal year or, in the case of a small company (sec. 267 para. 1 of the Commercial Code), by the expiration of the first eleven months. ²The articles of association may not extend the deadline. ³The provisions that govern the preparation of the annual financial statements are to be applied with respect to their formal approval.

(3) If an auditor of annual financial statements has audited the annual financial statements, he shall, upon the request of

handlungen über die Feststellung des Jahresabschlusses teilzunehmen.

(4) ¹Ist die Gesellschaft zur Aufstellung eines Konzernabschlusses und eines Konzernlageberichts verpflichtet, so sind die Absätze 1 bis 3 entsprechend anzuwenden. ²Das Gleiche gilt hinsichtlich eines Einzelabschlusses nach § 325 Abs. 2a des Handelsgesetzbuchs, wenn die Gesellschafter die Offenlegung eines solchen beschlossen haben.

§ 43 Haftung der Geschäftsführer.

(1) Die Geschäftsführer haben in den Angelegenheiten der Gesellschaft die Sorgfalt eines ordentlichen Geschäftsmannes anzuwenden.

(2) Geschäftsführer, welche ihre Obliegenheiten verletzen, haften der Gesellschaft solidarisch für den entstandenen Schaden.

(3) ¹Insbesondere sind sie zum Ersatze verpflichtet, wenn den Bestimmungen des § 30 zuwider Zahlungen aus dem zur Erhaltung des Stammkapitals erforderlichen Vermögen der Gesellschaft gemacht oder den Bestimmungen des § 33 zuwider eigene Geschäftsanteile der Gesellschaft erworben worden sind. ²Auf den Ersatzanspruch finden die Bestimmungen in § 9b Abs. 1 entsprechende Anwendung. ³Soweit der Ersatz zur Befriedigung der Gläubiger der Gesellschaft erforderlich ist, wird die Verpflichtung der Geschäftsführer dadurch nicht aufgehoben, daß dieselben in Befolgung eines Beschlusses der Gesellschafter gehandelt haben.

(4) Die Ansprüche auf Grund der vorstehenden Bestimmungen verjähren in fünf Jahren.

§ 43a Kreditgewährung aus Gesellschaftsvermögen.

¹Den Geschäftsführern, anderen gesetzlichen Vertretern, Prokuristen oder zum

a shareholder, participate in the discussions concerning the formal approval of the annual financial statements.

(4) ¹If the company is obligated to prepare consolidated annual financial statements and a group management report, paras. 1 to 3 shall apply accordingly. ²The same shall apply with respect to individual annual financial statements pursuant to sec. 325 para. 2a of the Commercial Code, if the shareholders have resolved the disclosure of such statements.

§ 43 Liability of the managing directors.

(1) In the affairs of the company, the managing directors shall apply the care of a prudent businessman.

(2) Managing directors who breach their duties are jointly and severally liable to the company for the damages that arise therefrom.

(3) ¹In particular, they are obligated to indemnify the company if payments are made in contravention of the provisions of sec. 30 from the assets of the company required for the maintenance of the registered share capital or if, in contravention of sec. 33, the company acquires its own shares. ²The provisions of sec. 9b para. 1 shall apply accordingly to the claim for indemnification. ³To the extent indemnification is required to satisfy the company's creditors, the obligation of the managing directors is not removed on account of their having acted pursuant to a resolution of the shareholders.

(4) The claims based on the preceding provisions become time-barred in five years.

§ 43a Granting loans from corporate assets.

¹The managing directors, other legal representatives, procuration officers,

gesamten Geschäftsbetrieb ermächtigten Handlungsbevollmächtigten darf Kredit nicht aus dem zur Erhaltung des Stammkapitals erforderlichen Vermögen der Gesellschaft gewährt werden. ²Ein entgegen Satz 1 gewährter Kredit ist ohne Rücksicht auf entgegenstehende Vereinbarungen sofort zurückzugewähren.

and authorized signatories may not be granted credit from the corporate assets required for the maintenance of the registered share capital. ²Credit granted in violation of sentence 1 shall be returned immediately, regardless of agreements to the contrary.

§ 44 Stellvertreter von Geschäftsführern.

Die für die Geschäftsführer gegebenen Vorschriften gelten auch für Stellvertreter von Geschäftsführern.

§ 44 Deputy managing directors.

The provisions relating to the managing directors apply to deputy managing directors as well.

§ 45 Rechte der Gesellschafter.

(1) Die Rechte, welche den Gesellschaftern in den Angelegenheiten der Gesellschaft, insbesondere in bezug auf die Führung der Geschäfte zustehen, sowie die Ausübung derselben bestimmen sich, soweit nicht gesetzliche Vorschriften entgegenstehen, nach dem Gesellschaftsvertrag.

(2) In Ermangelung besonderer Bestimmungen des Gesellschaftsvertrages finden die Vorschriften der §§ 46 bis 51 Anwendung.

§ 45 Rights of the shareholders.

(1) The rights of the shareholders in the affairs of the company, in particular with regard to the management of the business and the exercise of these rights, are determined according to the articles of association to the extent statutory provisions do not provide otherwise.

(2) In the absence of specific provisions in the articles of association, the provisions of sec. 46 to 51 apply.

§ 46 Aufgabenkreis der Gesellschafter.

Der Bestimmung der Gesellschafter unterliegen:

1. die Feststellung des Jahresabschlusses und die Verwendung des Ergebnisses;
1a. die Entscheidung über die Offenlegung eines Einzelabschlusses nach internationalen Rechnungslegungsstandards (§ 325 Abs. 2a des Handelsgesetzbuchs) und über die Billigung des von den Geschäftsführern aufgestellten Abschlusses;
1b. die Billigung eines von den Geschäftsführern aufgestellten Konzernabschlusses;
2. die Einforderung der Einlagen;

§ 46 Scope of responsibilities of the shareholders.

The shareholders decide upon the following:

1. the formal approval of the annual financial statements and the appropriation of profits;
1a. the decision on the disclosure of individual annual financial statements pursuant to international accounting standards (sec. 325 para. 2a of the Commercial Code) and on the approval of the financial statements drawn up by the managing directors;
1b. the approval of the consolidated annual financial statements drawn up by the managing directors;
2. the calling in of contributions;

3. die Rückzahlung von Nachschüssen;
4. die Teilung, die Zusammenlegung sowie die Einziehung von Geschäftsanteilen;
5. die Bestellung und die Abberufung von Geschäftsführern sowie die Entlastung derselben;
6. die Maßregeln zur Prüfung und Überwachung der Geschäftsführung;
7. die Bestellung von Prokuristen und von Handlungsbevollmächtigten zum gesamten Geschäftsbetrieb;
8. die Geltendmachung von Ersatzansprüchen, welche der Gesellschaft aus der Gründung oder Geschäftsführung gegen Geschäftsführer oder Gesellschafter zustehen, sowie die Vertretung der Gesellschaft in Prozessen, welche sie gegen die Geschäftsführer zu führen hat.

§ 47 Abstimmung.

(1) Die von den Gesellschaftern in den Angelegenheiten der Gesellschaft zu treffenden Bestimmungen erfolgen durch Beschlußfassung nach der Mehrheit der abgegebenen Stimmen.

(2) Jeder Euro eines Geschäftsanteils gewährt eine Stimme.

(3) Vollmachten bedürfen zu ihrer Gültigkeit der Textform.

(4) [1]Ein Gesellschafter, welcher durch die Beschlußfassung entlastet oder von einer Verbindlichkeit befreit werden soll, hat hierbei kein Stimmrecht und darf ein solches auch nicht für andere ausüben. [2]Dasselbe gilt von einer Beschlußfassung, welche die Vornahme eines Rechtsgeschäfts oder die Einleitung oder Erledigung eines Rechtsstreites gegenüber einem Gesellschafter betrifft.

§ 48 Gesellschafterversammlung.

(1) Die Beschlüsse der Gesellschafter werden in Versammlungen gefaßt.

3. the repayment of additional contributions;
4. the division, the joinder and the redemption of shares;
5. the appointment and dismissal of managing directors, as well as the ratification of their acts;
6. the measures for reviewing and supervising the management of the company;
7. the appointment of procuration officers and authorized signatories;
8. the assertion of indemnification claims against managing directors or shareholders to which the company is entitled on the basis of the way the company was founded or managed, as well as the representation of the company in actions against the managing directors.

§ 47 Voting.

(1) The decisions to be reached by the shareholders in respect of the affairs of the company are made by resolutions passed by the majority of votes cast.

(2) Every euro of a share grants one vote.

(3) Powers of attorney must be in text form in order to be valid.

(4) [1]A shareholder whose acts are to be ratified or who is to be released from a liability in the resolution is excluded from voting on the resolution and may not exercise a voting right for others. [2]The same applies to a resolution concerning the conclusion of a legal transaction or the initiation or termination of a legal action vis-à-vis a shareholder.

§ 48 Shareholder meeting.

(1) The shareholder resolutions are adopted in meetings.

(2) Der Abhaltung einer Versammlung bedarf es nicht, wenn sämtliche Gesellschafter in Textform mit der zu treffenden Bestimmung oder mit der schriftlichen Abgabe der Stimmen sich einverstanden erklären.

(3) Befinden sich alle Geschäftsanteile der Gesellschaft in der Hand eines Gesellschafters oder daneben in der Hand der Gesellschaft, so hat er unverzüglich nach der Beschlußfassung eine Niederschrift aufzunehmen und zu unterschreiben.

§ 49 Einberufung der Versammlung.

(1) Die Versammlung der Gesellschafter wird durch die Geschäftsführer berufen.

(2) Sie ist außer den ausdrücklich bestimmten Fällen zu berufen, wenn es im Interesse der Gesellschaft erforderlich erscheint.

(3) Insbesondere muß die Versammlung unverzüglich berufen werden, wenn aus der Jahresbilanz oder aus einer im Laufe des Geschäftsjahres aufgestellten Bilanz sich ergibt, daß die Hälfte des Stammkapitals verloren ist.

§ 50 Minderheitsrechte.

(1) Gesellschafter, deren Geschäftsanteile zusammen mindestens dem zehnten Teil des Stammkapitals entsprechen, sind berechtigt, unter Angabe des Zwecks und der Gründe die Berufung der Versammlung zu verlangen.

(2) In gleicher Weise haben die Gesellschafter das Recht zu verlangen, daß Gegenstände zur Beschlußfassung der Versammlung angekündigt werden.

(3) [1]Wird dem Verlangen nicht entsprochen oder sind Personen, an welche dasselbe zu richten wäre, nicht vorhanden, so können die in Absatz 1 bezeichneten Gesellschafter unter Mitteilung des Sachverhältnisses die Berufung oder Ankündigung selbst bewirken. [2]Die Versammlung beschließt, ob die ent-

(2) A meeting need not be held if all the shareholders consent in text form to the decision to be taken or to the casting of votes in writing.

(3) If all shares of the company are held by one shareholder or by one shareholder and the company, the shareholder shall prepare minutes without undue delay after the adoption of the resolution and sign such minutes.

§ 49 Convening of the meeting.

(1) The meeting of shareholders is convened by the managing directors.

(2) It is to be convened, in addition to the cases expressly set forth, when it appears necessary in the interest of the company.

(3) The meeting shall in particular be convened without undue delay when the annual balance sheet or a balance sheet prepared in the course of the fiscal year shows that half of the registered share capital has been lost.

§ 50 Minority rights.

(1) Shareholders who hold shares representing in the aggregate at least a tenth of the registered share capital are entitled, upon indicating its purpose and reasons, to request the convening of a meeting.

(2) In the same way, the shareholders have the right to request that items to be resolved by the meeting are announced.

(3) [1]If this request is not complied with or if persons do not exist to whom such request would have to be addressed, the shareholders set forth in para. 1 may convene the meeting or make the announcement themselves with communication of the relevant facts. [2]The meeting

standenen Kosten von der Gesellschaft zu tragen sind.

§ 51 Form der Einberufung.

(1) ¹Die Berufung der Versammlung erfolgt durch Einladung der Gesellschafter mittels eingeschriebener Briefe. ²Sie ist mit einer Frist von mindestens einer Woche zu bewirken.

(2) Der Zweck der Versammlung soll jederzeit bei der Berufung angekündigt werden.

(3) Ist die Versammlung nicht ordnungsmäßig berufen, so können Beschlüsse nur gefaßt werden, wenn sämtliche Gesellschafter anwesend sind.

(4) Das gleiche gilt in bezug auf Beschlüsse über Gegenstände, welche nicht wenigstens drei Tage vor der Versammlung in der für die Berufung vorgeschriebenen Weise angekündigt worden sind.

§ 51a Auskunfts- und Einsichtsrecht.

(1) Die Geschäftsführer haben jedem Gesellschafter auf Verlangen unverzüglich Auskunft über die Angelegenheiten der Gesellschaft zu geben und die Einsicht der Bücher und Schriften zu gestatten.

(2) ¹Die Geschäftsführer dürfen die Auskunft und die Einsicht verweigern, wenn zu besorgen ist, daß der Gesellschafter sie zu gesellschaftsfremden Zwecken verwenden und dadurch der Gesellschaft oder einem verbundenen Unternehmen einen nicht unerheblichen Nachteil zufügen wird. ²Die Verweigerung bedarf eines Beschlusses der Gesellschafter.

(3) Von diesen Vorschriften kann im Gesellschaftsvertrag nicht abgewichen werden.

decides whether the costs that arose are to be borne by the company.

§ 51 Form of convening.

(1) ¹The meeting shall be convened by invitation of the shareholders by registered letters. ²At least one week's notice shall be given.

(2) The purpose of the meeting should always be announced when convening the meeting.

(3) If the meeting is not properly convened, resolutions can be adopted only when all shareholders are present.

(4) The same applies with respect to resolutions concerning items that were not announced at least three days prior to the meeting according to the procedures specified for convening a meeting.

§ 51a Right to information and inspection.

(1) The managing directors shall provide each shareholder with information regarding the affairs of the company without undue delay upon request and shall allow such shareholder to inspect the books and records.

(2) ¹The managing directors may refuse to provide information and allow inspection when there is reason to fear that the shareholder will use this for purposes not related to the company and thereby inflict a not inconsiderable harm on the company or an affiliated enterprise. ²Such refusal requires a resolution of the shareholders.

(3) The articles of association may not provide otherwise.

§ 51b Gerichtliche Entscheidung über das Auskunfts- und Einsichtsrecht.

¹Für die gerichtliche Entscheidung über das Auskunfts- und Einsichtsrecht findet § 132 Abs. 1, 3 und 4 des Aktiengesetzes entsprechende Anwendung. ²Antragsberechtigt ist jeder Gesellschafter, dem die verlangte Auskunft nicht gegeben oder die verlangte Einsicht nicht gestattet worden ist.

§ 52 Aufsichtsrat.

(1) Ist nach dem Gesellschaftsvertrag ein Aufsichtsrat zu bestellen, so sind § 90 Abs. 3, 4, 5 Satz 1 und 2, § 95 Satz 1, § 100 Abs. 1 und 2 Nr. 2 und Abs. 5, § 101 Abs. 1 Satz 1, § 103 Abs. 1 Satz 1 und 2, §§ 105, 107 Abs. 4, §§ 110 bis 114, 116 des Aktiengesetzes in Verbindung mit § 93 Abs. 1 und 2 Satz 1 und 2 des Aktiengesetzes, § 124 Abs. 3 Satz 2, §§ 170, 171, 394 und 395 des Aktiengesetzes entsprechend anzuwenden, soweit nicht im Gesellschaftsvertrag ein anderes bestimmt ist.

(2) ¹Ist nach dem Drittelbeteiligungsgesetz ein Aufsichtsrat zu bestellen, so legt die Gesellschafterversammlung für den Frauenanteil im Aufsichtsrat und unter den Geschäftsführern Zielgrößen fest, es sei denn, sie hat dem Aufsichtsrat diese Aufgabe übertragen. ²Ist nach dem Mitbestimmungsgesetz, dem Montan-Mitbestimmungsgesetz oder dem Mitbestimmungsergänzungsgesetz ein Aufsichtsrat zu bestellen, so legt der Aufsichtsrat für den Frauenanteil im Aufsichtsrat und unter den Geschäftsführern Zielgrößen fest. ³Liegt der Frauenanteil bei Festlegung der Zielgrößen unter 30 Prozent, so dürfen die Zielgrößen den jeweils erreichten Anteil nicht mehr unterschreiten. ⁴Gleichzeitig sind Fristen zur Erreichung der Zielgrößen festzulegen. ⁵Die Fristen dürfen jeweils nicht länger als fünf Jahre sein.

§ 51b Court decisions regarding the right to information and inspection.

¹Sec. 132 paras. 1,3 and 4 of the Stock Corporation Act shall apply accordingly to court decisions regarding the right to information and inspection. ²Every shareholder who is not provided with the information requested or who is not permitted the inspection requested is entitled to submit an application.

§ 52 Supervisory board.

(1) If a supervisory board is to be appointed under the articles of association, sec. 90 paras. 3, 4, 5 sentences 1 and 2, sec. 95 sentence 1, sec. 100 paras. 1 and 2 no. 2 and para. 5, sec. 101 para. 1 sentence 1, sec. 103 para. 1 sentences 1 and 2, sec. 105, 107 para. 3 sentences 2 and 3 and para. 4, sec. 110 to 114 and 116 of the Stock Corporation Act in connection with sec. 93 paras. 1 and 2 sentences 1 and 2 of the Stock Corporation Act, sec. 124 para. 3 sentence 2, sec. 170, 171, 394 and 395 of the Stock Corporation Act shall apply accordingly, unless the articles of association provide otherwise.

(2) ¹If a supervisory board is to be appointed pursuant to the One Third Participation Act, the shareholder meeting shall determine targets for the proportion of women in the supervisory board and among the managing directors, unless it has delegated this task to the supervisory board. ²If a supervisory board is to be appointed pursuant to the Codetermination Act, the Coal, Iron and Steel Codetermination Act or the Supplementary Codetermination Act, the supervisory board shall determine the targets for the proportion of women in the supervisory board and among the managing directors. ³If the proportion of women is below 30 percent at the time the targets are determined, the targets may not fall below the achieved percentage in each case. ⁴At the same time, deadlines for achieving the targets are

(3) ¹Werden die Mitglieder des Aufsichtsrats vor der Eintragung der Gesellschaft in das Handelsregister bestellt, gilt § 37 Abs. 4 Nr. 3 und 3a des Aktiengesetzes entsprechend. ²Die Geschäftsführer haben bei jeder Änderung in den Personen der Aufsichtsratsmitglieder unverzüglich eine Liste der Mitglieder des Aufsichtsrats, aus welcher Name, Vorname, ausgeübter Beruf und Wohnort der Mitglieder ersichtlich ist, zum Handelsregister einzureichen; das Gericht hat nach § 10 des Handelsgesetzbuchs einen Hinweis darauf bekannt zu machen, dass die Liste zum Handelsregister eingereicht worden ist.

(4) Schadensersatzansprüche gegen die Mitglieder des Aufsichtsrats wegen Verletzung ihrer Obliegenheiten verjähren in fünf Jahren.

Abschnitt 4. Abänderungen des Gesellschaftsvertrages

§ 53 Form der Satzungsänderung.

(1) Eine Abänderung des Gesellschaftsvertrages kann nur durch Beschluß der Gesellschafter erfolgen.

(2) ¹Der Beschluß muß notariell beurkundet werden, derselbe bedarf einer Mehrheit von drei Vierteilen der abgegebenen Stimmen. ²Der Gesellschaftsvertrag kann noch andere Erfordernisse aufstellen.

(3) Eine Vermehrung der den Gesellschaftern nach dem Gesellschaftsvertrag obliegenden Leistungen kann nur mit Zustimmung sämtlicher beteiligter Gesellschafter beschlossen werden.

§ 54 Anmeldung und Eintragung der Satzungsänderung.

(1) ¹Die Abänderung des Gesellschaftsvertrages ist zur Eintragung in das Handelsregister anzumelden. ²Der Anmel-

to be set. ⁵None of these deadlines may exceed five years.

(3) ¹If the members of the supervisory board are appointed prior to registration of the company in the commercial register, sec. 37 para. 4 nos. 3 and 3a of the Stock Corporation Act shall apply accordingly. ²Upon every change of the members of the supervisory board, the managing directors shall, without undue delay, submit to the commercial register a list of the members of the supervisory board, providing the surname, first name, profession and place of residence; the court shall publicly announce pursuant to sec. 10 of the Commercial Code that the list was submitted to the commercial register.

(4) Claims for damages against members of the supervisory board for violation of their duties become time-barred in five years.

Part 4. Amendments to the Articles of Association

§ 53 Form of amendments to the articles of association.

(1) The articles of association can only be amended by shareholder resolution.

(2) ¹The resolution shall be notarized, and requires a majority of three quarters of the votes cast. ²The articles of association can impose additional requirements as well.

(3) An increase in the payments required to be paid by the shareholders under the articles of association can be decided only with the consent of all the shareholders involved.

§ 54 Application and registration of amendments to the articles of association.

(1) ¹An application shall be made for the amendment to the articles of association to be registered in the commercial reg-

dung ist der vollständige Wortlaut des Gesellschaftsvertrags beizufügen; er muß mit der Bescheinigung eines Notars versehen sein, daß die geänderten Bestimmungen des Gesellschaftsvertrags mit dem Beschluß über die Änderung des Gesellschaftsvertrags und die unveränderten Bestimmungen mit dem zuletzt zum Handelsregister eingereichten vollständigen Wortlaut des Gesellschaftsvertrags übereinstimmen.

(2) Bei der Eintragung genügt, sofern nicht die Abänderung die in § 10 bezeichneten Angaben betrifft, die Bezugnahme auf die bei dem Gericht eingereichten Dokumente über die Abänderung.

(3) Die Abänderung hat keine rechtliche Wirkung, bevor sie in das Handelsregister des Sitzes der Gesellschaft eingetragen ist.

§ 55 Erhöhung des Stammkapitals.

(1) Wird eine Erhöhung des Stammkapitals beschlossen, so bedarf es zur Übernahme jedes Geschäftsanteils an dem erhöhten Kapital einer notariell aufgenommenen oder beglaubigten Erklärung des Übernehmers.

(2) [1]Zur Übernahme eines Geschäftsanteils können von der Gesellschaft die bisherigen Gesellschafter oder andere Personen, welche durch die Übernahme ihren Beitritt zu der Gesellschaft erklären, zugelassen werden. [2]Im letzteren Falle sind außer dem Nennbetrag des Geschäftsanteils auch sonstige Leistungen, zu welchen der Beitretende nach dem Gesellschaftsvertrage verpflichtet sein soll, in der in Absatz 1 bezeichneten Urkunde ersichtlich zu machen.

(3) Wird von einem der Gesellschaft bereits angehörenden Gesellschafter ein Geschäftsanteil an dem erhöhten Kapital übernommen, so erwirbt derselbe einen weiteren Geschäftsanteil.

ister. [2]The entire wording of the articles of association shall be attached to the application; it shall be accompanied by a notary's certification that the amended provisions of the articles of association agree with the resolution on the amendment of the articles of association and that the unamended provisions agree with the wording of the articles of association most recently submitted to the commercial register.

(2) At registration it is sufficient to refer to the documents concerning the amendment which were submitted to the court, unless the amendment concerns the matters referred to in sec. 10.

(3) The amendment legally does not become effective until it is registered in the commercial register of the registered office of the company.

§ 55 Increase of the registered share capital.

(1) If an increase of the registered share capital is resolved, the subscription to each share in the increased capital requires a declaration of the subscriber recorded or certified by a notary.

(2) [1]The present shareholders may be permitted to subscribe to a share, as may other persons who declare their membership in the company through such a subscription. [2]In the latter case, other than the nominal amount of the share, other obligations to which the joining member shall be obligated pursuant to the articles of association are to be evidenced in the document referred to in para. 1 as well.

(3) If a share in the increased capital is subscribed to by an existing shareholder of the company, such shareholder acquires an additional share.

(4) Die Bestimmungen in § 5 Abs. 2 und 3 über die Nennbeträge der Geschäftsanteile sowie die Bestimmungen in § 19 Abs. 6 über die Verjährung des Anspruchs der Gesellschaft auf Leistung der Einlagen sind auch hinsichtlich der an dem erhöhten Kapital übernommenen Geschäftsanteile anzuwenden.

(4) The provisions in sec. 5 paras. 2 and 3 regarding the nominal amounts of the shares as well as the provisions of sec. 19 para. 6 regarding the time limitation of the claim of the company to the rendering of the contributions shall also apply with respect to the subscribed shares in the increased capital.

§ 55a Genehmigtes Kapital.

(1) ¹Der Gesellschaftsvertrag kann die Geschäftsführer für höchstens fünf Jahre nach Eintragung der Gesellschaft ermächtigen, das Stammkapital bis zu einem bestimmten Nennbetrag (genehmigtes Kapital) durch Ausgabe neuer Geschäftsanteile gegen Einlagen zu erhöhen. ²Der Nennbetrag des genehmigten Kapitals darf die Hälfte des Stammkapitals, das zur Zeit der Ermächtigung vorhanden ist, nicht übersteigen.

§ 55a Authorized capital.

(1) ¹The articles of association may authorize the managing directors for up to five years from the registration of the company to increase the registered share capital up to a specified nominal amount (authorized capital) through issuance of new shares against contributions. ²The nominal amount of the authorized capital may not exceed half of the registered share capital which is present at the time of the authorization.

(2) Die Ermächtigung kann auch durch Abänderung des Gesellschaftsvertrages für höchstens fünf Jahre nach deren Eintragung erteilt werden.

(2) The authorization may also be granted through an amendment of the articles of association for up to five years after its registration.

(3) Gegen Sacheinlagen (§ 56) dürfen Geschäftsanteile nur ausgegeben werden, wenn die Ermächtigung es vorsieht.

(3) Against contributions in kind (sec. 56), shares may be issued only if the authorization so provides.

§ 56 Kapitalerhöhung mit Sacheinlagen.

(1) ¹Sollen Sacheinlagen geleistet werden, so müssen ihr Gegenstand und der Nennbetrag des Geschäftsanteils, auf den sich die Sacheinlage bezieht, im Beschluß über die Erhöhung des Stammkapitals festgesetzt werden. ²Die Festsetzung ist in die in § 55 Abs. 1 bezeichnete Erklärung des Übernehmers aufzunehmen.

§ 56 Capital increase with contributions in kind.

(1) ¹If contributions in kind are to be made, the type of assets and the nominal amount of the share to which the contribution in kind relates shall be stipulated in the resolution on the increase of the registered share capital. ²The stipulation is to be included in the subscriber's declaration described in sec. 55 para. 1.

(2) Die §§ 9 und 19 Abs. 2 Satz 2 und Abs. 4 finden entsprechende Anwendung.

(2) Sec. 9 and 19 para. 2 sentence 2 and para. 4 shall apply accordingly.

§ 56a Leistungen auf das neue Stammkapital.

Für die Leistungen der Einlagen auf das neue Stammkapital finden § 7 Abs. 2

§ 56a Contributions to the new registered share capital.

Sec. 7 para. 2 sentence 1 and para. 3 as well as sec. 19 para. 5 shall apply accord-

Satz 1 und Abs. 3 sowie § 19 Abs. 5 entsprechende Anwendung.

§ 57 Anmeldung der Erhöhung.

(1) Die beschlossene Erhöhung des Stammkapitals ist zur Eintragung in das Handelsregister anzumelden, nachdem das erhöhte Kapital durch Übernahme von Geschäftsanteilen gedeckt ist.

(2) ¹In der Anmeldung ist die Versicherung abzugeben, daß die Einlagen auf das neue Stammkapital nach § 7 Abs. 2 Satz 1 und Abs. 3 bewirkt sind und daß der Gegenstand der Leistungen sich endgültig in der freien Verfügung der Geschäftsführer befindet. ²§ 8 Abs. 2 Satz 2 gilt entsprechend.

(3) Der Anmeldung sind beizufügen:

1. die in § 55 Abs. 1 bezeichneten Erklärungen oder eine beglaubigte Abschrift derselben;
2. eine von den Anmeldenden unterschriebene Liste der Personen, welche die neuen Geschäftsanteile übernommen haben; aus der Liste müssen die Nennbeträge der von jedem übernommenen Geschäftsanteile ersichtlich sein;
3. bei einer Kapitalerhöhung mit Sacheinlagen die Verträge, die den Festsetzungen nach § 56 zugrunde liegen oder zu ihrer Ausführung geschlossen worden sind.

(4) Für die Verantwortlichkeit der Geschäftsführer, welche die Kapitalerhöhung zur Eintragung in das Handelsregister angemeldet haben, finden § 9a Abs. 1 und 3, § 9b entsprechende Anwendung.

ingly to the rendering of contributions to the new registered share capital.

§ 57 Application for registration of the increase.

(1) An application shall be made for the resolved increase of the registered share capital to be registered in the commercial register after the increased capital has been covered by subscription to the shares.

(2) ¹In the application, assurances shall be provided that the contributions to the new registered share capital have been made in accordance with sec. 7 para. 2 sentence 1 and para. 3, and that the assets contributed have been placed definitively at the free disposal of the managing directors. ²Sec. 8 para. 2 sentence 2 shall apply accordingly.

(3) The following shall be attached to the application:

1. the declarations described in sec. 55 para. 1 or a certified copy of the same;
2. a list of the persons who have subscribed to the new shares which list is to be signed by the persons submitting the application; the nominal amounts of each subscribed share shall be apparent from the list;
3. in the event of a capital increase with contributions in kind, the contracts on which the stipulations in accordance with sec. 56 are based, or which were concluded for their implementation.

(4) Sec. 9a paras. 1 and 3 and sec. 9b shall apply accordingly with respect to the responsibility of the managing directors who have applied for the capital increase to be registered in the commercial register.

§ 57a Ablehnung der Eintragung.

Für die Ablehnung der Eintragung durch das Gericht findet § 9c Abs. 1 entsprechende Anwendung.

§ 57b *(aufgehoben)*

§ 57c Kapitalerhöhung aus Gesellschaftsmitteln.

(1) Das Stammkapital kann durch Umwandlung von Rücklagen in Stammkapital erhöht werden (Kapitalerhöhung aus Gesellschaftsmitteln).

(2) Die Erhöhung des Stammkapitals kann erst beschlossen werden, nachdem der Jahresabschluß für das letzte vor der Beschlußfassung über die Kapitalerhöhung abgelaufene Geschäftsjahr (letzter Jahresabschluß) festgestellt und über die Ergebnisverwendung Beschluß gefaßt worden ist.

(3) Dem Beschluß über die Erhöhung des Stammkapitals ist eine Bilanz zugrunde zu legen.

(4) Neben den §§ 53 und 54 über die Abänderung des Gesellschaftsvertrags gelten die §§ 57d bis 57o.

§ 57d Ausweisung von Kapital- und Gewinnrücklagen.

(1) Die Kapital- und Gewinnrücklagen, die in Stammkapital umgewandelt werden sollen, müssen in der letzten Jahresbilanz und, wenn dem Beschluß eine andere Bilanz zugrunde gelegt wird, auch in dieser Bilanz unter „Kapitalrücklage" oder „Gewinnrücklagen" oder im letzten Beschluß über die Verwendung des Jahresergebnisses als Zuführung zu diesen Rücklagen ausgewiesen sein.

(2) Die Rücklagen können nicht umgewandelt werden, soweit in der zugrunde gelegten Bilanz ein Verlust, einschließlich eines Verlustvortrags, ausgewiesen ist.

(3) Andere Gewinnrücklagen, die einem bestimmten Zweck zu dienen bestimmt

§ 57a Rejection of registration.

Sec. 9c para. 1 shall apply accordingly with respect to the rejection of the registration by the court.

§ 57b *(repealed)*

§ 57c Capital increase from company resources.

(1) The registered share capital may be increased through the conversion of reserves into registered share capital (capital increase from company resources).

(2) The increase of the registered share capital cannot be resolved until the annual financial statements for the last completed fiscal year prior to the resolution on the capital increase (last annual financial statements) have been approved and a resolution on the appropriation of the profits has been adopted.

(3) The resolution on the increase of the registered share capital is to be based on a balance sheet.

(4) In addition to sec. 53 and 54 regarding the amendment to the articles of association, sec. 57d to 57o shall apply.

§ 57d Showing of capital and revenue reserves.

(1) The capital and revenue reserves to be converted into registered share capital shall be shown in the last annual balance sheet and, if the resolution is based on another balance sheet, in this balance sheet as well under "Capital Reserves" or "Revenue Reserves" or in the last resolution on the use of the annual profits as allocation to these reserves.

(2) The reserves cannot be converted to the extent a loss, including a loss carried forward, is shown in the balance sheet serving as a basis.

(3) Other revenue reserves that are designated to serve a specific purpose may

sind, dürfen nur umgewandelt werden, soweit dies mit ihrer Zweckbestimmung vereinbar ist.

be converted only to the extent this is compatible with their designated purpose.

§ 57e Zugrundelegung der letzten Jahresbilanz; Prüfung.

(1) Dem Beschluß kann die letzte Jahresbilanz zugrunde gelegt werden, wenn die Jahresbilanz geprüft und die festgestellte Jahresbilanz mit dem uneingeschränkten Bestätigungsvermerk der Abschlußprüfer versehen ist und wenn ihr Stichtag höchstens acht Monate vor der Anmeldung des Beschlusses zur Eintragung in das Handelsregister liegt.

(2) Bei Gesellschaften, die nicht große im Sinne des § 267 Abs. 3 des Handelsgesetzbuchs sind, kann die Prüfung auch durch vereidigte Buchprüfer erfolgen; die Abschlußprüfer müssen von der Versammlung der Gesellschafter gewählt sein.

§ 57f Anforderungen an die Bilanz.

(1) [1]Wird dem Beschluß nicht die letzte Jahresbilanz zugrunde gelegt, so muß die Bilanz den Vorschriften über die Gliederung der Jahresbilanz und über die Wertansätze in der Jahresbilanz entsprechen. [2]Der Stichtag der Bilanz darf höchstens acht Monate vor der Anmeldung des Beschlusses zur Eintragung in das Handelsregister liegen.

(2) [1]Die Bilanz ist, bevor über die Erhöhung des Stammkapitals Beschluß gefaßt wird, durch einen oder mehrere Prüfer darauf zu prüfen, ob sie dem Absatz 1 entspricht. [2]Sind nach dem abschließenden Ergebnis der Prüfung keine Einwendungen zu erheben, so haben die Prüfer dies durch einen Vermerk zu bestätigen. [3]Die Erhöhung des Stammkapitals kann nicht ohne diese Bestätigung der Prüfer beschlossen werden.

§ 57e Using last annual balance sheet as basis; audit.

(1) The last annual balance sheet can be used as a basis for the resolution if the annual balance sheet has been audited and the formally approved annual balance sheet has been furnished with the unqualified certification of the auditor of annual financial statements, and if its record date is no more than eight months prior to the application of the resolution for registration with the commercial register.

(2) For companies that are not large in terms of sec. 267 para. 3 of the Commercial Code, the audit can also be performed by registered bookkeepers; the auditors of annual financial statements shall be elected by the shareholder meeting.

§ 57f Requirements of the balance sheet.

(1) [1]If the resolution is not based on the last annual balance sheet, the balance sheet shall conform to the rules regarding the structure of the annual balance sheet and regarding the valuation in the annual balance sheet. [2]The record date of the balance sheet may be no more than eight months prior to the application of the resolution for registration with the commercial register.

(2) [1]Before a resolution is adopted regarding the increase of the registered share capital, the balance sheet shall be audited by one or more auditors as to whether it complies with para. 1. [2]If after the final results of the audit there are no objections to be raised, the auditors shall confirm this by means of a certification. [3]The increase of the registered share capital cannot be resolved without this confirmation of the auditors.

(3) ¹Die Prüfer werden von den Gesellschaftern gewählt; falls nicht andere Prüfer gewählt werden, gelten die Prüfer als gewählt, die für die Prüfung des letzten Jahresabschlusses von den Gesellschaftern gewählt oder vom Gericht bestellt worden sind. ²Im übrigen sind, soweit sich aus der Besonderheit des Prüfungsauftrags nichts anderes ergibt, § 318 Abs. 1 Satz 2, § 319 Abs. 1 bis 4, § 319a Abs. 1, § 319b Abs. 1, § 320 Abs. 1 Satz 2, Abs. 2 und die §§ 321 und 323 des Handelsgesetzbuchs anzuwenden. ³Bei Gesellschaften, die nicht große im Sinne des § 267 Abs. 3 des Handelsgesetzbuchs sind, können auch vereidigte Buchprüfer zu Prüfern bestellt werden.

§ 57g Vorherige Bekanntgabe des Jahresabschlusses.

Die Bestimmungen des Gesellschaftsvertrags über die vorherige Bekanntgabe des Jahresabschlusses an die Gesellschafter sind in den Fällen des § 57f entsprechend anzuwenden.

§ 57h Arten der Kapitalerhöhung.

(1) ¹Die Kapitalerhöhung kann vorbehaltlich des § 57l Abs. 2 durch Bildung neuer Geschäftsanteile oder durch Erhöhung des Nennbetrags der Geschäftsanteile ausgeführt werden. ²Die neuen Geschäftsanteile und die Geschäftsanteile, deren Nennbetrag erhöht wird, müssen auf einen Betrag gestellt werden, der auf volle Euro lautet.

(2) ¹Der Beschluß über die Erhöhung des Stammkapitals muß die Art der Erhöhung angeben. ²Soweit die Kapitalerhöhung durch Erhöhung des Nennbetrags der Geschäftsanteile ausgeführt werden soll, ist sie so zu bemessen, daß durch sie auf keinen Geschäftsanteil, dessen Nennbetrag erhöht wird, Beträge entfallen, die durch die Erhöhung des Nennbetrags des Geschäftsanteils nicht gedeckt werden können.

(3) ¹The auditors shall be elected by the shareholders; if no other auditors are elected, the auditors who were elected by the shareholders or appointed by the court for the auditing of the last annual financial statements shall be deemed elected. ²In addition, to the extent nothing else results from the special nature of the audit assignment, sec. 318 para. 1 sentence 2, sec. 319 paras. 1 to 4, sec. 319a para. 1, sec. 319b para. 1, sec. 320 para. 1 sentence 2 and para. 2, and sec. 321 and 323 of the Commercial Code shall apply. ³For companies that are not large in terms of sec. 267 para. 3 of the Commercial Code, registered bookkeepers can also be appointed.

§ 57g Advanced disclosure of the annual financial statements.

The provisions of the articles of association regarding the prior disclosure of the annual financial statements to the shareholders are to be applied accordingly in the cases of sec. 57f.

§ 57h Kinds of capital increase.

(1) ¹Subject to sec. 57l para. 2, the capital increase can be effected by the creation of new shares or by increasing the nominal value of the shares. ²The new shares and the shares whose nominal value is increased shall be set to an even euro amount.

(2) ¹The resolution on the increase of the registered share capital shall indicate the kind of increase. ²To the extent the capital increase shall be carried out by an increase in the nominal value of the shares, the increase shall be calculated in such a way that it does not lead to the allotment of amounts to shares whose nominal value is being increased, which amounts cannot be covered by the increase in the nominal value of the share.

§ 57i Anmeldung und Eintragung des Erhöhungsbeschlusses.

(1) ¹Der Anmeldung des Beschlusses über die Erhöhung des Stammkapitals zur Eintragung in das Handelsregister ist die der Kapitalerhöhung zugrunde gelegte, mit dem Bestätigungsvermerk der Prüfer versehene Bilanz, in den Fällen des § 57f außerdem die letzte Jahresbilanz, sofern sie noch nicht nach § 325 Abs. 1 des Handelsgesetzbuchs eingereicht ist, beizufügen. ²Die Anmeldenden haben dem Registergericht gegenüber zu erklären, daß nach ihrer Kenntnis seit dem Stichtag der zugrunde gelegten Bilanz bis zum Tag der Anmeldung keine Vermögensminderung eingetreten ist, die der Kapitalerhöhung entgegenstünde, wenn sie am Tag der Anmeldung beschlossen worden wäre.

(2) Das Registergericht darf den Beschluß nur eintragen, wenn die der Kapitalerhöhung zugrunde gelegte Bilanz für einen höchstens acht Monate vor der Anmeldung liegenden Zeitpunkt aufgestellt und eine Erklärung nach Absatz 1 Satz 2 abgegeben worden ist.

(3) Zu der Prüfung, ob die Bilanzen den gesetzlichen Vorschriften entsprechen, ist das Gericht nicht verpflichtet.

(4) Bei der Eintragung des Beschlusses ist anzugeben, daß es sich um eine Kapitalerhöhung aus Gesellschaftsmitteln handelt.

§ 57j Verteilung der Geschäftsanteile.

¹Die neuen Geschäftsanteile stehen den Gesellschaftern im Verhältnis ihrer bisherigen Geschäftsanteile zu. ²Ein entgegenstehender Beschluß der Gesellschafter ist nichtig.

§ 57i Application for registration and registration of the resolution on increase.

(1) ¹The balance sheet that is used as a basis for the capital increase and is furnished with the certification of the auditors – in cases under sec. 57f the last annual balance sheet as well, to the extent as it has not yet been submitted pursuant to sec. 325 para. 1 of the Commercial Code – shall be attached to the application for registration in the commercial register of the resolution on the increase of the registered share capital. ²The persons making the application shall declare to the register court that, to their knowledge, from the record date of the balance sheet being used as a basis up to the date of the application, there has been no reduction in assets that would contravene the capital increase if it were resolved on such application date.

(2) The register court may register the resolution only if the balance sheet on which the capital increase is based was prepared as of a date at most eight months prior to the application and a declaration pursuant to para. 1 sentence 2 has been made.

(3) The court is not obligated to examine whether the balance sheets comply with legal requirements.

(4) It is to be indicated with the registration of the resolution that it pertains to a capital increase from company resources.

§ 57j Allocation of shares.

¹The shareholders are entitled to the new shares in proportion to their previous shareholdings. ²Any resolution of the shareholders to the contrary is null and void.

§ 57k Teilrechte; Ausübung der Rechte.

(1) Führt die Kapitalerhöhung dazu, daß auf einen Geschäftsanteil nur ein Teil eines neuen Geschäftsanteils entfällt, so ist dieses Teilrecht selbständig veräußerlich und vererblich.

(2) Die Rechte aus einem neuen Geschäftsanteil, einschließlich des Anspruchs auf Ausstellung einer Urkunde über den neuen Geschäftsanteil, können nur ausgeübt werden, wenn Teilrechte, die zusammen einen vollen Geschäftsanteil ergeben, in einer Hand vereinigt sind oder wenn sich mehrere Berechtigte, deren Teilrechte zusammen einen vollen Geschäftsanteil ergeben, zur Ausübung der Rechte (§ 18) zusammenschließen.

§ 57l Teilnahme an der Erhöhung des Stammkapitals.

(1) Eigene Geschäftsanteile nehmen an der Erhöhung des Stammkapitals teil.

(2) ¹Teileingezahlte Geschäftsanteile nehmen entsprechend ihrem Nennbetrag an der Erhöhung des Stammkapitals teil. ²Bei ihnen kann die Kapitalerhöhung nur durch Erhöhung des Nennbetrags der Geschäftsanteile ausgeführt werden. ³Sind neben teileingezahlten Geschäftsanteilen vollständig eingezahlte Geschäftsanteile vorhanden, so kann bei diesen die Kapitalerhöhung durch Erhöhung des Nennbetrags der Geschäftsanteile und durch Bildung neuer Geschäftsanteile ausgeführt werden. ⁴Die Geschäftsanteile, deren Nennbetrag erhöht wird, können auf jeden Betrag gestellt werden, der auf volle Euro lautet.

§ 57m Verhältnis der Rechte; Beziehungen zu Dritten.

(1) Das Verhältnis der mit den Geschäftsanteilen verbundenen Rechte zueinander wird durch die Kapitalerhöhung nicht berührt.

§ 57k Partial rights; exercise of rights.

(1) If the capital increase leads to only a part of a new share being allotted to a share, this partial right is independently transferable and heritable.

(2) The rights stemming from a new share, including the claim to issuance of a document regarding the new share, can be exercised only when partial rights that together result in a full share become consolidated in the hands of a single owner or when several entitled persons whose partial rights together result in a full share join together to exercise the rights (sec. 18).

§ 57l Participation in the increase of the registered share capital.

(1) Own shares participate in the increase of the registered share capital.

(2) ¹Shares that are partially paid in participate in the increase of the registered share capital according to their nominal value. ²With respect to such shares, the capital increase can be effected only by means of increasing the nominal value of the shares. ³If shares that are completely paid in are available in addition to shares partly paid in, in the case of such shares, the capital increase can be effected by increasing the nominal value of the shares and by creating new shares. ⁴The shares whose nominal value is being increased can be set at any even euro amount.

§ 57m Relationship of rights; relationships to third parties.

(1) The relationship of the rights attached to the shares to each other is not affected by the capital increase.

(2) ¹Soweit sich einzelne Rechte teileingezahlter Geschäftsanteile, insbesondere die Beteiligung am Gewinn oder das Stimmrecht, nach der je Geschäftsanteil geleisteten Einlage bestimmen, stehen diese Rechte den Gesellschaftern bis zur Leistung der noch ausstehenden Einlagen nur nach der Höhe der geleisteten Einlage, erhöht um den auf den Nennbetrag des Stammkapitals berechneten Hundertsatz der Erhöhung des Stammkapitals, zu. ²Werden weitere Einzahlungen geleistet, so erweitern sich diese Rechte entsprechend.

(3) Der wirtschaftliche Inhalt vertraglicher Beziehungen der Gesellschaft zu Dritten, die von der Gewinnausschüttung der Gesellschaft, dem Nennbetrag oder Wert ihrer Geschäftsanteile oder ihres Stammkapitals oder in sonstiger Weise von den bisherigen Kapital- oder Gewinnverhältnissen abhängen, wird durch die Kapitalerhöhung nicht berührt.

§ 57n Gewinnbeteiligung der neuen Geschäftsanteile.

(1) Die neuen Geschäftsanteile nehmen, wenn nichts anderes bestimmt ist, am Gewinn des ganzen Geschäftsjahres teil, in dem die Erhöhung des Stammkapitals beschlossen worden ist.

(2) ¹Im Beschluß über die Erhöhung des Stammkapitals kann bestimmt werden, daß die neuen Geschäftsanteile bereits am Gewinn des letzten vor der Beschlußfassung über die Kapitalerhöhung abgelaufenen Geschäftsjahrs teilnehmen. ²In diesem Fall ist die Erhöhung des Stammkapitals abweichend von § 57c Abs. 2 zu beschließen, bevor über die Ergebnisverwendung für das letzte vor der Beschlußfassung abgelaufene Geschäftsjahr Beschluß gefaßt worden ist. ³Der Beschluß über die Ergebnisverwendung für das letzte vor der Beschlußfassung über die Kapitalerhöhung abgelaufene Geschäftsjahr wird erst wirksam, wenn das Stammkapital

(2) ¹To the extent individual rights, in particular sharing in profits or voting rights, of shares that have been partially paid in are determined according to the contribution made per share, the shareholders are, up until the still outstanding contributions have been made, entitled to these rights only in proportion with the amount of the contribution already made, increased by the percentage of the increase of the registered share capital over the nominal value of the registered share capital. ²If additional payments are made, these rights expand accordingly.

(3) The commercial terms of contractual relationships of the company vis-à-vis third parties, which relationships rely on the distribution of profits of the company, the nominal value or value of its shares or its registered share capital, or in any other way on pre-existing capital or profit relations, are not affected by the capital increase.

§ 57n Profit participation of new shares.

(1) If nothing has been stipulated to the contrary, the new shares participate in the profits of the entire fiscal year in which the increase of the registered share capital was resolved.

(2) ¹In the resolution on the increase of the registered share capital, it may be stipulated that the new shares shall participate in the profits of the last completed fiscal year prior to the adoption of the resolution. ²In this case, the increase of the registered share capital shall be resolved, in deviation from sec. 57c para. 2, before the appropriation of profits has been resolved for the last completed fiscal year prior to the adoption of the resolution. ³The resolution on the appropriation of profits for the last completed fiscal year prior to the adoption of the resolution on the capital increase does not become effective until the registered share capital has been increased. ⁴The

erhöht worden ist. [4]Der Beschluß über die Erhöhung des Stammkapitals und der Beschluß über die Ergebnisverwendung für das letzte vor der Beschlußfassung über die Kapitalerhöhung abgelaufene Geschäftsjahr sind nichtig, wenn der Beschluß über die Kapitalerhöhung nicht binnen drei Monaten nach der Beschlußfassung in das Handelsregister eingetragen worden ist; der Lauf der Frist ist gehemmt, solange eine Anfechtungs- oder Nichtigkeitsklage rechtshängig ist.

resolution on the increase of the registered share capital and the resolution on the appropriation of profits for the last completed fiscal year prior to the adoption of the resolution on the capital increase are null and void if the resolution on the capital increase has not been registered in the commercial register within three months of the adoption of the resolution; the running of such time period is suspended so long as an action to set aside or an action for the declaration of nullity is pending.

§ 57o Anschaffungskosten.

[1]Als Anschaffungskosten der vor der Erhöhung des Stammkapitals erworbenen Geschäftsanteile und der auf sie entfallenden neuen Geschäftsanteile gelten die Beträge, die sich für die einzelnen Geschäftsanteile ergeben, wenn die Anschaffungskosten der vor der Erhöhung des Stammkapitals erworbenen Geschäftsanteile auf diese und auf die auf sie entfallenden neuen Geschäftsanteile nach dem Verhältnis der Nennbeträge verteilt werden. [2]Der Zuwachs an Geschäftsanteilen ist nicht als Zugang auszuweisen.

§ 57o Acquisition costs.

[1]The acquisition costs of the shares acquired prior to the increase of the registered share capital and those of the new shares allotted to them are deemed to be those amounts that relate to the individual shares when the acquisition costs of the shares acquired prior to the increase of the registered share capital are allocated to these and to the new shares allotted to them in proportion to their nominal value. [2]The increase in shares is not to be shown as an addition.

§ 58 Herabsetzung des Stammkapitals.

(1) Eine Herabsetzung des Stammkapitals kann nur unter Beobachtung der nachstehenden Bestimmungen erfolgen:

1. der Beschluß auf Herabsetzung des Stammkapitals muß von den Geschäftsführern in den Gesellschaftsblättern bekanntgemacht werden; in dieser Bekanntmachung sind zugleich die Gläubiger der Gesellschaft aufzufordern, sich bei derselben zu melden; die aus den Handelsbüchern der Gesellschaft ersichtlichen oder in anderer Weise bekannten Gläubiger sind durch besondere Mitteilung zur Anmeldung aufzufordern;

2. die Gläubiger, welche sich bei der Gesellschaft melden und der Her-

§ 58 Reduction of the registered share capital.

(1) A reduction of the registered share capital can take place only in accordance with the following provisions:

1. the resolution on the reduction of the registered share capital shall be announced by the managing directors in the company's designated journals; at the same time in this announcement, the creditors of the company shall be called upon to register with the company; the creditors that are apparent from the commercial books of the company or that are otherwise known are to be called upon via special notice to register with the company;

2. the creditors that register with the company and do not agree to the

absetzung nicht zustimmen, sind wegen der erhobenen Ansprüche zu befriedigen oder sicherzustellen;

3. die Anmeldung des Herabsetzungsbeschlusses zur Eintragung in das Handelsregister erfolgt nicht vor Ablauf eines Jahres seit dem Tage, an welchem die Aufforderung der Gläubiger in den Gesellschaftsblättern stattgefunden hat;

4. mit der Anmeldung ist die Bekanntmachung des Beschlusses einzureichen; zugleich haben die Geschäftsführer die Versicherung abzugeben, daß die Gläubiger, welche sich bei der Gesellschaft gemeldet und der Herabsetzung nicht zugestimmt haben, befriedigt oder sichergestellt sind.

(2) ¹Die Bestimmung in § 5 Abs. 1 über den Mindestbetrag des Stammkapitals bleibt unberührt. ²Erfolgt die Herabsetzung zum Zweck der Zurückzahlung von Einlagen oder zum Zweck des Erlasses zu leistender Einlagen, dürfen die verbleibenden Nennbeträge der Geschäftsanteile nicht unter den in § 5 Abs. 2 und 3 bezeichneten Betrag herabgehen.

§ 58a Vereinfachte Kapitalherabsetzung.

(1) Eine Herabsetzung des Stammkapitals, die dazu dienen soll, Wertminderungen auszugleichen oder sonstige Verluste zu decken, kann als vereinfachte Kapitalherabsetzung vorgenommen werden.

(2) ¹Die vereinfachte Kapitalherabsetzung ist nur zulässig, nachdem der Teil der Kapital- und Gewinnrücklagen, der zusammen über zehn vom Hundert des nach der Herabsetzung verbleibenden Stammkapitals hinausgeht, vorweg aufgelöst ist. ²Sie ist nicht zulässig, solange ein Gewinnvortrag vorhanden ist.

(3) ¹Im Beschluß über die vereinfachte Kapitalherabsetzung sind die Nennbeträge der Geschäftsanteile dem herabge-

reduction are to have their asserted claims satisfied or secured;

3. the application for registration in the commercial register of the resolution on the capital reduction shall not occur prior to the expiration of one year from the date on which the calling of the creditors in the company's designated journals has taken place;

4. the announcement of the resolution shall be submitted with the application; at the same time, the managing directors shall provide assurance that the creditors that have registered with the company and have not agreed to the reduction have been satisfied or secured.

(2) ¹The provision in sec. 5 para. 1 regarding the minimum amount of the registered share capital remains unaffected. ²If the reduction takes place for the purpose of repaying contributions or for the purpose of waiving contributions to be rendered, the remaining nominal amounts of the shares may not decrease below the amount indicated in sec. 5 paras. 1 and 3.

§ 58a Simplified capital reduction.

(1) A reduction of the registered share capital that is to serve the purpose of compensating for declines in value or covering other losses can be performed as a simplified capital reduction.

(2) ¹The simplified capital reduction is permissible only after the portion of capital reserves and revenue reserves that in the aggregate exceeds ten percent of the registered share capital remaining after the reduction has been released in advance. ²It is not permissible so long as there is profit carried forward.

(3) ¹In the resolution on the simplified capital reduction, the nominal value of the shares shall be adjusted to the

setzten Stammkapital anzupassen. ²Die Geschäftsanteile müssen auf einen Betrag gestellt werden, der auf volle Euro lautet.

(4) ¹Das Stammkapital kann unter den in § 5 Abs. 1 bestimmten Mindestnennbetrag herabgesetzt werden, wenn dieser durch eine Kapitalerhöhung wieder erreicht wird, die zugleich mit der Kapitalherabsetzung beschlossen ist und bei der Sacheinlagen nicht festgesetzt sind. ²Die Beschlüsse sind nichtig, wenn sie nicht binnen drei Monaten nach der Beschlußfassung in das Handelsregister eingetragen worden sind. ³Der Lauf der Frist ist gehemmt, solange eine Anfechtungs- oder Nichtigkeitsklage rechtshängig ist. ⁴Die Beschlüsse sollen nur zusammen in das Handelsregister eingetragen werden.

(5) Neben den §§ 53 und 54 über die Abänderung des Gesellschaftsvertrags gelten die §§ 58b bis 58f.

§ 58b Beträge aus Rücklagenauflösung und Kapitalherabsetzung.

(1) Die Beträge, die aus der Auflösung der Kapital- oder Gewinnrücklagen und aus der Kapitalherabsetzung gewonnen werden, dürfen nur verwandt werden, um Wertminderungen auszugleichen und sonstige Verluste zu decken.

(2) ¹Daneben dürfen die gewonnenen Beträge in die Kapitalrücklage eingestellt werden, soweit diese zehn vom Hundert des Stammkapitals nicht übersteigt. ²Als Stammkapital gilt dabei der Nennbetrag, der sich durch die Herabsetzung ergibt, mindestens aber der nach § 5 Abs. 1 zulässige Mindestnennbetrag.

(3) Ein Betrag, der auf Grund des Absatzes 2 in die Kapitalrücklage eingestellt worden ist, darf vor Ablauf des fünften nach der Beschlußfassung über die Kapitalherabsetzung beginnenden Geschäftsjahrs nur verwandt werden

reduced registered share capital. ²The shares shall be set to an even euro amount.

(4) ¹The registered share capital may be reduced below the minimum nominal value stipulated in sec. 5 para. 1 if this amount is restored again by a capital increase which is resolved at the same time as the capital reduction and for which no contributions in kind are stipulated. ²Resolutions are null and void if they are not registered in the commercial register within three months of the adoption of the resolution. ³The running of the time period is suspended so long as an action to set aside or an action for the declaration of nullity is pending. ⁴The resolutions should be registered in the commercial register only together.

(5) In addition to sec. 53 and 54 with respect to the amendment to the articles of association, sec. 58b to 58f shall apply.

§ 58b Amounts from the release of reserves and from capital reduction.

(1) Amounts obtained from the release of capital reserves or revenue reserves and from capital reductions may only be used to compensate for declines in value and to cover other losses.

(2) ¹Additionally, the amounts obtained may be placed in capital reserves to the extent such amounts do not exceed ten percent of the registered share capital. ²For this purpose, the nominal value resulting from the reduction is to be counted as registered share capital, but this shall be at least the minimum nominal value permitted in accordance with sec. 5 para. 1.

(3) An amount that is transferred to the capital reserves on the basis of para. 2 may be used prior to the end of the fifth fiscal year after the adoption of the resolution on the capital reduction only

1. zum Ausgleich eines Jahresfehlbetrags, soweit er nicht durch einen Gewinnvortrag aus dem Vorjahr gedeckt ist und nicht durch Auflösung von Gewinnrücklagen ausgeglichen werden kann;
2. zum Ausgleich eines Verlustvortrags aus dem Vorjahr, soweit er nicht durch einen Jahresüberschuß gedeckt ist und nicht durch Auflösung von Gewinnrücklagen ausgeglichen werden kann;
3. zur Kapitalerhöhung aus Gesellschaftsmitteln.

§ 58c Nichteintritt angenommener Verluste.

[1]Ergibt sich bei Aufstellung der Jahresbilanz für das Geschäftsjahr, in dem der Beschluß über die Kapitalherabsetzung gefaßt wurde, oder für eines der beiden folgenden Geschäftsjahre, daß Wertminderungen und sonstige Verluste in der bei der Beschlußfassung angenommenen Höhe tatsächlich nicht eingetreten oder ausgeglichen waren, so ist der Unterschiedsbetrag in die Kapitalrücklage einzustellen. [2]Für einen nach Satz 1 in die Kapitalrücklage eingestellten Betrag gilt § 58b Abs. 3 sinngemäß.

§ 58d Gewinnausschüttung.

(1) [1]Gewinn darf vor Ablauf des fünften nach der Beschlußfassung über die Kapitalherabsetzung beginnenden Geschäftsjahrs nur ausgeschüttet werden, wenn die Kapital- und Gewinnrücklagen zusammen zehn vom Hundert des Stammkapitals erreichen. [2]Als Stammkapital gilt dabei der Nennbetrag, der sich durch die Herabsetzung ergibt, mindestens aber der nach § 5 Abs. 1 zulässige Mindestnennbetrag.

(2) [1]Die Zahlung eines Gewinnanteils von mehr als vier vom Hundert ist erst für ein Geschäftsjahr zulässig, das später als zwei Jahre nach der Beschlußfassung über die Kapitalherab-

1. to compensate for an annual net loss to the extent not covered by profit carried forward from the preceding year and cannot be compensated for by release of revenue reserves;
2. to compensate for a loss carried forward from the preceding year to the extent not covered by annual net income and which cannot be compensated for by release of revenue reserves;
3. to increase capital from company resources.

§ 58c Nonmaterialization of assumed losses.

[1]If, in the preparation of the annual balance sheet for the fiscal year in which the resolution on the capital reduction was passed or for one of the two subsequent fiscal years, it turns out that declines in value and other losses in the amount assumed at the time of the adoption of the resolution did not actually materialize or were compensated for, then the difference in such amounts shall be transferred to the capital reserves. [2]Sec. 58b para. 3 shall apply accordingly to any amount placed in the capital reserves in accordance with sentence 1.

§ 58d Distribution of profits.

(1) [1]Profits may be distributed prior to the expiration of the fifth fiscal year after the adoption of the resolution on the capital reduction only if the aggregate amount of capital reserves and revenue reserves together reach ten percent of the registered share capital. [2]For this purpose, the nominal value remaining from the reduction is to be counted as registered share capital, but this shall be at least the minimum nominal value permitted according to sec. 5 para. 1.

(2) [1]The payment of a profit share of more than four percent is permissible only for a fiscal year that begins later than two years after the adoption of the resolution on the capital reduction. [2]This

setzung beginnt. ²Dies gilt nicht, wenn die Gläubiger, deren Forderungen vor der Bekanntmachung der Eintragung des Beschlusses begründet worden waren, befriedigt oder sichergestellt sind, soweit sie sich binnen sechs Monaten nach der Bekanntmachung des Jahresabschlusses, auf Grund dessen die Gewinnverteilung beschlossen ist, zu diesem Zweck gemeldet haben. ³Einer Sicherstellung der Gläubiger bedarf es nicht, die im Fall des Insolvenzverfahrens ein Recht auf vorzugsweise Befriedigung aus einer Deckungsmasse haben, die nach gesetzlicher Vorschrift zu ihrem Schutz errichtet und staatlich überwacht ist. ⁴Die Gläubiger sind in der Bekanntmachung nach § 325 Abs. 2 des Handelsgesetzbuchs auf die Befriedigung oder Sicherstellung hinzuweisen.

does not apply if the creditors whose claims arose prior to the announcement of the registration of the resolution have been satisfied or secured, as long as they registered for this purpose within six months of the announcement of the annual financial statements on the basis of which the distribution of profits has been resolved. ³Creditors need not be provided with security who in the case of insolvency proceedings have a right to preferential satisfaction from a covering fund that is set up for their protection in accordance with statutory provisions and monitored by the state. ⁴The creditors shall be notified of such satisfaction or provision of security in the announcement in accordance with sec. 325 para. 2 of the Commercial Code.

§ 58e Beschluss über die Kapitalherabsetzung.

§ 58e Resolution on the capital reduction.

(1) ¹Im Jahresabschluß für das letzte vor der Beschlußfassung über die Kapitalherabsetzung abgelaufene Geschäftsjahr können das Stammkapital sowie die Kapital- und Gewinnrücklagen in der Höhe ausgewiesen werden, in der sie nach der Kapitalherabsetzung bestehen sollen. ²Dies gilt nicht, wenn der Jahresabschluß anders als durch Beschluß der Gesellschafter festgestellt wird.

(1) ¹In the annual financial statements for the last completed fiscal year prior to the adoption of the resolution on the capital reduction, the registered share capital as well as the capital reserves and revenue reserves may be shown in the amount they should have after giving effect to the capital reduction. ²This does not apply if the annual financial statements are formally approved in a way other than through resolution of the shareholders.

(2) Der Beschluß über die Feststellung des Jahresabschlusses soll zugleich mit dem Beschluß über die Kapitalherabsetzung gefaßt werden.

(2) The resolution on the formal approval of the annual financial statements should be adopted at the same time as the resolution on the capital reduction.

(3) ¹Die Beschlüsse sind nichtig, wenn der Beschluß über die Kapitalherabsetzung nicht binnen drei Monaten nach der Beschlußfassung in das Handelsregister eingetragen worden ist. ²Der Lauf der Frist ist gehemmt, solange eine Anfechtungs- oder Nichtigkeitsklage rechtshängig ist.

(3) ¹The resolutions are null and void if the resolution on the capital reduction has not been registered in the commercial register within three months after the adoption of the resolution. ²The running of the time limit is suspended so long as an action to set aside or an action for the declaration of nullity is pending.

(4) Der Jahresabschluß darf nach § 325 des Handelsgesetzbuchs erst nach Eintragung des Beschlusses über die Kapitalherabsetzung offengelegt werden.

§ 58f Kapitalherabsetzung bei gleichzeitiger Erhöhung des Stammkapitals.

(1) ¹Wird im Fall des § 58e zugleich mit der Kapitalherabsetzung eine Erhöhung des Stammkapitals beschlossen, so kann auch die Kapitalerhöhung in dem Jahresabschluß als vollzogen berücksichtigt werden. ²Die Beschlussfassung ist nur zulässig, wenn die neuen Geschäftsanteile übernommen, keine Sacheinlagen festgesetzt sind und wenn auf jeden neuen Geschäftsanteil die Einzahlung geleistet ist, die nach § 56a zur Zeit der Anmeldung der Kapitalerhöhung bewirkt sein muss. ³Die Übernahme und die Einzahlung sind dem Notar nachzuweisen, der den Beschluß über die Erhöhung des Stammkapitals beurkundet.

(2) ¹Sämtliche Beschlüsse sind nichtig, wenn die Beschlüsse über die Kapitalherabsetzung und die Kapitalerhöhung nicht binnen drei Monaten nach der Beschlußfassung in das Handelsregister eingetragen worden sind. ²Der Lauf der Frist ist gehemmt, solange eine Anfechtungs- oder Nichtigkeitsklage rechtshängig ist oder eine zur Kapitalherabsetzung. ³Die Beschlüsse sollen nur zusammen in das Handelsregister eingetragen werden.

(3) Der Jahresabschluß darf nach § 325 des Handelsgesetzbuchs erst offengelegt werden, nachdem die Beschlüsse über die Kapitalherabsetzung und Kapitalerhöhung eingetragen worden sind.

§ 59 *(aufgehoben)*

(4) According to sec. 325 of the Commercial Code, the annual financial statements may not be disclosed until registration of the resolution on the capital reduction.

§ 58f Capital reduction in event of simultaneous increase of registered share capital.

(1) ¹If in a case under sec. 58e an increase in the registered share capital is resolved simultaneously with the reduction of the registered share capital, the capital increase as well can be regarded as completed in the annual financial statements. ²The adoption of the resolution is permissible only if the new shares have been subscribed to, no contributions in kind have been stipulated, and if payment has been made on each new share which payment shall, according to sec. 56a, have been effected at the time of the registration of the capital increase. ³The subscription and the payment are to be proved to the notary who notarizes the resolution on the increase of the registered share capital.

(2) ¹All resolutions are null and void if the resolutions on the capital reduction and the capital increase have not been registered in the commercial register within three months after the adoption of the resolution. ²The running of the time limit is suspended so long as an action to set aside or an action for the declaration of nullity is pending. ³The resolutions should be registered in the commercial register only together.

(3) The annual financial statements may not be disclosed according to sec. 325 of the Commercial Code until the resolutions on the capital reduction and the capital increase have been registered.

§ 59 *(repealed)*

Abschnitt 5. Auflösung und Nichtigkeit der Gesellschaft

§ 60 Auflösungsgründe.

(1) Die Gesellschaft mit beschränkter Haftung wird aufgelöst:

1. durch Ablauf der im Gesellschaftsvertrag bestimmten Zeit;
2. durch Beschluß der Gesellschafter; derselbe bedarf, sofern im Gesellschaftsvertrag nicht ein anderes bestimmt ist, einer Mehrheit von drei Vierteilen der abgegebenen Stimmen;
3. durch gerichtliches Urteil oder durch Entscheidung des Verwaltungsgerichts oder der Verwaltungsbehörde in den Fällen der §§ 61 und 62;
4. durch die Eröffnung des Insolvenzverfahrens; wird das Verfahren auf Antrag des Schuldners eingestellt oder nach der Bestätigung eines Insolvenzplans, der den Fortbestand der Gesellschaft vorsieht, aufgehoben, so können die Gesellschafter die Fortsetzung der Gesellschaft beschließen;
5. mit der Rechtskraft des Beschlusses, durch den die Eröffnung des Insolvenzverfahrens mangels Masse abgelehnt worden ist;
6. mit der Rechtskraft einer Verfügung des Registergerichts, durch welche nach § 399 des Gesetzes über das Verfahren in Familiensachen und in den Angelegenheiten der freiwilligen Gerichtsbarkeit ein Mangel des Gesellschaftsvertrags festgestellt worden ist;
7. durch die Löschung der Gesellschaft wegen Vermögenslosigkeit nach § 394 des Gesetzes über das Verfahren in Familiensachen und in den Angelegenheiten der freiwilligen Gerichtsbarkeit.

(2) Im Gesellschaftsvertrag können weitere Auflösungsgründe festgesetzt werden.

Part 5. Dissolution and Nullity of the Company

§ 60 Grounds for dissolution.

(1) A limited liability company is dissolved:

1. by virtue of expiration of the period of its existence set forth in the articles of association;
2. by resolution of the shareholders; this requires a majority of three fourths of the votes cast, unless otherwise provided in the articles of association;
3. by court judgment or by decision of the administrative court or of the administrative authorities in cases under sec. 61 and 62;
4. by virtue of the commencement of insolvency proceedings; if the proceedings are discontinued upon application of the debtor or repealed after affirmation of an insolvency plan providing for the continued existence of the company, the shareholders can resolve the continuation of the company;
5. upon an order rejecting the opening of insolvency proceedings for insufficient assets becoming res judicata;
6. upon an order of the register court becoming res judicata by means of which, in accordance with sec. 399 of the Act on Procedure in Family Matters and Matters of Non-Contentious Jurisdiction, a defect in the articles of association has been determined;
7. by the cancellation of the company due to insufficient assets in accordance with sec. 394 of the Act on Procedure in Family Matters and Matters of Non-Contentious Jurisdiction.

(2) The articles of association may stipulate additional grounds for dissolution.

§ 61 Dissolution by judgment.

(1) The company may be dissolved by court judgment if the attainment of the purpose of the company becomes impossible to achieve, or if other good cause for dissolution pertaining to the circumstances of the company exists.

(2) [1]The action for dissolution is to be brought against the company. [2]It can be filed only by shareholders whose shares in the aggregate represent at least a tenth of the registered share capital.

(3) The regional court in whose district the company has its registered office has exclusive jurisdiction over the action.

§ 62 Dissolution by an administrative authority.

(1) If a company endangers the public interest by reason of its shareholders adopting unlawful resolutions or knowingly allowing unlawful actions by managing directors to occur, it can be dissolved without thereby providing grounds for a claim to compensation.

(2) The procedures and the jurisdiction of the authorities depend on the regulations applicable to contentious administrative matters in each state.

§ 63 *(repealed)*

§ 64 Liability for payments after illiquidity or over-indebtedness.

[1]The managing directors are obligated to reimburse the company for payments made after the company became illiquid or after its over-indebtedness was ascertained. [2]This does not apply to payments that are consistent with the care of a prudent businessman. [3]The managing directors shall incur the same obligation for payments to shareholders to the extent they had to result in the illiquidity of the company unless

soweit diese zur Zahlungsunfähigkeit der Gesellschaft führen mussten, es sei denn, dies war auch bei Beachtung der in Satz 2 bezeichneten Sorgfalt nicht erkennbar. [4]Auf den Ersatzanspruch finden die Bestimmungen in § 43 Abs. 3 und 4 entsprechende Anwendung.

this was not recognizable even when applying the care set forth in sentence 2. [4]The provisions of sec. 43 paras. 3 and 4 shall apply accordingly to the claim for reimbursement.

§ 65 Anmeldung und Eintragung der Auflösung.

(1) [1]Die Auflösung der Gesellschaft ist zur Eintragung in das Handelsregister anzumelden. [2]Dies gilt nicht in den Fällen der Eröffnung oder der Ablehnung der Eröffnung des Insolvenzverfahrens und der gerichtlichen Feststellung eines Mangels des Gesellschaftsvertrags. [3]In diesen Fällen hat das Gericht die Auflösung und ihren Grund von Amts wegen einzutragen. [4]Im Falle der Löschung der Gesellschaft (§ 60 Abs. 1 Nr. 7) entfällt die Eintragung der Auflösung.

(2) [1]Die Auflösung ist von den Liquidatoren in den Gesellschaftsblättern bekanntzumachen. [2]Durch die Bekanntmachung sind zugleich die Gläubiger der Gesellschaft aufzufordern, sich bei derselben zu melden.

§ 66 Liquidatoren.

(1) In den Fällen der Auflösung außer dem Fall des Insolvenzverfahrens erfolgt die Liquidation durch die Geschäftsführer, wenn nicht dieselbe durch den Gesellschaftsvertrag oder durch Beschluß der Gesellschafter anderen Personen übertragen wird.

(2) Auf Antrag von Gesellschaftern, deren Geschäftsanteile zusammen mindestens dem zehnten Teil des Stammkapitals entsprechen, kann aus wichtigen Gründen die Bestellung von Liquidatoren durch das Gericht erfolgen.

(3) [1]Die Abberufung von Liquidatoren kann durch das Gericht unter derselben Voraussetzung wie die Bestellung stattfinden. [2]Liquidatoren, welche nicht vom Gericht ernannt sind, können auch

§ 65 Application for registration and registration of the dissolution.

(1) [1]The dissolution of the company shall be filed for registration in the commercial register. [2]This does not apply in the case of the commencement or the rejection of the commencement of insolvency proceedings, or in the case of judicial determination of a defect in the articles of association. [3]In these cases, the court shall register the dissolution and its grounds ex officio. [4]In the case of the cancellation of the company (sec. 60 para. 1 no. 7), there is no registration of the dissolution.

(2) [1]The dissolution shall be announced by the liquidators in the company's designated journals. [2]The announcement shall, at the same time, call upon the creditors of the company to register with the company.

§ 66 Liquidators.

(1) In cases of dissolution other than in the case of insolvency proceedings, the liquidation shall be performed by the managing directors, unless it is entrusted to other persons by the articles of association or by shareholder resolution.

(2) Upon application of shareholders whose shares in the aggregate represent at least one tenth of the registered share capital, the court may appoint liquidators if good cause exists.

(3) [1]The liquidators can be dismissed by the court under the same prerequisites as apply to their appointment. [2]Liquidators not appointed by the court can also be dismissed by shareholder resolution

durch Beschluß der Gesellschafter vor Ablauf des Zeitraums, für welchen sie bestellt sind, abberufen werden.

(4) Für die Auswahl der Liquidatoren findet § 6 Abs. 2 Satz 2 und 3 entsprechende Anwendung.

(5) ¹Ist die Gesellschaft durch Löschung wegen Vermögenslosigkeit aufgelöst, so findet eine Liquidation nur statt, wenn sich nach der Löschung herausstellt, daß Vermögen vorhanden ist, das der Verteilung unterliegt. ²Die Liquidatoren sind auf Antrag eines Beteiligten durch das Gericht zu ernennen.

§ 67 Anmeldung der Liquidatoren.

(1) Die ersten Liquidatoren sowie ihre Vertretungsbefugnis sind durch die Geschäftsführer, jeder Wechsel der Liquidatoren und jede Änderung ihrer Vertretungsbefugnis sind durch die Liquidatoren zur Eintragung in das Handelsregister anzumelden.

(2) Der Anmeldung sind die Urkunden über die Bestellung der Liquidatoren oder über die Änderung in den Personen derselben in Urschrift oder öffentlich beglaubigter Abschrift beizufügen.

(3) ¹In der Anmeldung haben die Liquidatoren zu versichern, daß keine Umstände vorliegen, die ihrer Bestellung nach § 66 Abs. 4 in Verbindung mit § 6 Abs. 2 Satz 2 Nr. 2 und 3 sowie Satz 3 entgegenstehen, und daß sie über ihre unbeschränkte Auskunftspflicht gegenüber dem Gericht belehrt worden sind. ²§ 8 Abs. 3 Satz 2 ist anzuwenden.

(4) Die Eintragung der gerichtlichen Ernennung oder Abberufung der Liquidatoren geschieht von Amts wegen.

§ 68 Zeichnung der Liquidatoren.

(1) ¹Die Liquidatoren haben in der bei ihrer Bestellung bestimmten Form ihre

prior to the expiration of the period for which they are appointed.

(4) Sec. 6 para. 2 sentences 2 and 3 shall apply accordingly to the selection of liquidators.

(5) ¹If the company is dissolved through cancellation due to insufficient assets, a liquidation shall take place only if it turns out after the cancellation that assets are available for distribution. ²The liquidators shall be appointed by the court upon petition of a party involved.

§ 67 Application for registration of liquidators.

(1) The managing directors shall apply for the first liquidators, as well as their representative authority, to be registered in the commercial register; the liquidators shall apply for every change in identity of the liquidators and every change in their representative authority to be registered in the commercial register.

(2) The documents pertaining to the appointment of the liquidators or to the change in their identities are to be attached to the application in original or in publicly certified copy.

(3) ¹In the application, the liquidators shall provide assurance that no circumstances exist that oppose their appointment pursuant to sec. 66 para. 4 in connection with sec. 6 para. 2 sentence 2 nos. 2 and 3 and sentence 3, and that such liquidators have been informed of their unlimited duty to provide information to the court. ²Sec. 8 para. 3 sentence 2 shall apply.

(4) The registration of the court appointment or dismissal of liquidators takes place ex officio.

§ 68 Signature of liquidators.

(1) ¹The liquidators shall make their declarations of intent in the form deter-

Willenserklärungen kundzugeben und für die Gesellschaft zu zeichnen. ²Ist nichts darüber bestimmt, so muß die Erklärung und Zeichnung durch sämtliche Liquidatoren erfolgen.

(2) Die Zeichnungen geschehen in der Weise, daß die Liquidatoren der bisherigen, nunmehr als Liquidationsfirma zu bezeichnenden Firma ihre Namensunterschrift beifügen.

§ 69 Rechtsverhältnisse von Gesellschaft und Gesellschaftern.

(1) Bis zur Beendigung der Liquidation kommen ungeachtet der Auflösung der Gesellschaft in bezug auf die Rechtsverhältnisse derselben und der Gesellschafter die Vorschriften des zweiten und dritten Abschnitts zur Anwendung, soweit sich aus den Bestimmungen des gegenwärtigen Abschnitts und aus dem Wesen der Liquidation nicht ein anderes ergibt.

(2) Der Gerichtsstand, welchen die Gesellschaft zur Zeit ihrer Auflösung hatte, bleibt bis zur vollzogenen Verteilung des Vermögens bestehen.

§ 70 Aufgaben der Liquidatoren.

¹Die Liquidatoren haben die laufenden Geschäfte zu beendigen, die Verpflichtungen der aufgelösten Gesellschaft zu erfüllen, die Forderungen derselben einzuziehen und das Vermögen der Gesellschaft in Geld umzusetzen; sie haben die Gesellschaft gerichtlich und außergerichtlich zu vertreten. ²Zur Beendigung schwebender Geschäfte können die Liquidatoren auch neue Geschäfte eingehen.

§ 71 Eröffnungsbilanz; Rechte und Pflichten.

(1) Die Liquidatoren haben für den Beginn der Liquidation eine Bilanz (Eröffnungsbilanz) und einen die Eröffnungsbilanz erläuternden Bericht sowie für den Schluß eines jeden Jahres einen

mined at the time of their appointment and shall sign for the company. ²Unless otherwise provided, the declaration and signing shall be made by all the liquidators.

(2) Signing takes place by means of the liquidators adding their signatures to the present name of the company, now to be referred to as a company in liquidation.

§ 69 Legal relationships of company and shareholders.

(1) Until completion of the liquidation, the provisions of the Second Part and the Third Part shall apply with respect to the legal relationships of the company and the shareholders, without regard to the dissolution of the company, unless otherwise provided in this Part or from the nature of the liquidation.

(2) The place of jurisdiction that the company had at the time of its dissolution remains in effect until the distribution of its assets has been completed.

§ 70 Responsibilities of liquidators.

¹The liquidators shall conclude the day to day business, fulfill the obligations of the company being dissolved, call in its receivables and monetize its assets; they shall represent the company in and out of court. ²In order to conclude pending transactions, the liquidators may enter into new transactions as well.

§ 71 Opening balance sheet; rights and duties.

(1) The liquidators shall prepare a balance sheet for the beginning of the liquidation (opening balance sheet) and a report explaining the opening balance sheet, as well as annual financial state-

Jahresabschluß und einen Lagebericht aufzustellen.

(2) ¹Die Gesellschafter beschließen über die Feststellung der Eröffnungsbilanz und des Jahresabschlusses sowie über die Entlastung der Liquidatoren. ²Auf die Eröffnungsbilanz und den erläuternden Bericht sind die Vorschriften über den Jahresabschluß entsprechend anzuwenden. ³Vermögensgegenstände des Anlagevermögens sind jedoch wie Umlaufvermögen zu bewerten, soweit ihre Veräußerung innerhalb eines übersehbaren Zeitraums beabsichtigt ist oder diese Vermögensgegenstände nicht mehr dem Geschäftsbetrieb dienen; dies gilt auch für den Jahresabschluß.

(3) ¹Das Gericht kann von der Prüfung des Jahresabschlusses und des Lageberichts durch einen Abschlußprüfer befreien, wenn die Verhältnisse der Gesellschaft so überschaubar sind, daß eine Prüfung im Interesse der Gläubiger und der Gesellschafter nicht geboten erscheint. ²Gegen die Entscheidung ist die Beschwerde zulässig.

(4) Im übrigen haben sie die aus §§ 37, 41, 43 Abs. 1, 2 und 4, § 49 Abs. 1 und 2, § 64 sich ergebenden Rechte und Pflichten der Geschäftsführer.

(5) Auf den Geschäftsbriefen ist anzugeben, dass sich die Gesellschaft in Liquidation befindet; im Übrigen gilt § 35a entsprechend.

§ 72 Vermögensverteilung.

¹Das Vermögen der Gesellschaft wird unter die Gesellschafter nach Verhältnis ihrer Geschäftsanteile verteilt. ²Durch den Gesellschaftsvertrag kann ein anderes Verhältnis für die Verteilung bestimmt werden.

§ 73 Sperrjahr.

(1) Die Verteilung darf nicht vor Tilgung oder Sicherstellung der Schulden der Gesellschaft und nicht vor Ablauf ei-

ments and a management report as of the end of each year.

(2) ¹The shareholders resolve on the formal approval of the opening balance sheet and the annual financial statements, as well as on the ratification of the acts of the liquidators. ²The provisions regarding annual financial statements are to be applied accordingly to the opening balance sheet and the explanatory report. ³Fixed assets are to be valued like current assets to the extent that the disposal of such fixed assets is intended within a foreseeable period of time or to the extent that such fixed assets are no longer used in the business operation of the company; this applies to the annual financial statements as well.

(3) ¹The court may waive the requirement that the annual financial statements and the management report be audited by an auditor of annual financial statements if the situation of the company is so apparent that an audit does not appear required in the interests of the creditors and the shareholders. ²The decision is subject to appeal.

(4) In other respects, they have the rights and duties of the managing directors provided in sec. 37, 41, 43 paras. 1, 2, and 4, sec. 49 paras. 1 and 2, and sec. 64.

(5) The business letters shall specify that the company is being liquidated; apart from that, sec. 35a shall apply accordingly.

§ 72 Distribution of assets.

¹The assets of the company shall be distributed among the shareholders on a pro rata basis in proportion to their shares. ²Another ratio for the distribution can be laid down in the articles of association.

§ 73 Restrictive year.

(1) The distribution may not occur before the debts of the company are repaid or secured and not before one year

nes Jahres seit dem Tage vorgenommen werden, an welchem die Aufforderung an die Gläubiger (§ 65 Abs. 2) in den Gesellschaftsblättern erfolgt ist.

(2) ¹Meldet sich ein bekannter Gläubiger nicht, so ist der geschuldete Betrag, wenn die Berechtigung zur Hinterlegung vorhanden ist, für den Gläubiger zu hinterlegen. ²Ist die Berichtigung einer Verbindlichkeit zur Zeit nicht ausführbar oder ist eine Verbindlichkeit streitig, so darf die Verteilung des Vermögens nur erfolgen, wenn dem Gläubiger Sicherheit geleistet ist.

(3) ¹Liquidatoren, welche diesen Vorschriften zuwiderhandeln, sind zum Ersatz der verteilten Beträge solidarisch verpflichtet. ²Auf den Ersatzanspruch finden die Bestimmungen in § 43 Abs. 3 und 4 entsprechende Anwendung.

§ 74 Schluss der Liquidation.

(1) ¹Ist die Liquidation beendet und die Schlußrechnung gelegt, so haben die Liquidatoren den Schluß der Liquidation zur Eintragung in das Handelsregister anzumelden. ²Die Gesellschaft ist zu löschen.

(2) ¹Nach Beendigung der Liquidation sind die Bücher und Schriften der Gesellschaft für die Dauer von zehn Jahren einem der Gesellschafter oder einem Dritten in Verwahrung zu geben. ²Der Gesellschafter oder der Dritte wird in Ermangelung einer Bestimmung des Gesellschaftsvertrags oder eines Beschlusses der Gesellschafter durch das Gericht bestimmt.

(3) ¹Die Gesellschafter und deren Rechtsnachfolger sind zur Einsicht der Bücher und Schriften berechtigt. ²Gläubiger der Gesellschaft können von dem Gericht zur Einsicht ermächtigt werden.

has passed since the date on which the calling of the creditors (sec. 65 para. 2) was made in the company's designated journals.

(2) ¹If a known creditor does not register with the company, the amount owed shall be deposited for the creditor if there is a right to deposit. ²If the settlement of a liability cannot be made for the time being, or if a liability is disputed, assets may only be distributed if the creditor has been provided with a security.

(3) ¹Liquidators who violate these regulations are jointly and severally obligated to reimburse distributed amounts. ²The provisions of sec. 43 paras. 3 and 4 shall apply accordingly to any claim for compensation.

§ 74 Completion of the liquidation.

(1) ¹If the liquidation has been completed and the final accounts have been prepared, the liquidators shall apply for the completion of the liquidation to be registered in the commercial register. ²The company is to be deleted from the commercial register.

(2) ¹After completion of the liquidation, the books and records of the company shall be given to one of the shareholders or a third party who shall retain them for a period of ten years. ²The shareholder or the third party shall be determined by the court in the absence of a provision of the articles of association or of a resolution of the shareholders.

(3) ¹The shareholders and their legal successors are entitled to inspect the books and documents. ²Creditors of the company may receive authorization for inspection from the court.

§ 75 Nichtigkeitsklage.

(1) Enthält der Gesellschaftsvertrag keine Bestimmungen über die Höhe des Stammkapitals oder über den Gegenstand des Unternehmens oder sind die Bestimmungen des Gesellschaftsvertrags über den Gegenstand des Unternehmens nichtig, so kann jeder Gesellschafter, jeder Geschäftsführer und, wenn ein Aufsichtsrat bestellt ist, jedes Mitglied des Aufsichtsrats im Wege der Klage beantragen, daß die Gesellschaft für nichtig erklärt werde.

(2) Die Vorschriften der §§ 246 bis 248 des Aktiengesetzes finden entsprechende Anwendung.

§ 76 Heilung von Mängeln durch Gesellschafterbeschluss.

Ein Mangel, der die Bestimmungen über den Gegenstand des Unternehmens betrifft, kann durch einstimmigen Beschluß der Gesellschafter geheilt werden.

§ 77 Wirkung der Nichtigkeit.

(1) Ist die Nichtigkeit einer Gesellschaft in das Handelsregister eingetragen, so finden zum Zwecke der Abwicklung ihrer Verhältnisse die für den Fall der Auflösung geltenden Vorschriften entsprechende Anwendung.

(2) Die Wirksamkeit der im Namen der Gesellschaft mit Dritten vorgenommenen Rechtsgeschäfte wird durch die Nichtigkeit nicht berührt.

(3) Die Gesellschafter haben die versprochenen Einzahlungen zu leisten, soweit es zur Erfüllung der eingegangenen Verbindlichkeiten erforderlich ist.

§ 75 Action for the declaration of nullity.

(1) If the articles of association do not contain any provisions regarding the amount of the registered share capital or the object of the enterprise, or if the provisions of the articles of association regarding the object of the enterprise are null and void, then any shareholder, any managing director, and, if a supervisory board has been appointed, any member of the supervisory board may bring an action for the declaration of nullity of the company.

(2) The provisions of sec. 246 to 248 of the Stock Corporation Act shall apply accordingly.

§ 76 Cure of defects by shareholder resolution.

A defect pertaining to the provisions regarding the object of the enterprise may be cured by unanimous resolution of the shareholders.

§ 77 Effect of nullity.

(1) Where the nullity of a company has been registered in the commercial register, the provisions with respect to the dissolution of the company shall apply accordingly with respect to the winding up of its affairs.

(2) The validity of legal transactions entered into with third parties in the name of the company is not affected by the nullity.

(3) The shareholders shall render the payments they promised to the extent necessary to settle any liabilities incurred.

Abschnitt 6. Ordnungs-, Straf- und Bußgeldvorschriften

§ 78 Anmeldepflichtige.

Die in diesem Gesetz vorgesehenen Anmeldungen zum Handelsregister sind durch die Geschäftsführer oder die Liquidatoren, die in § 7 Abs. 1, § 57 Abs. 1, § 57i Abs. 1, § 58 Abs. 1 Nr. 3 vorgesehenen Anmeldungen sind durch sämtliche Geschäftsführer zu bewirken.

§ 79 Zwangsgelder.

(1) ¹Geschäftsführer oder Liquidatoren, die §§ 35a, 71 Abs. 5 nicht befolgen, sind hierzu vom Registergericht durch Festsetzung von Zwangsgeld anzuhalten; § 14 des Handelsgesetzbuchs bleibt unberührt. ²Das einzelne Zwangsgeld darf den Betrag von fünftausend Euro nicht übersteigen.

(2) In Ansehung der in §§ 7, 54, 57 Abs. 1, § 58 Abs. 1 Nr. 3 bezeichneten Anmeldungen zum Handelsregister findet, soweit es sich um die Anmeldung zum Handelsregister des Sitzes der Gesellschaft handelt, eine Festsetzung von Zwangsgeld nach § 14 des Handelsgesetzbuchs nicht statt.

§§ 80–81a *(aufgehoben)*

§ 82 Falsche Angaben.

(1) Mit Freiheitsstrafe bis zu drei Jahren oder mit Geldstrafe wird bestraft, wer

1. als Gesellschafter oder als Geschäftsführer zum Zweck der Eintragung der Gesellschaft über die Übernahme der Geschäftsanteile, die Leistung der Einlagen, die Verwendung eingezahlter Beträge, über Sondervorteile, Gründungsaufwand und Sacheinlagen,
2. als Gesellschafter im Sachgründungsbericht,

Part 6. Administrative, penal and administrative fine provisions

§ 78 Persons subject to filing obligations.

The applications to the commercial register provided for in this Act shall be effected by the managing directors or the liquidators; the applications provided for in sec. 7 para. 1, sec. 57 para. 1, sec. 57i para. 1, sec. 58 para. 1 no. 3 shall be effected by all managing directors.

§ 79 Administrative fines.

(1) ¹Managing directors or liquidators who do not comply with sec. 35a and 71 para. 5 shall be compelled by the register court to comply by the levying of administrative fines; sec. 14 of the Commercial Code remains unaffected. ²A single administrative fine may not exceed the amount of five thousand euros.

(2) With respect to the applications indicated in sec. 7, 54, 57 para. 1, sec. 58 para. 1 no. 3, administrative fines pursuant to sec. 14 of the Commercial Code may not be imposed if the application relates to the registration with the commercial register of the registered office of the company.

§§ 80–81a *(repealed)*

§ 82 False information.

(1) Imprisonment for a period of up to three years or a fine shall be imposed as punishment on any person who provides false information

1. as shareholder or as a managing director, for the purpose of the registration of the company, regarding the subscription of shares, the rendering of contributions, the use of amounts paid in, regarding special benefits, formation expenses and contributions in kind,
2. as a shareholder in the report on formation through contributions in kind,

3. als Geschäftsführer zum Zweck der Eintragung einer Erhöhung des Stammkapitals über die Zeichnung oder Einbringung des neuen Kapitals oder über Sacheinlagen,
4. als Geschäftsführer in der in § 57i Abs. 1 Satz 2 vorgeschriebenen Erklärung oder
5. als Geschäftsführer einer Gesellschaft mit beschränkter Haftung oder als Geschäftsleiter einer ausländischen juristischen Person in der nach § 8 Abs. 3 Satz 1 oder § 39 Abs. 3 Satz 1 abzugebenden Versicherung oder als Liquidator in der nach § 67 Abs. 3 Satz 1 abzugebenden Versicherung falsche Angaben macht.

(2) Ebenso wird bestraft, wer

1. als Geschäftsführer zum Zweck der Herabsetzung des Stammkapitals über die Befriedigung oder Sicherstellung der Gläubiger eine unwahre Versicherung abgibt oder
2. als Geschäftsführer, Liquidator, Mitglied eines Aufsichtsrats oder ähnlichen Organs in einer öffentlichen Mitteilung die Vermögenslage der Gesellschaft unwahr darstellt oder verschleiert, wenn die Tat nicht in § 331 Nr. 1 oder Nr. 1a des Handelsgesetzbuchs mit Strafe bedroht ist.

§ 83 *(aufgehoben)*

§ 84 Verletzung der Verlustanzeigepflicht.

(1) Mit Freiheitsstrafe bis zu drei Jahren oder mit Geldstrafe wird bestraft, wer es als Geschäftsführer unterläßt, den Gesellschaftern einen Verlust in Höhe der Hälfte des Stammkapitals anzuzeigen.

(2) Handelt der Täter fahrlässig, so ist die Strafe Freiheitsstrafe bis zu einem Jahr oder Geldstrafe.

3. as a managing director, for the purpose of registration of an increase in the registered share capital, regarding the subscription to or contribution of the new capital or regarding contributions in kind,
4. as a managing director, in the declaration prescribed in sec. 57i para. 1 sentence 2, or
5. as a managing director of a limited liability company or as manager of a foreign legal person, in the assurance to be made pursuant to sec. 8 para. 3 sentence 1 or sec. 39 para. 3 sentence 1 or, as a liquidator, in the assurance to be made pursuant to sec. 67 para. 3 sentence 1.

(2) The same punishment exists for those who

1. as a managing director, for the purpose of the reduction of the registered share capital, provides false assurance that creditors have been satisfied or secured, or
2. as a managing director, liquidator, member of the supervisory board or a similar corporate body misrepresents or conceals the financial position of the company in a public announcement unless the offense is punishable pursuant to sec. 331 no. 1 or no. 1a of the Commercial Code.

§ 83 *(repealed)*

§ 84 Violation of the duty to inform of losses.

(1) Anyone who as a managing director fails to inform the shareholders of a loss amounting to half of the registered share capital shall be punished with imprisonment for a period of up to three years or with a fine.

(2) If the person acts negligently, the punishment shall be imprisonment for a period of up to one year or a fine.

§ 85 Verletzung der Geheimhaltungspflicht.

(1) Mit Freiheitsstrafe bis zu einem Jahr oder mit Geldstrafe wird bestraft, wer ein Geheimnis der Gesellschaft, namentlich ein Betriebs- oder Geschäftsgeheimnis, das ihm in seiner Eigenschaft als Geschäftsführer, Mitglied des Aufsichtsrats oder Liquidator bekanntgeworden ist, unbefugt offenbart.

(2) ^{1}Handelt der Täter gegen Entgelt oder in der Absicht, sich oder einen anderen zu bereichern oder einen anderen zu schädigen, so ist die Strafe Freiheitsstrafe bis zu zwei Jahren oder Geldstrafe. ^{2}Ebenso wird bestraft, wer ein Geheimnis der in Absatz 1 bezeichneten Art, namentlich ein Betriebs- oder Geschäftsgeheimnis, das ihm unter den Voraussetzungen des Absatzes 1 bekanntgeworden ist, unbefugt verwertet.

(3) ^{1}Die Tat wird nur auf Antrag der Gesellschaft verfolgt. ^{2}Hat ein Geschäftsführer oder ein Liquidator die Tat begangen, so sind der Aufsichtsrat und, wenn kein Aufsichtsrat vorhanden ist, von den Gesellschaftern bestellte besondere Vertreter antragsberechtigt. ^{3}Hat ein Mitglied des Aufsichtsrats die Tat begangen, so sind die Geschäftsführer oder die Liquidatoren antragsberechtigt.

§ 86 Verletzung der Pflichten bei Abschlussprüfungen

Mit Freiheitsstrafe bis zu einem Jahr oder mit Geldstrafe wird bestraft, wer als Mitglied eines Aufsichtsrats oder als Mitglied eines Prüfungsausschusses einer Gesellschaft, die kapitalmarktorientiert im Sinne des § 264d des Handelsgesetzbuchs, die CRR-Kreditinstitut im Sinne des § 1 Absatz 3d Satz 1 des Kreditwesengesetzes, mit Ausnahme der in § 2 Absatz 1 Nummer 1 und 2

§ 85 Breach of the duty of secrecy.

(1) Any person who, without authorization, reveals a secret of the company, particularly an operational or business secret, that became known to such person in his capacity as managing director, member of the supervisory board or liquidator shall be subject to imprisonment for a period of up to one year or a fine.

(2) ^{1}If the person acts in return for payment or with the intention of personal enrichment or enrichment of a third party or of harming a third party, such person shall be subject to imprisonment for a period of up to two years or a fine. ^{2}Any person who, without authorization, utilizes a secret of the kind indicated in para. 1, particularly an operational or business secret, that became known to such person under the circumstances described in para. 1, shall be subject to the same punishment.

(3) ^{1}The offense shall be prosecuted only upon application of the company. ^{2}If a managing director or a liquidator committed the offense, the supervisory board or, if no supervisory board is present, special representatives appointed by the shareholders, are authorized to apply for prosecution. ^{3}If a member of the supervisory board committed the offense, the managing directors or the liquidators are authorized to file the application.

§ 86 Violation of duties during audits

Imprisonment for a period of up to one year or a fine shall be imposed on any person who, as a member of a supervisory board or as a member of an audit committee of a company that is a capital market-oriented company in terms of sec. 264d of the Commercial Code, a CRR credit institute in terms of sec. 1 para. 3d sentence 1 of the Banking Act, with the exception of the institutes mentioned in sec. 2 para. 1 no. 1 and 2 of the

des Kreditwesengesetzes genannten Institute, oder die Versicherungsunternehmen ist im Sinne des Artikels 2 Absatz 1 der Richtlinie 91/674/EWG des Rates vom 19. Dezember 1991 über den Jahresabschluß und den konsolidierten Abschluß von Versicherungsunternehmen (ABl. L 374 vom 31.12.1991, S. 7), die zuletzt durch die Richtlinie 2006/46/EG (ABl. L 224 vom 16.8.2006, S. 1) geändert worden ist,

1. eine in § 87 Absatz 1, 2 oder Absatz 3 bezeichnete Handlung begeht und dafür einen Vermögensvorteil erhält oder sich versprechen lässt oder
2. eine in § 87 Absatz 1, 2 oder Absatz 3 bezeichnete Handlung beharrlich wiederholt.

§ 87 Bußgeldvorschriften

(1) Ordnungswidrig handelt, wer als Mitglied eines Aufsichtsrats oder als Mitglied eines Prüfungsausschusses einer Gesellschaft, die kapitalmarktorientiert im Sinne des § 264d des Handelsgesetzbuchs, die CRR-Kreditinstitut im Sinne des § 1 Absatz 3d Satz 1 des Kreditwesengesetzes, mit Ausnahme der in § 2 Absatz 1 Nummer 1 und 2 des Kreditwesengesetzes genannten Institute, oder die Versicherungsunternehmen ist im Sinne des Artikels 2 Absatz 1 der Richtlinie 91/674/EWG des Rates vom 19. Dezember 1991 über den Jahresabschluß und den konsolidierten Abschluß von Versicherungsunternehmen (ABl. L 374 vom 31.12.1991, S. 7), die zuletzt durch die Richtlinie 2006/46/EG (ABl. L 224 vom 16.8.2006, S. 1) geändert worden ist,

1. die Unabhängigkeit des Abschlussprüfers oder der Prüfungsgesellschaft nicht nach Maßgabe des Artikels 4 Absatz 3 Unterabsatz 2, des Artikels 5 Absatz 4 Unterabsatz 1 Satz 1 oder des Artikels 6 Absatz 2 der Verordnung (EU) Nr. 537/2014 des Europäischen Parlaments und des Rates vom 16. April 2014 über spezifische Anforderungen an die

Banking Act, or an insurance company in terms of Art. 2 para. 1 of the Council Directive 91/674 EEC of December 19, 1991 on the annual accounts and consolidated accounts of insurance undertakings (OJ L 374/7 of December 31, 1991) in the version of the Directive 2006/46/EC (OJ L 224/1 of August 16, 2006),

1. commits any of the actions listed in sec. 87 para. 1, 2 or 3 and accepts pecuniary advantages or a corresponding pledge, or
2. persistently repeats any of the actions listed in sec. 87 para. 1, 2 or 3.

§ 87 Fines.

(1) A regulatory offence is committed by a person who, as a member of a supervisory board or as a member of an audit committee of a company that is a capital market-oriented company in terms of sec. 264d of the Commercial Code, a CRR credit institute in terms of sec. 1 para. 3d sentence 1 of the Banking Act, with the exception of the institutes mentioned in sec. 2 para. 1 no. 1 and 2 of the Banking Act, or that is an insurance company in terms of Art. 2 para. 1 of the Council Directive 91/674 EEC of December 19, 1991 on the annual accounts and consolidated accounts of insurance undertakings (OJ L 374/7 of December 31, 1991) in the version of Directive 2006/46/ EC (OJ L 224/1 of August 16, 2006),

1. does not supervise the independence of the auditor or the audit firm in accordance with Art. 4 para. 3 subpara. 2, Art. 5 para. 4 subpara. 1 sentence 1 or Art. 6 para. 2 of Regulation (EU) no. 537/2014 of the European Parliament and of the Council of April 16, 2014 on specific requirements regarding statutory audit of public-interest entities and repealing

Abschlussprüfung bei Unternehmen von öffentlichem Interesse und zur Aufhebung des Beschlusses 2005/909/EG der Kommission (ABl. L 158 vom 27.5.2014, S. 77, L 170 vom 11.6.2014, S. 66) überwacht oder
2. eine Empfehlung für die Bestellung eines Abschlussprüfers oder einer Prüfungsgesellschaft vorlegt, die den Anforderungen nach Artikel 16 Absatz 2 Unterabsatz 2 oder 3 der Verordnung (EU) Nr. 537/2014 nicht entspricht oder der ein Auswahlverfahren nach Artikel 16 Absatz 3 Unterabsatz 1 der Verordnung (EU) Nr. 537/2014 nicht vorangegangen ist.

(2) Ordnungswidrig handelt, wer als Mitglied eines Aufsichtsrats, der einen Prüfungsausschuss nicht bestellt hat, einer in Absatz 1 genannten Gesellschaft den Gesellschaftern einen Vorschlag für die Bestellung eines Abschlussprüfers oder einer Prüfungsgesellschaft vorlegt, der den Anforderungen nach Artikel 16 Absatz 5 Unterabsatz 1 der Verordnung (EU) Nr. 537/2014 nicht entspricht.

(3) Ordnungswidrig handelt, wer als Mitglied eines Aufsichtsrats, der einen Prüfungsausschuss bestellt hat, einer in Absatz 1 genannten Gesellschaft den Gesellschaftern einen Vorschlag für die Bestellung eines Abschlussprüfers oder einer Prüfungsgesellschaft vorlegt, der den Anforderungen nach Artikel 16 Absatz 5 Unterabsatz 1 oder Unterabsatz 2 Satz 1 oder Satz 2 der Verordnung (EU) Nr. 537/2014 nicht entspricht.

(4) Die Ordnungswidrigkeit kann mit einer Geldbuße bis zu fünfzigtausend Euro geahndet werden.

(5) Verwaltungsbehörde im Sinne des § 36 Absatz 1 Nummer 1 des Gesetzes über Ordnungswidrigkeiten ist bei CRR-Kreditinstituten im Sinne des § 1 Absatz 3d Satz 1 des Kreditwesengesetzes, mit Ausnahme der in § 2 Absatz 1 Nummer 1 und 2 des Kreditwesengesetzes genannten Institute, und bei Versicherungsunternehmen im Sinne

Commission Decision 2005/909/EC, or
2. submits a recommendation for the appointment of an auditor or an audit firm that does not comply with the requirements set out in Art. 16 para. 2 subpara. 2 or 3 of Regulation (EU) no. 537/2014 or that has not been preceded by a selection procedure pursuant to Art. 16 para. 3 subpara. 1 of Regulation (EU) 537/2014.

(2) A regulatory offence is committed by a person who, as a member of a supervisory board that has not appointed an audit committee, submits a proposal to the shareholders of a company pursuant to para. 1 to appoint an auditor or an audit firm that does not comply with the requirements set out in Art. 16 para. 5 subpara. 1 of Regulation (EU) 537/2014.

(3) A regulatory offence is committed by a person who, as a member of a supervisory board that has appointed an audit committee, submits a proposal to the shareholders of a company listed in para. 1 to appoint an auditor or an audit firm that does not comply with the requirements pursuant to Art. 16 para. 5 subpara. 1 or subpara. 2 sentence 1 or sentence 2 of Regulation (EU) 537/2014.

(4) The regulatory offence can be punished with a fine of up to fifty-thousand euros.

(5) The administrative authority in terms of sec. 36 para. 1 no. 1 of the Act on Regulatory Offences for CRR credit institutes in terms of sec. 1 para. 3d sentence 1 of the Banking Act, with the exception of the institutes mentioned in sec. 2 para. 1 no. 1 and 2 of the Banking Act, and for insurance companies in terms of Art. 2 para. 1 Council Direc-

des Artikels 2 Absatz 1 der Richtlinie 91/674/EWG die Bundesanstalt für Finanzdienstleistungsaufsicht, im Übrigen das Bundesamt für Justiz.

§ 88 Mitteilungen an die Abschlussprüferaufsichtsstelle

(1) Die nach § 87 Absatz 5 zuständige Verwaltungsbehörde übermittelt der Abschlussprüferaufsichtsstelle beim Bundesamt für Wirtschaft und Ausfuhrkontrolle alle Bußgeldentscheidungen nach § 87 Absatz 1 bis 3.

(2) In Strafverfahren, die eine Straftat nach § 86 zum Gegenstand haben, übermittelt die Staatsanwaltschaft im Falle der Erhebung der öffentlichen Klage der Abschlussprüferaufsichtsstelle die das Verfahren abschließende Entscheidung. Ist gegen die Entscheidung ein Rechtsmittel eingelegt worden, ist die Entscheidung unter Hinweis auf das eingelegte Rechtsmittel zu übermitteln.

Anlage (zu § 2 Abs. 1a)

a) **Musterprotokoll für die Gründung einer Einpersonengesellschaft**

UR. Nr. . . . .

Heute, den . . . . ,

erschien vor mir, ... ,

Notar/in mit dem Amtssitz in

. . . . ,

Herr/Frau[1] . . . .[2]

1. Der Erschienene errichtet hiermit nach § 2 Abs. 1a GmbHG eine Gesellschaft mit beschränkter Haftung

unter der Firma . . . .

mit dem Sitz in. . . . .

2. Gegenstand des Unternehmens ist

. . . .

3. Das Stammkapital der Gesellschaft beträgt . . . . €

---

tive 91/674 EEC is the Federal Financial Supervisory Authority, and in all other cases the Federal Office of Justice.

§ 88 Notification of the Auditor Oversight Body

(1) The competent authority pursuant to sec. 87 para. 5 submits all decisions on fines pursuant to sec. 87 paras. 1 to 3 to the Auditor Oversight Body within the Federal Office for Economic Affairs and Export Control.

(2) [1]In criminal proceedings concerning an offence in terms of sec. 86, the public prosecutor's office submits the final decision to the Auditor Oversight Body in case an action is filed. [2]If the decision has been appealed, the decision is to be submitted with reference to the filed appeal.

Annex (to sec. 2 para. 1a)

a) **Model protocol for the incorporation of a single shareholder company**

Deed roll no.. . . . .

Today, the. . . . . ,

appeared before me, ... ,

Notary with official residence in

. . . . ,

Mr./Ms.[1] . . . .[2]

1. The person appearing hereby establishes, pursuant to sec. 2 para. 1 of the Limited Liability Company Act, a limited liability company with the

company name . . . .

with registered office in. . . . .

2. The object of the enterprise is

. . . .

3. The registered share capital amounts to . . . . €

(i.W. . . . . Euro) und wird vollständig	(in words . . . . euro) and is subscribed in whole
von Herrn/Frau[1] . . . . (Geschäftsanteil Nr. 1) übernommen.	by Mr./Ms. . . . . (share no. 1).
Die Einlage ist in Geld zu erbringen, und zwar sofort in voller Höhe/zu 50 Prozent sofort, im Übrigen sobald die Gesellschafterversammlung ihre Einforderung beschließt[3].	The contribution is to be rendered in cash and immediately in the full amount/in an amount equal to fifty percent immediately, the rest immediately after the shareholder meeting has resolved to call it in[3].
4. Zum Geschäftsführer der Gesellschaft wird	4.
Herr/Frau[4]. . . . . ,	Mr./Ms.[4]. . . . . ,
geboren am. . . . . ,	born on . . . . ,
wohnhaft in . . . . , bestellt.	residing in . . . . , is appointed managing director of the company.
Der Geschäftsführer ist von den Beschränkungen des § 181 des Bürgerlichen Gesetzbuchs befreit.	The managing director is released from the restrictions of sec. 181 of the Civil Code.
5. Die Gesellschaft trägt die mit der Gründung verbundenen Kosten bis zu einem Gesamtbetrag von 300 €, höchstens jedoch bis zum Betrag ihres Stammkapitals. Darüber hinausgehende Kosten trägt der Gesellschafter.	5. The company bears the costs in connection with its incorporation up to a total amount of 300 €, but at most up to the amount of its registered share capital. Any further costs are borne by the shareholder.
6. Von dieser Urkunde erhält eine Ausfertigung der Gesellschafter, beglaubigte Ablichtungen die Gesellschaft und das Registergericht (in elektronischer Form) sowie eine einfache Abschrift das Finanzamt – Körperschaftsteuerstelle.	6. Of this deed, the shareholder receives an original, the company and the register court (in electronic form) certified copies and the tax office (corporate income tax office) a simple copy.
7. Der Erschienene wurde vom Notar/von der Notarin insbesondere auf Folgendes hingewiesen:	7. The person appearing was instructed of the following by the notary:
Hinweise:	Remarks:
1) Nicht Zutreffendes streichen. Bei juristischen Personen ist die Anrede Herr/Frau wegzulassen.	1) Cross out what is not applicable. In case of legal persons, the address Mr./Ms. is to be omitted.
2) Hier sind neben der Bezeichnung des Gesellschafters und den Angaben zur notariellen Identitätsfeststellung ggf.	2) Beside the specification of the shareholder and the information on personal identification by the notary, the matri-

der Güterstand und die Zustimmung des Ehegatten sowie die Angaben zu einer etwaigen Vertretung zu vermerken.

3) Nicht Zutreffendes streichen. Bei der Unternehmergesellschaft muss die zweite Alternative gestrichen werden.

4) Nicht Zutreffendes streichen.

b) Musterprotokoll für die Gründung einer Mehrpersonengesellschaft mit bis zu drei Gesellschaftern

UR. Nr. . . . .,

Heute, den . . . .,

erschien vor mir, ...,

Notar/in mit dem Amtssitz in

. . . .,

Herr/Frau[1] . . . .[2]

Herr/Frau[1] . . . .[2]

Herr/Frau[1] . . . .[2]

1. Die Erschienen errichten hiermit nach § 2 Abs. 1a GmbHG eine Gesellschaft mit beschränkter Haftung

unter der Firma . . . .

. . . .

mit dem Sitz in. . . . .

. . . .

2. Gegenstand des Unternehmens ist

. . . .

3. Das Stammkapital der Gesellschaft beträgt . . . . €

(i.W. . . . . Euro)

und wird vollständig

und wird wie folgt übernommen:

Herr/Frau[1] . . . .

übernimmt einen Geschäftsanteil mit einem Nennbetrag in Höhe von . . . . €

monial property regime and the approval of the spouse as well as information about a possible representation shall be noted here if applicable.

3) Cross out what is not applicable. In case of an entrepreneur company, the second alternative must to be crossed out.

4) Cross out what is not applicable.

b) Model protocol for the incorporation of a multiple shareholder company with up to three shareholders

Deed roll no. . . . .,

Today, the . . . .,

Appeared before me . . . .,

Notary with official residence in

. . . .,

Mr./Ms.[1] . . . .[2]

Mr./Ms.[1] . . . .[2]

Mr./Ms.[1] . . . .[2]

1. The persons appearing hereby establish a limited liability company pursuant to sec. 2 para. 1a Limited Liability Company Act

with the company name . . . .

. . . .

with registered office in. . . . .

. . . .

2. The object of the enterprise is

. . . .

3. The registered share capital amounts to . . . . €

(in words. . . . . euro)

and is subscribed as follows:

Mr./Ms.[1] . . . .

subscribes a share with a nominal amount of . . . . €

(i.W. .... Euro) (Geschäftsanteil Nr. 1),	(in words. .... euro) (share no. 1)
Herr/Frau[1]	Mr./Ms.[1] ....
übernimmt einen Geschäftsanteil mit einem Nennbetrag in Höhe von .... €	subscribes a share with a nominal amount of .... €
(i.W. .... Euro) (Geschäftsanteil Nr. 2),	(in words. .... euro) (share no. 2)
Herr/Frau[1]	Mr./Ms.[1] ....
übernimmt einen Geschäftsanteil mit einem Nennbetrag in Höhe von .... €	subscribes a share with a nominal amount of .... €
(i.W. .... Euro) (Geschäftsanteil Nr. 3).	(in words. .... euro) (share no.3)
Die Einlagen sind in Geld zu erbringen, und zwar sofort in voller Höhe/zu 50 Prozent sofort, im Übrigen sobald die Gesellschafterversammlung ihre Einforderung beschließt.[3]	The contributions are to be rendered in cash and immediately in the full amount / in an amount equal to fifty percent immediately, the rest immediately after the shareholder meeting has resolved to call them in [3].

4. Zum Geschäftsführer der Gesellschaft wird

Herr/Frau[4] .... ,

geboren am. .... ,

wohnhaft in .... ,

bestellt.

Der Geschäftsführer ist von den Beschränkungen des § 181 des Bürgerlichen Gesetzbuchs befreit.

4.

Mr./Ms. [4] .... ,

born on .... ,

residing in .... ,

is appointed as a managing director.

The managing director is released from the restrictions of sec. 181 of the Civil Code.

5. Die Gesellschaft trägt die mit der Gründung verbundenen Kosten bis zu einem Gesamtbetrag von 300 €, höchstens jedoch bis zum Betrag ihres Stammkapitals. Darüber hinausgehende Kosten tragen die Gesellschafter im Verhältnis der Nennbeträge ihrer Geschäftsanteile.

5. The company bears the costs in connection with its incorporation up to a total amount of 300 €, but at most up to the amount of its registered share capital. Any further costs are borne by the shareholders.

6. Von dieser Urkunde erhält eine Ausfertigung jeder Gesellschafter, beglaubigte Ablichtungen die Gesellschaft und das Registergericht (in elektronischer Form) sowie eine einfache Abschrift das Finanzamt – Körperschaftsteuerstelle.

6 Of this deed, each shareholder receives an original, the company and the register court (in electronic form) a certified copy and the tax office (corporate income tax office) a simple copy.

7. Die Erschienenen wurden vom Notar/von der Notarin insbesondere auf Folgendes hingewiesen:

Hinweise:

1) Nicht Zutreffendes streichen. Bei juristischen Personen ist die Anrede Herr/Frau wegzulassen.

2) Hier sind neben der Bezeichnung des Gesellschafters und den Angaben zur notariellen Identitätsfeststellung ggf. der Güterstand und die Zustimmung des Ehegatten sowie die Angaben zu einer etwaigen Vertretung zu vermerken.

3) Nicht Zutreffendes streichen. Bei der Unternehmergesellschaft muss die zweite Alternative gestrichen werden.

4) Nicht Zutreffendes streichen.

7. The persons appearing were instructed of the following by the notary:

Remarks:

1) Cross out what is not applicable. In case of legal persons, the address Mr./Ms. is to be omitted.

2) Beside the specification of the shareholder and the information on personal identification by the notary, the matrimonial property regime and the approval of the spouses as well as information about a possible representation shall be noted here if applicable.

3) Cross out what is not applicable. In case of the entrepreneur company the second alternative must be crossed out.

4) Cross out what is not applicable.

B. Stock Corporation Act

Stock Corporation Act
(Aktiengesetz)

| Vom 6. September 1965 | Enacted on September 6, 1965 |
| (BGBl. I S. 1089) | (Federal Law Gazette, Vol. I, p. 1089) |

BGBl. III/ FNA 4121-1   Federal Law Gazette, Vol. III/ FNA 4121-1

Zuletzt geänd. durch Art. 73 Achte ZuständigkeitsanpassungsVO v. 25. 11. 2003 (BGBl. I S. 2304), Art. 5 Nr. 3 Zweites G zur Vereinfachung der Wahl der Arbeitnehmervertreter in den Aufsichtsrat v. 18. 5. 2004 (BGBl. I S. 974), Art. 12e Erstes JustizmodernisierungsG v. 24. 8. 2004 (BGBl. I S. 2198), Art. 4 BilanzrechtsreformG v. 4. 12. 2004 (BGBl. I S. 3166), Art. 11 G zur Anpassung von Verjährungsvorschriften an das SchuldrechtsmodernisierungsG v. 9. 12. 2004 (BGBl. I S. 3214), Art. 5 BilanzkontrollG v. 15. 12. 2004 (BGBl. I S. 3408), Art. 1 G zur Unternehmensintegrität und Modernisierung des AnfechtungsR (UMAG) v. 22. 9. 2005 (BGBl. I S. 2802), Art. 6 ÜbernahmeRL-UmsetzungsG v. 8. 7. 2006 (BGBl. I S. 1426), Art. 103 Neunte ZuständigkeitsanpassungsVO v. 31. 10. 2006 (BGBl. I S. 2407), Art. 9 G über elektronische Handelsregister und Genossenschaftsregister sowie das Unternehmensregister v. 10. 11. 2006 (BGBl. I S. 2553), Art. 3 G zur Umsetzung der Regelungen über die Mitbestimmung der Arbeitnehmer bei einer Verschmelzung von Kapitalgesellschaften aus verschiedenen Mitgliedstaaten v. 21. 12. 2006 (BGBl. I S. 3332), Art. 13 TransparenzRL-UmsetzungsG v. 5. 1. 2007 (BGBl. I S. 10), Art. 3 Zweites G zur Änd. des UmwandlungsG v. 19. 4. 2007 (BGBl. I S. 542), Art. 11 FinanzmarktRL-UmsetzungsG v. 16. 7. 2007 (BGBl. I S. 1330),

Last amended by Art. 73 of the Eighth Ordinance on the Adjustment of Jurisdiction dated November 25, 2003 (Federal Law Gazette Vol. I, p. 3422); Art. 5 of the Second Act on the Simplification of the Election of Employee Representatives to the Supervisory Board, dated May 18, 2004 (Federal Law Gazette Vol. I, p. 974), Art. 12e of the First Act on the Modernization of the Judiciary, dated August 24, 2004 (Federal Law Gazette Vol. I, p. 2198), Art. 4 of the Act on Accounting Reform, dated December 4, 2004 (Federal Law Gazette, Vol. I, p. 3166), Art. 11 of the Act on the Adjustment of Time Limitation Provisions to the Act to Modernize the Law of Obligations, dated December 9, 2004 (Federal Law Gazette, Vol. I, p. 3214), Art. 5 of the Act on Accounting Review, dated December 15, 2004 (Federal Law Gazette Vol. I, p. 3408), Art. 1 of the Act on Business Integrity and Modernization of the Law of Actions to Set Aside dated September 9, 2005 (Federal Law Gazette Vol. I, p. 2802), Art. 6 of the Act on Implementation of the Acquisition Directive, dated July 8, 2006, (Federal Law Gazette Vol. I, p. 1426), Art. 103 of the Ninth Ordinance on the Adjustment of Jurisdiction dated October 31, 2006 (Federal Law Gazette Vol. I, p. 2407), Art. 9 of the Act on the Electronic Commercial Register and Cooperative Society Register as well as the Company Reg-

Art. 3 RisikobegrenzungsG v. 12. 8. 2008 (BGBl. I S. 1666), Art. 5 G zur Modernisierung des GmbH-Rechts u. zur Bekämpfung von Missbräuchen v. 23. 10. 2008 (BGBl. I S. 2026), Art. 2 G zur Änd. des G über die Überführung der Anteilsrechte an der VW-Werk GmbH in private Hand v. 8. 12. 2008 (BGBl. I S. 2369), Art. 74 G zur Reform des Verfahrens in Familiensachen und in den Angelegenheiten der freiwilligen Gerichtsbarkeit v. 17. 12. 2008 (BGBl. I S. 2586), Art. 5 G zur Modernisierung des Bilanzrechts v. 25. 5. 2009 (BGBl. I S. 1102), Art. 1 G zur Umsetzung der Aktionärsrechterichtlinie v. 30. 7. 2009 (BGBl. I S. 2479), Art. 1 G zur Angemessenheit der Vorstandsvergütung v. 31. 7. 2009 (BGBl. I S. 2509), Art. 6 RestrukturierungsG v. 09.12.2010 (BGBl. I S. 1900), Art. 2 Abs. 49 G zur Änd. von Vorschriften über Verkündung und Bekanntmachungen sowie der ZPO, des EGZPO und der AO v. 22.12.2011 (BGBl. I S. 3044), Art. 3 Kleinstkapitalgesellschaften-BilanzrechtsänderungsG v. 20.12.2012 (BGBl. I S. 2751), Art. 12 AIFM-Umsetzungsgesetz v. 04.07.2013 (BGBl. I S. 1981), Art. 26 2. KostenrechtsmodernisierungsG v. 23.07.2013 (BGBl. I S. 2586), Art. 2 Abs. 53 G zur Modernisierung der Finanzaufsicht über Versicherungen v. 01.04.2015 (BGBl. I S. 434), Art. 3 G für die gleichberechtigte Teilhabe von Frauen und Männern an Führungspositionen in der Privatwirtschaft und im öffentlichen Dienst v. 24.04.2015 (BGBl. I S. 642), Art. 4 Bilanzrichtlinie-Umsetzungsgesetz v. 17.07.2015 (BGBl. I S. 1245), Art. 198 Zehnte ZuständigkeitsanpassungsVO v. 31.08.2015 (BGBl. I S. 1474), Art. 7 G zur Umsetzung der TransparenzRL-ÄndRL v. 20.11.2015 (BGBl. I S. 2029), Art. 1 Aktienrechtsnovelle 2016 v. 22.12.2015 (BGBl. I S. 2565), Art. 5 Abschlussprüfungsreformgesetz v. 10.05.2016 (BGBl. I S. 1142).

ister dated November 10, 2006 (Federal Law Gazette, Vol. I, p. 2553), Art. 3 of the Act on the Implementation of Provisions on Employee Codetermination in Case of Mergers of Corporations from Different Member States, dated December 21, 2006 (Federal Law Gazette, Vol. I, p. 3332), Art. 13 of the Act on the Transformation of the Transparency Directive dated January 5, 2007 (Federal Law Gazette Vol. I, p. 10), Art. 3 of the Second Act on the Amendment of the Transformation Act, dated April 19, 2007 (Federal Law Gazette, Vol. I, p. 542), Art. 11 of the Act on the Transformation of the Financial Market Directive, dated July 16, 2007 (Federal Law Gazette, Vol. I, p. 1330), Art. 3 of the Risk Limitation Act, dated August 12, 2008 (Federal Law Gazette Vol. I, p. 1666), Art. 5 of the Act to Modernize Limited Liability Company Law and to Combat Abuses dated October 23, 2008 (Federal Law Gazette, Vol. I, p. 2026), Art. 2 of the Act on the Transfer of Participation Rights in the VW-Works Limited Liability Company to Private Hands, dated December 8, 2008 (Federal Law Gazette, Vol. I, p. 2369), Art. 74 of the Act on the Reform of the Act on Matters in Non-Contentious Jurisdiction, dated December 17, 2008 (Federal Law Gazette, Vol. I, p. 2586), Art. 5 of the Act on the Modernization of Accounting Law, dated May 25, 2009 (Federal Law Gazette, Vol. I, p. 1102), Art. 1 of the Act to Implement the Shareholders' Rights Directive (Shareholders' Rights Act) dated July 30, 2009 (Federal Law Gazette, Vol. I, p. 2479), Art. 1 of the Act on the Reasonableness of the Remuneration of the Members of the Management Board, dated July 31, 2009 (Federal Law Gazette, Vol. I, p. 2509), Art. 6 of the Restructing Law, dated December 9, 2010 (Federal Law Gazette, Vol. I, p. 1900), Art. 2 para. 49, of the Act amending the Proclamation and the Announcement as well as the Code of Civil Procedure, Introductory Act to the Code of Civil Procedure and the Regulation of Taxation, dated December 22, 2011 (Federal

Law Gazette, Vol. I, p. 3044), Art. 3 of the German Micro-Enterprises Amending Accounting Law, dated December 20, 2012 (Federal Law Gazette, Vol. I, p. 2751), Art. 12 of the AIFM- implementation Act, dated July 4, 2013 (Federal Law Gazette, Vol. I, p. 1981), Art. 26 of the Modernisation of Costs Law, dated July 23, 2013 (Federal Law Gazette, Vol. I, p. 2586), Art. 2 para. 53 Modernisation of the Insurances' Financial Supervision Act, dated April 1, 2015 (Federal Law Gazette, Vol. I, p. 434), Art.3 of the Act of equal Participation of Women and Men in leading Positions in the Private and Public Sector, dated April 24, 2015 (Federal Law Gazette, Vol. I, p. 642), Art. 4 of the Accounting Directive- Implementation Law, dated July 17, 2015 (Federal Law Gazette, Vol. I, p. 1245), Art. 198 of the tenth Competence Reassignment Ordinance, dated August 31, 2015 (Federal Law Gazette, Vol. I, p. 1474), Art. 7 of the Transparency Directive Implementing Act-Amending Directive, dated November 20, 2015 (Federal Law Gazette, Vol. I, p. 2029), Art.1 Amendment of the Law on Stock Companies 2016, dated December 22, 2015 (Federal Law Gazette, Vol. I, p. 2565), Art. 5 of the Act on the Reform of Financial Statement Law, dated May 10, 2016 (Federal Law Gazette, Vol. I, p. 1142).

Inhaltsübersicht	§§	Summary of contents	§§
Erstes Buch. **Aktiengesellschaft (§§ 1–277)**		**First Book.** **Stock Corporation (§§ 1–277)**	
Erster Teil. Allgemeine Vorschriften	1–22	Part One. General Provisions	1–22
Zweiter Teil. Gründung der Gesellschaft	23–53	Part Two. Formation of the Company	23–53
Dritter Teil. Rechtsverhältnisse der Gesellschaft und der Gesellschafter	53a–75	Part Three. Legal Relationships of the Company and the Shareholders	53a–75
Vierter Teil. Verfassung der Aktiengesellschaft	76–149	Part Four. Constitution of the Stock Corporation	76–149
1. Abschnitt. Vorstand	76–94	Section One. Management Board	76–94

2. Abschnitt. Aufsichtsrat	95–116	Section Two. Supervisory Board	95–116
3. Abschnitt. Benutzung des Einflusses auf die Gesellschaft	117	Section Three. Exertion of Influence on the Company	117
4. Abschnitt. Hauptversammlung	118–149	Section Four. General Meeting	118–149
1. Unterabschnitt. Rechte der Hauptversammlung	118–120	Subsection One. Rights of the General Meeting	118–120
2. Unterabschnitt. Einberufung der Hauptversammlung	121–128	Subsection Two. Convening of the General Meeting	121–128
3. Unterabschnitt. Verhandlungsniederschrift. Auskunftsrecht	129–132	Subsection Three. Minutes of Proceedings. Right to Information	129–132
4. Unterabschnitt. Stimmrecht	133–137	Subsection Four. Voting Right	133–137
5. Unterabschnitt. Sonderbeschluß	138	Subsection Five. Special Resolution	138
6. Unterabschnitt. Vorzugsaktien ohne Stimmrecht	139–141	Subsection Six. Preference Shares without Voting Right	139–141
7. Unterabschnitt. Sonderprüfung. Geltendmachung von Ersatzansprüchen	142–149	Subsection Seven. Special Audit. Asserting of Claims for Damages	142–149
Fünfter Teil. Rechnungslegung. Gewinnverwendung	150–178	Part Five. Accounting. Appropriation of Profits	150–178
1. Abschnitt. Jahresabschluss und Lagebericht. Entsprechenserklärung	150–161	Section One. Annual Financial Statements and Management Report. Declaration of Compliance	150–161
2. Abschnitt. Prüfung des Jahresabschlusses	162–171	Section Two. Audit of Annual Financial Statements	162-171
1. Unterabschnitt. Prüfung durch Abschlußprüfer (aufgehoben)		Subsection One. Audit by the Auditor of Annual Financial Statements (repealed)	
2. Unterabschnitt. Prüfung durch den Aufsichtsrat	170, 171	Subsection Two. Audit by the Supervisory Board	170–171
3. Abschnitt. Feststellung des Jahresabschlusses. Gewinnverwendung	172–176	Section Three. Formal Approval of Annual Financial Statements. Appropriation of Profits	172–176
1. Unterabschnitt. Feststellung des Jahresabschlusses	172, 173	Subsection One. Formal Approval of the Annual Financial Statements	172, 173
2. Unterabschnitt. Gewinnverwendung	174	Subsection Two. Appropriation of Profits	174

3. Unterabschnitt. Ordentliche Hauptversammlung	175, 176	Subsection Three. Ordinary General Meeting 175, 176
4. Abschnitt. Bekanntmachung des Jahresabschlusses (aufgehoben)		Section Four. Announcement of Annual Financial Statements (repealed)
Sechster Teil. Satzungsänderung. Maßnahmen der Kapitalbeschaffung und Kapitalherabsetzung	179–240	Part Six. Amendment of the Articles of Association. Capital Increases and Capital Reductions 179–240
1. Abschnitt. Satzungsänderung	179–181	Section One. Amendment of the Articles of Association 179–181
2. Abschnitt. Maßnahmen der Kapitalbeschaffung	182–221	Section Two. Capital Increases 182–221
1. Unterabschnitt. Kapitalerhöhung gegen Einlagen	182–191	Subsection One. Capital Increase against Contributions 182–191
2. Unterabschnitt. Bedingte Kapitalerhöhung	192–201	Subsection Two. Contingent Capital Increase 192–201
3. Unterabschnitt. Genehmigtes Kapital	202–206	Subsection Three. Authorized Capital 202–206
4. Unterabschnitt. Kapitalerhöhung aus Gesellschaftsmitteln	207–220	Subsection Four. Capital Increase from Company Resources 207–220
5. Unterabschnitt. Wandelschuldverschreibungen. Gewinnschuldverschreibungen	221	Subsection Five. Convertible Bonds. Dividend Bonds 221
3. Abschnitt. Maßnahmen der Kapitalherabsetzung	222–240	Section Three. Capital Reductions 222–240
1. Unterabschnitt. Ordentliche Kapitalherabsetzung	222–228	Subsection One. Ordinary Capital Reduction 222–228
2. Unterabschnitt. Vereinfachte Kapitalherabsetzung	229–236	Subsection Two. Simplified Capital Reduction 229–236
3. Unterabschnitt. Kapitalherabsetzung durch Einziehung von Aktien. Ausnahme für Stückaktien	237–239	Subsection Three. Capital Reduction by Redemption of Shares. Exception of Non-Par Value Shares 237–239
4. Unterabschnitt. Ausweis der Kapitalherabsetzung	240	Subsection Four. The Capital Reduction in the Financial Statements 240

Siebenter Teil. Nichtigkeit von Hauptversammlungsbeschlüssen und des festgestellten Jahresabschlusses. Sonderprüfung wegen unzulässiger Unterbewertung	241–261	Part Seven. Nullity of Resolutions of the General Meeting and of the Formally Approved Annual Financial Statements. Special Audit for Unlawful Undervaluation	241–261
1. Abschnitt. Nichtigkeit von Hauptversammlungsbeschlüssen	241–255	Section One. Nullity of Resolutions of the General Meeting	241–255
1. Unterabschnitt. Allgemeines	241–249	Subsection One. General Provisions	241–249
2. Unterabschnitt. Nichtigkeit bestimmter Hauptversammlungsbeschlüsse	250–255	Subsection Two. Nullity of Specific Resolutions of the General Meeting	250–255
2. Abschnitt. Nichtigkeit des festgestellten Jahresabschlusses	256, 257	Section Two. Nullity of the Formally Approved Annual Financial Statements	256, 257
3. Abschnitt. Sonderprüfung wegen unzulässiger Unterbewertung	258–261a	Section Three. Special Audit Due to Unlawful Undervaluation	258–261a
Achter Teil. Auflösung und Nichtigerklärung der Gesellschaft	262–277	Part Eight. Dissolution and Declaration of Nullity of the Company	262–277
1. Abschnitt. Auflösung	262–274	Section One. Dissolution	262–274
1. Unterabschnitt. Auflösungsgründe und Anmeldung	262, 263	Subsection One. Reasons for Dissolution and Application	262, 263
2. Unterabschnitt. Abwicklung	264–274	Subsection Two. Liquidation	264–274
2. Abschnitt. Nichtigerklärung der Gesellschaft	275–277	Section Two. Declaration of Nullity of the Company	275–277

Zweites Buch.
Kommanditgesellschaft auf Aktien (§§ 278–290)

Second Book.
Partnership Limited by Shares (§§ 278–290)

Drittes Buch.
Verbundene Unternehmen (§§ 291–328)

Third Book.
Affiliated Enterprises (§§ 291–328)

Erster Teil. Unternehmensverträge	291–307	Part One. Enterprise Agreements	291–307
1. Abschnitt. Arten von Unternehmensverträgen	291, 292	Section One. Types of Enterprise Agreements	291, 292
2. Abschnitt. Abschluß, Änderung und Beendigung von Unternehmensverträgen	293–299	Section Two. Conclusion, Amendment and Termination of Enterprise Agreements	293–299

3. Abschnitt. Sicherung der Gesellschaft und der Gläubiger	300–303	Section Three. Security for the Company and Creditors	300–303
4. Abschnitt. Sicherung der außenstehenden Aktionäre bei Beherrschungs- und Gewinnabführungsverträgen	304–307	Section Four. Security for External Shareholders in the Case of Domination and Profit Transfer Agreements	304–307
Zweiter Teil. Leitungsmacht und Verantwortlichkeit bei Abhängigkeit von Unternehmen	308–318	Part Two. Power of Direction and Liability in the Case of Controlled Enterprises	308–318
1. Abschnitt. Leitungsmacht und Verantwortlichkeit bei Bestehen eines Beherrschungsvertrags	308–310	Section One. Power of Direction and Liability in the Case of a Domination Agreement	308–310
2. Abschnitt. Verantwortlichkeit bei Fehlen eines Beherrschungsvertrags	311–318	Section Two. Liability in the Absence of a Domination Agreement	311–318
Dritter Teil. Eingegliederte Gesellschaften	319–327	Part Three. Integrated Companies	319–327
Vierter Teil. Ausschluss von Minderheitsaktionären	327a–327f	Part Four. Expulsion of Minority Shareholders	327a–327f
Fünfter Teil. Wechselseitig beteiligte Unternehmen	328	Part Five. Enterprises with Cross-Shareholdings	328
Sechster Teil. Rechnungslegung im Konzern (aufgehoben)		Part Six. Accounting in Groups of Companies (repealed)	

Viertes Buch.
Sonder-, Straf- und Schlußvorschriften (§§ 394–410)

Fourth Book.
Special, Penal and Final Provisions (§§ 394–410)

Erster Teil. Sondervorschriften bei Beteiligung von Gebietskörperschaften	394, 395	Part One. Special Provisions Relating to Participation of Municipal Authorities	394, 395
Zweiter Teil. Gerichtliche Auflösung	396–398	Part Two. Dissolution by Order of the Court	396–398
Dritter Teil. Straf- und Bußgeldvorschriften. Schlußvorschriften	399–410	Part Three. Penal Provisions and Fines. Final Provisions	399–410

Der Bundestag hat mit Zustimmung des Bundesrates das folgende Gesetz beschlossen:

With the consent of the upper house of parliament, the lower house of parliament passed the following law:

Erstes Buch. Aktiengesellschaft

Erster Teil. Allgemeine Vorschriften

§ 1 Wesen der Aktiengesellschaft.

(1) ¹Die Aktiengesellschaft ist eine Gesellschaft mit eigener Rechtspersönlichkeit. ²Für die Verbindlichkeiten der Gesellschaft haftet den Gläubigern nur das Gesellschaftsvermögen.

(2) Die Aktiengesellschaft hat ein in Aktien zerlegtes Grundkapital.

§ 2 Gründerzahl.

An der Feststellung des Gesellschaftsvertrags (der Satzung) müssen sich eine oder mehrere Personen beteiligen, welche die Aktien gegen Einlagen übernehmen.

§ 3 Formkaufmann; Börsennotierung.

(1) Die Aktiengesellschaft gilt als Handelsgesellschaft, auch wenn der Gegenstand des Unternehmens nicht im Betrieb eines Handelsgewerbes besteht.

(2) Börsennotiert im Sinne dieses Gesetzes sind Gesellschaften, deren Aktien zu einem Markt zugelassen sind, der von staatlich anerkannten Stellen geregelt und überwacht wird, regelmäßig stattfindet und für das Publikum mittelbar oder unmittelbar zugänglich ist.

§ 4 Firma.

Die Firma der Aktiengesellschaft muß, auch wenn sie nach § 22 des Handelsgesetzbuchs oder nach anderen gesetzlichen Vorschriften fortgeführt wird, die Bezeichnung „Aktiengesellschaft" oder eine allgemein verständliche Abkürzung dieser Bezeichnung enthalten.

First Book. Stock Corporation

Part One. General Provisions

§ 1 Nature of the stock corporation.

(1) ¹The stock corporation is a company which constitutes a separate legal person. ²Only the corporate assets are available to the creditors to satisfy the liabilities of the company.

(2) The stock corporation has a registered share capital divided into shares.

§ 2 Number of founders.

The articles of association shall be established by one or more persons who subscribe to shares in return for contributions.

§ 3 Company with merchant status; listing on the stock exchange.

(1) The stock corporation qualifies as a commercial company even if the object of the enterprise does not consist of operating a commercial business.

(2) Companies whose shares are admitted to a market which is regulated and monitored by state recognized authorities, takes place regularly and is accessible to the public directly or indirectly are defined as being listed within the meaning of this Act.

§ 4 Name.

The name of the stock corporation shall include the term "Aktiengesellschaft" ("stock corporation") or a commonly understood abbreviation of this term even if it is a name which is continuing to be used within the meaning of sec. 22 Commercial Code or any other legal provisions.

§ 5 Sitz.

Sitz der Gesellschaft ist der Ort im Inland, den die Satzung bestimmt.

§ 6 Grundkapital.

Das Grundkapital muß auf einen Nennbetrag in Euro lauten.

§ 7 Mindestnennbetrag des Grundkapitals.

Der Mindestnennbetrag des Grundkapitals ist fünfzigtausend Euro.

§ 8 Form und Mindestbeträge der Aktien.

(1) Die Aktien können entweder als Nennbetragsaktien oder als Stückaktien begründet werden.

(2) [1]Nennbetragsaktien müssen auf mindestens einen Euro lauten. [2]Aktien über einen geringeren Nennbetrag sind nichtig. [3]Für den Schaden aus der Ausgabe sind die Ausgeber den Inhabern als Gesamtschuldner verantwortlich. [4]Höhere Aktiennennbeträge müssen auf volle Euro lauten.

(3) [1]Stückaktien lauten auf keinen Nennbetrag. [2]Die Stückaktien einer Gesellschaft sind am Grundkapital in gleichem Umfang beteiligt. [3]Der auf die einzelne Aktie entfallende anteilige Betrag des Grundkapitals darf einen Euro nicht unterschreiten. [4]Absatz 2 Satz 2 und 3 findet entsprechende Anwendung.

(4) Der Anteil am Grundkapital bestimmt sich bei Nennbetragsaktien nach dem Verhältnis ihres Nennbetrags zum Grundkapital, bei Stückaktien nach der Zahl der Aktien.

(5) Die Aktien sind unteilbar.

(6) Diese Vorschriften gelten auch für Anteilscheine, die den Aktionären vor

§ 5 Registered office.

The registered office of the company shall be the location in Germany stipulated in the articles of association.

§ 6 Registered share capital.

The nominal value of the registered share capital shall be stated in euros.

§ 7 Minimum nominal value of registered share capital.

The minimum nominal value of the registered share capital shall be fifty thousand euros.

§ 8 Form and minimum value of the shares.

(1) The shares can either take the form of par value shares or non-par value shares.

(2) [1]Par value shares shall have a value of at least one euro. [2]Shares having a lower par value are invalid. [3]The issuers of the shares shall be jointly and severally liable to the holders thereof for any damage arising from the issue. [4]Higher nominal values for shares shall be stated in even euro amounts.

(3) [1]Non-par value shares do not have a nominal value. [2]The non-par value shares of a company participate equally in the registered share capital. [3]The part of the registered share capital attributable to an individual share shall not be less than one euro. [4]Para. 2 sentences 2 and 3 shall apply accordingly.

(4) The part of the registered share capital attributable to each share is determined for par value shares on the basis of the ratio of their nominal value to the registered share capital and for non-par value shares according to the number of the shares.

(5) Shares are indivisible.

(6) The above provisions shall also apply to certificates issued to sharehold-

der Ausgabe der Aktien erteilt werden (Zwischenscheine).

§ 9 Ausgabebetrag der Aktien.

(1) Für einen geringeren Betrag als den Nennbetrag oder den auf die einzelne Stückaktie entfallenden anteiligen Betrag des Grundkapitals dürfen Aktien nicht ausgegeben werden (geringster Ausgabebetrag).

(2) Für einen höheren Betrag ist die Ausgabe zulässig.

§ 10 Aktien und Zwischenscheine.

(1) ¹Die Aktien lauten auf Namen. ²Sie können auf den Inhaber lauten, wenn

1. die Gesellschaft börsennotiert ist oder
2. der Anspruch auf Einzelverbriefung ausgeschlossen ist und die Sammelurkunde bei einer der folgenden Stellen hinterlegt wird:

   a) einer Wertpapiersammelbank im Sinne des § 1 Absatz 3 Satz 1 des Depotgesetzes,
   b) einem zugelassenen Zentralverwahrer oder einem anerkannten Drittland-Zentralverwahrer gemäß der Verordnung (EU) Nr. 909/2014 des Europäischen Parlaments und des Rates vom 23. Juli 2014 zur Verbesserung der Wertpapierlieferungen und -abrechnungen in der Europäischen Union und über Zentralverwahrer sowie zur Änderung der Richtlinien 98/26/EG und 2014/65/EU und der Verordnung (EU) Nr. 236/2012 (ABl. L 257 vom 28.8.2014, S. 1) oder
   c) einem sonstigen ausländischen Verwahrer, der die Voraussetzungen des § 5 Absatz 4 Satz 1 des Depotgesetzes erfüllt.

ers before the shares are issued (interim certificates).

§ 9 Issue price of shares.

(1) Shares shall not be issued for an amount below the nominal value or the part of the registered share capital attributable to the individual non-par value shares (lowest issue price).

(2) Shares may be issued for a higher amount.

§ 10 Share certificates and interim certificates.

(1) ¹All shares are registered shares. ²They can only be issued as bearer shares, if

1. the company is listed at a stock exchange or
2. the entitlement to the individual certification of the shares shall be excluded and the global certificate is deposited with one of the following depositories:

   a) a securities depository within the meaning of sec. 1 para. 3 sentence 1 of the Securities Deposit Act;
   b) an authorised central depository or an accepted third country securities depository in accordance with the Regulation (EU) No. 909/2014 of the European Parliament and the Council of July 23, 2014 on Improving Securities Settlement in the European Union and on Central Securities Depositories as well as Amending Directives 98/26/EG and 204/65/EU and Regulation (EU) No. 236/2012 (ABl. L 257 dated August 28, 2014, sentence 1) or
   c) an other foreign depository, which fulfills the conditions of sec. 5 para. 4 sentence 1 Securities Deposit Act.

³Solange im Fall des Satzes 2 Nummer 2 die Sammelurkunde nicht hinterlegt ist, ist § 67 entsprechend anzuwenden.

(2) ¹Die Aktien müssen auf Namen lauten, wenn sie vor der vollen Leistung des Ausgabebetrags ausgegeben werden. ²Der Betrag der Teilleistungen ist in der Aktie anzugeben.

(3) Zwischenscheine müssen auf Namen lauten.

(4) ¹Zwischenscheine auf den Inhaber sind nichtig. ²Für den Schaden aus der Ausgabe sind die Ausgeber den Inhabern als Gesamtschuldner verantwortlich.

(5) In der Satzung kann der Anspruch des Aktionärs auf Verbriefung seines Anteils ausgeschlossen oder eingeschränkt werden.

§ 11 Aktien besonderer Gattung.

¹Die Aktien können verschiedene Rechte gewähren, namentlich bei der Verteilung des Gewinns und des Gesellschaftsvermögens. ²Aktien mit gleichen Rechten bilden eine Gattung.

§ 12 Stimmrecht. Keine Mehrstimmrechte.

(1) ¹Jede Aktie gewährt das Stimmrecht. ²Vorzugsaktien können nach den Vorschriften dieses Gesetzes als Aktien ohne Stimmrecht ausgegeben werden.

(2) Mehrstimmrechte sind unzulässig.

§ 13 Unterzeichnung der Aktien.

¹Zur Unterzeichnung von Aktien und Zwischenscheinen genügt eine vervielfältigte Unterschrift. ²Die Gültigkeit der Unterzeichnung kann von der Beachtung einer besonderen Form abhängig gemacht werden. ³Die Formvorschrift muß in der Urkunde enthalten sein.

³ While in the case of sentence 2 number 2 the global certificate is not deposit, sec. 67 shall apply accordingly.

(2) ¹If issued before the issue price has been paid in full, the shares shall be issued as registered shares. ²The share certificate shall state the amount of the partial payments which have been made.

(3) Interim certificates shall take the form of registered shares.

(4) ¹Interim certificates issued as bearer shares are null and void. ²The issuers of the shares shall be jointly and severally liable to the holders thereof for any damage arising from the issue.

(5) The shareholder's claim of having a share certificate issued for his share may be excluded or limited in the articles of association.

§ 11 Shares of special classes.

¹The shares may grant various rights especially to the distribution of profits and corporate assets. ²Shares granting the same rights form one class of shares.

§ 12 Voting right. No multiple voting rights.

(1) ¹Each share confers a voting right. ²Preference shares may be issued as shares without a voting right in accordance with the provisions of this Act.

(2) Multiple voting rights are not permitted.

§ 13 Signing of share certificates.

¹Share certificates and interim certificates may be signed using a facsimile signature. ²It may be stipulated that the signature shall take a certain form in order to be valid. ³The requirement for a certain form shall be included in the certificate.

§ 14 Jurisdiction.

Unless stipulated otherwise, references to the court made within this Act shall refer to the court at the place the company has its registered office.

§ 15 Affiliated enterprises.

Affiliated enterprises are legally independent enterprises which, in relation to each other, are either majority-held and majority holding enterprises (sec. 16), controlled and controlling enterprises (sec. 17), group enterprises (sec. 18), enterprises with cross-shareholdings (sec. 19) or parties to an enterprise agreement (sec. 291, 292).

§ 16 Majority-held and majority holding enterprises.

(1) If the majority of the shares in a legally independent enterprise are held by another enterprise or if another enterprise holds the majority of the voting rights (majority holding), then the enterprise is a majority-held enterprise and the other enterprise a majority holding enterprise.

(2) [1]The part of the shares held by one enterprise shall be determined in the case of corporations according to the ratio of the total nominal value of the shares held by the enterprise to the nominal capital, and in the case of companies with non-par value shares according to the number of shares. [2]Own shares shall, in the case of corporations, be deducted from the nominal capital and in the case of companies with non-par value shares from the number of shares. [3]Shares in an enterprise held by another party for account of the enterprise are deemed to be equivalent to own shares.

(3) [1]The part of voting rights allocated to an enterprise shall be determined in accordance with the ratio of the number

---

§ 14 Zuständigkeit.

Gericht im Sinne dieses Gesetzes ist, wenn nichts anderes bestimmt ist, das Gericht des Sitzes der Gesellschaft.

§ 15 Verbundene Unternehmen.

Verbundene Unternehmen sind rechtlich selbständige Unternehmen, die im Verhältnis zueinander in Mehrheitsbesitz stehende Unternehmen und mit Mehrheit beteiligte Unternehmen (§ 16), abhängige und herrschende Unternehmen (§ 17), Konzernunternehmen (§ 18), wechselseitig beteiligte Unternehmen (§ 19) oder Vertragsteile eines Unternehmensvertrags (§§ 291, 292) sind.

§ 16 In Mehrheitsbesitz stehende Unternehmen und mit Mehrheit beteiligte Unternehmen.

(1) Gehört die Mehrheit der Anteile eines rechtlich selbständigen Unternehmens einem anderen Unternehmen oder steht einem anderen Unternehmen die Mehrheit der Stimmrechte zu (Mehrheitsbeteiligung), so ist das Unternehmen ein in Mehrheitsbesitz stehendes Unternehmen, das andere Unternehmen ein an ihm mit Mehrheit beteiligtes Unternehmen.

(2) [1]Welcher Teil der Anteile einem Unternehmen gehört, bestimmt sich bei Kapitalgesellschaften nach dem Verhältnis des Gesamtnennbetrags der ihm gehörenden Anteile zum Nennkapital, bei Gesellschaften mit Stückaktien nach der Zahl der Aktien. [2]Eigene Anteile sind bei Kapitalgesellschaften vom Nennkapital, bei Gesellschaften mit Stückaktien von der Zahl der Aktien abzusetzen. [3]Eigenen Anteilen des Unternehmens stehen Anteile gleich, die einem anderen für Rechnung des Unternehmens gehören.

(3) [1]Welcher Teil der Stimmrechte einem Unternehmen zusteht, bestimmt sich nach dem Verhältnis der Zahl der

Stimmrechte, die es aus den ihm gehörenden Anteilen ausüben kann, zur Gesamtzahl aller Stimmrechte. ²Von der Gesamtzahl aller Stimmrechte sind die Stimmrechte aus eigenen Anteilen sowie aus Anteilen, die nach Absatz 2 Satz 3 eigenen Anteilen gleichstehen, abzusetzen.

(4) Als Anteile, die einem Unternehmen gehören, gelten auch die Anteile, die einem von ihm abhängigen Unternehmen oder einem anderen für Rechnung des Unternehmens oder eines von diesem abhängigen Unternehmens gehören und, wenn der Inhaber des Unternehmens ein Einzelkaufmann ist, auch die Anteile, die sonstiges Vermögen des Inhabers sind.

§ 17 Abhängige und herrschende Unternehmen.

(1) Abhängige Unternehmen sind rechtlich selbständige Unternehmen, auf die ein anderes Unternehmen (herrschendes Unternehmen) unmittelbar oder mittelbar einen beherrschenden Einfluß ausüben kann.

(2) Von einem in Mehrheitsbesitz stehenden Unternehmen wird vermutet, daß es von dem an ihm mit Mehrheit beteiligten Unternehmen abhängig ist.

§ 18 Konzern und Konzernunternehmen.

(1) ¹Sind ein herrschendes und ein oder mehrere abhängige Unternehmen unter der einheitlichen Leitung des herrschenden Unternehmens zusammengefaßt, so bilden sie einen Konzern; die einzelnen Unternehmen sind Konzernunternehmen. ²Unternehmen, zwischen denen ein Beherrschungsvertrag (§ 291) besteht oder von denen das eine in das andere eingegliedert ist (§ 319), sind als unter einheitlicher Leitung zusammengefaßt anzusehen. ³Von einem abhängigen Unternehmen wird vermutet, daß es mit dem herrschenden Unternehmen einen Konzern bildet.

of the voting rights it can exercise on the basis of the shares it holds to the total number of all voting rights. ²Voting rights from own shares and from shares deemed equivalent to own shares pursuant to para. 2 sentence 3 are deducted from the total number of all voting rights.

(4) Shares held by a controlled enterprise or by another party for account of the enterprise or another enterprise controlled by it and, if the owner of the enterprise is a sole proprietor, those shares which constitute other property of the owner are also deemed to be shares held by the enterprise.

§ 17 Controlled and controlling enterprises.

(1) Controlled enterprises are legally separate enterprises over which another enterprise (controlling enterprise) is able to exercise, directly or indirectly, a controlling influence.

(2) It is assumed that the majority-held enterprise is controlled by the enterprise having the majority holding therein.

§ 18 Group and group enterprises.

(1) ¹If a controlling enterprise and one or more controlled enterprises are under the common direction of the controlling enterprise, they shall form a group, with the individual enterprises constituting group enterprises. ²Enterprises shall also be deemed to be under common direction if they are parties to a domination agreement (sec. 291) or one has been integrated into the other (sec. 319). ³It is assumed that a controlled enterprise forms a group together with the controlling enterprise.

(2) Sind rechtlich selbständige Unternehmen, ohne daß das eine Unternehmen von dem anderen abhängig ist, unter einheitlicher Leitung zusammengefaßt, so bilden sie auch einen Konzern; die einzelnen Unternehmen sind Konzernunternehmen.

§ 19 Wechselseitig beteiligte Unternehmen.

(1) ¹Wechselseitig beteiligte Unternehmen sind Unternehmen mit Sitz im Inland in der Rechtsform einer Kapitalgesellschaft, die dadurch verbunden sind, daß jedem Unternehmen mehr als der vierte Teil der Anteile des anderen Unternehmens gehört. ²Für die Feststellung, ob einem Unternehmen mehr als der vierte Teil der Anteile des anderen Unternehmens gehört, gilt § 16 Abs. 2 Satz 1, Abs. 4.

(2) Gehört einem wechselseitig beteiligten Unternehmen an dem anderen Unternehmen eine Mehrheitsbeteiligung oder kann das eine auf das andere Unternehmen unmittelbar oder mittelbar einen beherrschenden Einfluß ausüben, so ist das eine als herrschendes, das andere als abhängiges Unternehmen anzusehen.

(3) Gehört jedem der wechselseitig beteiligten Unternehmen an dem anderen Unternehmen eine Mehrheitsbeteiligung oder kann jedes auf das andere unmittelbar oder mittelbar einen beherrschenden Einfluß ausüben, so gelten beide Unternehmen als herrschend und als abhängig.

(4) § 328 ist auf Unternehmen, die nach Absatz 2 oder 3 herrschende oder abhängige Unternehmen sind, nicht anzuwenden.

§ 20 Mitteilungspflichten.

(1) ¹Sobald einem Unternehmen mehr als der vierte Teil der Aktien einer Aktiengesellschaft mit Sitz im Inland gehört, hat es dies der Gesellschaft unverzüglich schriftlich mitzuteilen. ²Für

(2) If legally independent enterprises are under common direction without either of the enterprises controlling the other, they also form a group, with the individual enterprises constituting group enterprises.

§ 19 Enterprises with cross-shareholdings.

(1) ¹Enterprises with cross-shareholdings are enterprises which have their registered office in Germany, take the legal form of a corporation and are affiliated by way of each enterprise holding more than one quarter of the shares in the other. ²Sec. 16 para. 2 sentence 1 and para. 4 shall apply when determining whether an enterprise holds more than a quarter of the shares in the other enterprise.

(2) If one of the enterprises with cross-shareholdings has a majority holding in the other enterprise or if one of the enterprises can exercise a controlling influence, directly or indirectly, over the other, then one enterprise shall be regarded as a controlling and the other enterprise as a controlled enterprise.

(3) If each of the enterprises with cross-shareholdings has a majority holding in the other or if each of the enterprises can exercise a controlling influence, directly or indirectly, over the other, then both enterprises shall be deemed controlling and controlled enterprises.

(4) Sec. 328 shall not apply to enterprises which are controlling or controlled enterprises pursuant to para. 2 or 3.

§ 20 Disclosure obligations.

(1) ¹An enterprise shall inform the company without undue delay in writing as soon as it acquires more than one quarter of the shares in a stock corporation with its registered office in Germany.

die Feststellung, ob dem Unternehmen mehr als der vierte Teil der Aktien gehört, gilt § 16 Abs. 2 Satz 1, Abs. 4.

(2) Für die Mitteilungspflicht nach Absatz 1 rechnen zu den Aktien, die dem Unternehmen gehören, auch Aktien,

1. deren Übereignung das Unternehmen, ein von ihm abhängiges Unternehmen oder ein anderer für Rechnung des Unternehmens oder eines von diesem abhängigen Unternehmens verlangen kann;
2. zu deren Abnahme das Unternehmen, ein von ihm abhängiges Unternehmen oder ein anderer für Rechnung des Unternehmens oder eines von diesem abhängigen Unternehmens verpflichtet ist.

(3) Ist das Unternehmen eine Kapitalgesellschaft, so hat es, sobald ihm ohne Hinzurechnung der Aktien nach Absatz 2 mehr als der vierte Teil der Aktien gehört, auch dies der Gesellschaft unverzüglich schriftlich mitzuteilen.

(4) Sobald dem Unternehmen eine Mehrheitsbeteiligung (§ 16 Abs. 1) gehört, hat es auch dies der Gesellschaft unverzüglich schriftlich mitzuteilen.

(5) Besteht die Beteiligung in der nach Absatz 1, 3 oder 4 mitteilungspflichtigen Höhe nicht mehr, so ist dies der Gesellschaft unverzüglich schriftlich mitzuteilen.

(6) [1]Die Gesellschaft hat das Bestehen einer Beteiligung, die ihr nach Absatz 1 oder 4 mitgeteilt worden ist, unverzüglich in den Gesellschaftsblättern bekanntzumachen; dabei ist das Unternehmen anzugeben, dem die Beteiligung gehört. [2]Wird der Gesellschaft mitgeteilt, daß die Beteiligung in der nach Absatz 1 oder 4 mitteilungspflichtigen Höhe nicht mehr besteht, so ist auch dies unverzüglich in den Gesellschaftsblättern bekanntzumachen.

(7) [1]Rechte aus Aktien, die einem nach Absatz 1 oder 4 mitteilungspflichtigen

[2]Sec. 16 para. 2 sentence 1, para. 4 apply when determining whether an enterprise holds more than a quarter of the shares in the other enterprise.

(2) For the purposes of the disclosure obligations pursuant to para. 1, shares held by the enterprise include shares

1. which the enterprise, an enterprise controlled by it or another party can demand to be transferred for account of the enterprise or an enterprise controlled by it;
2. which the enterprise, an enterprise controlled by it or another party is obligated to acquire for account of the enterprise or an enterprise controlled by it.

(3) If the enterprise is a corporation it shall also inform the company without undue delay in writing as soon as it acquires more than a quarter of the shares, excluding any shares pursuant to para. 2.

(4) The enterprise shall also inform the company without undue delay in writing as soon as it gains a majority holding (sec. 16 para. 1).

(5) The company shall be informed without undue delay in writing if the holding ceases to be of a level requiring disclosure pursuant to paras. 1, 3 or 4.

(6) [1]The company shall without undue delay publish the existence of a holding of which it is informed pursuant to paras. 1 or 4 in the company's designated journals; the name of the enterprise to which the holding belongs has to be stated. [2]Notice shall also be given without undue delay in the company's designated journals if the company is informed that the holding no longer exists at a level requiring disclosure pursuant to paras. 1 or 4.

(7) [1]Rights arising from shares belonging to an enterprise with an obligation

Unternehmen gehören, bestehen für die Zeit, für die das Unternehmen die Mitteilungspflicht nicht erfüllt, weder für das Unternehmen noch für ein von ihm abhängiges Unternehmen oder für einen anderen, der für Rechnung des Unternehmens oder eines von diesem abhängigen Unternehmens handelt. ²Dies gilt nicht für Ansprüche nach § 58 Abs. 4 und § 271, wenn die Mitteilung nicht vorsätzlich unterlassen wurde und nachgeholt worden ist.

(8) Die Absätze 1 bis 7 gelten nicht für Aktien eines Emittenten im Sinne des § 21 Abs. 2 des Wertpapierhandelsgesetzes.

§ 21 Mitteilungspflichten der Gesellschaft.

(1) ¹Sobald der Gesellschaft mehr als der vierte Teil der Anteile einer anderen Kapitalgesellschaft mit Sitz im Inland gehört, hat sie dies dem Unternehmen, an dem die Beteiligung besteht, unverzüglich schriftlich mitzuteilen. ²Für die Feststellung, ob der Gesellschaft mehr als der vierte Teil der Anteile gehört, gilt § 16 Abs. 2 Satz 1, Abs. 4 sinngemäß.

(2) Sobald der Gesellschaft eine Mehrheitsbeteiligung (§ 16 Abs. 1) an einem anderen Unternehmen gehört, hat sie dies dem Unternehmen, an dem die Mehrheitsbeteiligung besteht, unverzüglich schriftlich mitzuteilen.

(3) Besteht die Beteiligung in der nach Absatz 1 oder 2 mitteilungspflichtigen Höhe nicht mehr, hat die Gesellschaft dies dem anderen Unternehmen unverzüglich schriftlich mitzuteilen.

(4) Rechte aus Anteilen, die einer nach Absatz 1 oder 2 mitteilungspflichtigen Gesellschaft gehören, bestehen nicht für die Zeit, für die sie die Mitteilungspflicht nicht erfüllt. 2§ 20 Abs. 7 Satz 2 gilt entsprechend.

(5) Die Absätze 1 bis 4 gelten nicht für Aktien eines Emittenten im Sinne des § 21 Abs. 2 des Wertpapierhandelsgesetzes.

to disclose pursuant to paras. 1 or 4 do not exist for the enterprise, an enterprise controlled by it or for any other party acting for account of the enterprise or an enterprise controlled by it until such time as the enterprise meets its disclosure obligations. ²The above does not apply for claims pursuant to sec. 58 para. 4 and sec. 271, provided the failure to disclose was not intentionally and has since been rectified.

(8) Paras. 1 to 7 do not apply to shares of an issuer within the meaning of sec. 21 para. 2 Securities Trading Act

§ 21 Disclosure obligations of the company.

(1) ¹As soon as the company acquires more than one quarter of the shares in another corporation with its registered office in Germany, it shall inform such enterprise in writing without undue delay. ²Sec. 16 para. 2 sentence 1, para. 4 shall apply accordingly when determining whether the company holds more than one quarter of the shares.

(2) As soon as the company acquires a majority holding (sec. 16 para. 1) in another enterprise, it shall inform such enterprise without undue delay in writing.

(3) If the holding ceases to be of a level requiring disclosure pursuant to paras. 1 or 2, the company shall inform the other enterprise without undue delay in writing.

(4) ¹Rights from shares held by a company obligated to make a disclosure pursuant to paras. 1 or 2 do not exist until such time as the company meets its disclosure obligations. ²Sec. 20 para. 7 sentence 2 shall apply accordingly.

(5) Paras. 1 to 4 shall not apply to shares of an issuer within the meaning of sec. 21 para. 2 Securities Trading Act.

§ 22 Nachweis mitgeteilter Beteiligungen.

Ein Unternehmen, dem eine Mitteilung nach § 20 Abs. 1, 3 oder 4, § 21 Abs. 1 oder 2 gemacht worden ist, kann jederzeit verlangen, daß ihm das Bestehen der Beteiligung nachgewiesen wird.

Zweiter Teil. Gründung der Gesellschaft

§ 23 Feststellung der Satzung.

(1) ¹Die Satzung muß durch notarielle Beurkundung festgestellt werden. ²Bevollmächtigte bedürfen einer notariell beglaubigten Vollmacht.

(2) In der Urkunde sind anzugeben

1. die Gründer;
2. bei Nennbetragsaktien der Nennbetrag, bei Stückaktien die Zahl, der Ausgabebetrag und, wenn mehrere Gattungen bestehen, die Gattung der Aktien, die jeder Gründer übernimmt;
3. der eingezahlte Betrag des Grundkapitals.

(3) Die Satzung muß bestimmen

1. die Firma und den Sitz der Gesellschaft;
2. den Gegenstand des Unternehmens; namentlich ist bei Industrie- und Handelsunternehmen die Art der Erzeugnisse und Waren, die hergestellt und gehandelt werden sollen, näher anzugeben;
3. die Höhe des Grundkapitals;
4. die Zerlegung des Grundkapitals entweder in Nennbetragsaktien oder in Stückaktien, bei Nennbetragsaktien deren Nennbeträge und die Zahl der Aktien jeden Nennbetrags, bei Stückaktien deren Zahl, außerdem, wenn mehrere Gattungen bestehen,

§ 22 Proof of disclosed holdings.

An enterprise to which a disclosure has been made pursuant to sec. 20 paras. 1, 3 or 4, sec. 21 paras. 1 or 2 may request at any time to be provided with proof of the existence of such holding.

Part Two. Formation of the Company

§ 23 Establishment of the articles of association.

(1) ¹The articles of association shall be established in the form of a notarial deed. ²Authorized representatives require a power of attorney certified by a notary.

(2) The deed shall state

1. the names of the founders;
2. for par value shares the nominal value and for non-par value shares the number, the issue price and, if there is more than one class of shares, the class of the shares subscribed to by each founder;
3. the paid-in amount of the registered share capital.

(3) The articles of association shall stipulate

1. the name and the registered office of the company;
2. the object of the enterprise, with details being given of the type of products and goods to be manufactured and traded in the case of industrial and trade enterprises;
3. the amount of the registered share capital;
4. the subdivision of the registered share capital either in par value shares or non-par value shares; in the case of par value shares the nominal value of the said shares and the number of shares issued for each nominal value shall be stated and in the case of non-par value shares the number thereof and, if there is more

than one class of shares, the class of the shares and the number of the shares in each class shall be stated;
5. whether the shares are issued as registered or bearer shares;
6. the number of members of the management board or the rules for determining this number.

(4) The articles of association shall include provisions concerning the form company announcements are to take.

(5) [1]The articles of association may only deviate from the provisions of this Act if expressly permitted. [2]Supplementary provisions may be included in the articles of association unless a regulation in this Act has conclusive effect.

§ 24 *(repealed)*

§ 25 Announcements by the company.

[1]If the law or the articles of association stipulate that an announcement of the company is to be made in the company's designated journals, such announcement shall be made in the Federal law Gazette.

§ 26 Special benefits. Formation expenses.

(1) Each special benefit granted to an individual shareholder or a third party shall be specified in the articles of association together with the name of the person granted the said benefit.

(2) The total expenses paid by the company to shareholders or to other persons as compensation or remuneration for the formation of the company or the preparation therefor shall be specified separately in the articles of association.

(3) [1]If not so specified, any contracts and transactions made in implementation thereof shall be invalid vis-à-vis the company. [2]Such invalidity cannot be cured by means of amending the ar-

delsregister kann die Unwirksamkeit nicht durch Satzungsänderung geheilt werden.

(4) Die Festsetzungen können erst geändert werden, wenn die Gesellschaft fünf Jahre im Handelsregister eingetragen ist.

(5) Die Satzungsbestimmungen über die Festsetzungen können durch Satzungsänderung erst beseitigt werden, wenn die Gesellschaft dreißig Jahre im Handelsregister eingetragen ist und wenn die Rechtsverhältnisse, die den Festsetzungen zugrunde liegen, seit mindestens fünf Jahren abgewickelt sind.

§ 27 Sacheinlagen. Sachübernahmen. Rückzahlungen von Einlagen.

(1) [1]Sollen Aktionäre Einlagen machen, die nicht durch Einzahlung des Ausgabebetrags der Aktien zu leisten sind (Sacheinlagen), oder soll die Gesellschaft vorhandene oder herzustellende Anlagen oder andere Vermögensgegenstände übernehmen (Sachübernahmen), so müssen in der Satzung festgesetzt werden der Gegenstand der Sacheinlage oder der Sachübernahme, die Person, von der die Gesellschaft den Gegenstand erwirbt, und der Nennbetrag, bei Stückaktien die Zahl der bei der Sacheinlage zu gewährenden Aktien oder die bei der Sachübernahme zu gewährende Vergütung. [2]Soll die Gesellschaft einen Vermögensgegenstand übernehmen, für den eine Vergütung gewährt wird, die auf die Einlage eines Aktionärs angerechnet werden soll, so gilt dies als Sacheinlage.

(2) Sacheinlagen oder Sachübernahmen können nur Vermögensgegenstände sein, deren wirtschaftlicher Wert feststellbar ist; Verpflichtungen zu Dienstleistungen können nicht Sacheinlagen oder Sachübernahmen sein.

(3) [1]Ist eine Geldeinlage eines Aktionärs bei wirtschaftlicher Betrachtung und

ticles of association once the company has been registered in the commercial register.

(4) Such matters specified in the articles of association may only be amended once the company has been registered in the commercial register for five years.

(5) The provisions in the articles of association concerning such specified matters may only be removed by means of amending the articles of association once the company has been registered in the commercial register for thirty years and all legal relationships underlying the said matters have been settled for at least five years.

§ 27 Contributions in kind. Acquisitions in kind. Repayment of Contributions.

(1) [1] If shareholders are to render contributions other than by paying the issue price of the shares (contributions in kind) or if the company is to acquire existing assets, assets which are to be created or any other property (acquisitions in kind), the articles of association shall specify the object of the contribution in kind or the acquisition in kind, the person from whom the company is to acquire the object and the nominal value or, in the case of non-par value shares, the number of shares to be issued in return for the contribution in kind or the remuneration to be granted in return for the acquisition in kind. [2] If the company is to acquire an asset in return for remuneration credited to the contribution made by a shareholder, this is deemed to be a contribution in kind.

(2) Only assets having an economic value which can be determined may constitute contributions in kind or acquisitions in kind; obligations to render services cannot constitute contributions in kind or acquisitions in kind.

(3) [1]If a cash contribution of a shareholder is, from an economic point of

aufgrund einer im Zusammenhang mit der Übernahme der Geldeinlage getroffenen Abrede vollständig oder teilweise als Sacheinlage zu bewerten (verdeckte Sacheinlage), so befreit dies den Aktionär nicht von seiner Einlageverpflichtung. ²Jedoch sind die Verträge über die Sacheinlage und die Rechtshandlungen zu ihrer Ausführung nicht unwirksam. ³Auf die fortbestehende Geldeinlagepflicht des Aktionärs wird der Wert des Vermögensgegenstandes im Zeitpunkt der Anmeldung der Gesellschaft zur Eintragung in das Handelsregister oder im Zeitpunkt seiner Überlassung an die Gesellschaft, falls diese später erfolgt, angerechnet. ⁴ Die Anrechnung erfolgt nicht vor Eintragung der Gesellschaft in das Handelsregister. ⁵Die Beweislast für die Werthaltigkeit des Vermögensgegenstandes trägt der Aktionär.

view and based on an understanding reached in connection with the promise of the contribution in cash, in fact a contribution in kind in whole or in part (hidden contribution in kind) then the shareholder shall not be released from his obligation to render a contribution. ²However, the contracts concerning the contribution in kind and the legal acts for its consummation shall not be invalid. ³The value of the asset at the time the application for registration of the company in the commercial register is made or at the time the asset is transferred to the company, if such transfer occurs later, shall be deducted from the continuing obligation of the shareholder to render the cash contribution. ⁴The deduction shall not take place prior to the registration of the company in the commercial register. ⁵The burden of proof for the value of the asset is on the shareholder.

(4) ¹Ist vor der Einlage eine Leistung an den Aktionär vereinbart worden, die wirtschaftlich einer Rückzahlung der Einlage entspricht und die nicht als verdeckte Sacheinlage im Sinne von Absatz 3 zu beurteilen ist, so befreit dies den Aktionär von seiner Einlageverpflichtung nur dann, wenn die Leistung durch einen vollwertigen Rückgewähranspruch gedeckt ist, der jederzeit fällig ist oder durch fristlose Kündigung durch die Gesellschaft fällig werden kann. ²Eine solche Leistung oder die Vereinbarung einer solchen Leistung ist in der Anmeldung nach § 37 anzugeben.

(4) ¹If, prior to the contribution, a performance to the shareholder was agreed upon which economically corresponds to a repayment of the contribution and which cannot be judged a hidden contribution in kind within the meaning of para. 3, the shareholder is only released from his obligation to render the contribution if the performance is matched by an unimpaired claim for return which is due at any time or which can be made due by termination without notice by the company. ²Such performance or the agreement on such performance shall be declared in the application pursuant to sec. 37.

(5) Für die Änderung rechtswirksam getroffener Festsetzungen gilt § 26 Abs. 4, für die Beseitigung der Satzungsbestimmungen § 26 Abs. 5.

(5) Sec. 26 para. 4 shall apply to the amendment of lawfully made stipulations, sec. 26 para. 5 shall apply to the deletion of provisions in the articles of association.

§ 28 Gründer.

Die Aktionäre, die die Satzung festgestellt haben, sind die Gründer der Gesellschaft.

§ 28 Founders.

The shareholders who have established the articles of association of the company are the founders of the company.

§ 29 Establishment of the company.

The company is established upon all shares being subscribed to by the founders.

§ 30 Appointment of the supervisory board, the management board and the auditor of annual financial statements.

(1) [1]The founders shall appoint the company's first supervisory board and the auditor of annual financial statements for the first full or partial fiscal year. [2]The appointment shall be notarized.

(2) The provisions concerning the appointment of employee representatives on the supervisory board shall not apply to the composition and appointment of the first supervisory board.

(3) [1]The members of the first supervisory board may not be appointed for any longer than until the conclusion of the general meeting which resolves on ratification regarding the first full or partial fiscal year. [2]The management board shall, within a reasonable time prior to expiry of the term of office of the first supervisory board, announce which legal provisions it believes ought to be taken as the basis when compiling the next supervisory board; sec. 96 to 99 shall apply.

(4) The supervisory board shall appoint the first management board.

§ 31 Appointment of supervisory board in case of formation through contributions in kind.

(1) [1]If the contribution or acquisition of an enterprise or part of an enterprise is specified in the articles of association as the object of a contribution in kind or an acquisition in kind, the founders shall only appoint the number of supervisory board members which are to be appointed by the general meeting, without being bound to nominations, on the basis of the legal provisions the founders be-

mensetzung des Aufsichtsrats maßgebend sind, von der Hauptversammlung ohne Bindung an Wahlvorschläge zu wählen sind. ²Sie haben jedoch, wenn dies nur zwei Aufsichtsratsmitglieder sind, drei Aufsichtsratsmitglieder zu bestellen.

(2) Der nach Absatz 1 Satz 1 bestellte Aufsichtsrat ist, soweit die Satzung nichts anderes bestimmt, beschlußfähig, wenn die Hälfte, mindestens jedoch drei seiner Mitglieder an der Beschlußfassung teilnehmen.

(3) ¹Unverzüglich nach der Einbringung oder Übernahme des Unternehmens oder des Unternehmensteils hat der Vorstand bekanntzumachen, nach welchen gesetzlichen Vorschriften nach seiner Ansicht der Aufsichtsrat zusammengesetzt sein muß. ²§§ 97 bis 99 gelten sinngemäß. ³Das Amt der bisherigen Aufsichtsratsmitglieder erlischt nur, wenn der Aufsichtsrat nach anderen als den von den Gründern für maßgebend gehaltenen Vorschriften zusammenzusetzen ist oder wenn die Gründer drei Aufsichtsratsmitglieder bestellt haben, der Aufsichtsrat aber auch aus Aufsichtsratsmitgliedern der Arbeitnehmer zu bestehen hat.

(4) Absatz 3 gilt nicht, wenn das Unternehmen oder der Unternehmensteil erst nach der Bekanntmachung des Vorstands nach § 30 Abs. 3 Satz 2 eingebracht oder übernommen wird.

(5) § 30 Abs. 3 Satz 1 gilt nicht für die nach Absatz 3 bestellten Aufsichtsratsmitglieder der Arbeitnehmer.

§ 32 Gründungsbericht.

(1) Die Gründer haben einen schriftlichen Bericht über den Hergang der Gründung zu erstatten (Gründungsbericht).

(2) ¹Im Gründungsbericht sind die wesentlichen Umstände darzulegen, von denen die Angemessenheit der Leistun-

lieve to apply to the composition of the supervisory board following such contribution or acquisition. ²If this means that only two members of the supervisory board would be appointed, however, they shall appoint three members of the supervisory board.

(2) Unless provided otherwise in the articles of association, the supervisory board appointed pursuant to para. 1 sentence 1 has a quorum if half, but at least three, of the members thereof participate in adopting the resolution.

(3) ¹Without undue delay after the contribution or acquisition of the enterprise or part of an enterprise, the management board shall announce which legal provisions it believes govern the composition of the supervisory board. ²Sec. 97 to 99 shall apply accordingly. ³The term of office of the then current supervisory board members expires only if the supervisory board is to be composed on the basis of regulations other than those the founders believed to be authoritative, or if the founders have appointed three members of the supervisory board, but employee representatives are also to be included on the supervisory board.

(4) Para. 3 shall not apply if the enterprise or part of an enterprise is contributed or acquired after the announcement is made by the management board pursuant to sec. 30 para. 3 sentence 2.

(5) Sec. 30 para. 3 sentence 1 shall not apply to the employee representatives on the supervisory board appointed pursuant to para. 3.

§ 32 Formation report.

(1) The founders shall draw up a written report concerning the procedure of the formation of the company (formation report).

(2) ¹The formation report shall set out the material circumstances on which the appropriateness of the consideration for

gen für Sacheinlagen oder Sachübernahmen abhängt. ²Dabei sind anzugeben

1. die vorausgegangenen Rechtsgeschäfte, die auf den Erwerb durch die Gesellschaft hingezielt haben;
2. die Anschaffungs- und Herstellungskosten aus den letzten beiden Jahren;
3. beim Übergang eines Unternehmens auf die Gesellschaft die Betriebserträge aus den letzten beiden Geschäftsjahren.

(3) Im Gründungsbericht ist ferner anzugeben, ob und in welchem Umfang bei der Gründung für Rechnung eines Mitglieds des Vorstands oder des Aufsichtsrats Aktien übernommen worden sind und ob und in welcher Weise ein Mitglied des Vorstands oder des Aufsichtsrats sich einen besonderen Vorteil oder für die Gründung oder ihre Vorbereitung eine Entschädigung oder Belohnung ausbedungen hat.

§ 33 Gründungsprüfung. Allgemeines.

(1) Die Mitglieder des Vorstands und des Aufsichtsrats haben den Hergang der Gründung zu prüfen.

(2) Außerdem hat eine Prüfung durch einen oder mehrere Prüfer (Gründungsprüfer) stattzufinden, wenn

1. ein Mitglied des Vorstands oder des Aufsichtsrats zu den Gründern gehört oder
2. bei der Gründung für Rechnung eines Mitglieds des Vorstands oder des Aufsichtsrats Aktien übernommen worden sind oder
3. ein Mitglied des Vorstands oder des Aufsichtsrats sich einen besonderen Vorteil oder für die Gründung oder ihre Vorbereitung eine Entschädigung oder Belohnung ausbedungen hat oder
4. eine Gründung mit Sacheinlagen oder Sachübernahmen vorliegt.

contributions in kind or acquisitions in kind depends. ²The report shall state:

1. the legal transactions made previously in order to arrange the acquisition by the company;
2. the acquisition and production costs from the two preceding years;
3. in the event of the transfer of an enterprise to the company the income from the two preceding fiscal years.

(3) The formation report shall also state whether and to what extent shares were subscribed to at the formation for the account of a member of the management board or the supervisory board and whether and how a member of the management board or the supervisory board has reached an agreement to receive a special benefit or any remuneration or reward for the formation or the preparation thereof.

§ 33 Formation audit. General provisions.

(1) The members of the management board and the supervisory board shall audit the formation procedure.

(2) In addition, an audit shall also be conducted by one or more auditors (formation auditors) if

1. one of the founders is a member of the management board or the supervisory board or
2. shares were subscribed to at formation for the account of a member of the management board or the supervisory board or
3. a member of the management board or the supervisory board has acquired a special benefit or has negotiated any remuneration or reward for the formation or the preparation thereof or
4. the formation involves contributions in kind or acquisitions in kind.

(3) ¹In den Fällen des Absatzes 2 Nr. 1 und 2 kann der beurkundende Notar (§ 23 Abs. 1 Satz 1) anstelle eines Gründungsprüfers die Prüfung im Auftrag der Gründer vornehmen; die Bestimmungen über die Gründungsprüfung finden sinngemäße Anwendung. ²Nimmt nicht der Notar die Prüfung vor, so bestellt das Gericht die Gründungsprüfer. ³Gegen die Entscheidung ist die Beschwerde zulässig.

(4) Als Gründungsprüfer sollen, wenn die Prüfung keine anderen Kenntnisse fordert, nur bestellt werden

1. Personen, die in der Buchführung ausreichend vorgebildet und erfahren sind;
2. Prüfungsgesellschaften, von deren gesetzlichen Vertretern mindestens einer in der Buchführung ausreichend vorgebildet und erfahren ist.

(5) ¹Als Gründungsprüfer darf nicht bestellt werden, wer nach § 143 Abs. 2 nicht Sonderprüfer sein kann. ²Gleiches gilt für Personen und Prüfungsgesellschaften, auf deren Geschäftsführung die Gründer oder Personen, für deren Rechnung die Gründer Aktien übernommen haben, maßgebenden Einfluß haben.

§ 33a Sachgründung ohne externe Gründungsprüfung.

(1) Von einer Prüfung durch Gründungsprüfer kann bei einer Gründung mit Sacheinlagen oder Sachübernahmen (§ 33 Abs. 2 Nr. 4) abgesehen werden, soweit eingebracht werden sollen:

1. übertragbare Wertpapiere oder Geldmarktinstrumente im Sinne des § 2 Absatz 1 und 1a des Wertpapierhandelsgesetzes, wenn sie mit dem gewichteten Durchschnittspreis bewertet werden, zu dem sie während der letzten drei Monate vor dem Tag ihrer tatsächlichen Einbringung auf einem oder mehreren organisierten

(3) ¹In the cases stipulated in para. 2 nos. 1 and 2, the recording notary (sec. 23 para. 1 sentence 1) may conduct the audit instead of the formation auditor at the founders' request; the provisions concerning the formation audit shall apply accordingly. ²If the audit is not conducted by the notary, the court shall appoint the formation auditors. ³The decision is subject to appeal.

(4) Provided the audit does not require any additional expertise, only the following may be appointed as formation auditors:

1. persons having sufficient training and experience in book-keeping;
2. auditing companies having at least one legal representative with sufficient training and experience in book-keeping.

(5) ¹Anyone who is barred from being a special auditor pursuant to sec. 143 para. 2 may not be appointed a formation auditor. ²The above shall also apply to persons and auditing companies whose management is under the decisive influence of the founders or persons on whose account the founders have subscribed to shares.

§ 33a Formation through contributions in kind without external formation audit.

(1) An audit by formation auditors may be omitted in the case of a formation involving contributions in kind or acquisitions in kind (sec. 33 para. 2 no. 4) to the extent that it is intended to contribute:

1. transferable securities or money market instruments within the meaning of sec. 2 para. 1 sentence 1 and para. 1a of the Securities Trading Act if they are valued at the weighted average price at which they were traded in one or more organized markets within the meaning of sec. 2 para. 5 of the Securities Trading Act

Märkten im Sinne von § 2 Abs. 5 des Wertpapierhandelsgesetzes gehandelt worden sind,

2. andere als die in Nummer 1 genannten Vermögensgegenstände, wenn eine Bewertung zu Grunde gelegt wird, die ein unabhängiger, ausreichend vorgebildeter und erfahrener Sachverständiger nach den allgemein anerkannten Bewertungsgrundsätzen mit dem beizulegenden Zeitwert ermittelt hat und wenn der Bewertungsstichtag nicht mehr als sechs Monate vor dem Tag der tatsächlichen Einbringung liegt.

(2) Absatz 1 ist nicht anzuwenden, wenn der gewichtete Durchschnittspreis der Wertpapiere oder Geldmarktinstrumente (Absatz 1 Nr. 1) durch außergewöhnliche Umstände erheblich beeinflusst worden ist oder wenn anzunehmen ist, dass der beizulegende Zeitwert der anderen Vermögensgegenstände (Absatz 1 Nr. 2) am Tag ihrer tatsächlichen Einbringung auf Grund neuer oder neu bekannt gewordener Umstände erheblich niedriger ist als der von dem Sachverständigen angenommene Wert.

§ 34 Umfang der Gründungsprüfung.

(1) Die Prüfung durch die Mitglieder des Vorstands und des Aufsichtsrats sowie die Prüfung durch die Gründungsprüfer haben sich namentlich darauf zu erstrecken,

1. ob die Angaben der Gründer über die Übernahme der Aktien, über die Einlagen auf das Grundkapital und über die Festsetzungen nach §§ 26 und 27 richtig und vollständig sind;

2. ob der Wert der Sacheinlagen oder Sachübernahmen den geringsten Ausgabebetrag der dafür zu gewährenden Aktien oder den Wert der dafür zu gewährenden Leistungen erreicht.

(2) ¹Über jede Prüfung ist unter Darlegung dieser Umstände schriftlich zu

during the last three months prior to the day of their actual contribution,

2. assets other than those set forth in no. 1, if their valuation was determined by an independent, sufficiently trained and experienced expert pursuant to generally accepted valuation principles and on the basis of the relevant present value and if the valuation date is not more than six months before the day of the actual contribution.

(2) Para. 1 shall not apply if the weighted average price of the securities or money market instruments (para. 1 no. 1) was substantially influenced by extraordinary circumstances or if it is to be assumed that the relevant present value of the other assets (para. 1 no. 2) is, on the day of their actual contribution and on the basis of new or newly known circumstances, substantially lower than the value assumed by the expert.

§ 34 Scope of formation audit.

(1) The audit conducted by the members of the management board and the supervisory board and the audit conducted by the formation auditors shall extend to the following:

1. whether the statements of the founders concerning the subscription to shares, the contributions to the registered share capital and the stipulations pursuant to sec. 26 and 27 are correct and complete;

2. whether the value of the contributions in kind or the acquisitions in kind reach the value of the lowest issue price of the shares issued in return or the value of the consideration to be paid therefor.

(2) ¹A written report shall be submitted concerning each audit, covering the

berichten. ²In dem Bericht ist der Gegenstand jeder Sacheinlage oder Sachübernahme zu beschreiben sowie anzugeben, welche Bewertungsmethoden bei der Ermittlung des Wertes angewandt worden sind. ³In dem Prüfungsbericht der Mitglieder des Vorstands und des Aufsichtsrats kann davon sowie von Ausführungen zu Absatz 1 Nr. 2 abgesehen werden, soweit nach § 33a von einer externen Gründungsprüfung abgesehen wird.

(3) ¹Je ein Stück des Berichts der Gründungsprüfer ist dem Gericht und dem Vorstand einzureichen. ²Jedermann kann den Bericht bei dem Gericht einsehen.

§ 35 Meinungsverschiedenheiten zwischen Gründern und Gründungsprüfern. Vergütung und Auslagen der Gründungsprüfer.

(1) Die Gründungsprüfer können von den Gründern alle Aufklärungen und Nachweise verlangen, die für eine sorgfältige Prüfung notwendig sind.

(2) ¹Bei Meinungsverschiedenheiten zwischen den Gründern und den Gründungsprüfern über den Umfang der Aufklärungen und Nachweise, die von den Gründern zu gewähren sind, entscheidet das Gericht. ²Die Entscheidung ist unanfechtbar. ³Solange sich die Gründer weigern, der Entscheidung nachzukommen, wird der Prüfungsbericht nicht erstattet.

(3) ¹Die Gründungsprüfer haben Anspruch auf Ersatz angemessener barer Auslagen und auf Vergütung für ihre Tätigkeit. ²Die Auslagen und die Vergütung setzt das Gericht fest. ³Gegen die Entscheidung ist die Beschwerde zulässig; die Rechtsbeschwerde ist ausgeschlossen. ⁴Aus der rechtskräftigen Entscheidung findet die Zwangsvollstreckung nach der Zivilprozeßordnung statt.

above circumstances. ²The report shall describe the object of each contribution in kind or acquisition in kind and shall state which evaluation methods were used to calculate the value. ³This as well as statements with respect to para. 1 no. 2, may be omitted from the audit report of the members of the management board and the supervisory board to the extent that an external formation audit is omitted pursuant to sec. 33a.

(3) ¹One copy of the formation auditors' report shall be submitted to the court and the management board respectively. ²The report shall be available for inspection by the public at the court.

§ 35 Differences of opinion between founders and formation auditors. Remuneration and expenses for formation auditors.

(1) The formation auditors can request that the founders provide all explanations and evidence required for a precise audit.

(2) ¹The court shall decide on differences of opinion between the founders and the formation auditors concerning the scope of the explanations and evidence to be supplied by the founders. ²No appeal may be filed against the decision. ³The audit report shall not be issued until the founders agree to honor the decision.

(3) ¹The formation auditors shall be entitled to the reimbursement of reasonable cash expenses and to remuneration for their services. ²The expenses and the remuneration shall be determined by the court. ³The decision is subject to appeal; no further appeal on a point of law may be made. ⁴A decision that has become res judicata shall be enforceable pursuant to the Code of Civil Procedure.

§ 36 Anmeldung der Gesellschaft.

(1) Die Gesellschaft ist bei dem Gericht von allen Gründern und Mitgliedern des Vorstands und des Aufsichtsrats zur Eintragung in das Handelsregister anzumelden.

(2) Die Anmeldung darf erst erfolgen, wenn auf jede Aktie, soweit nicht Sacheinlagen vereinbart sind, der eingeforderte Betrag ordnungsgemäß eingezahlt worden ist (§ 54 Abs. 3) und, soweit er nicht bereits zur Bezahlung der bei der Gründung angefallenen Steuern und Gebühren verwandt wurde, endgültig zur freien Verfügung des Vorstands steht.

§ 36a Leistung der Einlagen.

(1) Bei Bareinlagen muß der eingeforderte Betrag (§ 36 Abs. 2) mindestens ein Viertel des geringsten Ausgabebetrags und bei Ausgabe der Aktien für einen höheren als diesen auch den Mehrbetrag umfassen.

(2) ^{1}Sacheinlagen sind vollständig zu leisten. ^{2}Besteht die Sacheinlage in der Verpflichtung, einen Vermögensgegenstand auf die Gesellschaft zu übertragen, so muß diese Leistung innerhalb von fünf Jahren nach der Eintragung der Gesellschaft in das Handelsregister zu bewirken sein. ^{3}Der Wert muß dem geringsten Ausgabebetrag und bei Ausgabe der Aktien für einen höheren als diesen auch dem Mehrbetrag entsprechen.

§ 37 Inhalt der Anmeldung.

(1) ^{1}In der Anmeldung ist zu erklären, daß die Voraussetzungen des § 36 Abs. 2 und des § 36a erfüllt sind; dabei sind der Betrag, zu dem die Aktien ausgegeben werden, und der darauf eingezahlte Betrag anzugeben. ^{2}Es ist nachzuweisen, daß der eingezahlte Betrag endgültig zur freien Verfügung des Vorstands steht. ^{3}Ist der Betrag gemäß § 54 Abs. 3 durch Gutschrift auf ein Konto eingezahlt worden, so ist der Nachweis durch

§ 36 Registration of the company.

(1) All founders and members of the management board and the supervisory board shall apply to the court for the company to be registered in the commercial register.

(2) The application may not be made until the amount called in, unless contributions in kind have been agreed, has been duly paid in for each share (sec. 54 para. 3), and, in so far as it has not already been used to pay the taxes and fees incurred at formation, is unconditionally at the free disposal of the management board.

§ 36a Payment of contributions.

(1) If cash contributions are made, the amount called in (sec. 36 para. 2) shall be at least one quarter of the lowest issue price and shall also cover the additional amount if shares are issued for a higher amount.

(2) ^{1}Contributions in kind shall be rendered in full. ^{2}If the contribution in kind consists of the obligation to transfer assets to the company, this obligation shall be fulfilled within a period of five years after the company is registered in the commercial register. ^{3}The value shall correspond to the lowest issue price and, if shares are issued for a higher amount, shall also cover such additional amount.

§ 37 Contents of the application.

(1) ^{1}The application shall declare that the requirements of sec. 36 para. 2 and sec. 36a have been met; the amount for which the shares are to be issued and the amount paid in shall be stated. ^{2}Evidence shall be provided of the fact that the amount paid in is unconditionally at the free disposal of the management board. ^{3}If the amount has been credited to a bank account (sec. 54 para. 3), evidence shall be provided in the form

eine Bestätigung des kontoführenden Instituts zu führen. ⁴Für die Richtigkeit der Bestätigung ist das Institut der Gesellschaft verantwortlich. ⁵Sind von dem eingezahlten Betrag Steuern und Gebühren bezahlt worden, so ist dies nach Art und Höhe der Beträge nachzuweisen.

(2) ¹In der Anmeldung haben die Vorstandsmitglieder zu versichern, daß keine Umstände vorliegen, die ihrer Bestellung nach § 76 Abs. 3 Satz 2 Nr. 2 und 3 sowie Satz 3 entgegenstehen, und daß sie über ihre unbeschränkte Auskunftspflicht gegenüber dem Gericht belehrt worden sind. ²Die Belehrung nach § 53 Abs. 2 des Bundeszentralregistergesetzes kann schriftlich vorgenommen werden; sie kann auch durch einen Notar oder einen im Ausland bestellten Notar, durch einen Vertreter eines vergleichbaren rechtsberatenden Berufs oder einen Konsularbeamten erfolgen.

(3) In der Anmeldung sind ferner anzugeben:

1. eine inländische Geschäftsanschrift,
2. Art und Umfang der Vertretungsbefugnis der Vorstandsmitglieder.

(4) Der Anmeldung sind beizufügen

1. die Satzung und die Urkunden, in denen die Satzung festgestellt worden ist und die Aktien von den Gründern übernommen worden sind;
2. im Fall der §§ 26 und 27 die Verträge, die den Festsetzungen zugrunde liegen oder zu ihrer Ausführung geschlossen worden sind, und eine Berechnung des der Gesellschaft zur Last fallenden Gründungsaufwands; in der Berechnung sind die Vergütungen nach Art und Höhe und die Empfänger einzeln anzuführen;
3. die Urkunden über die Bestellung des Vorstands und des Aufsichtsrats;

of written confirmation from the bank where the account is kept. ⁴The bank shall be responsible vis-à-vis the company for the accuracy of the confirmation. ⁵If taxes and fees have been paid using the amount paid in, evidence shall be provided as to the nature and amount of such payments.

(2) ¹In the application, the members of the management board shall provide assurance that no circumstances exist that, according to sec. 76 para. 3 sentence 2 nos. 2 and 3 as well as sentence 3, present an obstacle to their appointment, and that they have been advised of their unlimited duty to furnish information to the court. ²Such advisement pursuant to sec. 53 para. 2 of the Federal Central Register Act may be performed in writing; it may also be performed by a notary or a notary appointed in a foreign country or a representative of a comparable profession providing legal advice or a consular officer.

(3) The application shall further state:

1. a business address in Germany,
2. the nature and extent of the power of representation of the members of the management board.

(4) The following shall be enclosed with the application:

1. the articles of association and the documents in which the articles of association have been established and the shares have been subscribed to by the founders;
2. if sec. 26 and 27 apply, the contracts on which the stipulations are based or which have been concluded for the execution thereof and a calculation of the formation expenses incurred by the company; such calculation shall list the remunerations individually, stating the kind, amount and recipients thereof;
3. the documents concerning the appointment of the management board and the supervisory board;

3a. eine Liste der Mitglieder des Aufsichtsrats, aus welcher Name, Vorname, ausgeübter Beruf und Wohnort der Mitglieder ersichtlich ist;
4. der Gründungsbericht und die Prüfungsberichte der Mitglieder des Vorstands und des Aufsichtsrats sowie der Gründungsprüfer nebst ihren urkundlichen Unterlagen.

(5) Für die Einreichung von Unterlagen nach diesem Gesetz gilt § 12 Abs. 2 des Handelsgesetzbuchs entsprechend.

§ 37a Anmeldung bei Sachgründung ohne externe Gründungsprüfung.

(1) ¹Wird nach § 33a von einer externen Gründungsprüfung abgesehen, ist dies in der Anmeldung zu erklären. ²Der Gegenstand jeder Sacheinlage oder Sachübernahme ist zu beschreiben. ³Die Anmeldung muss die Erklärung enthalten, dass der Wert der Sacheinlagen oder Sachübernahmen den geringsten Ausgabebetrag der dafür zu gewährenden Aktien oder den Wert der dafür zu gewährenden Leistungen erreicht. ⁴Der Wert, die Quelle der Bewertung sowie die angewandte Bewertungsmethode sind anzugeben.

(2) In der Anmeldung haben die Anmeldenden außerdem zu versichern, dass ihnen außergewöhnliche Umstände, die den gewichteten Durchschnittspreis der einzubringenden Wertpapiere oder Geldmarktinstrumente im Sinne von § 33a Abs. 1 Nr. 1 während der letzten drei Monate vor dem Tag ihrer tatsächlichen Einbringung erheblich beeinflusst haben könnten, oder Umstände, die darauf hindeuten, dass der beizulegende Zeitwert der Vermögensgegenstände im Sinne von § 33a Abs. 1 Nr. 2 am Tag ihrer tatsächlichen Einbringung aufgrund neuer oder neu bekannt gewordener Umstände erheblich niedriger ist als der von dem Sachverständigen angenommene Wert, nicht bekannt geworden sind.

3a. a list of the members of the supervisory board providing the surname, first name, profession and place of residence of the members;
4. the formation report and the audit reports from the members of the management board, the supervisory board and the formation auditors together with the relevant documents.

(5) Sec. 12 para. 2 of the Commercial Code shall apply accordingly to the submission of documents pursuant to this Act.

§ 37a Application in case of formation through contributions in kind without external formation audit.

(1) ¹If an external formation audit is omitted pursuant to sec. 33a, this shall be declared in the application. ²The object of each contribution in kind or acquisition in kind shall be described. ³The application shall contain the declaration that the value of the contributions in kind or acquisitions in kind is equal to the lowest issue price of the shares to be issued in return or to the value of the remuneration to be granted in return. ⁴The value, the source of the valuation as well as the valuation method applied shall be stated.

(2) The applicants shall further assure in the application that they have not become aware of extraordinary circumstances which may have substantially influenced the weighted average price of the securities or money market instruments within the meaning of sec. 33a para. 1 no. 1 during the three months prior to the day of their actual contribution or of circumstances which indicate that the relevant present value of the assets within the meaning of sec. 33a para. 1 no. 2 is, on the day of their actual contribution and based on new or newly known circumstances, substantially lower than the value assumed by the expert.

(3) Der Anmeldung sind beizufügen:

1. Unterlagen über die Ermittlung des gewichteten Durchschnittspreises, zu dem die einzubringenden Wertpapiere oder Geldmarktinstrumente während der letzten drei Monate vor dem Tag ihrer tatsächlichen Einbringung auf dem organisierten Markt gehandelt worden sind,
2. jedes Sachverständigengutachten, auf das sich die Bewertung in den Fällen des § 33a Abs. 1 Nr. 2 stützt.

§ 38 Prüfung durch das Gericht.

(1) ¹Das Gericht hat zu prüfen, ob die Gesellschaft ordnungsgemäß errichtet und angemeldet ist. ²Ist dies nicht der Fall, so hat es die Eintragung abzulehnen.

(2) ¹Das Gericht kann die Eintragung auch ablehnen, wenn die Gründungsprüfer erklären oder es offensichtlich ist, daß der Gründungsbericht oder der Prüfungsbericht der Mitglieder des Vorstands und des Aufsichtsrats unrichtig oder unvollständig ist oder den gesetzlichen Vorschriften nicht entspricht. ²Gleiches gilt, wenn die Gründungsprüfer erklären oder das Gericht der Auffassung ist, daß der Wert der Sacheinlagen oder Sachübernahmen nicht unwesentlich hinter dem geringsten Ausgabebetrag der dafür zu gewährenden Aktien oder dem Wert der dafür zu gewährenden Leistungen zurückbleibt.

(3) ¹Enthält die Anmeldung die Erklärung nach § 37a Abs. 1 Satz 1, hat das Gericht hinsichtlich der Werthaltigkeit der Sacheinlagen oder Sachübernahmen ausschließlich zu prüfen, ob die Voraussetzungen des § 37a erfüllt sind. ²Lediglich bei einer offenkundigen und erheblichen Überbewertung kann das Gericht die Eintragung ablehnen.

(4) Wegen einer mangelhaften, fehlenden oder nichtigen Bestimmung der Satzung darf das Gericht die Eintragung nach Absatz 1 nur ablehnen, soweit die-

(3) The following shall be attached to the application:

1. documents concerning the determination of the weighted average price at which the securities or money market instruments which are to be contributed were traded in the organized market during the three months prior to the day of their actual contribution,
2. every expert opinion on which the valuation in the cases of sec. 33a para. 1 no. 2 is based.

§ 38 Inspection by the court.

(1) ¹The court shall inspect whether the company has been duly established and the application duly made. ²If this is not the case, the court shall refuse registration.

(2) ¹The court may also refuse registration if the formation auditors declare or it is apparent that the formation report or the audit report of the members of the management board and the supervisory board is incorrect or incomplete or does not comply with legal provisions. ²The same shall apply if the formation auditors declare or the court is of the opinion that the value of the contributions in kind or acquisitions in kind is not inconsiderably lower than the lowest issue price of the shares to be issued in return or the value of the consideration to be given therefor.

(3) ¹If the application contains the declaration pursuant to sec. 37a para. 1 sentence 1, the court shall, with regard to the unimpairedness of the contributions in kind or acquisitions in kind, review only whether the requirements of sec. 37a are fulfilled. ²The court may only refuse registration in the case of an obvious and substantial overvaluation.

(4) The court may reject registration according to para. 1 because of a defective, missing, or null and void provision of the articles of association only to the

se Bestimmung, ihr Fehlen oder ihre Nichtigkeit	extent such provision, its absence, or its nullity

1. Tatsachen oder Rechtsverhältnisse betrifft, die nach § 23 Abs. 3 oder auf Grund anderer zwingender gesetzlicher Vorschriften in der Satzung bestimmt sein müssen oder die in das Handelsregister einzutragen oder von dem Gericht bekanntzumachen sind,
2. Vorschriften verletzt, die ausschließlich oder überwiegend zum Schutze der Gläubiger der Gesellschaft oder sonst im öffentlichen Interesse gegeben sind, oder
3. die Nichtigkeit der Satzung zur Folge hat.

§ 39 Inhalt der Eintragung.

(1) ¹Bei der Eintragung der Gesellschaft sind die Firma und der Sitz der Gesellschaft, eine inländische Geschäftsanschrift, der Gegenstand des Unternehmens, die Höhe des Grundkapitals, der Tag der Feststellung der Satzung und die Vorstandsmitglieder anzugeben. ²Wenn eine Person, die für Willenserklärungen und Zustellungen an die Gesellschaft empfangsberechtigt ist, mit einer inländischen Anschrift zur Eintragung in das Handelsregister angemeldet wird, sind auch diese Angaben einzutragen; Dritten gegenüber gilt die Empfangsberechtigung als fortbestehend, bis sie im Handelsregister gelöscht und die Löschung bekannt gemacht worden ist, es sei denn, dass die fehlende Empfangsberechtigung dem Dritten bekannt war. ³Ferner ist einzutragen, welche Vertretungsbefugnis die Vorstandsmitglieder haben.

(2) Enthält die Satzung Bestimmungen über die Dauer der Gesellschaft oder über das genehmigte Kapital, so sind auch diese Bestimmungen einzutragen.

1. pertains to facts or legal matters that, according to sec. 23 para. 3 or on the basis of other statutory legal regulations, have to be determined in the articles of association, or that have to be registered in the commercial register or announced by the court,
2. violates regulations that are exclusively or preliminarily for the protection of the creditors of the company or are otherwise in the public interest, or
3. has the nullity of the articles of association as a consequence.

§ 39 Contents of the registration.

(1) ¹The name and registered office of the company, a business address in Germany, the object of the enterprise, the amount of the registered share capital, the date of establishment of the articles of association and the names of the members of the management board shall be stated in the registration of the company. ²If a person, who is authorized to receive declarations of intent and deliveries addressed to the company, files for registration in the commercial register with a business address in Germany, this information shall be registered as well; in relation to third parties, the authorization to receive shall be deemed to continue until it is deleted from the commercial register and the deletion has been publicly notified, unless the third party was aware of the lack of the authorization to receive. ³Furthermore, the extent to which the members of the management board have power of representation shall be registered.

(2) If the articles of association contain provisions relating to the duration of the company or to the authorized capital, such provisions shall also be registered.

§ 40 *(aufgehoben)*

§ 40 *(repealed)*

§ 41 Handeln im Namen der Gesellschaft vor der Eintragung. Verbotene Aktienausgabe.

§ 41 Actions in the name of the company prior to registration. Prohibited issuance of shares.

(1) ¹Vor der Eintragung in das Handelsregister besteht die Aktiengesellschaft als solche nicht. ²Wer vor der Eintragung der Gesellschaft in ihrem Namen handelt, haftet persönlich; handeln mehrere, so haften sie als Gesamtschuldner.

(1) ¹Prior to the registration in the commercial register, the stock corporation does not exist as such. ²Anyone acting in the name of the company prior to registration shall be personally liable; in the case of more than one person acting, they are jointly and severally liable.

(2) Übernimmt die Gesellschaft eine vor ihrer Eintragung in ihrem Namen eingegangene Verpflichtung durch Vertrag mit dem Schuldner in der Weise, daß sie an die Stelle des bisherigen Schuldners tritt, so bedarf es zur Wirksamkeit der Schuldübernahme der Zustimmung des Gläubigers nicht, wenn die Schuldübernahme binnen drei Monaten nach der Eintragung der Gesellschaft vereinbart und dem Gläubiger von der Gesellschaft oder dem Schuldner mitgeteilt wird.

(2) If the company assumes an obligation entered into in its name prior to registration by agreement with the relevant debtor by substituting itself for such debtor, the validity of such assumption of obligation does not require the creditor's consent provided such assumption of obligation is agreed and the creditor is informed by the company or the debtor within three months of the company being registered.

(3) Verpflichtungen aus nicht in der Satzung festgesetzten Verträgen über Sondervorteile, Gründungsaufwand, Sacheinlagen oder Sachübernahmen kann die Gesellschaft nicht übernehmen.

(3) The company may not assume obligations arising from contracts pertaining to special benefits, formation expenses, contributions in kind or acquisitions in kind not specified in the articles of association.

(4) ¹Vor der Eintragung der Gesellschaft können Anteilsrechte nicht übertragen, Aktien oder Zwischenscheine nicht ausgegeben werden. ²Die vorher ausgegebenen Aktien oder Zwischenscheine sind nichtig. ³Für den Schaden aus der Ausgabe sind die Ausgeber den Inhabern als Gesamtschuldner verantwortlich.

(4) ¹Shares may not be transferred and share certificates and interim certificates may not be issued before the company is registered. ²Share certificates or interim certificates issued previously shall be null and void. ³The issuers of the shares are jointly and severally liable to the holders thereof for any damage arising from the issue.

§ 42 Einpersonen-Gesellschaft.

§ 42 Single shareholder company.

Gehören alle Aktien allein oder neben der Gesellschaft einem Aktionär, ist unverzüglich eine entsprechende Mitteilung unter Angabe von Name, Vorname, Geburtsdatum und Wohnort des alleinigen Aktionärs zum Handelsregister einzureichen.

If all the shares are held by one shareholder either on his own or together with the company, notification of this shall be submitted without undue delay to the commercial register, stating the sole shareholder's surname, first name, date of birth, and place of residence.

§§ 43, 44 *(aufgehoben)*

§ 45 Sitzverlegung.

(1) Wird der Sitz der Gesellschaft im Inland verlegt, so ist die Verlegung beim Gericht des bisherigen Sitzes anzumelden.

(2) ¹Wird der Sitz aus dem Bezirk des Gerichts des bisherigen Sitzes verlegt, so hat dieses unverzüglich von Amts wegen die Verlegung dem Gericht des neuen Sitzes mitzuteilen. ²Der Mitteilung sind die Eintragungen für den bisherigen Sitz sowie die bei dem bisher zuständigen Gericht aufbewahrten Urkunden beizufügen; bei elektronischer Registerführung sind die Eintragungen und die Dokumente elektronisch zu übermitteln. ³Das Gericht des neuen Sitzes hat zu prüfen, ob die Verlegung ordnungsgemäß beschlossen und § 30 des Handelsgesetzbuchs beachtet ist. ⁴Ist dies der Fall, so hat es die Sitzverlegung einzutragen und hierbei die ihm mitgeteilten Eintragungen ohne weitere Nachprüfung in sein Handelsregister zu übernehmen. ⁵Mit der Eintragung wird die Sitzverlegung wirksam. ⁶Die Eintragung ist dem Gericht des bisherigen Sitzes mitzuteilen. ⁷Dieses hat die erforderlichen Löschungen von Amts wegen vorzunehmen.

(3) ¹Wird der Sitz an einen anderen Ort innerhalb des Bezirks des Gerichts des bisherigen Sitzes verlegt, so hat das Gericht zu prüfen, ob die Sitzverlegung ordnungsgemäß beschlossen und § 30 des Handelsgesetzbuchs beachtet ist. ²Ist dies der Fall, so hat es die Sitzverlegung einzutragen. ³Mit der Eintragung wird die Sitzverlegung wirksam.

§ 46 Verantwortlichkeit der Gründer.

(1) ¹Die Gründer sind der Gesellschaft als Gesamtschuldner verantwortlich für

§§ 43, 44 *(repealed)*

§ 45 Change of registered office.

(1) If the registered office is relocated within Germany, such relocation shall be notified with the court at the previous registered office.

(2) ¹If the registered office is relocated to a location outside the district of the court responsible for the previous registered office, such court shall ex officio and without undue delay notify the court at the new registered office. ²The registration entries for the previous registered office and the documents retained by the court previously having jurisdiction shall be attached to such notification; if the register is kept electronically, the registrations and the documents shall be transmitted electronically. ³The court at the new registered office shall check whether the relocation of the registered office has been duly resolved and sec. 30 Commercial Code duly complied with. ⁴If this is the case, it shall register the relocation of registered office and shall enter the registration entries notified to it in its commercial register without making any further investigations. ⁵The change of registered office becomes effective upon registration. ⁶The court at the previous registered office shall be informed of the registration. ⁷Such court shall make the necessary deletions ex officio.

(3) ¹If the registered office is relocated within the district of the court at the previous registered office, the court shall check whether the relocation of the registered office has been duly resolved and sec. 30 Commercial Code duly complied with. ²If this is the case, it shall register the change of registered office. ³The change of registered office becomes effective upon registration.

§ 46 Liability of founders.

(1) ¹The founders are jointly and severally liable vis-à-vis the company for

die Richtigkeit und Vollständigkeit der Angaben, die zum Zwecke der Gründung der Gesellschaft über Übernahme der Aktien, Einzahlung auf die Aktien, Verwendung eingezahlter Beträge, Sondervorteile, Gründungsaufwand, Sacheinlagen und Sachübernahmen gemacht worden sind. ²Sie sind ferner dafür verantwortlich, daß eine zur Annahme von Einzahlungen auf das Grundkapital bestimmte Stelle (§ 54 Abs. 3) hierzu geeignet ist und daß die eingezahlten Beträge zur freien Verfügung des Vorstands stehen. ³Sie haben, unbeschadet der Verpflichtung zum Ersatz des sonst entstehenden Schadens, fehlende Einzahlungen zu leisten und eine Vergütung, die nicht unter den Gründungsaufwand aufgenommen ist, zu ersetzen.

(2) Wird die Gesellschaft von Gründern durch Einlagen, Sachübernahmen oder Gründungsaufwand vorsätzlich oder aus grober Fahrlässigkeit geschädigt, so sind ihr alle Gründer als Gesamtschuldner zum Ersatz verpflichtet.

(3) Von diesen Verpflichtungen ist ein Gründer befreit, wenn er die die Ersatzpflicht begründenden Tatsachen weder kannte noch bei Anwendung der Sorgfalt eines ordentlichen Geschäftsmannes kennen mußte.

(4) Entsteht der Gesellschaft ein Ausfall, weil ein Aktionär zahlungsunfähig oder unfähig ist, eine Sacheinlage zu leisten, so sind ihr zum Ersatz als Gesamtschuldner die Gründer verpflichtet, welche die Beteiligung des Aktionärs in Kenntnis seiner Zahlungsunfähigkeit oder Leistungsunfähigkeit angenommen haben.

(5) ¹Neben den Gründern sind in gleicher Weise Personen verantwortlich, für deren Rechnung die Gründer Aktien übernommen haben. ²Sie können sich auf ihre eigene Unkenntnis nicht wegen solcher Umstände berufen, die ein

the accuracy and completeness of the information given for the purpose of the formation of the company pertaining to subscription to shares, payment in respect of shares, appropriation of amounts paid in, special benefits, formation expenses, contributions in kind and acquisitions in kind. ²They shall also be also liable for ensuring that an agency designated to accept payments towards the registered share capital (sec. 54 para. 3) is duly qualified to such purpose and that the amounts paid in are unconditionally at the free disposal of the management board. ³Without prejudice to their obligation to compensate for other damage, they shall make any payments which are lacking and reimburse any remuneration which was not included in the formation expenses.

(2) If any of the founders either intentionally or by gross negligence cause damage to the company via contributions, acquisitions in kind or formation expenses, all founders shall be jointly and severally liable to provide the company compensation therefor.

(3) A founder is released from such obligation if he was not actually aware of the facts giving rise to liability, nor should have been aware of such facts had he exercised the care of a prudent businessman.

(4) If the company suffers a loss due to a shareholder being illiquid or unable to make a contribution in kind, those founders who agreed to the shareholder obtaining a shareholding in spite of being aware of his insolvency or inability to make the contribution shall be jointly and severally liable to the company.

(5) ¹Persons for whose account the founders have subscribed to shares shall have the same liability as the founders. ²Those persons cannot appeal to their own ignorance regarding such circumstances that a founder acting for their

für ihre Rechnung handelnder Gründer kannte oder kennen mußte.

§ 47 Verantwortlichkeit anderer Personen neben den Gründern.

Neben den Gründern und den Personen, für deren Rechnung die Gründer Aktien übernommen haben, ist als Gesamtschuldner der Gesellschaft zum Schadenersatz verpflichtet,

1. wer bei Empfang einer Vergütung, die entgegen den Vorschriften nicht in den Gründungsaufwand aufgenommen ist, wußte oder nach den Umständen annehmen mußte, daß die Verheimlichung beabsichtigt oder erfolgt war, oder wer zur Verheimlichung wissentlich mitgewirkt hat;
2. wer im Fall einer vorsätzlichen oder grobfahrlässigen Schädigung der Gesellschaft durch Einlagen oder Sachübernahmen an der Schädigung wissentlich mitgewirkt hat;
3. wer vor Eintragung der Gesellschaft in das Handelsregister oder in den ersten zwei Jahren nach der Eintragung die Aktien öffentlich ankündigt, um sie in den Verkehr einzuführen, wenn er die Unrichtigkeit oder Unvollständigkeit der Angaben, die zum Zwecke der Gründung der Gesellschaft gemacht worden sind (§ 46 Abs. 1), oder die Schädigung der Gesellschaft durch Einlagen oder Sachübernahmen kannte oder bei Anwendung der Sorgfalt eines ordentlichen Geschäftsmannes kennen mußte.

§ 48 Verantwortlichkeit des Vorstands und des Aufsichtsrats.

[1]Mitglieder des Vorstands und des Aufsichtsrats, die bei der Gründung ihre Pflichten verletzen, sind der Gesellschaft zum Ersatz des daraus entstehenden Schadens als Gesamtschuldner verpflichtet; sie sind namentlich dafür verantwortlich, daß eine zur Annah-

account was aware or should have been aware of.

§ 47 Liability of persons other than founders.

In addition to the founders and other persons for whose account the founders have subscribed to shares, the following persons shall be jointly and severally liable to the company for damages:

1. any person when receiving any remuneration which, contrary to the provisions, was not included in the formation expenses and who knew, or who ought to have known under the circumstances, that the concealment thereof was intended or had occurred or who knowingly participated in the concealment thereof;
2. any person who, in case of damage to the company caused intentionally or by gross negligence via contributions or acquisitions in kind, knowingly participated in causing such damage;
3. any person who, before the company is registered in the commercial register or in the first two years following registration, publicly advertises the shares for the purpose of introducing them onto the market if he was actually aware or should have been aware had he exercised the care of a prudent businessman that the information given for the purpose of formation of the company (sec. 46 para. 1) is incorrect or incomplete or that the company will be damaged by contributions or acquisitions in kind.

§ 48 Liability of the management board and the supervisory board.

[1]Members of the management board and the supervisory board who breach their obligations pertaining to the formation of the company shall be jointly and severally liable to the company for any resulting damage; they shall be liable for ensuring that an agency desig-

me von Einzahlungen auf die Aktien bestimmte Stelle (§ 54 Abs. 3) hierzu geeignet ist, und daß die eingezahlten Beträge zur freien Verfügung des Vorstands stehen. ²Für die Sorgfaltspflicht und Verantwortlichkeit der Mitglieder des Vorstands und des Aufsichtsrats bei der Gründung gelten im übrigen §§ 93 und 116 mit Ausnahme von § 93 Abs. 4 Satz 3 und 4 und Abs. 6.

nated to accept payments towards the registered share capital (sec. 54 para. 3) is duly authorized to such purpose and that the amounts paid in are unconditionally at the free disposal of the management board. ²In addition, sec. 93 and sec. 116 with the exception of sec. 93 para. 4 sentences 3 and 4 and para. 6 shall apply to the duty to take due care and the liability of the members of the management board and the supervisory board with regard to the formation of the company.

§ 49 Verantwortlichkeit der Gründungsprüfer.

§ 323 Abs. 1 bis 4 des Handelsgesetzbuchs über die Verantwortlichkeit des Abschlußprüfers gilt sinngemäß.

§ 49 Liability of the formation auditors.

Sec. 323 para. 1 to 4 Commercial Code pertaining to the liability of the auditor of annual accounts shall apply accordingly.

§ 50 Verzicht und Vergleich.

¹Die Gesellschaft kann auf Ersatzansprüche gegen die Gründer, die neben diesen haftenden Personen und gegen die Mitglieder des Vorstands und des Aufsichtsrats (§§ 46 bis 48) erst drei Jahre nach der Eintragung der Gesellschaft in das Handelsregister und nur dann verzichten oder sich über sie vergleichen, wenn die Hauptversammlung zustimmt und nicht eine Minderheit, deren Anteile zusammen den zehnten Teil des Grundkapitals erreichen, zur Niederschrift Widerspruch erhebt. ²Die zeitliche Beschränkung gilt nicht, wenn der Ersatzpflichtige zahlungsunfähig ist und sich zur Abwendung des Insolvenzverfahrens mit seinen Gläubigern vergleicht oder wenn die Ersatzpflicht in einem Insolvenzplan geregelt wird.

§ 50 Waiver and composition.

¹The company may only waive or compromise claims for damages against the founders, any other persons having liability and the members of the management board and the supervisory board (sec. 46 to 48) three years after the company has been registered in the commercial register, and then only if the general meeting grants its consent and no objection is raised in the minutes by a minority of shareholders whose aggregate holding amounts to at least one tenth of the registered share capital. ²The time limit shall not apply if the party liable for the damage is illiquid and enters into a composition with his creditors in order to avert insolvency proceedings or if the liability for damages is regulated in an insolvency plan.

§ 51 Verjährung der Ersatzansprüche.

¹Ersatzansprüche der Gesellschaft nach den §§ 46 bis 48 verjähren in fünf Jahren. ²Die Verjährung beginnt mit der Eintragung der Gesellschaft in das Handelsregister oder, wenn die zum Ersatz verpflichtende Handlung später began-

§ 51 Statute of limitation for damage claims.

¹The company's claims for damages pursuant to sec. 46 to 48 become time-barred after five years. ²The period of limitation commences upon registration of the company in the commercial register or, if the act giving rise to the indem-

gen worden ist, mit der Vornahme der Handlung.

nification was committed later, upon the performance of the act.

§ 52 Nachgründung.

§ 52 Post-formation acquisitions.

(1) ¹Verträge der Gesellschaft mit Gründern oder mit mehr als 10 vom Hundert des Grundkapitals an der Gesellschaft beteiligten Aktionären, nach denen sie vorhandene oder herzustellende Anlagen oder andere Vermögensgegenstände für eine den zehnten Teil des Grundkapitals übersteigende Vergütung erwerben soll, und die in den ersten zwei Jahren seit der Eintragung der Gesellschaft in das Handelsregister geschlossen werden, werden nur mit Zustimmung der Hauptversammlung und durch Eintragung in das Handelsregister wirksam. ²Ohne die Zustimmung der Hauptversammlung oder die Eintragung im Handelsregister sind auch die Rechtshandlungen zu ihrer Ausführung unwirksam.

(1) ¹Contracts concluded in the first two years following the registration of the company in the commercial register by the company and founders or shareholders holding more than ten percent of the registered share capital of the company which stipulate that the company shall acquire existing installations, installations to be constructed or any other assets in return for remuneration amounting to more than one tenth of the registered share capital shall only take effect upon being registered in the commercial register after obtaining the approval of the general meeting. ²Absent such consent of the general meeting and registration, any transaction in execution of such agreements shall be invalid.

(2) ¹Ein Vertrag nach Absatz 1 bedarf der schriftlichen Form, soweit nicht eine andere Form vorgeschrieben ist. ²Er ist von der Einberufung der Hauptversammlung an, die über die Zustimmung beschließen soll, in dem Geschäftsraum der Gesellschaft zur Einsicht der Aktionäre auszulegen. ³Auf Verlangen ist jedem Aktionär unverzüglich eine Abschrift zu erteilen. ⁴Die Verpflichtungen nach den Sätzen 2 und 3 entfallen, wenn der Vertrag für denselben Zeitraum über die Internetseite der Gesellschaft zugänglich ist. ⁵In der Hauptversammlung ist der Vertrag zugänglich zu machen. ⁶Der Vorstand hat ihn zu Beginn der Verhandlung zu erläutern. ⁷Der Niederschrift ist er als Anlage beizufügen.

(2) ¹The written form is required for a contract pursuant to para. 1, unless some other form is prescribed. ²Such contract shall be displayed for inspection by the shareholders at the offices of the company as of the date notice is given of the general meeting which is to resolve on approval therefor. ³A copy shall be supplied without undue delay to each shareholder upon request. ⁴The obligations pursuant to the sentences 2 and 3 shall cease to exist if the contract is accessible during the same period of time on the website of the company. ⁵The contract shall be made accessible at the general meeting. ⁶The management board shall explain the contract at the beginning of proceedings. ⁷The contract shall be attached to the minutes.

(3) ¹Vor der Beschlußfassung der Hauptversammlung hat der Aufsichtsrat den Vertrag zu prüfen und einen schriftlichen Bericht zu erstatten (Nachgründungsbericht). ²Für den Nachgründungsbericht gilt sinngemäß § 32 Abs. 2 und 3 über den Gründungsbericht.

(3) ¹The supervisory board shall inspect the contract and submit a written report (post-formation report) before the resolution is adopted by the general meeting. ²Sec. 32 paras. 2 and 3 pertaining to the formation report shall apply accordingly to the post-formation report.

(4) ¹Außerdem hat vor der Beschlussfassung eine Prüfung durch einen oder mehrere Gründungsprüfer stattzufinden. ²§ 33 Abs. 3 bis 5, §§ 34, 35 über die Gründungsprüfung gelten sinngemäß. ²Unter den Voraussetzungen des § 33a kann von einer Prüfung durch Gründungsprüfer abgesehen werden.

(5) ¹Der Beschluß der Hauptversammlung bedarf einer Mehrheit, die mindestens drei Viertel des bei der Beschlußfassung vertretenen Grundkapitals umfaßt. ²Wird der Vertrag im ersten Jahre nach der Eintragung der Gesellschaft in das Handelsregister geschlossen, so müssen außerdem die Anteile der zustimmenden Mehrheit mindestens ein Viertel des gesamten Grundkapitals erreichen. ³Die Satzung kann an Stelle dieser Mehrheiten größere Kapitalmehrheiten und weitere Erfordernisse bestimmen.

(6) ¹Nach Zustimmung der Hauptversammlung hat der Vorstand den Vertrag zur Eintragung in das Handelsregister anzumelden. ²Der Anmeldung ist der Vertrag mit dem Nachgründungsbericht und dem Bericht der Gründungsprüfer mit den urkundlichen Unterlagen beizufügen. ³Wird nach Absatz 4 Satz 3 von einer externen Gründungsprüfung abgesehen, gilt § 37a entsprechend.

(7) ¹Bestehen gegen die Eintragung Bedenken, weil die Gründungsprüfer erklären oder weil es offensichtlich ist, daß der Nachgründungsbericht unrichtig oder unvollständig ist oder den gesetzlichen Vorschriften nicht entspricht oder daß die für die zu erwerbenden Vermögensgegenstände gewährte Vergütung unangemessen hoch ist, so kann das Gericht die Eintragung ablehnen. ²Enthält die Anmeldung die Erklärung nach § 37a Abs. 1 Satz 1, gilt § 38 Abs. 3 entsprechend.

(8) Einzutragen sind der Tag des Vertragsschlusses und der Zustimmung

(4) ¹In addition, an inspection shall be carried out by one or several formation auditors before the resolution is adopted. ²Sec. 33 paras. 3 to 5, sec. 34, 35 pertaining to the formation audit shall apply accordingly. ²An audit by formation auditors may be omitted if the requirements of sec. 33a are met.

(5) ¹The resolution of the general meeting shall be adopted with a majority of at least three quarters of the registered share capital represented at the adopting of the resolution. ²In addition, if the contract is concluded in the first year following the registration of the company in the commercial register, the shares of the majority granting approval for such contract shall amount to at least one quarter of the entire registered share capital. ³The articles of association may provide for larger capital majorities and for further requirements in place of the above majorities.

(6) ¹After approval has been granted by the general meeting, the management board shall file an application for the contract to be registered in the commercial register. ²The contract together with the post-formation report and the report from the formation auditors and the relevant documents shall be attached to the application. ³If an external formation audit is omitted pursuant to para. 4 sentence 3, sec. 37a shall apply accordingly.

(7) ¹The court may refuse registration if there are any objections to the registration because the formation auditors state or it is apparent that the post-formation report is incorrect, incomplete or fails to comply with the relevant legal provisions or that the consideration granted for the assets which are to be acquired is inappropriately high. ²If the application contains the declaration pursuant to sec. 37a para. 1 sentence 1, sec. 38 para. 3 shall apply accordingly.

(8) The date the contract was concluded, the date the general meeting granted its

der Hauptversammlung sowie der oder die Vertragspartner der Gesellschaft.

(9) Vorstehende Vorschriften gelten nicht, wenn der Erwerb der Vermögensgegenstände im Rahmen der laufenden Geschäfte der Gesellschaft, in der Zwangsvollstreckung oder an der Börse erfolgt.

§ 53 Ersatzansprüche bei der Nachgründung.

¹Für die Nachgründung gelten die §§ 46, 47, 49 bis 51 über die Ersatzansprüche der Gesellschaft sinngemäß. ²An die Stelle der Gründer treten die Mitglieder des Vorstands und des Aufsichtsrats. ³Sie haben die Sorgfalt eines ordentlichen und gewissenhaften Geschäftsleiters anzuwenden. ⁴Soweit Fristen mit der Eintragung der Gesellschaft in das Handelsregister beginnen, tritt an deren Stelle die Eintragung des Vertrags über die Nachgründung.

Dritter Teil. Rechtsverhältnisse der Gesellschaft und der Gesellschafter

§ 53a Gleichbehandlung der Aktionäre.

Aktionäre sind unter gleichen Voraussetzungen gleich zu behandeln.

§ 54 Hauptverpflichtung der Aktionäre.

(1) Die Verpflichtung der Aktionäre zur Leistung der Einlagen wird durch den Ausgabebetrag der Aktien begrenzt.

(2) Soweit nicht in der Satzung Sacheinlagen festgesetzt sind, haben die Aktionäre den Ausgabebetrag der Aktien einzuzahlen.

(3) ¹Der vor der Anmeldung der Gesellschaft eingeforderte Betrag kann nur in gesetzlichen Zahlungsmitteln oder durch Gutschrift auf ein Konto bei einem Kreditinstitut oder einem nach § 53 Abs. 1 Satz 1 oder § 53b Abs. 1 Satz 1

approval and the contractual partners of the company shall be registered.

(9) The above provisions do not apply if the assets are acquired in the company's normal course of business, during enforcement proceedings or on the stock exchange.

§ 53 Post-formation claims for damages.

¹Sec. 46, 47, 49 to 51 concerning the company's claims for damages shall apply accordingly to post-formation acquisitions. ²The members of the management board and the supervisory board shall be substituted for the founders. ³They shall apply the due care of a diligent and conscientious manager. ⁴Where time periods commence upon the registration of the company in the commercial register, the date the post-formation contract is registered shall apply instead of such registration.

Part Three. Legal Relationships of the Company and the Shareholders

§ 53a Equal treatment of shareholders.

Shareholders shall be treated equally under equivalent circumstances.

§ 54 Main obligation of shareholders.

(1) The shareholders' obligation to make the contributions shall be limited by the issue price of the shares.

(2) Unless contributions in kind are stipulated in the articles of association, the shareholders shall pay in the issue price of the shares.

(3) ¹The amount called in before the application for the company to be registered in the commercial register is filed may only be paid in and placed at the free disposal of the management board in legal tender or by being credited to

oder Abs. 7 des Gesetzes über das Kreditwesen tätigen Unternehmen der Gesellschaft oder des Vorstands zu seiner freien Verfügung eingezahlt werden. ²Forderungen des Vorstands aus diesen Einzahlungen gelten als Forderungen der Gesellschaft.

(4) ¹Der Anspruch der Gesellschaft auf Leistung der Einlagen verjährt in zehn Jahren von seiner Entstehung an. ²Wird das Insolvenzverfahren über das Vermögen der Gesellschaft eröffnet, so tritt die Verjährung nicht vor Ablauf von sechs Monaten ab dem Zeitpunkt der Eröffnung ein.

§ 55 Nebenverpflichtungen der Aktionäre.

(1) ¹Ist die Übertragung der Aktien an die Zustimmung der Gesellschaft gebunden, so kann die Satzung Aktionären die Verpflichtung auferlegen, neben den Einlagen auf das Grundkapital wiederkehrende, nicht in Geld bestehende Leistungen zu erbringen. ²Dabei hat sie zu bestimmen, ob die Leistungen entgeltlich oder unentgeltlich zu erbringen sind. ³Die Verpflichtung und der Umfang der Leistungen sind in den Aktien und Zwischenscheinen anzugeben.

(2) Die Satzung kann Vertragsstrafen für den Fall festsetzen, daß die Verpflichtung nicht oder nicht gehörig erfüllt wird.

§ 56 Keine Zeichnung eigener Aktien; Aktienübernahme für Rechnung der Gesellschaft oder durch ein abhängiges oder in Mehrheitsbesitz stehendes Unternehmen.

(1) Die Gesellschaft darf keine eigenen Aktien zeichnen.

(2) ¹Ein abhängiges Unternehmen darf keine Aktien der herrschenden Gesellschaft, ein in Mehrheitsbesitz stehendes

an account maintained by the company or the management board with a credit institution or an enterprise active according to sec. 53 para. 1 sentence 1 or sec. 53b para. 1 sentence 1 or para. 7 Banking Act. ²Claims of the management board concerning such payments are deemed to constitute claims of the company.

(4) ¹The claim of the company to the rendering of the contributions shall become time-barred ten years after the claim has come into being. ²If insolvency proceedings are commenced over the assets of the company, the claim shall not become time-barred during the six months following the commencement of the proceedings.

§ 55 Ancillary duties of shareholders.

(1) ¹If the transfer of shares requires the consent of the company, the articles of association may obligate the shareholders to make recurring contributions not involving the payment of money in addition to their contributions towards the registered share capital. ²The articles of association shall stipulate whether such contributions are to be made in return for consideration or not. ³The obligation and the scope of the contributions shall be stated in the share certificates and interim certificates.

(2) The articles of association may stipulate contractual penalties in the event that such obligation is not, or not duly, met.

§ 56 No subscription of own shares; acquisition of shares on behalf of the company or by a controlled or majority held enterprise.

(1) The company may not subscribe to its own shares.

(2) ¹A controlled enterprise may not acquire shares in the controlling company and a majority-held enterprise may not

Unternehmen keine Aktien der an ihm mit Mehrheit beteiligten Gesellschaft als Gründer oder Zeichner oder in Ausübung eines bei einer bedingten Kapitalerhöhung eingeräumten Umtausch- oder Bezugsrechts übernehmen. ²Ein Verstoß gegen diese Vorschrift macht die Übernahme nicht unwirksam.

(3) ¹Wer als Gründer oder Zeichner oder in Ausübung eines bei einer bedingten Kapitalerhöhung eingeräumten Umtausch- oder Bezugsrechts eine Aktie für Rechnung der Gesellschaft oder eines abhängigen oder in Mehrheitsbesitz stehenden Unternehmens übernommen hat, kann sich nicht darauf berufen, daß er die Aktie nicht für eigene Rechnung übernommen hat. ²Er haftet ohne Rücksicht auf Vereinbarungen mit der Gesellschaft oder dem abhängigen oder in Mehrheitsbesitz stehenden Unternehmen auf die volle Einlage. ³Bevor er die Aktie für eigene Rechnung übernommen hat, stehen ihm keine Rechte aus der Aktie zu.

(4) ¹Werden bei einer Kapitalerhöhung Aktien unter Verletzung der Absätze 1 oder 2 gezeichnet, so haftet auch jedes Vorstandsmitglied der Gesellschaft auf die volle Einlage. ²Dies gilt nicht, wenn das Vorstandsmitglied beweist, daß es kein Verschulden trifft.

§ 57 Keine Rückgewähr, keine Verzinsung der Einlagen.

(1) ¹Den Aktionären dürfen die Einlagen nicht zurückgewährt werden. ²Als Rückgewähr gilt nicht die Zahlung des Erwerbspreises beim zulässigen Erwerb eigener Aktien. ³Satz 1 gilt nicht bei Leistungen, die bei Bestehen eines Beherrschungs- oder Gewinnabführungsvertrags (§ 291) erfolgen oder durch einen vollwertigen Gegenleistungs- oder Rückgewähranspruch gegen den Aktionär gedeckt sind. ⁴Satz 1 ist zudem nicht anzuwenden auf die Rückgewähr eines Aktionärsdarlehens und Leistungen auf Forderungen aus Rechtshand-

acquire shares in its majority holding company as a founder or subscriber or by exercising a conversion or subscription right granted in connection with a contingent capital increase. ²Failure to comply with this provision shall not render the acquisition invalid.

(3) ¹Anyone acquiring a share for the account of the company, a controlled enterprise or a majority held enterprise, whether as a founder or subscriber or by exercising a conversion or subscription right granted in connection with a contingent capital increase, shall not be able to plead that he did not acquire the share for his own account. ²He is liable for the full contribution, regardless of any agreements with the company, the controlled enterprise or the majority held enterprise. ³He is not be entitled to any rights arising from the share until he has acquired the share for his own account.

(4) ¹If, in the case of a capital increase, shares are subscribed to in violation of paras. 1 or 2, each member of the management board of the company shall also be liable for the full contribution. ²The above does not apply if the member of the management board proves that he was not at fault.

§ 57 No repayment of contributions, no interest on contributions.

(1) ¹Contributions may not be repaid to the shareholders. ²Payment of the purchase price in the case of a permitted acquisition by the company of its own shares shall not constitute a repayment. ³Sentence 1 shall not apply to performances which are made while a domination or profit transfer agreement (sec. 291) is in existence or which are matched by an unimpaired claim against the shareholder for consideration or for return. Sentence 1 shall also not apply to the repayment of a shareholder loan and to performances on claims result-

lungen, die einem Aktionärsdarlehen wirtschaftlich entsprechen.

(2) Den Aktionären dürfen Zinsen weder zugesagt noch ausgezahlt werden.

(3) Vor Auflösung der Gesellschaft darf unter die Aktionäre nur der Bilanzgewinn verteilt werden.

§ 58 Verwendung des Jahresüberschusses.

(1) ¹Die Satzung kann nur für den Fall, daß die Hauptversammlung den Jahresabschluß feststellt, bestimmen, daß Beträge aus dem Jahresüberschuß in andere Gewinnrücklagen einzustellen sind. ²Auf Grund einer solchen Satzungsbestimmung kann höchstens die Hälfte des Jahresüberschusses in andere Gewinnrücklagen eingestellt werden. ³Dabei sind Beträge, die in die gesetzliche Rücklage einzustellen sind, und ein Verlustvortrag vorab vom Jahresüberschuß abzuziehen.

(2) ¹Stellen Vorstand und Aufsichtsrat den Jahresabschluß fest, so können sie einen Teil des Jahresüberschusses, höchstens jedoch die Hälfte, in andere Gewinnrücklagen einstellen. ²Die Satzung kann Vorstand und Aufsichtsrat zur Einstellung eines größeren oder kleineren Teils des Jahresüberschusses ermächtigen. ³Auf Grund einer solchen Satzungsbestimmung dürfen Vorstand und Aufsichtsrat keine Beträge in andere Gewinnrücklagen einstellen, wenn die anderen Gewinnrücklagen die Hälfte des Grundkapitals übersteigen oder soweit sie nach der Einstellung die Hälfte übersteigen würden. ⁴Absatz 1 Satz 3 gilt sinngemäß.

(2a) ¹Unbeschadet der Absätze 1 und 2 können Vorstand und Aufsichtsrat den Eigenkapitalanteil von Wertaufholungen bei Vermögensgegenständen des Anlage- und Umlaufvermögens in an-

ing from legal acts which correspond in economic terms to a shareholder loan.

(2) Interest may neither be promised nor paid to shareholders.

(3) Only the balance sheet profit may be distributed among shareholders prior to the dissolution of the company.

§ 58 Use of annual net income.

(1) ¹The articles of association may stipulate that amounts from the annual net income are to be allocated to other revenue reserves only in the event that the general meeting formally approves the annual financial statements. ²At most half of the annual net income may be allocated to other revenue reserves on the basis of such a provision in the articles of association. ³Amounts which are to be allocated to the statutory reserve and any loss carried forward shall be deducted from the balance sheet profit for the year beforehand.

(2) ¹If the annual financial statements are formally approved by the management board and the supervisory board, they may allocate part of the annual net income, but at the most half thereof, to other revenue reserves. ²The articles of association may authorize the management board and the supervisory board to allocate a larger or smaller part of the annual net income to revenue reserves. ³The management board and supervisory board may not allocate any amounts to other revenue reserves on the basis of such a provision in the articles of association if the other revenue reserves amount to more than half of the registered share capital or to such an extent that they would amount to more than half thereof after the allocation is made. ⁴Para. 1 sentence 3 applies accordingly.

(2a) ¹Without prejudice to paras. 1 and 2, the management board and the supervisory board may allocate to other revenue reserves the capitalized part of restorations in value of fixed assets and

dere Gewinnrücklagen einstellen. ²Der Betrag dieser Rücklagen ist in der Bilanz gesondert auszuweisen; er kann auch im Anhang angegeben werden.

(3) ¹Die Hauptversammlung kann im Beschluss über die Verwendung des Bilanzgewinns weitere Beträge in Gewinnrücklagen einstellen oder als Gewinn vortragen. ²Sie kann ferner, wenn die Satzung sie hierzu ermächtigt, auch eine andere Verwendung als nach Satz 1 oder als die Verteilung unter die Aktionäre beschließen.

(4) Die Aktionäre haben Anspruch auf den Bilanzgewinn, soweit er nicht nach Gesetz oder Satzung, durch Hauptversammlungsbeschluss nach Absatz 3 oder als zusätzlicher Aufwand auf Grund des Gewinnverwendungsbeschlusses von der Verteilung unter die Aktionäre ausgeschlossen ist.

(5) Sofern die Satzung dies vorsieht, kann die Hauptversammlung auch eine Sachausschüttung beschließen.

§ 59 Abschlagszahlung auf den Bilanzgewinn.

(1) Die Satzung kann den Vorstand ermächtigen, nach Ablauf des Geschäftsjahrs auf den voraussichtlichen Bilanzgewinn einen Abschlag an die Aktionäre zu zahlen.

(2) ¹Der Vorstand darf einen Abschlag nur zahlen, wenn ein vorläufiger Abschluß für das vergangene Geschäftsjahr einen Jahresüberschuß ergibt. ²Als Abschlag darf höchstens die Hälfte des Betrags gezahlt werden, der von dem Jahresüberschuß nach Abzug der Beträge verbleibt, die nach Gesetz oder Satzung in Gewinnrücklagen einzustellen sind. ³Außerdem darf der Abschlag nicht die Hälfte des vorjährigen Bilanzgewinns übersteigen.

current assets ²The amount of such reserves shall be shown separately in the balance sheet; but may also be stated in the notes.

(3) ¹The general meeting may allocate in the resolution on the appropriation of balance sheet profit further amounts to revenue reserves or carry forward such amounts as profit. ²In addition, if permitted to do so by the articles of association, the general meeting may also resolve on appropriation other than stipulated in sentence 1 or other than by distribution to the shareholders.

(4) The shareholders are entitled to the balance sheet profit to the extent that such profit is not excluded from distribution to shareholders by law, by the articles of association, by a resolution of the general meeting pursuant to para. 3 or as an additional expense pursuant to the resolution on the appropriation of profits.

(5) If so provided in the articles of association, the general meeting may also adopt a resolution stipulating a distribution in kind.

§ 59 Advance payment of balance sheet profit.

(1) The articles of association may authorize the management board to pay the shareholders an advance payment on account of the expected balance sheet profit after the end of the fiscal year.

(2) ¹The management board may only pay out an advance payment if preliminary financial statements for the preceding fiscal year show an annual net income for the year. ²An advance payment shall amount at most to half the amount remaining from the annual net income after deducting therefrom the amounts which are to be allocated to the revenue reserves pursuant to the law or the articles of association. ³In addition, the advance payment may not exceed half of the balance sheet profit from the preceding year.

(3) Die Zahlung eines Abschlags bedarf der Zustimmung des Aufsichtsrats.

(3) The consent of the supervisory board is required before an advance payment is made.

§ 60 Gewinnverteilung.

(1) Die Anteile der Aktionäre am Gewinn bestimmen sich nach ihren Anteilen am Grundkapital.

(2) ¹Sind die Einlagen auf das Grundkapital nicht auf alle Aktien in demselben Verhältnis geleistet, so erhalten die Aktionäre aus dem verteilbaren Gewinn vorweg einen Betrag von vier vom Hundert der geleisteten Einlagen. ²Reicht der Gewinn dazu nicht aus, so bestimmt sich der Betrag nach einem entsprechend niedrigeren Satz. ³Einlagen, die im Laufe des Geschäftsjahrs geleistet wurden, werden nach dem Verhältnis der Zeit berücksichtigt, die seit der Leistung verstrichen ist.

(3) Die Satzung kann eine andere Art der Gewinnverteilung bestimmen.

§ 61 Vergütung von Nebenleistungen.

Für wiederkehrende Leistungen, zu denen Aktionäre nach der Satzung neben den Einlagen auf das Grundkapital verpflichtet sind, darf eine den Wert der Leistungen nicht übersteigende Vergütung ohne Rücksicht darauf gezahlt werden, ob ein Bilanzgewinn ausgewiesen wird.

§ 62 Haftung der Aktionäre beim Empfang verbotener Leistungen.

(1) ¹Die Aktionäre haben der Gesellschaft Leistungen, die sie entgegen den Vorschriften dieses Gesetzes von ihr empfangen haben, zurückzugewähren. ²Haben sie Beträge als Gewinnanteile bezogen, so besteht die Verpflichtung nur, wenn sie wußten oder infolge von Fahrlässigkeit nicht wußten, daß sie zum Bezuge nicht berechtigt waren.

§ 60 Distribution of profits.

(1) The shareholders' shares in the profits are determined according to the parts they hold in the registered share capital.

(2) ¹If the contributions to the registered share capital have not been made in the same ratio for all shares, the shareholders shall initially receive from the distributable profit an amount equal to four percent of the contributions made. ²If the profit is not sufficient for such payments to be made, the amount shall be determined on the basis of a correspondingly lower rate. ³Contributions made in the course of the fiscal year shall be taken into consideration pro rata according to the time which has passed since the contribution was made.

(3) The articles of association may determine another method for the distribution of profits.

§ 61 Consideration for ancillary obligations.

Consideration may be paid for recurring obligations which shareholders are obligated to render pursuant to the articles of association in addition to the contributions to the registered share capital irrespective of whether or not there is a balance sheet profit, provided such consideration does not exceed the value of such recurring contributions.

§ 62 Liability of shareholders who receive prohibited payments.

(1) ¹The shareholders shall repay to the company any payments they have received from the company contrary to the provisions of this Act. ²If they have received payments by way of dividends, the above obligation shall only apply if they knew or as a result of negligence did not know that they were not entitled to such receipt.

(2) ¹Der Anspruch der Gesellschaft kann auch von den Gläubigern der Gesellschaft geltend gemacht werden, soweit sie von dieser keine Befriedigung erlangen können. ²Ist über das Vermögen der Gesellschaft das Insolvenzverfahren eröffnet, so übt während dessen Dauer der Insolvenzverwalter oder der Sachwalter das Recht der Gesellschaftsgläubiger gegen die Aktionäre aus.

(3) Die Ansprüche nach diesen Vorschriften verjähren in zehn Jahren seit dem Empfang der Leistung. ²§ 54 Abs. 4 Satz 2 findet entsprechende Anwendung.

§ 63 Folgen nicht rechtzeitiger Einzahlung.

(1) ¹Die Aktionäre haben die Einlagen nach Aufforderung durch den Vorstand einzuzahlen. ²Die Aufforderung ist, wenn die Satzung nichts anderes bestimmt, in den Gesellschaftsblättern bekanntzumachen.

(2) ¹Aktionäre, die den eingeforderten Betrag nicht rechtzeitig einzahlen, haben ihn vom Eintritt der Fälligkeit an mit fünf vom Hundert für das Jahr zu verzinsen. ²Die Geltendmachung eines weiteren Schadens ist nicht ausgeschlossen.

(3) Für den Fall nicht rechtzeitiger Einzahlung kann die Satzung Vertragsstrafen festsetzen.

§ 64 Ausschluß säumiger Aktionäre.

(1) Aktionären, die den eingeforderten Betrag nicht rechtzeitig einzahlen, kann eine Nachfrist mit der Androhung gesetzt werden, daß sie nach Fristablauf ihrer Aktien und der geleisteten Einzahlungen für verlustig erklärt werden.

(2) ¹Die Nachfrist muß dreimal in den Gesellschaftsblättern bekanntgemacht werden. ²Die erste Bekanntmachung

(2) ¹The claim of the company can also be asserted by creditors of the company to the extent that said creditors are unable to obtain settlement of their claims from the company. ²If insolvency proceedings have been instituted against the company's assets, the insolvency administrator or the custodian shall exercise the rights of the company's creditors against the shareholders for the duration of such insolvency proceedings.

(3) ¹The claims pursuant to the above provisions shall become time-barred ten years after receipt of the payment. ²Sec. 54 para. 4 sentence 2 shall apply accordingly.

§ 63 Consequences of late payments.

(1) ¹The shareholders shall pay the contributions after being requested to do so by the management board. ²Unless stipulated otherwise in the articles of association, the demand for payment shall be published in the company's designated journals.

(2) ¹Shareholders who fail to pay the amount called in on time shall pay interest thereon at a rate of five percent per annum with effect from the due date. ²Claims may be made for further damages.

(3) The articles of association may stipulate contractual penalties in the event of late payment.

§ 64 Expulsion of defaulting shareholders.

(1) Shareholders who fail to pay the amount called in on time may be granted a grace period accompanied by a warning that their shares and any contributions already made shall be declared forfeited upon the expiration of such period.

(2) ¹The grace period shall be published three times in the company's designated journals. ²The first announcement shall

muß mindestens drei Monate, die letzte mindestens einen Monat vor Fristablauf ergehen. ³Zwischen den einzelnen Bekanntmachungen muß ein Zeitraum von mindestens drei Wochen liegen. ⁴Ist die Übertragung der Aktien an die Zustimmung der Gesellschaft gebunden, so genügt an Stelle der öffentlichen Bekanntmachungen die einmalige Einzelaufforderung an die säumigen Aktionäre; dabei muß eine Nachfrist gewährt werden, die mindestens einen Monat seit dem Empfang der Aufforderung beträgt.

(3) ¹Aktionäre, die den eingeforderten Betrag trotzdem nicht zahlen, werden durch Bekanntmachung in den Gesellschaftsblättern ihrer Aktien und der geleisteten Einzahlungen zugunsten der Gesellschaft für verlustig erklärt. ²In der Bekanntmachung sind die für verlustig erklärten Aktien mit ihren Unterscheidungsmerkmalen anzugeben.

(4) ¹An Stelle der alten Urkunden werden neue ausgegeben; diese haben außer den geleisteten Teilzahlungen den rückständigen Betrag anzugeben. ²Für den Ausfall der Gesellschaft an diesem Betrag oder an den später eingeforderten Beträgen haftet ihr der ausgeschlossene Aktionär.

§ 65 Zahlungspflicht der Vormänner.

(1) ¹Jeder im Aktienregister verzeichnete Vormann des ausgeschlossenen Aktionärs ist der Gesellschaft zur Zahlung des rückständigen Betrags verpflichtet, soweit dieser von seinen Nachmännern nicht zu erlangen ist. ²Von der Zahlungsaufforderung an einen früheren Aktionär hat die Gesellschaft seinen unmittelbaren Vormann zu benachrichtigen. ³Daß die Zahlung nicht zu erlangen ist, wird vermutet, wenn sie nicht innerhalb eines Monats seit der Zahlungsaufforderung und der Benachrichtigung des Vormanns eingegangen ist. ⁴Gegen Zahlung des rückständigen

be published at least three months and the last at least one month before the expiration date of the grace period. ³There shall be a period of at least three weeks between the individual announcements. ⁴If the company's consent is required for the transfer of the shares, it shall suffice for a single individual demand to be made to the defaulting shareholders instead of a public announcement; in this case a grace period of at least one month following receipt of the demand shall be granted.

(3) ¹Shareholders who nevertheless fail to pay the amount called in shall be declared by announcement in the company's designated journals to have forfeited their shares and the contributions made, for the benefit of the company. ²Such announcement shall specify the forfeited shares and the distinguishing features thereof.

(4) ¹New certificates shall be issued in place of the old and shall specify the contribution in arrears as well as the partial payments which have been made. ²The expelled shareholder shall be liable to the company for the loss of such amount or of the amounts called in at a later date.

§ 65 Payment obligations of predecessors.

(1) ¹Each predecessor of the expelled shareholder listed in the share register shall be obligated to pay the company the contribution in arrears to the extent that his successors are unable to do so. ²The company shall notify the immediate predecessor of any demand for payment made to a previous shareholder. ³It shall be assumed that payment cannot be obtained if such payment has not been received within one month from the date payment was requested and the predecessor notified. ⁴The new share certificate shall be issued in return for payment of the contribution in arrears.

Betrags wird die neue Urkunde ausgehändigt.

(2) ¹Jeder Vormann ist nur zur Zahlung der Beträge verpflichtet, die binnen zwei Jahren eingefordert werden. ²Die Frist beginnt mit dem Tage, an dem die Übertragung der Aktie zum Aktienregister der Gesellschaft angemeldet wird.

(3) ¹Ist die Zahlung des rückständigen Betrags von Vormännern nicht zu erlangen, so hat die Gesellschaft die Aktie unverzüglich zum Börsenpreis und beim Fehlen eines Börsenpreises durch öffentliche Versteigerung zu verkaufen. ²Ist von der Versteigerung am Sitz der Gesellschaft kein angemessener Erfolg zu erwarten, so ist die Aktie an einem geeigneten Ort zu verkaufen. ³Zeit, Ort und Gegenstand der Versteigerung sind öffentlich bekanntzumachen. ⁴Der ausgeschlossene Aktionär und seine Vormänner sind besonders zu benachrichtigen; die Benachrichtigung kann unterbleiben, wenn sie untunlich ist. ⁵Bekanntmachung und Benachrichtigung müssen mindestens zwei Wochen vor der Versteigerung ergehen.

§ 66 Keine Befreiung der Aktionäre von ihren Leistungspflichten.

(1) ¹Die Aktionäre und ihre Vormänner können von ihren Leistungspflichten nach den §§ 54 und 65 nicht befreit werden. ²Gegen eine Forderung der Gesellschaft nach den §§ 54 und 65 ist die Aufrechnung nicht zulässig.

(2) Absatz 1 gilt entsprechend für die Verpflichtung zur Rückgewähr von Leistungen, die entgegen den Vorschriften dieses Gesetzes empfangen sind, für die Ausfallhaftung des ausgeschlossenen Aktionärs sowie für die Schadenersatzpflicht des Aktionärs wegen nicht gehöriger Leistung einer Sacheinlage.

(3) Durch eine ordentliche Kapitalherabsetzung oder durch eine Kapitalherabsetzung durch Einziehung von

(2) ¹Each predecessor shall only be obligated to pay those amounts which are called in within a period of two years. ²Such period shall commence on the day on which application was made for the transfer of the share to be entered in the company's share register.

(3) ¹If payment of the contribution in arrears cannot be obtained from the predecessors, the company shall without undue delay sell the share at the stock exchange price and, in the absence of a stock exchange price, by public auction. ²If a reasonably successful outcome is not to be expected from an auction at the place where the company has its registered office, the share shall be sold at a suitable location. ³A public announcement shall be made stating the time, place and object of the auction. ⁴The expelled shareholder and his predecessors shall be notified separately; such notification need not be made if impracticable. ⁵The above announcement and notification shall be made at least two weeks prior to the auction.

§ 66 No release of shareholders from obligations to make contributions.

(1) ¹The shareholders and their predecessors may not be released from their obligations to render contributions pursuant to sec. 54 and 65. ²A set-off against a claim to which the company is entitled pursuant to sec. 54 and 65 may not be made.

(2) Para. 1 shall apply accordingly to the obligation to repay payments which have been received contrary to the provisions of this Act, to the expelled shareholder's contingent liability and to the shareholder's obligation to pay damages resulting from failure to make a contribution in kind correctly.

(3) The shareholders may be released from the obligation to render contributions on account of an ordinary capital

Aktien können die Aktionäre von der Verpflichtung zur Leistung von Einlagen befreit werden, durch eine ordentliche Kapitalherabsetzung jedoch höchstens in Höhe des Betrags, um den das Grundkapital herabgesetzt worden ist.

§ 67 Eintragung im Aktienregister.

(1) ¹Namensaktien sind unabhängig von einer Verbriefung unter Angabe des Namens, Geburtsdatums und der Adresse des Aktionärs sowie der Stückzahl oder der Aktiennummer und bei Nennbetragsaktien des Betrags in das Aktienregister der Gesellschaft einzutragen. ²Der Aktionär ist verpflichtet, der Gesellschaft die Angaben nach Satz 1 mitzuteilen. ³Die Satzung kann Näheres dazu bestimmen, unter welchen Voraussetzungen Eintragungen im eigenen Namen für Aktien, die einem anderen gehören, zulässig sind. ⁴Aktien, die zu einem inländischen, EU- oder ausländischen Investmentvermögen nach dem Kapitalanlagegesetzbuch gehören, dessen Anteile oder Aktien nicht ausschließlich von professionellen und semiprofessionellen Anlegern gehalten werden, gelten als , Aktien des inländischen, EU- oder ausländischen Investmentvermögens, auch wenn sie im Miteigentum der Anleger stehen; verfügt das Investmentvermögen über keine eigene Rechtspersönlichkeit, gelten sie als Aktien der Verwaltungsgesellschaft des Investmentvermögens.

(2) ¹Im Verhältnis zur Gesellschaft gilt als Aktionär nur, wer als solcher im Aktienregister eingetragen ist. ²Jedoch bestehen Stimmrechte aus Eintragungen nicht, die eine nach Absatz 1 Satz 3 bestimmte satzungsmäßige Höchstgrenze überschreiten oder hinsichtlich derer eine satzungsmäßige Pflicht zur Offenlegung, dass die Aktien einem anderen gehören, nicht erfüllt wird. ³Ferner bestehen Stimmrechte aus Aktien nicht, solange ein Auskunftsverlangen

reduction or a capital reduction involving the redemption of shares, but in the case of an ordinary capital reduction the amount of such release may not exceed the amount by which the registered share capital has been reduced.

§ 67 Entry in share register.

(1) ¹Registered shares shall be entered in the company's share register, regardless of their securitization, where the name, date of birth and address of the shareholder , the number of shares held or the identification number of the share and, in the case of par value shares, the par value thereof shall be stated. ²The shareholder shall disclose to the company the information pursuant to sentence 1. ³The articles of association may specify in more detail the prerequisites under which registrations in one's own name for shares which belong to someone else are permitted. ⁴Shares which belong to a domestic, EU or foreign financial investment estate pursuant to the (capital) investment code (Kapitalanlagegesetzbuch-KAGB), whose shares are not exclusively held by professional or semiprofessional investors , shall be deemed to be shares of the domestic, EU or foreign financial investment estate even if they are co-owned by the investors; if the financial investment estate is not a legal person, such shares shall be deemed to be shares of the management company of the financial investment estate.

(2) ¹In relation to the company, only those persons who are registered in the share register shall be deemed to be shareholders. ²However, such voting rights arising from registrations which exceed an upper limit set forth in the articles of association pursuant to para. 1 sentence 3 or in respect of which a duty set forth in the articles of association to disclose that the shares belong to someone else is not fulfilled shall be suspended. ³Further, voting rights of shares shall

gemäß Absatz 4 Satz 2 oder Satz 3 nach Fristablauf nicht erfüllt ist.

(3) Geht die Namensaktie auf einen anderen über, so erfolgen Löschung und Neueintragung im Aktienregister auf Mitteilung und Nachweis.

(4) ¹Die bei Übertragung oder Verwahrung von Namensaktien mitwirkenden Kreditinstitute sind verpflichtet, der Gesellschaft die für die Führung des Aktienregisters erforderlichen Angaben gegen Erstattung der notwendigen Kosten zu übermitteln. ²Der Eingetragene hat der Gesellschaft auf ihr Verlangen innerhalb einer angemessenen Frist mitzuteilen, inwieweit ihm die Aktien, als deren Inhaber er im Aktienregister eingetragen ist, auch gehören; soweit dies nicht der Fall ist, hat er die in Absatz 1 Satz 1 genannten Angaben zu demjenigen zu übermitteln, für den er die Aktien hält. ³Dies gilt entsprechend für denjenigen, dessen Daten nach Satz 2 oder diesem Satz übermittelt werden. ⁴Absatz 1 Satz 4 gilt entsprechend; für die Kostentragung gilt Satz 1. ⁵Wird der Inhaber von Namensaktien nicht in das Aktienregister eingetragen, so ist das depotführende Institut auf Verlangen der Gesellschaft verpflichtet, sich gegen Erstattung der notwendigen Kosten durch die Gesellschaft an dessen Stelle gesondert in das Aktienregister eintragen zu lassen. ⁶§ 125 Abs. 5 gilt entsprechend. ⁷Wird ein Kreditinstitut im Rahmen eines Übertragungsvorgangs von Namensaktien nur vorübergehend gesondert in das Aktienregister eingetragen, so löst diese Eintragung keine Pflichten infolge des Absatzes 2 und nach § 128 aus und führt nicht zur Anwendung von satzungsmäßigen Beschränkungen nach Absatz 1 Satz 3.

(5) ¹Ist jemand nach Ansicht der Gesellschaft zu Unrecht als Aktionär in das Aktienregister eingetragen worden, so

be suspended so long as a request for information pursuant to para. 4 sentence 2 or sentence 3 is not fulfilled after the time limit has expired.

(3) If the registered share is transferred to another person, the deletion and renewed entry in the share register shall be effected upon the submission of notification and evidence to this effect.

(4) ¹Credit institutions involved in the transfer or custody of registered shares shall be obligated to provide the company with the details required for entry in the share register in return for payment of the necessary costs. ² The registered person shall disclose to the company upon its request within an adequate period of time the extent to which the shares registered in the share register in his name are actually owned by him; so long as this is not the case, he shall communicate the information specified in para. 1 sentence 1 concerning the person for which he holds the shares. ³This shall apply to anyone whose information is communicated pursuant to sentence 2 or this sentence. ⁴Para. 1 sentence 4 shall apply accordingly; sentence 1 shall apply to the bearing of costs. ⁵If the holder of registered shares is not registered in the share register, the depositary credit institution shall, upon request by the company, cause itself to be registered separately in his place in the share register against reimbursement of necessary costs. ⁶Sec. 125 para. 5 shall apply accordingly. ⁷If a credit institution is only temporarily registered separately in the share register in the context of a transfer of registered shares, this registration shall not give rise to obligations pursuant to para. 2 and sec. 128 and shall not result in the application of restrictions set forth in the articles of association pursuant to para. 1 sentence 3.

(5) ¹If, in the opinion of the company, someone has been wrongfully entered as a shareholder in the share register,

kann die Gesellschaft die Eintragung nur löschen, wenn sie vorher die Beteiligten von der beabsichtigten Löschung benachrichtigt und ihnen eine angemessene Frist zur Geltendmachung eines Widerspruchs gesetzt hat. [2]Widerspricht ein Beteiligter innerhalb der Frist, so hat die Löschung zu unterbleiben.

(6) [1]Der Aktionär kann von der Gesellschaft Auskunft über die zu seiner Person in das Aktienregister eingetragenen Daten verlangen. [2]Bei nichtbörsennotierten Gesellschaften kann die Satzung Weiteres bestimmen. [3]Die Gesellschaft darf die Registerdaten sowie die nach Absatz 4 Satz 2 und 3 mitgeteilten Daten für ihre Aufgaben im Verhältnis zu den Aktionären verwenden. [4]Zur Werbung für das Unternehmen darf sie die Daten nur verwenden, soweit der Aktionär nicht widerspricht. [5]Die Aktionäre sind in angemessener Weise über ihr Widerspruchsrecht zu informieren.

(7) Diese Vorschriften gelten sinngemäß für Zwischenscheine.

§ 68 Übertragung von Namensaktien. Vinkulierung.

(1) [1]Namensaktien können auch durch Indossament übertragen werden. [2]Für die Form des Indossaments, den Rechtsausweis des Inhabers und seine Verpflichtung zur Herausgabe gelten sinngemäß Artikel 12, 13 und 16 des Wechselgesetzes.

(2) [1]Die Satzung kann die Übertragung an die Zustimmung der Gesellschaft binden. [2]Die Zustimmung erteilt der Vorstand. [3]Die Satzung kann jedoch bestimmen, daß der Aufsichtsrat oder die Hauptversammlung über die Erteilung der Zustimmung beschließt. [4]Die Satzung kann die Gründe bestimmen, aus denen die Zustimmung verweigert werden darf.

(3) Bei Übertragung durch Indossament ist die Gesellschaft verpflichtet, die

the company may only delete the entry after first informing the persons concerned of the intended deletion and granting them an appropriate period in which to file an objection. [2]If one of the persons concerned objects within such period, the deletion may not be made.

(6) [1]The shareholder may demand information from the company as to what data relating to his person is entered in the share register. [2]In the case of unlisted companies, the articles of association may stipulate further provisions. [3]The company may use the data in the share register as well as the information disclosed pursuant to para. 4 sentences 2 and 3 in connection with its duties vis-à-vis the shareholders. [4]It may only use such data for the purposes of advertising the enterprise if the shareholder does not object. [5]The shareholders shall be given reasonable notice as to their right to object.

(7) The above provisions shall apply accordingly to interim certificates.

§ 68 Transfer of registered shares. Restrictions on transferability.

(1) [1]Registered shares may also be transferred via endorsement. [2]Art. 12, 13 and 16 of the Bills of Exchange Act shall apply accordingly to the form of the endorsement, the legal title of the holder and the holder's obligation to surrender the share.

(2) [1]The articles of association may stipulate that the company's consent is required for the transfer of the share. [2]Consent shall be granted by the management board. [3]The articles of association may stipulate, however, that the supervisory board or the general meeting is to resolve on the granting of consent. [4]The articles of association may stipulate the reasons for which consent may be withheld.

(3) In the event of a transfer by endorsement, the company shall be obligated to

Ordnungsmäßigkeit der Reihe der Indossamente, nicht aber die Unterschriften zu prüfen.

(4) Diese Vorschriften gelten sinngemäß für Zwischenscheine.

§ 69 Rechtsgemeinschaft an einer Aktie.

(1) Steht eine Aktie mehreren Berechtigten zu, so können sie die Rechte aus der Aktie nur durch einen gemeinschaftlichen Vertreter ausüben.

(2) Für die Leistungen auf die Aktie haften sie als Gesamtschuldner.

(3) [1]Hat die Gesellschaft eine Willenserklärung dem Aktionär gegenüber abzugeben, so genügt, wenn die Berechtigten der Gesellschaft keinen gemeinschaftlichen Vertreter benannt haben, die Abgabe der Erklärung gegenüber einem Berechtigten. [2]Bei mehreren Erben eines Aktionärs gilt dies nur für Willenserklärungen, die nach Ablauf eines Monats seit dem Anfall der Erbschaft abgegeben werden.

§ 70 Berechnung der Aktienbesitzzeit.

[1]Ist die Ausübung von Rechten aus der Aktie davon abhängig, daß der Aktionär während eines bestimmten Zeitraums Inhaber der Aktie gewesen ist, so steht dem Eigentum ein Anspruch auf Übereignung gegen ein Kreditinstitut, Finanzdienstleistungsinstitut oder ein nach § 53 Abs. 1 Satz 1 oder § 53b Abs. 1 Satz 1 oder Abs. 7 des Gesetzes über das Kreditwesen tätiges Unternehmen gleich. [2]Die Eigentumszeit eines Rechtsvorgängers wird dem Aktionär zugerechnet, wenn er die Aktie unentgeltlich, von seinem Treuhänder, als Gesamtrechtsnachfolger, bei Auseinandersetzung einer Gemeinschaft oder bei einer Bestandsübertragung nach § 13 des Versicherungsaufsichtsgesetzes oder § 14 des Gesetzes über Bausparkassen erworben hat.

check the properness of the sequence of endorsements but need not check signatures.

(4) The above provisions shall apply accordingly to interim certificates.

§ 69 Co-ownership of a share.

(1) If more than one person is entitled to a share, the rights arising from the share may only be exercised by a common representative.

(2) They shall be jointly and severally liable for the obligations in respect of the share.

(3) [1]If the company is to submit a declaration of intent to the shareholder, it shall suffice for the declaration to be submitted to one of the persons entitled to the share if such persons have failed to name a common representative to the company. [2]If a shareholder has several heirs, the above shall only apply to declarations of intent made after the expiration of one month following the succession to the inheritance.

§ 70 Calculation of the period of share ownership.

[1]If the shareholder is required to have held the share for a certain period before being able to exercise the rights arising therefrom, a claim to assignment against a credit institution, a financial services institution or an enterprise acting pursuant to sec. 53 para. 1 sentence 1 or sec. 53b para. 1 sentence 1 or para. 7 of the Banking Act shall be deemed equivalent to ownership. [2]The period of ownership of a legal predecessor shall be attributed to a shareholder if he acquired the share free of charge from his trustee, as universal successor, upon severance of co-ownership or as a result of a transfer of assets pursuant to sec. 14 of the Insurance Supervisory Act or sec. 14 of the Savings and Loan Association Act.

§ 71 Erwerb eigener Aktien.

(1) ¹Die Gesellschaft darf eigene Aktien nur erwerben,

1. wenn der Erwerb notwendig ist, um einen schweren, unmittelbar bevorstehenden Schaden von der Gesellschaft abzuwenden,
2. wenn die Aktien Personen, die im Arbeitsverhältnis zu der Gesellschaft oder einem mit ihr verbundenen Unternehmen stehen oder standen, zum Erwerb angeboten werden sollen,
3. wenn der Erwerb geschieht, um Aktionäre nach § 305 Abs. 2, § 320b oder nach § 29 Abs. 1, § 125 Satz 1 in Verbindung mit § 29 Abs. 1, § 207 Abs. 1 Satz 1 des Umwandlungsgesetzes abzufinden,
4. wenn der Erwerb unentgeltlich geschieht oder ein Kreditinstitut mit dem Erwerb eine Einkaufskommission ausführt,
5. durch Gesamtrechtsnachfolge,
6. auf Grund eines Beschlusses der Hauptversammlung zur Einziehung nach den Vorschriften über die Herabsetzung des Grundkapitals,
7. wenn sie ein Kreditinstitut, Finanzdienstleistungsinstitut oder Finanzunternehmen ist, aufgrund eines Beschlusses der Hauptversammlung zum Zwecke des Wertpapierhandels. ²Der Beschluß muß bestimmen, daß der Handelsbestand der zu diesem Zweck zu erwerbenden Aktien fünf vom Hundert des Grundkapitals am Ende jeden Tages nicht übersteigen darf; er muß den niedrigsten und höchsten Gegenwert festlegen. ³Die Ermächtigung darf höchstens fünf Jahre gelten; oder
8. aufgrund einer höchstens fünf Jahre geltenden Ermächtigung der Hauptversammlung, die den niedrigsten und höchsten Gegenwert sowie den Anteil am Grundkapital, der zehn vom Hundert nicht übersteigen darf,

§ 71 Acquisition of own shares.

(1) ¹The company may only acquire its own shares:

1. if the acquisition is necessary in order to avert serious and imminent harm to the company,
2. if the shares are to be offered to former or current employees of the company or an affiliate enterprise thereof,
3. if the acquisition is made in order to compensate shareholders pursuant to sec. 305 para. 2, sec. 320b or sec. 29 para. 1, sec. 125 sentence 1 in connection with sec. 29 para. 1, sec. 207 para. 1 sentence 1 of the Transformation Act,
4. if the acquisition is made without consideration or a credit institution executes a purchase commission by effecting the acquisition,
5. by way of universal succession,
6. on the basis of a resolution adopted by the general meeting to redeem shares pursuant to the provisions concerning the reduction of the registered share capital,
7. if it is a credit institution, a financial services institution or a financial enterprise, on the basis of a resolution adopted by the general meeting for the purposes of trading in securities. ²The resolution shall stipulate that the trading portfolio of the shares to be acquired for this purpose may not exceed five percent of the registered share capital at the end of each day and shall specify the lowest and highest price. ³The authorization may not be valid for longer than five years; or
8. on the basis of an authorization granted by the general meeting valid for no more than five years which specifies the lowest and highest price and the portion of the registered share capital attributable

festlegt. ²Als Zweck ist der Handel in eigenen Aktien ausgeschlossen. ³§ 53a ist auf Erwerb und Veräußerung anzuwenden. ⁴Erwerb und Veräußerung über die Börse genügen dem. ⁵Eine andere Veräußerung kann die Hauptversammlung beschließen; § 186 Abs. 3, 4 und § 193 Abs. 2 Nr. 4 sind in diesem Fall entsprechend anzuwenden. ⁶Die Hauptversammlung kann den Vorstand ermächtigen, die eigenen Aktien ohne weiteren Hauptversammlungsbeschluß einzubeziehen.

(2) ¹Auf die zu den Zwecken nach Absatz 1 Nr. 1 bis 3, 7 und 8 erworbenen Aktien dürfen zusammen mit anderen Aktien der Gesellschaft, welche die Gesellschaft bereits erworben hat und noch besitzt, nicht mehr als zehn vom Hundert des Grundkapitals entfallen. ²Dieser Erwerb ist ferner nur zulässig, wenn die Gesellschaft im Zeitpunkt des Erwerbs eine Rücklage in Höhe der Aufwendungen für den Erwerb bilden könnte, ohne das Grundkapital oder eine nach Gesetz oder Satzung zu bildende Rücklage zu mindern, die nicht zur Zahlung an die Aktionäre verwandt werden darf. ³In den Fällen des Absatzes 1 Nr. 1, 2, 4, 7 und 8 ist der Erwerb nur zulässig, wenn auf die Aktien der Ausgabebetrag voll geleistet ist.

(3) ¹In den Fällen des Absatzes 1 Nr. 1 und 8 hat der Vorstand die nächste Hauptversammlung über die Gründe und den Zweck des Erwerbs, über die Zahl der erworbenen Aktien und den auf sie entfallenden Betrag des Grundkapitals, über deren Anteil am Grundkapital sowie über den Gegenwert der Aktien zu unterrichten. ²Im Falle des Absatzes 1 Nr. 2 sind die Aktien innerhalb eines Jahres nach ihrem Erwerb an die Arbeitnehmer auszugeben.

(4) ¹Ein Verstoß gegen die Absätze 1 oder 2 macht den Erwerb eigener Akti-

thereto, which may not exceed ten percent. ²The purpose may not consist of trading in the company's own shares. ³Sec. 53a shall apply to the acquisition and disposal thereof. ⁴Acquisition and disposal on the stock exchange shall suffice. ⁵The general meeting can resolve another method of disposal; in this case, sec. 186 paras. 3, 4 and sec. 193 para. 2 no. 4 shall apply accordingly. ⁶The general meeting can authorize the management board to redeem the company's own shares without a further resolution of the general meeting being adopted.

(2) ¹The shares acquired for the purposes stipulated in para. 1 nos. 1 to 3, 7 and 8 together with other shares in the company already acquired and still held by the company may not account for more than ten percent of the registered share capital. ²Furthermore, such acquisition shall only be permitted if the company could, at the time of the acquisition, provide for a reserve in the amount of the expenditures for the acquisition without reducing the registered share capital or any reserve to be provided pursuant to the law or the articles of association which may not be used to make payment to shareholders. ³In the case of para. 1 nos. 1, 2, 4, 7 and 8, the acquisition shall only be permitted if the issue price of the shares has been paid in full.

(3) ¹In the case of para. 1 nos. 1 and 8, the management board shall inform the next general meeting of the reasons for and purpose of the acquisition, the number of shares acquired and the amount of the registered share capital attributable thereto, the portion of the registered share capital accounted for by such shares and the price thereof. ²In the case of para. 1 no. 2, the shares shall be issued to the employees within one year of being acquired.

(4) ¹A violation of paras. 1 or 2 shall not render the company's acquisition of its

en nicht unwirksam. ²Ein schuldrechtliches Geschäft über den Erwerb eigener Aktien ist jedoch nichtig, soweit der Erwerb gegen die Absätze 1 oder 2 verstößt.

§ 71a Umgehungsgeschäfte.

(1) ¹Ein Rechtsgeschäft, das die Gewährung eines Vorschusses oder eines Darlehens oder die Leistung einer Sicherheit durch die Gesellschaft an einen anderen zum Zweck des Erwerbs von Aktien dieser Gesellschaft zum Gegenstand hat, ist nichtig. ²Dies gilt nicht für Rechtsgeschäfte im Rahmen der laufenden Geschäfte von Kreditinstituten oder Finanzdienstleistungsinstituten sowie für die Gewährung eines Vorschusses oder eines Darlehens oder für die Leistung einer Sicherheit zum Zweck des Erwerbs von Aktien durch Arbeitnehmer der Gesellschaft oder eines mit ihr verbundenen Unternehmens; auch in diesen Fällen ist das Rechtsgeschäft jedoch nichtig, wenn die Gesellschaft im Zeitpunkt des Erwerbs eine Rücklage in Höhe der Aufwendungen für den Erwerb nicht bilden könnte, ohne das Grundkapital oder eine nach Gesetz oder Satzung zu bildende Rücklage zu mindern, die nicht zur Zahlung an die Aktionäre verwandt werden darf. ³Satz 1 gilt zudem nicht für Rechtsgeschäfte bei Bestehen eines Beherrschungs- oder Gewinnabführungsvertrags (§ 291).

(2) Nichtig ist ferner ein Rechtsgeschäft zwischen der Gesellschaft und einem anderen, nach dem dieser berechtigt oder verpflichtet sein soll, Aktien der Gesellschaft für Rechnung der Gesellschaft oder eines abhängigen oder eines in ihrem Mehrheitsbesitz stehenden Unternehmens zu erwerben, soweit der Erwerb durch die Gesellschaft gegen § 71 Abs. 1 oder 2 verstoßen würde.

§ 71b Rechte aus eigenen Aktien.

Aus eigenen Aktien stehen der Gesellschaft keine Rechte zu.

own shares invalid. ²A transaction creating the obligation to such acquisition by the company of its own shares shall, however, be null and void to the extent that the acquisition violates paras. 1 or 2.

§ 71a Circumventive transactions.

(1)¹Any transaction by way of which the company grants an advance payment, a loan or security to another person for the purpose of acquiring shares in such company shall be null and void. ²The above shall not apply to transactions in the ordinary course of business of credit institutions or financial services institutions or to the granting of an advance payment or a loan or security for the purpose of employees of the company or an affiliate thereof acquiring shares; the transaction shall also be null and void in such instances, however, if the company could not, at the time of the acquisition, provide for a reserve in the amount of the expenditures for the acquisition without reducing the registered share capital or any reserve to be provided pursuant to the law or the articles of association which may not be used to make payment to shareholders. ³Sentence 1 also shall not apply to legal transactions performed while a domination or profit transfer agreement (sec. 291) is in existence.

(2) A transaction between the company and another party entitling or obligating the latter to acquire shares in the company on behalf of the company or an enterprise controlled by the company or in which the company has a majority holding shall also be null and void to the extent that such acquisition by the company would violate sec. 71 paras. 1 or 2.

§ 71b Rights from own shares.

The company shall not be entitled to any rights arising from its own shares.

§ 71c Veräußerung und Einziehung eigener Aktien.

(1) Hat die Gesellschaft eigene Aktien unter Verstoß gegen § 71 Abs. 1 oder 2 erworben, so müssen sie innerhalb eines Jahres nach ihrem Erwerb veräußert werden.

(2) Entfallen auf die Aktien, welche die Gesellschaft nach § 71 Abs. 1 in zulässiger Weise erworben hat und noch besitzt, mehr als zehn vom Hundert des Grundkapitals, so muß der Teil der Aktien, der diesen Satz übersteigt, innerhalb von drei Jahren nach dem Erwerb der Aktien veräußert werden.

(3) Sind eigene Aktien innerhalb der in den Absätzen 1 und 2 vorgesehenen Fristen nicht veräußert worden, so sind sie nach § 237 einzuziehen.

§ 71d Erwerb eigener Aktien durch Dritte.

[1]Ein im eigenen Namen, jedoch für Rechnung der Gesellschaft handelnder Dritter darf Aktien der Gesellschaft nur erwerben oder besitzen, soweit dies der Gesellschaft nach § 71 Abs. 1 Nr. 1 bis 5, 7 und 8 und Abs. 2 gestattet wäre. [2]Gleiches gilt für den Erwerb oder den Besitz von Aktien der Gesellschaft durch ein abhängiges oder ein im Mehrheitsbesitz der Gesellschaft stehendes Unternehmen sowie für den Erwerb oder den Besitz durch einen Dritten, der im eigenen Namen, jedoch für Rechnung eines abhängigen oder eines im Mehrheitsbesitz der Gesellschaft stehenden Unternehmens handelt. [3]Bei der Berechnung des Anteils am Grundkapital nach § 71 Abs. 2 Satz 1 und § 71c Abs. 2 gelten diese Aktien als Aktien der Gesellschaft. [4]Im übrigen gelten § 71 Abs. 3 und 4, §§ 71a bis 71c sinngemäß. [5]Der Dritte oder das Unternehmen hat der Gesellschaft auf ihr Verlangen das Eigentum an den Aktien zu verschaffen. [6]Die Gesellschaft hat den Gegenwert der Aktien zu erstatten.

§ 71c Sale and redemption of own shares.

(1) If the company has acquired its own shares in violation of sec. 71 paras. 1 or 2, such shares shall be sold within one year of being acquired.

(2) If shares the company has lawfully acquired and still holds pursuant to sec. 71 para. 1 account for more than ten percent of the registered share capital, the portion of the shares exceeding such rate shall be sold within three years of the acquisition of the shares.

(3) If own shares fail to be sold within the time periods stipulated in paras. 1 and 2, they shall be redeemed pursuant to sec. 237.

§ 71d Acquisition of own shares by third parties.

[1]A third party acting in his own name but for account of the company may only acquire or hold shares in the company to the extent that the company would be permitted to do so pursuant to sec. 71 para. 1 nos. 1 to 5, 7 and 8 and para. 2. [2]The same shall also apply to the acquisition or holding of shares in the company by an enterprise controlled by the company or in which the company has a majority holding as well as to the acquisition or holding of shares by a third party acting in his own name but for account of an enterprise controlled by the company or in which the company has a majority holding. [3]Such shares shall be deemed to be shares held by the company for the purposes of calculating the part of the registered share capital pursuant to sec. 71 para. 2 sentence 1 and sec. 71c para. 2. [4]Incidentally, sec. 71 paras. 3 and 4, sec. 71a to 71c shall apply accordingly. [5]The third party or the enterprise shall grant the company ownership of the shares upon the company's request. [6]The company shall reimburse the purchase price of the shares.

§ 71e Inpfandnahme eigener Aktien.

(1) ¹Dem Erwerb eigener Aktien nach § 71 Abs. 1 und 2, § 71d steht es gleich, wenn eigene Aktien als Pfand genommen werden. ²Jedoch darf ein Kreditinstitut oder Finanzdienstleistungsinstitut im Rahmen der laufenden Geschäfte eigene Aktien bis zu dem in § 71 Abs. 2 Satz 1 bestimmten Anteil am Grundkapital als Pfand nehmen. ³§ 71a gilt sinngemäß.

(2) ¹Ein Verstoß gegen Absatz 1 macht die Inpfandnahme eigener Aktien unwirksam, wenn auf sie der Ausgabebetrag noch nicht voll geleistet ist. ²Ein schuldrechtliches Geschäft über die Inpfandnahme eigener Aktien ist nichtig, soweit der Erwerb gegen Absatz 1 verstößt.

§ 72 Kraftloserklärung von Aktien im Aufgebotsverfahren.

(1) ¹Ist eine Aktie oder ein Zwischenschein abhanden gekommen oder vernichtet, so kann die Urkunde im Aufgebotsverfahren nach dem Gesetz über das Verfahren in Familiensachen und in den Angelegenheiten der freiwilligen Gerichtsbarkeit für kraftlos erklärt werden. ²§ 799 Abs. 2 und § 800 des Bürgerlichen Gesetzbuchs gelten sinngemäß.

(2) Sind Gewinnanteilscheine auf den Inhaber ausgegeben, so erlischt mit der Kraftloserklärung der Aktie oder des Zwischenscheins auch der Anspruch aus den noch nicht fälligen Gewinnanteilscheinen.

(3) Die Kraftloserklärung einer Aktie nach §§ 73 oder 226 steht der Kraftloserklärung der Urkunde nach Absatz 1 nicht entgegen.

§ 73 Kraftloserklärung von Aktien durch die Gesellschaft.

(1) ¹Ist der Inhalt von Aktienurkunden durch eine Veränderung der rechtlichen Verhältnisse unrichtig geworden,

§ 71e Pledging of own shares.

(1) ¹It shall be deemed equivalent to an acquisition of own shares pursuant to sec. 71 paras. 1 and 2, sec. 71d if the company pledges its own shares. ²A credit institution or a financial service institution may take a pledge of its own shares in the normal course of business to an extent not exceeding the part of the registered share capital stipulated in sec. 71 para. 2 sentence 1. ³Sec. 71a shall apply accordingly.

(2) ¹A violation of para. 1 shall render the pledging of own shares invalid if the issue price thereof has not yet been paid in full. ²A contract creating an obligation for the pledge of own shares to the company shall be null and void if the acquisition of such shares would violate para. 1.

§ 72 Cancellation of share certificates by means of invalidation proceedings.

(1) ¹If a share certificate or an interim certificate is lost or destroyed, such certificate may be cancelled by means of invalidation proceedings pursuant to the Act on Procedure in Family Matters and Matters of Non-Contentious Jurisdiction . ²Sec. 799 para. 2 and sec. 800 of the Civil Code shall apply accordingly.

(2) If bearer dividend coupons have been issued, any claims from such coupons which are not yet due become extinct upon the date the share certificate or interim certificate is cancelled.

(3) The cancellation of a share pursuant to sec. 73 or 226 does not impede the certificate being declared invalid pursuant to para. 1.

§ 73 Cancellation of share certificates by the company.

(1) ¹If the contents of share certificates become inaccurate as a result of a change in legal circumstances, the

so kann die Gesellschaft die Aktien, die trotz Aufforderung nicht zur Berichtigung oder zum Umtausch bei ihr eingereicht sind, mit Genehmigung des Gerichts für kraftlos erklären. ²Beruht die Unrichtigkeit auf einer Änderung des Nennbetrags der Aktien, so können sie nur dann für kraftlos erklärt werden, wenn der Nennbetrag zur Herabsetzung des Grundkapitals herabgesetzt ist. ³Namensaktien können nicht deshalb für kraftlos erklärt werden, weil die Bezeichnung des Aktionärs unrichtig geworden ist. ⁴Gegen die Entscheidung des Gerichts ist die Beschwerde zulässig; eine Anfechtung der Entscheidung, durch die die Genehmigung erteilt wird, ist ausgeschlossen.

(2) ¹Die Aufforderung, die Aktien einzureichen, hat die Kraftloserklärung anzudrohen und auf die Genehmigung des Gerichts hinzuweisen. ²Die Kraftloserklärung kann nur erfolgen, wenn die Aufforderung in der in § 64 Abs. 2 für die Nachfrist vorgeschriebenen Weise bekanntgemacht worden ist. ³Die Kraftloserklärung geschieht durch Bekanntmachung in den Gesellschaftsblättern. ⁴In der Bekanntmachung sind die für kraftlos erklärten Aktien so zu bezeichnen, daß sich aus der Bekanntmachung ohne weiteres ergibt, ob eine Aktie für kraftlos erklärt ist.

(3) ¹An Stelle der für kraftlos erklärten Aktien sind, vorbehaltlich einer Satzungsregelung nach § 10 Abs. 5, neue Aktien auszugeben und dem Berechtigten auszuhändigen oder, wenn ein Recht zur Hinterlegung besteht, zu hinterlegen. ²Die Aushändigung oder Hinterlegung ist dem Gericht anzuzeigen.

(4) Soweit zur Herabsetzung des Grundkapitals Aktien zusammengelegt werden, gilt § 226.

company may, if a court consents, cancel those share certificates which have not been submitted to the company for correction or exchange in spite of a request being made to this effect. ²If the inaccuracy pertains to a change in the par value of the shares, such share certificates may only be cancelled if the par value has been reduced for the purposes of reducing the registered share capital. ³Registered shares may not be cancelled as a result of the name of the shareholder having become incorrect. ⁴The decision of the court is subject to appeal; an appeal may not be filed against the decision granting consent.

(2) ¹The request to surrender the share certificates shall give warning of the cancellation thereof and shall refer to the consent granted by the court. ²The shares may only be cancelled if the request is announced in the manner prescribed in sec. 64 para. 2 for the period of grace. ³The cancellation shall be effected by way of announcement in the company's designated journals. ⁴In such announcement, the cancelled shares shall be defined in such a manner that it is perfectly clear from the announcement whether or not a share has been cancelled.

(3) ¹Subject to any provisions included in the articles of association pursuant to sec. 10 para. 5, new share certificates shall be issued in place of cancelled share certificates and delivered to the persons entitled thereto or deposited if the company is entitled to make such deposit. ²The court shall be notified of such deposit or delivery.

(4) Sec. 226 shall apply if shares are consolidated in order to effect a capital reduction.

§ 74 Neue Urkunden an Stelle beschädigter oder verunstalteter Aktien oder Zwischenscheine.

¹Ist eine Aktie oder ein Zwischenschein so beschädigt oder verunstaltet, daß die Urkunde zum Umlauf nicht mehr geeignet ist, so kann der Berechtigte, wenn der wesentliche Inhalt und die Unterscheidungsmerkmale der Urkunde noch sicher zu erkennen sind, von der Gesellschaft die Erteilung einer neuen Urkunde gegen Aushändigung der alten verlangen. ²Die Kosten hat er zu tragen und vorzuschießen.

§ 75 Neue Gewinnanteilscheine.

Neue Gewinnanteilscheine dürfen an den Inhaber des Erneuerungsscheins nicht ausgegeben werden, wenn der Besitzer der Aktie oder des Zwischenscheins der Ausgabe widerspricht; sie sind dem Besitzer der Aktie oder des Zwischenscheins auszuhändigen, wenn er die Haupturkunde vorlegt.

Vierter Teil .Verfassung der Aktiengesellschaft

Erster Abschnitt. Vorstand

§ 76 Leitung der Aktiengesellschaft.

(1) Der Vorstand hat unter eigener Verantwortung die Gesellschaft zu leiten.

(2) ¹Der Vorstand kann aus einer oder mehreren Personen bestehen. ²Bei Gesellschaften mit einem Grundkapital von mehr als drei Millionen Euro hat er aus mindestens zwei Personen zu bestehen, es sei denn, die Satzung bestimmt, daß er aus einer Person besteht. ³Die Vorschriften über die Bestellung eines Arbeitsdirektors bleiben unberührt.

(3) ¹Mitglied des Vorstands kann nur eine natürliche, unbeschränkt ge-

§ 74 New certificates in place of damaged or defaced share certificates or interim certificates.

¹If a share certificate or an interim certificate has been damaged or defaced to such an extent that the certificate is no longer suitable for circulation, the person entitled thereto may request from the company that a new certificate be issued against surrender of the previous certificate, provided that the essential contents and the distinguishing features of the certificate are still clearly recognizable. ²The costs incurred shall be borne and paid in advance by the shareholder.

§ 75 New dividend coupons.

New dividend coupons may not be issued to the holder of the renewal coupon if the holder of the share certificate or interim certificate objects; they shall be issued to the holder of the share certificate or the interim certificate upon submission of the main certificate.

Part Four. Constitution of the Stock Corporation

Section One. Management Board

§ 76 Management of the stock corporation.

(1) The management board shall manage the company under its own responsibility.

(2) ¹The management board may comprise one or more persons. ²For companies with a registered share capital of more than three million euros, it shall comprise at least two persons, unless the articles of association stipulate that it shall comprise one person. ³The provisions concerning the appointment of a works director shall remain unaffected.

(3) ¹Only a natural person of full legal capacity may be a member of the management board. ²Member of the man-

schäftsfähige Person sein. ²Mitglied des Vorstands kann nicht sein, wer

1. als Betreuer bei der Besorgung seiner Vermögensangelegenheiten ganz oder teilweise einem Einwilligungsvorbehalt (§ 1903 des Bürgerlichen Gesetzbuchs) unterliegt,

2. aufgrund eines gerichtlichen Urteils oder einer vollziehbaren Entscheidung einer Verwaltungsbehörde einen Beruf, einen Berufszweig, ein Gewerbe oder einen Gewerbezweig nicht ausüben darf, sofern der Unternehmensgegenstand ganz oder teilweise mit dem Gegenstand des Verbots übereinstimmt,

3. wegen einer oder mehrerer vorsätzlich begangener Straftaten

   a) des Unterlassens der Stellung des Antrags auf Eröffnung des Insolvenzverfahrens (Insolvenzverschleppung),
   b) nach den §§ 283 bis 283d des Strafgesetzbuchs (Insolvenzstraftaten),
   c) der falschen Angaben nach § 399 dieses Gesetzes oder § 82 des Gesetzes betreffend die Gesellschaften mit beschränkter Haftung,
   d) der unrichtigen Darstellung nach § 400 dieses Gesetzes, § 331 des Handelsgesetzbuchs, § 313 des Umwandlungsgesetzes oder § 17 des Publizitätsgesetzes,
   e) nach den §§ 263 bis 264a oder den §§ 265b bis 266a des Strafgesetzbuchs zu einer Freiheitsstrafe von mindestens einem Jahr

verurteilt worden ist; dieser Ausschluss gilt für die Dauer von fünf Jahren seit der Rechtskraft des Urteils, wobei die Zeit nicht eingerechnet wird, in welcher der Täter auf behördliche Anordnung in einer Anstalt verwahrt worden ist.

³Satz 2 Nr. 3 gilt entsprechend bei einer Verurteilung im Ausland wegen einer

agement board may not be someone who,

1. as a ward, with regard to the handling of his financial affairs, is partially or completely subject to a requirement that any transactions entered into by him be approved by a third party (sec. 1903 of the Civil Code),

2. is due to a court judgment or by an enforceable decision of an administrative body prohibited from exercising a profession, a branch of a profession, a trade or a branch of a trade to the extent that the object of the enterprise matches the subject matter of the prohibition in whole or in part,

3. has been convicted of one or more intentionally committed criminal offenses

   a) of failure to file the application for the commencement of insolvency proceedings (delay in filing a petition in insolvency),
   b) pursuant to sec. 283 to 283d of the Criminal Code (criminal offenses related to insolvency),
   c) of making false statements pursuant to sec. 399 of this Act or sec. 82 of the Limited Liability Company Act,
   d) of misrepresentation pursuant to sec. 400 of this Act , 331 of the Commercial Code, sec. 313 of the Transformation Act or sec. 17 of the Disclosure Act,
   e) pursuant to sec. 263 to 264a or sec. 265b to 266a of the Criminal Code resulting in a prison sentence of one year or longer;

this exclusion applies for five years from when the conviction has become res judicata, excluding the period of time during which the offender was confined to an institution by official order.

³Sentence 2 no. 3 shall apply accordingly in the case of a conviction abroad for

Tat, die mit den in Satz 2 Nr. 3 genannten Taten vergleichbar ist.	an offense which is comparable to the offenses mentioned in sentence 2 no. 3.
(4) ¹Der Vorstand von Gesellschaften, die börsennotiert sind oder der Mitbestimmung unterliegen, legt für den Frauenanteil in den beiden Führungsebenen unterhalb des Vorstands Zielgrößen fest. ²Liegt der Frauenanteil bei Festlegung der Zielgrößen unter 30 Prozent, so dürfen die Zielgrößen den jeweils erreichten Anteil nicht mehr unterschreiten. ³Gleichzeitig sind Fristen zur Erreichung der Zielgrößen festzulegen. ⁴Die Fristen dürfen jeweils nicht länger als fünf Jahre sein.	(4) ¹The management board of companies, which are listed at a stock exchange or are under the statute of employee codetermination, states a target for the women's representation at the top two layers of management beneath the management board. ²If the percentage of women's representation below 30 percent when setting the target, the target must not fall below the reached percentage. ³Time limits for achieving the target have to be set at the same time. ⁴The time limits shall not exceed five years.

§ 77 Geschäftsführung.   § 77 Management.

(1) ¹Besteht der Vorstand aus mehreren Personen, so sind sämtliche Vorstandsmitglieder nur gemeinschaftlich zur Geschäftsführung befugt. ²Die Satzung oder die Geschäftsordnung des Vorstands kann Abweichendes bestimmen; es kann jedoch nicht bestimmt werden, daß ein oder mehrere Vorstandsmitglieder Meinungsverschiedenheiten im Vorstand gegen die Mehrheit seiner Mitglieder entscheiden.

(1) ¹If the management board comprises more than one person, all members of the management board shall manage the company jointly. ²The articles of association or the rules of procedure for the management board may provide otherwise; however, it cannot be stipulated that one or several members of the management board may decide on differences in opinion among the members of the management board against the majority of the members thereof.

(2) ¹Der Vorstand kann sich eine Geschäftsordnung geben, wenn nicht die Satzung den Erlaß der Geschäftsordnung dem Aufsichtsrat übertragen hat oder der Aufsichtsrat eine Geschäftsordnung für den Vorstand erläßt. ²Die Satzung kann Einzelfragen der Geschäftsordnung bindend regeln. ³Beschlüsse des Vorstands über die Geschäftsordnung müssen einstimmig gefaßt werden.

(2) ¹The management board may issue rules of procedure for itself, provided the articles of association have not transferred responsibility for issuing rules of procedure to the supervisory board or the supervisory board has decreed rules of procedure for the management board. ²The articles of association may make binding provisions in respect of individual matters relating to the rules of procedure. ³Resolutions adopted by the management board concerning the rules of procedure shall be adopted unanimously.

§ 78 Vertretung.   § 78 Representation.

(1) ¹Der Vorstand vertritt die Gesellschaft gerichtlich und außergerichtlich. ²Hat eine Gesellschaft keinen Vorstand

(1) ¹The management board shall represent the company in and out of court. ²If a company does not have a management

(Führungslosigkeit), wird die Gesellschaft für den Fall, dass ihr gegenüber Willenserklärungen abgegeben oder Schriftstücke zugestellt werden, durch den Aufsichtsrat vertreten.

(2) ¹Besteht der Vorstand aus mehreren Personen, so sind, wenn die Satzung nichts anderes bestimmt, sämtliche Vorstandsmitglieder nur gemeinschaftlich zur Vertretung der Gesellschaft befugt. ²Ist eine Willenserklärung gegenüber der Gesellschaft abzugeben, so genügt die Abgabe gegenüber einem Vorstandsmitglied oder im Fall des Absatzes 1 Satz 2 gegenüber einem Aufsichtsratsmitglied. ³An die Vertreter der Gesellschaft nach Absatz 1 können unter der im Handelsregister eingetragenen Geschäftsanschrift Willenserklärungen gegenüber der Gesellschaft abgegeben und Schriftstücke für die Gesellschaft zugestellt werden. ⁴Unabhängig hiervon können die Abgabe und die Zustellung auch unter der eingetragenen Anschrift der empfangsberechtigten Person nach § 39 Abs. 1 Satz 2 erfolgen.

(3) ¹Die Satzung kann auch bestimmen, daß einzelne Vorstandsmitglieder allein oder in Gemeinschaft mit einem Prokuristen zur Vertretung der Gesellschaft befugt sind. ²Dasselbe kann der Aufsichtsrat bestimmen, wenn die Satzung ihn hierzu ermächtigt hat. 3Absatz 2 Satz 2 gilt in diesen Fällen sinngemäß.

(4) ¹Zur Gesamtvertretung befugte Vorstandsmitglieder können einzelne von ihnen zur Vornahme bestimmter Geschäfte oder bestimmter Arten von Geschäften ermächtigen. ²Dies gilt sinngemäß, wenn ein einzelnes Vorstandsmitglied in Gemeinschaft mit einem Prokuristen zur Vertretung der Gesellschaft befugt ist.

board (lack of leadership), it is represented by the supervisory board in the case that declarations of intent are made vis-à-vis the company or documents are delivered to the company.

(2) ¹If the management board comprises several persons, all members of the management board shall only be able to represent the company jointly, unless provided otherwise in the articles of association. ²If a declaration of intent is to be made vis-à-vis the company, it is sufficient to make such declaration vis-à-vis one member of the management board or, in the case of para. 1 sentence 2, one member of the supervisory board. ³Declarations of intent may be made and writings may be delivered for the company to the representatives pursuant to para. 1 at the business address registered in the commercial register. ⁴Independent of this, declarations may also be made and deliveries may also be effected to the registered address of the person authorized to receive pursuant to sec. 39 para. 1 sentence 2.

(3) ¹The articles of association may stipulate that individual members of the management board are authorized to represent the company alone or together with a procuration officer. ²The same may also be stipulated by the supervisory board if it has been authorized to do so by the articles of association. ³Para. 2 sentence 2 shall apply accordingly in these instances.

(4) ¹Members of the management board authorized to represent the company jointly may authorize a single member to engage in certain transactions or types of transactions. ²This shall apply accordingly if an individual member of the management board is authorized to represent the company together with a procuration officer.

§ 79 *(aufgehoben)*

§ 79 *(repealed)*

§ 80 Angaben auf Geschäftsbriefen.

§ 80 Information on business letters.

(1) ¹Auf allen Geschäftsbriefen gleichviel welcher Form, die an einen bestimmten Empfänger gerichtet werden, müssen die Rechtsform und der Sitz der Gesellschaft, das Registergericht des Sitzes der Gesellschaft und die Nummer, unter der die Gesellschaft in das Handelsregister eingetragen ist, sowie alle Vorstandsmitglieder und der Vorsitzende des Aufsichtsrats mit dem Familiennamen und mindestens einem ausgeschriebenen Vornamen angegeben werden. ²Der Vorsitzende des Vorstands ist als solcher zu bezeichnen. ³Werden Angaben über das Kapital der Gesellschaft gemacht, so müssen in jedem Falle das Grundkapital sowie, wenn auf die Aktien der Ausgabebetrag nicht vollständig eingezahlt ist, der Gesamtbetrag der ausstehenden Einlagen angegeben werden.

(1) ¹All business letters, regardless of their form, directed to a specific recipient shall state the legal form and the registered office of the company, the register court at the registered office of the company, the number under which the company is registered in the commercial register and the surname and at least one full first name of all members of the management board and the chairman of the supervisory board. ²The chairman of the management board shall be designated as such. ³If details are given concerning the company's capital, the registered share capital and, if the issue price has not been fully paid in, the aggregate amount of the outstanding contributions shall be stated in any event.

(2) Der Angaben nach Absatz 1 Satz 1 und 2 bedarf es nicht bei Mitteilungen oder Berichten, die im Rahmen einer bestehenden Geschäftsverbindung ergehen und für die üblicherweise Vordrucke verwendet werden, in denen lediglich die im Einzelfall erforderlichen besonderen Angaben eingefügt zu werden brauchen.

(2) The details stipulated in para. 1 sentences 1 and 2 shall not be required for communications or reports which are made in the course of an existing business relationship and for which forms are generally used in which only the particulars of the specific transaction need be inserted.

(3) Bestellscheine gelten als Geschäftsbriefe im Sinne des Absatzes 1. ²Absatz 2 ist auf sie nicht anzuwenden.

(3) ¹Order forms shall constitute business letters within the meaning of para. 1. ²Para. 2 shall not apply to them.

(4) ¹Auf allen Geschäftsbriefen und Bestellscheinen, die von einer Zweigniederlassung einer Aktiengesellschaft mit Sitz im Ausland verwendet werden, müssen das Register, bei dem die Zweigniederlassung geführt wird, und die Nummer des Registereintrags angegeben werden; im übrigen gelten die Vorschriften der Absätze 1 bis 3 für die Angaben bezüglich der Haupt- und der Zweigniederlassung, soweit nicht das ausländische Recht Abweichungen nötig macht. ²Befindet sich die ausländische Gesellschaft in Abwicklung, so

(4) ¹All business letters and order forms which are used by a branch office of a stock corporation with its registered office abroad shall state the register in which the branch office is registered and the number of the registration; in other respects, the provisions of paras. 1 to 3 shall apply to information with respect to the head office and the branch office, to the extent that foreign law does not require deviations. ²If the foreign company is being liquidated, this shall also be stated, as shall the names of all liquidators.

sind auch diese Tatsache sowie alle Abwickler anzugeben.

§ 81 Änderung des Vorstands und der Vertretungsbefugnis seiner Mitglieder.

(1) Jede Änderung des Vorstands oder der Vertretungsbefugnis eines Vorstandsmitglieds hat der Vorstand zur Eintragung in das Handelsregister anzumelden.

(2) Der Anmeldung sind die Urkunden über die Änderung in Urschrift oder öffentlich beglaubigter Abschrift beizufügen.

(3) ¹Die neuen Vorstandsmitglieder haben in der Anmeldung zu versichern, daß keine Umstände vorliegen, die ihrer Bestellung nach § 76 Abs. 3 Satz 2 Nr. 2 und 3 sowie Satz 3 entgegenstehen, und daß sie über ihre unbeschränkte Auskunftspflicht gegenüber dem Gericht belehrt worden sind. ²§ 37 Abs. 2 Satz 2 ist anzuwenden.

§ 82 Beschränkungen der Vertretungs- und Geschäftsführungsbefugnis.

(1) Die Vertretungsbefugnis des Vorstands kann nicht beschränkt werden.

(2) Im Verhältnis der Vorstandsmitglieder zur Gesellschaft sind diese verpflichtet, die Beschränkungen einzuhalten, die im Rahmen der Vorschriften über die Aktiengesellschaft die Satzung, der Aufsichtsrat, die Hauptversammlung und die Geschäftsordnungen des Vorstands und des Aufsichtsrats für die Geschäftsführungsbefugnis getroffen haben.

§ 83 Vorbereitung und Ausführung von Hauptversammlungsbeschlüssen.

(1) ¹Der Vorstand ist auf Verlangen der Hauptversammlung verpflichtet, Maß-

§ 81 Changes in the management board and power of representation of the members thereof.

(1) The management board shall apply for any change in the management board or the power of representation of the members thereof to be registered in the commercial register.

(2) The documents regarding the change are to be attached in the original or as certified copies to the application.

(3) ¹The new members of the management board shall provide assurance in the application that there are no circumstances which would prevent them from being appointed pursuant to sec. 76 para. 3 sentence 2 nos. 2 and 3 as well as sentence 3 and that they have been informed as to their unrestricted obligation to provide information to the court. ²Sec. 37 para. 2 sentence 2 shall apply.

§ 82 Restrictions on the power of representation and the authority to manage.

(1) The management board's power of representation may not be made subject to any restrictions.

(2) The members of the management board shall be bound in relation to the company to comply with the restrictions concerning their authority to manage the company stipulated in accordance with the provisions governing the stock corporation by the articles of association, the supervisory board, the general meeting and the rules of procedure for the management board and the supervisory board.

§ 83 Preparation and implementation of resolutions adopted by the general meeting.

(1) ¹The management board shall, at the request of the general meeting, prepare

nahmen, die in die Zuständigkeit der Hauptversammlung fallen, vorzubereiten. ²Das gleiche gilt für die Vorbereitung und den Abschluß von Verträgen, die nur mit Zustimmung der Hauptversammlung wirksam werden. ³Der Beschluß der Hauptversammlung bedarf der Mehrheiten, die für die Maßnahmen oder für die Zustimmung zu dem Vertrag erforderlich sind.

(2) Der Vorstand ist verpflichtet, die von der Hauptversammlung im Rahmen ihrer Zuständigkeit beschlossenen Maßnahmen auszuführen.

§ 84 Bestellung und Abberufung des Vorstands.

(1) ¹Vorstandsmitglieder bestellt der Aufsichtsrat auf höchstens fünf Jahre. ²Eine wiederholte Bestellung oder Verlängerung der Amtszeit, jeweils für höchstens fünf Jahre, ist zulässig. ³Sie bedarf eines erneuten Aufsichtsratsbeschlusses, der frühestens ein Jahr vor Ablauf der bisherigen Amtszeit gefaßt werden kann. ⁴Nur bei einer Bestellung auf weniger als fünf Jahre kann eine Verlängerung der Amtszeit ohne neuen Aufsichtsratsbeschluß vorgesehen werden, sofern dadurch die gesamte Amtszeit nicht mehr als fünf Jahre beträgt. ⁵Dies gilt sinngemäß für den Anstellungsvertrag; er kann jedoch vorsehen, daß er für den Fall einer Verlängerung der Amtszeit bis zu deren Ablauf weitergilt.

(2) Werden mehrere Personen zu Vorstandsmitgliedern bestellt, so kann der Aufsichtsrat ein Mitglied zum Vorsitzenden des Vorstands ernennen.

any matter falling within the competence of the general meeting. ²The foregoing shall also apply to the preparation and execution of contracts which are only valid if approved by the general meeting. ³In order to be valid, the resolution of the general meeting shall be adopted with the majorities which are required for the matters in question or for approval to be granted for the contract.

(2) The management board shall be obligated to implement any measures falling within the scope of the competence of the general meeting which are resolved by the general meeting.

§ 84 Appointment and dismissal of the management board.

(1) ¹Members of the management board shall be appointed by the supervisory board for a period of at most five years. ²Such appointment may be renewed or the term of office extended, in each instance for a maximum of five years. ³Such renewed appointment or extension of the term of office shall require a new resolution to be adopted by the supervisory board, which may be adopted no earlier than one year before the end of the previous term of office. ⁴The term of office may only be extended without a new resolution being adopted by the supervisory board if the appointment is for a term of less than five years, providing the resulting aggregate term of office is no longer than five years. ⁵This shall apply accordingly to the employment contract; such contract may, however, stipulate that in the event of an extension of the term of office it shall continue to apply until the expiration of such term.

(2) If the management board consists of more than one member, the supervisory board may designate one of the members as chairman of the management board.

(3) ¹Der Aufsichtsrat kann die Bestellung zum Vorstandsmitglied und die Ernennung zum Vorsitzenden des Vorstands widerrufen, wenn ein wichtiger Grund vorliegt. ²Ein solcher Grund ist namentlich grobe Pflichtverletzung, Unfähigkeit zur ordnungsmäßigen Geschäftsführung oder Vertrauensentzug durch die Hauptversammlung, es sei denn, daß das Vertrauen aus offenbar unsachlichen Gründen entzogen worden ist. ³Dies gilt auch für den vom ersten Aufsichtsrat bestellten Vorstand. ⁴Der Widerruf ist wirksam, bis seine Unwirksamkeit rechtskräftig festgestellt ist. ⁵Für die Ansprüche aus dem Anstellungsvertrag gelten die allgemeinen Vorschriften.

(4) Die Vorschriften des Gesetzes über die Mitbestimmung der Arbeitnehmer in den Aufsichtsräten und Vorständen der Unternehmen des Bergbaus und der Eisen und Stahl erzeugenden Industrie in der im Bundesgesetzblatt Teil III, Gliederungsnummer 801-2, veröffentlichten bereinigten Fassung – Montan-Mitbestimmungsgesetz – über die besonderen Mehrheitserfordernisse für einen Aufsichtsratsbeschluß über die Bestellung eines Arbeitsdirektors oder den Widerruf seiner Bestellung bleiben unberührt.

§ 85 Bestellung durch das Gericht.

(1) ¹Fehlt ein erforderliches Vorstandsmitglied, so hat in dringenden Fällen das Gericht auf Antrag eines Beteiligten das Mitglied zu bestellen. ²Gegen die Entscheidung ist die Beschwerde zulässig.

(2) Das Amt des gerichtlich bestellten Vorstandsmitglieds erlischt in jedem Fall, sobald der Mangel behoben ist.

(3) ¹Das gerichtlich bestellte Vorstandsmitglied hat Anspruch auf Ersatz angemessener barer Auslagen und auf Vergütung für seine Tätigkeit. ²Einigen sich das gerichtlich bestellte Vorstands-

(3) ¹The supervisory board may revoke the appointment of a member of the management board or the designation of a member as chairman for good cause. ²Such good cause shall include in particular a gross breach of duty, inability to manage the company properly or a withdrawal of confidence on the part of the general meeting, unless such withdrawal of confidence was made for manifestly arbitrary reasons. ³The above provisions shall also apply to the management board appointed by the first supervisory board. ⁴The revocation shall be valid until such time as the invalidity thereof is established by a court decision being res judicata. ⁵Claims arising from the employment contract shall be governed by the general provisions of law.

(4) The provisions on the Act on the Co-determination of Employees in the Supervisory and Management Boards of Enterprises in the Mining and Iron and Steel Producing Industries published in the Federal Law Gazette Part III, sec. 801-2 in the revised version "Coal, Iron and Steel Codetermination Act" – pertaining to the special majority requirements for a supervisory board resolution on the appointment of a works director or the revocation of his appointment shall not be affected by the above.

§ 85 Appointment by the court.

(1) ¹If the management board does not have the required number of members, the court shall in urgent cases appoint the member upon application by one of the parties concerned. ²The decision is subject to appeal.

(2) The term of office of the member appointed by the court shall terminate as soon as the vacancy is filled.

(3) ¹The member of the management board appointed by the court shall be entitled to reimbursement of reasonable cash expenses and to remuneration for his services. ²If the member appointed

mitglied und die Gesellschaft nicht, so setzt das Gericht die Auslagen und die Vergütung fest. ³Gegen die Entscheidung ist die Beschwerde zulässig; die Rechtsbeschwerde ist ausgeschlossen. ⁴Aus der rechtskräftigen Entscheidung findet die Zwangsvollstreckung nach der Zivilprozeßordnung statt.

by the court and the company fail to come to an agreement, the court shall fix the amount of expenses and remuneration due. ³The decision is subject to appeal; no further appeal on a point of law may be made. ⁴A decision being res judicata may be enforced in accordance with the provisions of the Code of Civil Procedure.

§ 86 *(aufgehoben)*

§ 86 *(repealed)*

§ 87 Grundsätze für die Bezüge der Vorstandsmitglieder.

§ 87 Principles governing the remuneration of management board members.

(1) ¹Der Aufsichtsrat hat bei der Festsetzung der Gesamtbezüge des einzelnen Vorstandsmitglieds (Gehalt, Gewinnbeteiligungen, Aufwandsentschädigungen, Versicherungsentgelte, Provisionen, anreizorientierte Vergütungszusagen wie zum Beispiel Aktienbezugsrechte und Nebenleistungen jeder Art) dafür zu sorgen, dass diese in einem angemessenen Verhältnis zu den Aufgaben und Leistungen des Vorstandsmitglieds sowie zur Lage der Gesellschaft stehen und die übliche Vergütung nicht ohne besondere Gründe übersteigen. ²Die Vergütungsstruktur ist bei börsennotierten Gesellschaften auf eine nachhaltige Unternehmensentwicklung auszurichten. ³Variable Vergütungsbestandteile sollen daher eine mehrjährige Bemessungsgrundlage haben; für außerordentliche Entwicklungen soll der Aufsichtsrat eine Begrenzungsmöglichkeit vereinbaren. ⁴Satz 1 gilt sinngemäß für Ruhegehalt, Hinterbliebenenbezüge und Leistungen verwandter Art.

(1) ¹When determining the total remuneration for the individual members of the management board (salary, participation in profits, reimbursement of expenses, insurance premiums, commission, incentive-based promises of compensation such as share subscription rights and side benefits of any kind), the supervisory board shall ensure that such total remuneration is reasonable in relation to the duties and performance of the member of the management board as well as in relation to the situation of the company and that it does not exceed the usual compensation without special reasons. ²The compensation structure of listed companies shall be aligned towards a sustainable corporate development. ³Fluctuating compensation components shall therefore have a multi-year basis for assessment; the supervisory board shall arrange for a possibility of limitation in case of extraordinary developments. ⁴Sentence 1 shall apply accordingly to pensions, payments to surviving dependants of the deceased and similar payments.

(2) ¹Verschlechtert sich die Lage der Gesellschaft nach der Festsetzung so, dass die Weitergewährung der Bezüge nach Absatz 1 unbillig für die Gesellschaft wäre, so soll der Aufsichtsrat oder im Falle des § 85 Absatz 3 das Gericht auf Antrag des Aufsichtsrats die Bezüge auf die angemessene Höhe herabsetzen. ²Ruhegehalt, Hinterbliebenenbezüge

(2) ¹If the situation of the company worsens after the determination such that the continued granting of the remuneration pursuant to para. 1 would be unreasonable for the company, the supervisory board or, in the case of sec. 85 para. 3, the court upon application by the supervisory board shall reduce the remuneration to a reasonable level. ²Pensions,

und Leistungen verwandter Art können nur in den ersten drei Jahren nach Ausscheiden aus der Gesellschaft nach Satz 1 herabgesetzt werden. ³Durch eine Herabsetzung wird der Anstellungsvertrag im übrigen nicht berührt. ⁴Das Vorstandsmitglied kann jedoch seinen Anstellungsvertrag für den Schluß des nächsten Kalendervierteljahrs mit einer Kündigungsfrist von sechs Wochen kündigen.

(3) Wird über das Vermögen der Gesellschaft das Insolvenzverfahren eröffnet und kündigt der Insolvenzverwalter den Anstellungsvertrag eines Vorstandsmitglieds, so kann es Ersatz für den Schaden, der ihm durch die Aufhebung des Dienstverhältnisses entsteht, nur für zwei Jahre seit dem Ablauf des Dienstverhältnisses verlangen.

§ 88 Wettbewerbsverbot.

(1) ¹Die Vorstandsmitglieder dürfen ohne Einwilligung des Aufsichtsrats weder ein Handelsgewerbe betreiben noch im Geschäftszweig der Gesellschaft für eigene oder fremde Rechnung Geschäfte machen. ²Sie dürfen ohne Einwilligung auch nicht Mitglied des Vorstands oder Geschäftsführer oder persönlich haftender Gesellschafter einer anderen Handelsgesellschaft sein. ³Die Einwilligung des Aufsichtsrats kann nur für bestimmte Handelsgewerbe oder Handelsgesellschaften oder für bestimmte Arten von Geschäften erteilt werden.

(2) ¹Verstößt ein Vorstandsmitglied gegen dieses Verbot, so kann die Gesellschaft Schadenersatz fordern. ²Sie kann statt dessen von dem Mitglied verlangen, daß es die für eigene Rechnung gemachten Geschäfte als für Rechnung der Gesellschaft eingegangen gelten läßt und die aus Geschäften für fremde Rechnung bezogene Vergütung herausgibt oder seinen Anspruch auf die Vergütung abtritt.

payments to surviving dependants of the deceased and similar payments may only be reduced pursuant to sentence 1 during the first three years following the exit from the company. ³The other provisions in the employment contract shall remain unaffected by such a reduction. ⁴The member of the management board may, however, terminate his employment contract with effect from the end of the next quarter upon giving six weeks notice.

(3) If insolvency proceedings are commenced over the company's assets and the insolvency administrator terminates the employment contract of a member of the management board, such member may only demand compensation for the damage he suffers as a result of the termination of such contract for a period of two years following termination thereof.

§ 88 Prohibition of competition.

(1) ¹The members of the management board may not engage in any trade or enter into any dealings in the same branch as the company either for their own account or for account of a third party without first obtaining the consent of the supervisory board. ²Nor may they without consent become a member of the management board, a managing director or a personally liable partner of another commercial company. ³The supervisory board may only grant its consent for specific trades or commercial companies or for specific types of dealings.

(2) ¹The company may claim for damages if a member of the management board violates this prohibition. ²If preferred, it may require the member to treat any dealing made for his own account as having been made for account of the company and to either surrender the remuneration received in return for dealings conducted for account of a third party or assign his rights to such remuneration.

(3) ¹Die Ansprüche der Gesellschaft verjähren in drei Monaten seit dem Zeitpunkt, in dem die übrigen Vorstandsmitglieder und die Aufsichtsratsmitglieder von der zum Schadensersatz verpflichtenden Handlung Kenntnis erlangen oder ohne grobe Fahrlässigkeit erlangen müssten. ²Sie verjähren ohne Rücksicht auf diese Kenntnis oder grob fahrlässige Unkenntnis in fünf Jahren von ihrer Entstehung an.

(3) ¹The company's claims shall become time-barred three months after the remaining members of the management board and the supervisory board obtain knowledge or would obtain knowledge without gross negligence of the action giving rise to the claim for damages. ²Such claims shall become time-barred five years after the occurrence giving rise thereto irrespective of such knowledge or grossly negligent lack of knowledge.

§ 89 Kreditgewährung an Vorstandsmitglieder.

§ 89 Granting of credit to members of the management board.

(1) ¹Die Gesellschaft darf ihren Vorstandsmitgliedern Kredit nur auf Grund eines Beschlusses des Aufsichtsrats gewähren. ²Der Beschluß kann nur für bestimmte Kreditgeschäfte oder Arten von Kreditgeschäften und nicht für länger als drei Monate im voraus gefaßt werden. ³Er hat die Verzinsung und Rückzahlung des Kredits zu regeln. ⁴Der Gewährung eines Kredits steht die Gestattung einer Entnahme gleich, die über die dem Vorstandsmitglied zustehenden Bezüge hinausgeht, namentlich auch die Gestattung der Entnahme von Vorschüssen auf Bezüge. ⁵Dies gilt nicht für Kredite, die ein Monatsgehalt nicht übersteigen.

(1) ¹The company may only grant the members of its management board credit on the basis of a supervisory board resolution. ²Such resolution may only authorize certain credit transactions or types of credit transaction and may not be adopted more than three months in advance. ³It shall stipulate interest rates and the repayment of the credit. ⁴Permission for a withdrawal in excess of the remuneration due to a member of the management board, including permission for a withdrawal of advance payments towards remuneration, shall be deemed to constitute granting of credit. ⁵This shall not apply to credits not exceeding the value of a monthly salary.

(2) ¹Die Gesellschaft darf ihren Prokuristen und zum gesamten Geschäftsbetrieb ermächtigten Handlungsbevollmächtigten Kredit nur mit Einwilligung des Aufsichtsrats gewähren. ²Eine herrschende Gesellschaft darf Kredite an gesetzliche Vertreter, Prokuristen oder zum gesamten Geschäftsbetrieb ermächtigte Handlungsbevollmächtigte eines abhängigen Unternehmens nur mit Einwilligung ihres Aufsichtsrats, eine abhängige Gesellschaft darf Kredite an gesetzliche Vertreter, Prokuristen oder zum gesamten Geschäftsbetrieb ermächtigte Handlungsbevollmächtigte des herrschenden Unternehmens nur mit Einwilligung des Aufsichtsrats des herrschenden Un-

(2) ¹Credit may only be granted by the company to its procuration officers and authorized signatories with authorization for actions with respect to all of the company's business activity if the supervisory board gives its consent. ²Credit may only be granted by a controlling company to legal representatives, procuration officers or authorized signatories with authorization for actions with respect to all of the company's business activity of a controlled enterprise if the supervisory board of the controlling company gives its consent, and a controlled company may only grant credit to legal representatives, procuration officers or authorized signatories with authorization for actions with respect to

ternehmens gewähren. ³Absatz 1 Satz 2 bis 5 gilt sinngemäß.

(3) ¹Absatz 2 gilt auch für Kredite an den Ehegatten, Lebenspartner oder an ein minderjähriges Kind eines Vorstandsmitglieds, eines anderen gesetzlichen Vertreters, eines Prokuristen oder eines zum gesamten Geschäftsbetrieb ermächtigten Handlungsbevollmächtigten. ²Er gilt ferner für Kredite an einen Dritten, der für Rechnung dieser Personen oder für Rechnung eines Vorstandsmitglieds, eines anderen gesetzlichen Vertreters, eines Prokuristen oder eines zum gesamten Geschäftsbetrieb ermächtigten Handlungsbevollmächtigten handelt.

(4) ¹Ist ein Vorstandsmitglied, ein Prokurist oder ein zum gesamten Geschäftsbetrieb ermächtigter Handlungsbevollmächtigter zugleich gesetzlicher Vertreter oder Mitglied des Aufsichtsrats einer anderen juristischen Person oder Gesellschafter einer Personenhandelsgesellschaft, so darf die Gesellschaft der juristischen Person oder der Personenhandelsgesellschaft Kredit nur mit Einwilligung des Aufsichtsrats gewähren; Absatz 1 Satz 2 und 3 gilt sinngemäß. ²Dies gilt nicht, wenn die juristische Person oder die Personenhandelsgesellschaft mit der Gesellschaft verbunden ist oder wenn der Kredit für die Bezahlung von Waren gewährt wird, welche die Gesellschaft der juristischen Person oder der Personenhandelsgesellschaft liefert.

(5) Wird entgegen den Absätzen 1 bis 4 Kredit gewährt, so ist der Kredit ohne Rücksicht auf entgegenstehende Vereinbarungen sofort zurückzugewähren, wenn nicht der Aufsichtsrat nachträglich zustimmt.

(6) Ist die Gesellschaft ein Kreditinstitut oder Finanzdienstleistungsinstitut, auf das § 15 des Gesetzes über das Kredit-

all of the company's business activity of the controlling enterprise if the supervisory board of the controlling enterprise grants its consent. ³Para. 1 sentences 2 to 5 shall apply accordingly.

(3) ¹Para. 2 shall also apply to a credit to the spouse, domestic partner or a minor child of a member of the management board, another legal representative, a procuration officer or an authorized signatory with authorization for actions with respect to all of the company's business activity. ²It shall also apply to credits to third parties acting for account of such persons or for account of a member of the management board, another legal representative, a procuration officer or an authorized signatory with authorization for actions with respect to all of the company's business activity.

(4) ¹If a member of the management board, a procuration officer or an authorized signatory with authorization for actions with respect to all of the company's business activity is at the same time the legal representative or a member of the supervisory board of another legal person or a partner in a commercial partnership, the company may only grant the legal person or the partnership credit if the supervisory board gives its consent; para. 1 sentences 2 and 3 shall apply accordingly. ²The above shall not apply if the legal person or the commercial partnership is affiliated to the company or if the credit is granted for the payment of goods supplied by the company to the legal person or the commercial partnership.

(5) If credit is granted contrary to the provisions in paras. 1 to 4, the credit shall be paid back immediately irrespective of agreements to the contrary unless the supervisory board grants its consent retrospectively.

(6) If the company is a credit institution or a financial services institution to which sec. 15 of the Banking Act applies,

wesen anzuwenden ist, gelten anstelle der Absätze 1 bis 5 die Vorschriften des Gesetzes über das Kreditwesen.

the provisions of the Banking Act shall apply in lieu of paras. 1 to 5.

§ 90 Berichte an den Aufsichtsrat.

§ 90 Reports to the supervisory board.

(1) ¹Der Vorstand hat dem Aufsichtsrat zu berichten über

(1) ¹The management board shall report to the supervisory board on the following:

1. die beabsichtigte Geschäftspolitik und andere grundsätzliche Fragen der Unternehmensplanung (insbesondere die Finanz-, Investitions- und Personalplanung), wobei auf Abweichungen der tatsächlichen Entwicklung von früher berichteten Zielen unter Angabe von Gründen einzugehen ist;
2. die Rentabilität der Gesellschaft, insbesondere die Rentabilität des Eigenkapitals;
3. den Gang der Geschäfte, insbesondere den Umsatz, und die Lage der Gesellschaft;
4. Geschäfte, die für die Rentabilität oder Liquidität der Gesellschaft von erheblicher Bedeutung sein können.

1. intended business policy and other fundamental matters relating to corporate policy (in particular financial, investment and human resource planning); such reports shall mention any deviations between actual developments and previously reported objectives, stating the reasons for such deviation;
2. the profitability of the company, in particular the return on shareholders' equity;
3. the progress of business, in particular turnover, and the situation of the company;
4. transactions which may be of considerable importance for the profitability or liquidity of the company.

²Ist die Gesellschaft Mutterunternehmen (§ 290 Abs. 1, 2 des Handelsgesetzbuchs), so hat der Bericht auch auf Tochterunternehmen und auf Gemeinschaftsunternehmen (§ 310 Abs. 1 des Handelsgesetzbuchs) einzugehen. ³Außerdem ist dem Vorsitzenden des Aufsichtsrats aus sonstigen wichtigen Anlässen zu berichten; als wichtiger Anlaß ist auch ein dem Vorstand bekanntgewordener geschäftlicher Vorgang bei einem verbundenen Unternehmen anzusehen, der auf die Lage der Gesellschaft von erheblichem Einfluß sein kann.

²If the company is a parent enterprise (sec. 290 paras. 1, 2 of the Commercial Code), the report shall also report on subsidiaries and joint ventures (sec. 310 para. 1 of the Commercial Code). ³Furthermore, reports shall be submitted to the chairman of the supervisory board on other significant developments; a business transaction concerning an affiliated enterprise which comes to the attention of the management board and which may have a considerable effect on the situation of the company shall also be deemed to constitute a significant development.

(2) Die Berichte nach Absatz 1 Satz 1 Nr. 1 bis 4 sind wie folgt zu erstatten:

(2) The reports pursuant to para. 1 sentence 1 nos. 1 to 4 shall be submitted as follows:

1. die Berichte nach Nummer 1 mindestens einmal jährlich, wenn nicht Änderungen der Lage oder neue

1. reports pursuant to no. 1 at least once a year, unless an immediate report is called for in view of changes to the situation or new issues;

Fragen eine unverzügliche Berichterstattung gebieten;
2. die Berichte nach Nummer 2 in der Sitzung des Aufsichtsrats, in der über den Jahresabschluß verhandelt wird;
3. die Berichte nach Nummer 3 regelmäßig, mindestens vierteljährlich;
4. die Berichte nach Nummer 4 möglichst so rechtzeitig, daß der Aufsichtsrat vor Vornahme der Geschäfte Gelegenheit hat, zu ihnen Stellung zu nehmen.

(3) ¹Der Aufsichtsrat kann vom Vorstand jederzeit einen Bericht verlangen über Angelegenheiten der Gesellschaft, über ihre rechtlichen und geschäftlichen Beziehungen zu verbundenen Unternehmen sowie über geschäftliche Vorgänge bei diesen Unternehmen, die auf die Lage der Gesellschaft von erheblichem Einfluß sein können. ²Auch ein einzelnes Mitglied kann einen Bericht, jedoch nur an den Aufsichtsrat, verlangen.

(4) ¹Die Berichte haben den Grundsätzen einer gewissenhaften und getreuen Rechenschaft zu entsprechen. ²Sie sind möglichst rechtzeitig und, mit Ausnahme des Berichts nach Absatz 1 Satz 3, in der Regel in Textform zu erstatten.

(5) ¹Jedes Aufsichtsratsmitglied hat das Recht, von den Berichten Kenntnis zu nehmen. ²Soweit die Berichte in Textform erstattet worden sind, sind sie auch jedem Aufsichtsratsmitglied auf Verlangen zu übermitteln, soweit der Aufsichtsrat nichts anderes beschlossen hat. ³Der Vorsitzende des Aufsichtsrats hat die Aufsichtsratsmitglieder über die Berichte nach Absatz 1 Satz 3 spätestens in der nächsten Aufsichtsratssitzung zu unterrichten.

§ 91 Organisation; Buchführung.

(1) Der Vorstand hat dafür zu sorgen, daß die erforderlichen Handelsbücher geführt werden.

2. reports pursuant to no. 2 in the supervisory board meeting dealing with the annual financial statements;
3. reports pursuant to no. 3 regularly, but at least once every quarter;
4. reports pursuant to no. 4 as far as possible in such good time that the supervisory board has an opportunity to comment on such transactions before they are implemented.

(3) ¹The supervisory board may at any time request a report from the management board on the affairs of the company, its legal and business relationships to affiliated enterprises and on any matters relating to the business of such enterprises which might have a considerable effect on the situation of the company. ²A report may also be requested by any individual member, but such report shall only be made available to the supervisory board.

(4) ¹The reports shall conform to the principles of conscientious and accurate accounting. ²They shall be delivered as promptly as possible and, with the exception of the report pursuant to para. 1 sentence 3, as a rule in text form.

(5) ¹Each member of the supervisory board shall be entitled to be informed of the contents of the reports. ²If the reports are submitted in text form, they shall be transmitted to each member of the supervisory board upon request, unless the supervisory board has resolved otherwise. ³The chairman of the supervisory board shall inform the members of the supervisory board of the reports made pursuant to para. 1 sentence 2 either prior to or during the next supervisory board meeting.

§ 91 Organization; Bookkeeping.

(1) The management board shall ensure that the required books of account are kept.

(2) Der Vorstand hat geeignete Maßnahmen zu treffen, insbesondere ein Überwachungssystem einzurichten, damit den Fortbestand der Gesellschaft gefährdende Entwicklungen früh erkannt werden.

§ 92 Vorstandspflichten bei Verlust, Überschuldung oder Zahlungsunfähigkeit.

(1) Ergibt sich bei Aufstellung der Jahresbilanz oder einer Zwischenbilanz oder ist bei pflichtmäßigem Ermessen anzunehmen, daß ein Verlust in Höhe der Hälfte des Grundkapitals besteht, so hat der Vorstand unverzüglich die Hauptversammlung einzuberufen und ihr dies anzuzeigen.

(2) [1]Nachdem die Zahlungsunfähigkeit der Gesellschaft eingetreten ist oder sich ihre Überschuldung ergeben hat, darf der Vorstand keine Zahlungen leisten. [2]Dies gilt nicht von Zahlungen, die auch nach diesem Zeitpunkt mit der Sorgfalt eines ordentlichen und gewissenhaften Geschäftsleiters vereinbar sind. [3]Die gleiche Verpflichtung trifft den Vorstand für Zahlungen an Aktionäre, soweit diese zur Zahlungsunfähigkeit der Gesellschaft führen mussten, es sei denn, dies war auch bei Beachtung der in § 93 Abs. 1 Satz 1 bezeichneten Sorgfalt nicht erkennbar.

§ 93 Sorgfaltspflicht und Verantwortlichkeit der Vorstandsmitglieder.

(1) [1]Die Vorstandsmitglieder haben bei ihrer Geschäftsführung die Sorgfalt eines ordentlichen und gewissenhaften Geschäftsleiters anzuwenden. [2]Eine Pflichtverletzung liegt nicht vor, wenn das Vorstandsmitglied bei einer unternehmerischen Entscheidung vernünftigerweise annehmen durfte, auf der Grundlage angemessener Information zum Wohle der Gesellschaft zu handeln. [3]Über vertrauliche Angaben und

(2) The management board shall introduce appropriate measures, in particular setting up a monitoring system, in order to ensure that any developments endangering the continued existence of the company may be identified early on.

§ 92 Duties of management board in the event of loss, over-indebtedness or illiquidity.

(1) If it becomes apparent when drawing up the annual balance sheet or an interim balance sheet or if it is to be assumed on the basis of a due assessment of the circumstances that the company has incurred a loss amounting to half of the registered share capital, the management board shall convene a general meeting without undue delay and inform the meeting thereof.

(2) [1]The management board may not make any payments once the company has become illiquid or over-indebted. [2]This shall not apply to payments made after such time if such payments are compatible with the due care of a diligent and conscientious manager. [3]The management board shall have the same obligation with respect to payments to shareholders to the extent such payments will lead to the illiquidity of the company, unless this was not recognizable even when observing the care set forth in sec. 93 para. 1 sentence 1.

§ 93 Duty of care and responsibility of members of the management board.

(1) [1]The members of the management board shall apply the due care of a diligent and conscientious manager in managing the company. [2]There is no breach of duty if the member of the management board, in the case of an entrepreneurial decision, could reasonably assume to be acting on the basis of adequate information and for the benefit of the company. [3]The members of the management board shall keep con-

Geheimnisse der Gesellschaft, namentlich Betriebs- oder Geschäftsgeheimnisse, die den Vorstandsmitgliedern durch ihre Tätigkeit im Vorstand bekanntgeworden sind, haben sie Stillschweigen zu bewahren. ⁴Die Pflicht des Satzes 3 gilt nicht gegenüber einer nach § 342b des Handelsgesetzbuchs anerkannten Prüfstelle im Rahmen einer von dieser durchgeführten Prüfung.

(2) ¹Vorstandsmitglieder, die ihre Pflichten verletzen, sind der Gesellschaft zum Ersatz des daraus entstehenden Schadens als Gesamtschuldner verpflichtet. ²Ist streitig, ob sie die Sorgfalt eines ordentlichen und gewissenhaften Geschäftsleiters angewandt haben, so trifft sie die Beweislast. ³Schließt die Gesellschaft eine Versicherung zur Absicherung eines Vorstandsmitglieds gegen Risiken aus dessen beruflicher Tätigkeit für die Gesellschaft ab, ist ein Selbstbehalt von mindestens 10 Prozent des Schadens mindestens bis zur Höhe des Eineinhalbfachen der festen jährlichen Vergütung des Vorstandsmitglieds vorzusehen.

(3) Die Vorstandsmitglieder sind namentlich zum Ersatz verpflichtet, wenn entgegen diesem Gesetz

1. Einlagen an die Aktionäre zurückgewährt werden,
2. den Aktionären Zinsen oder Gewinnanteile gezahlt werden,
3. eigene Aktien der Gesellschaft oder einer anderen Gesellschaft gezeichnet, erworben, als Pfand genommen oder eingezogen werden,
4. Aktien vor der vollen Leistung des Ausgabebetrags ausgegeben werden,
5. Gesellschaftsvermögen verteilt wird,
6. Zahlungen entgegen § 92 Abs. 2 geleistet werden,
7. Vergütungen an Aufsichtsratsmitglieder gewährt werden,
8. Kredit gewährt wird,
9. bei der bedingten Kapitalerhöhung außerhalb des festgesetzten Zwecks

fidential information and secrets of the company, namely trade or business secrets, which they obtained knowledge of from their activity on the management board. ⁴The duty set forth in sentence 3 shall not apply to an auditing agency accredited pursuant to sec. 342b of the Commercial Code in the context of an audit performed by it.

(2) ¹Members of the management board who fail to comply with their duties shall be jointly and severally liable to the company for any resulting damage. ²In the event of a dispute as to whether or not they applied the due care of a diligent and conscientious manager, they shall bear the burden of proof. ³If the company obtains insurance covering a member of the management board against risks from their professional activity for the company, a deductible of at least ten percent of the damage at least up to the level of one-and-a-half times the fixed yearly compensation of the member of the management board shall be provided for.

(3) The members of the management board shall in particular be liable if, contrary to the provisions of this Act,

1. contributions are repaid to shareholders,
2. the shareholders are paid interest or granted a share in the profits,
3. own shares of the company or another company are subscribed to, acquired, pledged or redeemed,
4. shares are issued before the issue price has been paid in full,
5. corporate assets are distributed,
6. payments are made in contravention of sec. 92 para. 2,
7. remunerations are paid to supervisory board members,
8. credit is granted,
9. new shares are issued at a contingent capital increase for a purpose oth-

oder vor der vollen Leistung des Gegenwerts Bezugsaktien ausgegeben werden.

(4) ¹Der Gesellschaft gegenüber tritt die Ersatzpflicht nicht ein, wenn die Handlung auf einem gesetzmäßigen Beschluß der Hauptversammlung beruht. ²Dadurch, daß der Aufsichtsrat die Handlung gebilligt hat, wird die Ersatzpflicht nicht ausgeschlossen. ³Die Gesellschaft kann erst drei Jahre nach der Entstehung des Anspruchs und nur dann auf Ersatzansprüche verzichten oder sich über sie vergleichen, wenn die Hauptversammlung zustimmt und nicht eine Minderheit, deren Anteile zusammen den zehnten Teil des Grundkapitals erreichen, zur Niederschrift Widerspruch erhebt. ⁴Die zeitliche Beschränkung gilt nicht, wenn der Ersatzpflichtige zahlungsunfähig ist und sich zur Abwendung des Insolvenzverfahrens mit seinen Gläubigern vergleicht oder wenn die Ersatzpflicht in einem Insolvenzplan geregelt wird.

(5) ¹Der Ersatzanspruch der Gesellschaft kann auch von den Gläubigern der Gesellschaft geltend gemacht werden, soweit sie von dieser keine Befriedigung erlangen können. ²Dies gilt jedoch in anderen Fällen als denen des Absatzes 3 nur dann, wenn die Vorstandsmitglieder die Sorgfalt eines ordentlichen und gewissenhaften Geschäftsleiters gröblich verletzt haben; Absatz 2 Satz 2 gilt sinngemäß. ³Den Gläubigern gegenüber wird die Ersatzpflicht weder durch einen Verzicht oder Vergleich der Gesellschaft noch dadurch aufgehoben, daß die Handlung auf einem Beschluß der Hauptversammlung beruht. ⁴Ist über das Vermögen der Gesellschaft das Insolvenzverfahren eröffnet, so übt während dessen Dauer der Insolvenzverwalter oder der Sachwalter das Recht der Gläubiger gegen die Vorstandsmitglieder aus.

(6) Die Ansprüche aus diesen Vorschriften verjähren bei Gesellschaften, die

er than that specified or before the price therefor has been paid in full.

(4) ¹The members of the management board shall not be liable to the company for damages if the action was taken on the basis of a lawful resolution of the general meeting. ²The fact that the supervisory board approved the action shall not exclude liability for damages. ³The company may only waive or compromise claims for damages three years after such claims arise and then only if the general meeting grants its consent and no objection is raised in the minutes by a minority of shareholders whose aggregate holding amounts to one tenth of the registered share capital. ⁴The time limit shall not apply if the party liable for the damage is illiquid and enters into a composition with his creditors in order to avert insolvency proceedings or if the liability for damages is regulated in an insolvency plan.

(5) ¹The company's claim for damages may also be asserted by creditors of the company to the extent that said creditors are unable to obtain fulfillment of their claims from the company. ²In cases other than those pursuant to para. 3, however, the foregoing shall only apply if the members of the management board have grossly breached the duty of care of a diligent and conscientious manager; para. 2 sentence 2 shall apply accordingly. ³The liability for damages is not excluded vis-à-vis the creditors by a waiver or composition by the company or by the fact that the act which caused the damage is based on a resolution of the general meeting. ⁴If insolvency proceedings have been commenced against the assets of the company, the insolvency administrator or the custodian shall exercise the company's rights against the members of the management board for the duration of such proceedings.

(6) Claims arising from these provisions shall become time barred after ten years

zum Zeitpunkt der Pflichtverletzung börsennotiert sind, in zehn Jahren, bei anderen Gesellschaften in fünf Jahren.

§ 94 Stellvertreter von Vorstandsmitgliedern.

Die Vorschriften für die Vorstandsmitglieder gelten auch für ihre Stellvertreter.

Zweiter Abschnitt. Aufsichtsrat

§ 95 Zahl der Aufsichtsratsmitglieder

[1]Der Aufsichtsrat besteht aus drei Mitgliedern. [2]Die Satzung kann eine bestimmte höhere Zahl festsetzen. [3]Die Zahl muß durch drei teilbar sein, wenn dies zur Erfüllung mitbestimmungsrechtlicher Vorgaben erforderlich ist. [4]Die Höchstzahl der Aufsichtsratsmitglieder beträgt bei Gesellschaften mit einem Grundkapital

bis zu 1.500.000 Euro neun,

von mehr als 1.500.000 Euro fünfzehn,

von mehr als 10.000.000 Euro einundzwanzig.

[5]Durch die vorstehenden Vorschriften werden hiervon abweichende Vorschriften des Mitbestimmungsgesetzes vom 4. Mai 1976 (BGBl. I S. 1153), des Montan-Mitbestimmungsgesetzes und des Gesetzes zur Ergänzung des Gesetzes über die Mitbestimmung der Arbeitnehmer in den Aufsichtsräten und Vorständen der Unternehmen des Bergbaus und der Eisen und Stahl erzeugenden Industrie in der im Bundesgesetzblatt Teil III, Gliederungsnummer 801-3, veröffentlichten bereinigten Fassung – Mitbestimmungsergänzungsgesetz – nicht berührt.

for companies, which are listed at a stock exchange at the time of the breach of duty, and for all other companies after five years.

§ 94 Deputies of members of the management board.

The provisions relating to members of the management board shall also apply to their deputies.

Section Two. Supervisory Board

§ 95 Number of supervisory board members.

[1]The supervisory board consists of three members. [2]The articles of association may stipulate a specific higher number. [3]Such number shall be divisible by three, if this is necessary for the fulfillment of the codetermination rules. [4]The maximum number of supervisory board members for companies with a registered share capital of

up to EUR 1,500,000 shall be nine,

more than EUR 1,500,000 shall be fifteen,

more than EUR 10,000,000 shall be twenty-one.

[5]The above provisions shall not affect provisions to the contrary contained in the Codetermination Act of May 4, 1976 (Federal Law Gazette, Vol. I, p. 1153), the Iron Coal and Steel Codetermination Act and the Supplementary Act on the Codetermination of Employees in Supervisory Boards and Management Boards of Enterprises in the Mining and Iron and Steel Producing Industries published in the Federal Law Gazette Part III, section 801-2 in the revised version "Coal, Iron and Steel Codetermination Act".

§ 96 Composition of the supervisory board.

(1) The supervisory board shall be composed as follows:

– in companies to which the Codetermination Act applies, the supervisory board shall consist of representatives of the shareholders and the employees,

– in companies to which the Coal, Iron and Steel Codetermination Act applies, the supervisory board shall consist of representatives of the shareholders, the employees and further members,

– in companies to which sec. 5 to 13 of the Codetermination Amendment Act apply, the supervisory board shall consist of representatives of the shareholders and the employees and one additional member,

– in companies to which the One-Third Participation Act applies, the supervisory board shall consist of representatives of the shareholders and the employees,

– in companies to which the Act on Codetermination by Employees in International Mergers of December 21, 2006 (Federal Law Gazette Part I, p. 3332) applies, the supervisory board shall consist of representatives of the shareholders and the employees,

– and in the case of all other companies, the supervisory board shall only consist of representatives of the shareholders.

(2) [1]In listed companies to which the Codetermination Act, the Coal, Iron and Steel Codetermination Act or the Codetermination Amendment Act applies, the supervisory board shall consist of at least 30 percent women and of at least 30 percent men. [2]The minimum percentage shall be met by the supervisory board as a whole. [3]In case either the majority of the shareholders' or employee representatives resolves by majority prior to the election to the chairman of the

ses vor der Wahl der Gesamterfüllung gegenüber dem Aufsichtsratsvorsitzenden, so ist der Mindestanteil für diese Wahl von der Seite der Anteilseigner und der Seite der Arbeitnehmer getrennt zu erfüllen. [4]Es ist in allen Fällen auf volle Personenzahlen mathematisch auf- beziehungsweise abzurunden. [5]Verringert sich bei Gesamterfüllung der höhere Frauenanteil einer Seite nachträglich und widerspricht sie nun der Gesamterfüllung, so wird dadurch die Besetzung auf der anderen Seite nicht unwirksam. [6]Eine Wahl der Mitglieder des Aufsichtsrats durch die Hauptversammlung und eine Entsendung in den Aufsichtsrat unter Verstoß gegen das Mindestanteilsgebot ist nichtig. [7]Ist eine Wahl aus anderen Gründen für nichtig erklärt, so verstoßen zwischenzeitlich erfolgte Wahlen insoweit nicht gegen das Mindestanteilsgebot. [8]Auf die Wahl der Aufsichtsratsmitglieder der Arbeitnehmer sind die in Satz 1 genannten Gesetze zur Mitbestimmung anzuwenden.

supervisory board to refuse to fulfill the requirements as a whole, for this election the shareholders as well as the employee representatives have to fulfill the minimum percentage separately. [4]In any event it has to be mathematically rounded up or down to a whole number of persons. [5]If, in case of an overall compliance, the higher proportion of women narrows subsequently on one side, and this contradicts the overall compliance, the other side's election does not become void. [6]An election of the supervisory board's members by the general meeting and a delegation to the Supervisory Board by violating the minimum requirement is void. [7]If an election is declared void for some other reason, an interim election does not violate the minimum requirement in this respect. [8]The statutes mentioned in sentence 1 about the codetermination do also apply to the election of the supervisory board members representing the employees.

(3) [1]Bei börsennotierten Gesellschaften, die aus einer grenzüberschreitenden Verschmelzung hervorgegangen sind und bei denen nach dem Gesetz über die Mitbestimmung der Arbeitnehmer bei einer grenzüberschreitenden Verschmelzung das Aufsichts- oder Verwaltungsorgan aus derselben Zahl von Anteilseigner- und Arbeitnehmervertretern besteht, müssen in dem Aufsichts- oder Verwaltungsorgan Frauen und Männer jeweils mit einem Anteil von mindestens 30 Prozent vertreten sein. [2]Absatz 2 Satz 2, 4, 6 und 7 gilt entsprechend.

(3) [1]In listed companies, which originate from a cross-border merger and in which the supervisory or administrative board consists of the same number of shareholder and employee representatives, women and men shall be represented in the supervisory or administrative body with at least 30%. [2]Para. 2 sentence 2, 4, 6 and 7 shall apply correspondingly.

(4) Nach anderen als den zuletzt angewandten gesetzlichen Vorschriften kann der Aufsichtsrat nur zusammengesetzt werden, wenn nach § 97 oder nach § 98 die in der Bekanntmachung des Vorstands oder in der gerichtlichen Entscheidung angegebenen gesetzlichen Vorschriften anzuwenden sind.

(4) The supervisory board may only be composed other than by the above mentioned rules, if corresponding to sec. 97 or sec. 98 the legal provisions stated by the management board`s announcement or by the court's decision shall apply.

§ 97 Bekanntmachung über die Zusammensetzung des Aufsichtsrats.

(1) ¹Ist der Vorstand der Ansicht, daß der Aufsichtsrat nicht nach den für ihn maßgebenden gesetzlichen Vorschriften zusammengesetzt ist, so hat er dies unverzüglich in den Gesellschaftsblättern und gleichzeitig durch Aushang in sämtlichen Betrieben der Gesellschaft und ihrer Konzernunternehmen bekanntzumachen. ²In der Bekanntmachung sind die nach Ansicht des Vorstands maßgebenden gesetzlichen Vorschriften anzugeben. ³Es ist darauf hinzuweisen, daß der Aufsichtsrat nach diesen Vorschriften zusammengesetzt wird, wenn nicht Antragsberechtigte nach § 98 Abs. 2 innerhalb eines Monats nach der Bekanntmachung im Bundesanzeiger das nach § 98 Abs. 1 zuständige Gericht anrufen.

(2) ¹Wird das nach § 98 Abs. 1 zuständige Gericht nicht innerhalb eines Monats nach der Bekanntmachung im Bundesanzeiger angerufen, so ist der neue Aufsichtsrat nach den in der Bekanntmachung des Vorstands angegebenen gesetzlichen Vorschriften zusammenzusetzen. ²Die Bestimmungen der Satzung über die Zusammensetzung des Aufsichtsrats, über die Zahl der Aufsichtsratsmitglieder sowie über die Wahl, Abberufung und Entsendung von Aufsichtsratsmitgliedern treten mit der Beendigung der ersten Hauptversammlung, die nach Ablauf der Anrufungsfrist einberufen wird, spätestens sechs Monate nach Ablauf dieser Frist insoweit außer Kraft, als sie den nunmehr anzuwendenden gesetzlichen Vorschriften widersprechen. ³Mit demselben Zeitpunkt erlischt das Amt der bisherigen Aufsichtsratsmitglieder. ⁴Eine Hauptversammlung, die innerhalb der Frist von sechs Monaten stattfindet, kann an Stelle der außer Kraft tretenden Satzungsbestimmungen mit

§ 97 Announcement concerning the composition of the supervisory board.

(1) ¹If the management board is of the opinion that the supervisory board has not been composed in accordance with the applicable statutory provisions, it shall make an announcement to this effect in the company's designated journals without undue delay and at the same time in notices displayed in all facilities of the company and group enterprises. ²The announcement shall state the statutory provisions the management board believes to be applicable. ³It shall be stated that the supervisory board shall be composed in accordance with these provisions unless persons entitled to make an application pursuant to sec. 98 para. 2 call on the court having jurisdiction pursuant to sec. 98 para. 1 within one month of the announcement being published in the Federal Law Gazette.

(2) ¹If the court having jurisdiction pursuant to sec. 98 para. 1 is not called on within one month of the announcement being published in the Federal Law Gazette, the new supervisory board shall be composed in accordance with the statutory provisions specified in the announcement made by the management board. ²The provisions in the articles of association concerning the composition of the supervisory board, the number of members of the supervisory board and on the election, dismissal and appointment of supervisory board members shall, insofar as they contradict the statutory provisions which are now applicable, cease to be effective upon the end of the first general meeting held after the expiration of the period in which an application may be made to the court, and at the latest six months after the expiration of such period. ³The term of office of the previous supervisory board members shall terminate on the same date. ⁴A general meeting held within the six-month period may pass, by simple majority of the

einfacher Stimmenmehrheit neue Satzungsbestimmungen beschließen.

(3) Solange ein gerichtliches Verfahren nach §§ 98, 99 anhängig ist, kann eine Bekanntmachung über die Zusammensetzung des Aufsichtsrats nicht erfolgen.

§ 98 Gerichtliche Entscheidung über die Zusammensetzung des Aufsichtsrats.

(1) Ist streitig oder ungewiss, nach welchen gesetzlichen Vorschriften der Aufsichtsrat zusammenzusetzen ist, so entscheidet darüber auf Antrag ausschließlich das Landgericht, in dessen Bezirk die Gesellschaft ihren Sitz hat.

(2) ¹Antragsberechtigt sind

1. der Vorstand,
2. jedes Aufsichtsratsmitglied,

3. jeder Aktionär,
4. der Gesamtbetriebsrat der Gesellschaft oder, wenn in der Gesellschaft nur ein Betriebsrat besteht, der Betriebsrat,
5. der Gesamt- oder Unternehmenssprecherausschuss der Gesellschaft oder, wenn in der Gesellschaft nur ein Sprecherausschuss besteht, der Sprecherausschuss,

6. der Gesamtbetriebsrat eines anderen Unternehmens, dessen Arbeitnehmer nach den gesetzlichen Vorschriften, deren Anwendung streitig oder ungewiß ist, selbst oder durch Delegierte an der Wahl von Aufsichtsratsmitgliedern der Gesellschaft teilnehmen, oder, wenn in dem anderen Unternehmen nur ein Betriebsrat besteht, der Betriebsrat,

7. der Gesamt- oder Unternehmenssprecherausschuss eines anderen Unternehmens, dessen Arbeitneh-

votes cast, a resolution stipulating new provisions to be included in the articles of association to replace those ceasing to have effect.

(3) An announcement concerning the composition of the supervisory board may not be made while court proceedings pursuant to sec. 98, 99 are pending.

§ 98 Court decision on the composition of the supervisory board.

(1) If it is in dispute or unclear which statutory provisions are to govern the composition of the supervisory board, the regional court in whose district the company has its registered office shall have exclusive jurisdiction to decide the matter upon application.

(2) ¹The following shall be entitled to make an application:

1. the management board,
2. each member of the supervisory board,
3. each shareholder,
4. the central works council of the company or, if the company only has one works council, such works council,
5. the central spokespersons' committee or enterprise-wide spokespersons' committee of the company, or, if only one spokespersons' committee exists in the company, the spokespersons' committee,
6. the central works council of another enterprise whose employees take part, according to legal regulations the application of which is in dispute or unclear, in the election of the members of the company's supervisory board either in person or via delegates pursuant to the provisions the application of which is in dispute or unclear or, if there is only one works council in the other enterprise, such works council,
7. the central spokespersons' committee or enterprise-wide spokespersons' committee of another enter-

mer nach den gesetzlichen Vorschriften, deren Anwendung streitig oder ungewiss ist, selbst oder durch Delegierte an der Wahl von Aufsichtsratsmitgliedern der Gesellschaft teilnehmen, oder, wenn in dem anderen Unternehmen nur ein Sprecherausschuss besteht, der Sprecherausschuss,

8. mindestens ein Zehntel oder einhundert der Arbeitnehmer, die nach den gesetzlichen Vorschriften, deren Anwendung streitig oder ungewiß ist, selbst oder durch Delegierte an der Wahl von Aufsichtsratsmitgliedern der Gesellschaft teilnehmen,
9. Spitzenorganisationen der Gewerkschaften, die nach den gesetzlichen Vorschriften, deren Anwendung streitig oder ungewiß ist, ein Vorschlagsrecht hätten,
10. Gewerkschaften, die nach den gesetzlichen Vorschriften, deren Anwendung streitig oder ungewiß ist, ein Vorschlagsrecht hätten.

²Ist die Anwendung des Mitbestimmungsgesetzes oder die Anwendung von Vorschriften des Mitbestimmungsgesetzes streitig oder ungewiß, so sind außer den nach Satz 1 Antragsberechtigten auch je ein Zehntel der wahlberechtigten in § 3 Abs. 1 Nr. 1 des Mitbestimmungsgesetzes bezeichneten Arbeitnehmer oder der wahlberechtigten leitenden Angestellten im Sinne des Mitbestimmungsgesetzes antragsberechtigt.

(3) Die Absätze 1 und 2 gelten sinngemäß, wenn streitig ist, ob der Abschlußprüfer das nach § 3 oder § 16 des Mitbestimmungsergänzungsgesetzes maßgebliche Umsatzverhältnis richtig ermittelt hat.

(4) ¹Entspricht die Zusammensetzung des Aufsichtsrats nicht der gerichtlichen Entscheidung, so ist der neue Aufsichtsrat nach den in der Entscheidung angegebenen gesetzlichen Vorschriften zusammenzusetzen. ²§ 97 Abs. 2 gilt

prise whose employees take part, according to legal regulations the application of which is in dispute or unclear, either in person or through delegates in the election of members of the supervisory board of the company, or, if only one spokespersons' committee exists in the other enterprise, the spokespersons' committee,

8. at least one tenth or one hundred of the employees who take part in the election of the members of the company's supervisory board either in person or via delegates pursuant to the provisions the application of which is in dispute or unclear,
9. leading organizations of the trade unions which would have a right to nominate members pursuant to the provisions the application of which is in dispute or unclear,
10. trade unions which would have a right to nominate members pursuant to the provisions the application of which is in dispute or unclear.

²If the application of the Codetermination Act or provisions thereof is in dispute or unclear, in addition to those persons entitled to make an application pursuant to sentence 1, one tenth of the employees designated in sec. 3 para. 1 no. 1 of the Codetermination Act who are entitled to vote or one tenth of the managerial employees within the meaning of the Codetermination Act who are entitled to vote shall also be entitled to make an application.

(3) Paras. 1 and 2 shall apply accordingly in case of a dispute as to whether the auditor of annual financial statement has correctly determined the decisive turnover proportion pursuant to sec. 3 or sec. 16 of the Codetermination Amendment Act.

(4) ¹If the composition of the supervisory board does not comply with the court decision, the new supervisory board shall be compiled in accordance with the legal provisions stated in the court decision. ²Sec. 97 para. 2 shall apply ac-

sinngemäß mit der Maßgabe, daß die Frist von sechs Monaten mit dem Eintritt der Rechtskraft beginnt.

cordingly, with the exception that the six-month period shall commence on the date on which the decision becomes res judicata.

§ 99 Verfahren.

(1) Auf das Verfahren ist das Gesetz über das Verfahren in Familiensachen und in den Angelegenheiten der freiwilligen Gerichtsbarkeit anzuwenden, soweit in den Absätzen 2 bis 5 nichts anderes bestimmt ist.

(2) [1]Das Landgericht hat den Antrag in den Gesellschaftsblättern bekanntzumachen. [2]Der Vorstand und jedes Aufsichtsratsmitglied sowie die nach § 98 Abs. 2 antragsberechtigten Betriebsräte, Sprecherausschüsse, Spitzenorganisationen und Gewerkschaften sind zu hören.

(3) [1]Das Landgericht entscheidet durch einen mit Gründen versehenen Beschluss. [2]Gegen die Entscheidung des Landgerichts findet die Beschwerde statt. [3]Sie kann nur auf eine Verletzung des Rechts gestützt werden; § 72 Abs. 1 Satz 2 und § 74 Abs. 2 und 3 des Gesetzes über das Verfahren in Familiensachen und in den Angelegenheiten der freiwilligen Gerichtsbarkeit sowie § 547 der Zivilprozessordnung gelten sinngemäß. [4]Die Beschwerde kann nur durch die Einreichung einer von einem Rechtsanwalt unterzeichneten Beschwerdeschrift eingelegt werden. [5]Die Landesregierung kann durch Rechtsverordnung die Entscheidung über die Beschwerde für die Bezirke mehrerer Oberlandesgerichte einem der Oberlandesgerichte oder dem Obersten Landesgericht übertragen, wenn dies der Sicherung einer einheitlichen Rechtsprechung dient. [6]Die Landesregierung kann die Ermächtigung auf die Landesjustizverwaltung übertragen.

(4) [1]Das Gericht hat seine Entscheidung dem Antragsteller und der Gesellschaft zuzustellen. [2]Es hat sie ferner ohne

§ 99 Proceedings.

(1) Unless stipulated otherwise in paras. 2 to 5, the Act on Procedure in Family Matters and Matters of Non-Contentious Jurisdiction shall apply to the court proceedings.

(2) [1]The regional court shall publish the application in the company's designated journals. [2]The management board, each member of the supervisory board and those works councils, spokespersons' committees, leading organizations and trade unions which are entitled to make an application pursuant to sec. 98 para. 2 shall be heard.

(3) [1]The regional court shall issue an order stating the reasons for its decision. [2]The decision of the regional court is subject to appeal. [3]Such appeal may only be based on a violation of the law; sec. 72 para. 1 sentence 2 and sec. 74 paras. 2 and 3 of the Act on Procedure in Family Matters and on Matters of Non-Contentious Jurisdiction as well as sec. 547 of the Code of Civil Procedure shall apply accordingly. [4]An appeal may only be made by submitting a notice of appeal signed by an attorney. [5]The state government may pass a regulation transferring the authority to decide on the appeal for the districts of several higher regional courts to one specific higher regional court or to the supreme regional court if this serves to ensure uniformity of court rulings. [6]The state government may transfer such authority to the body responsible for the administration of justice in the state.

(4) [1]The court shall serve its decision to the party making the application and to the company. [2]Furthermore, it shall

Gründe in den Gesellschaftsblättern bekanntzumachen. ³Die Beschwerde steht jedem nach § 98 Abs. 2 Antragsberechtigten zu. ⁴Die Beschwerdefrist beginnt mit der Bekanntmachung der Entscheidung im Bundesanzeiger, für den Antragsteller und die Gesellschaft jedoch nicht vor der Zustellung der Entscheidung.

(5) ¹Die Entscheidung wird erst mit der Rechtskraft wirksam. ²Sie wirkt für und gegen alle. ³Der Vorstand hat die rechtskräftige Entscheidung unverzüglich zum Handelsregister einzureichen.

(6) ¹Die Kosten können ganz oder zum Teil dem Antragsteller auferlegt werden, wenn dies der Billigkeit entspricht. ²Kosten der Beteiligten werden nicht erstattet.

§ 100 Persönliche Voraussetzungen für Aufsichtsratsmitglieder.

(1) ¹Mitglied des Aufsichtsrats kann nur eine natürliche, unbeschränkt geschäftsfähige Person sein. ²Ein Betreuer, der bei der Besorgung seiner Vermögensangelegenheiten ganz oder teilweise einem Einwilligungsvorbehalt (§ 1903 des Bürgerlichen Gesetzbuchs) unterliegt, kann nicht Mitglied des Aufsichtsrats sein.

(2) ¹Mitglied des Aufsichtsrats kann nicht sein, wer

1. bereits in zehn Handelsgesellschaften, die gesetzlich einen Aufsichtsrat zu bilden haben, Aufsichtsratsmitglied ist,
2. gesetzlicher Vertreter eines von der Gesellschaft abhängigen Unternehmens ist,
3. gesetzlicher Vertreter einer anderen Kapitalgesellschaft ist, deren Aufsichtsrat ein Vorstandsmitglied der Gesellschaft angehört, oder

publish the decision in the company's designated journals without stating the reasons therefor. ³An appeal may be filed by any of the parties entitled to file an application pursuant to sec. 98 para. 2. ⁴The period in which an appeal may be filed shall commence upon the date the decision is announced in the Federal Law Gazette, but, in the case of the party making the application and the company, not prior to the service of the decision.

(5) ¹The decision shall only take effect once it becomes res judicata. ²It shall be effective for and against all parties. ³The management board shall submit the decision being res judicata to the commercial register without undue delay.

(6) ¹The petitioner may, however, be ordered to pay all or a part of the costs if this is fair under the circumstances. ²Costs incurred by the parties concerned shall not be reimbursed.

§ 100 Personal requirements for supervisory board members.

(1) ¹Only a natural person with full legal capacity may be a member of the supervisory board. ²Anyone under the care of a custodian who is partially or entirely subject to a requirement to obtain consent concerning the management of his financial affairs (sec. 1903 of the Civil Code) may not be a member of the supervisory board.

(2) ¹Member of the supervisory board may not be someone who

1. he is already a member of the supervisory board in ten commercial enterprises under a legal obligation to form a supervisory board,
2. he is the legal representative of an enterprise controlled by the company,
3. he is the legal representative of another corporation whose supervisory board includes a member of the company's management board, or

4. in den letzten zwei Jahren Vorstandsmitglied derselben börsennotierten Gesellschaft war, es sei denn, seine Wahl erfolgt auf Vorschlag von Aktionären, die mehr als 25 Prozent der Stimmrechte an der Gesellschaft halten.

²Auf die Höchstzahl nach Satz 1 Nr. 1 sind bis zu fünf Aufsichtsratssitze nicht anzurechnen, die ein gesetzlicher Vertreter (beim Einzelkaufmann der Inhaber) des herrschenden Unternehmens eines Konzerns in zum Konzern gehörenden Handelsgesellschaften, die gesetzlich einen Aufsichtsrat zu bilden haben, inne hat. ³Auf die Höchstzahl nach Satz 1 Nr. 1 sind Aufsichtsratsämter im Sinne der Nummer 1 doppelt anzurechnen, für die das Mitglied zum Vorsitzenden gewählt worden ist.

(3) Die anderen persönlichen Voraussetzungen der Aufsichtsratsmitglieder der Arbeitnehmer sowie der weiteren Mitglieder bestimmen sich nach dem Mitbestimmungsgesetz, dem Montan-Mitbestimmungsgesetz, dem Mitbestimmungsergänzungsgesetz, dem Drittelbeteiligungsgesetz und dem Gesetz über die Mitbestimmung der Arbeitnehmer bei einer grenzüberschreitenden Verschmelzung.

(4) Die Satzung kann persönliche Voraussetzungen nur für Aufsichtsratsmitglieder fordern, die von der Hauptversammlung ohne Bindung an Wahlvorschläge gewählt oder auf Grund der Satzung in den Aufsichtsrat entsandt werden.

(5) Bei Gesellschaften, die kapitalmarktorientiert im Sinne des § 264d des Handelsgesetzbuchs, die CRR-Kreditinstitute im Sinne des § 1 Absatz 3d Satz 1 des Kreditwesengesetzes, mit Ausnahme der in § 2 Absatz 1 Nummer 1 und 2 des Kreditwesengesetzes genannten Institute, oder die Versicherungsunter-

4. if he was, during the last two years, a member of the management board of the same listed company unless he was elected upon nomination by shareholders holding more than 25 percent of the voting rights in the company.

²Up to five seats held by a legal representative (in the case of a sole proprietor, the owner) of the controlling enterprise of a group on the supervisory boards of commercial enterprises belonging to the group which are under a legal obligation to form a supervisory board shall not be taken into account when determining the maximum number of seats pursuant to sentence 1 no. 1. ³Supervisory board seats within the meaning of no. 1 shall be counted twice when determining the maximum number of seats pursuant to sentence 1 no. 1 if the member has been elected to the position of chairman.

(3) The remaining personal requirements for the employee representatives on the supervisory board and the further members of the supervisory board shall be determined in accordance with the Codetermination Act, the Coal, Iron and Steel Codetermination Act, the Codetermination Amendment Act, the One-Third Participation Act and the Act on the Codetermination by Employees in International Mergers applies,

(4) The articles of association may stipulate personal requirements only for members of the supervisory board who are elected by the general meeting without being bound to nominations or for members who are appointed to the supervisory board on the basis of the articles of association.

(5) In companies within the meaning of sec. 264d of the Commercial Code, the CRR-credit institutions within the meaning of sec. 1 para. 3d sentence 1 of the German Banking Act, with the exception of the institutions mentioned in sec. 2 para. 1 number 1 and 2 of the German Banking Act or the insurance

nehmen im Sinne des Artikels 2 Absatz 1 der Richtlinie 91/674/EWG des Rates vom 19. Dezember 1991 über den Jahresabschluß und den konsolidierten Abschluß von Versicherungsunternehmen (ABl. L 374 vom 31.12.1991, S. 7), die zuletzt durch die Richtlinie 2006/46/EG (ABl. L 224 vom 16.8.2006, S. 1) geändert worden ist, sind, muss mindestens ein Mitglied des Aufsichtsrats über Sachverstand auf den Gebieten Rechnungslegung oder Abschlussprüfung verfügen; die Mitglieder müssen in ihrer Gesamtheit mit dem Sektor, in dem die Gesellschaft tätig ist, vertraut sein.

companies within the meaning of Article 2 para. 1 of Council Directive 91/674/EWG of 19 December 1991 on the Annual Accounts and Consolidated Accounts of Insurance Undertakings (ABl. L 374, 31.12.1991, p.7) as last amended by Directive 2006/46/EG (ABl. L 224, 16.08.2006, p.1) at least one independent member of the supervisory board shall have expert knowledge in the fields of financial accounting or the auditing of financial statements; the members as a whole have to be familiar with the sector, in which the company is operating.

§ 101 Bestellung der Aufsichtsratsmitglieder.

§ 101 Appointment of supervisory board members.

(1) [1]Die Mitglieder des Aufsichtsrats werden von der Hauptversammlung gewählt, soweit sie nicht in den Aufsichtsrat zu entsenden oder als Aufsichtsratsmitglieder der Arbeitnehmer nach dem Mitbestimmungsgesetz, dem Mitbestimmungsergänzungsgesetz, dem Drittelbeteiligungsgesetz oder dem Gesetz über die Mitbestimmung der Arbeitnehmer bei einer grenzüberschreitenden Verschmelzung zu wählen sind. [2]An Wahlvorschläge ist die Hauptversammlung nur gemäß §§ 6 und 8 des Montan-Mitbestimmungsgesetzes gebunden.

(1) [1]The members of the supervisory board shall be elected by the general meeting unless they are to be appointed to the supervisory board or are to be elected as employee representatives on the supervisory board pursuant to the Codetermination Act, the Codetermination Amendment Act, the One-Third Participation Act or the Act on the Codetermination by Employees in International Mergers. [2]The general meeting shall only be bound to nominations pursuant to sec. 6 and 8 of the Coal, Iron and Steel Codetermination Act.

(2) [1]Ein Recht, Mitglieder in den Aufsichtsrat zu entsenden, kann nur durch die Satzung und nur für bestimmte Aktionäre oder für die jeweiligen Inhaber bestimmter Aktien begründet werden. [2]Inhabern bestimmter Aktien kann das Entsendungsrecht nur eingeräumt werden, wenn die Aktien auf Namen lauten und ihre Übertragung an die Zustimmung der Gesellschaft gebunden ist. [3]Die Aktien der Entsendungsberechtigten gelten nicht als eine besondere Gattung. [4]Die Entsendungsrechte können insgesamt höchstens für ein Drittel der sich aus dem Gesetz oder der Satzung ergebenden Zahl der Aufsichtsratsmit-

(2) [1]The right to appoint members to the supervisory board may only be granted by the articles of association and only for certain shareholders or the respective holders of specific shares. [2]The holders of specific shares may only be granted a right to appoint members to the supervisory board if the shares are in registered form and the company's consent is required for the transfer thereof. [3]The shares of those entitled to appoint members to the supervisory board shall not be deemed to constitute a special class of share. [4]The right of appointment may only be granted to a total of at most one third of the number of shareholder members the supervisory board is to

glieder der Aktionäre eingeräumt werden.

(3) ¹Stellvertreter von Aufsichtsratsmitgliedern können nicht bestellt werden. ²Jedoch kann für jedes Aufsichtsratsmitglied mit Ausnahme des weiteren Mitglieds, das nach dem Montan-Mitbestimmungsgesetz oder dem Mitbestimmungsergänzungsgesetz auf Vorschlag der übrigen Aufsichtsratsmitglieder gewählt wird, ein Ersatzmitglied bestellt werden, das Mitglied des Aufsichtsrats wird, wenn das Aufsichtsratsmitglied vor Ablauf seiner Amtszeit wegfällt. ³Das Ersatzmitglied kann nur gleichzeitig mit dem Aufsichtsratsmitglied bestellt werden. ⁴Auf seine Bestellung sowie die Nichtigkeit und Anfechtung seiner Bestellung sind die für das Aufsichtsratsmitglied geltenden Vorschriften anzuwenden.

have pursuant to the law or the articles of association.

(3) ¹Deputies of supervisory board members may not be appointed. ²Nevertheless, a substitute member who shall become a member of the supervisory board should the relevant supervisory board member cease to hold office before the end of his term of office may be appointed for each member of the supervisory board with the exception of the additional member to be appointed after being nominated by the other supervisory board members pursuant to the Coal, Iron and Steel Codetermination Act or the Codetermination Amendment Act. ³The substitute member may only be appointed simultaneously with the member of the supervisory board. ⁴The appointment, nullity and contestation of the appointment of the substitute member shall be governed by the provisions applicable to the supervisory board member.

§ 102 Amtszeit der Aufsichtsratsmitglieder.

(1) ¹Aufsichtsratsmitglieder können nicht für längere Zeit als bis zur Beendigung der Hauptversammlung bestellt werden, die über die Entlastung für das vierte Geschäftsjahr nach dem Beginn der Amtszeit beschließt. ²Das Geschäftsjahr, in dem die Amtszeit beginnt, wird nicht mitgerechnet.

(2) Das Amt des Ersatzmitglieds erlischt spätestens mit Ablauf der Amtszeit des weggefallenen Aufsichtsratsmitglieds.

§ 102 Term of office of supervisory board members.

(1) ¹Members of the supervisory board may only be appointed for a term lasting no longer than until the end of the general meeting granting ratification in the fourth fiscal year following the commencement of the term of office. ²The fiscal year in which the term of office commences shall not be counted.

(2) The term of office of the substitute member shall terminate at the latest upon the expiration of the original term of office of the member who has ceased to hold office.

§ 103 Abberufung der Aufsichtsratsmitglieder.

(1) ¹Aufsichtsratsmitglieder, die von der Hauptversammlung ohne Bindung an einen Wahlvorschlag gewählt worden sind, können von ihr vor Ablauf der Amtszeit abberufen werden. ²Der Beschluß bedarf einer Mehrheit, die mindestens drei Viertel der abgegebenen

§ 103 Dismissal of supervisory board members.

(1) ¹Supervisory board members who have been elected by the general meeting without such meeting being bound to a nomination may be dismissed by the general meeting before the expiration of their term of office. ²The resolution to this effect shall require a major-

Stimmen umfaßt. ³Die Satzung kann eine andere Mehrheit und weitere Erfordernisse bestimmen.

(2) ¹Ein Aufsichtsratsmitglied, das auf Grund der Satzung in den Aufsichtsrat entsandt ist, kann von dem Entsendungsberechtigten jederzeit abberufen und durch ein anderes ersetzt werden. ²Sind die in der Satzung bestimmten Voraussetzungen des Entsendungsrechts weggefallen, so kann die Hauptversammlung das entsandte Mitglied mit einfacher Stimmenmehrheit abberufen.

(3) ¹Das Gericht hat auf Antrag des Aufsichtsrats ein Aufsichtsratsmitglied abzuberufen, wenn in dessen Person ein wichtiger Grund vorliegt. ²Der Aufsichtsrat beschließt über die Antragstellung mit einfacher Mehrheit. ³Ist das Aufsichtsratsmitglied auf Grund der Satzung in den Aufsichtsrat entsandt worden, so können auch Aktionäre, deren Anteile zusammen den zehnten Teil des Grundkapitals oder den anteiligen Betrag von einer Million Euro erreichen, den Antrag stellen. ⁴Gegen die Entscheidung ist die Beschwerde zulässig.

(4) Für die Abberufung der Aufsichtsratsmitglieder, die weder von der Hauptversammlung ohne Bindung an einen Wahlvorschlag gewählt worden sind noch auf Grund der Satzung in den Aufsichtsrat entsandt sind, gelten außer Absatz 3 das Mitbestimmungsgesetz, das Montan-Mitbestimmungsgesetz, das Mitbestimmungsergänzungsgesetz, das Drittelbeteiligungsgesetz, das SE-Beteiligungsgesetz und das Gesetz über die Mitbestimmung der Arbeitnehmer bei einer grenzüberschreitenden Verschmelzung.

(5) Für die Abberufung eines Ersatzmitglieds gelten die Vorschriften über die

ity of at least three quarters of the votes cast. ³The articles of association may stipulate another majority and further requirements.

(2) ¹A member of the supervisory board who has been appointed to the supervisory board on the basis of the articles of association may at any time be dismissed by the person entitled to make the appointment and replaced by another member. ²If the requirements for the right of appointment stipulated in the articles of association have ceased to apply, the general meeting can dismiss the appointed member with a simple majority of votes cast.

(3) ¹The court shall dismiss a member of the supervisory board upon application by the supervisory board if there is good cause relating to his person. ²The supervisory board shall decide whether or not to make such an application with a simple majority of votes cast. ³If the member of the supervisory board has been appointed to the supervisory board on the basis of the articles of association, the application may also be made by shareholders holding shares with an aggregate value of one tenth of the registered share capital or a proportionate amount of one million euros. ⁴The decision is subject to appeal.

(4) In addition to para. 3, the Codetermination Act, the Coal, Iron and Steel Codetermination Act, the Codetermination Amendment Act, the One-Third Participation Act, the SE Participation Act and the Act on the Codetermination by Employees in International Mergers shall apply to the dismissal of supervisory board members who are neither elected by the general meeting without such meeting being bound to a nomination nor appointed to the supervisory board on the basis of the articles of association.

(5) The dismissal of a substitute member shall be governed by the provisions applying to the dismissal of the super-

Abberufung des Aufsichtsratsmitglieds, für das es bestellt ist.

§ 104 Bestellung durch das Gericht.

(1) ¹Gehört dem Aufsichtsrat die zur Beschlußfähigkeit nötige Zahl von Mitgliedern nicht an, so hat ihn das Gericht auf Antrag des Vorstands, eines Aufsichtsratsmitglieds oder eines Aktionärs auf diese Zahl zu ergänzen. ²Der Vorstand ist verpflichtet, den Antrag unverzüglich zu stellen, es sei denn, daß die rechtzeitige Ergänzung vor der nächsten Aufsichtsratssitzung zu erwarten ist. ³Hat der Aufsichtsrat auch aus Aufsichtsratsmitgliedern der Arbeitnehmer zu bestehen, so können auch den Antrag stellen

1. der Gesamtbetriebsrat der Gesellschaft oder, wenn in der Gesellschaft nur ein Betriebsrat besteht, der Betriebsrat, sowie, wenn die Gesellschaft herrschendes Unternehmen eines Konzerns ist, der Konzernbetriebsrat,
2. der Gesamt- oder Unternehmenssprecherausschuss der Gesellschaft oder, wenn in der Gesellschaft nur ein Sprecherausschuss besteht, der Sprecherausschuss sowie, wenn die Gesellschaft herrschendes Unternehmen eines Konzerns ist, der Konzernsprecherausschuss,
3. der Gesamtbetriebsrat eines anderen Unternehmens, dessen Arbeitnehmer selbst oder durch Delegierte an der Wahl teilnehmen, oder, wenn in dem anderen Unternehmen nur ein Betriebsrat besteht, der Betriebsrat,
4. der Gesamt- oder Unternehmenssprecherausschuss eines anderen Unternehmens, dessen Arbeitnehmer selbst oder durch Delegierte an der Wahl teilnehmen, oder, wenn in dem anderen Unternehmen nur ein Sprecherausschuss besteht, der Sprecherausschuss.

visory board member for whom such substitute has been appointed.

§ 104 Appointment by the court.

(1) ¹If the supervisory board does not have the number of members required to constitute a quorum, the court shall make it up to such number upon application by the management board, a member of the supervisory board or a shareholder. ²The management board is obligated to file an application without undue delay, unless it is to be expected that the supervisory board will consist of the correct number of members before the next sitting of the supervisory board. ³If the supervisory board is to include employee members, the application may also be filed by

1. the central works council of the company, or if the company only has one works council, such works council and, if the company is the controlling enterprise in a group, the group works council,
2. the central spokespersons' committee or enterprise-wide spokespersons' committee of the company, or, if only one spokespersons' committee exists in the company, the spokespersons' committee, as well as the group spokespersons' committee if the company is the controlling enterprise of a group,
3. the central works council of another enterprise whose employees take part in the election either in person or via delegates or, if there is only one works council in such enterprise, that works council,
4. the central spokespersons' committee or enterprise-wide spokespersons' committee of another enterprise whose employees take part either in person or via delegates in the election, or, if only one spokespersons' committee exists in the other enterprise, the spokespersons' committee,

5. mindestens ein Zehntel oder einhundert der Arbeitnehmer, die selbst oder durch Delegierte an der Wahl teilnehmen,
6. Spitzenorganisationen der Gewerkschaften, die das Recht haben, Aufsichtsratsmitglieder der Arbeitnehmer vorzuschlagen,
7. Gewerkschaften, die das Recht haben, Aufsichtsratsmitglieder der Arbeitnehmer vorzuschlagen.

[4]Hat der Aufsichtsrat nach dem Mitbestimmungsgesetz auch aus Aufsichtsratsmitgliedern der Arbeitnehmer zu bestehen, so sind außer den nach Satz 3 Antragsberechtigten auch je ein Zehntel der wahlberechtigten in § 3 Abs. 1 Nr. 1 des Mitbestimmungsgesetzes bezeichneten Arbeitnehmer oder der wahlberechtigten leitenden Angestellten im Sinne des Mitbestimmungsgesetzes antragsberechtigt. [5]Gegen die Entscheidung ist die Beschwerde zulässig.

(2) [1]Gehören dem Aufsichtsrat länger als drei Monate weniger Mitglieder als die durch Gesetz oder Satzung festgesetzte Zahl an, so hat ihn das Gericht auf Antrag auf diese Zahl zu ergänzen. [2]In dringenden Fällen hat das Gericht auf Antrag den Aufsichtsrat auch vor Ablauf der Frist zu ergänzen. [3]Das Antragsrecht bestimmt sich nach Absatz 1. [4]Gegen die Entscheidung ist die Beschwerde zulässig.

(3) Absatz 2 ist auf einen Aufsichtsrat, in dem die Arbeitnehmer ein Mitbestimmungsrecht nach dem Mitbestimmungsgesetz, dem Montan-Mitbestimmungsgesetz oder dem Mitbestimmungsergänzungsgesetz haben, mit der Maßgabe anzuwenden,

1. daß das Gericht den Aufsichtsrat hinsichtlich des weiteren Mitglieds, das nach dem Montan-Mitbestimmungsgesetz oder dem Mitbestimmungsergänzungsgesetz auf

5. at least one tenth or one hundred of the employees taking part in the election either in person or via delegates,
6. leading organizations of trade unions which are entitled to nominate employee representatives on the supervisory board,
7. trade unions which are entitled to nominate employee representatives on the supervisory board.

[4]If the supervisory board is to include employee members pursuant to the Codetermination Act, in addition to those persons entitled to file an application pursuant to sentence 3 one tenth of the employees designated in sec. 3 para. 1 no. 1 of the Codetermination Act who are entitled to vote or one tenth of the managerial employees within the meaning of the Codetermination Act who are entitled to vote shall also be entitled to file an application. [5]The decision is subject to appeal.

(2) [1]If the supervisory board consists of fewer members than the number stipulated by law or in the articles of association for longer than three months, the court shall appoint the missing number of members upon application. [2]In urgent cases the court shall also appoint the missing members to the supervisory board upon application before the expiration of such period. [3]The right to file an application shall be governed by para. 1. [4]The decision is subject to appeal.

(3) Para. 2 shall apply to a supervisory board in which the employees have a right of codetermination pursuant to the Codetermination Act, the Coal, Iron and Steel Codetermination Act or the Codetermination Amendment Act subject to the provisions

1. that the court cannot appoint the member of the supervisory board who is to be elected upon nomination by the other supervisory board members pursuant to the Coal, Iron

Vorschlag der übrigen Aufsichtsratsmitglieder gewählt wird, nicht ergänzen kann,
2. daß es stets ein dringender Fall ist, wenn dem Aufsichtsrat, abgesehen von dem in Nummer 1 genannten weiteren Mitglied, nicht alle Mitglieder angehören, aus denen er nach Gesetz oder Satzung zu bestehen hat.

(4) ¹Hat der Aufsichtsrat auch aus Aufsichtsratsmitgliedern der Arbeitnehmer zu bestehen, so hat das Gericht ihn so zu ergänzen, daß das für seine Zusammensetzung maßgebende zahlenmäßige Verhältnis hergestellt wird. ²Wenn der Aufsichtsrat zur Herstellung seiner Beschlußfähigkeit ergänzt wird, gilt dies nur, soweit die zur Beschlußfähigkeit nötige Zahl der Aufsichtsratsmitglieder die Wahrung dieses Verhältnisses möglich macht. ³Ist ein Aufsichtsratsmitglied zu ersetzen, das nach Gesetz oder Satzung in persönlicher Hinsicht besonderen Voraussetzungen entsprechen muß, so muß auch das vom Gericht bestellte Aufsichtsratsmitglied diesen Voraussetzungen entsprechen. ⁴Ist ein Aufsichtsratsmitglied zu ersetzen, bei dessen Wahl eine Spitzenorganisation der Gewerkschaften, eine Gewerkschaft oder die Betriebsräte ein Vorschlagsrecht hätten, so soll das Gericht Vorschläge dieser Stellen berücksichtigen, soweit nicht überwiegende Belange der Gesellschaft oder der Allgemeinheit der Bestellung des Vorgeschlagenen entgegenstehen; das gleiche gilt, wenn das Aufsichtsratsmitglied durch Delegierte zu wählen wäre, für gemeinsame Vorschläge der Betriebsräte der Unternehmen, in denen Delegierte zu wählen sind.

(5) Die Ergänzung durch das Gericht ist bei börsennotierten Gesellschaften, für die das Mitbestimmungsgesetz, das Montan-Mitbestimmungsgesetz oder das Mitbestimmungsergänzungsgesetz gilt, nach Maßgabe des § 96 Absatz 2 Satz 1 bis 5 vorzunehmen.

and Steel Codetermination Act or the Codetermination Amendment Act,
2. that it shall always be deemed to be an urgent case if, with the exception of the further member mentioned in no. 1, the supervisory board does not consist of all members stipulated by law or the articles of association.

(4) ¹If the supervisory board is required to include employee members, the court shall appoint members in such a manner that the numerical ratio required for the composition of the supervisory board is established. ²If additional members are appointed to the supervisory board in order to constitute a quorum, the foregoing shall only apply to the extent that the number of supervisory board members required for a quorum to be constituted permits such ratio to be maintained. ³If a supervisory board member is to be replaced who is subject to particular requirements in view of his person pursuant to the law or the articles of association, the member appointed by the court shall also comply with such requirements. ⁴If a supervisory board member is to be replaced for whom a leading organization of the trade unions, a trade union or the works councils have a right of nomination, the court shall take nominations made by such bodies into account unless appointment of the nominated person would contravene the overriding interests of the company or the general public; this shall also apply, if the supervisory board member is to be elected by delegates, for joint nominations made by the works councils of the enterprises in which delegates are to be elected.

(5) For listed companies that are subject to the Codetermination Act, the Coal, Iron and Steel Codetermination Act or the Codetermination Amendment Act, the appointment by the court shall be in accordance with sec. 96 para. 2 sentence 1 to 5.

(6) Das Amt des gerichtlich bestellten Aufsichtsratsmitglieds erlischt in jedem Fall, sobald der Mangel behoben ist.

(7) ¹Das gerichtlich bestellte Aufsichtsratsmitglied hat Anspruch auf Ersatz angemessener barer Auslagen und, wenn den Aufsichtsratsmitgliedern der Gesellschaft eine Vergütung gewährt wird, auf Vergütung für seine Tätigkeit. ²Auf Antrag des Aufsichtsratsmitglieds setzt das Gericht die Auslagen und die Vergütung fest. ³Gegen die Entscheidung ist die Beschwerde zulässig; die Rechtsbeschwerde ist ausgeschlossen. ⁴Aus der rechtskräftigen Entscheidung findet die Zwangsvollstreckung nach der Zivilprozeßordnung statt.

§ 105 Unvereinbarkeit der Zugehörigkeit zum Vorstand und zum Aufsichtsrat.

(1) Ein Aufsichtsratsmitglied kann nicht zugleich Vorstandsmitglied, dauernd Stellvertreter von Vorstandsmitgliedern, Prokurist oder zum gesamten Geschäftsbetrieb ermächtigter Handlungsbevollmächtigter der Gesellschaft sein.

(2) ¹Nur für einen im voraus begrenzten Zeitraum, höchstens für ein Jahr, kann der Aufsichtsrat einzelne seiner Mitglieder zu Stellvertretern von fehlenden oder verhinderten Vorstandsmitgliedern bestellen. ²Eine wiederholte Bestellung oder Verlängerung der Amtszeit ist zulässig, wenn dadurch die Amtszeit insgesamt ein Jahr nicht übersteigt. ³Während ihrer Amtszeit als Stellvertreter von Vorstandsmitgliedern können die Aufsichtsratsmitglieder keine Tätigkeit als Aufsichtsratsmitglied ausüben. ⁴Das Wettbewerbsverbot des § 88 gilt für sie nicht.

(6) The term of office of the member appointed by the court shall terminate as soon as the defect has been remedied.

(7) ¹The supervisory board member appointed by the court shall be entitled to the reimbursement of reasonable cash expenses and, if remuneration is paid to the members of the company's supervisory board, to remuneration for his services. ²Upon application by the supervisory board member, the court shall fix the amount of expenses and remuneration. ³The decision is subject to appeal; no further appeal on a point of law may be made. ⁴A decision being res judicata shall be enforceable pursuant to the Code of Civil Procedure.

§ 105 Incompatibility of membership on the management board and the supervisory board.

(1) A member of the supervisory board may not at the same time be a member of the management board, a permanent deputy of management board members, a procuration officer of the company or an authorized signatory with authorization for actions with respect to all of the company's business activity.

(2) ¹The supervisory board may only appoint individual members thereof as deputies for missing members of the management board or members being unable to act for a predetermined period of time of no longer than one year. ²A renewed appointment or extension of the term of office is permissible, providing the total term of office does not amount to more than one year as a result. ³The supervisory board members may not fulfill their duties as a member of the supervisory board during their term of office as deputies of management board members. ⁴The prohibition of competition pursuant to sec. 88 shall not apply to them.

§ 106 Bekanntmachung der Änderungen im Aufsichtsrat.

Der Vorstand hat bei jeder Änderung in den Personen der Aufsichtsratsmitglieder unverzüglich eine Liste der Mitglieder des Aufsichtsrats, aus welcher Name, Vorname, ausgeübter Beruf und Wohnort der Mitglieder ersichtlich ist, zum Handelsregister einzureichen; das Gericht hat nach § 10 des Handelsgesetzbuchs einen Hinweis darauf bekannt zu machen, dass die Liste zum Handelsregister eingereicht worden ist.

§ 107 Innere Ordnung des Aufsichtsrats.

(1) ¹Der Aufsichtsrat hat nach näherer Bestimmung der Satzung aus seiner Mitte einen Vorsitzenden und mindestens einen Stellvertreter zu wählen. ²Der Vorstand hat zum Handelsregister anzumelden, wer gewählt ist. ³Der Stellvertreter hat nur dann die Rechte und Pflichten des Vorsitzenden, wenn dieser verhindert ist.

(2) ¹Über die Sitzungen des Aufsichtsrats ist eine Niederschrift anzufertigen, die der Vorsitzende zu unterzeichnen hat. ²In der Niederschrift sind der Ort und der Tag der Sitzung, die Teilnehmer, die Gegenstände der Tagesordnung, der wesentliche Inhalt der Verhandlungen und die Beschlüsse des Aufsichtsrats anzugeben. ³Ein Verstoß gegen Satz 1 oder Satz 2 macht einen Beschluß nicht unwirksam. ⁴Jedem Mitglied des Aufsichtsrats ist auf Verlangen eine Abschrift der Sitzungsniederschrift auszuhändigen.

(3) ¹Der Aufsichtsrat kann aus seiner Mitte einen oder mehrere Ausschüsse bestellen, namentlich, um seine Verhandlungen und Beschlüsse vorzubereiten oder die Ausführung seiner Beschlüsse zu überwachen. ²Er kann insbesondere einen Prüfungsausschuss bestellen, der sich mit der Überwachung des Rechnungslegungsprozesses, der Wirksamkeit des internen Kontrollsys-

§ 106 Announcement of changes in the supervisory board.

Upon each change of the members of the supervisory board, the managing board shall without undue delay submit to the commercial register a list of the members of the supervisory board providing the surname, first name, profession and place of residence; the court shall provide public notice pursuant to sec. 10 of the Commercial Code that the list was submitted to the commercial register.

§ 107 Internal organization of the supervisory board.

(1) ¹The supervisory board shall appoint a chairman and at least one deputy from among its members in accordance with the relevant provisions in the articles of association. ²The management board shall notify the commercial register of the persons elected. ³The deputy shall only have the rights and obligations of the chairman if the chairman is unable to act.

(2) ¹Minutes shall be kept of the supervisory board meetings and signed by the chairman. ²The minutes shall state the date and place of the meeting, the persons present, the items of the agenda, the essential contents of proceedings and the resolutions adopted by the supervisory board. ³A violation of sentence 1 or sentence 2 shall not render the resolution invalid. ⁴A copy of the minutes of the meeting shall be distributed to each member of the supervisory board upon demand.

(3) ¹The supervisory board may appoint one or several committees from among its members for the purposes of preparing the proceedings and resolutions or monitoring the implementation of the resolutions. ²It may in particular appoint an audit committee which is responsible for the supervision of the financial accounting process, the effectiveness of the system of internal controls, the risk

tems, des Risikomanagementsystems und des internen Revisionssystems sowie der Abschlussprüfung, hier insbesondere der Auswahl und der Unabhängigkeit des Abschlussprüfers und der vom Abschlussprüfer zusätzlich erbrachten Leistungen, befasst. ³Der Prüfungsausschuss kann Empfehlungen oder Vorschläge zur Gewährleistung der Integrität des Rechnungslegungsprozesses unterbreiten ⁴Die Aufgaben nach Absatz 1 Satz 1, § 59 Abs. 3, § 77 Abs. 2 Satz 1, § 84 Abs. 1 Satz 1 und 3, Abs. 2 und Abs. 3 Satz 1, § 87 Abs. 1 und Abs. 2 Satz 1 und 2, § 111 Abs. 3, §§ 171, 314 Abs. 2 und 3 sowie Beschlüsse, daß bestimmte Arten von Geschäften nur mit Zustimmung des Aufsichtsrats vorgenommen werden dürfen, können einem Ausschuß nicht an Stelle des Aufsichtsrats zur Beschlußfassung überwiesen werden. ⁵Dem Aufsichtsrat ist regelmäßig über die Arbeit der Ausschüsse zu berichten.

(4) Richtet der Aufsichtsrat einer Gesellschaft, die kapitalmarktorientiert im Sinne des § 264d des Handelsgesetzbuchs, die CRR-Kreditinstitut im Sinne des § 1 Absatz 3d Satz 1 des Kreditwesengesetzes, mit Ausnahme der in § 2 Absatz 1 Nummer 1 und 2 des Kreditwesengesetzes genannten Institute, oder die Versicherungsunternehmen im Sinne des Artikels 2 Absatz 1 der Richtlinie 91/674/EWG ist, einen Prüfungsausschuss im Sinn des Absatzes 3 Satz 2 ein, so müssen die Voraussetzungen des § 100 Absatz 5 erfüllt sein.

§ 108 Beschlußfassung des Aufsichtsrats.

(1) Der Aufsichtsrat entscheidet durch Beschluß.

(2) ¹Die Beschlußfähigkeit des Aufsichtsrats kann, soweit sie nicht gesetzlich geregelt ist, durch die Satzung bestimmt werden. ²Ist sie weder gesetzlich noch durch die Satzung geregelt, so ist der Aufsichtsrat nur beschlußfähig, wenn

management systems and the internal audit system as well as for the auditing of financial statements, in particular the selection and independence of the auditor of financial statements and the performances which are additionally rendered by the auditor. ³The audit committee may issue recommendation proposals to ensure the integrity of the accounting process. ⁴A committee may not be granted responsibility in place of the supervisory board for adopting resolutions relating to the tasks pursuant to para. 1 sentence 1, sec. 59 para. 3, sec. 77 para. 2 sentence 1, sec. 84 para. 1 sentences 1 and 3, para. 2 and para. 3 sentence 1, sec. 87 para. 1 and para. 2 sentences 1 and 2, sec. 111 para. 3, sec. 171, sec. 314 paras. 2 and 3 or resolutions stipulating that certain types of transactions may only be made with the consent of the supervisory board. ⁵Reports on the work of the committees shall be submitted regularly to the supervisory board.

(4) If the supervisory board of a company that is capital market oriented within the meaning of sec. 264d of the Commercial Code, a CRR- credit institution within the meaning of sec. 1 para. 3d sentence 1 of the German Banking Act, with the exception of the institutions mentioned in sec. 2 para. 1 number 1 and 2 of the German Banking Act or an insurance company within the meaning of Article 2 para. 1 of Council Directive 91/674/EWG, establishes an audit committee within the meaning of para. 3 sentence 2, the requirements of sec. 100 para. 5 have to be met.

§ 108 Resolutions of the supervisory board.

(1) The supervisory board shall make decisions by resolution.

(2) ¹The requirements for a quorum in the supervisory board may, to the extent not regulated by law, be stipulated in the articles of association. ²If the requirements for such quorum are neither regulated by law nor stipulated in the

mindestens die Hälfte der Mitglieder, aus denen er nach Gesetz oder Satzung insgesamt zu bestehen hat, an der Beschlußfassung teilnimmt. ³In jedem Fall müssen mindestens drei Mitglieder an der Beschlußfassung teilnehmen. ⁴Der Beschlußfähigkeit steht nicht entgegen, daß dem Aufsichtsrat weniger Mitglieder als die durch Gesetz oder Satzung festgesetzte Zahl angehören, auch wenn das für seine Zusammensetzung maßgebende zahlenmäßige Verhältnis nicht gewahrt ist.

(3) ¹Abwesende Aufsichtsratsmitglieder können dadurch an der Beschlußfassung des Aufsichtsrats und seiner Ausschüsse teilnehmen, daß sie schriftliche Stimmabgaben überreichen lassen. ²Die schriftlichen Stimmabgaben können durch andere Aufsichtsratsmitglieder überreicht werden. ³Sie können auch durch Personen, die nicht dem Aufsichtsrat angehören, übergeben werden, wenn diese nach § 109 Abs. 3 zur Teilnahme an der Sitzung berechtigt sind.

(4) Schriftliche, fernmündliche oder andere vergleichbare Formen der Beschlussfassung des Aufsichtsrats und seiner Ausschüsse sind vorbehaltlich einer näheren Regelung durch die Satzung oder eine Geschäftsordnung des Aufsichtsrats nur zulässig, wenn kein Mitglied diesem Verfahren widerspricht.

§ 109 Teilnahme an Sitzungen des Aufsichtsrats und seiner Ausschüsse.

(1) ¹An den Sitzungen des Aufsichtsrats und seiner Ausschüsse sollen Personen, die weder dem Aufsichtsrat noch dem Vorstand angehören, nicht teilnehmen. ²Sachverständige und Auskunftspersonen können zur Beratung über einzelne Gegenstände zugezogen werden.

(2) Aufsichtsratsmitglieder, die dem Ausschuß nicht angehören, können an

articles of association, there shall only be a quorum in the supervisory board if at least half of the total number of supervisory board members stipulated by the law or the articles of association participate in the adopting of the resolution. ³At least three members shall participate in the adopting of the resolution in all instances. ⁴The quorum shall not be affected by the fact that the supervisory board has fewer members than the number determined by law or in the articles of association, even if the requisite numerical ratio is not maintained.

(3) ¹Absent supervisory board members may participate in the adopting of resolutions by the supervisory board and the committees thereof by submitting their votes in writing. ²The written votes may be submitted by other members of the supervisory board. ³They may also be submitted by persons who do not belong to the supervisory board if such persons are entitled to attend the meeting pursuant to sec. 109 para. 3.

(4) Subject to more detailed provisions in the articles of association or the rules of procedure of the supervisory board, resolutions may only be adopted in writing, by telephone or by any other comparable method if no member objects to this procedure.

§ 109 Attendance of meetings of the supervisory board and its committees.

(1) ¹Persons who belong to neither the supervisory board nor the management board ought not to attend meetings of the supervisory board and its committees. ²Experts and persons needed to give information may be called upon to attend in order to give advice on individual matters.

(2) Members of the supervisory board who do not belong to the committee

den Ausschußsitzungen teilnehmen, wenn der Vorsitzende des Aufsichtsrats nichts anderes bestimmt.

(3) Die Satzung kann zulassen, daß an den Sitzungen des Aufsichtsrats und seiner Ausschüsse Personen, die dem Aufsichtsrat nicht angehören, an Stelle von verhinderten Aufsichtsratsmitgliedern teilnehmen können, wenn diese sie hierzu in Textform ermächtigt haben.

(4) Abweichende gesetzliche Vorschriften bleiben unberührt.

§ 110 Einberufung des Aufsichtsrats.

(1) ¹Jedes Aufsichtsratsmitglied oder der Vorstand kann unter Angabe des Zwecks und der Gründe verlangen, daß der Vorsitzende des Aufsichtsrats unverzüglich den Aufsichtsrat einberuft. ²Die Sitzung muß binnen zwei Wochen nach der Einberufung stattfinden.

(2) Wird dem Verlangen nicht entsprochen, so kann das Aufsichtsratsmitglied oder der Vorstand unter Mitteilung des Sachverhalts und der Angabe einer Tagesordnung selbst den Aufsichtsrat einberufen.

(3) ¹Der Aufsichtsrat muss zwei Sitzungen im Kalenderhalbjahr abhalten. ²In nichtbörsennotierten Gesellschaften kann der Aufsichtsrat beschließen, dass eine Sitzung im Kalenderhalbjahr abzuhalten ist.

§ 111 Aufgaben und Rechte des Aufsichtsrats.

(1) Der Aufsichtsrat hat die Geschäftsführung zu überwachen.

(2) ¹Der Aufsichtsrat kann die Bücher und Schriften der Gesellschaft sowie die Vermögensgegenstände, namentlich die Gesellschaftskasse und die Bestände an Wertpapieren und Waren, einsehen und prüfen. ²Er kann damit auch einzelne Mitglieder oder für bestimmte Aufgaben besondere Sachverständige

may attend committee meetings unless stipulated otherwise by the chairman of the supervisory board.

(3) The articles of association may allow persons who do not belong to the supervisory board to attend meetings of the supervisory board and its committees in place of incapacitated supervisory board members if the latter have given them authority to do so in text form.

(4) Diverging statutory provisions shall not be affected.

§ 110 Convening of the supervisory board.

(1) ¹The management board or any member of the supervisory board can, stating the purpose and reasons for such request, request the chairman of the supervisory board to convene a meeting of the supervisory board without undue delay. ²The meeting shall be held within two weeks of being convened.

(2) If a request is not met, the member of the supervisory board or the management board may convene the supervisory board themselves, stating the facts of the case and the agenda of the meeting.

(3) ¹The supervisory board shall meet twice every six months. ²In the case of companies which are not listed, the supervisory board may decide to hold one meeting every six months.

§ 111 Duties and rights of the supervisory board.

(1) The supervisory board shall supervise the management of the company.

(2) ¹The supervisory board may view and examine the books, records and assets of the company, in particular the company's cash and inventories of securities and goods. ²It may commission individual members or, in the case of specific duties, special experts to do so. ³It shall commission the auditor of

beauftragen. ³Er erteilt dem Abschlußprüfer den Prüfungsauftrag für den Jahres- und den Konzernabschluß gemäß § 290 des Handelsgesetzbuchs.

(3) ¹Der Aufsichtsrat hat eine Hauptversammlung einzuberufen, wenn das Wohl der Gesellschaft es fordert. ²Für den Beschluß genügt die einfache Mehrheit.

(4) ¹Maßnahmen der Geschäftsführung können dem Aufsichtsrat nicht übertragen werden. ²Die Satzung oder der Aufsichtsrat hat jedoch zu bestimmen, daß bestimmte Arten von Geschäften nur mit seiner Zustimmung vorgenommen werden dürfen. ³Verweigert der Aufsichtsrat seine Zustimmung, so kann der Vorstand verlangen, daß die Hauptversammlung über die Zustimmung beschließt. ⁴Der Beschluß, durch den die Hauptversammlung zustimmt, bedarf einer Mehrheit, die mindestens drei Viertel der abgegebenen Stimmen umfaßt. ⁵Die Satzung kann weder eine andere Mehrheit noch weitere Erfordernisse bestimmen.

(5) ¹Der Aufsichtsrat von Gesellschaften, die börsennotiert sind oder der Mitbestimmung unterliegen, legt für den Frauenanteil im Aufsichtsrat und im Vorstand Zielgrößen fest. ²Liegt der Frauenanteil bei Festlegung der Zielgrößen unter 30 Prozent, so dürfen die Zielgrößen den jeweils erreichten Anteil nicht mehr unterschreiten. ³Gleichzeitig sind Fristen zur Erreichung der Zielgrößen festzulegen. ⁴Die Fristen dürfen jeweils nicht länger als fünf Jahre sein. ⁵Soweit für den Aufsichtsrat bereits eine Quote nach § 96 Absatz 2 gilt, sind die Festlegungen nur für den Vorstand vorzunehmen.

(6) Die Aufsichtsratsmitglieder können ihre Aufgaben nicht durch andere wahrnehmen lassen.

annual financial statement to conduct the audit for the annual financial statements and the consolidated financial statements pursuant to sec. 290 of the Commercial Code.

(3) ¹The supervisory board shall call a general meeting if so required by the interests of the company. ²A simple majority shall suffice for the resolution to be adopted.

(4) ¹Management measures may not be transferred to the supervisory board. ²The articles of association or the supervisory board shall, however, stipulate that certain types of transactions may only be entered into after receiving the consent of the supervisory board. ³If the supervisory board withholds its consent, the management board may request that the general meeting adopt a resolution on the granting of such consent. ⁴The resolution in which the general meeting grants its consent shall require a majority of at least three quarters of the votes cast. ⁵The articles of association may not stipulate another majority nor any further requirements.

(5) ¹The supervisory board of companies, which are listed or under the statute of employee codetermination, shall set a target for the women's representation on the supervisory and the management board. ²If the percentage of women below 30 percent when setting the target, the target must not fall below the reached percentage. ³Time limits for achieving the target shall be set at the same time. ⁴The time limits shall not exceed five years. ⁴Insofar as a quota within the meaning of sec. 96 para. 2 does already apply for the supervisory board the targets shall be set only for the management board.

(6) The members of the supervisory board may not entrust their duties to any other person.

§ 112 Vertretung der Gesellschaft gegenüber Vorstandsmitgliedern.

[1]Vorstandsmitgliedern gegenüber vertritt der Aufsichtsrat die Gesellschaft gerichtlich und außergerichtlich. [2]§ 78 Abs. 2 Satz 2 gilt entsprechend.

§ 113 Vergütung der Aufsichtsratsmitglieder.

(1) [1]Den Aufsichtsratsmitgliedern kann für ihre Tätigkeit eine Vergütung gewährt werden. [2]Sie kann in der Satzung festgesetzt oder von der Hauptversammlung bewilligt werden. [3]Sie soll in einem angemessenen Verhältnis zu den Aufgaben der Aufsichtsratsmitglieder und zur Lage der Gesellschaft stehen. [4]Ist die Vergütung in der Satzung festgesetzt, so kann die Hauptversammlung eine Satzungsänderung, durch welche die Vergütung herabgesetzt wird, mit einfacher Stimmenmehrheit beschließen.

(2) [1]Den Mitgliedern des ersten Aufsichtsrats kann nur die Hauptversammlung eine Vergütung für ihre Tätigkeit bewilligen. [2]Der Beschluß kann erst in der Hauptversammlung gefaßt werden, die über die Entlastung der Mitglieder des ersten Aufsichtsrats beschließt.

(3) [1]Wird den Aufsichtsratsmitgliedern ein Anteil am Jahresgewinn der Gesellschaft gewährt, so berechnet sich der Anteil nach dem Bilanzgewinn, vermindert um einen Betrag von mindestens vier vom Hundert der auf den geringsten Ausgabebetrag der Aktien geleisteten Einlagen. [2]Entgegenstehende Festsetzungen sind nichtig.

§ 114 Verträge mit Aufsichtsratsmitgliedern.

(1) Verpflichtet sich ein Aufsichtsratsmitglied außerhalb seiner Tätigkeit im Aufsichtsrat durch einen Dienstvertrag, durch den ein Arbeitsverhältnis nicht begründet wird, oder durch einen

§ 112 Representation of the company vis-à-vis members of the management board.

[1]The supervisory board shall represent the company both in and out of court vis-à-vis members of the management board. [2]Sec. 78 para. 2 sentence 2 shall apply accordingly.

§ 113 Remuneration for supervisory board members.

(1) [1]The members of the supervisory board may be paid remuneration for their duties. [2]Such remuneration may be stipulated in the articles of association or approved by the general meeting. [3]It ought to be reasonable in relation to the duties of the supervisory board member and the situation of the company. [4]If the remuneration is stipulated in the articles of association, the general meeting may, with a simple majority of votes cast, resolve an amendment of the articles of association reducing the remuneration.

(2) [1]Remuneration for the members of the first supervisory board may only be approved by the general meeting. [2]The resolution may only be adopted in the general meeting resolving on ratification of the acts of the members of the first supervisory board and not before.

(3) [1]If the members of the supervisory board are granted a share in the company's annual profits, such share shall be calculated according to the balance sheet profit minus an amount of at least four percent of the contributions paid in respect of the lowest issue price of the shares. [2]Any provisions to the contrary shall be null and void.

§ 114 Contracts with supervisory board members.

(1) If, in addition to his services within the supervisory board, a supervisory board member commits himself to undertaking a certain professional service by entering into either a service

Werkvertrag gegenüber der Gesellschaft zu einer Tätigkeit höherer Art, so hängt die Wirksamkeit des Vertrags von der Zustimmung des Aufsichtsrats ab.

(2) ¹Gewährt die Gesellschaft auf Grund eines solchen Vertrags dem Aufsichtsratsmitglied eine Vergütung, ohne daß der Aufsichtsrat dem Vertrag zugestimmt hat, so hat das Aufsichtsratsmitglied die Vergütung zurückzugewähren, es sei denn, daß der Aufsichtsrat den Vertrag genehmigt. ²Ein Anspruch des Aufsichtsratsmitglieds gegen die Gesellschaft auf Herausgabe der durch die geleistete Tätigkeit erlangten Bereicherung bleibt unberührt; der Anspruch kann jedoch nicht gegen den Rückgewähranspruch aufgerechnet werden.

§ 115 Kreditgewährung an Aufsichtsratsmitglieder.

(1) ¹Die Gesellschaft darf ihren Aufsichtsratsmitgliedern Kredit nur mit Einwilligung des Aufsichtsrats gewähren. ²Eine herrschende Gesellschaft darf Kredite an Aufsichtsratsmitglieder eines abhängigen Unternehmens nur mit Einwilligung ihres Aufsichtsrats, eine abhängige Gesellschaft darf Kredite an Aufsichtsratsmitglieder des herrschenden Unternehmens nur mit Einwilligung des Aufsichtsrats des herrschenden Unternehmens gewähren. ³Die Einwilligung kann nur für bestimmte Kreditgeschäfte oder Arten von Kreditgeschäften und nicht für länger als drei Monate im voraus erteilt werden. ⁴Der Beschluß über die Einwilligung hat die Verzinsung und Rückzahlung des Kredits zu regeln. ⁵Betreibt das Aufsichtsratsmitglied ein Handelsgewerbe als Einzelkaufmann, so ist die Einwilligung nicht erforderlich, wenn der Kredit für die Bezahlung von Waren gewährt wird, welche die Gesellschaft seinem Handelsgeschäft liefert.

agreement which does not create an employment relationship or a contract for works and services with the company, the validity of such contract shall depend on consent being granted by the supervisory board.

(2) ¹If the company grants the member of the supervisory board remuneration on the basis of such a contract without the supervisory board having granted its consent, the member of the supervisory board shall reimburse the company such remuneration unless the supervisory board subsequently approves the contract. ²Any claim the member of the supervisory board has against the company for the return of any enrichment gained as a result of the services rendered shall not be affected; such claim may not, however, be offset against the company's claim for the repayment of the remuneration.

§ 115 Granting of credit to supervisory board members.

(1) ¹The company may only grant credit to the members of its supervisory board if the supervisory board gives its consent. ²A controlling company may only grant credit to members of the supervisory board of a controlled enterprise if the supervisory board of the controlling company gives its consent, and a controlled company may only grant credit to members of the supervisory board of the controlling enterprise if the supervisory board of the controlling enterprise grants its consent. ³Consent may only be granted for specific credit transactions or types of credit transaction and no earlier than three months in advance. ⁴The resolution granting consent shall stipulate the terms for the payment of interest and the repayment of the credit. ⁵If the supervisory board member operates a business as a sole proprietor, consent shall not be necessary if the credit is granted for the payment of goods supplied by the company to his business.

(2) Absatz 1 gilt auch für Kredite an den Ehegatten, Lebenspartner oder an ein minderjähriges Kind eines Aufsichtsratsmitglieds und für Kredite an einen Dritten, der für Rechnung dieser Personen oder für Rechnung eines Aufsichtsratsmitglieds handelt.

(3) [1]Ist ein Aufsichtsratsmitglied zugleich gesetzlicher Vertreter einer anderen juristischen Person oder Gesellschafter einer Personenhandelsgesellschaft, so darf die Gesellschaft der juristischen Person oder der Personenhandelsgesellschaft Kredit nur mit Einwilligung des Aufsichtsrats gewähren; Absatz 1 Satz 3 und 4 gilt sinngemäß. [2]Dies gilt nicht, wenn die juristische Person oder die Personenhandelsgesellschaft mit der Gesellschaft verbunden ist oder wenn der Kredit für die Bezahlung von Waren gewährt wird, welche die Gesellschaft der juristischen Person oder der Personenhandelsgesellschaft liefert.

(4) Wird entgegen den Absätzen 1 bis 3 Kredit gewährt, so ist der Kredit ohne Rücksicht auf entgegenstehende Vereinbarungen sofort zurückzugewähren, wenn nicht der Aufsichtsrat nachträglich zustimmt.

(5) Ist die Gesellschaft ein Kreditinstitut oder Finanzdienstleistungsinstitut, auf das § 15 des Gesetzes über das Kreditwesen anzuwenden ist, gelten anstelle der Absätze 1 bis 4 die Vorschriften des Gesetzes über das Kreditwesen.

§ 116 Sorgfaltspflicht und Verantwortlichkeit der Aufsichtsratsmitglieder.

[1]Für die Sorgfaltspflicht und Verantwortlichkeit der Aufsichtsratsmitglieder gilt § 93 mit Ausnahme des Absatzes 2 Satz 3 über die Sorgfaltspflicht und Verantwortlichkeit der Vorstandsmitglieder sinngemäß. [2]Die Aufsichtsratsmitglieder sind insbesondere zur Verschwiegenheit über erhaltene vertrauliche Berichte und vertrauliche Beratungen

(2) Para. 1 shall also apply to credits granted to the spouse, domestic partner or minor child of a supervisory board member and to credits to third parties acting for account of these persons or for account of the supervisory board member.

(3) [1]If a member of the supervisory board is at the same time the legal representative of another legal person or a partner in a commercial partnership, the company may only grant credit to the legal person or the commercial partnership if the supervisory board gives its consent; para. 1 sentences 3 and 4 shall apply accordingly. [2]The foregoing shall not apply if the legal person or the commercial partnership is affiliated to the company or if the credit is granted for the payment of goods supplied by the company to the legal person or the commercial partnership.

(4) If credit is granted contrary to the provisions in para. 1 to 3, the credit shall be repaid immediately irrespective of any agreements to the contrary unless the supervisory board grants its consent retrospectively.

(5) If the company is a credit institution or a financial services institution to which sec. 15 of the Banking Act applies, the provisions of the Banking Act shall apply instead of paras. 1 to 4.

§ 116 Duty of care and responsibility of supervisory board members.

[1]Sec. 93 with the exception of para. 2 sentence 3 on the duty of care and responsibility of the members of the management board shall apply accordingly to the duty of care and responsibility of the members of the supervisory board. [2]The members of the supervisory board are under a particular obligation not to disclose any details concerning confi-

verpflichtet. ³Sie sind namentlich zum Ersatz verpflichtet, wenn sie eine unangemessene Vergütung festsetzen (§ 87 Absatz 1).

dential reports they obtain and confidential discussions. ³They shall in particular be liable for damages if they determine an unreasonable compensation (sec. 87 para. 1).

Dritter Abschnitt. Benutzung des Einflusses auf die Gesellschaft

Section Three. Exertion of Influence on the Company

§ 117 Schadenersatzpflicht.

§ 117 Liability for damages.

(1) ¹Wer vorsätzlich unter Benutzung seines Einflusses auf die Gesellschaft ein Mitglied des Vorstands oder des Aufsichtsrats, einen Prokuristen oder einen Handlungsbevollmächtigten dazu bestimmt, zum Schaden der Gesellschaft oder ihrer Aktionäre zu handeln, ist der Gesellschaft zum Ersatz des ihr daraus entstehenden Schadens verpflichtet. ²Er ist auch den Aktionären zum Ersatz des ihnen daraus entstehenden Schadens verpflichtet, soweit sie, abgesehen von einem Schaden, der ihnen durch Schädigung der Gesellschaft zugefügt worden ist, geschädigt worden sind.

(1) ¹Anyone who intentionally exerts his influence over the company to induce a member of the management board or the supervisory board, a procuration officer or an authorized signatory to act to the detriment of the company or its shareholders shall be liable to the company for any resulting damage. ²He shall also be liable to the shareholders for any resulting damage to the extent that they have suffered damage in addition to any damage caused by the damage of the company.

(2) ¹Neben ihm haften als Gesamtschuldner die Mitglieder des Vorstands und des Aufsichtsrats, wenn sie unter Verletzung ihrer Pflichten gehandelt haben. ²Ist streitig, ob sie die Sorgfalt eines ordentlichen und gewissenhaften Geschäftsleiters angewandt haben, so trifft sie die Beweislast. ³Der Gesellschaft und auch den Aktionären gegenüber tritt die Ersatzpflicht der Mitglieder des Vorstands und des Aufsichtsrats nicht ein, wenn die Handlung auf einem gesetzmäßigen Beschluß der Hauptversammlung beruht. ⁴Dadurch, daß der Aufsichtsrat die Handlung gebilligt hat, wird die Ersatzpflicht nicht ausgeschlossen.

(2) ¹In addition to such person, the members of the management board and the supervisory board shall be jointly and severally liable if they acted in breach of their duties. ²In the event of a dispute as to whether or not they applied the due care of a diligent and conscientious manager, they shall bear the burden of proof. ³The members of the management board and the supervisory board shall not be liable to the company for damages if their acts were based on a lawful resolution adopted by the general meeting. ⁴The fact that the supervisory board has approved the action shall not mean that liability for damages is excluded.

(3) Neben ihm haftet ferner als Gesamtschuldner, wer durch die schädigende Handlung einen Vorteil erlangt hat, sofern er die Beeinflussung vorsätzlich veranlaßt hat.

(3) In addition to such person, any person who gains an advantage from the damaging action shall also be jointly and severally liable insofar as he intentionally caused the influence to be exerted.

(4) Für die Aufhebung der Ersatzpflicht gegenüber der Gesellschaft gilt sinngemäß § 93 Abs. 4 Satz 3 und 4.

(5) ¹Der Ersatzanspruch der Gesellschaft kann auch von den Gläubigern der Gesellschaft geltend gemacht werden, soweit sie von dieser keine Befriedigung erlangen können. ²Den Gläubigern gegenüber wird die Ersatzpflicht weder durch einen Verzicht oder Vergleich der Gesellschaft noch dadurch aufgehoben, daß die Handlung auf einem Beschluß der Hauptversammlung beruht. ³Ist über das Vermögen der Gesellschaft das Insolvenzverfahren eröffnet, so übt während dessen Dauer der Insolvenzverwalter oder der Sachwalter das Recht der Gläubiger aus.

(6) Die Ansprüche aus diesen Vorschriften verjähren in fünf Jahren.

(7) Diese Vorschriften gelten nicht, wenn das Mitglied des Vorstands oder des Aufsichtsrats, der Prokurist oder der Handlungsbevollmächtigte durch Ausübung

1. der Leitungsmacht auf Grund eines Beherrschungsvertrags oder
2. der Leitungsmacht einer Hauptgesellschaft (§ 319), in die die Gesellschaft eingegliedert ist,

zu der schädigenden Handlung bestimmt worden ist.

(4) Sec. 93 para. 4 sentences 3 and 4 shall apply accordingly to the cancellation of the liability for damages vis-à-vis the company.

(5) ¹The company's claim for damages may also be asserted by creditors of the company to the extent that said creditors are unable to obtain settlement of their claims from the company. ²The liability for damages vis-à-vis the creditors shall not be cancelled by a waiver or composition by the company, nor by the fact that the action was based on a resolution adopted by the general meeting. ³If insolvency proceedings have been commenced against the company's assets, the insolvency administrator or the custodian shall exercise the rights of the creditors for the duration of such proceedings.

(6) Claims arising from the above provisions shall become time-barred after five years.

(7) The above provisions shall not apply if the member of the management board or the supervisory board, a procuration officer or an authorized signatory was induced to engage in the act causing damage by the exercise of

1. the power to give directives under a domination agreement or
2. the power to give directives of a principal company (sec. 319) into which the company has been integrated.

Vierter Abschnitt. Hauptversammlung

Erster Unterabschnitt. Rechte der Hauptversammlung

§ 118 Allgemeines.

(1) ¹Die Aktionäre üben ihre Rechte in den Angelegenheiten der Gesellschaft in der Hauptversammlung aus, soweit

Section Four. General Meeting

Subsection One. Rights of the General Meeting

§ 118 General provisions.

(1) ¹The shareholders exercise their rights relating to the matters of the company in the general meeting unless

das Gesetz nichts anderes bestimmt. ²Die Satzung kann vorsehen oder den Vorstand dazu ermächtigen vorzusehen, dass die Aktionäre an der Hauptversammlung auch ohne Anwesenheit an deren Ort und ohne einen Bevollmächtigten teilnehmen und sämtliche oder einzelne ihrer Rechte ganz oder teilweise im Wege elektronischer Kommunikation ausüben können.

(2) Die Satzung kann vorsehen oder den Vorstand dazu ermächtigen vorzusehen, dass Aktionäre ihre Stimmen, auch ohne an der Versammlung teilzunehmen, schriftlich oder im Wege elektronischer Kommunikation abgeben dürfen (Briefwahl).

(3) ¹Die Mitglieder des Vorstands und des Aufsichtsrats sollen an der Hauptversammlung teilnehmen. ²Die Satzung kann jedoch bestimmte Fälle vorsehen, in denen die Teilnahme von Mitgliedern des Aufsichtsrats im Wege der Bild- und Tonübertragung erfolgen darf.

(4) Die Satzung oder die Geschäftsordnung gemäß § 129 Abs. 1 kann vorsehen oder den Vorstand oder den Versammlungsleiter dazu ermächtigen vorzusehen, die Bild- und Tonübertragung der Versammlung zuzulassen.

§ 119 Rechte der Hauptversammlung.

(1) Die Hauptversammlung beschließt in den im Gesetz und in der Satzung ausdrücklich bestimmten Fällen, namentlich über

1. die Bestellung der Mitglieder des Aufsichtsrats, soweit sie nicht in den Aufsichtsrat zu entsenden oder als Aufsichtsratsmitglieder der Arbeitnehmer nach dem Mitbestimmungsgesetz, dem Mitbestimmungsergänzungsgesetz, dem Drittelbeteiligungsgesetz oder dem Gesetz über die Mitbestimmung der Arbeitnehmer bei einer grenzüber-

otherwise provided for by law. ²The articles of association may provide or may authorize the management board to provide that the shareholders may participate in the general meeting without being present and without a proxy and may exercise all or individual rights in whole or in part by way of electronic communication.

(2) The articles of association may provide or may authorize the management board to provide that shareholders may cast their votes in writing or by way of electronic communication without participating in the meeting (absentee voting).

(3) ¹The members of the management board and the supervisory board shall attend the general meeting. ²The articles of association may, however, stipulate certain cases in which members of the supervisory board may participate via audio-visual transmission.

(4) The articles of association or the rules of procedure pursuant to sec. 129 para. 1 may provide or may authorize the management board or the chairman of the meeting to provide that the audio-visual transmission of the meeting is permitted.

§ 119 Rights of the general meeting.

(1) The general meeting shall adopt resolutions in the cases expressly stipulated by law and in the articles of association, in particular

1. the appointment of supervisory board members, unless such members are to be appointed to the supervisory board or elected as employee representatives in accordance with the Codetermination Act, the Codetermination Amendment Act , the One-Third Participation Act or the Act on the Codetermination by Employees in International Mergers.

schreitenden Verschmelzung zu wählen sind;
2. die Verwendung des Bilanzgewinns;
3. die Entlastung der Mitglieder des Vorstands und des Aufsichtsrats;
4. die Bestellung des Abschlußprüfers;
5. Satzungsänderungen;
6. Maßnahmen der Kapitalbeschaffung und der Kapitalherabsetzung;
7. die Bestellung von Prüfern zur Prüfung von Vorgängen bei der Gründung oder der Geschäftsführung;
8. die Auflösung der Gesellschaft.

(2) Über Fragen der Geschäftsführung kann die Hauptversammlung nur entscheiden, wenn der Vorstand es verlangt.

§ 120 Entlastung, Votum zum Vergütungssystem.

(1) ¹Die Hauptversammlung beschließt alljährlich in den ersten acht Monaten des Geschäftsjahrs über die Entlastung der Mitglieder des Vorstands und über die Entlastung der Mitglieder des Aufsichtsrats. ²Über die Entlastung eines einzelnen Mitglieds ist gesondert abzustimmen, wenn die Hauptversammlung es beschließt oder eine Minderheit es verlangt, deren Anteile zusammen den zehnten Teil des Grundkapitals oder den anteiligen Betrag von einer Million Euro erreichen.

(2) ¹Durch die Entlastung billigt die Hauptversammlung die Verwaltung der Gesellschaft durch die Mitglieder des Vorstands und des Aufsichtsrats. ²Die Entlastung enthält keinen Verzicht auf Ersatzansprüche.

(3) Die Verhandlung über die Entlastung soll mit der Verhandlung über die Verwendung des Bilanzgewinns verbunden werden.

2. the appropriation of the balance sheet profit;
3. ratification of the acts of the members of the management board and the supervisory board;
4. the appointment of the auditor of annual financial statements;
5. amendments to the articles of association;
6. measures to increase or reduce the registered share capital;
7. the appointment of auditors for the examination of procedures relating to the formation or management of the company;
8. the dissolution of the company.

(2) The general meeting may only resolve on matters relating to the management of the company if requested to do so by the management board.

§ 120 Ratification, vote on compensation system.

(1) ¹The general meeting shall resolve in the first eight months of each fiscal year on the ratification of the acts of the members of the management board and on the ratification of the acts of the members of the supervisory board. ²A separate vote shall be held concerning the ratification of the acts of one individual member if so resolved by the general meeting or so requested by a minority having an aggregate shareholding amounting to one tenth of the registered share capital or the proportionate amount of one million euros.

(2) ¹By granting its ratification, the general meeting approves the administration of the company by the members of the management board and the supervisory board. ²Such ratification shall not entail a waiver of claims for damages.

(3) Proceedings concerning the granting of ratification shall be combined with the proceedings concerning the appro-

(4) ¹Die Hauptversammlung der börsennotierten Gesellschaft kann über die Billigung des Systems zur Vergütung der Vorstandsmitglieder beschließen. ²Der Beschluss begründet weder Rechte noch Pflichten; insbesondere lässt er die Verpflichtung des Aufsichtsrates nach § 87 unberührt. ³Der Beschluss ist nicht nach § 243 anfechtbar.

(4) ¹The general meeting of the listed company may resolve on the approval of the system of compensation of the members of the management board. ² The resolution does not give rise to either rights or duties; in particular, the obligation of the supervisory board pursuant to sec. 87 remains unaffected. ³The resolution cannot be contested pursuant to sec. 243.

Zweiter Unterabschnitt. Einberufung der Hauptversammlung

Subsection Two. Convening of the General Meeting

§ 121 Allgemeines.

§ 121 General provisions.

(1) Die Hauptversammlung ist in den durch Gesetz oder Satzung bestimmten Fällen sowie dann einzuberufen, wenn das Wohl der Gesellschaft es fordert.

(1) The general meeting shall be convened in those cases stipulated by law or in the articles of association and whenever necessary in the interests of the company.

(2) ¹Die Hauptversammlung wird durch den Vorstand einberufen, der darüber mit einfacher Mehrheit beschließt. ²Personen, die in das Handelsregister als Vorstand eingetragen sind, gelten als befugt. ³Das auf Gesetz oder Satzung beruhende Recht anderer Personen, die Hauptversammlung einzuberufen, bleibt unberührt.

(2) ¹The general meeting shall be convened by the management board, which shall decide on the convening of the general meeting by a simple majority of the votes. ²Persons registered in the commercial register as members of the management board shall be deemed to have the necessary authorization. ³The foregoing shall not affect the right of other persons to convene the general meeting pursuant to the law or the articles of association.

(3) ¹Die Einberufung muss die Firma, den Sitz der Gesellschaft sowie Zeit und Ort der Hauptversammlung enthalten. ²Zudem ist die Tagesordnung anzugeben. ³Bei börsennotierten Gesellschaften hat der Vorstand oder, wenn der Aufsichtsrat die Versammlung einberuft, der Aufsichtsrat in der Einberufung ferner anzugeben:

(3) ¹The notification of convening of the meeting shall state the name and registered office of the company as well as the time and place of the general meeting. ²Furthermore, the agenda shall be stated. ³In the case of listed companies, the management board or, if the supervisory board convenes the meeting, the supervisory board, shall further state in the notification of convening of the meeting:

1. die Voraussetzungen für die Teilnahme an der Versammlung und die Ausübung des Stimmrechts sowie gegebenenfalls den Nachweisstich-

1. the requirements for participation in the meeting and the exercise of the voting right as well as, if applicable, the record date for the proof pursu-

tag nach § 123 Absatz 4 Satz 2 und dessen Bedeutung;
2. das Verfahren für die Stimmabgabe
   a) durch einen Bevollmächtigten unter Hinweis auf die Formulare, die für die Erteilung einer Stimmrechtsvollmacht zu verwenden sind, und auf die Art und Weise, wie der Gesellschaft ein Nachweis über die Bestellung eines Bevollmächtigten elektronisch übermittelt werden kann sowie
   b) durch Briefwahl oder im Wege der elektronischen Kommunikation gemäß § 118 Abs. 1 Satz 2, soweit die Satzung eine entsprechende Form der Stimmrechtsausübung vorsieht;
3. Die Rechte der Aktionäre nach § 122 Abs. 2, § 126 Abs. 1, den §§ 127, 131 Abs. 1; die Angaben können sich auf die Fristen für die Ausübung der Rechte beschränken, wenn in der Einberufung im Übrigen auf weitergehende Erläuterungen auf der Internetseite der Gesellschaft hingewiesen wird;
4. die Internetseite der Gesellschaft, über die die Informationen nach § 124a zugänglich sind.

(4) ¹Die Einberufung ist in den Gesellschaftsblättern bekannt zu machen. ² Sind die Aktionäre der Gesellschaft namentlich bekannt, so kann die Hauptversammlung mit eingeschriebenem Brief einberufen werden, wenn die Satzung nichts anderes bestimmt; der Tag der Absendung gilt als Tag der Bekanntmachung.

(4a) Bei börsennotierten Gesellschaften, die nicht ausschließlich Namensaktien ausgegeben haben oder welche die Einberufung den Aktionären nicht unmittelbar nach Absatz 4 Satz 2 und 3 übersenden, ist die Einberufung spätestens zum Zeitpunkt der Bekanntmachung solchen Medien zur Veröffentlichung zuzuleiten, bei denen davon

ant to sec. 123 para. 4 sentence 2 and its significance;
2. the procedure for casting a vote
   a) by a proxy, indicating the forms which are to be used for the granting of a proxy to exercise a voting right and indicating the manner in which a proof of the appointment of a proxy can be transmitted electronically to the company as well as
   b) by absentee voting or by way of electronic communication pursuant to sec. 118 para. 1 sentence 2 to the extent the articles of association provide for a corresponding manner of the exercise of voting rights;
3. the rights of shareholders pursuant to sec. 122 para. 2, sec. 126 para. 1, sec. 127, 131 para. 1; the information may be limited to the time periods for the exercise of the rights if the notification of convening of the meeting otherwise refers to further information on the website of the company;
4. the website of the company on which the information pursuant to sec. 124a can be accessed.

(4) ¹The convening of the meeting shall be announced in the company's designated journals. ²If the shareholders of the company are known by name, the general meeting may be convened by registered letter; the date of posting shall constitute the day the announcement is made.

(4a) In the case of listed companies which did not exclusively issue registered shares or which do not send the notification of convening of the meeting directly to the shareholders pursuant to para. 4 sentences 2 and 3, the notification of convening of the meeting shall, by the time of the announcement, be sent to such media for publication who

ausgegangen werden kann, dass sie die Information in der gesamten Europäischen Union verbreiten.

(5) ¹Wenn die Satzung nichts anderes bestimmt, soll die Hauptversammlung am Sitz der Gesellschaft stattfinden. ²Sind die Aktien der Gesellschaft an einer deutschen Börse zum Handel im regulierten Markt zugelassen, so kann, wenn die Satzung nichts anderes bestimmt, die Hauptversammlung auch am Sitz der Börse stattfinden.

(6) Sind alle Aktionäre erschienen oder vertreten, kann die Hauptversammlung Beschlüsse ohne Einhaltung der Bestimmungen dieses Unterabschnitts fassen, soweit kein Aktionär der Beschlußfassung widerspricht.

(7) ¹Bei Fristen und Terminen, die von der Versammlung zurückberechnet werden, ist der Tag der Versammlung nicht mitzurechnen. ²Eine Verlegung von einem Sonntag, einem Sonnabend oder einem Feiertag auf einen zeitlich vorausgehenden oder nachfolgenden Werktag kommt nicht in Betracht. ³Die §§ 187 bis 193 des Bürgerlichen Gesetzbuchs sind nicht entsprechend anzuwenden. ⁴Bei nichtbörsennotierten Gesellschaften kann die Satzung eine andere Berechnung der Frist bestimmen.

§ 122 Einberufung auf Verlangen einer Minderheit.

(1) ¹Die Hauptversammlung ist einzuberufen, wenn Aktionäre, deren Anteile zusammen den zwanzigsten Teil des Grundkapitals erreichen, die Einberufung schriftlich unter Angabe des Zwecks und der Gründe verlangen; das Verlangen ist an den Vorstand zu richten. ²Die Satzung kann das Recht, die Einberufung der Hauptversammlung zu verlangen, an eine andere Form und an den Besitz eines geringeren Anteils am Grundkapital knüpfen. ³Die Antragsteller haben nachzuweisen, dass sie seit

can be expected to distribute the information within the whole of the European Union.

(5) ¹Unless stipulated otherwise in the articles of association, the general meeting shall be held at the registered office of the company. ²If the company's shares are admitted for trading in the regulated market at a German stock exchange, the general meeting may also be held at the seat of such stock exchange, unless stipulated otherwise in the articles of association.

(6) If all shareholders are present or represented, the general meeting may adopt resolutions without complying to the provisions in this subsection provided none of the shareholders object to the resolution.

(7) ¹In the case of time periods and dates which are calculated backwards from the meeting, the day of the meeting shall not be included in the calculation. ²A relocation from a Sunday, a Saturday or a public holiday to a preceding or subsequent business day shall not take place. ³Sec. 187 to 193 of the Civil Code shall not apply accordingly. ⁴In the case of companies which are not listed, the articles of association may provide for a different manner of calculation of time periods.

§ 122 Convening at the request of a minority.

(1) ¹A general meeting shall be convened if shareholders having an aggregate shareholding amounting to one twentieth of the registered share capital file a written request for such meeting to be held, stating the purpose and the reasons therefor; such request shall be directed to the management board. ²The articles of association may link the right to request that the general meeting be convened to another form and to a lesser share in the registered share capital. ³The petitioners must prove that they

mindestens 90 Tagen vor dem Tag des Zugangs des Verlangens Inhaber der Aktien sind und dass sie die Aktien bis zur Entscheidung des Vorstands über den Antrag halten. [4]§ 121 Absatz 7 ist entsprechend anzuwenden.

(2) [1]In gleicher Weise können Aktionäre, deren Anteile zusammen den zwanzigsten Teil des Grundkapitals oder den anteiligen Betrag von 500.000 Euro erreichen, verlangen, daß Gegenstände auf die Tagesordnung gesetzt und bekanntgemacht werden. [2]Jedem neuen Gegenstand muss eine Begründung oder eine Beschlussvorlage beiliegen. [3]Das Verlangen im Sinne des Satzes 1 muss der Gesellschaft mindestens 24 Tage, bei börsennotierten Gesellschaften mindestens 30 Tage vor der Versammlung zugehen; der Tag des Zugangs ist nicht mitzurechnen.

(3) [1]Wird dem Verlangen nicht entsprochen, so kann das Gericht die Aktionäre, die das Verlangen gestellt haben, ermächtigen, die Hauptversammlung einzuberufen oder den Gegenstand bekanntzumachen. [2]Zugleich kann das Gericht den Vorsitzenden der Versammlung bestimmen. [3]Auf die Ermächtigung muß bei der Einberufung oder Bekanntmachung hingewiesen werden. [4]Gegen die Entscheidung ist die Beschwerde zulässig. [5]Die Antragsteller haben nachzuweisen, dass sie die Aktien bis zur Entscheidung des Gerichts halten.

(4) Die Gesellschaft trägt die Kosten der Hauptversammlung und im Fall des Absatzes 3 auch die Gerichtskosten, wenn das Gericht dem Antrag stattgegeben hat.

§ 123 Frist, Anmeldung zur Hauptversammlung, Nachweis.

(1) [1]Die Hauptversammlung ist mindestens dreißig Tage vor dem Tage der Versammlung einzuberufen. [2]Der Tag der Einberufung ist nicht mitzurechnen.

have held their shares for a period of at least 90 days prior to the date the demand is received and that they will hold the shares until a decision is taken on the motion by the management board. [4]Sec. 121 para. 7 shall apply accordingly.

(2) [1]In the same way, shareholders with an aggregate shareholding of one twentieth of the registered share capital or the proportionate amount of EUR 500,000 may request that items are put on the agenda and are announced as items on the agenda. [2]Each new item shall be accompanied by a statement of reasons or a draft resolution. [3]The request pursuant to sentence 1 must be received by the company at least 24 days, or in the case of listed companies at least 30 days, prior to the meeting; the date of receipt shall not be included in the calculation.

(3) [1]If such request is not met, the court may authorize those shareholders who filed the request to convene the general meeting or to publish the item. [2]The court may also appoint the chairman of the meeting at the same time. [3]Reference shall be made to the authorization granted by the court and the convening or the publication. [4]The decision shall be subject to appeal. [5]The petitioners must prove that they will hold their shares until a decision is taken by the court.

(4) The company shall bear the costs of the general meeting and, in the case of para. 3, the court costs if the court grants the application.

§ 123 Time period, application to attend the general meeting, proof.

(1) [1]The general meeting shall be convened at least thirty days before the day of the meeting. [2]The day of the convening of the meeting shall not be included in the calculation.

(2) ¹Die Satzung kann die Teilnahme an der Hauptversammlung oder die Ausübung des Stimmrechts davon abhängig machen, dass die Aktionäre sich vor der Versammlung anmelden. ²Die Anmeldung muss der Gesellschaft unter der in der Einberufung hierfür mitgeteilten Adresse mindestens sechs Tage vor der Versammlung zugehen. ³In der Satzung oder in der Einberufung aufgrund einer Ermächtigung durch die Satzung kann eine kürzere, in Tagen zu bemessende Frist vorgesehen werden. ⁴Der Tag des Zugangs ist nicht mitzurechnen. ⁵Die Mindestfrist des Absatzes 1 verlängert sich um die Tage der Anmeldungsfrist.

(3) Die Satzung kann bestimmen, wie die Berechtigung zur Teilnahme an der Versammlung oder zur Ausübung des Stimmrechts nachzuweisen ist; Absatz 2 Satz 5 gilt in diesem Fall entsprechend.

(4) ¹Bei Inhaberaktien börsennotierter Gesellschaften reicht ein durch das depotführende Institut in Textform erstellter besonderer Nachweis des Anteilsbesitzes aus. ²Der Nachweis hat sich bei börsennotierten Gesellschaften auf den Beginn des 21. Tages vor der Versammlung zu beziehen und muss der Gesellschaft unter der in der Einberufung hierfür mitgeteilten Adresse mindestens sechs Tage vor der Versammlung zugehen. ³In der Satzung oder in der Einberufung auf Grund einer Ermächtigung durch die Satzung kann eine kürzere, in Tagen zu bemessende Frist vorgesehen werden. ⁴Der Tag des Zugangs ist nicht mitzurechnen. ⁵Im Verhältnis zur Gesellschaft gilt für die Teilnahme an der Versammlung oder für die Ausübung des Stimmrechts als Aktionär nur, wer den Nachweis erbracht hat.

(5) Bei Namensaktien börsennotierter Gesellschaften folgt die Berechtigung zur Teilnahme an der Versammlung oder zur Ausübung des Stimmrechts

(2) ¹The articles of association may make attendance of the general meeting or exercising of the right to vote conditional upon the shareholders applying to attend the meeting. ²The application must be received by the company at the address set forth for this purpose in the meeting invitation at least six days prior to the meeting. ³The articles of association or, on the basis of an authorization by the articles of association, the notification of convening of the meeting may provide for a shorter time period to be measured in days. ⁴The day of receipt shall not be included in the calculation. ⁵The minimum time period pursuant to para. 1 shall be prolonged by the days of the time period for the application.

(3) ¹The articles of association may determine, how the entitlement to participate in the meeting or the exercise of voting rights shall be proven; para. 2 sentence 5 shall apply in this case accordingly.

(4) ¹In the case of bearer shares of listed companies, a special proof of share ownership issued in text form by the depository bank shall be sufficient. ²In the case of listed companies, the proof shall pertain to the beginning of the twenty first day prior to the meeting and shall be received by the company at least six days prior to the meeting. ³The articles of association or, on the basis of an authorization by the articles of association, the notification of convening of the meeting may provide for a shorter time period to be measured in days. ⁴The day of receipt shall not be included in the calculation. ⁵Only those persons who have furnished proof shall be considered shareholders in relation to the company with respect to attendance of the meeting or exercise of the voting right.

(5) In the case of registered shares of listed companies the entitlement to participate in the meeting or to exercise the voting rights results from the registra-

gemäß § 67 Absatz 2 Satz 1 aus der Eintragung im Aktienregister.

§ 124 Bekanntmachung von Ergänzungsverlangen, Vorschläge zur Beschlussfassung.

(1) ¹Hat die Minderheit nach § 122 Abs. 2 verlangt, dass Gegenstände auf die Tagesordnung gesetzt werden, so sind diese entweder bereits mit der Einberufung oder andernfalls unverzüglich nach Zugang des Verlangens bekannt zu machen. ²§ 121 Abs. 4 gilt sinngemäß; zudem gilt bei börsennotierten Gesellschaften § 121 Abs. 4a entsprechend. ³Bekanntmachung und Zuleitung haben dabei in gleicher Weise wie bei der Einberufung zu erfolgen.

(2) ¹Steht die Wahl von Aufsichtsratsmitgliedern auf der Tagesordnung, so ist in der Bekanntmachung anzugeben, nach welchen gesetzlichen Vorschriften sich der Aufsichtsrat zusammensetzt; ist die Hauptversammlung an Wahlvorschläge gebunden, so ist auch dies anzugeben.. ²Die Bekanntmachung muss bei einer Wahl von Aufsichtsratsmitgliedern börsennotierter Gesellschaften, für die das Mitbestimmungsgesetz, das Montan-Mitbestimmungsgesetz oder das Mitbestimmungsergänzungsgesetz gilt, ferner enthalten:

1. Angabe, ob der Gesamterfüllung nach § 96 Absatz 2 Satz 3 widersprochen wurde, und

2. Angabe, wie viele der Sitze im Aufsichtsrat mindestens jeweils von Frauen und Männern besetzt sein müssen, um das Mindestanteilsgebot nach § 96 Absatz 2 Satz 1 zu erfüllen.

³Soll die Hauptversammlung über eine Satzungsänderung oder über einen Vertrag beschließen, der nur mit Zustimmung der Hauptversammlung wirksam wird, so ist auch der Wortlaut der vorgeschlagenen Satzungsänderung

tion in the share register in accordance with sec. 67 para. 2 sentence 1.

§ 124 Announcement of requests for amendment, proposals for resolution.

(1) ¹If the minority pursuant to sec. 122 para. 2 has requested that items be placed on the agenda, these shall be announced either together with the convening of the meeting or otherwise without undue delay after receipt of the request. ²Sec. 121 para. 4 shall apply accordingly; furthermore, in the case of listed companies, sec. 121 para. 4a shall apply accordingly. ³Announcement and sending shall in this case take place in the same manner as with the convening of a meeting.

(2) ¹If the election of supervisory board members is on the agenda, the announcement shall state the statutory provisions governing the composition of the supervisory board; if the general meeting bound by nominations, it shall also disclose that fact. ²In the case of an election of supervisory board members in listed companies, which are subject to the Codetermination Act, the Coal, Iron and Steel Codetermination Act or the Codetermination Amendment Act, the announcement has to contain the following:

1. a declaration on whether the overall fulfillment according to sec. 96 para. 2 sentence 3 has been contradicted, and

2. a declaration on how many seats in the supervisory board need to be filled by women and men, to achieve the respective minimum fulfillment according to sec. 96 para. 2 sentence 1.

³If the general meeting is to decide on an amendment to the articles of association or on a contract which is only valid if the general meeting grants its consent, the text of the proposed amendment to the articles of association or the essen-

oder der wesentliche Inhalt des Vertrags bekanntzumachen.

(3) ¹Zu jedem Gegenstand der Tagesordnung, über den die Hauptversammlung beschließen soll, haben der Vorstand und der Aufsichtsrat, zur Wahl von Aufsichtsratsmitgliedern und Prüfern nur der Aufsichtsrat, in der Bekanntmachung Vorschläge zur Beschlußfassung zu machen. ²Bei Gesellschaften, die kapitalmarktorientiert im Sinne des § 264d des Handelsgesetzbuchs, die CRR-Kreditinstitute im Sinne des § 1 Absatz 3d Satz 1 des Kreditwesengesetzes, mit Ausnahme der in § 2 Absatz 1 Nummer 1 und 2 des Kreditwesengesetzes genannten Institute, oder die Versicherungsunternehmen im Sinne des Artikels 2 Absatz 1 der Richtlinie 91/674/EWG sind, ist der Vorschlag des Aufsichtsrats zur Wahl des Abschlussprüfers auf die Empfehlung des Prüfungsausschusses zu stützen. ³Satz 1 findet keine Anwendung, wenn die Hauptversammlung bei der Wahl von Aufsichtsratsmitgliedern nach § 6 des Montan-Mitbestimmungsgesetzes an Wahlvorschläge gebunden ist, oder wenn der Gegenstand der Beschlußfassung auf Verlangen einer Minderheit auf die Tagesordnung gesetzt worden ist. ⁴Der Vorschlag zur Wahl von Aufsichtsratsmitgliedern oder Prüfern hat deren Namen, ausgeübten Beruf und Wohnort anzugeben. ⁵Hat der Aufsichtsrat auch aus Aufsichtsratsmitgliedern der Arbeitnehmer zu bestehen, so bedürfen Beschlüsse des Aufsichtsrats über Vorschläge zur Wahl von Aufsichtsratsmitgliedern nur der Mehrheit der Stimmen der Aufsichtsratsmitglieder der Aktionäre; § 8 des Montan-Mitbestimmungsgesetzes bleibt unberührt.

(4) ¹Über Gegenstände der Tagesordnung, die nicht ordnungsgemäß bekanntgemacht sind, dürfen keine Beschlüsse gefaßt werden. ²Zur Be-

tial contents of the contract respectively shall also be published.

(3) ¹The management board and the supervisory board, or in the case of the election of supervisory board members and auditors of the annual financial statements, only the supervisory board, shall make proposals for the resolution for each item on the agenda which is to be decided by the general meeting in the announcement. ²In the case of companies within the meaning of sec. 264d of the Commercial Code, the CRR- credit institutions within the meaning of sec. 1 para. 3d sentence 1 of the German Banking Act, with the exception of the institutions mentioned in sec. 2 para. 1 number 1 and 2 of the German Banking Act or the insurance companies within the meaning of Article 2 para. 1 of Council Directive 91/674/EWG, the proposal of the supervisory board for the election of the auditor of financial statements shall be based on the recommendation of the audit committee. ³Sentence 1 shall not apply if the general meeting is bound to nominations for the election of supervisory board members pursuant to sec. 6 of the Coal, Iron and Steel Codetermination Act or if the item on which a resolution is to be adopted was placed on the agenda at the request of a minority. ⁴The proposal for the election of supervisory board members or auditors of the annual financial statements shall state their name, practiced profession and place of residence. ⁵If employee representatives are also to be included on the supervisory board, resolutions adopted by the supervisory board concerning nominations of supervisory board members shall only require the majority of votes cast by the shareholder members of the supervisory board; sec. 8 of the Coal, Iron and Steel Codetermination Act shall not be affected.

(4) ¹No resolution may be adopted on any items on the agenda which have not been duly published. ²No announcement shall be required for resolutions

schlußfassung über den in der Versammlung gestellten Antrag auf Einberufung einer Hauptversammlung, zu Anträgen, die zu Gegenständen der Tagesordnung gestellt werden, und zu Verhandlungen ohne Beschlußfassung bedarf es keiner Bekanntmachung.

§ 124a Veröffentlichungen auf der Internetseite der Gesellschaft.

¹Bei börsennotierten Gesellschaften müssen alsbald nach der Einberufung der Hauptversammlung über die Internetseite der Gesellschaft zugänglich sein:

1. der Inhalt der Einberufung;
2. eine Erläuterung, wenn zu einem Gegenstand der Tagesordnung kein Beschluss gefasst werden soll;
3. die der Versammlung zugänglich zu machenden Unterlagen;
4. die Gesamtzahl der Aktien und der Stimmrechte im Zeitpunkt der Einberufung, einschließlich getrennter Angaben zur Gesamtzahl für jede Aktiengattung;
5. gegebenenfalls die Formulare, die bei Stimmabgabe durch Vertretung oder bei Stimmabgabe mittels Briefwahl zu verwenden sind, sofern diese Formulare den Aktionären nicht direkt übermittelt werden.

²Ein nach Einberufung der Versammlung bei der Gesellschaft eingegangenes Verlangen von Aktionären im Sinne von § 122 Abs. 2 ist unverzüglich nach seinem Eingang bei der Gesellschaft in gleicher Weise zugänglich zu machen.

§ 125 Mitteilungen für die Aktionäre und an Aufsichtsratsmitglieder.

(1) ¹Der Vorstand hat mindestens 21 Tage vor der Versammlung den Kreditinstituten und den Vereinigungen von Aktionären, die in der letzten Hauptversammlung Stimmrechte für Aktionäre ausgeübt oder die die Mitteilung verlangt haben, die Einberufung der

concerning a motion put forward during the meeting for the convening of a general meeting, motions put forward concerning items on the agenda and proceedings which do not lead to a resolution being adopted.

§ 124 a Announcements on the website of the company.

¹In the case of listed companies, the following shall be accessible on the website of the company shortly after the convening of the general meeting:

1. the contents of the notification of convening of the meeting;
2. an explanation with respect to a certain item of the agenda no resolution is to be adopted;
3. the documents to be made accessible to the meeting;
4. the aggregate number of shares and voting rights at the time of the convening of the meeting, including separate information on the aggregate number for each class of shares;
5. if applicable, the forms which are to be used for the casting of a vote by proxy or for the casting of a vote by absentee voting, to the extent these forms were not sent directly to the shareholders.

²A request by shareholders within the meaning of sec. 122 para. 2 which was received after the convening of the meeting by the company shall be made accessible in the same manner by the company without undue delay after receipt.

§ 125 Information for shareholders and supervisory board members.

(1) ¹The management board shall notify the credit institutions and the shareholder associations which exercised voting rights for shareholders in the previous general meeting or which have requested that they be so notified of the convening of the general meeting at

Hauptversammlung mitzuteilen. ²Der Tag der Mitteilung ist nicht mitzurechnen. ³Ist die Tagesordnung nach § 122 Abs. 2 zu ändern, so ist bei börsennotierten Gesellschaften die geänderte Tagesordnung mitzuteilen. ⁴In der Mitteilung ist auf die Möglichkeiten der Ausübung des Stimmrechts durch einen Bevollmächtigten, auch durch eine Vereinigung von Aktionären, hinzuweisen. ⁵Bei börsennotierten Gesellschaften sind einem Vorschlag zur Wahl von Aufsichtsratsmitgliedern Angaben zu deren Mitgliedschaft in anderen gesetzlich zu bildenden Aufsichtsräten beizufügen; Angaben zu ihrer Mitgliedschaft in vergleichbaren in- und ausländischen Kontrollgremien von Wirtschaftsunternehmen sollen beigefügt werden.	least twenty-one days prior to the meeting. ²The day of such notification shall not be included in the calculation. ³If the agenda is to be modified pursuant to sec. 122 para. 2 then, in the case of listed companies, the modified agenda shall be notified. ⁴Such notification shall refer to the possibilities for the exercising of the voting right by a proxy, including by a shareholder association. ⁵In the case of listed companies, information concerning membership of nominated supervisory board members in other supervisory boards required by law shall be attached to a nomination of supervisory board members; information concerning their membership in comparable domestic and foreign authorities responsible for supervising commercial enterprises shall also be attached.
(2) ¹Die gleiche Mitteilung hat der Vorstand den Aktionären zu machen, die es verlangen oder zu Beginn des 14. Tages vor der Versammlung als Aktionär im Aktienregister der Gesellschaft eingetragen sind. ²Die Satzung kann die Übermittlung auf den Weg elektronischer Kommunikation beschränken.	(2) ¹The management board shall provide the same notification to shareholders who request it or who are entered as a shareholder in the company's share register at the beginning of the fourteenth day prior to the date of the general meeting. ²The articles of association may limit the transmission to the method of electronic communication.
(3) Jedes Aufsichtsratsmitglied kann verlangen, daß ihm der Vorstand die gleichen Mitteilungen übersendet.	(3) Each member of the supervisory board may request the same information from the management board.
(4) Jedem Aufsichtsratsmitglied und jedem Aktionär sind auf Verlangen die in der Hauptversammlung gefassten Beschlüsse mitzuteilen.	(4) Each member of the supervisory board and each shareholder shall be informed upon request of the resolutions adopted in the general meeting.
(5) Finanzdienstleistungsinstitute und die nach § 53 Abs. 1 Satz 1 oder § 53b Abs. 1 Satz 1 oder Abs. 7 des Gesetzes über das Kreditwesen tätigen Unternehmen sind den Kreditinstituten gleichgestellt.	(5) Financial service institutions and enterprises acting pursuant to sec. 53 para. 1 sentence 1 or sec. 53b para. 1 sentence 1 or para. 7 of the Banking Act shall be deemed to be equivalent to credit institutions.

§ 126 Anträge von Aktionären.

(1) ¹Anträge von Aktionären einschließlich des Namens des Aktionärs, der Begründung und einer etwaigen Stellungnahme der Verwaltung sind den in

§ 126 Motions brought by shareholders.

(1) ¹Motions put forward by a shareholder stating the name of the shareholder, the reasons for the motion and any comments on the part of the administration

§ 125 Abs. 1 bis 3 genannten Berechtigten unter den dortigen Voraussetzungen zugänglich zu machen, wenn der Aktionär mindestens 14 Tage vor der Versammlung der Gesellschaft einen Gegenantrag gegen einen Vorschlag von Vorstand und Aufsichtsrat zu einem bestimmten Punkt der Tagesordnung mit Begründung an die in der Einberufung hierfür mitgeteilte Adresse übersandt hat. ²Der Tag des Zugangs ist nicht mitzurechnen. ³Bei börsennotierten Gesellschaften hat das Zugänglichmachen über die Internetseite der Gesellschaft zu erfolgen. ⁴§ 125 Abs. 3 gilt entsprechend.

shall be made accessible to the entitled persons named in sec. 125 para. 1 to 3 subject to the conditions stated therein if, at least fourteen days prior to the meeting, the shareholder sends a counter motion against a proposal made by the management board and the supervisory board on a particular item on the agenda to the company at the address given for this purpose in the notification of convening the meeting together with his reasons for such motion. ²The day of receipt shall not be included in the calculation. ³ In the case of listed companies, access shall be provided via the website of the company. ⁴Sec. 125 para. 3 shall apply accordingly.

(2) ¹Ein Gegenantrag und dessen Begründung brauchen nicht zugänglich gemacht zu werden,

(2) ¹The counter motion and the reasons therefor need not be made accessible

1. soweit sich der Vorstand durch das Zugänglichmachen strafbar machen würde,

2. wenn der Gegenantrag zu einem gesetz- oder satzungswidrigen Beschluß der Hauptversammlung führen würde,

3. wenn die Begründung in wesentlichen Punkten offensichtlich falsche oder irreführende Angaben oder wenn sie Beleidigungen enthält,

4. wenn ein auf denselben Sachverhalt gestützter Gegenantrag des Aktionärs bereits zu einer Hauptversammlung der Gesellschaft nach § 125 zugänglich gemacht worden ist,

5. wenn derselbe Gegenantrag des Aktionärs mit wesentlich gleicher Begründung in den letzten fünf Jahren bereits zu mindestens zwei Hauptversammlungen der Gesellschaft nach § 125 zugänglich gemacht worden ist und in der Hauptversammlung weniger als der zwanzigste Teil des vertretenen Grundkapitals für ihn gestimmt hat,

1. if the management board would render itself liable to prosecution by making such counter motion and reasons accessible,

2. if the counter motion would result in a resolution of the general meeting which is either unlawful or in breach of the articles of association,

3. if the reasons contain key statements which are manifestly incorrect or misleading or if they are slanderous,

4. if a counter motion of the shareholder based on the same subject matter has already been made accessible in connection with a general meeting of the company pursuant to sec. 125,

5. if the same counter motion of the shareholder with essentially the same reasons has within the previous five years already been made accessible in the context of at least two general meetings of the company pursuant to sec. 125 and less than one-twentieth of the registered share capital represented at the general meeting voted in favor of such counter motion,

6. wenn der Aktionär zu erkennen gibt, daß er an der Hauptversammlung nicht teilnehmen und sich nicht vertreten lassen wird, oder
7. wenn der Aktionär in den letzten zwei Jahren in zwei Hauptversammlungen einen von ihm mitgeteilten Gegenantrag nicht gestellt hat oder nicht hat stellen lassen.

²Die Begründung braucht nicht zugänglich gemacht zu werden, wenn sie insgesamt mehr als 5.000 Zeichen beträgt.

(3) Stellen mehrere Aktionäre zu demselben Gegenstand der Beschlußfassung Gegenanträge, so kann der Vorstand die Gegenanträge und ihre Begründungen zusammenfassen.

§ 127 Wahlvorschläge von Aktionären.

¹Für den Vorschlag eines Aktionärs zur Wahl von Aufsichtsratsmitgliedern oder von Abschlußprüfern gilt § 126 sinngemäß. ²Der Wahlvorschlag braucht nicht begründet zu werden. ³Der Vorstand braucht den Wahlvorschlag auch dann nicht zugänglich zu machen, wenn der Vorschlag nicht die Angaben nach § 124 Absatz 3 Satz 4 und § 125 Abs. 1 Satz 5 enthält. ⁴Der Vorstand hat den Vorschlag eines Aktionärs zur Wahl von Aufsichtsratsmitgliedern börsennotierter Gesellschaften, für die das Mitbestimmungsgesetz, das Montan-Mitbestimmungsgesetz oder das Mitbestimmungsergänzungsgesetz gilt, mit folgenden Inhalten zu versehen:

1. Hinweis auf die Anforderungen des § 96 Absatz 2,
2. Angabe, ob der Gesamterfüllung nach § 96 Absatz 2 Satz 3 widersprochen wurde und
3. Angabe, wie viele der Sitze im Aufsichtsrat mindestens jeweils von Frauen und Männern besetzt sein müssen, um das Mindestanteilsge-

6. if the shareholder indicates that he shall neither attend the general meeting nor arrange for a representative to attend on his behalf, or
7. if in the previous two years the shareholder has failed in two general meetings to make or cause to be made on his behalf a counter motion communicated by him.

²The reasons need not be made available if the text thereof exceeds a total of 5,000 characters.

(3) If several shareholders file a counter motion in respect of the same resolution, the management board may combine the counter motions and reasons.

§ 127 Nominations brought by shareholders.

¹Sec. 126 shall apply accordingly to nominations made by shareholders for the election of supervisory board members or auditors of annual financial statements. ²There is no need for reasons to be given for the nomination. ³Furthermore, the management board need not make the nomination available if the nomination does not contain the information pursuant to sec. 124 para. 3 sentence 3 and sec. 125 para. 1 sentence 5. ⁴The management board shall add to the shareholder's proposal regarding the election of supervisory board members in listed companies, which are subject to the Codetermination Act, the Coal, Iron and Steel Codetermination Act or the Codetermination Amendment Act the following Information:

1. reference to sec. 96 para. 2,
2. a declaration on whether the overall fulfillment according to sec. 96 para. 2 sentence 3 has been contradicted, and
3. a declaration on how many seats in the supervisory board need to be filled by women and men, to achieve

bot nach § 96 Absatz 2 Satz 1 zu erfüllen.

§ 127a Aktionärsforum.

(1) Aktionäre oder Aktionärsvereinigungen können im Aktionärsforum des Bundesanzeigers andere Aktionäre auffordern, gemeinsam oder in Vertretung einen Antrag oder ein Verlangen nach diesem Gesetz zu stellen oder in einer Hauptversammlung das Stimmrecht auszuüben.

(2) Die Aufforderung hat folgende Angaben zu enthalten:

1. den Namen und eine Anschrift des Aktionärs oder der Aktionärsvereinigung,
2. die Firma der Gesellschaft,
3. den Antrag, das Verlangen oder einen Vorschlag für die Ausübung des Stimmrechts zu einem Tagesordnungspunkt,
4. den Tag der betroffenen Hauptversammlung.

(3) Die Aufforderung kann auf eine Begründung auf der Internetseite des Auffordernden und dessen elektronische Adresse hinweisen.

(4) Die Gesellschaft kann im Bundesanzeiger auf eine Stellungnahme zu der Aufforderung auf ihrer Internetseite hinweisen.

(5) Das Bundesministerium der Justiz und für Verbraucherschutz wird ermächtigt, durch Rechtsverordnung die äußere Gestaltung des Aktionärsforums und weitere Einzelheiten insbesondere zu der Aufforderung, dem Hinweis, den Entgelten, zu Löschungsfristen, Löschungsanspruch, zu Missbrauchsfällen und zur Einsichtnahme zu regeln.

§ 128 Übermittlung der Mitteilungen.

(1) ¹Hat ein Kreditinstitut zu Beginn des 21. Tages vor der Versammlung für Aktionäre Inhaberaktien der Gesellschaft in Verwahrung oder wird es für

the minimum fulfillment according to sec. 96 para. 2 sentence 1.

Sec. 127a Shareholders' forum.

(1) Shareholders or associations of shareholders may request other shareholders in the shareholders' forum of the Federal Law Gazette to, jointly or as representatives, file an application or make a demand pursuant to this Act or to exercise the right to vote in the general meeting.

(2) The request must set forth the following information:

1. The name and the address of the shareholder or of the association of shareholders,
2. the name of the company,
3. the application, the demand or the proposal for the exercise of the voting right concerning an agenda item,
4. the date of the relevant general meeting.

(3) The request may refer to an explanatory statement on the website of the requesting person and to its electronic address.

(4) The company may, in the Federal Law Gazette, point to a statement concerning the request on its website.

(5) The Federal Ministry of Justice and Consumer Protection is authorized to regulate by ordinance the design of the shareholders' forum and further details, in particular with regard to the request, the reference, the fees, the removal periods, the right to removal, the cases of abuse and the inspection.

§ 128 Transmission of notifications.

(1) ¹If at the beginning of the twenty-first day prior to the meeting a credit institution takes bearer shares of the company into custody for shareholders or if it is

Namensaktien, die ihm nicht gehören, im Aktienregister eingetragen, so hat es die Mitteilungen nach § 125 Abs. 1 unverzüglich an die Aktionäre zu übermitteln. ²Die Satzung der Gesellschaft kann die Übermittlung auf den Weg elektronischer Kommunikation beschränken; in diesem Fall ist das Kreditinstitut auch aus anderen Gründen nicht zu mehr verpflichtet.

(2) Die Verpflichtung des Kreditinstituts zum Ersatz eines aus der Verletzung des Absatzes 1 entstehenden Schadens kann im voraus weder ausgeschlossen noch beschränkt werden.

(3) ¹Das Bundesministerium der Justiz und für Verbraucherschutz wird ermächtigt, im Einvernehmen mit dem Bundesministerium für Wirtschaft und Energie und dem Bundesministerium der Finanzen durch Rechtsverordnung vorzuschreiben, dass die Gesellschaft den Kreditinstituten die Aufwendungen für

1. die Übermittlung der Angaben gemäß § 67 Abs. 4 und
2. die Vervielfältigung der Mitteilungen und für ihre Übersendung an die Aktionäre zu ersetzen hat. ²Es können Pauschbeträge festgesetzt werden. ³Die Rechtsverordnung bedarf nicht der Zustimmung des Bundesrates.

(4) § 125 Abs. 5 gilt entsprechend.

Dritter Unterabschnitt. Verhandlungsniederschrift. Auskunftsrecht

§ 129 Geschäftsordnung; Verzeichnis der Teilnehmer.

(1) ¹Die Hauptversammlung kann sich mit einer Mehrheit, die mindestens drei Viertel des bei der Beschlußfassung vertretenen Grundkapitals umfaßt, eine Geschäftsordnung mit Regeln für die Vorbereitung und Durchführung der Hauptversammlung geben. ²In der Hauptversammlung ist ein Verzeich-

entered in the share register for registered shares which do not belong to it, it shall transmit the notifications pursuant to sec. 125 para. 1 to the shareholders without undue delay. ²The articles of association of the company may limit the transmission to electronic communication; in this case the credit institution shall not be obligated to do any more.

(2) The obligation of the credit institution to compensate for damages resulting from a violation of para. 1 can neither be excluded nor limited in advance.

(3) ¹The Federal Ministry of Justice and Consumer Protection shall be authorized, in agreement with the Federal Ministry of Economics and Energy and the Federal Ministry of Finance, to issue a regulation decreeing that the company reimburse the credit institutions expenses incurred for

1. forwarding the information pursuant to sec. 67 para. 4 and
2. copying the communications and sending them to the shareholders. ²Flat rate amounts may be stipulated. ³The consent of the Federal Council shall not be required for such regulation.

(4) Sec. 125 para. 5 shall apply accordingly.

Subsection Three. Minutes of Proceedings. Right to Information.

§ 129 Rules of procedure; list of attendees.

(1) ¹The general meeting may adopt rules of procedure stipulating rules for the preparation and conducting of the general meeting if so agreed by a majority amounting to at least three quarters of the registered share capital represented at the adopting of the resolution. ²A list shall be drawn up at the

nis der erschienenen oder vertretenen Aktionäre und der Vertreter von Aktionären mit Angabe ihres Namens und Wohnorts sowie bei Nennbetragsaktien des Betrags, bei Stückaktien der Zahl der von jedem vertretenen Aktien unter Angabe ihrer Gattung aufzustellen.

(2) ¹Sind einem Kreditinstitut oder einer in § 135 Abs. 8 bezeichneten Person Vollmachten zur Ausübung des Stimmrechts erteilt worden und übt der Bevollmächtigte das Stimmrecht im Namen dessen, den es angeht, aus, so sind bei Nennbetragsaktien der Betrag, bei Stückaktien die Zahl und die Gattung der Aktien, für die ihm Vollmachten erteilt worden sind, zur Aufnahme in das Verzeichnis gesondert anzugeben. ²Die Namen der Aktionäre, welche Vollmachten erteilt haben, brauchen nicht angegeben zu werden.

(3) ¹Wer von einem Aktionär ermächtigt ist, im eigenen Namen das Stimmrecht für Aktien auszuüben, die ihm nicht gehören, hat bei Nennbetragsaktien den Betrag, bei Stückaktien die Zahl und die Gattung dieser Aktien zur Aufnahme in das Verzeichnis gesondert anzugeben. ²Dies gilt auch für Namensaktien, als deren Aktionär der Ermächtigte im Aktienregister eingetragen ist.

(4) ¹Das Verzeichnis ist vor der ersten Abstimmung allen Teilnehmern zugänglich zu machen. ²Jedem Aktionär ist auf Verlangen bis zu zwei Jahren nach der Hauptversammlung Einsicht in das Teilnehmerverzeichnis zu gewähren.

(5) § 125 Abs. 5 gilt entsprechend.

§ 130 Niederschrift.

(1) ¹Jeder Beschluß der Hauptversammlung ist durch eine über die Verhandlung notariell aufgenommene Niederschrift zu beurkunden. ²Gleiches

general meeting of those shareholders attending or represented at the meeting and of shareholder representatives, stating their name and place of residence and in the case of par value shares the amount or in the case of non-par value shares the number of each of the shares represented together with the class thereof.

(2) ¹If a credit institution or a person designated in sec. 135 para. 8 has been granted a proxy for the exercising of the voting right and if the proxy holder exercises the voting right without disclosing the name of the shareholder, in the case of par value shares the amount and in the case of non-par value shares the number and class of the shares for which the proxy has been granted shall be stated separately in the list. ²The names of shareholders who have granted a proxy need not be stated.

(3) ¹Anyone who has been authorized by a shareholder to exercise in his own name the voting right for shares he does not hold shall state in the case of par value shares the amount and in the case of non-par value shares the number and class of these shares for inclusion in the list. ²This shall also apply to registered shares for which the holder of the authorization is entered in the share register as the shareholder.

(4) ¹The list shall be made available to all attendees before the first vote is cast. ²Each shareholder shall be allowed to inspect the list of attendees upon request within two years after the general meeting being held.

(5) Sec. 125 para. 5 shall apply accordingly.

§ 130 Minutes.

(1) ¹Each resolution adopted in the general meeting shall be recorded in minutes of the proceedings taking the form of a notarial deed. ²This shall also apply

gilt für jedes Verlangen einer Minderheit nach § 120 Abs. 1 Satz 2, § 137. ³Bei nichtbörsennotierten Gesellschaften reicht eine vom Vorsitzenden des Aufsichtsrats zu unterzeichnende Niederschrift aus, soweit keine Beschlüsse gefaßt werden, für die das Gesetz eine Dreiviertel- oder größere Mehrheit bestimmt.

(2) ¹In der Niederschrift sind der Ort und der Tag der Verhandlung, der Name des Notars sowie die Art und das Ergebnis der Abstimmung und die Feststellung des Vorsitzenden über die Beschlußfassung anzugeben. ²Bei börsennotierten Gesellschaften umfasst die Feststellung über die Beschlussfassung für jeden Beschluss auch

1. die Zahl der Aktien, für die gültige Stimmen abgegeben wurden,
2. den Anteil des durch die gültigen Stimmen vertretenen Grundkapitals am eingetragenen Grundkapital,
3. die Zahl der für einen Beschluss abgegebenen Stimmen, Gegenstimmen und gegebenenfalls die Zahl der Enthaltungen.

³Abweichend von Satz 2 kann der Versammlungsleiter die Feststellung über die Beschlussfassung für jeden Beschluss darauf beschränken, dass die erforderliche Mehrheit erreicht wurde, falls kein Aktionär eine umfassende Feststellung gemäß Satz 2 verlangt.

(3) Die Belege über die Einberufung der Versammlung sind der Niederschrift als Anlage beizufügen, wenn sie nicht unter Angabe ihres Inhalts in der Niederschrift aufgeführt sind.

(4) ¹Die Niederschrift ist von dem Notar zu unterschreiben. ²Die Zuziehung von Zeugen ist nicht nötig.

(5) Unverzüglich nach der Versammlung hat der Vorstand eine öffentlich beglaubigte, im Falle des Absatzes 1 Satz 3 eine vom Vorsitzenden des Aufsichtsrats unterzeichnete Abschrift der

to each request brought by a minority pursuant to sec. 120 para. 1 sentence 2, sec. 137. ³In the case of listed companies, minutes signed by the chairman of the supervisory board shall suffice provided no resolutions are adopted for which a majority of three quarters or greater is prescribed by law.

(2) ¹The minutes shall state the place and date of the proceedings, the name of the notary, the form and result of voting and the determination made by the chairman regarding the resolutions. ²In the case of listed companies, the determination for each resolution shall also include

1. the number of shares for which valid votes were cast,
2. the registered share capital`s proportion of the registered share capital which was represented by valid votes,
3. the number of votes cast in favor of a resolution, the number of votes against and, if applicable, the number of abstentions.

³Sentence 2 notwithstanding, the chairman of the meeting may limit the determination regarding the resolution for each resolution to a statement that the necessary majority was attained, if no shareholder requests a comprehensive determination pursuant to sentence 2.

(3) The documents relating to the convening of the general meeting shall be appended to the minutes if the contents thereof have not been recorded in the minutes.

(4) ¹The minutes shall be signed by the notary. ²The presence of witnesses shall not be required.

(5) Without undue delay following the general meeting, the management board shall submit a certified copy of the minutes and the appendices or, in the case of para. 1 sentence 3, signed by

Niederschrift und ihrer Anlagen zum Handelsregister einzureichen.

(6) Börsennotierte Gesellschaften müssen innerhalb von sieben Tagen nach der Versammlung die festgestellten Abstimmungsergebnisse einschließlich der Angaben nach Absatz 2 Satz 2 auf ihrer Internetseite veröffentlichen.

§ 131 Auskunftsrecht des Aktionärs.

(1) [1]Jedem Aktionär ist auf Verlangen in der Hauptversammlung vom Vorstand Auskunft über Angelegenheiten der Gesellschaft zu geben, soweit sie zur sachgemäßen Beurteilung des Gegenstands der Tagesordnung erforderlich ist. [2]Die Auskunftspflicht erstreckt sich auch auf die rechtlichen und geschäftlichen Beziehungen der Gesellschaft zu einem verbundenen Unternehmen. [3]Macht eine Gesellschaft von den Erleichterungen nach § 266 Absatz 1 Satz 3, § 276 oder § 288 des Handelsgesetzbuchs Gebrauch, so kann jeder Aktionär verlangen, dass ihm in der Hauptversammlung über den Jahresabschluss der Jahresabschluss in der Form vorgelegt wird, die er ohne diese Erleichterungen hätte. [4]Die Auskunftspflicht des Vorstands eines Mutterunternehmens (§ 290 Abs. 1, 2 des Handelsgesetzbuchs) in der Hauptversammlung, der der Konzernabschluss und der Konzernlagebericht vorgelegt werden, erstreckt sich auch auf die Lage des Konzerns und der in den Konzernabschluss einbezogenen Unternehmen.

(2) [1]Die Auskunft hat den Grundsätzen einer gewissenhaften und getreuen Rechenschaft zu entsprechen. [2]Die Satzung oder die Geschäftsordnung gemäß § 129 kann den Versammlungsleiter ermächtigen, das Frage- und Rederecht des Aktionärs zeitlich angemessen zu beschränken, und Näheres dazu bestimmen.

the chairman of the supervisory board, to the commercial register.

(6) Listed companies shall publish the voting results that were determined including the information pursuant to para. 2 sentence 2 on their website within seven days after the meeting.

§ 131 Shareholder's right to information.

(1) [1]Each shareholder shall upon request be given information from the management board in the general meeting regarding the company's affairs to the extent required to allow a proper assessment of the items on the agenda. [2]The obligation to provide information shall also extend to the legal and business relationships between the company and an affiliated enterprise. [3]If a company makes use of the simplifications pursuant to sec. 266 para. 1 sentence 3, sec. 276 or sec. 288 of the Commercial Code, each shareholder may request that the annual financial statements be presented to him at the general meeting dealing with the annual financial statements in the form they would take if such facilitations were not applied. [4]The obligation on the part the management board of a parent enterprise (sec. 290 paras. 1, 2 of the Commercial Code) to provide information in the general meeting in which the consolidated financial statements and consolidated management report are presented shall also extend to the situation of the group of companies and the enterprises included in the consolidated financial statements.

(2) [1]The information shall comply with the principles of conscientious and true accounting. [2]The articles of association or the rules of procedure pursuant to sec. 129 may authorize the chairman of the meeting to restrict the rights of the shareholders to ask questions and to speak to an adequate period of time and to regulate other details.

(3) ¹Der Vorstand darf die Auskunft verweigern,

1. soweit die Erteilung der Auskunft nach vernünftiger kaufmännischer Beurteilung geeignet ist, der Gesellschaft oder einem verbundenen Unternehmen einen nicht unerheblichen Nachteil zuzufügen;
2. soweit sie sich auf steuerliche Wertansätze oder die Höhe einzelner Steuern bezieht;
3. über den Unterschied zwischen dem Wert, mit dem Gegenstände in der Jahresbilanz angesetzt worden sind, und einem höheren Wert dieser Gegenstände, es sei denn, daß die Hauptversammlung den Jahresabschluß feststellt;
4. über die Bilanzierungs- und Bewertungsmethoden, soweit die Angabe dieser Methoden im Anhang ausreicht, um ein den tatsächlichen Verhältnissen entsprechendes Bild der Vermögens-, Finanz- und Ertragslage der Gesellschaft im Sinne des § 264 Abs. 2 des Handelsgesetzbuchs zu vermitteln; dies gilt nicht, wenn die Hauptversammlung den Jahresabschluß feststellt;
5. soweit sich der Vorstand durch die Erteilung der Auskunft strafbar machen würde;
6. soweit bei einem Kreditinstitut oder Finanzdienstleistungsinstitut Angaben über angewandte Bilanzierungs- und Bewertungsmethoden sowie vorgenommene Verrechnungen im Jahresabschluß, Lagebericht, Konzernabschluß oder Konzernlagebericht nicht gemacht zu werden brauchen;
7. soweit die Auskunft auf der Internetseite der Gesellschaft über mindestens sieben Tage vor Beginn und in der Hauptversammlung durchgängig zugänglich ist.

²Aus anderen Gründen darf die Auskunft nicht verweigert werden.

(3) ¹The management board may refuse to provide information

1. insofar as according to reasonable business judgment the providing of such information is likely to cause not inconsiderable damage to the company or an affiliated enterprise;
2. insofar as it pertains to tax valuations or the amount of individual taxes;
3. concerning the difference between the value at which items are shown in the annual balance sheet and a higher value of such items, unless the general meeting formally approves the annual financial statements;
4. concerning the accounting and evaluation methods, provided that the details given in the notes concerning such methods are sufficient to give an accurate portrayal of the situation regarding the assets, finances and profits of the company within the meaning of sec. 264 para. 2 of the Commercial Code; this shall not apply if the general meeting formally approves the annual financial statements;
5. insofar as the management board would make itself liable to prosecution by giving such information;
6. insofar as, in the case of a credit institution or a financial services institute, there is no requirement for information concerning the accounting and valuation methods used and set-offs made to be given in the annual financial statements, management report, consolidated financial statement or consolidated management report;
7. insofar as the information is continuously accessible on the website of the company from the seventh day prior to the general meeting through and during the general meeting.

²Information may not be denied for any other reason.

(4) ¹Ist einem Aktionär wegen seiner Eigenschaft als Aktionär eine Auskunft außerhalb der Hauptversammlung gegeben worden, so ist sie jedem anderen Aktionär auf dessen Verlangen in der Hauptversammlung zu geben, auch wenn sie zur sachgemäßen Beurteilung des Gegenstands der Tagesordnung nicht erforderlich ist. ²Der Vorstand darf die Auskunft nicht nach Absatz 3 Satz 1 Nr. 1 bis 4 verweigern. ³Sätze 1 und 2 gelten nicht, wenn ein Tochterunternehmen (§ 290 Abs. 1, 2 des Handelsgesetzbuchs), ein Gemeinschaftsunternehmen (§ 310 Abs. 1 des Handelsgesetzbuchs) oder ein assoziiertes Unternehmen (§ 311 Abs. 1 des Handelsgesetzbuchs) die Auskunft einem Mutterunternehmen (§ 290 Abs. 1, 2 des Handelsgesetzbuchs) zum Zwecke der Einbeziehung der Gesellschaft in den Konzernabschluß des Mutterunternehmens erteilt und die Auskunft für diesen Zweck benötigt wird.

(5) Wird einem Aktionär eine Auskunft verweigert, so kann er verlangen, daß seine Frage und der Grund, aus dem die Auskunft verweigert worden ist, in die Niederschrift über die Verhandlung aufgenommen werden.

§ 132 Gerichtliche Entscheidung über das Auskunftsrecht.

(1) Ob der Vorstand die Auskunft zu geben hat, entscheidet auf Antrag ausschließlich das Landgericht, in dessen Bezirk die Gesellschaft ihren Sitz hat.

(2) ¹Antragsberechtigt ist jeder Aktionär, dem die verlangte Auskunft nicht gegeben worden ist, und, wenn über den Gegenstand der Tagesordnung, auf den sich die Auskunft bezog, Beschluß gefaßt worden ist, jeder in der Hauptversammlung erschienene Aktionär, der in der Hauptversammlung Widerspruch zur Niederschrift erklärt hat. ²Der Antrag ist binnen zwei Wochen nach der

(4) ¹If a shareholder has been given information outside of the general meeting as a result of him being a shareholder, such information shall be given to any other shareholder in the general meeting upon request, even if such information is not necessary for a proper assessment of the item on the agenda. ²The management board may not refuse to give the information pursuant to para. 3 sentence 1 nos. 1 to 4. ³Sentences 1 and 2 shall not apply if a subsidiary (sec. 290 paras. 1, 2 of the Commercial Code), a joint venture (sec. 310 para. 1 of the Commercial Code) or an associated enterprise (sec. 311 para. 1 of the Commercial Code) provides the information to a parent enterprise (sec. 290 paras. 1, 2 of the Commercial Code) for the purpose of the inclusion of the company in the parent enterprise's consolidated annual financial statements and the information is required for this purpose.

(5) If information is denied a shareholder, such shareholder may request that his question and the reason given for the refusal of the information be recorded in the minutes of the proceedings.

§ 132 Court decision on the right to information.

(1) The regional court of the district in which the company has its registered office shall have sole jurisdiction for deciding, upon application, whether the management board is obligated to provide information.

(2) ¹Each shareholder who has been denied the requested information and, if a resolution has been adopted concerning the item on the agenda, each shareholder present at the general meeting who raised his objection in the minutes of the general meeting, shall be entitled to file an application. ²Such application shall be filed within two weeks of the general meeting in which the information was denied.

Hauptversammlung zu stellen, in der die Auskunft abgelehnt worden ist.

(3) ¹§ 99 Abs. 1, 3 Satz 1, 2 und 4 bis 6 sowie Abs. 5 Satz 1 und 3 gilt entsprechend. ²Die Beschwerde findet nur statt, wenn das Landgericht sie in der Entscheidung für zulässig erklärt. ³§ 70 Abs. 2 des Gesetzes über das Verfahren in Familiensachen und in den Angelegenheiten der freiwilligen Gerichtsbarkeit ist entsprechend anzuwenden.

(4) ¹Wird dem Antrag stattgegeben, so ist die Auskunft auch außerhalb der Hauptversammlung zu geben. ²Aus der Entscheidung findet die Zwangsvollstreckung nach den Vorschriften der Zivilprozeßordnung statt.

(5) Das mit dem Verfahren befaßte Gericht bestimmt nach billigem Ermessen, welchem Beteiligten die Kosten des Verfahrens aufzuerlegen sind.

Vierter Unterabschnitt.
Stimmrecht

§ 133 Grundsatz der einfachen Stimmenmehrheit.

(1) Die Beschlüsse der Hauptversammlung bedürfen der Mehrheit der abgegebenen Stimmen (einfache Stimmenmehrheit), soweit nicht Gesetz oder Satzung eine größere Mehrheit oder weitere Erfordernisse bestimmen.

(2) Für Wahlen kann die Satzung andere Bestimmungen treffen.

§ 134 Stimmrecht.

(1) ¹Das Stimmrecht wird nach Aktiennennbeträgen, bei Stückaktien nach deren Zahl ausgeübt. ²Für den Fall, daß einem Aktionär mehrere Aktien gehören, kann bei einer nichtbörsennotierten Gesellschaft die Satzung das Stimmrecht durch Festsetzung eines Höchstbetrags oder von Abstufungen beschränken. ³Die Satzung kann außerdem bestimmen, daß zu den Aktien, die dem Aktionär gehören, auch die Aktien rechnen, die einem anderen für seine

(3) ¹Sec. 99 paras. 1, 3 sentences 1, 2 and 4 to 6 as well as para. 5 sentences 1 and 3 shall apply accordingly. ²The decision shall only be subject to appeal if the regional court permits such appeal in its decision. ³Sec. 70 para. 2 of the Act on Procedure in Family Matters and Matters of Non-Contentious Jurisdiction shall apply accordingly.

(4) ¹If the application is granted, the information shall be provided even outside the general meeting. ²A final and binding decision shall be enforceable pursuant to the Code of Civil Procedure.

(5) The court dealing with the proceedings shall determine which party shall be ordered to pay the costs after making a fair assessment of the circumstances.

Subsection Four.
Voting Right

§ 133 Principle of simple majority of votes.

(1) The resolutions of the general meeting shall require a majority of the votes cast (simple majority) unless a greater majority or other requirements are prescribed by law or stipulated in the articles of association.

(2) The articles of association may make other provisions for elections.

§ 134 Voting right.

(1) ¹The voting right shall be exercised according to the par value of shares, or in the case of non-par value shares according to the number of shares. ²In the case of a company which is not listed, the articles of association may limit voting rights with respect to shareholders holding more than one share by stipulating a maximum par value or a sliding scale. ³The articles of association may also stipulate that those shares held by another person on behalf of a sharehold-

Rechnung gehören. ⁴Für den Fall, daß der Aktionär ein Unternehmen ist, kann sie ferner bestimmen, daß zu den Aktien, die ihm gehören, auch die Aktien rechnen, die einem von ihm abhängigen oder ihn beherrschenden oder einem mit ihm konzernverbundenen Unternehmen oder für Rechnung solcher Unternehmen einem Dritten gehören. ⁵Die Beschränkungen können nicht für einzelne Aktionäre angeordnet werden. ⁶Bei der Berechnung einer nach Gesetz oder Satzung erforderlichen Kapitalmehrheit bleiben die Beschränkungen außer Betracht.

(2) ¹Das Stimmrecht beginnt mit der vollständigen Leistung der Einlage. ²Entspricht der Wert einer verdeckten Sacheinlage nicht dem in § 36a Abs. 2 Satz 3 genannten Wert, so steht dies dem Beginn des Stimmrechts nicht entgegen; das gilt nicht, wenn der Wertunterschied offensichtlich ist. ³Die Satzung kann bestimmen, daß das Stimmrecht beginnt, wenn auf die Aktie die gesetzliche oder höhere satzungsmäßige Mindesteinlage geleistet ist. ⁴In diesem Fall gewährt die Leistung der Mindesteinlage eine Stimme; bei höheren Einlagen richtet sich das Stimmenverhältnis nach der Höhe der geleisteten Einlagen. ⁵Bestimmt die Satzung nicht, daß das Stimmrecht vor der vollständigen Leistung der Einlage beginnt, und ist noch auf keine Aktie die Einlage vollständig geleistet, so richtet sich das Stimmenverhältnis nach der Höhe der geleisteten Einlagen; dabei gewährt die Leistung der Mindesteinlage eine Stimme. ⁶Bruchteile von Stimmen werden in diesen Fällen nur berücksichtigt, soweit sie für den stimmberechtigten Aktionär volle Stimmen ergeben. ⁷Die Satzung kann Bestimmungen nach diesem Absatz nicht für einzelne Aktionäre oder für einzelne Aktiengattungen treffen.

er shall be counted as belonging to the shareholder. ⁴Furthermore, the articles of association may stipulate that in the event of the shareholder being an enterprise, those shares held by a controlled enterprise, a controlling enterprise, or an enterprise belonging to the same group or by a third person on behalf of such enterprises shall be counted as belonging to the shareholder. ⁵Such limitations may not be implemented for individual shareholders. ⁶The limitations shall not apply when calculating a capital majority required by law or pursuant to the articles of association.

(2) ¹Voting rights shall arise once the contribution has been paid in full. ²If the value of a hidden contribution in kind does not correspond to the value set forth in sec. 36a para. 2 sentence 3, this shall not prevent the voting right from coming into being; this shall not apply if the discrepancy in value is obvious. ³The articles of association may stipulate that the voting rights shall arise upon payment of the minimum contribution required by law or a higher minimum contribution stipulated in the articles of association. ⁴In this case, payment of the minimum contribution shall entitle the shareholder to one vote; if payments exceed the minimum contribution, voting rights shall be determined in accordance with the contributions made. ⁵If the articles of association do not stipulate that voting rights arise before the contribution has been paid in full and if contributions have not yet been paid in full towards any of the shares, the voting rights shall be determined in accordance with the amount of contributions paid, with payment of the minimum contribution entailing one vote. ⁶In these cases, fractions of votes shall only be taken into account to the extent that they result in full votes for the shareholder entitled to vote. ⁷The articles of association may not make provisions pursuant to this para. for individual shareholders or individual classes of shares.

(3) ¹Das Stimmrecht kann durch einen Bevollmächtigten ausgeübt werden. ²Bevollmächtigt der Aktionär mehr als eine Person, so kann die Gesellschaft eine oder mehrere von diesen zurückweisen. ³Die Erteilung der Vollmacht, ihr Widerruf und der Nachweis der Bevollmächtigung gegenüber der Gesellschaft bedürfen der Textform, wenn in der Satzung oder in der Einberufung aufgrund einer Ermächtigung durch die Satzung nichts Abweichendes und bei börsennotierten Gesellschaften nicht eine Erleichterung bestimmt wird. ⁴Die börsennotierte Gesellschaft hat zumindest einen Weg elektronischer Kommunikation für die Übermittlung des Nachweises anzubieten. ⁵Werden von der Gesellschaft benannte Stimmrechtsvertreter bevollmächtigt, so ist die Vollmachtserklärung von der Gesellschaft drei Jahre nachprüfbar festzuhalten; § 135 Abs. 5 gilt entsprechend.

(4) Die Form der Ausübung des Stimmrechts richtet sich nach der Satzung.

§ 135 Ausübung des Stimmrechts durch Kreditinstitute und geschäftsmäßig Handelnde.

(1) ¹Ein Kreditinstitut darf das Stimmrecht für Aktien, die ihm nicht gehören und als deren Inhaber es nicht im Aktienregister eingetragen ist, nur ausüben, wenn es bevollmächtigt ist. ²Die Vollmacht darf nur einem bestimmten Kreditinstitut erteilt werden und ist von diesem nachprüfbar festzuhalten. ³Die Vollmachtserklärung muss vollständig sein und darf nur mit der Stimmrechtsausübung verbundene Erklärungen enthalten. ⁴Erteilt der Aktionär keine ausdrücklichen Weisungen, so kann eine generelle Vollmacht nur die Berechtigung des Kreditinstituts zur Stimmrechtsausübung

1. entsprechend eigenen Abstimmungsvorschlägen (Absätze 2 und 3) oder

---

(3) ¹The voting right may be exercised by a proxy. ²If the shareholder appoints more than one person as proxy, the company may reject one or more of the holders of such proxy. ³The granting of the proxy, its revocation and the proof of appointment as proxy vis-à-vis the company require text form, unless the articles of association or, on the basis of an authorization in the articles of association, the notification of convening of the meeting provides otherwise or, in the case of listed companies, provides for an easing of this requirement. ⁴The listed company shall offer at least one method of electronic communication for the transmission of the proof. ⁵If proxies for the exercising of the voting right named by the company are appointed, the company shall maintain a verifiable record of the declaration of proxy for a period of three years; sec. 135 para. 5 shall apply accordingly.

(4) The method of exercising the voting rights shall be stipulated in the articles of association.

§ 135 Exercising of voting rights by credit institutions and professional agents.

(1) ¹A credit institution may only exercise voting rights attached to shares which it does not hold and for which it is not entered in the share register as the holder if it has been authorized to do so. ²The proxy may only be issued to a specific credit institution and such institution shall record it in a verifiable way. ³The proxy statement shall be complete and may only contain statements relating to the exercise of the voting right. ⁴If the shareholder does not issue explicit instructions, a general proxy may only provide for the authorization of the credit institution to exercise the voting right

1. in accordance with its own proposals for voting (paras. 2 and 3) or

2. entsprechend den Vorschlägen des Vorstands oder des Aufsichtsrats oder für den Fall voneinander abweichender Vorschläge den Vorschlägen des Aufsichtsrats (Absatz 4) vorsehen.

⁵Bietet das Kreditinstitut die Stimmrechtsausübung gemäß Satz 4 Nr. 1 oder Nr. 2 an, so hat es sich zugleich zu erbieten, im Rahmen des Zumutbaren und bis auf Widerruf einer Aktionärsvereinigung oder einem sonstigen Vertreter nach Wahl des Aktionärs die zur Stimmrechtsausübung erforderlichen Unterlagen zuzuleiten. ⁶Das Kreditinstitut hat den Aktionär jährlich und deutlich hervorgehoben auf die Möglichkeiten des jederzeitigen Widerrufs der Vollmacht und der Änderung des Bevollmächtigten hinzuweisen. ⁷Die Erteilung von Weisungen zu den einzelnen Tagesordnungspunkten, die Erteilung und der Widerruf einer generellen Vollmacht nach Satz 4 und eines Auftrags nach Satz 5 einschließlich seiner Änderung sind dem Aktionär durch ein Formblatt oder Bildschirmformular zu erleichtern.

(2) ¹Ein Kreditinstitut, das das Stimmrecht auf Grund einer Vollmacht nach Absatz 1 Satz 4 Nr. 1 ausüben will, hat dem Aktionär rechtzeitig eigene Vorschläge für die Ausübung des Stimmrechts zu den einzelnen Gegenständen der Tagesordnung zugänglich zu machen. ²Bei diesen Vorschlägen hat sich das Kreditinstitut vom Interesse des Aktionärs leiten zu lassen und organisatorische Vorkehrungen dafür zu treffen, dass Eigeninteressen aus anderen Geschäftsbereichen nicht einfließen; es hat ein Mitglied der Geschäftsleitung zu benennen, das die Einhaltung dieser Pflichten sowie die ordnungsgemäße Ausübung des Stimmrechts und deren Dokumentation zu überwachen hat. ³Zusammen mit seinen Vorschlägen hat das Kreditinstitut darauf hinzuweisen, dass es das Stimmrecht entsprechend den eigenen Vorschlägen ausüben wer-

2. in accordance with the proposals of the management board or the supervisory board or, in the case of proposals which deviate from each other, the proposals of the supervisory board (para. 4).

⁵If the credit institution offers to exercise the voting right pursuant to sentence 4 no. 1 or no. 2, it shall at the same time offer to, within reasonable bounds and subject to revocation, send the documents required for the exercise of the voting right to a shareholder association or another representative chosen by the shareholder. ⁶The credit institution shall notify the shareholder every year of, and shall clearly highlight the possibilities of revoking, the proxy at any time and of appointing a different proxy. ⁷The issuance of instructions with respect to the individual agenda items, the issuance and the revocation of a general proxy pursuant to sentence 4 and of a mandate pursuant to sentence 5 including its modification shall be facilitated for the shareholder through a paper or screen form.

(2) ¹A credit institution which intends to exercise the voting right on the basis of a proxy pursuant to para. 1 sentence 4 no. 1 shall timely make accessible to the shareholder its own proposals for the exercise of the voting right with respect to the individual agenda items. ²In making these proposals, the credit institution shall be guided by the interest of the shareholder and shall make organizational arrangements such that interests of its own from other business areas are not incorporated; it shall nominate a member of the management who shall supervise the observance of these obligations as well as the proper exercise of the voting right and their documentation. ³Together with its proposals, the credit institution shall point out that it will exercise the voting right in accordance with its own proposals unless the shareholder timely issues a

de, wenn der Aktionär nicht rechtzeitig eine andere Weisung erteilt. ⁴Gehört ein Vorstandsmitglied oder ein Mitarbeiter des Kreditinstituts dem Aufsichtsrat der Gesellschaft oder ein Vorstandsmitglied oder ein Mitarbeiter der Gesellschaft dem Aufsichtsrat des Kreditinstituts an, so hat das Kreditinstitut hierauf hinzuweisen. ⁵Gleiches gilt, wenn das Kreditinstitut an der Gesellschaft eine Beteiligung hält, die nach § 21 des Wertpapierhandelsgesetzes meldepflichtig ist, oder einem Konsortium angehörte, das die innerhalb von fünf Jahren zeitlich letzte Emission von Wertpapieren der Gesellschaft übernommen hat.

(3) ¹Hat der Aktionär dem Kreditinstitut keine Weisung für die Ausübung des Stimmrechts erteilt, so hat das Kreditinstitut im Falle des Absatzes 1 Satz 4 Nr. 1 das Stimmrecht entsprechend seinen eigenen Vorschlägen auszuüben, es sei denn, dass es den Umständen nach annehmen darf, dass der Aktionär bei Kenntnis der Sachlage die abweichende Ausübung des Stimmrechts billigen würde. ²Ist das Kreditinstitut bei der Ausübung des Stimmrechts von einer Weisung des Aktionärs oder, wenn der Aktionär keine Weisung erteilt hat, von seinem eigenen Vorschlag abgewichen, so hat es dies dem Aktionär mitzuteilen und die Gründe anzugeben. ³In der eigenen Hauptversammlung darf das bevollmächtigte Kreditinstitut das Stimmrecht auf Grund einer Vollmacht nur ausüben, soweit der Aktionär eine ausdrückliche Weisung zu den einzelnen Gegenständen der Tagesordnung erteilt hat. ⁴Gleiches gilt in der Versammlung einer Gesellschaft, an der es mit mehr als 20 Prozent des Grundkapitals unmittelbar oder mittelbar beteiligt ist; für die Berechnung der Beteiligungsschwelle bleiben mittelbare Beteiligungen im Sinne des § 22a Absatz 3 bis 6 des Wertpapierhandelsgesetzes außer Betracht.

(4) ¹Ein Kreditinstitut, das in der Hauptversammlung das Stimmrecht auf

different instruction. ⁴If a member of the management board or an employee of the credit institution belongs to the supervisory board of the company or if a member of the management board or an employee of the company belongs to the supervisory board of the credit institution then the credit institution shall point this out. ⁵The same shall apply if the credit institution holds a share of the company which is to be notified pursuant to sec. 21 of the Securities Trading Act or if it belonged to a syndicate which carried out the most recent issuance of securities of the company, provided that such issuance took place during the previous five years.

(3) ¹If the shareholder has not issued an instruction to the credit institution with respect to the exercise of the voting right, the credit institution shall in the case of para. 1 sentence 4 no. 1 exercise the voting right in accordance with its own proposals, unless it may assume under the circumstances that the shareholder would, if he knew the circumstances, approve the different exercise of the voting right. ²If the credit institution deviated from an instruction of the shareholder in the exercise of the voting right or, if the shareholder did not issue an instruction, from its own proposal, then it shall so notify the shareholder and give reasons. ³The credit institution appointed as a proxy may only exercise the voting right in its own general meeting on the basis of a proxy to the extent that the shareholder has issued an explicit instruction with respect to the individual items of the agenda. ⁴The same shall apply in the meeting of a company in which the credit institution directly or indirectly holds more than twenty percent of the registered share capital; to calculate the participation, indirect interests within the meaning of sec. 22a para. 3 to 6 of the German Securities Act shall be disregarded.

(4) ¹A credit institution that intends to exercise the voting right in the general

Grund einer Vollmacht nach Absatz 1 Satz 4 Nr. 2 ausüben will, hat den Aktionären die Vorschläge des Vorstands und des Aufsichtsrats zugänglich zu machen, sofern dies nicht anderweitig erfolgt. ²Absatz 2 Satz 3 sowie Absatz 3 Satz 1 bis 3 gelten entsprechend.

(5) ¹Wenn die Vollmacht dies gestattet, darf das Kreditinstitut Personen, die nicht seine Angestellten sind, unterbevollmächtigen. ²Wenn es die Vollmacht nicht anders bestimmt, übt das Kreditinstitut das Stimmrecht im Namen dessen aus, den es angeht. ³Ist die Briefwahl bei der Gesellschaft zugelassen, so darf das bevollmächtigte Kreditinstitut sich ihrer bedienen. ⁴Zum Nachweis seiner Stimmberechtigung gegenüber der Gesellschaft genügt bei börsennotierten Gesellschaften die Vorlegung eines Berechtigungsnachweises gemäß § 123 Abs. 3; im Übrigen sind die in der Satzung für die Ausübung des Stimmrechts vorgesehenen Erfordernisse zu erfüllen.

(6) ¹Ein Kreditinstitut darf das Stimmrecht für Namensaktien, die ihm nicht gehören, als deren Inhaber es aber im Aktienregister eingetragen ist, nur auf Grund einer Ermächtigung ausüben. ²Auf die Ermächtigung sind die Absätze 1 bis 5 entsprechend anzuwenden.

(7) Die Wirksamkeit der Stimmabgabe wird durch einen Verstoß gegen Absatz 1 Satz 2 bis 7, die Absätze 2 bis 6 nicht beeinträchtigt.

(8) Die Absätze 1 bis 7 gelten sinngemäß für Aktionärsvereinigungen und für Personen, die sich geschäftsmäßig gegenüber Aktionären zur Ausübung des Stimmrechts in der Hauptversammlung erbieten; dies gilt nicht, wenn derjenige, der das Stimmrecht ausüben will, gesetzlicher Vertreter, Ehegatte oder Lebenspartner des Aktionärs oder mit ihm bis zum vierten Grad verwandt oder verschwägert ist.

meeting on the basis of a proxy pursuant to para. 1 sentence 4 no. 2 shall make accessible to the shareholders the proposals of the management board and the supervisory board, unless this has already taken place otherwise. ²Para. 2 sentence 3 as well as para. 3 sentences 1 to 3 shall apply accordingly.

(5) ¹If the proxy so allows, the credit institution may delegate its authority by way of sub-proxy to persons who are not its employees. ²Unless the proxy provides otherwise, the credit institution exercises the voting right on behalf of the person who is concerned. ³If absentee voting is allowed with the company, the credit institution appointed as proxy may make use of it. ⁴In the case of listed companies, the presentation of a proof of authorization pursuant to sec. 123 para. 3 shall be sufficient vis-à-vis the company to prove the voting right; in all other cases the requirements for the exercise of the voting right set forth in the articles of association shall be met.

(6) ¹A credit institution may exercise the voting right for registered shares which it does not own but which it is registered in the share register as the owner only on the basis of an authorization. ²Paras. 1 to 5 shall apply accordingly to such authorization.

(7) The validity of the casting of a vote shall not be affected by a violation of para. 1 sentences 2 to 7, paras. 2 to 6.

(8) Paras. 1 to 7 shall apply accordingly to shareholder associations and to persons professionally offering the shareholders their services for the exercising of the voting right in the general meeting; this shall not apply if the person who wishes to exercise the voting right is the legal representative, spouse or domestic partner of the shareholder or is related to him by blood or marriage within the fourth degree.

(9) Die Verpflichtung des Kreditinstituts zum Ersatz eines aus der Verletzung der Absätze 1 bis 6 entstehenden Schadens kann im Voraus weder ausgeschlossen noch beschränkt werden.

(10) § 125 Abs. 5 gilt entsprechend.

§ 136 Ausschluß des Stimmrechts.

(1) [1]Niemand kann für sich oder für einen anderen das Stimmrecht ausüben, wenn darüber Beschluß gefaßt wird, ob er zu entlasten oder von einer Verbindlichkeit zu befreien ist oder ob die Gesellschaft gegen ihn einen Anspruch geltend machen soll. [2]Für Aktien, aus denen der Aktionär nach Satz 1 das Stimmrecht nicht ausüben kann, kann das Stimmrecht auch nicht durch einen anderen ausgeübt werden.

(2) [1]Ein Vertrag, durch den sich ein Aktionär verpflichtet, nach Weisung der Gesellschaft, des Vorstands oder des Aufsichtsrats der Gesellschaft oder nach Weisung eines abhängigen Unternehmens das Stimmrecht auszuüben, ist nichtig. [2]Ebenso ist ein Vertrag nichtig, durch den sich ein Aktionär verpflichtet, für die jeweiligen Vorschläge des Vorstands oder des Aufsichtsrats der Gesellschaft zu stimmen.

§ 137 Abstimmung über Wahlvorschläge von Aktionären.

Hat ein Aktionär einen Vorschlag zur Wahl von Aufsichtsratsmitgliedern nach § 127 gemacht und beantragt er in der Hauptversammlung die Wahl des von ihm Vorgeschlagenen, so ist über seinen Antrag vor dem Vorschlag des Aufsichtsrats zu beschließen, wenn es eine Minderheit der Aktionäre verlangt, deren Anteile zusammen den zehnten Teil des vertretenen Grundkapitals erreichen.

(9) The obligation of the credit institution to compensate damages arising from the violation of paras. 1 to 6 can neither be excluded nor limited in advance.

(10) Sec. 125 para. 5 shall apply accordingly.

§ 136 Exclusion of voting rights.

(1) [1]No person may exercise voting rights for himself or another if a resolution is being adopted as to whether ratification is to be granted for his acts, whether he is to be released from an obligation or whether the company is to assert a claim against him. [2]The voting rights arising from shares for which the shareholder may not exercise the voting right pursuant to sentence 1 may not be exercised by another person either.

(2) [1]A contract whereby a shareholder enters into an obligation to exercise the voting right in accordance with instructions issued by the company, the management board or the supervisory board of the company or in accordance with the instructions issued by a controlled enterprise shall be null and void. [2]A contract whereby a shareholder enters into an obligation to vote for the respective proposals of the management board or supervisory board of the company shall likewise be null and void.

§ 137 Voting on nominations made by shareholders.

If a shareholder has made a nomination for the election of supervisory board members pursuant to sec. 127 and proposes at the general meeting the election of the person nominated by him, a resolution shall be adopted concerning such proposal prior to the proposal of the supervisory board if a minority of shareholders having an aggregate shareholding of one tenth of the registered share capital represented at the meeting so requests.

Fünfter Unterabschnitt. Sonderbeschluß	**Subsection Five. Special Resolutions**
§ 138 Gesonderte Versammlung. Gesonderte Abstimmung.	**§ 138 Separate meeting. Separate vote.**
[1]In diesem Gesetz oder in der Satzung vorgeschriebene Sonderbeschlüsse gewisser Aktionäre sind entweder in einer gesonderten Versammlung dieser Aktionäre oder in einer gesonderten Abstimmung zu fassen, soweit das Gesetz nichts anderes bestimmt. [2]Für die Einberufung der gesonderten Versammlung und die Teilnahme an ihr sowie für das Auskunftsrecht gelten die Bestimmungen über die Hauptversammlung, für die Sonderbeschlüsse die Bestimmungen über Hauptversammlungsbeschlüsse sinngemäß. [3]Verlangen Aktionäre, die an der Abstimmung über den Sonderbeschluß teilnehmen können, die Einberufung einer gesonderten Versammlung oder die Bekanntmachung eines Gegenstands zur gesonderten Abstimmung, so genügt es, wenn ihre Anteile, mit denen sie an der Abstimmung über den Sonderbeschluß teilnehmen können, zusammen den zehnten Teil der Anteile erreichen, aus denen bei der Abstimmung über den Sonderbeschluß das Stimmrecht ausgeübt werden kann.	[1]Special resolutions of certain shareholders prescribed in this Act or in the articles of association shall be adopted either in a separate meeting of these shareholders or in a separate vote, unless prescribed otherwise by law. [2]The provisions governing the general meeting shall apply accordingly to the convening of the separate meeting, attendance thereof and the right to information, and the provisions governing resolutions adopted by the general meeting shall apply accordingly to the special resolutions. [3]If shareholders who are entitled to participate in the voting on the special resolution require the convening of a separate meeting or the announcement of an item to be voted on separately, it shall suffice if the aggregate total of shares entitling them to participate in voting on the special resolution is at least one tenth of the shares entitled to vote on such special resolution.
Sechster Unterabschnitt. Vorzugsaktien ohne Stimmrecht	**Subsection Six. Preference Shares without Voting Right**
§ 139 Wesen.	**§ 139 Nature.**
(1) Für Aktien, die mit einem Vorzug bei der Verteilung des Gewinns ausgestattet sind, kann das Stimmrecht ausgeschlossen werden (Vorzugsaktien ohne Stimmrecht). [2]Der Vorzug kann insbesondere in einem auf die Aktie vorweg entfallenden Gewinnanteil (Vorabdividende) oder einem erhöhten Gewinnanteil (Mehrdividende) bestehen. [3]Wenn die Satzung nichts anderes bestimmt, ist eine Vorabdividende nachzuzahlen.	(1) [1]Shares which carry the benefit of a preference right with respect to the distribution of profits may be issued without voting rights (preference shares without voting right). [2]The preference may, in particular, consist of a dividend per share allocated beforhand (advance dividend) or an increased dividend (additional dividend). [3]Unless provided otherwise in the articles of association, an advance dividend has to be re-margined.
(2) Vorzugsaktien ohne Stimmrecht dürfen nur bis zur Hälfte des Grundkapitals ausgegeben werden.	(2) Preference shares without voting right may only be issued for up to half of the registered share capital.

§ 140 Rechte der Vorzugsaktionäre.

(1) Die Vorzugsaktien ohne Stimmrecht gewähren mit Ausnahme des Stimmrechts die jedem Aktionär aus der Aktie zustehenden Rechte.

(2) [1]Ist der Vorzug nachzuzahlen und wird der Vorzugsbetrag in einem Jahr nicht oder nicht vollständig gezahlt und im nächsten Jahr nicht neben dem vollen Vorzug für dieses Jahres nachgezahlt, so haben die Aktionäre das Stimmrecht, bis die Rückstände gezahlt sind. [2]Ist der Vorzug nicht nachzuzahlen und wird der Vorzugsbetrag in einem Jahr nicht oder nicht vollständig gezahlt, so haben die Vorzugsaktionäre das Stimmrecht, bis der Vorzug in einem Jahr vollständig gezahlt ist. [3]Solange das Stimmrecht besteht, sind die Vorzugsaktien auch bei der Berechnung einer nach Gesetz oder Satzung erforderlichen Kapitalmehrheit zu berücksichtigen.

(3) Soweit die Satzung nichts anderes bestimmt, entsteht dadurch, dass der nachzuzahlende Vorzugsbetrag in einem Jahr nicht oder nicht vollständig gezahlt wird, noch kein durch spätere Beschlüsse über die Gewinnverteilung bedingter Anspruch auf den rückständigen Vorzugsbetrag.

§ 141 Aufhebung oder Beschränkung des Vorzugs.

(1) Ein Beschluß, durch den der Vorzug aufgehoben oder beschränkt wird, bedarf zu seiner Wirksamkeit der Zustimmung der Vorzugsaktionäre.

(2) [1]Ein Beschluß über die Ausgabe von Vorzugsaktien, die bei der Verteilung des Gewinns oder des Gesellschaftsvermögens den Vorzugsaktien ohne Stimmrecht vorgehen oder gleichstehen, bedarf gleichfalls der Zustimmung der Vorzugsaktionäre. [2]Der Zustimmung bedarf es nicht, wenn die Ausgabe bei Einräumung des Vorzugs oder, falls das

§ 140 Rights of holders of preference shares.

(1) The preference shares without voting right shall convey the same rights as those enjoyed by other shareholders with the exception of the voting right.

(2) [1]If the preference has to be re-margined and if the preference dividend is not paid or not paid in full in any given year and if it is not made up in the following year together with the full amount of the preference dividend for that year, the shareholders shall have a voting right until such time as the shortfall has been paid. [2]If the preference does not to be re-margined and if the preference amount is not paid or not paid in full in any given year, the preference shareholders shall have a voting right until such time as the shortfall has been paid. [3]As long as the voting right exists, the preference shares shall also be taken into account when calculating a capital majority required by law or pursuant to the articles of association.

(3) Unless provided otherwise in the articles of association, the fact that the preference amount is not re-margined or not paid in full in any given year shall not give rise to a claim to the preference dividend in arrears contingent upon resolutions concerning the distribution of profits adopted at a later date.

§ 141 Cancellation or restriction of preference rights.

(1) A resolution canceling or restricting the preference rights shall require the consent of the holders of the preference shares in order to be effective.

(2) [1]A resolution on the issue of preference shares which are to enjoy priority over or to rank equally with the preference shares without voting right in respect of the distribution of profits or corporate assets shall also require the consent of the holders of the existing preference shares. [2]Consent shall not be required if the right to issue such

Stimmrecht später ausgeschlossen wurde, bei der Ausschließung ausdrücklich vorbehalten worden war und das Bezugsrecht der Vorzugsaktionäre nicht ausgeschlossen wird.

(3) ¹Über die Zustimmung haben die Vorzugsaktionäre in einer gesonderten Versammlung einen Sonderbeschluß zu fassen. ²Er bedarf einer Mehrheit, die mindestens drei Viertel der abgegebenen Stimmen umfaßt. ³Die Satzung kann weder eine andere Mehrheit noch weitere Erfordernisse bestimmen. ⁴Wird in dem Beschluß über die Ausgabe von Vorzugsaktien, die bei der Verteilung des Gewinns oder des Gesellschaftsvermögens den Vorzugsaktien ohne Stimmrecht vorgehen oder gleichstehen, das Bezugsrecht der Vorzugsaktionäre auf den Bezug solcher Aktien ganz oder zum Teil ausgeschlossen, so gilt für den Sonderbeschluß § 186 Abs. 3 bis 5 sinngemäß.

(4) Ist der Vorzug aufgehoben, so gewähren die Aktien das Stimmrecht.

Siebenter Unterabschnitt.
Sonderprüfung. Geltendmachung von Ersatzansprüchen

§ 142 Bestellung der Sonderprüfer.

(1) ¹Zur Prüfung von Vorgängen bei der Gründung oder der Geschäftsführung, namentlich auch bei Maßnahmen der Kapitalbeschaffung und Kapitalherabsetzung, kann die Hauptversammlung mit einfacher Stimmenmehrheit Prüfer (Sonderprüfer) bestellen. ²Bei der Beschlußfassung kann ein Mitglied des Vorstands oder des Aufsichtsrats weder für sich noch für einen anderen mitstimmen, wenn die Prüfung sich auf Vorgänge erstrecken soll, die mit der Entlastung eines Mitglieds des Vorstands oder des Aufsichtsrats oder der Einleitung eines Rechtsstreits zwischen der Gesellschaft und einem Mitglied

shares was expressly reserved upon the granting of the preference rights or, if voting rights were excluded at a later date, upon the exclusion thereof and if the subscription right of the holders of the existing preference shares is not excluded.

(3) ¹The holders of the preference shares shall adopt a special resolution as to whether or not to grant such consent in a separate meeting. ²Such resolution shall require a majority of at least three quarters of the votes cast. ³The articles of association may not stipulate another majority nor other requirements. ⁴If a resolution on the issue of preference shares which are to enjoy priority over or to rank equally with the preference shares without voting right in respect of the distribution of profits or corporate assets wholly or partially excludes the subscription right of the existing holders of preference shares to such shares, sec. 186 paras. 3 to 5 shall apply accordingly.

(4) If the preference rights are revoked, the shares shall grant a voting right.

Subsection Seven.
Special Audit. Asserting of Claims for Damages

§ 142 Appointment of special auditors.

(1) ¹The general meeting may, by simple majority, appoint auditors (special auditors) to investigate matters relating to the formation or management of the company, in particular measures relating to a capital increase or reduction. ²A member of the management board or the supervisory board may neither vote on his own behalf nor on behalf of another person if the audit is to extend to procedures relating to ratification of the acts of a member of the management board or the supervisory board or to the instituting of a legal dispute between the company and a member of the management board or the supervi-

des Vorstands oder des Aufsichtsrats zusammenhängen. ³Für ein Mitglied des Vorstands oder des Aufsichtsrats, das nach Satz 2 nicht mitstimmen kann, kann das Stimmrecht auch nicht durch einen anderen ausgeübt werden.

(2) ¹Lehnt die Hauptversammlung einen Antrag auf Bestellung von Sonderprüfern zur Prüfung eines Vorgangs bei der Gründung oder eines nicht über fünf Jahre zurückliegenden Vorgangs bei der Geschäftsführung ab, so hat das Gericht auf Antrag von Aktionären, deren Anteile bei Antragstellung zusammen den hundertsten Teil des Grundkapitals oder einen anteiligen Betrag von 100.000 Euro erreichen, Sonderprüfer zu bestellen, wenn Tatsachen vorliegen, die den Verdacht rechtfertigen, dass bei dem Vorgang Unredlichkeiten oder grobe Verletzungen des Gesetzes oder der Satzung vorgekommen sind; dies gilt auch für nicht über zehn Jahre zurückliegende Vorgänge, sofern die Gesellschaft zur Zeit des Vorgangs börsennotiert war. ²Die Antragsteller haben nachzuweisen, dass sie seit mindestens drei Monaten vor dem Tag der Hauptversammlung Inhaber der Aktien sind und dass sie die Aktien bis zur Entscheidung über den Antrag halten. ³Für eine Vereinbarung zur Vermeidung einer solchen Sonderprüfung gilt § 149 entsprechend.

(3) Die Absätze 1 und 2 gelten nicht für Vorgänge, die Gegenstand einer Sonderprüfung nach § 258 sein können.

(4) ¹Hat die Hauptversammlung Sonderprüfer bestellt, so hat das Gericht auf Antrag von Aktionären, deren Anteile bei Antragstellung zusammen den hundertsten Teil des Grundkapitals oder einen anteiligen Betrag von 100.000 Euro erreichen, einen anderen Sonderprüfer zu bestellen, wenn dies aus einem in der Person des bestellten Sonderprüfers liegenden Grund geboten erscheint, insbesondere, wenn der bestellte Sonderprüfer nicht die für den Gegenstand der Sonderprüfung erforderlichen Kenntnisse hat, seine Befangenheit zu besor-

sory board. ³The voting right may not be exercised by another person on behalf of a member of the management board or the supervisory board who is not entitled to participate in the voting pursuant to sentence 2.

(2) ¹If the general meeting rejects an application for the appointment of special auditors to investigate a matter relating to the formation of the company or a matter relating to the management of the company occurring less than five years previously, the court shall, upon application by shareholders with an aggregate holding amounting to one-hundredth of the registered share capital or the proportionate amount of 100,000 euros at the time the application is made, appoint special auditors if there are facts which give reason to suspect that improprieties or serious violations of the law or the articles of association occurred in connection with the matter; this also applies to events which date back not more than ten years, if the company had been listed at that time. ²The applicants shall establish that they have held the shares for at least three months prior to the date of the general meeting and that they will hold the shares until the application is decided on. ³Sec. 149 shall apply accordingly to an agreement intended to avoid such a special audit.

(3) Paras. 1 and 2 shall not apply to matters which are permitted to be the object of a special audit pursuant to sec. 258.

(4) ¹If the general meeting has appointed special auditors, the court shall appoint another special auditor upon application by shareholders with an aggregate holding amounting to one-hundredth of the registered share capital or the proportionate amount of 100,000 euros at the time the application is made, if this appears necessary for reasons relating to the person of the special auditor who has been appointed, in particular if the special auditor lacks the expertise required for the object of the special audit, if there are concerns as to his impartial-

gen ist oder Bedenken wegen seiner Zuverlässigkeit bestehen. ²Der Antrag ist binnen zwei Wochen seit dem Tage der Hauptversammlung zu stellen.

(5) ¹Das Gericht hat außer den Beteiligten auch den Aufsichtsrat und im Fall des Absatzes 4 den von der Hauptversammlung bestellten Sonderprüfer zu hören. ²Gegen die Entscheidung ist die Beschwerde zulässig. ³Über den Antrag gemäß den Absätzen 2 und 4 entscheidet das Landgericht, in dessen Bezirk die Gesellschaft ihren Sitz hat.

(6) ¹Die vom Gericht bestellten Sonderprüfer haben Anspruch auf Ersatz angemessener barer Auslagen und auf Vergütung für ihre Tätigkeit. ²Die Auslagen und die Vergütung setzt das Gericht fest. ³Gegen die Entscheidung ist die Beschwerde zulässig; die Rechtsbeschwerde ist ausgeschlossen. ⁴Aus der rechtskräftigen Entscheidung findet die Zwangsvollstreckung nach der Zivilprozeßordnung statt.

(7) Hat die Gesellschaft Wertpapiere im Sinne des § 2 Absatz 1 des Wertpapierhandelsgesetzes ausgegeben, die an einer inländischen Börse zum Handel im regulierten Markt zugelassen sind, so hat im Falle des Absatzes 1 Satz 1 der Vorstand und im Falle des Absatzes 2 Satz 1 das Gericht der Bundesanstalt für Finanzdienstleistungsaufsicht die Bestellung des Sonderprüfers und dessen Prüfungsbericht mitzuteilen; darüber hinaus hat das Gericht den Eingang eines Antrags auf Bestellung eines Sonderprüfers mitzuteilen.

(8) Auf das gerichtliche Verfahren nach den Absätzen 2 bis 6 sind die Vorschriften des Gesetzes über das Verfahren in Familiensachen und in den Angelegenheiten der freiwilligen Gerichtsbarkeit anzuwenden, soweit in diesem Gesetz nichts anderes bestimmt ist.

§ 143 Auswahl der Sonderprüfer.

(1) Als Sonderprüfer sollen, wenn der Gegenstand der Sonderprüfung keine

ity or doubts as to his reliability. ²The application shall be brought within two weeks following the date of the general meeting.

(5) ¹In addition to the parties concerned, the court shall hear the supervisory board and, in the case of para. 4, the special auditor appointed by the general meeting. ²The decision is subject to appeal. ³The regional court in the district of which the company has its registered office shall decide on the application pursuant to paras. 2 and 4.

(6) ¹The special auditors appointed by the court shall be entitled to the reimbursement of reasonable cash expenses and to remuneration for their services. ²The expenses and the remuneration shall be fixed by the court. ³The decision is subject to appeal; no further appeal on a point of law may be made. ⁴A decision being res judicata shall be enforceable pursuant to the Code of Civil Procedure.

(7) If the company has issued securities within the meaning of sec. 2 para. 1 of the Securities Trading Act which are admitted for trading in the regulated market at a German stock exchange, the management board, in the case of para. 1 sentence 1, and the court, in the case of para. 2 sentence 1, shall notify the Federal Financial Supervisory Authority of the appointment of the special auditor and their accounting report; furthermore, the court shall be notified of the receipt of an application for appointment of a special auditor.

(8) The provisions of the Act on Procedure in Family Matters and Matters of Non-Contentious Jurisdiction shall apply to the court proceedings pursuant to paras. 2 to 6 unless set forth otherwise in this Act.

§ 143 Selection of special auditors.

(1) Unless the object of the special audit requires particular expertise, only the

anderen Kenntnisse fordert, nur bestellt werden

1. Personen, die in der Buchführung ausreichend vorgebildet und erfahren sind;
2. Prüfungsgesellschaften, von deren gesetzlichen Vertretern mindestens einer in der Buchführung ausreichend vorgebildet und erfahren ist.

(2) ¹Sonderprüfer darf nicht sein, wer nach § 319 Abs. 2, 3, § 319a Abs. 1, § 319b des Handelsgesetzbuchs nicht Abschlußprüfer sein darf oder während der Zeit, in der sich der zu prüfende Vorgang ereignet hat, hätte sein dürfen. ²Eine Prüfungsgesellschaft darf nicht Sonderprüfer sein, wenn sie nach § 319 Abs. 2, 4, § 319a Abs. 1, § 319b des Handelsgesetzbuchs nicht Abschlußprüfer sein darf oder während der Zeit, in der sich der zu prüfende Vorgang ereignet hat, hätte sein dürfen.

following persons may be appointed as special auditors:

1. persons having sufficient training and experience in bookkeeping;
2. auditing companies having at least one legal representative with sufficient training and experience in bookkeeping.

(2) ¹Anyone who pursuant to sec. 319 paras. 2, 3, sec. 319a para. 1, sec. 319b of the Commercial Code is not qualified or who at the time the matter upon investigation occurred would not have been qualified to act as an auditor of annual financial statements may not be appointed as a special auditor. ²An auditing company may not be a special auditor if, pursuant to sec. 319 paras. 2, 4, sec. 319a para. 1, sec. 319b of the Commercial Code, it is not qualified or at the time the matter upon investigation occurred would not have been qualified to act as an auditor of annual financial statements.

§ 144 Verantwortlichkeit der Sonderprüfer.

§ 323 des Handelsgesetzbuchs über die Verantwortlichkeit des Abschlußprüfers gilt sinngemäß.

§ 144 Liability of special auditors.

Sec. 323 of the Commercial Code concerning the liability of auditors of the annual financial statements shall apply accordingly.

§ 145 Rechte der Sonderprüfer. Prüfungsbericht.

(1) Der Vorstand hat den Sonderprüfern zu gestatten, die Bücher und Schriften der Gesellschaft sowie die Vermögensgegenstände, namentlich die Gesellschaftskasse und die Bestände an Wertpapieren und Waren, zu prüfen.

(2) Die Sonderprüfer können von den Mitgliedern des Vorstands und des Aufsichtsrats alle Aufklärungen und Nachweise verlangen, welche die sorgfältige Prüfung der Vorgänge notwendig macht.

(3) Die Sonderprüfer haben die Rechte nach Absatz 2 auch gegenüber einem

§ 145 Rights of special auditors. Audit report.

(1) The management board shall allow the special auditors to inspect all books and records of the company as well as its assets, in particular cash and inventories of securities and goods.

(2) The special auditors may request all explanations and evidence necessary for a diligent inspection of the matters from the members of the management board and the supervisory board.

(3) The special auditors shall also be entitled to the rights pursuant to para. 2

Konzernunternehmen sowie gegenüber einem abhängigen oder herrschenden Unternehmen.

(4) Auf Antrag des Vorstands hat das Gericht zu gestatten, dass bestimmte Tatsachen nicht in den Bericht aufgenommen werden, wenn überwiegende Belange der Gesellschaft dies gebieten und sie zur Darlegung der Unredlichkeiten oder groben Verletzungen gemäß § 142 Abs. 2 nicht unerlässlich sind.

(5) [1]Über den Antrag gemäß Absatz 4 entscheidet das Landgericht, in dessen Bezirk die Gesellschaft ihren Sitz hat. [2]§ 142 Abs. 5 Satz 2, Abs. 8 gilt entsprechend.

(6) [1]Die Sonderprüfer haben über das Ergebnis der Prüfung schriftlich zu berichten. [2]Auch Tatsachen, deren Bekanntwerden geeignet ist, der Gesellschaft oder einem verbundenen Unternehmen einen nicht unerheblichen Nachteil zuzufügen, müssen in den Prüfungsbericht aufgenommen werden, wenn ihre Kenntnis zur Beurteilung des zu prüfenden Vorgangs durch die Hauptversammlung erforderlich ist. [3]Die Sonderprüfer haben den Bericht zu unterzeichnen und unverzüglich dem Vorstand und zum Handelsregister des Sitzes der Gesellschaft einzureichen. [4]Auf Verlangen hat der Vorstand jedem Aktionär eine Abschrift des Prüfungsberichts zu erteilen. [5]Der Vorstand hat den Bericht dem Aufsichtsrat vorzulegen und bei der Einberufung der nächsten Hauptversammlung als Gegenstand der Tagesordnung bekanntzumachen.

vis-à-vis a group enterprise, a controlled enterprise or a controlling enterprise.

(4) Upon application of the management board, the court shall allow certain facts to be excluded from the report if preponderant interests of the company so command and if such facts are not indispensable to the determination of the dishonesties or gross violations pursuant to sec. 142 para 2.

(5) [1]The regional court in the district of which the company has its registered office shall decide on the application pursuant to para. 4. [2]Sec. 142 para 5 sentence 2, para. 8 shall apply accordingly.

(6) [1]The special auditors shall provide a written report of their findings. [2]Facts which are capable of causing the company or an affiliated enterprise not inconsiderable damage if they become known shall also be included in the audit report if knowledge thereof is necessary for the general meeting to be able to assess the matter under investigation. [3]The special auditors shall sign the report and shall submit it without undue delay to the management board and the commercial register of the registered office of the company. [4]The management board shall provide each shareholder with a copy of the audit report upon request. [5]The management board shall submit the report to the supervisory board and shall announce it as an item on the agenda when the next general meeting is convened.

§ 146 Kosten.

[1]Bestellt das Gericht Sonderprüfer, so trägt die Gesellschaft die Gerichtskosten und die Kosten der Prüfung. [2]Hat der Antragsteller die Bestellung durch vorsätzlich oder grob fahrlässig unrichtigen Vortrag erwirkt, so hat der Antragsteller der Gesellschaft die Kosten zu erstatten.

§ 146 Costs.

[1]If special auditors are appointed by the court, the company shall bear the court costs and the costs for the audit. [2]If the applicant has caused the appointment by pleadings which were willfully or grossly negligently incorrect, he shall reimburse the costs to the company.

§ 147 Geltendmachung von Ersatzansprüchen.

(1) ¹Die Ersatzansprüche der Gesellschaft aus der Gründung gegen die nach den §§ 46 bis 48, 53 verpflichteten Personen oder aus der Geschäftsführung gegen die Mitglieder des Vorstands und des Aufsichtsrats oder aus § 117 müssen geltend gemacht werden, wenn es die Hauptversammlung mit einfacher Stimmenmehrheit beschließt. ²Der Ersatzanspruch soll binnen sechs Monaten seit dem Tage der Hauptversammlung geltend gemacht werden.

(2) ¹Zur Geltendmachung des Ersatzanspruchs kann die Hauptversammlung besondere Vertreter bestellen. ²Das Gericht (§ 14) hat auf Antrag von Aktionären, deren Anteile zusammen den zehnten Teil des Grundkapitals oder den anteiligen Betrag von einer Million Euro erreichen, als Vertreter der Gesellschaft zur Geltendmachung des Ersatzanspruchs andere als die nach den §§ 78, 112 oder nach Satz 1 zur Vertretung der Gesellschaft berufenen Personen zu bestellen, wenn ihm dies für eine gehörige Geltendmachung zweckmäßig erscheint. ³Gibt das Gericht dem Antrag statt, so trägt die Gesellschaft die Gerichtskosten. ⁴Gegen die Entscheidung ist die Beschwerde zulässig. ⁵Die gerichtlich bestellten Vertreter können von der Gesellschaft den Ersatz angemessener barer Auslagen und eine Vergütung für ihre Tätigkeit verlangen. ⁶Die Auslagen und die Vergütung setzt das Gericht fest. ⁷Gegen die Entscheidung ist die Beschwerde zulässig; die Rechtsbeschwerde ist ausgeschlossen. ⁸Aus der rechtskräftigen Entscheidung findet die Zwangsvollstreckung nach der Zivilprozeßordnung statt.

§ 148 Klagezulassungsverfahren.

(1) ¹Aktionäre, deren Anteile im Zeitpunkt der Antragstellung zusammen den einhundertsten Teil des Grundkapitals oder einen anteiligen Betrag von

§ 147 Asserting of claims for compensation.

(1) ¹Any claims for compensation of the company against persons liable pursuant to sec. 46 to 48, 53 arising from the formation of the company or against members of the management board and the supervisory board arising from the management of the company or pursuant to sec. 117 shall be asserted if the general meeting so resolves with a simple majority. ²The claim for damages shall be asserted within six months of the date of the general meeting.

(2) ¹The general meeting may appoint special representatives for asserting the claim for compensation. ²The court (sec. 14) shall, upon application by shareholders with an aggregate holding amounting to one tenth of the registered share capital or the proportionate amount of one million euros, appoint persons other than those entitled to represent the company pursuant to sec. 78, 112 or sentence 1 if the court believes that this is appropriate to ensure the proper assertion of the claim. ³If the court grants the application, the court costs shall be borne by the company. ⁴The decision is subject to appeal. ⁵The representatives appointed by the court may request from the company the reimbursement of reasonable cash expenses and remuneration for their services. ⁶The expenses and remuneration shall be fixed by the court. ⁷The decision is subject to appeal; no further appeal on a point of law may be made. ⁸A decision being res judicata shall be enforceable pursuant to the Code of Civil Procedure.

§ 148 Complaint admission proceedings.

(1) ¹Shareholders with an aggregate holding amounting to one hundredth of the registered share capital or a proportionate amount of 100,000 euros at

100.000 Euro erreichen, können die Zulassung beantragen, im eigenen Namen die in § 147 Abs. 1 Satz 1 bezeichneten Ersatzansprüche der Gesellschaft geltend zu machen. ²Das Gericht lässt die Klage zu, wenn

1. die Aktionäre nachweisen, dass sie die Aktien vor dem Zeitpunkt erworben haben, in dem sie oder im Falle der Gesamtrechtsnachfolge ihre Rechtsvorgänger von den behaupteten Pflichtverstößen oder dem behaupteten Schaden auf Grund einer Veröffentlichung Kenntnis erlangen mussten,
2. die Aktionäre nachweisen, dass sie die Gesellschaft unter Setzung einer angemessenen Frist vergeblich aufgefordert haben, selbst Klage zu erheben,
3. Tatsachen vorliegen, die den Verdacht rechtfertigen, dass der Gesellschaft durch Unredlichkeit oder grobe Verletzung des Gesetzes oder der Satzung ein Schaden entstanden ist, und
4. der Geltendmachung des Ersatzanspruchs keine überwiegenden Gründe des Gesellschaftswohls entgegenstehen.

(2) ¹Über den Antrag auf Klagezulassung entscheidet das Landgericht, in dessen Bezirk die Gesellschaft ihren Sitz hat, durch Beschluss. ²Ist bei dem Landgericht eine Kammer für Handelssachen gebildet, so entscheidet diese anstelle der Zivilkammer. ³Die Landesregierung kann die Entscheidung durch Rechtsverordnung für die Bezirke mehrerer Landgerichte einem der Landgerichte übertragen, wenn dies der Sicherung einer einheitlichen Rechtsprechung dient. ⁴Die Landesregierung kann die Ermächtigung auf die Landesjustizverwaltung übertragen. ⁵Die Antragstellung hemmt die Verjährung des streitgegenständlichen Anspruchs bis zur rechtskräftigen Antragsabweisung oder bis zum Ablauf der Frist für die Klageerhebung. ⁶Vor der Entscheidung hat das Gericht

the time the application is made may apply for the admission of an action to enforce the damage claims of the company pursuant to sec. 147 para. 1 sentence 1 in their own name. ²The court shall approve the complaint if

1. the shareholders prove that they have acquired the shares before the point in time at which they or, in the case of universal succession, their legal predecessors had obtained knowledge of the asserted breaches of duty or the asserted damage from a public announcement,
2. the shareholders prove that they have requested the company in vain to set an adequate deadline for it to bring an action itself,
3. there are facts justifying the suspicion that the company suffered a damage caused by dishonesty or gross violation of the law or of the articles of association, and
4. there are no preponderant reasons of the interest of the company opposing the assertion of the damage claim.

(2) ¹The Regional Court in whose district the company has its registered office shall decide on the application by resolution. ²If there is a commercial division established at that Regional Court, it shall decide instead of the civil division. ³The state government may delegate the decision for the districts of several Regional Courts to one of the Regional Courts by ordinance if this serves to ensure a unified case law. ⁴The state government may delegate the authorization to the state administration of the judiciary. ⁵The submission of an application shall suspend the running of the statute of limitations for the claim in issue until the rejection of the application has become res judicata or until the time limit for bringing an action has expired. ⁶Prior to the decision,

dem Antragsgegner Gelegenheit zur Stellungnahme zu geben. ⁷Gegen die Entscheidung findet die sofortige Beschwerde statt. ⁸Die Rechtsbeschwerde ist ausgeschlossen. ⁹Die Gesellschaft ist im Zulassungsverfahren und im Klageverfahren beizuladen.

(3) ¹Die Gesellschaft ist jederzeit berechtigt, ihren Ersatzanspruch selbst gerichtlich geltend zu machen; mit Klageerhebung durch die Gesellschaft wird ein anhängiges Zulassungs- oder Klageverfahren von Aktionären über diesen Ersatzanspruch unzulässig. ²Die Gesellschaft ist nach ihrer Wahl berechtigt, ein anhängiges Klageverfahren über ihren Ersatzanspruch in der Lage zu übernehmen, in der sich das Verfahren zur Zeit der Übernahme befindet. ³Die bisherigen Antragsteller oder Kläger sind in den Fällen der Sätze 1 und 2 beizuladen.

(4) ¹Hat das Gericht dem Antrag stattgegeben, kann die Klage nur binnen drei Monaten nach Eintritt der Rechtskraft der Entscheidung und sofern die Aktionäre die Gesellschaft nochmals unter Setzung einer angemessenen Frist vergeblich aufgefordert haben, selbst Klage zu erheben, vor dem nach Absatz 2 zuständigen Gericht erhoben werden. ²Sie ist gegen die in § 147 Abs. 1 Satz 1 genannten Personen und auf Leistung an die Gesellschaft zu richten. ³Eine Nebenintervention durch Aktionäre ist nach Zulassung der Klage nicht mehr möglich. ⁴Mehrere Klagen sind zur gleichzeitigen Verhandlung und Entscheidung zu verbinden.

(5) ¹Das Urteil wirkt, auch wenn es auf Klageabweisung lautet, für und gegen die Gesellschaft und die übrigen Aktionäre. ²Entsprechendes gilt für einen nach § 149 bekannt zu machenden Vergleich; für und gegen die Gesellschaft wirkt dieser aber nur nach Klagezulassung.

(6) ¹Die Kosten des Zulassungsverfahrens hat der Antragsteller zu tragen,

the court shall provide the defendant with an opportunity to comment. ⁷The decision shall be subject to immediate appeal. ⁸No further appeal on a point of law may be made. ⁹The company shall be summoned to join the admission and complaint proceedings.

(3) ¹The company may at any time enforce its damage claim in court; pending admission or complaint proceedings concerning this damage claim brought by shareholders become inadmissible once the company files the complaint. ²The company may at its election assume pending complaint proceedings concerning its damage claim in the state which the proceedings are in at the time of the assumption . ³The former applicants or plaintiffs shall, in the cases of sentences 1 and 2, be summoned to join.

(4) ¹If the court grants the application, the complaint may be brought only within three months after the decision has become res judicata and, if the shareholders have again requested the company in vain to set an adequate deadline for it to bring an action itself, only before the court competent pursuant to para. 2. ²The complaint shall be directed against the persons mentioned in sec. 147 para. 1 sentence 1 and for performance to the company. ³An intervention by shareholders after admission of the complaint is not possible. ⁴Several complaints shall be joined for simultaneous trial and decision.

(5) ¹The judgment shall be effective for and against the company and the other shareholders, also if it dismisses the complaint. ²This shall apply accordingly to a settlement to be announced pursuant to sec. 149; such settlement shall, however, be effective for and against the company only after admission of the complaint.

(6) ¹The applicant shall bear the costs of the admission proceedings to the ex-

soweit sein Antrag abgewiesen wird. ²Beruht die Abweisung auf entgegenstehenden Gründen des Gesellschaftswohls, die die Gesellschaft vor Antragstellung hätte mitteilen können, aber nicht mitgeteilt hat, so hat sie dem Antragsteller die Kosten zu erstatten. ³Im Übrigen ist über die Kostentragung im Endurteil zu entscheiden. ⁴Erhebt die Gesellschaft selbst Klage oder übernimmt sie ein anhängiges Klageverfahren von Aktionären, so trägt sie etwaige bis zum Zeitpunkt ihrer Klageerhebung oder Übernahme des Verfahrens entstandene Kosten des Antragstellers und kann die Klage nur unter den Voraussetzungen des § 93 Abs. 4 Satz 3 und 4 mit Ausnahme der Sperrfrist zurücknehmen. ⁵Wird die Klage ganz oder teilweise abgewiesen, hat die Gesellschaft den Klägern die von diesen zu tragenden Kosten zu erstatten, sofern nicht die Kläger die Zulassung durch vorsätzlich oder grob fahrlässig unrichtigen Vortrag erwirkt haben. ⁶Gemeinsam als Antragsteller oder als Streitgenossen handelnde Aktionäre erhalten insgesamt nur die Kosten eines Bevollmächtigten erstattet, soweit nicht ein weiterer Bevollmächtigter zur Rechtsverfolgung unerlässlich war.

tent his application is rejected. ²If the rejection is based on opposing reasons of the interest of the company which the company could have notified but did not notify prior to the application, it shall reimburse the costs to the applicant. ³In other respects, the distribution of costs shall be determined in the final judgment. ⁴If the company itself brings a complaint or assumes pending complaint proceedings of shareholders, it shall bear any costs of the applicant incurred until the complaint was brought or the proceedings were assumed and it may withdraw the complaint only pursuant to the requirements of sec. 93 para. 4 sentence 3 and 4 with the exception of the blocking period. ⁵If the complaint is dismissed in whole or in part, the company shall reimburse to the plaintiffs the costs to be borne by them unless the plaintiffs have caused the admission by pleadings which were willfully or grossly negligently incorrect. ⁶Shareholders acting jointly as applicants or co-plaintiffs shall in the aggregate receive only the costs of one representative unless a further representative was indispensable for the enforcement of rights.

§ 149 Bekanntmachungen zur Haftungsklage.

(1) Nach rechtskräftiger Zulassung der Klage gemäß § 148 sind der Antrag auf Zulassung und die Verfahrensbeendigung von der börsennotierten Gesellschaft unverzüglich in den Gesellschaftsblättern bekannt zu machen.

(2) ¹Die Bekanntmachung der Verfahrensbeendigung hat deren Art, alle mit ihr im Zusammenhang stehenden Vereinbarungen einschließlich Nebenabreden im vollständigen Wortlaut sowie die Namen der Beteiligten zu enthalten. ²Etwaige Leistungen der Gesellschaft und ihr zurechenbare Leistungen Dritter sind gesondert zu beschreiben und

§ 149 Announcements concerning the complaint for damages.

(1) After the admission of the complaint pursuant to sec. 148 has become res judicata, the application for admission and the termination of the proceedings shall be announced by the listed company in the company's designated journals without undue delay.

(2) ¹The announcement of the termination of the proceedings shall set forth its nature, all agreements connected to it including side agreements with their complete wording as well as the names of the persons involved. ²Any performances by the company and performances by third parties attributable to it shall be described and highlighted sep-

hervorzuheben. ³Die vollständige Bekanntmachung ist Wirksamkeitsvoraussetzung für alle Leistungspflichten. ⁴Die Wirksamkeit von verfahrensbeendigenden Prozesshandlungen bleibt hiervon unberührt. ⁵Trotz Unwirksamkeit bewirkte Leistungen können zurückgefordert werden.

(3) Die vorstehenden Bestimmungen gelten entsprechend für Vereinbarungen, die zur Vermeidung eines Prozesses geschlossen werden.

arately. ³The complete announcement is a condition for the effectiveness of all obligations to perform. ⁴The effectiveness of procedural acts terminating the proceedings shall remain unaffected. ⁵Performances made in spite of ineffectiveness may be reclaimed.

(3) The preceding provisions shall apply accordingly to agreements which were entered into in order to avoid complaint proceedings.

Fünfter Teil. Rechnungslegung. Gewinnverwendung

Part Five. Accounting. Appropriation of Profits

Erster Abschnitt. Jahresabschluss und Lagebericht. Entsprechenserklärung

Section One. Annual Financial Statements and Management Report. Declaration of Compliance

§ 150 Gesetzliche Rücklage. Kapitalrücklage.

§ 150 Statutory reserve. Capital reserve.

(1) In der Bilanz des nach den §§ 242, 264 des Handelsgesetzbuchs aufzustellenden Jahresabschlusses ist eine gesetzliche Rücklage zu bilden.

(2) In diese ist der zwanzigste Teil des um einen Verlustvortrag aus dem Vorjahr geminderten Jahresüberschusses einzustellen, bis die gesetzliche Rücklage und die Kapitalrücklagen nach § 272 Abs. 2 Nr. 1 bis 3 des Handelsgesetzbuchs zusammen den zehnten oder den in der Satzung bestimmten höheren Teil des Grundkapitals erreichen.

(3) Übersteigen die gesetzliche Rücklage und die Kapitalrücklagen nach § 272 Abs. 2 Nr. 1 bis 3 des Handelsgesetzbuchs zusammen nicht den zehnten oder den in der Satzung bestimmten höheren Teil des Grundkapitals, so dürfen sie nur verwandt werden

1. zum Ausgleich eines Jahresfehlbetrags, soweit er nicht durch einen Gewinnvortrag aus dem Vorjahr gedeckt ist und nicht durch Auflösung anderer Gewinnrücklagen ausgeglichen werden kann;

(1) A statutory reserve shall be provided in the balance sheet of the annual financial statements to be drawn up pursuant to sec. 242, 264 of the Commercial Code.

(2) One-twentieth of the annual net income after deduction of any loss carried forward from the previous year shall be allocated to such reserve until the statutory reserve and the capital reserves pursuant to sec. 272 para. 2 nos. 1 to 3 of the Commercial Code together reach one tenth or a higher proportion of the registered share capital stipulated in the articles of association.

(3) If the statutory reserve and the capital reserves pursuant to sec. 272 para. 2 nos. 1 to 3 of the Commercial Code fail together to reach one tenth or a higher proportion of the registered share capital stipulated in the articles of association, they may only be used

1. to balance out an annual net loss provided such loss is not covered by profit carried forward from the previous year and cannot be balanced out by releasing other revenue reserves;

2. zum Ausgleich eines Verlustvortrags aus dem Vorjahr, soweit er nicht durch einen Jahresüberschuß gedeckt ist und nicht durch Auflösung anderer Gewinnrücklagen ausgeglichen werden kann.

(4) ¹Übersteigen die gesetzliche Rücklage und die Kapitalrücklagen nach § 272 Abs. 2 Nr. 1 bis 3 des Handelsgesetzbuchs zusammen den zehnten oder den in der Satzung bestimmten höheren Teil des Grundkapitals, so darf der übersteigende Betrag verwandt werden

1. zum Ausgleich eines Jahresfehlbetrags, soweit er nicht durch einen Gewinnvortrag aus dem Vorjahr gedeckt ist;
2. zum Ausgleich eines Verlustvortrags aus dem Vorjahr, soweit er nicht durch einen Jahresüberschuß gedeckt ist;
3. zur Kapitalerhöhung aus Gesellschaftsmitteln nach den §§ 207 bis 220.

²Die Verwendung nach den Nummern 1 und 2 ist nicht zulässig, wenn gleichzeitig Gewinnrücklagen zur Gewinnausschüttung aufgelöst werden.

§§ 150a, 151 *(aufgehoben)*

§ 152 Vorschriften zur Bilanz.

(1) ¹Das Grundkapital ist in der Bilanz als gezeichnetes Kapital auszuweisen. ²Dabei ist der auf jede Aktiengattung entfallende Betrag des Grundkapitals gesondert anzugeben. ³Bedingtes Kapital ist mit dem Nennbetrag zu vermerken. ⁴Bestehen Mehrstimmrechtsaktien, so sind beim gezeichneten Kapital die Gesamtstimmenzahl der Mehrstimmrechtsaktien und die der übrigen Aktien zu vermerken.

(2) Zu dem Posten „Kapitalrücklage" sind in der Bilanz oder im Anhang gesondert anzugeben

2. to balance out a loss carried forward from the previous year provided such loss is not covered by annual net income and cannot be balanced out by releasing other revenue reserves.

(4) ¹If the statutory reserve and the capital reserves pursuant to sec. 272 para. 2 nos. 1 to 3 of the Commercial Code together exceed one tenth or a higher proportion of the registered share capital stipulated in the articles of association, the excess amount may be used

1. to balance out an annual net loss provided it is not covered by profit carried forward from the previous year;
2. to balance out a loss carried forward from the previous year provided it is not covered by annual net income;
3. for a capital increase from company resources pursuant to sec. 207 to 220.

²A use pursuant to nos. 1 and 2 shall not be permitted if revenue reserves are at the same time released for the distribution of profits.

§§ 150a, 151 *(repealed)*

§ 152 Provisions regarding the balance sheet.

(1) ¹The registered share capital shall be shown in the balance sheet as subscribed capital. ²The amount of the registered share capital accounted for by each class of share shall be stated separately. ³Contingent capital shall be shown at its par value. ⁴If there are shares with multiple voting rights, the total number of votes accounted for by the shares with multiple voting rights and that of the remaining shares shall be stated with the subscribed capital.

(2) Separate entries shall be made in the balance sheet or the notes under the item "capital reserve" for the following:

1. der Betrag, der während des Geschäftsjahrs eingestellt wurde;
2. der Betrag, der für das Geschäftsjahr entnommen wird.

(3) Zu den einzelnen Posten der Gewinnrücklagen sind in der Bilanz oder im Anhang jeweils gesondert anzugeben

1. die Beträge, die die Hauptversammlung aus dem Bilanzgewinn des Vorjahrs eingestellt hat;
2. die Beträge, die aus dem Jahresüberschuß des Geschäftsjahrs eingestellt werden;
3. die Beträge, die für das Geschäftsjahr entnommen werden.

(4) ¹Die Absätze 1 bis 3 sind nicht anzuwenden auf Aktiengesellschaften, die Kleinstkapitalgesellschaften im Sinne des § 267a des Handelsgesetzbuchs sind, wenn sie von der Erleichterung nach § 266 Absatz 1 Satz 4 des Handelsgesetzbuchs Gebrauch machen. ²Kleine Aktiengesellschaften im Sinne des § 267 Absatz 1 des Handelsgesetzbuchs haben die Absätze 2 und 3 mit der Maßgabe anzuwenden, dass die Angaben in der Bilanz zu machen sind.

§§ 153–157 *(aufgehoben)*

§ 158 Vorschriften zur Gewinn- und Verlustrechnung.

(1) ¹Die Gewinn- und Verlustrechnung ist nach dem Posten „Jahresüberschuß/Jahresfehlbetrag" in Fortführung der Nummerierung um die folgenden Posten zu ergänzen:

1. Gewinnvortrag/Verlustvortrag aus dem Vorjahr
2. Entnahmen aus der Kapitalrücklage
3. Entnahmen aus Gewinnrücklagen
   a) aus der gesetzlichen Rücklage
   b) aus der Rücklage für Anteile an einem herrschenden oder mehrheitlich beteiligten Unternehmen
   c) aus satzungsmäßigen Rücklagen
   d) aus anderen Gewinnrücklagen

1. the amount allocated to such reserves during the fiscal year;
2. the amount withdrawn for the fiscal year.

(3) Separate entries shall be made in the balance sheet or the notes under the individual items relating to revenue reserves for the following:

1. the amounts allocated to reserves by the general meeting from balance sheet profit for the previous year;
2. the amounts allocated to reserves from the annual net income for the fiscal year;
3. the amounts withdrawn for the fiscal year.

(4) ¹The paragraphs 1 to 3 do not apply to stock corporations which are small corporations within the meaning of sec. 267a of the Commercial Code, if they made use of the option provided for in sec. 266 para. 1 sentence 4 of the Commercial Code. ²Small stock corporations within the meaning of sec. 267 para. 1 of the Commercial Code apply to the paragraphs 2 and 3 provided that details are presented in the balance sheet.

§§ 153–157 *(repealed)*

§ 158 Provisions concerning the profit and loss statement.

(1) ¹The following consecutively numbered items shall be included in the profit and loss statement after the item "annual net income/annual net loss":

1. profit/loss carried forward from the previous year
2. withdrawals from the capital reserve
3. withdrawals from revenue reserves
   a) from the statutory reserve
   b) from the reserve for shares in a controlling enterprise or an enterprise with majority ownership
   c) from reserves pursuant to the articles of association
   d) from other revenue reserves

4. Einstellungen in Gewinnrücklagen
   a) in die gesetzliche Rücklage
   b) in die Rücklage für Anteile an einem herrschenden oder mehrheitlich beteiligten Unternehmen
   c) in satzungsmäßige Rücklagen
   d) in andere Gewinnrücklagen
5. Bilanzgewinn/Bilanzverlust.
	4. transfers to revenue reserves
	   a) to the statutory reserve
	   b) to the reserve for shares in a controlling enterprise or an enterprise with majority ownership
	   c) to reserves pursuant to the articles of association
	   d) to other revenue reserves
	5. balance sheet profit/net loss.

²Die Angaben nach Satz 1 können auch im Anhang gemacht werden.	²The information pursuant to sentence 1 may also be provided in the notes.
(2) ¹Von dem Ertrag aus einem Gewinnabführungs- oder Teilgewinnabführungsvertrag ist ein vertraglich zu leistender Ausgleich für außenstehende Gesellschafter abzusetzen; übersteigt dieser den Ertrag, so ist der übersteigende Betrag unter den Aufwendungen aus Verlustübernahme auszuweisen. ²Andere Beträge dürfen nicht abgesetzt werden.	(2) ¹Any compensation due on the basis of a contract to outside shareholders shall be deducted from the income arising from profit transfer agreements or partial profit transfer agreement; if such compensation exceeds the income, the excess shall be shown under expenses from losses. ² No other amounts may be deducted.
(3) Die Absätze 1 und 2 sind nicht anzuwenden auf Aktiengesellschaften, die Kleinstkapitalgesellschaften im Sinne des § 267a des Handelsgesetzbuchs sind, wenn sie von der Erleichterung nach § 275 Absatz 5 des Handelsgesetzbuchs Gebrauch machen.	(3) ¹The paragraphs 1 and 2 do not apply to stock corporations which are small corporations within the meaning of sec. 267a of the Commercial Code, if they made use of the option provided for in sec. 275 para. 5 of the Commercial Code.

§ 159 *(aufgehoben)*	**§ 159** *(repealed)*
§ 160 Vorschriften zum Anhang.	**§ 160 Provisions concerning the notes.**
(1) In jedem Anhang sind auch Angaben zu machen über	(1) Information relating to the following shall also be given in each set of notes:
1. den Bestand und den Zugang an Aktien, die ein Aktionär für Rechnung der Gesellschaft oder eines abhängigen oder eines im Mehrheitsbesitz der Gesellschaft stehenden Unternehmens oder ein abhängiges oder im Mehrheitsbesitz der Gesellschaft stehendes Unternehmen als Gründer oder Zeichner oder in Ausübung eines bei einer bedingten Kapitalerhöhung eingeräumten Umtausch- oder Bezugsrechts übernommen hat; sind solche Aktien im Geschäftsjahr verwertet worden, so ist auch über die	1. the number of shares held and acquired by a shareholder on behalf of the company or of an enterprise controlled by the company or an enterprise in which the company has a majority holding or an enterprise controlled by the company or in which the company has a majority holding as a founder or subscriber or by exercising a transfer or subscription right granted in connection with a contingent capital increase; if such shares were disposed during the fiscal year, the disposal shall be

Verwertung unter Angabe des Erlöses und die Verwendung des Erlöses zu berichten;	reported, stating the income and the manner in which they are to be used;
2. den Bestand an eigenen Aktien der Gesellschaft, die sie, ein abhängiges oder im Mehrheitsbesitz der Gesellschaft stehendes Unternehmen oder ein anderer für Rechnung der Gesellschaft oder eines abhängigen oder eines im Mehrheitsbesitz der Gesellschaft stehenden Unternehmens erworben oder als Pfand genommen hat; dabei sind die Zahl dieser Aktien und der auf sie entfallende Betrag des Grundkapitals sowie deren Anteil am Grundkapital, für erworbene Aktien ferner der Zeitpunkt des Erwerbs und die Gründe für den Erwerb anzugeben. Sind solche Aktien im Geschäftsjahr erworben oder veräußert worden, so ist auch über den Erwerb oder die Veräußerung unter Angabe der Zahl dieser Aktien, des auf sie entfallenden Betrags des Grundkapitals, des Anteils am Grundkapital und des Erwerbs- oder Veräußerungspreises, sowie über die Verwendung des Erlöses zu berichten;	2. the number of own shares held by the company which it, an enterprise controlled by the company or an enterprise in which the company has a majority holding or another party acting on behalf of the company or an enterprise controlled by the company or an enterprise in which the company has a majority holding has acquired or taken as a pledge; the number of such shares and the amount of the registered share capital attributed to them as well as their share in the registered share capital shall be stated, and in the case of acquired shares also the date of acquisition and the reasons for the acquisition. ²If such shares have been acquired or sold during the fiscal year, a report shall also be given regarding the acquisition or sale, stating the number of these shares, the amount of the registered share capital attributed to them, their share in the registered share capital and the purchase or sale price, as well as the manner in which income have been or are to be used;
3. die Zahl der Aktien jeder Gattung, wobei zu Nennbetragsaktien der Nennbetrag und zu Stückaktien der rechnerische Wert für jede von ihnen anzugeben ist, sofern sich diese Angaben nicht aus der Bilanz ergeben; davon sind Aktien, die bei einer bedingten Kapitalerhöhung oder einem genehmigten Kapital im Geschäftsjahr gezeichnet wurden, jeweils gesondert anzugeben;	3. the number of the shares of each class, whereby in case of par value shares, the par value of the shares and in case of registered shares the accounting par value for each shall be indicated, to the extent that this information cannot be derived from the balance sheet; shares subscribed during the fiscal year in connection with a contingent capital increase or an issue of authorized capital shall be stated separately;
4. das genehmigte Kapital;	4. authorized capital;
5. die Zahl der Bezugsrechte gemäß § 192 Absatz 2 Nummer 3	5. the number of subscription rights pursuant to sec. 192 para. 2 no. 3
6. (weggefallen)	6. (repealed)
7. das Bestehen einer wechselseitigen Beteiligung unter Angabe des Unternehmens;	7. the existence of a cross-shareholding, stating the enterprise concerned;

8. das Bestehen einer Beteiligung, die nach § 20 Abs. 1 oder Abs. 4 dieses Gesetzes oder nach § 21 Abs. 1 oder Abs. 1a des Wertpapierhandelsgesetzes mitgeteilt worden ist; dabei ist der nach § 20 Abs. 6 dieses Gesetzes oder der nach § 26 Abs. 1 des Wertpapierhandelsgesetzes veröffentlichte Inhalt der Mitteilung anzugeben.

(2) Die Berichterstattung hat insoweit zu unterbleiben, als es für das Wohl der Bundesrepublik Deutschland oder eines ihrer Länder erforderlich ist.

(3) ¹Absatz 1 Nummer 1 und 3 bis 8 ist nicht anzuwenden auf Aktiengesellschaften, die kleine Kapitalgesellschaften im Sinne des § 267 Absatz 1 des Handelsgesetzbuchs sind. ²Absatz 1 Nummer 2 ist auf diese Aktiengesellschaften mit der Maßgabe anzuwenden, dass die Gesellschaft nur Angaben zu von ihr selbst oder durch eine andere Person für Rechnung der Gesellschaft erworbenen und gehaltenen eigenen Aktien machen muss und über die Verwendung des Erlöses aus der Veräußerung eigener Aktien nicht zu berichten braucht.

§ 161 Erklärung zum Corporate Governance Kodex.

(1) ¹Vorstand und Aufsichtsrat der börsennotierten Gesellschaft erklären jährlich, dass den vom Bundesministerium der Justiz und für Verbraucherschutz im amtlichen Teil des Bundesanzeigers bekannt gemachten Empfehlungen der „Regierungskommission Deutscher Corporate Governance Kodex" entsprochen wurde und wird oder welche Empfehlungen nicht angewendet wurden oder werden und warum nicht. ²Gleiches gilt für Vorstand und Aufsichtsrat einer Gesellschaft, die ausschließlich andere Wertpapiere als Aktien zum Handel an einem organisierten Markt im Sinn des § 2 Abs. 5 des Wertpapierhandelsgesetzes ausgegeben hat und deren ausgegebene Aktien auf eigene

8. the existence of a shareholding which has been notified pursuant to sec. 20 paras. 1 or 4 of this Act or pursuant to sec. 21 para. 1 or para. 1a of the Securities Trading Act; the contents of the notification publicized pursuant to sec. 20 para. 6 of this Act or pursuant to sec. 26 para. 1 of the Securities Trading Act shall be stated.

(2) Such information shall not be reported if reporting thereof would damage the Federal Republic of Germany or one of its states.

(3) ¹Paragraph 1a number 1 and 3 to 8 do not apply to stock corporations which are small within the meaning of sec. 267a of the Commercial Code. ²Paragraph 1 number 2 applies to the above mentioned companies to the extent that the company should only present the information concerning their own participation in shares or their participation through a person acting on the company's behalf; concerning the use of proceeds from the sale of treasury stock there is no report necessary.

§ 161 Declaration on Corporate Governance Codex.

(1) ¹The management board and the supervisory board of listed companies shall declare annually that the recommendations of the "Government Commission German Corporate Governance Codex" published by the Federal Ministry of Justice and Consumer Protection in the official section of the Federal Law Gazette have been and are complied with or which recommendations have not been or are not applied and why not. ²The same shall apply to the management board and supervisory board of a company which exclusively issued securities other than shares for trading in an organized market within the meaning of sec. 2 para. 5 of the Securities Trading Act and whose issued shares are traded

Veranlassung über ein multilaterales Handelssystem im Sinn des § 2 Abs. 3 Satz 1 Nr. 8 des Wertpapierhandelsgesetzes gehandelt werden.

(2) Die Erklärung ist auf der Internetseite der Gesellschaft dauerhaft öffentlich zugänglich zu machen.

Zweiter Abschnitt. Prüfung des Jahresabschlusses

Erster Unterabschnitt. Prüfung durch Abschlußprüfer

§§ 162–169 *(aufgehoben)*

Zweiter Unterabschnitt. Prüfung durch den Aufsichtsrat

§ 170 Vorlage an den Aufsichtsrat.

(1) ¹Der Vorstand hat den Jahresabschluß und den Lagebericht unverzüglich nach ihrer Aufstellung dem Aufsichtsrat vorzulegen. ²Satz 1 gilt entsprechend für einen Einzelabschluss nach § 325 Abs. 2a des Handelsgesetzbuchs sowie bei Mutterunternehmen (§ 290 Abs. 1, 2 des Handelsgesetzbuchs) für den Konzernabschluss und den Konzernlagebericht.

(2) ¹Zugleich hat der Vorstand dem Aufsichtsrat den Vorschlag vorzulegen, den er der Hauptversammlung für die Verwendung des Bilanzgewinns machen will. ²Der Vorschlag ist, sofern er keine abweichende Gliederung bedingt, wie folgt zu gliedern:

1. Verteilung an die Aktionäre
2. Einstellung in Gewinnrücklagen
3. Gewinnvortrag
4. Bilanzgewinn

(3) ¹Jedes Aufsichtsratsmitglied hat das Recht, von den Vorlagen und Prüfungs-

at its own instigation via a multi-lateral trading system within the meaning of sec. 2 para. 3 sentence 1 no. 8 of the Securities Trading Act.

(2) The declaration shall be made publicly accessible on the website of the company on a permanent basis.

Section Two. Audit of Annual Financial Statements

Subsection One. Audit by the Auditor of Annual Financial Statements

§§ 162–169 *(repealed)*

Subsection Two. Audit by the Supervisory Board

§ 170 Submission to the supervisory board.

(1) ¹The management board shall submit the annual financial statements and the management report to the supervisory board without undue delay after they have been drawn up. ²Sentence 1 shall apply accordingly to individual financial statements pursuant to sec. 325 para. 2a of the Commercial Code as well as, in the case of parent companies (sec. 290 paras. 1 and 2 of the Commercial Code), to the consolidated financial statements and the consolidated management report.

(2) ¹At the same time, the management board shall submit to the supervisory board the proposal it intends to make to the general meeting for the appropriation of the balance sheet profit. ²Unless another format is required under the circumstances, the proposal shall be set out as follows:

1. distribution to shareholders
2. allocation to revenue reserves
3. profit carried forward
4. balance sheet profit

(3) ¹Each supervisory board member shall be entitled to take note of the

berichten Kenntnis zu nehmen. ²Die Vorlagen und Prüfungsberichte sind auch jedem Aufsichtsratsmitglied oder, soweit der Aufsichtsrat dies beschlossen hat, den Mitgliedern eines Ausschusses zu übermitteln.

§ 171 Prüfung durch den Aufsichtsrat.

(1) ¹Der Aufsichtsrat hat den Jahresabschluß, den Lagebericht und den Vorschlag für die Verwendung des Bilanzgewinns zu prüfen, bei Mutterunternehmen (§ 290 Abs. 1, 2 des Handelsgesetzbuchs) auch den Konzernabschluß und den Konzernlagebericht. ²Ist der Jahresabschluß oder der Konzernabschluss durch einen Abschlußprüfer zu prüfen, so hat dieser an den Verhandlungen des Aufsichtsrats oder des Prüfungsausschusses über diese Vorlagen teilzunehmen und über die wesentlichen Ergebnisse seiner Prüfung, insbesondere wesentliche Schwächen des internen Kontroll- und des Risikomanagementsystems bezogen auf den Rechnungslegungsprozess, zu berichten. ³Er informiert über Umstände, die seine Befangenheit besorgen lassen und über Leistungen, die er zusätzlich zu den Abschlussprüfungsleistungen erbracht hat.

(2) ¹Der Aufsichtsrat hat über das Ergebnis der Prüfung schriftlich an die Hauptversammlung zu berichten. ²In dem Bericht hat der Aufsichtsrat auch mitzuteilen, in welcher Art und in welchem Umfang er die Geschäftsführung der Gesellschaft während des Geschäftsjahrs geprüft hat; bei börsennotierten Gesellschaften hat er insbesondere anzugeben, welche Ausschüsse gebildet worden sind, sowie die Zahl seiner Sitzungen und die der Ausschüsse mitzuteilen. ³Ist der Jahresabschluß durch einen Abschlußprüfer zu prüfen, so hat der Aufsichtsrat ferner zu dem Er-

documents and audit reports. ²Such documents and audit reports shall be transmitted to each member of the supervisory board or, if so resolved by the supervisory board, to the members of a committee.

§ 171 Inspection by the supervisory board.

(1) ¹The supervisory board shall inspect the annual financial statements, the management report and the proposal for the appropriation of the balance sheet profit, as well as in the case of parent companies (sec. 290 paras. 1 and 2 of the Commercial Code) the consolidated annual financial statements and the group management report. ²If the annual financial statements or the consolidated annual financial statements are to be audited by an auditor of annual financial statements, such auditor shall take part in the proceedings of the supervisory board or the audit committee concerning these documents and report on the essential findings of his audit, in particular substantial weaknesses of the internal control and the risk management system with regard to the financial accounting process. ³He shall report on circumstances which cause concern over bias as well as on performances which he has rendered in addition to the performances concerning the audit of the financial statements.

(2) ¹The supervisory board shall submit a written report on the result of the audit to the general meeting. ²In the report, the supervisory board shall also state in what manner and to what extent it has supervised the management of the company during the fiscal year; in the case of listed companies it shall in particular state which committees have been formed and the number of meetings held by the supervisory board and by the committees. ³If the annual financial statements are to be audited by an auditor of annual financial statements, the supervisory board shall also comment

gebnis der Prüfung des Jahresabschlusses durch den Abschlußprüfer Stellung zu nehmen. ⁴Am Schluß des Berichts hat der Aufsichtsrat zu erklären, ob nach dem abschließenden Ergebnis seiner Prüfung Einwendungen zu erheben sind und ob er den vom Vorstand aufgestellten Jahresabschluß billigt. ⁵Bei Mutterunternehmen (§ 290 Abs. 1, 2 des Handelsgesetzbuchs) finden die Sätze 3 und 4 entsprechende Anwendung auf den Konzernabschluss.

(3) ¹Der Aufsichtsrat hat seinen Bericht innerhalb eines Monats, nachdem ihm die Vorlagen zugegangen sind, dem Vorstand zuzuleiten. ²Wird der Bericht dem Vorstand nicht innerhalb der Frist zugeleitet, hat der Vorstand dem Aufsichtsrat unverzüglich eine weitere Frist von nicht mehr als einem Monat zu setzen. ³Wird der Bericht dem Vorstand nicht vor Ablauf der weiteren Frist zugeleitet, gilt der Jahresabschluss als vom Aufsichtsrat nicht gebilligt; bei Mutterunternehmen (§ 290 Abs. 1, 2 des Handelsgesetzbuchs) gilt das Gleiche hinsichtlich des Konzernabschlusses.

(4) ¹Die Absätze 1 bis 3 gelten auch hinsichtlich eines Einzelabschlusses nach § 325 Abs. 2a des Handelsgesetzbuchs. ²Der Vorstand darf den in Satz 1 genannten Abschluss erst nach dessen Billigung durch den Aufsichtsrat offen legen.

on the results of the audit of the annual financial statements conducted by the auditor of annual financial statements. ⁴At the end of the report, the supervisory board shall declare whether after its conclusive examination objections are to be raised and whether it approves the annual financial statements drawn up by the management board. ⁵In the case of parent companies (sec. 290 paras. 1 and 2 of the Commercial Code) sentences 3 and 4 shall apply accordingly to the consolidated annual financial statements.

(3) ¹The supervisory board shall forward its report to the management board within one month of receiving the documents. ²If the report is not forwarded to the management board within this period, the management board shall without undue delay set the supervisory board a grace period of no more than one month. ³If the report is not forwarded to the management board before the expiration of such grace period, the annual financial statements shall be deemed not to have been approved by the supervisory board; in the case of parent companies (sec. 290 paras. 1 and 2 of the Commercial Code) the same shall apply with regard to the consolidated annual financial statements.

(4) ¹Paras. 1 to 3 shall also apply with respect to individual financial statements pursuant to sec. 325 para. 2a of the Commercial Code. ²The management board may disclose the financial statements designated in sentence 1 only after their approval by the supervisory board.

Dritter Abschnitt. Feststellung des Jahresabschlusses. Gewinnverwendung

Erster Unterabschnitt. Feststellung des Jahresabschlusses

§ 172 Feststellung durch Vorstand und Aufsichtsrat.

¹Billigt der Aufsichtsrat den Jahresabschluß, so ist dieser festgestellt, sofern nicht Vorstand und Aufsichtsrat beschließen, die Feststellung des Jahresabschlusses der Hauptversammlung zu überlassen. ²Die Beschlüsse des Vorstands und des Aufsichtsrats sind in den Bericht des Aufsichtsrats an die Hauptversammlung aufzunehmen.

§ 173 Feststellung durch die Hauptversammlung.

(1) ¹Haben Vorstand und Aufsichtsrat beschlossen, die Feststellung des Jahresabschlusses der Hauptversammlung zu überlassen, oder hat der Aufsichtsrat den Jahresabschluß nicht gebilligt, so stellt die Hauptversammlung den Jahresabschluß fest. ²Hat der Aufsichtsrat eines Mutterunternehmens (§ 290 Abs. 1, 2 des Handelsgesetzbuchs) den Konzernabschluss nicht gebilligt, so entscheidet die Hauptversammlung über die Billigung.

(2) ¹Auf den Jahresabschluß sind bei der Feststellung die für seine Aufstellung geltenden Vorschriften anzuwenden. ²Die Hauptversammlung darf bei der Feststellung des Jahresabschlusses nur die Beträge in Gewinnrücklagen einstellen, die nach Gesetz oder Satzung einzustellen sind.

Third Section. Formal Approval of Annual Financial Statements. Appropriation of Profits

Subsection One. Formal Approval of the Annual Financial Statements

§ 172 Formal approval by the management board and the supervisory board.

¹If the supervisory board approves the annual financial statements, they shall be deemed to have been formally approved unless the management board and the supervisory board adopt a resolution to the effect that the general meeting shall be responsible for granting formal approval. ²The resolutions adopted by the management board and the supervisory board shall be included in the supervisory board's report to the general meeting.

§ 173 Formal approval by the general meeting.

(1) ¹If the management board and the supervisory board have resolved that the general meeting is to be responsible for granting formal approval of the annual financial statements or if the supervisory board has failed to approve the annual financial statements, formal approval shall be granted by the general meeting. ²If the supervisory board of a parent enterprise (sec. 290 paras. 1 and 2 of the Commercial Code has failed to approve the consolidated annual financial statements, the general meeting shall decide on approval.

(2) ¹The provisions governing the drawing up of the annual financial statements shall apply to its formal approval. ²When granting formal approval for the annual financial statements, the general meeting may only allocate those amounts to the revenue reserves which are to be allocated in accordance with the law or the articles of association.

(3) ¹Ändert die Hauptversammlung einen von einem Abschlußprüfer auf Grund gesetzlicher Verpflichtung geprüften Jahresabschluß, so werden vor der erneuten Prüfung nach § 316 Abs. 3 des Handelsgesetzbuchs von der Hauptversammlung gefaßte Beschlüsse über die Feststellung des Jahresabschlusses und die Gewinnverwendung erst wirksam, wenn auf Grund der erneuten Prüfung ein hinsichtlich der Änderungen uneingeschränkter Bestätigungsvermerk erteilt worden ist. ²Sie werden nichtig, wenn nicht binnen zwei Wochen seit der Beschlußfassung ein hinsichtlich der Änderungen uneingeschränkter Bestätigungsvermerk erteilt wird.

(3) ¹If the general meeting amends annual financial statements audited by an auditor of annual financial statements in accordance with legal requirements, resolutions adopted by the general meeting concerning formal approval of the annual financial statements and the appropriation of profits before a renewed audit is conducted pursuant to sec. 316 para. 3 of the Commercial Code shall only become effective if an unqualified certification of the auditor of annual financial statements has been given regarding the amendments. ²They shall become null and void if an unqualified certification of the auditor of annual financial statements is not given regarding the amendments within two weeks of the resolution being adopted.

Zweiter Unterabschnitt. Gewinnverwendung

Subsection Two. Appropriation of Profits

§ 174 Beschluss über Gewinnverwendung.

§ 174 Resolution on Appropriation of Profits.

(1) ¹Die Hauptversammlung beschließt über die Verwendung des Bilanzgewinns. ²Sie ist hierbei an den festgestellten Jahresabschluß gebunden.

(1) ¹The general meeting shall resolve on the appropriation of balance sheet profit. ²It is bound to the formally approved annual financial statements in this regard.

(2) In dem Beschluß ist die Verwendung des Bilanzgewinns im einzelnen darzulegen, namentlich sind anzugeben

1. der Bilanzgewinn;
2. der an die Aktionäre auszuschüttende Betrag oder Sachwert;
3. die in Gewinnrücklagen einzustellenden Beträge;
4. ein Gewinnvortrag;
5. der zusätzliche Aufwand auf Grund des Beschlusses.

(2) The resolution shall give details of the appropriation of the balance sheet profit, in particular stating the following

1. balance sheet profit;
2. the amount or payment in kind which is to be distributed to shareholders;
3. the amounts to be allocated to revenue reserves;
4. any profits carried forward;
5. additional expenses incurred on the basis of the resolution.

(3) Der Beschluß führt nicht zu einer Änderung des festgestellten Jahresabschlusses.

(3) The resolution shall not lead to an amendment of the approved annual financial statements.

Dritter Unterabschnitt.
Ordentliche Hauptversammlung

§ 175 Einberufung.

(1) ¹Unverzüglich nach Eingang des Berichts des Aufsichtsrats hat der Vorstand die Hauptversammlung zur Entgegennahme des festgestellten Jahresabschlusses und des Lageberichts, eines vom Aufsichtsrat gebilligten Einzelabschlusses nach § 325 Abs. 2a des Handelsgesetzbuchs sowie zur Beschlußfassung über die Verwendung eines Bilanzgewinns, bei einem Mutterunternehmen (§ 290 Abs. 1, 2 des Handelsgesetzbuchs) auch zur Entgegennahme des vom Aufsichtsrat gebilligten Konzernabschlusses und des Konzernlageberichts, einzuberufen. ²Die Hauptversammlung hat in den ersten acht Monaten des Geschäftsjahrs stattzufinden.

(2) ¹Der Jahresabschluss, ein vom Aufsichtsrat gebilligter Einzelabschluss nach § 325 Absatz 2a des Handelsgesetzbuchs, der Lagebericht, der Bericht des Aufsichtsrats und der Vorschlag des Vorstands für die Verwendung des Bilanzgewinns sind von der Einberufung an in dem Geschäftsraum der Gesellschaft zur Einsicht durch die Aktionäre auszulegen. ²Auf Verlangen ist jedem Aktionär unverzüglich eine Abschrift der Vorlagen zu erteilen. ³Bei einem Mutterunternehmen (§ 290 Abs. 1, 2 des Handelsgesetzbuchs) gelten die Sätze 1 und 2 auch für den Konzernabschluss, den Konzernlagebericht und den Bericht des Aufsichtsrats hierüber. ⁴Die Verpflichtungen nach den Sätzen 1 bis 3 entfallen, wenn die dort bezeichneten Dokumente für denselben Zeitraum über die Internetseite der Gesellschaft zugänglich sind.

Subsection Three.
Ordinary General Meeting

§ 175 Convening.

(1) ¹Without undue delay upon receiving the report from the supervisory board, the management board shall convene the general meeting in order to receive the formally approved annual financial statements and the management report, individual financial statements approved by the supervisory board pursuant to sec. 325 para. 2a of the Commercial Code and to adopt a resolution on the appropriation of any balance sheet profit, and in the case of a parent enterprise (sec. 290 paras. 1 and 2 of the Commercial Code) also to receive the consolidated annual financial statements approved by the supervisory board and the group management report. ²The general meeting shall be held in the first eight months of the fiscal year.

(2) ¹The annual financial statements, individual financial statements approved by the supervisory board pursuant to sec. 325 para. 2a of the Commercial Code, the management report, the report from the supervisory board and the proposal made by the management board concerning the appropriation of balance sheet profit shall be displayed in the company's offices for inspection by the shareholders as of the date the general meeting is convened. ²Each shareholder shall be given a copy of the documents without undue delay upon request. ³In the case of a parent enterprise (sec. 290 paras. 1 and 2 of the Commercial Code), sentences 1 and 2 shall also apply to the consolidated annual financial statements, the group management report and the report from the supervisory board thereupon. ⁴The obligations pursuant to sentences 1 to 3 shall not apply if the documents designated therein are accessible on the website of the company during the same period of time.

(3) ¹Hat die Hauptversammlung den Jahresabschluss festzustellen oder hat sie über die Billigung des Konzernabschlusses zu entscheiden, so gelten für die Einberufung der Hauptversammlung zur Feststellung des Jahresabschlusses oder zur Billigung des Konzernabschlusses und für das Zugänglichmachen der Vorlagen und die Erteilung von Abschriften die Absätze 1 und 2 sinngemäß. ²Die Verhandlungen über die Feststellung des Jahresabschlusses und über die Verwendung des Bilanzgewinns sollen verbunden werden.

(4) ¹Mit der Einberufung der Hauptversammlung zur Entgegennahme des festgestellten Jahresabschlusses oder, wenn die Hauptversammlung den Jahresabschluß festzustellen hat, der Hauptversammlung zur Feststellung des Jahresabschlusses sind Vorstand und Aufsichtsrat an die in dem Bericht des Aufsichtsrats enthaltenen Erklärungen über den Jahresabschluß (§§ 172, 173 Abs. 1) gebunden. ²Bei einem Mutterunternehmen (§ 290 Abs. 1, 2 des Handelsgesetzbuchs) gilt Satz 1 für die Erklärung des Aufsichtsrats über die Billigung des Konzernabschlusses entsprechend.

§ 176 Vorlagen. Anwesenheit des Abschlußprüfers.

(1) ¹Der Vorstand hat der Hauptversammlung die in § 175 Abs. 2 genannten Vorlagen sowie bei börsennotierten Gesellschaften einen erläuternden Bericht zu den Angaben nach § 289 Abs. 4, § 315 Abs. 4 des Handelsgesetzbuchs zugänglich zu machen. ²Zu Beginn der Verhandlung soll der Vorstand seine Vorlagen, der Vorsitzende des Aufsichtsrats den Bericht des Aufsichtsrats erläutern. ³Der Vorstand soll dabei auch zu einem Jahresfehlbetrag oder einem

(3) ¹If the general meeting is to formally approve the annual financial statements or decide on approval for the consolidated annual financial statements, paras. 1 and 2 shall apply accordingly to the convening of the general meeting which is to formally approve the annual financial statements or to approve the consolidated annual financial statements and to the granting of access to documents and the furnishing of copies. ²The proceedings concerning the formal approval of the annual financial statements and the appropriation of the balance sheet profit shall be combined.

(4) ¹The management board and the supervisory board shall be bound to the statements regarding the annual financial statements made in the report of the supervisory board (sec. 172, 173 para. 1) as of the date the general meeting which is to receive the formally approved annual financial statements or, if the general meeting is to formally approve the annual financial statements, the general meeting which is to formally approve the annual financial statements is convened. ²In the case of a parent enterprise (sec. 290 paras. 1 and 2 of the Commercial Code), sentence 1 shall apply accordingly to the declaration made by the supervisory board concerning the approval for the consolidated annual financial statements.

§ 176 Documents. Presence of the auditor of annual financial statements.

(1) ¹The management board shall make accessible to the general meeting the templates set forth in sec. 175 para. 2 as well as, in the case of listed companies, an explanatory report on the information pursuant to sec. 289 para. 4, sec. 315 para. 4 of the Commercial Code. ²At the beginning of the proceedings, the management board shall comment on the presented documents and the chairman of the supervisory board shall comment on the supervisory board's report. ³The

Verlust Stellung nehmen, der das Jahresergebnis wesentlich beeinträchtigt hat. ⁴Satz 3 ist auf Kreditinstitute nicht anzuwenden.

(2) ¹Ist der Jahresabschluß von einem Abschlußprüfer zu prüfen, so hat der Abschlußprüfer an den Verhandlungen über die Feststellung des Jahresabschlusses teilzunehmen. ²Satz 1 gilt entsprechend für die Verhandlungen über die Billigung eines Konzernabschlusses. ³Der Abschlußprüfer ist nicht verpflichtet, einem Aktionär Auskunft zu erteilen.

Vierter Abschnitt. Bekanntmachung des Jahresabschlusses

§§ 177, 178 *(aufgehoben)*

Sechster Teil. Satzungsänderung. Maßnahmen der Kapitalbeschaffung und Kapitalherabsetzung

Erster Abschnitt. Satzungsänderung

§ 179 Beschluß der Hauptversammlung.

(1) ¹Jede Satzungsänderung bedarf eines Beschlusses der Hauptversammlung. ²Die Befugnis zu Änderungen, die nur die Fassung betreffen, kann die Hauptversammlung dem Aufsichtsrat übertragen.

(2) ¹Der Beschluß der Hauptversammlung bedarf einer Mehrheit, die mindestens drei Viertel des bei der Beschlußfassung vertretenen Grundkapitals umfaßt. ²Die Satzung kann eine andere Kapitalmehrheit, für eine Änderung des Gegenstands des Unternehmens jedoch nur eine größere Kapitalmehrheit bestimmen. ³Sie kann weitere Erfordernisse aufstellen.

(3) ¹Soll das bisherige Verhältnis mehrerer Gattungen von Aktien zum Nach-

management board shall also comment on any annual net loss or a loss which has seriously impaired the results for the year. ⁴Sentence 3 shall not apply to credit institutions.

(2) ¹If the annual financial statements are to be audited by an auditor of annual financial statements, the auditor of annual financial statements shall attend proceedings concerning formal approval for the annual financial statements. ²Sentence 1 shall apply accordingly to proceedings concerning the approval of consolidated financial statements. ³The auditor of annual financial statements shall not be obligated to provide a shareholder with information.

Section Four. Announcement of Annual Financial Statements

§§ 177, 178 *(repealed)*

Part Six. Amendment of the Articles of Association. Capital Increases and Capital Reductions.

Section One. Amendment of the Articles of Association

§ 179 Resolution of the general meeting.

(1) ¹Any amendment to the articles of association shall require a resolution of the general meeting. ²The general meeting may delegate authority to amend merely the wording of the articles of association to the supervisory board.

(2) ¹The resolution of the general meeting requires a majority of at least three quarters of the registered share capital represented at the adoption of the resolution. ²The articles of association may provide for another majority, although if the object of the enterprise is to be amended, only a larger majority may be stipulated. ³The articles of association may establish additional requirements.

(3) ¹If the current relationship among several classes of shares is to be altered

teil einer Gattung geändert werden, so bedarf der Beschluß der Hauptversammlung zu seiner Wirksamkeit der Zustimmung der benachteiligten Aktionäre. ²Über die Zustimmung haben die benachteiligten Aktionäre einen Sonderbeschluß zu fassen. ³Für diesen gilt Absatz 2.

§ 179a Verpflichtung zur Übertragung des ganzen Gesellschaftsvermögens.

(1) ¹Ein Vertrag, durch den sich eine Aktiengesellschaft zur Übertragung des ganzen Gesellschaftsvermögens verpflichtet, ohne daß die Übertragung unter die Vorschriften des Umwandlungsgesetzes fällt, bedarf auch dann eines Beschlusses der Hauptversammlung nach § 179, wenn damit nicht eine Änderung des Unternehmensgegenstandes verbunden ist. ²Die Satzung kann nur eine größere Kapitalmehrheit bestimmen.

(2) ¹Der Vertrag ist von der Einberufung der Hauptversammlung an, die über die Zustimmung beschließen soll, in dem Geschäftsraum der Gesellschaft zur Einsicht der Aktionäre auszulegen. ²Auf Verlangen ist jedem Aktionär unverzüglich eine Abschrift zu erteilen. ³Die Verpflichtungen nach den Sätzen 1 und 2 entfallen, wenn der Vertrag für denselben Zeitraum über die Internetseite der Gesellschaft zugänglich ist. ⁴In der Hauptversammlung ist der Vertrag zugänglich zu machen. ⁵Der Vorstand hat ihn zu Beginn der Verhandlung zu erläutern. ⁶Der Niederschrift ist er als Anlage beizufügen.

(3) Wird aus Anlaß der Übertragung des Gesellschaftsvermögens die Gesellschaft aufgelöst, so ist der Anmeldung der Auflösung der Vertrag in Ausfertigung oder öffentlich beglaubigter Abschrift beizufügen.

to the relative disadvantage of one class, the resolution of the general meeting shall require the consent of those adversely affected shareholders in order to be valid. ²This shall require adoption of a special resolution to be voted on solely by the adversely affected shareholders. ³Para. 2 shall apply to such resolution.

§ 179a Obligation to transfer the entire corporate assets.

(1) ¹An agreement under which a stock corporation obligates itself to transfer its entire corporate assets shall require, if said transaction does not fall within the Transformation Act, the adoption of a resolution by the general meeting pursuant to sec. 179, even where it is not undertaken in conjunction with amending the object of the enterprise. ²The articles of association may stipulate that a greater, but not a smaller, majority of capital shall be required in order for the resolution to be adopted.

(2) ¹The agreement shall be displayed in the company's office for inspection by the shareholders from the date of the convening of the general meeting that is to vote on the agreement. ²Each shareholder shall be given a copy of the agreement without undue delay upon request. ³The obligations pursuant to sentences 1 and 2 shall cease to exist if the agreement is accessible during the same period of time on the website of the company. ⁴The agreement shall be made accessible in the general meeting. ⁵The management board shall explain it at the outset of the proceedings. ⁶The agreement shall be appended to the minutes.

(3) In the event that the company is dissolved as a result of the transfer of the corporate assets, an executed copy or certified copy of the agreement shall be appended to the application for registration of the dissolution.

§ 180 Zustimmung der betroffenen Aktionäre.

(1) Ein Beschluß, der Aktionären Nebenverpflichtungen auferlegt, bedarf zu seiner Wirksamkeit der Zustimmung aller betroffenen Aktionäre.

(2) Gleiches gilt für einen Beschluß, durch den die Übertragung von Namensaktien oder Zwischenscheinen an die Zustimmung der Gesellschaft gebunden wird.

§ 181 Eintragung der Satzungsänderung.

(1) ¹Der Vorstand hat die Satzungsänderung zur Eintragung in das Handelsregister anzumelden. ²Der Anmeldung ist der vollständige Wortlaut der Satzung beizufügen; er muß mit der Bescheinigung eines Notars versehen sein, daß die geänderten Bestimmungen der Satzung mit dem Beschluß über die Satzungsänderung und die unveränderten Bestimmungen mit dem zuletzt zum Handelsregister eingereichten vollständigen Wortlaut der Satzung übereinstimmen.

(2) Soweit nicht die Änderung Angaben nach § 39 betrifft, genügt bei der Eintragung die Bezugnahme auf die beim Gericht eingereichten Urkunden.

(3) Die Änderung wird erst wirksam, wenn sie in das Handelsregister des Sitzes der Gesellschaft eingetragen worden ist.

Zweiter Abschnitt. Maßnahmen der Kapitalbeschaffung

Erster Unterabschnitt. Kapitalerhöhung gegen Einlagen

§ 182 Voraussetzungen.

(1) ¹Eine Erhöhung des Grundkapitals gegen Einlagen kann nur mit einer Mehrheit beschlossen werden, die mindestens drei Viertel des bei der Be-

§ 180 Consent of affected shareholders.

(1) A resolution imposing ancillary duties on shareholders shall require the consent of all the affected shareholders in order to be effective.

(2) The foregoing shall also apply to resolutions that make the transfer of registered shares or interim certificates subject to the consent of the company.

§ 181 Registration of amendments to the articles of association.

(1) ¹The management board shall apply for the registration of the amendment of the articles of association in the commercial register. ²The application shall be accompanied by the complete text of the articles of association; a certificate from a notary shall be submitted therewith, verifying that the amended provisions in the articles of association accurately reflect the contents of the adopted resolution, and that the unamended provisions correspond to the text of the articles of association previously registered in the commercial register.

(2) If the amendments do not concern those details stipulated in sec. 39, it is sufficient for the registration to merely make reference to the documents that have been submitted to the court.

(3) An amendment shall only take effect upon its registration in the commercial register responsible for the registered office of the company.

Section Two. Capital Increases

Subsection One. Capital Increase against Contributions

§ 182 General provisions.

(1) ¹A resolution to increase the registered share capital against contributions may only be adopted with a majority of at least three quarters of the regis-

schlußfassung vertretenen Grundkapitals umfaßt. ²Die Satzung kann eine andere Kapitalmehrheit, für die Ausgabe von Vorzugsaktien ohne Stimmrecht jedoch nur eine größere Kapitalmehrheit bestimmen. ³Sie kann weitere Erfordernisse aufstellen. ⁴Die Kapitalerhöhung kann nur durch Ausgabe neuer Aktien ausgeführt werden. ⁵Bei Gesellschaften mit Stückaktien muß sich die Zahl der Aktien in demselben Verhältnis wie das Grundkapital erhöhen.

(2) ¹Sind mehrere Gattungen von stimmberechtigten Aktien vorhanden, so bedarf der Beschluß der Hauptversammlung zu seiner Wirksamkeit der Zustimmung der Aktionäre jeder Gattung. ²Über die Zustimmung haben die Aktionäre jeder Gattung einen Sonderbeschluß zu fassen. ³Für diesen gilt Absatz 1.

(3) Sollen die neuen Aktien für einen höheren Betrag als den geringsten Ausgabebetrag ausgegeben werden, so ist der Mindestbetrag, unter dem sie nicht ausgegeben werden sollen, im Beschluß über die Erhöhung des Grundkapitals festzusetzen.

(4) ¹Das Grundkapital soll nicht erhöht werden, solange ausstehende Einlagen auf das bisherige Grundkapital noch erlangt werden können. ²Für Versicherungsgesellschaften kann die Satzung etwas anderes bestimmen. ³Stehen Einlagen in verhältnismäßig unerheblichem Umfang aus, so hindert dies die Erhöhung des Grundkapitals nicht.

§ 183 Kapitalerhöhung mit Sacheinlagen. Rückzahlung von Einlagen.

(1) ¹Wird eine Sacheinlage (§ 27 Abs. 1 und 2) gemacht, so müssen ihr Gegenstand, die Person, von der die Gesellschaft den Gegenstand erwirbt, und der Nennbetrag, bei Stückaktien die Zahl

tered share capital represented at the adoption of the resolution. ²The articles of association may provide for another majority, but in the case of issue of preference shares without voting right, only a larger majority may be stipulated. ³The articles of association may establish additional requirements. ⁴The capital increase may only be achieved through the issue of new shares. ⁵For companies with non-par value shares, the number of shares shall be increased in the same proportion as the registered share capital.

(2) ¹If there is more than one class of voting shares, a resolution of the general meeting shall require the separate consent of the shareholders of each class of shares in order to be validly adopted. ²The shareholders of each class shall adopt a special resolution granting their consent. ³Para. 1 shall apply in this case.

(3) If the new shares are to be issued for a higher price than the lowest issue price, the minimum acceptable contribution in consideration thereof shall be fixed in the resolution on the capital increase.

(4) ¹The registered share capital shall not be increased while outstanding contributions to the current registered share capital are still obtainable. ²The articles of association may stipulate otherwise for insurance companies. ³If the amount of outstanding contributions is, with regard to the circumstances, insignificant, this shall not preclude an increase of the registered share capital.

§ 183 Capital increase against contributions in kind. Repayment of contributions.

(1) ¹If a contribution in kind is to be made (sec. 27 para. 1 and 2), the resolution increasing the registered share capital shall stipulate the object of the contribution, the party from whom the

der bei der Sacheinlage zu gewährenden Aktien im Beschluß über die Erhöhung des Grundkapitals festgesetzt werden. ²Der Beschluß darf nur gefaßt werden, wenn die Einbringung von Sacheinlagen und die Festsetzungen nach Satz 1 ausdrücklich und ordnungsgemäß bekanntgemacht worden sind.

(2) § 27 Abs. 3 und 4 gilt entsprechend.

(3) ¹Bei der Kapitalerhöhung mit Sacheinlagen hat eine Prüfung durch einen oder mehrere Prüfer stattzufinden. ²§ 33 Abs. 3 bis 5, die §§ 34, 35 gelten sinngemäß.

§ 183a Kapitalerhöhung mit Sacheinlagen ohne Prüfung.

(1) ¹Von einer Prüfung der Sacheinlage (§ 183 Abs. 3) kann unter den Voraussetzungen des § 33a abgesehen werden. ²Wird hiervon Gebrauch gemacht, so gelten die folgenden Absätze.

(2) ¹Der Vorstand hat das Datum des Beschlusses über die Kapitalerhöhung sowie die Angaben nach § 37a Abs. 1 und 2 in den Gesellschaftsblättern bekannt zu machen. ²Die Durchführung der Erhöhung des Grundkapitals darf nicht in das Handelsregister eingetragen werden vor Ablauf von vier Wochen seit der Bekanntmachung.

(3) ¹Liegen die Voraussetzungen des § 33a Abs. 2 vor, hat das Amtsgericht auf Antrag von Aktionären, die am Tag der Beschlussfassung über die Kapitalerhöhung gemeinsam fünf vom Hundert des Grundkapitals hielten und am Tag der Antragsstellung noch halten, einen oder mehrere Prüfer zu bestellen. ²Der Antrag kann bis zum Tag der Eintragung der Durchführung der Erhöhung des Grundkapitals (§ 189) gestellt werden. ³Das Gericht hat vor der Entscheidung über den Antrag den Vorstand zu hören. ⁴Gegen die Entscheidung ist die Beschwerde gegeben.

company is to receive it, and the nominal value, or in the case of non-par value shares, the number of shares to be granted in consideration of the contribution. ²The resolution shall only be adopted if the contributions in kind and the stipulations specified in sentence 1 have been explicitly and duly announced.

(2) Sec. 27 paras. 3 and 4 shall apply accordingly.

(3) ¹A capital increase against contributions in kind shall require an audit by one or more auditors. ²Sec. 33 paras. 3 to 5, sec. 34, 35 shall apply accordingly.

§ 183a Capital increase from contributions in kind without audit.

(1) ¹An audit of the contribution in kind (sec. 183 para. 3) may be omitted if the requirements of sec. 33a are met. ²If this is made use of, the following paragraphs shall apply.

(2) ¹The management board shall announce the date of the resolution on the capital increase as well as the information pursuant to sec. 37a paras. 1 and 2 in the company's designated journals. ²The implementation of the increase of the registered share capital may not be registered in the commercial register until four weeks have expired since the announcement.

(3) ¹If the requirements of sec. 33a para. 2 are met, the local court shall, upon application by shareholders who held on the day of the adoption of the resolution on the capital increase together five percent of the registered share capital and who still hold such share on the day of the application, appoint one or more auditors. ²The application may be made until the day of the registration of the implementation of the increase of the registered share capital (sec. 189). ³The court shall hear the management board prior to deciding on the application. ⁴The decision may be appealed.

(4) Für das weitere Verfahren gelten § 33 Abs. 4 und 5, die §§ 34, 35 entsprechend.

§ 184 Anmeldung des Beschlusses.

(1) ¹Der Vorstand und der Vorsitzende des Aufsichtsrats haben den Beschluss über die Erhöhung des Grundkapitals zur Eintragung in das Handelsregister anzumelden. ²In der Anmeldung ist anzugeben, welche Einlagen auf das bisherige Grundkapital noch nicht geleistet sind und warum sie nicht erlangt werden können. ³Soll von einer Prüfung der Sacheinlage abgesehen werden und ist das Datum des Beschlusses der Kapitalerhöhung vorab bekannt gemacht worden (§ 183a Abs. 2), müssen die Anmeldenden in der Anmeldung nur noch versichern, dass ihnen seit der Bekanntmachung keine Umstände im Sinne von § 37a Abs. 2 bekannt geworden sind.

(2) Der Anmeldung sind der Bericht über die Prüfung von Sacheinlagen (§ 183 Abs. 3) oder die in § 37a Abs. 3 bezeichneten Anlagen beizufügen.

(3) ¹Das Gericht kann die Eintragung ablehnen, wenn der Wert der Sacheinlage nicht unwesentlich hinter dem geringsten Ausgabebetrag der dafür zu gewährenden Aktien zurückbleibt. ²Wird von einer Prüfung der Sacheinlage nach § 183a Abs. 1 abgesehen, gilt § 38 Abs. 3 entsprechend.

§ 185 Zeichnung der neuen Aktien.

(1) ¹Die Zeichnung der neuen Aktien geschieht durch schriftliche Erklärung (Zeichnungsschein), aus der die Beteiligung nach der Zahl und bei Nennbetragsaktien dem Nennbetrag und, wenn mehrere Gattungen ausgegeben werden, der Gattung der Aktien hervorgehen muß. ²Der Zeichnungsschein soll doppelt ausgestellt werden. ³Er hat zu enthalten:

1. den Tag, an dem die Erhöhung des Grundkapitals beschlossen worden ist;

(4) Sec. 33 paras. 4 and 5, sec. 34, 35 shall apply accordingly to the further proceedings.

§ 184 Application for the resolution.

(1) ¹The management board and the chairman of the supervisory board shall submit the application for the resolution on the capital increase to be registered in the commercial register. ²In such application, the current outstanding capital contributions shall be stated along with an explanation as to why these cannot be obtained. ³If an audit of the contribution in kind is to be omitted and if the date of the resolution on the capital increase has been announced in advance (sec. 183a para. 2), the applicants shall further set forth in their application that since the announcement they have not become aware of circumstances within the meaning of sec. 37a para. 2.

(2) The report on the audit of contributions in kind (sec. 183 para. 3) or the attachments set forth in sec. 37a para. 3 shall be attached to the application.

(3) ¹The court may refuse the registration if the value of the contribution in kind substantially falls short of the lowest issue price of the shares which are to be granted in return. ²If an audit of the contribution in kind pursuant to sec. 183a para. 1 is omitted, sec. 38 para. 3 shall apply accordingly.

§ 185 Subscription to new shares.

(1) ¹The subscription to new shares shall be effected by means of a written declaration ("subscription certificate"), which shall specify the number, and, for par value shares, the nominal value of the shares, and, if more than one class is being issued, the particular class of shares to be subscribed. ²The subscription certificate shall be drawn up in duplicate. ³It shall contain:

1. the date on which the capital increase was resolved;

2. den Ausgabebetrag der Aktien, den Betrag der festgesetzten Einzahlungen sowie den Umfang von Nebenverpflichtungen;
3. die bei einer Kapitalerhöhung mit Sacheinlagen vorgesehenen Festsetzungen und, wenn mehrere Gattungen ausgegeben werden, den auf jede Aktiengattung entfallenden Betrag des Grundkapitals;
4. den Zeitpunkt, an dem die Zeichnung unverbindlich wird, wenn nicht bis dahin die Durchführung der Erhöhung des Grundkapitals eingetragen ist.

(2) Zeichnungsscheine, die diese Angaben nicht vollständig oder die außer dem Vorbehalt in Absatz 1 Nr. 4 Beschränkungen der Verpflichtung des Zeichners enthalten, sind nichtig.

(3) Ist die Durchführung der Erhöhung des Grundkapitals eingetragen, so kann sich der Zeichner auf die Nichtigkeit oder Unverbindlichkeit des Zeichnungsscheins nicht berufen, wenn er auf Grund des Zeichnungsscheins als Aktionär Rechte ausgeübt oder Verpflichtungen erfüllt hat.

(4) Jede nicht im Zeichnungsschein enthaltene Beschränkung ist der Gesellschaft gegenüber unwirksam.

§ 186 Bezugsrecht.

(1) ¹Jedem Aktionär muß auf sein Verlangen ein seinem Anteil an dem bisherigen Grundkapital entsprechender Teil der neuen Aktien zugeteilt werden. ²Für die Ausübung des Bezugsrechts ist eine Frist von mindestens zwei Wochen zu bestimmen.

(2) ¹Der Vorstand hat den Ausgabebetrag oder die Grundlagen für seine Festlegung und zugleich eine Bezugsfrist gemäß Absatz 1 in den Gesellschaftsblättern bekannt zu machen. ²Sind nur die Grundlagen der Festlegung angegeben, so hat er spätestens drei Tage vor Ablauf der Bezugsfrist den Ausgabebe-

2. the issue price of the shares, the stipulated consideration to be paid in, as well as the extent of any ancillary duties;
3. the stipulations provided for in the event of a capital increase with contributions in kind, and if several classes of shares are being issued, a breakdown of the registered share capital allocated to each class;
4. the point in time at which the subscription shall become non-binding, if at this time the implementation of the capital increase has not yet to be registered.

(2) Subscription certificates that do not contain all the required information, or those that contain limitations relating to the obligations of the subscriber, apart from the reservation permissible under para. 1 no. 4, shall be null and void.

(3) Once the implementation of the capital increase has been registered, the subscriber may not assert that such certificate is null and void or unenforceable if he has exercised any rights or fulfilled any obligations as a shareholder by virtue of the subscription certificate.

(4) Any limitation that is not stated in the subscription certificate shall be invalid vis-à-vis the company.

§ 186 Subscription right.

(1) ¹Each shareholder shall be entitled, upon demand, to subscribe the number of new shares in proportion to his holdings in the current registered share capital. ²A period of at least two weeks shall be fixed during which such subscription right may be exercised.

(2) ¹The management board shall announce the issue price or the basis on which it is to be determined and the exercise period pursuant to para. 1 in the company's designated journals. ²If only the basis on which the issue price is to be determined is announced, the management board shall announce the

trag in den Gesellschaftsblättern und über ein elektronisches Informationsmedium bekannt zu machen.

(3) ¹Das Bezugsrecht kann ganz oder zum Teil nur im Beschluß über die Erhöhung des Grundkapitals ausgeschlossen werden. ²In diesem Fall bedarf der Beschluß neben den in Gesetz oder Satzung für die Kapitalerhöhung aufgestellten Erfordernissen einer Mehrheit, die mindestens drei Viertel des bei der Beschlußfassung vertretenen Grundkapitals umfaßt. ³Die Satzung kann eine größere Kapitalmehrheit und weitere Erfordernisse bestimmen. ⁴Ein Ausschluß des Bezugsrechts ist insbesondere dann zulässig, wenn die Kapitalerhöhung gegen Bareinlagen zehn vom Hundert des Grundkapitals nicht übersteigt und der Ausgabebetrag den Börsenpreis nicht wesentlich unterschreitet.

(4) ¹Ein Beschluß, durch den das Bezugsrecht ganz oder zum Teil ausgeschlossen wird, darf nur gefaßt werden, wenn die Ausschließung ausdrücklich und ordnungsgemäß bekanntgemacht worden ist. ²Der Vorstand hat der Hauptversammlung einen schriftlichen Bericht über den Grund für den teilweisen oder vollständigen Ausschluß des Bezugsrechts zugänglich zu machen; in dem Bericht ist der vorgeschlagene Ausgabebetrag zu begründen.

(5) ¹Als Ausschluß des Bezugsrechts ist es nicht anzusehen, wenn nach dem Beschluß die neuen Aktien von einem Kreditinstitut oder einem nach § 53 Abs. 1 Satz 1 oder § 53b Abs. 1 Satz 1 oder Abs. 7 des Gesetzes über das Kreditwesen tätigen Unternehmen mit der Verpflichtung übernommen werden sollen, sie den Aktionären zum Bezug anzubieten. ²Der Vorstand hat dieses Bezugsangebot mit den Angaben gemäß Absatz 2 Satz 1 und einen endgültigen Ausgabebetrag gemäß Absatz 2 Satz 2 bekannt zu machen; gleiches gilt, wenn die neuen Aktien von einem anderen als

issue price in the company's designated journals and an electronic source of information no later than three days before the expiry of the exercise period.

(3) ¹The subscription right may be limited or excluded only in the resolution on the capital increase. ²In order for such a resolution to be adopted, a majority of at least three quarters of the registered share capital represented at the adoption of the resolution shall be required in addition to meeting all the requirements mandated by law or the articles of association. ³The articles of association may stipulate a greater majority and establish additional requirements. ⁴An exclusion of the subscription right is permissible particularly in the situation where the capital increase against cash contribution does not exceed ten percent of the current registered share capital and the issue price is not substantially below the price on the stock exchange.

(4) ¹A resolution limiting or excluding the subscription right may only be adopted if the proposed modifications are duly and explicitly announced. ²The management board shall make accessible to the general meeting with a written report stating the reasons for the limitation or exclusion of the subscription right; this report shall also explain how the proposed issue price was determined.

(5) ¹A resolution stipulating that the new shares are to be acquired by a credit institution or a similar business entity within the definition of sec. 53 para. 1 sentence 1 or sec. 53b para. 1 sentence 1 or para. 7 of the Banking Act, with the obligation to offer them for subscription to the shareholders, shall not be construed as an exclusion of the subscription right. ²The management board shall announce this subscription offer, stating the details pursuant to para. 2 sentence 1 and a final issue price pursuant to para. 2 sentence 2; the foregoing shall also apply if the new shares are to

einem Kreditinstitut oder Unternehmen im Sinne des Satzes 1 mit der Verpflichtung übernommen werden sollen, sie den Aktionären zum Bezug anzubieten.

§ 187 Zusicherung von Rechten auf den Bezug neuer Aktien.

(1) Rechte auf den Bezug neuer Aktien können nur unter Vorbehalt des Bezugsrechts der Aktionäre zugesichert werden.

(2) Zusicherungen vor dem Beschluß über die Erhöhung des Grundkapitals sind der Gesellschaft gegenüber unwirksam.

§ 188 Anmeldung und Eintragung der Durchführung.

(1) Der Vorstand und der Vorsitzende des Aufsichtsrats haben die Durchführung der Erhöhung des Grundkapitals zur Eintragung in das Handelsregister anzumelden.

(2) ¹Für die Anmeldung gelten sinngemäß § 36 Abs. 2, § 36a und § 37 Abs. 1. ²Durch Gutschrift auf ein Konto des Vorstands kann die Einzahlung nicht geleistet werden.

(3) Der Anmeldung sind beizufügen

1. die Zweitschriften der Zeichnungsscheine und ein vom Vorstand unterschriebenes Verzeichnis der Zeichner, das die auf jeden entfallenden Aktien und die auf sie geleisteten Einzahlungen angibt;
2. bei einer Kapitalerhöhung mit Sacheinlagen die Verträge, die den Festsetzungen nach § 183 zugrunde liegen oder zu ihrer Ausführung geschlossen worden sind;
3. eine Berechnung der Kosten, die für die Gesellschaft durch die Ausgabe der neuen Aktien entstehen werden.

be acquired by any party, other than a credit institution or business entity as defined in sentence 1, who assumes an obligation to offer the new shares to the shareholders.

§ 187 Guaranteeing subscription rights to new shares.

(1) Rights to subscribe new shares may only be guaranteed subject to the subscription right of the shareholders.

(2) Any such guarantee issued prior to the adoption of the resolution increasing the registered share capital are invalid vis-à-vis the company.

§ 188 Application for and registration of the implementation of the increase.

(1) The management board and the chairman of the supervisory board shall apply for the implementation of the increase of the registered share capital to be registered in the commercial register.

(2) ¹Sec. 36 para. 2, sec. 36a and sec. 37 para. 1 shall apply accordingly to the application. ²Crediting an account held in the name of the management board shall not constitute effective payment of the contribution.

(3) The following documents shall be submitted together with the application

1. the duplicates of the subscription certificates and a list of the subscribers, signed by the management board, stating the number of shares allotted to each and the respective contributions therefor;
2. in the case of a capital increase against contributions in kind, the agreements which are the basis of the stipulations required under sec. 183, or agreements concluded due to the implementation thereof;
3. a computation of the costs to be incurred by the company as a result of the issue of the new shares.

(4) Anmeldung und Eintragung der Durchführung der Erhöhung des Grundkapitals können mit Anmeldung und Eintragung des Beschlusses über die Erhöhung verbunden werden.	(4) The application for the registration of the implementation of the capital increase and the subsequent registration thereof may be made in conjunction with the application for the registration of the resolution on the increase and the subsequent registration thereof.
§ 189 Wirksamwerden der Kapitalerhöhung.	**§ 189 Effectiveness of the capital increase.**
Mit der Eintragung der Durchführung der Erhöhung des Grundkapitals ist das Grundkapital erhöht.	The capital increase shall be deemed effective as soon as the implementation of the increase is registered.
§ 190 *(aufgehoben)*	**§ 190** *(repealed)*
§ 191 Verbotene Ausgabe von Aktien und Zwischenscheinen.	**§ 191 Prohibition on issue of share certificates and interim certificates.**
[1]Vor der Eintragung der Durchführung der Erhöhung des Grundkapitals können die neuen Anteilsrechte nicht übertragen, neue Aktien und Zwischenscheine nicht ausgegeben werden. [2]Die vorher ausgegebenen neuen Aktien und Zwischenscheine sind nichtig. [3]Für den Schaden aus der Ausgabe sind die Ausgeber den Inhabern als Gesamtschuldner verantwortlich.	[1]New share certificates and interim certificates may not be issued, and no rights thereto may be transferred, prior to the registration of the implementation of the capital increase. [2]The share certificates and interim certificates issued prior to such registration shall be null and void. [3]The issuers shall be jointly and severally liable to the holders for damages arising from the issue.
Zweiter Unterabschnitt. Bedingte Kapitalerhöhung	**Subsection Two. Contingent Capital Increase**
§ 192 Voraussetzungen.	**§ 192 Requirements.**
(1) Die Hauptversammlung kann eine Erhöhung des Grundkapitals beschließen, die nur so weit durchgeführt werden soll, wie von einem Umtausch- oder Bezugsrecht Gebrauch gemacht wird, das die Gesellschaft hat oder auf die neuen Aktien (Bezugsaktien) einräumt (bedingte Kapitalerhöhung).	(1) The general meeting may adopt a resolution increasing the registered share capital that will be implemented only to the extent that conversion or subscription rights held or granted by the company for new shares ("preemptive shares") are exercised ("contingent capital increase").
(2) Die bedingte Kapitalerhöhung soll nur zu folgenden Zwecken beschlossen werden:	(2) A contingent capital increase may be resolved only for the following purposes:
1. zur Gewährung von Umtausch- oder Bezugsrechten auf Grund von Wandelschuldverschreibungen; 2. zur Vorbereitung des Zusammenschlusses mehrerer Unternehmen;	1. to grant conversion or subscription rights on the basis of convertible bonds; 2. in preparation of a merger of several business entities;

3. zur Gewährung von Bezugsrechten an Arbeitnehmer und Mitglieder der Geschäftsführung der Gesellschaft oder eines verbundenen Unternehmens im Wege des Zustimmungs- oder Ermächtigungsbeschlusses.

(3) [1]Der Nennbetrag des bedingten Kapitals darf die Hälfte und der Nennbetrag des nach Absatz 2 Nr. 3 beschlossenen Kapitals den zehnten Teil des Grundkapitals, das zur Zeit der Beschlußfassung über die bedingte Kapitalerhöhung vorhanden ist, nicht übersteigen. [2]§ 182 Abs. 1 Satz 5 gilt sinngemäß. [3]Satz 1 gilt nicht für eine bedingte Kapitalerhöhung nach Absatz 2 Nummer 1, die nur zu dem Zweck beschlossen wird, der Gesellschaft einen Umtausch zu ermöglichen, zu dem sie für den Fall ihrer drohenden Zahlungsunfähigkeit oder zum Zweck der Abwendung einer Überschuldung berechtigt ist. [4]Ist die Gesellschaft ein Institut im Sinne des § 1 Absatz 1b des Kreditwesengesetzes, gilt Satz 1 ferner nicht für eine bedingte Kapitalerhöhung nach Absatz 2 Nummer 1, die zu dem Zweck beschlossen wird, der Gesellschaft einen Umtausch zur Erfüllung bankaufsichtsrechtlicher oder zum Zweck der Restrukturierung oder Abwicklung erlassener Anforderungen zu ermöglichen. [5]Eine Anrechnung von bedingtem Kapital, auf das Satz 3 oder Satz 4 Anwendung findet, auf sonstiges bedingtes Kapital erfolgt nicht.

(4) Ein Beschluß der Hauptversammlung, der dem Beschluß über die bedingte Kapitalerhöhung entgegensteht, ist nichtig.

(5) Die folgenden Vorschriften über das Bezugsrecht gelten sinngemäß für das Umtauschrecht.

§ 193 Erfordernisse des Beschlusses.

(1) [1]Der Beschluß über die bedingte Kapitalerhöhung bedarf einer Mehrheit, die mindestens drei Viertel des bei der Beschlußfassung vertretenen Grundka-

3. to grant subscription rights to employees and members of the management of the company or an affiliated enterprise via a consent or authorization resolution.

(3) [1]The nominal amount of the contingent capital shall not be greater than one-half and the nominal amount of the capital resolved pursuant to para. 2 no. 3 not greater than ten percent of the registered share capital available at the time the resolution on the contingent capital increase is adopted. [2]Sec. 182 para. 1 sentence 5 shall apply accordingly. [3]Sentence 1 shall not apply to a contingent capital increase pursuant to para. 2 number 1, that is only resolved for the purpose of allowing the company an exchange to which it is entitled in the event of pending illiquidity or of avoiding a possible over-indebtedness. [4]If the company is an institute within the meaning of sec. 1 para. 1b of the German Banking Act, sentence 1 does not apply to a contingent capital increase according to para. 2 number 1, which is resolved for the purpose of allowing the company an exchange to fulfill bank regulatory requirements or for restructuring or the fulfillment of imposed requirements. [5]A crediting of contingent capital, which applies to sentence 3 or 4, to other conditional capital shall not be made.

(4) Any resolution of the general meeting that contravenes the resolution on the contingent capital increase shall be null and void.

(5) The following regulations concerning the subscription right shall apply accordingly to conversion rights.

§ 193 Requirements of the resolution

(1) [1]A resolution on a contingent capital increase requires a majority of at least three quarters of the registered share capital represented at the adoption of

pitals umfaßt. ²Die Satzung kann eine größere Kapitalmehrheit und weitere Erfordernisse bestimmen. ³§ 182 Abs. 2 und § 187 Abs. 2 gelten.

(2) Im Beschluß müssen auch festgestellt werden

1. der Zweck der bedingten Kapitalerhöhung;
2. der Kreis der Bezugsberechtigten;
3. der Ausgabebetrag oder die Grundlagen, nach denen dieser Betrag errechnet wird; bei einer bedingten Kapitalerhöhung für die Zwecke des § 192 Abs. 2 Nr. 1 genügt es, wenn in dem Beschluss oder in dem damit verbundenen Beschluss nach § 221 der Mindestausgabebetrag oder die Grundlagen für die Festlegung des Ausgabebetrags oder des Mindestausgabebetrags bestimmt werden; sowie
4. bei Beschlüssen nach § 192 Abs. 2 Nr. 3 auch die Aufteilung der Bezugsrechte auf Mitglieder der Geschäftsführungen und Arbeitnehmer, Erfolgsziele, Erwerbs- und Ausübungszeiträume und Wartezeit für die erstmalige Ausübung (mindestens vier Jahre).

§ 194 Bedingte Kapitalerhöhung mit Sacheinlagen. Rückzahlung von Einlagen.

(1) ¹Wird eine Sacheinlage gemacht, so müssen ihr Gegenstand, die Person, von der die Gesellschaft den Gegenstand erwirbt, und der Nennbetrag, bei Stückaktien die Zahl der bei der Sacheinlage zu gewährenden Aktien im Beschluß über die bedingte Kapitalerhöhung festgesetzt werden. ²Als Sacheinlage gilt nicht der Umtausch von Schuldverschreibungen gegen Bezugsaktien. ³Der Beschluß darf nur gefaßt werden, wenn die Einbringung von Sacheinlagen ausdrücklich und ordnungsgemäß bekanntgemacht worden ist.

the resolution. ²The articles of association may stipulate a larger capital majority and further requirements. ³Sec. 182 para. 2 and sec. 187 para. 2 shall apply.

(2) The following shall also be stated in the resolution:

1. the purpose of the contingent capital increase;
2. the parties having subscription rights;
3. the issue price or the basis upon which it shall be calculated; in the case of a contingent capital increase for the purposes of sec. 192 para. 2 no. 1 it shall be sufficient if the minimum issue price or the basis for the determination of the issue price or of the minimum issue price are set forth in the resolution or in the resolution pursuant to sec. 221 connected therewith; and
4. for resolutions pursuant to sec. 192 para. 2 no. 3, the allocation of subscription rights to members of the management and employees, performance targets, acquisition and option periods, and the waiting period prior to the initial exercise of rights (minimum four years).

§ 194 Contingent capital increase against contributions in kind. Repayment of contributions.

(1) ¹In the case of a contribution in kind, the object of the contribution, the party from whom the company shall receive it, and the nominal amount, or, for non-par value shares, the number of shares to be issued in consideration thereof shall be stipulated in the resolution on the contingent capital increase. ²The transfer of bonds in exchange for preemptive shares shall not be construed as a contribution in kind. ³The resolution may only be adopted if the proposed contribution in kind has been explicitly and duly announced.

(2) ¹§ 27 Abs. 3 und 4 gilt entsprechend; an die Stelle des Zeitpunkts der Anmeldung nach § 27 Abs. 3 Satz 3 und der Eintragung nach § 27 Abs. 3 Satz 4 tritt jeweils der Zeitpunkt der Ausgabe der Bezugsaktien.

(3) Die Absätze 1 und 2 gelten nicht für die Einlage von Geldforderungen, die Arbeitnehmern der Gesellschaft aus einer ihnen von der Gesellschaft eingeräumten Gewinnbeteiligung zustehen.

(4) ¹Bei der Kapitalerhöhung mit Sacheinlagen hat eine Prüfung durch einen oder mehrere Prüfer stattzufinden. ²§ 33 Abs. 3 bis 5, die §§ 34, 35 gelten sinngemäß.

(5) § 183a gilt entsprechend.

§ 195 Anmeldung des Beschlusses.

(1) ¹Der Vorstand und der Vorsitzende des Aufsichtsrats haben den Beschluß über die bedingte Kapitalerhöhung zur Eintragung in das Handelsregister anzumelden. ²§ 184 Abs. 1 Satz 3 gilt entsprechend.

(2) Der Anmeldung sind beizufügen

1. bei einer bedingten Kapitalerhöhung mit Sacheinlagen die Verträge, die den Festsetzungen nach § 194 zugrunde liegen oder zu ihrer Ausführung geschlossen worden sind, und der Bericht über die Prüfung von Sacheinlagen (§ 194 Abs. 4) oder die in § 37a Abs. 3 bezeichneten Anlagen;
2. eine Berechnung der Kosten, die für die Gesellschaft durch die Ausgabe der Bezugsaktien entstehen werden.

(3) ¹Das Gericht kann die Eintragung ablehnen, wenn der Wert der Sacheinlage nicht unwesentlich hinter dem geringsten Ausgabebetrag der dafür zu gewährenden Aktien zurückbleibt. ²Wird von einer Prüfung der Sacheinlage nach § 183a Abs. 1 abgesehen, gilt § 38 Abs. 3 entsprechend.

(2) ¹Sec. 27 paras. 3 and 4 shall apply accordingly; the time of the application pursuant to sec. 27 para. 3 sentence 3 and of the registration pursuant to sec. 27 para. 3 sentence 4 shall in each case be replaced by the time of issuance of the preemptive shares.

(3) Paras. 1 and 2 shall not apply to contributions of accounts receivables of the employees of the company by virtue of a profit-sharing plan established by the company for their benefit.

(4) ¹One or more auditors shall conduct an audit when there is to be a capital increase against contributions in kind. ²Sec. 33 paras. 3 to 5, sec. 34, 35 shall apply accordingly.

(5) Sec. 183a shall apply accordingly.

§ 195 Application for the resolution.

(1) ¹The management board and the chairman of the supervisory board shall apply for the resolution on the contingent capital increase to be registered in the commercial register. ²Sec. 184 para. 1 sentence 3 shall apply accordingly.

(2) The application shall be accompanied by:

1. in the case of a contingent capital increase against a contribution in kind, the agreements that lay the basis for the stipulations pursuant to sec. 194 or those concluded in execution thereof, and the audit report pertaining to such contribution in kind (sec. 194 para. 4) or the attachments set forth in sec. 37a para. 3;
2. a computation of the costs to be incurred by the company as a result of the issue of the preemptive shares.

(3) ¹The court may refuse the registration if the value of the contribution in kind substantially falls short of the lowest issue price of the shares to be granted in return. ²If an audit of the contribution in kind is omitted pursuant to sec. 183a para. 1, sec. 38 para. 3 shall apply accordingly.

§ 196 *(aufgehoben)*

§ 196 *(repealed)*

§ 197 Verbotene Aktienausgabe.

¹Vor der Eintragung des Beschlusses über die bedingte Kapitalerhöhung können die Bezugsaktien nicht ausgegeben werden. ²Ein Anspruch des Bezugsberechtigten entsteht vor diesem Zeitpunkt nicht. ³Die vorher ausgegebenen Bezugsaktien sind nichtig. ⁴Für den Schaden aus der Ausgabe sind die Ausgeber den Inhabern als Gesamtschuldner verantwortlich.

§ 197 Prohibited issue of shares.

¹Preemptive shares may not be issued prior to the registration of the resolution on the contingent capital increase. ² No claim pertaining to the shares shall accrue to a party with subscription rights prior to such registration. ³Any certificates for preemptive shares issued previously shall be null and void. ⁴The issuers of such shares shall be jointly and severally liable to the holders for damages arising from the issue.

§ 198 Bezugserklärung.

(1) ¹Das Bezugsrecht wird durch schriftliche Erklärung ausgeübt. ²Die Erklärung (Bezugserklärung) soll doppelt ausgestellt werden. ³Sie hat die Beteiligung nach der Zahl und bei Nennbetragsaktien dem Nennbetrag und, wenn mehrere Gattungen ausgegeben werden, der Gattung der Aktien, die Feststellungen nach § 193 Abs. 2, die nach § 194 bei der Einbringung von Sacheinlagen vorgesehenen Festsetzungen sowie den Tag anzugeben, an dem der Beschluß über die bedingte Kapitalerhöhung gefaßt worden ist.

(2) ¹Die Bezugserklärung hat die gleiche Wirkung wie eine Zeichnungserklärung. ²Bezugserklärungen, deren Inhalt nicht dem Absatz 1 entspricht oder die Beschränkungen der Verpflichtung des Erklärenden enthalten, sind nichtig.

(3) Werden Bezugsaktien ungeachtet der Nichtigkeit einer Bezugserklärung ausgegeben, so kann sich der Erklärende auf die Nichtigkeit nicht berufen, wenn er auf Grund der Bezugserklärung als Aktionär Rechte ausgeübt oder Verpflichtungen erfüllt hat.

(4) Jede nicht in der Bezugserklärung enthaltene Beschränkung ist der Gesellschaft gegenüber unwirksam.

§ 198 Exercise notice.

(1) ¹The subscription right shall be exercised by submitting a written notice to such effect. ²Such notice (exercise notice) shall be executed in duplicate. ³It shall state the number, and in the case of par value shares, the nominal value, and if more than one class is being issued, the class of the shares, the stipulations pursuant to sec. 193 para. 2, the stipulations required under sec. 194 for contributions in kind, as well as the date on which the resolution on the contingent capital increase was adopted.

(2) ¹The exercise notice shall have the same effect as a subscription declaration. ²An exercise notice whose contents are not in compliance with para. 1, or one containing limitations on the obligations of the shareholder submitting the exercise notice shall be null and void.

(3) Where preemptive shares are issued despite the nullity of the exercise notice, the person submitting the exercise notice may not claim relief by reason of the nullity of such notice if he has either exercised rights or discharged obligations as a shareholder by virtue of that exercise notice.

(4) Any limitation not stated in the exercise notice shall be invalid vis-à-vis the company.

§ 199 Ausgabe der Bezugsaktien.

(1) Der Vorstand darf die Bezugsaktien nur in Erfüllung des im Beschluß über die bedingte Kapitalerhöhung festgesetzten Zwecks und nicht vor der vollen Leistung des Gegenwerts ausgeben, der sich aus dem Beschluß ergibt.

(2) ¹Der Vorstand darf Bezugsaktien gegen Wandelschuldverschreibungen nur ausgeben, wenn der Unterschied zwischen dem Ausgabebetrag der zum Umtausch eingereichten Schuldverschreibungen und dem höheren geringsten Ausgabebetrag der für sie zu gewährenden Bezugsaktien aus einer anderen Gewinnrücklage, soweit sie zu diesem Zweck verwandt werden kann, oder durch Zuzahlung des Umtauschberechtigten gedeckt ist. ²Dies gilt nicht, wenn der Gesamtbetrag, zu dem die Schuldverschreibungen ausgegeben sind, den geringsten Ausgabebetrag der Bezugsaktien insgesamt erreicht oder übersteigt.

§ 200 Wirksamwerden der bedingten Kapitalerhöhung.

Mit der Ausgabe der Bezugsaktien ist das Grundkapital erhöht.

§ 201 Anmeldung der Ausgabe von Bezugsaktien.

(1) Der Vorstand meldet ausgegebene Bezugsaktien zur Eintragung in das Handelsregister mindestens einmal jährlich bis spätestens zum Ende des auf den Ablauf des Geschäftsjahrs folgenden Kalendermonats an.

(2) ¹Der Anmeldung sind die Zweitschriften der Bezugserklärungen und ein vom Vorstand unterschriebenes Verzeichnis der Personen, die das Bezugsrecht ausgeübt haben, beizufügen. ²Das Verzeichnis hat die auf jeden Aktionär entfallenden Aktien und die auf sie gemachten Einlagen anzugeben.

§ 199 Issue of preemptive shares.

(1) The management board may only issue preemptive shares in order to achieve the purpose stipulated in the resolution on the contingent capital increase, and may not issue such shares before full payment of the consideration provided for in such resolution.

(2) ¹The management board may issue preemptive shares against convertible bonds only if the difference between the issue price of the bonds surrendered for conversion and the higher lowest issue price of the preemptive shares is covered by another revenue reserve which may be used for such purpose or by an additional payment from the person entitled to conversion. ²The foregoing shall not apply if the aggregate amount for which the bonds were issued equals or exceeds the lowest issue price for the preemptive shares.

§ 200 Effectiveness of the contingent capital increase.

The capital increase shall become effective upon the issue of preemptive shares.

§ 201 Application for the issue of preemptive shares.

(1) Within one month after the end of the fiscal year, the management board shall at least once a year apply for registration with the commercial register to what extent in the foregoing fiscal year preemptive shares were issued.

(2) ¹The application shall be accompanied by duplicates of the exercise notices and a complete list of the names of all those who have exercised subscription rights, signed by the management board. ²The list shall the specify the shares issued to each party and the respective contribution made in consideration thereof.

(3) In der Anmeldung hat der Vorstand zu erklären, daß die Bezugsaktien nur in Erfüllung des im Beschluß über die bedingte Kapitalerhöhung festgesetzten Zwecks und nicht vor der vollen Leistung des Gegenwerts ausgegeben worden sind, der sich aus dem Beschluß ergibt.

(3) In the application, the management board shall state that the shares were issued only in order to achieve the purpose stipulated in the resolution on the contingent capital increase, and that no shares were issued prior to the full payment of the consideration provided for in such resolution.

**Dritter Unterabschnitt.
Genehmigtes Kapital**

**Subsection Three.
Authorized Capital**

§ 202 Voraussetzungen.

§ 202 Requirements.

(1) Die Satzung kann den Vorstand für höchstens fünf Jahre nach Eintragung der Gesellschaft ermächtigen, das Grundkapital bis zu einem bestimmten Nennbetrag (genehmigtes Kapital) durch Ausgabe neuer Aktien gegen Einlagen zu erhöhen.

(1) The articles of association may authorize the management board, for a period not exceeding five years after the date of registration of the company, to increase the registered share capital up to a specified nominal value ("authorized capital") by the issue of new shares against contributions.

(2) [1]Die Ermächtigung kann auch durch Satzungsänderung für höchstens fünf Jahre nach Eintragung der Satzungsänderung erteilt werden. [2]Der Beschluß der Hauptversammlung bedarf einer Mehrheit, die mindestens drei Viertel des bei der Beschlußfassung vertretenen Grundkapitals umfaßt. [3]Die Satzung kann eine größere Kapitalmehrheit und weitere Erfordernisse bestimmen. [4]§ 182 Abs. 2 gilt.

(2) [1]Such authorization may also be granted via an amendment to the articles of association for a period not exceeding five years after the date of registration of the amendment. [2]The resolution of the general meeting requires a majority of at least three quarters of the registered share capital represented at the adoption of the resolution. [3]The articles of association may stipulate a larger capital majority and further requirements. [4]Sec. 182 para. 2 shall apply.

(3) [1]Der Nennbetrag des genehmigten Kapitals darf die Hälfte des Grundkapitals, das zur Zeit der Ermächtigung vorhanden ist, nicht übersteigen. [2]Die neuen Aktien sollen nur mit Zustimmung des Aufsichtsrats ausgegeben werden. [3]§ 182 Abs. 1 Satz 5 gilt sinngemäß.

(3) [1]The nominal value of the authorized capital may not exceed one half of the registered share capital available at the time the authorization is granted. [2]The new shares shall only be issued with the consent of the supervisory board. [3]Sec. 182 para. 1 sentence 5 shall apply accordingly.

(4) Die Satzung kann auch vorsehen, daß die neuen Aktien an Arbeitnehmer der Gesellschaft ausgegeben werden.

(4) The articles of association may also provide for new shares to be issued to employees of the company.

§ 203 Ausgabe der neuen Aktien.

§ 203 Issue of new shares.

(1) [1]Für die Ausgabe der neuen Aktien gelten sinngemäß, soweit sich aus den

(1) [1]Unless provided otherwise in the following provisions, sec. 185 to 191 re-

folgenden Vorschriften nichts anderes ergibt, §§ 185 bis 191 über die Kapitalerhöhung gegen Einlagen. ²An die Stelle des Beschlusses über die Erhöhung des Grundkapitals tritt die Ermächtigung der Satzung zur Ausgabe neuer Aktien.

(2) ¹Die Ermächtigung kann vorsehen, daß der Vorstand über den Ausschluß des Bezugsrechts entscheidet. ²Wird eine Ermächtigung, die dies vorsieht, durch Satzungsänderung erteilt, so gilt § 186 Abs. 4 sinngemäß.

(3) ¹Die neuen Aktien sollen nicht ausgegeben werden, solange ausstehende Einlagen auf das bisherige Grundkapital noch erlangt werden können. ²Für Versicherungsgesellschaften kann die Satzung etwas anderes bestimmen. ³Stehen Einlagen in verhältnismäßig unerheblichem Umfang aus, so hindert dies die Ausgabe der neuen Aktien nicht. ⁴In der ersten Anmeldung der Durchführung der Erhöhung des Grundkapitals ist anzugeben, welche Einlagen auf das bisherige Grundkapital noch nicht geleistet sind und warum sie nicht erlangt werden können.

(4) Absatz 3 Satz 1 und 4 gilt nicht, wenn die Aktien an Arbeitnehmer der Gesellschaft ausgegeben werden.

§ 204 Bedingungen der Aktienausgabe.

(1) ¹Über den Inhalt der Aktienrechte und die Bedingungen der Aktienausgabe entscheidet der Vorstand, soweit die Ermächtigung keine Bestimmungen enthält. ²Die Entscheidung des Vorstands bedarf der Zustimmung des Aufsichtsrats; gleiches gilt für die Entscheidung des Vorstands nach § 203 Abs. 2 über den Ausschluß des Bezugsrechts.

(2) Sind Vorzugsaktien ohne Stimmrecht vorhanden, so können Vorzugsaktien,

lating to a capital increase against contributions shall apply accordingly to the issue of new shares. ²In applying such provisions, the resolution increasing the registered share capital shall be substituted by the authorization to issue new shares stipulated in the articles of association.

(2) ¹The authorization may grant the management board discretionary power to exclude the subscription right. ²If such authorization is granted via an amendment to the articles of association, sec. 186 para. 4 shall apply accordingly.

(3) ¹The new shares shall not be issued as long as outstanding contributions to the current registered share capital are still obtainable. ²The articles of association may provide otherwise in the case of insurance companies. ³If the amount of such outstanding contributions is relatively insignificant, this shall not preclude the issue of new shares. ⁴In the initial application for registration of the implementation of the capital increase, the outstanding contributions to the current registered share capital shall be stated, with an explanation as to why they are unobtainable.

(4) Para. 3 sentences 1 and 4 shall not apply if the shares have been issued to company employees.

§ 204 Conditions of the share issue.

(1) ¹Unless the authorization provides otherwise, the management board shall determine the shareholder rights and the conditions to which the issue of the shares shall be subject. ²The decision of the management board shall require the consent of the supervisory board; the same shall apply to the management board's decision pertaining to the exclusion of the subscription right pursuant to sec. 203 para. 2.

(2) If preference shares without voting rights have previously been issued,

die bei der Verteilung des Gewinns oder des Gesellschaftsvermögens ihnen vorgehen oder gleichstehen, nur ausgegeben werden, wenn die Ermächtigung es vorsieht.

(3) ¹Weist ein Jahresabschluß, der mit einem uneingeschränkten Bestätigungsvermerk versehen ist, einen Jahresüberschuß aus, so können Aktien an Arbeitnehmer der Gesellschaft auch in der Weise ausgegeben werden, daß die auf sie zu leistende Einlage aus dem Teil des Jahresüberschusses gedeckt wird, den nach § 58 Abs. 2 Vorstand und Aufsichtsrat in andere Gewinnrücklagen einstellen können. ²Für die Ausgabe der neuen Aktien gelten die Vorschriften über eine Kapitalerhöhung gegen Bareinlagen, ausgenommen § 188 Abs. 2. ³Der Anmeldung der Durchführung der Erhöhung des Grundkapitals ist außerdem der festgestellte Jahresabschluß mit Bestätigungsvermerk beizufügen. ⁴Die Anmeldenden haben ferner die Erklärung nach § 210 Abs. 1 Satz 2 abzugeben.

new preference shares which entitle the holder to the same or superior rights to dividends and distributions of the corporate assets may only be issued if the authorization so provides.

(3) ¹If annual financial statements furnished with an unqualified certification of the auditor of annual financial statements reveal an annual net income, shares may be issued to employees in such a manner that the contributions due in consideration thereof are covered by that portion of annual net income which, pursuant to sec. 58 para. 2, may be allocated at the discretion of the management board and the supervisory board to other revenue reserves. ²With the exception of sec. 188 para. 2, all provisions pertaining to a capital increase against cash contributions shall apply to the issue of new shares. ³The application for registration of the implementation of the capital increase shall be accompanied by the annual financial statements furnished with a certification of the auditor of annual financial statements. ⁴The applicants shall also make a declaration as stipulated in sec. 210 para. 1 sentence 2.

§ 205 Ausgabe gegen Sacheinlagen. Rückzahlung von Einlagen.

(1) Gegen Sacheinlagen dürfen Aktien nur ausgegeben werden, wenn die Ermächtigung es vorsieht.

(2) ¹Der Gegenstand der Sacheinlage, die Person, von der die Gesellschaft den Gegenstand erwirbt, und der Nennbetrag, bei Stückaktien die Zahl der bei der Sacheinlage zu gewährenden Aktien sind, wenn sie nicht in der Ermächtigung festgesetzt sind, vom Vorstand festzusetzen und in den Zeichnungsschein aufzunehmen. ²Der Vorstand soll die Entscheidung nur mit Zustimmung des Aufsichtsrats treffen.

(3) § 27 Abs. 3 und 4 gilt entsprechend.

§ 205 Issue against contributions in kind. Repayment of contributions.

(1) Shares may only be issued against contributions in kind if the authorization so provides.

(2) ¹To the extent that they have not been stipulated in the authorization, the management board shall stipulate the object of the contribution in kind, the party from whom the company is to receive it, its nominal value, and in the case of non-par value shares, the number of shares to be granted in consideration thereof, and this information shall be stated in the subscription certificate. ²The management board's decision shall require the consent of the supervisory board.

(3) Sec. 27 paras. 3 and 4 shall apply accordingly.

(4) Die Absätze 2 und 3 gelten nicht für die Einlage von Geldforderungen, die Arbeitnehmern der Gesellschaft aus einer ihnen von der Gesellschaft eingeräumten Gewinnbeteiligung zustehen.

(5) ¹Bei Ausgabe der Aktien gegen Sacheinlagen hat eine Prüfung durch einen oder mehrere Prüfer stattzufinden; § 33 Abs. 3 bis 5, die §§ 34, 35 gelten sinngemäß. ²§ 183a ist entsprechend anzuwenden. ³Anstelle des Datums des Beschlusses über die Kapitalerhöhung hat der Vorstand seine Entscheidung über die Ausgabe neuer Aktien gegen Sacheinlagen sowie die Angaben nach § 37a Abs. 1 und 2 in den Geschäftsblättern bekannt zu machen.

(6) Soweit eine Prüfung der Sacheinlage nicht stattfindet, gilt für die Anmeldung der Durchführung der Kapitalerhöhung zur Eintragung in das Handelsregister (§ 203 Abs. 1 Satz 1, § 188) auch § 184 Abs. 1 Satz 3 und Abs. 2 entsprechend.

(7) ¹Das Gericht kann die Eintragung ablehnen, wenn der Wert der Sacheinlage nicht unwesentlich hinter dem geringsten Ausgabebetrag der dafür zu gewährenden Aktien zurückbleibt. ²Wird von einer Prüfung der Sacheinlage nach § 183a Abs. 1 abgesehen, gilt § 38 Abs. 3 entsprechend.

§ 206 Verträge über Sacheinlagen vor Eintragung der Gesellschaft.

¹Sind vor Eintragung der Gesellschaft Verträge geschlossen worden, nach denen auf das genehmigte Kapital eine Sacheinlage zu leisten ist, so muß die Satzung die Festsetzungen enthalten, die für eine Ausgabe gegen Sacheinlagen vorgeschrieben sind. ²Dabei gelten sinngemäß § 27 Abs. 3 und 5, die §§ 32 bis 35, 37 Abs. 4 Nr. 2, 4 und 5, die §§ 37a, 38 Abs. 2 und 3 sowie § 49 über die Gründung der Gesellschaft. ³An die Stelle der

(4) Paras. 2 and 3 shall not apply to the contribution of claims for money which are due to employees of the company from a profit participation granted to them by the company.

(5) ¹For the issue of shares against contributions in kind, an audit shall be conducted by one or more auditors; sec. 33 paras. 3 to 5, sec. 34, 35 shall apply accordingly. ²Sec. 183a shall apply accordingly. ³Instead of announcing the date of the resolution on the capital increase, the management board shall announce its decision concerning the issuance of new shares against contributions in kind as well as the information pursuant to sec. 37a paras. 1 and 2 in the company's designated journals.

(6) To the extent that an audit of the contribution in kind does not take place, sec. 184 para. 1 sentence 3 and para. 2 shall also apply accordingly to the application for registration in the commercial register of the implementation of the capital increase (sec. 203 para. 1 sentence 1, sec. 188).

(7) ¹The court may refuse registration if the value of the contribution in kind is not inconsiderably lower than the lowest issue price of the shares granted in return. ²If an audit of the contribution in kind pursuant to sec. 183a para. 1 is omitted, sec. 38 para. 3 shall apply accordingly.

§ 206 Agreements on contributions in kind prior to the registration of the company.

¹If any agreements requiring a contribution in kind to be made towards authorized capital are concluded prior to the registration of the company, the articles of association shall contain those stipulations prescribed in the event of an issue of shares against contributions in kind. ²In this regard, sec. 27 paras. 3 and 5, sec. 32 to 35, 37 para. 4 no. 2, 4 and 5, sec. 37a, 38 paras. 2 and 3 as well as sec. 49 pertaining to the formation of

Gründer tritt der Vorstand und an die Stelle der Anmeldung und Eintragung der Gesellschaft die Anmeldung und Eintragung der Durchführung der Erhöhung des Grundkapitals.	the company shall apply accordingly. ³In applying such provisions, the founders shall be substituted by the management board, and the application and registration of the company shall be substituted by the application and registration of the implementation of the capital increase.

Vierter Unterabschnitt. Kapitalerhöhung aus Gesellschaftsmitteln

Subsection Four. Capital Increase from Company Resources

§ 207 Voraussetzungen.

§ 207 Requirements.

(1) Die Hauptversammlung kann eine Erhöhung des Grundkapitals durch Umwandlung der Kapitalrücklage und von Gewinnrücklagen in Grundkapital beschließen.

(1) The general meeting may resolve to increase the registered share capital by converting the capital reserve and revenue reserves into registered share capital.

(2) ¹Für den Beschluß und für die Anmeldung des Beschlusses gelten § 182 Abs. 1, § 184 Abs. 1 sinngemäß. ²Gesellschaften mit Stückaktien können ihr Grundkapital auch ohne Ausgabe neuer Aktien erhöhen; der Beschluß über die Kapitalerhöhung muß die Art der Erhöhung angeben.

(2) ¹Sec. 182 para. 1, sec. 184 para. 1 shall apply accordingly with regard to both the resolution and the application for the registration of the resolution. ²Companies with non-par value shares may increase their registered share capital without the issue of new shares; the resolution on the capital increase shall specify the type of increase to be effected.

(3) Dem Beschluß ist eine Bilanz zugrunde zu legen.

(3) The resolution shall be based on a balance sheet.

§ 208 Umwandlungsfähigkeit von Kapital- und Gewinnrücklagen.

§ 208 Capital and revenue reserves that may be converted.

(1) ¹Die Kapitalrücklage und die Gewinnrücklagen, die in Grundkapital umgewandelt werden sollen, müssen in der letzten Jahresbilanz und, wenn dem Beschluß eine andere Bilanz zugrunde gelegt wird, auch in dieser Bilanz unter „Kapitalrücklage" oder „Gewinnrücklagen" oder im letzten Beschluß über die Verwendung des Jahresüberschusses oder des Bilanzgewinns als Zuführung zu diesen Rücklagen ausgewiesen sein. ²Vorbehaltlich des Absatzes 2 können andere Gewinnrücklagen und deren Zuführungen in voller Höhe, die Kapitalrücklage und die gesetzliche Rücklage sowie deren Zuführungen nur, soweit sie zusammen den zehnten oder

(1) ¹The capital reserve and the revenue reserves which are to be converted into registered share capital shall have been designated as "capital reserve" or "revenue reserves" in the latest annual balance sheet, and if the resolution is based on another balance, in such other balance sheet on which the resolution is to be based, or they shall have appeared in the latest resolution on the appropriation of the annual net income or balance sheet profit as amounts to be allocated to such reserves. ²Subject to the provisions of para. 2, the full amount of other revenue reserves and allocations thereto, the capital reserve, and the statutory reserve along with allocations thereto

den in der Satzung bestimmten höheren Teil des bisherigen Grundkapitals übersteigen, in Grundkapital umgewandelt werden.

(2) ¹Die Kapitalrücklage und die Gewinnrücklagen sowie deren Zuführungen können nicht umgewandelt werden, soweit in der zugrunde gelegten Bilanz ein Verlust einschließlich eines Verlustvortrags ausgewiesen ist. ²Gewinnrücklagen und deren Zuführungen, die für einen bestimmten Zweck bestimmt sind, dürfen nur umgewandelt werden, soweit dies mit ihrer Zweckbestimmung vereinbar ist.

§ 209 Zugrunde gelegte Bilanz.

(1) Dem Beschluß kann die letzte Jahresbilanz zugrunde gelegt werden, wenn die Jahresbilanz geprüft und die festgestellte Jahresbilanz mit dem uneingeschränkten Bestätigungsvermerk des Abschlußprüfers versehen ist und wenn ihr Stichtag höchstens acht Monate vor der Anmeldung des Beschlusses zur Eintragung in das Handelsregister liegt.

(2) ¹Wird dem Beschluß nicht die letzte Jahresbilanz zugrunde gelegt, so muß die Bilanz §§ 150, 152 dieses Gesetzes, §§ 242 bis 256a, 264 bis 274a des Handelsgesetzbuchs entsprechen. ²Der Stichtag der Bilanz darf höchstens acht Monate vor der Anmeldung des Beschlusses zur Eintragung in das Handelsregister liegen.

(3) ¹Die Bilanz muß durch einen Abschlußprüfer darauf geprüft werden, ob sie §§ 150, 152 dieses Gesetzes, §§ 242 bis 256a, 264 bis 274a des Handelsgesetzbuchs entspricht. ²Sie muß mit einem uneingeschränkten Bestätigungsvermerk versehen sein.

may be converted into registered share capital only if the aggregate amount thereof exceeds one tenth, or such higher proportion as may be stipulated in the articles of association, of the existing registered share capital.

(2) ¹Neither the capital reserve nor the revenue reserves and allocations thereto may be converted if the relevant balance sheet shows a loss, including a loss carried forward. ²Revenue reserves and allocations thereto that have been designated for a specific purpose may only be converted in so far as a conversion is compatible with such designated purpose.

§ 209 Relevant balance sheet.

(1) The latest annual balance sheet can be used as a basis for the resolution if the annual balance sheet has been audited and the formally approved annual balance sheet has been furnished with an unqualified certification of the auditor of annual financial statements, and if its record date is no more than eight months prior to the application for registration of the resolution with the commercial register.

(2) ¹If the resolution is not based on the latest annual balance sheet, the relevant balance sheet shall comply with sec. 150, 152 of this Act, sec. 242 to 256a, sec. 264 to 274a of the Commercial Code. ²The record date of such balance sheet may not be more than eight months prior to the application for registration of the resolution in the commercial register.

(3) ¹The balance sheet shall be audited by an auditor of annual financial statements to ascertain whether it complies with the sec. 150 and 152 of this Act, and sec. 242 to 256a, sec. 264 to 274a of the Commercial Code. ²Such balance sheet shall be furnished with an unqualified certification of the auditor of annual financial statements.

(4) ¹Wenn die Hauptversammlung keinen anderen Prüfer wählt, gilt der Prüfer als gewählt, der für die Prüfung des letzten Jahresabschlusses von der Hauptversammlung gewählt oder vom Gericht bestellt worden ist. ²Soweit sich aus der Besonderheit des Prüfungsauftrags nichts anderes ergibt, sind auf die Prüfung § 318 Abs. 1 Satz 3 und 4, § 319 Abs. 1 bis 4, § 319a Abs. 1, § 319b Abs. 1, § 320 Abs. 1, 2, §§ 321, 322 Abs. 7 und § 323 des Handelsgesetzbuchs entsprechend anzuwenden.

(5) ¹Bei Versicherungsgesellschaften wird der Prüfer vom Aufsichtsrat bestimmt; Absatz 4 Satz 1 gilt sinngemäß. ²Soweit sich aus der Besonderheit des Prüfungsauftrags nichts anderes ergibt, ist auf die Prüfung § 341k des Handelsgesetzbuchs anzuwenden.

(6) Im Fall der Absätze 2 bis 5 gilt für das Zugänglichmachen der Bilanz und für die Erteilung von Abschriften § 175 Abs. 2 sinngemäß.

§ 210 Anmeldung und Eintragung des Beschlusses.

(1) ¹Der Anmeldung des Beschlusses zur Eintragung in das Handelsregister ist die der Kapitalerhöhung zugrunde gelegte Bilanz mit Bestätigungsvermerk, im Fall des § 209 Abs. 2 bis 6 außerdem die letzte Jahresbilanz, sofern sie noch nicht nach § 325 Abs. 1 des Handelsgesetzbuchs eingereicht ist, beizufügen. ²Die Anmeldenden haben dem Gericht gegenüber zu erklären, daß nach ihrer Kenntnis seit dem Stichtag der zugrunde gelegten Bilanz bis zum Tag der Anmeldung keine Vermögensminderung eingetreten ist, die der Kapitalerhöhung entgegenstünde, wenn sie am Tag der Anmeldung beschlossen worden wäre.

(2) Das Gericht darf den Beschluß nur eintragen, wenn die der Kapitalerhöhung zugrunde gelegte Bilanz auf einen höchstens acht Monate vor der An-

(4) ¹If the general meeting does not elect another auditor, the auditor who was elected by the general meeting to audit the last annual financial statements or who was appointed by the court for that purpose shall be deemed to have been elected. ²Unless the special nature of the audit requires otherwise, sec. 318 para. 1 sentences 3 and 4, sec. 319 paras. 1 to 4, sec. 319a para. 1, sec. 319b para. 1, sec. 320 paras. 1, 2, sec. 321 and 322 para. 7 and sec. 323 of the Commercial Code shall apply accordingly to the audit.

(5) ¹In the case of insurance companies, the auditor shall be appointed by the supervisory board; para. 4 sentence 1 shall apply accordingly. ²Unless the special nature of the audit requires otherwise, sec. 341k of the Commercial Code shall apply to the audit.

(6) In the case of paras. 2 to 5, sec. 175 para. 2 shall apply accordingly to the granting of access to the balance sheet and the furnishing of copies thereof.

§ 210 Application and registration of the resolution.

(1) ¹The application for the registration of the resolution in the commercial register shall be accompanied by the balance sheet furnished with a certification of the auditor on which the capital increase is based and, in the case of sec. 209 paras. 2 to 6, the latest annual balance sheet, if not previously submitted pursuant to sec. 325 para. 1 of the Commercial Code. ²The applicants shall declare before the court that, to their knowledge, no decline in the value of company assets has occurred between the record date of the relevant balance sheet and the date of the application to such extent as would preclude the capital increase if such resolution were to be adopted on the date of application.

(2) The court may register the resolution only if the record date of the balance sheet on which the capital increase is based is no more than eight months

meldung liegenden Stichtag aufgestellt und eine Erklärung nach Absatz 1 Satz 2 abgegeben worden ist.

(3) Das Gericht braucht nicht zu prüfen, ob die Bilanzen den gesetzlichen Vorschriften entsprechen.

(4) Bei der Eintragung des Beschlusses ist anzugeben, daß es sich um eine Kapitalerhöhung aus Gesellschaftsmitteln handelt.

§ 211 Wirksamwerden der Kapitalerhöhung.

(1) Mit der Eintragung des Beschlusses über die Erhöhung des Grundkapitals ist das Grundkapital erhöht.

(2) (aufgehoben)

§ 212 Aus der Kapitalerhöhung Berechtigte.

[1]Neue Aktien stehen den Aktionären im Verhältnis ihrer Anteile am bisherigen Grundkapital zu. [2]Ein entgegenstehender Beschluß der Hauptversammlung ist nichtig.

§ 213 Teilrechte.

(1) Führt die Kapitalerhöhung dazu, daß auf einen Anteil am bisherigen Grundkapital nur ein Teil einer neuen Aktie entfällt, so ist dieses Teilrecht selbständig veräußerlich und vererblich.

(2) Die Rechte aus einer neuen Aktie einschließlich des Anspruchs auf Ausstellung einer Aktienurkunde können nur ausgeübt werden, wenn Teilrechte, die zusammen eine volle Aktie ergeben, in einer Hand vereinigt sind oder wenn sich mehrere Berechtigte, deren Teilrechte zusammen eine volle Aktie ergeben, zur Ausübung der Rechte zusammenschließen.

§ 214 Aufforderung an die Aktionäre.

(1) [1]Nach der Eintragung des Beschlusses über die Erhöhung des Grundkapi-

prior to the date of application and a declaration in accordance with para. 1 sentence 2 has been made.

(3) The court does not need to review whether the balance sheets comply with statutory provisions.

(4) The registration of the resolution shall state that it pertains to a capital increase from company resources.

§ 211 Effectiveness of the capital increase.

(1) The increase of registered share capital shall become effective upon registration of the resolution on the capital increase.

(2) (repealed)

§ 212 Persons entitled to new shares resulting from the capital increase.

[1]New shares shall be allocated to the shareholders in proportion to their holdings in the previous registered share capital. [2]Any resolution of the general meeting to the contrary shall be null and void.

§ 213 Fractional shares.

(1) If the capital increase results in only a fraction of a new share being allocated to a holding in the previous registered share capital, such fractional share may be separately disposed of or inherited.

(2) The rights deriving from a new share, including the claim to issue a share certificate, can be exercised only when fractional shares that together comprise a full share become consolidated in the hands of a single owner or when several entitled persons whose fractional shares together result in a full share join together to exercise the rights.

§ 214 Call to the shareholders.

(1) [1]After the resolution on increasing the registered share capital by issue

tals durch Ausgabe neuer Aktien hat der Vorstand unverzüglich die Aktionäre aufzufordern, die neuen Aktien abzuholen. ²Die Aufforderung ist in den Gesellschaftsblättern bekanntzumachen. ³In der Bekanntmachung ist anzugeben,

1. um welchen Betrag das Grundkapital erhöht worden ist,
2. in welchem Verhältnis auf die alten Aktien neue Aktien entfallen.

⁴In der Bekanntmachung ist ferner darauf hinzuweisen, daß die Gesellschaft berechtigt ist, Aktien, die nicht innerhalb eines Jahres seit der Bekanntmachung der Aufforderung abgeholt werden, nach dreimaliger Androhung für Rechnung der Beteiligten zu verkaufen.

(2) ¹Nach Ablauf eines Jahres seit der Bekanntmachung der Aufforderung hat die Gesellschaft den Verkauf der nicht abgeholten Aktien anzudrohen. ²Die Androhung ist dreimal in Abständen von mindestens einem Monat in den Gesellschaftsblättern bekanntzumachen. ³Die letzte Bekanntmachung muß vor dem Ablauf von achtzehn Monaten seit der Bekanntmachung der Aufforderung ergehen.

(3) ¹Nach Ablauf eines Jahres seit der letzten Bekanntmachung der Androhung hat die Gesellschaft die nicht abgeholten Aktien für Rechnung der Beteiligten zum Börsenpreis und beim Fehlen eines Börsenpreises durch öffentliche Versteigerung zu verkaufen. ²§ 226 Abs. 3 Satz 2 bis 6 gilt sinngemäß.

(4) ¹Die Absätze 1 bis 3 gelten sinngemäß für Gesellschaften, die keine Aktienurkunden ausgegeben haben. ²Die Gesellschaften haben die Aktionäre aufzufordern, sich die neuen Aktien zuteilen zu lassen.

of new shares has been registered, the management board shall without undue delay call on the shareholders to collect the new share certificates. ²The call shall be announced in the company's designated journals. ³The announcement shall state:

1. the amount by which the registered share capital has been increased,
2. the proportion in which the new shares have been allocated to previously existing shares.

⁴The announcement shall further state that the company may, after three warnings, sell any shares for the account of the persons entitled thereto which have not been collected within one year of the announcement of the call.

(2) ¹After expiration of one year from the date the call is announced, the company shall issue a warning that it may sell any uncollected shares. ²Such warning shall be announced three times at intervals of not less than one month in the company's designated journals. ³The final announcement of the warning shall be announced no later than eighteen months after the date of announcement of the call.

(3) ¹After expiration of one year from the date of the final announcement of the warning, the company shall sell for the account of the persons entitled thereto any uncollected shares at the stock exchange price, and if there is no applicable stock exchange price, by public auction. ²Sec. 226 para. 3 sentences 2 to 6 shall apply accordingly.

(4) ¹Paras. 1 to 3 shall apply accordingly to companies that have not issued share certificates. ²Such companies shall call on the shareholders to accept the allocation of new shares.

§ 215 Eigene Aktien. Teileingezahlte Aktien.

(1) Eigene Aktien nehmen an der Erhöhung des Grundkapitals teil.

(2) ¹Teileingezahlte Aktien nehmen entsprechend ihrem Anteil am Grundkapital an der Erhöhung des Grundkapitals teil. ²Bei ihnen kann die Kapitalerhöhung nicht durch Ausgabe neuer Aktien ausgeführt werden, bei Nennbetragsaktien wird deren Nennbetrag erhöht. ³Sind neben teileingezahlten Aktien volleingezahlte Aktien vorhanden, so kann bei volleingezahlten Nennbetragsaktien die Kapitalerhöhung durch Erhöhung des Nennbetrags der Aktien und durch Ausgabe neuer Aktien ausgeführt werden; der Beschluß über die Erhöhung des Grundkapitals muß die Art der Erhöhung angeben. ⁴Soweit die Kapitalerhöhung durch Erhöhung des Nennbetrags der Aktien ausgeführt wird, ist sie so zu bemessen, daß durch sie auf keine Aktie Beträge entfallen, die durch eine Erhöhung des Nennbetrags der Aktien nicht gedeckt werden können.

§ 216 Wahrung der Rechte der Aktionäre und Dritter.

(1) Das Verhältnis der mit den Aktien verbundenen Rechte zueinander wird durch die Kapitalerhöhung nicht berührt.

(2) ¹Soweit sich einzelne Rechte teileingezahlter Aktien, insbesondere die Beteiligung am Gewinn oder das Stimmrecht, nach der auf die Aktie geleisteten Einlage bestimmen, stehen diese Rechte den Aktionären bis zur Leistung der noch ausstehenden Einlagen nur nach der Höhe der geleisteten Einlage, erhöht um den auf den Nennbetrag des Grundkapitals berechneten Hundertsatz der Erhöhung des Grundkapitals zu. ²Werden weitere Einzahlungen geleistet, so erweitern sich diese Rechte entsprechend. ³Im Fall des § 271 Abs. 3 gelten die Erhöhungsbeträge als voll eingezahlt.

§ 215 Own shares. Partially paid shares.

(1) Own shares shall participate in any increase of the registered share capital.

(2) ¹Partially paid shares shall participate in any increase in the registered share capital in proportion to their share in the registered share capital. ²If such shares exist, a capital increase may not be carried out by the issue of new shares, if they are par value shares, their par value may be increased for this purpose. ³If fully paid shares exist in addition to partially paid shares, the capital increase in respect of such fully paid par value shares may be carried out by increasing the par value of the shares and the issue of new shares; the resolution on the capital increase shall specify the manner of the increase. ⁴If the capital increase is effected by increasing the par value of the shares, the capital increase shall be calculated in such a manner that no share shall be allocated an amount which cannot be covered by increasing the par value of the shares.

§ 216 Protection of the rights of shareholders and third parties.

(1) ¹The relationship of the rights attached to the shares to each other is not affected by the capital increase.

(2) ¹To the extent that specific rights arising from partially paid shares, in particular the right to participate in the profits or the voting right, are determined by the contribution made in respect of each share, the shareholders are, until the still outstanding contributions have been made, entitled to these rights only in proportion to the amount of the contribution already made, increased by the percentage of the increase of the registered share capital over the nominal value of the registered share capital. ²If further contributions are made, such rights shall increase proportionately. ³In the case of sec. 271 para. 3 the amounts

(3) ¹Der wirtschaftliche Inhalt vertraglicher Beziehungen der Gesellschaft zu Dritten, die von der Gewinnausschüttung der Gesellschaft, dem Nennbetrag oder Wert ihrer Aktien oder ihres Grundkapitals oder sonst von den bisherigen Kapital- oder Gewinnverhältnissen abhängen, wird durch die Kapitalerhöhung nicht berührt. ²Gleiches gilt für Nebenverpflichtungen der Aktionäre.

§ 217 Beginn der Gewinnbeteiligung.

(1) Neue Aktien nehmen, wenn nichts anderes bestimmt ist, am Gewinn des ganzen Geschäftsjahrs teil, in dem die Erhöhung des Grundkapitals beschlossen worden ist.

(2) ¹Im Beschluß über die Erhöhung des Grundkapitals kann bestimmt werden, daß die neuen Aktien bereits am Gewinn des letzten vor der Beschlußfassung über die Kapitalerhöhung abgelaufenen Geschäftsjahrs teilnehmen. ²In diesem Fall ist die Erhöhung des Grundkapitals zu beschließen, bevor über die Verwendung des Bilanzgewinns des letzten vor der Beschlußfassung abgelaufenen Geschäftsjahrs Beschluß gefaßt ist. ³Der Beschluß über die Verwendung des Bilanzgewinns des letzten vor der Beschlußfassung über die Kapitalerhöhung abgelaufenen Geschäftsjahrs wird erst wirksam, wenn das Grundkapital erhöht ist. ⁴Der Beschluß über die Erhöhung des Grundkapitals und der Beschluß über die Verwendung des Bilanzgewinns des letzten vor der Beschlußfassung über die Kapitalerhöhung abgelaufenen Geschäftsjahrs sind nichtig, wenn der Beschluß über die Kapitalerhöhung nicht binnen drei Monaten nach der Beschlußfassung in das Handelsregister eingetragen worden ist. ⁵Der Lauf der Frist ist gehemmt, solange eine Anfechtungs- oder Nichtigkeitsklage rechtshängig ist.

of the increase shall be deemed to have been paid in full.

(3) ¹The commercial terms of agreements between the company and third parties which depend on the distribution of the company's profits, the nominal value or market value of its shares or registered share capital, or any other way on the previous situation as to capital or profitability, shall not be affected by the capital increase. ²The foregoing shall also apply to the ancillary duties of the shareholders.

§ 217 Commencement of participation in profits.

(1) Unless otherwise provided, the new shares shall participate in profits of the entire fiscal year in which the resolution on the capital increase was adopted.

(2) ¹The resolution on the capital increase may provide that the new shares shall also participate in the profits of the last fiscal year ending prior to the adoption of the resolution on the capital increase. ²In that case the resolution on the capital increase shall be adopted prior to the adoption of the resolution on the appropriation of the balance sheet profit of the last fiscal year ending prior to the adoption of such resolution on the capital increase. ³The resolution on the appropriation of the balance sheet profit of the latest fiscal year ending prior to adoption of the resolution on the capital increase shall become effective only after the registered share capital has been increased. ⁴The resolution on the increase of the registered share capital and the resolution on the appropriation of the balance sheet profit of the latest fiscal year ending prior to the adoption of the resolution on the capital increase shall be null and void if the resolution on the capital increase has not been registered in the commercial register within three months following the adoption of the resolution. ⁵The running of such period shall be suspended for such time

as an action to set aside a resolution or an action for the declaration of nullity of a resolution is pending.

§ 218 Bedingtes Kapital.

¹Bedingtes Kapital erhöht sich im gleichen Verhältnis wie das Grundkapital. ²Ist das bedingte Kapital zur Gewährung von Umtauschrechten an Gläubiger von Wandelschuldverschreibungen beschlossen worden, so ist zur Deckung des Unterschieds zwischen dem Ausgabebetrag der Schuldverschreibungen und dem höheren geringsten Ausgabebetrag der für sie zu gewährenden Bezugsaktien insgesamt eine Sonderrücklage zu bilden, soweit nicht Zuzahlungen der Umtauschberechtigten vereinbart sind.

§ 219 Verbotene Ausgabe von Aktien und Zwischenscheinen.

Vor der Eintragung des Beschlusses über die Erhöhung des Grundkapitals in das Handelsregister dürfen neue Aktien und Zwischenscheine nicht ausgegeben werden.

§ 220 Wertansätze.

¹Als Anschaffungskosten der vor der Erhöhung des Grundkapitals erworbenen Aktien und der auf sie entfallenen neuen Aktien gelten die Beträge, die sich für die einzelnen Aktien ergeben, wenn die Anschaffungskosten der vor der Erhöhung des Grundkapitals erworbenen Aktien auf diese und auf die auf sie entfallenen neuen Aktien nach dem Verhältnis der Anteile am Grundkapital verteilt werden. ²Der Zuwachs an Aktien ist nicht als Zugang auszuweisen.

§ 218 Contingent capital.

¹Contingent capital shall increase in the same proportion as the registered share capital. ²If the contingent capital has been approved by resolution in order to grant conversion rights to holders of convertible bonds, a special reserve shall be provided in an amount equal to the difference between the issue price of bonds and the higher aggregate minimum issue price of the preemptive shares to be issued therefor, to the extent that additional payments by the persons entitled to conversion have not been agreed.

§ 219 Prohibited issue of share certificates and interim certificates.

New share certificates and interim certificates may not be issued prior to the registration of the resolution on the capital increase in the commercial register.

§ 220 Valuation.

¹The acquisition costs for shares acquired prior to the capital increase and for new shares attributable thereto shall be deemed to be the amounts attributable to the individual shares if the acquisition costs of the shares acquired prior to the capital increase are allocated to such shares and the new shares attributable thereto in proportion to their respective percentage in the registered share capital. ²The increase in number of shares may not be shown as an increase in value.

Fünfter Unterabschnitt. Wandelschuldverschreibungen. Gewinnschuldverschreibungen

§ 221 Wandel-, Gewinnschuldverschreibungen.

(1) ¹Schuldverschreibungen, bei denen den Gläubigern oder der Gesellschaft ein Umtausch- oder Bezugsrecht auf Aktien eingeräumt wird (Wandelschuldverschreibungen), und Schuldverschreibungen, bei denen die Rechte der Gläubiger mit Gewinnanteilen von Aktionären in Verbindung gebracht werden (Gewinnschuldverschreibungen), dürfen nur auf Grund eines Beschlusses der Hauptversammlung ausgegeben werden. ²Der Beschluß bedarf einer Mehrheit, die mindestens drei Viertel des bei der Beschlußfassung vertretenen Grundkapitals umfaßt. ³Die Satzung kann eine andere Kapitalmehrheit und weitere Erfordernisse bestimmen. ⁴§ 182 Abs. 2 gilt.

(2) ¹Eine Ermächtigung des Vorstandes zur Ausgabe von Wandelschuldverschreibungen kann höchstens für fünf Jahre erteilt werden. ²Der Vorstand und der Vorsitzende des Aufsichtsrats haben den Beschluß über die Ausgabe der Wandelschuldverschreibungen sowie eine Erklärung über deren Ausgabe beim Handelsregister zu hinterlegen. ³Ein Hinweis auf den Beschluß und die Erklärung ist in den Gesellschaftsblättern bekanntzumachen.

(3) Absatz 1 gilt sinngemäß für die Gewährung von Genußrechten.

(4) ¹Auf Wandelschuldverschreibungen, Gewinnschuldverschreibungen und Genußrechte haben die Aktionäre ein Bezugsrecht. ²Die §§ 186 und 193 Abs. 2 Nr. 4 gelten sinngemäß.

Subsection Five. Convertible Bonds. Dividend Bonds

§ 221. Convertible, Dividend Bonds.

(1) ¹Bonds providing holders or the company with a right to obtain shares via conversion or subscription (convertible bonds) and bonds in which the rights of the holders are connected to dividends paid to shareholders (dividend bonds) may only be issued on the basis of a resolution of the general meeting. ²Such resolution requires a majority of at least three quarters of the registered share capital represented at the adoption of the resolution. ³The articles of association may stipulate a different capital majority and further requirements. ⁴Sec. 182 para. 2 shall apply.

(2) ¹The management board may be authorized to issue convertible bonds for a period of not more than five years. ²The management board and the chairman of the supervisory board shall submit to the commercial register the resolution on the issue of convertible bonds and a confirmation of the issue thereof. ³Notice of the resolution and of the confirmation of issue shall be announced in the company's designated journals.

(3) Para. 1 shall apply accordingly to the granting of jouissance rights.

(4) ¹Shareholders shall have subscription rights with respect to convertible bonds, dividend bonds and jouissance rights. ²Sec. 186 and sec. 193 para. 2 no. 4 shall apply accordingly.

Dritter Abschnitt. Maßnahmen der Kapitalherabsetzung	**Section Three. Capital Reductions**
Erster Unterabschnitt. Ordentliche Kapitalherabsetzung	**Subsection One. Ordinary Capital Reduction**
§ 222 Voraussetzungen.	**§ 222 Requirements.**
(1) ¹Eine Herabsetzung des Grundkapitals kann nur mit einer Mehrheit beschlossen werden, die mindestens drei Viertel des bei der Beschlußfassung vertretenen Grundkapitals umfaßt. ²Die Satzung kann eine größere Kapitalmehrheit und weitere Erfordernisse bestimmen.	(1) ¹A reduction of the registered share capital shall require the consent of a majority of at least three quarters of the registered share capital represented at the adoption of the resolution. ²The articles of association may stipulate a larger capital majority and additional requirements.
(2) ¹Sind mehrere Gattungen von stimmberechtigten Aktien vorhanden, so bedarf der Beschluß der Hauptversammlung zu seiner Wirksamkeit der Zustimmung der Aktionäre jeder Gattung. ²Über die Zustimmung haben die Aktionäre jeder Gattung einen Sonderbeschluß zu fassen. ³Für diesen gilt Absatz 1.	(2) ¹If there is more than one class of voting shares, the resolution of the general meeting shall require the individual consent of each class in order to be effective. ²Such consent shall be obtained by means of special resolutions to be adopted by each class of shareholders separately. ³Para. 1 shall apply to such resolutions.
(3) In dem Beschluß ist festzusetzen, zu welchem Zweck die Herabsetzung stattfindet, namentlich ob Teile des Grundkapitals zurückgezahlt werden sollen.	(3) The resolution shall stipulate the purpose of the capital reduction, in particular whether any of the registered share capital is to be repaid.
(4) ¹Die Herabsetzung des Grundkapitals erfordert bei Gesellschaften mit Nennbetragsaktien die Herabsetzung des Nennbetrags der Aktien. ²Soweit der auf die einzelne Aktie entfallende anteilige Betrag des herabgesetzten Grundkapitals den Mindestbetrag nach § 8 Abs. 2 Satz 1 oder Abs. 3 Satz 3 unterschreiten würde, erfolgt die Herabsetzung durch Zusammenlegung der Aktien. ³Der Beschluß muß die Art der Herabsetzung angeben.	(4) ¹If the company has issued par value shares, a reduction of the registered share capital shall require a reduction of the par value of such shares. ²If the proportionate amount of the reduced registered share capital attributable to an individual share would be less than the minimum amount set out in sec. 8 para. 2 sentence 1 or para. 3 sentence 3, the reduction shall be effected by means of a consolidation of the shares. ³The resolution shall stipulate in which manner the capital reduction is to be made.
§ 223 Anmeldung des Beschlusses.	**§ 223 Application for the resolution.**
Der Vorstand und der Vorsitzende des Aufsichtsrats haben den Beschluß über die Herabsetzung des Grundkapitals zur Eintragung in das Handelsregister anzumelden.	The management board and the chairman of the supervisory board shall apply for the resolution on the reduction of the registered share capital being registered in the commercial register.

§ 224 Wirksamwerden der Kapitalherabsetzung.

Mit der Eintragung des Beschlusses über die Herabsetzung des Grundkapitals ist das Grundkapital herabgesetzt.

§ 225 Gläubigerschutz.

(1) ¹Den Gläubigern, deren Forderungen begründet worden sind, bevor die Eintragung des Beschlusses bekanntgemacht worden ist, ist, wenn sie sich binnen sechs Monaten nach der Bekanntmachung zu diesem Zweck melden, Sicherheit zu leisten, soweit sie nicht Befriedigung verlangen können. ²Die Gläubiger sind in der Bekanntmachung der Eintragung auf dieses Recht hinzuweisen. ³Das Recht, Sicherheitsleistung zu verlangen, steht Gläubigern nicht zu, die im Fall des Insolvenzverfahrens ein Recht auf vorzugsweise Befriedigung aus einer Deckungsmasse haben, die nach gesetzlicher Vorschrift zu ihrem Schutz errichtet und staatlich überwacht ist.

(2) ¹Zahlungen an die Aktionäre dürfen auf Grund der Herabsetzung des Grundkapitals erst geleistet werden, nachdem seit der Bekanntmachung der Eintragung sechs Monate verstrichen sind und nachdem den Gläubigern, die sich rechtzeitig gemeldet haben, Befriedigung oder Sicherheit gewährt worden ist. ²Auch eine Befreiung der Aktionäre von der Verpflichtung zur Leistung von Einlagen wird nicht vor dem bezeichneten Zeitpunkt und nicht vor Befriedigung oder Sicherstellung der Gläubiger wirksam, die sich rechtzeitig gemeldet haben.

(3) Das Recht der Gläubiger, Sicherheitsleistung zu verlangen, ist unabhängig davon, ob Zahlungen an die Aktionäre auf Grund der Herabsetzung des Grundkapitals geleistet werden.

§ 224 Effectiveness of the capital reduction.

The reduction of the registered share capital shall become effective upon registration of the resolution on the reduction of the registered share capital.

§ 225 Protection of creditors.

(1) ¹Creditors whose claims arose prior to the date of the announcement of the registration of the resolution shall, if the request is made within six months following the date of such announcement, be granted security to the extent that they may not demand satisfaction. ²The creditors shall be advised of this right in the announcement of the registration. ³Creditors having a right in the event of insolvency proceedings to the preferential settlement of their claims from covering funds created for their protection in accordance with legal provisions and monitored by the state shall not be entitled to a right to demand security.

(2) ¹Payments to the shareholders on the basis of a reduction of the registered share capital may be made only after a six-month period has elapsed since the announcement of this registration and those creditors who made timely demands have had their claims satisfied or secured. ²Additionally, no shareholder having an outstanding obligation to contribute shall be relieved of such obligation prior to the lapse of the aforementioned period or before those creditors who made timely demands have had their claims satisfied or secured.

(3) Whether or not any payments are made to shareholders on the basis of a capital reduction shall have no bearing on the right of creditors to demand security.

§ 226 Kraftloserklärung von Aktien.

(1) ¹Sollen zur Durchführung der Herabsetzung des Grundkapitals Aktien durch Umtausch, Abstempelung oder durch ein ähnliches Verfahren zusammengelegt werden, so kann die Gesellschaft die Aktien für kraftlos erklären, die trotz Aufforderung nicht bei ihr eingereicht worden sind. ²Gleiches gilt für eingereichte Aktien, welche die zum Ersatz durch neue Aktien nötige Zahl nicht erreichen und der Gesellschaft nicht zur Verwertung für Rechnung der Beteiligten zur Verfügung gestellt sind.

(2) ¹Die Aufforderung, die Aktien einzureichen, hat die Kraftloserklärung anzudrohen. ²Die Kraftloserklärung kann nur erfolgen, wenn die Aufforderung in der in § 64 Abs. 2 für die Nachfrist vorgeschriebenen Weise bekanntgemacht worden ist. ³Die Kraftloserklärung geschieht durch Bekanntmachung in den Gesellschaftsblättern. ⁴In der Bekanntmachung sind die für kraftlos erklärten Aktien so zu bezeichnen, daß sich aus der Bekanntmachung ohne weiteres ergibt, ob eine Aktie für kraftlos erklärt ist.

(3) ¹Die neuen Aktien, die an Stelle der für kraftlos erklärten Aktien auszugeben sind, hat die Gesellschaft unverzüglich für Rechnung der Beteiligten zum Börsenpreis und beim Fehlen eines Börsenpreises durch öffentliche Versteigerung zu verkaufen. ²Ist von der Versteigerung am Sitz der Gesellschaft kein angemessener Erfolg zu erwarten, so sind die Aktien an einem geeigneten Ort zu verkaufen. ³Zeit, Ort und Gegenstand der Versteigerung sind öffentlich bekanntzumachen. ⁴Die Beteiligten sind besonders zu benachrichtigen; die Benachrichtigung kann unterbleiben, wenn sie untunlich ist. ⁵Bekanntmachung und Benachrichtigung müssen mindestens zwei Wochen vor der Versteigerung ergehen. ⁶Der Erlös ist den Beteiligten auszuzahlen oder, wenn ein

§ 226 Cancellation of share certificates.

(1) ¹Should the implementation of the reduction of registered share capital entail the consolidating of share certificates by exchange, stamping or similar procedures, the company may declare those share certificates that have not been turned in, despite a demand for their surrender, to be cancelled. ²The foregoing shall also apply to surrendered share certificates that are insufficient in number for replacement by new share certificates and have not been made available to the company for sale on behalf of the parties concerned.

(2) ¹The notice to surrender share certificates shall warn that they are subject to cancellation. ²Cancellation may only be effected if the notice to surrender has been announced as prescribed in sec. 64 para. 2 with respect to the grace period. ³The shares shall be cancelled upon an announcement to this effect being made in the company's designated journals. ⁴The cancelled shares shall be sufficiently identified in the announcement so as to make clear, without any further information, whether a particular share certificate is to be cancelled.

(3) ¹The new share certificates which are to be issued in place of cancelled share certificates shall be, without undue delay, sold by the company on behalf of the parties concerned at the stock exchange price, and in the absence of a stock exchange price, by public auction. ²If adequate results cannot be expected from an auction at the company's registered office, the shares shall be sold at a suitable location. ³The time, place and subject matter of the auction shall be publicly announced. ⁴The parties concerned shall be notified separately; such notification may be omitted if it is infeasible. ⁵The announcement and notification shall be made at least two weeks prior to the auction. ⁶The income shall be paid to

Recht zur Hinterlegung besteht, zu hinterlegen.

§ 227 Anmeldung der Durchführung.

(1) Der Vorstand hat die Durchführung der Herabsetzung des Grundkapitals zur Eintragung in das Handelsregister anzumelden.

(2) Anmeldung und Eintragung der Durchführung der Herabsetzung des Grundkapitals können mit Anmeldung und Eintragung des Beschlusses über die Herabsetzung verbunden werden.

§ 228 Herabsetzung unter den Mindestnennbetrag.

(1) Das Grundkapital kann unter den in § 7 bestimmten Mindestnennbetrag herabgesetzt werden, wenn dieser durch eine Kapitalerhöhung wieder erreicht wird, die zugleich mit der Kapitalherabsetzung beschlossen ist und bei der Sacheinlagen nicht festgesetzt sind.

(2) ¹Die Beschlüsse sind nichtig, wenn sie und die Durchführung der Erhöhung nicht binnen sechs Monaten nach der Beschlußfassung in das Handelsregister eingetragen worden sind. ²Der Lauf der Frist ist gehemmt, solange eine Anfechtungs- oder Nichtigkeitsklage rechtshängig ist. ³Die Beschlüsse und die Durchführung der Erhöhung des Grundkapitals sollen nur zusammen in das Handelsregister eingetragen werden.

Zweiter Unterabschnitt. Vereinfachte Kapitalherabsetzung

§ 229 Voraussetzungen.

(1) ¹Eine Herabsetzung des Grundkapitals, die dazu dienen soll, Wertminderungen auszugleichen, sonstige Verluste zu decken oder Beträge in die Kapitalrücklage einzustellen, kann in

the persons concerned, or if a right to deposit exists, be deposited.

§ 227 Application for the implementation.

(1) The management board shall apply for the implementation of the capital reduction to be registered in the commercial register.

(2) The application and registration of the implementation of the capital reduction may be made together with the application and registration of the resolution on the reduction.

§ 228 Reduction to less than the minimum nominal value.

(1) The registered share capital may be reduced to less than the minimum nominal value required under sec. 7 if the nominal value is restored to at least such minimum by adoption of a resolution on a capital increase in which no contributions in kind are stipulated at the same time as the resolution on the capital reduction.

(2) ¹Resolutions shall be null and void if they, and the implementation of the increase, have not been registered in the commercial register within six months of the date of adoption of the resolutions. ²The running of such period shall be suspended for as long as an action to set aside a resolution or an action for the declaration of nullity of a resolution is pending. ³The resolutions and the implementation of the capital increase shall only be registered together in the commercial register.

Subsection Two. Simplified Capital Reduction

§ 229 Requirements.

(1) ¹A capital reduction for the purpose of compensating for a decline in the value of assets, offsetting other losses, or allocating amounts to the capital reserve may be accomplished through a

vereinfachter Form vorgenommen werden. ²Im Beschluß ist festzusetzen, daß die Herabsetzung zu diesen Zwecken stattfindet.

(2) ¹Die vereinfachte Kapitalherabsetzung ist nur zulässig, nachdem der Teil der gesetzlichen Rücklage und der Kapitalrücklage, um den diese zusammen über zehn vom Hundert des nach der Herabsetzung verbleibenden Grundkapitals hinausgehen, sowie die Gewinnrücklagen vorweg aufgelöst sind. ²Sie ist nicht zulässig, solange ein Gewinnvortrag vorhanden ist.

(3) § 222 Abs. 1, 2 und 4, §§ 223, 224, 226 bis 228 über die ordentliche Kapitalherabsetzung gelten sinngemäß.

§ 230 Verbot von Zahlungen an die Aktionäre.

¹Die Beträge, die aus der Auflösung der Kapital- oder Gewinnrücklagen und aus der Kapitalherabsetzung gewonnen werden, dürfen nicht zu Zahlungen an die Aktionäre und nicht dazu verwandt werden, die Aktionäre von der Verpflichtung zur Leistung von Einlagen zu befreien. ²Sie dürfen nur verwandt werden, um Wertminderungen auszugleichen, sonstige Verluste zu decken und Beträge in die Kapitalrücklage oder in die gesetzliche Rücklage einzustellen. ³Auch eine Verwendung zu einem dieser Zwecke ist nur zulässig, soweit sie im Beschluß als Zweck der Herabsetzung angegeben ist.

§ 231 Beschränkte Einstellung in die Kapitalrücklage und in die gesetzliche Rücklage.

¹Die Einstellung der Beträge, die aus der Auflösung von anderen Gewinnrücklagen gewonnen werden, in die gesetzliche Rücklage und der Beträge, die aus der Kapitalherabsetzung gewonnen werden, in die Kapitalrücklage ist nur zulässig, soweit die Kapitalrücklage und die gesetzliche Rücklage zusammen zehn vom Hundert des Grundka-

simplified procedure. ²The resolution shall stipulate that the reduction is being made for one of these purposes.

(2) ¹A simplified reduction of registered share capital is only permissible after any amount by which the sum of the statutory reserve and the capital reserve exceeds ten per cent of the registered share capital remaining after such reduction and any amounts in the revenue reserves have been released. ²The simplified procedure is not permissible so long as there is any profit carried forward.

(3) Sec. 222 paras. 1, 2 and 4, sec. 223, 224, 226 to 228 concerning the ordinary capital reduction shall apply accordingly.

§ 230 Prohibition on payments to shareholders.

¹The amounts obtained from the release of the capital reserves and revenue reserves and from the capital reduction may not be utilized for payments to shareholders or to relieve shareholders from their obligations to make contributions. ²Such amounts may only be utilized to compensate for declines in value of assets, to cover other losses and to allocate amounts to the capital reserve or the statutory reserve. ³The utilization of such sums for these purposes shall only be permitted to the extent that the resolution states that this was the purpose of the capital reduction.

§ 231 Limited transfer to the capital reserve and statutory reserve.

¹The transfer of amounts obtained from the release of other revenue reserves to the statutory reserve, and the transfer of amounts obtained from the capital reduction to the capital reserve, may be made only if the capital reserve and the statutory reserve combined do not exceed ten percent of the registered share capital. ²The registered share cap-

pitals nicht übersteigen. ²Als Grundkapital gilt dabei der Nennbetrag, der sich durch die Herabsetzung ergibt, mindestens aber der in § 7 bestimmte Mindestnennbetrag. ³Bei der Bemessung der zulässigen Höhe bleiben Beträge, die in der Zeit nach der Beschlußfassung über die Kapitalherabsetzung in die Kapitalrücklage einzustellen sind, auch dann außer Betracht, wenn ihre Zahlung auf einem Beschluß beruht, der zugleich mit dem Beschluß über die Kapitalherabsetzung gefaßt wird.

ital shall in that case be deemed to be the nominal value resulting from the capital reduction, but not less than the minimum nominal value prescribed in sec. 7. ³In assessing the amounts allowed to be transferred, those amounts which are to be allocated to the capital reserve after the adoption of the resolution on the capital reduction shall not be taken into account, even if such allocation is based on a resolution adopted at the same time as the resolution on the capital reduction.

§ 232 Einstellung von Beträgen in die Kapitalrücklage bei zu hoch angenommenen Verlusten.

§ 232 Transfer of amounts to the capital reserve in the case of overestimated losses.

Ergibt sich bei Aufstellung der Jahresbilanz für das Geschäftsjahr, in dem der Beschluß über die Kapitalherabsetzung gefaßt wurde, oder für eines der beiden folgenden Geschäftsjahre, daß Wertminderungen und sonstige Verluste in der bei der Beschlußfassung angenommenen Höhe tatsächlich nicht eingetreten oder ausgeglichen waren, so ist der Unterschiedsbetrag in die Kapitalrücklage einzustellen.

If it becomes apparent in connection with the preparation of the annual balance sheet for the fiscal year in which the resolution on the capital reduction was adopted or for one of the two following fiscal years that declines in the value of the assets or other losses have not in fact occurred in the amount estimated when the resolution was adopted, or they have been offset, the amount of such difference shall be allocated to the capital reserves.

§ 233 Gewinnausschüttung. Gläubigerschutz.

§ 233 Distribution of profits. Protection of creditors.

(1) ¹Gewinn darf nicht ausgeschüttet werden, bevor die gesetzliche Rücklage und die Kapitalrücklage zusammen zehn vom Hundert des Grundkapitals erreicht haben. ²Als Grundkapital gilt dabei der Nennbetrag, der sich durch die Herabsetzung ergibt, mindestens aber der in § 7 bestimmte Mindestnennbetrag.

(1) ¹Profits may not be distributed until the statutory reserve and the capital reserve combined have reached the level of ten percent of the registered share capital. ²In this context, the registered share capital shall be deemed to be the nominal value resulting from the capital reduction, but not less than the minimum nominal value prescribed in sec. 7.

(2) ¹Die Zahlung eines Gewinnanteils von mehr als vier vom Hundert ist erst für ein Geschäftsjahr zulässig, das später als zwei Jahre nach der Beschlußfassung über die Kapitalherabsetzung beginnt. ²Dies gilt nicht, wenn die Gläubiger, deren Forderungen vor der Bekanntmachung der Eintragung des Beschlusses begründet worden wa-

(2) ¹The payment of a dividend exceeding four percent shall only be permitted for a fiscal year beginning at least two years after the resolution on the capital reduction has been adopted. ²The foregoing shall not apply if the claims of creditors which arose prior to the announcement of the registration of such resolution have been satisfied or

ren, befriedigt oder sichergestellt sind, soweit sie sich binnen sechs Monaten nach der Bekanntmachung des Jahresabschlusses, auf Grund dessen die Gewinnverteilung beschlossen ist, zu diesem Zweck gemeldet haben. ³Einer Sicherstellung der Gläubiger bedarf es nicht, die im Fall des Insolvenzverfahrens ein Recht auf vorzugsweise Befriedigung aus einer Deckungsmasse haben, die nach gesetzlicher Vorschrift zu ihrem Schutz errichtet und staatlich überwacht ist. ⁴Die Gläubiger sind in der Bekanntmachung nach § 325 Abs. 2 des Handelsgesetzbuchs auf die Befriedigung oder Sicherstellung hinzuweisen.

(3) Die Beträge, die aus der Auflösung von Kapital- und Gewinnrücklagen und aus der Kapitalherabsetzung gewonnen sind, dürfen auch nach diesen Vorschriften nicht als Gewinn ausgeschüttet werden.

§ 234 Rückwirkung der Kapitalherabsetzung.

(1) Im Jahresabschluß für das letzte vor der Beschlußfassung über die Kapitalherabsetzung abgelaufene Geschäftsjahr können das gezeichnete Kapital sowie die Kapital- und Gewinnrücklagen in der Höhe ausgewiesen werden, in der sie nach der Kapitalherabsetzung bestehen sollen.

(2) ¹In diesem Fall beschließt die Hauptversammlung über die Feststellung des Jahresabschlusses. ²Der Beschluß soll zugleich mit dem Beschluß über die Kapitalherabsetzung gefaßt werden.

(3) ¹Die Beschlüsse sind nichtig, wenn der Beschluß über die Kapitalherabsetzung nicht binnen drei Monaten nach der Beschlußfassung in das Handelsregister eingetragen worden ist. ²Der Lauf der Frist ist gehemmt, solange eine Anfechtungs- oder Nichtigkeitsklage rechtshängig ist.

secured, provided they applied for this purpose within the six months following the announcement of the annual financial statements that served as the basis of the resolution on the dividend. ³It shall not be necessary to grant security to creditors having a right in the event of insolvency proceedings to the preferential settlement of their claims from covering funds created for their protection in accordance with legal provisions and monitored by the state. ⁴In an announcement made pursuant to sec. 325 para. 2 of the Commercial Code, the creditors shall be advised of such satisfaction or provision of security.

(3) The foregoing provisions do not permit the distribution of profits out of amounts gained from the release of capital reserves and revenue reserves or out of amounts obtained by virtue of the capital reduction.

§ 234 Retroactive effect of the capital reduction.

(1) In the annual financial statements for the last fiscal year ending prior to the adoption of the resolution on the capital reduction, subscribed capital, capital reserves and revenue reserves may be shown in the respective amounts that will prevail upon completion of the capital reduction.

(2) ¹In this case, the general meeting shall resolve on formal approval of the annual financial statements. ²Such resolution shall be adopted together with the resolution on the capital reduction.

(3) ¹The resolutions shall be null and void if the resolution on the capital reduction has not been registered in the commercial register within three months of the adoption thereof. ²The running of such period shall be suspended for as long as an action to set aside a resolution or an action for the declaration of nullity of a resolution is pending.

§ 235 Rückwirkung einer gleichzeitigen Kapitalerhöhung.

(1) ¹Wird im Fall des § 234 zugleich mit der Kapitalherabsetzung eine Erhöhung des Grundkapitals beschlossen, so kann auch die Kapitalerhöhung in dem Jahresabschluß als vollzogen berücksichtigt werden. ²Die Beschlußfassung ist nur zulässig, wenn die neuen Aktien gezeichnet, keine Sacheinlagen festgesetzt sind und wenn auf jede Aktie die Einzahlung geleistet ist, die nach § 188 Abs. 2 zur Zeit der Anmeldung der Durchführung der Kapitalerhöhung bewirkt sein muß. ³Die Zeichnung und die Einzahlung sind dem Notar nachzuweisen, der den Beschluß über die Erhöhung des Grundkapitals beurkundet.

(2) ¹Sämtliche Beschlüsse sind nichtig, wenn die Beschlüsse über die Kapitalherabsetzung und die Kapitalerhöhung und die Durchführung der Erhöhung nicht binnen drei Monaten nach der Beschlußfassung in das Handelsregister eingetragen worden sind. ²Der Lauf der Frist ist gehemmt, solange eine Anfechtungs- oder Nichtigkeitsklage rechtshängig ist. ³Die Beschlüsse und die Durchführung der Erhöhung des Grundkapitals sollen nur zusammen in das Handelsregister eingetragen werden.

§ 236 Offenlegung.

Die Offenlegung des Jahresabschlusses nach § 325 des Handelsgesetzbuchs darf im Fall des § 234 erst nach Eintragung des Beschlusses über die Kapitalherabsetzung, im Fall des § 235 erst ergehen, nachdem die Beschlüsse über die Kapitalherabsetzung und Kapitalerhöhung und die Durchführung der Kapitalerhöhung eingetragen worden sind.

§ 235 Retroactive effect of a simultaneous capital increase.

(1) ¹If in the case of sec. 234, a resolution is adopted concerning an increase of the registered share capital at the same time as the resolution on the capital reduction, the capital increase may also be deemed to have been completed when drawing up the annual financial statements. ²The resolution shall only be valid if the new shares have been subscribed to, no contributions in kind have been stipulated and the contribution which shall have been paid at the date of registration of the implementation of the capital increase pursuant to sec. 188 para. 2 has been paid for each share. ³Evidence of the subscription and payment of contributions shall be furnished to the notary who is to notarize the resolution on the capital increase.

(2) ¹All resolutions shall be null and void if the resolutions on the capital reduction, the capital increase and the implementation of the increase have not been registered in the commercial register within three months of the adoption thereof. ²The running of such period shall be suspended for as long as an action to set aside a resolution or an action for the declaration of nullity of a resolution is pending. ³The resolutions and the implementation of the capital increase shall only be registered together in the commercial register.

§ 236 Disclosure.

Disclosure of the annual financial statements pursuant to sec. 325 of the Commercial Code may, in the case of sec. 234, only be made after registration of the resolution on the capital reduction, and in the case of sec. 235, only after the resolutions on the capital reduction, capital increase and the implementation of the capital increase have been registered.

Dritter Unterabschnitt. Kapitalherabsetzung durch Einziehung von Aktien. Ausnahme für Stückaktien

§ 237 Voraussetzungen.

(1) [1]Aktien können zwangsweise oder nach Erwerb durch die Gesellschaft eingezogen werden. [2]Eine Zwangseinziehung ist nur zulässig, wenn sie in der ursprünglichen Satzung oder durch eine Satzungsänderung vor Übernahme oder Zeichnung der Aktien angeordnet oder gestattet war.

(2) [1]Bei der Einziehung sind die Vorschriften über die ordentliche Kapitalherabsetzung zu befolgen. [2]In der Satzung oder in dem Beschluß der Hauptversammlung sind die Voraussetzungen für eine Zwangseinziehung und die Einzelheiten ihrer Durchführung festzulegen. [3]Für die Zahlung des Entgelts, das Aktionären bei einer Zwangseinziehung oder bei einem Erwerb von Aktien zum Zwecke der Einziehung gewährt wird, und für die Befreiung dieser Aktionäre von der Verpflichtung zur Leistung von Einlagen gilt § 225 Abs. 2 sinngemäß.

(3) Die Vorschriften über die ordentliche Kapitalherabsetzung brauchen nicht befolgt zu werden, wenn Aktien, auf die der Ausgabebetrag voll geleistet ist,

1. der Gesellschaft unentgeltlich zur Verfügung gestellt oder
2. zu Lasten des Bilanzgewinns oder einer anderen Gewinnrücklage, soweit sie zu diesem Zweck verwandt werden können, eingezogen werden oder
3. Stückaktien sind und der Beschluss der Hauptversammlung bestimmt, dass sich durch die Einziehung der Anteil der übrigen Aktien am Grundkapital gemäß § 8 Abs. 3 erhöht; wird der Vorstand zur Einziehung ermächtigt, so kann er auch zur Anpassung der Angabe der Zahl in der Satzung ermächtigt werden.

Subsection Three. Capital Reduction by Redemption of Shares. Exception for Non-Par Value Shares

§ 237 Requirements.

(1) [1]Shares may be cancelled by compulsory redemption or upon acquisition by the company. [2]A compulsory redemption is only permissible if prescribed or provided for in the original articles of association or as a result of an amendment to the articles of association effected prior to the acquisition of or subscription to the shares.

(2) [1]The provisions regarding an ordinary capital reduction shall govern such redemption. [2]The conditions governing a compulsory redemption and the details as to the implementation thereof shall be stipulated in the articles of association or the resolution of the general meeting. [3]Sec. 225 para. 2 shall apply accordingly to the payment of the consideration which is to be granted to the shareholders in the case of a compulsory redemption or an acquisition of shares for the purpose of cancellation, and to the relieve of such shareholders from the obligation to make contributions.

(3) The provisions regarding an ordinary capital reduction need not be observed if shares with respect to which the issue price has been fully paid

1. are surrendered to the company free of charge or
2. are redeemed by change to balance sheet profit or other revenue reserves, to the extent they may be used for such purpose or
3. are non-par value shares and the resolution of the general meeting stipulates that the amount of the registered share capital accounted for by the remaining shares shall be increased pursuant to sec. 8 para. 3 as a result of the redemption of the shares; if the management board is permitted to redeem shares, it may

(4) ¹Auch in den Fällen des Absatzes 3 kann die Kapitalherabsetzung durch Einziehung nur von der Hauptversammlung beschlossen werden. ²Für den Beschluß genügt die einfache Stimmenmehrheit. ³Die Satzung kann eine größere Mehrheit und weitere Erfordernisse bestimmen. ⁴Im Beschluß ist der Zweck der Kapitalherabsetzung festzusetzen. ⁵Der Vorstand und der Vorsitzende des Aufsichtsrats haben den Beschluß zur Eintragung in das Handelsregister anzumelden.

(5) In den Fällen des Absatzes 3 Nr. 1 und 2 ist in die Kapitalrücklage ein Betrag einzustellen, der dem auf die eingezogenen Aktien entfallenden Betrag des Grundkapitals gleichkommt.

(6) ¹Soweit es sich um eine durch die Satzung angeordnete Zwangseinziehung handelt, bedarf es eines Beschlusses der Hauptversammlung nicht. ²In diesem Fall tritt für die Anwendung der Vorschriften über die ordentliche Kapitalherabsetzung an die Stelle des Hauptversammlungsbeschlusses die Entscheidung des Vorstands über die Einziehung.

§ 238 Wirksamwerden der Kapitalherabsetzung.

¹Mit der Eintragung des Beschlusses oder, wenn die Einziehung nachfolgt, mit der Einziehung ist das Grundkapital um den auf die eingezogenen Aktien entfallenden Betrag herabgesetzt. ²Handelt es sich um eine durch die Satzung angeordnete Zwangseinziehung, so ist, wenn die Hauptversammlung nicht über die Kapitalherabsetzung beschließt, das Grundkapital mit der Zwangseinziehung herabgesetzt. ³Zur Einziehung bedarf es einer Handlung der Gesellschaft, die auf Vernichtung

also be permitted to adjust the number stipulated in the articles of association.

(4) ¹Also in cases stipulated in para. 3 a capital reduction by means of redemption of shares shall in any event require a resolution of the general meeting ²A simple majority of votes cast shall suffice for such a resolution. ³The articles of association may stipulate a larger majority and further requirements. ⁴The purpose of the capital reduction shall be stated in the resolution. ⁵The management board and the chairman of the supervisory board shall apply for the resolution to be registered in the commercial register.

(5) In the cases stipulated in para. 3 nos. 1 and 2, an amount shall be allocated to the capital reserve which is equal to the amount of the registered share capital attributable to the redeemed shares.

(6) ¹If a compulsory redemption is prescribed by the articles of association, a resolution of the general meeting shall not be required. ²In that case, with respect to the applicability of the provisions regarding an ordinary capital reduction, the decision of the management board regarding the redemption shall replace the resolution of the general meeting.

§ 238 Effectiveness of the capital reduction.

¹The reduction of the registered share capital by the amount attributable to the shares redeemed shall become effective upon registration of the resolution or, in the case of subsequent redemption, upon redemption. ²In the case of a compulsory redemption prescribed by the articles of association, the reduction of the share capital shall become effective upon such compulsory redemption, unless the general meeting resolves on such capital reduction. ³The redemption shall require an act of the company which has the purpose of nullifying the

§ 239 Anmeldung der Durchführung.

(1) ¹Der Vorstand hat die Durchführung der Herabsetzung des Grundkapitals zur Eintragung in das Handelsregister anzumelden. ²Dies gilt auch dann, wenn es sich um eine durch die Satzung angeordnete Zwangseinziehung handelt.

(2) Anmeldung und Eintragung der Durchführung der Herabsetzung können mit Anmeldung und Eintragung des Beschlusses über die Herabsetzung verbunden werden.

Vierter Unterabschnitt. Ausweis der Kapitalherabsetzung

§ 240 Gesonderte Ausweisung.

¹Der aus der Kapitalherabsetzung gewonnene Betrag ist in der Gewinn- und Verlustrechnung als „Ertrag aus der Kapitalherabsetzung" gesondert, und zwar hinter dem Posten „Entnahmen aus Gewinnrücklagen", auszuweisen. ²Eine Einstellung in die Kapitalrücklage nach § 229 Abs. 1 und § 232 ist als „Einstellung in die Kapitalrücklage nach den Vorschriften über die vereinfachte Kapitalherabsetzung" gesondert auszuweisen. ³Im Anhang ist zu erläutern, ob und in welcher Höhe die aus der Kapitalherabsetzung und aus der Auflösung von Gewinnrücklagen gewonnenen Beträge

1. zum Ausgleich von Wertminderungen,
2. zur Deckung von sonstigen Verlusten oder
3. zur Einstellung in die Kapitalrücklage

verwandt werden. ⁴Ist die Gesellschaft eine kleine Kapitalgesellschaft (§ 267 Absatz 1 des Handelsgesetzbuchs), braucht sie Satz 3 nicht anzuwenden.

der Rechte aus bestimmten Aktien gerichtet ist.

rights arising with respect to specific shares.

§ 239 Application for the implementation of the capital reduction.

(1) ¹The management board shall apply for the implementation of the capital reduction to be registered in the commercial register. ²The foregoing shall also apply in the case of a compulsory redemption prescribed by the articles of association.

(2) The application and registration of the implementation of the reduction may be combined with the application and registration of the resolution on the reduction.

Subsection Four. The Capital Reduction in the Financial Statements

§ 240 Separate Entry.

¹The amount obtained in connection with the capital reduction shall be shown separately in the profit and loss statement as "income from capital reduction" after the item "withdrawals from revenue reserves". ²A transfer to the capital reserve pursuant to sec. 229 para. 1 and sec. 232 shall be shown separately as "transfer to the capital reserve pursuant to the provisions governing simplified procedure for capital reduction". ³The notes shall explain whether and to what extent the amounts received in connection with the capital reduction and the release of revenue reserves have been utilized:

1. to compensate a decline in the value of assets,
2. to cover other losses, or
3. for transfer to the capital reserve.

⁴Sentence 3 does not apply to small corporations within the meaning of sec. 267 para. 1 of the Commercial Code.

Siebenter Teil. Nichtigkeit von Hauptversammlungsbeschlüssen und des festgestellten Jahresabschlusses. Sonderprüfung wegen unzulässiger Unterbewertung

Part Seven. Nullity of Resolutions of the General Meeting and of the Formally Approved Annual Financial Statements. Special Audit for Unlawful Undervaluation

Erster Abschnitt. Nichtigkeit von Hauptversammlungsbeschlüssen

Section One. Nullity of Resolutions of the General Meeting.

Erster Unterabschnitt. Allgemeines

Subsection One. General Provisions

§ 241 Nichtigkeitsgründe.

§ 241 Grounds for nullity.

Ein Beschluß der Hauptversammlung ist außer in den Fällen des § 192 Abs. 4, §§ 212, 217 Abs. 2, § 228 Abs. 2, § 234 Abs. 3 und § 235 Abs. 2 nur dann nichtig, wenn er

In addition to the cases pursuant to sec. 192 para. 4, sec. 212, 217 para. 2, sec. 228 para. 2, sec. 234 para. 3 and sec. 235 para. 2, a resolution of a general meeting shall be null and void only if it:

1. in einer Hauptversammlung gefaßt worden ist, die unter Verstoß gegen § 121 Abs. 2 und 3 Satz 1 oder Abs. 4 einberufen war,
2. nicht nach § 130 Abs. 1 und 2 Satz 1 und Abs. 4 beurkundet ist,
3. mit dem Wesen der Aktiengesellschaft nicht zu vereinbaren ist oder durch seinen Inhalt Vorschriften verletzt, die ausschließlich oder überwiegend zum Schutze der Gläubiger der Gesellschaft oder sonst im öffentlichen Interesse gegeben sind,
4. durch seinen Inhalt gegen die guten Sitten verstößt,
5. auf Anfechtungsklage durch Urteil rechtskräftig für nichtig erklärt worden ist,
6. nach § 398 des Gesetzes über das Verfahren in Familiensachen und in den Angelegenheiten der freiwilligen Gerichtsbarkeit auf Grund rechtskräftiger Entscheidung als nichtig gelöscht worden ist.

1. has been adopted by a general meeting convened in violation of sec. 121 paras. 2 and 3 sentence 1 or para. 4,
2. has not been notarized in accordance with sec. 130 paras. 1 and 2 sentence 1 and para. 4,
3. cannot be reconciled with the nature of a stock corporation or by its terms violates regulations which exclusively or primarily serve to protect creditors of the company or otherwise serve the public interest,
4. is by its terms in violation of public policy,
5. has been declared null and void by a binding court judgment issued in favor of an action to set aside a resolution,
6. has been cancelled as null and void by virtue of a decision being res judicata pursuant to sec. 398 of the Act on Procedure in Family Matters and Matters of Non-Contentious Jurisdiction.

§ 242 Heilung der Nichtigkeit.

§ 242 Curing of Nullity.

(1) Die Nichtigkeit eines Hauptversammlungsbeschlusses, der entgegen § 130 Abs. 1 und 2 Satz 1 und Abs. 4 nicht oder nicht gehörig beurkundet

(1) The nullity of a resolution of the general meeting that has either not been notarized or not properly notarized as prescribed in sec. 130 paras. 1 and 2 sen-

worden ist, kann nicht mehr geltend gemacht werden, wenn der Beschluß in das Handelsregister eingetragen worden ist.

(2) ¹Ist ein Hauptversammlungsbeschluß nach § 241 Nr. 1, 3 oder 4 nichtig, so kann die Nichtigkeit nicht mehr geltend gemacht werden, wenn der Beschluß in das Handelsregister eingetragen worden ist und seitdem drei Jahre verstrichen sind. ²Ist bei Ablauf der Frist eine Klage auf Feststellung der Nichtigkeit des Hauptversammlungsbeschlusses rechtshängig, so verlängert sich die Frist, bis über die Klage rechtskräftig entschieden ist oder sie sich auf andere Weise endgültig erledigt hat. ³Eine Löschung des Beschlusses von Amts wegen nach § 398 des Gesetzes über das Verfahren in Familiensachen und in den Angelegenheiten der freiwilligen Gerichtsbarkeit wird durch den Zeitablauf nicht ausgeschlossen. ⁴Ist ein Hauptversammlungsbeschluß wegen Verstoßes gegen § 121 Abs. 4 Satz 2 nach § 241 Nr. 1 nichtig, so kann die Nichtigkeit auch dann nicht mehr geltend gemacht werden, wenn der nicht geladene Aktionär den Beschluß genehmigt. ⁵Ist ein Hauptversammlungsbeschluss nach § 241 Nr. 5 oder § 249 nichtig, so kann das Urteil nach § 248 Abs. 1 Satz 3 nicht mehr eingetragen werden, wenn gemäß § 246a Abs. 1 rechtskräftig festgestellt wurde, dass Mängel des Hauptversammlungsbeschlusses die Wirkung der Eintragung unberührt lassen; § 398 des Gesetzes über das Verfahren in Familiensachen und in den Angelegenheiten der freiwilligen Gerichtsbarkeit findet keine Anwendung.

(3) Absatz 2 gilt entsprechend, wenn in den Fällen des § 217 Abs. 2, § 228 Abs. 2, § 234 Abs. 3 und § 235 Abs. 2 die erforderlichen Eintragungen nicht fristgemäß vorgenommen worden sind.

tence 1 and para. 4 cannot be asserted once it has been registered in the commercial register.

(2) ¹If the resolution of the general meeting is null and void pursuant to sec. 241 paras. 1, 3 or 4, the nullity may not be asserted if a period of three years has passed from the date the resolution was registered in the commercial register. ²If an action for the declaration of nullity of the resolution of the general meeting is still pending upon expiration of the three year period, the running of the limitation period shall be suspended until a decision being res judicata has been reached regarding the claim or such claim has been ultimately resolved through other means. ³A cancellation ex officio of the resolution pursuant to sec. 398 of the Act on Procedure in Family Matters and Matters of Non-Contentious Jurisdiction shall not be excluded by virtue of the expiration of the limitation period. ⁴Should a resolution of the general meeting be null and void pursuant to sec. 241 no. 1 due to a violation of sec. 121 para. 4 sentence 2, its nullity may not be asserted even if the resolution is approved by those shareholders who were not invited to the meeting. ⁵If a resolution of the general meeting pursuant to sec. 241 no. 5 or sec. 249 is null and void, the judgment pursuant to sec. 248 para. 1 sentence 3 may not be registered any more if it was determined pursuant to sec. 246a para. 1 that defects in the resolution of the general meeting do not affect the registration and if such determination has become res judicata; sec. 398 of the Act on Procedure in Family Matters and Matters of Non-Contentious Jurisdiction shall not apply.

(3) Para. 2 shall apply accordingly if the prescribed registrations have not been made within the appropriate time periods in the cases described in sec. 217 para. 2, sec. 228 para. 2, sec. 234 para. 3 and sec. 235 para. 2.

§ 243 Anfechtungsgründe.

(1) Ein Beschluß der Hauptversammlung kann wegen Verletzung des Gesetzes oder der Satzung durch Klage angefochten werden.

(2) [1]Die Anfechtung kann auch darauf gestützt werden, daß ein Aktionär mit der Ausübung des Stimmrechts für sich oder einen Dritten Sondervorteile zum Schaden der Gesellschaft oder der anderen Aktionäre zu erlangen suchte und der Beschluß geeignet ist, diesem Zweck zu dienen. [2]Dies gilt nicht, wenn der Beschluß den anderen Aktionären einen angemessenen Ausgleich für ihren Schaden gewährt.

(3) Die Anfechtung kann nicht gestützt werden:

1. auf die durch eine technische Störung verursachte Verletzung von Rechten, die nach § 118 Abs. 1 Satz 2, Abs. 2 und § 134 Abs. 3 auf elektronischem Wege wahrgenommen worden sind, es sei denn, der Gesellschaft ist grobe Fahrlässigkeit oder Vorsatz vorzuwerfen; in der Satzung kann ein strengerer Verschuldensmaßstab bestimmt werden,
2. auf eine Verletzung des § 121 Abs. 4a, des § 124 a oder des § 128,
3. auf Gründe, die ein Verfahren nach § 318 Abs. 3 des Handelsgesetzbuchs rechtfertigen.

(4) [1]Wegen unrichtiger, unvollständiger oder verweigerter Erteilung von Informationen kann nur angefochten werden, wenn ein objektiv urteilender Aktionär die Erteilung der Information als wesentliche Voraussetzung für die sachgerechte Wahrnehmung seiner Teilnahme- und Mitgliedschaftsrechte angesehen hätte. [2]Auf unrichtige, unvollständige oder unzureichende Informationen in der Hauptversammlung über die Ermittlung, Höhe oder Angemessenheit von Ausgleich, Abfindung, Zuzahlung oder über sonstige Kompensationen kann eine Anfechtungsklage

§ 243 Grounds for an action to set aside.

(1) The validity of a resolution of the general meeting may be set aside upon an action based on violation of law or of the articles of association.

(2) [1]An action to set aside a resolution may also be based upon the grounds that, when exercising the voting right, a shareholder was seeking to acquire special benefits for himself or a third party to the detriment of the company, and the said resolution is suited to this purpose. [2]The foregoing shall not apply if the resolution guarantees fair compensation to the other shareholders.

(3) An action to set aside cannot be based upon:

1. a violation of rights which were exercised electronically pursuant to sec. 118 para. 1 sentence 2, para. 2 and sec. 134 para. 3 and which violation was caused by a technical disruption, unless the company is guilty of gross negligence or intent; the articles of association may provide for a stricter standard of culpability,
2. a violation of sec. 121 para. 4a, sec. 124a or sec. 128,
3. reasons which justify proceedings pursuant to sec. 318 para. 3 of the Commercial Code.

(4) [1]Actions to set aside may only be based on an incorrect, incomplete or refused grant of information if a shareholder judging objectively would have regarded the granting of such information as an essential requirement for the proper exercise of their rights of his participation and membership rights. [2]An action to set aside may not be based on incorrect, incomplete or insufficient information in the general meeting concerning the determination, amount or adequacy of a settlement, an additional payment or other compensation if the Act Concerning Valuation Objections

nicht gestützt werden, wenn das Gesetz für Bewertungsrügen ein Spruchverfahren vorsieht.

provides for legal challenge proceedings.

§ 244 Bestätigung anfechtbarer Hauptversammlungsbeschlüsse.

¹Die Anfechtung kann nicht mehr geltend gemacht werden, wenn die Hauptversammlung den anfechtbaren Beschluß durch einen neuen Beschluß bestätigt hat und dieser Beschluß innerhalb der Anfechtungsfrist nicht angefochten oder die Anfechtung rechtskräftig zurückgewiesen worden ist. ²Hat der Kläger ein rechtliches Interesse, daß der anfechtbare Beschluß für die Zeit bis zum Bestätigungsbeschluß für nichtig erklärt wird, so kann er die Anfechtung weiterhin mit dem Ziel geltend machen, den anfechtbaren Beschluß für diese Zeit für nichtig zu erklären.

§ 244 Affirmation of a contestable resolution of the general meeting.

¹An action to set aside a resolution may no longer be brought if the general meeting has affirmed the contestable resolution by subsequent resolution and an action to set aside such resolution has not been brought within the statute of limitations for such action or such action to set aside a resolution has not been dismissed in a decision being res judicata. ²If the plaintiff has a legal interest in having the contestable resolution declared null and void for the period until its adoption by subsequent affirmation, he may proceed with the action for the purpose of having such contestable resolution declared null and void for such period.

§ 245 Anfechtungsbefugnis.

Zur Anfechtung ist befugt

1. jeder in der Hauptversammlung erschienene Aktionär, wenn er die Aktien schon vor der Bekanntmachung der Tagesordnung erworben hatte und gegen den Beschluß Widerspruch zur Niederschrift erklärt hat;
2. jeder in der Hauptversammlung nicht erschienene Aktionär, wenn er zu der Hauptversammlung zu Unrecht nicht zugelassen worden ist oder die Versammlung nicht ordnungsgemäß einberufen oder der Gegenstand der Beschlußfassung nicht ordnungsgemäß bekanntgemacht worden ist;
3. im Fall des § 243 Abs. 2 jeder Aktionär, wenn er die Aktien schon vor der Bekanntmachung der Tagesordnung erworben hatte;
4. der Vorstand;

§ 245 Authority to file an action to set aside a resolution.

The following parties shall have the authority to file an action to set aside a resolution:

1. each shareholder present at the general meeting if he had acquired the shares prior to the announcement of the meeting agenda and if he has raised objections against the resolution in the minutes;
2. each shareholder not present at the general meeting if he was wrongly disallowed from attending the general meeting, if the meeting was not duly convened, or if the subject matter of the resolution was not duly and properly announced;
3. in the case of sec. 243 para. 2, every shareholder if he had acquired the shares prior to the announcement of the meeting agenda;
4. the management board;

5. jedes Mitglied des Vorstands und des Aufsichtsrats, wenn durch die Ausführung des Beschlusses Mitglieder des Vorstands oder des Aufsichtsrats eine strafbare Handlung oder eine Ordnungswidrigkeit begehen oder wenn sie ersatzpflichtig werden würden.

§ 246 Anfechtungsklage.

(1) Die Klage muß innerhalb eines Monats nach der Beschlußfassung erhoben werden.

(2) ¹Die Klage ist gegen die Gesellschaft zu richten. ²Die Gesellschaft wird durch Vorstand und Aufsichtsrat vertreten. ³Klagt der Vorstand oder ein Vorstandsmitglied, wird die Gesellschaft durch den Aufsichtsrat, klagt ein Aufsichtsratsmitglied, wird sie durch den Vorstand vertreten.

(3) ¹Zuständig für die Klage ist ausschließlich das Landgericht, in dessen Bezirk die Gesellschaft ihren Sitz hat. ²Ist bei dem Landgericht eine Kammer für Handelssachen gebildet, so entscheidet diese an Stelle der Zivilkammer. ³§ 148 Abs. 2 Satz 3 und 4 gilt entsprechend. ⁴Die mündliche Verhandlung findet nicht vor Ablauf der Monatsfrist des Absatzes 1 statt. ⁵ Die Gesellschaft kann unmittelbar nach Ablauf der Monatsfrist des Absatzes 1 eine eingereichte Klage bereits vor Zustellung einsehen und sich von der Geschäftsstelle Auszüge und Abschriften erteilen lassen. ⁶Mehrere Anfechtungsprozesse sind zur gleichzeitigen Verhandlung und Entscheidung zu verbinden.

(4) ¹Der Vorstand hat die Erhebung der Klage unverzüglich in den Gesellschaftsblättern bekanntzumachen. ²Ein Aktionär kann sich als Nebenintervenient nur innerhalb eines Monats nach

5. each member of the management board and supervisory board, if by implementation of the resolution, members of either board would be committing punishable offenses or violating an ordinance or would become liable for damages.

§ 246 Action to set aside a resolution.

(1) The action shall be filed within one month of the adoption of the resolution.

(2) ¹The action shall be brought against the company. ²The company shall be represented by the management board and the supervisory board. ³If the action is brought by the management board or a member thereof, the company shall be represented by the supervisory board and, if the action is brought by a member of the supervisory board, it shall be represented by the management board.

(3) ¹Only the Regional Court in whose district the company has its registered office has jurisdiction over the action. ² If a commercial division is established at the Regional Court, it shall decide instead of the civil division. ³Sec. 148 para. 2 sentences 3 and 4 shall apply accordingly. ⁴Oral proceedings shall not take place prior to the expiration of the one month limitation period specified in para. 1. ⁵The company may inspect a complaint that was filed immediately after the expiration of the one-month time period of para. 1 already before it is served and may request to be furnished with excerpts and copies by the office of the court. ⁶Multiple actions shall be consolidated in order to be heard and decided together.

(4) ¹The management board shall without undue delay announce the filing of the action in the company's designated journals. ²A shareholder may join the complaint as an intervener only within one month from the announcement.

der Bekanntmachung an der Klage beteiligen.

§ 246a Freigabeverfahren.

(1) ¹Wird gegen einen Hauptversammlungsbeschluss über eine Maßnahme der Kapitalbeschaffung, der Kapitalherabsetzung (§§ 182 bis 240) oder einen Unternehmensvertrag (§§ 291 bis 307) Klage erhoben, so kann das Gericht auf Antrag der Gesellschaft durch Beschluss feststellen, dass die Erhebung der Klage der Eintragung nicht entgegensteht und Mängel des Hauptversammlungsbeschlusses die Wirkung der Eintragung unberührt lassen. ²Auf das Verfahren sind § 247, die §§ 82, 83 Abs. 1 und § 84 der Zivilprozessordnung sowie die im ersten Rechtszug für das Verfahren vor dem Landgerichten geltenden Vorschriften der Zivilprozessordnung entsprechend anzuwenden, soweit nichts Abweichendes bestimmt ist. ³Über den Antrag entscheidet ein Senat des Oberlandesgerichts, in dessen Bezirk die Gesellschaft ihren Sitz hat.

(2) Ein Beschluss nach Absatz 1 ergeht, wenn

1. die Klage unzulässig oder offensichtlich unbegründet ist,
2. der Kläger nicht binnen einer Woche nach Zustellung des Antrags durch Urkunden nachgewiesen hat, dass er seit Bekanntmachung der Einberufung einen anteiligen Betrag von mindestens 1.000 Euro hält oder
3. das alsbaldige Wirksamwerden des Hauptversammlungsbeschlusses vorrangig erscheint, weil die vom Antragsteller dargelegten wesentlichen Nachteile für die Gesellschaft und ihre Aktionäre nach freier Überzeugung des Gerichts die Nachteile für den Antragsgegner überwiegen, es sei denn, es liegt eine besondere Schwere des Rechtsverstoßes vor.

(3) ¹Eine Übertragung auf den Einzelrichter ist ausgeschlossen; einer Güte-

§ 246a Release proceedings

(1) ¹If a complaint is filed against a resolution of the general meeting concerning a measure to raise capital (sec. 182 to 240) or an enterprise agreement (sec. 291 to 307), the court may, upon application of the company, determine by resolution that the filing of the complaint does not impede registration and that defects of the resolution of the general meeting do not affect the registration. ²Sec. 247 as well as sec. 82, 83 para. 1 and sec. 84 of the Code of Civil Procedure and the provisions of the Code of Civil Procedure applicable to proceedings of the first instance before the regional courts shall apply accordingly to the present proceedings, unless explicitly provided otherwise. ³The application shall be decided upon by a senate of the higher regional court in whose district the company has its registered office.

(2) A resolution pursuant to para. 1 is issued if

1. the complaint is inadmissible or apparently unsubstantiated,
2. the plaintiff has not demonstrated within one week from the service of the application by written documents that since the announcement of the convening of the meeting he has held a proportionate amount of at least 1,000 euros or
3. the resolution of the general meeting subject to the complaint will take priority if, in the free conviction of the court, the substantial disadvantages to the company and its shareholders which are argued by the applicant outweigh the disadvantages for the respondent, unless the violation of the law is particularly severe.

(3) ¹A transfer to a single judge is excluded; a conciliation hearing is not re-

verhandlung bedarf es nicht. ²In dringenden Fällen kann auf eine mündliche Verhandlung verzichtet werden. ³Die vorgebrachten Tatsachen, auf Grund deren der Beschluss ergehen kann, sind glaubhaft zu machen. ⁴Der Beschluss ist unanfechtbar. ⁵Er ist für das Registergericht bindend; die Feststellung der Bestandskraft der Eintragung wirkt für und gegen jedermann. ⁶Der Beschluss soll spätestens drei Monate nach Antragstellung ergehen; Verzögerungen der Entscheidung sind durch unanfechtbaren Beschluss zu begründen.

(4) ¹Erweist sich die Klage als begründet, so ist die Gesellschaft, die den Beschluss erwirkt hat, verpflichtet, dem Antragsgegner den Schaden zu ersetzen, der ihm aus einer auf dem Beschluss beruhenden Eintragung des Hauptversammlungsbeschlusses entstanden ist. ²Nach der Eintragung lassen Mängel des Beschlusses seine Durchführung unberührt; die Beseitigung dieser Wirkung der Eintragung kann auch nicht als Schadensersatz verlangt werden.

§ 247 Streitwert.

(1) ¹Den Streitwert bestimmt das Prozeßgericht unter Berücksichtigung aller Umstände des einzelnen Falles, insbesondere der Bedeutung der Sache für die Parteien, nach billigem Ermessen. ²Er darf jedoch ein Zehntel des Grundkapitals oder, wenn dieses Zehntel mehr als 500.000 Euro beträgt, 500.000 Euro nur insoweit übersteigen, als die Bedeutung der Sache für den Kläger höher zu bewerten ist.

(2) ¹Macht eine Partei glaubhaft, daß die Belastung mit den Prozeßkosten nach dem gemäß Absatz 1 bestimmten Streitwert ihre wirtschaftliche Lage erheblich gefährden würde, so kann das Prozeßgericht auf ihren Antrag anordnen, daß ihre Verpflichtung zur Zahlung von Gerichtskosten sich nach einem ihrer Wirtschaftslage angepaßten Teil des Streitwerts bemißt. ²Die Anordnung hat

quired. ²In urgent cases, oral proceedings may be waived. ³The facts pleaded based on which the resolution can be issued shall be made credible. ⁴The resolution is unappealable. ⁵It shall be binding on the register court; the determination that the registration cannot be appealed shall be effective for and against everybody. ⁶The resolution shall be issued at the latest three months after the application is made; delays of the decision shall be justified in an unappealable resolution.

(4) ¹If the complaint proves to be substantiated, the company which has procured the resolution shall compensate the respondent for the damages resulting from a registration of the resolution of the general meeting that was based on the resolution of the court. ²After registration, defects of the resolution shall not affect its implementation; the removal of this effect of the registration can also not be claimed as compensation for damages.

§ 247 Value of the matter in dispute.

(1) ¹The court hearing the case shall have discretion in determining the value of the matter in dispute, taking into account all circumstances of the particular case, particularly the significance of the issue for the parties. ²Such value shall, however, only exceed one tenth of the value of the registered share capital or if such one tenth exceeds 500,000 euros, 500,000 euros if the importance of the subject matter for the plaintiff is such that a higher valuation is required.

(2) ¹Should a party furnish evidence that his financial situation would be considerably jeopardized as a result of having to bear the court costs based on the value of the matter in dispute determined pursuant to para. 1, the court may upon application by that party order that his obligation to pay court costs shall be calculated on the basis of a part of the value of the matter in dispute which

zur Folge, daß die begünstigte Partei die Gebühren ihres Rechtsanwalts ebenfalls nur nach diesem Teil des Streitwerts zu entrichten hat. ³Soweit ihr Kosten des Rechtsstreits auferlegt werden oder soweit sie diese übernimmt, hat sie die von dem Gegner entrichteten Gerichtsgebühren und die Gebühren seines Rechtsanwalts nur nach dem Teil des Streitwerts zu erstatten. ⁴Soweit die außergerichtlichen Kosten dem Gegner auferlegt oder von ihm übernommen werden, kann der Rechtsanwalt der begünstigten Partei seine Gebühren von dem Gegner nach dem für diesen geltenden Streitwert beitreiben.

(3) ¹Der Antrag nach Absatz 2 kann vor der Geschäftsstelle des Prozeßgerichts zur Niederschrift erklärt werden. ²Er ist vor der Verhandlung zur Hauptsache anzubringen. ³Später ist er nur zulässig, wenn der angenommene oder festgesetzte Streitwert durch das Prozeßgericht heraufgesetzt wird. ⁴Vor der Entscheidung über den Antrag ist der Gegner zu hören.

§ 248 Urteilswirkung.

(1) ¹Soweit der Beschluß durch rechtskräftiges Urteil für nichtig erklärt ist, wirkt das Urteil für und gegen alle Aktionäre sowie die Mitglieder des Vorstands und des Aufsichtsrats, auch wenn sie nicht Partei sind. ²Der Vorstand hat das Urteil unverzüglich zum Handelsregister einzureichen. ³War der Beschluß in das Handelsregister eingetragen, so ist auch das Urteil einzutragen. ⁴Die Eintragung des Urteils ist in gleicher Weise wie die des Beschlusses bekanntzumachen.

(2) Hatte der Beschluß eine Satzungsänderung zum Inhalt, so ist mit dem Urteil der vollständige Wortlaut der Satzung, wie er sich unter Berücksichtigung des

takes account of his financial situation. ²As a result of such order, the benefiting party shall also only be required to pay attorneys' fees on the basis of that part of the value of the matter in dispute. ³Insofar as such party is ordered to pay or assumes costs incurred by the action, it shall only reimburse the court costs and attorney's fees incurred by the opposing party on the basis of that part of the value of the matter in dispute. ⁴If the opposing party is ordered to pay or assumes the extra-judicial costs, the attorney acting on behalf of the benefiting party may collect his fees from the opposing party in accordance with the value of the matter in dispute applicable to this opposing party.

(3) ¹An application pursuant to para. 2 may be made to the record of the court clerk of the court hearing the case. ²Such application shall be made prior to the hearing of the subject matter. ³A subsequent application may only be made if the assumed or fixed value of the matter in dispute is increased by the court hearing the case. ⁴The opposing party shall be heard prior to any decision on such application.

§ 248 Effect of judgment.

(1) ¹If the resolution is declared null and void by judgment being res judicata, such judgment shall be effective in favor of and against all shareholders as well as members of the management board and supervisory board, even if they were not parties to the action. ²The management board shall submit the judgment to the commercial register without undue delay. ³If the resolution was registered in the commercial register, the judgment shall also be registered. ⁴The registration of the judgment shall be announced in the same manner as the registration of the resolution.

(2) If the resolution concerned an amendment to the articles of association, the judgment shall be submitted to the commercial register together with

Urteils und aller bisherigen Satzungsänderungen ergibt, mit der Bescheinigung eines Notars über diese Tatsache zum Handelsregister einzureichen.

§ 248a Bekanntmachungen zur Anfechtungsklage.

¹Wird der Anfechtungsprozess beendet, hat die börsennotierte Gesellschaft die Verfahrensbeendigung unverzüglich in den Gesellschaftsblättern bekannt zu machen. ²§ 149 Abs. 2 und 3 ist entsprechend anzuwenden.

§ 249 Nichtigkeitsklage.

(1) ¹Erhebt ein Aktionär, der Vorstand oder ein Mitglied des Vorstands oder des Aufsichtsrats Klage auf Feststellung der Nichtigkeit eines Hauptversammlungsbeschlusses gegen die Gesellschaft, so finden § 246 Abs. 2, Abs. 3 Satz 1 bis 5, Abs. 4, §§ 246a, 247, 248 und 248a entsprechende Anwendung. ²Es ist nicht ausgeschlossen, die Nichtigkeit auf andere Weise als durch Erhebung der Klage geltend zu machen. ³Schafft der Hauptversammlungsbeschluss Voraussetzungen für eine Umwandlung nach § 1 des Umwandlungsgesetzes und ist der Umwandlungsbeschluss eingetragen, so gilt § 20 Abs. 2 des Umwandlungsgesetzes für den Hauptversammlungsbeschluss entsprechend.

(2) ¹Mehrere Nichtigkeitsprozesse sind zur gleichzeitigen Verhandlung und Entscheidung zu verbinden. ²Nichtigkeits- und Anfechtungsprozesse können verbunden werden.

the full text of the articles of association taking into account the judgment and all previous amendments to the articles of association and certificated by a notary with respect to the completeness of such text.

§ 248a Announcements concerning the action to set aside.

¹If the proceedings concerning the action to set aside are terminated, the listed company shall announce the termination of the proceedings in the company's designated journals without undue delay. ²Sec. 149 paras. 2 and 3 shall apply accordingly.

§ 249 Action for the declaration of nullity of a resolution.

(1) ¹If a shareholder, the management board or a member of the management board or supervisory board brings an action for the declaration of nullity of a resolution of the general meeting against the company, sec. 246 paras. 2, 3 sentences 1 to 5, para. 4, sec. 246a, 247, 248 and 248a shall apply accordingly. ²The assertion of nullity via means other than by such action shall not be precluded. ³If the resolution of the general meeting creates the premises for a transformation pursuant to sec. 1 of the Transformation Act and if the transformation resolution is registered, sec. 20 para. 2 of the Transformation Act shall apply accordingly to the resolution of the general meeting.

(2) ¹Multiple actions seeking to declare the same resolution null and void shall be consolidated in order to be heard and decided together. ²Actions to set aside a resolution and actions for the declaration of nullity of a resolution may be consolidated.

Zweiter Unterabschnitt. Nichtigkeit bestimmter Hauptversammlungsbeschlüsse

§ 250 Nichtigkeit der Wahl von Aufsichtsratsmitgliedern.

(1) Die Wahl eines Aufsichtsratsmitglieds durch die Hauptversammlung ist außer im Falle des § 241 Nr. 1, 2 und 5 nur dann nichtig, wenn

1. der Aufsichtsrat unter Verstoß gegen § 96 Absatz 4 , § 97 Abs. 2 Satz 1 oder § 98 Abs. 4 zusammengesetzt wird;

2. die Hauptversammlung, obwohl sie an Wahlvorschläge gebunden ist (§§ 6 und 8 des Montan-Mitbestimmungsgesetzes), eine nicht vorgeschlagene Person wählt;

3. durch die Wahl die gesetzliche Höchstzahl der Aufsichtsratsmitglieder überschritten wird (§ 95);

4. die gewählte Person nach § 100 Abs. 1 und 2 bei Beginn ihrer Amtszeit nicht Aufsichtsratsmitglied sein kann;

5. die Wahl gegen § 96 Absatz 2 verstößt.

(2) Für die Klage auf Feststellung, daß die Wahl eines Aufsichtsratsmitglieds nichtig ist, sind parteifähig

1. der Gesamtbetriebsrat der Gesellschaft oder, wenn in der Gesellschaft nur ein Betriebsrat besteht, der Betriebsrat, sowie, wenn die Gesellschaft herrschendes Unternehmen eines Konzerns ist, der Konzernbetriebsrat,

2. der Gesamt- oder Unternehmenssprecherausschuss der Gesellschaft oder, wenn in der Gesellschaft nur ein Sprecherausschuss besteht, der Sprecherausschuss sowie, wenn die Gesellschaft herrschendes Unternehmen eines Konzerns ist, der Konzernsprecherausschuss,

Subsection Two. Nullity of Specific Resolutions of the General Meeting

§ 250 Nullity of the election of supervisory board members.

(1) The election of a member of the supervisory board by the general meeting shall, in addition to the case of sec. 241 nos. 1, 2 and 5, be null and void only if:

1. the composition of the supervisory board is in violation of sec. 96 para. 4, sec. 97 para. 2 sentence 1 or sec. 98 para. 4;

2. the general meeting, although bound by nominations (sec. 6 and 8 of the Coal, Iron and Steel Codetermination Act), has elected a person who was not nominated;

3. as a result of the election, the legal maximum number of supervisory board members has been exceeded (sec. 95);

4. the person elected does not meet the qualifications for supervisory board membership pursuant to sec. 100 paras. 1 and 2 upon commencement of his term of office;

5. the election violates sec. 96 para.2.

(2) The following shall have capacity to be party to an action to declare the election of a member of the supervisory board to be null and void:

1. the central works council of the company or, if only one works council exists in the company, the works council as well as, if the company is the controlling enterprise of a group of companies, the group works council,

2. the central or enterprise spokespersons' committee of the company or, if only one spokespersons' committee exists in the company, the spokespersons' committee as well as, if the company is the controlling enterprise of a group, the group spokespersons' committee,

3. der Gesamtbetriebsrat eines anderen Unternehmens, dessen Arbeitnehmer selbst oder durch Delegierte an der Wahl von Aufsichtsratsmitgliedern der Gesellschaft teilnehmen, oder, wenn in dem anderen Unternehmen nur ein Betriebsrat besteht, der Betriebsrat,
4. der Gesamt- oder Unternehmenssprecherausschuss eines anderen Unternehmens, dessen Arbeitnehmer selbst oder durch Delegierte an der Wahl von Aufsichtsratsmitgliedern der Gesellschaft teilnehmen, oder, wenn in dem anderen Unternehmen nur ein Sprecherausschuss besteht, der Sprecherausschuss,
5. jede in der Gesellschaft oder in einem Unternehmen, dessen Arbeitnehmer selbst oder durch Delegierte an der Wahl von Aufsichtsratsmitgliedern der Gesellschaft teilnehmen, vertretene Gewerkschaft sowie deren Spitzenorganisation.

(3) [1]Erhebt ein Aktionär, der Vorstand, ein Mitglied des Vorstands oder des Aufsichtsrats oder eine in Absatz 2 bezeichnete Organisation oder Vertretung der Arbeitnehmer gegen die Gesellschaft Klage auf Feststellung, dass die Wahl eines Aufsichtsratsmitglieds nichtig ist, so gelten § 246 Abs. 2, Abs. 3 Satz 1 bis 4, Abs. 4, §§ 247, 248 Abs. 1 Satz 2, §§ 248a und 249 Abs. 2 sinngemäß. [2]Es ist nicht ausgeschlossen, die Nichtigkeit auf andere Weise als durch Erhebung der Klage geltend zu machen.

§ 251 Anfechtung der Wahl von Aufsichtsratsmitgliedern.

(1) [1]Die Wahl eines Aufsichtsratsmitglieds durch die Hauptversammlung kann wegen Verletzung des Gesetzes oder der Satzung durch Klage angefochten werden. [2]Ist die Hauptversammlung an Wahlvorschläge gebunden, so kann die Anfechtung auch darauf gestützt werden, daß der Wahlvorschlag gesetz-

3. the central works council of another company whose employees take part either in person or via delegates in the election of members of the supervisory board of the company, or, if only one works council exists in the other enterprise, the works council,
4. the central or enterprise spokespersons' committee of another enterprise whose employees take part either in person or via delegates in the election of members of the supervisory board of the company, or, if only one spokespersons' committee exists in the other enterprise, the spokespersons' committee,
5. each trade union represented in the company or in an enterprise the employees of which take part either in person or via delegates in the election of members of the supervisory board of the company and the leading organization of the trade union.

(3) [1]If a shareholder, the management board, a member of the management board or supervisory board or an organization or employee representative specified in para. 2 brings an action against the company seeking to declare the election of a member to the supervisory board null and void, sec. 246 para. 2, para. 3 sentences 1 to 4, para. 4, sec. 247, sec. 248 para. 1 sentence 2, sec. 248a and sec. 249 para. 2 shall apply accordingly. [2]The assertion of nullity by means other than such an action shall not be precluded.

§ 251 Action to set aside the election of supervisory board members.

(1) [1]An action to set aside the election of a member of the supervisory board by the general meeting may be based on a violation of the law or the articles of association. [2]If the general meeting is bound by nominations, such action may also be based on the fact that such nomination was made illegally. [3]Sec. 243 para. 4 and sec. 244 shall apply.

widrig zustande gekommen ist. ³§ 243 Abs. 4 und § 244 gelten.

(2) ¹Für die Anfechtungsbefugnis gilt § 245 Nr. 1, 2 und 4. ²Die Wahl eines Aufsichtsratsmitglieds, das nach dem Montan-Mitbestimmungsgesetz auf Vorschlag der Betriebsräte gewählt worden ist, kann auch von jedem Betriebsrat eines Betriebs der Gesellschaft, jeder in den Betrieben der Gesellschaft vertretenen Gewerkschaft oder deren Spitzenorganisation angefochten werden. ³Die Wahl eines weiteren Mitglieds, das nach dem Montan-Mitbestimmungsgesetz oder dem Mitbestimmungsergänzungsgesetz auf Vorschlag der übrigen Aufsichtratsmitglieder gewählt worden ist, kann auch von jedem Aufsichtsratsmitglied angefochten werden.

(3) Für das Anfechtungsverfahren gelten die §§ 246, 247, 248 Abs. 1 Satz 2 und § 248a.

§ 252 Urteilswirkung.

(1) Erhebt ein Aktionär, der Vorstand, ein Mitglied des Vorstands oder des Aufsichtsrats oder eine in § 250 Abs. 2 bezeichnete Organisation oder Vertretung der Arbeitnehmer gegen die Gesellschaft Klage auf Feststellung, daß die Wahl eines Aufsichtsratsmitglieds durch die Hauptversammlung nichtig ist, so wirkt ein Urteil, das die Nichtigkeit der Wahl rechtskräftig feststellt, für und gegen alle Aktionäre und Arbeitnehmer der Gesellschaft, alle Arbeitnehmer von anderen Unternehmen, deren Arbeitnehmer selbst oder durch Delegierte an der Wahl von Aufsichtsratsmitgliedern der Gesellschaft teilnehmen, die Mitglieder des Vorstands und des Aufsichtsrats sowie die in § 250 Abs. 2 bezeichneten Organisationen und Vertretungen der Arbeitnehmer, auch wenn sie nicht Partei sind.

(2) ¹Authority to bring an action to set aside a resolution shall be governed by sec. 245 nos. 1, 2 and 4. ²An action to set aside the election of a member of the supervisory board whose election was made pursuant to the Coal, Iron and Steel Codetermination Act upon nomination by the works council may also be brought by any works council in any of the company's facilities, any trade union represented in the company's facilities or the leading organization of such trade union. ³An action to set aside the election of a further member who is elected upon nomination by the other members of the supervisory board pursuant to the Coal, Iron and Steel Codetermination Act or the Codetermination Amendment Act may also be brought by any member of the supervisory board.

(3) The procedure for an action to set aside the election shall be governed by sec. 246, 247, 248 para. 1 sentence 2 and sec. 248a.

§ 252 Effect of judgment.

(1) If a shareholder, the management board, a member of the management board or the supervisory board, an organization or an employee representative specified in sec. 250 para. 2 brings an action to declare the election by the general meeting of a member of the supervisory board to be null and void, a judgment being res judicata which declares such election to be null and void shall for all purposes be binding on the shareholders and company employees, all employees of other enterprises who participate directly or through a representative in the election of supervisory board members, the members of the management board and the supervisory board, as well as the organizations and employee representatives specified in sec. 250 para. 2, even if they were not parties to the action.

(2) ¹Wird die Wahl eines Aufsichtsratsmitglieds durch die Hauptversammlung durch rechtskräftiges Urteil für nichtig erklärt, so wirkt das Urteil für und gegen alle Aktionäre sowie die Mitglieder des Vorstands und Aufsichtsrats, auch wenn sie nicht Partei sind. ²Im Fall des § 251 Abs. 2 Satz 2 wirkt das Urteil auch für und gegen die nach dieser Vorschrift anfechtungsberechtigten Betriebsräte, Gewerkschaften und Spitzenorganisationen, auch wenn sie nicht Partei sind.

§ 253 Nichtigkeit des Beschlusses über die Verwendung des Bilanzgewinns.

(1) ¹Der Beschluß über die Verwendung des Bilanzgewinns ist außer in den Fällen des § 173 Abs. 3, des § 217 Abs. 2 und des § 241 nur dann nichtig, wenn die Feststellung des Jahresabschlusses, auf dem er beruht, nichtig ist. ²Die Nichtigkeit des Beschlusses aus diesem Grunde kann nicht mehr geltend gemacht werden, wenn die Nichtigkeit der Feststellung des Jahresabschlusses nicht mehr geltend gemacht werden kann.

(2) Für die Klage auf Feststellung der Nichtigkeit gegen die Gesellschaft gilt § 249.

§ 254 Anfechtung des Beschlusses über die Verwendung des Bilanzgewinns.

(1) Der Beschluß über die Verwendung des Bilanzgewinns kann außer nach § 243 auch angefochten werden, wenn die Hauptversammlung aus dem Bilanzgewinn Beträge in Gewinnrücklagen einstellt oder als Gewinn vorträgt, die nicht nach Gesetz oder Satzung von der Verteilung unter die Aktionäre ausgeschlossen sind, obwohl die Einstellung oder der Gewinnvortrag bei vernünftiger kaufmännischer Beurteilung nicht notwendig ist, um die Lebens- und Widerstandsfähigkeit der Gesellschaft

(2) ¹If the election of a member of the supervisory board by the general meeting has been declared null and void by a judgment being res judicata, such judgment shall be binding for all purposes on all shareholders and members of the management board and the supervisory board, even if they were not parties to the action. ²Where the action falls within sec. 251 para. 2 sentence 2, the judgment shall also be binding on the works councils, trade unions and leading organizations that were entitled to bring an action, even if they were not parties to the action in the case in question.

§ 253 Nullity of a resolution on the appropriation of the balance sheet profit.

(1) ¹In addition to the cases of sec. 173 para. 3, sec. 217 para. 2 and sec. 241, a resolution on the appropriation of the balance sheet profit shall only be null and void if the formal approval of the annual financial statement upon which it is based is null and void. ²The nullity of such resolution on this basis may not be asserted if the nullity of the formal approval of the related annual financial statements may no longer be asserted.

(2) Sec. 249 shall apply to an action for the declaration of nullity of a resolution brought against the company.

§ 254 Action to set aside a resolution on the appropriation of the balance sheet profit.

(1) In addition to sec. 243, an action to set aside a resolution on the appropriation of the balance sheet profit may also be brought if the general meeting allocates to revenue reserves or carries forward as profit amounts taken from the balance sheet profit which are not excluded from distribution to shareholders by act of law or pursuant to the articles of association, even though the allocation or the profit carried forward is not, according to the judgment of a reasonable businessman, necessary in

für einen hinsichtlich der wirtschaftlichen und finanziellen Notwendigkeiten übersehbaren Zeitraum zu sichern und dadurch unter die Aktionäre kein Gewinn in Höhe von mindestens vier vom Hundert des Grundkapitals abzüglich von noch nicht eingeforderten Einlagen verteilt werden kann.

(2) ¹Für die Anfechtung gelten die §§ 244 bis 246, 247 bis 248a. ²Die Anfechtungsfrist beginnt auch dann mit der Beschlußfassung, wenn der Jahresabschluß nach § 316 Abs. 3 des Handelsgesetzbuchs erneut zu prüfen ist. ³Zu einer Anfechtung nach Absatz 1 sind Aktionäre nur befugt, wenn ihre Anteile zusammen den zwanzigsten Teil des Grundkapitals oder den anteiligen Betrag von 500.000 Euro erreichen.

§ 255 Anfechtung der Kapitalerhöhung gegen Einlagen.

(1) Der Beschluß über eine Kapitalerhöhung gegen Einlagen kann nach § 243 angefochten werden.

(2) ¹Die Anfechtung kann, wenn das Bezugsrecht der Aktionäre ganz oder zum Teil ausgeschlossen worden ist, auch darauf gestützt werden, daß der sich aus dem Erhöhungsbeschluß ergebende Ausgabebetrag oder der Mindestbetrag, unter dem die neuen Aktien nicht ausgegeben werden sollen, unangemessen niedrig ist. ²Dies gilt nicht, wenn die neuen Aktien von einem Dritten mit der Verpflichtung übernommen werden sollen, sie den Aktionären zum Bezug anzubieten.

(3) Für die Anfechtung gelten die §§ 244 bis 248a.

order to ensure the viability and resilience of the company for a period during which economic and financial needs are foreseeable, and as a result no profits of at least four percent of the registered share capital less any contributions not yet called in may be distributed to the shareholders.

(2) ¹Sec. 244 to 246, sec. 247 to sec. 248a shall apply to the action to set aside a resolution. ²The period for bringing the action shall commence on the date the resolution is adopted even if the annual financial statements are to be re-audited pursuant to sec. 316 para. 3 of the Commercial Code. ³Shareholders may only bring an action pursuant to para. 1 if their shareholdings together amount to one-twentieth of the registered share capital or represent a proportionate amount of not less than 500,000 euros.

§ 255 Action to set aside a capital increase against contributions.

(1) An action to set aside a resolution on a capital increase against contributions may be brought pursuant to sec. 243.

(2) ¹If the subscription right of the shareholders has been wholly or partially excluded, the action to set aside a resolution may also be based on the ground that the amount of the issue price arising from the resolution on the capital increase or the lowest amount below which new shares may not be issued is unreasonably low. ²This shall not apply if the new shares are to be acquired by a third party with the obligation to offer them to shareholders for subscription.

(3) Sec. 244 to 248a shall apply to the action to set aside a resolution.

Zweiter Abschnitt. Nichtigkeit des festgestellten Jahresabschlusses

§ 256 Nichtigkeit.

(1) Ein festgestellter Jahresabschluß ist außer in den Fällen des § 173 Abs. 3, § 234 Abs. 3 und § 235 Abs. 2 nichtig, wenn

1. er durch seinen Inhalt Vorschriften verletzt, die ausschließlich oder überwiegend zum Schutze der Gläubiger der Gesellschaft gegeben sind,
2. er im Falle einer gesetzlichen Prüfungspflicht nicht nach § 316 Abs. 1 und 3 des Handelsgesetzbuchs geprüft worden ist,
3. er im Falle einer gesetzlichen Prüfungspflicht von Personen geprüft worden ist, die nach § 319 Absatz 1 des Handelsgesetzbuchs oder nach Artikel 25 des Einführungsgesetzes zum Handelsgesetzbuch nicht Abschlussprüfer sind oder aus anderen Gründen als den folgenden nicht zum Abschlussprüfer bestellt sind:

   a) Verstoß gegen § 319 Absatz 2, 3 oder 4 des Handelsgesetzbuchs,
   b) Verstoß gegen § 319a Absatz 1 oder 3 des Handelsgesetzbuchs,
   c) Verstoß gegen § 319b Absatz 1 des Handelsgesetzbuchs,
   d) Verstoß gegen die Verordnung (EU) Nr. 537/2014 des Europäischen Parlaments und des Rates vom 16. April 2014 über spezifische Anforderungen an die Abschlussprüfung bei Unternehmen von öffentlichem Interesse und zur Aufhebung des Beschlusses 2005/909/EG der Kommission (ABl. L 158 vom 27.5.2014, S. 77, L 170 vom 11.6.2014, S. 66)
4. bei seiner Feststellung die Bestimmungen des Gesetzes oder der

Section Two. Nullity of the Formally Approved Annual Financial Statements

§ 256 Nullity.

(1) In addition to the cases of sec. 173 para. 3, sec. 234 para. 3 and sec. 235 para. 2, formally approved annual financial statements shall be null and void if

1. by virtue of their contents, they infringe provisions which are exclusively or primarily for the protection of creditors of the company,
2. in a case where there is a legal requirement for audit, they have not been audited in accordance with sec. 316 paras. 1 and 3 of the Commercial Code,
3. in a case where there is a legal requirement for an audit, they have been audited by persons who according to sec. 319 para. 1 of the Commercial Code or Article 25 of the Introductory Act to the Commercial Code are not auditors of annual financial statements or which are not appointed as auditors of annual financial statements for reasons other than:

   a) a violation of sec. 319 paras. 2, 3 or 4 of the Commercial Code,
   b) a violation of sec. 319a para. 1 or 3 of the Commercial Code,
   c) a violation of sec. 319b para. 1 of the Commercial Code,
   d) a violation of the regulation (EU) No. 537/2014 of the European Parliament and the Council of April, 16, 2014 on Specific Requirements Regarding Statutory Audit of Public-Interest Entities And Repealing Commission Decision 2005/909/EC (ABl. L 158 dated on the 27.05.2014, pg. 77, L 170 dated 11.06.2014, pg. 66),
4. the formal approval thereof constituted a breach of provisions of the

Satzung über die Einstellung von Beträgen in Kapital- oder Gewinnrücklagen oder über die Entnahme von Beträgen aus Kapital- oder Gewinnrücklagen verletzt worden sind.

(2) Ein von Vorstand und Aufsichtsrat festgestellter Jahresabschluß ist außer nach Absatz 1 nur nichtig, wenn der Vorstand oder der Aufsichtsrat bei seiner Feststellung nicht ordnungsgemäß mitgewirkt hat.

(3) Ein von der Hauptversammlung festgestellter Jahresabschluß ist außer nach Absatz 1 nur nichtig, wenn die Feststellung

1. in einer Hauptversammlung beschlossen worden ist, die unter Verstoß gegen § 121 Abs. 2 und 3 Satz 1 oder Abs. 4 einberufen war,
2. nicht nach § 130 Abs. 1 und 2 Satz 1 und Abs. 4 beurkundet ist,
3. auf Anfechtungsklage durch Urteil rechtskräftig für nichtig erklärt worden ist.

(4) Wegen Verstoßes gegen die Vorschriften über die Gliederung des Jahresabschlusses sowie wegen der Nichtbeachtung von Formblättern, nach denen der Jahresabschluß zu gliedern ist, ist der Jahresabschluß nur nichtig, wenn seine Klarheit und Übersichtlichkeit dadurch wesentlich beeinträchtigt sind.

(5) ¹Wegen Verstoßes gegen die Bewertungsvorschriften ist der Jahresabschluß nur nichtig, wenn

1. Posten überbewertet oder
2. Posten unterbewertet sind und dadurch die Vermögens- und Ertragslage der Gesellschaft vorsätzlich unrichtig wiedergegeben oder verschleiert wird.

law or articles of association concerning the allocation of amounts to capital reserves or revenue reserves or the withdrawal of amounts from capital reserves or revenue reserves.

(2) In addition to those cases pursuant to para. 1, annual financial statements formally approved by the management board and the supervisory board shall only be null and void if the management board or the supervisory board did not duly take part in the formal approval thereof.

(3) In addition to those cases pursuant to para. 1, annual financial statements formally approved by the general meeting shall only be null and void if the formal approval thereof

1. has been resolved upon by a general meeting which was convened in breach of sec. 121 paras. 2 and 3 sentence 1 or para. 4,
2. has not been notarized pursuant to sec. 130 paras. 1 and 2 sentence 1 and para. 4,
3. has been declared null and void by a judgment being res judicata in an action to set aside a resolution.

(4) The annual financial statements shall only be null and void on the ground of breach of the provisions regarding the structure of annual financial statements and on the ground of non-compliance with forms to be used when drawing up the annual financial statements if their clarity and readability has been significantly impaired as a result.

(5) ¹The annual financial statements shall be null and void for breach of the provisions on valuation only if:

1. items have been overvalued or
2. items have been undervalued and in consequence the assets situation and profitability of the company have been intentionally misrepresented or concealed.

²Überbewertet sind Aktivposten, wenn sie mit einem höheren Wert, Passivposten, wenn sie mit einem niedrigeren Betrag angesetzt sind, als nach §§ 253 bis 256a des Handelsgesetzbuchs zulässig ist. ³Unterbewertet sind Aktivposten, wenn sie mit einem niedrigeren Wert, Passivposten, wenn sie mit einem höheren Betrag angesetzt sind, als nach §§ 253 bis 256a des Handelsgesetzbuchs zulässig ist. ⁴Bei Kreditinstituten oder Finanzdienstleistungsinstituten sowie bei Kapitalanlagegesellschaften im Sinn des § 17 des Kapitalanlagegesetzbuchs liegt ein Verstoß gegen die Bewertungsvorschriften nicht vor, soweit die Abweichung nach den für sie geltenden Vorschriften, insbesondere den §§ 340e bis 340g des Handelsgesetzbuchs, zulässig ist; dies gilt entsprechend für Versicherungsunternehmen nach Maßgabe der für sie geltenden Vorschriften, insbesondere der §§ 341b bis 341h des Handelsgesetzbuchs.

(6) ¹Die Nichtigkeit nach Absatz 1 Nr. 1, 3 und 4, Absatz 2, Absatz 3 Nr. 1 und 2, Absatz 4 und 5 kann nicht mehr geltend gemacht werden, wenn seit der Bekanntmachung nach § 325 Abs. 2 des Handelsgesetzbuchs in den Fällen des Absatzes 1 Nr. 3 und 4, des Absatzes 2 und des Absatzes 3 Nr. 1 und 2 sechs Monate, in den anderen Fällen drei Jahre verstrichen sind. ²Ist bei Ablauf der Frist eine Klage auf Feststellung der Nichtigkeit des Jahresabschlusses rechtshängig, so verlängert sich die Frist, bis über die Klage rechtskräftig entschieden ist oder sie sich auf andere Weise endgültig erledigt hat.

(7) ¹Für die Klage auf Feststellung der Nichtigkeit gegen die Gesellschaft gilt § 249 sinngemäß. ²Hat die Gesellschaft Wertpapiere im Sinne des § 2 Absatz 1 des Wertpapierhandelsgesetzes ausgegeben, die an einer inländischen Börse zum Handel im regulierten Markt zugelassen sind, so hat das Gericht der Bundesanstalt für Finanzdienstleistungsaufsicht den Eingang einer Klage

²Assets shall be deemed to be overvalued if they are shown at a higher value and debit items if they are shown at a lower value than permitted pursuant to sec. 253 to 256 of the Commercial Code. ³Assets shall be deemed to be undervalued if they are shown at a lower value and debit items if they are shown at a higher value than permitted pursuant to sec. 253 to 256 of the Commercial Code. ⁴In the case of credit institutions and financial services institutions as well as capital investment companies within the meaning of sec. 2 para. 6 of the Financial Investment Act there shall be no breach of valuation provisions insofar as the divergence is permitted in accordance with the provisions applicable to them, in particular sec. 340e to 340g of the Commercial Code; this applies accordingly to insurance companies according to the provisions applicable to them, in particular sec. 341b to 341h of the Commercial Code.

(6) ¹Nullity in accordance with para. 1 nos. 1, 3 and 4, para. 2, para. 3 nos. 1 and 2, paras. 4 and 5 may no longer be asserted if, in the case of para. 1 nos. 3 and 4, para. 2 and para. 3 nos. 1 and 2, six months or, in other cases, three years have elapsed since the announcement pursuant to sec. 325 para. 2 of the Commercial Code. ²If upon expiration of such period an action for the declaration of nullity of the annual financial statements is pending, such period shall be extended until a decision being res judicata has been reached on the action or the action has been finally settled in another manner.

(7) ¹Sec. 249 shall apply accordingly to an action for the declaration of nullity of the annual financial statements against the company. ²If the company has issued securities within the meaning of sec. 17 of the capital Investment code which are admitted for trading in a regulated market at a German stock exchange, the court shall notify the Federal Financial Supervisory Authority of the filing of a

auf Feststellung der Nichtigkeit sowie jede rechtskräftige Entscheidung über diese Klage mitzuteilen.

§ 257 Anfechtung der Feststellung des Jahresabschlusses durch die Hauptversammlung.

(1) ¹Die Feststellung des Jahresabschlusses durch die Hauptversammlung kann nach § 243 angefochten werden. ²Die Anfechtung kann jedoch nicht darauf gestützt werden, daß der Inhalt des Jahresabschlusses gegen Gesetz oder Satzung verstößt.

(2) ¹Für die Anfechtung gelten die §§ 244 bis 246, 247 bis 248a. ²Die Anfechtungsfrist beginnt auch dann mit der Beschlußfassung, wenn der Jahresabschluß nach § 316 Abs. 3 des Handelsgesetzbuchs erneut zu prüfen ist.

Dritter Abschnitt. Sonderprüfung wegen unzulässiger Unterbewertung

§ 258 Bestellung der Sonderprüfer.

(1) ¹Besteht Anlaß für die Annahme, daß

1. in einem festgestellten Jahresabschluß bestimmte Posten nicht unwesentlich unterbewertet sind (§ 256 Abs. 5 Satz 3) oder

2. der Anhang die vorgeschriebenen Angaben nicht oder nicht vollständig enthält und der Vorstand in der Hauptversammlung die fehlenden Angaben, obwohl nach ihnen gefragt worden ist, nicht gemacht hat und die Aufnahme der Frage in die Niederschrift verlangt worden ist,

so hat das Gericht auf Antrag Sonderprüfer zu bestellen. ²Die Sonderprüfer

complaint for declaration of nullity and every decision regarding this complaint which becomes res judicata.

§ 257 Action to set aside the formal approval of the annual financial statements by the general meeting.

(1) ¹An action to set aside the formal approval of the annual financial statements by the general meeting may be brought pursuant to sec. 243. ²However, such action may not be based on the ground that the contents of the annual financial statements are in breach of the law or the articles of association.

(2) ¹Sec. 244 to 246, 247 to 248a shall apply to the action to set aside a resolution. ²The period for bringing such action shall commence on the date the resolution is adopted, even in the case where the annual financial statements are to be re-audited pursuant to sec. 316 para. 3 of the Commercial Code.

Section Three. Special Audit Due to Unlawful Undervaluation

§ 258 Appointment of special auditors.

(1) ¹The court shall upon application appoint special auditors if there is reason to suppose that:

1. specific items in the formally approved financial statements have been undervalued (sec. 256 para. 5 sentence 3) to a not immaterial extent, or

2. that the notes do not contain or do not contain in full the required information and the management board has not, despite a question pertaining to the matter being raised, supplied the missing information at the general meeting, and a formal request was made to record such question in the minutes.

²The special auditors shall examine the allegedly defective items as to whether

haben die bemängelten Posten darauf zu prüfen, ob sie nicht unwesentlich unterbewertet sind. ³Sie haben den Anhang darauf zu prüfen, ob die vorgeschriebenen Angaben nicht oder nicht vollständig gemacht worden sind und der Vorstand in der Hauptversammlung die fehlenden Angaben, obwohl nach ihnen gefragt worden ist, nicht gemacht hat und die Aufnahme der Frage in die Niederschrift verlangt worden ist.

(1a) Bei Kreditinstituten oder Finanzdienstleistungsinstituten sowie bei Kapitalverwaltungsgesellschaften im Sinn des § 17 des Kapitalanlagegesetzbuchs kann ein Sonderprüfer nach Absatz 1 nicht bestellt werden, soweit die Unterbewertung oder die fehlenden Angaben im Anhang auf der Anwendung des § 340f des Handelsgesetzbuchs beruhen.

(2) ¹Der Antrag muß innerhalb eines Monats nach der Hauptversammlung über den Jahresabschluß gestellt werden. ²Dies gilt auch, wenn der Jahresabschluß nach § 316 Abs. 3 des Handelsgesetzbuchs erneut zu prüfen ist. ³Er kann nur von Aktionären gestellt werden, deren Anteile zusammen den Schwellenwert des § 142 Abs. 2 erreichen. ⁴Die Antragsteller haben die Aktien bis zur Entscheidung über den Antrag zu hinterlegen oder eine Versicherung des depotführenden Instituts vorzulegen, dass die Aktien so lange nicht veräußert werden, und glaubhaft zu machen, daß sie seit mindestens drei Monaten vor dem Tage der Hauptversammlung Inhaber der Aktien sind. ⁵Zur Glaubhaftmachung genügt eine eidesstattliche Versicherung vor einem Notar.

(3) ¹Vor der Bestellung hat das Gericht den Vorstand, den Aufsichtsrat und den Abschlußprüfer zu hören. ²Gegen die Entscheidung ist die Beschwerde zulässig. ³Über den Antrag gemäß Absatz 1 entscheidet das Landgericht, in dessen Bezirk die Gesellschaft ihren Sitz hat.

they have been undervalued to a not immaterial extent. ³They shall examine the notes as to whether the required information has not been supplied, or has not been supplied in full, and whether the management board did not, despite a question pertaining to the matter being raised, supply the missing information at the general meeting, and a formal request was made to record such question in the minutes.

(1a) In the case of credit institutions or financial services institutions as well as capital management companies within the meaning of sec. 17 of the Capital Investment Act, a special auditor cannot be appointed pursuant to para. 1 insofar as the undervaluation or the information missing from the notes depends upon application of sec. 340f of the Commercial Code.

(2) ¹The application shall be made within one month of the general meeting dealing with the annual financial statements. ²This shall also apply if the annual financial statements are to be re-audited pursuant to sec. 316 para. 3 of the Commercial Code. ³It may only be made by shareholders whose shares taken together reach the threshold set forth in sec. 142 para. 2. ⁴The applicants shall either deposit their shares until the decision on the application is reached or shall provide an assurance of the custodian bank that the shares will not be sold until such time, and shall further furnish evidence that they have held the shares for not less than three months prior to the date of the general meeting. ⁵A sworn affidavit made before a notary shall be sufficient evidence.

(3) ¹Prior to appointing an auditor, the court shall hear the management board, the supervisory board and the auditor of annual financial statements. ²The decision is subject to appeal. ³The Regional Court in the district where the company has its registered office shall decide on the application pursuant to para. 1.

(4) ¹Sonderprüfer nach Absatz 1 können nur Wirtschaftsprüfer und Wirtschaftsprüfungsgesellschaften sein. ²Für die Auswahl gelten § 319 Abs. 2 bis 4, § 319a Abs. 1 und § 319b Abs. 1 des Handelsgesetzbuchs sinngemäß. ³Der Abschlußprüfer der Gesellschaft und Personen, die in den letzten drei Jahren vor der Bestellung Abschlußprüfer der Gesellschaft waren, können nicht Sonderprüfer nach Absatz 1 sein.

(5) ¹§ 142 Abs. 6 über den Ersatz angemessener barer Auslagen und die Vergütung gerichtlich bestellter Sonderprüfer, § 145 Abs. 1 bis 3 über die Rechte der Sonderprüfer, § 146 über die Kosten der Sonderprüfung und § 323 des Handelsgesetzbuchs über die Verantwortlichkeit des Abschlußprüfers gelten sinngemäß. ²Die Sonderprüfer nach Absatz 1 haben die Rechte nach § 145 Abs. 2 auch gegenüber dem Abschlußprüfer der Gesellschaft.

§ 259 Prüfungsbericht. Abschließende Feststellungen.

(1) ¹Die Sonderprüfer haben über das Ergebnis der Prüfung schriftlich zu berichten. ²Stellen die Sonderprüfer bei Wahrnehmung ihrer Aufgaben fest, daß Posten überbewertet sind (§ 256 Abs. 5 Satz 2), oder daß gegen die Vorschriften über die Gliederung des Jahresabschlusses verstoßen ist oder Formblätter nicht beachtet sind, so haben sie auch darüber zu berichten. ³Für den Bericht gilt § 145 Abs. 4 bis 6 sinngemäß.

(2) ¹Sind nach dem Ergebnis der Prüfung die bemängelten Posten nicht unwesentlich unterbewertet (§ 256 Abs. 5 Satz 3), so haben die Sonderprüfer am Schluß ihres Berichts in einer abschließenden Feststellung zu erklären,

1. zu welchem Wert die einzelnen Aktivposten mindestens und mit welchem Betrag die einzelnen Pas-

(4) ¹A special auditor pursuant to para. 1 shall be either a certified public accountant or a firm of certified public accountants. ²The selection shall be subject to the analogous application of sec. 319 paras. 2 to 4, sec. 319a para. 1 and sec. 319b para. 1 of the Commercial Code. ³The company's current auditor of annual financial statements and parties that have acted in this capacity within three years of such appointment may not serve as special auditor pursuant to para. 1.

(5) ¹Sec. 142 para. 6 regarding reimbursement of reasonable cash expenses and remuneration of special auditors appointed by the court, sec. 145 paras. 1 to 3 regarding the rights of special auditors, sec. 146 regarding the costs of the special audit and sec. 323 of the Commercial Code pertaining to the responsibilities of the special auditor shall apply accordingly. ²A special auditor appointed pursuant to para. 1 can also enforce rights granted under sec. 145 para. 2 against the company's auditor of annual financial statements.

§ 259 Audit report. Final assessment.

(1) ¹The special auditors shall report the results of the audit in writing. ²Should the special auditors determine in carrying out their duties that items have been overvalued (sec. 256 para. 5 sentence 2), or that provisions governing the structure of the annual financial statements have been violated or standard forms have not been observed, this shall also be reported. ³Sec. 145 paras. 4 to 6 shall apply accordingly to such report.

(2) ¹If the audit finds that the disputed items have indeed been undervalued to a not immaterial extent (sec. 256 para. 5 sentence 3), the special auditors shall state the following as a final assessment in the conclusion to the report:

1. the minimum value which ought to have been shown for each individual asset item and the maximum value

sivposten höchstens anzusetzen waren;
2. um welchen Betrag der Jahresüberschuß sich beim Ansatz dieser Werte oder Beträge erhöht oder der Jahresfehlbetrag sich ermäßigt hätte.

²Die Sonderprüfer haben ihrer Beurteilung die Verhältnisse am Stichtag des Jahresabschlusses zugrunde zu legen. ³Sie haben für den Ansatz der Werte und Beträge nach Nummer 1 diejenige Bewertungs- und Abschreibungsmethode zugrunde zu legen, nach der die Gesellschaft die zu bewertenden Gegenstände oder vergleichbare Gegenstände zuletzt in zulässiger Weise bewertet hat.

(3) Sind nach dem Ergebnis der Prüfung die bemängelten Posten nicht oder nur unwesentlich unterbewertet (§ 256 Abs. 5 Satz 3), so haben die Sonderprüfer am Schluß ihres Berichts in einer abschließenden Feststellung zu erklären, daß nach ihrer pflichtmäßigen Prüfung und Beurteilung die bemängelten Posten nicht unzulässig unterbewertet sind.

(4) ¹Hat nach dem Ergebnis der Prüfung der Anhang die vorgeschriebenen Angaben nicht oder nicht vollständig enthalten und der Vorstand in der Hauptversammlung die fehlenden Angaben, obwohl nach ihnen gefragt worden ist, nicht gemacht und ist die Aufnahme der Frage in die Niederschrift verlangt worden, so haben die Sonderprüfer am Schluß ihres Berichts in einer abschließenden Feststellung die fehlenden Angaben zu machen. ²Ist die Angabe von Abweichungen von Bewertungs- oder Abschreibungsmethoden unterlassen worden, so ist in der abschließenden Feststellung auch der Betrag anzugeben, um den der Jahresüberschuß oder Jahresfehlbetrag ohne die Abweichung, deren Angabe unterlassen wurde, höher oder niedriger gewesen wäre. ³Sind nach dem Ergebnis der Prüfung keine Angaben nach Satz 1 unterlassen worden, so haben die Sonderprüfer in ei-

which ought to have been shown for each individual debit item;
2. the amount by which the annual net income would have increased or the annual net loss would have decreased had these figures been used.

²The special auditors shall base their judgments on the closing date of the annual financial statements. ³In determining the values and amounts referred to in no. 1, the same valuation and depreciation methods should be applied as were applied by the company the last time it valued the items which are to be assessed or similar items in a permissible manner.

(3) If the audit finds that the disputed items have not been undervalued or have only been undervalued to an immaterial extent (sec. 256 para. 5 sentence 3), the special auditors shall state their final assessment in the conclusion to the report that after having carried out the audit with due professional diligence, they are of the opinion that the disputed items have not been unlawfully undervalued.

(4) ¹If the audit finds that the notes do not contain or do not contain in full the required information and the management board has not, despite a question pertaining to the matter being raised, supplied the missing information at the general meeting, and a formal request was made to record such question in the minutes, the special auditors shall provide the missing information in their final assessment at the conclusion of the report. ²If information has failed to be given concerning inconsistencies in the valuation or depreciation methods, the final assessment shall also state the amount by which the annual net income or annual net loss would have been higher or lower without the unmentioned inconsistencies. ³If the audit finds that no information pursuant to para. 1 has been omitted, the special auditors shall state in a final assessment that after having carried out the audit

ner abschließenden Feststellung zu erklären, daß nach ihrer pflichtmäßigen Prüfung und Beurteilung im Anhang keine der vorgeschriebenen Angaben unterlassen worden ist.

(5) Der Vorstand hat die abschließenden Feststellungen der Sonderprüfer nach den Absätzen 2 bis 4 unverzüglich in den Gesellschaftsblättern bekanntzumachen.

§ 260 Gerichtliche Entscheidung über die abschließenden Feststellungen der Sonderprüfer.

(1) ¹Gegen abschließende Feststellungen der Sonderprüfer nach § 259 Abs. 2 und 3 können die Gesellschaft oder Aktionäre, deren Anteile zusammen den zwanzigsten Teil des Grundkapitals oder den anteiligen Betrag von 500.000 Euro erreichen, innerhalb eines Monats nach der Veröffentlichung im Bundesanzeiger den Antrag auf Entscheidung durch das nach § 132 Abs. 1 zuständige Gericht stellen. ²§ 258 Abs. 2 Satz 4 und 5 gilt sinngemäß. ³Der Antrag muß auf Feststellung des Betrags gerichtet sein, mit dem die im Antrag zu bezeichnenden Aktivposten mindestens oder die im Antrag zu bezeichnenden Passivposten höchstens anzusetzen waren. ⁴Der Antrag der Gesellschaft kann auch auf Feststellung gerichtet sein, daß der Jahresabschluß die in der abschließenden Feststellung der Sonderprüfer festgestellten Unterbewertungen nicht enthielt.

(2) ¹Über den Antrag entscheidet das Gericht unter Würdigung aller Umstände nach freier Überzeugung. ²§ 259 Abs. 2 Satz 2 und 3 ist anzuwenden. ³Soweit die volle Aufklärung aller maßgebenden Umstände mit erheblichen Schwierigkeiten verbunden ist, hat das Gericht die anzusetzenden Werte oder Beträge zu schätzen.

with due professional diligence, they are of the opinion that no information which is required to be given has been omitted in the notes.

(5) The management board shall have the final assessments made by the special auditors pursuant to paras. 2 to 4 announced in the company's designated journals without undue delay.

§ 260 Court decision on the final assessment of the special auditors.

(1) ¹Both the company and shareholders whose aggregate shares represent at least one-twentieth of the registered share capital or the proportionate amount of 500,000 euros shall be entitled to file an application seeking a court decision against the final assessment reached by the special auditors pursuant to sec. 259 paras. 2 and 3 with the court having jurisdiction pursuant to sec. 132 para. 1 within one month of such final assessment being published in the Federal Law Gazette. ²Sec. 258 para. 2 sentences 4 and 5 shall apply accordingly. ³The application shall request determination of the minimum value which ought to have been shown for each individual asset item and the maximum value which ought to have been shown for each individual debit item specified therein. ⁴An application filed by the company may also seek determination that the annual financial statements did not contain the undervaluations stated in the final assessment of the special auditors.

(2) ¹The court shall decide on the application at its own discretion, giving due regard to all circumstances. ² Sec. 259 para. 2 sentences 2 and 3 shall apply. ³Insofar as a complete investigation of all pertinent circumstances would entail substantial difficulties, the values or amounts to be shown shall be estimated by the court.

(3) ¹§ 99 Abs. 1, Abs. 2 Satz 1, Abs. 3 und 5 gilt sinngemäß. ²Das Gericht hat seine Entscheidung der Gesellschaft und, wenn Aktionäre den Antrag nach Absatz 1 gestellt haben, auch diesen zuzustellen. ³Es hat sie ferner ohne Gründe in den Gesellschaftsblättern bekanntzumachen. ⁴Die Beschwerde steht der Gesellschaft und Aktionären zu, deren Anteile zusammen den zwanzigsten Teil des Grundkapitals oder den anteiligen Betrag von 500.000 Euro erreichen. ⁵§ 258 Abs. 2 Satz 4 und 5 gilt sinngemäß. ⁶Die Beschwerdefrist beginnt mit der Bekanntmachung der Entscheidung im Bundesanzeiger, jedoch für die Gesellschaft und, wenn Aktionäre den Antrag nach Absatz 1 gestellt haben, auch für diese nicht vor der Zustellung der Entscheidung.

(4) ¹Die Kosten sind, wenn dem Antrag stattgegeben wird, der Gesellschaft, sonst dem Antragsteller aufzuerlegen. ²§ 247 gilt sinngemäß.

§ 261 Entscheidung über den Ertrag auf Grund höherer Bewertung.

(1) ¹Haben die Sonderprüfer in ihrer abschließenden Feststellung erklärt, daß Posten unterbewertet sind, und ist gegen diese Feststellung nicht innerhalb der in § 260 Abs. 1 bestimmten Frist der Antrag auf gerichtliche Entscheidung gestellt worden, so sind die Posten in dem ersten Jahresabschluß, der nach Ablauf dieser Frist aufgestellt wird, mit den von den Sonderprüfern festgestellten Werten oder Beträgen anzusetzen. ²Dies gilt nicht, soweit auf Grund veränderter Verhältnisse, namentlich bei Gegenständen, die der Abnutzung unterliegen, auf Grund der Abnutzung, nach §§ 253 bis 256a des Handelsgesetzbuchs oder nach den Grundsätzen ordnungsmäßiger Buchführung für Aktivposten ein niedrigerer Wert oder für Passivposten ein höherer Betrag

(3) ¹Sec. 99 para. 1, para. 2 sentence 1, para. 3 and para. 5 shall apply accordingly. ²The court shall serve a copy of the decision on the company and, if shareholders brought the application pursuant to para. 1, also on such shareholders. ³The court shall also announce its decision without the reasons therefor in the company's designated journals. ⁴An appeal may be filed by the company and shareholders whose aggregate shares represent at least one-twentieth of the registered share capital or the proportionate amount of 500,000 euros. ⁵Sec. 258 para. 2 sentences 4 and 5 shall apply accordingly. ⁶The period for filing an appeal shall commence upon the announcement of the decision in the Federal Law Gazette, but, in the case of the company and the shareholders who applied pursuant to para. 1, not prior to the service of the decision.

(4) ¹If the application is successful, the costs shall be borne by the company, and otherwise by the party bringing the application. ²Sec. 247 shall apply accordingly.

§ 261 Decision on income resulting from higher evaluation.

(1) ¹If the special auditors stated in their final assessment that items were undervalued and if no application seeking a decision to be made by the court against this final assessment is filed within the period stipulated in sec. 260 para. 1, the items shall be shown in the first annual financial statements drawn up after the expiration of such period at the value or amount determined by the special auditors. ²This shall not apply if as a result of a change in circumstances, in particular as a result of depreciation in the case of objects subject to depreciation, a lower value is to be shown for asset items or a higher amount for debit items pursuant to sec. 253 to 256a of the Commercial Code or in accordance with proper accounting principles. ³In this case, the reasons shall be stated in the

anzusetzen ist. ³In diesem Fall sind im Anhang die Gründe anzugeben und in einer Sonderrechnung die Entwicklung des von den Sonderprüfern festgestellten Wertes oder Betrags auf den nach Satz 2 angesetzten Wert oder Betrag darzustellen. ⁴Sind die Gegenstände nicht mehr vorhanden, so ist darüber und über die Verwendung des Ertrags aus dem Abgang der Gegenstände im Anhang zu berichten. ⁵Bei den einzelnen Posten der Jahresbilanz sind die Unterschiedsbeträge zu vermerken, um die auf Grund von Satz 1 und 2 Aktivposten zu einem höheren Wert oder Passivposten mit einem niedrigeren Betrag angesetzt worden sind. ⁶Die Summe der Unterschiedsbeträge ist auf der Passivseite der Bilanz und in der Gewinn- und Verlustrechnung als „Ertrag auf Grund höherer Bewertung gemäß dem Ergebnis der Sonderprüfung" gesondert auszuweisen. ⁷Ist die Gesellschaft eine kleine Kapitalgesellschaft (§ 267 Absatz 1 des Handelsgesetzbuchs), hat sie die Sätze 3 und 4 nur anzuwenden, wenn die Voraussetzungen des § 264 Absatz 2 Satz 2 des Handelsgesetzbuchs unter Berücksichtigung der nach diesem Abschnitt durchgeführten Sonderprüfung vorliegen.

(2) ¹Hat das gemäß § 260 angerufene Gericht festgestellt, daß Posten unterbewertet sind, so gilt für den Ansatz der Posten in dem ersten Jahresabschluß, der nach Rechtskraft der gerichtlichen Entscheidung aufgestellt wird, Absatz 1 sinngemäß. ²Die Summe der Unterschiedsbeträge ist als „Ertrag auf Grund höherer Bewertung gemäß gerichtlicher Entscheidung" gesondert auszuweisen.

(3) ¹Der Ertrag aus höherer Bewertung nach Absätzen 1 und 2 rechnet für die Anwendung des § 58 nicht zum Jahresüberschuß. ²Über die Verwendung des Ertrags abzüglich der auf ihn zu entrichtenden Steuern entscheidet die Hauptversammlung, soweit nicht in dem Jahresabschluß ein Bilanzverlust ausgewiesen wird, der nicht durch Ka-

notes and a separate calculation shall be provided indicating the development of the value or amount determined by the auditors against the value or amount shown pursuant to sentence 2. ⁴If the objects are no longer available, this shall be reported in the notes, where a report shall also be included on how the income gained from the sale of the objects has been used. ⁵The amount by which asset items have been shown at a higher value and debit items have been shown at a lower amount on the basis of sentences 1 and 2 shall be indicated at the individual entries in the annual financial statements. ⁶The sum of such amounts shall be shown separately on the liabilities side of the balance sheet and in the profit and loss statement as "income resulting from higher valuation pursuant to the findings of the special audit". ⁷Sentences 3 and 4 do only apply to small corporations within the meaning of sec. 267a of the Commercial Code, if the conditions of sec. 264 para. 2 sentence 2 of the Commercial Code are satisfied by taking into account of the special audit conducted under the provisions of this section.

(2) ¹If the court applied to pursuant to sec. 260 declares that items have been undervalued, para. 1 shall apply accordingly to the values to be shown for the items in the first annual financial statements drawn up after the court decision becomes res judicata. ²The sum of the differences shall be indicated separately as "income resulting from higher valuation pursuant to court decision".

(3) ¹The income from higher valuation pursuant to para. 1 and 2 shall not be counted towards the annual net income for the purposes of sec. 58. ²The general meeting shall decide on the appropriation of the income minus the tax due thereon, unless a balance sheet loss which is not covered by capital reserves

pital- oder Gewinnrücklagen gedeckt ist.

§ 261a Mitteilungen an die Bundesanstalt für Finanzdienstleistungsaufsicht.

Das Gericht hat der Bundesanstalt für Finanzdienstleistungsaufsicht den Eingang eines Antrags auf Bestellung eines Sonderprüfers, jede rechtskräftige Entscheidung über die Bestellung von Sonderprüfern, den Prüfungsbericht sowie eine rechtskräftige gerichtliche Entscheidung über abschließende Feststellungen der Sonderprüfer nach § 260 mitzuteilen, wenn die Gesellschaft Wertpapiere im Sinne des § 2 Absatz 1 des Wertpapierhandelsgesetzes ausgegeben hat, die an einer inländischen Börse zum Handel im regulierten Markt zugelassen sind.

**Achter Teil.
Auflösung und Nichtigerklärung der Gesellschaft**

Erster Abschnitt. Auflösung

Erster Unterabschnitt. Auflösungsgründe und Anmeldung

§ 262 Auflösungsgründe.

(1) Die Aktiengesellschaft wird aufgelöst

1. durch Ablauf der in der Satzung bestimmten Zeit;

2. durch Beschluß der Hauptversammlung; dieser bedarf einer Mehrheit, die mindestens drei Viertel des bei der Beschlußfassung vertretenen Grundkapitals umfaßt; die Satzung kann eine größere Kapitalmehrheit und weitere Erfordernisse bestimmen;

3. durch die Eröffnung des Insolvenzverfahrens über das Vermögen der Gesellschaft;

or revenue reserves is shown in the annual financial statements.

§ 261a Notifications to the Federal Financial Supervisory Authority.

If the company has issued securities within the meaning of sec. 2 para. 1 sentence 1 of the Securities Trading Act which are admitted for trading in the regulated market at a German stock exchange, the court shall notify the Federal Financial Supervisory Authority of the filing of an application for the appointment of special auditors, of every decision concerning the application of special auditors which becomes res judicata, of the audit report as well as of every decision about the closing determinations of the special auditors pursuant to sec. 260 which has become res judicata.

Part Eight. Dissolution and Declaration of Nullity of the Company

Section One. Dissolution

Subsection One. Grounds for Dissolution and Application

§ 262 Grounds for dissolution.

(1) The stock corporation shall be dissolved

1. upon expiration of the period of time stipulated in the articles of association;

2. upon a resolution to this effect being adopted by the general meeting; such resolution requires a majority of at least three quarters of the registered share capital represented at the adoption of the resolution; the articles of association may stipulate a larger capital majority and further requirements;

3. upon the commencement of insolvency proceedings against the company's assets;

4. mit der Rechtskraft des Beschlusses, durch den die Eröffnung des Insolvenzverfahrens mangels Masse abgelehnt wird;
5. mit der Rechtskraft einer Verfügung des Registergerichts, durch welche nach § 399 des Gesetzes über das Verfahren in Familiensachen und in den Angelegenheiten der freiwilligen Gerichtsbarkeit ein Mangel der Satzung festgestellt worden ist;
6. durch Löschung der Gesellschaft wegen Vermögenslosigkeit nach § 394 des Gesetzes über das Verfahren in Familiensachen und in den Angelegenheiten der freiwilligen Gerichtsbarkeit.

(2) Dieser Abschnitt gilt auch, wenn die Aktiengesellschaft aus anderen Gründen aufgelöst wird.

§ 263 Anmeldung und Eintragung der Auflösung.

¹Der Vorstand hat die Auflösung der Gesellschaft zur Eintragung in das Handelsregister anzumelden. ²Dies gilt nicht in den Fällen der Eröffnung und der Ablehnung der Eröffnung des Insolvenzverfahrens (§ 262 Abs. 1 Nr. 3 und 4) sowie im Falle der gerichtlichen Feststellung eines Mangels der Satzung (§ 262 Abs. 1 Nr. 5). ³In diesen Fällen hat das Gericht die Auflösung und ihren Grund von Amts wegen einzutragen. ⁴Im Falle der Löschung der Gesellschaft (§ 262 Abs. 1 Nr. 6) entfällt die Eintragung der Auflösung.

Zweiter Unterabschnitt. Abwicklung

§ 264 Notwendigkeit der Abwicklung.

(1) Nach der Auflösung der Gesellschaft findet die Abwicklung statt, wenn nicht über das Vermögen der Gesellschaft das Insolvenzverfahren eröffnet worden ist.

4. upon the decision rejecting the commencement of insolvency proceedings due to a lack of assets becoming res judicata;
5. upon a ruling issued by the register court determining a defect in the articles of association pursuant to sec. 399 of the Act on Procedure in Family Matters and Matters of Non-Contentious Jurisdiction becoming res judicata;
6. upon the company being cancelled due to a lack of assets pursuant to sec. 394 of the Act on Procedure in Family Matters and Matters of Non-Contentious Jurisdiction.

(2) This section shall also apply if the stock corporation is dissolved for any other reason.

§ 263 Application and registration of the dissolution.

¹The management board shall apply for the dissolution of the company to be registered with the commercial register. ²This shall not apply in the case of the commencement or rejection of the commencement of insolvency proceedings (sec. 262 para. 1 nos. 3 and 4) nor in the event of a court determining a defect in the articles of association (sec. 262 para. 1 no. 5). ³In these instances, the dissolution and the reason therefor shall be registered ex officio by the court. ⁴In the event of the cancellation of the company (sec. 262 para. 1 no. 6) the requirement for the dissolution to be registered shall not apply.

Subsection Two. Liquidation

§ 264 Necessity of liquidation.

(1) Liquidation shall commence after the company has been dissolved unless insolvency proceedings have been commenced against the assets of the company.

(2) ¹Ist die Gesellschaft durch Löschung wegen Vermögenslosigkeit aufgelöst, so findet eine Abwicklung nur statt, wenn sich nach der Löschung herausstellt, daß Vermögen vorhanden ist, das der Verteilung unterliegt. ²Die Abwickler sind auf Antrag eines Beteiligten durch das Gericht zu ernennen.

(3) Soweit sich aus diesem Unterabschnitt oder aus dem Zweck der Abwicklung nichts anderes ergibt, sind auf die Gesellschaft bis zum Schluß der Abwicklung die Vorschriften weiterhin anzuwenden, die für nicht aufgelöste Gesellschaften gelten.

§ 265 Abwickler.

(1) Die Abwicklung besorgen die Vorstandsmitglieder als Abwickler.

(2) ¹Die Satzung oder ein Beschluß der Hauptversammlung kann andere Personen als Abwickler bestellen. ²Für die Auswahl der Abwickler gilt § 76 Abs. 3 Satz 2 und 3 sinngemäß. ³Auch eine juristische Person kann Abwickler sein.

(3) ¹Auf Antrag des Aufsichtsrats oder einer Minderheit von Aktionären, deren Anteile zusammen den zwanzigsten Teil des Grundkapitals oder den anteiligen Betrag von 500.000 Euro erreichen, hat das Gericht bei Vorliegen eines wichtigen Grundes die Abwickler zu bestellen und abzuberufen. ²Die Aktionäre haben glaubhaft zu machen, daß sie seit mindestens drei Monaten Inhaber der Aktien sind. ³Zur Glaubhaftmachung genügt eine eidesstattliche Versicherung vor einem Gericht oder Notar. ⁴Gegen die Entscheidung ist die Beschwerde zulässig.

(4) ¹Die gerichtlich bestellten Abwickler haben Anspruch auf Ersatz angemessener barer Auslagen und auf Vergütung für ihre Tätigkeit. ²Einigen sich der gerichtlich bestellte Abwickler und die Gesellschaft nicht, so setzt das Ge-

(2) ¹If the company has been dissolved by means of cancellation due to a lack of assets, liquidation shall only take place if it becomes apparent after the cancellation that there are assets which are subject to distribution. ²The liquidators shall be appointed by the court upon one of the parties concerned filing a request to this effect.

(3) Unless indicated otherwise by this subsection or the purpose of the liquidation, the provisions which apply to companies which have not been dissolved shall continue to apply to the company until such time as the liquidation has been completed.

§ 265 Liquidators.

(1) The management board members shall arrange the liquidation in the capacity of liquidators.

(2) ¹Other persons may be appointed liquidators by the articles of association or a resolution of the general meeting. ²Sec. 76 para. 3 sentences 2 and 3 shall apply accordingly to the selection of liquidators. ³A legal entity may also be a liquidator.

(3) ¹Upon application by the supervisory board or a minority of shareholders having an aggregate shareholding amounting to one twentieth of the registered share capital or the proportionate amount of 500,000 euros, the court shall appoint and dismiss the liquidators if there is good cause for doing so. ²The shareholders shall provide evidence that they have held the shares for at least three months. ³An affidavit sworn before a court or a notary shall suffice as such evidence. ⁴The decision is subject to appeal.

(4) ¹The liquidators appointed by the court shall be entitled to reimbursement of reasonable cash expenses and to remuneration for their services. ²If the liquidator appointed by the court and the company fail to come to an agreement,

richt die Auslagen und die Vergütung fest. ³Gegen die Entscheidung ist die Beschwerde zulässig; die Rechtsbeschwerde ist ausgeschlossen. ⁴Aus der rechtskräftigen Entscheidung findet die Zwangsvollstreckung nach der Zivilprozeßordnung statt.

(5) ¹Abwickler, die nicht vom Gericht bestellt sind, kann die Hauptversammlung jederzeit abberufen. ²Für die Ansprüche aus dem Anstellungsvertrag gelten die allgemeinen Vorschriften.

(6) Die Absätze 2 bis 5 gelten nicht für den Arbeitsdirektor, soweit sich seine Bestellung und Abberufung nach den Vorschriften des Montan-Mitbestimmungsgesetzes bestimmen.

§ 266 Anmeldung der Abwickler.

(1) Die ersten Abwickler sowie ihre Vertretungsbefugnis hat der Vorstand, jeden Wechsel der Abwickler und jede Änderung ihrer Vertretungsbefugnis haben die Abwickler zur Eintragung in das Handelsregister anzumelden.

(2) Der Anmeldung sind die Urkunden über die Bestellung oder Abberufung sowie über die Vertretungsbefugnis in Urschrift oder öffentlich beglaubigter Abschrift beizufügen.

(3) ¹In der Anmeldung haben die Abwickler zu versichern, daß keine Umstände vorliegen, die ihrer Bestellung nach § 265 Abs. 2 Satz 2 entgegenstehen, und daß sie über ihre unbeschränkte Auskunftspflicht gegenüber dem Gericht belehrt worden sind. ²§ 37 Abs. 2 Satz 2 ist anzuwenden.

(4) Die Bestellung oder Abberufung von Abwicklern durch das Gericht wird von Amts wegen eingetragen.

the expenses and the remuneration shall be determined by the court. ³The decision is subject to appeal; no further appeal on a point of law may be made. ⁴A decision being res judicata shall be enforceable pursuant to the Code of Civil Procedure.

(5) ¹Liquidators who are not appointed by the court may be removed from office at any time by the general meeting. ²The general provisions shall apply to claims arising from the employment contract.

(6) Paras. 2 to 5 shall not apply to the works director, provided the appointment and dismissal of such director is stipulated in accordance with the provisions of the Coal, Iron and Steel Co-determination Act.

§ 266 Application for registration of liquidators.

(1) The management board shall apply for the first liquidators and the representative authority they hold to be registered in the commercial register, and the liquidators shall apply for each change to the liquidators or their representative authority to be registered in the commercial register.

(2) An original or certified copy of the documents relating to the appointment or dismissal and to the representative authority shall be attached to the application.

(3) ¹The liquidators shall confirm in the application that there are no circumstances preventing them from being appointed pursuant to sec. 265 para. 2 sentence 2 and that they have been informed as to their unrestricted obligation to provide information to the court. ²Sec. 37 para. 2 sentence 2 shall apply.

(4) The appointment or dismissal of liquidators shall be registered by the court ex officio.

§ 267 Aufruf der Gläubiger.

¹Die Abwickler haben unter Hinweis auf die Auflösung der Gesellschaft die Gläubiger der Gesellschaft aufzufordern, ihre Ansprüche anzumelden. ²Die Aufforderung ist in den Gesellschaftsblättern bekanntzumachen.

§ 268 Pflichten der Abwickler.

(1) ¹Die Abwickler haben die laufenden Geschäfte zu beenden, die Forderungen einzuziehen, das übrige Vermögen in Geld umzusetzen und die Gläubiger zu befriedigen. ²Soweit es die Abwicklung erfordert, dürfen sie auch neue Geschäfte eingehen.

(2) ¹Im übrigen haben die Abwickler innerhalb ihres Geschäftskreises die Rechte und Pflichten des Vorstands. ²Sie unterliegen wie dieser der Überwachung durch den Aufsichtsrat.

(3) Das Wettbewerbsverbot des § 88 gilt für sie nicht.

(4) ¹Auf allen Geschäftsbriefen, die an einen bestimmten Empfänger gerichtet werden, müssen die Rechtsform und der Sitz der Gesellschaft, die Tatsache, daß die Gesellschaft sich in Abwicklung befindet, das Registergericht des Sitzes der Gesellschaft und die Nummer, unter der die Gesellschaft in das Handelsregister eingetragen ist, sowie alle Abwickler und der Vorsitzende des Aufsichtsrats mit dem Familiennamen und mindestens einem ausgeschriebenen Vornamen angegeben werden. ²Werden Angaben über das Kapital der Gesellschaft gemacht, so müssen in jedem Falle das Grundkapital sowie, wenn auf die Aktien der Ausgabebetrag nicht vollständig eingezahlt ist, der Gesamtbetrag der ausstehenden Einlagen angegeben werden. ³Der Angaben nach Satz 1 bedarf es nicht bei Mitteilungen oder Berichten, die im Rahmen einer bestehenden Geschäftsverbindung ergehen und für die üblicherweise Vor-

§ 267 Call to creditors.

¹The liquidators shall, referring to the dissolution of the company, call upon the creditors to register their claims. ²Such request shall be announced in the company's designated journals.

§ 268 Duties of liquidators.

(1) ¹The liquidators shall wind up current transactions, convert claims, turn the remaining assets into cash and satisfy the claims of the creditors. ²They may enter into new business transactions to the extent required for the liquidation of the company.

(2) ¹Otherwise, the liquidators shall have the same rights and duties of the management board within their field of business. ²Like the management board, they are subject to supervision by the supervisory board.

(3) The prohibition of competition stipulated in sec. 88 shall not apply to the liquidators.

(4) ¹All business letters addressed to a specific recipient shall state the legal form and registered office of the company, the fact that the company is in the process of being liquidated, the register court having jurisdiction for the registered office of the company and the number under which the company is registered in the commercial register, as well as the surnames and at least one full first name of all liquidators and the chairman of the supervisory board. ²If details are given concerning the capital of the company, the registered share capital and, if the issue price has not been paid in full on the shares, the total amount of the outstanding contributions shall be stated in all instances. ³The information pursuant to sentence 1 shall not be required for communications or reports made in the course of an existing business relationship and for which forms are generally used in which only the particulars of the specif-

drucke verwendet werden, in denen lediglich die im Einzelfall erforderlichen besonderen Angaben eingefügt zu werden brauchen. ⁴Bestellscheine gelten als Geschäftsbriefe im Sinne des Satzes 1; Satz 3 ist auf sie nicht anzuwenden.

ic transaction need be inserted. ⁴Order forms shall constitute business letters within the meaning of sentence 1; sentence 3 shall not apply to them.

§ 269 Vertretung durch die Abwickler.

§ 269 Representation by liquidators.

(1) Die Abwickler vertreten die Gesellschaft gerichtlich und außergerichtlich.

(1) The liquidators shall represent the company both in and out of court.

(2) ¹Sind mehrere Abwickler bestellt, so sind, wenn die Satzung oder die sonst zuständige Stelle nichts anderes bestimmt, sämtliche Abwickler nur gemeinschaftlich zur Vertretung der Gesellschaft befugt. ²Ist eine Willenserklärung gegenüber der Gesellschaft abzugeben, so genügt die Abgabe gegenüber einem Abwickler.

(2) ¹If more than one liquidator has been appointed, all liquidators shall only be authorized to represent the company jointly, unless provided otherwise by the articles of association or any other responsible authority. ²If a declaration of intent is to be submitted to the company, it shall suffice for it to be submitted to one of the liquidators.

(3) ¹Die Satzung oder die sonst zuständige Stelle kann auch bestimmen, daß einzelne Abwickler allein oder in Gemeinschaft mit einem Prokuristen zur Vertretung der Gesellschaft befugt sind. ²Dasselbe kann der Aufsichtsrat bestimmen, wenn die Satzung oder ein Beschluß der Hauptversammlung ihn hierzu ermächtigt hat. ³Absatz 2 Satz 2 gilt in diesen Fällen sinngemäß.

(3) ¹The articles of association or the other responsible authority may also stipulate that individual liquidators are authorized to represent the company alone or together with a procuration officer. ²The same may also be stipulated by the supervisory board if it has been authorized to do so by the articles of association or a resolution adopted by the general meeting. ³Para. 2 sentence 2 shall apply accordingly in these cases.

(4) ¹Zur Gesamtvertretung befugte Abwickler können einzelne von ihnen zur Vornahme bestimmter Geschäfte oder bestimmter Arten von Geschäften ermächtigen. ²Dies gilt sinngemäß, wenn ein einzelner Abwickler in Gemeinschaft mit einem Prokuristen zur Vertretung der Gesellschaft befugt ist.

(4) ¹Liquidators who are authorized to represent the company jointly may authorize certain of their number to effect certain transactions or certain types of transaction. ²This shall apply accordingly if a single liquidator is authorized to represent the company together with a procuration officer.

(5) Die Vertretungsbefugnis der Abwickler kann nicht beschränkt werden.

(5) The representative authority of the liquidators may not be restricted.

(6) Abwickler zeichnen für die Gesellschaft, indem sie der Firma einen die Abwicklung andeutenden Zusatz und ihre Namensunterschrift hinzufügen.

(6) Liquidators sign on behalf of the company by adding their signature and a component indicating that the company is in the process of liquidation to the company name.

§ 270 Opening balance sheet. Annual financial statements and management report.

(1) For the commencement of liquidation proceedings, the liquidators shall draw up a balance sheet (opening balance sheet) and a report explaining the opening balance sheet, as well as annual financial statements and a management report for the end of each year.

(2) ¹The general meeting shall resolve on formal approval for the opening balance sheet and the annual financial statements as well as on ratification of the actions of the liquidators and the members of the supervisory board. ²The provisions relating to annual financial statements shall apply accordingly to the opening balance sheet and the explanatory report. ³Fixed assets shall, however, be treated as current assets, provided they are intended to be sold within a foreseeable period or are no longer required for the conducting of business; this shall also apply to the annual financial statements.

(3) ¹The court may release the company from the obligation of having the annual financial statements and the management report inspected by an auditor of annual financial statements if the company's situation is so transparent that it does not appear necessary for an audit to be carried out in the interests of the creditors and shareholders. ²The decision is subject to appeal.

§ 271 Distribution of assets.

(1) The company's assets remaining after the adjustment of liabilities shall be distributed among the shareholders.

(2) The assets shall be distributed according to the share held in the registered share capital, unless shares granting different rights relating to the distribution of the corporate assets exist.

(3) ¹Sind die Einlagen auf das Grundkapital nicht auf alle Aktien in demselben Verhältnis geleistet, so werden die geleisteten Einlagen erstattet und ein Überschuß nach den Anteilen am Grundkapital verteilt. ²Reicht das Vermögen zur Erstattung der Einlagen nicht aus, so haben die Aktionäre den Verlust nach ihren Anteilen am Grundkapital zu tragen; die noch ausstehenden Einlagen sind, soweit nötig, einzuziehen.

§ 272 Gläubigerschutz.

(1) Das Vermögen darf nur verteilt werden, wenn ein Jahr seit dem Tage verstrichen ist, an dem der Aufruf der Gläubiger bekanntgemacht worden ist.

(2) Meldet sich ein bekannter Gläubiger nicht, so ist der geschuldete Betrag für ihn zu hinterlegen, wenn ein Recht zur Hinterlegung besteht.

(3) Kann eine Verbindlichkeit zur Zeit nicht berichtigt werden oder ist sie streitig, so darf das Vermögen nur verteilt werden, wenn dem Gläubiger Sicherheit geleistet ist.

§ 273 Schluß der Abwicklung.

(1) ¹Ist die Abwicklung beendet und die Schlußrechnung gelegt, so haben die Abwickler den Schluß der Abwicklung zur Eintragung in das Handelsregister anzumelden. ²Die Gesellschaft ist zu löschen.

(2) Die Bücher und Schriften der Gesellschaft sind an einen vom Gericht bestimmten sicheren Ort zur Aufbewahrung auf zehn Jahre zu hinterlegen.

(3) Das Gericht kann den Aktionären und den Gläubigern die Einsicht der Bücher und Schriften gestatten.

(4) ¹Stellt sich nachträglich heraus, daß weitere Abwicklungsmaßnahmen nötig sind, so hat auf Antrag eines Beteiligten das Gericht die bisherigen Abwickler

(3) ¹If the contributions to the registered share capital have not been paid in the same ratio on all shares, the contributions which have been made shall be reimbursed and any excess distributed according to the share held in the registered capital. ²If the assets are not sufficient for the contributions to be reimbursed, the shareholders shall bear the loss in accordance with the share they hold in the registered share capital; the outstanding contributions shall, as far as necessary, be collected.

§ 272 Protection of creditors.

(1) The assets may only be distributed after one year has passed since the day the creditors were called on.

(2) If a known creditor fails to register his claim, the amount owed shall be deposited for him if a right to the deposit of such amount exists.

(3) If a liability cannot be adjusted at the present time or if it is disputed, the assets may only be distributed if the creditor has been provided with security.

§ 273 Completion of liquidation.

(1) ¹The liquidators shall apply for the completion of liquidation to be registered in the commercial register once the liquidation has been completed and the final accounts rendered. ²The company shall be deleted.

(2) The books and records of the company shall be retained for a period of ten years at a safe place determined by the court.

(3) The court may allow shareholders and creditors to view the books and records.

(4) ¹If it becomes apparent at a later date that further liquidation measures are required, the previous liquidators shall be re-appointed or new liquidators shall be appointed by the court upon appli-

neu zu bestellen oder andere Abwickler zu berufen. ²§ 265 Abs. 4 gilt.

(5) Gegen die Entscheidungen nach den Absätzen 2, 3 und 4 Satz 1 ist die Beschwerde zulässig.

§ 274 Fortsetzung einer aufgelösten Gesellschaft.

(1) ¹Ist eine Aktiengesellschaft durch Zeitablauf oder durch Beschluß der Hauptversammlung aufgelöst worden, so kann die Hauptversammlung, solange noch nicht mit der Verteilung des Vermögens unter die Aktionäre begonnen ist, die Fortsetzung der Gesellschaft beschließen. ²Der Beschluß bedarf einer Mehrheit, die mindestens drei Viertel des bei der Beschlußfassung vertretenen Grundkapitals umfaßt. ³Die Satzung kann eine größere Kapitalmehrheit und weitere Erfordernisse bestimmen.

(2) Gleiches gilt, wenn die Gesellschaft

1. durch die Eröffnung des Insolvenzverfahrens aufgelöst, das Verfahren aber auf Antrag des Schuldners eingestellt oder nach der Bestätigung eines Insolvenzplans, der den Fortbestand der Gesellschaft vorsieht, aufgehoben worden ist;

2. durch die gerichtliche Feststellung eines Mangels der Satzung nach § 262 Abs. 1 Nr. 5 aufgelöst worden ist, eine den Mangel behebende Satzungsänderung aber spätestens zugleich mit der Fortsetzung der Gesellschaft beschlossen wird.

(3) ¹Die Abwickler haben die Fortsetzung der Gesellschaft zur Eintragung in das Handelsregister anzumelden. ²Sie haben bei der Anmeldung nachzuweisen, daß noch nicht mit der Verteilung des Vermögens der Gesellschaft unter die Aktionäre begonnen worden ist.

cation by one of the parties concerned. ²Sec. 265 para. 4 shall apply.

(5) The decisions pursuant to paras. 2, 3 and 4 sentence 1 are subject to appeal.

§ 274 Continuation of a dissolved company.

(1) ¹If a stock corporation has been dissolved due to the expiration of the time period or on the basis of a resolution of the general meeting, the general meeting may adopt a resolution stipulating the continuation of the company, provided the distribution of the assets among the shareholders has not yet been commenced. ²Such resolution shall require a majority of at least three quarters of the registered share capital represented at the adoption of the resolution. ³The articles of association may stipulate a larger capital majority and further requirements.

(2) The foregoing shall also apply if the company

1. has been dissolved as a result of insolvency proceedings being commenced, but such proceedings have since been suspended at the request of the debtor or have been terminated after confirmation of an insolvency plan providing for the continuation of the company;

2. has been dissolved due to a court determining a defect in the articles of association pursuant to sec. 262 para. 1 no. 5, but an amendment remedying the defect is resolved at the latest together with the continuation of the company.

(3) ¹The liquidators shall apply for the continuation of the company to be registered in the commercial register. ²They shall provide evidence with the application that the distribution of the assets to the shareholders has not yet commenced.

(4) ¹Der Fortsetzungsbeschluß wird erst wirksam, wenn er in das Handelsregister des Sitzes der Gesellschaft eingetragen worden ist. ²Im Falle des Absatzes 2 Nr. 2 hat der Fortsetzungsbeschluß keine Wirkung, solange er und der Beschluß über die Satzungsänderung nicht in das Handelsregister des Sitzes der Gesellschaft eingetragen worden sind; die beiden Beschlüsse sollen nur zusammen in das Handelsregister eingetragen werden.

(4) ¹The resolution on the continuation of the company shall only take effect once it has been registered in the commercial register responsible for the registered office of the company. ²In the case stipulated in para. 2 no. 2, the continuation resolution shall not take effect until it and the resolution on the amendment to the articles of association have been registered in the commercial register responsible for the registered office of the company; the two resolutions shall only be registered together in the commercial register.

Zweiter Abschnitt. Nichtigerklärung der Gesellschaft

Section Two. Declaration of Nullity of the Company

§ 275 Klage auf Nichtigerklärung.

§ 275 Action for the declaration of nullity of a resolution.

(1) ¹Enthält die Satzung keine Bestimmungen über die Höhe des Grundkapitals oder über den Gegenstand des Unternehmens oder sind die Bestimmungen der Satzung über den Gegenstand des Unternehmens nichtig, so kann jeder Aktionär und jedes Mitglied des Vorstands und des Aufsichtsrats darauf klagen, daß die Gesellschaft für nichtig erklärt werde. ²Auf andere Gründe kann die Klage nicht gestützt werden.

(1) ¹If the articles of association do not contain any provisions relating to the amount of the registered share capital or the object of the enterprise or if the provisions in the articles of association concerning the object of the enterprise are null and void, each shareholder and each member of the management board and the supervisory board may bring an action for the company to be declared null and void. ²Such action may not be based on any other reasons.

(2) Kann der Mangel nach § 276 geheilt werden, so kann die Klage erst erhoben werden, nachdem ein Klageberechtigter die Gesellschaft aufgefordert hat, den Mangel zu beseitigen, und sie binnen drei Monaten dieser Aufforderung nicht nachgekommen ist.

(2) If the defect can be cured pursuant to sec. 276, the action may only be brought once a party entitled to bring the action has called upon the company to remedy the defect and the company has failed to meet such request within three months.

(3) ¹Die Klage muß binnen drei Jahren nach Eintragung der Gesellschaft erhoben werden. ²Eine Löschung der Gesellschaft von Amts wegen nach § 397 Abs. 1 des Gesetzes über das Verfahren in Familiensachen und in den Angelegenheiten der freiwilligen Gerichtsbarkeit wird durch den Zeitablauf nicht ausgeschlossen.

(3) ¹The action shall be brought within three years of the company being registered. ²The expiration of such period shall not exclude the possibility of the company being cancelled officially pursuant to sec. 397 para. 1 of the Act on Procedure in Family Matters and Matters of Non-Contentious Jurisdiction.

(4) ¹Für die Anfechtung gelten § 246 Abs. 2 bis 4, §§ 247, 248 Abs. 1 Satz 1, §§ 248a, 249 Abs. 2 sinngemäß. ²Der Vorstand hat eine beglaubigte Abschrift der Klage und das rechtskräftige Urteil zum Handelsregister einzureichen. ³Die Nichtigkeit der Gesellschaft auf Grund rechtskräftigen Urteils ist einzutragen.

(4) ¹Sec. 246 paras. 2 to 4, sec. 247, 248 para. 1 sentence 1, sec. 248a, 249 para. 2 shall apply accordingly to the action to set aside. ²The management board shall submit a certified copy of the action and the judgment being res judicata to the commercial register. ³It shall be registered in the commercial register that the company has been declared null and void on the basis of a judgment being res judicata.

§ 276 Heilung von Mängeln.

Ein Mangel, der die Bestimmungen über den Gegenstand des Unternehmens betrifft, kann unter Beachtung der Bestimmungen des Gesetzes und der Satzung über Satzungsänderungen geheilt werden.

§ 276 Curing of defects.

A defect in the provisions relating to the object of the enterprise can be cured in compliance with the legal provisions and provisions in the articles of association concerning amendments to the articles of association.

§ 277 Wirkung der Eintragung der Nichtigkeit.

(1) Ist die Nichtigkeit einer Gesellschaft auf Grund rechtskräftigen Urteils oder einer Entscheidung des Registergerichts in das Handelsregister eingetragen, so findet die Abwicklung nach den Vorschriften über die Abwicklung bei Auflösung statt.

(2) Die Wirksamkeit der im Namen der Gesellschaft vorgenommenen Rechtsgeschäfte wird durch die Nichtigkeit nicht berührt.

(3) Die Gesellschafter haben die Einlagen zu leisten, soweit es zur Erfüllung der eingegangenen Verbindlichkeiten nötig ist.

§ 277 Effect of registration of nullity.

(1) If it has been registered in the commercial register that the company has been declared null and void on the basis of a judgment being res judicata or a decision of the register court, the company shall be liquidated in accordance with the provisions concerning liquidation in the event of dissolution.

(2) The validity of transactions effected in the name of the company shall not be effected by the nullity of such company.

(3) The shareholders shall provide contributions to the extent necessary for settling the obligations which have been entered into.

Zweites Buch. Kommanditgesellschaft auf Aktien

Second Book. Partnership Limited by Shares

§ 278 Wesen der Kommanditgesellschaft auf Aktien.

(1) Die Kommanditgesellschaft auf Aktien ist eine Gesellschaft mit eigener Rechtspersönlichkeit, bei der min-

§ 278 Nature of the partnership limited by shares.

(1) A partnership limited by shares is a company with its own legal personality in which at least one of the share-

destens ein Gesellschafter den Gesellschaftsgläubigern unbeschränkt haftet (persönlich haftender Gesellschafter) und die übrigen an dem in Aktien zerlegten Grundkapital beteiligt sind, ohne persönlich für die Verbindlichkeiten der Gesellschaft zu haften (Kommanditaktionäre).

(2) Das Rechtsverhältnis der persönlich haftenden Gesellschafter untereinander und gegenüber der Gesamtheit der Kommanditaktionäre sowie gegenüber Dritten, namentlich die Befugnis der persönlich haftenden Gesellschafter zur Geschäftsführung und zur Vertretung der Gesellschaft, bestimmt sich nach den Vorschriften des Handelsgesetzbuchs über die Kommanditgesellschaft.

(3) Im übrigen gelten für die Kommanditgesellschaft auf Aktien, soweit sich aus den folgenden Vorschriften oder aus dem Fehlen eines Vorstands nichts anderes ergibt, die Vorschriften des Ersten Buchs über die Aktiengesellschaft sinngemäß.

§ 279 Firma.

(1) Die Firma der Kommanditgesellschaft auf Aktien muß, auch wenn sie nach § 22 des Handelsgesetzbuchs oder nach anderen gesetzlichen Vorschriften fortgeführt wird, die Bezeichnung „Kommanditgesellschaft auf Aktien" oder eine allgemein verständliche Abkürzung dieser Bezeichnung enthalten.

(2) Wenn in der Gesellschaft keine natürliche Person persönlich haftet, muß die Firma, auch wenn sie nach § 22 des Handelsgesetzbuchs oder nach anderen gesetzlichen Vorschriften fortgeführt wird, eine Bezeichnung enthalten, welche die Haftungsbeschränkung kennzeichnet.

§ 280 Feststellung der Satzung. Gründer.

(1) [1]Die Satzung muß durch notarielle Beurkundung festgestellt werden. [2]In der Urkunde sind bei Nennbetragsakti-

holders has unrestricted liability vis-à-vis the creditors of the company (personally liable partner) and the others have a shareholding in the registered share capital which is divided into shares, without being personally liable for the obligations of the company (limited liability shareholders).

(2) The legal relationships of the personally liable partners among each other and towards all limited liability shareholders as well as towards third parties, in particular the authorization of the personally liable partners to manage and represent the company, shall be defined in accordance with the provisions on limited partnerships in the Commercial Code.

(3) In other respects, the provisions on stock corporations contained in the First Book of this Act shall apply accordingly to partnerships limited by shares unless required otherwise on the basis of the following provisions or due to the lack of a management board.

§ 279 Name.

(1) The name of the partnership limited by shares shall include the designation "partnership limited by shares" (Kommanditgesellschaft auf Aktien) or a commonly understood abbreviation of this designation, even if the name is continued according to sec. 22 of the Commercial Code or other legal regulations.

(2) If no natural person is personally liable for the company, the company name shall include a designation indicating the limitation on liability, even if the name is continued according to sec. 22 of the Commercial Code or other legal regulations.

§ 280 Establishment of the articles of association. Founders.

(1) [1]The articles of association shall be established by way of notarization. [2]The deed shall state, in the case of par

en der Nennbetrag, bei Stückaktien die Zahl, der Ausgabebetrag und, wenn mehrere Gattungen bestehen, die Gattung der Aktien anzugeben, die jeder Beteiligte übernimmt. [3]Bevollmächtigte bedürfen einer notariell beglaubigten Vollmacht.

(2) [1]Alle persönlich haftenden Gesellschafter müssen sich bei der Feststellung der Satzung beteiligen. [2]Außer ihnen müssen die Personen mitwirken, die als Kommanditaktionäre Aktien gegen Einlagen übernehmen.

(3) Die Gesellschafter, die die Satzung festgestellt haben, sind die Gründer der Gesellschaft.

§ 281 Inhalt der Satzung.

(1) Die Satzung muß außer den Festsetzungen nach § 23 Abs. 3 und 4 den Namen, Vornamen und Wohnort jedes persönlich haftenden Gesellschafters enthalten.

(2) Vermögenseinlagen der persönlich haftenden Gesellschafter müssen, wenn sie nicht auf das Grundkapital geleistet werden, nach Höhe und Art in der Satzung festgesetzt werden.

§ 282 Eintragung der persönlich haftenden Gesellschafter.

[1]Bei der Eintragung der Gesellschaft in das Handelsregister sind statt der Vorstandsmitglieder die persönlich haftenden Gesellschafter anzugeben. [2]Ferner ist einzutragen, welche Vertretungsbefugnis die persönlich haftenden Gesellschafter haben.

§ 283 Persönlich haftende Gesellschafter.

Für die persönlich haftenden Gesellschafter gelten sinngemäß die für den Vorstand der Aktiengesellschaft geltenden Vorschriften über

1. die Anmeldungen, Einreichungen, Erklärungen und Nachweise zum

value shares, the par value, and in the case of non-par value shares, the number, issue price and, if there are several classes thereof, the class of the shares subscribed to by each party. [3]Proxies require a power of attorney certified by a notary.

(2) [1]All personally liable partners shall participate in the establishing of the articles of association. [2]In addition, those persons subscribing to shares as limited liability shareholders against making contributions shall also participate.

(3) The partners who establish the articles of association are the founders of the company.

§ 281 Contents of the articles of association.

(1) In addition to the information stipulated in sec. 23 paras. 3 and 4, the articles of association shall also state the surname, first name and place of residence of each of the personally liable partners.

(2) If not paid to the registered share capital, the amount and nature of the capital contributions of the personally liable partners shall be stated in the articles of association.

§ 282 Registration on personally liable partners.

[1]When entering the company in the commercial register, the personally liable partners shall be stated in place of the members of the management board. [2]The representative authority of the personally liable partners shall also be registered in the commercial register.

§ 283 Personally liable partners.

The provisions applicable to the management board of the stock corporation concerning

1. applications for registration, submissions, declarations and evidence to

Handelsregister sowie über Bekanntmachungen;
2. die Gründungsprüfung;
3. die Sorgfaltspflicht und Verantwortlichkeit;
4. die Pflichten gegenüber dem Aufsichtsrat;
5. die Zulässigkeit einer Kreditgewährung;
6. die Einberufung der Hauptversammlung;
7. die Sonderprüfung;
8. die Geltendmachung von Ersatzansprüchen wegen der Geschäftsführung;
9. die Aufstellung, Vorlegung und Prüfung des Jahresabschlusses und des Vorschlags für die Verwendung des Bilanzgewinns;
10. die Vorlegung und Prüfung des Lageberichts sowie eines Konzernabschlusses und eines Konzernlageberichts;
11. die Vorlegung, Prüfung und Offenlegung eines Einzelabschlusses nach § 325 Abs. 2a des Handelsgesetzbuchs;
12. die Ausgabe von Aktien bei bedingter Kapitalerhöhung, bei genehmigtem Kapital und bei Kapitalerhöhung aus Gesellschaftsmitteln;
13. die Nichtigkeit und Anfechtung von Hauptversammlungsbeschlüssen;
14. den Antrag auf Eröffnung des Insolvenzverfahrens.

be provided to the commercial register and announcements;
2. the formation audit;
3. the duty of care and responsibility;
4. duties vis-à-vis the supervisory board;
5. whether or not credit may be granted;
6. the convening of the general meeting;
7. the special audit;
8. the asserting of claims for damages arising from the management of the company;
9. the drawing up, submission and auditing of the annual financial statements and the proposal for the appropriation of the balance sheet profit;
10. the submission and auditing of the management report as well as of the consolidated financial statements and the consolidated management report;
11. the submission, auditing and disclosure of individual financial statements pursuant to sec. 325 para. 2a of the Commercial Code;
12. the issue of shares in connection with a contingent capital increase, authorized capital and a capital increase from company resources;
13. the nullity and setting aside of resolutions adopted by the general meeting;
14. the application for commencement of insolvency proceedings shall apply accordingly to the personally liable partners.

§ 284 Wettbewerbsverbot.

(1) ¹Ein persönlich haftender Gesellschafter darf ohne ausdrückliche Einwilligung der übrigen persönlich haftenden Gesellschafter und des Aufsichtsrats weder im Geschäftszweig der Gesellschaft für eigene oder fremde Rechnung Geschäfte machen noch Mitglied des Vorstands oder Geschäftsführer oder persönlich haftender Ge-

§ 284 Prohibition on competition.

(1) ¹A personally liable partner may neither engage in business in the company's branch of business for his own or another's account nor be a member of the management board or the managing director or a personally liable partner of another comparable commercial company without first obtaining the explicit consent of the other personally liable

sellschafter einer anderen gleichartigen Handelsgesellschaft sein. ²Die Einwilligung kann nur für bestimmte Arten von Geschäften oder für bestimmte Handelsgesellschaften erteilt werden.

(2) ¹Verstößt ein persönlich haftender Gesellschafter gegen dieses Verbot, so kann die Gesellschaft Schadenersatz fordern. ²Sie kann statt dessen von dem Gesellschafter verlangen, daß er die für eigene Rechnung gemachten Geschäfte als für Rechnung der Gesellschaft eingegangen gelten läßt und die aus Geschäften für fremde Rechnung bezogene Vergütung herausgibt oder seinen Anspruch auf die Vergütung abtritt.

(3) ¹Die Ansprüche der Gesellschaft verjähren in drei Monaten seit dem Zeitpunkt, in dem die übrigen persönlich haftenden Gesellschafter und die Aufsichtsratsmitglieder von der zum Schadensersatz verpflichtenden Handlung Kenntnis erlangen oder ohne grobe Fahrlässigkeit erlangen müssten. ²Sie verjähren ohne Rücksicht auf diese Kenntnis oder grob fahrlässige Unkenntnis in fünf Jahren von ihrer Entstehung an.

§ 285 Hauptversammlung.

(1) ¹In der Hauptversammlung haben die persönlich haftenden Gesellschafter nur ein Stimmrecht für ihre Aktien. ²Sie können das Stimmrecht weder für sich noch für einen anderen ausüben bei Beschlußfassungen über

1. die Wahl und Abberufung des Aufsichtsrats;
2. die Entlastung der persönlich haftenden Gesellschafter und der Mitglieder des Aufsichtsrats;
3. die Bestellung von Sonderprüfern;
4. die Geltendmachung von Ersatzansprüchen;
5. den Verzicht auf Ersatzansprüche;
6. die Wahl von Abschlußprüfern.

partners and the supervisory board. ²Consent may only be granted for certain types of transactions or for certain commercial companies.

(2) ¹If a personally liable partner violates this prohibition, the company may demand damages. ²Alternatively, the company may demand that the shareholder agrees that the transactions he effected for his own account shall be deemed to have been effected for the company's account and that he returns any remuneration gained for transactions effected for the account of another or that he assigns his claim to remuneration.

(3) ¹The company's claims shall become time-barred three months after the other personally liable partners and the members of the supervisory board obtain knowledge of or would have obtained knowledge without gross negligence of the actions creating the liability for damages. ²The claims shall become time-barred five years after their coming into being irrespective of such knowledge or grossly negligent lack of knowledge.

§ 285 General meeting.

(1) ¹The personally liable partners shall only have one voting right for their shares in the general meeting. ²They may not exercise the voting right on their own behalf or on the behalf of another when resolutions are adopted concerning:

1. the election and dismissal of the supervisory board;
2. ratification of the acts of the personally liable partners and the members of the supervisory board;
3. the appointment of special auditors;
4. the assertion of claims to damages;
5. the waiver of claims to damages;
6. the selection of auditors of annual financial statements.

³Bei diesen Beschlußfassungen kann ihr Stimmrecht auch nicht durch einen anderen ausgeübt werden.

(2) ¹Die Beschlüsse der Hauptversammlung bedürfen der Zustimmung der persönlich haftenden Gesellschafter, soweit sie Angelegenheiten betreffen, für die bei einer Kommanditgesellschaft das Einverständnis der persönlich haftenden Gesellschafter und der Kommanditisten erforderlich ist. ²Die Ausübung der Befugnisse, die der Hauptversammlung oder einer Minderheit von Kommanditaktionären bei der Bestellung von Prüfern und der Geltendmachung von Ansprüchen der Gesellschaft aus der Gründung oder der Geschäftsführung zustehen, bedarf nicht der Zustimmung der persönlich haftenden Gesellschafter.

(3) ¹Beschlüsse der Hauptversammlung, die der Zustimmung der persönlich haftenden Gesellschafter bedürfen, sind zum Handelsregister erst einzureichen, wenn die Zustimmung vorliegt. ²Bei Beschlüssen, die in das Handelsregister einzutragen sind, ist die Zustimmung in der Verhandlungsniederschrift oder in einem Anhang zur Niederschrift zu beurkunden.

§ 286 Jahresabschluß. Lagebericht.

(1) ¹Die Hauptversammlung beschließt über die Feststellung des Jahresabschlusses. ²Der Beschluß bedarf der Zustimmung der persönlich haftenden Gesellschafter.

(2) ¹In der Jahresbilanz sind die Kapitalanteile der persönlich haftenden Gesellschafter nach dem Posten „Gezeichnetes Kapital" gesondert auszuweisen. ²Der auf den Kapitalanteil eines persönlich haftenden Gesellschafters für das Geschäftsjahr entfallende Verlust ist von dem Kapitalanteil abzuschreiben. ³Soweit der Verlust den Kapitalanteil übersteigt, ist er auf der Aktivseite unter der Bezeichnung

³Their voting right may not be exercised by another for such resolutions either.

(2) ¹The resolutions of the general meeting require the consent of the personally liable partners if they concern matters for which the agreement of the personally liable partners and the limited partners is required in a limited partnership. ²The consent of the personally liable partners is not required for the exercising of powers held by the general meeting or a minority of limited liability shareholders concerning the appointment of auditors and the asserting of the company's claims arising from the formation or the management of the company.

(3) ¹Resolutions of the general meeting requiring the consent of the personally liable partners shall only be submitted to the commercial register once such consent has been obtained. ²In the case of resolutions which are subject to registration in the commercial register, the granting of such consent shall be notarized in the minutes of the meeting or in an appendix to the minutes.

§ 286 Annual financial statements. Management report.

(1) ¹The general meeting shall resolve on formal approval of the annual financial statements. ²The resolution requires the consent of the personally liable partners.

(2) ¹The capital interests of the personally liable partners shall be stated separately in the annual balance sheet after the item "subscribed capital". ²Losses attributable to the capital interest of a personally liable partner for the fiscal year shall be deducted from such capital interest. ³If such loss exceeds the value of the capital interest, it shall be shown separately under the accounts receivable on the assets side under the heading

„Einzahlungsverpflichtungen persönlich haftender Gesellschafter" unter den Forderungen gesondert auszuweisen, soweit eine Zahlungsverpflichtung besteht; besteht keine Zahlungsverpflichtung, so ist der Betrag als „Nicht durch Vermögenseinlagen gedeckter Verlustanteil persönlich haftender Gesellschafter" zu bezeichnen und gemäß § 268 Abs. 3 des Handelsgesetzbuchs auszuweisen. [4]Unter § 89 fallende Kredite, die die Gesellschaft persönlich haftenden Gesellschaftern, deren Ehegatten, Lebenspartnern oder minderjährigen Kindern oder Dritten, die für Rechnung dieser Personen handeln, gewährt hat, sind auf der Aktivseite bei den entsprechenden Posten unter der Bezeichnung „davon an persönlich haftende Gesellschafter und deren Angehörige" zu vermerken.

(3) In der Gewinn- und Verlustrechnung braucht der auf die Kapitalanteile der persönlich haftenden Gesellschafter entfallende Gewinn oder Verlust nicht gesondert ausgewiesen zu werden.

(4) § 285 Nr. 9 Buchstabe a und b des Handelsgesetzbuchs gilt für die persönlich haftenden Gesellschafter mit der Maßgabe, daß der auf den Kapitalanteil eines persönlich haftenden Gesellschafters entfallende Gewinn nicht angegeben zu werden braucht.

§ 287 Aufsichtsrat.

(1) Die Beschlüsse der Kommanditaktionäre führt der Aufsichtsrat aus, wenn die Satzung nichts anderes bestimmt.

(2) [1]In Rechtsstreitigkeiten, die die Gesamtheit der Kommanditaktionäre gegen die persönlich haftenden Gesellschafter oder diese gegen die Gesamtheit der Kommanditaktionäre führen, vertritt der Aufsichtsrat die Kommanditaktionäre, wenn die Hauptversammlung keine besonderen Vertreter gewählt hat. [2]Für die Kosten des Rechtsstreits, die den Kommandit-

"payment obligations of personally liable partners" if a payment obligation exists; if there is no payment obligation, the amount shall be defined as "share in losses attributable to personally liable partners not covered by capital contributions" and shown pursuant to sec. 268 para. 3 of the Commercial Code. [4]Credits covered by sec. 89 granted by the company to personally liable partners, their spouses, partners or minor children or third parties acting on behalf of such persons shall be noted on the assets side at the relevant entries under the heading "of which to personally liable partners and their relatives".

(3) The profits or loss attributed to the capital interests of the personally liable partners need not be shown separately in the profit and loss statement.

(4) Sec. 285 no. 9 lit. a and b of the Commercial Code shall apply to personally liable partners with the exception that there is no requirement for the profits allocated to the capital interest of a personally liable partner to be stated.

§ 287 Supervisory board.

(1) The supervisory board shall implement the resolutions of the limited liability shareholders, unless provided otherwise in the articles of association.

(2) [1]In legal disputes brought by all limited liability shareholders against the personally liable partners or by the latter against all limited liability shareholders, the supervisory board shall represent the limited liability shareholders if the general meeting has not elected any particular representatives. [2]The company shall be liable for the costs of the legal dispute to be borne by the limited liabil-

aktionären zur Last fallen, haftet die Gesellschaft unbeschadet ihres Rückgriffs gegen die Kommanditaktionäre.

(3) Persönlich haftende Gesellschafter können nicht Aufsichtsratsmitglieder sein.

§ 288 Entnahmen der persönlich haftenden Gesellschafter. Kreditgewährung.

(1) ¹Entfällt auf einen persönlich haftenden Gesellschafter ein Verlust, der seinen Kapitalanteil übersteigt, so darf er keinen Gewinn auf seinen Kapitalanteil entnehmen. ²Er darf ferner keinen solchen Gewinnanteil und kein Geld auf seinen Kapitalanteil entnehmen, solange die Summe aus Bilanzverlust, Einzahlungsverpflichtungen, Verlustanteilen persönlich haftender Gesellschafter und Forderungen aus Krediten an persönlich haftende Gesellschafter und deren Angehörige die Summe aus Gewinnvortrag, Kapital- und Gewinnrücklagen sowie Kapitalanteilen der persönlich haftenden Gesellschafter übersteigt.

(2) ¹Solange die Voraussetzung von Absatz 1 Satz 2 vorliegt, darf die Gesellschaft keinen unter § 286 Abs. 2 Satz 4 fallenden Kredit gewähren. ²Ein trotzdem gewährter Kredit ist ohne Rücksicht auf entgegenstehende Vereinbarungen sofort zurückzugewähren.

(3) ¹Ansprüche persönlich haftender Gesellschafter auf nicht vom Gewinn abhängige Tätigkeitsvergütungen werden durch diese Vorschriften nicht berührt. ²Für eine Herabsetzung solcher Vergütungen gilt § 87 Abs. 2 Satz 1 und 2 sinngemäß.

§ 289 Auflösung

(1) Die Gründe für die Auflösung der Kommanditgesellschaft auf Aktien und das Ausscheiden eines von mehreren persönlich haftenden Gesellschaftern aus der Gesellschaft richten sich, soweit in den Absätzen 2 bis 6 nichts anderes

ity shareholders, without prejudice to its right of recourse to the limited liability shareholders.

(3) Personally liable partners may not be members of the supervisory board.

§ 288 Withdrawals by personally liable partners. Granting of credit.

(1) ¹If a personally liable partner is attributed a loss exceeding his capital interest, he may not withdraw any profits due on his capital interest. ²Furthermore, he may not withdraw any such share in profits or any cash due on his capital interest as long as the sum of the balance sheet loss, obligations of shareholders to make contributions, shares in losses attributable to personally liable partners and accounts receivable from credits to personally liable partners and their relatives exceed the sum of the profit carried forward, capital reserves and revenue reserves and the capital interests of the personally liable partners.

(2) ¹The company may not grant a credit pursuant to sec. 286 para. 2 sentence 4 while the requirement stipulated in para. 1 sentence 2 applies. ²Any credit granted nevertheless shall be returned immediately, irrespective of any agreements to the contrary.

(3) ¹Claims of personally liable partners to non-profit-related remuneration for services rendered shall not be affected by the above provisions. ²Sec. 87 para. 2 sentences 1 and 2 shall apply accordingly to the reduction of such remuneration.

§ 289 Dissolution.

(1) The reasons for a dissolution of the partnership limited by shares and the withdrawal of one of several personally liable partners from the company shall, unless stipulated otherwise in para. 2 to 6, comply with the provisions in the

bestimmt ist, nach den Vorschriften des Handelsgesetzbuchs über die Kommanditgesellschaft.

(2) Die Kommanditgesellschaft auf Aktien wird auch aufgelöst

1. mit der Rechtskraft des Beschlusses, durch den die Eröffnung des Insolvenzverfahrens mangels Masse abgelehnt wird;
2. mit der Rechtskraft einer Verfügung des Registergerichts, durch welche nach § 399 des Gesetzes über das Verfahren in Familiensachen und in den Angelegenheiten der freiwilligen Gerichtsbarkeit ein Mangel der Satzung festgestellt worden ist;
3. durch die Löschung der Gesellschaft wegen Vermögenslosigkeit nach § 394 des Gesetzes über das Verfahren in Familiensachen und in den Angelegenheiten der freiwilligen Gerichtsbarkeit.

(3) ¹Durch die Eröffnung des Insolvenzverfahrens über das Vermögen eines Kommanditaktionärs wird die Gesellschaft nicht aufgelöst. ²Die Gläubiger eines Kommanditaktionärs sind nicht berechtigt, die Gesellschaft zu kündigen.

(4) ¹Für die Kündigung der Gesellschaft durch die Kommanditaktionäre und für ihre Zustimmung zur Auflösung der Gesellschaft ist ein Beschluß der Hauptversammlung nötig. ²Gleiches gilt für den Antrag auf Auflösung der Gesellschaft durch gerichtliche Entscheidung. ³Der Beschluß bedarf einer Mehrheit, die mindestens drei Viertel des bei der Beschlußfassung vertretenen Grundkapitals umfaßt. ⁴Die Satzung kann eine größere Kapitalmehrheit und weitere Erfordernisse bestimmen.

(5) Persönlich haftende Gesellschafter können außer durch Ausschließung nur ausscheiden, wenn es die Satzung für zulässig erklärt.

(6) ¹Die Auflösung der Gesellschaft und das Ausscheiden eines persönlich

Commercial Code relating to limited partnerships.

(2) The partnership limited by shares shall also be dissolved

1. upon the decision rejecting the commencement of insolvency proceedings due to a lack of assets becoming res judicata;
2. upon a ruling issued by the register court determining a defect in the articles of association pursuant to sec. 399 of the Act on Procedure in Family Matters and Matters of Non-Contentious Jurisdiction becoming res judicata;
3. upon the company being cancelled due to a lack of assets pursuant to sec. 394 of the Act on Procedure in Family Matters and Matters of Non-Contentious Jurisdiction.

(3) ¹The company shall not be dissolved as a result of insolvency proceedings being commenced against the assets of one of the limited liability shareholders. ²The creditors of a limited liability shareholder are not entitled to terminate the company.

(4) ¹A resolution of the general meeting shall be required for the termination of the company by the limited liability shareholders and for their consent to the dissolution of the company. ²This also applies to an application for the company to be dissolved by order of the court. ³The resolution requires a majority of at least three quarters of the registered share capital represented at the adoption of the resolution. ⁴The articles of association may stipulate a larger capital majority and further requirements.

(5) Other than by expulsion, personally liable partners may only withdraw from the company if permitted to do so by the articles of association.

(6) ¹All personally liable partners shall apply for the dissolution of the company

haftenden Gesellschafters ist von allen persönlich haftenden Gesellschaftern zur Eintragung in das Handelsregister anzumelden. ²§ 143 Abs. 3 des Handelsgesetzbuchs gilt sinngemäß. ³In den Fällen des Absatzes 2 hat das Gericht die Auflösung und ihren Grund von Amts wegen einzutragen. ⁴Im Falle des Absatzes 2 Nr. 3 entfällt die Eintragung der Auflösung.

and the withdrawal of one of the personally liable partners to be registered in the commercial register. ²Sec. 143 para. 3 of the Commercial Code shall apply accordingly. ³In cases pursuant to para. 2, the court shall enter the dissolution of the company and the reasons therefor ex officio. ⁴There is no requirement for the dissolution to be registered in the commercial register in the case of para. 2 no. 3.

§ 290 Abwicklung.

(1) Die Abwicklung besorgen alle persönlich haftenden Gesellschafter und eine oder mehrere von der Hauptversammlung gewählte Personen als Abwickler, wenn die Satzung nichts anderes bestimmt.

(2) Die Bestellung oder Abberufung von Abwicklern durch das Gericht kann auch jeder persönlich haftende Gesellschafter beantragen.

(3) ¹Ist die Gesellschaft durch Löschung wegen Vermögenslosigkeit aufgelöst, so findet eine Abwicklung nur statt, wenn sich nach der Löschung herausstellt, daß Vermögen vorhanden ist, das der Verteilung unterliegt. ²Die Abwickler sind auf Antrag eines Beteiligten durch das Gericht zu ernennen.

§ 290 Liquidation.

(1) All personally liable partners and one or more persons elected by the general meeting shall arrange for liquidation in the capacity of liquidators, unless provided otherwise in the articles of association.

(2) Each personally liable partner may request the appointment or dismissal of liquidators by the court.

(3) ¹If the company has been dissolved by means of cancellation due to a lack of assets, liquidation shall only take place if it becomes apparent after the cancellation that there are assets which are subject to distribution. ²The liquidators shall be appointed by the court upon one of the parties concerned filing a request to this effect.

Drittes Buch.
Verbundene Unternehmen

Erster Teil. Unternehmensverträge

Erster Abschnitt. Arten von Unternehmensverträgen

§ 291 Beherrschungsvertrag. Gewinnabführungsvertrag.

(1) ¹Unternehmensverträge sind Verträge, durch die eine Aktiengesellschaft oder Kommanditgesellschaft auf Aktien die Leitung ihrer Gesellschaft einem anderen Unternehmen unterstellt (Beherr-

Third Book.
Affiliated Enterprises

Part One. Enterprise Agreements

Section One. Types of Enterprise Agreements

§ 291 Domination agreement. Profit transfer agreement.

(1) ¹Enterprise agreements are contracts by way of which a stock corporation or a partnership limited by shares transfers the management of such company to another enterprise (domination

schungsvertrag) oder sich verpflichtet, ihren ganzen Gewinn an ein anderes Unternehmen abzuführen (Gewinnabführungsvertrag). ²Als Vertrag über die Abführung des ganzen Gewinns gilt auch ein Vertrag, durch den eine Aktiengesellschaft oder Kommanditgesellschaft auf Aktien es übernimmt, ihr Unternehmen für Rechnung eines anderen Unternehmens zu führen.

agreement) or undertakes to transfer its entire profits to another enterprise (profit transfer agreement). ²A contract in which a stock corporation or a partnership limited by shares undertakes to operate its enterprise for the account of another shall also constitute a contract for the transfer of the entire profits.

(2) Stellen sich Unternehmen, die voneinander nicht abhängig sind, durch Vertrag unter einheitliche Leitung, ohne daß dadurch eines von ihnen von einem anderen vertragschließenden Unternehmen abhängig wird, so ist dieser Vertrag kein Beherrschungsvertrag.

(2) If enterprises which are not controlled by one another conclude an agreement placing them under common direction without one of these enterprises thereby becoming controlled by another contracting enterprise, such contract shall not constitute a domination agreement.

(3) Leistungen der Gesellschaft bei Bestehen eines Beherrschungs- oder eines Gewinnabführungsvertrags gelten nicht als Verstoß gegen die §§ 57, 58 und 60.

(3) Services rendered by the company while a domination agreement or a profit transfer agreement is in force shall not constitute a violation of sec. 57, 58 and 60.

§ 292 Andere Unternehmensverträge.

§ 292 Other enterprise agreements.

(1) Unternehmensverträge sind ferner Verträge, durch die eine Aktiengesellschaft oder Kommanditgesellschaft auf Aktien

(1) Enterprise agreements are also contracts by way of which a stock corporation or a partnership limited by shares

1. sich verpflichtet, ihren Gewinn oder den Gewinn einzelner ihrer Betriebe ganz oder zum Teil mit dem Gewinn anderer Unternehmen oder einzelner Betriebe anderer Unternehmen zur Aufteilung eines gemeinschaftlichen Gewinns zusammenzulegen (Gewinngemeinschaft),
2. sich verpflichtet, einen Teil ihres Gewinns oder den Gewinn einzelner ihrer Betriebe ganz oder zum Teil an einen anderen abzuführen (Teilgewinnabführungsvertrag),
3. den Betrieb ihres Unternehmens einem anderen verpachtet oder sonst überläßt (Betriebspachtvertrag, Betriebsüberlassungsvertrag).

1. undertakes to combine its profits or the profits from certain of its facilities with the profits from other enterprises or individual facilities of other enterprises for the purposes of distributing a joint profit (profit pool),
2. undertakes to transfer part of its profit or the profit from certain of its facilities in whole or in part to another (partial profit transfer agreement),
3. leases or otherwise surrenders the operating of its enterprise to another (lease of undertaking, agreement to relinquish undertaking).

(2) Ein Vertrag über eine Gewinnbeteiligung mit Mitgliedern von Vorstand und

(2) A contract with members of the management board and the supervisory

Aufsichtsrat oder mit einzelnen Arbeitnehmern der Gesellschaft sowie eine Abrede über eine Gewinnbeteiligung im Rahmen von Verträgen des laufenden Geschäftsverkehrs oder Lizenzverträgen ist kein Teilgewinnabführungsvertrag.

(3) [1]Ein Betriebspacht- oder Betriebsüberlassungsvertrag und der Beschluß, durch den die Hauptversammlung dem Vertrag zugestimmt hat, sind nicht deshalb nichtig, weil der Vertrag gegen die §§ 57, 58 und 60 verstößt. [2]Satz 1 schließt die Anfechtung des Beschlusses wegen dieses Verstoßes nicht aus.

board or with individual employees of the company concerning participation in profits and an arrangement concerning participation in profits made within the framework of license agreements or routine business shall not constitute a partial profit transfer agreement.

(3) [1]A lease of undertaking or an agreement to relinquish undertaking and the resolution in which the general meeting has granted its consent for such agreement shall not be null and void on the grounds that the agreement violates sec. 57, 58 and 60. [2]The possibility of bringing an action to set aside the resolution on the basis of such a violation shall not be excluded as a result of sentence 1.

Zweiter Abschnitt. Abschluß, Änderung und Beendigung von Unternehmensverträgen

§ 293 Zustimmung der Hauptversammlung.

(1) [1]Ein Unternehmensvertrag wird nur mit Zustimmung der Hauptversammlung wirksam. [2]Der Beschluß bedarf einer Mehrheit, die mindestens drei Viertel des bei der Beschlußfassung vertretenen Grundkapitals umfaßt. [3]Die Satzung kann eine größere Kapitalmehrheit und weitere Erfordernisse bestimmen. [4]Auf den Beschluß sind die Bestimmungen des Gesetzes und der Satzung über Satzungsänderungen nicht anzuwenden.

(2) [1]Ein Beherrschungs- oder ein Gewinnabführungsvertrag wird, wenn der andere Vertragsteil eine Aktiengesellschaft oder Kommanditgesellschaft auf Aktien ist, nur wirksam, wenn auch die Hauptversammlung dieser Gesellschaft zustimmt. [2]Für den Beschluß gilt Absatz 1 Satz 2 bis 4 sinngemäß.

(3) Der Vertrag bedarf der schriftlichen Form.

Section Two. Conclusion, Amendment and Termination of Enterprise Agreements

§ 293 Approval of general meeting.

(1) [1]An enterprise agreement only becomes effective upon being approved by the general meeting. [2]The resolution requires a majority of at least three quarters of the registered share capital represented at the adoption of the resolution. [3]The articles of association may stipulate a larger capital majority and further requirements. [4]Legal provisions and provisions contained in the articles of association concerning amendments to the articles of association shall not apply to this resolution.

(2) [1]A domination agreement or profit transfer agreement concluded with a stock corporation or a partnership limited by shares shall only be effective if the general meeting of such company also grants its consent. [2]Para. 1 sentences 2 to 4 shall apply accordingly to this resolution.

(3) The agreement shall require the written form.

§ 293a Bericht über den Unternehmensvertrag.

(1) ¹Der Vorstand jeder an einem Unternehmensvertrag beteiligten Aktiengesellschaft oder Kommanditgesellschaft auf Aktien hat, soweit die Zustimmung der Hauptversammlung nach § 293 erforderlich ist, einen ausführlichen schriftlichen Bericht zu erstatten, in dem der Abschluß des Unternehmensvertrags, der Vertrag im einzelnen und insbesondere Art und Höhe des Ausgleichs nach § 304 und der Abfindung nach § 305 rechtlich und wirtschaftlich erläutert und begründet werden; der Bericht kann von den Vorständen auch gemeinsam erstattet werden. ²Auf besondere Schwierigkeiten bei der Bewertung der vertragschließenden Unternehmen sowie auf die Folgen für die Beteiligungen der Aktionäre ist hinzuweisen.

(2) ¹In den Bericht brauchen Tatsachen nicht aufgenommen zu werden, deren Bekanntwerden geeignet ist, einem der vertragschließenden Unternehmen oder einem verbundenen Unternehmen einen nicht unerheblichen Nachteil zuzufügen. ²In diesem Falle sind in dem Bericht die Gründe, aus denen die Tatsachen nicht aufgenommen worden sind, darzulegen.

(3) Der Bericht ist nicht erforderlich, wenn alle Anteilsinhaber aller beteiligten Unternehmen auf seine Erstattung durch öffentlich beglaubigte Erklärung verzichten.

§ 293b Prüfung des Unternehmensvertrags.

(1) Der Unternehmensvertrag ist für jede vertragschließende Aktiengesellschaft oder Kommanditgesellschaft auf Aktien durch einen oder mehrere sachverständige Prüfer (Vertragsprüfer) zu prüfen, es sei denn, daß sich alle Aktien der abhängigen Gesellschaft in der Hand des herrschenden Unternehmens befinden.

§ 293a Report on the enterprise agreement.

(1) ¹If the approval of the general meeting is required pursuant to sec. 293, the management board of each stock corporation or partnership limited by shares which is party to an enterprise agreement shall submit a comprehensive written report giving an explanation of the conclusion of the enterprise agreement, details of the agreement and in particular the nature and amount of the compensation pursuant to sec. 304 and the consideration pursuant to sec. 305 from both the legal and the economic point of view; such report may also be made jointly by the management boards. ²Mention shall be made of any particular difficulties concerning the valuation of the enterprises which are party to the contract and to the consequences for the shareholders.

(2) ¹Facts which, if they become known, are capable of causing not inconsiderable damage to one of the enterprises which is party to the agreement or an affiliated enterprise thereof need not be included in the report. ²In this case, the report shall state the reasons why such facts have not been included.

(3) The report is not required if all the shareholders of all the enterprises concerned submit a certified declaration stating that they dispense with such report.

§ 293b Inspection of the enterprise agreement.

(1) The enterprise agreement shall be inspected by one or more specialist auditors (contract auditors) for each stock corporation or partnership limited by shares which is party to the agreement, unless all shares in the controlled company are held by the controlling enterprise.

(2) § 293a Abs. 3 ist entsprechend anzuwenden.

§ 293c Bestellung der Vertragsprüfer.

(1) ¹Die Vertragsprüfer werden jeweils auf Antrag der Vorstände der vertragschließenden Gesellschaften vom Gericht ausgewählt und bestellt. ²Sie können auf gemeinsamen Antrag der Vorstände für alle vertragschließenden Gesellschaften gemeinsam bestellt werden. ³Zuständig ist das Landgericht, in dessen Bezirk die abhängige Gesellschaft ihren Sitz hat. ⁴Ist bei dem Landgericht eine Kammer für Handelssachen gebildet, so entscheidet deren Vorsitzender an Stelle der Zivilkammer. ⁵Für den Ersatz von Auslagen und für die Vergütung der vom Gericht bestellten Prüfer gilt § 318 Abs. 5 des Handelsgesetzbuchs.

(2) § 10 Abs. 3 bis 5 des Umwandlungsgesetzes gilt entsprechend.

§ 293d Auswahl, Stellung und Verantwortlichkeit der Vertragsprüfer.

(1) ¹Für die Auswahl und das Auskunftsrecht der Vertragsprüfer gelten § 319 Abs. 1 bis 4, § 319a Abs. 1, § 319b Abs. 1, § 320 Abs. 1 Satz 2 und Abs. 2 Satz 1 und 2 des Handelsgesetzbuchs entsprechend. ²Das Auskunftsrecht besteht gegenüber den vertragschließenden Unternehmen und gegenüber einem Konzernunternehmen sowie einem abhängigen und einem herrschenden Unternehmen.

(2) ¹Für die Verantwortlichkeit der Vertragsprüfer, ihrer Gehilfen und der bei der Prüfung mitwirkenden gesetzlichen Vertreter einer Prüfungsgesellschaft gilt § 323 des Handelsgesetzbuchs entsprechend. ²Die Verantwortlichkeit besteht gegenüber den vertragschließenden Unternehmen und deren Anteilsinhabern.

(2) Sec. 293a para. 3 shall apply accordingly.

§ 293c Appointment of contract auditors.

(1) ¹Each of the contract auditors shall be selected and appointed by the court at the petition of the management boards of the companies which are party to the agreement. ²They may be appointed upon joint application of the management boards jointly for all companies which are party to the agreement. ³The regional court in the district of which the controlled company has its registered office shall have jurisdiction. ⁴If such regional court has a chamber for commercial matters, the presiding judge thereof shall decide in lieu of the civil chamber. ⁵The reimbursement of expenses and the remuneration of the auditors appointed by the court shall be governed by sec. 318 para. 5 of the Commercial Code.

(2) Sec. 10 paras. 3 to 5 of the Transformation Act shall apply accordingly.

§ 293d Selection, status and liability of contract auditors.

(1) ¹ Sec. 319 paras. 1 to 4, sec. 319a para. 1, sec. 319b para. 1, sec. 320 para. 1 sentence 2 and para. 2 sentences 1 and 2 of the Commercial Code shall apply accordingly to the selection and right to information of the contract auditors. ²The right to information shall apply vis-à-vis the enterprises which are party to the contract, an enterprise in the same group, a controlled and a controlling enterprise.

(2) ¹Sec. 323 of the Commercial Code shall apply accordingly to the responsibility of the contract auditors, their assistants and the legal representatives of an auditing company involved in the inspection. ²Responsibility applies vis-à-vis the enterprises which are party to the contract and the shareholders thereof.

§ 293e Prüfungsbericht.

(1) ¹Die Vertragsprüfer haben über das Ergebnis der Prüfung schriftlich zu berichten. ²Der Prüfungsbericht ist mit einer Erklärung darüber abzuschließen, ob der vorgeschlagene Ausgleich oder die vorgeschlagene Abfindung angemessen ist. ³Dabei ist anzugeben,

1. nach welchen Methoden Ausgleich und Abfindung ermittelt worden sind;
2. aus welchen Gründen die Anwendung dieser Methoden angemessen ist;
3. welcher Ausgleich oder welche Abfindung sich bei der Anwendung verschiedener Methoden, sofern mehrere angewandt worden sind, jeweils ergeben würde; zugleich ist darzulegen, welches Gewicht den verschiedenen Methoden bei der Bestimmung des vorgeschlagenen Ausgleichs oder der vorgeschlagenen Abfindung und der ihnen zugrunde liegenden Werte beigemessen worden ist und welche besonderen Schwierigkeiten bei der Bewertung der vertragschließenden Unternehmen aufgetreten sind.

(2) § 293a Abs. 2 und 3 ist entsprechend anzuwenden.

§ 293f Vorbereitung der Hauptversammlung.

(1) Von der Einberufung der Hauptversammlung an, die über die Zustimmung zu dem Unternehmensvertrag beschließen soll, sind in dem Geschäftsraum jeder der beteiligten Aktiengesellschaften oder Kommanditgesellschaften auf Aktien zur Einsicht der Aktionäre auszulegen

1. der Unternehmensvertrag;
2. die Jahresabschlüsse und die Lageberichte der vertragschließenden Unternehmen für die letzten drei Geschäftsjahre;

§ 293e Audit report.

(1) ¹The contract auditors shall provide a written report on the results of their audit. ²The audit report shall conclude with a declaration as to whether the proposed compensation or proposed consideration is appropriate. ³The following shall be stated:

1. the methods used to determine the compensation and consideration;
2. the reasons why it is appropriate for such methods to be applied;
3. if several methods have been used, the compensation or consideration which would be due as a result of each of the various methods; the weighting given to the various methods when determining the proposed consideration or the proposed compensation and the values upon which they are based shall also be stated, as shall any particular difficulties which arose when valuating the enterprises which are party to the contract.

(2) Sec. 293a paras. 2 and 3 shall apply accordingly.

§ 293f Preparation of the general meeting.

(1) From such time as the general meeting which is to resolve on approval for the enterprise agreement has been convened, the following shall be displayed for inspection by the shareholders in the offices of each of the stock corporations or partnerships limited by shares concerned:

1. the enterprise agreement;
2. the annual financial statements and the management reports of the enterprises which are party to the contract for the three preceding fiscal years;

3. die nach § 293a erstatteten Berichte der Vorstände und die nach § 293e erstatteten Berichte der Vertragsprüfer.

(2) Auf Verlangen ist jedem Aktionär unverzüglich und kostenlos eine Abschrift der in Absatz 1 bezeichneten Unterlagen zu erteilen.

(3) Die Verpflichtungen nach den Absätzen 1 und 2 entfallen, wenn die in Absatz 1 bezeichneten Unterlagen für denselben Zeitraum über die Internetseite der Gesellschaft zugänglich sind.

§ 293g Durchführung der Hauptversammlung.

(1) In der Hauptversammlung sind die in § 293f Abs. 1 bezeichneten Unterlagen zugänglich zu machen.

(2) ¹Der Vorstand hat den Unternehmensvertrag zu Beginn der Verhandlung mündlich zu erläutern. ²Er ist der Niederschrift als Anlage beizufügen.

(3) Jedem Aktionär ist auf Verlangen in der Hauptversammlung Auskunft auch über alle für den Vertragschluß wesentlichen Angelegenheiten des anderen Vertragsteils zu geben.

§ 294 Eintragung. Wirksamwerden.

(1) ¹Der Vorstand der Gesellschaft hat das Bestehen und die Art des Unternehmensvertrages sowie den Namen des anderen Vertragsteils zur Eintragung in das Handelsregister anzumelden; beim Bestehen einer Vielzahl von Teilgewinnabführungsverträgen kann anstelle des Namens des anderen Vertragsteils auch eine andere Bezeichnung eingetragen werden, die den jeweiligen Teilgewinnabführungsvertrag konkret bestimmt. ²Der Anmeldung sind der Vertrag sowie, wenn er nur mit Zustimmung der Hauptversammlung des anderen Vertragsteils wirksam wird, die Niederschrift dieses Beschlus-

3. the reports of the management board submitted pursuant to sec. 293a and the reports of the contract auditors submitted pursuant to sec. 293e.

(2) A copy of the documents stated in para. 1 shall be provided without undue delay and free of charge to any shareholder who so requests.

(3) The obligations pursuant to paras. 1 and 2 shall cease to exist if the documents set forth in para. 1 are accessible during the same time period on the website of the company.

§ 293g Conducting of the general meeting.

(1) The documents pursuant to sec. 293f para. 1 shall be made accessible during the general meeting.

(2) ¹The management board shall explain the content of the enterprise agreement at the beginning of the proceedings. ²Such agreement shall be attached to the minutes as an appendix.

(3) Each shareholder shall, upon request, be given information in the general meeting on all matters relating to the other party of the contract which are of relevance to the conclusion of the agreement.

§ 294 Registration. Effectiveness.

(1) ¹The management board of the company shall apply for the existence and nature of the enterprise agreement and the name of the other party to the contract to be registered in the commercial register; if a multitude of partial profit transfer agreements exists, another designation which specifies the particular partial profit transfer agreement may be registered in place of the name of the other party to the contract. ²An original, executed copy or certified copy of the agreement and, if it is only effective if approved by the general meeting of the other party to the contract, the minutes of this resolution and the appendices

ses und ihre Anlagen in Urschrift, Ausfertigung oder öffentlich beglaubigter Abschrift beizufügen.

(2) Der Vertrag wird erst wirksam, wenn sein Bestehen in das Handelsregister des Sitzes der Gesellschaft eingetragen worden ist.

§ 295 Änderung.

(1) [1]Ein Unternehmensvertrag kann nur mit Zustimmung der Hauptversammlung geändert werden. [2]§§ 293 bis 294 gelten sinngemäß.

(2) [1]Die Zustimmung der Hauptversammlung der Gesellschaft zu einer Änderung der Bestimmungen des Vertrags, die zur Leistung eines Ausgleichs an die außenstehenden Aktionäre der Gesellschaft oder zum Erwerb ihrer Aktien verpflichten, bedarf, um wirksam zu werden, eines Sonderbeschlusses der außenstehenden Aktionäre. [2]Für den Sonderbeschluß gilt § 293 Abs. 1 Satz 2 und 3. [3]Jedem außenstehenden Aktionär ist auf Verlangen in der Versammlung, die über die Zustimmung beschließt, Auskunft auch über alle für die Änderung wesentlichen Angelegenheiten des anderen Vertragsteils zu geben.

§ 296 Aufhebung.

(1) [1]Ein Unternehmensvertrag kann nur zum Ende des Geschäftsjahrs oder des sonst vertraglich bestimmten Abrechnungszeitraums aufgehoben werden. [2]Eine rückwirkende Aufhebung ist unzulässig. [3]Die Aufhebung bedarf der schriftlichen Form.

(2) [1]Ein Vertrag, der zur Leistung eines Ausgleichs an die außenstehenden Aktionäre oder zum Erwerb ihrer Aktien verpflichtet, kann nur aufgehoben werden, wenn die außenstehenden Aktionäre durch Sonderbeschluß zustimmen. [2]Für den Sonderbeschluß gilt § 293 Abs. 1 Satz 2 und 3, § 295 Abs. 2 Satz 3 sinngemäß.

thereto shall be attached to the application filed with the commercial register.

(2) The agreement shall only take effect once the existence thereof has been registered in the commercial register responsible for the registered office of the company.

§ 295 Amendment.

(1) [1]An enterprise agreement may only be amended if the general meeting grants its consent. [2]Sec. 293 to 294 shall apply accordingly.

(2) [1]The consent of the general meeting for an amendment to the provisions in the agreement placing the company under an obligation to pay compensation to the external shareholders of the company or to purchase their shares shall require a special resolution to be adopted by the external shareholders before it takes effect. [2]Sec. 293 para. 1 sentences 2 and 3 shall apply to such special resolution. [3]Each external shareholder shall, upon request, be given information in the general meeting on all matters relating to the other party to the contract which are of relevance to the amendment.

§ 296 Termination by agreement.

(1) [1]An enterprise agreement may only be terminated by agreement with effect from the end of the fiscal year or another accounting period defined in the agreement. [2]The agreement may not be terminated by agreement retroactively. [3]Termination by agreement requires the written form.

(2) [1]An agreement placing the company under an obligation to pay compensation to the external shareholders of the company or to purchase their shares may only be terminated by agreement if the external shareholders grant their approval in a special resolution. [2]Sec. 293 para. 1 sentences 2 and 3, sec. 295 para. 2 sentence 3 shall apply accordingly to the special resolution.

§ 297 Kündigung.

(1) ¹Ein Unternehmensvertrag kann aus wichtigem Grunde ohne Einhaltung einer Kündigungsfrist gekündigt werden. ²Ein wichtiger Grund liegt namentlich vor, wenn der andere Vertragsteil voraussichtlich nicht in der Lage sein wird, seine auf Grund des Vertrags bestehenden Verpflichtungen zu erfüllen.

(2) ¹Der Vorstand der Gesellschaft kann einen Vertrag, der zur Leistung eines Ausgleichs an die außenstehenden Aktionäre der Gesellschaft oder zum Erwerb ihrer Aktien verpflichtet, ohne wichtigen Grund nur kündigen, wenn die außenstehenden Aktionäre durch Sonderbeschluß zustimmen. ²Für den Sonderbeschluß gilt § 293 Abs. 1 Satz 2 und 3, § 295 Abs. 2 Satz 3 sinngemäß.

(3) Die Kündigung bedarf der schriftlichen Form.

§ 298 Anmeldung und Eintragung.

Der Vorstand der Gesellschaft hat die Beendigung eines Unternehmensvertrags, den Grund und den Zeitpunkt der Beendigung unverzüglich zur Eintragung in das Handelsregister anzumelden.

§ 299 Ausschluß von Weisungen.

Auf Grund eines Unternehmensvertrags kann der Gesellschaft nicht die Weisung erteilt werden, den Vertrag zu ändern, aufrechtzuerhalten oder zu beendigen.

Dritter Abschnitt. Sicherung der Gesellschaft und der Gläubiger

§ 300 Gesetzliche Rücklage.

In die gesetzliche Rücklage sind an Stelle des in § 150 Abs. 2 bestimmten Betrags einzustellen,

1. wenn ein Gewinnabführungsvertrag besteht, aus dem ohne die Gewinnabführung entstehenden, um

§ 297 Termination.

(1) ¹An enterprise agreement may be terminated without notice for good cause. ²Such good cause shall be deemed to exist when the other party to the contract shall in all probability not be in a position to meet its obligations in accordance with the agreement.

(2) ¹The management board of the company may only terminate a contract placing the company under an obligation to pay compensation to the external shareholders or to purchase their shares without good cause if the external shareholders grant their consent in a special resolution. ²Sec. 293 para. 1 sentences 2 and 3, sec. 295 para. 2 sentence 3 shall apply accordingly to the special resolution.

(3) Any termination requires the written form.

§ 298 Application and registration.

The management board of the company shall apply without undue delay for the completion of the enterprise agreement, the reason and the date of the completion to be registered in the commercial register.

§ 299 Exclusion of instructions.

The company may not be instructed on the basis of an enterprise agreement to amend, maintain or complete the agreement.

Section Three. Security for the Company and Creditors

§ 300 Statutory reserve.

The following shall be allocated to the statutory reserve in place of the amount stipulated in sec. 150 para. 2:

1. in the case of a profit transfer agreement, the amount from the annual net income arising without the

einen Verlustvortrag aus dem Vorjahr geminderten Jahresüberschuß der Betrag, der erforderlich ist, um die gesetzliche Rücklage unter Hinzurechnung einer Kapitalrücklage innerhalb der ersten fünf Geschäftsjahre, die während des Bestehens des Vertrags oder nach Durchführung einer Kapitalerhöhung beginnen, gleichmäßig auf den zehnten oder den in der Satzung bestimmten höheren Teil des Grundkapitals aufzufüllen, mindestens aber der in Nummer 2 bestimmte Betrag;
2. wenn ein Teilgewinnabführungsvertrag besteht, der Betrag, der nach § 150 Abs. 2 aus dem ohne die Gewinnabführung entstehenden, um einen Verlustvortrag aus dem Vorjahr geminderten Jahresüberschuß in die gesetzliche Rücklage einzustellen wäre;
3. wenn ein Beherrschungsvertrag besteht, ohne daß die Gesellschaft auch zur Abführung ihres ganzen Gewinns verpflichtet ist, der zur Auffüllung der gesetzlichen Rücklage nach Nummer 1 erforderliche Betrag, mindestens aber der in § 150 Abs. 2 oder, wenn die Gesellschaft verpflichtet ist, ihren Gewinn zum Teil abzuführen, der in Nummer 2 bestimmte Betrag.

§ 301 Höchstbetrag der Gewinnabführung.

¹Eine Gesellschaft kann, gleichgültig welche Vereinbarungen über die Berechnung des abzuführenden Gewinns getroffen worden sind, als ihren Gewinn höchstens den ohne die Gewinnabführung entstehenden Jahresüberschuß, vermindert um einen Verlustvortrag aus dem Vorjahr und um den Betrag, der nach § 300 in die gesetzlichen Rücklagen einzustellen ist, und den nach § 268 Abs. 8 des Handelsgesetzbuchs ausschüttungsgesperrten Betrag, abführen. ²Sind während der Dauer des Vertrags Beträge in andere Gewinnrücklagen eingestellt worden,

transfer of profit and after deduction of any loss carried forward from the previous year which is required in order to fill up the statutory reserve equally, including any capital reserve, to one tenth or any higher percentage stipulated in the articles of association of the registered share capital within the first five fiscal years beginning during the existence of the agreement or after the implementation of a capital increase, but at least the amount stipulated in no. 2;
2. in the case of a partial profit transfer agreement, the amount which would be allocated to the statutory reserve pursuant to sec. 150 para. 2 from the annual net income arising without the transfer of profit and after deduction of any loss carried forward from the previous year;
3. in the case of a domination agreement which does not obligate the company to transfer its entire profit, the amount required in order to fill the statutory reserve pursuant to no. 1, but at least the amount stipulated in sec. 150 para. 2 or, if the company is obligated to transfer part of its profits, the amount stipulated in no. 2.

§ 301 Highest amount of transferable profit.

¹Irrespective of what agreements have been made concerning the calculation of the profit which is to be transferred, a company may at most transfer the annual net income arising without the profit transfer and after deduction of any loss carried forward from the previous year and the amount which is to be allocated to the statutory reserves pursuant to sec. 300 and the amount which may not be distributed pursuant to sec. 268 para. 8 of the Commercial Code. ²If other amounts have been allocated to other revenue reserves during the term of the agreement, such amounts may be with-

so können diese Beträge den anderen Gewinnrücklagen entnommen und als Gewinn abgeführt werden.

§ 302 Verlustübernahme.

(1) Besteht ein Beherrschungs- oder ein Gewinnabführungsvertrag, so hat der andere Vertragsteil jeden während der Vertragsdauer sonst entstehenden Jahresfehlbetrag auszugleichen, soweit dieser nicht dadurch ausgeglichen wird, daß den anderen Gewinnrücklagen Beträge entnommen werden, die während der Vertragsdauer in sie eingestellt worden sind.

(2) Hat eine abhängige Gesellschaft den Betrieb ihres Unternehmens dem herrschenden Unternehmen verpachtet oder sonst überlassen, so hat das herrschende Unternehmen jeden während der Vertragsdauer sonst entstehenden Jahresfehlbetrag auszugleichen, soweit die vereinbarte Gegenleistung das angemessene Entgelt nicht erreicht.

(3) [1]Die Gesellschaft kann auf den Anspruch auf Ausgleich erst drei Jahre nach dem Tage, an dem die Eintragung der Beendigung des Vertrags in das Handelsregister nach § 10 des Handelsgesetzbuchs bekannt gemacht worden ist, verzichten oder sich über ihn vergleichen. [2]Dies gilt nicht, wenn der Ausgleichspflichtige zahlungsunfähig ist und sich zur Abwendung des Insolvenzverfahrens mit seinen Gläubigern vergleicht oder wenn die Ersatzpflicht in einem Insolvenzplan geregelt wird. [3]Der Verzicht oder Vergleich wird nur wirksam, wenn die außenstehenden Aktionäre durch Sonderbeschluß zustimmen und nicht eine Minderheit, deren Anteile zusammen den zehnten Teil des bei der Beschlußfassung vertretenen Grundkapitals erreichen, zur Niederschrift Widerspruch erhebt.

(4) Die Ansprüche aus diesen Vorschriften verjähren in zehn Jahren seit dem Tag, an dem die Eintragung der Beendigung des Vertrags in das Handelsregis-

drawn from the other revenue reserves and transferred as profit.

§ 302 Assumption of losses.

(1) In the case of a domination or profit transfer agreement, the other party to the contract shall compensate for any other annual net loss occurring during the term of the agreement, unless such annual net loss is compensated for by withdrawing amounts which have been paid into other revenue reserves during the term of the agreement from such reserves.

(2) If a controlled company has leased or otherwise surrendered the operation of its business to the controlling enterprise, the controlling enterprise shall compensate for all other annual net losses occurring during the term of the agreement, to the extent the agreed consideration fails to reach the appropriate amount.

(3) [1]The company may not waive or compound its claim to compensation until three years have passed from the day on which the registration of the termination of the agreement in the commercial register was announced pursuant to sec. 10 of the Commercial Code. [2]This shall not apply if the party which is obligated to make the compensatory payments is illiquid and enters into a composition with its creditors in order to avert insolvency proceedings or if the liability for damages is regulated in an insolvency plan. [3]The waiver or composition shall only take effect if the external shareholders grant their approval in a special resolution and no objection is raised in the minutes by a minority with an aggregate shareholding of one tenth of the registered share capital represented at the adoption of the resolution.

(4) The claims pursuant to these provisions shall become time-barred ten years after the day on which the registration of the termination of the contract was

ter nach § 10 des Handelsgesetzbuchs bekannt gemacht worden ist.

§ 303 Gläubigerschutz.

(1) ¹Endet ein Beherrschungs- oder ein Gewinnabführungsvertrag, so hat der andere Vertragsteil den Gläubigern der Gesellschaft, deren Forderungen begründet worden sind, bevor die Eintragung der Beendigung des Vertrags in das Handelsregister nach § 10 des Handelsgesetzbuchs bekannt gemacht worden ist, Sicherheit zu leisten, wenn sie sich binnen sechs Monaten nach der Bekanntmachung der Eintragung zu diesem Zweck bei ihm melden. ²Die Gläubiger sind in der Bekanntmachung der Eintragung auf dieses Recht hinzuweisen.

(2) Das Recht, Sicherheitsleistung zu verlangen, steht Gläubigern nicht zu, die im Fall des Insolvenzverfahrens ein Recht auf vorzugsweise Befriedigung aus einer Deckungsmasse haben, die nach gesetzlicher Vorschrift zu ihrem Schutz errichtet und staatlich überwacht ist.

(3) ¹Statt Sicherheit zu leisten, kann der andere Vertragsteil sich für die Forderung verbürgen. ²§ 349 des Handelsgesetzbuchs über den Ausschluß der Einrede der Vorausklage ist nicht anzuwenden.

Vierter Abschnitt. Sicherung der außenstehenden Aktionäre bei Beherrschungs- und Gewinnabführungsverträgen

§ 304 Angemessener Ausgleich.

(1) ¹Ein Gewinnabführungsvertrag muß einen angemessenen Ausgleich für die außenstehenden Aktionäre durch eine auf die Anteile am Grundkapital bezogene wiederkehrende Geldleistung (Ausgleichszahlung) vorsehen. ²Ein Beherrschungsvertrag muß, wenn die Gesellschaft nicht auch zur Abführung ihres ganzen Gewinns verpflichtet ist, den außenstehenden Aktionären als an-

announced pursuant to sec. 10 of the Commercial Code.

§ 303 Protection of creditors.

(1) ¹If a domination or profit transfer agreement ends, the other party to the contract shall provide security to those creditors of the company whose claims arose before the registration of the termination of the agreement in the commercial register was announced pursuant to sec. 10 of the Commercial Code, provided such creditors contact such party for this purpose within six months of the announcement of such registration. ²The creditors shall be advised of this right in the announcement of the registration.

(2) Creditors having a right to the preferential settlement of their claims in the event of insolvency proceedings from covering funds created for their protection in accordance with legal provisions and monitored by the state shall not be entitled to a right to demand security.

(3) ¹In lieu of rendering security, the other party to the contract may grant a guarantee for the claim. ²Sec. 349 of the Commercial Code which excludes the defense of failure to pursue remedy against the principal debtor, shall not apply.

Section Four. Security for External Shareholders in the Case of Domination and Profit Transfer Agreements

§ 304 Appropriate compensation.

(1) ¹A profit transfer agreement shall provide for an appropriate compensation for the external shareholders via a recurring cash payment relating to the shares in the registered share capital (compensation payment). ²A domination agreement, if the company is not also obligated to transfer its entire profit, shall guarantee the external shareholders an appropriate compensation

gemessenen Ausgleich einen bestimmten jährlichen Gewinnanteil nach der für die Ausgleichszahlung bestimmten Höhe garantieren. ³Von der Bestimmung eines angemessenen Ausgleichs kann nur abgesehen werden, wenn die Gesellschaft im Zeitpunkt der Beschlußfassung ihrer Hauptversammlung über den Vertrag keinen außenstehenden Aktionär hat.

(2) ¹Als Ausgleichszahlung ist mindestens die jährliche Zahlung des Betrags zuzusichern, der nach der bisherigen Ertragslage der Gesellschaft und ihren künftigen Ertragsaussichten unter Berücksichtigung angemessener Abschreibungen und Wertberichtigungen, jedoch ohne Bildung anderer Gewinnrücklagen, voraussichtlich als durchschnittlicher Gewinnanteil auf die einzelne Aktie verteilt werden könnte. ²Ist der andere Vertragsteil eine Aktiengesellschaft oder Kommanditgesellschaft auf Aktien, so kann als Ausgleichszahlung auch die Zahlung des Betrags zugesichert werden, der unter Herstellung eines angemessenen Umrechnungsverhältnisses auf Aktien der anderen Gesellschaft jeweils als Gewinnanteil entfällt. ³Die Angemessenheit der Umrechnung bestimmt sich nach dem Verhältnis, in dem bei einer Verschmelzung auf eine Aktie der Gesellschaft Aktien der anderen Gesellschaft zu gewähren wären.

(3) ¹Ein Vertrag, der entgegen Absatz 1 überhaupt keinen Ausgleich vorsieht, ist nichtig. ²Die Anfechtung des Beschlusses, durch den die Hauptversammlung der Gesellschaft dem Vertrag oder einer unter § 295 Abs. 2 fallenden Änderung des Vertrags zugestimmt hat, kann nicht auf § 243 Abs. 2 oder darauf gestützt werden, daß der im Vertrag bestimmte Ausgleich nicht angemessen ist. ³Ist der im Vertrag bestimmte Ausgleich nicht angemessen, so hat das in § 2 des Spruchverfahrensgesetzes bestimmte Gericht auf Antrag den vertraglich geschuldeten Ausgleich zu bestimmen,

consisting of an annual share in profits of the amount determined for the compensation payment. ³The obligation to determine an appropriate compensation may only be dispensed with if the company has no external shareholders at the time the general meeting adopts the resolution on the agreement.

(2) ¹The minimum promised compensation payment shall consist of the annual payment of the amount which could be expected to be distributed as the average dividend on the individual shares in view of the operating results of the company to date and its future prospects, taking reasonable depreciation and value adjustments into account but without allowing for the creation of other revenue reserves. ²If the other party to the contract is a stock corporation or a partnership limited by shares, the promised compensation payment may also consist of the amount due as a dividend when a reasonable conversion rate to shares in the other company is created. ³The reasonableness of such conversion shall be determined by the ratio in which shares in the other company would be granted in return for one share in the company in the event of a merger.

(3) ¹An agreement which fails to provide for any compensation whatsoever in violation of para. 1 shall be null and void. ²An action to set aside the resolution in which the general meeting of the company has granted its approval for the agreement or an amendment to the agreement pursuant to sec. 295 para. 2 may not be based on sec. 243 para. 2 or on the claim that the compensation stipulated in the agreement is not appropriate. ³If the compensation stipulated in the agreement is not appropriate, the court stipulated in sec. 2 of the Act on Legal Challenge Proceed-

wobei es, wenn der Vertrag einen nach Absatz 2 Satz 2 berechneten Ausgleich vorsieht, den Ausgleich nach dieser Vorschrift zu bestimmen hat.

(4) Bestimmt das Gericht den Ausgleich, so kann der andere Vertragsteil den Vertrag binnen zwei Monaten nach Rechtskraft der Entscheidung ohne Einhaltung einer Kündigungsfrist kündigen.

§ 305 Abfindung.

(1) Außer der Verpflichtung zum Ausgleich nach § 304 muß ein Beherrschungs- oder ein Gewinnabführungsvertrag die Verpflichtung des anderen Vertragsteils enthalten, auf Verlangen eines außenstehenden Aktionärs dessen Aktien gegen eine im Vertrag bestimmte angemessene Abfindung zu erwerben.

(2) Als Abfindung muß der Vertrag,

1. wenn der andere Vertragsteil eine nicht abhängige und nicht in Mehrheitsbesitz stehende Aktiengesellschaft oder Kommanditgesellschaft auf Aktien mit Sitz in einem Mitgliedstaat der Europäischen Union oder in einem anderen Vertragsstaat des Abkommens über den Europäischen Wirtschaftsraum ist, die Gewährung eigener Aktien dieser Gesellschaft,
2. wenn der andere Vertragsteil eine abhängige oder in Mehrheitsbesitz stehende Aktiengesellschaft oder Kommanditgesellschaft auf Aktien und das herrschende Unternehmen eine Aktiengesellschaft oder Kommanditgesellschaft auf Aktien mit Sitz in einem Mitgliedstaat der Europäischen Union oder in einem anderen Vertragsstaat des Abkommens über den Europäischen Wirtschaftsraum ist, entweder die Gewährung

ings shall, upon application, determine the compensation due under contract; if the agreement provides for a compensation calculated pursuant to para. 2 sentence 2, the court shall determine the compensation in accordance with this provision.

(4) If the compensation is determined by the court, the other party to the contract may terminate the agreement without notice within two months of the decision becoming res judicata.

§ 305 Consideration.

(1) In addition to the obligation to provide a compensation pursuant to sec. 304, a domination agreement or profit transfer agreement shall also include the obligation on the part of the other party to the contract to acquire the shares of an external shareholder in return for appropriate consideration stipulated in the agreement if so requested by such shareholder.

(2) The agreement shall provide for consideration as follows:

1. if the other party to the contract is a stock corporation or a partnership limited by shares with its registered office in a European Union member state or in another contracting state of the Treaty on the European Economic Area which is neither a controlled nor a majority-owned enterprise, by granting shares in such company which are held by the company itself,
2. if the other party to the contract is a controlled or a majority-owned stock corporation or partnership limited by shares and the controlling enterprise is a stock corporation or a partnership limited by shares with its registered office in a European Union member state or in another contracting state of the Treaty on the European Economic Area, either by granting shares in the controlling enterprise or the enterprise which

von Aktien der herrschenden oder mit Mehrheit beteiligten Gesellschaft oder eine Barabfindung,

3. in allen anderen Fällen eine Barabfindung

vorsehen.

(3) ¹Werden als Abfindung Aktien einer anderen Gesellschaft gewährt, so ist die Abfindung als angemessen anzusehen, wenn die Aktien in dem Verhältnis gewährt werden, in dem bei einer Verschmelzung auf eine Aktie der Gesellschaft Aktien der anderen Gesellschaft zu gewähren wären, wobei Spitzenbeträge durch bare Zuzahlungen ausgeglichen werden können. ²Die angemessene Barabfindung muß die Verhältnisse der Gesellschaft im Zeitpunkt der Beschlußfassung ihrer Hauptversammlung über den Vertrag berücksichtigen. ³Sie ist nach Ablauf des Tages, an dem der Beherrschungs- oder Gewinnabführungsvertrag wirksam geworden ist, mit jährlich fünf Prozentpunkten über dem jeweiligen Basiszinssatz nach § 247 des Bürgerlichen Gesetzbuchs zu verzinsen; die Geltendmachung eines weiteren Schadens ist nicht ausgeschlossen.

(4) ¹Die Verpflichtung zum Erwerb der Aktien kann befristet werden. ²Die Frist endet frühestens zwei Monate nach dem Tage, an dem die Eintragung des Bestehens des Vertrags im Handelsregister nach § 10 des Handelsgesetzbuchs bekannt gemacht worden ist. ³Ist ein Antrag auf Bestimmung des Ausgleichs oder der Abfindung durch das in § 2 des Spruchverfahrensgesetzes bestimmte Gericht gestellt worden, so endet die Frist frühestens zwei Monate nach dem Tage, an dem die Entscheidung über den zuletzt beschiedenen Antrag im Bundesanzeiger bekanntgemacht worden ist.

(5) ¹Die Anfechtung des Beschlusses, durch den die Hauptversammlung der Gesellschaft dem Vertrag oder einer unter § 295 Abs. 2 fallenden Änderung des Vertrags zugestimmt hat, kann nicht

has the majority interest in the company or a cash consideration,

3. in all other cases, a cash consideration.

(3) ¹If shares in another company are offered as consideration, such consideration shall be deemed appropriate if the shares are granted in the ratio in which shares in the other company would be granted for one share in the company in the event of a merger, with fractional amounts being able to be equalized with additional cash payments. ²The appropriate cash consideration shall take into account the situation of the company at the time the resolution on the agreement is adopted by its general meeting. ³Annual interest of five percentage points above the relevant risk free rate as stated in sec. 247 of the Civil Code shall be due on the cash consideration with effect from the expiry of the day on which the domination or profit transfer agreement takes effect; claims may be brought for more extensive damages.

(4) ¹A time limit may be imposed on the obligation to acquire shares. ²The period shall end no sooner than two months after the date on which the registration in the commercial register of the existence of the agreement has been announced pursuant to sec. 10 of the Commercial Code. ³If an application has been filed for the court stipulated in sec. 2 of the Act on Legal Challenge Proceedings to determine the compensation or consideration, the period shall end no sooner than two months after the date in which the decision on the final application to be decided on is announced in the Federal Law Gazette.

(5) ¹An action to set aside the resolution in which the general meeting of the company has granted its approval for the agreement or an amendment to the agreement pursuant to sec. 295 para. 2

darauf gestützt werden, daß der Vertrag keine angemessene Abfindung vorsieht. ²Sieht der Vertrag überhaupt keine oder eine den Absätzen 1 bis 3 nicht entsprechende Abfindung vor, so hat das in § 2 des Spruchverfahrensgesetzes bestimmte Gericht auf Antrag die vertraglich zu gewährende Abfindung zu bestimmen. ³Dabei hat es in den Fällen des Absatzes 2 Nr. 2, wenn der Vertrag die Gewährung von Aktien der herrschenden oder mit Mehrheit beteiligten Gesellschaft vorsieht, das Verhältnis, in dem diese Aktien zu gewähren sind, wenn der Vertrag nicht die Gewährung von Aktien der herrschenden oder mit Mehrheit beteiligten Gesellschaft vorsieht, die angemessene Barabfindung zu bestimmen. ⁴§ 304 Abs. 4 gilt sinngemäß.

may not be based on the claim that the agreement does not provide for appropriate consideration. ²If the agreement fails to provide for any consideration whatsoever or provides for consideration which is not in accordance with paras. 1 to 3, the court stipulated in sec. 2 of the Act on Legal Challenge Proceedings shall, upon application, determine the consideration to be granted by contract. ³In the cases stated in para. 2 no. 2, if the agreement provides for shares to be granted in the controlling enterprise or the enterprise with the majority shareholding, the court shall determine the ratio according to which such shares are to be granted and if the agreement does not provide for the granting of shares in the controlling enterprise or the enterprise with the majority shareholding, the court shall determine the appropriate cash consideration. ⁴Sec. 304 para. 4 shall apply accordingly.

§ 306 *(aufgehoben)*

§ 306 *(repealed)*

§ 307 Vertragsbeendigung zur Sicherung außenstehender Aktionäre.

§ 307 Termination of agreement for the protection of external shareholders.

Hat die Gesellschaft im Zeitpunkt der Beschlußfassung ihrer Hauptversammlung über einen Beherrschungs- oder Gewinnabführungsvertrag keinen außenstehenden Aktionär, so endet der Vertrag spätestens zum Ende des Geschäftsjahrs, in dem ein außenstehender Aktionär beteiligt ist.

If a company has no external shareholders at the time its general meeting adopts a resolution on a domination or profit transfer agreement, the contract shall end automatically at the latest at the end of the fiscal year in which an external shareholder acquires an interest in the company.

Zweiter Teil. Leitungsmacht und Verantwortlichkeit bei Abhängigkeit von Unternehmen

Part Two. Power of Direction and Responsibility in the Case of Controlled Enterprises

Erster Abschnitt. Leitungsmacht und Verantwortlichkeit bei Bestehen eines Beherrschungsvertrags

Section One. Power of Direction and Responsibility in the Case of a Domination Agreement

§ 308 Leitungsmacht.

§ 308 Power of direction.

(1) ¹Besteht ein Beherrschungsvertrag, so ist das herrschende Unternehmen berechtigt, dem Vorstand der Gesellschaft hinsichtlich der Leitung der Ge-

(1) ¹If a domination agreement exists, the controlling enterprise shall be entitled to issue instructions to the management board of the company concerning the

sellschaft Weisungen zu erteilen. ²Bestimmt der Vertrag nichts anderes, so können auch Weisungen erteilt werden, die für die Gesellschaft nachteilig sind, wenn sie den Belangen des herrschenden Unternehmens oder der mit ihm und der Gesellschaft konzernverbundenen Unternehmen dienen.

(2) ¹Der Vorstand ist verpflichtet, die Weisungen des herrschenden Unternehmens zu befolgen. ²Er ist nicht berechtigt, die Befolgung einer Weisung zu verweigern, weil sie nach seiner Ansicht nicht den Belangen des herrschenden Unternehmens oder der mit ihm und der Gesellschaft konzernverbundenen Unternehmen dient, es sei denn, daß sie offensichtlich nicht diesen Belangen dient.

(3) ¹Wird der Vorstand angewiesen, ein Geschäft vorzunehmen, das nur mit Zustimmung des Aufsichtsrats der Gesellschaft vorgenommen werden darf, und wird diese Zustimmung nicht innerhalb einer angemessenen Frist erteilt, so hat der Vorstand dies dem herrschenden Unternehmen mitzuteilen. ²Wiederholt das herrschende Unternehmen nach dieser Mitteilung die Weisung, so ist die Zustimmung des Aufsichtsrats nicht mehr erforderlich; die Weisung darf, wenn das herrschende Unternehmen einen Aufsichtsrat hat, nur mit dessen Zustimmung wiederholt werden.

§ 309 Verantwortlichkeit der gesetzlichen Vertreter des herrschenden Unternehmens.

(1) Besteht ein Beherrschungsvertrag, so haben die gesetzlichen Vertreter (beim Einzelkaufmann der Inhaber) des herrschenden Unternehmens gegenüber der Gesellschaft bei der Erteilung von Weisungen an diese die Sorgfalt eines ordentlichen und gewissenhaften Geschäftsleiters anzuwenden.

(2) ¹Verletzen sie ihre Pflichten, so sind sie der Gesellschaft zum Ersatz des daraus entstehenden Schadens als Gesamt-

management of the company. ²Unless provided otherwise in the agreement, instructions which are disadvantageous for the company may also be issued if they are in the interests of the controlling enterprise or enterprises in the same group as the company and the controlling enterprise.

(2) ¹The management board is obligated to heed the instructions issued by the controlling enterprise. ²It is not entitled to refuse to heed instructions which it believes are not in the interests of the controlling enterprise or enterprises in the same group as the company and the controlling enterprise, unless it is apparent that the instructions do not serve such interests.

(3) ¹If the management board is instructed to effect a transaction which may only be effected with the approval of the company's supervisory board, and if such approval is not granted within a reasonable period of time, the management board shall notify the controlling enterprise. ²If the controlling enterprise repeats the instruction after having been given such notification, the approval of the supervisory board shall no longer be required; if the controlling enterprise has a supervisory board, the instruction may only be repeated if such supervisory board grants its approval.

§ 309 Liability of the legal representatives of the controlling enterprise.

(1) If a domination agreement exists, the legal representatives (in the case of a sole proprietor, the owner) of the controlling enterprise shall apply the due care of a prudent and conscientious businessman when issuing instructions to the company.

(2) ¹If the legal representatives fail to comply with their duties, they shall be jointly and severally liable to the compa-

schuldner verpflichtet. ²Ist streitig, ob sie die Sorgfalt eines ordentlichen und gewissenhaften Geschäftsleiters angewandt haben, so trifft sie die Beweislast.

(3) ¹Die Gesellschaft kann erst drei Jahre nach der Entstehung des Anspruchs und nur dann auf Ersatzansprüche verzichten oder sich über sie vergleichen, wenn die außenstehenden Aktionäre durch Sonderbeschluß zustimmen und nicht eine Minderheit, deren Anteile zusammen den zehnten Teil des bei der Beschlußfassung vertretenen Grundkapitals erreichen, zur Niederschrift Widerspruch erhebt. ²Die zeitliche Beschränkung gilt nicht, wenn der Ersatzpflichtige zahlungsunfähig ist und sich zur Abwendung des Insolvenzverfahrens mit seinen Gläubigern vergleicht oder wenn die Ersatzpflicht in einem Insolvenzplan geregelt wird.

(4) ¹Der Ersatzanspruch der Gesellschaft kann auch von jedem Aktionär geltend gemacht werden. ²Der Aktionär kann jedoch nur Leistung an die Gesellschaft fordern. ³Der Ersatzanspruch kann ferner von den Gläubigern der Gesellschaft geltend gemacht werden, soweit sie von dieser keine Befriedigung erlangen können. ⁴Den Gläubigern gegenüber wird die Ersatzpflicht durch einen Verzicht oder Vergleich der Gesellschaft nicht ausgeschlossen. ⁵Ist über das Vermögen der Gesellschaft das Insolvenzverfahren eröffnet, so übt während dessen Dauer der Insolvenzverwalter oder der Sachwalter das Recht der Aktionäre und Gläubiger, den Ersatzanspruch der Gesellschaft geltend zu machen, aus.

(5) Die Ansprüche aus diesen Vorschriften verjähren in fünf Jahren.

ny for the resulting damage. ²They shall bear the burden of proof in the event of a dispute as to whether or not they applied the due care of a prudent and conscientious businessman.

(3) ¹The company may only waive or compound its claims to damages three years after such claims arise and then only if the external shareholders grant their approval in a special resolution and a minority with an aggregate shareholding of one tenth of the registered share capital represented at the adoption of the resolution does not raise an objection in the minutes. ²The time restriction shall not apply if the party under an obligation to pay damages is illiquid and enters into a composition with its creditors in order to avert insolvency proceedings or if the liability for damages is regulated in an insolvency plan.

(4) ¹The company's claim to damages may also be asserted by any shareholder. ²The shareholder may, however, only demand payment to the company. ³The claim to damages may also be asserted by the creditors of the company, to the extent that said creditors are unable to obtain settlement of their claims from the company. ⁴The liability for damages shall not be excluded vis-à-vis the creditors by a waiver or composition by the company. ⁵If insolvency proceedings have been commenced against the assets of the company, the insolvency administrator or the custodian shall exercise the rights of the shareholders and the creditors to assert the company's claim to damages for the duration of such proceedings.

(5) Claims arising from the above provisions shall become time-barred after five years.

§ 310 Verantwortlichkeit der Verwaltungsmitglieder der Gesellschaft.

(1) ¹Die Mitglieder des Vorstands und des Aufsichtsrats der Gesellschaft haften neben dem Ersatzpflichtigen nach § 309 als Gesamtschuldner, wenn sie unter Verletzung ihrer Pflichten gehandelt haben. ²Ist streitig, ob sie die Sorgfalt eines ordentlichen und gewissenhaften Geschäftsleiters angewandt haben, so trifft sie die Beweislast.

(2) Dadurch, daß der Aufsichtsrat die Handlung gebilligt hat, wird die Ersatzpflicht nicht ausgeschlossen.

(3) Eine Ersatzpflicht der Verwaltungsmitglieder der Gesellschaft besteht nicht, wenn die schädigende Handlung auf einer Weisung beruht, die nach § 308 Abs. 2 zu befolgen war.

(4) § 309 Abs. 3 bis 5 ist anzuwenden.

Zweiter Abschnitt. Verantwortlichkeit bei Fehlen eines Beherrschungsvertrags

§ 311 Schranken des Einflusses.

(1) Besteht kein Beherrschungsvertrag, so darf ein herrschendes Unternehmen seinen Einfluß nicht dazu benutzen, eine abhängige Aktiengesellschaft oder Kommanditgesellschaft auf Aktien zu veranlassen, ein für sie nachteiliges Rechtsgeschäft vorzunehmen oder Maßnahmen zu ihrem Nachteil zu treffen oder zu unterlassen, es sei denn, daß die Nachteile ausgeglichen werden.

(2) ¹Ist der Ausgleich nicht während des Geschäftsjahrs tatsächlich erfolgt, so muß spätestens am Ende des Geschäftsjahrs, in dem der abhängigen Gesellschaft der Nachteil zugefügt worden ist, bestimmt werden, wann und durch welche Vorteile der Nachteil ausgeglichen werden soll. ²Auf die zum Ausgleich bestimmten Vorteile ist der abhängigen Gesellschaft ein Rechtsanspruch zu gewähren.

§ 310 Liability of the company's administration.

(1) ¹The members of the company's management board and supervisory board shall be jointly and severally liable together with the party liable for damages pursuant to sec. 309 if they have failed to comply with their duties. ²They shall bear the burden of proof in the event of a dispute as to whether or not they applied the due care of a prudent and conscientious businessman.

(2) Liability for damages shall not be excluded by the fact that the supervisory board has approved the action.

(3) The members of the company's administration shall not be liable for damages if the damaging action is based on instructions which were to be followed pursuant to sec. 308 para. 2.

(4) Sec. 309 paras. 3 to 5 shall apply.

Section Two. Liability in the Absence of a Domination Agreement

§ 311 Restriction on influence.

(1) If no domination agreement exists, a controlling enterprise may not exploit its influence in order to cause a controlled stock corporation or partnership limited by shares to effect a transaction which is detrimental to itself or to take or refrain from taking measures if by doing so it places itself at a disadvantage unless such disadvantages are compensated.

(2) ¹If such disadvantages are not actually compensated during the fiscal year, a resolution shall be adopted no later than at the end of the fiscal year in which the controlled company suffers the disadvantage stating when and via which advantages the disadvantage is to be compensated. ²The controlled company shall be granted a legal claim to the advantages intended to compensate the disadvantages it has suffered.

§ 312 Bericht des Vorstands über Beziehungen zu verbundenen Unternehmen.	**§ 312 Management board report on relations to affiliated enterprises.**
(1) ¹Besteht kein Beherrschungsvertrag, so hat der Vorstand einer abhängigen Gesellschaft in den ersten drei Monaten des Geschäftsjahrs einen Bericht über die Beziehungen der Gesellschaft zu verbundenen Unternehmen aufzustellen. ²In dem Bericht sind alle Rechtsgeschäfte, welche die Gesellschaft im vergangenen Geschäftsjahr mit dem herrschenden Unternehmen oder einem mit ihm verbundenen Unternehmen oder auf Veranlassung oder im Interesse dieser Unternehmen vorgenommen hat, und alle anderen Maßnahmen, die sie auf Veranlassung oder im Interesse dieser Unternehmen im vergangenen Geschäftsjahr getroffen oder unterlassen hat, aufzuführen. ³Bei den Rechtsgeschäften sind Leistung und Gegenleistung, bei den Maßnahmen die Gründe der Maßnahme und deren Vorteile und Nachteile für die Gesellschaft anzugeben. ⁴Bei einem Ausgleich von Nachteilen ist im einzelnen anzugeben, wie der Ausgleich während des Geschäftsjahrs tatsächlich erfolgt ist, oder auf welche Vorteile der Gesellschaft ein Rechtsanspruch gewährt worden ist.	(1) ¹If no domination agreement exists, the management board of a controlled company shall draw up a report on the relations between the company and affiliated enterprises in the first three months of the fiscal year. ²The report shall state all legal transactions effected by the company in the previous fiscal year with the controlling enterprise or an affiliated enterprise thereof or at the request or in the interests of such enterprises and all other measures it has taken or refrained from taking in the past fiscal year at the request or in the interests of such enterprises. ³Performance and counter-performance shall be stated for the legal transactions and the reasons for the measures and the advantages and disadvantages entailed for the company shall be stated for the measures. ⁴If disadvantages subject to compensation were incurred, details shall either be given as to how such disadvantages have been compensated during the fiscal year or regarding the individual advantages to which the company has been granted a legal claim.
(2) Der Bericht hat den Grundsätzen einer gewissenhaften und getreuen Rechenschaft zu entsprechen.	(2) The report shall comply with the principles of conscientious and accurate accounting.
(3) ¹Am Schluß des Berichts hat der Vorstand zu erklären, ob die Gesellschaft nach den Umständen, die ihm in dem Zeitpunkt bekannt waren, in dem das Rechtsgeschäft vorgenommen oder die Maßnahme getroffen oder unterlassen wurde, bei jedem Rechtsgeschäft eine angemessene Gegenleistung erhielt und dadurch, daß die Maßnahme getroffen oder unterlassen wurde, nicht benachteiligt wurde. ²Wurde die Gesellschaft benachteiligt, so hat er außerdem zu erklären, ob die Nachteile ausgeglichen worden sind. ³Die Erklärung ist auch in den Lagebericht aufzunehmen.	(3) ¹At the end of the report, the management board shall state whether, in view of the circumstances known to the management board at the time the transaction was effected or the measure taken or refrained from being taken, the company received reasonable counter-performance for each legal transaction and no detriment was caused to the company by taking or refraining from taking the measure. ²If the company was placed at a disadvantage, the management board shall also state whether such disadvantages have been compensated. ³This statement shall also be included in the management report.

§ 313 Prüfung durch den Abschlußprüfer.

(1) ¹Ist der Jahresabschluß durch einen Abschlußprüfer zu prüfen, so ist gleichzeitig mit dem Jahresabschluß und dem Lagebericht auch der Bericht über die Beziehungen zu verbundenen Unternehmen dem Abschlußprüfer vorzulegen. ²Er hat zu prüfen, ob

1. die tatsächlichen Angaben des Berichts richtig sind,
2. bei den im Bericht aufgeführten Rechtsgeschäften nach den Umständen, die im Zeitpunkt ihrer Vornahme bekannt waren, die Leistung der Gesellschaft nicht unangemessen hoch war; soweit sie dies war, ob die Nachteile ausgeglichen worden sind,
3. bei den im Bericht aufgeführten Maßnahmen keine Umstände für eine wesentlich andere Beurteilung als die durch den Vorstand sprechen.

³§ 320 Abs. 1 Satz 2 und Abs. 2 Satz 1 und 2 des Handelsgesetzbuchs gilt sinngemäß. ⁴Die Rechte nach dieser Vorschrift hat der Abschlußprüfer auch gegenüber einem Konzernunternehmen sowie gegenüber einem abhängigen oder herrschenden Unternehmen.

(2) ¹Der Abschlußprüfer hat über das Ergebnis der Prüfung schriftlich zu berichten. ²Stellt er bei der Prüfung des Jahresabschlusses, des Lageberichts und des Berichts über die Beziehungen zu verbundenen Unternehmen fest, daß dieser Bericht unvollständig ist, so hat er auch hierüber zu berichten. ³Der Abschlussprüfer hat seinen Bericht zu unterzeichnen und dem Aufsichtsrat vorzulegen; dem Vorstand ist vor der Zuleitung Gelegenheit zur Stellungnahme zu geben.

§ 313 Examination by the auditor of annual financial statements.

(1) ¹If the annual financial statements are to be examined by an auditor of annual financial statements, the report on relations to affiliated enterprises shall be submitted to the auditor of annual financial statements together with the annual financial statements and the management report. ²The auditor of annual financial statements shall examine whether

1. the facts stated in the report are accurate,
2. the performance rendered by the company was not inappropriately high for the legal transactions listed in the report in view of the circumstances which were known at the time such transactions were effected and, if it was inappropriately high, whether the disadvantages have since been compensated,
3. in view of the measures listed in the report there are no circumstances which would indicate an assessment which differs essentially from that made by the management board.

³Sec. 320 para. 1 sentence 2 and para. 2 sentences 1 and 2 of the Commercial Code shall apply accordingly. ⁴The auditor of annual financial statements shall also be entitled to the rights pursuant to this provision vis-à-vis a company in the same group as well as vis-à-vis a controlled or controlling enterprise.

(2) ¹The auditor of annual financial statements shall report on the findings of his examination in writing. ²He shall also report if he ascertains that the report on relations to affiliated enterprises is incomplete when examining the annual financial statements, the management report and the report on relations to affiliated enterprises. ³The auditor of annual financial statements shall sign his report and submit it to the supervisory board; the management board shall be given an opportunity to comment on the report before it is forwarded.

(3) ¹Sind nach dem abschließenden Ergebnis der Prüfung keine Einwendungen zu erheben, so hat der Abschlußprüfer dies durch folgenden Vermerk zum Bericht über die Beziehungen zu verbundenen Unternehmen zu bestätigen:

Nach meiner/unserer pflichtmäßigen Prüfung und Beurteilung bestätige ich/bestätigen wir, daß

1. die tatsächlichen Angaben des Berichts richtig sind,
2. bei den im Bericht aufgeführten Rechtsgeschäften die Leistung der Gesellschaft nicht unangemessen hoch war oder Nachteile ausgeglichen worden sind,
3. bei den im Bericht aufgeführten Maßnahmen keine Umstände für eine wesentlich andere Beurteilung als die durch den Vorstand sprechen.

²Führt der Bericht kein Rechtsgeschäft auf, so ist Nummer 2, führt er keine Maßnahme auf, so ist Nummer 3 des Vermerks fortzulassen. ³Hat der Abschlußprüfer bei keinem im Bericht aufgeführten Rechtsgeschäft festgestellt, daß die Leistung der Gesellschaft unangemessen hoch war, so ist Nummer 2 des Vermerks auf diese Bestätigung zu beschränken.

(4) ¹Sind Einwendungen zu erheben oder hat der Abschlußprüfer festgestellt, daß der Bericht über die Beziehungen zu verbundenen Unternehmen unvollständig ist, so hat er die Bestätigung einzuschränken oder zu versagen. ²Hat der Vorstand selbst erklärt, daß die Gesellschaft durch bestimmte Rechtsgeschäfte oder Maßnahmen benachteiligt worden ist, ohne daß die Nachteile ausgeglichen worden sind, so ist dies in dem Vermerk anzugeben und der Vermerk auf die übrigen Rechtsgeschäfte oder Maßnahmen zu beschränken.

(5) ¹Der Abschlußprüfer hat den Bestätigungsvermerk mit Angabe von Ort

(3) ¹If the final conclusion of the report is that no objections are to be raised, the auditor of annual financial statements shall confirm this with the following certification on the report on relations to affiliated enterprises:

After duly examining and assessing the report, I/we hereby confirm that

1. the details given in the report are correct,
2. the performance rendered by the company in relation to the legal transactions listed in the report was not inappropriately high or any disadvantages have been compensated,
3. in view of the measures listed in the report there are no circumstances which would indicate an assessment which differs essentially from that made by the management board.

²No. 2 of the certificate shall be omitted if the report does not list any legal transactions, and no. 3 if it does not list any measures. ³If the auditor of annual financial statements ascertained that the performance rendered by the company was not inappropriately high for any of the legal transactions listed in the report, no. 2 of the certificate shall be restricted to confirmation of this.

(4) ¹If any objections are to be raised or if the auditor of annual financial statements ascertains that the report on relations to affiliated enterprises is incomplete, the auditor shall either give confirmation subject to reservations or withhold it altogether. ²If the management board has itself declared that the company has been placed at a disadvantage due to certain legal transactions or measures and that such disadvantages have not been compensated, this shall be stated in the certificate, and the certificate restricted to the remaining legal transactions or measures.

(5) ¹The auditor of annual financial statements shall sign the certification,

und Tag zu unterzeichnen. ²Der Bestätigungsvermerk ist auch in den Prüfungsbericht aufzunehmen.

§ 314 Prüfung durch den Aufsichtsrat.

(1) ¹Der Vorstand hat den Bericht über die Beziehungen zu verbundenen Unternehmen unverzüglich nach dessen Aufstellung dem Aufsichtsrat vorzulegen. ²Dieser Bericht und, wenn der Jahresabschluss durch einen Abschlussprüfer zu prüfen ist, der Prüfungsbericht des Abschlussprüfers sind auch jedem Aufsichtsratsmitglied oder, wenn der Aufsichtsrat dies beschlossen hat, den Mitgliedern eines Ausschusses zu übermitteln.

(2) ¹Der Aufsichtsrat hat den Bericht über die Beziehungen zu verbundenen Unternehmen zu prüfen und in seinem Bericht an die Hauptversammlung (§ 171 Abs. 2) über das Ergebnis der Prüfung zu berichten. ²Ist der Jahresabschluß durch einen Abschlußprüfer zu prüfen, so hat der Aufsichtsrat in diesem Bericht ferner zu dem Ergebnis der Prüfung des Berichts über die Beziehungen zu verbundenen Unternehmen durch den Abschlußprüfer Stellung zu nehmen. ³Ein von dem Abschlußprüfer erteilter Bestätigungsvermerk ist in den Bericht aufzunehmen, eine Versagung des Bestätigungsvermerks ausdrücklich mitzuteilen.

(3) Am Schluß des Berichts hat der Aufsichtsrat zu erklären, ob nach dem abschließenden Ergebnis seiner Prüfung Einwendungen gegen die Erklärung des Vorstands am Schluß des Berichts über die Beziehungen zu verbundenen Unternehmen zu erheben sind.

(4) Ist der Jahresabschluss durch einen Abschlussprüfer zu prüfen, so hat dieser an den Verhandlungen des Auf-

stating the place and date. ²The certification shall also be included in the audit report.

§ 314 Examination by supervisory board.

(1)¹The management board shall submit the report on relations to affiliated enterprises to the supervisory board without undue delay after it has been drawn up. ²A copy of this report and, if the annual financial statements are to be examined by an auditor of annual financial statements, the audit report provided by the auditor of annual financial statements shall also be transmitted to each member of the supervisory board or, if so resolved by the supervisory board, to the members of a committee.

(2) ¹The supervisory board shall examine the report on the relations to affiliated enterprises and report on the findings of such examination in its report to the general meeting (sec. 171 para. 2). ²If the annual financial statements are to be examined by an auditor of annual financial statements, the supervisory board shall also in this report state its position on the findings of the examination of the report on the relations to affiliated enterprises by the auditor of annual financial statements. ³A certification granted by the auditor of annual financial statements shall be included in the report, and it shall be explicitly stated if the auditor of annual financial statements refused to issue such certification.

(3) At the end of the report, the supervisory board shall state whether, after having finally completed their examination, there are any objections to be raised against the statement made by the management board at the conclusion of the report on relations to affiliated enterprises.

(4)⁾ If the annual financial statements are to be examined by an auditor of annual financial statements, such auditor shall

sichtsrats oder eines Ausschusses über den Bericht über die Beziehungen zu verbundenen Unternehmen teilzunehmen und über die wesentlichen Ergebnisse seiner Prüfung zu berichten.

§ 315 Sonderprüfung.

¹Auf Antrag eines Aktionärs hat das Gericht Sonderprüfer zur Prüfung der geschäftlichen Beziehungen der Gesellschaft zu dem herrschenden Unternehmen oder einem mit ihm verbundenen Unternehmen zu bestellen, wenn

1. der Abschlußprüfer den Bestätigungsvermerk zum Bericht über die Beziehungen zu verbundenen Unternehmen eingeschränkt oder versagt hat,
2. der Aufsichtsrat erklärt hat, daß Einwendungen gegen die Erklärung des Vorstands am Schluß des Berichts über die Beziehungen zu verbundenen Unternehmen zu erheben sind,
3. der Vorstand selbst erklärt hat, daß die Gesellschaft durch bestimmte Rechtsgeschäfte oder Maßnahmen benachteiligt worden ist, ohne daß die Nachteile ausgeglichen worden sind.

²Liegen sonstige Tatsachen vor, die den Verdacht einer pflichtwidrigen Nachteilszufügung rechtfertigen, kann der Antrag auch von Aktionären gestellt werden, deren Anteile zusammen den Schwellenwert des § 142 Abs. 2 erreichen, wenn sie glaubhaft machen, dass sie seit mindestens drei Monaten vor dem Tage der Antragstellung Inhaber der Aktien sind. ³Über den Antrag entscheidet das Landgericht, in dessen Bezirk die Gesellschaft ihren Sitz hat. ⁴§ 142 Abs. 8 gilt entsprechend. ⁵Gegen die Entscheidung ist die Beschwerde zulässig. ⁶Hat die Hauptversammlung zur Prüfung derselben Vorgänge Sonderprüfer bestellt, so kann jeder Aktionär den Antrag nach § 142 Abs. 4 stellen.

participate in the meetings of the supervisory board or a committee concerning the report on the relations to affiliated enterprises and shall report on the essential results of his examination.

§ 315 Special audit.

¹Upon application by a shareholder, the court shall appoint special auditors to examine the business relations between the company and the controlling enterprise or an affiliate thereof if

1. the auditor of annual financial statements has either withheld the certification on the report on relations to affiliated enterprises or has issued it subject to restrictions,
2. the supervisory board has declared that objections are to be raised to the declaration made by the management board at the end of the report on relations to affiliated enterprises,
3. the management board itself has declared that the company has been made to suffer disadvantages as a result of certain legal transactions or measures and such disadvantages have not been compensated.

²If there are any other circumstances justifying the suspicion that the company has been made to suffer disadvantages unduly, the application may also be filed by shareholders with an aggregate shareholding that reaches the threshold set forth in sec. 142 para. 2 if they provide evidence that they have held the shares for at least three months before filing such application. ³The Regional Court in the district where the company has its registered office shall decide on the application. ⁴Sec. 142 para. 8 shall apply accordingly. ⁵The decision is subject to appeal. ⁶If the general meeting has appointed special auditors to examine the same matters, any shareholder may file the application pursuant to sec. 142 para. 4.

§ 316 Kein Bericht über Beziehungen zu verbundenen Unternehmen bei Gewinnabführungsvertrag.

§§ 312 bis 315 gelten nicht, wenn zwischen der abhängigen Gesellschaft und dem herrschenden Unternehmen ein Gewinnabführungsvertrag besteht.

§ 317 Verantwortlichkeit des herrschenden Unternehmens und seiner gesetzlichen Vertreter.

(1) ¹Veranlaßt ein herrschendes Unternehmen eine abhängige Gesellschaft, mit der kein Beherrschungsvertrag besteht, ein für sie nachteiliges Rechtsgeschäft vorzunehmen oder zu ihrem Nachteil eine Maßnahme zu treffen oder zu unterlassen, ohne daß es den Nachteil bis zum Ende des Geschäftsjahrs tatsächlich ausgleicht oder der abhängigen Gesellschaft einen Rechtsanspruch auf einen zum Ausgleich bestimmten Vorteil gewährt, so ist es der Gesellschaft zum Ersatz des ihr daraus entstehenden Schadens verpflichtet. ²Es ist auch den Aktionären zum Ersatz des ihnen daraus entstehenden Schadens verpflichtet, soweit sie, abgesehen von einem Schaden, der ihnen durch Schädigung der Gesellschaft zugefügt worden ist, geschädigt worden sind.

(2) Die Ersatzpflicht tritt nicht ein, wenn auch ein ordentlicher und gewissenhafter Geschäftsleiter einer unabhängigen Gesellschaft das Rechtsgeschäft vorgenommen oder die Maßnahme getroffen oder unterlassen hätte.

(3) Neben dem herrschenden Unternehmen haften als Gesamtschuldner die gesetzlichen Vertreter des Unternehmens, die die Gesellschaft zu dem Rechtsgeschäft oder der Maßnahme veranlaßt haben.

(4) § 309 Abs. 3 bis 5 gilt sinngemäß.

§ 316 No report on relations to affiliated enterprises in the case of profit transfer agreement.

Sec. 312 to 315 shall not apply if a profit transfer agreement has been concluded between the controlled company and the controlling enterprise.

§ 317 Responsibility of the controlling enterprise and its legal representatives.

(1) ¹If a controlling enterprise causes a controlled company with which it has not concluded a domination agreement to effect a legal transaction to the detriment of itself or to take or refrain from taking a measure, thereby placing itself at a disadvantage, and if the controlling enterprise fails to compensate such disadvantage by the end of the fiscal year or grant the controlled company a legal claim to an advantage intended to compensate such disadvantage, the controlling enterprise shall be liable to the company for the damage suffered by the company as a result. ²It shall also be liable to the shareholders for the damage they suffer as a result if they have suffered damage other than that suffered as a result of the damage to the company.

(2) The liability to compensate damages shall not apply if a prudent and conscientious manager of an independent company would also have effected the legal transaction or taken or refrained from taking the measure.

(3) The legal representatives of the enterprise who caused the company to effect the legal transaction or take the measure shall be jointly and severally liable together with the controlling enterprise.

(4) Sec. 309 paras. 3 to 5 shall apply accordingly.

§ 318 Verantwortlichkeit der Verwaltungsmitglieder der Gesellschaft.

(1) ¹Die Mitglieder des Vorstands der Gesellschaft haften neben den nach § 317 Ersatzpflichtigen als Gesamtschuldner, wenn sie es unter Verletzung ihrer Pflichten unterlassen haben, das nachteilige Rechtsgeschäft oder die nachteilige Maßnahme in dem Bericht über die Beziehungen der Gesellschaft zu verbundenen Unternehmen aufzuführen oder anzugeben, daß die Gesellschaft durch das Rechtsgeschäft oder die Maßnahme benachteiligt wurde und der Nachteil nicht ausgeglichen worden war. ²Ist streitig, ob sie die Sorgfalt eines ordentlichen und gewissenhaften Geschäftsleiters angewandt haben, so trifft sie die Beweislast.

(2) Die Mitglieder des Aufsichtsrats der Gesellschaft haften neben den nach § 317 Ersatzpflichtigen als Gesamtschuldner, wenn sie hinsichtlich des nachteiligen Rechtsgeschäfts oder der nachteiligen Maßnahme ihre Pflicht, den Bericht über die Beziehungen zu verbundenen Unternehmen zu prüfen und über das Ergebnis der Prüfung an die Hauptversammlung zu berichten (§ 314), verletzt haben; Absatz 1 Satz 2 gilt sinngemäß.

(3) Der Gesellschaft und auch den Aktionären gegenüber tritt die Ersatzpflicht nicht ein, wenn die Handlung auf einem gesetzmäßigen Beschluß der Hauptversammlung beruht.

(4) § 309 Abs. 3 bis 5 gilt sinngemäß.

§ 318 Responsibility of the members of the company's administration.

(1) ¹The members of the management board of the company shall be jointly and severally liable together with the parties liable for damages pursuant to sec. 317 if they, in breach of their duties, have failed to list the detrimental legal transaction or the detrimental measures in the report on the relations of the company to affiliated enterprises or to disclose that the company suffered a disadvantage as a result of the legal transaction or the measure and that such disadvantage has not been compensated. ²They shall bear the burden of proof in the event of a dispute as to whether or not they applied the due care of a prudent and conscientious businessman.

(2) The members of the supervisory board of the company shall be jointly and severally liable together with the parties liable for damages pursuant to sec. 317 if, with regard to the detrimental legal transaction or the detrimental measure, they have failed to comply with their duty to examine the report on relations to affiliated enterprises and to report on the findings of such report to the general meeting (sec. 314); para. 1 sentence 2 shall apply accordingly.

(3) The liability for damages vis-à-vis the company and the shareholders shall not apply if the action was based on a lawful resolution of the general meeting.

(4) Sec. 309 para. 3 to 5 shall apply accordingly.

Dritter Teil. Eingegliederte Gesellschaften

§ 319 Eingliederung.

(1) ¹Die Hauptversammlung einer Aktiengesellschaft kann die Eingliederung der Gesellschaft in eine andere Aktiengesellschaft mit Sitz im Inland (Hauptgesellschaft) beschließen, wenn sich alle

Part Three. Integrated Companies

§ 319 Integration.

(1) ¹The general meeting of a stock corporation may resolve on the integration of the company into another stock corporation having its registered office in Germany (main company) if all shares

Aktien der Gesellschaft in der Hand der zukünftigen Hauptgesellschaft befinden. ²Auf den Beschluß sind die Bestimmungen des Gesetzes und der Satzung über Satzungsänderungen nicht anzuwenden.

(2) ¹Der Beschluß über die Eingliederung wird nur wirksam, wenn die Hauptversammlung der zukünftigen Hauptgesellschaft zustimmt. ²Der Beschluß über die Zustimmung bedarf einer Mehrheit, die mindestens drei Viertel des bei der Beschlußfassung vertretenen Grundkapitals umfaßt. ³Die Satzung kann eine größere Kapitalmehrheit und weitere Erfordernisse bestimmen. ⁴Absatz 1 Satz 2 ist anzuwenden.

(3) ¹Von der Einberufung der Hauptversammlung der zukünftigen Hauptgesellschaft an, die über die Zustimmung zur Eingliederung beschließen soll, sind in dem Geschäftsraum dieser Gesellschaft zur Einsicht der Aktionäre auszulegen

1. der Entwurf des Eingliederungsbeschlusses;
2. die Jahresabschlüsse und die Lageberichte der beteiligten Gesellschaften für die letzten drei Geschäftsjahre;
3. ein ausführlicher schriftlicher Bericht des Vorstands der zukünftigen Hauptgesellschaft, in dem die Eingliederung rechtlich und wirtschaftlich erläutert und begründet wird (Eingliederungsbericht).

²Auf Verlangen ist jedem Aktionär der zukünftigen Hauptgesellschaft unverzüglich und kostenlos eine Abschrift der in Satz 1 bezeichneten Unterlagen zu erteilen. ³Die Verpflichtungen nach den Sätzen 1 und 2 entfallen, wenn die in Satz 1 bezeichneten Unterlagen für denselben Zeitraum über die Internetseite der zukünftigen Hauptgesellschaft zugänglich sind. ⁴In der Hauptversammlung sind diese Unterlagen zugänglich zu machen. ⁵Jedem Aktionär ist in der Hauptversammlung auf

in the company are held by the future main company. ²The legal provisions and provisions in the articles of association concerning amendments to the articles of association shall not apply to such resolution.

(2) ¹The resolution on integration shall only take effect if the general meeting of the future main company grants its approval. ²The resolution on the approval requires a majority of at least three quarters of the registered share capital represented at the adoption of the resolution. ³The articles of association may stipulate a larger capital majority and further requirements. ⁴Para. 1 sentence 2 shall apply.

(3) ¹The following shall be displayed for inspection by the shareholders in the offices of the future main company as of the date the general meeting of the company which is to decide on approval for integration is convened:

1. the draft of the integration resolution;
2. the annual financial statements and the management reports of the companies concerned from the three preceding fiscal years;
3. a comprehensive written report from the management board of the future main company describing and giving the reasons for the integration from a legal and economic point of view (integration report).

²Each shareholder in the future main company shall, upon request, be provided without undue delay and free of charge with a copy of the documents listed in sentence 1. ³The obligations pursuant to sentences 1 and 2 shall cease to exist if the documents set forth in sentence 1 are accessible during the same time period on the website of the future main company. ⁴These documents shall be made accessible during the general meeting. ⁵Each shareholder shall, upon request, be given information in

Verlangen Auskunft auch über alle im Zusammenhang mit der Eingliederung wesentlichen Angelegenheiten der einzugliedernden Gesellschaft zu geben.

(4) ¹Der Vorstand der einzugliedernden Gesellschaft hat die Eingliederung und die Firma der Hauptgesellschaft zur Eintragung in das Handelsregister anzumelden. ²Der Anmeldung sind die Niederschriften der Hauptversammlungsbeschlüsse und ihre Anlagen in Ausfertigung oder öffentlich beglaubigter Abschrift beizufügen.

(5) ¹Bei der Anmeldung nach Absatz 4 hat der Vorstand zu erklären, daß eine Klage gegen die Wirksamkeit eines Hauptversammlungsbeschlusses nicht oder nicht fristgemäß erhoben oder eine solche Klage rechtskräftig abgewiesen oder zurückgenommen worden ist; hierüber hat der Vorstand dem Registergericht auch nach der Anmeldung Mitteilung zu machen. ²Liegt die Erklärung nicht vor, so darf die Eingliederung nicht eingetragen werden, es sei denn, daß die klageberechtigten Aktionäre durch notariell beurkundete Verzichtserklärung auf die Klage gegen die Wirksamkeit des Hauptversammlungsbeschlusses verzichten.

(6) ¹Der Erklärung nach Absatz 5 Satz 1 steht es gleich, wenn nach Erhebung einer Klage gegen die Wirksamkeit eines Hauptversammlungsbeschlusses das Gericht auf Antrag der Gesellschaft, gegen deren Hauptversammlungsbeschluß sich die Klage richtet, durch Beschluß festgestellt hat, daß die Erhebung der Klage der Eintragung nicht entgegensteht. ²Auf das Verfahren sind § 247, die §§ 82, 83 Abs. 1 und § 84 der Zivilprozeßordnung sowie die im ersten Rechtszug für das Verfahren vor den Landgerichten geltenden Vorschriften der Zivilprozeßordnung entsprechend anzuwenden, soweit nichts Abweichen-

the general meeting pertaining to all matters of the company to be integrated which are of fundamental relevance to the integration.

(4) ¹The management board of the company which is to be integrated shall apply for the integration and the name of the main company to be registered in the commercial register. ²The executed copy or certified copies of the minutes of the resolutions of the general meeting and the appendices thereto shall be attached to the application to the commercial register.

(5) ¹When making the application pursuant to para. 4, the management board shall state that a legal action against the validity of the resolution of the general meeting has not been brought or not been brought within the specified time or that such an action has been dismissed by a judgment being res judicata or withdrawn; the management board shall also inform the register court if this happens after the application has been filed. ²If such declaration has not been made, the integration may not be registered unless those shareholders who are entitled to bring a legal action waive their right to bring an action against the effectiveness of the resolution of the general meeting by submitting a notarized waiver.

(6) ¹It shall be deemed equivalent to the declaration pursuant to para. 5 sentence 1 if, after an action is brought against the validity of the resolution of the general meeting, the court has issued an order upon the application of the company whose general meeting adopted the resolution in dispute that the bringing of such action shall not prevent the integration from being registered in the commercial register. ²Sec. 247 as well as sec. 82, 83 para. 1 and sec. 84 of the Code of Civil Procedure and the provisions of the Code of Civil Procedure applicable to proceedings of the first instance before the regional courts shall apply accordingly to the proceed-

des bestimmt ist. ³ Ein Beschluss nach Satz 1 ergeht, wenn

1. die Klage unzulässig oder offensichtlich unbegründet ist,
2. der Kläger nicht binnen einer Woche nach Zustellung des Antrags durch Urkunden nachgewiesen hat, dass er seit der Bekanntmachung der Einberufung einen anteiligen Betrag von mindestens 1.000 Euro hält oder
3. das alsbaldige Wirksamwerden des Hauptversammlungsbeschlusses vorrangig erscheint, weil die vom Antragsteller dargelegten wesentlichen Nachteile für die Gesellschaft und ihre Aktionäre nach freier Überzeugung des Gerichts die Nachteile für den Antragsgegner überwiegen, es sei denn, es liegt eine besondere Schwere des Rechtsverstoßes vor.

⁴Der Beschluß kann in dringenden Fällen ohne mündliche Verhandlung ergehen. ⁵Der Beschluss soll spätestens drei Monate nach Antragstellung ergehen; Verzögerungen der Entscheidung sind durch unanfechtbaren Beschluss zu begründen. ⁶Die vorgebrachten Tatsachen, aufgrund derer der Beschluß nach Satz 3 ergehen kann, sind glaubhaft zu machen. ⁷Über den Antrag entscheidet ein Senat des Oberlandesgerichts, in dessen Bezirk die Gesellschaft ihren Sitz hat. ⁸Eine Übertragung auf den Einzelrichter ist ausgeschlossen; einer Güteverhandlung bedarf es nicht. ⁹Der Beschluss ist unanfechtbar. ¹⁰Erweist sich die Klage als begründet, so ist die Gesellschaft, die den Beschluß erwirkt hat, verpflichtet, dem Antragsgegner den Schaden zu ersetzen, der ihm aus einer auf dem Beschluß beruhenden Eintragung der Eingliederung entstanden ist. ¹¹Nach der Eintragung lassen Mängel des Beschlusses seine Durchführung unberührt; die Beseitigung dieser Wirkung der Eintragung kann auch nicht als Schadenersatz verlangt werden.

ings here, unless explicitly provided for otherwise. ³A resolution pursuant to sentence 1 is issued if

1. the complaint is inadmissible or apparently unsubstantiated,
2. the plaintiff has not demonstrated within one week from the service of the application by written documents that since the announcement of the convening of the meeting he has held a proportionate amount of at least 1,000 euros,
3. the resolution of the general meeting subject to the complaint appears to take priority because, in the free conviction of the court, the substantial disadvantages to the company and its shareholders which are argued by the applicant outweigh the disadvantages for the respondent, unless the violation of the law is particularly severe.

⁴In urgent cases, the order may be issued without oral proceedings being held. ⁵The resolution should be issued at the latest three months after the application is made; delays shall be justified in an unappealable decision. ⁶Evidence shall be provided for the facts submitted on the basis of which the order may be issued pursuant to sentence 3. ⁷The application shall be decided upon by a senate of the Higher Regional Court in whose district the company has its registered office. ⁸A transfer to a single judge is excluded; a conciliation hearing is not required. ⁹The resolution is unappealable. ¹⁰If the action turns out to be justified, the company which obtained the order is obligated to compensate the opponent for the damage caused him by the integration being registered in the commercial register on the basis of such order. ¹¹Defects of the resolution shall not affect its implementation after the registration; the elimination of this effect of the registration can also not be demanded as compensation for damages.

(7) Mit der Eintragung der Eingliederung in das Handelsregister des Sitzes der Gesellschaft wird die Gesellschaft in die Hauptgesellschaft eingegliedert.

§ 320 Eingliederung durch Mehrheitsbeschluß.

(1) ¹Die Hauptversammlung einer Aktiengesellschaft kann die Eingliederung der Gesellschaft in eine andere Aktiengesellschaft mit Sitz im Inland auch dann beschließen, wenn sich Aktien der Gesellschaft, auf die zusammen fünfundneunzig vom Hundert des Grundkapitals entfallen, in der Hand der zukünftigen Hauptgesellschaft befinden. ²Eigene Aktien und Aktien, die einem anderen für Rechnung der Gesellschaft gehören, sind vom Grundkapital abzusetzen. ³Für die Eingliederung gelten außer § 319 Abs. 1 Satz 2, Abs. 2 bis 7 die Absätze 2 bis 4.

(2) ¹Die Bekanntmachung der Eingliederung als Gegenstand der Tagesordnung ist nur ordnungsgemäß, wenn

1. sie die Firma und den Sitz der zukünftigen Hauptgesellschaft enthält,
2. ihr eine Erklärung der zukünftigen Hauptgesellschaft beigefügt ist, in der diese den ausscheidenden Aktionären als Abfindung für ihre Aktien eigene Aktien, im Falle des § 320b Abs. 1 Satz 3 außerdem eine Barabfindung anbietet.

²Satz 1 Nr. 2 gilt auch für die Bekanntmachung der zukünftigen Hauptgesellschaft.

(3) ¹Die Eingliederung ist durch einen oder mehrere sachverständige Prüfer (Eingliederungsprüfer) zu prüfen. ²Diese werden auf Antrag des Vorstands der zukünftigen Hauptgesellschaft vom Gericht ausgewählt und bestellt. ³§ 293a Abs. 3, §§ 293c bis 293e sind sinngemäß anzuwenden.

(4) ¹Die in § 319 Abs. 3 Satz 1 bezeichneten Unterlagen sowie der Prüfungs-

(7) The company shall be integrated into the main company upon the integration being registered in the commercial register at the company's registered office.

§ 320 Integration by majority resolution.

(1) ¹The general meeting of a stock corporation may also decide on integrating the company into another stock corporation registered in Germany if shares in the company accounting for ninety five percent of the registered share capital are held by the future main company. ²Own shares and shares held by another party on account of the company shall be deducted from the registered share capital. ³In addition to sec. 319 para. 1 sentence 2 and para. 2 to 7, para. 2 to 4 shall also apply to the integration.

(2) ¹The integration shall only be deemed to have been duly announced as an item on the agenda if

1. the name and the registered office of the future main company are stated,
2. a declaration of the future main company is attached in which such company offers the withdrawing shareholders consideration for their shares consisting of own shares plus, in the case of para. sec. 320b para. 1 sentence 3, an additional cash consideration.

²Sentence 1 no. 2 shall also apply to the announcement made by the future main company.

(3) ¹The integration shall be examined by one or more expert auditors (integration auditors). ²These auditors shall be selected and appointed by the court at the application of the management board of the future main company. ³Sec. 293a para. 3, sec. 293c to 293e shall apply accordingly.

(4) ¹The documents stipulated in sec. 319 para. 3 sentence 1 and the audit report

bericht nach Absatz 3 sind jeweils von der Einberufung der Hauptversammlung an, die über die Zustimmung zur Eingliederung beschließen soll, in dem Geschäftsraum der einzugliedernden Gesellschaft und der Hauptgesellschaft zur Einsicht der Aktionäre auszulegen. [2]In dem Eingliederungsbericht sind auch Art und Höhe der Abfindung nach § 320b rechtlich und wirtschaftlich zu erläutern und zu begründen; auf besondere Schwierigkeiten bei der Bewertung der beteiligten Gesellschaften sowie auf die Folgen für die Beteiligungen der Aktionäre ist hinzuweisen. [3]§ 319 Abs. 3 Satz 2 bis 5 gilt sinngemäß für die Aktionäre beider Gesellschaften.

pursuant to para. 3 shall be displayed for inspection by the shareholders in the offices of both the company which is to be integrated and the main company as of the convening of the general meeting which is to decide on approval for integration. [2]The integration report shall also describe and give the reasons for the nature and amount of the consideration pursuant to sec. 320b from a legal and economic point of view; mention shall be made of any particular difficulties pertaining to the valuation of the companies concerned and of the consequences for the shareholders' interests. [3]Sec. 319 para. 3 sentences 2 to 4 shall apply accordingly to the shareholders of both companies.

§ 320a Wirkungen der Eingliederung.

[1]Mit der Eintragung der Eingliederung in das Handelsregister gehen alle Aktien, die sich nicht in der Hand der Hauptgesellschaft befinden, auf diese über. [2]Sind über diese Aktien Aktienurkunden ausgegeben, so verbriefen sie bis zu ihrer Aushändigung an die Hauptgesellschaft nur den Anspruch auf Abfindung.

§ 320a Effects of integration.

[1]Upon the entering of the integration in the commercial register, all shares not already held by the main company shall be transferred to such company. [2]Until they are submitted to the main company, share certificates which have been issued for these shares shall only represent the claim of the holder thereof to consideration.

§ 320b Abfindung der ausgeschiedenen Aktionäre.

(1) [1]Die ausgeschiedenen Aktionäre der eingegliederten Gesellschaft haben Anspruch auf angemessene Abfindung. [2]Als Abfindung sind ihnen eigene Aktien der Hauptgesellschaft zu gewähren. [3]Ist die Hauptgesellschaft eine abhängige Gesellschaft, so sind den ausgeschiedenen Aktionären nach deren Wahl eigene Aktien der Hauptgesellschaft oder eine angemessene Barabfindung zu gewähren. [4]Werden als Abfindung Aktien der Hauptgesellschaft gewährt, so ist die Abfindung als angemessen anzusehen, wenn die Aktien in dem Verhältnis gewährt werden, in dem bei einer Verschmelzung auf eine Aktie der Gesellschaft Aktien der Hauptgesellschaft zu gewähren wären, wobei

§ 320b Consideration for former shareholders.

(1) [1]The former shareholders of the company which has been integrated shall be entitled to appropriate consideration. [2]They shall be granted own shares in the main company as consideration. [3]If the main company is a controlled company, the former shareholders shall be granted the choice of own shares in the main company or an appropriate cash consideration. [4]If shares in the main company are granted as consideration, such consideration shall be deemed to be reasonable if the shares are granted in the ratio in which shares in the main company would be granted to one share in the company in the case of a merger; fractional amounts may be balanced out with additional cash payments.

Spitzenbeträge durch bare Zuzahlungen ausgeglichen werden können. ⁵Die Barabfindung muß die Verhältnisse der Gesellschaft im Zeitpunkt der Beschlußfassung ihrer Hauptversammlung über die Eingliederung berücksichtigen. ⁶Die Barabfindung sowie bare Zuzahlungen sind von der Bekanntmachung der Eintragung der Eingliederung an mit jährlich 5 Prozentpunkten über dem jeweiligen Basiszinssatz nach § 247 des Bürgerlichen Gesetzbuchs zu verzinsen; die Geltendmachung eines weiteren Schadens ist nicht ausgeschlossen.

(2) ¹Die Anfechtung des Beschlusses, durch den die Hauptversammlung der eingegliederten Gesellschaft die Eingliederung der Gesellschaft beschlossen hat, kann nicht auf § 243 Abs. 2 oder darauf gestützt werden, daß die von der Hauptgesellschaft nach § 320 Abs. 2 Nr. 2 angebotene Abfindung nicht angemessen ist. ²Ist die angebotene Abfindung nicht angemessen, so hat das in § 2 des Spruchverfahrensgesetzes bestimmte Gericht auf Antrag die angemessene Abfindung zu bestimmen. ³Das gleiche gilt, wenn die Hauptgesellschaft eine Abfindung nicht oder nicht ordnungsgemäß angeboten hat und eine hierauf gestützte Anfechtungsklage innerhalb der Anfechtungsfrist nicht erhoben oder zurückgenommen oder rechtskräftig abgewiesen worden ist.

⁵The cash consideration shall take into account the situation of the company at the time its general meeting adopted the resolution on integration. ⁶Annual interest of five percentage points above the relevant risk free rate as stated in sec. 247 of the Civil Code shall be due on the cash consideration and any additional cash payments with effect from the date the registration of the integration in the commercial register is announced; further damages may be claimed.

(2) ¹An action to set aside the resolution in which the general meeting of the company which has been integrated decided on the integration of the company may not be based on sec. 243 para. 2 or on the claim that the consideration offered by the main company pursuant to sec. 320 para. 2 no. 2 is not appropriate. ²If the consideration offered is not appropriate, the court stipulated in sec. 2 of the Act on Legal Challenge Proceedings shall, upon request, determine the appropriate consideration. ³This shall also apply if the main company has failed to offer or to duly offer consideration and an action to set aside a resolution based on such fact has not been brought, has been withdrawn or has been dismissed by a judgment being res judicata within statutory time limit for an action to set aside a resolution.

§ 321 Gläubigerschutz.

(1) ¹Den Gläubigern der eingegliederten Gesellschaft, deren Forderungen begründet worden sind, bevor die Eintragung der Eingliederung in das Handelsregister bekanntgemacht worden ist, ist, wenn sie sich binnen sechs Monaten nach der Bekanntmachung zu diesem Zweck melden, Sicherheit zu leisten, soweit sie nicht Befriedigung verlangen können. ²Die Gläubiger sind in der Bekanntmachung der Eintragung auf dieses Recht hinzuweisen.

§ 321 Protection of creditors.

(1) ¹Those creditors of the company which has been integrated whose claims arose before the registration of the integration in the commercial register was announced shall be provided security if they contact the company for this purpose within six months of such announcement to such extent that they are unable to obtain settlement of their claims. ²The announcement of the registration in the commercial register shall advise the creditors of this right.

(2) Das Recht, Sicherheitsleistung zu verlangen, steht Gläubigern nicht zu, die im Falle des Insolvenzverfahrens ein Recht auf vorzugsweise Befriedigung aus einer Deckungsmasse haben, die nach gesetzlicher Vorschrift zu ihrem Schutz errichtet und staatlich überwacht ist.

§ 322 Haftung der Hauptgesellschaft.

(1) [1]Von der Eingliederung an haftet die Hauptgesellschaft für die vor diesem Zeitpunkt begründeten Verbindlichkeiten der eingegliederten Gesellschaft den Gläubigern dieser Gesellschaft als Gesamtschuldner. [2]Die gleiche Haftung trifft sie für alle Verbindlichkeiten der eingegliederten Gesellschaft, die nach der Eingliederung begründet werden. [3]Eine entgegenstehende Vereinbarung ist Dritten gegenüber unwirksam.

(2) Wird die Hauptgesellschaft wegen einer Verbindlichkeit der eingegliederten Gesellschaft in Anspruch genommen, so kann sie Einwendungen, die nicht in ihrer Person begründet sind, nur insoweit geltend machen, als sie von der eingegliederten Gesellschaft erhoben werden können.

(3) [1]Die Hauptgesellschaft kann die Befriedigung des Gläubigers verweigern, solange der eingegliederten Gesellschaft das Recht zusteht, das ihrer Verbindlichkeit zugrunde liegende Rechtsgeschäft anzufechten. [2]Die gleiche Befugnis hat die Hauptgesellschaft, solange sich der Gläubiger durch Aufrechnung gegen eine fällige Forderung der eingegliederten Gesellschaft befriedigen kann.

(4) Aus einem gegen die eingegliederte Gesellschaft gerichteten vollstreckbaren Schuldtitel findet die Zwangsvollstreckung gegen die Hauptgesellschaft nicht statt.

(2) Creditors having a right to the preferential settlement of their claims in the event of insolvency proceedings from covering funds created for their protection in accordance with legal provisions and monitored by the state shall not be entitled to a right to demand security.

§ 322 Liability of the main company.

(1) [1]With effect from the integration, the main company shall be jointly and severally liable to the creditors of the integrated company for liabilities entered into before this time by such company. [2]It shall also be liable in the same way for all liabilities of the integrated company entered into after integration. [3]An agreement to the contrary shall be invalid vis-à-vis third parties.

(2) If the main company is claimed upon for a liability of the integrated company, it may only assert objections not founded in its own person to the extent that they may be raised by the integrated company.

(3) [1]The main company may refuse satisfaction of the creditor as long as the integrated company is entitled to contest the legal transaction on which its liability is based. [2]The main company shall have the same authority as long as the creditor may obtain satisfaction by way of offset against a claim of the integrated company which is due for payment.

(4) An executory title against the integrated company shall not be enforceable against the main company.

§ 323 Leitungsmacht der Hauptgesellschaft und Verantwortlichkeit der Vorstandsmitglieder.

(1) ¹Die Hauptgesellschaft ist berechtigt, dem Vorstand der eingegliederten Gesellschaft hinsichtlich der Leitung der Gesellschaft Weisungen zu erteilen. ²§ 308 Abs. 2 Satz 1, Abs. 3, §§ 309, 310 gelten sinngemäß. ³§§ 311 bis 318 sind nicht anzuwenden.

(2) Leistungen der eingegliederten Gesellschaft an die Hauptgesellschaft gelten nicht als Verstoß gegen die §§ 57, 58 und 60.

§ 324 Gesetzliche Rücklage. Gewinnabführung. Verlustübernahme.

(1) Die gesetzlichen Vorschriften über die Bildung einer gesetzlichen Rücklage, über ihre Verwendung und über die Einstellung von Beträgen in die gesetzliche Rücklage sind auf eingegliederte Gesellschaften nicht anzuwenden.

(2) ¹Auf einen Gewinnabführungsvertrag, eine Gewinngemeinschaft oder einen Teilgewinnabführungsvertrag zwischen der eingegliederten Gesellschaft und der Hauptgesellschaft sind die §§ 293 bis 296, 298 bis 303 nicht anzuwenden. ²Der Vertrag, seine Änderung und seine Aufhebung bedürfen der schriftlichen Form. ³Als Gewinn kann höchstens der ohne die Gewinnabführung entstehende Bilanzgewinn abgeführt werden. ⁴Der Vertrag endet spätestens zum Ende des Geschäftsjahrs, in dem die Eingliederung endet.

(3) Die Hauptgesellschaft ist verpflichtet, jeden bei der eingegliederten Gesellschaft sonst entstehenden Bilanzverlust auszugleichen, soweit dieser den Betrag der Kapitalrücklagen und der Gewinnrücklagen übersteigt.

§ 325 *(aufgehoben)*

§ 323 Power of direction of the main company and responsibility of members of the management board.

(1) ¹The main company shall be entitled to issue instructions regarding the management of the company to the management board of the integrated company. ²Sec. 308 para. 2 sentence 1, para. 3, sec. 309, 310 shall apply accordingly. ³Sec. 311 to 318 shall not apply.

(2) Services rendered by the integrated company to the main company shall not be deemed to constitute a violation of sec. 57, 58 and 60.

§ 324 Statutory reserve. Transfer of profit. Assumption of loss.

(1) The legal provisions governing the providing of the statutory reserve, the appropriation thereof and the allocation of amounts to the statutory reserve shall not apply to integrated companies.

(2) ¹Sec. 293 to 296, 298 to 303 shall not apply to a profit transfer agreement, a profit pool or a partial profit transfer agreement concluded between the integrated company and the main company. ²The written form shall be required for the agreement, amendments thereto and the termination by agreement thereof. ³The most profit which may be transferred shall be the balance sheet profit arising without the transfer of profit. ⁴The agreement shall terminate at the latest with effect from the end of the fiscal year in which the integration ends.

(3) The main company is obligated to balance out any balance sheet losses incurred by the integrated company to the extent that such losses exceed the amount of the capital reserves and revenue reserves.

§ 325 *(repealed)*

§ 326 Auskunftsrecht der Aktionäre der Hauptgesellschaft.

Jedem Aktionär der Hauptgesellschaft ist über Angelegenheiten der eingegliederten Gesellschaft ebenso Auskunft zu erteilen wie über Angelegenheiten der Hauptgesellschaft.

§ 327 Ende der Eingliederung.

(1) Die Eingliederung endet

1. durch Beschluß der Hauptversammlung der eingegliederten Gesellschaft,
2. wenn die Hauptgesellschaft nicht mehr eine Aktiengesellschaft mit Sitz im Inland ist,
3. wenn sich nicht mehr alle Aktien der eingegliederten Gesellschaft in der Hand der Hauptgesellschaft befinden,
4. durch Auflösung der Hauptgesellschaft.

(2) Befinden sich nicht mehr alle Aktien der eingegliederten Gesellschaft in der Hand der Hauptgesellschaft, so hat die Hauptgesellschaft dies der eingegliederten Gesellschaft unverzüglich schriftlich mitzuteilen.

(3) Der Vorstand der bisher eingegliederten Gesellschaft hat das Ende der Eingliederung, seinen Grund und seinen Zeitpunkt unverzüglich zur Eintragung in das Handelsregister des Sitzes der Gesellschaft anzumelden.

(4) ¹Endet die Eingliederung, so haftet die frühere Hauptgesellschaft für die bis dahin begründeten Verbindlichkeiten der bisher eingegliederten Gesellschaft, wenn sie vor Ablauf von fünf Jahren nach dem Ende der Eingliederung fällig und daraus Ansprüche gegen die frühere Hauptgesellschaft in einer in § 197 Abs. 1 Nr. 3 bis 5 des Bürgerlichen Gesetzbuchs bezeichneten Art festgestellt sind oder eine gerichtliche oder behördliche Vollstreckungshandlung vorgenommen oder beantragt wird; bei

§ 326 Right to information of shareholders of the main company.

Each shareholder in the main company shall be provided with information on matters relating to the integrated company as well as matters relating to the main company.

§ 327 End of integration.

(1) The integration shall end

1. due to a resolution to this effect being adopted by the general meeting of the integrated company,
2. if the main company ceases to be a stock corporation registered in Germany,
3. if the main company no longer holds all shares in the integrated company,
4. as a result of the dissolution of the main company.

(2) The main company shall without undue delay inform the integrated company in writing if the main company no longer holds all shares in the integrated company.

(3) The management board of the previously integrated company shall apply without undue delay for the end of the integration, the reason therefor and the date on which such integration ended to be registered in the commercial register at the registered office of the company.

(4) ¹If the integration ends, the former main company shall be liable for the liabilities that have previously arisen of the previously integrated company if they become due within five years after the end of the integration and if claims against the former main company are determined in a way set forth in sec. 197 para. 1 nos. 3 to 5 of the Civil Code or if a judicial or administrative enforcement action has been effected or applied for; in case of public law liabilities, the issuance of an administrative act is suffi-

öffentlich-rechtlichen Verbindlichkeiten genügt der Erlass eines Verwaltungsakts. ²Die Frist beginnt mit dem Tag, an dem die Eintragung des Endes der Eingliederung in das Handelsregister nach § 10 des Handelsgesetzbuchs bekannt gemacht worden ist. ³Die für die Verjährung geltenden §§ 204, 206, 210, 211 und 212 Abs. 2 und 3 des Bürgerlichen Gesetzbuchs sind entsprechend anzuwenden. ⁴Einer Feststellung in einer in § 197 Abs. 1 Nr. 3 bis 5 des Bürgerlichen Gesetzbuchs bezeichneten Art bedarf es nicht, soweit die frühere Hauptgesellschaft den Anspruch schriftlich anerkannt hat.

cient. ²The limitation period begins with the day on which the registration in the commercial register of the end of the integration has been announced pursuant to sec. 10 of the Commercial Code. ³The provisions on time limitations in sec. 204, 206, 210, 211 and 212 paras. 2 and 3 of the Civil Code shall apply accordingly. ⁴A determination in a way set forth in sec. 197 para. 1 nos. 3 to 5 of the Civil Code is not required to the extent the former main company has acknowledged the claim in writing.

Vierter Teil. Ausschluss von Minderheitsaktionären

Part Four. Expulsion of Minority Shareholders

§ 327a Übertragung von Aktien gegen Barabfindung.

§ 327a Transfer of shares in return for cash consideration.

(1) ¹Die Hauptversammlung einer Aktiengesellschaft oder einer Kommanditgesellschaft auf Aktien kann auf Verlangen eines Aktionärs, dem Aktien der Gesellschaft in Höhe von 95 vom Hundert des Grundkapitals gehören (Hauptaktionär), die Übertragung der Aktien der übrigen Aktionäre (Minderheitsaktionäre) auf den Hauptaktionär gegen Gewährung einer angemessenen Barabfindung beschließen. ²§ 285 Abs. 2 Satz 1 findet keine Anwendung.

(1) ¹At the request of a shareholder holding shares in the company which account for ninety-five percent of the registered share capital (main shareholder), the general meeting of a stock corporation or a partnership limited by shares can adopt a resolution stipulating the transfer of the shares held by the other shareholders (minority shareholders) to the principal shareholder in return for appropriate cash consideration. ²Sec. 285 para. 2 sentence 1 shall not apply.

(2) Für die Feststellung, ob dem Hauptaktionär 95 vom Hundert der Aktien gehören, gilt § 16 Abs. 2 und 4.

(2) Sec. 16 paras. 2 and 4 shall apply when determining whether ninety-five percent of the shares are held by the main shareholder.

§ 327b Barabfindung.

§ 327b Cash consideration.

(1) ¹Der Hauptaktionär legt die Höhe der Barabfindung fest; sie muss die Verhältnisse der Gesellschaft im Zeitpunkt der Beschlussfassung ihrer Hauptversammlung berücksichtigen. ²Der Vorstand hat dem Hauptaktionär alle dafür notwendigen Unterlagen zur Verfügung zu stellen und Auskünfte zu erteilen.

(1) ¹The principal shareholder shall stipulate the amount of the cash consideration; such consideration shall take into account the company's situation at the time the resolution is adopted. ²The management board shall provide the principal shareholder with all necessary documents and information.

(2) Die Barabfindung ist von der Bekanntmachung der Eintragung des

(2) Annual interest of five percentage points above the relevant risk free rate

Übertragungsbeschlusses in das Handelsregister an mit jährlich 5 Prozentpunkten über dem jeweiligen Basiszinssatz nach § 247 des Bürgerlichen Gesetzbuchs zu verzinsen; die Geltendmachung eines weiteren Schadens ist nicht ausgeschlossen.

(3) Vor Einberufung der Hauptversammlung hat der Hauptaktionär dem Vorstand die Erklärung eines im Geltungsbereich dieses Gesetzes zum Geschäftsbetrieb befugten Kreditinstituts zu übermitteln, durch die das Kreditinstitut die Gewährleistung für die Erfüllung der Verpflichtung des Hauptaktionärs übernimmt, den Minderheitsaktionären nach Eintragung des Übertragungsbeschlusses unverzüglich die festgelegte Barabfindung für die übergegangenen Aktien zu zahlen.

§ 327c Vorbereitung der Hauptversammlung.

(1) Die Bekanntmachung der Übertragung als Gegenstand der Tagesordnung hat folgende Angaben zu enthalten:

1. Firma und Sitz des Hauptaktionärs, bei natürlichen Personen Name und Adresse;

2. die vom Hauptaktionär festgelegte Barabfindung.

(2) ¹Der Hauptaktionär hat der Hauptversammlung einen schriftlichen Bericht zu erstatten, in dem die Voraussetzungen für die Übertragung dargelegt und die Angemessenheit der Barabfindung erläutert und begründet werden. ²Die Angemessenheit der Barabfindung ist durch einen oder mehrere sachverständige Prüfer zu prüfen. ³Diese werden auf Antrag des Hauptaktionärs vom Gericht ausgewählt und bestellt. ⁴§ 293a Abs. 2 und 3, § 293c Abs. 1 Satz 3 bis 5, Abs. 2 sowie die §§ 293d und 293e sind sinngemäß anzuwenden.

(3) Von der Einberufung der Hauptversammlung an sind in dem Geschäfts-

as stated in sec. 247 of the Civil Code shall be due on the cash consideration with effect from the date the registration in the commercial register of the resolution on the transfer of the shares is announced; further damages may be claimed.

(3) Before the general meeting is convened, the main shareholder shall submit to the management board a declaration from a credit institution authorized to operate in the area of validity of this Act warranting performance of the main shareholder's obligation to pay the minority shareholders the agreed cash consideration for the transferred shares without undue delay once the resolution on the transfer of such shares has been registered.

§ 327c Preparation of the general meeting.

(1) The announcement that the transfer is to be an item on the agenda shall contain the following information:

1. name and registered office of the main shareholder or if the main shareholder is a natural person, his name and address;

2. the cash consideration stipulated by the main shareholder.

(2) ¹The main shareholder shall provide the general meeting with a written report which presents the requirements for the transfer and describes and justifies the appropriateness of the cash consideration. ²The appropriateness of the cash consideration shall be assessed by one or more expert auditors. ³Such auditors shall be selected and appointed by the court upon the request of the main shareholder. ⁴Sec. 293a paras. 2 and 3, sec. 293c para. 1 sentences 3 to 5, para. 2 and sec. 293d and 293e shall apply accordingly.

(3) The following shall be displayed for inspection by the shareholders in the

raum der Gesellschaft zur Einsicht der Aktionäre auszulegen

1. der Entwurf des Übertragungsbeschlusses;
2. die Jahresabschlüsse und Lageberichte für die letzten drei Geschäftsjahre;
3. der nach Absatz 2 Satz 1 erstattete Bericht des Hauptaktionärs;
4. der nach Absatz 2 Satz 2 bis 4 erstattete Prüfungsbericht.

(4) Auf Verlangen ist jedem Aktionär unverzüglich und kostenlos eine Abschrift der in Absatz 3 bezeichneten Unterlagen zu erteilen.

(5) Die Verpflichtungen nach den Absätzen 3 und 4 entfallen, wenn die in Absatz 3 bezeichneten Unterlagen für denselben Zeitraum über die Internetseite der Gesellschaft zugänglich sind.

§ 327d Durchführung der Hauptversammlung.

¹In der Hauptversammlung sind die in § 327c Abs. 3 bezeichneten Unterlagen zugänglich zu machen. ²Der Vorstand kann dem Hauptaktionär Gelegenheit geben, den Entwurf des Übertragungsbeschlusses und die Bemessung der Höhe der Barabfindung zu Beginn der Verhandlung mündlich zu erläutern.

§ 327e Eintragung des Übertragungsbeschlusses.

(1) ¹Der Vorstand hat den Übertragungsbeschluss zur Eintragung in das Handelsregister anzumelden. ²Der Anmeldung sind die Niederschrift des Übertragungsbeschlusses und seine Anlagen in Ausfertigung oder öffentlich beglaubigter Abschrift beizufügen.

(2) § 319 Abs. 5 und 6 gilt sinngemäß.

(3) ¹Mit der Eintragung des Übertragungsbeschlusses in das Handelsregister gehen alle Aktien der Minderheitsaktionäre auf den Hauptaktionär über.

office of the company as of the date the general meeting is convened:

1. the draft of the resolution on the transfer;
2. the annual financial statements and management reports for the three preceding fiscal years;
3. the main shareholder's report pursuant to para. 2 sentence 1;
4. the audit report pursuant to para. 2 sentences 2 to 4.

(4) Each shareholder shall be supplied without undue delay and free of charge with a copy of the documents listed in para. 3 upon request.

(5) The obligations pursuant to paras. 3 and 4 shall cease to exist if the documents set forth in para. 3 are accessible during the same period of time on the website of the company.

§ 327d Conducting of the general meeting.

¹The documents set forth in sec. 327c para. 3 shall be made accessible during the general meeting. ²The management board can give the main shareholder the opportunity to explain the draft of the resolution on the transfer and the calculation of the amount of the cash consideration at the commencement of proceedings.

§ 327e Registration of the resolution on the transfer of shares.

(1) ¹The management board shall apply for the resolution on the transfer to be registered in the commercial register. ²An executed copy or a certified copy of the minutes of the resolution and the appendices thereto shall be attached to the application.

(2) Sec. 319 paras. 5 and 6 shall apply accordingly.

(3) ¹All shares held by the minority shareholders shall be transferred to the main shareholder upon the registration in the commercial register of the resolu-

²Sind über diese Aktien Aktienurkunden ausgegeben, so verbriefen sie bis zu ihrer Aushändigung an den Hauptaktionär nur den Anspruch auf Barabfindung.

§ 327f Gerichtliche Nachprüfung der Abfindung.

¹Die Anfechtung des Übertragungsbeschlusses kann nicht auf § 243 Abs. 2 oder darauf gestützt werden, dass die durch den Hauptaktionär festgelegte Barabfindung nicht angemessen ist. ²Ist die Barabfindung nicht angemessen, so hat das in § 2 des Spruchverfahrensgesetzes bestimmte Gericht auf Antrag die angemessene Barabfindung zu bestimmen. ³Das Gleiche gilt, wenn der Hauptaktionär eine Barabfindung nicht oder nicht ordnungsgemäß angeboten hat und eine hierauf gestützte Anfechtungsklage innerhalb der Anfechtungsfrist nicht erhoben, zurückgenommen oder rechtskräftig abgewiesen worden ist.

Fünfter Teil Wechselseitig beteiligte Unternehmen

§ 328 Beschränkung der Rechte.

(1) ¹Sind eine Aktiengesellschaft oder Kommanditgesellschaft auf Aktien und ein anderes Unternehmen wechselseitig beteiligte Unternehmen, so können, sobald dem einen Unternehmen das Bestehen der wechselseitigen Beteiligung bekannt geworden ist oder ihm das andere Unternehmen eine Mitteilung nach § 20 Abs. 3 oder § 21 Abs. 1 gemacht hat, Rechte aus den Anteilen, die ihm an dem anderen Unternehmen gehören, nur für höchstens den vierten Teil aller Anteile des anderen Unternehmens ausgeübt werden. ²Dies gilt nicht für das Recht auf neue Aktien bei einer Kapitalerhöhung aus Gesellschaftsmitteln. ³§ 16 Abs. 4 ist anzuwenden.

tion on the transfer. ²If share certificates have been issued for such shares, they shall only represent the claim of the holder thereof to a cash consideration until they are submitted to the principal shareholder.

§ 327f Subsequent court inspection of the consideration.

¹An action to set aside the resolution on the transfer of shares may not be based upon sec. 243 para. 2 or on the claim that the cash consideration determined by the main shareholder is not appropriate. ²If the cash consideration is not appropriate, the court stipulated in sec. 2 of the Act on Legal Challenge Proceedings shall, upon application, determine the appropriate cash consideration. ³The same shall apply if the main shareholder has failed to offer or to duly offer a cash consideration and an action to set aside a resolution based on such fact has not been brought, has been withdrawn or has been dismissed by a judgment being res judicata within the statutory time limit for an action to set aside a resolution.

Part Five. Enterprises with Cross-Shareholdings

§ 328 Limitations on rights.

(1) ¹If a stock corporation or a partnership limited by shares and another enterprise have cross-shareholdings, as soon as one of the enterprises realizes that they have a cross-shareholding or receives notification pursuant to sec. 20 para. 3 or sec. 21 para. 1 from the other enterprise, rights from shares held by such enterprise in the other enterprise may at most be exercised for one quarter of all shares of the other enterprise. ²This shall not apply to the right to new shares in the event of a capital increase from company resources. ³Sec. 16 para. 4 shall apply.

(2) Die Beschränkung des Absatzes 1 gilt nicht, wenn das Unternehmen seinerseits dem anderen Unternehmen eine Mitteilung nach § 20 Abs. 3 oder § 21 Abs. 1 gemacht hatte, bevor es von dem anderen Unternehmen eine solche Mitteilung erhalten hat und bevor ihm das Bestehen der wechselseitigen Beteiligung bekannt geworden ist.

(3) In der Hauptversammlung einer börsennotierten Gesellschaft kann ein Unternehmen, dem die wechselseitige Beteiligung gemäß Absatz 1 bekannt ist, sein Stimmrecht zur Wahl von Mitgliedern in den Aufsichtsrat nicht ausüben.

(4) Sind eine Aktiengesellschaft oder Kommanditgesellschaft auf Aktien und ein anderes Unternehmen wechselseitig beteiligte Unternehmen, so haben die Unternehmen einander unverzüglich die Höhe ihrer Beteiligung und jede Änderung schriftlich mitzuteilen.

(2) The limitation stipulated in para. 1 shall not apply if the enterprise has itself issued notification to the other enterprise pursuant to sec. 20 para. 3 or sec. 21 para. 1 before receiving such notification from the other enterprise and before it became aware of the cross-shareholding.

(3) An enterprise which has learnt of the cross-shareholding pursuant to para. 1 may not exercise its voting right for the election of members of the supervisory board in the general meeting of a listed company.

(4) If a stock corporation or a partnership limited by shares and another enterprise have cross-shareholdings, the enterprises shall without undue delay inform each other in writing of the amount of their shareholding and any changes thereto.

Sechster Teil. Rechnungslegung im Konzern

§§ 329–393 *(aufgehoben)*

Part Six. Accounting in Groups of Companies

§§ 329–393 *(repealed)*

Viertes Buch. Sonder-, Straf- und Schlußvorschriften

Fourth Book. Special, Penal and Final Provisions

Erster Teil. Sondervorschriften bei Beteiligung von Gebietskörperschaften

Part One. Special Provisions Relating to Participation of Municipal Authorities

§ 394 Berichte der Aufsichtsratsmitglieder.

§ 394 Reports by supervisory board members.

[1]Aufsichtsratsmitglieder, die auf Veranlassung einer Gebietskörperschaft in den Aufsichtsrat gewählt oder entsandt worden sind, unterliegen hinsichtlich der Berichte, die sie der Gebietskörperschaft zu erstatten haben, keiner Verschwiegenheitspflicht. [2]Für vertrauliche Angaben und Geheimnisse der Gesellschaft, namentlich Betriebs- oder Geschäftsgeheimnisse, gilt dies nicht, wenn ihre Kenntnis für die Zwecke

[1]Supervisory board members who have been elected or appointed to the supervisory board at the instigation of a municipal authority shall not be subject to a confidentiality obligation with regard to the reports they are obligated to make to the municipal authority. [2]This shall not apply to confidential information and company secrets, namely trade or business secrets, if knowledge thereof is of no significance for the purpose of

der Berichte nicht von Bedeutung ist. ³Die Berichtspflicht nach Satz 1 kann auf Gesetz, auf Satzung oder auf dem Aufsichtsrat in Textform mitgeteiltem Rechtsgeschäft beruhen.

§ 395 Verschwiegenheitspflicht.

(1) Personen, die damit betraut sind, die Beteiligungen einer Gebietskörperschaft zu verwalten oder für eine Gebietskörperschaft die Gesellschaft, die Betätigung der Gebietskörperschaft als Aktionär oder die Tätigkeit der auf Veranlassung der Gebietskörperschaft gewählten oder entsandten Aufsichtsratsmitglieder zu prüfen, haben über vertrauliche Angaben und Geheimnisse der Gesellschaft, namentlich Betriebs- oder Geschäftsgeheimnisse, die ihnen aus Berichten nach § 394 bekanntgeworden sind, Stillschweigen zu bewahren; dies gilt nicht für Mitteilungen im dienstlichen Verkehr.

(2) Bei der Veröffentlichung von Prüfungsergebnissen dürfen vertrauliche Angaben und Geheimnisse der Gesellschaft, namentlich Betriebs- oder Geschäftsgeheimnisse, nicht veröffentlicht werden.

Zweiter Teil. Gerichtliche Auflösung

§ 396 Voraussetzungen.

(1) ¹Gefährdet eine Aktiengesellschaft oder Kommanditgesellschaft auf Aktien durch gesetzwidriges Verhalten ihrer Verwaltungsträger das Gemeinwohl und sorgen der Aufsichtsrat und die Hauptversammlung nicht für eine Abberufung der Verwaltungsträger, so kann die Gesellschaft auf Antrag der zuständigen obersten Landesbehörde des Landes, in dem die Gesellschaft ihren Sitz hat, durch Urteil aufgelöst werden. ²Ausschließlich zuständig für die Klage ist das Landgericht, in dessen Bezirk die Gesellschaft ihren Sitz hat.

the reports. ³The reporting obligation pursuant to sentence 1 can be based on legislation, the articles of association or on a legal transaction announced to the supervisory board in writing.

§ 395 Confidentiality obligation.

(1) Persons entrusted with administrating the interests of a municipal authority or with examining the company, the activity of the municipal authority as a shareholder or the actions of the supervisory board members elected or appointed by the municipal authority on behalf of the municipal authority shall not disclose confidential information and secrets of the company, namely trade or business secrets, which they learn of from reports pursuant to sec. 394; this shall not apply to communications made for official purposes.

(2) Confidential information and secrets of the company, namely trade or business secrets, may not be published when publishing the findings of examinations.

Part Two. Dissolution by Order of the Court

§ 396 Requirements.

(1) ¹If a stock corporation or a partnership limited by shares is a threat to the public interest due to the illegal actions of its administrative bodies and if the supervisory board and the general meeting fail to have the administrative bodies dismissed, the company may be dissolved by court judgment upon application by the competent highest state authority of the state in which the company has its registered office. ²The regional court responsible for the district in which the company is registered shall have sole jurisdiction.

(2) ¹Nach der Auflösung findet die Abwicklung nach den §§ 264 bis 273 statt. ²Den Antrag auf Abberufung oder Bestellung der Abwickler aus einem wichtigen Grund kann auch die in Absatz 1 Satz 1 bestimmte Behörde stellen.

(2) ¹Liquidation pursuant to sec. 264 to 273 shall take place after dissolution. ²An application for liquidators to be dismissed or appointed for good cause may also be brought by the authority stipulated in para. 1 sentence 1.

§ 397 Anordnungen bei der Auflösung.

§ 397 Orders relating to dissolution.

Ist die Auflösungsklage erhoben, so kann das Gericht auf Antrag der in § 396 Abs. 1 Satz 1 bestimmten Behörde durch einstweilige Verfügung die nötigen Anordnungen treffen.

If an action has been brought for the dissolution of the company, the court may also issue the necessary orders by injunction on application by the authorities stipulated in sec. 396 para. 1 sentence 1.

§ 398 Eintragung.

§ 398 Registration.

¹Die Entscheidungen des Gerichts sind dem Registergericht mitzuteilen. ²Dieses trägt sie, soweit sie eintragungspflichtige Rechtsverhältnisse betreffen, in das Handelsregister ein.

¹The register court shall be informed of the court's decisions. ²If such decisions concern legal relations which are subject to registration, it shall enter them in the commercial register.

Dritter Teil. Straf- und Bußgeldvorschriften. Schlußvorschriften

Part Three. Penal Provisions and Fines. Final Provisions

§ 399 Falsche Angaben.

§ 399 False statements.

(1) Mit Freiheitsstrafe bis zu drei Jahren oder mit Geldstrafe wird bestraft, wer

(1) Any person who

1. als Gründer oder als Mitglied des Vorstands oder des Aufsichtsrats zum Zweck der Eintragung der Gesellschaft oder eines Vertrags nach § 52 Absatz1 Satz 1 über die Übernahme der Aktien, die Einzahlung auf Aktien, die Verwendung eingezahlter Beträge, den Ausgabebetrag der Aktien, über Sondervorteile, Gründungsaufwand, Sacheinlagen und Sachübernahmen oder in der nach § 37a Absatz 2, auch in Verbindung mit § 52 Absatz 6 Satz 3,abzugebenden Versicherung,

1. as a founder or as a member of the management board or the supervisory board makes false statements or fails to disclose relevant circumstances regarding the subscription to shares, payment of contributions, the use of amounts paid in, the issue price of the shares, special benefits, formation expenses, contributions in kind and acquisitions in kind or in the assurance to be given pursuant to sec. 37a para. 2 for the purpose of having the company or a contract within the meaning of sec. 52 para. 1 sentence 1 registered in the commercial register,

2. als Gründer oder als Mitglied des Vorstands oder des Aufsichtsrats imGründungsbericht, im Nachgründungsbericht oder im Prüfungsbericht,

2. as a founder or as a member of the management board or the supervisory board makes false statements or fails to disclose relevant circumstances in the formation report, the

3. in der öffentlichen Ankündigung nach § 47 Nr. 3,

4. als Mitglied des Vorstands oder des Aufsichtsrats zum Zweck der Eintragung einer Erhöhung des Grundkapitals (§§ 182 bis 206) über die Einbringung des bisherigen, die Zeichnung oder Einbringung des neuen Kapitals, den Ausgabebetrag der Aktien, die Ausgabe der Bezugsaktien, über Sacheinlagen, in der Bekanntmachung nach § 183a Abs. 2 Satz 1 in Verbindung mit § 37a Abs. 2 oder in der nach § 184 Abs. 1 Satz 3 abzugebenden Versicherung,

5. als Abwickler zum Zweck der Eintragung der Fortsetzung der Gesellschaft in dem nach § 274 Abs. 3 zu führenden Nachweis oder

6. als Mitglied des Vorstands einer Aktiengesellschaft oder des Leitungsorganseiner ausländischen juristischen Person in der nach § 37 Abs. 2 Satz 1 oder § 81 Abs. 3 Satz 1 abzugebenden Versicherung oder als Abwickler in der nach § 266 Abs. 3 Satz 1 abzugebenden Versicherung

falsche Angaben macht oder erhebliche Umstände verschweigt.

(2) Ebenso wird bestraft, wer als Mitglied des Vorstands oder des Aufsichtsrats zum Zweck der Eintragung einer Erhöhung des Grundkapitals die in § 210 Abs. 1 Satz 2 vorgeschriebene Erklärung der Wahrheit zuwider abgibt.

3. makes false statements or fails to disclose relevant circumstances in the public announcement pursuant to sec. 47 para. 3,

4. as a member of the management board or the supervisory board makes false statements or fails to disclose relevant circumstances relating to the contribution of the previous capital, subscription or contribution of the new capital, the issue price of the shares, the issue of new shares, contributions in kind, in the announcement pursuant to sec. 183a para. 2 sentence 1 in connection with sec. 37a para. 2 or in the assurance to be given pursuant to sec. 184 para. 1 sentence 3 for the purpose of having an increase in the registered share capital (sec. 182 to 206) registered in the commercial register or,

5. as a liquidator makes false statements or fails to disclose relevant circumstances in the evidence to be furnished pursuant to sec. 274 para. 3 for the purpose of having the continuation of the company registered in the commercial register, or

6. as a member of the management board of a stock company or a management body of a foreign legal person makes false statements or fails to disclose relevant circumstances in the statement to be made pursuant to sec. 37 para. 2 sentence 1 or sec. 81 para. 3 sentence 1 or as a liquidator

post-formation report or the audit report,

makes false statements or fails to disclose relevant circumstances in the statement to be made pursuant to sec. 266 para. 3 sentence 1 shall be punished with imprisonment of up to three years or a fine.

(2) The same punishment shall also be incumbent upon any person who in his position as a member of the management board or the supervisory board makes a false statement in the declaration pursuant to sec. 210 para. 1 sen-

tence 2 for the purposes of having an increase in the registered share capital registered in the commercial register.

§ 400 Unrichtige Darstellung.

(1) Mit Freiheitsstrafe bis zu drei Jahren oder mit Geldstrafe wird bestraft, wer als Mitglied des Vorstands oder des Aufsichtsrats oder als Abwickler

1. die Verhältnisse der Gesellschaft einschließlich ihrer Beziehungen zu verbundenen Unternehmen in Darstellungen oder Übersichten über den Vermögensstand, in Vorträgen oder Auskünften in der Hauptversammlung unrichtig wiedergibt oder verschleiert, wenn die Tat nicht in § 331 Nr. 1 oder 1a des Handelsgesetzbuchs mit Strafe bedroht ist, oder
2. in Aufklärungen oder Nachweisen, die nach den Vorschriften dieses Gesetzes einem Prüfer der Gesellschaft oder eines verbundenen Unternehmens zu geben sind, falsche Angaben macht oder die Verhältnisse der Gesellschaft unrichtig wiedergibt oder verschleiert, wenn die Tat nicht in § 331 Nr. 4 des Handelsgesetzbuchs mit Strafe bedroht ist.

(2) Ebenso wird bestraft, wer als Gründer oder Aktionär in Aufklärungen oder Nachweisen, die nach den Vorschriften dieses Gesetzes einem Gründungsprüfer oder sonstigen Prüfer zu geben sind, falsche Angaben macht oder erhebliche Umstände verschweigt.

§ 401 Pflichtverletzung bei Verlust, Überschuldung oder Zahlungsunfähigkeit.

(1) Mit Freiheitsstrafe bis zu drei Jahren oder mit Geldstrafe wird bestraft, wer es als Mitglied des Vorstands entgegen § 92 Abs. 1 unterläßt, bei einem Verlust in Höhe der Hälfte des Grundkapitals

§ 400 Misrepresentation.

(1) Any person who as a member of the management board or the supervisory board or as a liquidator

1. misrepresents or conceals the situation of the company including its relations to affiliated enterprises in presentations or overviews of the financial situation, in speeches or information delivered to the general meeting unless such act constitutes a criminal offense pursuant to sec. 331 nos. 1 or 1a of the Commercial Code, or
2. makes false statements or misrepresents or conceals the situation of the company in disclosures or statements which are to be given to an auditor of the company or an affiliated enterprise in accordance with the provisions of this Act, unless such act constitutes a criminal offense pursuant to sec. 331 no. 4 of the Commercial Code, shall be punished with imprisonment of up to three years or a fine.

(2) The same punishment shall also be incumbent on any person who as a founder or shareholder makes false statements or conceals significant facts in disclosures or statements to be made to a formation auditor or any other auditor pursuant to the provisions of this Act.

§ 401 Violation of duties in the event of loss, over-indebtedness or illiquidity.

(1) Any person who, as a member of the management board and in violation of sec. 92 para. 1, fails to convene and inform the general meeting after losses of more than one half of the registered share capital have occurred shall be

B. Stock Corporation Act

die Hauptversammlung einzuberufen und ihr dies anzuzeigen.

(2) Handelt der Täter fahrlässig, so ist die Strafe Freiheitsstrafe bis zu einem Jahr oder Geldstrafe.

§ 402 Falsche Ausstellung von Berechtigungsnachweisen.

(1) Wer Bescheinigungen, die zum Nachweis des Stimmrechts in einer Hauptversammlung oder in einer gesonderten Versammlung dienen sollen, falsch ausstellt oder verfälscht, wird mit Freiheitsstrafe bis zu drei Jahren oder mit Geldstrafe bestraft, wenn die Tat nicht in anderen Vorschriften über Urkundenstraftaten mit schwererer Strafe bedroht ist.

(2) Ebenso wird bestraft, wer von einer falschen oder verfälschten Bescheinigung der in Absatz 1 bezeichneten Art zur Ausübung des Stimmrechts Gebrauch macht.

(3) Der Versuch ist strafbar.

§ 403 Verletzung der Berichtspflicht.

(1) Mit Freiheitsstrafe bis zu drei Jahren oder mit Geldstrafe wird bestraft, wer als Prüfer oder als Gehilfe eines Prüfers über das Ergebnis der Prüfung falsch berichtet oder erhebliche Umstände im Bericht verschweigt.

(2) Handelt der Täter gegen Entgelt oder in der Absicht, sich oder einen anderen zu bereichern oder einen anderen zu schädigen, so ist die Strafe Freiheitsstrafe bis zu fünf Jahren oder Geldstrafe.

§ 404 Verletzung der Geheimhaltungspflicht.

(1) Mit Freiheitsstrafe bis zu einem Jahr, bei börsennotierten Gesellschaften bis zu zwei Jahren, oder mit Geldstrafe wird bestraft, wer ein Geheimnis der Gesellschaft, namentlich ein Betriebs-

punished with imprisonment of up to three years or a fine.

(2) If the offender acts negligently, the punishment shall be imprisonment of up to one year or a fine.

§ 402 False issuing of credentials.

(1) Any person who issues certificates which are to serve as evidence of the voting right in a general meeting or a separate meeting or who falsifies such certificates shall be punished with imprisonment of up to three years or a fine unless a more severe punishment is stipulated for the act in other criminal provisions relating to documents.

(2) Any person who uses a false or falsified certificate of the type stated in para. 1 for the exercising of the voting right shall also be punished.

(3) An attempt shall be punishable.

§ 403 Violation of the duty to report.

(1) Any person who as an auditor or auditor's assistant makes a false report on the result of the audit or who fails to mention significant circumstances in the report shall be punished with imprisonment of up to three years or a fine.

(2) If the offender acts in return for payment or with the intention of enriching himself or another person or damaging another person, the punishment shall be imprisonment of up to five years or a fine.

§ 404 Violation of duty to observe confidentiality.

(1) Any person who, without authority to do so, discloses a secret of the company, in particular a trade or business secret, which became known to him in his capacity as

oder Geschäftsgeheimnis, das ihm in seiner Eigenschaft als

1. Mitglied des Vorstands oder des Aufsichtsrats oder Abwickler,
2. Prüfer oder Gehilfe eines Prüfers

bekanntgeworden ist, unbefugt offenbart; im Falle der Nummer 2 jedoch nur, wenn die Tat nicht in § 333 des Handelsgesetzbuchs mit Strafe bedroht ist.

(2) ¹Handelt der Täter gegen Entgelt oder in der Absicht, sich oder einen anderen zu bereichern oder einen anderen zu schädigen, so ist die Strafe Freiheitsstrafe bis zu zwei Jahren, bei börsennotierten Gesellschaften bis zu drei Jahren, oder Geldstrafe. ²Ebenso wird bestraft, wer ein Geheimnis der in Absatz 1 bezeichneten Art, namentlich ein Betriebs- oder Geschäftsgeheimnis, das ihm unter den Voraussetzungen des Absatzes 1 bekanntgeworden ist, unbefugt verwertet.

(3) ¹Die Tat wird nur auf Antrag der Gesellschaft verfolgt. ²Hat ein Mitglied des Vorstands oder ein Abwickler die Tat begangen, so ist der Aufsichtsrat, hat ein Mitglied des Aufsichtsrats die Tat begangen, so sind der Vorstand oder die Abwickler antragsberechtigt.

§ 404a Verletzung der Pflichten bei Abschlussprüfungen

Mit Freiheitsstrafe bis zu einem Jahr oder mit Geldstrafe wird bestraft, wer als Mitglied des Aufsichtsrats oder als Mitglied eines Prüfungsausschusses einer Gesellschaft, die kapitalmarktorientiert im Sinne des § 264d des Handelsgesetzbuchs, die CRR-Kreditinstitut im Sinne des § 1 Absatz 3d Satz 1 des Kreditwesengesetzes, mit Ausnahme der in § 2 Absatz 1 Nummer 1 und 2

1. a member of the management board or the supervisory board or as a liquidator,
2. an auditor or an auditor's assistant

shall be punished by imprisonment of up to one year, in the case of listed companies up to two years, or a fine; in the case of no. 2, however, this shall only apply if the act does not constitute a criminal offense pursuant to sec. 333 of the Commercial Code.

(2) ¹If the offender acts in return for payment or with the intention of enriching himself or another person or damaging another person, the punishment shall be imprisonment of up to two years, in the case of listed companies up to three years, or a fine. ²The same punishment shall also be incumbent upon any person who without authority to do so exploits a secret of the type stipulated in para. 1, namely a trade or business secret, which became known to him in the circumstances stated in para. 1.

(3) ¹The offense shall only be pursued upon application by the company. ²If the offense has been committed by a member of the management board or a liquidator, the supervisory board shall be entitled to file the application, and if the offense has been committed by a member of the supervisory board, the management board or the liquidators shall be entitled to file the application.

§ 404a Violation of the duties during closure audits

Any person who as a member of the supervisory board or as a member of the audit committee of a company within the meaning of sec. 264d of the Commercial Code, the CRR- credit institutions within the meaning of sec. 1 para. 3d sentence 1 of the German Banking Act, with the exception of the institutions mentioned in sec. 2 para. 1 number 1 and 2 of the German Banking Act

des Kreditwesengesetzes genannten Institute, oder die Versicherungsunternehmen ist im Sinne des Artikels 2 Absatz 1 der Richtlinie 91/674/EWG des Rates vom 19. Dezember 1991 über den Jahresabschluß und den konsolidierten Abschluß von Versicherungsunternehmen (ABl. L 374 vom 31.12.1991, S. 7), die zuletzt durch die Richtlinie 2006/46/EG (ABl. L 224 vom 16.8.2006, S. 1) geändert worden ist,

1. eine in § 405 Absatz 3b, 3c oder Absatz 3d bezeichnete Handlung begeht und dafür einen Vermögensvorteil erhält oder sich versprechen lässt oder
2. eine in § 405 Absatz 3b, 3c oder Absatz 3d bezeichnete Handlung beharrlich wiederholt.

§ 405 Ordnungswidrigkeiten.

(1) Ordnungswidrig handelt, wer als Mitglied des Vorstands oder des Aufsichtsrats oder als Abwickler

1. Namensaktien ausgibt, in denen der Betrag der Teilleistung nicht angegeben ist, oder Inhaberaktien ausgibt, bevor auf sie der Ausgabebetrag voll geleistet ist,
2. Aktien oder Zwischenscheine ausgibt, bevor die Gesellschaft oder im Fall einer Kapitalerhöhung die Durchführung der Erhöhung des Grundkapitals oder im Fall einer bedingten Kapitalerhöhung oder einer Kapitalerhöhung aus Gesellschaftsmitteln der Beschluß über die bedingte Kapitalerhöhung oder die Kapitalerhöhung aus Gesellschaftsmitteln eingetragen ist,
3. Aktien oder Zwischenscheine ausgibt, die auf einen geringeren als den nach § 8 Abs. 2 Satz 1 zulässigen Mindestnennbetrag lauten oder auf die bei einer Gesellschaft mit Stückaktien ein geringerer anteiliger Betrag des Grundkapitals als der

or the insurance companies within the meaning of Article 2 para. 1 of Council Directive 91/674/EWG of 19 December 1991 on the Annual Accounts and Consolidated Accounts of Insurance undertakings (ABl. L 374, 31.12.1991, p.7) as last amended by Directive 2006/46/EG (ABl. L 224, 16.08.2006, p.1) shall be punished with imprisonment of up to one year or a fine

1. if the person commits an action mentioned in sec. 405 paras. 3b, 3c or para. 3d and gains a pecuniary advantage or obtains such a promise or
2. if the person persistently repeated an action mentioned in sec. 405 paras. 3b, 3c or para. 3d.

§ 405 Administrative offenses.

(1) An administrative offense shall be deemed to have been committed by any person who as a member of the management board or the supervisory board or as a liquidator

1. issues registered share certificates which fail to state the amount of the partial contribution or issues bearer share certificates before the issue price thereof has been paid in full,
2. issues share certificates or interim certificates before the company or in the event of a capital increase the implementation of the increase of the registered share capital or in the event of a contingent capital increase or a capital increase from company resources the resolution on the contingent capital increase or the capital increase from company resources has been registered,
3. issues share certificates or interim certificates for an amount less than the minimum nominal amount pursuant to sec. 8 para. 2 sentence 1 or, in the case of a company with non-par value shares, issues share certificates or interim certificates which have been allocated a pro-

nach § 8 Abs. 3 Satz 3 zulässige Mindestbetrag entfällt, oder

4. a) entgegen § 71 Abs. 1 Nr. 1 bis 4 oder Abs. 2 eigene Aktien der Gesellschaft erwirbt oder, in Verbindung mit § 71e Abs. 1, als Pfand nimmt,
   b) zu veräußernde eigene Aktien (§ 71c Abs. 1 und 2) nicht anbietet oder
   c) die zur Vorbereitung der Beschlußfassung über die Einziehung eigener Aktien (§ 71c Abs. 3) erforderlichen Maßnahmen nicht trifft.

(2) Ordnungswidrig handelt auch, wer als Aktionär oder als Vertreter eines Aktionärs die nach § 129 in das Verzeichnis aufzunehmenden Angaben nicht oder nicht richtig macht.

(2a) Ordnungswidrig handelt, wer entgegen § 67 Abs. 4 Satz 2, auch in Verbindung mit Satz 3, eine Mitteilung nicht oder nicht richtig macht.

(3) Ordnungswidrig handelt ferner, wer

1. Aktien eines anderen, zu dessen Vertretung er nicht befugt ist, ohne dessen Einwilligung zur Ausübung von Rechten in der Hauptversammlung oder in einer gesonderten Versammlung benutzt,
2. zur Ausübung von Rechten in der Hauptversammlung oder in einer gesonderten Versammlung Aktien eines anderen benutzt, die er sich zu diesem Zweck durch Gewähren oder Versprechen besonderer Vorteile verschafft hat,
3. Aktien zu dem in Nummer 2 bezeichneten Zweck gegen Gewähren

portionate amount of the registered share capital which is lower than the minimum amount pursuant to sec. 8 para. 3 sentence 3, or

4. a) acquires own shares in violation of sec. 71 para. 1 nos. 1 to 4 or para. 2 or, in connection with sec. 71e para. 1, takes such shares in pledge,
   b) fails to offer own shares which are to be sold (sec. 71c paras. 1 and 2) or
   c) fails to take the necessary measures for the preparation of the adoption of a resolution on the withdrawal of own shares (sec. 71c para. 3).

(2) An administrative offense shall also be deemed to have been committed by any person who as a shareholder or the representative of a shareholder fails to give or to give correctly the information which is to be included in the register pursuant to sec. 129.

(2a) An administrative offense shall also be deemed to have been committed by any person who, contrary to sec. 67 para. 4 sentence 2, also in connection with sentence 3, does not make a notification or makes it incorrectly.

(3) Furthermore, an administrative offense shall be deemed to have been committed by anyone who

1. uses shares belonging to another person whom he is not entitled to represent in order to exercise rights in the general meeting or in a separate meeting without first obtaining the consent of such person,
2. uses shares belonging to another person which he has obtained for this purpose by granting or promising special benefits in order to exercise rights in the general meeting or in a separate meeting,
3. lets another use shares for the purpose stipulated in no. 2 in return for

oder Versprechen besonderer Vorteile einem anderen überläßt,
4. Aktien eines anderen, für die er oder der von ihm Vertretene das Stimmrecht nach § 135 nicht ausüben darf, zur Ausübung des Stimmrechts benutzt,

5. Aktien, für die er oder der von ihm Vertretene das Stimmrecht nach § 20 Abs. 7, § 21 Abs. 4, §§ 71b, 71d Satz 4, § 134 Abs. 1, §§ 135, 136, 142 Abs. 1 Satz 2, § 285 Abs. 1 nicht ausüben darf, einem anderen zum Zweck der Ausübung des Stimmrechts überläßt oder solche ihm überlassene Aktien zur Ausübung des Stimmrechts benutzt,

6. besondere Vorteile als Gegenleistung dafür fordert, sich versprechen läßt oder annimmt, daß er bei einer Abstimmung in der Hauptversammlung oder in einer gesonderten Versammlung nicht oder in einem bestimmten Sinne stimme oder

7. besondere Vorteile als Gegenleistung dafür anbietet, verspricht oder gewährt, daß jemand bei einer Abstimmung in der Hauptversammlung oder in einer gesonderten Versammlung nicht oder in einem bestimmten Sinne stimme.

(3a) Ordnungswidrig handelt, wer vorsätzlich oder leichtfertig

1. entgegen § 121 Abs. 4a Satz 1, auch in Verbindung mit § 124 Abs. 1 Satz 3, die Einberufung nicht, nicht richtig, nicht vollständig oder nicht rechtzeitig zuleitet oder

2. entgegen § 124a Angaben nicht, nicht richtig oder nicht vollständig zugänglich macht.

(3b) Ordnungswidrig handelt, wer als Mitglied des Aufsichtsrats oder als Mitglied eines Prüfungsausschusses einer Gesellschaft, die kapitalmarkto-

granting or promising special benefits,
4. uses shares belonging to another person for which he or the person represented by him may not exercise the voting right pursuant to sec. 135 for the purpose of exercising the voting right,

5. lets another use shares for which he or the person represented by him may not exercise the voting right pursuant to sec. 20 para. 7, sec. 21 para. 4, sec. 71b, 71d sentence 4, sec. 134 para. 1, sec. 135, 136, 142 para. 1 sentence 2, sec. 285 para. 1 for the purpose of exercising the voting right or uses such shares which have been transferred to him in order to exercise the voting right,

6. demands, is promised or accepts special benefits in return for not voting or voting in a certain way in a vote held in the general meeting or a separate meeting or

7. offers, promises or grants special benefits in return for someone not voting or voting in a certain way in a vote held in the general meeting or a separate meeting.

(3a) An administrative offense shall be deemed to have been committed by any person who intentionally or recklessly

1. contrary to sec. 121 para. 4a sentence 1, also in connection with sec. 124 para. 1 sentence 3, fails to send the notification of convening of the meeting incorrectly, incompletely or not in time or

2. contrary to sec. 124a fails to make accessible information incorrectly or incompletely.

(3b) An administrative offense shall be deemed to have been committed by any person who as a member of the supervisory board or member of the audit com-

rientiert im Sinne des § 264d des Handelsgesetzbuchs, die CRR-Kreditinstitut im Sinne des § 1 Absatz 3d Satz 1 des Kreditwesengesetzes, mit Ausnahme der in § 2 Absatz 1 Nummer 1 und 2 des Kreditwesengesetzes genannten Institute, oder die Versicherungsunternehmen ist im Sinne des Artikels 2 Absatz 1 der Richtlinie 91/674/EWG des Rates vom 19. Dezember 1991 über den Jahresabschluß und den konsolidierten Abschluß von Versicherungsunternehmen (ABl. L 374 vom 31.12.1991, S. 7), die zuletzt durch die Richtlinie 2006/46/EG (ABl. L 224 vom 16.8.2006, S. 1) geändert worden ist,

1. die Unabhängigkeit des Abschlussprüfers oder der Prüfungsgesellschaft nicht nach Maßgabe des Artikels 4 Absatz 3 Unterabsatz 2, des Artikels 5 Absatz 4 Unterabsatz 1 Satz 1 oder des Artikels 6 Absatz 2 der Verordnung (EU) Nr. 537/2014 des Europäischen Parlaments und des Rates vom 16. April 2014 über spezifische Anforderungen an die Abschlussprüfung bei Unternehmen von öffentlichem Interesse und zur Aufhebung des Beschlusses 2005/909/EG der Kommission (ABl. L 158 vom 27.5.2014, S. 77, L 170 vom 11.6.2014, S. 66) überwacht oder
2. eine Empfehlung für die Bestellung eines Abschlussprüfers oder einer Prüfungsgesellschaft vorlegt, die den Anforderungen nach Artikel 16 Absatz 2 Unterabsatz 2 oder 3 der Verordnung (EU) Nr. 537/2014 nicht entspricht oder der ein Auswahlverfahren nach Artikel 16 Absatz 3 Unterabsatz 1 der Verordnung (EU) Nr. 537/2014 nicht vorangegangen ist.

(3c) Ordnungswidrig handelt, wer als Mitglied eines Aufsichtsrats, der einen Prüfungsausschuss nicht bestellt hat, einer in Absatz 3b genannten Gesellschaft der Hauptversammlung einen Vorschlag für die Bestellung eines Abschlussprüfers oder einer Prü-

mittee of a company within the meaning of sec. 264d of the Commercial Code, the CRR- credit institutions within the meaning of sec. 1 para. 3d sentence 1 of the German Banking Act, with the exception of the institutions mentioned in sec. 2 para. 1 number 1 and 2 of the German Banking Act or the insurance companies within the meaning of Article 2 para. 1 of Council Directive 91/674/EWG of 19 December 1991 on the Annual Accounts and Consolidated Accounts of Insurance undertakings (ABl. L 374, 31.12.1991, p.7) as last amended by Directive 2006/46/EG (ABl. L 224, 16.08.2006, p.1)

1. does not monitor the auditor's or audit firm's independence in accordance with the second subparagraph of Article 4(3), the first subparagraph sentence 1 of Article 5(4) or Article 6(2) of Regulation (EU) No. 537/2014 of the European Parliament and the Council of April, 16, 2014 on Specific Requirements Regarding Statutory Audit of Public-Interest Entities and repealing Commission Decision 2005/909/EC (ABl. L 158 dated 27.05.2014, pg. 77, L 170 dated 11.06.2014, pg. 66) or

2. presents a recommendation for an auditor or an audit firm, which does not satisfy the requirements named in the second or third subparagraph of Article 16(2) of Regulation (EU) No. 537/2014 or to which no selection process within the meaning of the first subparagraph of article 16(3) of Regulation (EU) No. 537/2014 has been conducted.

(3c) An administrative offense shall be deemed to have been committed by any person who as a member of the supervisory board, who has not appointed the audit committee, submits a proposal concerning the appointment of the auditor or an audit firm to a company

fungsgesellschaft vorlegt, der den Anforderungen nach Artikel 16 Absatz 5 Unterabsatz 1 der Verordnung (EU) Nr. 537/2014 nicht entspricht.

(3d) Ordnungswidrig handelt, wer als Mitglied eines Aufsichtsrats, der einen Prüfungsausschuss bestellt hat, einer in Absatz 3b genannten Gesellschaft der Hauptversammlung einen Vorschlag für die Bestellung eines Abschlussprüfers oder einer Prüfungsgesellschaft vorlegt, der den Anforderungen nach Artikel 16 Absatz 5 Unterabsatz 1 oder Unterabsatz 2 Satz 1 oder Satz 2 der Verordnung (EU) Nr. 537/2014 nicht entspricht.

(4) Die Ordnungswidrigkeit kann in den Fällen der Absätze 3b bis 3d mit einer Geldbuße bis zu fünfzigtausend f Euro; in den übrigen Fällen mit einer Geldbuße bis zu fünfundzwanzigtausend Euro geahndet werden.

(5) Verwaltungsbehörde im Sinne des § 36 Absatz 1 Nummer 1 des Gesetzes über Ordnungswidrigkeiten ist in den Fällen der Absätze 3b bis 3d bei CRR-Kreditinstituten im Sinne des § 1 Absatz 3d Satz 1 des Kreditwesengesetzes, mit Ausnahme der in § 2 Absatz 1 Nummer 1 und 2 des Kreditwesengesetzes genannten Institute, und bei Versicherungsunternehmen im Sinne des Artikels 2 Absatz 1 der Richtlinie 91/674/EWG die Bundesanstalt für Finanzdienstleistungsaufsicht, im Übrigen das Bundesamt für Justiz.

mentioned in paragraph 3b, which does not fulfill the requirements of the first subparagraph of Article 16(5) or the first or second sentence of the second subparagraph of Article 16(5) of Regulation (EC) No. 537/2014.

(3d) An administrative offense shall be deemed to have been committed by any person who as a member of the supervisory board, who has appointed the audit committee, submits a proposal concerning the appointment of the auditor or an audit firm to a company mentioned in paragraph 3b, which does not fulfill the requirements of the first subparagraph of Article 16(5) of Regulation (EC) No. 537/2014.

(4) The administrative offense may be punished in the cases of paragraphes 3b to 3d by a fine of up to fifty thousand euros; in all other cases by a fine of up to twenty five thousand euros

(5) The administrative authority in the sense of sec. 36 para. 1 no. 1 of the Code of Administrative Offences is in the cases of paragraphs 3b to 3d on CRR- credit institutions within the meaning of sec. 1 para. 3d sentence 1 of the German Banking Act, with the exception of the institutions mentioned in sec. 2 para. 1 number 1 and 2 of the German Banking Act or the insurance companies within the meaning of Article 2 para. 1 of Council Directive 91/674/EWG, the Federal Agency for Financial Services Supervision, in all other cases the Federal Office of Justice.

§ 406 *(aufgehoben)*

§ 407 Zwangsgelder.

(1) ¹Vorstandsmitglieder oder Abwickler, die § 52 Abs. 2 Satz 2 bis 4, § 71c, § 73 Abs. 3 Satz 2, §§ 80, 90, 104 Abs. 1, § 111 Abs. 2, § 145, §§ 170, 171 Abs. 3 oder Abs. 4 Satz 1 in Verbindung mit Abs. 3, §§ 175, 179a Abs. 2 Satz 1 bis 3,

§ 406 *(repealed)*

§ 407 Administrative fines.

(1) ¹The register court shall impose administrative fines on members of the management board or liquidators who fail to comply with sec. 52 para. 2 sentences 2 to 4, sec. 71c, sec. 73 para. 3 sentence 2, sec. 80, 90, 104 para. 1, sec. 111

214 Abs. 1, § 246 Abs. 4, §§ 248a, 259 Abs. 5, § 268 Abs. 4, § 270 Abs. 1, § 273 Abs. 2, §§ 293f, 293g Abs. 1, § 312 Abs. 1, § 313 Abs. 1, § 314 Abs. 1 nicht befolgen, sind hierzu vom Registergericht durch Festsetzung von Zwangsgeld anzuhalten; § 14 des Handelsgesetzbuchs bleibt unberührt. ²Das einzelne Zwangsgeld darf den Betrag von fünftausend Euro nicht übersteigen.

(2) Die Anmeldungen zum Handelsregister nach den §§ 36, 45, 52, 181 Abs. 1, §§ 184, 188, 195, 210, 223, 237 Abs. 4, §§ 274, 294 Abs. 1, § 319 Abs. 3 werden durch Festsetzung von Zwangsgeld nicht erzwungen.

§ 407a Mitteilungen an die Abschlussprüferaufsichtsstelle

(1) Die nach § 405 Absatz 5 zuständige Verwaltungsbehörde übermittelt der Abschlussprüferaufsichtsstelle beim Bundesamt für Wirtschaft und Ausfuhrkontrolle alle Bußgeldentscheidungen nach § 405 Absatz 3b bis 3d.

(2) ¹In Strafverfahren, die eine Straftat nach § 404a zum Gegenstand haben, übermittelt die Staatsanwaltschaft im Falle der Erhebung der öffentlichen Klage der Abschlussprüferaufsichtsstelle die das Verfahren abschließende Entscheidung. ²Ist gegen die Entscheidung ein Rechtsmittel eingelegt worden, ist die Entscheidung unter Hinweis auf das eingelegte Rechtsmittel zu übermitteln.

§ 408 Strafbarkeit persönlich haftender Gesellschafter einer Kommanditgesellschaft auf Aktien.

¹Die §§ 399 bis 407 gelten sinngemäß für die Kommanditgesellschaft auf Aktien. ²Soweit sie Vorstandsmitglieder betreffen, gelten sie bei der Kommanditgesellschaft auf Aktien für die persönlich haftenden Gesellschafter.

para. 2, sec. 145, sec. 170, 171 para. 3 or para. 4 sentence 1 in connection with para. 3, sec. 175, 179a para. 2 sentences 1 to 3, 214 para. 1, sec. 246 para. 4, sec. 248a, sec. 259 para. 5, sec. 268 para. 4, sec. 270 para. 1, sec. 273 para. 2, sec. 293f, 293g para. 1, sec. 312 para. 1, sec. 313 para. 1, sec. 314 para. 1; sec. 14 of the Commercial Code shall remain unaffected. ²Each individual administrative fine may not exceed the amount of five thousand euros.

(2) Applications to the commercial register pursuant to sec. 36, 45, 52, 181 para. 1, sec. 184, 188, 195, 210, 223, 237 para. 4, sec. 274, 294 para. 1, sec. 319 para. 3 shall not be enforced by imposing of administrative fines.

§ 407a Notification to the Agency for auditor's supervision

(1) The administrative authority referred to in sec. 405 para. 5 shall convey all fines decisions referring to sec. 405 paras. 3b to 3d to the Federal Office of Economics and Export Control.

(2) ¹In criminal proceedings, which involve an offence referring to sec. 404a, shall the public prosecutor's office convey the decision closing the procedure to the agency for auditor' supervision, in the event of public charges. ²If an appeal has been lodged against the court's decision, the decision shall be conveyed referring to the lodged appeal.

§ 408 Criminal liability of personally liable partners of a partnership limited by shares.

¹Sec. 399 to 407 shall apply accordingly to a partnership limited by shares. ²Those provisions that apply to members of the management board shall apply to the personally liable partners in the case of a partnership limited by shares.

§ 409 Geltung in Berlin.
(gegenstandslos)

§ 410 Inkrafttreten.

Dieses Gesetz tritt am 1. Januar 1966 in Kraft.

§ 409 Applicability in Berlin.
(obsolete)

§ 410 Effective date.

This Act shall come into force on January 1, 1966.

Appendix 1

Comparison between the Legal Forms of an AG and a GmbH

	GmbH[1]		AG[2]	
General	– Simple form of a corporation, relatively easy to set up and operate. – Shareholder has far-reaching influence on management, in particular comprehensive rights to issue instructions and obtain information. – Management may be dismissed at any time. – Shares not admissible to stock exchange trading.		– Typical legal form for a larger scale enterprise. – Shares admissible to stock exchange trading. – Stricter and more formal requirements than for a *GmbH*. – Management is not bound by instructions issued by shareholders. – Right of shareholders to obtain information more limited.	
Own Shares	– As a general rule, a *GmbH* may hold its own shares.	sec. 33	– An *AG* may acquire and hold its own shares only in exceptional cases and on a limited scale.	sec. 71
Assignment of Shares	– Shares may be sold and assigned by notarized agreement. – Articles of association may impose an impediment to assignment (e.g., by stipulating the need for the consent of the company or shareholders).	sec. 15	– As a general rule, informal assignment of shares is possible. – The company's articles of association may impose restrictions (e.g., the need for approval by the company).	
Liability of the Shareholders for Contributions	– Joint and several liability of the shareholders for contributions in arrears.	sec. 24	– Each shareholder is only liable for his own contribution. – No joint and several liability. – Release from liability not possible.	sec. 54 sec. 66

[1] References are to the Limited Liability Company Act, unless otherwise indicated.
[2] References are to the Stock Corporation Act, unless otherwise indicated.

	GmbH[1]		AG[2]	
Codetermination	– Up to 500 employees: no codetermination. – More than 500 but at most 2,000 employees: One third of supervisory board made up of employee representatives (special requirements if Coal, Iron and Steel Codetermination Act applies). – More than 2,000 employees: Half of supervisory board made up of employee representatives (board chairman has casting vote).	sec. 1, sec. 4 of the One-Third Participation Act sec. 1 para. 1 of the Codetermination Act	– Codetermination is the rule. – Up to 2,000 employees: One third of supervisory board made up of employee representatives (special requirements if Coal, Iron and Steel Codetermination Act applies). Exception: No codetermination if AG has less than 500 employees and was registered after August 9, 1994. – More than 2,000 employees: Half of supervisory board made up of employee representatives (board chairman has casting vote).	sec. 1, sec. 4 of the One-Third Participation Act sec. 1 para. 1 of the Codetermination Act
Corporate Bodies	– Managing director(s) – Supervisory board (optional in general but required in the case of a codetermined *GmbH*) – Shareholder meeting		– Management board – Supervisory board – General meeting	
Managing Directors/ Management Board				
– Appointment	– One or more managing directors. – By the shareholder meeting, unless an obligatory supervisory board exists pursuant to the Codetermination Act. – The shareholder meeting is also competent to conclude employment contracts. – No limits as to the term of office.	sec. 6 para. 1 sec. 46 no. 5	– One or more members of the management board. – By the supervisory board for terms of up to five years. – This power of appointment may not be delegated to a committee of the supervisory board. – The supervisory board is also competent to conclude employment contracts. – Reappointments are permitted.	sec. 76 para. 2 sec. 84 para. 1 sec. 107 para. 3 sentence 4

Appendix 1

	GmbH[1]		AG[2]	
- Dismissal	- By the shareholder meeting, unless an obligatory supervisory board exists pursuant to the Codetermination Act. - If the Codetermination Act does not apply, dismissal is possible at any time. - If the Codetermination Act applies, the supervisory board may dismiss only for good cause.	sec. 38, sec. 46 no. 5 sec. 31 of the Codetermination Act, sec. 84 para. 3 of the Stock Corporation Act	- By the supervisory board. - Only for good cause. - Examples of good cause: gross breach of duty, vote of no confidence by general meeting.	sec. 84 para. 3
- Duties	**Representation** - The managing directors' power of representation vis-à-vis third parties is, as a rule, unlimited and non-restrictable. - If there is more than one managing director, the managing directors are only authorized to represent the company jointly. Sole power of representation may be granted.	sec. 35 para. 1, sec. 37 sec. 35 para. 2	**Representation** - The power of representation of the management board members vis-à-vis third parties is, as a general rule, unlimited and non-restrictable. - If there is more than one member of the management board, the members are only authorized to represent the company jointly, unless the articles of association provide otherwise.	sec. 78, sec. 82 exceptions: sec. 50, sec. 52, sec. 89, sec. 112. sec. 78 para. 2, sec. 78 para. 3, 4

	GmbH[1]		AG[2]	
	Management – Joint management, but division of responsibilities customary. Appointment of a chairman possible. – Authority to manage may be restricted and (to a great extent) withdrawn in the articles of association or by instructions contained in shareholder resolutions.	sec. 45 para. 1	**Management** – Joint management, but division of responsibilities customary. Appointment of a chairman possible. – The authority to manage is, as a general rule, unrestricted and may not be withdrawn. It may, however, be subject to limitations, in particular by implementing a provision in the articles of association, or, in the absence of such provision, by a resolution of the supervisory board, according to which certain management acts require the consent of the supervisory board.	sec. 76 para. 1, sec. 77 sec. 111 para. 4 sentence 2
– Instructions	– The shareholder meeting or the sole shareholder has extensive power to issue instructions to the managing directors.	sec. 37 para. 1, sec. 45	– The management board is responsible for managing the company in its own discretion. – The shareholders do not have the power to issue binding instructions. – The authority to manage may be limited only through consent requirements in favor of the supervisory board (see above).	sec. 76 sec. 111 para. 4
Supervisory Board	– Optional if not more than 500 employees, otherwise obligatory. – As a general rule, the provisions of the Stock Corporation Act apply to an obligatory supervisory board.	sec. 1 of the One-Third Participation Act sec. 1 para. 1 of the Codetermination Act	– Obligatory	sec. 95 et seq.

	GmbH[1]		AG[2]	
– Composition	– More than 500 but at most 2,000 employees: 2/3 representatives of the shareholders, 1/3 representatives of the employees (special requirements if Coal, Iron and Steel Codetermination Act applies). – More than 2,000 employees: Half of supervisory board made up of employee representatives (board chairman has casting vote).	sec. 1, sec. 4 of the One-Third Participation Act sec. 1 para. 1, sec. 7 of the Codetermination Act	– Up to 500 employees: If the AG was registered after August 9, 1994, the supervisory board is made up of shareholder representatives only. – More than 500 but at most 2,000 employees: 2/3 representatives of the shareholders, 1/3 representatives of the employees (special requirements if Coal, Iron and Steel Codetermination Act applies). – More than 2,000 employees: Half of supervisory board made up of employee representatives (board chairman has casting vote).	sec. 1 para. 1 no. 1 of the One-Third Participation Act sec. 1, sec. 4 of the One-Third Participation Act sec. 1 para. 1, sec. 7 of the Codetermination Act
– Appointment	– Shareholder representatives are elected by the shareholder meeting. – Employee representatives are elected in accordance with the relevant law governing codetermination. – The articles of association may provide for a right of certain shareholders to delegate up to one third of the members of the supervisory board.	sec. 101 of the Stock Corporation Act	– Shareholder representatives are elected by the general meeting for terms of up to five years. – The articles of association may provide for a right of certain shareholders to delegate up to one third of the members of the supervisory board.	sec. 101, sec. 102 para. 1
– Dismissal	– Dismissal possible at any time by those with a power of delegation. – By shareholder meeting with a majority of 75% of the votes cast (or a different majority stipulated in the articles of association).	sec. 103 of the Stock Corporation Act	– Dismissal possible at any time by those with a power of delegation. – By general meeting at any time with a majority of 75% of the votes cast (or a different majority stipulated in the articles of association).	sec. 103

	GmbH[1]		AG[2]	
– Duties	– In the case of an obligatory supervisory board, stock corporation law applies to a great extent (important exception: shareholder meeting still competent to appoint and dismiss the managing directors). – In the case of an optional supervisory board, the rights and duties are governed by the articles of association. – The supervisory board must as a minimum be competent to supervise the managing directors.	sec. 52 para. 1	– Appointment and dismissal of the members of the management board. – Supervision of the management board, in particular making use of the right to obtain information and to inspect the books of the AG. – Representation of the AG vis-à-vis members of the management board. – Review of the annual financial statements. – Convening of the general meeting if the interests of the company so require. – No authority to manage the company but consent requirements may exist (see above).	sec. 84 sec. 90, sec. 111 para. 1 sec. 89, sec. 112 sec. 171 sec. 111 para. 3 sec. 111 para. 4 sentence 2
Gender Quota				
– Supervisory Board			– If the AG has more than 2,000 employees and is admitted to stock exchange trading: A fixed gender quota of 30% must be observed for both male and female supervisory board members.	sec. 96 para. 2

Appendix 1

	GmbH[1]		AG[2]	
Managing Directors/ Management Board	– More than 500 but at most 2,000 employees: The shareholder meeting must determine target figures for the proportion of women in the supervisory board and amongst the managing directors. – More than 2,000 employees: The supervisory board must determine target figures for the proportion of women in the supervisory board and amongst the managing directors. – If the proportion of women at the time of determination is below 30%, the target figures may not be lower than the respective status quo.	sec. 52 para. 2	– The supervisory board must determine target figures for the proportion of women in the supervisory board and the management board. If the proportion of women at the time of determination is below 30%, the target figures may not be lower than the respective status quo. – Exception: No target figures required if the AG has less than 500 employees *and* is not admitted to stock exchange trading.	sec. 111 para. 5
Senior Management	– If the *GmbH* has more than 500 employees, the managing directors must determine target figures for the proportion of women in the two levels of senior management below the managing directors. If the proportion of women at the time of determination is below 30%, the target figures may not be lower than the respective status quo.	sec. 36	– The management board must determine target figures for the proportion of women in the two levels of senior management below the management board. If the proportion of women at the time of determination is below 30%, the target figures may not be lower than the respective status quo. – Exception: No target figures required if the *AG* has less than 500 employees *and* is not admitted to stock exchange trading.	sec. 76 para. 4
Shareholder Meeting/ General Meeting				

	GmbH[1]		AG[2]	
– Convening	– Meetings of the shareholders are convened by one or more of the managing directors.	sec. 49 para. 1	– General meetings are in general convened by the management board; by individual shareholders if the articles of association so provide; by the supervisory board in exceptional cases.	sec. 121 para. 2 sentence 1,2, sec. 121 para. 2 sentence 3, sec. 111 para. 3
	– Convening by registered letter at least one week in advance stating the items on the agenda.	sec. 51	– Meetings must be convened at least 30 days in advance, stating the items of the agenda.	sec. 123 et seq.
	– Time limit on convening and announcing the shareholder meeting may be waived.			
– Decision Making	– In general through shareholder resolutions, requiring a simple majority of the registered share capital voting at the meeting.	sec. 47, sec. 48 para. 1	– By way of resolutions and, as a general rule, with simple majority of the registered share capital present at the meeting.	sec. 133 para. 1
	– Amendments of the articles of association generally require notarization and a 75% majority.	sec. 53 para. 2	– If the articles of association are to be amended (or other important measures are to be decided, such as enterprise agreements or mergers) a 75% majority is required.	sec. 179 para. 2
	– Resolutions may be voted on in writing outside of a physical meeting if all shareholders agree.	sec. 48 para. 2	– Notarization only required for AGs which are admitted to stock exchange trading or if resolutions are adopted for which the law requires a majority of 75% or a larger majority.	sec. 130 para. 1
	– Unanimous resolutions may also be adopted by facsimile or e-mail.	sec. 48 para. 2		

Appendix 1   591

	GmbH[1]		AG[2]	
– Rights and Competencies	– Set forth in articles of association and in statute. – Authority to issue binding instructions to the managing directors. – In general no authority to represent and act on behalf of the company.	sec. 46, sec. 37 para. 1	– Competence for all fundamental decisions, such as: Amendments of the articles of association. Election and dismissal of the shareholder representatives on the supervisory board. Ratification of acts of the management board and the supervisory board. Adoption of resolutions on the appropriation of profits. – As a general rule, no competence for questions regarding the course of business, unless the management board requests a decision of the general meeting.	sec. 119 sec. 179 sec. 101 para. 1, sec. 103 sec. 120 sec. 174 sec. 119 para. 2
Right of Shareholders to Information	– Right to obtain information from managing directors in all company matters. – Right to inspect the company's books and records.	sec. 51a	– Right to demand information from the management board only at general meetings and only insofar as the information is necessary to allow a proper evaluation of an agenda item. – Special reporting obligations of the management board in connection with the exclusion of subscription rights and the conclusion of an enterprise agreement, squeeze outs, mergers etc.	sec. 131 para. 1 sec. 186 para. 4 sentence 2, sec. 293a para. 1, sec. 327c para. 2, sec. 63 of the Transformation Act

	GmbH[1]		AG[2]	
Appropriation and Distribution of Profit and Loss	– The shareholder meeting decides on the appropriation of profits. – As a general rule, the shareholders are entitled to the annual net income plus profit carried forward and minus loss carried forward or to the balance sheet profit. – If the articles of association do not specify otherwise, funds may be allocated to the revenue reserves by shareholder resolution or carried forward as profit. – The prevailing view holds that interim or advance dividends are permitted.	sec. 29 para. 2 sec. 29 para. 1 sec. 29 para. 2	– The management board and supervisory board may allocate a maximum of 50% of the annual net income to other revenue reserves unless the articles of association provide for a greater or smaller amount, however, only insofar as the other revenue reserves do not exceed 50% of the registered share capital. – The formally approved annual financial statements are the basis for the resolution on the appropriation of the balance sheet profit. – Upon proposal of the management board, the general meeting resolves on the appropriation of the balance sheet profit. – Minimum distribution to the shareholders: 4% of the registered share capital. A lower dividend may be contested by the shareholders. – Interim dividends after each fiscal year are possible up to a certain amount if provided for in the articles of association and approved by the supervisory board, provided that the interim financial statements show an annual net income.	sec. 58 para. 2 sec. 174 para. 1 sec. 119 para. 1 no. 2, sec. 170 para. 2, sec. 174 sec. 254 para. 1 sec. 59 para. 2

Appendix 1

	GmbH[1]		AG[2]	
Annual Financial Statements	– To be prepared within three months after the end of the fiscal year (six months in the case of tiny and small corporations). – To be formally approved by the shareholder meeting within eight months after the end of the fiscal year (eleven months in the case of tiny and small corporations).	sec. 264 para. 1 of the Commercial Code sec. 42a para. 2	– Preparation of annual financial statement follows same principles as in case of a *GmbH*. – Formal approval by the management board and supervisory board jointly or the general meeting, at latest within eight months after the end of the fiscal year.	sec. 264 para. 1 of the Commercial Code sec. 172, sec. 173, sec. 175 para. 1
Duty to Have Annual Financial Statements and the Management Report Audited	No difference.			
Duty to Disclose and Announce Annual Financial Statements and Management Report	No difference. Stock corporations listed on a stock exchange may be obliged to issue annual and biannual finance reports as well as interim notifications pursuant to sec. 37v et seq. of the Securities Trading Act.			

Appendix 2

A. Glossary
English – German

English	German	Brief Description
Action for the declaration of nullity of a resolution	Nichtigkeitsklage	Action which can be brought by a shareholder, the management board, the supervisory board and members of both corporate bodies to the Regional Court (*Landgericht*) with respect to a resolution of the general meeting. If the action is successful, the Regional Court states that the resolution is null and void.
Action to set aside a resolution	Anfechtungsklage	Action by which any resolution of the general meeting can be set aside by a shareholder, by the management board and, in certain cases, by members of the supervisory board within a term of one month of the adoption of the resolution. If the action is successful, the Regional Court declares the resolution null and void.
Annual financial statements	Jahresabschluss	Annual accounts of an *AG* or a *GmbH* which are drawn up by the management board (*AG*) or the managing directors (*GmbH*), reviewed by auditors and formally approved by the management board and the supervisory board or, in exceptional cases, by the general meeting (*AG*) or by the shareholder meeting (*GmbH*). The annual financial statements consist of the balance sheet, the profit and loss statement and the notes. Depending on the size of the corporation, a management report may be required in addition. The annual financial statements form the basis for the appropriation of the balance sheet profit. See also balance sheet profit.
Annual net income	Jahresüberschuss	Profit and loss statement position reflecting the income remaining after the deduction of interest, tax and depreciation. The management board and the supervisory board decide on its appropriation before the general meeting resolves on the appropriation of the balance sheet profit.
Annual net loss	Jahresfehlbetrag	Profit and loss statement position reflecting the loss remaining after the deduction of interest, tax and depreciation.

English	German	Brief Description
Approval of the annual financial statements	Billigung des Jahresabschlusses	The supervisory board grants its approval if it has no objections to the annual financial statements and the consolidated financial statements. See also formal approval.
Articles of association	Satzung	Articles of association of an *AG* or a *GmbH* which are determined by the founders and amended by the general meeting (*AG*) or the shareholder meeting (*GmbH*) from time to time thereafter. Amendments of the articles of association require, as a rule, a qualified majority of 75%.
Authorized capital	Genehmigtes Kapital	One of the methods to increase the registered share capital of an *AG* or a *GmbH*. The management board can be authorized by the general meeting or the shareholder meeting for a period of up to five years to increase the registered share capital by up to half of the amount of the existing capital through issuance of new shares against contributions. See also capital increase.
Balance sheet	Bilanz	Part of the annual financial statements.
Balance sheet profit	Bilanzgewinn	A position in the profit and loss statement. The balance sheet profit is the profit that is available for distribution to the shareholders by way of payment of dividends. In an *AG*, the general meeting, which is bound by the formally approved annual financial statements, resolves on the appropriation of the balance sheet profit. In a *GmbH*, the shareholder meeting both approves the annual financial statements and determines the use of the balance sheet profit. See also dividend.
Capital increase	Kapitalerhöhung	Increase of the registered share capital of an *AG* or a *GmbH* against cash contributions or contributions in kind. The general meeting (*AG*) or the shareholder meeting (*GmbH*) is competent to resolve on a capital increase with a majority of generally 75%. The registered share capital of an *AG* can be increased by way of an ordinary capital increase, by making use of authorized capital and contingent capital as well as by a capital increase from company resources. The registered share capital of a *GmbH* can be increased by way of an ordinary capital increase, by making use of authorized capital and by a capital increase from company resources. See also authorized capital, capital increase from company resources and contingent capital.

English	German	Brief Description
Capital increase from company resources	Kapitalerhöhung aus Gesellschaftsmitteln	Capital increase of an *AG* or a *GmbH* where the registered share capital is increased by converting reserves into registered share capital. The corporation therefore does not receive new funds. See also capital increase.
Capital market-oriented corporation	Kapitalmarkt-orientierte Kapitalgesellschaft	Stock corporation which is listed on a stock exchange or has applied for a listing on a stock exchange.
Capital reduction	Kapitalherabsetzung	Reduction of the registered share capital of an *AG* or a *GmbH* where the registered share capital is reduced either by partial distribution of the registered share capital to the shareholders or by adjustment of the registered share capital without distribution to cover losses in the case of a crisis of the company. In the latter case, a so-called simplified capital reduction is also possible and common.
Cash contribution	Bareinlage	Cash payment made by a subscriber to new shares in the context of the formation of a company or a capital increase.
Certified by a notary	notariell beglaubigt	German notaries issue certificates in which they testify that a document has been signed in their presence and that the person signing the document is identical with the person named in the document. See also notarized by a notary.
Codetermination	Mitbestimmung	Participation of the employees in the decision-making process of larger *AGs* or, also, larger *GmbHs*. Such participation is effected by the appointment of employee representatives as full members of the supervisory board.
Commercial register	Handelsregister	Publicly accessible register kept by the Local Courts (*Amtsgerichte*) as register courts which records, inter alia, a set of basic data about every German *AG* and *GmbH*. See also Register Court.
Common direction	Einheitliche Leitung	Common direction is assumed to exist if an enterprise is controlled by a controlling enterprise. See also controlling and controlled enterprise.

English	German	Brief Description
Consolidated financial statements	Konzernabschluss	The consolidated financial statements present the financial situation of a group of companies by reflecting the profitability of the included enterprises in the way in which they would be presented if they formed a single enterprise. The consolidated financial statements consist of a consolidated balance sheet, a consolidated profit and loss statement and consolidated notes. Furthermore, a consolidated management report is required. They are drawn up by the management board and approved by the supervisory board. See also approval of the annual financial statements.
Contingent capital increase	Bedingte Kapitalerhöhung	One of four methods to increase the registered share capital of an *AG*. The scope of application of the contingent capital increase is restricted to a small number of specific situations. Contingent capital can be created, for example, to service convertible and warrant-linked bonds or stock options. Contingent capital cannot be used in a *GmbH*.
Contribution in kind	Sacheinlage	A transfer of assets or rights effected by a subscriber to new shares in the context of the formation of a company or a capital increase.
Controlling and controlled enterprise	Herrschendes und abhängiges Unternehmen	The controlling enterprise can, directly or indirectly, exert dominant influence on the controlled enterprise. If one enterprise holds a majority of the shares of another, it is assumed that the latter is controlled by the former.
Convertible bond	Wandelschuldverschreibung/ Wandelanleihe	Convertible bonds are issued by an *AG* and can be exchanged, after expiry of a certain period of time, for shares in the issuing company.
Dissolution	Auflösung	First stage of the termination process of a corporation. The dissolution must be registered with the commercial register. Following dissolution, the liquidation process commences. See also liquidation.
Dividend	Dividende	The participation of a shareholder in the balance sheet profit of an *AG*.
Domination agreement	Beherrschungsvertrag	Enterprise agreement under which the controlled enterprise submits to the direction of the controlling enterprise which can issue binding instructions to it. The domination agreement leads to an obligation of the controlling enterprise to compensate for any annual net loss of the controlled enterprise, to pay compensation to any co-shareholders and to make a purchase offer against appropriate consideration to co-shareholders. See also enterprise agreement.

English	German	Brief Description
Enterprise agreement	Unternehmensvertrag	Domination agreements, profit transfer agreements, partial profit transfer agreements, profit pool agreements, lease of undertaking agreements and agreements to relinquish undertakings are all forms of enterprise agreements. See also domination agreement and profit transfer agreement.
Entrepreneur Company	Unternehmergesellschaft (UG)	A *GmbH* with a registered share capital of less than EUR 25,000 can be formed but must then call itself "Unternehmergesellschaft (haftungsbeschränkt)" or "UG (haftungsbeschränkt)". A *UG* is in general subject to the same laws as a *GmbH*. Special provisions apply, however, with regard to formation and the appropriation of profits.
Formal approval of the annual financial statements	Feststellung des Jahresabschlusses	The annual financial statements of an *AG* are drawn up by the management board and, afterwards, reviewed by the supervisory board. If the supervisory board has no objections to the annual financial statements, it approves them. If the supervisory board approves the annual financial statements, the annual financial statements are formally approved unless the management board and supervisory board decide that the general meeting has to formally approve the annual financial statements. In the case of a *GmbH*, the shareholder meeting is responsible for formal approval of the annual financial statements.
General meeting	Hauptversammlung	Depending on the context, the term general meeting may have two meanings: (i) one of the three corporate bodies of an *AG* with specific powers provided for in the statutes or (ii) the physical meeting of the shareholders of an *AG*.
German Corporate Governance Code	Deutscher Corporate Governance Kodex	Self-regulatory rules that were designed by an expert committee.
GmbH & Co. KG	GmbH & Co. KG	A *GmbH & Co. KG* is a limited partnership with one or more limited partners and a general partner. The general partner has unlimited liability and is a *GmbH* rather than a natural person.
Group of companies/Group	Konzern	A group of companies exists when one or more controlled enterprises are under the common direction of a controlling enterprise. As a rule, a group of companies is created when an enterprise acquires a majority holding in an *AG* or a *GmbH*. The conclusion of an enterprise agreement may also result in the creation of a group of companies.
Higher Regional Court	Oberlandesgericht (OLG)	Third level in the German four-level hierarchy of civil law courts.

English	German	Brief Description
Indirect subscription right	Mittelbares Bezugsrecht	Subscription rights granted to the shareholders of an *AG* in the case of a capital increase by involving an underwriting syndicate. The underwriting syndicate offers the shares to the holders of the subscription rights on the same terms and conditions as if the shares had been offered directly by the issuing *AG*.
Limited Liability Company	Gesellschaft mit beschränkter Haftung (GmbH)	Separate legal entity for whose liabilities towards third parties the shareholders are generally not liable and the shares of which cannot be admitted to stock exchange trading.
Limited Liability Company Act	GmbH-Gesetz (GmbHG)	Main statute governing the *GmbH*.
Liquidation	Liquidation	After dissolution, the corporation enters the liquidation stage. In this stage, the corporation remains intact as a legal entity but the previous object of the enterprise is replaced by the purpose of liquidation. When liquidation is complete, the company ceases to exist. The liquidator must file for registration of the company's termination with the commercial register.
Local Court	Amtsgericht (AG)	Lowest court in the German four-level hierarchy of civil law courts.
Managing director	Geschäftsführer	Corporate body of a *GmbH*. The managing directors are responsible for the management and representation of the company. A *GmbH* may have one or more managing directors. The managing directors are appointed by the shareholder meeting.
Management board	Vorstand	One of the three corporate bodies of an *AG*. The management board is responsible for the management and representation of the *AG*. The members of the management board are appointed by the supervisory board.
Non-par value shares	Stückaktien	In contrast to par value shares, the participation of non-par value shares is defined as a fraction of the registered share capital of the *AG*, i.e., not by an individual nominal amount. The nominal value of a non-par value share is equal to the total registered share capital divided by the total number of existing shares. See also par value shares.

English	German	Brief Description
Notarized by a notary	notariell beurkundet	Some types of contracts and declarations which are of particular relevance to the respective parties require notarization. Here and in contrast to a mere certification, the notary draws up a notarial deed in which the declarations of the parties are recorded and which is read aloud, word by word, to the parties. The notary reviews the validity of the declarations contained in the notarial deed and advises the parties of their consequences and any dangers attached to them. See also certified by a notary.
Notes	Anhang	Appendix to the annual financial statements of an *AG* or a *GmbH* in which the management must explain positions on the balance sheet and the profit and loss statement.
Par value shares	Nennbetragsaktien	Shares with an individual nominal value printed on the certificate and stated in the articles of association.
Post-formation acquisition	Nachgründung	If the *AG*, within the first two years after its initial registration in the commercial register, concludes a contract concerning the acquisition of assets from founders or from shareholders with a shareholding of more than 10% and if the value of the consideration for such assets exceeds 10% of the registered share capital, such arrangement is called a post-formation acquisition. The contract concerned becomes valid only when the general meeting has granted its consent and when it is registered in the commercial register.
Preference shares	Vorzugsaktien	Shares of a special class which usually do not carry voting rights as long as a preferred dividend is paid.
Pre-registered company (pre-AG / pre-GmbH)	Vorgesellschaft	The pre-registered company (pre-*AG* or pre-*GmbH*) comes into being upon the establishment of the articles of association. It is a sui generis legal entity which corresponds to the future *GmbH* or *AG*. Upon registration in the commercial register, the pre-registered company turns into a corporation with full legal capacity.
Profit transfer agreement	Gewinnabführungsvertrag	Enterprise agreement under which one enterprise must transfer its entire profits to another enterprise. See also enterprise agreement.
Ratification	Entlastung	Resolution of the general meeting (*AG*) or the shareholder meeting (*GmbH*) approving the acts of the management board and the supervisory board (*AG*) or of the managing directors (*GmbH*). For the corporate bodies of *GmbHs*, but not of *AGs*, ratification results in a waiver of any liability claims of the corporation against them.

English	German	Brief Description
Regional Court	Landgericht (LG)	Second level in the German four-level hierarchy of civil law courts.
Register court	Registergericht	Department of the Local Courts (*Amtsgerichte*) which maintains the commercial register. See also commercial register.
Registered share capital	Grundkapital	Nominal share capital of an *AG* which must amount to at least EUR 50,000 and which is divided into shares. See also share.
Registered share capital	Stammkapital	Nominal share capital of a *GmbH* which must amount to at least EUR 25,000 if the company name is to include the designation "GmbH" and which is split into one or more shares. A *GmbH* with a registered share capital of less than EUR 25,000 must call itself *Unternehmergesellschaft* (*UG*). See also share.
Release proceedings	Freigabeverfahren	Proceedings in which a court may decide that a resolution of the general meeting of an *AG* may be registered in the commercial register and thus become effective even though actions to set aside the resolution are still pending.
Share	Geschäftsanteil	The participation in a *GmbH* acquired through subscription. It is not embodied in a share certificate and cannot be admitted to stock exchange trading. The shareholdings are recorded in a shareholder list deposited in the commercial register.
Share	Aktie	Within the Stock Corporation Act, the term share may have one of three meanings: (i) the physical share certificate; (ii) the representation of the membership in the *AG*; (iii) the fraction of the registered share capital.
Shareholder meeting	Gesellschafterversammlung	The shareholder meeting is the *GmbH*'s highest corporate body for the formulation of the objectives of the company in which the shareholders regularly exercise their rights.
Special representative	Besonderer Vertreter	The general meeting of an *AG* may appoint a special representative to assert claims on behalf of the company against founders, members of the management or supervisory board and against persons who have exercised influence on the company to its detriment.
Stock Corporation	Aktiengesellschaft (AG)	The *AG* is a separate legal entity whose registered share capital is divided into shares. The shares in an *AG* can be admitted to stock exchange trading. Only the assets of the *AG* are available to the creditors to satisfy the liabilities of the company.
Subscription right	Bezugsrecht	Right of every shareholder of an *AG* to participate in a capital increase by subscribing to shares on a pro rata basis. This right can be fully or partially excluded under certain conditions.

English	German	Brief Description
Supervisory board	Aufsichtsrat	One of the three corporate bodies of an *AG*. Has responsibility for supervising the activity of the management board of the *AG*. In the case of codetermined *AGs*, its members are elected partly by the general meeting and partly by the employees and, in the case of non-codetermined *AGs*, by the general meeting only. A *GmbH* will form a supervisory board if its articles of association so provide or if it is forced to do so by codetermination law.
Underwriting syndicate	Emissionskonsortium	A group of investment companies which jointly underwrite new shares resulting from a capital increase for the purpose of making such shares available on the capital markets.
Warrant-linked bond	Optionsschuldverschreibungen/ Optionsanleihen	Warrant-linked bonds are issued by an *AG* with warrants that entitle the bearer to buy shares in the issuing company at a predetermined price, usually after a predetermined period of time.

B. Glossary
German – English

Abberufung	dismissal
Abhängiges Unternehmen	controlled enterprise
Abhängigkeitsbericht	report on intra-group relations
Abschlagszahlung	advance payment
Abschlussprüfer	auditor of annual financial statements
Abtretung	assignment
Abwickler	liquidator
Aktie	share
Aktiengattung	class of shares
Aktiengesellschaft (AG)	stock corporation
Aktienregister	share register
Amtsgericht (AG)	Local Court
Amtszeit	term of office
andere Gewinnrücklage	other revenue reserve
Anfechtungsklage	action to set aside a resolution
angemessene Abfindung (i.S.d. § 305 AktG)	appropriate consideration
Anhang	notes
Anlagevermögen	fixed assets
Anschaffungskosten	acquisition costs
Antrag (eines Aktionärs in der Hauptversammlung)	motion
Arbeitnehmervertreter im Aufsichtsrat	employee representative on the supervisory board
Arbeitsrecht	labor law
Auflösung der Gesellschaft	dissolution of the company
Auflösung	dissolution
Aufsichtsrat	supervisory board
Aufwand	expenses
Ausfallhaftung	contingent liability
Ausfertigung	executed copy
Ausgabe einer Aktie	issuance of a share
Auslagenersatz	reimbursement of expenses
Ausschluss (von Aktionären)	expulsion (of shareholders)
außergerichtlich	out of court

Barabfindung (i.S.d. § 305 AktG)	cash consideration
Bareinlage	cash contribution
Bedingte Kapitalerhöhung	contingent capital increase
bedingtes Kapital	contingent capital
beglaubigen	to certify
beglaubigte Abschrift	certified copy
Beherrschungsvertrag	domination agreement
Bekanntmachung	announcement
(gerichtlicher) Beschluss	(court) order
beschlussfähig sein	to have a quorum
Beschwerde	appeal
besonderer Vertreter	special representative
(uneingeschränkter) Bestätigungsvermerk des Abschlussprüfers	(unqualified) certification of the auditor of annual financial statements
Betriebspachtvertrag	lease of undertaking
Betriebsrat	works council
Betriebsüberlassungsvertrag	agreement to relinquish undertaking
beurkunden	to notarize
Bezugserklärung	exercise notice
Bezugsrecht	subscription right
Bilanz	balance sheet
Bilanzgewinn	balance sheet profit
Billigung des Jahresabschlusses	approval of the annual financial statements
börsennotiert	listed (or: admitted to stock exchange trading)
Bundesanzeiger	Federal Gazette
Bundesgerichtshof	Federal Supreme Court
Deutscher Corporate Governance Kodex	German Corporate Governance Code
Dividende	dividend
Dividendenschein, Gewinnanteilschein	dividend coupon
Drittelbeteiligungsgesetz	One-Third Participation Act
eigene Anteile	own shares
einen Beschluss fassen	to adopt a resolution
einen Mangel heilen	to cure a defect
einfordern (von Leistungen/Einlagen)	to call in (performances/contributions)
Einheitliche Leitung	common direction

Einlagen	contributions
Ein-Mann Gesellschaft	single-shareholder company
Einzahlen des Ausgabebetrags	to pay in the issue price
Einzelkaufmann	sole proprietor
Einziehung von Aktien	redemption of shares
Emissionskonsortium	underwriting syndicate
Entlastung (des Vorstands, Aufsichtsrats, von Geschäftsführern)	ratification of the acts (of the management board, supervisory board, managing directors)
Entlastung	ratification
entsprechend	accordingly
Errichtung	establishment
Ersatzmitglieder	substitute members
Ertrag / Erträge	income
Feststellung der Satzung	establishment of the articles of association
Feststellung des Jahresabschlusses	formal approval of the annual financial statements
Freigabeverfahren	release proceedings
Freiheitsstrafe	imprisonment
fristlose Kündigung	termination without notice
Gegenantrag (eines Aktionärs in der Hauptversammlung)	counter motion (of a shareholder in the general meeting)
Gegenstand des Unternehmens	object of the enterprise
Geldstrafe	fine
Gemeinwohl	public interest
Genehmigtes Kapital	authorized capital
Genussrecht	jouissance right
gerichtlich	in court
gerichtliche Entscheidung	court decision
gerichtliche Verfügung	court ruling
geringster Ausgabebetrag	lowest issue price
Geschäftsanteil	share
Geschäftsführer	managing director
Geschäftsjahr	fiscal year
Geschäftsordnung	rules of procedure
Geschäftsräume	offices
Geschäftssitz	registered office
Gesellschaft mit beschränkter Haftung (GmbH)	Limited Liability Company

Gesellschafterbeschluss	shareholder resolution
Gesellschafterversammlung	shareholder meeting
Gesellschaftsblätter	the company's designated journals
Gesellschaftsbücher	company's books
Gesellschaftsmittel	company resources
Gesellschaftsvermögen	corporate assets
Gesellschaftsvertrag	articles of association
gesetzliche Rücklage	statutory reserve
Gewinn- und Verlustrechnung	profit and loss statement
Gewinn	profit
Gewinnabführungsvertrag	profit transfer agreement
Gewinnausschüttung	distribution of profits
Gewinngemeinschaft	profit pool
Gewinnrücklage	revenue reserve
Gewinnschuldverschreibung	dividend bond
Gewinnverwendung	appropriation of profits
Gewinnverwendungsbeschluss	resolution on the appropriation of profits
Gewinnvortrag	profit carried forward
GmbH & Co. KG	*GmbH & Co. KG* (limited partnership with a *GmbH* as general partner)
GmbH-Gesetz (GmbHG)	Limited Liability Company Act
grobe Fahrlässigkeit	gross negligence
Grundbuch	land register
Gründer	founder
Grundkapital	registered share capital
Gründung	formation
Gründungsbericht	formation report
Gründungsprüfer	formation auditor
Handelsregister	commercial register
Handlungsbevollmächtigter	authorized signatory
Hauptversammlung	general meeting
herrschende Meinung	prevailing view
herrschendes Unternehmen	controlling enterprise
Herstellungskosten	production costs
in Rücklagen einstellen	to allocate to reserves
Inhaber einer Anleihe	holder of a bond
Insolvenz	insolvency
Insolvenzverwalter	insolvency administrator

Jahresabschluss	annual financial statements
Jahresfehlbetrag	annual net loss
Jahresüberschuss	annual net income
Kaduzierung	forfeiture of shares
Kapitalerhöhung	capital increase
Kapitalerhöhung aus Gesellschaftsmitteln	capital increase from company resources
Kapitalgesellschaft	corporation
Kapitalherabsetzung	capital reduction
Konzern	group of companies
Konzernabschluss	consolidated financial statements
Kreditinstitut	credit institution
Kündigung	termination
Lagebericht	management report
Landgericht (LG)	Regional Court
Liquidation	liquidation
Liquidationserlös	liquidation proceeds
Maßnahme der Geschäftsführung	management measure
Mehrstimmrechte	multiple voting rights
Mitbestimmung	codetermination
Mitbestimmungsgesetz	Codetermination Act
Mittelbares Bezugsrecht	indirect subscription right
Muttergesellschaft	parent company
Nachgründung	post-formation acquisition
Nachgründungsbericht	post-formation report
Nachschuss	additional contribution
Namensaktie	registered share
Nebenverpflichtung	ancillary duty
Nennbetrag	nominal value
Nennbetragsaktien	par value shares
Nichtigkeit des Gesellschaftsvertrags	nullity of the articles of association
Nichtigkeitsklage	action for declaration of nullity of a resolution
Niederschrift	minutes
notariell beglaubigt	certified by a notary
notariell beurkundet	notarized by a notary

Oberlandesgericht (OLG)	Higher Regional Court
Optionsschuldverschreibung/ Optionsanleihe	warrant-linked bond
ordentliche Kündigung	ordinary termination with notice
ordentlicher Geschäftsmann	prudent businessman
ordentlicher und gewissenhafter Geschäftsleiter	diligent and conscientious manager
Organ (einer Gesellschaft)	corporate body
Passivposten (Bilanz)	debit item
Prokurist	procuration officer
Rechtskraft	res judicata
rechtskräftig (sein)	(being) res judicata
Registergericht	Register Court
Rücklagen auflösen	to release a reserve
Rücklagen bilden	to provide a reserve
Rückstellung auflösen	to reverse an accrual
Rückstellung	accrual
Rückstellungen bilden	to set up an accrual
Rumpfgeschäftsjahr	partial fiscal year
Sacheinlage	contribution in kind
Sachgründungsbericht	report on formation through contributions in kind
Sachübernahme	acquisition of assets (with the economic effect of a contribution in kind)
Sammelverwahrung	collective custody
Satzung	articles of association
sinngemäß	analogously
sofortige Beschwerde	immediate appeal
Sonderbeschluss	special resolution
Sonderverwahrung	separate custody
Sondervorteil	special benefit
Stammkapital	registered share capital
stellvertretendes Mitglied	deputy member
stille Beteiligung	silent participation
Streifbandverwahrung	jacket custody
Stückaktien	non-par value shares

Teilgewinnabführungsvertrag	partial profit transfer agreement
Textform	text form
überschuldet	over-indebted
Umlaufvermögen	current assets
Umwandlungsgesetz	Transformation Act
unbeschränkt geschäftsfähige Person	natural person of full legal capacity
Unternehmensvertrag	enterprise agreement
Unwirksam	invalid
Urteil	judgment
verbundene Unternehmen	affiliated enterprises
Vererblich	inheritable
Verjähren	to become time-barred
Verlustrücktrag	loss carried back
Verlustvortrag	loss carried forward
Vertragsstrafe	contractual penalty
Vertretungsbefugnis	power of representation (authority to represent and act on behalf of another person)
Verwahrung	custody
vinkulierte Namensaktie	registered share with restricted transferability
Vinkulierung	restriction on transferability (of shares)
von Amts wegen	ex officio
Vorgesellschaft	pre-registered company (pre-*AG*/pre-*GmbH*)
vorsätzlich	intentionally
Vorstand	management board
Vorzugsaktien	preference shares
Wahlvorschlag	nomination
Wandelschuldverschreibung/Wandelanleihe	convertible bond
wechselseitige Beteiligung	cross-shareholding
Wertaufholungen	restorations in value
Wertminderung	decline in value of assets
wichtiger Grund	good cause
Widerspruch zur Niederschrift erheben	to raise an objection in the minutes
wiederkehrende Leistungen	recurring contributions
Willenserklärung	declaration of intent

zahlungsunfähig	illiquid
Zeichnung	subscription
zur Einsicht auslegen	to display for inspection
zur freien Verfügung der Geschäftsführer	at the free disposal of the managing directors
Zwangsgeld	administrative fine
Zwangsvollstreckung	enforcement proceedings
Zwischenschein	interim certificate